KT-210-716

CONTEMPORARY BRITISH DRAMATISTS

CONTEMPORARY LITERATURE SERIES

Contemporary American Dramatists
Contemporary British Dramatists
Contemporary Women Dramatists

CONTEMPORARY BRITISH DRAMATISTS

INTRODUCTION BY
MICHAEL BILLINGTON

EDITOR
K.A. BERNEY

ASSOCIATE EDITOR
N.G. TEMPLETON

St J
St James Press

LONDON   DETROIT   WASHINGTON DC

Gale Research International Ltd.
PO Box 699
Cheriton House
North Way
Andover
Hants SP10 5YE
United Kingdom

or

Gale Research Inc.
835 Penobscot Bldg.
Detroit, MI 48226–4094
U.S.A.

ST. JAMES PRESS is an imprint of Gale Research International Ltd.
An Affiliated Company of Gale Research Inc.

A CIP catalogue record for this book is available from the British Library

ISBN 1–55862–213–6

Typeset by Florencetype Ltd, Kewstoke, Avon
Printed in the United Kingdom by Unwin Brothers Ltd, Woking

Published simultaneously in the United Kingdom and the United States of America

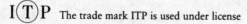 I⟨T⟩P   The trade mark ITP is used under license

CONTENTS

EDITOR'S NOTE

The main part of *Contemporary British Dramatists* contains entries on British and Irish writers for the stage.

The selection of writers included in this book is based on the recommendations of the advisers listed on page xv and is intended to reflect the best and most prominent of contemporary playwrights from the United Kingdom and Ireland (those who are currently active, as well as some who have died since 1950, but whose reputations remain essentially contemporary).

The entry for each writer consists of a biography, a complete list of published and/or produced plays and all other separately published books, a selected list of bibliographies and critical studies on the writer, and a signed essay. In addition, entrants were invited to comment on their work.

We have listed plays that were produced but not published; librettos and musical plays are listed along with other plays. The dates given are those of first publication/performance.

Some of the entries in the Dramatists section are supplemented in the Works section, which provides essays on a selection of the best-known plays written by the entrants.

The book concludes with a play, radio play, television play and screenplay title index.

ACKNOWLEDGEMENTS

We would like to thank the following for their help with this project: all the advisers and contributors; Barbara Archer; Deirdre Clark; Jackie Griffin; Lesley Henderson; Jane Kellock; Daniel Kirkpatrick; Roda Morrison, Humanities Publisher, Thomas Nelson; the staff of the London Theatre Museum; the staff of the British Library and Westminster Reference Library; and our friends and colleagues at St. James.

INTRODUCTION

Myth, after a certain time, becomes reality. Legend has it that post-war British drama really began on 8 May, 1956 when John Osborne's *Look Back in Anger* erupted onto the stage of the Royal Court Theatre. Of course it's only a half-truth. Plays were still being written in the decade after 1945. T.S. Eliot and Christopher Fry attempted to revive poetic drama, though they increasingly looked like swimming-instructors in an empty pool. N.C. Hunter wrote sub-Chekhovian comedies (*Waters of the Moon, A Day by the Sea*) that attracted glittering star-casts. Terence Rattigan continued to turn out well-fashioned plays one of which, *The Deep Blue Sea*, now looks like a minor classic. And John Whiting in *Saint's Day* anticipated the theatrical revolution to come. But, by and large, British drama was a pretty comatose affair until the foundation of the English Stage Company at the Royal Court in the mid-1950s. British theatre in the immediate post-war decade boasted great actors and showed a shrewd eye for French and American imports. But the West End, in particular, was dominated by an endless succession of country-house comedies and feeble thrillers leading the *Observer's* critic, Kenneth Tynan, to comment that to qualify as a dramatic hero you had to be earning at least £1,000 a year (then a sizeable sum) or be murdered in the house of someone who was. The British theatre, in a resonant phrase of Arthur Miller's seemed to be "hermetically sealed off from life."

All that changed with the arrival of *Look Back in Anger*: a structurally traditional but thematically radical play that opened the floodgates to a new generation of talent. Osborne brought eloquence, passion, rage, and youth to a theatre shrouded in gentlemanly good taste. What is more, the commercial success of his first play helped to put the Royal Court on a secure footing and proved to countless other writers that the British stage could cope with the tormented realities of life.

But what has happened to British drama in the almost four decades since we first encountered Jimmy Porter's incandescent tirades? It is difficult to sum up the work of the over 200 diverse writers found in the ensuing pages but a few common threads may be discerned. First and foremost is British drama's constant willingness to address the state of the nation. The story of post-war Britain is one of imperial decline ("Britain" as Dean Acheson famously said, "has lost an Empire without having found a role"), economic uncertainty, social tension, and agonizing introspection: out of our 40-year quest for an identity, however, has sprung much first-rate drama. The theatre has become the place where we examine who we are as a people and a few examples will prove my point. John Arden's *The Workhouse Donkey* is a superb Dionysiac spectacle about civic corruption. Alan Bennett's *Forty Years On* is a wry and witty examination, by one of nature's nostalgic reformers, about the break-up of the old order. Peter Barnes's *The Ruling Class* is about the demented excesses of a self-perpetuating aristocracy. David Edgar's *Destiny* memorably traces the persistent undercurrent of Fascism that has accompanied the loss of Empire. Alan Ayckbourn's *A Small Family Business* hilariously shows how the emphasis on entrepreneurial values leads directly to murder. And David Hare in his recent trilogy, comprising *Racing Demon, Murmuring Judges*, and *The Absence of War*, has examined the institutional decay affecting the church, the law, and the Labour Party.

A second common factor, much less remarked, is a fascination with stage language. In the 1950s you more or less had a straight choice between the exuberant metaphors of Christopher Fry and the dry understatement of Terence Rattigan. But over the last 40 years there has been an increasing alliance between poetry and colloquial prose: an area that has traditionally been the preserve of Irish dramatists. Arguably the greatest exemplar has been Harold Pinter whose writing career spans the whole period. Indeed when I asked Peter Hall what Pinter's contribution to our drama had been he unhesitatingly replied that "he made us realise that poetic drama can be mined out of real demotic speech." For proof you only have to look at any page of *The Caretaker, The Homecoming*, or *No Man's Land*. I would argue that most of our best dramatists have a poetic instinct. John Osborne re-introduced rhetoric to a verbally impoverished medium. Tom Stoppard's plays are a riotous cascade of puns, epigrams, *aperçus*, and witty explications of the seemingly abstruse. Edward Bond, in a very different way, produced a Brechtian poetry excavated from the language of everyday speech. And a writer like Howard Barker, possibly to excess, creates drama out of flinty, gnarled, muscular exchanges. Poetry and prose in the English language have, for several hundred years, been undergoing a prolonged separation: one of the achievements of post-war British drama has been to prove that they are neither irreconcilable nor incompatible. Indeed one of the most heartening signs, in recent years, has been the incorporation of professional poets like Tony Harrison and Derek Walcott—not least with their idiosyncratic versions of *The Oresteia* and *The Odyssey*—into mainstream drama.

A third quality you find in most British dramatists is a fascination with comedy and farce. My own view is that this is something to do with the native temperament: go back to the medieval Mystery plays and the tragedies of Shakespeare and you will find that the most sombre and terrifying material is flickeringly illuminated with laughter. In the second half of the 20th century it has become standard practice for British dramatists to deal with serious things comically. Beckett, of course, led the way in *Waiting for Godot*: the very purpose of existence explored through music-hall cross-talk. Other writers have followed the same path. Joe Orton used black comedy to attack conventional moral values and the hypocrisies of English life. Peter Nichols, reared like so many of his generation on music-hall and Variety, used their rhythms to explore a whole series of painful subjects: famously, in *A Day in the Death of Joe Egg*, the daily hazards of looking after a handicapped child. Tom Stoppard expanded the frontiers of farce in *Jumpers* and *Travesties* to embrace everything under the sun from metaphysics to the fallibility of memory. More recently Terry Johnson has come up with one of the most audacious plays of the 1990s in *Hysteria*: a work that invokes the plot-devices and structures of

Ben Travers's *Rookery Nook* to debate Freud's suppression of evidence of Viennese child-abuse. There seems no subject that British dramatists cannot handle comically; though Peter Barnes pushed that idea to its limits with *Laughter* which attempted to wrest a wild, brackish comedy from the tyrannies of Ivan the Terrible and Hitler.

But possibly the most significant quality of British drama over the past four decades has been its capacity for self-renewal. Not only has a new generation of dramatists emerged with each decade but the catchment area has constantly expanded. It's fair to say that the new British dramatists who emerged in 1956 were, with the striking exceptions of Shelagh Delaney and Ann Jellicoe, predominantly white and male though certainly not middle-class: Osborne, Pinter, and Wesker all came from working or lower middle-class backgrounds. Since then the picture has radically changed. A whole new generation of black dramatists has emerged spearheaded by Michael Abbensetts, Mustapha Matura and Derek Walcott. Women dramatists, who were barely visible when I started writing regularly about the theatre in 1971, are now numerous and ubiquitous: Caryl Churchill, Pam Gems, Louise Page, Sarah Daniels, Clare McIntyre, Winsome Pinnock, Rona Munro are as diverse in their themes, styles, and origins as any group of men. Ireland, which has historically injected passion and linguistic virtuosity into the sometimes anaemic veins of British drama, has also yielded a rich crop of writers from both North and South including Brian Friel, Tom Murphy, Frank McGuinness, and Billy Roche.

It's fascinating to speculate about the source of this self-renewal, which without being chauvinist, could not easily be matched in any other European country. Obviously it has a lot to do with social and political factors: the advance of black consciousness, the rise of feminism, the formation of separatist theatre groups to promote a particular cause. It may also be linked with the nature of the entertainment industry: radio has always been a nursery of dramatic talent but the advance of multi-channel television over the past four decades has also bred an insatiable hunger for writers. At root, however, I suspect it is the growing acceptance of the subsidy principle that explains the constant regeneration of British drama. In 1956 the Royal Court was the prime—almost the sole—outlet for new British writing. Now the National Theatre and the Royal Shakespeare Company, metropolitan venues like the Bush Theatre, Hampstead Theatre, the Tricycle, the Theatre Royal, Stratford East, and regional theatres like Manchester's Royal Exchange, Scarborough's Stephen Joseph Theatre-in-the-Round, Leeds' West Yorkshire Playhouse, Southampton's Nuffield Theatre and many more are all in the hunt for new plays. Writers need homes like everyone else; and the number of places where a dramatist can place his or her work has multiplied enormously. Which makes it all the sadder that, as I write in 1994, the Government is actually cutting back on subsidy to the performing arts and indirectly penalising new writing.

Granted this capacity for self-renewal, how would one characterise the different decades? The 1950s was the period that saw the initial explosion of energy, and words like "Angry Young Man" and "Kitchen Sink Realism" and "Comedy of Menace" were variously applied to Osborne, Wesker, and Pinter. In retrospect, what strikes one is the variety of voices and styles on offer. After all this was also the decade that saw the emergence of John Arden with his great poetic parable, *Serjeant Musgrave's Dance*, and of Peter Shaffer with his immaculately tailored study of family tensions, *Five Finger Exercise*. If there was any common thread, it was a fascination with the possibilities of theatrical language and a rumbling dissatisfaction with a class-ridden Britain still clinging on to its imperialist pretensions.

The breakthrough achieved in the 1950s led to a wealth of discovery in the 1960s: a decade it is now fashionable to rubbish as the source of all our social ills. But in the arts, as in so much else, it was a heady period of expansion and liberalisation. It saw the foundation of the Royal Shakespeare Company at Stratford-upon-Avon and the Aldwych Theatre in London and the National Theatre Company at the Old Vic. New theatres sprang up all over the regions. The seeds of what we now call the Fringe were sown in a multiplicity of small venues. Above all, the passing of the Theatre Act in 1968 meant that the Lord Chamberlain lost his arbitrary and historic power of censorship over living writers: a landmark event that made dramatists thereafter subject to the laws of the land. I suspect you would have to go back to the 1590s to find a more exciting decade in British theatre: it was a period that saw the emergence of talents as various as Alan Ayckbourn, Alan Bennett, Edward Bond, Peter Nichols, David Storey, and Tom Stoppard. It was also a decade of great plays that are still in the repertory: *The Homecoming, Saved, Rosencrantz and Guildenstern are Dead, A Patriot For Me, How the Other Half Loves.* I don't believe this is pure accident. It was something to do with the spirit of an age that believed anything was possible, that saw a loosening of the state's hold over private morality and that, with the election of a Labour Government in 1964, saw both a temporary upsurge in hope and an investment in the future of the arts.

Division by decade is, of course, arbitrary. The year 1968, a year of incipient revolution throughout Europe and America, also witnessed the growth of a new form of political theatre in Britain. But although there was a new militancy abroad—and an increasing impatience with the whole process of parliamentary democracy—it was only in the 1970s that the dramatists of that period reached maturity: most especially, David Hare, Howard Brenton, Trevor Griffiths, Howard Barker, David Edgar, and Caryl Churchill. Though arguably the most durable of them all, Christopher Hampton, adopted standard bourgeois forms to explore classic liberal dilemmas. For once, however, a decade does have a collective identity. It was a period of intensely political drama that threw up any number of plays about Britain's seeming imperviousness to radical or revolutionary change: works like Griffiths's *The Party*, Hare's *Plenty*, Brenton's *Magnificence* and, more obliquely, Edgar's *Destiny*.

Equally importantly, it was a decade that saw a widening of the writing community. Women wrestled openly with questions of gender, sexuality, and self-definition in works like *Owners* and *Cloud Nine* by Caryl Churchill and *Dusa, Fish, Stas and Vi* and *Piaf* by Pam Gems: they also showed a much greater willingness to experiment with theatrical forms than male dramatists. Black dramatists likewise showed a readiness to shake up both the style and substance of British Drama: Mustapha Matura's *Play Mas* dealt with life in pre- and post-independence Trinidad with appropriately carnivalesque fervour and Michael Abbensetts's *Alterations* vividly showed the pressures on a West Indian tailor to alter and shape a vast number of trousers for export to Japan. The foundation of the Black Theatre Co-Operative in 1978 also meant that

Afro-Caribbean dramatists at last had an institution dedicated to promoting and performing their work. The social and political upheavals of the late 1960s permeated the 1970s; and one positive gain was that British drama became more representative of the nation.

What emerges quite strongly is that British drama inevitably mirrors and reflects the character of the age. The period post-1979 is imperishably the Thatcher decade: one in which long cherished assumptions about state intervention, the liberal consensus, and collective power were held up to the light and ruthlessly examined. In many ways, the re-definition of Britain produced interesting plays. Doug Lucie, one of our sharpest social observers, piercingly analysed the development of a new amoral, apolitical, style-conscious generation in *Hard Feelings*. Caryl Churchill in *Top Girls* suggested that a feminism that did not embrace compassion and generosity was not worthy of the name. And David Hare in *The Secret Rapture* optimistically implied that the 1980s adulation of individualism and greed was but a temporary blip in the cycle of history. But while playwrights strongly criticized the ethos of the age, British drama's capacity for self-renewal came into question. At the end of the decade one could point only to a small handful of dramatists—Timberlake Wertenbaker, Jim Cartwright, Anthony Minghella—who had, in any real sense, emerged and prospered during a period that made words like "community" and "society" taboo.

The great strength of British drama today is that it has a rich forty-year past on which to build. Writers like Pinter, Shaffer, Stoppard, Ayckbourn, and Hare continue to write plays without any diminution of energy or ability: indeed recent works like Pinter's *Moonlight*, Stoppard's *Arcadia* and Hare's *Racing Demon* are amongst the very best things they have done. New writers still emerge from Fringe and studio theatres, though they now tend to be devoured by television with indecent speed. And, when one looks at other countries, one has cause to be grateful for the prodigality of British drama. But its future course will, I suspect, be determined by practical matters like the state of the economy, the ability to maintain the subsidised network and the affordability of theatre-tickets. No-one can predict with certainty where we go from here. We can, however, look back not with anger but with a certain modest pride at what has been accomplished over four decades: at the range of voices on offer, at the emergence of a handful of durable modern classics, at the re-invention of theatrical poetry and, above all, at our drama's ability to reflect the form and pressure of the time. Future historians who want to know what Britain was like in the second half of the 20th century will find in the drama an accurate and possibly indispensable guide. And what more can one ask of the theatre than that?

—Michael Billington

ADVISERS

Judith E. Barlow
C.W.E. Bigsby
Michael Billington
Katharine Brisbane
Ned Chaillet
Ruby Cohn

Tish Dace
Lizbeth Goodman
Anthony Graham-White
Nick Hern
Holly Hill
Joel Schechter

CONTRIBUTORS

Frances Rademacher Anderson
Roger Baker
Carol Banks
Gene A. Barnett
Clive Barker
Joss Bennathon
Gerald M. Berkowitz
Michael Billington
John Bowen
Christina Britzolakis
John Russell Brown
Joseph Bruchac
John Bull
Susan Carlson
Alasdair Cameron
Ned Chaillet
Ruby Cohn
Clare Colvin
Judy Cooke
Tish Dace
W. A. Darlington
Terence Dawson
Tony Dunn
Jane Edwardes
John Elsom
Richard Foulkes
S. E. Gontarski
Lizbeth Goodman
Lois Gordon
Robert Gordon
Anthony Graham-White
Steve Grant
Frances Gray
Prabhu S. Guptara
Paul Hadfield
Jonathan Hammond
James Hansford
Carole Hayman
Ronald Hayman
Harold Hobson

Christopher Innes
David E. Kemp
Burton S. Kendle
H. Gustav Klaus
Bernd-Peter Lange
Paul Lawley
Michael T. Leech
Matthew Lloyd
Felicia Hardison Londré
James MacDonald
Frank Marcus
Arthur E. McGuinness
Howard McNaughton
Christian H. Moe
Christopher Murray
Benedict Nightingale
Garry O'Connor
Marion O'Connor
John O'Leary
Malcolm Page
Rosemary Pountney
David Ian Rabey
Henry Raynor
Leslie du S. Read
Kenneth Richards
James Roose-Evans
Geoff Sadler
Arthur Sainer
Bernice Schrank
Adrienne Scullion
Christopher Smith
John Spurling
Carol Simpson Stern
Alan Strachan
Ronald W. Strang
J. L. Styan
Peter Thomson
Elaine Turner
Michelene Wandor
B. A. Young

LIST OF DRAMATISTS

Michael Abbensetts
Paul Ableman
Dannie Abse
Rodney Ackland
John Antrobus
Jane Arden
John Arden
Alan Ayckbourn

Enid Bagnold
Howard Barker
Peter Barnes
Neil Bartlett
Samuel Beckett
Brendan Behan
Alan Bennett
Eric Bentley
Steven Berkoff
Barry Bermange
Stephen Bill
Alan Bleasdale
Bridget Boland
Robert Bolt
Chris Bond
Edward Bond
John Bowen
Howard Brenton
Brigid Brophy
John Burrows
John Byrne

David Campton
Denis Cannan
Jim Cartwright
David Caute
Agatha Christie
Caryl Churchill
Brian Clark
John Clifford
Barry Collins
Stewart Conn
Ray Cooney
Noël Coward
Richard Crane
David Cregan
Martin Crimp
Beverley Cross

Sarah Daniels
Margaretta D'Arcy
Nick Darke
Nick Dear
Shelagh Delaney
Keith Dewhurst
J.P. Donleavy
Maureen Duffy
Andrea Dunbar
Nell Dunn
Charles Dyer

David Edgar
T.S. Eliot
Barry England
Marcella Evaristi
Stanley Eveling

Peter Flannery
James Forsyth
Michael Frayn
Brian Friel
Terence Frisby
Christopher Fry

Tom Gallacher
Shirley Gee
Jonathan Gems
Pam Gems
Peter Gill
John Godber
Steve Gooch
Ronald Gow
Simon Gray
Graham Greene
Walter Greenwood
Trevor Griffiths
John Grillo

Wilson John Haire
John Hale
Willis Hall
David Halliwell
Christopher Hampton
James Hanley
Chris Hannan
John Harding

David Hare
Richard Harris
Tony Harrison
Ronald Harwood
Michael Hastings
Robert Holman
John Hopkins
Debbie Horsfield
Roger Howard
Donald Howarth
Dusty Hughes
Ron Hutchinson

Debbie Isitt

Stephen Jeffreys
Ann Jellicoe
Terry Johnson
Keith Johnstone

John B. Keane
Charlotte Keatley
Barrie Keeffe
Tom Kempinski
Thomas Kilroy
Bernard Kops
Hanif Kureishi

Kevin Laffan
Bryony Lavery
Mike Leigh
Hugh Leonard
Doris Lessing
Deborah Levy
Henry Livings
Liz Lochhead
Stephen Lowe
Doug Lucie
Peter Luke

Sharman MacDonald
Wolf Mankowitz
Tony Marchant
Frank Marcus
Eugene McCabe
John McGrath
Tom McGrath
Frank McGuinness
Clare McIntyre

David Mercer
Ronald Millar
Anthony Minghella
Adrian Mitchell
Julian Mitchell
M.J. Molloy
Daniel Mornin
Bill Morrison
John Mortimer
Gregory Motton
David Mowat
Rona Munro
Iris Murdoch
Tom Murphy

G.F. Newman
Peter Nichols
Lewis Nkosi

Sean O'Casey
Mary O'Malley
Michael O'Neill
Joe Orton
John Osborne
Alun Owen

Louise Page
Stewart Parker
Caryl Phillips
David Pinner
Winsome Pinnock
Harold Pinter
Alan Plater
Stephen Poliakoff
Dennis Potter
David Pownall
J.B.Priestley

Peter Ransley
Terence Rattigan
Christina Reid
Anne Ridler
Billy Roche
David Rudkin
Willy Russell

James A. Saunders
Jeremy Seabrook
David Selbourne

Anthony Shaffer
Peter Shaffer
N.F. Simpson
Dodie Smith
Johnny Speight
Colin Spencer
John Spurling
Tom Stoppard
David Storey
Mike Stott

George Tabori
Cecil P. Taylor
Peter Terson
Sue Townsend
Ben Travers
William Trevor
David Turner

Peter Ustinov

Derek Walcott
Michelene Wandor
Keith Waterhouse
Timberlake Wertenbaker
Arnold Wesker
Peter Whelan
Ted Whitehead
Hugh Whitemore
John Whiting
Christopher Wilkinson
Heathcote Williams
Nigel Williams
Ted Willis
Snoo Wilson
Charles Wood
Nicholas Wright

LIST OF WORKS

CONTEMPORARY
BRITISH DRAMATISTS

A

ABBENSETTS, Michael.

Born in British Guiana (now Guyana), 8 June 1938; became British citizen, 1974. Educated at Queen's College, Guyana, 1952–56; Stanstead College, Quebec; Sir George Williams University, Montreal, 1960–61. Security attendant, Tower of London, 1963–67; staff member, Sir John Soane Museum, London, 1968–71. Resident playwright, Royal Court Theatre, London, 1974; visiting professor of drama, Carnegie Mellon University, Pittsburgh, 1981. Recipient: George Devine award, 1973; Arts Council bursary, 1977; Afro-Caribbean award, 1979. Address: c/o Heinemann Educational Books Ltd., Halley Court, Jordan Hill, Oxford OX2 8EJ, England.

Publications

PLAYS

Sweet Talk (produced 1973). 1976.
Alterations (produced 1978; revised version produced 1985).
Samba (produced 1980).1980.
In the Mood (produced 1981).
Outlaw (produced 1983).
El Dorado (produced 1984).
Living Together (includes *Roystony's Day, The Street Party*). 1988.
The Lion (produced 1993).

RADIO PLAYS: *Home Again*, 1975; *The Sunny Side of the Street*, 1977; *Brothers of the Sword*, 1978; *The Fast Lane*, 1980; *The Dark Horse*, 1981; *Summer Passions*, 1985.

TELEVISION PLAYS: *The Museum Attendant*, 1973; *Inner City Blues*, 1975; *Crime and Passion*, 1976; *Black Christmas*, 1977; *Roadrunner*, 1977; *Empire Road* series, 1977, 1979; *Easy Money*, 1982; *Big George Is Dead*, 1987.

NOVEL

Empire Road (novelization of television series). 1979.

Michael Abbensetts comments:

(1982) I once read something a black American playwright had written: he said his plays could not be understood by a white person. That is not the way I

1

feel about my plays. It seems to me that if a play is good enough it should have something to say to everybody, once they are prepared to look for that something. However, having said that, I would like to add that I would never want to write a play that a black audience did not like, no matter how popular it was with a white audience. When my stage play *Alterations* was praised by critics of the *Sunday Times* and the *Financial Times*, it made me feel very pleased, but I was equally pleased that the reviewer in the *Jamaica Gleaner* liked the play as well.

Which brings me to the question I am sometimes asked. Why do I write so much for television? First, BBC-TV pays me well—okay, *reasonably* well—and second, my TV plays are bound to reach a larger black audience than my stage plays ever do.

Yet originally I had never even thought of writing for the theatre. Originally I wanted to be a novelist. Then while I was at university in Canada I saw a version of Osborne's *Look Back in Anger*, and suddenly I knew what I wanted to be—a playwright. So then I came to England. Other West Indians were coming to the UK to find jobs, I came here to find theatre. I'd read of a place called the Royal Court Theatre, and I vowed to myself to get one of my plays on there, even though, at that time, I hadn't even written a single play. Yet in time I did get a play on at the Royal Court, and I was made resident dramatist at the Court. A lot has happened to me since those first, heady days at the Royal Court Theatre.

The majority of black British playwrights emerged in the 1970s. Michael Abbensetts is quite simply the best of these. His first work to be widely noticed, a 1973 television play *The Museum Attendant*, struck the two notes that characterize all of his output. First, it worked out a tragic situation within a broad tradition of comedy; the humour arises primarily from incongruity, though there are fine instances of verbal felicity and wit. In the juxtaposition of tragedy and comedy Abbensetts goes back to English Renaissance drama, though the more immediate mentor is probably Albee. Second, his work stood out because it was practically the first time that television drama had shown an accurate slice of immigrant life. A whole generation of television sitcoms (*Love Thy Neighbour* and *Mixed Blessings* were then the latest) had taken race as their main, if not sole, theme. With their appalling racialist jokes, shown on the dubious grounds of "therapeutic value," these plays were deeply upsetting to many people. *The Fosters*, the only previous all-black comedy series, was welcomed by black people but showed its American origins too clearly to be more than an aperitif. *Gangsters*, another television series, also with racialist jokes and in an American blood-and-thunder movie tradition, was more controversial. Condemned as "vicious and vacuous," it was also praised for "somehow managing to suggest more of the corruption and reasons for racial tension than a score of more balanced and realistic programmes." It did not, however, affect the convention of cardboard blacks who were a "problem," or were pawns in arguments about British politics—e.g., in the automatic coupling of racism and fascism. Generally, blacks in plays were just plain stupid, as in *Curry and Chips* or *Till Death Us Do Part*. At best, the presence of blacks on television consoled a liberal conscience.

Abbensetts's achievement in presenting a black viewpoint on black life in Britain allowed his characters to emerge as fully human beings for the very first time in the history of British performing media. He provides an honest picture of the diversity of black people, with individuals as sincere, muddled, feckless, wicked, or wonderful as might come from any other group. In contrast to the work of otherwise fine black playwrights such as Mustapha Matura, Abbensetts's work is free from defensive clowning.

Abbensetts has said that *Black Christmas* constitutes his claim to be taken seriously as a writer. In it a West Indian family under the peculiar strains of life in Britain holds together only by sheer will; Abbensetts can be seen, then, as working also in a tradition of domestic drama, though "domestic" needs to be understood in its extended Third World rather than nuclear Western sense. The concentrated impact of the concerns of *Black Christmas* was spun out into two series called *Empire Road*. Slicker if slighter than the single play, this established Abbensetts with the public. In the second series, especially, he was able to match his writing to the personality and strength of the actors. *D.I.V.O.R.C.E.*, the seventh episode of the second series, is generally considered the best; and in its most praised section two of the characters, now drunk, reminisce about their life in Britain, and especially those experiences that are traumatic or hideous. Abbensetts often presents middle-aged characters haunted by memory, a device that enables him to add irony and bite to his plays. In *D.I.V.O.R.C.E.* that haunted hinterland of memory has a rich dramatic impact that itself comes to haunt viewers.

It is, however, the stage play *Alterations* that is Abbensetts's best complete work. Walker, a West Indian tailor, is desperately racing against the clock, trying to alter an immense number of trousers to sizes suitable for export to Japan: if he can finish this work, he will earn enough money in time to pay the deposit and begin to realize a life-long ambition of having his own shop. The pressures created by the situation impose a series of alterations in the lives, attitudes, and expectations of all the characters in the play: Walker himself, Horace and Buster, who intermittently help and hinder Walker, and Walker's discarded wife Darlene, to whom he is still attached in a strange West Indian way. All of Abbensetts's plays are, to a certain extent, parables. Though he tends to pack too much into his stage plays, they seem generally to be better constructed than his television plays.

His best television play is *Big George Is Dead*. At Big George's funeral Tony appears, having returned prosperous from Tobago, to repay the money he owes his former friend Boogie. For old times' sake, Tony and Boogie decide to relive their glorious past: back in the swinging sixties Boogie, Tony, and Big George were three black desperadoes calling themselves "the wild bunch." Identities forged on the frontline of Soho nightlife are tested in a London that now has punks, muggers, drug dealers. As the night wears on, the two become more and more immersed in the tragic sense of loss in their lives—particularly Tony, whose girlfriend married Boogie when Tony was forced to disappear to Tobago. Tony's son has been adopted by Boogie, and no-one wants the boy to realize the truth. Here is an understated, atmospheric play, finely testifying to Abbensetts's reluctant cleavage from his earlier comic mode, making it possible for him richly to explore the muted tragedies of everyday people, everyday lives.

Abbensetts was criticized earlier, by black and white activists, for his lack of political commitment. Over the years it has become clear that he does have a political vision, though it is not of course rendered in terms of British political allegiances. He has a larger vision of immigrant groups as incipiently one community, an all-embracing refuge which strengthens black people to tackle the problems presented by the alien white man's world in which they live. But Abbensetts also portrays the actualities of the relations between the different immigrant groups, as well as between generations, and raises the question of where this community is headed.

—Prabhu S. Guptara

ABLEMAN, Paul.

Born in Leeds, Yorkshire, 13 June 1927; brought up in New York. Educated at King's College, University of London. Military service: 3 years. Married; one son. Agent: Peters, Fraser, and Dunlop Group, 503/4 The Chambers, Chelsea Harbour, Lots Road, London SW10 0XF. Address: 36 Duncan House, Fellows Road, London N.W.3, England.

Publications

PLAYS

Even His Enemy, with Gertrude Macauley (as *Letters to a Lady*, produced 1951). 1948.
Help! (revue; produced 1963).
One Hand Clapping (revue; produced 1964).
Dialogues (produced 1965).
Green Julia (produced 1965). 1966.
Tests (sketches). 1966.
Emily and Heathcliff (produced 1967).
Blue Comedy, Madly in Love, Hank's Night (produced 1968). 1968; *Madly in Love* in *Modern Short Comedies from Broadway and London*, edited by Stanley Richards, 1969.
The Black General, adaptation of *Othello* by Shakespeare (produced 1969).
And Hum Our Sword (produced 1973).
Little Hopping Robin (produced 1973).
The Visitor (produced 1974).
Windsor All-Sorts (produced 1977).

RADIO PLAY: *The Infant*, 1974.

TELEVISION PLAYS: *Barlowe of the Car Park*, 1961; *That Woman Is Wrecking Our Marriage*, 1969; *Visits from a Stranger*, 1970; *The Catch in a Cold*, 1970; *The Wrong 'Un*, from a work by Michael Brett, 1983; *Love Song*, from a novel by Jeffrey Archer, 1985; *A Killing on the Exchange* series, 1987.

NOVELS

I Hear Voices. 1957.
As Near as I Can Get. 1962.

Vac. 1968.
The Twilight of the Vilp. 1969.
Tornado Pratt. 1977.
Shoestring (novelization of television play). 1979.
Porridge (novelization of screenplay). 1979.
Shoestring's Finest Hour. 1980.
County Hall (novelization of television series). 1981.
Hi-De-Hi (novelization of television series). 1983.
A Killing on the Exchange (novelization of television series). 1987.
Dad's Army (novelization of the television series by Jimmy Perry and David
    Croft). 1989.

Verse

Bits: Some Prose Poems. 1969.

Other

The Mouth and Oral Sex. 1969; as *The Mouth,* 1972; as *The Sensuous Mouth,*
    1972.
Anatomy of Nakedness. 1982; as *The Banished Body,* 1984.
The Doomed Rebellion. 1983.
Straight Up: The Autobiography of Arthur Daley, As Told to Paul Ableman.
    1992.

Translator, with Veronica Hall, *Egypt,* by Simonne Lacourture. 1963.

Paul Ableman's dramatic output is small, but striking, both for the unpretentious wit of its dialogue and for the moral concern implicit in its characterization and plot. One central concern would seem to be the difficulty of
reconciling sexual fulfilment with good conscience and consideration for
others. Certainly this is so in *Green Julia,* probably his most impressive piece to
date, and as thoughtful a study of the hypocrisies of male sexuality as the
modern theatre has produced.

   There are only two characters onstage, Jake and Bob: the Julia of the title
remains offstage throughout, a presence constantly invoked by them and, by
the end of the play, a substantial one. Jake is leaving England, probably for a
long time, and feels a faint guilt about Julia, the erratic, self-absorbed but
generous divorcée he has made his mistress. Gradually, it becomes clear that he
wants Bob, his best friend, to take her off his mind by taking her over. But Bob,
who is the more morally pretentious of the two, affects both to despise her
("the most depraved old whore in Southern England") and to have a woman of
his own. Not only will he reject the idea, he appears to resent it; and the verbal
games the two men constantly play with each other (in which they imitate
army officers, psychiatrists, university professors, anything capable of easy
parody) become increasingly hostile. It is no longer possible to continue
camouflaging their true feelings in such a way. Bob comes right out with:
"What is your relationship with Julia? You never treat her, never help her or
worry about her, hardly ever think about her except on the odd evenings when
you happen to feel randy and she's available." This is clearly true; and yet, as
we also gradually discover, Bob's stance is a fraud. He is inexperienced,
anxious for sexual discovery, and likely to prove as unscrupulous as Jake in
achieving it. The curtain falls on the arrival of Julia, who is evidently destined

to be exploited by others until what promises to be a raddled and lonely old age.

By the end, the contrast between the jocular, harmless manner of these very ordinary young men and the callousness of their intentions is unmissable, and makes the play more than the light comedy it has at times pretended to be. With Ableman's other pieces on the same theme, however, there is no question of pretence. Both *Hank's Night* and *Madly in Love* leave a less bitter aftertaste, presumably because in each case mutual consent replaces exploitation and the tone can therefore remain good-humoured and amused. In *Madly in Love* an eccentric poet poses as a psychiatrist in the hope of losing his virginity by seducing a girl whose quirk is to obey every order she is given: the irony is that the shock of being told "make love to me" cures her, whereupon she freely gives herself to him in gratitude for his help. In *Hank's Night* two couples try to persuade themselves and each other to start an orgy, and fail lamentably until they gave up the attempt, whereupon the thing actually happens, spontaneously and unselfconsciously. The moral of both plays, and perhaps also of *Green Julia*, may be that those who do not seek to manipulate others and bend them to their will may receive something the more satisfying for being offered freely and without constraint. In the most unpretentious way, Ableman's work is a criticism of the earnestness and anxiety that attaches to sex nowadays, with so many people regarding it, not as a means of cementing genuine relationships or even as a form of enjoyment, but as a mere proof of personal adequacy.

All these pieces are naturalistic, or nearly so: Ableman has also written some 50 surrealist sketches under the general title of *Tests*, some of which have been performed in *One Hand Clapping* and other revues, and most of which prove to have little more to offer than verbal invention and a vague aura of "absurdism." One speech, typical both in the apparent arbitrariness of its language and in its facetiousness, reads: "A mammal of an estuary saluted a kindly laundryman. With a yelp the match teetered. Pickle all laundrymen. Toast archipelagos as if to pronounce renounce." A few "tests" do, however, seem to have a subject, notably *Johnson*, a parody of military conventions, *She's Dead*, in which two characters parrot cliché responses to violence and death, and *Another Lovely Day*, in which the speakers seek to fox each other by shifting their names and personae. However he develops as a dramatist (and since the 1970's he has applied himself more to the novel), it seems clear that Ableman is strongest when he is handling material that, at least to some extent, engages him as a moralist.

—Benedict Nightingale

ABSE, Dannie.

Born in Cardiff, Glamorgan, 22 September 1923. Educated at Marlborough Road Elementary School, Cardiff; St. Illtyd's College, Cardiff; University of South Wales and Monmouthshire, Cardiff; King's College, London; Westminster Hospital, London; qualified as physician 1950, M.R.C.S., L.R.C.P. Served in the Royal Air Force, 1951–54: squadron leader. Married Joan Mercer in 1951; one son and two daughters. Specialist in charge of the chest clinic, Central London Medical Establishment 1954–89. Senior Fellow in

Humanities, Princeton University, New Jersey, 1973–74. Editor, *Poetry and Poverty* magazine, London, 1949–54. President, Poetry Society 1978–92. Recipient: Foyle award, 1960; Welsh Arts Council award, 1971, 1987, for play, 1980; Cholmondeley award, 1985. D. Litt.: University of Wales, Cardiff, 1989. Fellow, Royal Society of Literature, 1983. Agent: Land Sheil Associates, 43 Doughty Street, London WC1N 2LF. Address: 85 Hodford Road, London NW11 8NH, England; or, Green Hollows, Craig-yr-Eos Road, Ogmore-by-Sea, Glamorgan, South Wales.

Publications

PLAYS

Fire in Heaven (produced 1948). 1956; revised version, as *Is the House Shut?* (produced 1964); revised version, as *In the Cage*, in *Three Questor Plays*, 1967.
Hands Around the Wall (produced 1950).
House of Cowards (produced 1960). In *Three Questor Plays*, 1967; in *Twelve Great Plays*, edited by Leonard F. Dean, 1970; revised version, in *The View from Row G*, 1990.
The Eccentric (produced 1961). 1961.
Gone (produced 1962). In *Three Questor Plays*, 1967; revised version, as *Gone in January* (produced 1977), in *Madog* 1981.
The Courting of Essie Glass (as *The Joker*, produced 1962; revised version, as *The Courting of Essie Glass*, broadcast 1975). In *Miscellany One*, 1981.
Three Questor Plays. 1967.
The Dogs of Pavlov (produced 1969). 1973.
Funland (produced 1975).
Pythagoras (produced 1976). 1979; as *Pythagoras Smith* in *The View from Row G*, 1990.
The View from Row G (includes *House of Cowards*, *The Dogs of Pavlov*, and *Pythagoras Smith*). 1990.

RADIO PLAYS: *Conform or Die*, 1957; *No Telegrams, No Thunder*, 1962; *You Can't Say Hello to Anybody*, 1964; *A Small Explosion*, 1964; *The Courting of Essie Glass*, 1975.

NOVELS

Ash on a Young Man's Sleeve. 1954.
Some Corner of an English Field. 1956.
O. Jones, O. Jones. 1970.
There Was a Young Man from Cardiff. 1991.

VERSE

After Every Green Thing. 1948.
Walking under Water. 1952.
Tenants of the House: Poems 1951–1956. 1957.
Poems, Golders Green. 1962.
Dannie Abse: A Selection. 1963.
A Small Desperation. 1968.
Demo. 1969.
Selected Poems. 1970.

Funland: A Poem in Nine Parts. 1971.
Corgi Modern Poets in Focus 4, with others, edited by Jeremy Robson. 1972.
Funland and Other Poems. 1973.
Lunchtime. 1974.
Penguin Modern Poets 26, with D.J. Enright and Michael Longley. 1975.
Collected Poems 1948–1976. 1977.
Way Out in the Centre. 1981; as *One-Legged on Ice*, 1983.
Ask the Bloody Horse. 1986; as *Sky in Narrow Streets*, in *Quarterly Review of Literature Poetry Series*, 28, 1987.
White Coat, Purple Coat: Collected Poems 1948–1988. 1989.
Remembrance of Crimes Past. 1990.
Recordings:
Poets of Wales, 1972; *The Poetry of Dannie Abse*, n.d.; *Dannie Abse*, 1984.

OTHER

Medicine on Trial. 1968.
A Poet in the Family (autobiography). 1974.
Miscellany One. 1981.
A Strong Dose of Myself (essays). 1983.
Under the Influence Of (lecture). 1984(?).
Journals from the Ant Heap. 1986.

Editor, with Elizabeth Jennings and Stephen Spender, *New Poems 1956.* 1956.
Editor, with Howard Sergeant, *Mavericks.* 1957.
Editor, *European Verse.* 1964.
Editor, *Corgi Modern Poets in Focus 1, 3, 5.* 1971–73.
Editor, *Thirteen Poets.* 1973.
Editor, *Poetry Dimension 2–5: The Best of the Poetry Year.* 1974–78.
Editor, *The Best of the Poetry Year 6–7.* 1979–80.
Editor, *Poetry Supplement, Christmas 1975.* 1975.
Editor, *My Medical School.* 1978.
Editor, *Wales in Verse.* 1983.
Editor, *Doctors and Patients.* 1984.
Editor, with Joan Abse, *Voices in the Gallery.* 1986.
Editor, with Joan Abse, *The Music Lover's Literary Companion.* 1988.
Editor, *The Hutchinson Book of Post-War British Poets.* 1989.

MANUSCRIPT COLLECTION: National Library of Wales, Aberystwyth, Dyfed.

CRITICAL STUDIES: *Dannie Abse* by Tony Curtis, 1985.

Dannie Abse comments:

Of a very early play of mine T.S. Eliot kindly remarked it was good for the stage and for the study. He was wrong. That play, alas, was not good for either; but I hope in later years some of my plays have earned Eliot's encomium. Anybody interested in my plays will find the three I'm most pleased with in a paperback, *The View from Row G.*

Dannie Abse's work explores the conflicting elements of the human psyche, showing man at war with his own self-destructive urges. As a practising doctor and a Jew, he sees clearly the limitations of the known, and the frightening depths of the subconscious, the irrational tyranny and subservience that underlie the apparent normality of the world. As one who wears both the white coat of the physician, and the magician's purple cloak, he remains wary of the system, and its threat to the individual. Abse sees in institutionalized obedience a force that reduces men and women to objects, detecting in the manipulation of medical experiments those same dark impulses that led to the gas ovens of Auschwitz and Belsen. Memory of the Nazi holocaust colours his writing, recalled in his plays with their potent themes of choice, delusion, the assertion and denial of self, and unquestioning obedience to evil.

Abse is a poet first and foremost and his earliest venture into drama was a verse play, *Fire in Heaven*. Set in an occupied country, it depicts the terrible choice placed before the main character, Christian, who is ordered to kill his family, or have the entire village massacred. After a painful struggle with his conscience, Christian murders his family. The appalling nature of the decision, and the horror of the killing itself, are ably—and shockingly—evoked by the author, although *Fire in Heaven* seems at times to be more akin to poetry than drama. Abse later rewrote it in two prose versions where the contrast is less stark, the occupying soldiers and their commander shown not as monsters, but as human beings caught in a fearful dilemma. Even so, some aspects of the work fail to satisfy completely, with Christian's character over-idealized, and an excess of dialogue betraying the story's poetic origins.

Choice and illusion also feature in *House of Cowards*, a drama based on Abse's poem "Meeting." It centres on the expected visit of the Speaker to a drab, uninteresting town whose inhabitants see him as the answer to their prayers. Eager at his promised coming, they recreate his image in their minds to fit their own requirements. But the Speaker, like Beckett's Godot, does not arrive, although expected the following day. Abse's story bears too close a resemblance to that of Beckett, while his everyday treatment of a symbolic theme renders the work less than effective.

Far better is *The Dogs of Pavlov*, where Abse continues his investigation of choice, and submission to evil. Taking his theme from an actual psychological experiment, he presents a horrifying picture of outwardly normal people only too easily persuaded to inflict pain on their fellows in the interests of "science." The fraught love relationship between Kurt and Sally, whom Abse casts in the roles of victim and torturer, gives pointed emphasis to their situation, while clothing the horror in human terms. The fact that the "pain" is simulated, and the experiment a sham, does nothing to dispel its sinister implications. Abse views the godlike power of the doctors, their arbitary manipulation of their subjects, as directly linked with the Nazi "experiments" and the concentration camps. Sally's final outburst, begging for death in the "electric chair," is a cry of anguish from a dehumanised victim whose own worst instincts have been realized. Abse displays assurance in the interplay and speech patterns of his characters, and in his use of the stage. *The Dogs of Pavlov* shows human beings operating to destructive effect inside the sheaths of their own illusory ideals.

Similar themes are explored in *Pythagoras*, perhaps Abse's finest play so far.

The scene is set in a mental hospital, where a power struggle takes place between the superintendent and an eccentric patient whose individuality constitutes a challenge to his authority. A former stage magician, Pythagoras sees himself as a reincarnation of the Greek sage, whose knowledge combined science, medicine, and religious magic, disciplines whose segregation is embodied in Dr. Aquillus, the superintendent. In the course of the play Pythagoras adopts the persona of his rival, and in one amusing but significant scene a reporter mistakes him for the superintendent and Pythagoras promptly "recreates" Dr. Aquillus as a psychopath. The play is derived from Abse's poem *Funland*, in which Pythagoras dies after a bungled rebellion by the inmates. Here there is a more profound and striking denouement, with Pythagoras collapsing at the moment of confrontation, and recuperating as a "normal" person, shorn of his individuality and powers. Deluded or not, his "fall" is tragic, a triumph of white-coated order over intuitive creation. Abse expands the theme with consummate skill, putting over his dark message with sharp exchanges of dialogue and frequent gems of humour. Here the symbolic and the natural fit together without strain, though their revelation is often bleak, as in the utterance of the patient being "demonstrated" to the medical students: "Yes, I am dead, and this is hell."

Pythagoras is matched on a smaller scale by some of Abse's shorter works. This is true of *Gone*, a one-act play whose basis is a prevented attempt at suicide. Similarly, *The Eccentric*, another one-acter, presents the idea of self-assertion through eccentricity, showing in the figure of the shopkeeper Goldstein a man fulfilled through his idiosyncrasies. His apparent stupidity in refusing to sell customers what they want is revealed as a principle of self-denial and as an ennobling act. "God doesn't say yes to everything," Goldstein tells his young protégé. "Maybe that's what makes a man." Though slight, *The Eccentric* is a poised, appealing work, whose deeper meanings are expressed in clear, individualised speech.

As the descendant of a persecuted race, Abse evokes the horrors of the past. As a writer and healer, he links them to the tyrannies of our own time. His plays, though secondary to his poetic works, sound a warning note that we ignore at our peril.

—Geoff Sadler

ACKLAND, Rodney.

Born in Westcliffe-on-Sea, Essex, 18 May 1908. Educated at Salesian College, 1915–16; Balham Grammar School, 1916–23; Central School of Speech Training and Dramatic Art, London. Married Mab Lonsdale (daughter of the playwright Frederick Lonsdale) in 1952 (died 1972). Salesman, Swan and Edgar, London, 1924; worked in the silks department, Stagg and Mantles, London, 1925, and in the advertising department, Vacuum Oil Company, London, 1925. Founder, with Roland Gillett, Kinsmen Pictures, 1946. *Died 6 December 1991.*

Publications

PLAYS

Improper People (produced 1929). 1930.
Marion-Ella (produced 1930).
Dance with No Music (produced 1930). 1933.
Strange Orchestra (produced 1931). 1932.
Ballerina, music by Henry Sullivan, lyrics by Desmond Carter, adaptation of the novel by Eleanor Smith (produced 1933).
Birthday (produced 1934). 1935.
The White Guard, adaptation of a play by Michael Bulgakov (produced 1934).
The Old Ladies, adaptation of the novel by Hugh Walpole (produced 1935; as *Night in the House*, produced 1935). 1935.
After October (produced 1936). 1936.
Plot Twenty-One (also director: produced 1936).
Yes, My Darling Daughter, adaptation of work by Mark Reed (produced 1937).
The Dark River (as *Remembrance of Things Past*, produced 1938; as *The Dark River*, produced 1941). 1942.
Sixth Floor, adaptation of a play by Alfred Ghéri (produced 1939).
Blossom Time, music by Schubert (produced 1942).
The Diary of a Scoundrel, adaptation of a play by A.N. Ostrovsky (produced 1942). 1948.
Crime and Punishment, adaptation of a novel by Dostoevsky (produced 1946). 1948.
Cupid and Mars, with Robert G. Newton, adaptation of a story by Newton (produced 1947).
Before the Party, adaptation of a story by W. Somerset Maugham (produced 1949). 1950.
A Multitude of Sins, with Robert G. Newton (produced 1951).
The Pink Room; or, *The Escapists* (produced 1952).
A Dead Secret (produced 1957) 1958.
Farewell, Farewell, Eugene, adaptation of a work by John Vari (produced 1959). 1960.
The Other Palace (produced 1964).
Smithereens (produced 1985).
Absolute Hell (produced 1987).
Too Clever by Half, adaptation of a work by Ostrovsky (produced 1988).

SCREENPLAYS: *Number Seventeen*, with Alfred Hitchcock and Alma Reville, 1931; *Yellow Sands*, with Michael Barringer, 1938; *Bank Holiday* (*Three on a Weekend*), with Roger Burford and Hans Wilhelm, 1938; *Keep Smiling* (*Smiling Along*), with Val Valentine, 1938; *The Silent Battle* (*Continental Express*), with Wolfgang Wilhelm, 1939; *Young Man's Fancy*, with Roland Pertwee, 1939; *An Englishman's Home*, with others, 1939; *George and Margaret*, with Brock Williams, 1940; *A Call for Arms*, 1940; *Miss Grant Goes to the Door*, 1940; *Under Your Hat*, with Anthony Kimmins and L. Green, 1940; *Rush Hour*, with Arthur Boys, 1941; *49th Parallel* (*The Invaders*) with Emeric Pressburger, 1941; *Lady Be Kind*, with Arthur Boys, 1941; *Night Watch*, with

Reg Graves, 1941; *Dangerous Moonlight (Suicide Squadron)*, with Terrence Young and Brian Desmond Hurst, 1941; *Hatter's Castle*, with Paul Merzbah and Rudolf Bernauer, 1941; *Uncensored*, with Terence Rattigan and Wolfgang Wilhelm, 1942; *The Hundred Pound Window*, with Abem Finkel and Brock Williams, 1943; *Thursday's Child*, with Donald Macardle, 1943; *The School Teacher*, 1944; *Love Story (A Lady Surrenders)*, with Leslie Arliss and Doreen Montgomery, 1944; *Wanted for Murder*, with Emeric Pressburger, 1946; *Temptation Harbour*, with Victor Skutezky and Frederic Gotfurt, 1947; *Bond Street*, with Terence Rattigan and Anatole de Grunwald, 1948; *The Queen of Spades*, with Arthur Boys, 1949.

OTHER

The Celluloid Mistress; or, The Custard Pie of Dr. Caligari (autobiography), with Elspeth Grant. 1954.

CRITICAL STUDIES: article in *Theatre World*, January 1939; preface by Romain Fanvic to *The Dark River*, 1942; interview with Frank Granville-Barker, in *Plays and Players*, September 1957; articles by Norman Marshall, in *London Magazine*, April 1965, Hilary Spurling in *Spectator*, 22 November 1968, and Raymond Marriott in *Stage*, November, 1968.

THEATRICAL ACTIVITIES

DIRECTOR: **Plays**—*Plot Twenty-One*, 1936; *The Belle of New York* by Hugh Morton, 1942; *The Dark River*, 1943; **Films**—*Lady Be Kind*, 1941; *A Letter from Home*, 1942; *Thursday's Child*, 1943; *The School Teacher*, 1944.
ACTOR: **Plays**—Medvedieff in *The Lower Depths* by Gorky, 1924; roles with the Oxford Players, and Lubin, Zozim and The He-Ancient in *Back to Methuselah* by Shaw, late 1920s; title role in *Young Woodley* by John van Druten, 1929; Young Man in *The Madonna of the Golden Hart* by Robert G. Newton, 1930; Charlie Clive in *The House with the Twisty Windows*, by May Parkington, 1930; in *Recipe for Murder* by Arnold Ridley, 1932; Joseph in *Musical Chairs* by Ronald Mackenzie, 1933; Paul in *Ballerina*, 1933; Karl Opal in *Take Heed* by Leslie Reade, 1934; Tony Willow in *Birthday*, 1934; Lariossik in *The White Guard*, 1934; Tony in *Battle Royal* by Kim Peacock, 1934; Oliver Nashwick in *After October*, 1936; Henry T. Warner in *A Case of Murder* by John Sheppard, 1939. **Films**—*The Case of Gabriel Perry*, 1935; *Alibi*, 1942.

Rodney Ackland was one of those artists who, temporarily at least, lose on the swings what they have already lost on the roundabouts. In the 1930s when much of his best work was written and performed in small theatre clubs or for short runs in West End theatres, he was highly praised by critics, referred to as "the English Chekhov", but considered too highbrow to become a popular success. The enthusiastic notices for *Strange Orchestra* cost Ackland his job with British International Pictures—the company saw no future in employing a serious writer. Now that fashions have changed and even Chekhov has become almost too respectable, Ackland is apt to be dismissed as "commercial", a practitioner of the "well-made play", for no better reason than that critics have learnt to so label a whole period in the English theatre.

His debt to Chekhov is unmistakable. Ackland's plays are organized as ant-heaps or hives in which a group of characters is arbitrarily gathered under one roof either by blood relationship (as in *Birthday* and *After October*) or by lodging together (as in *Strange Orchestra*), by belonging to the same club (*The Pink Room*), working on the same film (*The Other Palace*) or deliberately attempting to reconstruct the past (*The Dark River*). His characters have the same tendency as Chekhov's to follow separate lines of thought which surface abruptly in the middle of someone else's conversation, giving the same complex effect of mental isolation in the midst of physical conglomeration. And Ackland, like Chekhov, uses this effect to exploit the subtle range of emotional tones between comedy and tragedy—egotism, eccentricity, insensitivity, over-sensitivity shading down to loneliness, pathos and despair—intrinsic to the relationship between individuals and the more-or-less closed society of which they are part.

But the comparison with Chekhov will not go far beyond generalities. English middle-class metropolitan society of the period between the two World Wars had little in common with Russian rural society at the end of the 19th century and Ackland was a writer too faithful to his subject matter to follow Chekhov where he cannot lead. Even to use the word "society" in connection with Ackland's work rings false, since his characters are almost without exception those who have been tossed off the central wheel of their time and left lying at the edges, slightly bruised and spattered with mud, likely if they try to stand up again, as they consistently do, to be flung down flatter than before.

In his early play *Strange Orchestra* this process is somewhat too crudely demonstrated: a pair of lovers whose mutual devotion amounts to narcissism try to gas themselves; a girl jilted by a con-man goes blind as well. But, behind the obtrusively engineered story-line, the insecure, neurotic atmosphere of genteel seediness in furnished rooms—the world of Eliot's Prufock and of the typist in *The Waste Land*—is created by a careful accumulation of authentic detail. The play, like so many of Ackland's later and better ones, revolves around one of those elderly mother-figures, raffish, stalwart, broad-minded but none-too-bright, a giver and still more a taker of energy, who are perhaps his most recognizable contributions to the gallery of dramatic types.

Ackland's next play, *Birthday*, has no equal for its overtly humorous but finally savage portrait of a certain kind of English family life. The impenetrable selfishness of these people, the way they mask it as devotion to one another's interests, is expressed even in their appalling dog Jelly—surely the best part ever written for a dog—which has established such a tyranny of habit that its half-gnawed bones cannot be removed from the armchair without causing a scene. The play is weakened only by its heroine, whose attempt to escape from her family is too schematic, whose character is too unexplored, too fairy-tale, to stand up among so many realistic monsters.

No such weakness mars *After October*. It is the hero this time who has to bear the burden of a would-be escape, but although he is in himself a scarcely more realised character than the heroine of *Birthday*, his escape is altogether more tangible. The heroine of *Birthday* is dependent on love to take her away from lovelessness. The theatre is a good place for showing lovelessness and no one is better at it than Ackland, but love is another matter: even Shakespeare is apt to take refuge in formal passages about love rather than attempt a direct demonstration of the thing in action. But in *After October* the means of escape for the hero and all other characters in his train is to be his success as a playwright. The essential tawdriness of this escape—to be rich and famous instead of poor and unknown—enables Ackland to treat his hero lightly and objectively, without in any way diminishing the pathos of his disillusionment. *After October* is alive with closely observed portraits of the hero's family and friends, including Oliver Nashwick, that doyen of surly poets, whose first words on entering through the window are: "You wish I hadn't come".

Ackland's masterpiece is undoubtedly *The Dark River*, originally entitled *Remembrance of Things Past*. Its themes and characters are easily recognizable from his earlier work, the plot still turns on a failed attempt at escape from a narrowly confined group of "throw-offs", but the play is somehow on a grander and more universal scale than his others. Is this simply because explosions and shouting fascists are heard off-stage, because the little boy spells out "Guernica" from a newspaper headline, because the hero is obsessed with persuading the British government to build deep air-raid shelters? Certainly one has more of a feeling of a large world beyond the wings than in Ackland's other plays. But the sense of sombre grandeur and universality is more intrinsic than this. The characters themselves, detailed, idiosyncratic portraits as always, seem to cover more ground than before, to compose less a spectacle than an experience, drawing an audience into losses and defeats which temporarily stand for the audience's own, suggesting not simply that some unfortunates get caught in stagnant backwaters from which there is no escape, but that life itself is such a backwater when it is not infinitely worse, the approaching maelstrom that can be heard offstage.

For all the vagaries of fashion, there is not an English playwright this century more certain of being understood and loved by posterity than Ackland.

—John Spurling

ANTROBUS, John.

Born in Woolwich, London, 2 July 1933. Educated at Bishop Wordsworth Grammar School, Salisbury, Wiltshire; Selhurst Grammar School, Croydon, Surrey; King Edward VII Nautical College; Royal Military Academy, Sandhurst, Camberley, Surrey. Served in the British Army, East Surrey Regiment, 1952–55. Married Margaret McCormick in 1958 (divorced 1980); two sons and one daughter. Apprentice deck officer, Merchant Navy, 1950–52; supply teacher and waiter, 1953–54. Since 1955 freelance writer. Recipient: George Devine award, 1970; Writers Guild award, 1971; Arts Council bursary, 1973, 1976, 1980, 1982; Banff Television Festival award, 1987. Lives in London. Agent: Rogers, Coleridge, and White, 20 Powis Mews, London W11 1JN, England.

Publications

PLAYS

The Bed-Sitting Room, with Spike Milligan (also co-director: produced 1963). 1970; revised version, as *The Bed-Sitting Room 2* (also director: produced 1983).

Royal Commission Review (produced 1964).
You'll Come to Love Your Sperm Test (also director: produced 1965). In *New Writers 4*, 1965.
Cane of Honour (produced 1965).
The Missing Links (televised 1965; produced 1977). In *Why Bournemouth? and Other Plays*, 1970.
Trixie and Baba (produced 1968). 1969.
Why Bournemouth? (produced 1968). In *Why Bournemouth? and Other Plays*, 1970.
Captain Oates' Left Sock (produced 1969). 1974.
An Evening with John Antrobus (produced 1969).
Why Bournemouth? and Other Plays. 1970.
An Apple a Day (televised 1971; produced 1974). In *Why Bournemouth? and Other Plays*, 1970.
Stranger in a Cafeteria, in *Christmas Present* (produced 1971).
The Looneys (produced 1971).
Crete and Sergeant Pepper (produced 1972).
The Dinosaurs, and Certain Humiliations (produced 1973).
The Illegal Immigrant (produced 1974).
Mrs. Grabowski's Academy (produced 1975).
They Sleep Together (produced 1976).
Sketches in *City Delights* (revue; produced 1978).
Jonah (also director: produced 1979).
Hitler in Liverpool, One Orange for the Baby, Up in the Hide (produced 1980). 1983.
When Did You Last See Your Trousers?, with Ray Galton, adaptation of a story by Galton and Alan Simpson (produced 1986). 1988.

SCREENPLAYS: *Carry on Sergeant*, with Norman Hudis, 1958; *Idol on Parade*, 1959; *Jazzboat*, with Ken Hughes, 1960; *The Wrong Arm of the Law*, with others, 1962; *The Big Job*, with Talbot Rothwell, 1965; *The Bed-Sitting Room*, with Charles Wood, 1969.

RADIO WRITING: *Idiot Weekly* and *The Goon Show* series; *Brandy, Brandy*, 1972; *LMF (Lack of Moral Fibre)*, 1976; *Haute Cuisine*, 1977; *The Lie*, 1978; *In a Dry Place*, 1986; *Looneys*, 1987; *The Milligan Papers* series, 1987.

TELEVISION WRITING: *Idiot Weekly* series; *A Show Called Fred* series; *The Army Game* series; *Bootsie and Snudge* series; for Eric Sykes, Arthur Haynes, Frankie Howerd, Jimmy Wheeler shows; *Lenny the Lion Show*, 1957; *Variety Inc. Show*, 1957; *For the Children Show*, 1957; *Early to Braden* series, 1957; *The April 8th Show (Seven Days Early)*, 1958; *The Deadly Game of Chess*, 1958; *The Missing Links*, 1965; *An Apple a Day*, 1971; *Don't Feed the Fish*, 1971; *Marty Feldman Show*, 1972; *A Milligan for All Seasons*, with Spike Milligan, 1974; episode in *Too Close for Comfort*, 1984; *The Last Laugh Before T.V. AM*, with Spike Milligan, 1985; *Room at the Bottom* series, with Ray Galton, 1986 and 1987; *Alfred Hitchcock Presents*, 1987.

OTHER (for children)
The Boy with Illuminated Measles. 1978.
Help! I Am a Prisoner in a Toothpaste Factory. 1978.
Ronnie and the Haunted Rolls Royce. 1982.
Ronnie and the Great Knitted Robbery. 1982.
Pirates, with Mike Wallis. 1990.
Polo Time, with Mike Wallis. 1990.
Spooky Time, with Mike Wallis. 1990.
Picnic, with Mike Wallis. 1990.
Ronnie and the High Rise. 1992.
Ronnie and the Flying Fitted Carpet. 1992.

MANUSCRIPT COLLECTION: Mugar Memorial Library, Boston University.

THEATRICAL ACTIVITIES
DIRECTOR: **Plays**—*The Bed-Sitting Room* (co-director, with Spike Milligan), 1963; *You'll Come to Love Your Sperm Test*, 1965; *Savages* by Christopher Hampton, 1973; *Jonah*, 1979; *One Orange for the Baby*, 1980; *The Bed-Sitting Room 2*, 1983.
ACTOR: **Plays**—*You'll Come to Love Your Sperm Test*, 1965; *An Evening with John Antrobus*, 1969; Glendenning in *The Contractor* by David Storey, 1970; *Hitler in Liverpool*, 1980. **Film**—*Raising the Wind (Roommates)*, 1961; *Carry on Columbus*, 1992. **Radio**—*The Missing Links*, 1986. **Television**—*A Milligan for All Seasons*, 1974; *Squaring the Circle* by Tom Stoppard, 1986.

John Antrobus wrote his first play, *The Bed-Sitting Room*, with Spike Milligan; and though Antrobus's range has broadened, all his work has retained characteristics which are as well examined through this first play as through any other.

World War III, apparently caused by a "Nuclear Misunderstanding," mutates Lord Fortnum of Alamein into the bed-sitting room of the title. His doctor moves into the premises instead of curing his patient, a trendy vicar in a Victorian bathing costume performs a marriage service by reading from *Lady Chatterley's Lover*, and Harold Wilson becomes a parrot. It is a surrealist mock-heroic fable, then, a shell-distorted mirror to an absurd society. The Milligan element is clearly crucial; like that of *The Goon Show*, its humour may or may not be tasteful, and its vaudeville cross-talk moves from brilliant lunacy to dead trivialities. It remains hilarious—indeed it must be one of the funniest plays to come out of modern England—and it cocktails gentleness with blasphemy, pathos, beauty, desperation, and innocent reverence. The exuberance of the play gives way to tenderness in the scene at the end in which a mother cries, "Give me back my baby." But Goonishness is a fraught context for simple or naive sincerity, especially where it leads to immediate wish-fulfilment. Muddling through the ineptitude of the protagonists and the play is a strong moral concern addressed to the perennially urgent question of human survival. The play's satire, directed against politicians, vicars, advertising men, and all other regulators of modern man, is clearly rooted in Britain—as is its refusal to take itself seriously.

Ambivalences and tensions are rife in all of Antrobus's plays, and it is unclear whether these result from mere self-indulgence or from a lack of critical sense. At its worst, Antrobus's indiscipline leads to monotony, flabbiness, and garrulity; at his best Antrobus bids fair to rival Pinter; and usually, in spite of his lack of clarity and faults of his dramatic structure, Antrobus manages to be profoundly disturbing and stimulating. From a formal or technical point of view, his best work has been for radio. He is among the half dozen radio dramatists who manage to produce work which both understands and exploits the distinctive nature of radio as a medium. Antrobus is best known, however, for his work on television where both *The Army Game* and *Bootsie and Snudge* have acquired immortality.

His Christian conversion, though a conversion to Jesus rather than to dogma or denomination, seemed out of character to observers who could only see in his work brilliant if anarchic satire of the Establishment. Lying just under that hard and polished surface has been a concern, usually expressed through irony, with the deepest issues of our time: the problems posed by the "advances" of science, the nature of militarism, whether anything differentiates normalcy from madness, pretence and honesty in human relationships, the wolfish and sheepish character of such religion as is tolerated (or connived at) by those in cultural and political power, However, his conversion seems to have had no discernible effect on his work—or is the relatively conservative form of *Crete and Sergeant Pepper* part of a search for a new synthesis that is as yet only partly evident? If Antrobus can find a structure for his pyrotechnic fluidity, and grow the body of his work from that inner womb or heart which is clearly sensitive to moral and even spiritual issues, we may find his genius properly revealed instead of the individual, energetic, and zany playwright whom we have seen so far.

—Prabhu S. Guptara

ARDEN, Jane.

Born in Wales. Has two children. Director of the women's theatre company Holocaust, since 1970. Address: c/o John Calder Ltd., 18 Brewer Street, London, W1R 4AS, England.

Publications

PLAYS

Conscience and Desire, and *Dear Liz* (produced 1954).
The Party (produced 1958). 1958.
Vagina Rex and the Gas Oven (produced 1969). 1971.
A New Communion—for Freaks, Prophets and Witches (produced 1971).

SCREENPLAYS: *The Logic Game*, 1966; *Separation* (as Jane Dewar), 1968; *The Other Side of the Underneath*, 1973; *Vibration*, 1974; *Anti-Clock*, 1979.

TELEVISION PLAY: *The Thug*, 1959.

VERSE
You Don't Know What You Want, Do You? 1978.

THEATRICAL ACTIVITIES
DIRECTOR: **Film**—*The Other Side of the Underneath*, 1973.
ACTOR: **Plays**—Betty Lewis in *Dear Liz*, and Conscience in *Conscience and Desire*, 1954; Julia Craven in *The Philanderer* by Shaw, 1966. **Films**—*A Gunman Has Escaped*, 1948; *The Logic Game*, 1966; *Separation*, 1968. **Television**—*Romeo and Juliet*, 1947; *The Logic Game*, 1965; Inez in *Huis Clos*, by Sartre.

Jane Arden comments:
Biology—physics—genetics—observation of phenomena—leading to self-discovery—opening of the inner world—books (rarely)—signpost the reader to a richer textured experience of the universe-arousing the reader from his slumber—awakening him to a more illuminating perception of "being" in the world.

   Reading can be as paralysing an act (even absorbing so-called erudite works) as Bingo, if the information does not recreate the being and radicalize the behaviour. There are no such things as creative writers—some people have better radio-sets for tuning in to the only creation.

   The world needs healers, not "artists". Some of my signposts: Gurdjieff: *All and Everything*; *Tibetan Book of the Dead*; Wilhelm Reich's *Sexual Revolution*; C. Jung's *Psychology and Alchemy* and *Modern Man in Search of a Soul*; *I Chiang*; Rumi (12th century Sufi poet-saint); writings of Malcolm X.

Jane Arden is an astonishing, and perhaps even unique, figure in contemporary drama. She is impossible to categorize, and would almost certainly rebel against any attempt to do so for her work is notable for its very wide range of technical resources harnessed to serve her one main theme, which is the oppression of women in our society.

   She is a social-political writer. There are, of course, many dramatists whose motivation is primarily political and whose dynamism is derived from an urgent need to put across a particular message. But unlike them, Jane Arden has never tried to conform to the conventional structures of the theatre; the three-walled box set, the need for careful in-depth characterization, the beginning-middle-end construction are irrelevant to her. Instead she has drawn on techniques and influences from the cinema, television, and other manifestations of contemporary media (light projection, pop music). Message and the way she puts it across are closely linked: she subverts the railway tracks of the mind and of theatrical expectations.

   But this was not always so. Early in her career, as a dramatist in the most conventional manner possible, she wrote a play that is not only constructed with all the formality of conventional drama, but which was produced at a major London theatre with a major commercial cast that included Charles Laughton, Elsa Lanchester, Albert Finney, and Joyce Redman. This was *The Party*, a penetrating and often touching exploration of adolescent conflicts, providing, incidentally, some very rewarding, if wordy, roles for the actors.

   It would strain the use of hindsight beyond viability to detect in this play the seeds of Jane Arden's later development. Here her concern was with the conflict between reality and the fantasy-aspirations of the teenage heroine Henrietta, who wishes to see herself as a glamorous, wealthy, perhaps even debby type of girl. Her family and circumstances deny her all of these aspirations: the father is an alcoholic just returned from a cure, the home is grim and dingy, the mother fighting a tough battle and taking in lodgers. The play shows Henrietta's cruelty in denying the reality of her existence and eventual reconciliation with a kind of truth.

It is indeed possible to see that the women in this play are oppressed, but this oppression is accepted and in the context of the play not overtly commented upon, though as a whole the play does make a strong comment on the way in which individuals are distorted, emotionally and socially, by attempting to conform to the expectations of society.

Jane Arden did not produce another stage work until more than ten years later. But in the intervening years she became well known as an actress, and also as a speaker on television programmes usually on women and politics. She also wrote screenplays. Her next stage play appeared in 1969, was in itself sensational, and revealed the radical change that had been going on. In 1966, Jane Arden had written a film called *The Logic Game* which is described as "a surrealist puzzle attempting to locate the isolation of woman in the context of bourgeois marriage", and this was the first creative result of her increasing interest in the position of women in society. A second film came in 1968 (directed by Jack Bond). This was *Separation*, in which "the nerve of exploitation [was] more exposed, as the woman's personal dilemma began to have a political context". In these works, or explorations, Jane Arden is revealed as one of the first major voices of Women's Liberation which began to take on coherence in the late 1960s.

Meanwhile, practical developments within the theatre itself had been happening. Writers, directors, and actors were becoming increasingly discontented with the conventional theatrical forms; also with the financial/commercial situation of the theatre. And during the last years of the 1960s a number of experimental theatre groups came into being. The work shown in this context was at once more liberated politically and more liberated in form. In Jane Arden the two themes met with a production of her next play, *Vagina Rex and the Gas Oven*, which was given at the London Arts Laboratory, directed by Jack Bond.

This remains so far the most direct and intense expression of women's oppression in the theatre. Technically, it used one actress playing Woman (Sheila Allen) and one actor playing The Man (Victor Spinetti), plus a chorus of Furies, young actors and actresses who commented, took many parts, and became a sort of choreographed background. There was a pop group and much use of projection, lights, and varying sounds. Throughout, the techniques and images are used with a sound dramatic fluency that makes *Vagina Rex* outstanding as a political tract that is also extremely compelling theatre.

In *Vagina Rex* Jane Arden exposes every nerve related to the inferior, passive position of women. It caused considerable comment, one of the most ironic being a trendy Sunday newspaper's piece called "Are Women oppressed?" — "as though there was still some doubt about the matter", Jane Arden comments. In 1971, Jane Arden's next play *A New Communion — for Freaks, Prophets and*

Witches was produced in Edinburgh and London. It had an all-female cast and explored the themes in more detail. *Vagina Rex* related women firmly to men and to the pre-ordained social role expected of women. *A New Communion* internalized the themes, and the expression "women's rage" was made real.

Jane Arden's later work is excellent to read and gripping to watch when superbly performed, but it is doubtful whether it will be possible to perform *Vagina Rex* or *A New Communion* outside the context of a specialist and committed company of players. These plays are essentially products of a time and a place.

—Roger Baker

ARDEN, John.

Born in Barnsley, Yorkshire, 26 October 1930. Educated at schools in Barnsley; Sedbergh School, Yorkshire, 1944–48; King's College, Cambridge, 1950–53, B.A. in architecture 1953; Edinburgh College of Art, 1953–55, diploma in architecture 1955. Served in the British Army Intelligence Corps, 1949–50: lance-corporal. Married the actress Margaretta Ruth D'Arcy, *q.v.*, in 1957; five sons (one deceased). Architectural assistant, London, 1955–57; full-time writer from 1958. Fellow in playwriting, Bristol University, 1959–60; visiting lecturer in politics and drama, New York University, 1967; Regents' lecturer, University of California, Davis, 1973; writer-in-residence, University of New England, Armidale, New South Wales, 1975. Founder, Committee of 100 anti-nuclear group, 1961; chair *Peace News* pacifist weekly, London, 1966–70; co-founder, Corrandulla Arts and Entertainment, County Galway, Ireland, 1973; founding member, Theatre Writers' Group (now Theatre Writers' Union), 1975. Recipient: BBC Northern Region prize, 1957; Encyclopaedia Britannica prize, 1959; *Evening Standard* award, 1960; Trieste Festival award, 1961; Vernon Rice award, 1966; John Whiting award, 1973 PEN Macmillan Silver Pen award, 1992. Lives in Galway. Agent: Casarotto Ramsay Ltd., National House, 60–66 Wardour Street, London W1V 3HP, England.

Publications

PLAYS

All Fall Down (produced 1955).

The Waters of Babylon (produced 1957). In *Three Plays*, 1964.

When Is a Door Not a Door? (produced 1958). In *Soldier, Soldier and Other Plays*, 1967.

Live Like Pigs (produced 1958). In *New English Dramatists 3*, 1961; in *Three Plays*, 1964.

Serjeant Musgrave's Dance: An Unhistorical Parable (produced 1959). 1960; revised version (produced 1972).

The Happy Haven, with Margaretta D'Arcy (produced 1960). In *New English Dramatists 4*, 1962; in *Three Plays*, 1964.

Soldier, Soldier (televised 1960). In *Soldier, Soldier and Other Plays*, 1967.

The Business of Good Government: A Christmas Play, with Margaretta

D'Arcy (also co-director: as *A Christmas Play*, produced 1960; as *The Business of Good Government*, produced 1978). 1963.

Wet Fish (televised 1961). In *Soldier, Soldier and Other Plays*, 1967.

The Workhouse Donkey: A Vulgar Melodrama (produced 1963). 1964.

Ironhand, adaptation of a play by Goethe (produced 1963). 1965.

Armstrong's Last Goodnight: An Exercise in Diplomacy (produced 1964). 1965.

Ars Longa, Vita Brevis (for children), with Margaretta D'Arcy (produced 1964). In *Eight Plays 1*, edited by Malcolm Stuart Fellows, 1965.

Three Plays. 1964.

Play Without Words (produced 1965).

Fidelio, adaptation of a libretto by Joseph Sonnleithner and Friedrich Treitschke, music by Beethoven (produced 1965).

Left-Handed Liberty: A Play about Magna Carta (produced 1965). 1965.

Friday's Hiding, with Margaretta D'Arcy (produced 1966). In *Soldier, Soldier and Other Plays*, 1967.

The Royal Pardon; or, The Soldier Who Became an Actor (for children), with Margaretta D'Arcy (also co-director: produced 1966). 1967.

Soldier, Soldier and Other Plays. 1967.

The True History of Squire Jonathan and His Unfortunate Treasure (produced 1968). In *Two Autobiographical Plays*, 1971.

The Hero Rises Up: A Romantic Melodrama, with Margaretta D'Arcy (also co-director: produced 1968). 1969.

The Soldier's Tale, adaptation of a libretto by Ramuz, music by Stravinsky (produced 1968).

Harold Muggins Is a Martyr, with Margaretta D'Arcy and the Cartoon Archetypical Slogan Theatre (produced 1968).

The Bagman; or, The Impromptu of Muswell Hill (broadcast 1970). In *Two Autobiographical Plays*, 1971.

Two Autobiographical Plays. 1971.

Two Hundred Years of Labour History, with Margaretta D'Arcy (produced 1971).

Granny Welfare and the Wolf, with Margaretta D'Arcy and Roger Smith (produced 1971).

My Old Man's a Tory, with Margaretta D'Arcy (produced 1971).

Rudi Dutschke Must Stay, with Margaretta D'Arcy (produced 1971).

The Ballygombeen Bequest, with Margaretta D'Arcy (produced 1972). In *Scripts 9*, September 1972; revised version, as *The Little Gray Home in the West: An Anglo-Irish Melodrama* (produced 1982), 1982.

The Island of the Mighty: A Play on a Traditional British Theme, with Margaretta D'Arcy (produced 1972; section produced, as *Handful of Watercress*, 1976). 1974; in *Performance* 1974.

The Devil and the Parish Pump, with Margaretta D'Arcy and Corrandulla Arts and Entertainment (produced 1974).

The Crown Strike Play, with Margaretta D'Arcy and the Galway Theatre Workshop (produced 1974).

The Non-Stop Connolly Show: A Dramatic Cycle of Continuous Struggle in Six Parts, with Margaretta D'Arcy (also co-director: produced 1975). 5 vols., 1977–78; 1 vol. edition, 1986.

Sean O'Scrudu, with Margaretta D'Arcy and the Galway Theatre Workshop (produced 1976).
The Mongrel Fox, with Margaretta D'Arcy and the Galway Theatre Workshop (produced 1976).
No Room at the Inn, with Margaretta D'Arcy (produced 1976).
Silence, with Margaretta D'Arcy and the Galway Theatre Workshop (produced 1977).
Mary's Name, with Margaretta D'Arcy and the Galway Theatre Workshop (produced 1977).
Blow-in Chorus for Liam Cosgrave, with Margaretta D'Arcy and the Galway Theatre Workshop (produced 1977).
Plays 1 (includes *Serjeant Musgrave's Dance, The Workhouse Donkey, Armstrong's Last Goodnight*). 1977.
Vandaleur's Folly: An Anglo-Irish Melodrama, with Margaretta D'Arcy (also co-director: produced 1978). 1981.
Pearl: A Play about a Play Within the Play (broadcast 1978). 1979.
The Old Man Sleeps Alone (broadcast 1982). In *Best Radio Plays of 1982*, 1983.
The Mother, with Margaretta D'Arcy, adaptation of a play by Brecht (produced 1984).
The Making of Muswell Hill, with Margaretta D'Arcy (produced 1984).
Whose Is the Kingdom?, with Margaretta D'Arcy (broadcast 1988). 1988.

RADIO PLAYS: *The Life of Man*, 1956; *The Bagman*, 1970; *Keep These People Moving!* (for children), with Margaretta D'Arcy, 1972; *Pearl*, 1978; *To Put It Frankly*, 1979; *Don Quixote*, from the novel by Cervantes, 1980; *The Winking Goose* (documentary), 1982; *Garland for a Hoar Head*, 1982; *The Old Man Sleeps Alone*, 1982; *The Manchester Enthusiasts*, (in two parts) with Margaretta D'Arcy, 1984, (in three parts), as *The Ralahine Experiment*, 1985; *Whose Is the Kingdom?*, with Margaretta D'Arcy, 1988.

TELEVISION PLAYS: *Soldier, Soldier*, 1960; *Wet Fish*, 1961; *Sean O'Casey: Portrait of a Rebel* (documentary), with Margaretta D'Arcy, 1973 (Ireland).

NOVELS

Silence among the Weapons: Some Events at the Time of the Failure of a Republic. 1982; as *Vox Pop: Last Days of the Roman Republic*, 1983.
Books of Bale: A Fiction of History. 1988.

SHORT STORIES
Cogs Tyrannic. 1991.

OTHER

To Present the Pretence: Essays on the Theatre and Its Public. 1977.
Awkward Corners: Essays, Papers, Fragments, with Margaretta D'Arcy. 1988.

BIBLIOGRAPHY: *Arden on File* edited by Malcolm Page, 1985.

CRITICAL STUDIES: *John Arden* by Ronald Hayman, 1968; *Theatre Language: A Study of Arden, Osborne, Pinter, and Wesker* by John Russell Brown, 1972; *John Arden* by Simon Trussler, 1973; *John Arden* by Glenda Leeming, 1974; *Arden: A Study of His Plays* by Albert Hunt, 1974; *Anger and Detachment: A Study of Arden, Osborne, and Pinter* by Michael Anderson, 1976; *John Arden* by Frances Gray, 1982; *John Arden* by Malcolm Page, 1984, and *Arden on File* edited by Page, 1985.

THEATRICAL ACTIVITIES
DIRECTOR with Margaretta D'Arcy: several of his own plays.
ACTOR: **Plays**—Wise Man in *A Christmas Play*, 1960; Constable in *The Royal Pardon*, 1966; Mr. Muggins in *Harold Muggins Is a Martyr*, 1968.

John Arden comments:

(1977) At the present time the gap between the playwright and the active life of the theatre seems as wide as it has ever been: and it shows no sign of closing. Figures such as the director and the scenic designer, whose relevance to good dramatic writing is at best marginal, have increased their power and influence in no small measure during the past few years: and they stand ominously between playwright and actors, inhibiting proper communication. The *content* of new plays is obscured and neutralized by over-emphasis on aesthetic theatrical *form*. The dependence of the dramatic art upon subsidies from public funds has given rise to a bureaucratic intransigence on the part of directors, who are too often administrators as well, and are becoming less and less inclined to take the necessary risks demanded by adventurous and expanding experiment. The problem is similar to that faced by Ben Jonson in the 1620's, when he struck out against the dominance of Inigo Jones as designer-director of court entertainment, and lost his battle. The result of Jones's victory was the securing by the monarchy of the complete allegiance of the theatrical profession, followed by the closure of the theatres during the Cromwellian revolution. The playwrights, as a trade-grouping, never again recaptured the position of artistic strength and poetic potency which they had attained at the beginning of the 17th century. To forestall an equivalent disaster today, the modern dramatists must attempt two apparently contradictory tasks. 1) They must abandon their solitary status and learn to combine together to secure conditions-of-work and artistic control over the products of their imagination. 2) They must be prepared to combine not only with their fellows, but also with *actors*. It is not enough for the occasional author to *direct*; playwrights should be members of theatrical troupes, and take part in all aspects of production. In order to achieve goal 2), goal 1) must first be arrived at. The authors together must establish the importance of their written work as an essential *internal* element of the theatre, and then, individually, they must become absorbed into the theatre themselves as co-workers.

I am aware that these requirements go against all current trends. But the current trends are running towards the complete death of the modern drama. Remember, Shakespeare and Molière regarded themselves as men of the theatre rather than *literary* figures: and I believe it to be no accident that their works remain unequalled in the Western tradition.

A glance at John Arden's bibliography suggests that the entire opus of his work rests in his collaboration with his wife, Margaretta D'Arcy, for they have together produced a wealth of plays for both stage and radio, and Arden himself has not written for the stage for nearly 20 years. However, his handful of plays are generally acknowledged, by both critics and contemporaries, to be seminal to the modern British theatre, arguably classics within the lifetime of their author.

Arden's plays break through the confinements of realism by using open staging; broad, poetic language; characters bordering on caricature; complex visual imagery; active social settings; and an appropriation of traditional "popular" forms, like music-hall and medieval theatre, to dramatise the interactive effects of concepts, ideas, and social organisation on social, personal, and political life.

The scope and complexity of the plays, however, have often given rise to critical confusion, arguably owing to the very elements that have led to their acclaim, for change in form necessarily signals changes in perspective and concern. Thus, "realist" readings of a non-realist play will invariably cause confusion and misunderstanding. Bemusement over Arden's plays seem to stem from the assumption that whatever the form of the work, a play will inevitably boil down to an elaboration of human emotion, eliciting sympathy for the individual and taking a clear, simple literal moral stance, especially if it deals with social and moral issues.

For example, critics became focused on deciding whether *Serjeant Musgrave's Dance* was "pro" pacifism. A more inclusive view of the play, however, renders the question irrelevant. The play patently is not promoting war. No argument is proposed to polarise pacifism against war-mongering; rather, pacifism serves as the context, not the content of the play. That is, the play assumes its audience finds war, per se, undesirable, and this premise establishes the terms by which the relationship between means and ends may be dramatised.

Since on the whole we will agree that war is, generally, undesirable, we will also agree that Musgrave's aim to put an end to all war is commendable. Assuming that the audience is in accordance with Musgrave's purpose, the play turns our attention from his intentions to his actions: from his desired goal, which we share, to the means by which he pursues it; means which, in turn, produce their own ends contradictory to his original goal. Hence, through Musgrave we experience the process by which even the finest of intentions becomes corrupted by the means employed for its accomplishment, and we are called to assess the terms of their validity.

Our introduction to Musgrave through the effect he has on others prepares us to look towards action and consequence rather than explanation, to judge by effect rather than rationale. His soldiers prepare us for a man to admire: organised, commanding, demanding respect. His uniform and his confident manner suggest qualities our society admires: order, organisation, "God-fearing," and, above all, logic and reason. Alas, these are the very qualities which drive him to his horrifying conclusion. When Musgrave—steeped in simple fundamental religious belief, a soldier's training and discipline, a life of careful order and authority, and, especially, a total faith in logical thought—is confronted with the horrible chaos of war (to which he has devoted his life), he inevitably uses the only means he has to create a plan to annihilate war. His solution is neat, ordered, completely logical, and has, in his eyes, the blessing of God. His intentions are good; the result is destructive and insane. Musgrave's insight that the source of war lies with ordinary people who let their husbands and sons become cannon fodder has a certain validity, but his plan for eliminating war is both unacceptable and futile.

The opposition set up in *Serjeant Musgrave's Dance* is not between war and peace but between social ideals of order, organisation, and logic in contrast to the "messy scribbling" of day-to-day existence; the erratic demands of emotion and need. The extreme opposite to Musgrave is the Bargee, an unattractive picture of daily survival unhampered by principle or design. Near Musgrave, the Mayor and Parson organize fumblingly for their own ends. In the middle, the women and the miners with their needs, passions, and inconsistencies, their morals based more on experience than ideals. The play provides an analysis of the social precepts of order and reason as they are superimposed on the chaos of ordinary life.

Serjeant Musgrave's Dance also challenges the realist premises that good intentions mitigate behavior and that reason can solve all human problems, by calling "reason" into question. Annie's importance, for example, is not that she will sleep with any man but that her act of lovemaking is an act of revivification. Arden neither promotes nor condemns promiscuity, but contrasts the effect of Annie's actions with the imposed purity of Musgrave's orderliness.

Arden's vision is essentially anarchic. Ideals of organisation and reason distort human life. War itself is the result of order imposed on human existence. The entrance of the Dragoons to restore "order" and save us all from Musgrave may bring some relief, but it also brings an inescapable sense of failure.

The playwright's organization subverts the audience's preconception of order. Arden's use of the open stage, his ballads and heightened language, his frequent placing of more than one character at the centre of the action are devices to turn attention away from personalisation and simple moralising towards an examination of the practical functioning of these moral precepts in the social context. In *The Workhouse Donkey*, for example, it is fruitless to complain that none of the politicians is blameless. "Misgoverned," says Sweetman, "Oh, it's not exactly misgoverned. It's just the wrong lot are the governers, that's all." The play assumes that power corrupts. The difference between Labour and Tory is not corruptibility, but the form their corruption takes and to what end. The involvement of Feng, the incorruptible policeman, in this cosily untidy world takes us into an examination of the consequences of obsessive morality imposed on an imperfect world. As Arden says, Feng's absolute integrity causes infinitely more damage than Butterthwaite's bumbling dishonesty could ever manage. Feng lacks warmth and compassion for the catch-as-catch-can bustle of ordinary life. Butterthwaite's warmth and human failings endear us to him despite his imperfections. Assuming a world of general imperfection, Arden attempts to turn attention away from abstract ideals of simplistic morality and towards the effect of these ideals when they are put into practice without regard for the fundamental anarchy of daily living.

Arden's theatrical devices distance the audience from the characters so they might be seen as active members of working societies. No better or worse than others, these societies run, as by implication all do, on moral precepts that have both weaknesses and strengths. When one of these little worlds is confronted by another which does not share its assumptions, the characters find themselves in extreme situations which threaten these social preconceptions. The consequences and effects of these actions dramatize the complex relationships between the individual and society, between social ideals and their practical application, between means and end.

Live Like Pigs can be read as a confrontation between two ways of living, acceptable enough in themselves, but mutually destructive in confrontation. This pattern is most richly and tragically elaborated in *Armstrong's Last Goodnight*. Through Lindsay and Armstrong, the weaknesses and inner workings of their societies are set in relief. Neither Armstrong nor Lindsay is a villain. Each is the perfect representative of his society, but their worlds are different, with different ways of ordering and interpreting life, different moral concepts, different ideals. Both can enlist our sympathy: Armstrong, leader in an individualist world of action; Lindsay, spokesman for the King in an integrated world of reason. Each society, in its own terms, is perfectly viable. However, they are entirely incompatible.

Though both live in Scotland, Lindsay and Armstrong inhabit realities so different they can hardly speak to each other. The way each sees and evaluates the world excludes the world of the other. (When Lindsay tells Armstrong's wife he has come from the King, she answers "What King would that be?" Even such a simple concept as "King" is not shared.) The play's scenes are juxtaposed to emphasize the misinterpretations and incompatibilities. The use of the stage itself—with James's court on one side and Armstrong's castle on the other—presents a visual image of the distance between the two worlds. Clothing imagery eleborates the social symbols of value and role and marks the opposing experiences of the characters. It is not that one is right and one wrong, but rather that each, though wholly consistent within itself, is incompatible with the other. Yet, Lindsay's quest is to integrate the two.

The moral precepts that have been the strengths of each society are shown to also be their weaknesses as they are forced to the surface in the confrontation. Armstrong's dashing individualism leads him to his death. Lindsay's belief in reason is destroyed as his reasonable, organised society destroys Armstrong and the world he represents. We are not asked to judge the moral precepts informing these worlds so much as to wonder at the fact that despite their opposing orders and moralities, they resort to the same exact manner of dealing with threats—Wamphrey and Armstrong are executed on the same tree, victims of the same kind of treachery. Attention is turned from the superficialities of abstract moral judgement to the exacting examination of the execution of moral ideals in an imperfect world.

Arden's formal changes in his plays demand a shift from simplistic moralising to dramatic investigation, a transfer from idealised expectations and easy judgements to responsible application and political analysis that transcends the simple taking of sides.

Since his disengagement with the conventional theatre, Arden has collaborated with Margaretta D'Arcy on a host of works for both theatre and radio, hard-hitting, energetic pieces which overtly draw on "popular" theatre forms—music-hall, melodrama, living theatre. Directly confronting socio-political issues, their most salient quality is their expression of community. The plays not only confront community issues but are often the product of community cooperation. Thus, both form and content reflect the socio-political commitments of their collaborators.

Arden has also written radio plays which make full use of the vast canvas offered by the medium and continue his unblinkered investigation of socio-political dynamics including, unsurprisingly, the question of the artist's function in his society.

—Elaine Turner

See the essay on *Serjeant Musgrave's Dance.*

AYCKBOURN, Alan.

Born in London, 12 April 1939. Educated at Haileybury, Hertford, 1952–56. Married Christine Roland in 1959; two sons. Stage manager and actor, Donald Wolfit's company, in Edinburgh, Worthing, Leatherhead, Scarborough, and Oxford, 1956–57; actor and stage manager, Stephen Joseph Theatre-in-the-Round, Scarborough, Yorkshire, 1957–62; associate director, Victoria Theatre, Stoke-on-Trent, Staffordshire, 1962–64; drama producer, BBC Radio, Leeds, 1964–70. Since 1970 artistic director, Stephen Joseph Theatre-in-the-Round; associate director, National Theatre, London, 1986–88; professor of contemporary theatre, Oxford University, 1991–92. Recipient: *Evening Standard* award, 1973, 1974, 1977, 1985, 1987, 1989, 1990; Olivier award, 1985; *Plays and Players* award, 1987. D.Litt.: University of Hull, Yorkshire, 1981; University of Keele, Staffordshire, 1987; University of Leeds, 1987. C.B.E. (Commander, Order of the British Empire), 1987. Agent: Casarotto Ramsay Ltd., National House, 60–66 Wardour Street, London WIV 3HP, England.

Publications

PLAYS

The Square Cat (as Roland Allen) (produced 1959).
Love after All (as Roland Allen) (produced 1959).
Dad's Tale (for children; as Roland Allen) (produced 1960).
Standing Room Only (as Roland Allen) (also director: produced 1961).
Xmas v. Mastermind (produced 1962).
Mr. Whatnot (also director: produced 1963; revised version produced 1964). 1992.
Relatively Speaking (as *Meet My Father*, produced 1965; as *Relatively Speaking*, produced 1967). 1968.
The Sparrow (also director: produced 1967).
How the Other Half Loves (also director: produced 1969). 1972.

Countdown, in *We Who Are about to . . .*, later called *Mixed Doubles* (produced 1969). 1970.

Ernie's Incredible Illucinations (for children; produced 1971). 1969; in *The Best Short Plays 1979*, edited by Stanley Richards, 1979.

The Story So Far (also director: produced 1970; revised version, as *Me Times Me Times Me*, produced 1971; revised version, as *Family Circles*, produced 1978).

Time and Time Again (also director: produced 1971). 1973.

Absurd Person Singular (also director: produced 1972). In *Three Plays*, 1977.

Mother Figure, in *Mixed Blessings* (produced 1973).

The Norman Conquests: Table Manners, Living Together, Round and Round the Garden (also director: produced 1973). 1975.

Absent Friends (also director: produced 1974). In *Three Plays*, 1977.

Confusions: Mother Figure, Drinking Companion, Between Mouthfuls, Gosforth's Fête, A Talk in the Park (also director: produced 1974). 1977.

Jeeves, music by Andrew Lloyd Webber, adaptation of works by P.G. Wodehouse (produced 1975).

Bedroom Farce (also director: produced 1975). In *Three Plays*, 1977.

Just Between Ourselves (also director: produced 1976). In *Joking Apart, Ten Times Table, Just Between Ourselves*, 1979.

Three Plays. 1977.

Ten Times Table (also director: produced 1977). In *Joking Apart, Ten Times Table, Just Between Ourselves*, 1979.

Joking Apart (also director: produced 1978). In *Joking Apart, Ten Times Table, Just Between Ourselves*, 1979.

Men on Women on Men, music by Paul Todd (produced 1978).

Joking Apart, Ten Times Table, Just Between Ourselves. 1979; augmented edition, as *Joking Apart and Other Plays* (includes *Sisterly Feelings*), 1982.

Sisterly Feelings (also director: produced 1979). With *Taking Steps*, 1981.

Taking Steps (also director: produced 1979). With *Sisterly Feelings*, 1981.

Suburban Strains, music by Paul Todd (also director: produced 1980). 1982.

First Course, music by Paul Todd (also director: produced 1980).

Second Helping, music by Paul Todd (also director: produced 1980).

Season's Greetings (also director: produced 1980; revised version, also director: produced 1982). 1982.

Way Upstream (also director: produced 1981). 1983.

Making Tracks, music by Paul Todd (also director: produced 1981).

Me, Myself, and I, music by Paul Todd (also director: produced 1981). 1989.

Intimate Exchanges (also director: produced 1982). 2 vols., 1985.

A Trip to Scarborough, adaptation of the play by Sheridan (also director: produced 1982).

Incidental Music (produced 1983).

It Could Be Any One of Us (also director: produced 1983).

The Seven Deadly Virtues, music by Paul Todd (also director: produced 1984).

A Cut in the Rates (televised 1984). 1991.

The Westwoods (also director: produced 1984).

A Game of Golf (produced 1984).

A Chorus of Disapproval (also director: produced 1984). 1986.

Woman in Mind (also director: produced 1985). 1986.

Boy Meets Girl, music by Paul Todd (also director: produced 1985).
Girl Meets Boy, music by Paul Todd (also director: produced 1985).
Mere Soup Songs, music by Paul Todd (also director: produced 1986).
Tons of Money, adaptation of the farce by Will Evans and Valentine (also
   director: produced 1986). 1986.
A Small Family Business (also director: produced 1987). 1988.
Henceforward (also director: produced 1987).1988.
Vaudeville (produced 1988).
Mr. A's Amazing Maze Plays (for children) (also director: produced 1988).
   1989.
Man of the Moment (also director: produced 1988). 1990.
The Revengers' Comedies (also director: produced 1989). 1991.
Invisible Friends (for children) (also director: produced 1989). 1991.
Body Language (also director: produced 1990).
This Is Where We Came In (for children) (also director: produced 1990).
Callis to 5 (for children) (also director: produced 1990).
My Very Own Story (for children) (also director: produced 1991).
Wildest Dreams (also director: produced 1991).
Time of My Life (also director: produced 1992). 1993.
Between the Lines, music by Paul Todd (produced 1992).
Dreams From a Summer House, music by John Pattison (produced 1992).
Wolf at the Door, adaptation of a play by Henry Becque. 1993.

TELEVISION PLAYS: *Service Not Included (Masquerade* series), 1974; *A Cut in
the Rates*, 1984.

OTHER
Conversations with Ayckbourn, with Ian Watson. 1981.

CRITICAL STUDIES: *Theatre in the Round* by Stephen Joseph, 1967; *The Second
Wave* by John Russell Taylor, 1971; *Post-War British Theatre* by John Elsom,
1976, revised edition, 1979; *The New British Drama* by Oleg Kerensky, 1977;
Alan Ayckbourn by Michael Billington, 1983, revised edition, 1990; *File on
Ayckbourn*, edited by Malcolm Page, 1989; *Alan Ayckbourn: A Casebook* by
Bernard F. Dukore, 1991.

THEATRICAL ACTIVITIES
DIRECTOR: **Plays**—numerous productions at Victoria Theatre, Stoke-on-Trent,
and Stephen Joseph Theatre, Scarborough, including *Miss Julie* by Strindberg,
Pygmalion by Shaw, *A Man for All Seasons* by Robert Bolt, *Patriotic Bunting*
and *Tishoo* by Brian Thompson, *Time and the Conways* by J. B. Priestley, *The
Crucible* by Arthur Miller, *The Seagull* by Chekhov, *Thark* and *Rookery Nook*
by Ben Travers, and many of his own plays; *Way Upstream*, 1982, *A Chorus
of Disapproval*, 1985, *Tons of Money* by Will Evans and Valentine, 1986, *A
View from the Bridge* by Arthur Miller, 1987, *A Small Family Business*, 1987,
'Tis Pity She's a Whore by John Ford, 1988, and *The Haunt of Mr. Fossett* by
Stephen Mallatratt, 1988. Radio—more than 100 productions, Leeds,
1964–70, and subsequently.

ACTOR: **Plays**—roles with Stephen Joseph's touring company: The Cook in *Little Brother, Little Sister* by David Campton, 1961; Victoria Theatre, Stoke-on-Trent: Fred in *The Birds and the Wellwishers* and Robert in *An Awkward Number* by William Norfolk, Aston in *The Caretaker*, James in *The Collection*, and Ben in *The Dumb Waiter*, by Harold Pinter, title role in *O'Flaherty, V.C.* by G. B. Shaw, Roderick Usher in *Usher* by David Campton, Bill Starbuck in *The Rainmaker* by N. Richard Nash, The Crimson Gollywog in *Xmas v. Mastermind*, The Count in *The Rehearsal* by Anouilh, Vladimir in *Waiting for Godot* by Beckett, Thomas More in *A Man for All Seasons* by Robert Bolt, Jordan in *The Rainbow Machine* and Anderson in *Ted's Cathedral* by Alan Plater, Jerry Ryan in *Two for the Seesaw* by William Gibson, Mr. Manningham in *Gaslight* by Patrick Hamilton, The Interrogator in *The Prisoner* by Bridget Boland, and A Jew and Martin del Bosco in *The Jew of Malta* by Marlowe, 1962–64.

In the early part of Alan Ayckbourn's career, discussion often turned on his method of playwriting, announcing a title and then, three or four days before rehearsals were due to start, shutting himself away to write. Ayckbourn responded by stressing that he was only a dramatist once a year, occasionally twice, and was primarily a director, of the Stephen Joseph Theatre-in-the-Round in Scarborough. (He cleverly, and uniquely, appeared in print, presenting his view of his writings, in *Conversations with Ayckbourn*, ahead of any books of criticism.)

Ayckbourn's early plays, such as *Relatively Speaking* and *Time and Time Again*, are polished and amusing. (As Ayckbourn's titles rarely point unmistakeably to the content, distinguishing between the plays is initially difficult.) His distinctive ingenuity is first shown in *How the Other Half Loves*, in which a couple attend two different dinner parties, on different days, at the same time. *Absurd Person Singular* has its three scenes on three consecutive Christmas Eves, in three different kitchens, featuring the same three married couples: a fastidious tidiness. *The Norman Conquests* is a trilogy about the events of one weekend; it shows what is happening in a dining-room, sitting-room, and garden. The plays are designed to make sense in any order, or indeed if only one is seen. *Bedroom Farce* somehow steers eight people into three onstage bedrooms. *Sisterly Feelings* has alternative second and third acts (the choice of which is to be played determined by tossing a coin at the end of Acts 1 and 2) leading to the same fourth act. *Taking Steps* is set on different floors of a three-storey house, but "really" there is only one floor. In *It Could Be Any One of Us* Ayckbourn essays the comedy thriller, with five different endings convicting each of the suspects. *Intimate Exchanges* has two first acts, four second acts, eight third acts, and 16 fourth acts. Each episode concludes with a choice, and Ayckbourn has written the scenes for both choices. Further, the time between acts is always five days, then five weeks and finally five years, and the fourth acts are all in a churchyard, variously following weddings, christenings, funerals, and Harvest Festivals. To make his task even harder, the whole is for one actor and one actress, playing two or three parts in every version.

Ayckbourn's first attempt to write, in his phrase, "a truly hilarious dark play" is *Absurd Person Singular*. In the middle act a woman attempts suicide by several methods, while a stream of kind visitors fail to see her misery and instead clean her oven and mend her light. The comic-sinister ending has an obnoxious man dictatorially imposing party games on a group who want nothing to do with him. In *Absent Friends*, Ayckbourn's most restrained and sombre work, five people gather for a Saturday afternoon tea party to cheer Colin, whom they have not seen for some years and whose fiancée drowned two months before. Colin proves to be cheerful, which exposes the unhappiness of the rest.

Just Between Ourselves was Ayckbourn's first "Winter Play," written for January production when "the pressure that had always been on me to produce a play suited primarily to a holiday audience was no longer there." In this work he shows how a well-meaning husband drives his wife to insanity through relentless cheerfulness and optimism. The second scene ends with a disastrous tea party at which everyone tries not to focus on the forgotten birthday cake and the likelihood of accidents by the tense wife. In the extraordinary climax of the third scene, wildly funny and deeply tragic, the wife goes insane. While her husband has become entangled inside the car with the steering-wheel, seat belts, and a neighbouring woman, to whom he is demonstrating it, his wife quarrels with her mother-in-law and pursues her with a roaring electric drill. The car horn "blasts loudly and continuously," then a birthday cake is carried in and lights are switched on "bathing the scene in a glorious technicolour." Four months later the wife is seen again, sitting silent in the garden in January. Throughout this chilling scene she stares out blankly, speechless, motionless, as grim an image as any in Beckett.

Joking Apart sets its four scenes on special occasions: Guy Fawkes Night, Boxing Day, an 18th-birthday party. The scenes are four years apart, so the seven characters are seen over 12 years, from their twenties to their thirties. *Joking Apart* studies winners and losers, a likeable, generous, hospitable couple (who, significantly, have never bothered to get married) and their circle. Ayckbourn illuminates the sadness intrinsic to the way the world has born winners, and the less obvious fact that other people shrink through contrasting themselves with the winners. Similar emotional bleakness, and the same misgivings about the married state, are found in *The Story So Far* and *Season's Greetings*.

Two plays represent changes of direction. *Way Upstream* is about three couples struggling with a cabin cruiser on a week's river trip. As their journey is to Armageddon Bridge, allegory is intended: the decent, unassertive moderates (perhaps Social Democrats) eventually realise they must fight authoritarianism, capitalism, and the idle rich. *Woman in Mind* extends what has been called Comedy of Pain. Hit on the head by a garden rake, a concussed wife copes with her unsympathetic family and fantasizes an ideal family as well—which may not be as delightful as it seems. As her husband is a vicar, Ayckbourn is alluding to the failings of religion, with central themes of dislocation and unfulfilled existences.

The darker vision, of society and of individuals, has dominated in the plays from 1986 on. Ayckbourn's recent plays for children (or for families) have been described as "Stoppard for tots," playful approaches to reality and the illusion of theatre. Michael Billington in 1974 tried to place Ayckbourn as "a left-wing writer using a right-wing form; even if there is nothing strident, obvious or noisy about his socialism, it is none the less apparent that he has a real detestation for the money-grubber, the status-seeker and the get-rich-quicker." Martin Bronstein emphasises the feminism: "He's the only contemporary playwright who shows the real plight of the average woman in today's world." Ayckbourn himself has never admitted to such intentions; instead he speaks of examining "the Chekhovian field, exploring attitudes to death, loneliness, etc. — themes not generally dealt with in comedy." All Ayckbourn's work is amusing and ingenious; his greatest moments are those that combine laughs and true seriousness about the human condition — or at least the present condition of the English middle classes.

—Malcolm Page

See the essay on *The Norman Conquests*.

B

BAGNOLD, Enid (Algerine).

Born in Rochester, Kent, 27 October 1889. Educated at Prior's Field, Godalming, Surrey, in Marburg, Germany, Lausanne, Switzerland, and at the Villa Leona, Paris; studied painting with Walter Sickert. Served as a driver with the French Army and as a nurse in a London hospital during World War I. Married Sir Roderick Jones in 1920 (died 1962); three sons and one daughter. Journalist, *Hearth and Home*, London, 1912. Recipient: Arts Theatre prize, 1951; American Academy Award of Merit, 1956. C.B.E. (Commander, Order of the British Empire), 1976. *Died 31 March 1981.*

Publications

Plays

Lottie Dundass (produced 1942). 1941.
National Velvet, from her own novel (produced 1946). 1961.
Poor Judas (produced 1946). In *Two Plays,* 1951.
Two Plays (includes *Lottie Dundass* and *Poor Judas*). 1951; as *Theatre: Two Plays,* 1951.
Gertie (produced 1952; as *Little Idiot,* produced 1953).
The Chalk Garden (produced 1955). 1956.
The Last Joke (produced 1960). In *Four Plays,* 1970.
The Chinese Prime Minister (produced 1964). 1964.
Call Me Jacky (produced 1968). In *Four Plays,* 1970; revised version, as *A Matter of Gravity* (produced 1975). 1978.
Four Plays (includes *The Chalk Garden, The Last Joke, The Chinese Prime Minister, Call Me Jacky*). 1970.

Novels

The Happy Foreigner. 1920.
Serena Blandish; or, The Difficulty of Getting Married. 1924.
National Velvet. 1935.
The Squire. 1938; as *The Door of Life,* 1938.
The Loved and Envied. 1951.
The Girl's Journey: Containing The Happy Foreigner and The Squire. 1954.

Verse

The Sailing Ships and Other Poems. 1918.
Poems. 1978.
Early Poems. 1987.

OTHER

A Diary Without Dates. 1918.
Alice and Thomas and Jane (for children). 1930.
Autobiography: From 1889. 1969; revised edition, 1985.
Letters to Frank Harris and Other Friends, edited by R.P. Lister. 1980.

Translator, *Alexander of Asia*, by Princess Marthe Bibesco. 1935.

CRITICAL STUDY: *Bagnold: The Authorized Biography* by Anne Sebba, 1986.

Enid Bagnold writes in her Foreword to *Serena Blandish*, 1946:

The Reader: This book of yours that you are now offering up again, when did you last read it?

The Author: I sent *Serena Blandish* to the publishers twenty-two years ago. On a day in November 1924 it came back to me, printed and bound. I handled it with rapture, with prayers for its success, with passionate self-pity that my father insisted on anonymity. I was too exhausted by having written it to read it.

The Reader: What happens when a book goes from its author? How soon, once more, do you receive pleasure from your work?

The Author: It left me as a wild animal leaves its mother, not again to be recognized: to be met, perhaps, as I meet it now, muzzle to stranger-muzzle, all thread of kinship snapped. For me, after that, it never freshened. The wind never blew in it. The angel never shouted in the landscape. I never read it—well I never read it for twenty-two years—not till this morning.

The Reader: Then what do you think of your work, Author?

The Author: That perhaps is a little private. But I reflect on it and how, by writing, one exorcises the devil or the angel in a stretch of life, till, the winged creature risen, the landscape which before had shaken with the bustle of his escape, is suddenly fixed, as with gum, unrevisitable. In the years preceding every book there's a hunt and a capture. But when the hunt is over the stirrup-cup is for the public. The Author cannot enjoy what he has caught. He must be off. He must shoot again. And when he shoots no more then he is old.

The Reader: But—some success—when he is old? Can't he sit back on that?

The Author: Success, to give pleasure, must be on the move. No, there's no laurel to wear that he notices is any different from his hat. And writing is like love: all that is past is ashes: and the thread snaps on every book that is done.

The Reader: The pleasure then is in the writing?

The Author (a little warm): Not at all! Writing is a condition of grinding anxiety. It is an operation in which the footwork, the balance, the knowledge of sun and shade, the alteration of slush and crust, the selection of surface at high speed is a matter of exquisite fineness. Heavens—a pleasure! when you are without judgement, and hallucinations look like the truth! When experience (which trails behind) and imagination (which runs in front) will only combine by a miracle! When the whole thing is an ambidexterity of memory and creation—of the front and back of the brain—a lethargy of inward dipping and a tiptoe of poise while the lasso is whirling for the words! (More heated.) It is a gamble, a toss-up, an unsure benevolence of God! No! It can't be called pleasure!

The Reader: One last obvious question. Why then do you write?

The Author (with a sigh): For the sake of a split second when I feel myself immortal . . .

The Reader: Yes?—And . . .

The Author: . . . and just before the impact with my want of skill.

Enid Bagnold quotes Walter Kerr's review
(New York *Herald-Tribune*, 3 January 1964) of *The Chinese Prime Minister*:

I find myself touched by *The Chinese Prime Minister* . . . I am touched, I think, because I have seen one whole play in which there is not a single careless line.

There are careless scenes, oh, yes. Quite a large proportion of the middle act is taken up with a crossfire of family quarrelling that has as its purpose the badgering of Miss Leighton until Miss Leighton is pushed into a vital, and mistaken, decision. The sequence is ratchety enough to badger you, too, and to make you wonder whether the silken strands of the evening can be gathered into one steady hand again. But even there "carelessness" is not quite the right word. For playwright Enid Bagnold never does anything merely because she cannot think of anything better to do. Whatever she does, she does on impulse, inspiration, with a jump and a dagger in her hand, eyes gleaming. The gleam, the mad glint of her inspiration, may indeed flash out of the untidiest of corners. But in itself it is marvellously pure.

The obvious word for a lofty, detached, unpredictably witty play of this sort is "civilized". But I think we should do Miss Bagnold the justice of trying to avoid obvious words. *The Chinese Prime Minister* might more nearly, more properly be called humanely barbaric.

Its comedy is barbaric in the sense that, for all the elegance of elbow-length blue gloves and for all the urbanity of precise syntax sounded against deep chocolate drapes, the minds of the people who make the comedy are essentially brutal minds, minds capable of caring for themselves . . . All of the contestants who speak Miss Bagnold's brisk, knobby, out-of-nowhere lines somehow or other become admirable. For the lines are thoughts not echoes, not borrowings. And they are so often so very funny because they come not from the stage or from remembered literature but from a head that has no patience with twilight cant.

Miss Bagnold does not construct a play that all audiences will settle to easily. That is clear enough . . . It shimmers on the stage—and wavers there, too—like a vast, insubstantial spider's web, sprung with bits of real rain. It is not conventional, and it is not altogether secure. But it is written. And what a blessing that is.

Enid Bagnold wrote four plays before *The Chalk Garden,* her first and only big success. They are *Lottie Dundass, National Velvet, Poor Judas* and *Gertie.* Yet in her autobiography Bagnold speaks of *Lottie Dundass* as her first play and

Gertie as her second, and as usual her discrimination is absolute. *National Velvet* is an adaptation of her successful novel; it was filmed (with the young Elizabeth Taylor) and gave birth to soap-opera spin-offs on radio and television, but the novel is the version to remember. *Poor Judas*, a play about a writer unable to come to terms with his own lack of talent, won a prize in 1951 but has not made a mark in the current repertory. *Lottie Dundass*, an anecdotal piece, had a five-month run during the War with Sybil Thorndike and Ann Todd in the cast. *Gertie*, a comedy, opened in New York on a Wednesday and came off the following Saturday; in England it was retitled *Little Idiot* but failed. To compensate for the disappointment, Bagnold concentrated on *The Chalk Garden*, which she worked on for the next two years. It initiated the mandarin style that characterizes her last four plays, of which only *The Chalk Garden* has had a success befitting its merit.

The most immediately perceptible quality of *The Chalk Garden* is a rich suggestion of artificiality in the dialogue—"speech of an exquisite candour", Kenneth Tynan has called it, "building ornamental bridges of metaphor, tiptoeing across frail causeways of simile, and vaulting over gorges impassable to the rational soul". The whole play is in fact a metaphor, comparing the development of a child starved of mother-love with the development of plants starved of compost. Bagnold claimed to have been unaware of this parallel when she was writing the play, but it must have been lurking near the surface of her mind, for it is all-pervasive; the garden, never actually seen, is almost as much a character as the old retainer lying upstairs in whose amateur advice Mrs St Maugham, the aristocratic widow at the centre of the play, has placed her mistaken trust for so long.

There is something larger than life about all the people in the play; they are not caricatured in the manner of Rowlandson but elegantly exaggerated in the manner of El Greco. Bagnold lived most of her life among exceptional people and she could draw an exceptional character with confidence and consistency, though her success lay mostly in those who can be described, in the broadest possible sense, as aristocratic. Her themes are aristocratic too, themes like breeding and courage and resolution. Oddly enough, though, *The Last Joke*, in which the principle characters are Balkan princes drawn from life, is the least aristocratic of the four late plays. Perhaps this is due to the fact that the princes, Ferdinand Cavanati and his brother Hugo, are modelled on somewhat eccentric originals whom Bagnold revealed as Prince Antoine Bibesco and his brother Emmanuel. Reproducing a live eccentric is a harder task than creating one; and the provision of a plot in *The Last Joke* that seems almost as capricious as its executants does nothing to mend matters.

Nevertheless there is something to be admired in this play. The conception of the philosopher who has worked out so much about God that he is determined to hasten their meeting is potentially a brave one. It is a pity that more is not done with it than its incorporation into a melodramatic story about the stealing of a picture; or that the story, if this is to be the one, is not more straightforwardly told. But Bagnold has had to include too much of real life in it, and the amalgam of life and romance has not worked out well. The play got poor notices when it opened in London and had only a short run. Its successor was in every way better; Bagnold herself rated *The Chinese*

Prime Minister more highly than *The Chalk Garden*. But this too, for reasons not entirely attributable to the qualities of the script, had only a modest success.

The Chinese Prime Minister is a play about the pleasures of old age (and to show that these are not available only to the wealthy the author has complemented her sixty-nine-year-old protagonist with a 100-year-old butler who dies twice during the play and finds the experience not at all unpleasant). "She"—the only name given to the heroine—is an actress on the verge of retiring who is suddenly reunited with the husband who left her many years before. She has a vision of retirement with a notional Chinese Prime Minister whose term of office is done, who writes poems to outlive his achievements, who goes up into the mountains with no baggage but a birdcage . . . . Her husband, having made a fortune in oil that has kept him permanently resident in Arabia, has other ideas; he thinks of summoning up anew all the joys of their youth. But oil calls him back to Arabia, and She is happily resigned to being her own Chinese Prime Minister and living her remaining years in the peaceful style she has mapped out for them.

There is a fine serenity about the play that is marred only by what seems to be Bagnold's uncertainty about what to do with her batch of subsidiary characters—the heroine's children and their friends of their own generation, who never quite get integrated into the main scheme. In New York, where She was played by Margaret Leighton, it was a success; in London where She was played by Edith Evans, the actress for whom it was written, it took on a sentimental patina foreign to the writing, and was not. Bagnold was given to blaming producers for the artistic failures of her plays; of the four last plays *The Chalk Garden* is the only one (rightly or wrongly) that has acquired a stable reputation. Her rating of *The Chinese Prime Minister* as a better play than this was probably wrong; *The Chalk Garden* had the advantage of formidable discussions over a long period with Irene Mayer Selznick, a producer in whom Bagnold had faith, and emerged a dramatic jewel. But *The Chinese Prime Minister* has not deserved the neglect into which it has fallen.

Enid Bagnold's last piece, *Call Me Jacky*, won its director a grudging "did his best" from the author, followed by a complaint that inadequate rehearsal time was given to it. Perhaps two years with Irene Selznick might have made something of it; but as played, and as published, the subtleties the author called for seemed to exist principally in her mind. Once more we have the rich old lady at the centre of the piece, playing on the destinies of the younger generation, represented by a cook extracted from a lunatic asylum (a reminiscence of *The Chalk Garden*), the lady's grandson, an Oxford student, and four friends of his, a male homosexual pair and a female. It seems to have been written to demonstrate how liberal this rich old lady (in which, as usual, a certain autobiographical element is unmistakable) can be when confronted with the problems that afflict the young.

Thus, she is undisturbed by the homosexual liaisons, or by her grandson's marriage to a black girl and siring of a black baby, or by communist accusations of depriving the poor of the use of her grounds to live in. But the theme appears to be that such open-mindedness is the result of the basically aristocratic nature of her character; and when, in the highly improbable conclusion, she asks to be admitted to the paying wing of the home where her cook comes from, and the cook asks her pathetically if she might then be called by her Christian name, she replies coldly, "I'll be buggered if I do".

The combination of this attitude and this choice of words to express it in is characteristic of the generally muddled feeling of the play. The author claimed that the piece worked on two levels, but it is more truthful to say that it exists on two levels and works on neither of them, neither the surface frivolity nor the deeper implications. Bagnold was accustomed to taking years over the writing of her plays; that *Call Me Jacky* doesn't work suggests that the two years she worked on it and the time taken in production were neither of them enough; for the theme, a 20th-century version of *noblesse oblige*, is a characteristic one, worth developing, capable of development. In spite of Gladys Cooper's much-quoted judgement during the rehearsals for *The Chalk Garden*, Enid Bagnold was incapable of writing nonsense.

—B. A. Young

BARKER, Howard.

Born in London, 28 June 1946. Educated at Battersea Grammar School, London, 1958–64; Sussex University, Brighton, 1964–68, M.A. in history 1968. Married Sandra Law in 1972; one son. Resident dramatist, Open Space Theatre, London, 1974–75, and since 1988, the Wrestling School, London. Recipient: Arts Council bursary, 1971; Sony award, Society of Authors award, and Italia prize, all for radio play, 1985. Agent: Judy Daish Associates, 83 Eastbourne Mews, London W2 6LQ, England.

Publications

PLAYS

Cheek (produced 1970). In *New Short Plays 3*, 1972.
No One Was Saved (produced 1971).
Edward: The Final Days (produced 1971).
Faceache (produced 1971).
Alpha Alpha (produced 1972).
Private Parts (produced 1972).
Skipper, and My Sister and I (produced 1973).
Rule Britannia (produced 1973).
Bang (produced 1973).
Claw (produced 1975). With *Stripwell*, 1977.
Stripwell (produced 1975). With *Claw*, 1977.
Wax (produced 1976).
Aces High (screenplay). 1976.
Fair Slaughter (produced 1977). 1978; with *Crimes in Hot Countries*, 1985.
That Good Between Us (produced 1977). With *Credentials of a Sympathizer*, 1980.
The Love of a Good Man (produced 1978). With *All Bleeding*, 1980.
The Hang of the Gaol (produced 1978). With *Heaven*, 1982.
The Loud Boy's Life (produced 1980). In *Two Plays for the Right*, 1982.

Birth on a Hard Shoulder (produced 1980). In *Two Plays for the Right*, 1982.
No End of Blame: Scenes of Overcoming (produced 1981). 1981.
The Poor Man's Friend (produced 1981).
Two Plays for the Right. 1982.
Victory: Choices in Reaction (produced 1983). 1983.
A Passion in Six Days (produced 1983). With *Downchild*, 1985.
The Power of the Dog (produced 1984). 1985.
Don't Exaggerate (produced 1984). 1985.
Scenes from an Execution (broadcast 1984; produced 1990). With *The Castle*, 1985.
Crimes in Hot Countries (produced 1985). With *Fair Slaughter*, 1984.
Downchild (produced 1985). With *A Passion in Six Days*, 1985.
The Castle (produced 1985). With *Scenes from an Execution*, 1985.
Pity in History (televised 1985; produced 1986). With *Women Beware Women*, 1987.
Women Beware Women, adaptation of the play by Thomas Middleton (produced 1986). 1986; with *Pity in History*, 1988.
The Last Supper (produced 1988). 1988.
The Bite of the Night (produced 1988). 1988.
The Possibilities (10 plays) (produced 1988). 1988.
Golgo (produced 1989). With *Seven Lears*, 1990.
Seven Lears (produced 1989). With *Golgo*, 1990.
The Europeans. With *Judith*, 1990.
Judith. With *The Europeans*, 1990.
Collected Plays 1 (includes *Claw, No End of Blame, Scenes from an Execution, The Castle, Victory*). 1990.
A Hard Heart (broadcast 1992; produced 1992). 1992.
All He Fears (produced 1993).

SCREENPLAYS: *Made*, 1972; *Rape of Tamar*, 1973; *Aces High*, 1976.

RADIO PLAYS: *One Afternoon on the North Face of the 63rd Level of the Pyramid of Cheops the Great*, 1970; *Henry V in Two Parts*, 1971; *Herman, with Millie and Mick*, 1972; *Scenes from an Execution*, 1984; *The Early Hours of a Reviled Man*, 1990; *A Hard Heart*, 1992.

TELEVISION PLAYS: *Cows*, 1972; *The Chauffeur and the Lady*, 1972; *Mutinies*, 1974; *Pity in History*, 1985.

VERSE

The Breath of the Crowd. 1986.
Gary the Thief/Gary Upright. 1987.
Lullabies for the Impatient. 1989.
The Ascent of Monte Grappa. 1991.

OTHER

Arguments for a Theatre (essays). 1989.

CRITICAL STUDIES: *The New British Drama* by Oleg Kerensky, 1977; *Stages in the Revolution* by Catherine Itzin, 1980; *Dreams and Deconstructions* edited by Sandy Craig, 1980; *Howard Barker: An Expository Study of His Poetry and Drama, 1969–1987* by David Ian Rabey, 1989.

THEATRICAL ACTIVITIES
DIRECTOR: **Play**—*Don't Exaggerate*, 1986.

Having provided the high point of contemporary, radical theatre in the mid-1980s with a trilogy of plays (*Scenes from an Execution, Downchild, The Castle*) for the Royal Shakespeare Company at the small Pit theatre in London, Howard Barker has continued to excoriate the pieties of art, sex, and politics in a series of dramatic works whose intransigence and theatrical inventiveness still appal the managements of our main subsidised theatres. No Barker play has yet been main stage at either the National Theatre or the RSC. Actors, however, recognise his talent and an actors' company, The Wrestling School, was founded in 1988 exclusively to perform Barker. By 1992 it had five productions to its credit. Other theatres, such as the Almeida and Greenwich (both in London), Sheffield, and Leicester, have hosted Barker's extensive output. BBC-Radio 3 has recently broadcast his characterisation of Céline as a splenetic doctor wandering the wastelands of Paris by night (*The Early Hours of a Reviled Man*), and his libretto for Nigel Osborne's music to an opera on Goya.

There is always a war on in Barker's plays and it is perhaps his emphasis on struggle, pain, and treachery that affronts, and affrights, the rational humanism of theatre directors. *The Possibilities*, an evening of 10 short pieces, delights in cruel and abrupt reversals of lives and ideologies and proposes that all history is contemporary. In the eighth piece, Judith, after beheading Holofernes, is lauded as the heroine of Israel. A patriot comes to persuade her to leave her retreat and return in triumph to Jerusalem. Judith grows hot again as she recalls sex with Holofernes; when the patriot is caustic about deriving private pleasure from state business, Judith's knife comes out again and slashes off the patriot's hand. Desire, as in so many Barker plays, tramples across politics. In the seventh piece a typist refuses to submit her body and her clothes to the dowdy dictates of puritanical feminism. In the third piece a young whore, while constructing herself through underwear, shoes, and a red dress, argues with an old, despairing, female Stalinist that the zig-zags of history show as well in the seams of falling stockings as in the sagas of liquidations, show-trials, and barricades. She, too, in servicing the Party *nomenklatura*, is a revolutionary. In another piece a torturer turns on a young admirer and kills him because the young man lacked the courage to move from flattering his elder to usurping his position. The old, with Barker, maintain their position through cunning, not traditional respect. *Only Some Can Take the Strain* satirises the position of the specialist bookseller in an era of populism. He remains so loyal to his stock that he refuses to sell any of his books, arguing that their knowledge will be misused in a time of censorship. The piece contains the most bitterly accurate exchange of the collection. "I'm from the Ministry of Education," says the censor. "There's no such thing," replies the bookseller.

The education of a king is the theme of *Seven Lears*, Barker's imaginative "version" of Shakespeare's original. Barker's Lear, trying desperately to be a good king in the midst of war and intrigue, shuttles between his lover Prudentia and his wife Clarissa, Prudentia's daughter. Prudentia bolsters Lear with her endless desire for him, Clarissa reassures him with her clarity of motive and her leadership in war. Lear veers wildly between conscience and cruelty. The gaol, a collective of the unjustly imprisoned, is always at hand to remind him of the poor, but he orders merciless slaughter after a battle. He confers the dukedom of Gloucester on a beggar, but orders his most able minister to become his Fool and sanctions the execution of Prudentia at the prompting of Clarissa. Building on an old legend, Barker has Lear attempt to fly, but he only causes the death of a boy whom he was very fond of. He tries to drown Cordelia in a vat of gin and finishes playing chess with Kent, whom he hates. His desire for truth and honesty have caused only mayhem and unhappiness.

The war continues in *A Hard Heart* where a Greek city is under siege and its queen, Praxis, appeals to the architect Riddler to save them. Riddler, like Clarissa in *Seven Lears*, is arrogant, imperious, and a rationalist. By the play's end she will have been, in some measure, humbled by Seemore, a man of the streets who challenges her self-sufficient coldness and, in a parody of the Pluto and Proserpine myth, tries to drag her into the sewers to escape and be reborn. But Riddler's descent does not signal a subtle misogyny by Barker. Riddler has been stage-centre throughout the play, with a series of daring schemes to fool the enemy. They fail, not through her stupidity, but through the treachery of her son, Attila, the only person she loves and whom, through special pleading, she has preserved from military service and starvation. No Barker characters are immune from the upheaval of passion into their ordered lives. Their hubris is that they imagine they are.

In *The Europeans*, male and female are equally matched. The Viennese siege of 1684 has been lifted. The Turks have been repulsed from Europe and the Emperor and his court have returned to hail Vienna's military commander, Starhemberg. But Starhemberg refuses honours. He is searching for another self, one that can love, and he finds it with Katrin. She has undergone the extreme suffering that, for Barker's typology, alone can create a character of knowledge and equality. She has been raped by the Turks and her breasts cut off, but she is in the line of Barker's clear-eyed, crisp-talking women. She insists on a public examination of her body by the city's leading doctors and wants a mass distribution of prints of her disfigurement around the city. The birth of the product of the rape, a girl named Concilia by the mocking Emperor, takes place in full public view. Katrin is in love with language and holds onto it even at moments of extreme stress: "Sometimes I find a flow and then the words go—torrent—cascade—cascade again. I used that word just now! I like that word now I have discovered it. I shall use it, probably ad nauseam, cascading!" But in the climatic scene three of Act II she and Starhemberg are largely silent. Both naked, they sit at a distance and gaze at one another in a shuttered room. Their bodies are imperfect but their endurance has been equal, as are their minds. This is not propaganda for safe sex, but rather a brief equilibrium between lust and intelligence which could only be envisaged after extensive experience of thwarted passion and defeated reason. The shutters are opened by Katrin's sister Susannah whose exasperated desire for the corrupt priest Orphuls has been blocked by his wilful celibacy. In the final scene Concilia is given to the Turks so there will be no false harmony between East and West. Katrin and Starhemberg, without children to distract them, finally kiss. The new Europe will be produced by war-weary adults.

—Tony Dunn

BARNES, Peter.

Born in London, 10 January 1931. Educated at Stroud Grammar School, Gloucestershire. Served in the Royal Air Force, 1949–50. Married Charlotte Beck in 1958. Worked for the London County Council, 1948 and 1950–53; critic, *Films and Filming*, London, 1954; story editor, Warwick Films, 1956. Recipient: John Whiting award, 1969; *Evening Standard* award, 1969; Olivier award, 1985; Royal Television Society award, 1989. Agent: Casarotto Ramsay Ltd., National House, 60–66 Wardour Street, London W1V 3HP. Address: 7 Archery Close, Connaught Street, London W2 2BE, England.

Publications

PLAYS

The Time of the Barracudas (produced 1963).
Sclerosis (produced 1965).
The Ruling Class: A Baroque Comedy (produced 1968). 1969.
Leonardo's Last Supper, and Noonday Demons (produced 1969; *Noonday Demons* produced 1977). 1970.
Lulu, adaptation of plays by Frank Wedekind, translated by Charlotte Beck (also co-director: produced 1970). 1971.
The Alchemist, with Trevor Nunn, adaptation of the play by Jonson (produced 1970; revised version produced 1977).
The Devil Is an Ass, adaptation of the play by Jonson (also co-director: produced 1973; revised version produced 1976).
The Bewitched (produced 1974). 1974.
The Frontiers of Farce, adaptation of the plays *The Purging* by Feydeau and *The Singer* by Wedekind (also director: produced 1976; *The Purging* produced 1980). 1977.
For All Those Who Get Despondent (cabaret), adaptation of works by Brecht and Wedekind (also director: produced 1976; revised version, as *The Two Hangmen: Brecht and Wedekind*, broadcast 1978).
Antonio, adaptation of the plays *Antonio and Mellida* and *Antonio's Revenge* by Marston (broadcast 1977; also co-director: produced 1979).
Laughter! (produced 1978). 1978.
The Devil Himself (revue), adaptation of a play by Wedekind, music by Carl Davis and Stephen Deutsch (also director: produced 1980).
Barnes' People: Seven Monologues (broadcast 1981). In *Collected Plays*, 1981.
Collected Plays (includes *The Ruling Class, Leonardo's Last Supper, Noonday Demons, The Bewitched, Laughter!, Barnes' People*).1981; as *Plays: One*, 1989.

Somersaults (revue; also director: produced 1981).
Barnes' People II: Seven Duologues (broadcast 1984). 1984.
Red Noses (produced 1985). 1985.
Scenes from a Marriage, adaptation of a play by Feydeau (produced 1986).
The Real Long John Silver and Other Plays: Barnes' People III (as *Barnes' People III*, broadcast 1986). 1986.
The Real Long John Silver (produced 1989). In *The Real Long John Silver and Other Plays*, 1986.
Nobody Here But Us Chickens (televised 1989). With *Revolutionary Witness*, 1989.
Revolutionary Witness (televised 1989). With *Nobody Here But Us Chickens*, 1989.
The Spirit of Man (includes *A Hand Witch of the Second Stage, From Sleep and Shadow, The Night of the Simhat Torah*) (televised 1989; produced 1991). With *More Barnes' People*, 1990.
More Barnes' People (broadcast 1989–90). With *The Spirit of Man*, 1990.
Sunsets and Glories (produced 1990). 1990.
Tango at the End of Winter, adaptation of the play by Kunio Shimizu (produced 1991).
Plays: Two (includes *Red Noses, Sunsets and Glories, Socrates*). 1993.

SCREENPLAYS: *Violent Moment*, 1959; *The White Trap*, 1959; *Breakout*, 1959; *The Professionals*, 1960; *Off-Beat*, 1961; *Ring of Spies* (*Ring of Treason*), with Frank Launder, 1963; *Not with My Wife You Don't*, with others, 1966; *The Ruling Class*, 1972; *Enchanted April*, 1991.

RADIO PLAYS: *My Ben Jonson*, 1973; *Eastward Ho!*, from the play by Jonson, Chapman, and Marston, 1973; *Antonio*, 1977; *The Two Hangmen: Brecht and Wedekind*, 1978; *A Chaste Maid in Cheapside*, from the play by Middleton, 1979; *Eulogy on Baldness*, from a work by Synesius of Cyrene, 1980; *For the Conveyance of Oysters*, from a work by Gorky, 1981; *The Soldier's Fortune*, from the play by Thomas Otway, 1981; *The Atheist*, from the play by Thomas Otway, 1981; *Barnes' People*, 1981; *The Singer*, from a work by Wedekind, 1981; *The Magician*, from a work by Gorky, 1982; *The Dutch Courtesan*, from the play by Marston, 1982; *A Mad World, My Masters*, from the play by Middleton, 1983; *Barnes' People II*, 1984; *The Primrose Path*, from a play by Feydeau, 1984; *A Trick to Catch the Old One*, from the play by Middleton, 1985; *The Old Law*, from the play by Middleton and Rowley, 1986; *Woman of Paris*, from a work by Henri Becque, 1986; *Barnes' People III*, 1986; *No End to Dreaming*, 1987; *The Magnetic Lady*, from the play by Jonson, 1987; *More Barnes' People* (series of monologues), 1989–90; *Billy and Me*, 1990; *Madame Zenobia*, 1990; *Slaughterman*, 1990; *The Road to Strome*, 1990; *Losing Myself*, 1990; *A True Born Englishman*, 1990; *Houdini's Heir*, 1991.

TELEVISION PLAYS: *The Man with a Feather in His Hat*, 1960; *Revolutionary Witness*, 1989; *Nobody Here But Us Chickens*, 1989; *More Than a Touch of Zen*, 1989; *Not as Bad as They Seem*, 1989; *The Spirit of Man*, 1990; *Bye Bye Columbus*, 1992.

CRITICAL STUDIES: *The Theatre of Peter Barnes* by Bernard F. Dukore, 1981; *Landmarks of Modern British Drama: The Plays of the Sixties* edited by Roger Cornish and Violet Ketels, 1986; *New Theatre Quarterly* (Cambridge), no.21, 1990; *The Gothic Impulse* by Marybeth Inveso, 1991.

THEATRICAL ACTIVITIES

DIRECTOR: **Plays**—several of his own plays; *Bartholomew Fair* by Jonson, 1978 and 1987. **Film**—*Leonardo's Last Supper*, 1977. **Television**—*Nobody Here But Us Chickens*, 1989; *The Spirit of Man*, 1990; *Bye Bye Columbus*, 1992.

Peter Barnes quotes:
from his programme note for *The Ruling Class*, 1968:

The aim is to create, by means of soliloquy, rhetoric, formalized ritual, slapstick, songs, and dances, a comic theatre of contrasting moods and opposites, where everything is simultaneously tragic and ridiculous. And we hope never to consent to the deadly servitude of naturalism or lose our hunger for true size, weight, and texture.

Peter Barnes is one of the most consistently exciting and inventive of contemporary playwrights, a savage satirist and a glorious free-booter of past theatrical styles. Some of the more obvious influences are discernible in the adaptations of work by Marston, Jonson, and Wedekind—and in particular a magnificent version of Wedekind's *Lulu* plays. He is as implacably opposed to the dominant theatrical mode of naturalism as he is to the perpetuation of the status quo in the world in which he writes. His chief weapon is comedy, but a comedy always on the verge of nightmare. He first came to prominence with *The Ruling Class* in 1968—a play in which the delusion of the latest in a long line of insane Earls of Gurney that he is Christ serves as a perfectly reasonable representation of the continued appropriation of power by a self-perpetuating ruling-class.

The play—the plot of which concerns the efforts of the Earl's relations to get a male heir from him before having him certified—is a free-wheeling farcical broadside on ruling-class excesses. However, a pervading sense of disgust at the way things are is never balanced by any suggestion of a way out of the impasse. The only character who might seriously threaten the perpetuation of the old order is the butler, an ill-defined revolutionary completely unable to leave the world of privilege he would destroy despite the acquisition of a substantial inheritance from the previous Earl. And this fascination with the ostensible object of attack is something that he shares with the play itself. For all its venom Barnes seemed at this juncture unable to do more than pick away at the scab.

Subsequently the humour would be increasingly less cosy and the visions of society far bleaker. His plays were to offer an excess of blood, vomit, and excrement, guaranteed to offend the conventional West End audience (as is clearly intended), without ever offering the kind of positive analysis that might appeal to a more politically engaged audience. His work thus falls between the two extremes of contemporary theatre, and as a result he has quite unfairly continued to struggle for productions. Indeed, it took him seven years to realise the 1985 production of *Red Noses*.

After *The Ruling Class* Barnes moved away from an albeit fantasy version of the contemporary world; and his later plays offer a series of nightmare visions of climactic moments of earlier "civilisation" inhabited by characters who speak a variety of inventive and historically unlocatable languages in ways which make the link between present crisis and past roots something never less than urgent and disturbing. In *Leonardo's Last Supper*, the great artist regains consciousness in a filthy charnel-house where he has been carried having been prematurely declared dead. His joy at his resurrection, and at the further works of genius he will now be able to leave the world, is not shared by the wretched family. They had seen their contract for the burial of the famous man as a way to worldly fame and success, and they simply carry on with the arrangements, having first ensured a real corpse by plunging Leonardo head first into a bucket of excrement, urine, and vomit. The wonders of the Renaissance mean nothing to this self-dependent family unit and the working model of the basic precepts of capitalist enterprise that they provide acts also as a demonstration of the way in which all that is represented by the aspirations of such as Leonardo is built on the usually mute sufferings of other such socially insignificant people.

In *The Bewitched* Barnes turned to a key moment in modern European history, the problems over the succession to the grotesquely inbred Philip IV of Spain. The effect of the transference of power on the lives of the powerless throughout Europe is heightened dramatically by the Court's own total lack of concern for them, all interest being centered on explanations of, and attempts to rectify, the ruler's impotence. It is a world in which spiritual salvation is sought for in the torture chamber and in the *auto-da-fé*, as the political fate of Europe is decided by the crazy attempts of the institutions of church and state to create a rightful heir from the seed of an impotent and degenerate imbecile. The central metaphor that links a mad incapacity with political power is here used to far more telling effect, and the result is one of the most thrillingly disturbing plays of the modern period.

In *Laughter!* Barnes was to push the process a stage further with a series of carefully prepared theatrical shocks. Part One takes us back to another account of the insanity of rule, this time in the court of Ivan the Terrible. Terrifyingly comic though it is, it leaves the audience quite unready for what is to follow. Part Two opens in an office which is dominated by an eight-foot-high stretch of filing cabinets and in which a poster of Hitler is prominent on the wall. As the dialogue develops, the audience is invited to laugh as the bureaucrats fight for power and status amongst themselves, even as it becomes increasingly apparent that the office is responsible for organising the finer details of the extermination programme at Auschwitz Concentration Camp.

And then the wall of filing cabinets opens to reveal an interior of gassed corpses being violently stripped of valuables by a Sanitation Squad in gas-masks—the dry statistics of the files are suddenly metamorphosed in a grotesque masque of death. The audience is forced to confront the reality behind the language of a petty officialdom that carries out the insane demands of its rulers without questioning or ever properly looking at what it is that is being administered. That Barnes should then finish his play with an epilogue in which two Jewish stand-up comedians go through their paces at the concentration camp Christmas concert is evidence of a writer who is prepared to tread a more dangerous tightrope than any of his contemporaries.

With *Red Noses* he moved back into more distant history, continuing his exploration of the potential of laughter as a weapon against oppression. In the midst of a plague-torn Europe a group of self-appointed, and papally sanctioned Red Noses take on the role of theatrical clowns—acting out their parts on a politically repressive stage. They form an alliance with other more politically active groups in response to Barnes's own question: "Can we ever get laughter from comedy which doesn't accept the miseries of life but actually helps to change them? . . . Laughter linked with revolution might be the best of both worlds." But by the end of this remarkable play the passing of the plague is accompanied by the inevitable restoration of the old order of church and state.

The question that Barnes raises ever more urgently about the ability of the writer to affect change remains an open one, which makes his continuing problems in finding theatres to take his work the more depressing, and in itself provides a reason for his continual use of past history as a source for his plots; a desire to write about the problems of the individual at odds with a corrupt society, confronted by the worry that by the time his plays are produced any obviously contemporary references will have become dated. It was thus both peculiarly appropriate and very much to be welcomed that Britain's newest theatre, the West Yorkshire Playhouse in Leeds, should have opened in June 1990 with Barnes's *Sunsets and Glories*—his latest trip back through time. For the first time the playwright presents the figure of a truly good man, the 13th-century Pope Celestine IV, and his struggles. The play is "about a man who was a saint, became pope, and because he was good, was bad for the job . . . the only pope ever voted out of office." The humour is as black as ever, and Barnes continues magnificently to write as he wants, rather than bowing to the economically diminishing demands of the theatre of the new monetarist age for small-cast, small-scale domestic drama. If the National Theatre's title is to be taken seriously it is to be hoped that before too long the idea of offering this, one of the most important contemporary playwrights, a full season of his work—both old and new—is suggested. As it is, his lack of regular productions is nothing short of a national disgrace.

—John Bull

BARTLETT, Neil.

Born in Hitchin, Hertfordshire, in 1958. Educated at Magdalen College, Oxford, 1979–81, B.A. in English literature 1981. Founder member, 1982 Theatre Company, London, 1982–84; staff member, Consenting Adults in Public, London, 1983, September in the Pink (London Lesbian and Gay Arts Festival), London, 1983, and International Aids Day, London, 1986; director, Théâtre de Complicité, London, 1985; M.C. for National Review of Live Art, London, Nottingham, and Glasgow, 1985–90; founder member, 1988, and since 1988 director, writer and performer, Gloria, London. Recipient: Perrier award, 1985; *Time Out/*Dance Umbrella award, 1989; Writers Guild of Great Britain award, 1991; *Time Out* award, 1992. Agent: Gloria, 16 Chenies Street, London WC1E 7EX, England.

Publications

PLAYS

Dressing Up (produced 1983).
Pornography (produced 1984).
The Magic Flute, adaptation of the opera by Mozart (produced 1985).
A Vision of Love Revealed in Sleep, 1 (produced 1986).
Lady Audley's Secret, adaptation of the novel by Mary E. Braddon (produced 1988).
Le Misanthrope, adaptation of the play by Molière (produced 1988). 1990.
A Vision of Love Revealed in Sleep, 2 (produced 1989).
A Vision of Love Revealed in Sleep, 3 (produced 1990). In *Gay Plays 3*, edited by Michael Wilcox, 1990.
The School for Wives, adaptation of the play by Molière (produced 1990). 1990.
Bérénice, adaptation of the play by Jean Racine (produced 1990). 1990.
Sarrasine, adaptation of the story by Honoré de Balzac (produced 1990).
Let Them Call It Jazz, adaptation of the story by Jean Rhys (produced 1991).
A Judgement in Stone, adaptation of the novel by Ruth Rendell, music by Nicolas Bloomfield (produced 1992).
Night After Night (produced 1993).

SCREENPLAY: *Now That It's Morning*, 1992.

TELEVISION PLAYS: *That's What Friends Are For*, 1988; *That's How Strong My Love Is*, 1989.
Video:
Where Is Love, 1988; *Pedagogue* with Stuart Marshall, 1988.

NOVEL
Ready to Catch Him Should He Fall. 1990.

SHORT STORIES
The Ten Commandments. 1992.

OTHER
Who Was That Man? A Present for Mr. Oscar Wilde. 1988.

THEATRICAL ACTIVITIES
DIRECTOR: **Plays**—all his own plays; *More Bigger Snacks Now* by Théâtre de Complicité, 1985; *The Avenging Woman*, 1991; *Twelfth Night*, 1992; *The Game of Love and Chance*, 1992.
ACTOR: **Plays**—role in *Pornography*, 1984; Robert Audley in *Lady Audley's Secret*, 1988. **Television**—roles in all his own television plays. **Video**—roles in all his videos.

Neil Bartlett comments:

I do not consider my work "playwriting" because my performance work has its professional roots in collectively devised small-scale work, physical theatre, and performance art. I regard script as the documentation rather than origin of performance. I regard all my work as gay theatre whether it is solo performance, music theatre, or the re-invention of classic texts. I characteristically write, direct, light, and design all my pieces. I have been particularly influenced by my collaborations with: Banuta Rubess in Toronto and Riga; painter Robin Whitmore; vaudevillian Bette Bourne; and my colleagues in Gloria, producer, Simon Mellor, choreographer, Leah Hausman, and composer, Nicolas Bloomfield. I am particularly influenced by the unique traditions of British gay theatre in musicals, pub drag, pantomime, and contemporary activism. My favourite performer is Ethyl Eichelberger, my favourite play Racine's *Athalie*. My ambition is to produce a commercial pantomime, a classical tragedy, and a spectacular revue in the same season, in the same building, and with the same company.

Although he has, as yet, completed only a few original dramatic texts, with them Neil Bartlett has established himself as one of the most interesting new writers for the theatre working in Britain. Perversely, he has earned this reputation precisely because he recognises the limitations of the dramatist within the theatre. It is his involvement with all aspects of a production which marks him out as unique. He acts, directs, designs, and stage manages shows with equal aplomb and always in the service of the performance as a complete work of art.

Bartlett draws his inspiration from many different forms of theatre, from opera to performance art. Fortunately though, he does not make the mistake of so many performance artists of reacting against the dominance of text-based theatre by devaluing the text. Bartlett loves the sound and the sensuality of words, but seeks to present them with as much help as he can, shrouding them in beautiful music, illuminating them with startling visual images. His is also a theatre of immediate and erotic impact and he revels in ornate Victorian theatres, lavish costumes, and shock. Much of this shock comes from his foregrounding of his gay sexuality. "I'm queer, I'm here, get used to it," is the message audiences have to accept before they can begin to appreciate Bartlett's work.

But Bartlett is, above all, the most fastidious of theatre artists and will constantly rework a play until he is satisfied with it, accepting the challenge of recreating a work for different venues and reshaping it until it seems to have been created as a site-specific piece of theatre. Yet though his plays are feasts for the eyes, the ears, and the mind, they are accessible, controlled, and immaculate works of art with a backbone of political steel. It is this mixture of challenging politics and aesthetics which won him his reputation in fringe theatre and which allowed him to move over into mainstream theatre.

After university and involvement as actor and director with the 1982 Theatre Company (where he made a memorable Cleopatra in a little black frock), Bartlett's first piece, *Dressing Up*, was presented in 1983 in London as part of a lesbian and gay festival called "September in the Pink." It was on the same bill as the first play about AIDS presented in Britain, Louise Kelly's *Antibody*. *Dressing Up* was a piece of postmodern theatre created before the term became fashionable. Weaving together fragments from the lives of gay men in London from 17th to the 19th centuries, the piece was played out before a rack of costumes which mingled leather and lace, crinolines and codpieces. Mixing historical research about the lives of gay men in London, it was claimed by Bartlett to be "a polemic guide to the splendours of the male body." Underlying the whole piece was a serious political purpose which might best, but rather drearily, be described as reclaiming history, and which revealed Bartlett as the marble fist in the gold lamé glove. The second part of *Dressing Up* was a series of reflections on the work and the words of the novelist Edmund White—an act of homage from disciple to master and one in which AIDS was touched upon at a time when it was hardly known in Britain.

Bartlett's next original piece was *Pornography*, created for the Institute of Contemporary Arts. This was, in part, a collective creation using monologues woven around the personal memories of the actors in the piece, a device he was later to use to devastating effect in the reworked version for drag queens and lavish set of *A Vision of Love Revealed in Sleep*. *Pornography* played with ideas of narrative, with memory, and with theatre. It introduced a touch of red plush theatricality into the rather grim confines of the Institute of Contemporary Arts, but at the heart of the piece were human stories of love and betrayal, raw and shocking, but delivered with such total honesty as to render them utterly compelling. *Pornography* began an association between Bartlett and the ICA which led to him producing a version of *The Magic Flute* for them. His gloss on Mozart's opera was his first step in what seems to have been his assured progress towards creating the all-embracing work of theatre which exploits all that the stage has to offer to create that one ultimate performance.

Bartlett's interest in the hidden history of gay men, also evident in his much-praised book of meditations on Oscar Wilde *Who Was that Man?*, was used to overwhelming theatrical effect in his first one-man show *A Vision of Love Revealed in Sleep*. Commissioned first by Nikki Milican for the Midland Group in Nottingham, it has since been staged on the ornate Edwardian staircase of the old Battersea Town Hall, in a Docklands warehouse, in studio theatres, and in the later incarnation mentioned above, as a large-scale theatre piece expanded to include a chorus of lavishly-costumed drag queens.

A Vision of Love is based round the life of the Victorian painter and poet Simeon Solomon whose blossoming career was destroyed when he was prosecuted for gross indecency. Bartlett draws parallels between his life and Solomon's and takes the audience through a series of variations on this theme. The play demonstrated Bartlett's combined virtuosity in writing and performing, and he gained some notoriety from performing in the nude, in order, he says, to prevent audiences from wasting time wondering whether he would take his clothes off. But while audiences cannot fail to appreciate the skill with which Bartlett performs in his chosen environment—floating candles in the warehouse, luminous murals in the studio theatres—his paralleling of the 19th century and now prevents the piece from ever becoming a cosy bio-pic. His chilling evocation of what it meant to be a gay man in a 1980's London threatened by AIDS and by queer-bashing made *A Vision of Love* as thought-provoking as it was entertaining.

This skilful mixture of history, comment upon history, and unnerving immediacy—for example the endless repetition of "young man, if you want to be happy, be careful," with its social and sexual message—was also a feature of *Sarrasine*, Bartlett's reworking of Balzac, which introduced the audience to a world of baroque intrigue amongst cardinals and castrati and used four actors and singers to evoke the murky interface between the glittering aristocracy and the infinitely more exciting underworld of 18th-century Rome. The piece is dominated by the figure of La Zambinella who when the play begins is over 200 years old. La Zambinella is kept alive, like a vampire, by the devotion of continuing generations to the perfection of his voice. Through this unlikely figure, a tale of love and murder is woven which in Bartlett's hands fused music hall and music theatre, exploring obsession, the human need for art and admiration, and the similarity in response of the connoisseur to 17th-century opera and the man in the pub to a raunchy drag number. Bartlett also gave the play a political subtext which explored the erotic attraction of art and the sinister undercurrents of our worship of the artists who fulfill our sexual fantasies.

Although he is a prolific writer, much of his stage work has been in translations from Molière and Racine and in adaptations of novels as diverse as *Lady Audley's Secret* and Ruth Rendell's *A Judgement in Stone*, as well as a story by Jean Rhys. Few other theatre practitioners manage to combine so successfully pleasure and politics, intellectual excitement and eroticism. Yet, as Bartlett would be the first to admit, although he may explore the heavens he is always rooted on the stage—preferably in an elaborate Edwardian Matcham theatre.

—Alasdair Cameron

BECKETT, Samuel (Barclay).

Born at Foxrock, near Dublin, Ireland, 13 April 1906. Educated at Ida Elsner's Academy, Stillorgan; Earlsfort House preparatory school; Portora Royal School, County Fermanagh; Trinity College, Dublin (foundation scholar), B.A. in French and Italian 1927, M.A. 1931. Married Suzanne Deschevaux-Dumesnil in 1961 (died 1989). French teacher, Campbell College, Belfast, 1928; lecturer in English, École Normale Supérieure, Paris, 1928–30; lecturer in French, Trinity College, Dublin, 1930–31; translator and writer in Paris in the 1920's and 1930's, and closely associated with James Joyce's circle; in Dublin and London, 1933–37; returned to Paris, 1937; joined French Resistance, 1940; fled to Roussillon in unoccupied France, where he remained 1942–45; worked at the Irish Red Cross Hospital, St. Lô, France, 1945; resumed literary activity in Paris after World War II; after 1945, published the majority of his work in both French and English versions; in later years directed several productions of his own plays, especially for the Schiller-Theater, Berlin. Recipient: Croix de Guerre and Médaille de la Résistance for war service, 1945; many literary and artistic awards, including: Obie award, 1958, 1960, 1962, 1964; Italia prize, 1959; Nobel prize for

literature, 1969; National Grand prize for theatre, 1975; New York Drama
Critics Circle citation, 1984. Member of the German Academy of Art;
Companion of Literature, Royal Society of Literature, 1984; Member,
Aosdána, 1986. *Died 22 December 1989.*

Publications

PLAYS

Le Kid, with Georges Pelorson (produced 1931).
En Attendant Godot (produced 1953). 1952; translated by Beckett as *Waiting
  for Godot: Tragicomedy* (produced 1955), 1954.
Fin de partie (produced in French, 1957). With *Acte sans paroles,* 1957;
  translated by Beckett as *Endgame* (produced 1958) with *Act Without
  Words,* 1958.
Acte sans paroles, with music by John Beckett (produced in French, 1957).
  With *Fin de partie,* 1957; translated by Becket as *Act Without Words,* with
  Endgame, 1958.
All That Fall, from the radio play (broadcast 1957; produced 1965). 1957.
From an Abandoned Work. 1958.
Krapp's Last Tape (produced 1958). With *Embers,* 1959.
Embers (broadcast 1959). In *Evergreen Review,* November–December, 1959;
  with *Krapp's Last Tape,* 1959.
Act Without Words II (produced 1960). In *New Directions,* 1, Summer 1959;
  in *Krapp's Last Tape and Other Dramatic Pieces,* 1960.
Krapp's Last Tape and Other Dramatic Pieces (includes *All That Fall; Embers;
  Act Without Words I and II*). 1960.
The Old Tune, from Robert Pinget's *La Manivelle* (broadcast 1960). In *La
  Manivelle/The Old Tune,* by Pinget, 1960; also in *Plays 1,* by Pinget, 1963.
Happy Days (produced 1961). 1961; translated by Beckett as *Oh Les Beaux
  Jours* (produced 1963). 1963; bilingual edition, edited by James Knowlson,
  1978.
Words and Music (broadcast 1962). In *Evergreen Review,* November–
  December 1962; in book form, in *Play and Two Short Pieces for Radio,*
  1964.
Play (in German, as *Spiel,* produced 1963; as *Play,* 1964). As *Spiel,* in *Theater
  heute,* July 1963; as *Play,* in *Play and Two Short Pieces for Radio,* 1964.
Cascando, music by Marcel Mihalovici (broadcast in French, 1963; in English,
  1964). In German, in *Dramatische Dichtungen,* 1, 1963; in English, in
  Evergreen Review, May–June, 1963; in book form, in *Play and Two Short
  Pieces for Radio,* 1964.
Play and Two Short Pieces for Radio (includes *Words and Music* and
  Cascando). 1964.
Film (screenplay 1965). In *Eh Joe and Other Writings,* 1967.
Va et vient: Dramaticule (in German as *Kommen und Gehen,* produced 1966;
  as *Va et vient,* produced 1966). 1966; translated by Beckett as *Come and
  Go: Dramaticule* (produced 1968), 1967.
Eh Joe (broadcast 1966; produced 1978). In *Eh Joe and Other Writings,* 1967.
Eh Joe and Other Writings (includes *Act Without Words II* and *Film*). 1967.
Cascando and Other Short Dramatic Pieces (includes *Words and Music; Eh
  Joe; Play; Come and Go; Film*). 1968.

Breath (produced as part of Kenneth Tynan's *Oh! Calcutta!*, 1969. In *Breath and Other Shorts*, 1971.

Breath and Other Shorts (includes *Come and Go; Act Without Words I and II*; and the prose piece *From an Abandoned Work*). 1971.

Not I (produced 1972). 1973.

Fragment de Théâtre. 1974. Translated by Beckett as *Theatre I and II*, in *Ends and Odds*, 1976.

That Time (produced 1976). 1976.

Footfalls (produced 1976). 1976.

Ghost Trio (broadcast 1977). In *Ends and Odds*, 1976.

. . . but the clouds . . . (broadcast 1977). In *Ends and Odds*, 1976.

Rough For Radio I. As *Sketch for a Radio Play*, in *Stereo Headphones*, 7, 1976; as *Radio I*, in *Ends and Odds*, 1976; as *Rough for Radio I*, in *Collected Shorter Plays*, 1984.

Rough for Radio II (broadcast as *Rough for Radio*, 1976). As *Radio II*, in *Ends and Odds*, 1976; as *Rough for Radio II*, in *Collected Shorter Plays*, 1976.

Ends and Odds: Eight New Dramatic Pieces (includes *Not I; That Time; Footfalls; Ghost Trio; Theatre I and II; Radio I and II*). 1976; as *Ends and Odds: Plays and Sketches* (includes *Not I; That Time; Footfalls; Ghost Trio; . . . but the clouds . . .; Theatre I and II; Radio I and II*), 1977.

A Piece of Monologue (produced 1980). In *Rockaby and Other Short Pieces*, 1981.

Rockaby and Other Short Pieces (includes *A Piece of Monologue* and *Ohio Impromptu*). 1981.

Rockaby (produced 1981). In *Rockaby and Other Short Pieces*, 1981.

Ohio Impromptu (produced 1981). In *Rockaby and Other Short Pieces*, 1981.

Catastrophe (produced 1982). In *Collected Shorter Plays*, 1984.

Three Occasional Pieces (includes *A Piece of Monologue; Rockaby; Ohio Impromptu*). 1982.

Catastrophe et autres dramaticules: Cette fois; Solo; Berceuse; Impromptu d'Ohio. 1982.

Nacht und Traüme (broadcast 1982). In *Collected Shorter Plays*, 1982.

Quad (broadcast as *Quadrat 1+2*, 1982). In *Collected Shorter Plays*, 1982.

What Where (in German, as *Was Wo*, produced 1983; as *What Where*, produced 1983). In *Collected Shorter Plays*, 1984.

Collected Shorter Plays. 1984.

Ohio Impromptu; Catastrophe; What Where. 1984.

The Complete Dramatic Works. 1986.

SCREENPLAY: *Film*, 1965.

RADIO PLAYS: *All That Fall*, 1957; *Embers*, 1959; *The Old Tune*, from Robert Pinget's *La Manivelle*, 1960; *Words and Music*, 1962; *Cascando*, music by Marcel Mihalovici, in French, 1963, in English, 1964; *Rough for Radio*, 1976.

TELEVISION PLAYS: *Eh Joe*, 1966; *Not I*, from the stage play 1977; *Ghost Trio*, 1977; *. . . but the clouds . . .*, 1977; *Quad*, as *Quadrat 1+2*, 1982; *Nacht und Traüme*, 1982.

NOVELS

Murphy. 1938.
Molloy. 1951; translated by Beckett and Patrick Bowles, 1955.
Malone meurt. 1951; translated by Beckett as *Malone Dies*, 1956.
L'Innommable. 1953; translated by Beckett as *The Unnamable*, 1958.
Watt (written in English). 1953.
Molloy; Malone Dies; The Unnamable. 1960.
Comment c'est. 1961; translated by Beckett as *How It Is*, 1964.
Mercier et Camier. 1970; translated by Beckett as *Mercier and Camier*, 1974.

SHORT STORIES AND TEXTS

More Pricks than Kicks. 1934.
Nouvelles et Textes pour rien. 1955; translated by Beckett and Richard Seaver
    as *Stories and Texts for Nothing*, 1967.
From an Abandoned Work. 1958.
Imagination morte imaginez. 1965; translated by Beckett as *Imagination Dead
    Imagine*, 1965.
Assez. 1966; translated by Beckett as *Enough*, in *No's Knife*, 1967.
Bing. 1966; translated by Beckett as *Ping*, in *No's Knife*, 1967.
Têtes-Mortes (includes *D'Un Ouvrage Abandonné; Assez, Bing; Imagination
    morte imaginez*). 1967; translated by Beckett in *No's Knife*, 1967.
No's Knife: Collected Shorter Prose 1945–1966 (includes *Stories and Texts for
    Nothing; From an Abandoned Work; Enough; Imagination Dead Imagine;
    Ping*). 1967.
L'Issue. 1968.
Sans. 1969; translated by Beckett as *Lessness*, 1971.
Séjour. 1970.
Premier Amour. 1970; translated by Beckett as *First Love*, 1973.
Le Dépeupleur. 1971; translated by Beckett as *The Lost Ones*, 1972.
The North. 1972.
Abandonné. 1972.
Au loin un oiseau. 1973.
First Love and Other Shorts. 1974.
Fizzles. 1976.
For to End Yet Again and Other Fizzles. 1976.
All Strange Away. 1976.
Four Novellas (First Love; The Expelled; The Calmative; The End). 1977; as
    The Expelled and Other Novellas, 1980.
Six Residua. 1978.
Company. 1980.
Mal vu mal dit. 1981; translated by Beckett as *Ill Seen Ill Said*, 1982.
Worstward Ho. 1983.
Stirrings Still. 1988.
Nohow On (includes *Company; Ill Seen Ill Said; Worstward Ho*). 1989.

VERSE

Whoroscope. 1930.
Echo's Bones and Other Precipitates. 1935.

Gedichte (collected poems in English and French, with German translations). 1959.
Poems in English. 1961.
Poèmes. 1968.
Collected Poems in English and French. 1977; revised edition, as *Collected Poems 1930–1978,* 1984.
Mirlitonnades. 1978.

OTHER

"Dante . . . Bruno. Vico . . . Joyce," in *Our Exagmination round His Factification for Incamination of Work in Progress.* 1929.
Proust. 1931; with *Three Dialogues with Georges Duthuit,* 1965.
Three Dialogues with Georges Duthuit. In *Transition 48,* 1949; in book form, with *Proust,* 1965.
Bram van Velde, with Georges Duthuit and Jacques Putman. 1958; translated by Beckett and Olive Classe, 1960.
A Becket Reader. 1967
I Can't Go On: A Selection from the Work of Beckett, edited by Richard Seacver. 1976.
Disjecta: Miscellaneous Writings and a Dramatic Fragment, edited by Ruby Cohn. 1983.
Collected Shorter Prose 1945–1980. 1984.
Happy Days: The Production Notebook, edited by James Knowlson, 1985.
As the Story Was Told: Uncollected and Late Prose. 1990.

Translator, *Negro: An Anthology,* compiled by Nancy Cunard. 1934.
Translator, *Seven Poems by Paul Éluard.* In *Thorns of Thunder,* 1936.
Translator, *Anthology of Mexican Poetry,* edited by Octavio Paz. 1958.
Translator, with others, *Selected Poems,* by Alain Bosquet. 1963.
Translator, *Zone,* by Guillaume Apollinaire. 1972.
Translator, *Drunken Boat,* by Arthur Rimbaud, edited by James Knowlson and Felix Leakey. 1977.
Translator, with others, *No Matter No Fact.* 1988.

BIBLIOGRAPHY: *Samuel Beckett: His Works and His Critics: An Essay in Bibliography,* by Raymond Federman and John Fletcher, 1970; *Samuel Beckett: Checklist and Index of His Published Works 1967–1976* by Robin John Davis, 1979; *Samuel Beckett: A Reference Guide* by Cathleen Culotta Andonian 1988.

MANUSCRIPT COLLECTIONS: University of Texas, Austin; Ohio State University, Columbus; Washington University, St. Louis; Dartmouth College, Hanover, New Hampshire; Reading University, England.

CRITICAL STUDIES (selection): *Samuel Beckett: The Comic Gamut* by Ruby Cohn, 1962; *Samuel Beckett* by Ronald Hayman, 1968; revised edition, 1980; *Samuel Beckett Now: Critical Approaches to His Novels, Poetry, and Plays* edited by Melvin J. Friedman, 1970; *Beckett: A Study of His Plays* by John Fletcher and John Spurling, 1972, revised as *Beckett the Playwright,* 1985; *Back to Beckett* by Ruby Cohn, 1974; *Samuel Beckett: A Collection of*

Criticism edited by Ruby Cohn, 1975; *A Student's Guide to the Plays of Samuel Beckett* by Beryl S. Fletcher, 1978, revised edition, with John Fletcher, 1985; *Just Play: Beckett's Theatre* by Ruby Cohn, 1980; *Samuel Beckett: Modern Critical Views* edited by Harold Bloom, 1985; *Beckett on File*, edited by Virginia Cooke, 1985; *Samuel Beckett* by Linda Ben-Zvi, 1986; *Understanding Beckett: A Study of Monologue and Gesture in the Works of Beckett* by Peter Gidal, 1986; *Myth and Ritual in the Plays of Beckett* by Katherine H. Burkman, 1988; *Theatre of Shadows: Beckett's Drama 1956–1976* by Rosemary Pountney, 1988; *The Humour of Samuel Beckett* by Valerie Topsfield, 1988; *Beckett in Performance* by Jonathan Kalb, 1989; *Beckett* by Andrew K. Kennedy, 1989; *Understanding Samuel Beckett* by Alan Astro, 1990; *Women in Beckett: Performance and Critical Perspectives* by Linda Ben-Zvi, 1990.

When Samuel Beckett's *En Attendant Godot* (*Waiting for Godot*) opened at the Théâtre Babylone in Paris on 5 January 1953, the French dramatist and critic Jean Anouilh compared the event to the historic opening of Pirandello's *Six Characters in Search of an Author* two decades earlier, and he astutely described this new work as "a music-hall sketch of Pascal's *Pensées* as played by the Fraterlini clowns". That combination of ontological enigma and vaude-ville comedy (much of the latter indebted to the American silent films of Charlie Chaplin and Buster Keaton), combined, as Vivian Mercier observed, "in a play where nothing happens—twice", would become the hallmark of Beckett's assault first on naturalism and then on modernism itself.

The shock to English audiences schooled in the drawing-room comedies of Noël Coward, Somerset Maugham, and Arthur Wing Pinero was captured by the drama critic Harold Hobson: *Godot*

> knocked the shackles of plot from off the English drama. It destroyed the notion that the dramatist is God, knowing everything about his charac-ters and master of a complete philosophy answerable to all of our problems. It showed that Archer's dictum that a good play imitates the audible and visible surface of life is not necessarily true. It revealed that the drama approximates or can approximate the condition of music, touching chords deeper than can be reached by reason and saying things beyond the grasp of logic. It renewed the English theater in a single night.

The American premiere, however, generated something less than a theatrical renewal. Mistakenly promoted as "the laugh hit of two continents", *Waiting for Godot* opened at the Coconut Grove Playhouse in Miami Beach, Florida on January 3, 1956, to audiences of vacationers looking for easy diversion, and they, to say the least, were not amused. But America also saw the most visceral production of *Godot* ever staged when, in 1957, the San Francisco Actors' Workshop brought its production into the maximum security prison of San Quentin. A group of America's most hardened criminals—sentenced, in a wonderfully Beckettian phrase, "to life"—seemed to have little difficulty with this tale of waiting which puzzled critics the world over. As the reviewer for *The San Quentin News* clearly saw on 28 November 1957: "We're still waiting for Godot, and shall continue to wait. When the scenery gets too drab and the action too slow, we'll call each other names and swear to part forever—

but then there's no place to go". "That's how it is on this bitch of an earth", says Pozzo.

Thus with his first theatrical production Beckett managed to strip the theater of its conventions, to deal uncompromisingly with the philosophical enigmas of existence, and yet to appeal to audiences both cerebrally and viscerally by mixing the discourse of philosophy with the imagery of the music hall and the comic silent cinema.

The success of *Godot*, however, did not ensure future productions. When in 1957 French director Roger Blin attempted to stage Beckett's *Fin de partie* (*Endgame*) in Paris, he encountered so many difficulties that the play was finally produced in French at the Royal Court Theatre in London, before being moved to Paris. The interplay of the culinary characters, Hamm and Clov—chess pieces in a cosmic endgame, within the claustrophobic space of a bunker, pill box, or bomb shelter, Hamm blind and immobile, Clov sighted but tied to his master as tightly as Lucky is to Pozzo—is a dialectic of need and torment. More austerely than in *Godot*, Beckett developed in *Endgame* his unique sense of theater as a dialéctic of mime and monologue.

In 1956 the BBC's Third Programme solicited a radio script from Beckett, and he was immediately intrigued with the possibilities of the medium; as he wrote to Nancy Cunard, he "got a nice gruesome idea full of cartwheels and dragging of feet and puffing and panting which may or may not lead to something". It did, and *All That Fall*, broadcast in January 1957, began Beckett's long association with the BBC and with media works in general. When the BBC sent Beckett a tape of the broadcast, he was again fascinated by the dramatic possibilities of a disembodied voice, this time captured on audio tape, and he set to work shortly thereafter to stage it, producing *Krapp's Last Tape*. This interplay of art and technology continued to fascinate Beckett, and he wrote a series of radio plays for the BBC: *Embers, Words and Music*, and *Cascando*. In 1963 Beckett's American publisher asked him to write a films-cript and Beckett responded with the generically entitled *Film*, the shooting of which he oversaw in New York in July of 1964. But it was television which would allow Beckett to reach yet a wider audience, and in 1966 Beckett wrote *Eh Joe*, which he directed himself for German television and then oversaw for the BBC production in June of 1966.

In the theatre proper, Beckett continued his preoccupation with the mono-logue, producing a female counterpart to *Krapp's Last Tape* (without the tapes), *Happy Days*, in 1961. Buried to her waist in scorched sand for the first act and to her neck in the shorter second, Winnie retains an optimism in the face of her post-nuclear calamity that evokes the sort of bitter irony and pathos that make the role one of the great female leads in the theatre. Actresses, however, have had difficulty memorizing the long, complex, repetitive, looping monologue. In the Lincoln Center (New York) Beckett festival in 1972, Jessica Tandy, for instance, needed a television monitor built into her mound which functioned as a teleprompter. That Lincoln Center festival also saw the world premiere of another gruelling monologue, this time for a set of staged lips (reminiscent of the Man Ray painting and the Salvador Dali sofa), entitled *Not I*, and soon afterwards Beckett wrote another pair of monologues, *Footfalls* and *That Time*, both of which were produced as part of the 70th birthday celebration at the Royal Court Theatre in 1976, the former directed by Beckett himself. In 1981 Beckett created another brace of monologues for symposia planned to celebrate his 80th birthday at American universities. *Rockaby* was performed at the State University at Buffalo in April and *Ohio Impromptu* had its premiere at the Ohio State University Beckett Symposium in May, with both staged by long-time Beckett director Alan Schneider.

In addition to becoming the modern period's dominant playwright, Beckett also developed into a complete theatre man, serving an apprenticeship at first by attending rehearsals and advising directors and then taking full charge of his productions, beginning with *Va et vient* (*Come and Go*) in Paris in 1966. That same year Beckett directed, with full credit this time, the German television production of *Eh, Joe*. In 1967 the Schiller-Theater Werkstatt invited him to come to Berlin and direct any of his plays. He chose *Endspiel* (*Endgame*), "the favourite of my plays". Subsequently, from 1967 to 1985, Beckett directed some 16 other productions of his work in Berlin, Paris, and London, and beginning with *Endspiel*, kept detailed directorial notebooks for each staging. In the process of directing, Beckett also rewrote his texts. Publication of Beckett's theatrical notebooks, along with revised texts for his major plays, will make Beckett one of the most documented playwrights in the history of the theatre.

—S. E. Gontarski

See the essay on *Waiting for Godot*.

BEHAN, Brendan (Francis).

Born in Dublin, Ireland, 9 February 1923. Educated at the French Sisters of Charity School, Dublin, 1928–34; Christian Brothers School, Dublin, 1934–37; Day Apprentice School, 1937. Married Beatrice ffrench-Salkeld in 1955; one daughter. Joined the Irish Republican Army in 1937; apprentice housepainter, 1937–39; sent to Hollesley Bay Borstal, England, 1939–41, and deported; served terms in Mountjoy, Arbour Hill, and Curragh prisons, 1942–46; housepainter, journalist, and seaman, 1946–50; broadcaster, Radio Eireann, 1951–53; columnist, *Irish Press*, Dublin, 1954–55. Recipient: Obie award, 1958; Paris Festival award, 1958; French Critics award, 1962. *Died 20 March 1964.*

Publications

PLAYS

Moving Out (broadcast 1952). In *Complete Plays*, 1978.
A Garden Party (broadcast 1952). In *Complete Plays*, 1978.
The Quare Fellow (produced 1954; revised version, 1956). 1956.
The Big House (broadcast 1957). In *Complete Plays*, 1978.
An Giall (produced 1958). In *Poems and a Play in Irish*, 1981; translated by Richard Wall, 1987.
The Hostage, with Joan Littlewood, from *An Giall* (produced 1958). 1958; revised version, 1962.
The Big House, from the radio play (produced 1958). In *Complete Plays*, 1978.
The New House, a two-act stage version of Behan's radio plays *Moving Out*

and *A Garden Party*, (produced 1958). In *Best Short Plays of the World Theater 1958–1967*, edited by Stanley Richards, 1968.
Richard's Cork Leg, edited and completed by Alan Simpson (produced 1972). 1973.
Time for a Gargle (produced 1973).
Complete Plays (includes *The Quare Fellow; The Hostage; The Big House; Moving Out; A Garden Party; Richard's Cork Leg*). 1978.

RADIO PLAYS: *Moving Out*, 1952; *A Garden Party*, 1952; *The Big House*, 1957.

NOVEL
The Scarperer. 1964.

VERSE
Life Styles: Poems, with Nine Translations from the Irish of Brendan Behan, translated by Ulick O'Connor. 1973.
Poems and Stories, edited by Denis Cotter. 1978.
Poems and a Play in Irish. 1981.

OTHER
Borstal Boy (autobiography). 1958.
Behan's Island: An Irish Sketch-Book. 1962.
Hold Your Hour and Have Another (articles). 1963.
Behan's New York. 1964.
Confessions of an Irish Rebel. 1965.
The Wit of Behan, edited by Sean McCann. 1968.
After the Wake: Twenty-One Prose Works, edited by Peter Fallon. 1981.

BIBLIOGRAPHY: E.H. Mikhail, *Brendan Behan: An Annotated Bibliography of Criticism*, 1980.

CRITICAL STUDIES: *Beckett and Behan and a Theatre in Dublin* by Alan Simpson, 1962; *With Breast Expanded* by Brian Behan, 1964; *My Brother Brendan* by Dominic Behan, 1965; *The World of Behan* edited by Sean McCann, 1965; *Behan: Man and Showman* by Rae Jeffs, 1966; *Brendan Behan* by Ted E. Boyle, 1969; *Brendan Behan* by Ulick O'Connor, 1970, as *Brendan*, 1971; *Brendan Behan: A Memoir* by Seamus de Burca, 1971; *My Life with Brendan* by Beatrice Behan, Des Hickey, and Gus Smith, 1973; *The Major Works of Behan* by Peter R. Gerdes, 1973; *Brendan Behan* by Raymond Porter, 1973; *The Writings of Behan* by Colbert Kearney, 1977; *The Art of Behan* edited by E.H. Mikhail, 1979; *With Behan* by Peter Arthurs, 1981; *Behan: Interviews and Recollections* edited by E.H. Mikhail, (2 vols.), 1982.

The place of Behan in the pantheon of heroic drunks of 20th-century literature has long been secure, and with it the concomitant quality of masculine sexism. But, apart from alcohol dependence, numerous influences converge on the production of the plays which he may—loosely—be regarded as having written. His membership of the IRA, his experience of imprisonment, his collaboration with Alan Simpson and Joan Littlewood as director and dramaturg, and his proclivity towards the retrieval of a lost Gaelic identity—all of these factors merge in most of his work. Whatever the complexities of his personality, as a writer he was eagerly—and carelessly—eclectic, absorbing and distorting influences with what often looks like the swagger of literary vandalism but is probably closer to the workings of misprision. Scraps of Shaw and O'Casey surface surprisingly in *The Big House*, and the popular novels of Liam O'Flaherty are echoed in *An Giall* and its reworking as *The Hostage*. His journalistic curiosity meant that, in his sober years, any social situation seems to have stimulated his imaginative energy. His prose writings reflect his prison experience as a constant process of research, which included snatching at every opportunity to learn more Gaelic.

Behan's two major plays, *The Quare Fellow* and *The Hostage*, are stylistically antithetical, representing extremes of naturalism and Brechtian stylisation. However, their focusing methods are fundamentally the same. In each case, the on-stage characters represent the periphery of a more momentous public action, in that they have their attention fixed on another, off-stage drama in another arena: a person who is to be executed at dawn. In neither play is this person seen, but the reality of his predicament seems unquestionable, so that it governs the focus of both characters and audience; theatre-goers find themselves viewing reality through fictitious eyes. In each case, this ultimate focus has a high level of urgency, using a countdown process to generate tension both on stage and in the auditorium. For the characters, the condemned man represents a yardstick by which they measure themselves, whether in terms of normality, morality, or heroism. This is particularly clear in *The Hostage*, where one character brags about his impossible heroics with the IRA, subconsciously measuring himself against the Irish martyr in the background; but in the earlier play, also, the execution serves as a catalyst which makes the characters look hard at their own stature.

In neither play is it possible to isolate the text from the life and character of the author, and Behan's habit of writing himself into his plays means that they can have no pretension to objectivity. In the original production of *The Quare Fellow*, Behan himself sang the part of the prisoner in the punishment cells, so that each act began or ended with the author's own voice, making its formal effect rather like that of a ballad: at times, there is just the voice of the singer, at other times the ballad is fleshed out and animated. In *The Hostage*, a similar effect is achieved by the presence of the pianist, who seems to be half a character in the play, half a function of the author. In that play, there is actually a reference to the author—"Brendan Behan, he's too anti-British". Coming immediately after the most inflammatory patriotic song in the play, the effect is of strong alienation, and it leads directly to the fulfilment of the play's parabolic form as the title character finds his name in a newspaper and reads that he is to be shot in reprisal.

Characteristically, Behan does not end his play at the point at which the parable realises itself, but adds a final act which works as a coda in which the reality of death is inescapable but the perception of it is blurred by the often ludicrous action in the brothel on stage.

The same absurd vision permeates Behan's last, incomplete play, *Richard's Cork Leg*, where one character echoes Donne: "The grave's a dark and silent place and none there are to there embrace". The setting, an Irish cemetery which is dominated by a chapel and a tomb, is the object of an annual pilgrimage by Irish prostitutes. The tomb, of Crystal Clear, a prostitute hero, broadly satirises Irish piety, especially as the pilgrims are met by a group of Open Brethren, an extreme form of puritanism, and there is an obvious parallel between their ethos and the grave. Every element in this play seems a travesty of what it initially appears to represent, a tendency which was already strong in the brothel of *The Hostage*, but here there is no off-stage referential focus to give the action urgency, and it frequently dissolves into the tone of a revue.

The prostitution theme in Behan may be seen as ambiguous. *An Giall*, the original Gaelic version of *The Hostage*, was much closer to the naturalism of *The Quare Fellow*, and Littlewood's involvement in reshaping it for the Theatre Workshop production obviously increased its stylisation very considerably. One Gaelic scholar has paradoxically termed *An Giall* a "naturalistic tragedy"—paradoxical because naturalism denies the attribution of blame—and it is not difficult to see the brothel as the context of a demonstration of the animalism of humanity. But it is also a more overtly ideological play than any of the plays in English, and although there seems little doubt that Littlewood did a lot of interpolation and rescripting, it is also arguable that Behan's choice of language reflected different senses of the function of theatre. All writing in Gaelic was essentially and inevitably political, but the English-speaking theatre was commonly the arena for Behan's imagined triumphs as a clown, vindicated by his perception of that theatre as culminating in music-hall.

—Howard McNaughton

See the essay on *The Hostage*.

BENNETT, Alan.

Born in Leeds, Yorkshire, 9 May 1934. Educated at Leeds Modern School, 1946–52; Exeter College, Oxford, 1954–57 (Open Scholar in History), B.A. (honours) 1957. National Service: Joint Services School for Linguists, Cambridge and Bodmin. Temporary junior lecturer in history, Magdalen College, Oxford, 1960–62. Recipient: *Evening Standard* award, 1961, 1968, 1971, 1985 (for screenplay); Tony award, 1963; Guild of Television Producers award, 1967; Broadcasting Press Guild award, for television play 1984, 1991; Royal Television Society award, 1984, 1986; Olivier award, 1990. D. Litt.: University of Leeds, 1990. Honorary Fellow, Exeter College, Oxford, 1987. Agent: Peters, Fraser, and Dunlop Group, 503/4 The Chambers, Chelsea Harbour, Lots Road, London SW10 0XF, England.

Publications

PLAYS

Beyond the Fringe, with others (produced 1960). 1963.
Forty Years On (produced 1968). 1969.
Sing a Rude Song (additional material), book by Caryl Brahms and Ned Sherrin, music by Ron Grainer (produced 1969).
Getting On (produced 1971). 1972.
Habeas Corpus (produced 1973). 1973.

The Old Country (produced 1977). 1978.

Office Suite (includes *Green Forms*, televised as *Doris and Doreen*, 1978, and *A Visit from Miss Prothero*, televised 1978; produced 1987). 1981.

Enjoy (produced 1980). 1980.

Objects of Affection and Other Plays for Television (includes *Objects of Affection: Our Winnie, A Woman of No Importance, Rolling Home, Marks*, and *Say Something Happened*; and *A Day Out, Intensive Care, An Englishman Abroad*). 1982.

Single Spies 1989; with *Talking Heads*, 1990.
   An Englishman Abroad (televised 1983; also director: produced 1988).
   A Question of Attribution (produced 1988).

A Private Function (screenplay). 1984.

Forty Years On, Getting On, Habeas Corpus. 1985.

The Writer in Disguise (television plays; includes *Me, I'm Afraid of Virginia Woolf; Afternoon Off; One Fine Day; All Day on the Sands; The Old Crowd*; and an essay). 1985.

Kafka's Dick (produced 1986). In *Two Kafka Plays*, 1987.

The Insurance Man (televised 1986). In *Two Kafka Plays*, 1987.

Prick Up Your Ears (screenplay). 1987.

Talking Heads (includes *A Chip in the Sugar, Bed Among the Lentils, A Lady of Letters, Her Big Chance, Soldiering On, A Cream Cracker Under the Settee*) (televised 1987; produced 1992).1987; with *Single Spies*, 1990.

Single Spies and Talking Heads: Two Plays and Six Monologues. 1990.

The Wind in the Willows (produced 1990). 1991.

Forty Years On and Other Plays (includes *Getting On, Habeas Corpus, Enjoy*). 1991.

The Madness of George III (produced 1991). 1992.

SCREENPLAYS: *A Private Function*, 1984; *Prick Up Your Ears*, 1987.

RADIO PLAYS: *Uncle Clarence* (a talk) 1986; *The Lady in the Van*, 1990.

TELEVISION PLAYS: *On the Margin* series, 1966; *A Day Out*, 1972; *Sunset Across the Bay*, 1975; *A Little Outing*, 1977; *A Visit from Miss Prothero*, 1978; *Me, I'm Afraid of Virginia Woolf*, 1978; *Doris and Doreen*, 1978; *The Old Crowd*, 1979; *Afternoon Off*, 1979; *One Fine Day*, 1979; *All Day on the Sands*, 1979; *Intensive Care*, 1982; *Objects of Affection* (5 plays), 1982; *An Englishman Abroad*, 1983; *The Insurance Man*, 1986; *Talking Heads* (6 monologues), 1987; *102 Boulevard Haussmann*, 1990; *A Question of Attribution*, 1991.

CRITICAL STUDY: *Beyond the Fringe . . . and Beyond: A Critical Biography of Alan Bennett, Peter Cook, Jonathan Miller, and Dudley Moore* by Roland Bergan, 1990.

THEATRICAL ACTIVITIES

DIRECTOR: **Plays**—*An Englishman Abroad*, 1988.

ACTOR: **Plays**—in *Better Late* (revue), 1959; in *Beyond the Fringe*, 1960, 1961, and 1962; Archbishop of Canterbury in *The Blood of the Bambergs* by John

Osborne, 1962; Reverend Sloley-Jones in *A Cuckoo in the Nest* by Ben
Travers, 1964; Tempest in *Forty Years On*, 1968; Mrs. Swabb in *Habeas
Corpus*, 1974; role in *Down Cemetery Road: The Landscape of Philip Larkin*,
1987; Tailor in *An Englishman Abroad*, 1988; Anthony Blunt in *A Question
of Attribution*, 1988. Films—*Long Shot*, 1980; *The Secret Policeman's Ball*,
1986. Radio—in *The Great Jowett* by Graham Greene, 1980; *Dragon* by Don
Haworth, 1982; Machiavelli in *Better Halves* by Christopher Hope, 1988.
Television—Augustus Hare in *Famous Gossips*, 1965; in *The Drinking Party*,
1965; in *Alice in Wonderland*, 1966; in *On the Margin*, 1966; Denis Midgley
in *Intensive Care*, 1982; Shallow in *The Merry Wives of Windsor*, 1982;
Housemaster in *Breaking Up*, 1986; narrator of *Man and Music*, 1986; in
Fortunes of War, 1987; narrator of *Dinner at Noon* (*By-Line* series), 1988; in
A Chip in the Sugar, 1988.

. . . when we play language games, we do so rather in order to find out
what game it is we are playing.

—*Beyond the Fringe*

Whatever their ostensible themes, Alan Bennett's plays ultimately dramatize
man's desire to define himself and his world through teasingly inadequate
language, whether folk adages, government jargon, pronouncements from TV
experts, or misapplied quotations from the "Greats." The resulting parodies
simultaneously mock and honor the impulse to erect linguistic defenses in a
frightening world. Bennett's comedy generally respects his characters, from
aspiring intellectuals to northern ladies for whom "conversation is a conspiracy." But some recent works, like the TV plays collected as *The Writer in
Disguise*, do not always resist the temptation to condescend: "Still our eldest
girl's a manicurist and we've got a son in West Germany, so we haven't done
too badly." Bennett's increasing reliance on scatological humor, which reduces
some characters to animals with pretensions to dignity, creates some easy
laughs. When focusing on professional writers like Kafka in later plays or Joe
Orton in the film *Prick Up Your Ears*, Bennett sometimes overworks the
audience's smug recognition of verbal and thematic allusions to these authors.
Such distractions threaten to overwhelm his serious aims.

In *Beyond the Fringe* both Bennett's monologues and sketches with Peter
Cook, Jonathan Miller, and Dudley Moore focus on the game cliché, which
trivializes the supposedly serious, yet suggests that even inane values are better
than none. A supposed lecture by the Duke of Edinburgh illustrates the
precariousness of metaphorical language as well as an underlying desire for
decency: "This business of international politics is a game. . . . It's a hard
game, it's a rough game . . . sometimes, alas, it's a dirty game, but the point
about a game, surely, is that there's no need to take it seriously. . . ." Other
Fringe sketches brilliantly question the limits of discourse: a prison governor
rebukes a condemned man who rejects an analogy between capital punishment
and public school caning, "Come along, now, you're playing with words." Just
as this semantic comedy foreshadows later plays like Hampton's *The
Philanthropist* and Stoppard's *Jumpers*, "Aftermyth," a *Fringe* sketch on
Britain during the Blitz, seems the spiritual parent of the many parodies of
wartime England during the early 1970's. Bennett illuminates both the hilar-

ious perversion of political rhetoric and the profound need to find attractive equivalents for painful reality.

The Headmaster in *Forty Years On*, an ingenious play-within-a-play focusing on the annual performance by the boys and faculty of Albion School, indulges in similar rhetoric: "The more observant among you will have noticed that one of Bombardier Tiffin's legs was not his own. The other one, God bless him, was lost in the Great War. Some people lost other things, less tangible perhaps than legs, but no less worthwhile—they lost illusions, they lost hope, they lost faith. . . ." *Forty Years On* organizes a series of skits, similar in tone to "Aftermyth," on the cultural and political life of 20th-century England. Wicked portraits of culture heroes like Virginia Woolf and T.E. Lawrence are both outrageously unfair and deadly accurate. The best sketch is the Wilde pastiche in which Lady Dundowne, played by one of the masters in drag, advises her nephew to marry his spinster mother: "the arrangement seems so tidy that I am surprised it does not happen more often in society"—a perfect spoof of the archetypal Wilde plot and wit. "But then all women dress like their mothers, that is their tragedy. No man ever does. That is his," a parody of Wildean paradox, resonates with additional meaning from the elaborate pattern of homosexual allusion in the play; in this representative public school world, witty hyperbole equals literal statement. Bennett exposes the simultaneous idiocy and seductiveness of language on all levels, from the folk-wisdom of a nanny to the devious rhetoric of Chamberlain, while the rude singing of the rugby team both undercuts and elevates the idealized game metaphor of the school anthem. Though only the Headmaster emerges as a character, the cast of stereotypes is suitable for what is essentially a comic allegory of English life.

Getting On, an ambitious Chekhovian comedy, involves a fortyish Labour MP, George Oliver, whose nostalgia for stability ("What we crave in life is order") and linguistic skill link him with the Headmaster. His precarious illusion of order depends on an innocence of the sexual and political realities of his world: his son by a first marriage, his young second wife, and a Conservative homosexual MP form a strange triangle; his West Indian constituent who claimed that neighbors were poisoning her dog is not mad, as he had believed. Reality seems too complex for his categorizing, analytical mind, and, despite his belief in logic and language, he concludes, after a hilariously unsuccessful attempt to order a taxi, "Words fail me." Though continually confronted with proof of the pointlessness of work, George persists with established values (his only radical action, from an English viewpoint, is throwing a bucket of water at a dog that perpetually fouls his doorstep). Yet, as the punning title suggests, the ultimate reward for hard work is aging and death.

Habeas Corpus, which focuses on a sadly lecherous, aging GP in Hove, somewhat uneasily balances a well-made farce plot with Bennett's verbal comedy, more elegiac than ever amid a frenzy of trouserless men, missed assignations, and a spinster with an artificial bust. The wit, frequently obsessed with the decline of England or of individual Englishmen, often slows down the crucial pacing of the farce, which, in turn, sometimes undercuts the impact of Bennett's parodies. The wistful tone of the comedy is apparent in the doctor's lament for his lacerated sensibility: "They parade before me bodies the color of tripe and the texture of junket. Is this the image of God, this sagging parcel of vanilla blancmange hoisted day after day on to the consulting table? Is this the precious envelope of the soul?" Though such disillusionment does not stop his pursuit of a nubile young patient, his later reference to "the long littleness of life" as he prepares to examine her attests to the general elegiac note of the play. This mood derives partly from the songs and verses, like those in Auden's verse plays, that allow characters to comment directly to the audience, as the action stops: "So if you get your heart's desire,/Your longings come to pass,-/Remember in each other's beds,/It isn't going to last." The resulting vaudeville atmosphere, however effective, softens the hard lines of the farce, a form that Bennett wisely abandoned in the plays that followed.

The Old Country, another comic elegy on the continuing decline of England, initially puzzles the viewer with its tricky setting, a country house outside Moscow in which a British defector, Hilary, and his wife, Bron, have tried to recreate the England he betrayed. A visit from Hilary's sister and her husband, Duff, ostensibly in Russia to lecture on Forster, brings the offer of a return to an England Hilary will no longer recognize. Hilary and Duff, former Oxbridge men like Bennett, conduct a typical loving yet satirical analysis of Forster *dicta* like "Only connect."

In the debate over the desirability of return, when Bron asks where in England they could leave their doors unlocked for long periods, her sister-in-law replies, "Wiltshire once. Not any more. There are muggers in Malmesbury." Hilary attempts a more balanced assessment of the overall situation: "No Gamages. No Pontins. No more trains from Kemble to Cirencester. No Lyons. On the other hand I read of the Renaissance of the small bakery; country breweries revive. Better bread, better beer. They come from Florence to shop in Marks and Spencer. It is not an easy decision." But Bron angrily rejects this supposed objectivity as another instance of his ability to argue both sides simultaneously. Certainly Hilary does seem the archetypal Bennett verbal juggler as he tries to define the English response to experience with a complex litany of familiar allusions: "Irony is inescapable. We're conceived in irony. We float in it from the womb. It's the amniotic fluid. It's the silver sea. It's the waters at their priestlike task washing away guilt and purpose and responsibility. Joking but not joking. Caring but not caring. Serious but not serious." *The Old Country*, Bennett's most successful play since *Forty Years On*, dramatizes the dangerous moral and political consequences of this semantic playfulness.

Green Forms, one of two television plays collected as *Office Suite*, satirizes the attempts of government workers to define the unknown with comforting jargon. Perplexed by the computerization of the system and the expendability of employees and whole offices, the workers display typical linguistic resourcefulness: "Southport is being wound down. . . . Wound down. Wound up. Phased out anyway. I hope she hasn't been made . . . you know. . . . Well . . . redundant. I wouldn't like to think she's been made redundant; she was very nicely spoken." *A Visit from Miss Prothero*, the second one-acter, abounds in cozy malice as a retired bureaucrat gradually realizes the worthlessness of his life's work. In his world, gossip masquerades as folk-wisdom (Miss Prothero comments on an associate's eczema: "The doctor thinks it's nerves. I think it's those tights. Man-made fibers don't do for everybody. I pay if I wear crimplene").

Enjoy depicts a typical northern family, the son a transsexual social worker, the daughter a prostitute ("She's exceptional. You won't find girls like Linda stood on every street corner"), while the parents await the demolition of their home and speculate on their future residence: "It's a maisonette. They're built more on the human scale. That's the latest thing now, the human scale." Unfortunately, no authentic unifying tone emerges from the play's blend of folk comedy, parody, and satire on deranged social planners. That the old life with its family betrayals and vulgarities does not merit preservation, except as an historical curiosity, weakens concern for the fates of the couple, though there are affecting moments.

The Writer in Disguise, a collection of plays Bennett wrote for television, is uneven in quality and sometimes relies on a familiar mixture of nostalgia for, and broad satire of British seaside life (*All Day on the Sands, Afternoon Off*) but does reveal his ability to write for film and videotape as well as the stage. The best of the collection, *Me, I'm Afraid of Virginia Woolf*, develops Bennett's ambiguous views of Woolf and of high culture in general and mocks the futility of "further education" through the career of a literature teacher. As is frequent with Bennett, the best lines are not necessarily those that reinforce the key themes but primarily display his impressive wit, as when the protagonist attempts to explain unorthodox sex to his mother: "Having tea in Marshall and Snelgrove's isn't lesbianism."

A series of monologues, *Talking Heads*, further displays Bennett's skill at conveying character through speech. Aside from the strained and *Her Big Chance*, these monologues magically fuse pathos with their comedy and generate sympathy even for upper-class ladies in decline (*Soldiering On*). The strongest is *Bed Among the Lentils*, a showcase for Maggie Smith as the alcoholic wife of a vicar saved by an affair with a Pakistani shopkeeper. Though it never quite transcends the stereotypes of warring female parishioners ("If you think squash is a competitive activity, try flower arrangement") and sexually adroit third-worlders, the monologue brilliantly balances its compassion for the trapped wife with a satire of Christian values.

Single Spies, a program of one-acters, raises disturbing questions about patriotism and personal integrity in terms reminiscent of E.M. Forster, whose life seems of obsessive interest in a number of Bennett works. *An Englishman Abroad* derives from actress Coral Browne's encounter with Guy Burgess in Moscow, and *A Question of Attribution* wittily analyzes ethics and loyalties through conversations between Anthony Blunt, the "4th man," and Elizabeth II ("I was talking about art. I'm not sure that she was.") The play more than satisfies the uneasy anticipation created by the promise of a royal portrait: "If I am doing nothing, I like to be doing nothing to some purpose. That is what leisure means." With its Wildean echoes, the dialogue balances mockery of narrowness with insight into an impossible role. These two plays, while clearly sympathetic to their protagonists, differentiate interestingly between the physically and emotionally unkempt Burgess, and the colder, more controlled, provocatively ambiguous Blunt, for whom espionage may have been merely an elaborate game enabling him to savor his intellectual superiority to his compatriots. *Single Spies* reveals Bennett's increasing interest in biographical drama, a tendency evident in early works with references to the private lives of

T.E. Lawrence or Forster and culminating in the plays on Kafka and George III.

The Insurance Man, written for television, wittily attempts to reconcile Kafka's career as both an insurance executive and partner in an asbestos factory with the view of the universe conveyed by his fiction. Kafka's concern for a laborer, Franz, suffering from a work-related malady, leads him to offer Franz a job in the factory. The bitter comedy of Bennett's version of Kafka's world ("Just because you're the injured party, it doesn't mean you are not the guilty party.") ingeniously reveals a system in which even well-meaning officials like Kafka are doomed to intensify human suffering.

Less successful is *Kafka's Dick*, which traces Kafka's anti-authoritarian themes to his relationship with his father. The play is long for what it accomplishes, brilliant in some set pieces, but more a series of vaudeville skits than a coherent work. The Kafka who returns to life to learn that his writings have not been destroyed as he wished tries futilely to balance posthumous fame and the attendant loss of privacy (the title allusion especially disturbs him) and rivalry with writers like Proust: "My room was noisy. It was next door to my parents. When I was trying to write I had to listen to them having sexual intercourse. I'm the one who needed the cork-lined room. And he's the greatest writer of the twentieth century. O God."

Even more ambitious is *The Madness of George III*. Bennett's earlier portrait of Elizabeth II demonstrated an ability to get inside the skin of unexpected characters, though George III's bad press makes him a special challenge. Bennett skillfully weaves in necessary exposition: "Pitt was on our side then. Now he has stitched himself into the flag and passed himself off as the spirit of the nation and the Tories as the collective virtue of England. . . ." though such speeches lack the force of parallel passages in Shakespeare's histories. Bennett's emphasis on scatological humor seems appropriate in an analysis of George's unfortunate physical symptoms, some of which result from the uninformed arrogance of his physicians and all of which reinforce his humanity, a humanity that seems especially vulnerable since his most private functions become matters of public interest and debate. Inviting comparison with such examples of royal madness as Lear and Caligula, George never approaches their tragic dimensions, despite Bennett's reference to "tragic hero" in the preface. Bennett's king is too limited intellectually and spiritually for tragic stature, and the audience's continual awareness of his unpleasant symptoms establishes him primarily as a physical man, a Job without the spiritual capacity. Bennett also errs in introducing long passages from Shakespeare's play, which, though touching in their picture of Lear's regeneration, underscore the limitations of Bennett's psychology and language. The curtailing of George's mad speeches, which Bennett justifies in the preface, tends to minimize any sense of the king's mental and emotional complexity; it is difficult to know whether Bennett might have transcended his talent for making jokes about doctors and politicians and presented a figure of real stature. Just as the copious prefaces and production notes for this play and others suggest another Shaw, so does Bennett's gift for debunking history: the portrait of a loquacious Burke who bored his auditors is especially amusing. Despite some problems, this play represents real development for Bennett in its attempt to define a character in the context of a complex society, when the character is a ruler and the society is that of 18th-century English politics.

Bennett's ability to subordinate his verbal flourishes to some larger purpose is evident in his film scripts *Prick Up Your Ears* and *A Private Function*. In fact, the former unnecessarily downplays Joe Orton's genius with language in order to highlight more cinematic material about his sexual antics, and thus Orton's core, the rich talent that justified the biography, seems missing, though the film has some brilliant episodes. Less ambitious, *A Private Function* succeeds in its treatment of the social hierarchy in a postwar northern town, as a chiropodist and his wife try to overcome class barriers and an unfair system of rationing with the help of an illegal pig for a dinner honoring the newly-wed Princess Elizabeth. The polished dialogue and comic atmosphere suggest Chaucer's fabliaux, and Bennett's signature scatological humor seems exactly right in a work involving a pig, a chiropodist, a butcher, and a bizarre farm family. Like Bennett's best comedy the film creates a believable social world, and the dialogue reaffirms his status as England's pre-eminent comic drama-tist. Impressively prolific and apparently eager to expand his thematic range, Bennett has, through a long career, continued to fulfill the dazzling promise of his early work.

—Burton S. Kendle

See the essay on *Forty Years On*.

BERKOFF, Steven.

Born in Stepney, London, 3 August 1937. Educated at schools in Stepney; Hackney Downs Grammar School, London; Webber-Douglas Academy of Dramatic Art, London, 1958–59; École Jacques Lecoq, Paris, 1965. Married Shelley Lee in 1976. Actor in repertory in Nottingham, Liverpool, Coventry, and at Citizens' Theatre Glasgow, for six years. Since 1973 founding director, London Theatre Group. Recipient: Los Angeles Drama Critics Circle award, for directing, 1983. Agent: Joanna Marston, Rosica Colin Ltd., 1 Clareville Grove Mews, London SW7 5AH, England.

Publications

PLAYS

In the Penal Colony, adaptation of a story by Kafka (produced 1968). In *The Trial, Metamorphosis, In the Penal Colony: Three Theatre Adaptations from Franz Kafka*, 1988.

Metamorphosis, adaptation of a story by Kafka (produced 1968). With *The Trial*, 1981.

The Trial, adaptation of a novel by Kafka (produced 1971). With *Metamorphosis*, 1981.

Agamemnon, adaptation of a play by Aeschylus (produced 1971; revised version produced 1976). In *East, Agamemnon, The Fall of the House of Usher*, 1977.

Knock at the Manor Gate, adaptation of a story by Kafka (produced 1972).

Miss Julie Versus Expressionism, adaptation of a play by Strindberg (produced 1973).

Lunch (as *Mr. Prufrock's Songs*, produced 1974; revised version, as *Lunch*, produced 1981). In *West, Lunch, Harry's Christmas*, 1985.

The Fall of the House of Usher, adaptation of the story by Poe (produced 1974). In *East, Agamemnon, The Fall of the House of Usher*, 1977.

East (produced 1975). In *East, Agamemnon, The Fall of the House of Usher*, 1977.

East, Agamemnon, The Fall of the House of Usher. 1977.

Greek (produced 1980). With *Decadence*, 1982.

West (produced 1980). In *West, Lunch, Harry's Christmas*, 1985.

Decadence (produced 1981). With *Greek*, 1982.

Harry's Christmas (produced 1985). In *West, Lunch, Harry's Christmas*, 1985.

The Tell-Tale Heart, adaptation of the story by Poe (produced 1985).

West, Lunch, Harry's Christmas. 1985.

Kvetch (produced 1986). With *Acapulco*, 1986.

Sink the Belgrano! (produced 1986). With *Massage*, 1987.

Acapulco (produced 1986). With *Kvetch*, 1986.

The Trial, Metamorphosis, In the Penal Colony: Three Theatre Adaptations from Franz Kafka. 1988.

Decadence and Other Plays (includes *East, West, Greek*). 1989.

Say a Prayer for Me/ Hell (produced 1993).

One Man (includes *The Tell-Tale Heart, The Actor, Dog*)(produced 1993).

SHORT STORIES

Gross Intrusion and Other Stories. 1979.

OTHER

Steven Berkoff's America. 1988.

A Prisoner in Rio. 1989.

I Am Hamlet. 1989.

Theatre of Steven Berkoff. 1992.

THEATRICAL ACTIVITIES

DIRECTOR: **Plays**—all his own plays; *Macbeth*, 1970; *The Zoo Story* by Edward Albee, 1973; *Coriolanus*, 1988; *Salome* by Oscar Wilde, 1988, 1989, 1992.

ACTOR: **Plays**—most of his own plays; Gentleman Caller in *The Glass Menagerie* by Tennessee Williams, 1971; title role in *Hamlet*, 1980; Herod in *Salome* by Oscar Wilde, 1988, 1989, 1992. **Films**—*A Clockwork Orange*, 1971; *Barry Lyndon*, 1975; *The Passenger*, 1975; *Joseph Andrews*, 1977; *McVicar*, 1980; *Outland*, 1981; *Octopussy*, 1983; *Beverly Hills Cop*, 1984; *Rambo: First Blood, Part II*, 1985; *Revolution*, 1985; *Absolute Beginners*, 1986; *Under the Cherry Moon*, 1986; *The Krays*, 1990. **Television**—*Charlie Was a Rich Man*, 1981; *Sins*, 1987; *War and Remembrance*, 1990; *Tell-Tale Heart*, 1991; *Silent Night*, adaptation of *Harry's Christmas*, 1991.

Through his appearances in three of Hollywood's most successful motion pictures—*Octopussy, Beverly Hills Cop*, and *Rambo*—Steven Berkoff became one of the cinema's favourite villains. For those who knew Berkoff through his stage work in Britain and Los Angeles it was an unexpected transformation, as unlikely for a theatrical outsider as his subsequent embrace by Britain's National Theatre.

Long before the films were made, Berkoff had established his own dedicated following, an audience primed to admire the violent flow of his language as a dramatist and the physicality of his theatrical style. Where realism struggled to represent the inarticulacy of ordinary life, Berkoff gave his characters pages of poetic diatribe driven by profane imagery and obscene rhyme. He combined the street language of London's East End with Shakespearean grandiloquence. His visual images shared the urgent violence of his language, through the threatening presence of motorcycles and muscular actors in leather and denim.

His debt to classical theatre in his original plays was made clear by his productions of classics, ranging from Aeschylus to Shakespeare, and his adaptations of Kafka and Edgar Allan Poe. But his originality was also poured in great measure into those plays. In Berkoff's *Agamemnon*, for instance, the arrival of the watchman at the beginning of the play required an actor to exhaust himself on a quarter-mile run before the play began, collapsing onto the stage with his message. When a chorus is required, in his original work or in his production of a classic, it is as organic as any of the leading characters.

Reassuringly for those who cherished his iconoclasm, Berkoff reinvested much of his Hollywood earnings in stage projects that remained faithful to his chosen theatrical prophets. Very early in his career he chose some difficult masters, admiring, for instance, the discipline and formal skills of Bertolt Brecht as playwright and director, and noting with particular interest the way in which Brecht was able to develop his technique and beliefs through his own company, the Berliner Ensemble. That was a lesson he applied when he formed his own company, the London Theatre Group, where a Berkoff school of acting and presentation was carefully developed.

His next master was Antonin Artaud. All Berkoff's theatrical work demonstrates Artaud's dedication to using the theatre as a visceral art, drawing its energy from "the lower echelons of the body," from sexual and primal urges which can unleash profound feelings in actor and spectator. He once described his relationship with Artaud in clearly sexual terms when he said, "since I started with Artaud I've never flirted with anyone else."

Like the Living Theatre of Julian Beck and Judith Malina, however, and rather unlike Artaud, he has found in the primal physicality of his theatre a means of expressing political ideas. His disgust at Britain's conduct during the Falklands War in 1982 was dramatized in his play *Sink the Belgrano!*, a diatribe in punk-Shakespearean verse. The play made no concessions to the sensibilities of his admirers who knew him only for his film work. He scourged the audience with typically violent language, and, as in his earliest work, demanded of his actors extreme physical acts, portraying the dying sailors of the Argentinian battleship Belgrano in screams and formalized agony while his indictment of the British government was expressed through coarse poetry and coarse comedy, burlesquing the conventions of polite society.

Having demonstrated with *Sink the Belgrano!* that success would not soften his theatre, Berkoff consolidated the achievements of his earlier plays. His adaptation of Kafka's *Metamorphosis*, originally tailored to his own athletic performance as the man who is transformed into a giant insect, has proved exceptionally durable and has been staged by Berkoff in several languages, including a notable French production starring Roman Polanski. That adaptation has paved the way for his particular use of the human body and voice as the prime elements in his productions, powerfully demonstrating his concern for the expression of text through physical images which imprint themselves on the audience's memory. Visionary as his adaptations might be, however (his use of Poe is nightmarish in the extreme), it is the original writing which has proved most influential.

East, the play in which he first gave a violent representation to his vision of London life, has become a model for younger playwrights seeking to escape the limits of conversational drama. In that play he first mingled a Cockney corruption of Elizabethan-styled verse with sexual and aggressive prose speeches. Structured as a story of growing up in London's East End, with fights and fornication as major themes, the extreme imagery frequently grew into lyrical fantasias. "If I write a bit rationally, I know I fail. For instance, when I talk about a motorbike in *East*, it has to be the best, the shiniest. When I talk about a phallus, it is the largest. . . . Everything has to be extreme." The extreme view of London working-class life continued with the sequel, *West*, a few years later.

His whole vision of drama is one of extremes, demonstrated again in his North London reworking of the *Oedipus Tyrannus* of Sophocles which he called *Greek*. "In *Greek* every speech is an extreme feeling; of tenderness, of passion, of hate." Typically, despite the extremity of feeling when his hero, Eddie, discovers he has married his mother, Berkoff dispenses with the tragic ending and lets Eddie continue as her husband. Love, wherever you find it, is something worth keeping. It is by borrowing such themes as the Oedipus story and submitting them to his own vision that Berkoff achieves much of his intensity.

Decadence was his first full-scale assault on the ruling classes, though his distaste for middle-class values was earlier evident in his comically vulgar portrayal of the insect's family in *Metamorphosis*. Gluttony and the buggery of public schools were indulgences ideally suited to gross physical imagery, and the coarse poetry he provided for his couple in evening dress was potently expressed by the man as if the words were vomit. The theatricality of the play was enhanced by his demand that the same actors portray a complementary working-class couple, hopelessly in awe of decadence.

In *Harry's Christmas* Berkoff supplied a bitter corrective to the holiday spirit with his one-man play about a man whose loneliness leads him each year to recycle the few Christmas cards he has ever collected. Like his other work, the play was designed for sharp physical interpretations of the world rather than representations, and despite his work in Hollywood, his plays are still intended to tap the full potentiality of actors and clear away the trivial routines and reenactments of ordinary activity. With the use of his dialogue and monologues, "acting becomes a compulsive medium because I can touch primeval forces and release them—madness and maybe enlightenment." Occasionally, he finds an inspiration for such expression in existing sources, such as his internationally successful version of Oscar Wilde's *Salome*, first produced for Dublin's Gate Theatre.

His Hollywood and other American experiences have been absorbed into his writing, both dramatically and in prose, notably in his published imaginative "screenplay" *A Prisoner in Rio* and the plays *Kvetch* and *Acapulco*. The latter, in particular, demonstrates Hollywood's vulnerability to individuals such as Berkoff. In the process of turning him into a star, it allowed him to bear close-range witness to the movie-making megalomania of actors such as Sylvester Stallone in *Rambo*. Those experiences have been digested with customary bile to become the harsher entertainment of a Berkoff play.

—Ned Chaillet

See the essay on *East*.

BERMANGE, Barry.

Born in London, 7 November 1933. Educated at an art school in Essex, 1947–52. National service, 1952–54. Married Maurine Jewel Bright in 1961. Assistant designer, Perth Repertory Company, Scotland, 1955; actor and assistant stage manager, Swansea Repertory Company, 1956, Recipient: Arts Council bursary, 1964; Ohio State University award, 1967; German Critics award, 1968; Karl Sczuka prize (Germany), 1981, 1987. Address: 35 Alexandra Park Road, London N10 2DD, England.

Publications

PLAYS

No Quarter (broadcast 1962; produced 1964). In *No Quarter and The Interview*, 1969.

Nathan and Tabileth (broadcast 1962; produced 1967). With *Oldenberg*, 1967.

The Cloud (produced 1964).

Four Inventions (includes *The Dreams, Amor Dei, The After-Life, The Evenings of Certain Lives*) (broadcast 1964–65; produced 1969).

Oldenberg (televised 1967; produced 1967). With *Nathan and Tabileth*, 1967.

The Interview (televised 1968; produced 1969). In *No Quarter and The Interview*, 1969.

Invasion (televised 1969). In *No Quarter and The Interview*, 1969.

No Quarter and The Interview (includes *Invasion*). 1969.

Scenes from Family Life (televised 1969; produced 1974). In *Collection: Literature for the Seventies*, edited by Gerald and Nancy S. Messner, 1972.

Warcries (broadcast 1981; produced 1981).

The Soldiers (broadcast 1985; produced 1985).

The Dreams, Warcries, Klänge am Mikrophon (produced 1987).

RADIO PLAYS: *The Voice of the Peanut*, 1960; *Never Forget a Face*, 1961; *No Quarter*, 1962; *A Glass of Lemonade*, 1962; *Nathan and Tabileth*, 1962; *The Imposters* series, 1962; *Four Inventions*, 1964–65; *The Mortification*, 1964; *The Detour*, 1964; *Paths of Glory*, from the novel by Humphrey Cobb, 1965; *Letters of a Portuguese Nun*, 1966; *As a Man Grows Older*, 1967; *Neues vom Krieg*, 1969; *S.O.S.*, 1977, 1978; *Social Welfare*, 1979; *Warcries*, 1981; *English Speaking People*, 1981; *Scenario*, 1981; *Four Inventions (Reconstruc-*

tion 1), 1983; *Klänge am Mikrophon*, 1985; *The Soldiers*, 1985 ; *Testament*, 1985; *Le Désir*, 1986; *Radioville*, 1987; *Der gelbe Klang*, 1987; *Annulamento*, 1987; *4-Channels*, 1989; *Big City Nightwork*, 1990; *Cielo y Tierra*, 1991.

TELEVISION PLAYS: *Oldenberg*, 1967; *The Interview*, 1968; *Tramp*, 1968; *Invasion*, 1969; *Scenes from Family Life*, 1969; *International*, 1976; *Stars*, 1976.

THEATRICAL ACTIVITIES
DIRECTOR: most of his own plays.

The most remarkable characteristic of Barry Bermange's style as a dramatist is his ability to convey a powerful, universal theme with the utmost economy of means. His early plays (originally written for the stage) were first produced on radio, a medium ideally suited to capture the full evocativeness of the language, the symbolic power of the stories and the graceful accuracy of each carefully calculated effect. Indeed a live audience sometimes seems to disturb the precise timing on which his plays depend: there is too little room for laughter or any other spontaneous reaction. Bermange has sometimes been compared to Beckett and Ionesco: and his plots are occasionally reminiscent of the Theatre of the Absurd. In *No Quarter*, for example, a fat man and a quiet man seek lodging in a mysterious collapsing hotel: and eventually huddle together in a dark upper storey room, hoping that nothing will happen to them if they stay quite still. But Bermange's dialogue, unlike Ionesco's, rarely exploits for its own sake. His images do not carry the logic-shattering irrelevace of Dadaism. The plain meaning of *No Quarter* is also too apparent: the fat man and the quiet man represent two recognizable human reactions to the fear that their world is disintegrating. Nor is Bermange an iconoclastic writer. The collapsing hotel is not symbolic, say, of religion falling apart. Unlike the writers of the Absurd, Bermange does not delight in pointing out the nonsense of cherished institutions: nor are his stories tantalizingly ridiculous. He doesn't attempt to give a pleasing *frisson* to the rational mind by rubbing it up the wrong way. The themes of his plays are usually coherent and indeed logical, although they may contain many ambiguities. Bermange is a writer who defies easy categorizing simply because he chooses each technique carefully to express most directly his underlying themes. His plays can be absurdist: they can be naturalistic: they can even include carefully manoeuvred "happenings." But the styles have always been selected for their appropriateness, not from any *a priori* assumptions about Theatre or Dramatic Art.

In the same way he chooses his different styles with care, so Bermange distils each effect to its essential elements. Like Marguerite Duras, he sometimes presents an apparently small incident observed in precise detail: and separates it from all the surrounding life until it exists in a significant isolation. In *The Interview* eight men wait in an outer office, before being interviewed for a job. The audience never learns what the job is or who is finally selected. The play is solely concerned with the applicants' reactions to each other: and the small details — one man reading a newspaper, another looking at a picture — manage to convey an almost intolerable atmosphere of suspicion and rivalry. In

Nathan and Tabileth, an elderly couple feed the pigeons in the park, return home and spend the evening by the fire. They are visited by a young man, Bernie, who says he is their grandson, although they do not recognize him, and who talks of relatives they have forgotten. When Bernie leaves, the couple go to bed: and "darkness comes." Bermange manages to capture in the rambling repetitive dialogue and in the intense short soliloquies the shifting concentration of the old. Certain details—the hired boats on the lake, the pigeons, and the glowing fire—emerge in sharp focus: others slide into a grey and closing background. The timing of the play is calculated to break up the normal pace of events: the old people do not think consecutively and the audience is not allowed to do so. Sometimes they ramble on about the past: sometimes they try to cope with the present, with the breaking of a plate, with a scratched hand. No other contemporary play—with the possible exception of Beckett's *Happy Days*—conveys with such agonizing plausibility the experience of old age.

The Interview and *Nathan and Tabileth* are both basically naturalistic plays: the observable details have been carefully selected and arranged to provide a particular impact—but these details are convincing on the level of external reality. In *Oldenberg*, however, Bermange caricatures the main characters. A man and a woman decide to let a room in their house. The tenant is a stranger, Oldenberg, whom they have never even met. At first they make considerable efforts to furnish the room comfortably: but then the possibility occurs to them that their tenant may not be *English*. In a fit of xenophobia, they destroy and desecrate the room they have so carefully prepared. But the stranger when he arrives is English—and blind. *Oldenberg* is an allegory about the way in which people long for change but are afraid of the unfamiliar—of invasion. By using some of the techniques of Absurdist writers, Bermange heightens the contradictory emotions caused by the intrusions of visitors.

But perhaps Bermange's most extraordinary achievement was to compile four "sound inventions," originally for radio, but which were afterwards presented at the Institute of Contemporary Arts in London—through loudspeakers in a darkened auditorium. The inventions were recorded extracts of interviews with ordinary men and women—about their dreams, their reflections on old age, their beliefs or scepticisms about God and the After-life. The speeches were carefully edited into short revealing phrases, "orchestrated" with electronic music and finally presented as totally original music-drama works. In these inventions, Bermange's remarkable gifts for ordering sound effectively—both ordinary speech patterns and electronic effects—were allied to themes which could scarcely have been expressed effectively any other way. He invented a new form of radio and theatrical experience: and the only possible contemporary parallel would be with Berio's music-drama for Italian radio. With equal ingenuity, Bermange also wrote an improvisatory work for television, *Invasion*, where a dinner party is gradually submerged by the images of Vietnam, flickering across a television screen. Bermange's inventiveness, his assurance in handling different styles and media, and the powerful intensity of his chosen themes have won him a unique position among British dramatists. No other writer can rival him for controlled daring and insight into the potentialities of experimental drama.

—John Elsom

BILL, Stephen.

Born in Birmingham, 16 January 1948. Educated at Handsworth and Hales Owen grammar schools, 1952–67; Royal Academy of Dramatic Art, London, 1968–70. Married Sheila Kelley in 1971; one son and one daughter. Commis chef, Norfolk Hotel, Birmingham, 1966; ward orderly, Romsley Sanatorium, Romsley, Worcestershire, 1967–68; grave digger, Hales Owen Council, 1967; civil servant in tax office, Birmingham, 1968; writer-in-residence, Crucible Theatre, Sheffield, 1977–78. Recipient: Thames Television award, 1977; John Whiting award, 1979; London *Evening Standard* award, 1987; *Plays and Players* award, 1987; *Drama* award, 1987; Writers Guild of Great Britain award, 1991. Agent: Judy Daish Associates, 83 Eastbourne Mews, London W2 6LQ, England.

Publications

PLAYS

Girl Talk (produced 1978).
Squeakers and Strags (produced 1978).
Final Wave (produced 1979).
The Old Order (produced 1979).
Piggy-Back Rider (produced 1981).
The Bottom Drawer (produced 1982).
Naked in the Bull Ring (produced 1985).
Over the Bar (produced 1985).
Crossing the Line (produced 1987).
Curtains (produced 1987). 1988.
Heartlanders, with David Edgar and Anne Devlin (produced 1989). 1989.
Over a Barrel (produced 1990).
Stitched Up (produced 1990).
The Antigone Project (produced 1992).

RADIO PLAY: *Worshipping the Ground*, 1988.

TELEVISION PLAYS: *Lyndsey*, 1980; *House Warming*, 1983; *Eh Brian, It's a Whopper* series, 1984; *Marjorie and the Preacher Man*, with Jim Broadbent, 1987; *Broke*, 1991.

THEATRICAL ACTIVITIES

ACTOR: **Plays**—in repertory theatres and in London including: *The Silent Majority* by Mike Leigh, 1974; *Blood Sports* by David Edgar, 1975; *Blisters* by Sheila Kelley and Sarah Pia Anderson, 1976. **Film**—*Prick Up Your Ears*, 1987. **Television**—*Nuts in May* by Mike Leigh, 1976; *Spend, Spend, Spend* by Jack Rosenthal, 1977; *Stepping Out* by Sheila Kelley and Sarah Pia Anderson, 1977; *Days at the Beach* by Malcolm Mowbray, 1978.

Stephen Bill comments:

I feel like I am just a storyteller giving voice to the characters and situations that I have come across in everyday life. A voice to "ordinary" people whose stories I don't feel are normally told. I grew up in Handsworth, Birmingham.

My father went from school into his father's small badge enamelling business in the jewellery quarter. They only employed women enamellers because they "couldn't pay enough to employ men". My mother died when I was about four and we never argued at home. I only mention these odd facts because everything I write relates back to upbringing. To pitting one set of values against another. To having the arguments in public that we didn't know how to have in private.

My theatre work falls into two categories: 1) intimate, character-based dramas; 2) broader, community based theatre. The character-based work often explores the values we hold in common—or don't. It looks at how "ordinary" people cope when placed in extraordinary situations. It tries to make sense of, or celebrate, the contradictions. My experience in community-based theatre stems from my time as resident writer at the Crucible Theatre, Sheffield. I worked with their Theatre Vanguard Company which toured the whole of South Yorkshire. The plays I wrote for them were specific to the area and were for specific audiences—children, teenagers, handicapped groups etc. This strand of my work continued with: 2nd City Theatre Company, Theatre Foundry—the touring company for the Black Country; the *Heartlanders* project—a community play for Birmingham's centenary, co-written with Anne Devlin and David Edgar, with a cast of over a hundred local people; and in 1992 with *The Antigone Project* for the Royal Shakespeare Company. This is a retelling of the Sophocles play, *Antigone*, by 26 young people in the Chelmsley Wood area of Solihull. The story we tell will be out of their experience and will be in a language that is real to them.

Stephen Bill was an actor before he was a dramatist, and his first plays were written as a member of a company: he was resident writer at the Sheffield Crucible Theatre. He applied himself diligently to his job as a community playwright, researching issues and turning them into drama. His early plays are above average but conventional theatre-in-education about pigeons, delinquent teenagers, and the generation gap, mainly based in South Yorkshire. One, *Final Wave*, is atypical of all Bill's other work, using folk song and folk ritual, set on the remote island of St. Kilda, most of the action taking place in the 18th century, and the characters frequently speaking Gaelic. No other Bill characters speak any foreign language. Though they are rooted in the past, it is a past which goes no further back than World War II, they are geographically located no further south than Birmingham, no further north than Doncaster, and they speak in the authentic voices of the British working class and petit bourgeoisie.

During the time at Sheffield, Bill's own voice was confident but not noticeably individual. Real Bill began with his three plays for the Birmingham Repertory Company, *The Old Order*, *Piggy-Back Rider*, and *Naked in the Bull Ring*, all set in the Birmingham area and all based on his own family experience. The characters of *The Old Order* are the workers and management of a small factory like that once run by his own father. In *Piggy-Back Rider* a young accountant has taken over just such a factory from his father, George, and is destroying the work of two generations, selling off the land in parcels and getting rid of the workforce. George and his wife, Connie, move on into

Naked in the Bull Ring as the son and daughter-in-law of a woman of 90, strong-willed but no longer confident in mind or of her ability to control the conditions of her own life, and only able to control the lives of her own family by making those lives a nightmare.

That old woman, based on Bill's grandmother, appeared again five years later in what may be his finest play, *Curtains*. She has repeatedly asked to be helped to die, and is killed at the beginning of the second act by one of her daughters, unable to cope with her any longer. The rest of the family then attempt to behave as if the murder didn't happen. The play was commissioned by the Hampstead Theatre Club, had a considerable critical success and transferred rather inappropriately to the Whitehall Theatre, home of the Whitehall farces. It may have bemused the regular Whitehall audience and did not run for long. Shamefully, it has never been produced professionally in Britain since, although it has been performed by amateurs all over the world.

Bill's interest in communities persists throughout his work. In collaboration with David Edgar and Anne Devlin he wrote a community play, *Heartlanders*, for a cast of over a 100—again performed in Birmingham. But usually his community is a family reacting to some family disaster—euthanasia in *Curtains* or the sudden announcement by a daughter that she intends to marry in *The Bottom Drawer* (the assumption is that she must be pregnant). Or it may be the community of the workplace. Besides his use of his father's factory in the Birmingham trilogy, he used a factory making ornamental barrels in *Over a Barrel* and the management of a football club in *Over the Bar*. His characters are invariably much concerned with possessions, either the accumulation of them or the encumbrance they represent.

He has a poet's concern with imagery—in *Stitched Up*, a householder, overwhelmed with debt, simply goes into the kitchen cupboard and refuses to come out. Bill sees plays as conversations with an audience, which is why he enjoys working in regional theatres—"I know who I'm talking to." He is more interested in character than in narrative and likes to bring a group of people up against an idea or an event (or both) to see what comes of it. Consequently the plays are more conversation than action. Though its subject may be of everyday concern, the locale an ordinary house or factory, the language, the costumes, the whole approach naturalistic, a Bill play has none of the self-indulgence of a semi-improvised piece by someone like Mike Leigh. Bill is only naturalistic in the sense that Pinter is naturalistic; he has a very sharp ear, and a delight in the extra-ordinariness of demotic speech. Of all the present crop of British dramatists, he is the playwright of the inarticulate and confused. The characters of his later plays rarely finish a sentence.

—John Bowen

BLEASDALE, Alan.

Born in Liverpool, Lancashire, 23 March 1946. Educated at St. Aloysius Infant and Junior schools, Huyton, Lancashire, 1951–57; Wade Deacon Grammar School, Widnes, Lancashire, 1957–64; Padgate Teachers Training College, teachers certificate 1967. Married Julia Moses in 1970; two sons and one daughter. Teacher, St. Columbus Secondary Modern School, Huyton, 1967–71, King George V School, Gilbert and Ellice Islands, 1971–74, and

Halewood Grange Comprehensive School, Lancashire, 1974–75; resident
playwright, Liverpool Playhouse, 1975–76, and Contact Theatre, Manchester,
1976–78; joint artistic director, 1981–84, and associate director, 1984–86,
Liverpool Playhouse. Recipient: Broadcasting Press Guild award, 1982; Royal
Television Society award, 1982; BAFTA award, 1982; *Evening Standard*
award, for musical, 1985; ITV Achievement of the Decade award, 1989;
Broadcasting Press Guild Television and Radio award, 1991. Lives in
Liverpool. Agent: Lemon, Unna, and Durbridge, 24 Pottery Lane, Holland
Park, London W11 4LZ, England.

Publications

PLAYS

Fat Harold and the Last 26 (produced 1975).
The Party's Over (produced 1975).
Scully, with others, adaptation of the novel by Bleasdale (produced 1975).
    1984.
Franny Scully's Christmas Stories, with Kenneth Alan Taylor (produced 1976).
Down the Dock Road (produced 1976).
It's a Madhouse (produced 1976). With *Having a Ball*, 1986.
Should Auld Acquaintance (produced 1976).
No More Sitting on the Old School Bench (produced 1977). 1979.
Crackers (produced 1978).
Pimples (produced 1978).
Love Is a Many Splendoured Thing (for children; produced 1986). In *Act I*,
    edited by David Self and Ray Speakman, 1979.
Having a Ball (produced 1981; revised version produced 1990). With *It's a
    Madhouse*, 1986.
Boys from the Blackstuff (televised 1982). 1985.
Young People Today (sketch), in *The Big One* (produced 1983).
Are You Lonesome Tonight? (produced 1985). 1985.
The Monocled Mutineer, adaptation of the book by William Allison and John
    Fairley (televised 1986). 1986.
No Surrender: A Deadpan Farce (screenplay). 1986.
On the Ledge (produced 1993). 1993.

SCREENPLAY: *No Surrender*, 1987.

TELEVISION PLAYS: *Early to Bed*, 1975; *Dangerous Ambition*, 1976; *Scully's
New Year's Eve*, 1978; *The Black Stuff*, 1980; *The Muscle Market*, 1981;
Boys from the Blackstuff series, 1982; *Scully* series, 1984; *The Monocled
Mutineer*, 1986; *G.B.H.* series, 1991.

NOVELS

Scully. 1975.
Who's Been Sleeping in My Bed? 1977; revised edition, as *Scully and Mooey*,
    1984.

CRITICAL STUDIES: *Boys from the Blackstuff: The Making of Television Drama*
by Bob Millington and Robin Nelson, 1986.

Alan Bleasdale comments:

I try *never* to look back and examine my work. I don't re-read the script or watch the video once the piece is finished. For what it's worth, I don't think a writer should know what he or she is doing! That's for the audience or critic to judge. I do know, however, that since I was a child all I have ever wanted was to be good and to do good. I should have been a social worker.

Notes such as these can sometimes become a playwright's first and last line of defence or explanation: "This is what my plays really mean!" My only explanation and defence lie between the first and last curtain.

Finally, the only three quotations I have ever managed to learn off by heart: "Any victim demands allegiance" (Graham Greene, *The Heart of the Matter*). "All my humor is based on destruction and despair. If the whole world was tranquil, without disease and violence, I'd be standing on the breadline, right behind J. Edgar Hoover" (Lenny Bruce). "Too much talking stinks up the room" (Duke Ellington).

Although he had been writing for the theatre since the mid-1970's, it was his television series *Boys from the Blackstuff* that brought Alan Bleasdale wide recognition. In five successive episodes he traced, with mordant irony, the despair and madness of a group of unemployed Liverpool men and their families. The central battle is between the individual and the state. The unemployed struggle to supplement their dole money with casual earnings on building sites and in dockyards; the Department of Employment, the social services, and the police combine to corral their clients within the government regulations. Farce turns into tragedy which reverts to farce. While cars skid, crash, and overturn on Malloy's illegal building site at the end of the first episode, Snowy Malone, the plasterer who takes pride in his skills, falls to his death trying to escape the dole officials. Elsewhere Chrissie Todd shoots his rabbits for food, Yosser Hughes is rescued from drowning by the police he's assaulted, and the sanctimonious priest at George Malone's funeral finishes up vomiting his whiskey down a grid after the reception. Bleasdale has no more sentimental regard for his characters than they have for each other. The children are as uncompromising as the parents. The scene where Yosser's daughter Ann Marie butts the social worker Veronica is as comic as it is shocking.

Snowy's death is echoed by that of his father in the last episode. George Malone is respected throughout the community as a socialist and a battler for citizens' rights, but the structure of Bleasdale's series questions radically whether the Malones' ideology of class solidarity is still relevant to 1980's Britain. The Malones have some analysis of why mass unemployment has returned. Chrissie, Yosser, Dixie, and the rest have only their native wits which, unsupported by any community or educational training, can flip over into hallucination. Yosser Hughes is a monomaniac, and his white face, staring red-rimmed eyes, and monotonous cry of "Gizza job" and "I can do that" immediately became the nation's most dramatic vision of unemployed misery. Chrissie's wife Angie sees clearly that jokes are not enough: "if you don't

laugh, you'll cry—I've heard it for years—this stupid soddin' city's full of it,"
but when she screams at her husband to fight back she has no more idea than
he about how it can be done.

Bleasdale's view of the professional classes is equally acerbic. *Having a Ball*,
a stage play of 1981, counterpoints the reactions of three men, Lenny, Ritchie,
and Malcolm, waiting in hospital for vasectomies. They are all middle class
and they are all terrified. With a woman surgeon and Malcolm's wife Doreen
contemptuous of his Territorial Army "bravery," the play exposes not woman,
but man, as victim. And with three simultaneous areas for stage action, the
Waiting Room, the Preparation Room, and the Operating Theatre, Bleasdale
exploits all the possibilities for farcical encounters and concealments. But there
is no harmonious resolution. The play ends with Lenny, like Yosser, screaming
in despair. Through wit, mockery, and a kind of trickster role-playing, he has
exposed his own and everyone else's pretensions to control and confidence.
"Most of us are cowards most of the time," he remarks. "Until we have no
choice. And all the choices seem to be going." This is Bleasdale's savage double
bind which Chrissie expresses in *Boys from the Blackstuff* as "It's a way of life.
The only trouble is, it's no way to live".

With *Are You Lonesome Tonight?*, Bleasdale moves away, to his cost, from
his familiar territory of the North West of England. Elvis Presley, in his last
hours at Graceland, has the successes and betrayals of life portrayed to him
upstage. He drools over his mother, curses Colonel Parker, and comes over as
a good ol' southern boy of musical genius who was led astray by unscrupulous
agents. Other accounts of Elvis's last years depict a drug-ridden, gun-obsessed
monster, but Bleasdale was determined that this should be a tribute to what he
called the "working class hero" of his youth. It was a West End hit, but it
remains unique among Bleasdale's plays for its sentimentality and uncritical
adulation. The London production was memorable, not for the writing, but
for the electrifyingly accurate rendition of Elvis's great early hits by Simon
Bowman.

In 1986 Bleasdale returned to his strengths, anti-heroism and farce, with a 4-
part television series *The Monocled Mutineer*, and a film *No Surrender*. The
tricky career of Percy Toplis, a World War I conscript, is the subject of the
series. He leads an uprising of conscripted men against their atrocious conditions in the Etaples training camp in 1917. But he also impersonates officers
and thoroughly enjoys their life of gambling, drinking, and whoring. Percy
Toplis is neither demogogue nor ideologue. On several occasions he refuses to
be called either a hero or a socialist. He is a working-class rebel who refuses all
the clichés of such a figure. And he doesn't "lead" the Etaples uprising in any
conventional way. Rather he finds himself in a situation where he can inflict
the maximum of mayhem on a class which he both hates and simulates. "Don't
get angry," he advises; "get even." Toplis is no Scarlet Pimpernel of the
workers. After the war he is a poor man still hunted for his role at Etaples. He
thinks he can live off a rich widow, but finds she's as big a poser as he is.
Naturally he falls in love with her. When he rejoins the army it's not just to get
rich by black-marketing army supplies. He admits he doesn't seem able to
function outside that structure of command. Its rigidity creates his flexibility.
He's not therefore the roving outsider of the romantic tradition. To be that you
have to have the money and class Toplis hasn't got and never will have. The

agents of the state finally eliminate this cultural hybrid on a deserted Cumbrian road, but his girlfriend's pregnancy indicates that he may be reborn. What Bleasdale has intuited is that Toplis's combination of cynicism, courage, and style is the true basis for oppositional politics in 1980's Britain. The man who invents himself from the debris all around him is the man who anticipates the new patterns of life.

No Surrender begins, continues, and ends in debris. A new manager comes to take over a decrepit nightclub in Liverpool and finds it has been double-booked by two parties of Old Age Pensioners, one Catholic and the other Protestant. Infiltrated into this gathering is a Loyalist gunman on the run. Insults escalate from the verbal to the physical, the geriatrics take strength from the fires of religious fanaticism, and the film finishes in a mayhem of fists, bottles, the police, and the Fancy Dress competition.

G.B.H. is not only about physical violence, although throughout this 10-hour, seven-episode series for Channel 4 Bleasdale certainly features back-street beatings and picket-line intimidation. The last episode culminates in the firing of the town hall of a Northern city by a mob of angry black citizens incited to revolt by a group of MI5 agents posing as Trotskyite *provocateurs*. The central incident in the life of Michael Murray, Bleasdale's rabid Labour council leader, is an unwarranted beating he received from his primary school headmaster. The narrative proposes that this has bred in him a detestation of authority which has been the driving force behind his own authoritarian assumption of power in local politics. He is unable to cope with a humane, liberal headmaster like Jim Nelson, who keeps his school open during a strike manoeuvered by Murray, and plays the good angel to Murray's devil through-out this political morality play. *G.B.H.*'s real interest, however, occurs when the personal and political collide without resolution. At these murky cross-roads all is deceit and doubling. Murray's real Nemesis is one Eileen Critchley, rich when he was poor, at the same school as Murray, and a sado-masochist even as a child. She wants him to strangle her. Her refrain is "You want to please me, don't you Michael?" But he cannot do her the violence she desires. Eileen, it emerges late in the series, committed suicide at Oxford in her twenties. But in a scene with her younger sister Barbara which repeats many times she hisses "Get Michael, he's easy," and Barbara, an upper-class blonde of cool sexuality, and a member of MI5, pursues, seduces, and confuses Murray at the height of his power. *The* theme of our times, the absent father, is dramatised several times over in the criss-crossing stories of sex and politics that make up the series.

Jim Nelson also has a pathology. He is a hypochondriac with an irrational fear of bridges and a tendency to sleepwalk naked. He and his family represent the compassionate, middle-class socialism that Bleasdale clearly prefers to the conspiratorial fanaticism of Murray and his heavies. But Nelson's delusions remain farcical rather than psychological. His family is supportive, his sex-life is pure, and his morality impeccable. He is therefore dull (and woodenly acted by Michael Palin) and only interesting when he is the occasion for such scenes of hilariously black comedy as his nth interview with his doctor, or his conversation in the storm with Grosvenor, a country gentleman with a bilious contempt for the guests at his holiday retreat, particularly if they are from the North.

G.B.H. is a many-layered narrative, full of the most abrupt cutting between farce and tragedy, childhood and adulthood, the personal and the political. It does not always succeed, but its ambition far outruns any recent television scripts and its reading of the nature of obsession among public figures is very sophisticated.

—Tony Dunn

BOLAND, Bridget.

Born in London, 13 March 1913. Educated at the Convent of the Sacred Heart, Roehampton, 1921–31; Oxford University, 1932–35, B.A. (honours) in politics, philosophy, and economics 1935. Served in the Auxiliary Territorial Service, 1941–46; senior commander; produced morale-orientated plays for the troops, with three companies of actors, 1943–46. Film writer from 1937. Died 19 January 1988.

Publications

PLAYS

The Arabian Nights (produced 1948).
Cockpit (produced 1948). In Plays of the Year 1, 1949.
The Damascus Blade (produced 1950).
Temple Folly (produced 1951). 1958.
The Return (as Journey to Earth, produced 1952; as The Return, produced 1953). 1954.
The Prisoner (produced 1954). In Plays of the Year 10, 1954. Gordon (produced 1961). In Plays of the Year 25, 1962.
The Zodiac in the Establishment (produced 1963; as Time Out of Mind, produced 1970). 1963.
A Juan by Degrees, adaptation of a play by Pierre Humblot (produced 1965).

SCREENPLAYS: Spies of the Air, with A.R. Rawlinson, 1939; Laugh It Off, with Austin Melford, 1940: Old Mother Riley in Society, with others, 1940; Gaslight (Angel Street), with A.R. Rawlinson, 1940; This England, with A.R. Rawlinson and Emlyn Williams, 1941; Freedom Radio (A Voice in the Night), with others, 1941; He Found a Star, with Austin Melford, 1941: The Lost People, with Muriel Box, 1949; Prelude to Fame, 1950; The Fake, with Patrick Kirwan, 1953; The Prisoner, 1955; War and Peace, with others, 1956; Constantino il Grande (Constantine and the Cross), with others, 1961; Damon and Pythias, 1962; Anne of the Thousand Days, with John Hale, 1970.

RADIO PLAY: Sheba, 1954.

TELEVISION PLAY: Forever Beautiful, 1965.

NOVELS

The Wild Geese. 1938.
Portrait of a Lady in Love. 1942.
Caterina. 1975.

OTHER

Old Wives' Lore for Gardeners, with Maureen Boland. 1976.
Gardener's Magic and Other Old Wives' Lore. 1977.
At My Mother's Knee. 1978.

Editor, *The Lisle Letters: An Abridgement* (from 6-vol. edition, edited by
 Muriel St. Clare Byrne). 1983.

Bridget Boland writes (1987):

Although I hold a British passport I am in fact Irish, and the daughter of an
Irish politician at that, which may account for a certain contrariness in my
work. Many playwrights have become screenwriters; so I was a screenwriter
and became a playwright. Most women writers excel on human stories in
domestic settings: so I am bored by domestic problems and allergic to domestic
settings. I succeed best with heavy drama (*The Prisoner*), so I can't resist trying
to write frothy comedy (*Temple Folly*).

By the time you have written half a dozen plays or so you began to realize
you are probably still trying to write the one you started with. However
different I begin by thinking is the theme of each, I find that in the end every
play is saying: "Belief is dangerous"—the theme of *Cockpit*. In *The Damascus
Blade*, which, produced by Laurence Olivier and with John Mills and Peter
Finch in the cast, yet contrived to fold on its short pre-London tour, I tried to
put across the theme by too complicated a paradox. An Irishman descended
from a long line of soldiers of fortune holds that you must not kill for what you
believe in, but that a man must be prepared to die for something, if only the
belief of someone else. Having offered his sword to the foreign forces of
extreme right and extreme left in turn, he ends by dying as bodyguard to the
child of a prostitute, trying to keep it for her from its father—and realizes that
in spite of all his/my theories he has come to believe in the justice of her cause:
man—alas, God—is like that.

In 1948 Bridget Boland was well ahead of her time as a playwright. *Cockpit*
was one of the early forerunners of the vogue for environmental theatre which
was to spread to England from off-Broadway in 1960s. It was a play
which boldly turned its back on everything that was normal in the English
theatre of the time, including insularity. Its way of coming to grips with the
problem of Displaced Persons in post-war Europe was to use the whole
auditorium to create a theatrical image of a D.P. assembly centre, which itself
served as an image of the chaos on the continent, with masses of bewildered
hopeless people uprooted from where they belonged. Unsuspecting London
theatregoers arriving at the Playhouse found themselves faced with a curtain
painted in Germanic style and with notices in various European languages
forbidding them to fight or carry firearms. The dialogue begins incomprehen-
sibly: a quarrel in Polish between two women fighting over a saucepan. Two
English soldiers then take charge, appearing from the back of the stalls,
shouting orders and questions, treating the whole audience like D.Ps, forcing
them to feel uncomfortably involved in the action.

The discomfort becomes most acute at the climax of the play. Behind the

drawn curtains of one of the boxes a man is gravely ill. A Polish Professor tells
the English Captain that it may be a case of bubonic plague. The theatre has to
be sealed off. Armed guards are stationed at the exits and the suspense is
sustained while they wait for a doctor to arrive and then while they wait for the
news that it was a false alarm. If the play ran for only 58 performances it
cannot have been because it failed to make an impact.

On the face of it, the subject of *The Return*, could hardly have been more
contrasted—a nun's return to the modern world after 36 years of seclusion in a
convent. This is difficult material, but well dramatized it could have produced
fascinating insights both into the mind of the woman and into the changes
which had overtaken the world that surrounded her since she last saw it—in
1913. The play is by no means a complete failure: it has some very touching
moments. But it fails to do justice to its subject because, unlike *Cockpit*, it fails
to find a way of making the audience participate in the raw experience. It relies
too much on dialogue which analyses and describes.

The part of the nun is quite well-written, but on leaving the convent she goes
to live with a nephew and his wife, who are both sentimentally and unconvincingly characterized, while the chaplain and the man who runs a youth club
where the nun does voluntary work are seen very superficially. The problem of
dramatizing the impact the modern world makes on the woman's mind is
largely side-stepped. What we get instead is a plot in which a series of
misunderstandings are peeled off to reveal an unrealistic core of human
goodness.

In spite of several forays into the past (like *Gordon*, an old-fashioned drama
about Gordon and the siege of Khartoum) Boland is at her best in writing
about post-war Europe, and her best play is still *The Prisoner*, which seems to
have been inspired partly by the trial of the Hungarian Cardinal Mindszenty
and partly perhaps by Arthur Koestler's novel *Darkness at Noon*, which
presents a similar relationship between a political prisoner in a Communist
country and his interrogator, though in Koestler the sympathetic interrogator
is replaced half way through the action by a callous and unintelligent party-
liner of peasant stock. In *The Prisoner* it is the Cardinal whose origins are
proletarian, while the Interrogator is a clever aristocrat who has joined the
Party. The dialogue gives clear definition to the stages in the close personal
relationship that develops between the two adversaries, who like and respect
each other. Most of the cut and thrust is verbal, but there are some highly
theatrical climaxes, as when a coffin is brought in containing the apparently
dead body of the Cardinal's mother. The revelation that she has only been
anaesthetized is followed by the threat that she will be killed if he does not sign
the confession his captors want.

Not only the two central parts but also that of the main warder provide
excellent opportunities for actors, and the physical breakdown of the Cardinal
is particularly rewarding. The main flaw in the writing is a lapse into sentimentality when the Interrogator is made to repent, revealing that in destroying his
victim he has also destroyed his faith in his own work. But the damage this
does to the play is almost compensated for by a fine twist at the end. The death
sentence is repealed and the Cardinal, whose confession has discredited him,
knows that it will be more difficult for him to live than to die.

—Ronald Hayman

BOLT, Robert (Oxton).

Born in Sale, Manchester, Lancashire, 15 August 1924. Educated at Manchester Grammar School, graduated 1940; Manchester University, 1943, 1946–49, B.A. (honours) in history 1949; Exeter University, 1949–50, teaching diploma 1950. Served in the Royal Air Force, 1943–44; in the Royal West African Frontier Force, 1944–46: lieutenant. Married 1) Celia Ann Roberts in 1949 (marriage dissolved 1967), one son and two daughters; 2) the actress Sarah Miles in 1967 (divorced 1976), one son; 3) Ann, Lady Queensberry in 1980 (divorced 1985). Office boy, Sun Life Assurance Company, Manchester, 1942; schoolmaster, Bishopsteignton, Devon, 1950–51, and Millfield School, Street, Somerset, 1952–58. Recipient: *Evening Standard* award, 1957, for screenplay, 1987; New York Drama Critics Circle award, 1962; BAFTA award, 1962, 1966; Oscar, 1966, 1967; New York Film Critics award, 1966; Golden Globe award, for screenplay, 1967, 1987. LL.D.: Exeter University, 1977. C.B.E. (Commander, Order of the British Empire), 1972. Agent: Casarotto Ramsay Ltd., National House, 60–66 Wardour Street, London W1V 3HP, England.

Publications

PLAYS

A Man for All Seasons (broadcast 1954; produced 1960). 1960.
The Last of the Wine (broadcast 1955; produced 1956).
The Critic and the Heart (produced 1957).
Flowering Cherry (produced 1957). 1958.
The Tiger and the Horse (produced 1960). 1961.
Gentle Jack (produced 1963). 1965.
The Thwarting of Baron Bolligrew (produced 1965). 1966.
Doctor Zhivago: The Screenplay Based on the Novel by Boris Pasternak. 1966.
Brother and Sister (produced 1967; revised version produced 1968).
Vivat! Vivat Regina! (produced 1970). 1971.
State of Revolution (produced 1977). 1977.
The Mission (screenplay). 1986.

SCREENPLAYS: *Lawrence of Arabia,* 1962; *Doctor Zhivago,* 1965; *A Man for All Seasons,* 1966; *Ryan's Daughter,* 1970; *Lady Caroline Lamb,* 1973; *The Bounty,* 1984; *The Mission,* 1986.

RADIO PLAYS: *The Master,* 1953; *Fifty Pigs,* 1953; *Ladies and Gentlemen,* 1954; *A Man for All Seasons,* 1954; *Mr. Sampson's Sundays,* 1955; *The Last of the Wine,* 1955; *The Window,* 1958; *The Drunken Sailor,* 1958; *The Banana Tree,* 1961.

CRITICAL STUDY: *Robert Bolt* by Ronald Hayman, 1969.

THEATRICAL ACTIVITIES
DIRECTOR: Film—*Lady Caroline Lamb,* 1973.

"Inevitable," as Robert Bolt pointed out in the introduction to his most recently produced play, *State of Revolution*, "is the favourite word of Marx and Lenin. Their pages are spattered with it. Yet they are spattered too with fervent praise and bitter blame and urgent exhortation." This tension between the ideal as incorporated in a detached, quasi-scientific viewpoint (or in other manifestations) and private needs for self-expression, links the otherwise diverse and apparently unrelated themes of Bolt's important plays. In his first stage play to be produced, *The Critic and the Heart*, over-contrived though it is in the Somerset Maugham mould (Bolt consciously adopted *The Circle* as his model) the issues raised by two similar couples in the pattern of dependent artist and suffering, supportive woman, resolve themselves into alternative courses of action: art, here, is the ideal, the demands it makes on those close to the artist, its lowering contradiction. Like Marx, artists want to embody a truth, but their lives are often tragic contradictions of this.

Flowering Cherry, Bolt's most resounding stage success prior to *A Man for All Seasons*, embodies the detachment of the dreamer who cannot relate to ordinary office life. Cherry, again, has to choose whether he wants just the substance of his dream to remain true, or the actual orchard itself to exist, with all its attendant, real problems. His wife, Isobel, is unable to understand this. Ultimately Cherry is found to be inadequate (it was Ralph Richardson's larger-than-life quality which realized the fantasy inherent in Bolt's intentionally ordinary and scaled-down conception of Cherry).

Bolt's next play, *The Tiger and the Horse*, is a far more intellectual exercise, hinging on whether the wife of a Master of a college should sign a petition against the atom bomb and thereby jeopardize her husband's hope to succeed as Vice-Chancellor (it mirrored Bolt's own experience as one of the original members of Bertrand Russell's Committee of 100, when he served a short prison sentence). In *A Man for All Seasons* the opposition of the ideal to the politics of the state carries further the notion of love as the only thing that can rescue people from isolation. Thomas More is perfection of behaviour—as Bolt said, "This is why people like the play. They think 'Thank Christ, somebody can do it. I may not be able to, but life *can* be that perfect.' And he didn't do anything that you or I couldn't have done." It is More's adamantine sense of his own self—he is a good, an irreproachable man—which makes him refuse to go beyond a certain point, as he himself says when arguing with Thomas Cromwell, "Yes, a man's soul is his self!"

Gentle Jack, *Vivat! Vivat Regina!*, and *State of Revolution* show Bolt developing his fastidious craftsmanship more and more along Brechtian lines, though totally repudiating, in spite of former Marxist beliefs, Brecht's political values. The first's fairy-tale methods confused and alienated audiences, but the second, with its stronger integration of theatrical effect and its return to a broad historical canvas, brought back Bolt's reputation nearly to the peak it enjoyed when Paul Scofield was playing Thomas More. *State of Revolution*, performed at the National Theatre in 1977, with Michael Bryant as Lenin, betrays in its uneasy title too great a concentration of effort made by Bolt to find popular qualities in Gorky, Stalin, Trotsky, and Lenin himself. The subject's size is daunting, but Bolt does, with a culminating effort of intellectual power, prove his point that Lenin was an admirable man, "possessed by a terribly wrong idea," as well as providing rich ironic side-lights to history. But to whom, exactly, is he proving it? *State of Revolution*, overstocked with giants, lacks those essentially witty and English qualities that inform Bolt's best work. We are not far enough away from Kronstadt to, as Shakespeare did with Rome, turn it into contemporary poetry.

—Garry O'Connor

BOND, Chris(topher Godfrey).

Born in Sussex in 1945. Child actor; educated at the Central School of Speech and Drama, and the Drama Centre, both London. Married to the writer Claire Luckham. Actor, 1968–70, and resident dramatist, 1970–71, Victoria Theatre, Stoke-on-Trent, Staffordshire; artistic director, Everyman Theatre, Liverpool, 1976–78; director, Liverpool Playhouse, 1981–83; director, Half Moon Theatre, London, 1984–89. Recipient: Arts Council grant, 1970. Agent: Blanche Marvin, 21–A St. John's Wood High Street, London NW8 7NG, England.

Publications

PLAYS

Sweeney Todd, The Demon Barber of Fleet Street (produced 1970). 1974.
Mutiny (produced 1970).
Shem's Boat (for children; produced 1971).
Downright Hooligan (produced 1972).
Tarzan's Last Stand (produced 1973).
Judge Jeffreys (produced 1973).
The Country Wife, adaptation of the play by William Wycherley (produced 1974).
Under New Management (produced 1975).
The Cantril Tales, with others (produced 1975).
George, in *Prompt One*, edited by Alan Durband. 1976.
Scum: Death, Destruction, and Dirty Washing, with Claire Luckham (produced 1976).
Good Soldier Scouse (produced 1976).
The Beggar's Opera, based on the play by John Gay (also director: produced 1977).
A Tale of Two Cities, adaptation of the novel by Dickens (produced 1981).
Dracula (also director: produced 1984).
Spend, Spend, Spend, with Claire Luckham, adaptation of the televison play by Jack Rosenthal (also director: produced 1985).
All the Fun of the Fair, with John McGrath and others (also director: produced 1986).
El Sid, music by Dave Watts, lyrics by Andrew Birtles, from an idea by Dave Barry (also director: produced 1988).
The Mysterie of Maria Marten (produced 1991).

NOVEL

You Want Drink Something Cold. 1969.

Theatrical activities

Director: **Plays**—*Flying Blind* by Bill Morrison, 1977, 1979; *The Beggar's Opera*, 1977; *Stags and Hens* by Willy Russell, 1978; *Trafford Tanzi* by Claire Luckham, 1981 (and U.S. version, *Teaneck Tanzi*, 1983); *Blood Brothers* by Willy Russell, 1983; *Dracula*, 1984; *Sweeney Todd* by Hugh Wheeler and Stephen Sondheim (musical adaptation of Bond's play), 1985; *Scrap!* by Bill Morrison, 1985; *Spend, Spend, Spend*, 1985; *Destiny* by David Edgar, 1985; *All the Fun of the Fair*, 1986; *Moll Flanders* by Claire Luckham, 1986; *Love on the Plastic* by Julia Schofield, 1987; *As Is* by William M. Hoffman, 1987; *Macbeth*, 1987; *El Sid*, 1988; *Poppy* by Peter Nichols, 1988; *Nativity* by Nigel Williams, 1989.

Chris Bond is one of several British dramatists who grew up under the spell of Joan Littlewood's Theatre Workshop in Stratford, East London. In his case, however, a primary attraction to the theatre began almost from his cradle. His parents had run a touring company after World War II, and Bond himself was a child actor, playing at the Shakespeare Memorial Theatre, Stratford-on-Avon, from the age of 11. He grew to love the rough-and-tumble of acting life, the performing skills and the ability to contact audiences at all levels of appreciation; and in his plays he loves to throw in effects which grab the attention—songs, dances, pieces of mime, and simple stage tricks, such as the enlarged washing machine in *Under New Management* which "Harold MacMillan" mistakes for a Mini car and thus gets spun around with the rest of the laundry.

But the direction of his work, its more serious side, derives from Littlewood. Bond has written social and historical documentaries, such as *Under New Management* and *Judge Jeffreys*, and he seeks his audiences primarily from the young, working-class, left-wing public. Although not an overtly political writer, there is a strong vein of socialist thought within his work, which sometimes emerges into didactic messages but more usually is reflected in the handling of his themes—the caricatures of establishment authority, the sympathies with the underprivileged and downtrodden.

The clearest and most striking example of this tendency is *Downright Hooligan*, first produced at the Victoria Theatre, Stoke-on-Trent, where Bond was resident dramatist. The central character, Ian Rigby, is a sort of contemporary Wozzeck, whose eyes, deep-set beneath a granite forehead, suggest a Neanderthal mentality. Permanently out of work, a fixture in the betting shop, Ian is surrounded by a society whose logical illogicalities he cannot comprehend. His mother bawls at him for masturbating in his bedroom, while her lover winks at him and tells him dirty jokes. He accidentally kills the school hamster and sticks drawing pins in its eyes to decorate the body. His headmaster is appalled by the atrocity—but he doesn't know that Ian has just paid his last respects to his grandmother, whose dead drawn face has been padded out with clutches of her own hair. One form of decorating the dead is socially acceptable—Ian's treatment of the hamster is not. Confronted by the unpredictability of society, Ian asserts himself by hitting out savagely at an elderly man and is brought before the courts as a downright hooligan.

Thus, Bond, without glamorising his hero-victim, places the blame for his behaviour upon society at large; and some critics have claimed that his impression of the repressive social forces is simplistic, belonging too much to a "them" and "us" mentality. While his portrait of Ian Rigby's background is telling and convincing, and was presented with marvellous detail by the Stoke company, *Under New Management* is almost a cartoon, agit-prop documentary, showing 12 cretinous general managers—one dressed as a schoolboy clutching a teddy bear—messing up the Fisher-Bendix factory on the outskirts of Liverpool, until the heroic workers, faced by mass redundancy, take over. It was a thoroughly lively, enjoyable production, but inevitably one-sided, partly because Bond had deliberately not interviewed anyone from the management while conducting his research.

By trying to make his plays immediately entertaining, Bond also falls into the trap which snared some of Littlewood's productions. There is too much outer fun, too little inner content. The scenes are short and sketch-like, sometimes extended by horseplay, separated by songs and little dances, and the connecting themes are either lost or so heavily stressed that they seem merely repetitive. In the hands of a highly disciplined company, such as that of Stoke or of the old Liverpool Everyman, where Bond became artistic director, this music-hall mixture could be pulled into a tight shape. His plays usually require the concentration supplied by a firm director and an experienced team.

While striving for a casual, easy-going and lighthearted approach to the theatre, Bond in fact usually demands great restraint and professionalism from his performers—an apparent contradiction which not all directors have realised. There was a luckless production of *Judge Jeffreys* at Stratford East, where the script seemed as banal as the performances; and *Tarzan's Last Stand*, about Enoch Powell the "ape man," seemed to miss its very broad, satirical target by not taking Powell's arguments sufficiently seriously. Bond (like a somewhat similar writer of social documentaries, Alan Plater) has yet to find perhaps that dramatic structure within which his talents and social insights can be best expressed.

—John Elsom

BOND, Edward.

Born in London, 18 July 1934. Educated at Crouch End Secondary Modern School, 1944–49. Served in the British Army, 1953–55. Married Elisabeth Pablé in 1971. Member of the English Stage Company Writers Group, Royal Court Theatre, London, from 1958. Founding member, Theatre Writers' Group (now Theatre Writers' Union), 1975; Northern Arts literary fellow, universities of Newcastle upon Tyne and Durham, 1977–79; resident writer, University of Essex, Colchester, 1982; visiting professor, University of Palermo, Italy, 1983. Recipient: George Devine award, 1968; John Whiting award, 1968; Obie award, 1976. D. Litt.: Yale University, New Haven, Connecticut, 1977. Agent: Casarotto Ramsay Ltd., National House, 60–66 Wardour Street, London W1V 3HP, England.

Publications

PLAYS

The Pope's Wedding (produced 1962). In *The Pope's Wedding* (collection), 1971.

Saved (produced 1965). 1966.
A Chaste Maid in Cheapside, adaptation of the play by Middleton (produced 1966).
Three Sisters, adaptation of a play by Chekhov (produced 1967).
Narrow Road to the Deep North (produced 1968). 1968.
Early Morning (produced 1968). 1968; revised version in *Plays 1*, 1977.
Sketch in *The Enoch Show* (produced 1969).
Black Mass, part of *Sharpeville Sequence: A Scene, A Story, and Three Poems* (produced 1970). In *The Pope's Wedding* (collection), 1971; in *The Best Short Plays 1972*, edited by Stanley Richards, 1972.
Passion (produced 1971). In *New York Times*, 15 August 1971; with *Bingo*, 1974.
Lear (produced 1971). 1972.
The Pope's Wedding (collection; includes *Sharpeville Sequence* and the stories "Mr. Dog" and "The King with Golden Eyes"). 1971.
The Sea (produced 1973). 1973; with *Bingo*, 1975.
Bingo: Scenes of Money and Death (and Passion) (produced 1973). 1974; with *The Sea*, 1975.
Spring Awakening, adaptation of a play by Wedekind (produced 1974). 1979.
The Fool: Scenes of Bread and Love (produced 1975). With *We Come to the River*, 1976; published separately, 1978.
We Come to the River: Actions for Music, music by Hans Werner Henze (produced 1976). With *The Fool*, 1976.
The White Devil, adaptation of the play by Webster (produced 1976).
A-A-America: Grandma Faust, and The Swing (produced 1976). In *A-A-America, and Stone*, 1976.
Stone (produced 1976). In *A-A-America, and Stone*, 1976; in *Performing Arts Journal*, Fall 1977.
A-A-America, and Stone. 1976; revised edition, 1981.
Plays (revised versions):
   1. *Saved, Early Morning, The Pope's Wedding*. 1977.
   2. *Lear, The Sea, Narrow Road to the Deep North, Black Mass, Passion*. 1978.
   3. *Bingo, The Fool, The Woman*. 1987.
   4. *The Worlds, The Activists Papers, Restoration, Summer*. 1992.
The Woman: Scenes of War and Freedom (also co-director: produced 1978). 1979 (includes stories); 1979.
The Bundle: Scenes of Right and Evil; or, New Narrow Road to the Deep North (produced 1978). 1978.
The Worlds (also director: produced 1979). With *The Activists Papers*, 1980.
Restoration: A Pastoral, music by Nick Bicât (also director: produced 1981). 1981; revised version, with *The Cat*, 1982; revised version, published separately, 1988.
Summer: A European Play (also director: produced 1982). 1982.
Summer, with Fables, and Service: A Story. 1982.
Derek (produced 1982). With *Choruses from After the Assassinations*, 1983.
The Cat (opera libretto), music by Hans Werner Henze, adaptation of a work by Balzac (as *Die englische Katze*, produced 1983; as *The English Cat*,

produced 1985). With *Restoration*, 1982; as *The English Cat: A Story for Singers and Instrumentalists*, 1983.
Choruses from after the Assassinations (produced 1983). With *Derek*, 1983.
The War Plays: A Trilogy (includes *Red, Black and Ignorant*; *The Tin Can People*; *Great Peace*) (*Red, Black and Ignorant* produced 1984; *The Tin Can People* produced 1984; also director: trilogy produced 1985). 2 vols., 1985; revised edition, 1991.
Human Cannon (produced 1986). 1985.
Burns (for children; produced 1986).
September (produced 1989). In *Two Post-Modern Plays*, 1989.
Jackets II (produced 1989). In *Two Post-Modern Plays*, 1989.
In the Company of Men (produced 1992). In *Two Post-Modern Plays*, 1989.
Two Post-Modern Plays (includes *Jackets I* and *II*, *In the Company of Men*, *September*: "Notes on Post Modernism"). 1989.
Olly's Prison (televised 1993). 1993.

SCREENPLAYS: *Blow-up*, with Michelangelo Antonioni and Tonino Guerra, 1967; *Laughter in the Dark*, 1969; *Michael Kohlhaas*, with others, 1969; *The Lady of Monza* (English dialogue), 1970; *Walkabout*, 1971; *Nicholas and Alexandra*, with James Goldman, 1971; *Fury*, with Antonio Calenda and Ugo Pirro, 1973.

TELEVISION PLAY: *Olly's Prison*, 1993.

BALLET SCENARIO: *Orpheus*, music by Hans Werner Henze, 1979.

VERSE
The Swing Poems. 1976.
Theatre Poems and Songs, edited by Malcolm Hay and Philip Roberts. 1978.
Poems 1978–1985. 1987.

CRITICAL STUDIES: *Edward Bond* by Simon Trussler, 1976; *The Plays of Edward Bond* by Richard Scharine, 1976; *The Plays of Edward Bond: A Study* by Tony Coult, 1977, revised edition, 1979; *Edward Bond: A Companion to the Plays*, 1978, and *Bond: A Study of His Plays*, 1980, both by Malcolm Hay and Philip Roberts, and *Bond on File* edited by Roberts, 1985; *Edward Bond: A Study of His Plays* by Delia Donahue, 1979; *Edward Bond* by David L. Hirst, 1985; *The Art and Politics of Edward Bond* by Lou Lappin, 1987.

THEATRICAL ACTIVITIES

DIRECTOR: **Plays**—*Lear*, 1973; *The Woman* (co-director, with Sebastian Graham-Jones), 1978; *The Worlds*, 1979; *Restoration*, 1981; *Summer*, 1982; *The War Plays*, 1985.
ACTOR: **Plays**—Aighard in *One Leg over the Wrong Wall* by Albert Bernel, 1960; Christ in *Black Mass*, 1970.

Edward Bond writes the most lapidary language of today's English theatre, absorbing dialects, pastiches, metaphors, and questions into a rich mineral vein. Pithy phrases, swift scenes, and vivid characters are his building-blocks for what he calls Rational Theatre, dedicated to the creation of a rational society. Far from agit-prop, however, his plays range through history and legend, as well as the contemporary scene.

The early plays of surface realism shock by their pointless murders: young Scopey throttles an old hermit at the end of *The Pope's Wedding*; a group of youths stone a baby to death in the middle of *Saved*; at the beginning of *The Sea* Colin drowns while Hatch watches idly from the shore. However, confrontation with these deaths involves radical action on the part of Bond's protagonists. Behind its provocative title *The Pope's Wedding* dramatizes a young man's vain effort fully to understand another human being. Step by step, Scopey abandons companions, wife, job, in order to spend his time with an old hermit to learn "What yoo 'ere for?" Even in the old man's coat, communing with his corpse, he never learns.

As the title *Saved* suggests, Len is more successful. A loner, Len does not share in the bored activities of London youths who gamble, steal, fornicate. They rub a baby's face in its diaper, then pitch stones into its carriage while Len, perhaps the baby's father, watches. The baby dies, and only later does Len admit: "Well, I should a stopped yer." Rejected by the baby's mother, flirting briefly with the grandmother, Len the loner is finally "saved" by the grandfather's barely articulate plea for him to remain in their household.

The Sea opens with Colin's drowning while his friend Willie pleads vainly for help from Evens, a drunken recluse, and Hatch, a paranoid coast-guard watchman. Later Willie barely escapes a murderous attack by Hatch, who believes him to be an enemy from outer space. Despite his grief at Colin's death, contrasted with the satirized indifference of the towns-people, Willie comes to see that "The dead don't matter." Cumulatively, through these apparently realistic plays "Life laughs at death."

For the most part, Bond resembles Brecht in analyzing contemporary social injustice through parables based on legend or history. Since both playwrights see war as the cruellest social injustice, Bond explores that violence in violent plays. *Narrow Road to the Deep North* takes place in 19th-century Japan. Basho, the protagonist, follows the narrow road to the deep north in order to study, but he learns that "enlightenment is where you are." And where he is necessitates a choice between two evils, an English invader or a homegrown warlord. As the play ends, Basho is Prime Minister, his disciple falls disembowelled, and a stranger emerges from the river. Each man must make his own decisions in a time of war, and life goes on.

Of all Bond's protagonists, his Lear experiences the hardest enlightenment. From Shakespeare Bond borrows the large tragic conception intensified by grotesque humor. By way of Shakespeare, Bond re-enforces his own dramatic concern with moral responsibility. As in Shakespeare, Lear is an absolute autocrat. Instead of dividing his kingdom, Bond's Lear encloses it within a wall built by forced labor. Lear's two daughters foment war, and both meet violent deaths. A composite of Kent and the Fool, Bond's Gravedigger's Boy has a wife named Cordelia. After the Boy is shot and his wife raped by the daughter's soldiers, his Ghost accompanies Lear on an infernal descent through madness and blindness. The Gravedigger's Boy's Ghost is slain, Lear attains wisdom, and Cordelia attains power as head of a new autocracy. In spite of Lear's age, he tries physically to dismantle Cordelia's wall, but he is shot. Like

Shakespeare's Lear, he has learned compassion, but he has also learned the necessity for socially responsible action.

In a later war parable Bond looks back to the cultural roots of the Western tradition—the Trojan War. *The Woman* (or "Scenes of War and Freedom") is a panoramic drama with Trojan Hecuba as its protagonist. Part 1, set at the walls of Troy, condenses and revises Homer's *Iliad* to show a capitalist Greece attacking a feudal Troy ruled by Hecuba. Ismene, wife of the Greek commander Hero, speaks out so passionately for peace and mercy that she is buried alive in the Trojan wall. Part 2, set on an unnamed island 12 years later, finds blind Hecuba caring for her adopted daughter, the mentally crippled Ismene. War encroaches upon freedom when the Greeks invade the island. After wise old Hecuba perpetrates a ruse for freedom, she is killed in a storm. Ismene, crippled in mind, and a miner, crippled in body, face the new day together, strangers on an island.

Bond's non-war plays deriving from history and legend zig-zag sharply from comic to tragic tone. *Early Morning* puns on mourning, but the play is grotesquely hilarious in its exposé of Victorian social injustice. Proper Queen Victoria has Siamese twin sons, Crown Prince George and the protagonist Arthur. The Queen matches the former to Florence Nightingale whom she then rapes. Prince Albert, Disraeli, and Gladstone all plot against the Queen. By mid-play the whole cast is dead in Heaven, where the main activity is cannibalism, but all flesh regenerates. Arthur alone refuses to accept heavenly habit, starving himself to a second death.

Suicide also closes the grimmer *Bingo*, whose protagonist is William Shakespeare in retirement at Stratford. Aware that the land enclosure spreads starvation for its victims, Shakespeare nevertheless fails to oppose enclosure so long as his own investments are guaranteed. After a visit from drunken Ben Jonson, Shakespeare's disgust at cruelties of his fellow men shifts to self-disgust at his own failure to act: "How long have I been dead?" He answers the question by taking poison.

Like *Bingo*, *The Fool* indicts the cruelties of an acquisitive society. But unlike *Bingo*'s Shakespeare, The Fool, poet John Clare, is exploited by his social "betters." Not only does he lose his money, his poems, and his evanescent mistress, but also his sanity. Though Bond only sketches his two protagonist poets, Shakespeare and Clare, he dramatizes their society with deft economy.

Restoration dramatizes the life and death of another kind of fool, the honest servant Bob in the world of Restoration fops. Elegant, witty Lord Are deigns to marry a businessman's daughter for her dowry. She in turn has married him for entrance into the social whirl—an entrance he refuses her. In a preposterous scene she haunts him as a sourly unblithe spirit; he stabs her dead and persuades faithful Bob to take the blame. In spite of the courage and protests of Bob's black wife, he is hanged for the crime he did not commit. *Summer* stages a private story and the trilogy *The War Plays* a post-atomic epic, in impassioned pleas for social responsibility.

Bond's violent scenes and cruel humor at first attracted attention rather than appreciation, but he has gradually gathered admirers of his moral commitment theatricalized with verve and economy. Speaking against the Theatre of the Absurd—"Life becomes meaningless when you stop *acting* on the things that concern you most" — Bond has called his work the Rational Theatre. Instead of preaching a rational gospel, however, he fills an almost bare stage with whole societies from which and against which heroes arise, who learn through their suffering to act responsibly. This resembles the *pathos-mathos* of classical tragedy, but it is translated into a modern godless world.

—Ruby Cohn

See the essay on *Saved*.

BOWEN, John (Griffith).

Born in Calcutta, India, 5 November 1924. Educated at Queen Elizabeth's Grammar School, Crediton, Devon; Pembroke College, Oxford (editor, *Isis*), 1948–51; St. Antony's College, Oxford (Frere Exhibitioner in Indian Studies), 1951–53, M.A. 1953; Ohio State University, Columbus, 1952–53. Served in the Mahratha Light Infantry, 1943–47: captain. Assistant editor, *Sketch* magazine, London, 1953–56; copywriter, J. Walter Thompson Company, London, 1956–58; head of the copy department, S.T. Garland Advertising, London, 1958–60; script consultant, Associated Television, London, 1960–67; drama producer, Thames Television, London, 1978–79, London Weekend Television, 1981–83, and BBC, 1984. Recipient: Society of Authors travelling scholarship, 1986. Agent: (fiction) Elaine Greene Ltd., 31 Newington Green, London N16 9PU; (theatre) Casarotto Ramsay Ltd., National House, 60–66 Wardour Street, London W1V 3HP. Address: Old Lodge Farm, Sugarswell Lane, Edgehill, Banbury, Oxfordshire OX15 6HP, England.

Publications

PLAYS

The Essay Prize, with A Holiday Abroad and The Candidate: Plays for Television. 1962.

I Love You, Mrs. Patterson (produced 1964). 1964.

The Corsican Brothers, based on the play by Dion Boucicault (televised 1965; revised version produced 1970). 1970.

After the Rain, adaptation of his own novel (produced 1966). 1966; revised version, 1972.

The Fall and Redemption of Man (as *Fall and Redemption*, produced 1967; as *The Fall and Redemption of Man*, produced 1974). 1968.

Silver Wedding (televised 1967; revised version, produced in *We Who Are about to . . .*, later called *Mixed Doubles*, 1969). 1970.

Little Boxes (includes *The Coffee Lace* and *Trevor*) (produced 1968). 1968.

The Disorderly Women, adaptation of a play by Euripides (produced 1969). 1969.

The Waiting Room (produced 1970). 1970.

Robin Redbreast (televised 1970; produced 1974). In *The Television Dramatist*, edited by Robert Muller, 1973.

Diversions (produced 1973). Excerpts in *Play Nine*, edited by Robin Rook, 1981.

Young Guy Seeks Part-Time Work (televised 1973; produced 1978).

Roger, in *Mixed Blessings* (produced 1973). In *London Magazine*, October-November 1976.

Florence Nightingale (as *Miss Nightingale*, televised 1974; revised version, as *Florence Nightingale*, produced 1975). 1976.

Heil Caesar!, adaptation of *Julius Caesar* by Shakespeare (televised 1974). 1974; revised version (produced 1974), 1975.

Which Way Are You Facing? (produced 1976). Excerpts in *Play Nine*, edited by Robin Rook, 1981.

Singles (produced 1977).

Bondage (produced 1978).

The Inconstant Couple, adaptation of a play by Marivaux (produced 1978).

Spot the Lady (produced 1981).

The Geordie Gentleman, adaptation of a play by Molière (produced 1987).

The Oak Tree Tea Room Siege (produced 1990).

RADIO PLAYS: *Digby* (as Justin Blake, with Jeremy Bullmore), 1959; *Varieties of Love* (revised version of television play *The First Thing You Think Of*), 1968; *The False Diaghilev*, 1988.

TELEVISION PLAYS: created the *Garry Halliday* series; episodes in *Front Page Story*, *The Power Game*, *Wylde Alliance*, and *The Villains* series; *A Holiday Abroad*, 1960; *The Essay Prize*, 1960; *The Jackpot Question*, 1961; *The Candidate*, 1961; *Nuncle*, from the story by John Wain, 1962; *The Truth about Alan*, 1963; *A Case of Character*, 1964; *Mr. Fowlds*, 1965; *The Corsican Brothers*, 1965; *Finders Keepers*, 1967; *The Whole Truth*, 1967; *Silver Wedding*, 1967; *A Most Unfortunate Accident*, 1968; *Flotsam and Jetsam*, 1970; *Robin Redbreast*, 1970; *The Guardians* series (7 episodes), 1971; *A Woman Sobbing*, 1972; *The Emergency Channel*, 1973; *Young Guy Seeks Part-Time Work*, 1973; *Miss Nightingale*, 1974; *Heil Caesar!*, 1974; *The Treasure of Abbott Thomas*, 1974; *The Snow Queen*, 1974; *A Juicy Case*, 1975; *Brief Encounter*, from the film by Noël Coward, 1976; *A Photograph*, 1977; *Rachel in Danger*, 1978; *A Dog's Ransom*, from the novel by Patricia Highsmith, 1978; *Games*, 1978; *The Ice House*, 1978; *The Letter of the Law*, 1979; *Dying Day*, 1980; *The Specialist*, 1980; *A Game for Two Players*, 1980; *Dark Secret*, 1981; *Honeymoon*, 1985.

NOVELS

The Truth Will Not Help Us: Embroidery on an Historical Theme. 1956.
After the Rain. 1958.
The Centre of the Green. 1959.
Storyboard. 1960.
The Birdcage. 1962.
A World Elsewhere. 1965.
Squeak: A Biography of NPA 1978A 203. 1983.
The McGuffin. 1984.
The Girls: A Story of Village Life. 1986.
Fighting Back. 1989.
The Precious Gift. 1992.
Other (for children)

Pegasus. 1957.
The Mermaid and the Boy. 1958.
Garry Halliday and the Disappearing Diamonds [*Ray of Death; Kidnapped Five; Sands of Time; Flying Foxes*] (as Justin Blake, with Jeremy Bullmore). 5 vols., 1960–64.

MANUSCRIPT COLLECTIONS: Mugar Memorial Library, Boston University; (television works) Temple University Library, Philadelphia.

THEATRICAL ACTIVITIES
DIRECTOR: **Plays**—at the London Academy of Music and Dramatic Art since 1967; *The Disorderly Women,* 1969; *Fall and Redemption,* 1969; *The Waiting Room,* 1970.
ACTOR: **Plays**—in repertory, summers 1950–51 and 1965.

John Bowen comments:

My plays, like my novels, are distinguished by a general preoccupation with myth (*The Truth Will Not Help Us, After the Rain, A World Elsewhere, Fall and Redemption, The Disorderly Women, Robin Redbreast*), and mainly with one particular myth, that of the Bacchae, which in my reading represents the conflict between Apollonian and Dionysiac ways of living more than the mere tearing to pieces of a Sacred King. This theme, the fight in every human being and between beings themselves, rationality against instinct, is to be found somewhere in almost everything I have written.

Another common theme is of manipulation, one person using another or others, not always consciously, and sometimes "for their good." This theme has been most clearly expressed politically in the episodes I wrote for the television series *The Guardians,* and in my novel *A World Elsewhere.* A third common theme, allied to the other two, is that of self-deceit.

I think of plays as constructions (as all literary forms are, but plays and poems perhaps most), and enjoy theatricality. I like movement; plays are not talk, but action, though the talk may *be* action. I think that the cinema and television have helped the theatre in the 20th century to rediscover some of the mobility it had in the 16th. Though I like above all naturalistic acting, I hate naturalistic settings, and try to avoid waits for scene changes: in most of my plays, the scenes flow into each other by a shift of light.

I have been influenced by Ibsen and Chekhov, probably by Coward, Anouilh, Pirandello and Shaw. Of 20th-century directors, I have most admired Sir Tyrone Guthrie.

Before his first major stage success, with *After the Rain* in 1966, John Bowen was already well known as a novelist and theatre critic for the then prestigious *London Magazine.* His theatre columns of that period reveal a sympathetic understanding of a large variety of dramatic modes, and so it is unsurprising that his own plays have been criticised for stylistic eclecticism. Though *After the Rain* was based on one of Bowen's novels, its theatricality was immediately seen to reflect Weiss's *Marat/Sade*, particularly in the way that each member of the cast is presented as being a criminal deviant hypnotised into the therapeutic re-enactment of events related to the great deluge of the late 20th century. The metatheatrical dimension is not developed at all, however, and Bowen's deeper interest emerges as lying in the use of archetype, particularly through sometimes startling diachronic collations. *After the Rain* displays the emblems of epic theatre from the start: a bare stage with a lectern, minimal props, placards identifying locations, and the first character (a Lecturer) delivering his opening lines to the lighting technician. All the barriers of the conventional theatre seem to have dissolved. But within a few seconds the Lecturer is referring to "life in 1968" as something prehistoric; elastic time has suddenly soared beyond the audience's experience. Early in the second act there appears a character whom audience members (but not the characters) recognise as Noah, and time bounces back violently in the other direction. The nine prisoner/characters, ostensibly drifting on a raft in the 1970's, find themselves in an arena in which the mythological merges with the futuristic, and a primitive theocracy is generated by necessity—although the Lecturer's scepticism is continually apparent. Satire of varying strengths has been directed at the figures on the raft—stock types from the 1960's—and Noah, on his first appearance, seems also a target for iconoclastic ridicule. However, it quickly becomes apparent that the Noah myth is not one of regeneration but of fossilisation; the ark is full of rotting animals, and Noah survives alone as a demented Ancient Mariner, persecuted by the anonymous gods, crazed by drinking the blood of the Shetland pony. For the protection of humanity, the ark is incinerated with Noah aboard. A new totalitarian myth is, of course, emerging, but for the audience there remains the question of whether Arthur, the autocrat of the raft society, has annihilated the Noah myth or assimilated it. The ending differs in the 1972 revised version, but essentially in both versions Arthur's divinity is challenged when he demands the sacrifice of the first baby born, and the result is a duel, with the death of the god and the birth of the new society which presents the play; at the same time, however, roles are also broken and the play ends with the insistence that the theatre has been invaded by reality.

Bowen's fascination with what he calls "myth" seems to derive from its defiance of chronology and conventional concepts of causation. His adaptation of Boucicault's *The Corsican Brothers* for television and then for the stage seems to have been stimulated by the telepathic link between the twins, and thus between Corsican and Parisian society; but the play also drops the morality of melodrama into a Brechtian limbo, heralded by the hobby-horses of the first episode and developed by numerous flippantly sardonic songs, culminating in a "Moral Finale." *Fall and Redemption* seems to consist of an iconoclastic pilfering of quaint details from the Mystery Cycles to create an acting exercise for LAMDA students, and its termination with the crucifixion (rather than Doomsday, where all the English cycles end) was interpreted as insensitivity to form; yet its Brechtian rationale is evident at least when Cain and Abel are joined by a talking horse, and inescapable in the ending, where the actors help Jesus off the cross and then come forward for applause. In another myth play for LAMDA, *The Disorderly Women*, Bowen knew that he was joining numerous playwrights of the 1960's in attempting a contemporary

adaptation of *The Bacchae*; yet he was also trying to give a relatively sympathetic portrayal of Pentheus, as a ruler committed to moderation, a principle
neither understood by his father nor respected by Dionysus, whose cynicism,
Bowen's introduction suggests, is substantiated by Auschwitz, Hiroshima, and
Vietnam.

In the 1970's Bowen's interests and techniques developed variously, with
Singles, a comedy about sexual mercenaries, achieving a modest London
critical success. The dilemma of Pentheus was expanded and domesticated in a
play which did not reach London, *Which Way Are You Facing?*, a cerebral but
aggressively theatrical contribution to the history of the problem play, from
the sympathetic perspective of the control room of the Samaritans, monitoring
the unloveliest of humanity in every corner of the auditorium. By contrast, in
the much-praised *Robin Redbreast* Bowen exploits the savagery of myth which
leaps from prehistory into the life of a television script editor; the dialogue of
the final scene even includes a reference to *The Golden Bough*, but the
structure of this play depends on psychological realism and its main impact is
that of a thriller. In fact, although Bowen is best known for plays based on
myth using techniques of epic theatre, he learned his dramatic craft writing for
television, and his early plays (notably *A Holiday Abroad*) show a mastery of
the subtleties of realism. One of his mature plays, *The Coffee Lace*, has even
been interpreted as naturalistic in its portrayal of six veteran actors who have
hermetically sealed themselves off from the world after a major theatrical
failure ten years previously; however, they are also fossilised grotesques, very
similar in their situation to the figures of *After the Rain*. Ambivalent it may be,
but the play, with its companion piece *Trevor*, must dispel the common
complaint that Bowen is a humourless writer; the gentle comedy in the
portrayal of the social cripples in *The Coffee Lace* is rich but compassionate.

In the 1980s, Bowen increasingly returned to his preferred early genre,
fiction.

—Howard McNaughton

BRENTON, Howard.

Born in Portsmouth, Hampshire, 13 December 1942. Educated at Chichester
High School; St. Catharine's College, Cambridge, B.A. (honours) in English
1965. Married Jane Fry in 1970; two sons. Stage manager in several repertory
companies; resident dramatist, Royal Court Theatre, London, 1972–73.
Recipient: Arts Council bursary, 1969, 1970; John Whiting award, 1970;
Evening Standard award, 1977, 1985. Agent: Casarotto Ramsay Ltd.,
National House, 60–66 Wardour Street, London W1V 3HP, England.

Publications

PLAYS

Ladder of Fools (produced 1965).
Winter, Daddykins (produced 1965).
It's My Criminal (produced 1966).
A Sky-Blue Life, adaptation of stories by Gorky (produced 1967; revised
    version produced 1971). In *Three Plays*, 1989.

Gargantua, adaptation of the novel by Rabelais (produced 1969).
Gum and Goo (produced 1969). In *Plays for Public Places*, 1972.
Revenge (produced 1969). 1970.
Heads, and The Education of Skinny Spew (produced 1969). In *Christie in Love and Other Plays*, 1970.
Christie in Love (produced 1969). In *Christie in Love and Other Plays*, 1970.
Christie in Love and Other Plays. 1970.
Fruit (produced 1970).
Wesley (produced 1970). In *Plays for Public Places*, 1972.
Scott of the Antarctic; or, What God Didn't See (produced 1971). In *Plays for Public Places*, 1972.
Lay By, with others (produced 1971). 1972.
Hitler Dances (produced 1972). 1982.
Plays for Public Places. 1972.
How Beautiful with Badges (produced 1972). In *Three Plays*, 1989.
England's Ireland, with others (produced 1972).
Measure for Measure, adaptation of the play by Shakespeare (produced 1972). In *Three Plays*, 1989.
A Fart for Europe, with David Edgar (produced 1973).
The Screens, adaptation of a play by Jean Genet (produced 1973).
Brassneck, with David Hare (produced 1973). 1974.
Magnificence (produced 1973). 1973.
Mug (produced 1973).
Jedefrau, adaptation of a play by Hugo von Hofmannsthal (produced 1974).
The Churchill Play: As It Will be Performed in the Winter of 1984 by the Internees of Churchill Camp Somewhere in England (produced 1974; revised version, produced 1988). In *Plays 1*, 1986.
The Saliva Milkshake, adaptation of the novel *Under Western Eyes* by Conrad (televised 1975; produced 1975). 1977.
Government Property (produced 1975).
Weapons of Happiness (produced 1976). 1977.
Epsom Downs (produced 1977). 1977.
Deeds, with others (produced 1978). In *Plays and Players*, May and June 1978.
Sore Throats (produced 1979). With *Sonnets of Love and Opposition*, 1979.
Warwickgate, with others (produced 1979).
The Life of Galileo, adaptation of a play by Brecht (produced 1980). 1980.
The Romans in Britain (produced 1980). 1980; revised version, 1982.
Plays for the Poor Theatre (includes *The Saliva Milkshake, Christie in Love, Heads, The Education of Skinny Spew, Gum and Goo*). 1980.
A Short Sharp Shock!, with Tony Howard (produced 1980). With *Thirteenth Night*, 1981.
Thirteenth Night (produced 1981). With *A Short Sharp Shock!*, 1981.
Nail Poems: 32 Haiku (produced 1981).
Danton's Death, adaptation of a play by Georg Büchner (produced 1982). 1982.
The Thing (for children; produced 1982).
Conversations in Exile, adaptation of a work by Brecht (produced 1982).
The Genius (produced 1983). 1983.

Sleeping Policemen, with Tunde Ikoli (produced 1983). 1984.
Bloody Poetry (produced 1984). 1985.
Pravda: A Fleet Street Comedy, with David Hare (produced 1985). 1985.
Plays 1 (includes *Christie in Love, Magnificence, The Churchill Play, Weapons of Happiness, Epsom Downs, Sore Throats*). 1986.
Dead Head (televised 1986). 1987.
Plays 2 (includes *The Romans in Britain, Thirteenth Night, The Genius, Bloody Poetry, Greenland*). 1988.
Greenland (produced 1988). 1988.
Iranian Nights, with Tariq Ali (produced 1989). 1989.
Three Plays (includes *A Sky-Blue Life, How Beautiful with Badges, Measure for Measure*). 1989.
H.I.D. (Hess Is Dead) (produced 1989). 1989.
Moscow Gold, with Tariq Ali (produced 1990). 1990.
The Wall Dog, with Jane Brenton, adaptation of the play by Manfred Karge (produced 1990).
Berlin Bertie (produced 1992). 1992.

SCREENPLAY: *Skin Flicker,* 1973.

TELEVISION PLAYS: *Lushly,* 1972; *The Saliva Milkshake,* 1975; *The Paradise Run,* 1976; *A Desert of Lies,* 1984; *Dead Head* serial, 1986.

NOVEL
Diving for Pearls. 1989.

VERSE
Notes from a Psychotic Journal and Other Poems. 1969.

CRITICAL STUDIES: *New British Political Dramatists* by John Bull, 1984; *File on Brenton* edited by Tony Mitchell, 1988; *Brenton the Playwright* by Richard Boon, 1991.

THEATRICAL ACTIVITIES
ACTOR: **Plays**—with the Brighton Combination, 1969.

"It took me a long time" said Howard Brenton, after reading English at Cambridge University, "to get over being taught literature in that way." While at Cambridge Brenton wrote a long unworkable play called *Ladder of Fools,* but it was not until joining Brighton Combination as an actor and writer in 1968 that he began to find his feet in the theatre. Adapting Rabelais's *Gargantua* for a group show led Brenton to experiment with style; and a shoestring budget while writing *Gum and Goo* in 1969 taught him to write with concentration. His first full-length play, *Revenge,* was produced by the Royal Court Theatre Upstairs in 1969 and he subsequently worked with Portable Theatre, writing *Lay By* and *Brassneck* in collaboration with David Hare and others.

In 1970 Brenton won the John Whiting award for *Christie in Love.* The Rillington Place murderer is treated naturalistically, as a lover in search of a love-object, while the police are essentially non-naturalistic, giving the audience "a sense of moral vertigo." *Magnificence* turns on the impossibility of taking effective action against the establishment. In the final scene a would-be revolutionary, newly released from prison, fails to assassinate a cabinet minister because his gelignite mask has fused. When he tosses the mask away it explodes, killing both himself and his victim, a final ineffectual act.

Brenton's early settings range from the South Pole (*Scott of the Antarctic*) to Epsom race course on Derby day (*Epsom Downs*), via an internment camp (*The Churchill Play*), and a crisp factory (*Weapons of Happiness*). The plays are anarchic: *The Churchill Play*, for example, shows an army-operated internment camp for recalcitrant trade union members, in the Britain of 1984. Warning against the possibility of a totalitarian Britain, *Weapons of Happiness* presents a black-and-white world of bosses and workers in which (heavily symbolic) the workers flee, literally down the drain. Brenton's characters become signposts for good and evil. He describes the costumes for *Scott of the Antarctic* as: "Huge, gangling, gaudy apparitions—like adverts stepped down from the billboards of some rubbish world." It is a strip-cartoon technique, Brechtian in style.

During the 1970's Brenton emerged as a major political dramatist, his work increasingly in demand by establishment theatres. The National Theatre's 1980 production of *The Romans in Britain* (which caused a furore, due to its prosecution by Mary Whitehouse on the grounds of indecency) is not a celebration of violence and degradation, but a serious exploration of the dubious nature of Empire-building. Brenton uses the homosexual rape of a Druid priest by a Roman soldier to demonstrate this theme and goes on to show the results of British incursions into Ireland.

Brenton's work includes the translation and adaptation of Brecht's *Galileo* and Büchner's *Danton's Death*, both for the National Theatre—for which he also wrote (with David Hare) the enormously successful Fleet Street satire *Pravda* (Russian for "Truth"—from "a foundry of lies"). Other plays have experimented with technique: in *Thirteenth Night* Brenton tried to "bury" the plot of *Macbeth*, while *The Genius* is a modern version of *Galileo*: a 20th-century mathematician, having discovered a formula (which, if used to make a bomb would destroy the universe), attempts to hide his knowledge. Brenton's most innovative experiment is his collaboration with Tunde Ikoli for Foco Novo. Both wrote entirely separate plays, set in Peckham, about the same six characters. Working with director Roland Rees, the two plays were intercut to form the curiously dreamlike play, *Sleeping Policemen*.

Iranian Nights was written with Tariq Ali early in 1989 in passionate support of free expression during the crisis over Salman Rushdie's *Satanic Verses*. It was followed by *H.I.D.*, commissioned by the Mickery Theatre, Amsterdam, debating whether Hess or another finally died in Spandau gaol and exploring the question: "What is History? . . . that we bend, that we distort? From which we want . . . the truth?"

Brenton's first attempt at a play about Utopia was *Sore Throats*: "the most violent writing I have ever done." Subsequently he made an unsuccessful attempt to adapt William Morris's *News from Nowhere* and then shelved ideas for Utopias until Roland Rees requested a play about Shelley—Brenton realised that Shelley and his circle were "would-be Utopians" (in both work and life), and wrote *Bloody Poetry* "to salute them." *Greenland* followed in 1988, the play Brenton had been meditating for a decade: "I have tried to dramatize how I hope my children or my children's children will live and think." Brenton realised it was "a reckless undertaking" to try to describe a new world culture 700 years hence, free of conflict and oppression, but finally found a model in Shakespearean Romantic Comedy (where characters get lost and find themselves in an "alternative reality"). Act 2 of *Greenland* catapults Brenton's characters from 1987 into a 2687 Utopia:

> Joan: How is it organised? . . . There are no policies! No-one decides anything! . . . I just die for some authority!

In the final scene Joan returns to 1987 with a jewel from 2687, from which "Light splinters across the stage and out over the auditorium"—a surprisingly hopeful portent from Brenton for the future.

—Rosemary Pountney

See the essay on *Pravda*.

BROPHY, Brigid (Antonia).

Born in London, 12 June, 1929. Educated at St. Paul's Girls' School, London; St Hugh's College, Oxford (Jubilee scholar), 1947–48. married Sir Michael Levey in 1954; one daughter. Co-organiser, Writers Action Group, 1972–82; executive councillor, Writers Guild of Great Britain, 1975–78; vice-chairman, British Copyright Council, 1976–80. Since 1974 vice-president, Anti-Vivisection Society of Great Britain. Since 1984 has suffered from multiple sclerosis. Recipient: Cheltenham Festival prize, 1954; *London Magazine* prize, 1962; Tony Godwin award, 1985. Fellow, Royal Society of Literature, 1973. Address: Flat 3, 185 Old Brompton Road, London SW5 0AN, England.

Publications

PLAYS

The Waste-Disposal Unit (broadcast 1964). In *London Magazine*, April 1964; in *Best Short Plays of the World Theatre 1965–67*, 1968.
The Burglar (produced 1967). 1968.

RADIO PLAY: *The Waste-Disposal Unit*, 1964.

NOVELS

Hackenfeller's Ape. 1953.
The King of a Rainy Country. 1956.
Flesh. 1962.
The Finishing Touch. 1963.
The Snow Ball. 1964.
The Snow Ball, with The Finishing Touch. 1964.
In Transit. 1969.
The Adventures of God in His Search for the Black Girl: A Novel and Some Fables. 1973.
Palace Without Chairs: A Baroque Novel. 1978.

SHORT STORIES
The Crown Princess and Other Stories. 1953.

OTHER
Black Ship to Hell. 1962.
Mozart the Dramatist: A New View of Mozart, His Operas, and His Age. 1964; revised edition, 1988.
Don't Never Forget: Collected Views and Reviews. 1966.
Religious Education in State Schools. 1967.
Fifty Works of English and American Literature We Could Do Without, with Michael Levey and Charles Osborne. 1967.
Black and White: A Portrait of Aubrey Beardsley. 1968.
The Longford Threat to Freedom. 1972.
Prancing Novelist: A Defence of Fiction in the form of a Critical Biography in Praise of Ronald Firbank. 1973.
Beardsley and His World. 1976.
Pussy Owl (for children). 1976.
The Prince and the Wild Geese. 1983.
A Guide to Public Lending Right. 1983.
Baroque-'n'-Roll and Other Essays. 1987.
Reads (essays). 1989.

MANUSCRIPT COLLECTION: Lilly Library, University of Indiana, Bloomington.

Brigid Brophy comments:

Between the ages of 6 and 10, I was a prolific playwright, mainly in blank verse. An elderly widow in the London suburb where I lived, being anxious to foster the arts, appointed herself my impresario. She assembled a cast (of local children) and a regular audience (of their parents) and, season by season, mounted my oeuvre in her drawing room.

This excellent arrangement was, like much else, disrupted in 1939 by the war, and when I eventually began my public literary career it was as an author of books. In 1961 or so I reverted to my original vocation as dramatist by writing *The Waste-Disposal Unit,* a brief, black and I hope funny *fleur du mal,* which I composed in two foreign languages (Italian and American), with a touch of free verse, and through which I expressed my Baudelairean fascination with the linguistic perversion that transforms English into American.

That was first performed, to approving notices, on BBC radio and has since been staged as a one-act play, by students and other amateurs, in London, Cambridge, and Hong Kong. In 1967 a full-length play of mine, *The Burglar,* was produced in the West End. It concerns the plight of a burglar who, thinking to break into merely an empty household in order to filch material objects, in fact irrupts into the close-woven relationships of four lovers. I hoped to produce theatrical amusement, a pleasing formal pattern, and some illumination of our social morality by shock confrontation of the burglar (an economic libertarian but a sexual puritan) with the lovers, who are sexual libertarians but conventionalists on the subject of property. The play displeased the London critics and was a moderately resounding flop. (I believe, however, it fared more happily in Dortmund, Germany). I subsequently published it with a long preface which begins as an ephemeral defence of myself but continues, more importantly, with a discussion of society's attitude, including its unconscious attitudes towards the behaviour it labels crime.

The play's commercial failure understandably warned impresarios against me and brought my public career as a dramatist to an end. I have naturally continued to pursue my vocation, enlarging and varying my expressive use of the theatrical medium, first to create an opera in words and then to incarnate, by expressionist means, a metaphor of the unconscious wish to die. These experiments, however, remain private because of the present shortage of elderly widows anxious to foster the arts.

Brigid Brophy's *The Burglar* is a very clever piece of writing which reads far better than it plays. As Brophy points out in the long Shavian preface, she learned her stagecraft "from thinking hard about the form of great operas and not from ASMing for ten years in provincial rep" and indeed the structure is more musical and logical than theatrical. As a piece of argument for five voices it is witty and well constructed. As a radio play it might work; in the theatre it is progressively disappointing after a highly theatrical opening—with the stage almost in darkness, a ladder heaving into view outside the bedroom window, a figure climbing stealthily into view and then into the room, a bigger man stepping out from behind a curtain to seize the intruder and then the lights coming on.

The burden of the unanimously hostile reviews was that after this promising beginning there was a lot of talk and no action. This is not, in fact, what is wrong with the play. There is the burglar's amusing feebleness when Roderick manhandles him. There is the well-phased revelation that Roderick is not Edwina's husband. The sustained anti-climax of the lovers' inability to call the police is developed when the puritanic burglar seizes the moral advantage this gives him to justify his own immorality by savaging theirs. There is a well-contrived climax to Act One when Edwina's husband is heard letting himself into the flat. Roderick and the burglar hide and William comes into the room with an attractive girlfriend. Act Two is equally full of twists and surprises. Act Three culminates in a crash which indicates the burglar's off-stage death.

If, then, the play fails to involve an audience, it is not through lack of action but because the characters and the events fail to come theatrically to life. It is a very Shavian play: moral and social attitudes are dressed up as people, and Brophy takes a Shaw-like delight in flaying the hide off sacred cows which are conventionally venerated. The burglar himself is descended from the burglar in *Heartbreak House* who makes the same point about the injustice of the equation between years of his life wasted in prison and the material value of what he steals. The four middle-class lovers are as wittily capable of stepping over the trip-wires of sexual jealousy as any Shaw hero, and as easy to make into mouthpieces for long arguments about social assumptions governing sex and property. Behind all this there is a Shavian balance in the play's moral structure which weighs the wrongness of stealing other people's property against the wrongness of sleeping with other people's marital partners. Brophy is no more guilty than Shaw of using the stage as a platform for debate, but she is less expert at creating characters to involve an audience's emotions. There is no Captain Shotover, no Ellie Dunn to be saved from marrying a middle-aged industrialist, no Mazzini Dunn to be disabused from thinking himself to be in the industrialist's debt. If the cast of *Heartbreak House* were reduced to Hector and Hesiane, Randall and Ariadne, and the Burglar, no-one would be very involved.

It becomes clear quite early on that we are not watching a naturalistic play, that we are not being asked to believe that a burglar would be more interested in delivering moral diatribes about middle-class sexual morality than in making his escape, or that four lovers would behave with as much wit and poise when trapped into such an embarrassing situation. In making her characters almost vulnerable to anything except argument, Brophy is creating a certain theatrical effect, but it is one which rules out a great many others. As the play proceeds we find that the surprises we are being given are all very much of the same quality and calibre, intellectual steps in an argument, musical modulations in a quintet. Theatrically, therefore, they are subject to a law of diminishing returns. This would matter less if it were a one-act play or even a two-act play, but to sustain an audience's interest over two intervals the play would need either to be more emotional or more farcical on a physical level to match up with Brophy's description of it as "bedroom farce".

On the other hand, her fifty-minute radio play, *The Waste Disposal Unit*, is thoroughly successful as a farce within its own non-visual terms. As in her novel *In Transit*, which it prefigures, the comedy and the conflict are bedded in the language itself. The villain of the piece is the American idiom, which mangles the English language rather in the way that the waste disposal unit of the title, installed by visiting Americans in a 16th century Italian palazzo, finally crunches up the two American women, overwhelming mother and puritanic, sentimental daughter. *La donne mobile*, sing the men. *E disponibile*. But the triumph of the piece is to use both the medium and the abhorred idiom so very well, creating a bizarre farce of non-communication between Virgil Knockerbicker, the lethargic homosexual poet, Homer, his worried brother, Merry, the sweet young all-American wife, and Angelo Lumaca, the accredited agent of the Atlantic Seaboard Waste Disposal Unit Corporation. Having made the mistake of moving into three-dimensionality, Brigid Brophy should have the courage to move back to radio, a medium in which her ingenuity comes near to genius.

—Ronald Hayman

BURROWS, John.

Born in London, 19 November 1945. Educated at Manchester University, B.A. in drama. Agent: Alan Brodie, Alan Brodie Representation, 91 Regent Street, London W1R 7TB, England.

Publications

PLAYS

For Sylvia, with John Harding (produced 1972). In *The Best Short Plays 1978*, edited by Stanley Richards, 1978.
The Golden Pathway Annual, with John Harding (produced 1973). 1975.

Loud Reports, with John Harding and Peter Skellern (produced 1975).
Dirty Giant, with John Harding, music by Peter Skellern (produced 1975).
The Manly Bit, with John Harding (produced 1976).
Son of a Gun, with Sidewalk Theatre Company (produced 1976).
Cash Street, with Sidewalk Theatre Company (produced 1977).
Sketches in *Some Animals Are More Equal* (produced 1977).
Restless Natives, music by Rick Lloyd (produced 1978).
Dole Queue Fever, music by Rick Lloyd (produced 1978).
Sketches in *City Delights* (produced 1978).
Freedom Point, music by Rick Lloyd (produced 1979).
The Last Benefit (produced 1980).
One Big Blow, music by Rick Lloyd (produced 1981).
The Checkpoint, with the People Show (produced 1983).
Wartime Stories, music by Andrew Dickson, lyrics by Burrows (produced 1984).
It's a Girl!, music by Andy Whitefield (produced 1987).1988.
Viva España (produced 1988).
Sweet Broken Heart, music by Andy Whitfield (produced 1991).

RADIO WRITINGS: *The Heath and Me*, 1985.

TELEVISION PLAYS: *Do you Dig It?* with John Harding, 1976; *Not the Nine O'Clock News* series, 1980.

THEATRICAL ACTIVITIES
DIRECTOR: **Plays**—all of his own plays, and *Big Square Fields* by John McGrath, 1979; *The Garden of England* by Peter Cox, 1985.
ACTOR: Several of his own plays, and television plays, including *Talkin' Blues* by Nigel Williams, 1977

John Burrows and John Harding are two actors who evolved a distinctive revue-style to look at British class society and the effect its various myths have had on some of the inhabitants of that society. *For Sylvia* satirises gently and almost nostalgically the post-war myth-making of such 1950s epics as *The Dam Busters* and *Reach for the Sky*. Burrows, in the original production, played the central part of the pilot hero while Harding played everybody else. It was a very accurate re-creation and parody of that genre of film, performed with sensitivity and affection.

But *The Golden Pathway Annual* is a more considerable work. It revolves around Michael Peters, a member of the postwar grammar school generation, and traces him from his childhood, the son of a working-class George and Enid, through primary school, the 11-plus examination, grammar school, university, and out to the prospect of graduate unemployment. Again, Burrows played the central role in the first production, while Mark Wing-Davey and Maggie McCarthy played his parents and Harding everybody else. It is written in a series of short scenes—"Dad comes home from the war," "Michael at school," "The Coronation," "The Famous Five." *The Golden Pathway Annual* is a motif for the whole play—an annual sold by a slick salesman to Michael's gullible parents for Michael's "education" and the trigger to

Michael's fantasies, both in boyhood and early adolescence. We see him imagine himself as one of Enid Blyton's very middle-class "Famous Five" and then, a few years later, ironically realize this fantasy's bourgeois content. The play is a gently ironic satire on the rise of the post-war meritocracy and is beautifully evocative for anyone (like me) of that generation.

Their third play, *Loud Reports*, done this time with pop singer Peter Skellern, is about a blimpish brigadier, CorfePrater, and his resolute refusal to come to terms with modern-day social realities, whether it be the depression in the 1930s, the advent of the Welfare State in the 1940s, or affluence in the 1950s. Suez is a brief reminder of former glories, while he staggers on into the 1960s. It is less original than *The Golden Pathway Annual*, though scarcely less entertaining.

—Jonathan Hammond

BYRNE, John.

Born in Paisley, Renfrewshire, Scotland, 6 January 1940. Educated at St. Mirin's Academy and Glasgow School of Art, 1958–63. Married Alice Simpson in 1964; one son and one daughter. Graphic designer, Scottish Television, Glasgow, 1964–66; designer, A.F. Stoddard, carpet manufacturers, Elderslie, 1966–68. Writer- in-residence, Borderline Theatre, Irvine, Ayrshire, 1978–79, and Duncan of Jordanstone College, Dundee, 1981; associate director, Haymarket Theatre, Leicester, 1984–85. Theatrical set and costume designer. Recipient: *Evening Standard* award, 1978. Agent: Casarotto Ramsay Ltd., National House, 60–66 Wardour Street, London W1V 3HP, England. Address: 3 Castle Brae, Newport-on-Tay, Fife, Scotland.

Publications

PLAYS

Writer's Cramp (produced 1977; revised version, produced 1980). In *Plays and Players*, December 1977.
The Slab Boys Trilogy (originally called *Paisley Patterns*). 1987.
  1. *The Slab Boys* (produced 1978). 1981; revised version, 1982.
  2. *Cuttin' a Rug* (as *The Loveliest Night of the Year*, produced 1979; revised version, as *Threads*, produced 1980; as *Cuttin' a Rug*, produced 1982). *Threads* in *A Decade's Drama: Six Scottish Plays*, edited by Richard and Susan Mellis, 1981; *Cuttin' A Rug*, 1982.
  3. *Still Life* (produced 1982). 1982.
Normal Service (produced 1979). In *Plays and Players*, May–June 1979.
Hooray for Hollywood (produced 1980).
Babes in the Wood, music by John Gould, lyrics by David Dearlove (produced 1980).
Cara Coco (produced 1981).
Candy Kisses (produced 1984).
The London Cuckolds, adaptation of the play by Edward Ravenscroft (produced 1985). 1986.
Colquhoun and Macbride (produced 1992). 1992.

RADIO PLAYS: *The Staffie* (version of *Cuttin' a Rug*); *A Night at the Alex*, 1981; *The Nitshill Writing Circle*, 1984.

TELEVISION PLAYS: *The Butterfly's Hoof*, 1978; *Big Deal* (*Crown Court* series), 1984; *Tutti Frutti* series, 1987; *Your Cheatin' Heart* series, 1990.

NOVELS

Tutti Frutti (novelization of television series). 1987.
Your Cheatin' Heart (novelization of television series). 1990.

THEATRICAL ACTIVITIES

DESIGNER (sets, costumes, and/or posters): Plays—*The Cheviot, The Stag, and the Black Black Oil* by John McGrath, 1973; *The Fantastical Feats of Finn MacCool* by Sean McCarthy, 1974; *Writer's Cramp*, 1980; *Heaven and Hell* by Dusty Hughes, 1981; *The Number of the Beast* by Snoo Wilson, 1982; *The Slab Boys Trilogy*, 1982; *Other Worlds* by Robert Holman, 1982; *La Colombe* by Gounod, 1983; *McQuin's Metamorphosis* by Martyn Hobbs, 1984; *The Cherry Orchard* by Chekhov, 1984; *A Midsummer Night's Dream*, 1984; *Candy Kisses*, 1984; *Dead Men* by Mike Stott, 1985; *The London Cuckolds*, 1985; *The Marriage of Figaro* by Mozart, 1986.

John Byrne comments:

(1982) I think I was 11 or 12 when I wrote my first piece . . . not for the theatre, although it was highly-dramatic . . . about a cat that gets squashed under a bus. Accompanied by a linocut showing the young master in tears alongside the open coffin, it appeared in the pages of the school magazine. A slow fuse had been lit. 25 years later (in 1976) I wrote my first stage play, *Writer's Cramp*, a scherzo in J Minor for trio. This was followed by *The Slab Boys* (part 1 of a trilogy) based (but heavily embroidered) upon my own experience of working as a retarded teenager in the design studio of a carpet factory. Next came *Normal Service*, in the original draft densely packed with all sorts of motley stuffs like the haggis, but subsequently "opened up" for the stage, again based (however loosely) on a working experience, this time in television. I was trying in *Normal Service* to write a comedy without jokes, a comedy of manners, of character, the relationships within and without the office, the characters' attitudes towards one another, towards their own and each others' spouses, to their work. I can't be certain I've got the skill to cram all of that into two hours or so, which is part of the reason for my writing the aforementioned trilogy (in which the protagonists in Parts 1 and 2 are moved on 20-odd years in Part 3). In effect *The Slab Boys* trilogy will be one long play in three acts. In *Hooray for Hollywood* I transplanted the hero (F.S. McDade) of *Writer's Cramp* from Paisley to Los Angeles and looked on with mounting alarm as he proceeded to behave quite predictably. This was a ten-minute piece (part of an anthology) commissioned by the Actors' Theatre of Louisville. The distaff side of *Writer's Cramp*, *Cara Coco* (at present being rewritten), was presented by Borderline Theatre Co. in Scotland. Just now I am working on a

play set in another country (other than Scotland, that is) and on one set in
another time (not based on personal experience).

John Byrne was born in Paisley, a suburb of Glasgow, in 1940 and draws
heavily on his past experiences and his Scottish upbringing and adolescence for
his stage writing. Unlike many of his contemporaries Byrne didn't have any
success as a writer until early middle age. This success came in 1977 with his
first play, *Writer's Cramp*, which transferred to London from the Edinburgh
Festival and was subsequently revived. Until then Byrne had earned his living
as a designer and painter, having studied art before spells in carpet manufacture and in television, periods on which he was to draw in subsequent plays.
Byrne had dealings with the trendy world of art and pop music, particularly in
the swinging 1960's when he had an exhibition in London and was even
accorded a profile in one of the Sunday supplements. Byrne also designed LP
covers and dust jackets for contemporaries such as comedian Billy Connolly
and singer Gerry Rafferty and worked as a scene painter with the celebrated
Scottish touring group 7:84. His contempt for the art world has led him to quit
it for good and embrace the theatrical world not only as an alternative source
of inspiration but, in his view, as a superior way of life. Nevertheless his
painter's preoccupation with detail and his gifts of observation are stamped
boldly on his work for the stage.

   Writer's Cramp is an often very funny and accurate extended literary joke
which parodies the styles and pretensions of arty Scotland, through the life and
times of one Francis Seneca McDade. McDade, a writer, painter, and belle
lettrist as well as a loveable but irredeemable mediocrity, is shown progressing
from disaster to disaster: prep school, prison, literary Oxford, and swinging
London, before his final demise clutching a hard-won but rather irrelevant wad
of bank notes. Included among the send-ups and satires which intersperse the
scenes in question are an article on Work-shy Pensioners and a disastrous
musical on Dr. Spock, the latter like much of McDade's canon not advanced
much further than the planning stage. However, McDade does acquire brief
fame in the 1960's as an artist following a typical review from the art critic of
the *Scottish Field*, one Dermot Pantalone: "When I quizzed the artist as to why
so many of his pictures were painted on Formica using household brushes, his
answer was to pick up a pot of Banana Yellow Deep Gloss Enamel and
proceed to draw the outline of a giraffe on my overcoat. . . ." McDade and his
world of poseurs and eccentrics were a rather easy target for Byrne's obvious
comic and linguistic gifts. His second play, first seen at the Traverse Theatre in
Edinburgh, and later in London and on television, was a very different affair.
The Slab Boys is a lively piece of social realism cum situation comedy set in the
paint-mixing room of a Glasgow carpet factory in 1957, and it draws heavily
on Byrne's own past as an apprentice. The play, fiercely idiomatic and full of
pungent one-liners and shop-floor banter, details a working day, in particular
that of three very different apprentices: Phil, the small young rebel with a
secret urge to be a painter; Spanky, the heavy and slow pal of Phil's; and
Hector, shy and domiciled with an over-protective mother. It is Hector's
attempt to make himself ready and presentable for the forthcoming staff dance
which provides the piece with most of its narrative drive, although it is Byrne's

gift for recreating the trends and preoccupations of the period (from hit parade to comic book heroes and hairstyles) and his raucous sense of character and speech which made the play such a success.

Certainly Byrne's subsequent plays have also revealed an interest in character over narrative. *Threads* (originally *The Loveliest Night of the Year*) takes the action of *The Slab Boys* on to the evening of the "staffie" or firm dance. The dialogue is similarly colloquial, strident, and often witheringly amusing, but the action runs out of steam and relies on a series of farcial encounters in the dark which are poor compensation for the loss of the setting of the marvelously evocative slab room in the first play. Nevertheless Byrne still manages to provide the occasional telling visual effect (such as the glaring imprint of a flat iron on the back of Phil's otherwise immaculate white tuxedo).

Normal Service, which equally obviously draws on Byrne's experiences (this time as a designer for Scottish Television in the early 1960's), is set in the design room of such an organisation during a weekend in 1963 when the station's special tenth anniversary programme is due to be recorded. It depicts the internecine strife of the assembled workers who range from a cowardly, trendy media man with a kilt, to a decrepit and hilariously unsuccessful repair man, a weedy expectant father to a demonic trade-union official of Italian descent who declares war every time he answers a ringing phone. Indeed in the resulting chaos the characters and their interplay hold more sway over the audience than any development of storyline or message about technology and the chaotically minded people who service it daily.

Byrne's last substantial stage work, *Candy Kisses*, shows that his comic terrain can extend beyond Glasgow or London. It is set in 1963 in Italy where the visit of Pope Paul VI to Perugia is greeted with murderous intent by a demented fascist professor and two youthful locals with differing degrees of commitment to a Trotskyist terror group. There are varying supports: an East Coast American art student meets a draft-dodging West Coast twerp; a German fraulein attempts restoration of a Perugino fresco. Cleverly the local Italians speak with either Scots, Welsh, or Irish accents, a device which further isolates the cultural imperialists and foreigners. The plot unravels like a plate of spaghetti, although the play is hardly as substantial.

Byrne may not have kept up his steady output for the stage (though there is an amusing but insubstantial radio satire, *The Nitshill Writing Circle* which takes us back to *Writer's Cramp* territory) but he was acclaimed in 1987 for his television series *Tutti Frutti*, a whacky saga of an ageing Scottish rock-soul band on the road which starred among others one of the original Slab Boys, Robbie Coltrane. Perhaps this is the future direction for one of Britain's more engaging and unpretentious comic talents.

—Steve Grant

C

CAMPTON, David.

Born in Leicester, 5 June 1924. Educated at Wyggeston Grammar School, 1935–41, matriculation 1940. Served in the Royal Air Force, 1942–45; in the Fleet Air Arm, 1945–46. Clerk, City of Leicester Education Department, 1941–49, and East Midlands Gas Board, Leicester, 1949–56. Recipient: Arts Council bursary, 1958; British Theatre Association Whitworth prize, 1975, 1978, 1985; Japan prize, for radio play, 1977. Agent: ACTAC (Theatrical and Cinematic) Ltd., 15 High Street, Ramsbury, Wiltshire SN8 2PA. Address: 35 Liberty Road, Glenfield, Leicester LE3 8JF, England.

Publications

PLAYS

Going Home (produced 1950). 1951.
Honeymoon Express (produced 1951). 1951.
Change Partners (produced 1952). 1951.
Sunshine on the Righteous (produced 1953). 1952.
The Laboratory (produced 1954). 1955.
Want a Bet? (produced 1954).
Ripple in the Pool (produced 1955).
The Cactus Garden (produced 1955). 1955.
Dragons Are Dangerous (produced 1955).
Idol in the Sky, with Stephen Joseph (produced 1956).
Doctor Alexander. 1956.
Cuckoo Song. 1956.
The Lunatic View: A Comedy of Menace (includes *A Smell of Burning, Then
    . . ., Memento Mori, Getting and Spending*) (produced 1957; *Then . . .*
    produced 1980). 1960; *A Smell of Burning,* and *Then . . .* published 1971.
Roses round the Door (as *Ring of Roses,* produced 1958). 1967.
Frankenstein: The Gift of Fire, adaptation of the novel by Mary Shelley
    (produced 1959). 1973.
Little Brother, Little Sister (produced 1961). 1960.
A View from the Brink (playlets: produced 1960). Section entitled *Out of the
    Flying Pan* in *Little Brother, Little Sister; and Out of the Flying Pan,* 1970.
Four Minute Warning (includes *Little Brother, Little Sister; Mutatis Mutandis;
    Soldier from the Wars Returning; At Sea*) (produced 1960; *Soldier from the
    Wars Returning* produced 1961; *Mutatis Mutandis* produced 1967). 4 vols.,
    1960.

Funeral Dance (produced 1960). 1962.

Sketches in *You, Me and the Gatepost* (produced 1960).

Sketches in *Second Post* (produced 1961).

Passport to Florence (as *Stranger in the Family*, produced 1961). 1967.

The Girls and the Boys (revue; produced 1961).

Silence on the Battlefield (produced 1961). 1967.

Sketches in *Yer What?* (produced 1962).

Usher, adaptation of the story "The Fall of the House of Usher" by Poe (also
    director: produced 1962). 1973.

Incident (produced 1962). 1967.

A Tinkle of Tiny Bells (broadcast 1963; produced 1971).

Comeback (produced 1963; revised version, as *Honey, I'm Home*, produced
    1964).

Don't Wait for Me (broadcast 1963; produced 1963). In *Worth a Hearing: A
    Collection of Radio Plays*, edited by Alfred Bradley, 1967.

Dead and Alive (produced 1964). 1983.

On Stage: Containing Seventeen Sketches and One Monologue. 1964.

Resting Place (broadcast 1964; in *We Who Are about to . . .*, later called
    Mixed Doubles, produced 1969). 1970.

The End of the Picnic (broadcast 1964; produced 1973). In *Laughter and Fear*,
    1969.

The Manipulator (broadcast 1964; shortened version, as *A Point of View*,
    produced 1964; as *The Manipulator*, produced 1968). 1967.

Cock and Bull Story (produced 1965).

Where Have All the Ghosts Gone? (broadcast 1965). In *Laughter and Fear*,
    1969.

Split Down the Middle (broadcast 1965; produced 1966). 1973.

Two Leaves and a Stalk (produced 1967). 1967.

Angel Unwilling (broadcast 1967; produced 1972). 1972.

More Sketches. 1967.

Ladies' Night: Four Plays for Women (includes *Two Leaves and a Stalk*,
    Silence on the Battlefield, Incident, The Manipulator). 1967.

Parcel (broadcast 1968). 1979.

The Right Place (produced 1970). 1969.

Laughter and Fear: 9 One-Act Plays (includes *Incident, Then . . ., Memento
    Mori, The End of the Picnic, The Laboratory, A Point of View, Soldier from
    the Wars Returning, Mutatis Mutandis, Where Have All the Ghosts Gone?*).
    1969.

On Stage Again: Containing Fourteen Sketches and Two Monologues. 1969.

The Life and Death of Almost Everybody (produced 1970). 1971.

Now and Then (produced 1970). 1973.

Little Brother, Little Sister; and Out of the Flying Pan. 1970.

Timesneeze (produced 1970). 1974.

Wonderchick (produced 1970).

Jonah (produced 1971). 1972.

The Cagebirds (produced 1971). 1972.

Provisioning (produced 1971).

Us and Them (produced 1972). 1972.

Carmilla, adaptation of a story by Le Fanu (produced 1972). 1973.

Come Back Tomorrow. 1972.

In Committee. 1972.

Three Gothic Plays (includes *Frankenstein, Usher, Carmilla*). 1973.

Eskimos, in *Mixed Blessings* (produced 1973). In *Pieces of Campton,* 1979.

Relics (produced 1973). 1974.

An Outline of History (produced 1974). 1981.

Everybody's Friend (broadcast 1974; produced 1975). 1979.

Ragerbo! (produced 1975). 1977.

The Do-It-Yourself Frankenstein Outfit (produced 1975). 1978.

George Davenport, The Wigston Highwayman (produced 1975).

What Are You Doing Here? 1976.

No Go Area. 1976.

One Possessed (broadcast 1977). 1977.

Oh, Yes It Is! (produced 1977).

Zodiac, music by John Whitworth (produced 1977). 1978.

The Great Little Tilley (produced 1978).

After Midnight, Before Dawn (produced 1978). 1978.

Dark Wings (produced 1978). 1980.

Pieces of Campton (dialogues; includes *According to the Book, At the Door, Drip, Eskimos, Expectation, Strong Man Act, Sunday Breakfast, Under the Bush, Where Were You Last Winter?*). 1979.

Who Calls? (produced 1979). 1980.

Under the Bush (produced 1980). In *Pieces of Campton,* 1979.

Attitudes (produced 1981). 1980.

Freedom Log. 1980.

Star-station Freedom (produced 1981).

Look—Sea, and Great Whales. 1981.

Who's a Hero, Then? 1981.

Apocalypse Now and Then (includes *Mutatis Mutandis* and *The View from Here*) (produced 1982).

Olympus (produced 1983).

But Not Here (produced 1983). 1984.

Two in the Corner (includes *Reserved, En attendant François, Overhearings*). 1983.

En attendant François (produced 1984). In *Two in the Corner,* 1983.

Who's Been Sitting in My Chair? (produced 1984).

So Why? 1984.

Mrs. Meadowsweet (as *Mrs. M.,* broadcast 1984; revised version, as *Mrs. Meadowsweet,* produced 1985). 1986.

Cards, Cups, and Crystal Ball (produced 1985). 1986.

Singing in the Wilderness (produced 1985). 1986.

Our Branch in Brussels. 1986.

The Spectre Bridegroom, adaptation of the play by W.T. Moncrieff (also director: produced 1987). 1987.

Can You Hear the Music? (produced 1988). 1988.

The Winter of 1917 (produced 1989). 1989.

Smile (produced 1990). 1990.

RADIO PLAYS: *A Tinkle of Tiny Bells*, 1963; *Don't Wait for Me*, 1963; *The Manipulator*, 1964; *Alison*, 1964; *Resting Place*, 1964; *The End of the Picnic*, 1964; *Split Down the Middle*, 1965; *Where Have All the Ghosts Gone?*, 1965; *Angel Unwilling*, 1967; *The Missing Jewel*, 1967; *Parcel*, 1968; *Boo!*, 1971; *Now You Know*, 1971 (Italy); *Ask Me No Questions* (Germany); *Holiday, As Others See Us, So You Think You're a Hero, We Did It for Laughs, Deep Blue Sea?, Isle of the Free, You Started It, Good Money, You're on Your Own, Mental Health, We Know What's Right, When the Wells Run Dry, Our Crowd, Nice Old Stick Really, On the Rampage, Victor, Little Boy Lost*, and *Tramps* (all in *Inquiry* series), from 1971; *Everybody's Friend*, 1974; *One Possessed*, 1977; *I'm Sorry, Mrs. Baxter*, 1977; *Our Friend Bimbo*, 1978, *Three Fairy Tales*, 1979, and *Bang! Wham!*, 1979 (all Denmark); *Community* series (5 episodes for schools), 1979; *Peacock Feathers*, 1982; *Kahani Apni Apni* series, 1983; *Mrs. M.*, 1984; *Cards, Cups, and Crystal Ball*, 1987.

TELEVISION PLAYS: *One Fight More*, with Stephen Joseph, 1956; *See What You Think* series, 1957; *Starr and Company* (serialization), 1958; *Tunnel under the World*, 1966; *Someone in the Lift*, 1967; *The Triumph of Death*, 1968; *A Private Place*, 1968; *Liar*, 1969; *Time for a Change*, 1969; *Slim John*, with others, 1971; *The Bellcrest Story*, 1972; *People You Meet*, 1972.

OTHER (for children)
Gulliver in Lilliput. 1970.
Gulliver in the Land of the Giants. 1970.
The Wooden Horse of Troy. 1970.
Modern Aesop Stories. 1976.
Vampyre, from a story by John Polidori. 1986.
Frankenstein. 1987.
Becoming a Playwright. 1992.

CRITICAL STUDIES: *Anger and After* by John Russell Taylor, 1962, revised edition, 1969, as *The Angry Theatre*, 1962, revised edition, 1969; *The Disarmers* by Christopher Driver, 1964; "Comedy of Menace" by Irving Wardle, in *The Encore Reader*, 1965; *Laughter and Fear* edited by Michael Marland, 1969; *Investigating Drama* by Kenneth Pickering, Bill Horrocks, and David Male, 1974.

THEATRICAL ACTIVITIES
DIRECTOR: **Play**—*Usher*, 1962; *The Spectre Bridegroom*, 1987.
ACTOR: **Plays**—roles with Stephen Joseph's Theatre in the Round, Scarborough and on tour, 1957–63, including Petey in *The Birthday Party* by Harold Pinter, 1959, Old Man in *Memento Mori*, 1960, Polonius in *Hamlet*, 1962, Noah in *The Ark* by James Saunders, 1962, and Harry Perkins in *Comeback*, 1963; Cinquemani in *The Shameless Professor* by Pirandello, 1959; Bread in *The Blue Bird* by Maeterlinck, 1963.

David Campton comments:

Realizing that a play in a drawer is of no use to anyone, and that, being an
ephemeral thing, it will not wait for posterity to catch up with it, I have always
written with production in mind.

The circumstances of production have varied from the village hall, through
radio and television, to the West End stage. (Though representation on that
last has been confined to one-act plays and sketches.) This has also meant that
my plays have varied in kind from domestic comedy, through costume melodrama to—as Irving Wardle coined the phrase—"comedy of menace."

My profession is playwriting, and I hope I approach it with a professional
mixture of art and business. The art of playwriting is of prime importance; I
hope I have never relegated it to second place. I have never written a play
"because it might sell." Everything I have written has been clamouring to be
written and as long as I have been able to make marks on paper, there has
always been a queue of a dozen or more ideas waiting their turn to achieve
solid form. But an idea can always be developed towards a particular medium,
be it experimental theatre in the round or an all-female group performing in a
converted schoolroom.

I dislike pigeonholes and object to being popped into one. However, one label
that might fit is the title of an anthology of my plays: *Laughter and Fear*. This is
not quite the same as comedy of menace, which has acquired a connotation of
theatre of the absurd. It is in fact present in my lightest domestic comedy. It
seems to me that the chaos affecting everyone today—political, technical,
sociological, religious, etc., etc.—is so all-pervading that it cannot be ignored,
yet so shattering that it can only be approached through comedy. Tragedy
demands firm foundations; today we are dancing among the ruins.

David Campton is a prolific writer of short plays. The nine plays in *Laughter
and Fear* include some of the best of them. *On Stage* and *On Stage Again* are
collections of revue-length sketches, and many of his short plays are slight,
akin to those traditional short stories that present two or three characters,
reveal some significant event in their past to explain their present eccentricities,
and end with an unexpected twist. In *Where Have All the Ghosts Gone?*, for
example, a sensible young man intrudes on a drunken widow looking for his
girlfriend, who has been too ashamed of her mother to bring him home. The
mother does her best to break their attachment with a suicide attempt. She is
dependent on her daughter, but also blames her for the death of her husband in
a car crash, though the daughter was only five years old at the time, and now
plays upon her sense of guilt. The young man, however, proposes to the
daughter, and in an epilogue the mother tells the audience that the house and
garden are restored and she is grandmother to twins. But the twist is still to
come: "Just one big happy family. In fact to see me now, you'd never imagine
. . . No, you'd never imagine that I was once a real person."

This is typical Campton territory: the crumbling house, or dowdy flat; the
middle-aged or elderly middle-class woman in reduced circumstances as central character; and for theme the fight to maintain independence and defend
one's individuality, sometimes successfully, as in *The Manipulator*, in which a

Volpone-like bedridden woman uses gossip to blackmail, manipulate, and ensure that her daughters do not move her out of her flat. Since Campton's plays exploit the aching articulacies of the middle classes rather than the working-class inarticulacies explored by Pinter, Bond, and Stephen Lowe, they have lent themselves to radio productions.

Yet from his earliest work with Stephen Joseph's Theatre-in-the-Round in Scarborough, Campton has played with the inherent theatricality of the stage experience. This is particularly true of some of his more recent plays. In *The Life and Death of Almost Everybody,* a stage sweeper conjures characters from his imagination whom he then has trouble controlling. The committee of *In Committee,* meeting onstage, becomes aware, but refuses to acknowledge, that there is an audience present—even when "audience members" one by one replace committee members. And in *Who's a Hero, Then?* the stage is divided into an area representing a club and an "imagination area." At the club Norm is criticized for apparently letting his friend drown; each of his critics enters the imagination area in turn—through which the drowning man's cries ring each time—and does no better. The artificiality of the theatre experience is also implicit in *Timesneeze,* a play for youth performed by the National Theatre in 1970, in which a time-machine moves the hero to different places and periods.

Another kind of theatricality that Campton exploits, more successfully, is linguistic. Like Pinter, he plays with proverbs, catch-phrases, and clichés. *On Stage* includes four sketches about teenagers in which such phrases as "See you around" are by their repetition filled with all that is not being expressed. The committee members in *In Committee* are so tangled in procedural jargon that we never learn what the committee is considering. And in the high-level diplomatic encounter of *Out of the Flying Pan* the words themselves become garbled.

Campton acknowledges the influence of the Theatre of the Absurd. Ionesco's Jack, who demands a bride who is well-endowed, is first cousin to the new father who in *Mutatis Mutandis* has to break the news to his wife of their baby's precocious development of a full head of hair (green), teeth (pointed), and tail. The baby has inherited his eyes—fine brown eyes, all three of them. Similarly reminiscent of Ionesco is *Getting and Spending,* which follows a couple's progress from marriage to old age, pursuing mutual dreams that lead to the offstage proliferation of cots and prams in the nursery, while their dreams distract them from ever actually producing offspring.

It is when the absurd serves Campton's social conscience that he produces his best plays. *Incident* is a parable on racial prejudice, in which an inn refuses admission to a weary traveller because no one named Smith is to be admitted. The most interesting aspect of the play is the way in which Campton shows how Miss Smith's companion is drawn into negotiating a compromise, only to be (rightly) abandoned by Miss Smith. In *Soldier from the Wars Returning* a soldier boasts to a barmaid of his exploits and she hands him an eye-patch, a crutch, and so on, until he leaves the bar a cripple: a parable about war and perhaps an externalizing of the hidden psychological wounds that war inflicts on all participants. *Then . . .* is a nuclear-holocaust play. A physics teacher and the reigning Miss Europe are the sole survivors; despite the social conventions that they strive to follow, feelings that neither has ever had time for flow between them, but they dare not remove the brown paper bags they wear over their heads. These absurdly slight means of protection, like children's masquerades, and their unperturbedly conventional responses to meeting, convey the frailty and limited vision of human beings, commenting more effectively in ten minutes on the threat of nuclear war than any large-scale television dramatization of the future.

Of Campton's full-length plays, the swift-moving *Jonah*, commissioned for performance at Chelmsford Cathedral in 1971, is the most interesting. Jonah is called on to warn everyone, from businessmen to the cathedral's cleaners, of the imminent destruction of their sinful city. He resists the call, knowing he will be laughed at, and the destruction occurs—though, he and the audience learn, only in a private vision for him. He calls upon people to reform, and they do. But they begin to demand when the destruction will occur and goad Jonah into declaring a date and time. No destruction occurs. No one blames Jonah for false prophecy but at the end of the play he feels humiliated: he has devoted his life to justice and punishment, not to the mercy God has shown.

Campton is a workman-like—and sometimes workaday—playwright. *Jonah*, for example, could easily be performed with one professional as Jonah and amateurs in the numerous other roles. In his hands, *Frankenstein* becomes an easily staged, almost domestic drama about Victor Frankenstein's complicated relationships with his fiancée and his best friend. He has also written a number of short plays for all-female casts. But these, unfortunately, range from the mechanical to the contrived. For example, in *Singing in the Wilderness* an ecologist and a folklorist come across Cobweb, Moth, Mustardseed, and their relatively new friend Tinkerbell, who are suffering from old age, pesticicide spraying, and the destruction of hedgerows.

Campton is an unfashionable playwright. In an age that finds critically interesting the tough-minded and difficult, the crabbed or elliptical, his inventions seem facile, especially in his full-length plays, and sometimes whimsical. His characters are usually articulate, understand each other fairly well, and his humane messages are clear. Some of his short plays deserve repeated production.

—Anthony Graham-White

CANNAN, Denis.

Born Dennis Pullein-Thompson in Oxford, 14 May 1919; son of the late writer Joanna Cannan; brother of the writers Christine, Diana, and Josephine Pullein-Thompson. Educated at Eton College. Served in the Queen's Royal Regiment, 1939–45: mentioned in despatches. Married 1) Joan Ross in 1946 (marriage dissolved), two sons and one daughter; 2) Rose Evansky in 1965. Worked in repertory companies, 1937–39; actor at Citizens' Theatre, Glasgow, 1946–48, Bristol Old Vic, and in the West End, London. Address: 43 Osmond Road, Hove, East Sussex BN3 1TF, England.

Publications

PLAYS

Max (produced 1949).
Captain Carvallo (produced 1950). 1952.

Colombe, adaptation of the play by Jean Anouilh (produced 1951). 1952.
Misery Me! A Comedy of Woe (produced 1955). 1956.
You and Your Wife (produced 1955). 1956.
The Power and the Glory, with Pierre Bost, adaptation of the novel by Graham
    Greene (produced 1956). 1959; revised version (produced 1980).
Who's Your Father? (produced 1958). 1959.
US, with others (produced 1966). As *US: The Book of the Royal Shakespeare
    Production US/Vietnam/US/Experiment/Politics* . . ., 1968; as *Tell Me Lies*
    . . ., 1968.
Ghosts, adaptation of the play by Ibsen (produced 1967).
One at Night (produced 1971).
Les Iks, with Colin Higgins, based on *The Mountain People* by Colin Turnbull
    (produced 1975; as *The Ik*, produced 1976). 1984.
Dear Daddy (produced 1976). 1978.

SCREENPLAYS: *The Beggar's Opera*, with Christopher Fry, 1953; *Alive and
Kicking*, 1959; *Don't Bother to Knock* (*Why Bother to Knock*), with Frederic
Raphael and Frederic Gotfurt, 1961; *Tamahine*, 1963; *Sammy Going South*
(*A Boy Ten Feet Tall*), 1963; *The Amorous Adventures of Moll Flanders*, with
Roland Kibbee, 1965; *A High Wind in Jamaica*, with Stanley Mann and
Ronald Harwood, 1965; *Mayerling*, with Terence Young, 1968.

RADIO PLAYS: *Headlong Hall*, from the novel by Peacock, 1950; *The Moth and
the Star*, from *Liber Amoris* by Hazlitt, 1950; *The Greeting*, from the work by
Osbert Sitwell, 1964.

TELEVISION PLAYS: *Heaven and Earth*, with Peter Brook, 1956; *One Day at a
Time*, 1977; *Home-Movies*, 1979; *Fat Chance*, from a story by Robert Bloch,
1980; *Picture of a Place*, from a work by Doug Morgan, 1980; *The Best of
Everything*, from the novel by Stanley Ellin, 1981; *Way to Do It*, from a work
by Jack Ritchie, 1981; *By George!*, 1982; *The Absence of Emily*, from a work
by Jack Ritchie, 1982; *The Memory Man*, from a story by Henry Slesar, 1983;
The Last Bottle in the World, from a story by Stanley Ellin, 1986.

THEATRICAL ACTIVITIES
ACTOR: **Plays**—Richard Hare in *East Lynne*, based on Mrs. Henry Wood's
novel, 1936; roles in repertory theatres, 1937–39; Hjalmar in *The Wild Duck*
by Ibsen, Valentine in *You Never Can Tell* by Shaw, Hsieh Ping Quei in *Lady
Precious Stream* by S.I. Hsiung, and other roles, 1946–48; Ajax and Reporter
in *These Mortals* by H.M. Harwood, 1949; Sempronius in *The Apple Cart* by
Shaw, 1949; Kneller in *In Good King Charles's Golden Days* by Shaw, 1949;
The Widower in *Buoyant Billions* by Shaw, 1949, Oliver in *As You Like It*,
1950; title role and Octavius in *Julius Caesar*, 1950; Samuel Breeze in *A Penny
for a Song* by John Whiting, 1951; Harold Trewitt in *All the Year Round* by
Neville Croft, 1951. **Film**—*The Beggar's Opera*, 1953. **Television**—*The Rose
Without a Thorn*, 1948; *Buoyant Billions*, 1949.

Denis Cannan is the kind of dramatist who always has a tough time of it in the
English theatre: one who attempts to mix the genres. His forte, particularly in

the early 1950s, was intelligent, satirical farce, much closer to the world of Giraudoux and Anouilh than that of Rattigan and Coward. After a period of prolonged silence, he dropped the comic mask and launched a couple of direct, frontal assaults on the values of our society; but he still seems a dramatist of manifest talent who has been critically undervalued and unfairly neglected by the public.

Like so many postwar English dramatists, he started out as an actor working his way round the quality repertory companies (Glasgow, Malvern, Bristol); and his first play, *Max*, was in fact staged at the 1949 Malvern Festival when he was also playing three key Shavian roles. The work is of interest now chiefly because it established the theme that was to preoccupy him for several years to come, the barren, life-destroying conflict between opposing ideologies. But it was an uncharacteristic work in that it explored the theme in slightly melo-dramatic terms.

Cannan really came into his own with *Captain Carvallo*, presented the following year at the St. James's under Laurence Olivier's management. This is an absolutely delightful play, a witty, bubbling farcical comedy about the absurdities of military conflict. Set behind the lines of an unspecified occupied territory, it confronts a pair of ineffectual, peace-loving partisans with a philandering enemy officer in a remote farmhouse. The enemy Captain is interested only in seducing the farm-owner's wife: the partisans, though ordered to kill the Captain, are concerned only with keeping him alive. But, although the tone of the play is light, it makes the perfectly serious point that the only sane attitude to life is to preserve it at all costs.

Misery Me!, which had a short run at the Duchess in 1955, is likewise the work of a man who, in Kenneth Tynan's words, "despises politics and is in no humour for war." And again Cannan puts to the test the English love of categorisation by encasing his theme within a light, semi-farcical framework. The setting is a moth-eaten Arcadian tavern: and the basic conflict is between a Communist and a Capitalist each determined to slay the other. Both hit on the idea of employing a suicidal young intellectual as a hired assassin and so we see two great powers forcing weapons on a man bent only on self-destruction: a resonant and neatly satirical idea in the cold-war atmosphere of mid-1950s Europe. The weakness of the play is that the characters are abstractions invented to illustrate a theme and that the play's affirmation of life boils down in the end to an endorsement of romantic love: but again Cannan shows himself capable of satirising the contemporary condition and of expressing ideas within a popular format.

His other plays of the 1950s were rather less ambitious. *You and Your Wife* was about two fractious married couples trying to sort out their problems while held captive by a couple of gangsters; *The Power and the Glory* was a proficient adaptation (done in conjunction with Pierre Bost) of the Graham Greene novel about a whiskey-priest; and *Who's Your Father?* was an ingenious farce about a snobbish nouveau-riche couple and their daughter's irresponsible fiancé.

But, after a long absence from the theatre, Cannan only surfaced again as joint writer of the Royal Shakespeare Company's corporately devised Vietnam show, *US*. His precise contribution is difficult to disentangle. But we do know that he was author of Glenda Jackson's scorching and passionate indictment of the non-involvement of the English in anything happening outside their shores and that he wrote a very specific attack on the fact that Vietnam is a "reasonable" war. "It is," he said, "the first intellectuals' war. It is run by statisticians, physicists, economists, historians, psychiatrists, mathematicians, experts on everything, theorists from everywhere. Even the atrocities can be justified by logic." In the 1950's Cannan's attack on war had been comic and oblique: now it was impassioned and direct.

One at Night attacks certain aspects of our society with punitive vigour and sharp intelligence, if not with the greatest technical skill. Its hero is a middle-aged ex-journalist and advertising man seeking discharge from a mental institution to which he has been committed after having sexual relations with a girl under 16. He argues to the middle-class hospital tribunal that, far from corrupting an innocent, he has enlarged the girl's emotional experience: but he is steadfastly refused a discharge after shattering the tribunal's complacency by uncovering the hidden fears and frailties of its individual members. What gives the play its urgency is the feeling that Cannan isn't simply exploring a fashionable intellectual thesis (only the mad are sane) but that he is sharing with us a lived-through experience. And he makes, with some power, the point that in our society it is the scramble for wealth and material possessions that increases the incidence of insanity, but that it's the self-same scramble that produces the instant cure-alls and panaceas. It's precisely the point made, in fact, by Ken Loach's film, *Family Life*.

As a dramatist, Cannan has obviously changed course radically. Where once he wrapped his message up in farce and fantasy, he now lays it right on the line. Where once he adopted a deliberately apolitical stance, he now writes with a definite sense of commitment. But, whatever the profound changes in his style and attitude, he still writes with a bristling intelligence and pungent wit. For that reason one hopes the theatre will hear more from him.

—Michael Billington

CARTWRIGHT, Jim.

Born in Farnsworth, near Manchester, Lancashire, 27 June 1958. Educated at local schools; Royal Academy of Dramatic Art, London. Married Angela Jones in 1984. Writer-in-residence, Octagon Theatre, Bolton, Lancashire, 1989–91. Recipient: George Devine award, 1986; Beckett award, 1987; *Drama* award, 1986; *Plays and Players* award, 1986; Monte Carlo Golden Nymph award for film, 1987; Manchester *Evening News* award, 1990: *Evening Standard* award, 1992. Agent: Judy Daish Associates, 83 Eastbourne Mews, London W2 6LQ, England.

Publications

PLAYS

Road (produced 1986). 1986; revised version, 1990.
Baths (broadcast 1987; produced 1990).
Bed (produced 1989; revised version produced 1990). 1991.

To (produced 1989). 1991; as *Two*, 1992.
Eight Miles High (produced 1991).
The Rise and Fall of Little Voice (produced 1992). 1992.

RADIO PLAY: *Baths*, 1987.

TELEVISION PLAYS: *Wedded*, 1990; *Vroom*, 1990.

Jim Cartwright was the British theatre's most exciting discovery of the 1980s: a genuinely original new voice. Comparisons have been made with Osborne, Bond, and, more fruitfully, Shelagh Delaney, but Cartwright is very much his own man: a shrewd observer of North Country working-class life, a poet of the under-classes, a re-activator of demotic speech. In the course of four plays he has moved, geographically, from the Royal Court's Theatre Upstairs to the West End and from a fragmented, episodic structure (*Road*) to something closely resembling a traditional, well-made comedy (*The Rise and Fall of Little Voice*). But, although the work has progressed, the voice remains distinctive: that of a largely self-taught writer who loves the quirks and oddities of everyday speech and who has an enormous fund of sympathy for the discarded, the dispossessed, and the victims of our abrasive society.

Cartwright emerged, virtually out of the blue, in 1986 with *Road* which was given a stunning promenade production (later televised) by the Royal Court. Under the guidance of a rum-soaked narrator, Scullery, it took us on a kaleidoscopic tour of a grotty Lancastrian street: last stop before the slagheap. One by one, it introduced us to the characters in the road: an old woman locked into sexual reverie; a fanatical, keep-fit skinhead now converted to Buddhism; an unemployed ex-Royal Air Force conscript wondering, while doing the ironing, what happened to the days of jobs, courting, and the pictures three times a week; and, most tragically of all, a young boy and girl who get into bed and jointly commit anorexic suicide.

Road was variously compared to early Osborne, *Coronation Street*, *Under Milk Wood*, and *Our Town*. But what made the play unusual was partly Cartwright's ability to mix the realism of the streets with a heightened poetic language: an out-of-work office-girl conveyed her desperation by crying "Every day's like swimming in ache." Even more remarkable was Cartwright's ability to cut through the spectator's intellectual defences and flood the stage with feeling: in the remarkable final scene an unfulfilled double tryst, fuelled by liquor and Otis Redding's recording of "Try a Little Tenderness," exploded into a song of desperate aspiration. Loose-knit the play may have been. What finally bound the episodes together was Cartwright's compassion both for the confused, bewildered young and for the old, nursing a collective memory of lost dignity and pleasure.

Cartwright's intuitive sympathy for the old was at the very heart of his next, slightly overwritten and whimsically surreal piece, *Bed*. This was a strange, dream-driven Dylanesque poem of a play showing us seven old people lying side-by-side in a vast bed and drifting through their memories: from a shelf above the bed a sleepless, red-eyed, disembodied head vituperatively abused, in a Beckettesque manner, the snoozing elders. As in *Road*, there were elegiac memories of a lost and better England and signs of Cartwright's gift for language. But although the play was full of weird, wild images—including the sight of an old married couple descending through a hole in the bed to fetch a glass of water—it lacked any sense of imaginative rigour: as Paul Taylor wrote, "if *anything* can happen in the world of a play, then what actually does is robbed of dramatic necessity."

Cartwright was back on much surer ground in the cryptically entitled *To*: a sharp, salty, quickfire evocation of the surface gaiety and underlying melancholia of English pub life, with two actors playing both the publicans and their clientèle. Once again, the structure was episodic. But Cartwright turned that to great advantage by catching, as in a series of lightning sketches, the oddity and pain behind the camaraderie of the saloon-bar. He provided some wonderfully eccentric portraits including that of a solitary widower summoning up his wife's departed spirit by touching a brown teapot and a vision of two Memphis-hooked fatties haunted by memories of the King ("Elvis died of a choked bum," one of them confidently asserts). But the Boltonian comic realism was counterpointed by a sense of the English pub as a place of gregarious solitude where, under the cheerful sluicing, you can hear the sound of breaking glass and relationships.

With *The Rise and Fall of Little Voice*, Cartwright finally harnessed all his familiar characteristics—rich language, sympathy for the underdog, streetwise wit—to a consecutive narrative. The "Little Voice" of the title is a painfully shy, waif-like agoraphobe with a hidden talent for doing impressions of Garland, Bassey, Fields, and Piaf in the privacy of her bedroom. Under pressure from her coarse, boozy, widowed mum and the mother's sleazy, spivvy agent-boyfriend, the heroine is forced to expose her peculiar talent in a tatty Northern night-club. But the irony is that, through imitating others, she finally finds her own voice.

There are obvious echoes of other plays in which a female protagonist discovers her true identity: *A Taste of Honey*, *Roots*, *Educating Rita*. But the particular appeal of this play lies in the contrast between the story's mythic, fairytale quality and the lewd, loud, lively language. Cartwright goes out of his way to emphasise the story's fable-like aspect, even showing Little Voice being rescued by a young engineer rising outside her window on a British Telecom crane. The mother is a richly-drawn vulgarian who curls her tongue round some choice Boltonian phrases: she remembers her late husband as "a length of dry stick that bored me bra-less." With *The Rise and Fall of Little Voice* Cartwright has come up with an affirmative and wholly theatrical play: one that depends on the audience's spine-tingling realization that the actress playing Little Voice is really doing her own singing. It is easily the most optimistic Cartwright has written; but, like its predecessors, it hinges on his rare ability to exploit the communal conspiracy of live theatre.

—Michael Billington

See the essay on *Road*.

CAUTE, (John) David.

Born in Alexandria, Egypt, 16 December 1936. Educated at Edinburgh
Academy; Wellington College, Crowthorne, Berkshire; Wadham College,
Oxford, M.A. in modern history, D.Phil. 1962; Harvard University,
Cambridge, Massachusetts (Henry Fellow), 1960–61. Served in the British
Army, in Africa, 1955–56. Married 1) Catherine Shuckburgh in 1961
(divorced 1970), two sons; 2) Martha Bates in 1973, two daughters. Fellow,
All Souls College, Oxford, 1959–65; visiting professor, New York University
and Columbia University, New York, 1966–67; reader in social and political
theory, Brunel University, Uxbridge, Middlesex, 1967–70; Regents' lecturer,
University of California, 1974; Benjamin Meaker visiting professor, University
of Bristol, 1985. Literary and arts editor, *New Statesman*, London, 1979–80.
Deputy chair, 1979–80, and co-chair, 1981–82, Writers Guild of Great
Britain. Recipient: London Authors' Club award, 1960; Rhys memorial prize,
1960. Address: 41 Westcroft Square, London W6 0TA, England.

Publications

PLAYS

Songs for an Autumn Rifle (produced 1961).
The Demonstration (produced 1969). 1970.
The Fourth World (produced 1973).

RADIO PLAYS: *Fallout*, 1972; *The Zimbabwe Tapes*, 1983; *Henry and the
Dogs*, 1986; *Sanctions*, 1988.

TELEVISION DOCUMENTARY: *Brecht & Co.*, 1979.

NOVELS

At Fever Pitch. 1959.
Comrade Jacob. 1961.
The Decline of the West. 1966.
The Occupation. 1971.
The Baby Sitters (as John Salisbury). 1978.
Moscow Gold (as John Salisbury). 1980.
The K-Factor. 1983.
News from Nowhere. 1986.
Veronica; or, The Two Nations. 1989.

OTHER

Communism and the French Intellectuals 1914–1960. 1964.
The Left in Europe since 1789. 1966.
Fanon. 1970.
The Illusion. 1971.
The Fellow-Travellers. 1973; revised edition, 1988.
Collisions: Essays and Reviews. 1974.
Cuba, Yes? 1974.
The Great Fear: The Anti-Communist Purge under Truman and Eisenhower.
  1978.

Under the Skin: The Death of White Rhodesia. 1983.
The Espionage of the Saints: Two Essays on Silence and the State. 1986.
Left Behind: Journeys into British Politics. 1987.
Sixty-Eight: The Year of the Barricades. 1988.
Editor, *Essential Writings,* by Karl Marx. 1967.

CRITICAL STUDIES: *Anger and After* by John Russell Taylor, 1962, revised edition, 1969, as *The Angry Theatre,* 1962, revised edition, 1969.

David Caute comments:

With one exception, my plays have all been public plays. A "public" play, like a "private" play, is of course populated by individual characters with distinctive personalities, but the real subject lies elsewhere, in some wider social or political issue. Obviously the most elementary problem for the public playwright is to present characters who are not merely ciphers or puppets—words much cherished by critics hostile to didactic theatre.

Songs for an Autumn Rifle, written in 1960, is shaped in the spirit of banal realism. By the time I wrote my next play, *The Demonstration,* seven years later, my attitude towards both fiction and drama had changed. While the necessity of commitment still imposed itself, the old forms of naturalism, realism, and illusionist mimesis seemed incompatible with our present-day knowledge about language and communication. (These ideas are developed more fully in *The Illusion,* 1971.) One is therefore working to achieve a form of self-aware or dialectical theatre which is not only about a subject, but also about the play itself as a presentation—an inevitably distorting one—of that subject. The intention is to stimulate in the audience a greater critical awareness, rather than to seduce it into empathy and catharsis. In my view, for example, the lasting impact of Brecht's *Arturo Ui* consists less in what the play tells us about Hitler than what it tells us about *knowing about Hitler.*

The kind of writing I have in mind must pay far more attention to the physical possibilities of the theatre than did the old realism or well-made play. But whereas the author was once dictator, the modern playwright finds his supremacy challenged by directors or groups of actors. Up to a point this is healthy. But only up to a point! (See my "Author's Theatre," the *Listener,* 3 June 1971.)

One of my plays, *The Fourth World,* is different: a very private play, and, I hope a funny one. It was conceived and delivered all within a week.

While concern with social and political issues is no longer as rare among English dramatists as it was in the 1940s and early 1950s, there are still very few who are as deeply committed as David Caute, or as deeply interested either in European politics or in committed European playwrights like Sartre. Caute's first play, *Songs for an Autumn Rifle,* was a direct response to the dilemma that the Russian treatment of the 1956 Hungarian uprising created for members of the Party. The central character is the editor of a British Communist newspaper torn between his duty to the Party and his duty to the truth as relayed to him by an honest correspondent. On a personal level he is being pressured by his wife, who is not a Party member, by the doctrinaire daughter of a Party leader who works on his paper and is in love with him, and—indirectly—by his son, a National Serviceman who brings the Cyprus question into the play, first going to military prison for refusing to serve there, then submitting to an Intelligence Officer's persuasions and later being killed.

The play plunges right into its subject matter, with several scenes set in Hungary, showing the disillusioned correspondent of the English paper in argument not only with the Hungarian rebels but with Russian soldiers, whose attitudes are not altogether at one with the orders they have to carry out.

The Demonstration is a much more sophisticated piece of playmaking dramatising the problems of student revolution in terms of drama students at a university who rebel against the play their Professor gives them to perform, insisting on substituting a play about their own experience of repressive authoritarianism at the university. Their play has the same title as the play we are watching, and we are often jerked from one level of theatrical reality to another, when, for instance, a scene between the Women's Dean and a student turns out to be a scene between two students, one of whom is playing the Woman's Dean but can come out of character to make comments on her.

There is a very funny scene of rehearsing a sequence of the Professor's play ironically representing a confrontation between a bearded guerrilla and a single peasant, with interruptions from the students playing the parts, objecting that a bourgeois audience could take comfort from the satire. There is also an effective climax to the whole play when the police constables fail to respond to the Professor's orders to remove the handcuffs from the students they have arrested and the Superintendent's moustache fails to come off when he pulls at it. Reality has taken over.

But there is more theatrical exploitation than dramatic exploration of the no-man's-land between reality and illusion, and the play is not fuelled to fulfil the Pirandellian promise of its first few scenes. There are three main flaws. One is that the basic statement it is making seems to have been too rigidly predetermined instead of being evolved during the course of the writing. The second is that while there is an admirable sympathy in general for the victims of our society—black women not admitted to hairdressing shops, students whose liberty is curtailed by rules that stem from pre-Victorian puritanism— there is not enough sympathy for the private predicaments of the characters, who remain too much like stereotypes. This applies even to the central character, Professor Bright. Caute (who himself resigned from All Souls the year after he helped to organise the Oxford Teach-In on Vietnam) has no difficulty in understanding the dilemma of a son who deplores the rule-worshipping bigotry of the university authorities but still cannot side with the rebellious students against them. So it may be a kind of personal modesty that makes him keep pulling Steven Bright away from the centre of the action. Or it may be the technical failure to provide a character Steven can confide in. Or it may be a determination to focus on social and political rather than personal problems. But his failure to project Steven's ambivalence results in the third flaw—the lack of a firm moral and structural centre. In Act 2 Steven keeps disappearing to leave the stage free for the student actors. He makes two reappearances as an actor himself, in disguise. In the first he is not recognized until after he has made a long speech—an effective *coup de théâtre*. But this does not reveal enough of what he is feeling. Instead he is crowded out by a host of peripheral characters. The stage direction at the beginning of Act 2 Scene 2 tells us that his "maliciously creative hand" can be detected in the presence on the stage of the hippies and drop-outs who reject the political aims of the student revolutionaries, and that he is seen prowling about taking occasional notes and photographs. This is not enough. He should be holding the play together and carrying it forward, even when he is left by the students who take the initiative away from him.

—Ronald Hayman

CHRISTIE, (Dame) Agatha (Mary Clarissa, née Miller).

Born in Torquay, Devon, 15 September 1890. Studied singing and piano in Paris 1906. Married 1) Colonel Archibald Christie in 1914 (divorced 1928), one daughter; 2) the archaeologist Max Mallowan in 1930. Served as a Voluntary Aid Detachment nurse in a Red Cross Hospital in Torquay during World War I, and worked in the dispensary of University College Hospital, London, during World War II; worked with Mallowan on excavations in Iraq and Syria and on Assyrian cities. President, Detection Club. Recipient: Mystery Writers of America Grand Master award, 1954; New York Drama Critics Circle award, 1955. D.Litt.: University of Exeter, Devon, 1961. Fellow, Royal Society of Literature, 1950. C.B.E. (Commander, Order of the British Empire), 1956; D.B.E. (Dame Commander, Order of the British Empire), 1971. Died 12 January 1976.

Publications

PLAYS

Black Coffee (produced 1930). 1934.
Ten Little Niggers, from her own novel (produced 1943). 1944; as Ten Little Indians (produced 1944), 1946.
Appointment with Death, from her own novel (produced 1945). 1956.
Murder on the Nile, from her novel Death on the Nile (as Little Horizon, produced 1945; as Murder on the Nile, produced 1946). 1948.
The Hollow, from her own novel (produced 1951). 1952.
The Mousetrap, from her story "Three Blind Mice" (broadcast 1952; produced 1952). 1954.
Witness for the Prosecution, from her own story (produced 1953). 1954.
Spider's Web (produced 1954). 1957.
Towards Zero, with Gerald Verner, from the novel by Christie (produced 1956). 1957.
Verdict (produced 1958). 1958.
The Unexpected Guest (produced 1958). 1958.
Go Back for Murder, from her novel Five Little Pigs (produced 1960). 1960.
Rule of Three: Afternoon at the Seaside, The Patient, The Rats (produced 1962). 3 vols., 1963.
Fiddlers Three (produced 1971).

Akhnaton (as *Akhnaton and Nefertiti*, produced 1979; as *Akhnaton*, produced 1980). 1973.
The Mousetrap and Other Plays (includes *Witness for the Prosecution, Ten Little Indians, Appointment with Death, The Hollow, Towards Zero, Verdict, Go Back for Murder*). 1978.

RADIO PLAYS: *Behind the Screen* (serial), with others, 1930; *The Scoop* (serial), with others, 1931; *The Mousetrap*, 1952; *Personal Call*, 1960.

TELEVISION PLAY: *The Wasp's Nest*, 1937.

NOVELS
The Mysterious Affair at Styles. 1920.
The Secret Adversary. 1922.
The Murder on the Links. 1923.
The Man in the Brown Suit. 1924.
The Secret of Chimneys. 1925.
The Murder of Roger Ackroyd. 1926.
The Big Four. 1927.
The Mystery of the Blue Train. 1928.
The Seven Dials Mystery. 1929.
The Murder at the Vicarage. 1930.
Giants' Bread (as Mary Westmacott). 1930.
The Floating Admiral, with others. 1931.
The Sittaford Mystery. 1931; as *The Murder at Hazelmoor*, 1931.
Peril at End House. 1932.
Lord Edgware Dies. 1933; as *Thirteen at Dinner*, 1933.
Why Didn't They Ask Evans? 1934; as *The Boomerang Clue*, 1935.
Murder on the Orient Express. 1934; as *Murder in the Calais Coach*, 1934.
Murder in Three Acts. 1934; as *Three Act Tragedy*, 1935.
Unfinished Portrait (as Mary Westmacott). 1934.
Death in the Clouds. 1935; as *Death in the Air*, 1935.
The A.B.C. Murders. 1936; as *The Alphabet Murders*, 1966.
Cards on the Table. 1936.
Murder in Mesopotamia. 1936.
Death on the Nile. 1937.
Dumb Witness. 1937; as *Poirot Loses a Client*, 1937.
Appointment with Death. 1938.
Hercule Poirot's Christmas. 1938; as *Murder for Christmas*, 1939; as *A Holiday for Murder*, 1947.
Murder Is Easy. 1939; as *Easy to Kill*, 1939.
Ten Little Niggers. 1939; as *And Then There Were None*, 1940; as *Ten Little Indians*, 1965.
One, Two, Buckle My Shoe. 1940; as *The Patriotic Murders*, 1941; as *An Overdose of Death*, 1953.
Sad Cypress. 1940.
Evil under the Sun. 1941.
N or M? 1941.
The Body in the Library. 1942.

The Moving Finger. 1942.
Five Little Pigs. 1942; as *Murder in Retrospect,* 1942.
Death Comes as the End. 1944.
Towards Zero. 1944.
Absent in the Spring (as Mary Westmacott). 1944.
Sparkling Cyanide. 1945; as *Remembered Death,* 1945.
The Hollow. 1946; as *Murder after Hours,* 1954.
Taken at the Flood. 1948; as *There Is a Tide . . . ,* 1948.
The Rose and the Yew Tree (as Mary Westmacott). 1948.
Crooked House. 1949.
A Murder Is Announced. 1950.
They Came to Baghdad. 1951.
Mrs. McGinty's Dead. 1952; as *Blood Will Tell,* 1952.
They Do It with Mirrors. 1952; as *Murder with Mirrors,* 1952.
A Daughter's a Daughter (as Mary Westmacott). 1952.
After the Funeral. 1953; as *Funerals Are Fatal,* 1953; as *Murder at the Gallop,*
    1963.
A Pocket Full of Rye. 1953.
Destination Unknown. 1954; as *So Many Steps to Death,* 1955.
Hickory, Dickory, Dock. 1955; as *Hickory, Dickory, Death,* 1955.
Dead Man's Folly. 1956.
The Burden (as Mary Westmacott). 1956.
4:50 from Paddington. 1957; as *What Mrs. McGillicuddy Saw!,* 1957; as
    Murder She Said, 1961.
Ordeal by Innocence. 1958.
Cat among the Pigeons. 1959.
The Pale Horse. 1961.
The Mirror Crack'd from Side to Side. 1962; as *The Mirror Crack'd,* 1963.
The Clocks. 1963.
A Caribbean Mystery. 1964.
At Bertram's Hotel. 1965.
Third Girl. 1966.
Endless Night. 1967.
By the Pricking of My Thumbs. 1968.
Hallowe'en Party. 1969.
Passenger to Frankfurt. 1970.
Nemesis. 1971.
Elephants Can Remember. 1972.
Postern of Fate. 1973.
Curtain: Hercule Poirot's Last Case. 1975.
Sleeping Murder. 1976.
The Scoop, and Behind the Screen, with others. 1983.

SHORT STORIES

Poirot Investigates. 1924.
Partners in Crime. 1929; selection, as *The Sunningdale Mystery,* 1933.
The Underdog. 1929.
The Mysterious Mr. Quin. 1930.
The Thirteen Problems. 1932; as *The Tuesday Club Murders,* 1933; selection,

as *The Mystery of the Blue Geranium and Other Tuesday Club Murders*, 1940.
The Hound of Death and Other Stories. 1933.
Parker Pyne Investigates. 1934; as *Mr. Parker Pyne, Detective*, 1934.
The Listerdale Mystery and Other Stories. 1934.
Murder in the Mews and Three Other Poirot Cases. 1937; as *Dead Man's Mirror and Other Stories*, 1937.
The Regatta Mystery and Other Stories. 1939.
The Mystery of the Baghdad Chest. 1943.
The Mystery of the Crime in Cabin 66. 1943.
Poirot and the Regatta Mystery. 1943.
Poirot on Holiday. 1943.
Problem at Pollensa Bay, and Christmas Adventure. 1943.
The Veiled Lady, and The Mystery of the Baghdad Chest. 1944.
Poirot Knows the Murderer. 1946.
Poirot Lends a Hand. 1946.
The Labours of Hercules. 1947.
The Witness for the Prosecution and Other Stories. 1948.
The Mousetrap and Other Stories. 1949; as *Three Blind Mice and Other Stories*, 1950.
The Under Dog and Other Stories. 1951.
The Adventure of the Christmas Pudding, and Selection of Entrées. 1960.
Double Sin and Other Stories. 1961.
13 for Luck! A Selection of Mystery for Young Readers. 1961.
Surprise! Surprise! A Collection of Mystery Stories with Unexpected Endings, edited by Raymond T. Bond. 1965.
Star over Bethlehem and Other Stories (as Agatha Christie Mallowan). 1965.
13 Clues for Miss Marple. 1966.
The Golden Ball and Other Stories. 1971.
Poirot's Early Cases. 1974; as *Hercule Poirot's Early Cases*, 1974.
Miss Marple's Final Cases and Two Other Stories. 1979.
The Agatha Christie Hour. 1982.
Hercule Poirot's Casebook: Fifty Stories. 1984.
Miss Marple: Complete Short Stories. 1985.

VERSE

The Road of Dreams. 1925.
Poems. 1973.

OTHER

Come, Tell Me How You Live (travel). 1946; revised edition, 1975.
An Autobiography. 1977.

CRITICAL STUDIES: *Studies in Christie's Writings* by Frank Behre, 1967; *Christie: Mistress of Mystery* by G.C. Ramsey, 1967, revised edition, 1968; *The Mysterious World of Christie*, 1975; *A Christie Chronology* by Nancy Blue Wynne, 1976; *The Christie Mystery* by Derrick Murdoch, 1976; *Christie: First Lady of Crime* edited by H.R.F. Keating, 1977; *The Mystery of Christie* by Gwyn Robyns, 1978; *The Bedside, Bathtub, and Armchair Companion to*

Christie edited by Dick Riley and Pam McAllister, 1979; *Christie and All That Mousetrap* by Hubert Gregg, 1980; *A Talent to Deceive: An Appreciation of Christie* by Robert Barnard, 1980 (includes bibliography by Louise Barnard); *The Christie Who's Who* by Randall Toye, 1980;*The Life and Crimes of Christie* by Charles Osborne, 1982; *The Christie Companion* by Dennis Sanders and Len Lovallo, 1984; *Christie: A Biography* by Janet Morgan, 1984.

Agatha Christie was a seasoned and experienced spinner of webs and yarns. Like most prolific and professional writers, the quality of her work varies considerably. A play like *Black Coffee* is contrived, an obvious juggling of plot, while in a play like *Verdict* we see Christie, with the exception of one scene, at her worst. Of all her plays this is the most one-dimensional in its characterization. The story concerns a crippled wife who whines so much it is obvious she will be murdered; Karl, her husband, who is so saintly and forbearing it is obvious he will be accused unjustly of her murder; and Helen, the daughter of a millionaire, who is out to have an affair with Karl and who is so grotesquely drawn it is obvious she will murder Lisa. The characters lurch clumsily about the stage of this creaking plot and yet, if only on the level of crude melodrama, it does work. Just as the average Victorian novelist knew how to keep the reader in suspense, how to wring an extra tear, Christie even at her lowest excels at telling a story. It is fashionable in intellectual circles to decry her as it once was fashionable to dismiss Noël Coward. Yet even in a clumsy piece of stage craft like *Verdict*, Christie is capable of surprising writing as in the final scene (marred only by a sentimental curtain) which is of an entirely different quality to the rest of the play, full of insight. It is the scene in which Lisa, the lifelong friend who has always secretly loved him, finally tells Karl the truth about himself, that he does not see people as they are but only as concepts. "You put ideas first, not people; ideas of loyalty and friendship and pity, and because of that people who are near suffer". Suddenly it is as though Christie were writing out of some personal experience so that the scene leaps off the page, as the characters assume an extra dimension.

Certain of her plays are destined to become minor classics, perfect examples of a particular genre. *The Mousetrap* remains an oddity, a social, perhaps even sociological phenomenon, but *Ten Little Niggers*, *Spider's Web*, and *The Unexpected Guest* are three good examples of her at her best.

In the latter play, the curtain rises on a man who that moment has been shot dead in his wheelchair. Nearby, hidden in the shadows, stands his wife. Is it she who has killed him? Through the french windows enters a motorist who has lost his way in the fog and proceeds at once to help the wife build up an alibi. Christie, with a cool assurance, leads us swiftly past this improbable beginning, introducing her characters one after the other, each sharply etched (providing just enough for an actor to fill out), building up the suspense all round and skilfully levelling out a fair share of suspicion all round, so that the audience is so engrossed it does not have time to suspect that the murderer is in fact the intruder, the outsider, the uninvited guest.

Spider's Web is a stylishly constructed thriller while at the same time a comedy of situation and of character. Clarissa, a scatty society woman, remarks how boring life is and says, jokingly, that one of these days she will surely walk into the drawing-room and find a corpse on the floor. Needless to say this is exactly what happens. The characters include a sinister figure involved with the international drug market; a small girl who is afraid of being kidnapped; a lesbian-like housekeeper; and a butler with a past. Like those recipes for old-fashioned Christmas pudding full of nuts and fruit and brandy and beer and magic charms, Christie's play is stuffed with all the right ingredients for a splendid evening out in the theatre. The essence of this particular play and its charm is perhaps best conveyed in the scene in which Clarissa's husband asks her what she has been doing all day, and when she replies, "I fell over a body", he answers, "Yes, darling, your stories are always enchanting, but really there isn't time now".

> Clarissa—But Henry, it's true. That's only the beginning. The police came and it was just one thing after another. There was a narcotic ring, and Miss Peake isn't Miss Peake, she's really Mrs Brown, and Jeremy turned out to be the murderer and he was trying to steal a stamp worth £14,000.
> Husband—Huh! Must have been a second Swedish yellow.
> Clarissa—That's just what it was!
> Husband—The things you imagine, Clarissa!
> Clarissa—But darling. I didn't imagine it. How extraordinary it is; all my life nothing has really happened to me and tonight I've had the lot, murder, police, drug addicts, invisible ink, secret writing, almost arrested for manslaughter, and very nearly murdered. You know, in a way, it's almost *too* much all in one evening.
> Husband—Do go and make the coffee, darling.

In that last speech of Clarissa is contained the secret of Agatha Christie's success as a writer. Her cosy, nice, middle-class audience (and they are not to be despised, fashionable though it is to decry the bourgeoisie) are able to identify with Clarissa. Their life, like that of Clarissa, is often full of boring routine and social trivia, and then after putting down the latest Agatha Christie thriller, or returning home to Forest Row after her latest play, they are able to say, Tonight I have had the lot: murder, police, drug addicts, etc.—It's almost too much in one evening!

—James Roose-Evans

CHURCHILL, Caryl.

Born in London, 3 September 1938. Educated at Trafalgar School, Montreal, 1948–55; Lady Margaret Hall, Oxford, 1957–60, B.A. in English 1960. Married David Harter in 1961; three sons. Resident dramatist, Royal Court Theatre, London, 1974–75. Recipient: Richard Hillary memorial prize, 1961; Obie award, 1982, 1983, 1988; Susan Smith Blackburn prize, 1983, 1988; *Time Out* award, 1987; Olivier award, 1987; *Plays and Players* award, 1987; *Evening Standard* award, 1987. Agent: Casarotto Ramsay Ltd., National House, 60–66 Wardour Street, London W1V 3HP. Address: 12 Thornhill Square, London N.1., England.

Publications

PLAYS

Downstairs (produced 1958).
Having a Wonderful Time (produced 1960).
Easy Death (produced 1962).
The Ants (broadcast 1962). In *New English Dramatists 12*, 1968.
Lovesick (broadcast 1967). In *Shorts*, 1990.
Abortive (broadcast 1971). In *Shorts*, 1990.
Not, Not, Not, Not, Not Enough Oxygen (broadcast 1971). In *Shorts*, 1990.
The Judge's Wife (televised 1972). In *Shorts*, 1990.
Schreber's Nervous Illness (broadcast 1972; produced 1972). In *Shorts*, 1990.
Owners (produced 1972). 1973.
Perfect Happiness (broadcast 1973; produced 1974).
Moving Clocks Go Slow (produced 1975).
Objections to Sex and Violence (produced 1975). In *Plays by Women 4*, edited by Michelene Wandor, 1985.
Light Shining in Buckinghamshire (produced 1976). 1978.
Vinegar Tom (produced 1976). 1978.
Traps (produced 1977). 1978.
The After Dinner Joke (televised 1978). In *Shorts*, 1990.
Floorshow, with others (produced 1978).
Cloud Nine (produced 1979). 1979.
Three More Sleepless Nights (produced 1980). In *Shorts*, 1990.
Top Girls (produced 1982). 1982; revised version, 1984.
Fen (produced 1983). 1983.
Softcops (produced 1984). 1984.
Midday Sun, with Geraldine Pilgrim, Pete Brooks and John Ashford (produced 1984).
Plays 1 (includes *Owners, Vinegar Tom, Traps, Light Shining in Buckinghamshire, Cloud Nine*). 1985.
A Mouthful of Birds, with David Lan (produced 1986). 1987.
Softcops, and Fen. 1986.
Serious Money (produced 1987). 1987; revised edition, 1990.
Icecream (produced 1989). 1989.
Hot Fudge (produced 1989). In *Shorts*, 1990.
Mad Forest (produced 1990). 1990.
Shorts (includes *Lovesick; Abortive; Not, Not, Not, Not, Not Enough Oxygen; Schreber's Nervous Illness; The Hospital at the Time of the Revolution; The Judge's Wife; The After-Dinner Joke, Seagulls; Three More Sleepless Nights; Hot Fudge*). 1990.
Plays 2 (includes *Softcops, Top Girls, Fen, Serious Money*). 1990.
Lives of the Great Poisoners (produced 1991). 1993.
The Skriker (produced 1994). 1994.

RADIO PLAYS: The Ants, 1962; *Lovesick*, 1967; *Identical Twins*, 1968; *Abortive*, 1971; *Not, Not, Not, Not, Not Enough Oxygen*, 1971; *Schreber's Nervous Illness*, 1972; *Henry's Past*, 1972; *Perfect Happiness*, 1973.

TELEVISION PLAYS: *The Judge's Wife*, 1972; *Turkish Delight*, 1974; *The After Dinner Joke*, 1978; *The Legion Hall Bombing*, 1978; *Crimes*, 1982.

CRITICAL STUDIES: *File on Churchill* edited by Linda Fitzsimmons, 1989; *Caryl Churchill: A Casebook* edited by Phyllis R. Randall, 1989; *Churchill the Playwright* by Geraldine Cousin, 1989; *The Plays of Churchill* by Amelia Howe Kritzer, 1991.

London-born and Oxford-educated, Caryl Churchill is a highly successful playwright whose plays are designed to startle and instruct. In *The Plays of the Seventies*, Roger Cornish and Violet Ketels note that she is in the unique and enviable position as a contemporary British playwright of having had three plays, *Fen*, *Cloud Nine*, and *Top Girls*, running simultaneously in New York in the same year, 1983. Her plays are often gutsy, outspoken, and sharp in their critique of societal institutions. They are influenced by experimental movements in British theatre growing up in the late 1960s. She writes an alternative theatre, but one that is highly commercial while also controversial.

She has been writing plays for the radio, stage, and television for more than thirty years. *Shorts* offers a representative sample of ten of her short plays written between 1965 and 1989. Two of them have never been performed; several, such as *Lovesick* and *Abortive*, were written for radio; *The Judge's Wife* and *The After Dinner Joke* were written for television; and the recent *Hot Fudge* was originally intended to be a companion to *Icecream*. One of her most successful early plays is *The Ants*, a profoundly disturbing work about identity and perspective, broadcast on the BBC Third Program in 1962. Her early stage play, *Owners*, produced by the Royal Court Theatre Upstairs in 1972 offered an indictment of the concept of property and ownership. In 1974 she became a writer-in-residence at the Royal Court and in 1975 *Objections to Sex and Violence* was performed on their main stage. In 1976 she became the first woman dramatist invited to join the Joint Stock Theatre Group where she began working closely with two directors, Max Stafford-Clark and Les Waters, who have played an important part in her career ever since. The majority of her subsequent plays have been produced either on the Royal Court's main stage or in the Theatre Upstairs. Joseph Papp's matching grant to the Joint Stock made it possible for Churchill's plays to be brought to his Public Theatre in New York. She also worked with the feminist theatre group, Monstrous Regiment, where she produced *Vinegar Tom*. Some of her best and most commercially profitable plays, *Light Shining in Buckinghamshire*, *Cloud Nine*, and *Fen*, as well as some less successful albeit very interesting experiments, *A Mouthful of Birds* and *Icecream*, have been developed for Joint Stock. *Fen*, a play about low-paid women potato pickers, won the distinguished Susan Smith Blackburn prize which is awarded to outstanding women writers in the English language. Her plays have been performed at the National Theatre, the Barbican Pit, and the Royal Court Theatre, as well as in repertory companies across England and Scotland and on stages across the United States.

Her plays usually take the British people, often working-class, for their subjects, but they travel well, in part because of her feminist interests, topical themes, and socialist politics. Recently, in *Icecream*, she charted the travels of an American couple to Britain in search of their ancestors followed by the travels of the British distant cousins to America. The clash of the two cultures forms the backdrop to a chilling tale of murders and deaths that connect the families. The socio-political concerns expressed in her plays draw upon the thinking of such diverse minds as R.D. Laing, Frantz Fanon, and Michel Foucault. Her plays offer trenchant social commentaries upon the greedy decade of mergers and acquisitions, the appalling practices of colonialism and apartheid, and the theme of women's oppression, whether worked out in the 17th century practice of witch-burning or the twentieth-century phenomenon of the battered wife or child. Others explore women's liberation, showing both its gains and its losses. She often treats her themes with antic humour, or ludicrous parody, while making her audience consider how race, women-hating, and homophobia express themselves in our culture.

Churchill is well-schooled in the craft of theatre, employing Brechtian devices, experimenting with the formal components of the play—the way it inhabits time and space—and most recently experimenting with dance and movement combined with music to enhance the theatricality of her stage images. Her experiences working in the medium of broadcast and with Joint Stock's method of writing have both contributed importantly to the unusual texture, the overlapping of voices, and the often episodic structure of many of her plays. In *Traps* she keeps rerunning the action while altering it, violating linear chronology, building a scene only to undercut its key elements, leaving the audience perplexed about the exact relationships between characters and the nature of the action while absorbed by the psychological reality of the play. *Cloud Nine* takes similar liberties with time and the conventions of realistic theatre.

Writing radio plays taught her much about narrative: how characters can speak themselves, evoking the visual landscape while using words almost as musical notes, amplifying or diminishing the hearer's sense of space and time, and heightening the sense of anticipation. Her work in broadcast paved the way for her technique of overlapping characters' speeches on stage, a device she relies upon heavily since the writing of *Top Girls*. It also schooled her in the writing of dialogue. She often relies upon the exchange of short, staccato lines and a sparse, minimalist use of language in stage dialogue. Occasionally she uses language lavishly, giving characters long monologues. She opens *Serious Money* with a scene from Thomas Shadwell's *The Volunteers, or The Stockjobbers*, written in 1692. She then dazzles her audience with her own Shadwellian rhymed couplets throughout her play. She can also write tough, often sexually explicit dialogue. *Cloud Nine* shocked its audience with its talk of females masturbating and its use of cross-dressing and racial cross-casting to heighten the sense of the constructedness of race and gender. One of its more outlandish stage pictures occurs when a young man crawls under the late-Victorian long gown of a woman in colonial Africa, grabbing at her parts while she tries to preserve genteel appearances, belied not only by the man under her dress but also by the whip she holds, a symbol of her none-too-latent desire to see men flogged.

Her writing owes much to the protracted workshop experiences involving playwrights, actors, directors, and designers provided by the Royal Court Theatre Upstairs and Joint Stock. This format allows Churchill to work with the actors and directors in exploratory research to learn about the play's subject over a four week period, followed by an interval of up to ten weeks in which she is left to script, and concluding with a six-week period of rehearsal prior to the play's opening. At other times she has scripted during the improvisational workshop stage, bringing in new text almost daily. In one instance, she scripted collaboratively with David Lan, a playwright and anthropologist interested in rites of possession amongst Zimbabwe tribes. He scripted *A Mouthful of Birds* alongside her, both producing texts simultaneously. She seems to flourish in this setting. The workshop provides her rich thematic material and also immerses her in an environment, as it did in *Fen*. It gives her access to a wide range of characters and enables her to examine public and personal narratives, presenting private experiences set against a backdrop of historical time, institutional forces, and public events.

Churchill is a playwright of ideas. Although socialist in her political leanings, her stance is not predictable. Her work is lauded by feminists. She does not shy away from depicting powerful women corrupted by greed and ambition and deriving pleasure from the infliction of violence. She embarked on *A Mouthful of Birds*, with David Lan, providing a modern-day *Bacchae* in order to show women in the thrall of violence. Responding to feminist environmentalists and women in the peace movement, Churchill explores images that show violence and pleasure as often integral to each other. Her play concludes with women who have known the power and pleasure of violence choosing not to use it. In *Owners* and *Serious Money*, her respective protagonists, Marion, Scilla Todd, and Mary Lou Barnes are property owners, London traders, and arbitrageurs. They thrill at the power of money; they like it to come fast, and their pursuit of it knows no limits.

Churchill's plays are often satiric. They explicitly condemn their characters and the capitalist social order, but they do it with gusto. Her women are brassy. While *Serious Money* questions traditional ideas about gender and mocks the crassly sexual way in which capitalists equate money with women, considering both something that ought to be exploited, it also shows women who have been thoroughly appropriated. The fast money "Futures Song," bawdily shouting about cunts and money, which concludes the first act of the play caused a sensation when the play opened. Vulgar it is; perhaps even, finally, not necessary to Churchill's romp through the corrupt world of insider-trading, but its theatrical effect is visceral. The image conflates a chorus line with a drag ball played out in the traders' pits. Vamping in an orgy of excess, thrusting fists like pricks at the audience, and screaming out dirty words, the floor-traders, the insider dealers, the corporate raiders, and the arbitrageurs catch the audience up in a frenzy. *Softcops* is another play that revels in a 19th century carnivalesque atmosphere where freakish side-shows are manipulated for their so-called instructional potential.

Often a topical matter of political importance is the impetus for Churchill's plays. *Serious Money* was her response to the financial scandals involving the takeover of Guinness and the arbitrageur Boesky, whose testimony finally led to the end of the era of insider-trading. Feminist concerns finding voice in the 1970s and 1980s inspired *Vinegar Tom* and *Light Shining in Buckinghamshire*. Cults of possession, demonic rites, the rise of alcoholism, particularly among women, and a growing concern with the abuse of the body—whether as the result of eating disorders or violence—led to plays like the two cited above as well as *A Mouthful of Birds*. In the case of *Vinegar Tom*, Churchill was working with a feminist group, created in 1975, which was committed to exploring socialist themes. This play not only examines witchcraft and the scapegoating of women in the 17th century, with its obvious implications for the present day, but it examined the forces behind collectivities. In *Top Girls* Churchill looks at the liberated woman, the woman freed from housework, domesticity, and child-bearing. Marlene, the managing director of the Top Girls Employment Agency, celebrates her recent promotion by throwing a party to which she invites the most unlikely cast of guests—all women over-achievers, some real, some invented. Pope Joan, Chaucer's Patient Griselda, Lady Nijo, a medieval courtesan-turned-nun, and Dull Gret, a figure from a Brueghel painting, all participate in Marlene's party. Their talk is trivial; they pay little attention to each other, speaking over each others' lines, and all seemingly talking about their achievements. The play richly exploits all the trademarks of gender-bending for which Churchill is famous. She also plays fast and loose with time. In the second act, in ways reminiscent of *Cloud Nine*, the guests of the first act reappear, transformed into job applicants and interviewers in the personnel office. The play actually reveals the failure of the dream of liberation. These women are unhappy and miscast; their stories are ones of suffering, not success. The play is finally not as bleak as *Fen*. The women's suffering and sacrifices leave them incomplete and largely alone. The play's social context heightens the awareness of how gender constructs roles. Marlene is more than a victim of contemporary times—her victimage is rooted in historical institutions.

Softcops was produced by the Royal Shakespeare Company at the Pit in 1984. As in many of her plays, it probes the mainsprings of theatre—spectacle, act, and audience—taking as its subject Foucault's examination of the spectacle of the scaffold and the modern institutions of discipline and punishment worked out so brilliantly in *Discipline and Punish: The Birth of the Prison*. The play contrasts different mechanisms of control: those brought about through the witnessing of terrible punishments inflicted upon the body of the transgressor and thereby teaching the public not to commit bad acts for fear that they will suffer the agonies of the body they have watched, and those produced by eliminating the audience of the spectacle and replacing it with a single central figure well positioned to conduct sur-veillance of guilty parties and exert control. This latter kind of control depends on men's terror of disobedience, a fear that they will be found out, which can be produced merely by curtaining off the surveillor, so that he cannot be seen but can always see. Jeremy Bentham's architecture of the Panopticon, with its high, central watch tower, provided the ideal form of punishment, one in which very few in fact have to be imprisoned and the multitudes do not have to witness the spectacle of punishment. The conse-quence of the latter mechanisms of control are demonstrated in the modern-day institutions of reformatories, prisons, hospitals, and school rooms. In a play that is often funny and sometimes rather preachy, Churchill explores the close interrelationships between criminals and law-enforcers, subverting the power of authority, and finally posing the possibility that the entire institution of repressive authority might be toppled. This is a theme that she has advanced in a number of other plays from as early as *Objections to Sex and Violence*.

After more than thirty years of successful writing for the stage, there are now two book-length collections of Churchill's plays and she is the subject of a spate of critical articles and a book by Geraldine Cousin. The latter examines her use of the workshop format to develop her writing and offers an overview of her writing, considering in particular her handling of the theme of time and the possibility for revolutionary change in her plays. Churchill continues to be a fine playwright, not only because of the combination of daring and craft that is characteristic of her writing, but also because of the keen intelligence behind her plays, coupled with a high degree of wit.

—Carol Simpson Stern

See the essay on *Top Girls*.

CLARK, Brian (Robert).

Born in Bournemouth, Hampshire, 3 June 1932. Educated at Merrywood Grammar School, Bristol; Redland College of Education, Bristol, teaching certificate 1954; Central School of Speech and Drama, London, 1954–55; Nottingham University, B.A. (honours) in English 1964. Served in the Royal Corps of Signals, 1950–52. Married 1) Margaret Paling in 1961, two sons; 2) Anita Modak in 1983, one stepson and one stepdaughter; 3) Cherry Potter in 1990. Schoolteacher, 1955–61 and 1964–66; staff tutor in drama, University of Hull, 1966–70. Founder, Amber Lane Press, Ashover, Derbyshire, 1978–79, Ambergate, Derbyshire, 1980–81, and Oxford since 1982. Recipient: Society of West End Theatres award, 1978; *Evening Standard* award, 1978; *Plays and Players* award, 1978; BAFTA Shell International Television award, 1979. Fellow, Royal Society of Literature, 1985. Agent: Judy Daish Associates, 83 Eastbourne Mews, London W2 6LQ, England.

Publications

PLAYS

Lay By, with others (produced 1971). 1972.
England's Ireland, with others (produced 1972).
Truth or Dare? (produced 1972).
Whose Life Is It Anyway? (televised 1972; revised version produced 1978). 1978.
Post Mortem (produced 1975). In *Three One-Act Plays*, 1979.
Campion's Interview (produced 1976).
Can You Hear Me at the Back? (produced 1979). 1979.
Switching in the Afternoon or, As the Screw Turns (produced 1980).
Kipling (produced 1984).
All Change at the Wells, with Stephen Clark, music by Andrew Peggie (produced 1985).
The Petition (produced 1986). 1986.
Hopping to Byzantium, with Kathy Levin (produced 1990).

SCREENPLAY: *Whose Life Is It Anyway?*, with Reginald Rose, 1981.

TELEVISION PLAYS: *Ten Torrey Canyons*, 1972; *Play in a Manger*, 1972; *Whose Life Is It Anyway?*, 1972; *Achilles Heel*, 1973; *Operation Magic Carpet*, 1973; *A Follower for Emily*, 1974; *Easy Go*, 1974; *An Evil Influence*, 1975; *The Saturday Party*, 1975; *The Eleventh Hour*, with Clive Exton and Hugh Whitemore, 1975; *Parole*, 1976; *A Working Girl*, 1976; *Or Was He Pushed*, 1976; *The Country Party*, 1977; *There's No Place . . .*, 1977; *Happy Returns*, 1977; *Cat and Mouse*, 1977; *A Swinging Couple* (*Crown Court* series), 1977; *Out of Bounds* series, with Jim Hawkins, 1977; *Mirage*, with Jim Hawkins, 1978; *Houston, We Have a Problem*, with Jim Hawkins, 1978; *Telford's Change* series, 1979; *Horse Sense* (*All Creatures Great and Small* series), 1979; *Late Starter*, 1985; *Lord Elgin and Some Stones of No Value*, with others, 1985; *House Games*, with Cherry Potter.

OTHER

Group Theatre. 1971.
Out of Bounds (for children; novelization of television series), with Jim Hawkins. 1979.

Having taught drama in a university and written on group theatre, Brian Clark began his career as a playwright by collaborating with a number of younger radical dramatists on the anti-establishment political shockers *Lay By* and *England's Ireland* for Portable Theatre. There is no little irony in the fact that at about the same time he was writing the original television version of *Whose Life Is It Anyway?*, a play which six years later was to become the great "serious" West End hit of the late 1970's. Such was the critical and popular success of this play that it may be considered to have representative status. Here, it seemed, was a serious writer whose handling of an issue of contemporary relevance was, however entertaining, uncompromised by commercial success.

Whose Life Is It Anyway? concerns the claim by a man who lies in a hospital bed after a road accident, paralyzed from the neck down, to his right to die—that is, to commit suicide by choosing to be taken off the life-support machine. As its title suggests, the play's interest is in the moral argument, which culminates in the good-humored legal confrontation between the specialist, for whom life is an absolute, and the patient, who claims the right to choose suicide (eventually winning his case). The personal relationships between the patient, Ken, and the hospital staff are economically handled and often touching, and the play provides the opportunity for a virtuoso performance of an unusual kind in the central role (Tom Conti's performance was a major factor in its success in London). The dialogue, alert, witty, and highly polished, is one of the play's most attractive features, yet its particular quality points to a major dramatic limitation. Clark is interested only in those elements of his chosen dramatic situation which can readily be verbalized. His dialectical resource is impressive, but the most interesting things about the paralyzed Ken's situation are those matters—most of them to do with psychological states—that are on the edges of the moral and legal dialectics. Ken has chosen to have his life ended and seeks to enforce his wishes with wit and pertinacity, but what of the frustration, anger, depression, and eventual self-resignation that he must be presumed to have experienced? The legal case turns on his mental state, yet psychology is unimportant to the play itself. The arguments are there, but what of the *experience* of being paralyzed?

The problem of verbalization is even more acute in Clark's second full-length stage play, *Can You Hear Me at the Back?*, though here, in a very different situation, the dramatist shows himself to be continually aware of that problem. The play deals with the attempts of the middle-aged chief architect of a New Town to break out of a professional and personal (marital) impasse. The professional planner feels that his life is "planned," devoid of spontaneity (his ideal is a "planned spontaneity"). Although he finally leaves his wife, he had previously refused to take the easy way out by going away with his best friend's wife, who has confessed her love for him. The character himself is aware that he fits only too well the self-pitying cliché of the discontented middle-class white-collar menopausal male, just as he acknowledges that the slickness and facility of his way of speaking is the verbal equivalent of what he abhors about his profession: in both cases a disorderly reality is made to submit to neat abstractions. Yet the necessary critique of the middle-class ethos represented—of which luxuriant self-scorn and guilt are an essential part—is entirely absent. Clark's own failure to reveal in the play a valid alternative way of speaking to that of his main character means that the only perspective on middle-class disillusionment offered by the work is that of the middle-class represented within it.

Implicit in Clark's attempts to combine moral argument with popular theatrical appeal is a keen awareness of an essentially middle-class liberal audience. This emerges explicitly in the quasi-biographical one-man show written for Alec McCowen, *Kipling*. Confronted by an audience composed largely of what he would term "wishy-washy liberals," and resisting crustily any demand for self-revelation, Kipling launches out on "a non-stop elegy of self-justification." The show invites the projected (liberal) audience to re-examine inherited assumptions about Kipling and to question its own beliefs and convictions; yet at least one reviewer saw it as an "accomplished exercise in audience ingratiation," carefully neutralizing a potentially disturbing subject.

Much the same could be said (and was) of Clark's two-hander *The Petition*. Here Clark returns to the issue-play mode of *Whose Life Is It Anyway?*, except that in this instance the connection between the public issue ("in a way, the Bomb is the only thing worth writing about") and the private context is not ready-made. Clark's way of making it is thoroughly conventional. The discovery by a retired General that his wife has signed an anti-nuclear petition published in the *Times* prompts disclosure of her terminal illness and of an old sexual infidelity. Arguments about nuclear confrontation and the threat of universal annihilation are thus seen within the context of a purgative conflict within marriage. The characteristic facility of the dialogue tends only to confirm the cosy domestication of a disturbing issue (though the performances of Rosemary Harris and John Mills in London were remarkable). Reviewers mentioned William Douglas-Home and Terence Rattigan.

—Paul Lawley

CLIFFORD, John.

Born in Derby, 22 March 1950. Educated at Clifton College, Bristol, 1963–71; University of Granada, Spain, 1971; University of St. Andrews, Fife, Scotland, 1968–76, M.A. (honours) in Spanish and Arabic 1971, Ph.D. 1976. Student nurse, Kirkcaldy, Fife, 1977–78; yoga instructor, Leven, Fife, 1978; lecturer in Spanish, University of St. Andrews, 1980; drama critic and dance critic, the *Scotsman*, Edinburgh, 1981–87; regular contributor and occasional presenter, Tuesday Review, BBC Radio Scotland, and Kaleidoscope, Radio 4, 1981–87; contributor to the Glasgow *Herald*, *Scotland on Sunday*, *Plays and Players*, *Nursing Times*, and the *Observer*, 1981–87; Thames Television writer-in-residence, 1986–87, and member of the play reading panel, since 1986, Traverse Theatre, Edinburgh; guest lecturer in textual studies, Queen Margaret College, Edinburgh, 1992. Recipient: Scottish Arts Council fellowship, 1983, grant, 1990; Edinburgh Festival fringe first, 1985; Spirit of Mayfest award, 1988; Gulbenkian grant, 1988; British Council grant, 1989, 1992. Agent: Alan Brodie Representation, 91 Regent Street, London W1R 7TB, England.

Publications

PLAYS

The House with Two Doors, adaptation of a play by Calderón (produced 1980).

The Doctor of Honour, adaptation of a play by Calderón (produced 1983).

Romeo and Juliet, adaptation of the play by Shakespeare (produced 1984).

Losing Venice (produced 1985). In *Scot-Free*, edited by Alasdair Cameron, 1990.

Lucy's Play (produced 1986).

Heaven Bent, Hell Bound, adaptation of a play by Tirso de Molina (produced 1987).

Playing with Fire (produced 1987).

How Like an Angel (produced 1987).

Great Expectations, adaptation of the novel by Dickens (produced 1988).

Schism in England, adaptation of the play by Calderón (produced 1989).

Inés de Castro (produced 1989). In *First Run 2*, edited by Kate Harwood, 1990.

The House of Bernarda Alba, adaptation of the play by Lorca (produced 1989).

The Magic Theatre, adaptation of the play by Cervantes (produced 1989).

Ten Minute Play (produced 1991).

Light in the Village (produced 1991). 1991.

The Girl who Fell to Earth (produced 1991).

Macbeth, adaptation of the play by Shakespeare (produced 1991).

SCREENPLAY: *Santiago*, 1992.

RADIO PLAYS: *Desert Places*, 1983; *Ending Time*, 1984; *Losing Venice*, 1986; *The Price of Everything*, 1992; *Inés de Castro*, 1992; *Celestina*, adaptation of the novel by Fernando de Rojas, 1992.

TELEVISION PLAYS: *Inés de Castro*, 1991; *Quevedo*, 1992.

John Clifford comments:

When they succeed, I like to think my plays operate like good science fiction: they take the audience somewhere else, in space or in time. They engage the imagination; also, hopefully, the senses, the emotions and the intellect.

When I write, I follow my instincts and my sense of stagecraft. I don't plan things out much, or have any particular theme in mind. What happens shouldn't come from me, but from the characters. So in a way, I don't write my plays. I try to listen out for them. I don't think much about what they mean. If they're a rich source of pleasure that is enough of an achievement.

In the end, writing's just a job. There's nothing that special about it: nothing that should single us out for special praise or exonerate us from blame. Our work does affect the world, even if only in ways we cannot measure; and we bear the responsibility for the things we write.

Certainly in these times to express just pain, disgust, and misery is something of a crime. But in any case, I don't think my plays have much to do with self-expression. I'd rather see them as small acts of resistance.

John Clifford's reputation rests on a highly successful series of original plays written for the Traverse Theatre in Edinburgh, and on a number of elegant translations and adaptations that have established him as one of Britain's leading interpreters of Spanish drama.

Losing Venice, the first of his plays to be produced at the Traverse, begins in the milieu of 17th century Spain and takes its principal characters on a journey across the Mediterranean to Crete and Venice before they finally return home. The free-wheeling and picaresque action of the play recounts the story of the Duke, who goes in search of winning fame by the sword. Clifford pokes fun at the vainglory of warfare and at the posturing of this military adventurer. The most beguiling qualities of all his later work are already in evidence in this piece. The handling of historical period is delicately controlled, investing the play with an air of universality that is never ponderously sought after, but which has enabled the script to travel to other parts of the world with notable success. It is characteristic of this writer's work that the drama is animated at heart by a challenging idealism, a strong sense of the light and dark in human affairs, and the need to invoke the former to combat the latter. Yet the linguistic wit is abundant, the narrative energy insatiable, and a self-deprecating comic spirit plays across the proceedings with unpredictable effect.

Lucy's Play, produced the following year, is set in Syracuse in 386 A.D. The roving, Cervantes-style dynamic of *Losing Venice* is exchanged for what is in some ways a more classical comic structure, observing a certain unity of location. The basic premises of the situation are deliberately kept simple and the comedy is woven with great purity from the interplay of relationships. The plot follows the fortunes of Lucy, whose lover Lucius departs to seek his fortune, leaving her prey to the attentions of Max, the Mayor, who is trying to raise funds that will allow him to start a war. Lucy is unable to prevent the war, but miracles ensure that after the carnage some hope survives. Clifford's improvisations and *coups de théâtre* sometimes run the risk of trading on a certain naïveté, yet they tend to work in performance by providing unique opportunities to actors and because they pursue the concerns of the play with breathtaking clarity. The wry jokes that pepper the dialogue and the sudden reversals and transformations experienced by the characters suggest a certain casualness in the composition, but this is undercut throughout: the writer pinpoints unsettling truths about economics and spirituality, about consumption and generosity.

Playing with Fire in 1987 was followed in 1989 by *Inés de Castro*. This play is inspired by a medieval story of love thwarted by politics. A Spanish princess is prevented from marrying the Portuguese heir to the throne. When he becomes King, he has her corpse dressed to preside over his court. Once again a dazzling felicity allows modern dilemmas of moral priority to leap forth from the historical source. A new maturity in the writing is signalled by the capacity to sustain a wider range of idiom: the colloquial speech of a tradesman, the wistful lyricism of the lovers, the cat-and-mouse discourse of the corridors of power—these idioms give way finally to an extraordinary speech of brutal objectivity that describes a public torture of agonizing complexity.

Inés de Castro is an original play in its own right, but of all the titles to Clifford's name as playwright, it is the one that is closest to his work as a translator. Since his version of *The House with Two Doors*, Clifford has done much to rehabilitate the Spanish Golden Age in the British theatre, and in particular to advance the reputation of Calderón as one of the great world dramatists. He has also translated Calderón's *The Doctor of Honour* and *Schism in England*, as well as providing the Actor's Touring Company with *Heaven Bent, Hell Bound*, his version of Tirso de Molina's *El condenado por desconfiado*. His translation of *The House of Bernarda Alba* was produced at the Royal Lyceum Theatre in Edinburgh. This body of work is characterized by its vigorous and always highly playable language and also by its refusal to falsify the distinct Hispanic sensibility of the originals.

His most recent Traverse play, *Light in the Village*, sees Clifford taking a brave but quite typical step into the unknown. The play is set in the Third World and confronts us with the plight of a woman seeking justice and equity in a life skewed by poverty. The impulse in the developing world towards the technology of the West is riddled with as many complications as the appeal to traditional dispensations. Indeed, by the time you get down to the local and individual level, the large global perspective has refracted into such a bewildering array of ironies that it is little more than a source of sick jokes. The play, in the end, may have fallen short of full dramatic integration, but the very scope that it aimed to take on board was impressive. It confirmed Clifford's status as one of our most important trailblazing playwrights, whose work may be leavened with humour and playfulness but is also charged with the urgency of addressing large questions. Not all of his gambles come off, but they are all unmistakably inspired by his conviction that the theatre must be a place in which we engage with fundamental issues and are made to invoke the biggest values we can lay our hands on.

—Matthew Lloyd

COLLINS, Barry.

Born in Halifax, Yorkshire, 21 September 1941. Educated at Heath School, Halifax, 1953–61; Queen's College, Oxford. Married Anne Collins in 1963; two sons and one daughter. Teacher, Halifax Education Committee, 1962–63; journalist, Halifax *Evening Courier*, 1963–71. Recipient: Arts Council bursary, 1974; Edinburgh Festival award, 1980. Agent: Lemon, Unna, and Durbridge, 24 Pottery Lane, Holland Park, London W11 4LZ, England.

Publications

PLAYS

And Was Jerusalem Builded Here? (produced 1972).
Beauty and the Beast (for children; produced 1973).
Judgement (produced 1974). 1974; revised version, 1980.
The Strongest Man in the World (produced 1978). 1980.
Toads (produced 1979).
The Ice Chimney (produced 1980).
King Canute (broadcast 1985). In *Best Radio Plays of 1985*, 1986.
Atonement (produced 1987).

RADIO PLAY: *King Canute*, 1985.

TELEVISION PLAYS: *The Lonely Man's Lover*, 1974; *The Witches of Pendle*, 1975; *The Hills of Heaven* series, 1978; *Dirty Washing*, 1985; *Nada*, 1986; *Land*, 1987; *Lovebirds*, 1988.

Any script for solo theatre makes extraordinary demands on the creative resources of the performer, especially when, as is common with the genre, there is a virtual absence of stage directions. So Barry Collins's major work, *Judgement*, is deservedly also associated with the actors who have turned the 150-minute monologue into an engrossing theatrical debate: Peter O'Toole, Colin Blakely, and Richard Monette, to name the most successful of those who have done it in a dozen countries. Collins explains that the genesis of *Judgement* lay in an anecdote in George Steiner's epilogue to *The Death of Tragedy* concerning a war atrocity that suggests that God has grown weary of the savagery of man, and, in withdrawing His presence, has precluded tragedy. In the anecdote, a group of imprisoned Russian officers during World War II, abandoned by the Germans, resort to cannibalism; two survivors found by the advancing Russian forces are given a good ("decent") meal and then shot, which, with the incineration of their monastery prison, obliterates the evidence of man's potential for bestiality. Collins infers (though Steiner does not say this) that the survivors were insane, and projects his play from the hypothesis that one of them preserved his sanity, to be able, "dressed in white hospital tunic and regulation slippers," to deliver his Socratic apology to his judges (the theatre audience). His implicit crime is not cannibalism (his fellow survivor would be equally culpable), but sanity: he will "defend obscenities that should strike reason dumb." At the end of the argument, the speaker insists on his right to return to active service, and speaks of himself as someone who has suffered greatly for his country.

That the play is polemical few would doubt; in fact, one way of responding to the speaker's sophistry is interpreting it as the manufacture of the warrior-hero. Theatrically, the play is also something of a milestone, in that it may be seen as an extreme form of naturalism, in which the laboratory animal finds a voice and articulates its experiences before its extermination. This reading is supported by the context that Steiner gives the story: before the Germans left, they released some of their starving police dogs on the prisoners, so that the behaviour is seen as conditioned on various animals. Read in this light, the play poses the question which obsessed writers from Cicero to Zola: what is there about man that places him above the brute beasts? That a taboo has been violated is taken for granted by the judges, whose tribal mentality insists that a scapegoat must be found so that the existence of the taboo may be reinforced, and the dignity of man reasserted; thus in the theatre there is the uncanny atmosphere of a voice coming from "the other side," voicing extraterrestrial mysteries, rather as was presented in the medieval Harrowing of Hell or *Danse Macabre* dramas.

Collins's second attempt at a full-length monologue, *The Ice Chimney*, deals with an attempt by Maurice Wilson at a solo assault on Everest in 1936, and is thus another case of human fortitude braced against superhuman afflictions. Wilson's stature as a man of principle allows a sustained expositional analysis of the circumstances that led to his heroics, but the play never generates the urgency of *Judgement*, and its development seems an awkward amalgam of Milton, Auden, and Golding. In this play, Collins's socialism is not organic to the action, and commitment appears to be to the self rather than to the society.

Though best known for monologues, Collins has also written several large-cast works of epic theatre which articulate dilemmas of socialism with a Brechtian flamboyance and a sometimes Hegelian complexity. His loose documentary about the Luddites, *And Was Jerusalem Builded Here?*, required two choruses, actors with circus skills and singing ability, projections, and costumes based on Tarot cards. Nevertheless, the play does focus on one key character, a pamphleteer, on whom is centred a perplexing array of social and domestic responsibilities. Collins's most successful large-cast play has been *The Strongest Man in the World*, a parable for the theatre about Ivan Shukhov, a Russian miner who wins an Olympic weight-lifting title as a consequence of being made to take steroids. The echoes of *Samson Agonistes* in *The Ice Chimney* become rather more explicit here, as the dissident protagonist is initially discovered back in the mines, considering the aetiology of his present condition of muscle-bound impotence, both physical and ideological. The argument of the play does have a close affinity with that of *Judgement*, because Shukhov is acutely conscious of his own state as a (former) Soviet hero descended from a line of such heroes; the retribution visited on him is, again, extreme, and critics have been, predictably, divided in interpreting this as either a portrait of normal Soviet practice or a black cartoon inflating a commonplace to an enormity. Collins's stagecraft would support the latter view.

—Howard McNaughton

CONN, Stewart.

Born in Glasgow, Scotland, 5 November 1936. Educated at Kilmarnock Academy and Glasgow University. National Service: Royal Air Force. Married Judith Clarke in 1963; two sons. Since 1962 radio drama producer, currently Head of Drama (Radio), BBC, Edinburgh. Literary adviser, Edinburgh Royal Lyceum Theatre, 1973–75. Recipient: Eric Gregory award, 1963; Scottish Arts Council poetry prize and publication award, 1968, award, 1978; Edinburgh Festival Fringe award, for drama, 1981, 1988; New York International Radio Festival drama award, 1991. Lives in Edinburgh. Agent: Lemon, Unna, and Durbridge, 24 Pottery Lane, Holland Park, London W11 4LZ, England.

Publications

PLAYS

Break-Down (produced 1961).

Birds in a Wilderness (produced 1964).

I Didn't Always Live Here (produced 1967). In The Aquarium, The Man in the Green Muffler, I Didn't Always Live Here, 1976.

The King (produced 1967). In New English Dramatists 14, 1970.

Broche (produced 1968).

Fancy Seeing You, Then (produced 1974). In Playbill Two, edited by Alan Durband, 1969.

Victims (includes The Sword, In Transit, and The Man in the Green Muffler) (produced 1970). In Transit, published 1972; The Man in the Green Muffler, included in The Aquarium, The Man in the Green Muffler, I Didn't Always Live Here, 1976.

The Burning (produced 1971). 1973.

A Slight Touch of the Sun (produced 1972).

The Aquarium (produced 1973). In The Aquarium, The Man in the Green Muffler, I Didn't Always Live Here, 1976.

Thistlewood (produced 1975). 1979.

Count Your Blessings (produced 1975).

The Aquarium, The Man in the Green Muffler, I Didn't Always Live Here. 1976.

Play Donkey (produced 1977). 1980.

Billy Budd, with Stephen Macdonald, adaptation of the novel by Melville (produced 1978).

Hecuba (produced 1979; revised version produced 1989).

Herman (produced 1981).

Hugh Miller (produced 1988).

By the Pool (produced 1988).

The Dominion of Fancy (produced 1992).

RADIO PLAYS: *Any Following Spring*, 1962; *Cadenza for Real*, 1963; *Song of the Clyde*, 1964; *The Canary Cage*, 1967; *Too Late the Phalarope*, from the novel by Alan Paton, 1984.

TELEVISION PLAYS: *Wally Dugs Go in Pairs*, 1973; *The Kite*, 1979; *Blood Hunt*, 1986.

VERSE
Thunder in the Air. 1967.
The Chinese Tower. 1967.
Stoats in the Sunlight. 1968; as *Ambush and Other Poems*, 1970.
Corgi Modern Poets in Focus 3, with others, edited by Dannie Abse. 1971.
An Ear to the Ground. 1972.
Under the Ice. 1978.
In the Kibble Palace: New and Selected Poems. 1987.
The Luncheon of the Boating Party. 1992.

OTHER
The Living Poet (radio broadcast). 1989.
Editor, *New Poems 1973–74*. 1974.

MANUSCRIPT COLLECTION:
Scottish National Library, Edinburgh.

CRITICAL STUDY: *Towards the Human* by Iain Crichton Smith, 1987.

THEATRICAL ACTIVITIES
DIRECTOR: **Radio**—many plays, including *Armstrong's Last Goodnight* by John Arden, 1964; *The Anatomist* by James Bridie, 1965; *My Friend Mr. Leakey* by J.B.S. Haldane, 1967; *Mr. Gillie* by James Bridie, 1967; *Happy Days Are Here Again*, 1967, and *Good*, 1989, both by Cecil P. Taylor; *Wedderburn's Slave*, 1980, *The Telescope Garden*, 1986, and *Andromache*, 1989, all by Douglas Dunn; *Losing Venice* by John Clifford, 1987; *Dirt under the Carpet* by Rona Munro, 1987; *Not About Heroes*, and *In the Summer of 1918*, both by Stephen MacDonald; *Potestad* by Eduardo Pavlovsky; *Carver* by John Purser, 1991.

Stewart Conn comments:

(1973) My plays are about human beings, and about the dilemma of human choice. I interpret this dilemma in moral terms, and visualize the characters in the plays, and their relationships, as revolving around it. As Camus wrote (in *The Plague*), "On this earth there are pestilences and there are victims, and it's up to us, so far as possible, not to join forces with the pestilences." If there is a through line in what I have written so far, it might be a reminder that we do not live our lives in isolation—but that how we behave involves, and may cause hurt to, other people. At the same time the plays are explorations: they pose questions, rather than pretending to provide any easy answers. I do not wish to impose a set of values on an audience; but like to think what I write might induce them to reassess their own. At the same time I am concerned with theatricality and with the use of words in the theatre, as also with the attempt to provide an instructive metaphor for the violence and betrayal, large and small, with which we must come to terms, within ourselves and in our society.

(1982) I find the above all rather pretentious—and rather than "comment" again I would prefer simply to get on with the plays: that is hard enough. "We must remember who we are . . ." (Lopakhin in *The Cherry Orchard*). Perhaps my main aim now is to send the audience out into the night, ideally both transformed and entertained, in time for the last bus!

Stewart Conn is a poet as well as a dramatist, and his best plays, like *The King, The Sword* and *The Burning*, reveal this lyrical side. Of his full-length plays, *Broche* and *I Didn't Always Live Here* are little more than solid, competent pieces of dramatic craftsmanship; but *The Aquarium* and *The Burning* are both of considerable merit.

The Aquarium is set in a lower-middle-class Scottish home and depicts a classical father-son confrontation. The father is imbued with the puritanical work ethic and has clearly defined attitudes and beliefs, based on an old-fashioned morality, that he attempts to impose on his teenage son. The son is restless, unsure of himself and tentative in his approach to life, an attitude which is reflected in his flitting from job to job. Not unnaturally, he resists his father's attempts to make him conform, and they needle and taunt each other, with the mother ineffectually intervening, until matters come to a head when the father attempts to give his son a beating. This action triggers the son into a final breakaway from his family environment. The oppressive family atmosphere is particularly well and truthfully observed in this play, and the characters have a depth and power to them that belie their slightly clichéd conception. More than any other play of his, *The Aquarium* reveals the influence of Arthur Miller, a playwright he greatly admires.

The Burning is perhaps his most impressive work to date. It deals with the 16th-century power struggle between James VI of Scotland and his cousin, the Earl of Bothwell, and its theme can be deduced from Bothwell's line to James near the end of the play: "We are the upper and nether millstones, you and I. One way or another, it is those trappt in the middle must pay the price." The play is essentially about the brutality exercised toward those caught in the middle of any struggle for religious or political power, James standing for the divine right of kings, Bothwell for self-expression and individual freedom. But both treat the people under them as expendable and use them as pawns to advance their own positions. A subsidiary theme is that of witchcraft and superstition, but it is firmly placed within the context of the battle between authority and anarchy. The characters are vibrant with life, and reflect the underlying moral and ethical problems posed by a commitment to one side or the other, in a powerful and an exact way. Another remarkable feature of the play is the hard, sinewy Scottish language, which cleverly contrives to give an impression of late 16th-century speech.

Count Your Blessings revolves around Stanley, a man on the brink of death looking back over his past life and regretting the lost opportunities for fulfilling his potentialities. A particularly powerful scene shows him as a boy berating his schoolmaster father for caving in to pressure from his headmaster employer and reneging on his commitment to address a Communist Party rally in the 1930's on the effect of government cuts in education. *Thistlewood* is an impressionistic study of the 1820 Cato Street conspiracy of a group of radicals to assassinate the British Cabinet. The play draws modern parallels in the continuing struggle between conservatism and radicalism in our society.

Of Conn's short plays *The King* is a beautifully observed picture of two men fighting each other for the same girl, with a seduction scene between Attie and Lena that is replete with an unsentimental lyricism in the language. His trio of short plays, *Victims* (*The Man in the Green Muffler*, *In Transit*, and *The Sword*), are sharply and concisely drawn pictures of situations whose implications reverberate in the mind. The first play deals with an encounter between two pavement artists, one of whom has replaced someone who has died; the second is a macabre, Pinteresque exercise in violence, between two men and an intruder whom they slowly dominate; and *The Sword*, the best of the three, is a spooky psychological study of a man and a boy, both obsessed, for different reasons, with the idea of military glory. The characterisation in all of the plays is minutely and precisely accurate, qualities reflected in the taut dialogue, with strong lyrical undertones (particularly in *The Sword*), and the craftsmanlike attention to form.

The metaphorical connotations of Conn's best plays are strengthened by his feeling for dramatic construction, his understanding of individual psychology, and his basic interest in violence and its causes, both individual and in society at large. Allied with his quality of lyricism, these give his plays a peculiar power and depth.

—Jonathan Hammond

COONEY, Ray(mond George Alfred).

Born in London, 30 May 1932. Educated at Alleyn's School, Dulwich, London. Served in the Royal Army Service Corps, 1950–52. Married Linda Ann Dixon in 1962; two sons. Actor from 1946; theatrical director and producer from 1965; since 1966, director, Ray Cooney Presentations Ltd., London; director and artistic director, Theatre of Comedy Company, London, 1983–91; since 1991 owner, with George Borwick, The Playhouse Theatre, London. Address: 1/3 Spring Gardens, London SW1A 2BD, England.

Publications

PLAYS

Dickory Dock, with Tony Hilton (produced 1959).
One for the Pot, with Tony Hilton (produced 1960). 1963.
Who Were You with Last Night?, with Tony Hilton (produced 1962).
How's Your Father? (produced 1963).
Chase Me, Comrade! (produced 1964). 1966.
Charlie Girl, with Hugh and Margaret Williams, music and lyrics by David Heneker and John Taylor (produced 1965). 1972.
Bang Bang Beirut; or, Stand by Your Bedouin, with Tony Hilton (produced 1966; as *Stand by Your Bedouin*, produced 1967). 1971.

Not Now, Darling, with John Chapman (produced 1967; also director: produced 1970). 1970.
My Giddy Aunt, with John Chapman (produced 1967). 1970; revised edition, 1987.
Move Over, Mrs. Markham, with John Chapman (produced 1969; also director: produced 1971). 1972.
Why Not Stay for Breakfast?, with Gene Stone (produced 1970; also director: produced 1973). 1974.
Come Back to My Place, with John Chapman (produced 1973).
There Goes the Bride, with John Chapman (produced 1974). 1975.
Her Royal Highness . . .?, with Royce Ryton (also director: produced 1981).
Two into One (produced 1981; also director: produced 1984). 1985.
Run for Your Wife (also director: produced 1983). 1984.
Wife Begins at Forty, with Arne Sultan and Earl Barret (also director: produced 1985). 1986.
An Italian Straw Hat, adaptation of a play by Eugène Labiche (also director: produced 1986).
It Runs in the Family (also director: produced 1987). 1990.
Out of Order (also director: produced 1990). 1991.
Screenplays:
Not Now Comrade, 1977; *There Goes the Bride*, with Terence Marcel, 1980; *Why Not Stay for Breakfast?*, with Terence Marcel, 1985.

RADIO PLAYS: *Tale of the Repertory Actor*, 1971; *Mr. Willow's Wife*, with John Chapman, 1972; *Starring Leslie Willey*, 1987.

TELEVISION PLAYS (with Tony Hilton): *Boobs in the Wood*, 1960; *Round the Bend* (*Dial Rix* series), 1962.

THEATRICAL ACTIVITIES

DIRECTOR: Plays—many of his own plays, and *Thark* by Ben Travers, 1965; *In at the Death* by Duncan Greenwood and Robert King, 1967; *Press Cuttings* by Shaw, 1970; *The Mating Game* by Robin Hawdon, 1972; *Birds of Paradise* by Gaby Bruyère, 1974; *See How They Run* by Philip King, 1984; *Pygmalion* by Shaw, 1984; *Three Piece Suite* by Richard Harris, 1986; *Holiday Snap* by Michael Pertwee, 1986. Films—*Not Now Darling*, with David Croft, 1973; *Not Now Comrade*, with Harold Snoad, 1977; *There Goes the Bride*, 1980.
ACTOR: Plays—role in *Song of Norway* by Milton Lazarus, Robert Wright, and George Forrest, 1946; *Calcutta in the Morning* by Geoffrey Thomas, 1947; Larkin in *The Hidden Years* by Travers Otway, 1948; roles in repertory companies, 1952–56; *Dry Rot* by John Chapman, 1956; Corporal Flight in *Simple Spymen* by John Chapman, 1958; *One for the Pot*, 1961; Detective-Sergeant Trotter in *The Mousetrap* by Agatha Christie, 1964; Simon Sparrow in *Doctor at Sea* by Ted Willis, 1966; David Prosser in *Uproar in the House* by Anthony Marriott and Alistair Foot, 1967; Nicholas Wainwright in *Charlie Girl*, 1968; Timothy Westerby in *There Goes the Bride*, 1975; Willoughby Pink in *Banana Ridge* by Ben Travers, 1976; *Two into One*, 1981 and 1985; *Run for Your Wife*, 1983 and 1989; *Out of Order*, 1990; *It Runs in the Family*, 1992. Films—*Not Now Darling*, 1973; *Not Now Comrade*, 1977.

From the time of his first success with *One for the Pot* in 1960, Ray Cooney has sought to perfect his "talent to amuse." As one who has mastered the techniques of farce in the role of actor and producer, as well as writer, he is perhaps more qualified than most; certainly his varied abilities enable him to assess the likely response from the market-place, as well as the ivory tower, and the past 20 years have seen an increasingly imaginative use of his craft.

Farce is Cooney's chosen medium, and one in which he excels. Traditionally, its success depends less on characterisation or psychological insight than on swift and continuous action. Cooney's plays invariably fulfil these technical demands. Starting with a humdrum situation—a forthcoming society wedding, the collection of a mink coat, the decorating of an upmarket flat—the plays rapidly develop into a maze of misunderstandings, with the impending threat of potentially disastrous confrontations. Cooney shows great skill with his plots, neatly gauging the accelerating pace and eventual climax, matching the action with a brittle, fragmented dialogue. He is also adept at exploiting such stock devices as the aside to the audience, Gilbert's comments on his partner Arnold in *Not Now, Darling* being a typical—and effective—example. A similar device is used in the same play, when Arnold, confronted by a succession of irate spouses and girlfriends about to discover "proof" of infidelity, is repeatedly reduced to hurling the "evidence"—usually underwear—out of the window. Read cold from a script, the effect appears tedious and mechanical. Onstage it works, lending added emphasis to the humour of the situation.

Repetition is a key element in Cooney's farces, the threat of discovery or catastrophic encounter continually recurring as the comic tension heightens and the possibilities grow more disastrous. *Run for Your Wife* has its bigamous taxi-driver hero striving desperately to prevent the meeting of his two wives, his position rendered more comic by the use of a split stage which reveals both women and their thoughts at the same time. *Run for Your Wife* is one of Cooney's most striking works, the action ably measured, the wit of the matching dialogue astute and keen. The same is true of *Not Now, Darling* and *Move Over, Mrs. Markham*, which show Cooney at his best. Like most of his plays, they are aimed at an upper-middle-class audience—"the tired businessman," as one reviewer puts it—and this is reflected in the locations, the former set in a high-class furrier's, the latter in "a very elegant top floor London flat." In *Not Now, Darling* Cooney contrasts the lecherous Gilbert and the prim Arnold in an escalating series of encounters as the former's amorous intrigues come home to roost. (Arnold's "I refuse to put all my bags in one exit!" must be one of Cooney's funniest lines.) *Move Over, Mrs. Markham* involves a publisher's family and friends and their liaisons, its climax a hilarious scene where a prudish best-selling author is persuaded to sign for the firm by the publisher's wife, while the publisher himself (as the butler) makes constant interruptions. All three plays are deftly executed, the interplay of character and situation sure and precise, the climaxes carefully weighted for maximum comic impact. *There Goes the Bride* is not quite equal to them. Polly Perkins, the 1920's flapper invisible to everyone but the dazed Timothy, is an overworked device, and the play lacks the "ordinariness" of Cooney's best settings. More effective is the Australian father-in-law, Babcock, in his role as that stock figure, the "funny foreigner."

Farce, like the "tired businessman," is not noted for its taste, and Cooney's plays are no exception. On the face of it, there would appear to be nothing very funny about Lebanon, but *Bang Bang Beirut* (produced in 1966) manages to wring comedy from the subject, much as Croft and Perry's *'Allo, 'Allo* has done with wartime France. Just as farce admits no un-funny locations, Cooney also regards minorities as fair game. The "funny foreigner" is repeatedly met with in his plays, either in person or by proxy, as with Linda's awful Austrian imitation in *Move Over, Mrs. Markham*. Cooney seems to find homosexuality unbelievably amusing, and makes repeated use of its possibilities. The apparent "relationship" of Philip Markham and his partner is milked for laughs, the irony being their "discovery" by the effetely dressed Alistair, of whom Cooney seems unduly anxious to reassure us that "underneath his slightly arty exterior lurks a virile male." The bigamous husband of *Run for Your Wife* pretends to be gay himself at one point, and another camp character also makes an appearance. Many would contend that this kind of humour is on a par with racist jokes, and that the author is playing for easy laughs. No doubt Cooney, as a performer, would contend that there is no such thing. Recent plays such as *It Runs in the Family*, *Wife Begins at Forty*, and *Out of Order* display all his familiar skills, and serve to confirm his reputation, *Out of Order* especially ranking with his finest work so far. A sequel to the earlier *Two into One*, its story centres on the thwarted attempt by a junior government minister to secure a night of passion with an opposition secretary. The discovery in their hotel room of what appears to be the body of an intruder, trapped by a faulty sash window, is only the start of their troubles. Their unavailing efforts at hiding the "corpse" with the help of a bumbling PPS are further complicated by the unexpected arrival of both their spouses, the intrusive manager, a bribe-seeking waiter, and a private nurse. Cooney's script leads them—and us—adroitly through a frantic succession of hilarious scenes in which a cupboard and the faulty window figure prominently, the characters confronting each other repeatedly in varying stages of undress and potentially outrageous situations, the action matched throughout by the barbed wit of the author's dialogue. *Out of Order* provides an excellent example of Cooney's mastery of his chosen form. Nor is his work confined to the stage. In past years he has written for radio, television, and film, and his recent radio play *Starring Leslie Willey* shows a rekindling of his interest, utilising his flair for words effectively in the medium of sound.

Cooney, one feels, is not a particularly innovative writer. Rather, he is a master technician, a skilled manipulator of the conventions of his medium, where he operates to best effect. Attempts to move outside, as in *Why Not Stay for Breakfast?*, have been less satisfying. Within the limitations of his form, Cooney is altogether more impressive. Whether one laughs quite as loudly as the average businessman, or winces on occasion, the fact remains that Cooney is one of the most capable, and consistently successful, writers in the medium of farce.

—Geoff Sadler

COWARD, (Sir) Noël (Pierce).

Born in Teddington, Middlesex, 16 December 1899. Educated at Chapel Road
School, Clapham, London, and privately. Served in the Artists' Rifles, British
Army, 1918; head of the British Information Service propaganda bureau,
Paris, 1939–40; entertained troops, 1943–44. Actor, producer, and director:
made London stage debut with Charles Hawtrey's company, 1911, and thereafter appeared on the London and New York (from 1925) stage, often in
productions of his own works; also composer, lyricist, night-club and cabaret
entertainer, and, from 1917, film actor; built house at Blue Harbour, Jamaica,
1948; lived in Bermuda, 1956–59, and part of the time in Switzerland from
1959. President, Actors' Orphanage, 1934–56. Recipient: New York Drama
Critics Circle award, 1942; Tony award, 1971. D.Litt.: University of Sussex,
Brighton, 1972. Fellow, Royal Society of Literature. Knighted, 1970. *Died 26
March 1973.*

Publications

PLAYS

Ida Collaborates, with Esmé Wynne (produced 1917).
Sketches in *Tails Up!* (produced 1918).
Woman and Whisky, with Esmé Wynne (produced 1919).
I'll Leave it to You (produced 1920). 1920.
Bottles and Bones (produced 1922).
The Better Half (produced 1922).
Sketches in *The Co-Optimists: A Pierrotic Entertainment* (produced 1922;
    revised version produced 1924).
The Young Idea: A Comedy of Youth (produced 1922). 1924.
London Calling!, with Ronald Jeans (revue: produced 1923; revised versions
    produced 1923, 1924). Some items in *The Collected Sketches and Lyrics,*
    1931, and *The Noël Coward Song-Book,* 1953.
The Vortex (produced 1924). 1925.
Sketches in *Charlot's London Revue of 1924* (produced 1924).
The Rat Trap (produced 1926). 1924.
Sketches in *Yoicks!* (produced 1924).
*Three Plays: The Rat Trap; The Vortex; Fallen Angels; With the Author's
    Reply to His Critics.* 1925.
Sketches in *Charlot's Revue of 1926* (produced 1925).
On with the Dance, music by Philip Braham (revue: produced 1925). Some
    items in *The Collected Sketches and Lyrics,* 1931, and *The Noël Coward
    Song-Book,* 1953.
Hay Fever (produced 1925). 1925.
Fallen Angels (produced 1925; revised version produced 1967). 1925.
Easy Virtue (produced 1925). 1926.
The Queen Was in the Parlour (produced 1926). 1926.
This Was a Man (produced 1926). 1926.
The Marquise (produced 1927). 1927.
Home Chat (produced 1927). 1927.
Sirocco (produced 1927). 1927.
Sketches in *White Birds* (produced 1927).

This Year of Grace! (revue: produced 1928). In *Play Parade 2*, 1939.

Bitter-Sweet, music by Coward (produced 1929). 1929.

Private Lives: An Intimate Comedy (produced 1930). 1930.

The Collected Sketches and Lyrics. 1931.

Sketches in *Charles B. Cochran's 1931 Revue* (produced 1931).

Sketches in *The Third Little Show* (produced 1931). 1931.

Parody of Private Lives (as *Some Other Private Lives*, produced 1931). In *The Collected Lyrics and Sketches*, 1931.

Post-Mortem (televised 1967). 1931.

Cavalcade (produced 1931). 1932.

Weatherwise (produced 1932). In *The Collected Sketches and Lyrics*, 1931.

Words and Music (revue; produced 1932; revised version, as *Set to Music*, produced 1939). In *Play Parade 2*, 1939.

Design for Living (produced 1933). 1933.

Play Parade 1 (includes: *Cavalcade; Bitter-Sweet; The Vortex; Hay Fever; Design for Living; Private Lives; Post-Mortem*). 1933.

Conversation Piece (produced 1934). 1934.

Point Valaine (produced 1935). 1935.

Tonight at 8:30 (includes *We Were Dancing, The Astonished Heart, Red Peppers: An Interlude with Music, Hands Across the Sea, Fumed Oak: An Unpleasant Comedy, Shadow Play, Family Album: A Victorian Comedy with Music, Star Chamber, Ways and Means, Still Life*) (produced in three programmes, 1936). 3 vols., 1936 (*Star Chamber* unpublished).

Operette, music by Coward (produced 1938). 1938.

Sketches in *All Clear* (produced 1939).

Play Parade 2 (includes: *This Year of Grace!; Words and Music; Operette; Conversation Piece*). 1939; augmented edition including *Fallen Angels* and *Easy Virtue*, 1950.

Blithe Spirit: An Improbable Farce (produced 1941). 1941.

Present Laughter (produced 1942). 1943.

This Happy Breed (produced 1942). 1943.

Sign No More (revue; produced 1945). Some items in *The Noël Coward Song-Book*, 1953.

Pacific 1860: A Musical Romance, music by Coward (produced 1946). In *Play Parade 5*, 1958.

Brief Encounter, with others (screenplay 1946). In *Three British Screenplays*, edited by Roger Manvell, 1950.

Peace in Our Time (produced 1947). 1947.

Ace of Clubs, music by Coward (produced 1950). In *Play Parade 6*, 1962.

Play Parade 3 (includes: *The Queen Was in the Parlour; I'll Leave It to You; The Young Idea; The Rat Trap; Sirocco; This Was a Man, Home Chat; The Marquise*). 1950.

Relative Values (produced 1951). 1952.

Sketches in *The Lyric Revue* (produced 1951).

South Sea Bubble (as *Island Fling*, produced 1951; as *South Sea Bubble*, produced 1956). 1956.

Quadrille (produced 1952). 1952.

Sketches in *The Globe Revue* (produced 1952).

After the Ball, music by Coward, from a play by Wilde (produced 1954). 1954.

Play Parade 4 (includes: *Tonight at 8:30; Present Laughter; This Happy Breed*). 1954.
Nude with Violin (produced 1956). 1957.
Play Parade 5 (includes: *Pacific 1860; Peace in Our Time; Relative Values; Quadrille; Blithe Spirit*). 1958.
Look after Lulu, from a play by Feydeau (produced 1959). 1959.
London Morning (ballet scenario; produced 1959).
Waiting in the Wings (produced 1960). 1960.
Sail Away, music by Coward (produced 1961).
Play Parade 6 (includes: *Point Valaine; South Sea Bubble; Ace of Clubs; Nude with Violin; Waiting in the Wings*). 1962.
The Girl Who Came to Supper, music and lyrics by Coward, from play *The Sleeping Prince* by Rattigan (produced 1963).
Suite in Three Keys: A Song at Twilight, Shadows of the Evening, Come into the Garden Maud (produced in two programmes 1966). 1966.
Semi-Monde (produced 1977).
Plays 1 (includes: *Hay Fever; The Vortex; Fallen Angels; Easy Virtue*). 1979.
Plays 2 (includes: *Private Lives; Bitter-Sweet; The Marquise; Post-Mortem*). 1979.
Plays 3 (includes: *Design for Living; Cavalcade; Conversation Piece; Tonight at 8.30 (I)*). 1979.
Plays 4 (includes: *Blithe Spirit; This Happy Breed; Present Laughter; Tonight at 8.30 (II)*). 1983.
Plays 5 (includes: *Relative Values; Look After Lulu; Waiting in the Wings; Suite in Three Keys*). 1983.

SCREENPLAYS: *In Which We Serve*, 1942; *This Happy Breed*, 1944; *Blithe Spirit*, with others, 1945; *Brief Encounter*, with others, 1946; *The Astonished Heart*, with others, 1949; *Meet Me Tonight*, 1952.

RADIO PLAYS: *The Kindness of Mrs. Redcliffe*, 1951.

NOVEL
Pomp and Circumstance. 1960.

SHORT STORIES
To Step Aside: Seven Short Stories. 1939.
Star Quality: Six Stories. 1951.
The Collected Short Stories. 1962.
Seven Stories. 1963.
"Pretty Polly Barlow" and Other Stories. 1964; as *"Pretty Polly" and Other Stories*, 1965.
"Bon Voyage" and Other Stories. 1967.

VERSE
Poems by Hernia Whittlebot. 1923.
Chelsea Buns (as Hernia Whittlebot). 1925.
Spangled Unicorn: An Anthology. 1932.
The Coward Song-Book. 1953.

The Lyrics of Coward. 1965.
"Not Yet the Dodo" and Other Verses. 1967.
Collected Verse, edited by Graham Payn and Martin Tickner. 1984.

OTHER

A Withered Nosegay: Imaginary Biographies. 1922; augmented edition, as
  Terribly Intimate Portraits, 1922.
Present Indicative. 1937.
Australian Broadcast. 1941; as *Australia Visited 1940,* 1941.
Middle East Diary, July to October 1943. 1944.
Future Indefinite. 1954.
Short Stories, Short Plays, and Songs, edited by Gilbert Millstein. 1955.
The Wit of Coward, edited by Dick Richards. 1968.
Cowardy Custard: The World of Coward, edited by John Hadfield. 1973.
Diaries, edited by Graham Payn and Sheridan Morley. 1982.
Autobiography (includes the unfinished *Past Conditional*). 1986.
Out in the Midday Sun: The Paintings of Coward, text by Sheridan Morley.
  1988.

Editor, *The Last Bassoon: From the Diaries of Fred Bason.* 1960.

THEATRICAL ACTIVITIES
DIRECTOR: of plays, film, and television.
ACTOR: in plays, film, television, and cabaret.

CRITICAL STUDIES (selection): *A Talent to Amuse: A Biography of Coward* by
Sheridan Morley, 1969; *Noël* by Charles Castle, 1972; *The Privilege of His
Company: Coward Remembered* by William Marchant, 1975; *The Life of
Coward* by Cole Lesley, 1976, as *Remembered Laughter,* 1976; *Coward and
His Friends* by Cole Lesley, 1979; *Coward the Playwright* by John Lahr, 1982;
Noël Coward by Robert F. Kiernan, 1986; *Noël Coward* by Frances Gray,
1987; *File on Coward* edited by Jacqui Russell, 1987.

Perhaps the most prolific and uniformly successful of the English dramatists
who wrote between the two World Wars. Noël Coward was more than a
dramatist, he was an *homme de théâtre* of great versatility, being author,
dramatist, actor, producer, director, scenarist, cinema director, and composer.
Even as a dramatist he was remarkably versatile in terms of the kinds of
material he produced, his *opus* including farce, social, domestic, and manners
comedy, serious bourgeois drama, satire, revue, musical and historical drama,
lyrics and sketches, and scenarios for documentary and fiction films. So various
were his talents that even those sceptical of their depth would not begrudge
him the title he bestowed on himself, and which later came to be worn as his of
right, "the Master".

    Coward first came to prominence with a piece that was, for the generation of
the 1920's, what 30 years later John Osborne's *Look Back in Anger* was to be
for the late 1950's. The play was *The Vortex,* which Coward not only wrote,
but starred in. It was a society domestic drama treating what, for its time, was
strong subject matter—promiscuity and drug addiction. Particularly effective

was the denouement, which brought together the mother, heartbroken at losing her young lover to the girlfriend of her son, and the son, himself a drug addict: the scene between them, first of mutual recrimination, then of reconciliation, was brilliantly played by Coward and Lillian Braithwaite, and was the highlight of a play that even today retains considerable power. Coward's stage dialogue was neither profound nor rich, but he had a brilliant theatrical sense, and was a master at manipulating situations to effect surprise or shock. His command of stagecraft was turned to fine account in *The Vortex*, as too was his skill at making the superficial and sentimental appear profound and moving.

The skills evident in such early work were capitalised on with particular effect in his light and sophisticated high-life social comedies of the 1920's, like *Hay Fever* and *Easy Virtue*. These were, in effect, social dramas translated into manners comedy for satirical purpose; in them, bourgeois society is castigated for its immorality, hypocrisy, and lack of tolerance, and the manners-comedy tone is qualified by a melodramatic note derived from 1890's and Edwardian society drama, for these pieces stand in a tradition of comic *drame* Coward took over from the early Wilde and the more astringent Maugham.

With *Private Lives*, however, produced in 1930, Coward's own very distinctive voice sounds unmistakably. Modern, debonaire, mildly astringent manners comedy in the vein of this play was henceforth to be his *forte*. *Private Lives* is a comedy of social and sexual relations, with engaging character psychology, witty dialogue, and a humorous satirical deflation of the pretentions of smart socialite living of the 1920's and 1930's. Its patterned plot-line indicates the degree of its artificiality: Elyot Chase and his second wife, Sybil, are in the south of France on their honeymoon. But staying at the same hotel with them, and in adjacent rooms, is Elyot's first wife, Amanda, and her new husband, Victor. Elyot and Amanda meet, when on their respective balconies, are attracted to one another again, and elope together to Amanda's flat in Paris. But ensconced there, they argue as of old, as too do Sybil and Victor, who pursue them to Paris and who are soon in the flat with them, quarrelling with all the gusto of a married couple. Elyot and Amanda, amused by the irony of this recurring love-hate situation, slip quietly away together. The manners comedy Coward evolved here is essentially a domestic drama: many of the principals are married or engaged, but the comedy is firmly in the manners tradition in that the emphasis in relationships is on individual freedom of action, and the ways in which emotional self-absorption and pursuit of self-gratification run counter to socially imposed restraints. It is a light, slick, poised comic drama of impressive durability, as is evidenced by recent re-stagings in London and elsewhere.

Much of Coward's best work, then, was done in varieties of sophisticated comedy, and his drama is nearly always informed by a confident and assured social style, a fine theatrical sense, brittle wit, and a dialogue rich in neat epigrams and engaging one-liners. But his talents were various. *Conversation Piece*, written in both French and English, was a brittle sophisticated comedy more of sentiment than manners, but a quasi-historical drama too, set in the fashionable Brighton of 1811. Coward was no less successful with several kinds of quasi-naturalistic drama: in *Cavalcade*, popular on both stage and screen, he presented a panoramic overview of English domestic and public life from the Boer War through to the Armistice night of World War I, and *In Which We Serve*, a semi-documentary film, expressly conceived as part of the war effort, he recounted the story of a British destroyer and her personnel, and the fortunes of the crew's families ashore. In both he mined an engaging, and at the time very appropriate, vein of patriotism and sentiment. The latter emotion was marked, too, in his one-act piece, *Still Life*, later the inspiration for an outstanding British film, *Brief Encounter*. This piece reminds one that Coward was a master of the one-act form: notable was his 1935 *Tonight at 8:30*, a collection of short pieces including *Red Peppers*, *Hands Across the Sea*, and *Fumed Oak*, written for himself and Gertrude Lawrence.

There is no doubt some truth in the charge that Coward wrote too much and too fast, was too anxious to capitalise on his early success, and that he too frequently sacrificed quality for quick commercial returns. But given the degree and range of his success, and the length of time he worked in the theatre, the number of his plays still holding a place in the repertory is impressive. Add the range and quality of his performing talent, and the combination makes of Coward one of the most interesting creative figures to have worked in the 20th-century English theatre.

—Kenneth Richards

See the essay on *Private Lives*.

CRANE, Richard (Arthur).

Born in York, 4 December 1944. Educated at St. John's School, Leatherhead, Surrey, 1958–63; Jesus College, Cambridge, 1963–66, B.A. (honours) in classics and English 1966, M.A. 1971. Married Faynia Jeffery Williams in 1975; two sons and two stepdaughters. Actor and director: founder member, Brighton Combination and Pool, Edinburgh. Fellow in theatre, University of Bradford, Yorkshire, 1972–74; resident dramatist, National Theatre, London, 1974–75; fellow in creative writing, University of Leicester, 1976, and University of East Anglia, Norwich, 1988; literary manager, Royal Court Theatre, London, 1978–79; dramaturg, Tron Theatre, Glasgow, 1983–84; associate director, Brighton Theatre, 1980–85; lecturer in English, University of Maryland, 1990; writer-in-residence, Birmingham Polytechnic, and tutor in playwriting, University of Birmingham, 1990–91. Member of the Board of Directors, Edinburgh Festival Fringe Society, 1973–89. Recipient: Edinburgh Festival Fringe award, 1973, 1974, 1975, 1977, 1980, 1986, 1987, 1988, 1989; Thames Television bursary, 1974; Arts Council bursary, 1974. Agent: Casarotto Ramsay Ltd., National House, 60–66 Wardour Street, London W1V 3HP, England.

Publications

PLAYS

Footlights Revue, with others (produced 1966).
Three Ugly Women (produced 1967).
The Tenant (produced 1971).
Crippen (produced 1971).
Tom Brown (produced 1971).

Decent Things (produced 1972).
The Blood Stream (produced 1972).
Mutiny on the Bounty, music by Chris Mitchell (produced 1972; revised version produced 1980).
Bleak Midwinter (produced 1972).
David, King of the Jews, music by Chris Mitchell (produced 1973).
Thunder: A Play of the Brontës (produced 1973). 1976.
Examination in Progress (produced 1973).
Secrets (produced 1973).
The Pied Piper, music by Chris Mitchell (produced 1973).
The Quest, music by Chris Mitchell (produced 1974).
The Route of All Evil (produced 1974).
Humbug; or, Christmas Carol Backwards, music by Milton Reame-James (produced 1974).
Mystery Plays (produced 1974).
The King (produced 1974).
The Bradford Revue (produced 1974).
Mean Time (produced 1975).
Venus and Superkid (for children), music by Milton Reame-James (produced 1975).
Clownmaker (produced 1975).
Bloody Neighbours (produced 1975).
Manchester Tales (produced 1975).
Gunslinger: A Wild West Show, music by Joss Buckley (produced 1976). 1979.
Nero and the Golden House (produced 1976).
The Perils of Bardfrod, with David Edgar (produced 1976).
Satan's Ball, adaptation of a novel by Mikhail Bulgakov (produced 1977).
Gogol (produced 1978).
Vanity, adaptation of *Eugene Onegin* by Pushkin (produced 1980).
Sand (produced 1981).
The Brothers Karamazov, adaptation of a novel by Dostoevsky (produced 1981).
Burke and Hare (produced 1983).
The Possessed, with Yuri Lyubimov, adaptation of a novel by Dostoevsky (produced 1985).
Mutiny!, with David Essex, music by Essex (produced 1985).
Envy, adaptation of a novel by Yuri Olesha (produced 1986).
Soldier Soldier, adaptation of a work by Tony Parker (produced 1986).
Pushkin (produced 1987).
Red Magic (produced 1988).
Rolling the Stone (produced 1989).
Phaedra, with Michael Glenny, adaptation of the play by Marina Tsvetayeva (produced 1990).
Baggage and Bombshells (produced 1991).
Under the Stars (produced 1993).

SCREENPLAY: *Sebastian and the Seawitch* (for children), 1976.

RADIO PLAYS: *Optimistic Tragedy*, with Faynia Williams, adaptation of the play by Vsevolod Vishnevsky, 1986; *Anna and Marina*, 1991; *Plutopia*, music by Donald Swann, 1992; *Understudies*, 1992.

TELEVISION PLAYS: *Nice Time* series, 1968–69; *The Billy West Show*, 1970; *Rottingdean*, 1980; *The Possessed*, with Yuri Lyubimov, 1986.

RECORDINGS: *Mutiny!*, 1983, (and singles *Tahiti*, 1983, and *Welcome*, 1984).

THEATRICAL ACTIVITIES

DIRECTOR: Director of plays in Bradford, Edinburgh, and London, and actor from 1966 in London and in repertory, on television, and in films.

For three weeks each year, Edinburgh is a world theatrical capital with hundreds of performances taking place both in the International Festival and on the Fringe. Many a premiere sinks into instant obscurity, but the plays of Richard Crane have left an indelible mark, taking nine coveted Edinburgh Festival Fringe awards by 1992. Over 20 years of dedication to the Edinburgh Fringe is an unusual route to dramatic success, but there is a logic to it: by collaborating with his wife, the director Faynia Williams, and working with dedicated students from universities in Bradford, Essex, and East Anglia, Crane was able to produce epic drama on a scale normally considered only by the National and Royal Shakespeare Companies. Vast themes and a large theatrical canvas became economically feasible, and his work ranged from a retelling of the Arthurian legend to the full breadth of Mikhail Bulgakov's great novel, *The Master and Margarita*.

It is interesting, then, that it was an intimate and intense play for four actors that finally elevated his reputation nationally and internationally, and many of his later plays are highly refined miniatures for perhaps no more than a single actor. Although he had already had important posts as a playwright-in-residence at the National Theatre and with the Royal Court, it was his dramatization of *The Brothers Karamazov* in 1981 that consolidated Crane's London reputation, and, indeed, a reputation in what was then the Soviet Union. It was no accident, however, that the play was quarried from Russian literature for he and Faynia Williams had begun their exploration of the Russian greats well before it was fashionable.

Before turning to *The Brothers Karamazov* and Dostoevsky, Crane had presented a string of confrontations with Russian writers, including Bulgakov, Gogol, and Pushkin. They had followed investigations into British legends, English literature and religion. At one point, he had even written a children's play called *Venus and Superkid* which was described as a "trans-galactic rock supershow based on Greek legend."

His dramatic interests have ranged from a music-hall impression of the murderer Crippen, to *Thunder*, a retelling of the Brontë family story, and *David, King of the Jews*, performed at Bradford Cathedral in 1973. His 1974 script for Bradford University, *The Quest*, offered the first serious rumblings of significant talent—in part because it was technically overambitious—and it was the Edinburgh Fringe success of that year. In the play he retold the legend of Arthurian England, with opposing factions divided into prose and poetry speakers while the audience witnessed the rise and destruction of Camelot as if watching a jousting tournament.

The following year, which also saw the production of *Bloody Neighbours* in the National Theatre's studio season at the ICA Theatre, produced *Clownmaker*. It tells the story of the relationship between Diaghilev and Nijinsky, and it was marked by shattering stage effects in Faynia Williams's production. The Ballets Russes forms the backdrop for the portrait of Diaghilev as puppet-master, and the struggles of Nijinsky to establish a separate existence create the dramatic moments. Diaghilev produces Nijinsky's first sign of animation, by providing the impetus to dance, and Nijinsky's rebellion against his homosexual relationship with Diaghilev provokes a virtual earthquake. Memorable scenes and moments of evocative dialogue did not quite jell into a total success, but the sheer theatricality was refreshing and unusual.

His adaptation of Bulgakov's novel *The Master and Margarita* appeared two years later, after a series of somewhat less ambitious works. Called *Satan's Ball*, the play marked his first serious use of Russian material and formed a vast satirical and erotic canvas for Williams's staging, again on the Edinburgh Fringe. The next collaboration was on a markedly reduced scale: a monologue, originally performed by Crane himself in a production by Williams for their own small company, the Brighton Actors' Workshop. Again, the subject was Russian, the title the name of the author, *Gogol*, with material taken from Gogol's writing, particularly "The Overcoat," and from Gogol's life. His intention was to contrast the inner life with the outer appearance, to present the spiritual substance simultaneously with the surface indications and contradictions of the body, the clothes, and the published writing.

Before *The Brothers Karamazov* promoted him to the official Edinburgh Festival, Crane and Williams produced *Vanity* on the Fringe in 1980. It was a further investigation of Russian writing, described as a "response to *Eugene Onegin*," and it cleared the way for the official invitation in 1981, which resulted in the London season and a tour of the Soviet Union.

The distinction of *The Brothers Karamazov* as an adaptation for the stage lies largely in the lucid retention of the moral and metaphysical ambiguities of Dostoevsky's novel. The originality of the work is largely in the ingenious structural emphases which significantly alter the tone of the original. Crane transforms introspective guilt into heady confessions, with each son eagerly displaying the reasons for which he might possibly have murdered his father. A familiarity with the novel helps clarify the multiple actions, but the multiple role-playing of each character is theatrically engaging on its own. There is a playfulness in giving each of the four actors a principal characterization, then diverting them to play old Fyodor (always in a fur coat) or lounging women, which provides moment to moment entertainment. Crane thrives on challenges, and more often than not meets them with original theatrical solutions.

The main developments of Crane's work remain his collaborations with Faynia Williams, both with students and latterly in radio. However, his most visible production was his collaboration with the pop star and actor David Essex on a West End musical based on *Mutiny on the Bounty*. *Mutiny!* had the merit of dispensing with the standard image of the leading mutineer, Fletcher Christian, as a recognizable hero. He was approached rather as a confused

Romantic, longing for equality between officers and enlisted men. Unfortunately, the starry contributions by Essex were all too visible, keeping him moodily in view as sailors were flogged and involving him in erotic caresses with his island lover at every available chance.

Crane's most important collaboration was perhaps his work with the exiled Soviet director Yuri Lyubimov on a European co-production of a dramatization of Dostoevsky's *The Possessed* in 1985. The version reflected the director's highly personal vision of the book, but Crane's use of language was equally personal and the heightened imagery was as evident in his concentrated English as in the director's vivid staging.

Other projects, from a lively dramatization of the Soviet classic *Envy*, for the 1986 Edinburgh Festival, to a radio version of the classic communist drama by Vsevolod Vishnevsky, *Optimistic Tragedy*, continued to explore the riches of Russian writing, finally establishing a more personal tone with his impressionistic and intense study of the filmmaker Sergei Eisenstein called *Red Magic*, written as the Soviet Union lumbered towards dissolution.

Many of Crane's plays have been designed for his own performances as an actor, from his Gogol in an overcoat to a pun-rich retelling of the Sysyphus legend in *Rolling the Stone*, proving his value as an entertainer as well as a serious actor. The backstage knowledge he has accumulated as a theatrical all-rounder has been reflected in plays such as his script for radio, *Understudies*, a play about the jealousies and ambitions of those actors waiting for terrible things to happen to the star. Naturally, the roles are tailor-made for those who are already stars.

Yet serious themes with political connotations have also made repeated appearances in his work, from his dramatization of Tony Parker's book about British soldiers and their wives, *Soldier Soldier* to his 1991 play, *Baggage and Bombshells* a typically dense and imagistic shocker about women and war drawn from the rhetoric and propaganda of the Gulf War. For all his vast and varied output over the first 25 years of his writing career, Crane shows little sign of flagging creativity even if a single undisputed masterpiece has so far eluded him.

—Ned Chaillet

CREGAN, David (Appleton Quartus).

Born in Buxton, Derbyshire, 30 September 1931. Educated at the Leys School, Cambridge, 1945–50; Clare College, Cambridge, 1952–55, B.A. in English 1955. Served as an acting corporal in the Royal Air Force, 1950–52. Married Ailsa Mary Wynne Willson in 1960; three sons and one adopted daughter. Head of English, Palm Beach Private School, Florida, 1955–57; assistant English master, Burnage Boys' Grammar School, Manchester, 1957; assistant English master and head of drama, 1958–62, and part-time drama teacher, 1962–67, Hatfield School, Hertfordshire; salesman, and clerk at the Automobile Association, 1958. Worked with Royal Court Theatre Studio, London, 1964, 1968, and Midlands Arts Centre, Birmingham, 1971; conducted three-week studio at the Royal Shakespeare Company Memorial Theatre, Stratford-on-Avon, 1971. Member of the Drama Panel, West

Midlands Arts Association, 1972, and Eastern Arts, 1980. Recipient: Arts
Council bursary, 1966, 1975, 1978, and grant, 1971; Foyle award, 1966;
Sony award for radio, 1987. Agent: Casarotto Ramsay Ltd., National House,
60–66 Wardour Street, London W1V 3HP. Address: 76 Wood Close,
Hatfield, Hertfordshire, England.

Publications

PLAYS

Miniatures (produced 1965). 1970.
Transcending, and The Dancers (produced 1966). 1967.
Three Men for Colverton (produced 1966). 1967.
The Houses by the Green (produced 1968). 1969.
A Comedy of the Changing Years (produced 1969).
Arthur, in *Playbill One*, edited by Alan Durband. 1969.
Tipper (produced 1969).
Liebestraum and Other Pieces (produced 1970). In *The Land of Palms and Other Plays*, 1973.
Jack in the Box; and If You Don't Laugh, You Cry (produced 1971). In *The Land of Palms and Other Plays*, 1973.
The Daffodil, and Sentimental Value (produced 1971).
How We Held the Square: A Play for Children (produced 1971). 1973.
The Land of Palms (produced 1972). In *The Land of Palms and Other Plays*, 1973.
George Reborn (televised 1973; produced 1973). In *The Land of Palms and Other Plays*, 1973.
Cast Off (produced 1973).
Pater Noster (in *Mixed Blessings*, produced 1973). In *Play Nine*, edited by Robin Rook, 1981.
The Land of Palms and Other Plays (includes *Liebestraum*; *George Reborn*; *The Problem*; *Jack in the Box*; *If You Don't Laugh, You Cry*). 1973.
The King (produced 1974).
Tina (produced 1975). With *Poor Tom*, 1976.
Poor Tom (produced 1976). With *Tina*, 1976.
Tigers (produced 1978).
Young Sir (produced 1979).
Red Riding Hood (produced 1979).
Getting It Right (produced 1980).
A Name Is More Than a Name, in *Play Nine*, edited by Robin Rook. 1981.
Jack and the Beanstalk (pantomime), music by Brian Protheroe (produced 1982). 1987.
The Sleeping Beauty (pantomime), music by Brian Protheroe (produced 1983). 1984.
Red Ridinghood (pantomime), music by Brian Protheroe (produced 1984). 1986.
Crackling Angels (produced 1987).
Beauty and the Beast (pantomime), music by Brian Protheroe (produced 1987).
Cinderella (pantomime), music by Brian Protheroe (produced 1989).
Nice Dorothy (produced 1993).

RADIO PLAYS: *The Latter Days of Lucy Trenchard*, 1974; *The Monument*, 1978; *Hope*, 1979; *Inventor's Corner*, 1979; *The Joking Habit*, 1980; *The True Story of the Public School Strike 1990*, 1981; *Diana's Uncle and Other Relatives*, 1982; *The Spectre*, 1983; *The Awful Insulation of Rage*, 1986; *A Butler Did It*, 1990; *From a Second Home in Picardy*, 1990; *What Happened with St. George*, 1991; *Eavesdropping*, 1992.

TELEVISION PLAYS: *That Time of Life*, 1972; *George Reborn*, 1973; *I Want to Marry Your Son*, 1973; *Pipkins*, with Susan Pleat, 1974; *Reluctant Chickens*, 1982; *Events in a Museum*, 1983; *Goodbye Days*, 1984; *A Still Small Shout*, 1985; *Goodbye, And I Hope We Meet Again*, 1989.

NOVEL
Ronald Rossiter. 1959.

CRITICAL STUDIES: *The Second Wave* by John Russell Taylor, 1971; article by Timothy J. Kidd, in *British Dramatists since World War II* edited by Stanley Weintraub, 1982.

David Cregan comments:

1. I am a socialist because there is no other reasonable thing to be. However, all problems, as well as all interesting thoughts, seem to stem from that one position. How much does the individual matter and how much the community? Can a contemporary community ever avoid becoming systematized, and anyway how much less traumatic is it living unsystematically than systematically? How simplistic can a government be before it must be opposed totally? If material poverty produces spiritual poverty, which, with special exceptions, it does, can material wealth produce spiritual wealth? How important *is* spiritual wealth, and on what does its value depend? Can the elevation of one working class be justified if it is achieved at the expense of another working class? If freedom is no longer a meaningful conception (and it only achieves any meaning by being opposed to some form of tyranny), which qualified freedom is the most important? Of thought or from hunger? If leaders are bad, are institutions worse? What is the basic nature of man as opposed to the animals, and can it be improved?

I doubt if any of this appears overtly in any of my writing, though the head of steam is always provided by acute anxieties felt on one score or another among these and similar peculiarly 20th-century questions.

2. Since for me the best plays seem to *be* rather than to be *about*, I personally prefer the episodic forms in which characters may be presented quickly and variously, so that the architecture provides the major insights.

3. Since I have this delight in form, I find no pleasure or virtue in personal rhetoric, self-indulgent self-revelation, or absolute naturalism.

4. Delight in construction also biases me against any form of expressionism or abstract symbolism, and increasingly I use songs, jazz, and a rough poetry spoken to music for various constructional purposes.

5. Since construction of the kind so far indicated is frequently a question of rhythm, there is a "playful" quality about my work. It has a musical quality,

each scene sounding forward to another. This means the plays should be acted with a care for their surface, and anyone who acts them for any individual significance, the same shall surely lose it. There are frequently large alterations in emotional stance needed between the giving and receiving of the words, and there is much pleasure in watching this.

6. I have been much influenced by farce, Ibsen, Brecht, Beckett, and the directors I have been associated with at the Royal Court. Also by the intensely magical understanding of comedy shown by Keith Johnstone.

7. I am the fourth and youngest son of an Irish shirt manufacturer. My father fought and was gassed in World War I, and sought peace and prosperity in a small Derbyshire town, where he pursued a quiet Protestant way of life. My brothers fought, and one died, in World War II. I was largely brought up by a young working-class nursemaid.

8. Writer's notes about himself are alas more revealing when they fail to confirm the impression of his work than when they succeed. This happens to more of us than is generally supposed.

In David Cregan's earliest play, *Miniatures*, the deputy headmaster says "If only one knew what every mind was thinking. If one had their habits of thought one could put in train the running of the school that way it ought to go. That's the way of achieving what is democratically best for everyone. One must have their minds, or else it is coercion." The common theme of Cregan's plays is the struggle for power and the manipulation of social conventions to achieve it. A more or less closed society that has developed its own conventions is often the setting: a school in *Miniatures* and again in *Tina*, a small town in *Three Men for Colverton*, an oasis in *The Land of Palms*, a boarding house in *Poor Tom*. In other plays the characters act as if in a closed society: in *The Dancers*, in which a middle-aged quintet dance and pair off in various combinations, and the "cozy circle" of two mutually adulterous couples of *Liesbestraum*—but where, when Jane does not find herself attracted to her husband's lover's husband, the others fear that she will seek a lover elsewhere, in which case "we'll find ourselves part of a larger community before we know where we are, with all the loss of sovereignty that will entail."

Often in Cregan's plays one set of conventions is brought into conflict with another. In his most complex play, *Three Men for Colverton*, the leader of a trio of evangelists seeks to take control of the town from the domineering Mrs. Carnock. She believes Colverton "was meant to be a stagnant pool . . . and stagnant it will remain." The uncompromising vision of the evangelists, who "hate every lubricant of living" and decry "the stern virility of man [etiolated] in the black night of consumer goods," threatens the indulgence and manipulation of human relationships by which she maintains her dominance. Other power-seekers are the liberal vicar and an Anglican monk who uses the confessional to his own advantage.

Where existing conventions are strained or broken, new conventions are invented. In *Liebestraum* the adulterous relationships are regularized. A strict alternation of days for sleeping with one's marriage partner and with one's lover is threatened by Jane's uncertain feelings; when she does fulfil everyone's expectations by completing the sexual cross-partnering she does so on the wrong day and is denounced for the carnality. In *The Land of Palms* some British have set up a community of peace and harmony at an oasis. Three British ex-Foreign Legionnaires arrive with their military values. In *Transcending*, a short play of wonderful verve, a teenage girl escapes from the world of her parents and two of her neighbours, a young man and an older widower, all of whom have a role to offer her, by appearing at the end of the play dressed as a nun—escaping by invoking a different set of conventions.

It would be interesting to produce *Transcending* alongside the very funny *Pater Noster*, in which husband and wife are saying their bedtime prayers when the husband decides he is God, for he has created the child in her womb, and begins praying to himself despite his wife's arguments that there are other influences on conception, such as the availability of family allowances. The voice of the foetus is heard, apprehensive about the world it is to enter. We see the mother use the child to manipulate her husband and then, at the end of the play, threatening the foetus, "I'll tell him when he comes upstairs, and then you'll catch it." Even an infant is doomed in our world of manipulative conventions.

There are in Cregan's plays instinctive nonconformists. In *Miniatures* the climactic scene reveals the music teacher sitting in his store closet surrounded by all the items that have been stolen around the school. He later tries to hang himself. In *The Land of Palms* the soldier who cannot adapt to the oasis community kills himself. In *Three Men for Colverton* one of the evangelists is homosexual. He declares, "One is one and all alone and ever more shall be so. Two bodies don't make one, two minds don't make one, and I'm one." In the last scene he throws himself from a clocktower and dies. Not borne up by angels, this individualist has unwittingly destroyed the leading evangelist's power. Meanwhile, Mrs. Carnock has died, and perhaps the play's other nonconformist, a teacher who fornicates with his pupils, will establish "that dreary venture, the Arts Centre," which Mrs. Carnock had opposed, as "an act of existential heroism." In much the same spirit he will marry his latest, pregnant teenage mistress.

In Cregan's more recent short plays the nonconformists are the central characters. Tina, a teacher, dresses in jeans and leather jacket to try to reach an abused ten-year-old, whom Cregan has ironically named Dawn. In *Poor Tom* Tom murders the owner of the boarding-house to prevent him selling it. In each play much of the interest is in how the other characters react to his tearing of the social fabric.

Cregan writes dry, wry comedies. Introducing *Three Men for Colverton* he writes that "the situations of most of the characters are too painful to make me laugh. However, most of the people are themselves aware of the silliness of their positions, and this frequently leads them to act in a sillier way than ever." So it is in all his plays. The characters' self-consciousness effects a certain distancing from the audience. They often introduce themselves to the audience and sing choruses together. In *Three Men for Colverton* they move the revolving platforms Cregan envisions as setting. In *The Dancers* different records are put on and taken off, accompanied by lighting changes, while in the brief comedy *George Reborn* the characters conduct an orchestra in snatches from well-known classical works.

The Houses by the Green is more farcical than his other full-length plays. It

is a Plautine or *commedia* farce, offering the battle of two elderly men, the
Commander and Mervyn Molyneux, who live in adjacent houses, for the hand
of Molyneux's adopted daughter Susan, and their besting by her young lover,
the servingman Oliver whom they share. Molyneux woos Susan disguised as
his own friend; the Commander does likewise. Neither is aware of the other's
deception. Disguised as a land developer, Oliver threatens both with their
community's destruction. Even Susan disguises herself, as the developer's
trollop; Oliver, puzzled, tells the audience "I must be impersonating a real
person." Traditional forgiveness and marriage promises end the play when
Susan, untraditionally pregnant, "is suddenly sick at the side of the stage."

—Anthony Graham-White

CRIMP, Martin (Andrew).

Born in the United Kingdom, in February 1956. Educated at Cambridge
University, graduated 1978. Married; three daughters. Thames Television
writer-in-residence, Orange Tree Theatre, Richmond, Surrey, 1988–89.
Recipient: *Radio Times* award, 1986; George Devine award, 1993. Agent:
Judy Daish Associates, 83 Eastbourne Mews, London W2 6LQ, England.

Publications

PLAYS

Living Remains (produced 1982).
Love Games, with Howard Curtis, adaptation of the work by Jerzy
    Przezdziecki, from the translation by Boguslav Lawendowski (produced
    1982).
Four Attempted Acts (produced 1984).
A Variety of Death-Defying Acts (produced 1985).
Three Attempted Acts (broadcast 1985). In *Best Radio Plays of 1985*, edited
    by Richard Imison, 1986.
Definitely the Bahamas (produced 1987).
A Kind of Arden (produced 1987).
Spanish Girls (produced 1987).
Dealing with Clair (produced 1988). 1988.
Play with Repeats (produced 1989). 1990.
No One Sees the Video (produced 1990). With *Getting Attention*, 1991.
Getting Attention (produced 1991). With *No One Sees the Video*, 1991.
The Treatment (produced 1993).

RADIO PLAYS: *Three Attempted Acts*, 1985; *Six Figures at the Base of the
Crucifixion*, 1986.

In the short story *Stage Kiss*, Martin Crimp's narrator, a well-known actor in
middle age, visits the wife from whom he is "notoriously" divorced:

> The last thing my wife says to me is "Are you happy?" to which I reply
> "Are you?". In the theatre, these lines could prove unplayable, and I'd
> suggest a cut.

And yet it is in the discomforting area uncovered by this fundamental question and evasive answer that the action of Crimp's plays is developed. The appurtenances of comfort are all in place—television sets, cassette recorders, microwaves—but they are at best a distraction from, at worst a substitute for, self-recognition. The emotional hollowness of the Thatcherite society of the 1980's is exposed catastrophically to the audience, whilst the characters in the play (those who survive the violation) struggle to keep their eyes closed to it.

Crimp characteristically sprinkles the closely observed dialogue of his plays with "faint laughs" and disconcerting pauses, enforcing a recognition of the unsaid beneath the generally civilized discourse of the brittle encounters of which the plays are composed. In *Dealing with Clair*, the ostensible subject is usually the house which Mike and Liz, a monumentally unpleasant pair of libidinous yuppies, are trying to sell. Clair is their young estate agent, already inured to avarice and deception but not yet corrupted by it. Patronized by both the vendors, she is an object of casual desire for Mike and of casual jealousy for Liz, but for the enigmatic cash-buyer James, desire is not enough. *Dealing with Clair* relates unavoidably to the disappearance (presumed dead) in 1986 of a young estate agent, Suzy Lamplugh. More significant theatrically is the brilliantly sinister scene in which the solitary James conducts a soupy telephone conversation with Clair's mother while sitting on Clair's bed, emptying her handbag. With Clair and the cash-buyer both gone, the vendors are pleased to learn from a colleague of Clair's that the house has been undervalued.

The craftsmanship of *Dealing with Clair*, its use of repetition and the aural *leitmotif* of train-sounds, is unobtrusive. In *Play with Repeats*, the playwright's craft is placed in the foreground. As he might have been in one of J.B. Priestley's time-plays, Tony Steadman is given a chance to replay two crucial incidents in his unimpressive life. Unsurprisingly, he makes a worse show of it second time round. The play is more interesting for its creation and study of a casualty of competitive values than for its theatrical trickery. Tony pines for affection but earns none. He begins the play as a buttonholing pub bore, a role in which, on the reprise of his life, he is stabbed to death. His disappearance, like that of Clair in the earlier play, makes little difference to his workmates.

The self-conscious theatricality of *Play with Repeats* suggests some striving after effect. In *No One Sees the Video*, message and medium are finely synchronised. Crimp himself thinks of it as a "post-consumer play . . . it describes a world in which the equation of consumption with happiness is no longer debated, but is simply as axiomatic to everyday life as Newtonian mechanics."

Intelligent and independent though she is, Liz is drawn into the confidence trickery of market research. The question of whether she can survive without self-hatred remains open at the end of the play. Crimp's ear for the quirks and blandnesses of contemporary speech is fully displayed. Under the barrage of consumerist interrogation and the intimidating technology of video-recording, a sense of personal identity proves fragile. *No One Sees the Video* is a powerful documenting of our times.

Liz's troublesome teenage daughter Joanna is more resistant to the blandishments of consumerism than anyone else. A concern, tinged with anger, for the new generation is a feature of Crimp's work. The off-stage crying of the daughter of Liz and Mike in *Dealing with Clair* signals the self-absorption of her repulsive parents. The future of even a daughter of privilege is bleak. For Sharon in *Getting Attention*, the story is one of abuse culminating, we have to assume, in death. This is a fine and deeply disturbing play. The setting is a block of South London flats, from any one of which the sounds that emanate eerily implicate the others. The configuration of the stage contributes crucially to the action. The main area is the interior of the flat in which Carol lives with her four-year-old daughter Sharon and her common-law husband, Nick. They have a patch of garden, in which Carol sunbathes and Nick does body-building exercises. At the bottom of the garden, where it stretches out into the audience, the invisible Sharon is sometimes allowed to play. From the balcony running alongside the flats above, the lonely Bob will look at the scantily dressed Carol and the lonely Milly will try to warn her that Sharon is eating mud. Most of the time, though, Sharon is locked in her room. The concrete evidence of her existence is the light that shows above her door when she is trying to attract her mother's attention. But the play is full of noises. Bob, drinking alone, falls over in his flat (or is it Nick dealing with Sharon?). Nick and Carol make love; Bob listens to them and to the birds scratching in his chimney (though this scratching, we will eventually learn, is Sharon's sad attempt to attract attention). Every Friday, Nick brings for Carol some new gadget for home comfort and when the scratching stops, Sharon is probably dead.

—Peter Thomson

CROSS, (Alan) Beverley.

Born in London, 13 April 1931; son of the theatrical manager George Cross and the actor Eileen Williams. Educated at the Nautical College, Pangbourne, Berkshire, 1944–47; Balliol College, Oxford, 1952–53. Served in the Royal Naval Reserve, 1944–48; British Army, 1948–50. Married 1) Elizabeth Clunies-Ross in 1955 (marriage dissolved), two daughters; 2) Gayden Collins in 1965 (marriage dissolved), one son; 3) the actress Maggie Smith in 1975. Seaman, Norwegian Merchant Service, 1950–52; actor, Shakespeare Memorial Theatre Company, 1954–56; production assistant for children's drama, BBC Television, 1956. Drama consultant, Stratford Festival Theatre, Ontario, 1975–80. Recipient: Arts Council grant, 1957, and award, 1960. Agent: Curtis Brown Group, 162–168 Regent Street, London W1R 5TB, England.

Publications

PLAYS

One More River (produced 1958). 1959.
The Singing Dolphin (for children), based on an idea by Kitty Black (produced 1959). With *The Three Cavaliers*, 1960.
Strip the Willow (produced 1960). 1961.
The Three Cavaliers (for children; produced 1960). With *The Singing Dolphin*, 1960.
Belle; or, The Ballad of Dr. Crippen, with Wolf Mankowitz, music by Monty Norman (produced 1961).
Boeing-Boeing, adaptation of a play by Marc Camoletti (produced 1961). 1967.
Wanted on Voyage, adaptation of a play by Jacques Deval (produced 1962).

Half a Sixpence, music by David Heneker, adaptation of the novel *Kipps* by H.G. Wells (produced 1963). 1967.

The Mines of Sulphur, music by Richard Rodney Bennett (produced 1965). In *Plays of the Year 30*, 1965.

The Pirates and the Inca Gold (produced 1966).

Jorrocks, music by David Heneker, adaptation of novels by R.S. Surtees (produced 1966). 1968.

All the King's Men (for children), music by Richard Rodney Bennett (produced 1969). 1969.

Phil the Fluter, with Donal Giltinan, music and lyrics by David Heneker and Percy French (produced 1969).

Victory, music by Richard Rodney Bennett, adaptation of the novel by Joseph Conrad (produced 1970). 1970.

The Rising of the Moon, music by Nicholas Maw (produced 1970). 1971.

Catherine Howard (televised 1970). In *The Six Wives of Henry VIII*, edited by J.C. Trewin, 1972; revised version (produced 1972), 1973.

The Crickets Sing (produced 1971). 1970.

The Owl on the Battlements (for children; produced 1971).

Where's Winkle? (for children; produced 1972).

The Great Society (produced 1974).

Hans Christian Andersen, with John Fearnley and Tommy Steele, music and lyrics by Frank Loesser (produced 1974; revised version produced 1976). 1978.

The Mask of Orpheus, music by Nicholas Maw. 1976.

Happy Birthday, adaptation of a play by Marc Camoletti (produced 1978). 1980.

Haworth: A Portrait of the Brontës (produced 1978). 1978.

The Scarlet Pimpernel, adaptation of the novel by Baroness Orczy (produced 1985). 1988.

Miranda, adaptation of a play by Goldoni (produced 1987).

SCREENPLAYS: *Jason and the Argonauts*, with Jan Read, 1963; *The Long Ships*, with Berkely Mather, 1964; *Genghis Khan*, with Clarke Reynolds and Berkely Mather, 1965; *Half a Sixpence*, 1967; *The Donkey Rustlers*, 1969; *Mussolini: Ultimo Atto (Mussolini: The Last Act)*, with Carlo Lizzani, 1972; *Sinbad and the Eye of the Tiger*, 1977; *The Clash of the Titans*, 1981.

TELEVISION PLAYS: *The Nightwalkers*, from his own novel, 1960; *The Dark Pits of War*, 1960; *Catherine Howard*, 1970; *March On, Boys!*, 1975; *A Bill of Mortality*, 1975; *Miss Sugar Plum*, 1976; *The World Turned Upside Down*, 1976.

NOVELS

Mars in Capricorn. 1955.

The Nightwalkers. 1956.

CRITICAL STUDIES: *Anger and After* by John Russell Taylor, 1962, revised edition, 1969, as *The Angry Theatre*, 1962, revised edition, 1969; introduction by J.C. Trewin to *The Mines of Sulphur*, in *Plays of the Year 30*, 1965.

THEATRICAL ACTIVITIES

DIRECTOR: Plays—*Boeing-Boeing*, 1964; *The Platinum Cat* by Roger Longrigg, 1965.

ACTOR: Plays—Agamemnon in *Troilus and Cressida*, 1953; Soldier in *Othello*, 1954; Mr. Fox in *Toad of Toad Hall* by A.A. Milne, 1954; Balthazar in *Much Ado about Nothing*, 1955; Herald in *King Lear*, 1955.

Beverley Cross comments:

Four main divisions of work: 1) for the commercial theatre, viz., books for musicals, boulevard comedies (i.e., *Boeing-Boeing*, *Half a Sixpence*); 2) librettos for modern opera (i.e., *The Mines of Sulphur*, *The Rising of the Moon*); 3) comedies and librettos for children (i.e., *The Three Cavaliers*, *All the King's Men*, *The Owl on the Battlements*); 4) fantasy movies (i.e., *Jason and the Argonauts*, *The Clash of the Titans*, etc).

Since 1969 has lived mostly abroad—in Greece, France, the US, and Canada —working on 4).

Beverley Cross has become best known as a writer of books for popular musicals (*Half a Sixpence*, *Jorrocks*) and of librettos for operas (*Victory*, *The Rising of the Moon*). He has also translated a highly successful boulevard farce (*Boeing-Boeing*), contributed one of the better episodes to a highly successful television series, *The Six Wives of Henry VIII* (*Catherine Howard*), written several lively, if less obviously successful, plays for children, and a small number of commercially unsuccessful plays for adults. What generalisations can be made on the basis of such a spread of work?

First, that at his best he is capable of writing a vigorous, muscular, masculine dialogue which many more pretentious writers might envy. Second, that he is particularly interested in a spirit of adventure that (he feels) no longer exists in the contemporary world, and, consequently, in the character of the adventurer himself. It is significant that many of his works are set in other periods: the light children's play, *The Singing Dolphin*, among pirates in the 18th century, the serious opera, *The Mines of Sulphur*, in a remote country house at about the same time. This latter work, with its forceful language and vivid portrayal of a murderer who traps a troupe of wandering actors and is then trapped by them, shows Cross at his strongest. Another work is set in the future:

> No planes to spoil the view. No trippers to litter the grass. No stinking petrol fumes to poison the air. No silly women to bitch away your time with their gossip and intrigue. Nothing to read, nothing to see. Complete freedom for the first time in my life. It's wonderful!

That is spoken by a character in *Strip the Willow*, a rather inconclusive quasi-Shavian comedy of ideas involving a tiny group of survivors of nuclear desolation, deep in the English countryside, living on their wits while the Russians and Americans divide the world between them; but the sentiment could be Cross's own.

He has written only one artistically successful play for adults; and that is his first, *One More River*, which occurs (characteristically) in a ship moored in a backwater on another continent and involves (characteristically) a mutiny. The seamen, among whom egalitarian notions have been circulating, turn on an unpopular officer and hang him, on false suspicion of having caused the death of one of their number. But they haven't the ability to exercise power, and are ignominiously forced to get an apprentice officer to navigate them upriver. The story is excitingly told, and some of the characterisation, notably of a self-satisfied, popularity-seeking bosun, is as good as some of it is melodramatic; but what makes the play interesting is its unfashionable viewpoint. Carefully, logically, it suggests that absolute democracy is mob-rule: some men are superior to others, and the others must submit to their authority. It is, of course, possible to pick holes in the argument as it emerges, for instance by pointing out that Cross does not face the possibility that the seaman's apparent inferiority may be less innate than the result of an unjust environment; but the achievement stands. *One More River* is one of the very few intelligent right-wing plays that the modern theatre has produced.

—Benedict Nightingale

D

DANIELS, Sarah.

Born in London in 1957. Writer-in-residence, Royal Court Theatre, London, 1984. Recipient: George Devine award, 1983. Agent: Judy Daish Associates, 83 Eastbourne Mews, London W2 6LQ, England.

Publications

PLAYS

Penumbra (produced 1981).
Ripen Our Darkness (produced 1981). With *The Devil's Gateway*, 1986.
Ma's Flesh Is Grass (produced 1981).
The Devil's Gateway (produced 1983). With *Ripen Our Darkness*, 1986.
Masterpieces (produced 1983). 1984; revised version (produced 1984), 1986.
Neaptide (produced 1986). 1986.
Byrthrite (produced 1986). 1987.
The Gut Girls (produced 1988). 1989.
Beside Herself (produced 1990). 1990.
Head-Rot Holiday (produced 1992).

Sarah Daniels has been accused of many things, but never of writing boring plays. There are some critics who find her work alarming in its representations of strong, confused, complicated, or angry women. Daniels's plays rarely portray strong men, unless we count men who abuse their positions of power. In this, she has been accused of misconstruing reality, of allowing her "feminist anger" to stand in the way of writing "good theatre." But Daniels's work is not purposefully angry or intentionally controversial in critical terms.

One suspects that a good deal of the critical alarm with which some of Daniels's work has been received is a reaction to the centrality of women in the plays and to Daniels's style, which tends to be informed by street-smart rather than academic ideas about aesthetic standards. Yet Daniels's plays need no apology, for her work is highly innovative in its self-consciously radical approach to the representation of social issues of relevance to her audiences. Daniels's work is powerful: sometimes raw, sometimes unpleasantly close to reality. Her writing is fuelled by her awareness of the complexity of life in the modern world, of different forms of sexual and racial discrimination, and of class difference. But most importantly, her writing is fuelled by two qualities rare in contemporary playwriting: a penchant for black humour, and a strength and depth of vision—unacademic, straightforward, biased, and determined—which allows Daniels to touch on subjects which others tend to gloss over or avoid altogether.

Daniels's work is often controversial, centering on themes such as pornography and violence (*Masterpieces*), rewriting of myth and reviewing of archetypal images of women (*Ripen Our Darkness*), male appropriation of women's bodies in the birthing process (*Byrthrite*), and the rights of lesbian mothers (*Neaptide*).

The best known and most controversial of her plays is *Masterpieces*, a play which deals with the issue of pornography. The central character is Rowena, a woman who watches a snuff film and who is so upset by it that she cannot separate the brutal sexual murder she has witnessed on the screen and the threat of real violence outside the cinema. When a stranger accosts her in the station, she reacts in automatic defense and shoves him; he dies on the subway line. The play shifts back and forth between exchanges with Rowena, her partner, and friends. All have different experiences of pornography, and all have difficulty seeing the issue objectively. Finally, Rowena is taken to trial for the murder of the stranger. She does not deny shoving him, but cites legal precedents of men found guilty of murder being let off with excuses such as "nagging wives." At the end of the play, Rowena describes the snuff film in graphic detail to the policewoman who waits with her for the verdict. Her final words are chilling:

> Rowena: I don't want anything to do with men who have knives or whips or men who look at photos of women tied and bound, or men who say relax and enjoy it. Or men who tell misogynist jokes.
>
> *Blackout.*

Masterpieces is unsettling, not only because it deals with the issue of pornography but because it challenges the distinction between soft and hard porn, and—in Rowena's final words—it suggests that the continuum from sexist jokes to real sexual violence against women is a real and dangerous one. In this way, the play depicts and challenges aspects of contemporary controversy over the pornography issue. Years after its first production *Masterpieces* is frequently produced, particularly by student and community theatre groups using it as an impetus to academic debate and social action.

Neaptide is, after *Masterpieces*, Daniels's best known and most important play, not least because it is the only play dealing with the subject of lesbianism to be produced at Britain's National Theatre. But more important is the play itself. In *Neaptide*, Daniels tells the story of Claire, a woman who finds it necessary to hide her sexual identity in order to protect her job and thereby support her young daughter. Claire is a teacher in a small secondary school, torn between defending the rights of a few lesbian pupils and remaining silent, thereby keeping the secret of her own sexuality from her peers. While she is involved in a potential child custody case, the pressure to "appear normal" is great. Meanwhile, she reads the myth of Persephone. The ending of the play is optimistic, but not overly so. Only individual women transcend such limitations: the lesbian pupils are saved when the principal of the school is embarrassed into a confession of her own homosexuality, the mother comes out of the proverbial closet and decides to fight for her child. The myth functions as a convenient analogue to contemporary problems, but not as an over-simplified model of a social corrective, nor as an all-encompassing statement about the function of roles.

Sarah Daniels often conducts research for her plays: for *Masterpieces*, she read feminist literature on the subject of pornography; for *Byrthrite* she investigated the role of midwives in the 17th century; for *The Gut Girls* she did local research into the history of women's work in the Deptford slaughter-houses. Before writing *Beside Herself*, Daniels contacted survivors of child sexual abuse, which is the play's underlying theme. *Beside Herself* is Daniels's latest full-length stage play, and her least realistic. It extends the earlier experimentation with myth and history into a complicated weaving of time frames, fiction, and "reality" in the world of one play. Her writing has taken another turn, however, in her most recent project, *Head-Rot Holiday*, a play for Clean Break Theatre Company involving the stories of women ex-prisoners and their children.

In all her plays, as in *Masterpieces*, Sarah Daniels takes issues of real importance to women's lives and puts them centre stage. Her plays are not easily pigeonholed: they don't quite fit the canon of great drama, and are difficult to argue for as replacements for any of the so-called classics on university reading lists. But they teach more about the power of the theatre and of the written word than do many of the texts found in the average classroom. Her work is difficult and controversial in the most positive, change-oriented sense. She is a playwright of courage and considerable talent.

—Lizbeth Goodman

See the essay on *Neaptide*.

D'ARCY, Margaretta Ruth.

Born in London, England, 14 June 1934. Educated at eight different schools in and around Dublin. Left school at age 15. Trained as an actress. Married the writer John Arden, *q.v.*, in 1957; five sons (one deceased). Founding member, Kirkby Moorside Entertainment, Yorkshire, and Norman Productions, Dublin, 1963. Regents' professor, University of California, Davis, 1973; co-founder, Corrandulla Arts and Entertainment, County Galway, Ireland, 1973–75; founding member, Galway Theare Workshp, 1976–77, Women in Media and Entertainment, from 1982, and Women's Sceal Radio and Radio Pirate Women, 1987, and from 1989, all County Galway, Ireland. Visiting lecturer, University of Bologna, Italy, 1986, and visiting examiner, University of Oran, Algeria, 1991. Recipient: Arts Council of Great Britain Playwright's award, 1972. Member, Aosdana, 1981, Time Off For Women, 1989, and honorary member, Trinidad and Tobago Domestic Workers' Union, 1989. Lives in Galway. Agent: Casarotto Ramsay Ltd., National House, 60–66 Wardour Street, London W1V 3HP, England.

Publications

PLAYS

The Happy Haven, with John Arden (produced 1960). In *New English Dramatists 4*, 1962; in *Three Plays*, 1964.

The Business of Good Government: A Christmas Play, with John Arden (also co-director: as *A Christmas Play*, produced 1960; as *The Business of Good Government*, produced 1978). 1963.

Ars Longa, Vita Brevis (for children), with John Arden (produced 1964). In *Eight Plays 1*, edited by Malcolm Stuart Fellows, 1965.

The Royal Pardon; or, The Soldier Who Became an Actor (for children), with John Arden (also co-director: produced 1966). 1967.

Friday's Hiding, with John Arden (produced 1966). In *Soldier, Soldier and Other Plays*, 1967.

The Vietnam War Game (produced 1967).

The Hero Rises Up: A Romantic Melodrama, with John Arden (also co-director: produced 1968). 1969.

Harold Muggins Is a Martyr, with John Arden and the Cartoon Archetypical Slogan Theatre (produced 1968).

Two Hundred Years of Labour History, with John Arden (produced 1971).

Granny Welfare and the Wolf, with John Arden and Roger Smith (produced 1971).

My Old Man's a Tory, with John Arden (produced 1971).

Rudi Dutschke Must Stay, with John Arden (produced 1971).

The Ballygombeen Bequest, with John Arden (produced 1972). In *Scripts 9*, September 1972; revised version, as *The Little Gray Home in the West: An Anglo-Irish Melodrama* (produced 1982), 1982.

The Island of the Mighty: A Play on a Traditional British Theme, with John Arden (produced 1972; section produced, as *Handful of Watercress*, 1976) 1974; in *Performance*, 1974.

The Henry Dubb Show (produced 1973).

The Devil and the Parish Pump, with John Arden and Corrandulla Arts and Entertainment (produced 1974).

The Crown Strike Play, with John Arden and the Galway Theatre Workshop (produced 1974).

The Non-Stop Connolly Show: A Dramatic Cycle of Continuous Struggle in Six Parts, with John Arden (also co-director; produced 1975). 5 vols., 1977–78; 1 vol. edition, 1986.

Sean O'Scrudu, with John Arden and the Galway Theatre Workshop (produced 1976).

The Mongrel Fox, with John Arden and the Galway Theatre Workshop (produced 1976).

No Room at the Inn, with John Arden (produced 1976).

A Pinprick of History (produced 1977).

Silence, with John Arden and the Galway Theatre Workshop (produced 1977).

Mary's Name, with John Arden and the Galway Theatre Workshop (produced 1977).

Blow-in Chorus for Liam Cosgrave, with John Arden and the Galway Theatre Workshop (produced 1977).

Voices of Rural Women (produced 1978).

Countess Markevicz' Incarceration (produced 1978).

The Poisoned Stream (produced 1979).

Vandaleur's Folly: An Anglo-Irish Melodrama, with John Arden (also co-director, produced 1978). 1981.

The Mother, with John Arden, adaptation of a play by Brecht (produced 1984).
The Making of Muswell Hill, with John Arden (produced 1984).
Opera Ag Obair (produced 1987).
Whose Is the Kingdom?, with John Arden (broadcast 1988). 1988.
Ducas Na Saoirse (produced annually, 1987–92). In *Theatre-Ireland*, 1993.
The Eleanor Mary Show (produced 1991).

DOCUMENTARIES: *The Kirkbymoorside Film*, 1963; *The Unfulfilled Dream*, 1969; *Galway Rent and Rate Strike*, 1972; *Sean O'Casey: Portrait of a Rebel*, with John Arden, 1973; *The St. Bridget's Place Lower Film*, 1990.

VIDEO: *The Corrandulla Film*, 1974; *Ireland for Nicaragua*, 1985; *Greenham for Libya*, 1987; *Circus Exposé*, 1988.

RADIO PLAYS: *Keep Those People Moving!* (for children), with John Arden, 1972; *The Manchester Enthusiasts*, (in two parts) with John Arden, 1984, (in three parts), as *The Ralahine Experiment*, 1985; *Whose Is the Kingdom?*, with John Arden, 1988.

OTHER
Tell Them Everything (autobiographical). 1981.
Awkward Corners: Essays, Papers, Fragments, with John Arden. 1988.

BIBLIOGRAPHY: *Arden on File* edited by Malcolm Page (for listing of collaborative work with John Arden), 1985.

THEATRICAL ACTIVITIES
DIRECTOR: **Plays**—with John Arden: several of their own plays. **Documentary and Video**—*The Kirkbymoorside Film*, 1963; *The Unfulfilled Dream*, 1969; *Galway Rent and Rate Strike*, 1972; *The Corrandulla Film*, 1972; *Ireland for Nicaragua*, 1985; *Greenham for Libya*, 1987; *Circus Exposé* , 1988; *The St. Bridget's Place Lower Film*, 1990.

Margaretta D'Arcy comments:

I was struck all of a heap a few years back, when I was invited to take part in an international theatre conference—upon looking through all the bumph outlining the sessions, I discovered that the word "play" had been dropped from the vocabulary of every item. Instead, there was "text", "performers", "plastic arts", "venues", "workshops", "symposia", "practitioners", etc., etc. I decided to use the occasion to query the disappearance of "play".

From *Webster's Dictionary*: "Brisk, lively, or light activity involving change". From *Amazons, Bluestockings and Crones* (a feminist dictionary): "Play is something women are encouraged to give up at puberty in exchange for dedication to the needs of others".

And yet I remember, when I was young, going to see "plays" by the "Garryowen Players"; although by that time the word "playhouse" had already been removed and we went to see them in a "theatre". I am not sure whether there is a connection between the loss of the concept of "play" and our present-day mechanistic bums-on-seats "task-profit" syndrome where the finished commodity off the cultural production-line is all that matters and to hell with the personal growth and vision of the workers.

But on the cover of the brochure for that international conference was a quote from Mayakovsky: "Today these are only stage prop doors but tomorrow reality will replace this theatrical trash."

He wrote that in 1921, and at the same period someone else was also exploring ways of breaking down the hierachic conventions of theatrical artificiality which mirror our society, ways to put human beings in the centre. She was Neva L. Boyd, a pioneer in the field of creative group play in Chicago. Her techniques were taken up by Viola Spolin, "to stimulate expression in both children and adults through self-discovery and personal experiencing". In Spolin's book, *Improvisation for the Theatre* (1963), summing up her 30 years' work, she states: "The game is a natural group form providing the involvement and personal freedom necessary for experiencing. There must be group agreement on the rules of the game, and group-interaction moving towards the objective if the game is to be played. The first step towards playing is personal freedom. Before we can play (and then experience) we must be free to do so. Our simplest move out into the environment is interrupted by our need for favourable comment, or interpretation by established authority. We either fear we will not get approval, or we accept outside comment and interpretation unquestionably. In a culture where approval/disapproval has become the predominant regulator of effort and position, and often the substitute for love, our personal freedoms are dissipated."

It is no accident that this was written by a woman. We women are the most conditioned of the species to accept, from birth, the culture of approval/disapproval, which automatically deprives us of play.

So how to reclaim play ?

Monitoring my own feelings and my own feelings of stress and contradiction throughout my career in the regular non-commercial theatre (whether community theatre, political theatre, street theatre, agitprop) — feelings caused by the tension of having to organise myself between child-rearing in the home and putting together my theatre outside the home — I finally resolved the contradictions in 1981 at a women's conference in Dublin where it became apparent that women's most enjoyable activity is neither to go to a theatre, nor to act in a theatre, but to talk and listen with women, telling each other stories, making fools of ourselves and laughing at ourselves.

In consequence I came also to realise that radio is the one medium that really fulfills these requirements for women: listening to it does not interrupt the natural rhythm of one's own life, one can still get on with one's work and yet receive everything that the radio is putting out to us.

A short step from this understanding: radio as potentially the cheapest and most flexible form for women's expression.

In 1987 I set up a short-range women's radio in my own home in Galway in the west of Ireland. Not a public service for people to consume, but a radio where women can be freely on the airwaves not caring whether anyone is listening or not. In other words we play on the airwaves.

Recently in the *Irish Times* I read an economic affairs article called "New Interest in Concept of Self-reliance". It said: "A new interactive emphasis between global and indigenous forces may be discerned in recent thinking. This can lay the intellectual groundwork for policies through which small, poor or weak states may find windows of opportunity to participate more equally in the world economy. Marginalisation and how to escape from it are increasingly urgent issues. The effort must be made to ensure that an international system in which the poor transfer money to the rich can be brought to an end."

In our radio/theatre this is exactly what happens. We combine tapes of women's expression from all over the world with our own indigenous impromptus of a small corner of a provincial city—the intellect and imagination coming together, the global and the local, all intermingled with trivial gossip from one or two neighbouring streets—as someone said to me, "It has all the fascination of overhearing women chat over a garden wall, you never know where it's going to take you."

No set programmes, no profit-directed tasks for the "service of others" or the "approval of others", no hidden agenda whereby such service and such approval must always assist the patriarchal military/industrial culture which envelops us—but simply play.

And of course our greatest problem—when women are trying to do something new in contradiction of the demands of the military/industrial culture, how can we have that work recognised, valued and counted?

First we must understand how to count it for ourselves; and only through the freedom of PLAY can we do so, only through the freedom of PLAY can we pass our understanding on to others.

Margaretta D'Arcy is the wife of, and collaborator with John Arden. It is customary for D'Arcy to be included as little more than a footnote in critical works on Arden. However, the plays they have written in collaboration are distinguishable in content, form, and intent from those that John Arden has written alone.

Born in Ireland, D'Arcy began acting in the fringe theatres in Dublin. Her active political commitment has been seen to stem from her Irish roots, struggling against the double bind between either being paternally absorbed by the British establishment or being marginalised. D'Arcy is too clear-minded, however, not to associate the relevance of Irish issues with other similar political structures and struggles. Her work confronts not only the patriarchal arrogance of the established hierarchy but also exposes the connections between capitalism, patriotism, and patriarchy, and the resulting misogyny.

For D'Arcy, "politics starts with the personal", describing the necessity to live with her political and social commitment in everyday life: "Had John Arden and I sorted out our values, in relation to one another, in relation to the way we thought theatre ought to be made, in relation to the relation between theatre and life?" (from *Arden/D'Arcy Plays One*, London, Methuen, 1991).

Wherever they lived, Arden and D'Arcy became active members of the community. In the winter of 1960, when D'Arcy herself was pregnant, they created a nativity play, *The Business of Good Government*, for and with the villagers of Brent Knol, where they were living. The nativity is placed in a familiar everyday context. By clearly offering the social, personal, and political perspectives of all the characters, the play retains the quality of a traditional nativity play while simultaneously opening the socio-political context for discussion.

This active commitment to community—creating theatrical events with the community about issues central to that community—is the hallmark of the D'Arcy-Arden collaboration. D'Arcy's contribution lies arguably in the firm link between the political and the personal, in finding political implications in personal experiences and exposing the personal consequences of political issues.

The plays are boisterous expressions of popular theatre with songs, verses, mime, and larger-than-life caricatures.

D'Arcy and Arden's denials of the rigid separation between performance and audience is a political expression in itself; a blow against established conventions and the "Arts" as the province of the elite.

The Royal Pardon deals openly with the workings of the theatrical world and how it reflects the social hierarchy. A bit player and a stage hand save a theatre company's performance, but the reward for their enterprise is to be fired before the company's Royal Command Performance.

The Little Gray Home in the West tells the story of a wealthy British businessman's unscrupulous handling of the property he has inherited in Ireland. The play spans the period from 1945, when Baker-Forescue inherits the property, to 1971 when internment and the British army prompt active resistance. The property includes a ramshackle small-holding inhabited by the impoverished Seamus, his wife Teresa, and their increasing family. The play opens with Padraic, son of Seamus and Teresa, aged 26, and dead. We later discover that he was murdered at a road block where he was tortured by British soldiers who describe themselves as "mercenaries". The ghosts of the dead haunt the British in Ireland.

The characters are drawn broadly, defined by their economic and social status which, in turn, forms their motives and desires. The play's Marxist position is unabashed, dividing its world between the haves and have-nots, even denoting a no man's land where a few have-nots, in this case Hagan, are willing to betray to get more. However, typical of all the Arden-D'Arcy plays, despite its clear though complex political analysis and critical perspective, the play is neither didactic nor sentimental. Each character is given ample opportunity to voice his/her reasons and explain his/her motives. In the end it is these motives, along with their practical implications for both personal experience and social morality, that are at stake. One empathises with the landlord's disappointment and anger when his friends holiday at his "chalet" and find it filthy and full of chickens, or when the high winds cause rack and ruin. But the greed and callousness that drive his feelings and form the guile with which he cheats his tenants turn our sympathies against him.

Seamus is forced to sign a document that gives Baker-Forescue ownership of the humble cottage when Seamus dies. As Seamus signs, he and Baker-Forescue take on the roles of Michael Collins and Lloyd George, clearly exposing the contract as an encapsulation of Anglo-Irish relations, a symbol of the greed and deceit practiced by the powerful on the powerless.

Caricature, song, verse, and music-hall asides give the performance a vibrant energy which gives the complex moral and political analysis emotional power by setting it in relief. *The Little Gray Home in the West* ends perversely with a custard pie fight, the climax of a Laurel and Hardy type antagonism between Hagan and Baker-Forescue initiated by the dead Padraic. The property is summarily blown up by the I.R.A., and Baker-Forescue takes his business methods to Europe.

It has been suggested that the fundamental antagonism between the West End theatre and D'Arcy-Arden plays (they have not had a play produced in the West End since 1972) lies in the form of the plays rather than directly with the content. This is a salient argument. If the theatre is "the world", a microcosm of the social context, then the structure of each play implies social structure. The formal, highly-structured conventional theatre with its audience firmly separated from the performance and the controlled, enclosed structure of the realistic play can be seen to reflect an image of a highly-structured hierachical society. Inevitably, the anarchic, varied structure of a D'Arcy-Arden play with its myriad of scenes, its songs and poems, its open stage where anything can happen, its cartoon characters and broad sweeps of time and space, and its direct relationship with the audience suggests an energetic rejection, if not ridicule, of the established hierarchies and offers a viable alternative.

In 1972 the *The Island of the Mighty* was produced by the Royal Shakespeare Company. The play presents the problems of the lame King Arthur against the poverty and suffering of his subjects. The text requires equal weight be given to Arthur's struggling subjects and his personal crisis, opening discussions regarding historical perspectives, national myth, patriotism, and storytelling. Without this balance the issues are aborted and the story becomes a shallow depiction of the romantic pathos of a failing hero.

D'Arcy and Arden expressed their commitment both to the macrocosm of socio-politics and the microcosm of theatre by literally picketing the Aldwych Theatre where the play was rehearsing. The RSC insisted the quarrel was personal rather than political or moral; ironically reflecting the onstage reduction of complex discussion of the political implications of national mythologising to a sentimental illustration of personal pathos. D'Arcy who had not been allowed to visit rehearsals until the run-throughs was dismissed as a "difficult woman".

Nothing could more explicitly illustrate the necessity and urgency in this talented, tireless woman's energetic fight against the patriarchal hierarchy.

— Elaine Turner

DARKE, Nick.

Born in Wadebridge, Cornwall, 29 August 1948. Educated at Newquay Grammar School, Cornwall; Rose Bruford College, Sidcup, Kent, 1967–70, diploma 1970. Has two sons. Actor in repertory, Belfast, 1970; actor and director, Victoria Theatre, Stoke-on-Trent, Staffordshire, 1971–79. Recipient: George Devine award, 1979. Agent: Casarotto Ramsay Ltd., National House, 60–66 Wardour Street, London W1V 3HP. Address: St. Julians, Sevenoaks, Kent TN15 0RX, England.

Publications

PLAYS

Mother Goose (pantomime; also director: produced 1977).
Never Say Rabbit in a Boat (produced 1978).
Landmarks (produced 1979).
A Tickle on the River's Back (produced 1979).
Summer Trade (produced 1979).
High Water (produced 1980). In *Plays Introduction*, 1984.
Say Your Prayers, music by Andrew Dickson (produced 1981).
The Catch (produced 1981).
The Lowestoft Man (produced 1982).
The Body, music by Guy Woolfenden (produced 1983). 1983.
Cider with Rosie, adaptation of the work by Laurie Lee (produced 1983).
The Earth Turned Inside Out (produced 1984).
Bud (produced 1985). In *Ting Tang Mine and Other Plays*, 1987.
The Oven Glove Murders (produced 1986).
The Dead Monkey (produced 1986). In *Ting Tang Mine and Other Plays*, 1987.
Ting Tang Mine (produced 1987; revised version produced 1987). In *Ting Tang Mine and Other Plays*, 1987.
Ting Tang Mine and Other Plays (includes *The Dead Monkey, Bud*). 1987.
Campesinos (produced 1989).
Kissing the Pope (produced 1989). In *Kissing the Pope: A Play and a Diary for Nicaragua*, 1990.

RADIO PLAYS: *Foggy Anniversary*, 1979; *Lifeboat*, 1981.

TELEVISION PLAY: *Farmers Arms*, 1983.

THEATRICAL ACTIVITIES

DIRECTOR: Plays—*Mother Goose, Man Is Man* by Brecht, *The Miser* by Molière, *Absurd Person Singular* by Alan Ayckbourn, *The Scarlet Pimpernel*, and *A Cuckoo in the Nest* by Ben Travers, 1977–79.
ACTOR: roles in more than 50 plays.

Nick Darke comments:

I consider my seven years as an actor to have been an apprenticeship for writing plays. By appearing in over 50 productions of new plays, classics, documentaries, children's plays, and community road-shows I learned first-hand the difference between good and bad dialogue, how to create characters and construct a world for the play to exist in. Most of my plays make people laugh, but I try to make an audience question its laughter. I have a low boredom threshold, and my interest in my plays lasts for exactly as long as it takes me to write them. I have strong ideas about how they should be cast and directed, and I watch them in performance to see how the audience reacts. After that my interest wanes and the next one has to be different in every respect to the last. I write quickly: the quicker it's written, the better the play. I think about a play for far longer than it takes me to write it. I type as fast as my brain works, so I dispense with the longhand stage and work straight onto the keyboard. I read my work out loud as I write it. For this reason I have to work entirely alone and out of earshot. I don't just mouth what I've written, if a scene demands decibels I supply them. If it's funny, I laugh. To see an audience laugh at something as much as I did when I first thought of it is a pleasure only another playwright could understand. I judge the success of my plays from the audience's response. My agent reads and sees my work, and I disregard her advice at my peril; she is my most valuable critic. I don't know what is a good play and what isn't. I don't know what makes some people like a play and others not. Some nights a whole audience will dislike a play, the next night they'll love it, with no perceptible change in the performance. My plays tend to be ambiguous, and because the style alters with each one, nobody knows what to expect. This makes for hair-raising volatility which I don't like, but can't help. My advice to a budding playwright: Cultivate your sense of rhythm, and never go into rehearsal without a good ending.

Nick Darke, who started his theatrical career as an actor at the Victoria Theatre, Stoke-on-Trent, seems to launch himself into writing plays rather as if he were working on new roles. Energetic, versatile, imaginative, inventive, eclectic, insatiably hungry for identifications which let him disappear into a disguise, he slips unrecognisably from one style, one period, one setting to another. *The Dead Monkey* is set in contemporary California, *Ting Tang Mine* goes back to an early 19th-century Cornish copper-mining community, *A Tickle on the River's Back* takes place on a Thames barge, while the setting for *The Oven Glove Murders* is a Soho film production company. Darke lodges himself in contrasting idioms like an actor who is good at accents.

His plays, almost without exception, contain sequences which are extremely suspenseful, and others which are extremely funny, but even in his best plays, such as *The Body* and *The Dead Monkey*, the writing sometimes sinks too far below the level he is capable of achieving. The funniest sequences in *The Body* occur in the first half, which climaxes in a hilarious scene involving a muddy, half-naked corpse, a farmer who is also muddy and half-naked because he is impersonating the corpse, a cat which has just been strangled, a rat-trap, an old man wearing a gas-mask, an old woman who believes she may have been touched by divinity, three farmers who speak verse in unison and a policeman who is trying to arrest all the villagers simultaneously. Less amusing and more suspenseful, the second half of the play, set in an American airbase, works towards a climax that centres on the probability of a nuclear explosion as a young Cornish farmer, brainwashed into believing he is an American soldier, brandishes a loaded machine gun and hesitates about whether to obey the orders of a sane sergeant or a demented lieutenant who has been tied up and blindfolded but not—this was the sergeant's mistake—gagged.

The plot also introduces a rector who dresses as a Mandarin, realising that his parishioners pay no more attention to him than they would to a Chinaman. They do listen if he harangues them in Chinese, but all this is not entirely irrelevant to the plot because it convinces the psychopathic lieutenant (who suspects reds under the unlikeliest of beds) that Chinese infiltration is converting the villagers to Maoism. The solution is to ask them whether they're Communist and shoot them if they deny it.

Darke's hostility to nuclear weapons, Americans, policemen, soldiers, and capitalism is rather generalised, and his writing sags under its heavy burden of literary influences and bizarre jokes. The most obvious debt is to Brecht, who was himself indebted to Kipling for the three soldiers in *Mann ist Mann* who brainwash a civilian into taking on the identity of a missing comrade. The play also seems to have been influenced by the Auden and Isherwood of *The Dog Beneath the Skin*, by the Stoppard of *After Magritte*, and by the T.S. Eliot of the verse plays.

The Dead Monkey is a funnier, more consistent play, more accomplished, less patchy, less eclectic, though the rhythms of Tennessee Williams and Edward Albee are sometimes audible. We also feel that, as in some of the morbid *coups de théâtre* of *The Body*, Darke is trying to make us shudder. The play opens with the monkey dead on the table. Later on in the act we learn that Dolores, the wife of an unsuccessful commercial traveller, has been supplementing her income by performing sexual tricks with the monkey. Towards the end of the act the monkey, which may have died from the physical strain, is cooked and eaten by husband and wife.

It must be conceded though, that even if Darke is trying too hard to shock, he is succeeding better than any young playwright since Stephen Poliakoff and that the play is still richer in surprising dramatic twists than in shock effects. The plot pulls the couple through a taxing series of changing situations so that, as in a play by Strindberg, they each become almost like a new person as they react to changes in their partner. Lingering love gradually gives way to implacable hatred, but the savagery of Hank's physical attack on Dolores takes us by surprise. Eventually we see her lying dead on the table in the same position as the monkey, but the aggressive husband then starts talking to his dead wife, apologising, pleading with her to come back, reminding her of what she said after the animal's death—perhaps it was looking down on them. Perhaps she is now, while he pulls the dead body off the table and clings to it as if dancing.

Like the imaginary child in Albee's *Who's Afraid of Virginia Woolf?* the monkey and the Macedonian curly pig they adopt to replace it are emblems of what is missing from their relationship, but the borrowing is unimportant in comparison with the success achieved in the sharply written sequences of marital bickering and in the chemical changes that occur in Dolores's personality and in the relationship when a well-paid job lifts her into a position financially superior to Hank's. An acute observer of the effects that money and social prestige have on sexual relationships, Darke is already starting to take his eclecticism into his stride.

—Ronald Hayman

DEAR, Nick.

Born in Portsmouth, Hampshire, 11 June 1955. Educated at various schools in Southampton; University of Essex, Colchester, B.A. (honours) 1977. Lives with Penny Downie; two children. Has worked as messenger boy, laundry van driver, bakery worker, garage attendant, town sergeant at Southampton Guildhall, film company administrator, and tutor in film and photography; playwright-in-residence, University of Essex, 1985; Arts Council play- wright-in-residence, Royal Exchange Theatre, Manchester, 1987–88. Recipient: Pye Radio award, 1980; John Whiting award, 1987. Agent: Rosica Colin Ltd., 1 Clareville Grove Mews, London SW7 5AH, England.

Publications

PLAYS

The Perfect Alibi (produced 1980).
Pure Science (broadcast 1983; revised version produced 1986).
Temptation (produced 1984).
In the Ruins (broadcast 1984; revised version produced 1989). With *The Art of Success*, 1989.
The Bed (produced 1985).
The Art of Success (produced 1986). With *In the Ruins*, 1989.
Food of Love (produced 1988).
A Family Affair, adaptation of a play by Ostrovsky (produced 1988). 1989.
The Last Days of Don Juan, adaptation of a play by Tirso de Molina (produced 1990). 1990.
Le Bourgeois Gentilhomme, adaptation of the play by Molière (produced 1992). 1992.

SCREENPLAYS: *Memo*, with Ann Foreman, 1980; *The Monkey Parade*, with Ann Foreman, 1982; *The Ranter*, 1988.

RADIO PLAYS: *Matter Permitted*, 1980; *Pure Science*, 1983; *In the Ruins*, 1984; *Jonathan Wild*, adaptation of the novel by Fielding, 1985; *Free*, 1986; *Swansong*, with David Sawer, 1989.

Nick Dear comments:

I mistrust writers' statements about their own work. I think there are two types of plays and of playwriting. One is concerned with money, glory, and a lot of invitations to dinner. The other is concerned with finding out something about oneself and one's place in the world—that old story—and attempting to communicate it honestly. Success is easily measured on the first count; less so on the second.

Sex, greed, disgust, and greatly heightened language are four of the basic elements which Nick Dear regularly mixes in his theatrical alchemy. His voice is a powerfully original one, at its most intense in his most famous play, *The Art of Success*, a savage portrait of the great painter, engraver, and caricaturist William Hogarth. But even in his minor plays, when he playfully borrows form and style from the likes of Steven Berkoff, Joe Orton, and Harold Pinter, as in *Pure Science*, there is no mistaking the fierceness of Dear's own vision.

Pure Science is particularly revealing of Dear's influences because it flirts with form. The elderly couple whose private life is invaded by a young Mr. Perkins could be the couple in Pinter's *A Slight Ache*, thrown off-balance by the presence of the Matchseller at their gate; or the flirtatious Mr. Perkins could be said to resemble Orton's Mr. Sloane, importing sexual and criminal danger into the house. When he speaks, Mr. Perkins uses the rough rhyme of a Berkoff Eastender, grandly elevating his larcenous inclinations through doggerel.

The moral arguments, however, are pure Dear. The chemical smells which have wafted up the stairs from the basement for the past 50 years are the evidence of unceasing experiments in alchemy—the time-honoured art of transmutating base elements into higher elements, such as lead into gold. It is that prospect which attracts the attention of Mr. Perkins, who fails to find interest in what has been achieved by his host—eternal life.

Although the latter was the grand aim of alchemy, Dear himself is clearly not convinced that scientific advancement will improve the lot of mankind; he calls on J. Robert Oppenheimer, the father of the atomic bomb, as a witness to the dangers of science and drives the four horsemen of the Apocalypse through the play. But it remains a comedy, with a workshop full of entrails for predicting the future, and it offers a cheerful reversal when the greedy, villainous, and seductive Mr. Perkins is drowned by the elderly wife—"There should be more comeuppance." The couple decide to take their secret knowledge into hiding, like many unknown others, rather than share it with a wicked world.

In Dear's play *Temptation*—where a schoolteacher hopelessly trots out examples of zoological variety to his pupils while reminding them that man destroys a species every month where evolution takes a thousand years—the bitter view of humanity is even more specific. On his way towards suicide, the teacher blurs his unspoken thoughts with his lessons, telling his children that the headmistress "has little knowledge of the world, she's not even frightened of it." His own state of mind is best summed up with the thought that he is "aware that there are 3,000 million starving and he has not gone mad." But perhaps he has, for his own grip on life has slipped through the ordinary muddle of an unwise affair and a damaged marriage.

Perhaps as evidence for the prosecution of humanity, Dear has turned to history more than once, providing a harrowing portrait of the declining George III in *In the Ruins*, but making his greatest impact with *The Art of Success*. Hogarth's chosen form of expression, the harsh morality pictures which made up such series as *The Rake's Progress*, *The Harlot's Progress*, and *Marriage à la Mode*, obviously found a sympathizer in Dear, but Hogarth's own morality was to face a rigorous test in the play.

Dear's great achievement in the play is to enter into Hogarth's world; by trawling with Hogarth through the whoring and hypocrisy of his era he etches his own series of images: Hogarth debasing a condemned murderer by sketching her in her cell against her will; Hogarth seeking degradation with prostitutes; Hogarth's wife uncovering a sheaf of drawings depicting her in sexual acts with other men. The murky desires of Hogarth's deepest imagining are shown dramatically as the force behind his own condemnations of corruption.

For all its power to shock and darkness of tone, for all the violent vigour of the language, *The Art of Success* is also comic and knowing. With its portrayal of the powers and movers of the time, of Hogarth's coup in achieving copyright for his work, it also comments on the 1980's and the commerce of art. For the duration of the play, author and subject seem to share a common vision.

Adaptation has also provided Dear with rich modes of expression, unleashing the extravagant theatrical gestures of Russian and Spanish drama through his extremely vivid English versions of classic plays. Although skilled in writing miniatures such as *Temptation*, he seems most at home when given the scope of classical drama. Perhaps the stunted theatricality of late 1980's English theatre, reduced in size commensurate with the reductions in subsidy, limited his original contributions to the theatre, but the beginning of the 1990's saw him immersed in a potentially rich collaboration, writing for the theatre of Peter Brook.

—Ned Chaillet

DELANEY, Shelagh.

Born in Salford, Lancashire, 25 November 1939. Educated at Broughton Secondary School. Has one daughter. Worked as salesgirl, usherette, and photographer's laboratory assistant. Recipient: Foyle New Play award, 1959; Arts Council bursary, 1959; New York Drama Critics Circle award, 1961; BAFTA award, 1962; Robert Flaherty award, for screenplay, 1962; Encyclopaedia Britannica award, 1963; Writers Guild award, for screenplay, 1969; Cannes Film Festival award, 1985. Fellow, Royal Society of Literature, 1985. Agent: Tessa Sayle, 11 Jubilee Place, London SW3 3TE, England.

Publications

PLAYS

A Taste of Honey (produced 1958). 1959.
The Lion in Love (produced 1960). 1961.
The House That Jack Built (televised 1977; produced 1979). 1977.
Don't Worry about Matilda (broadcast 1983; produced 1987).

SCREENPLAYS: *A Taste of Honey*, with Tony Richardson, 1961; *The White Bus*, 1966; *Charlie Bubbles*, 1968; *Dance with a Stranger*, 1985.

RADIO PLAYS: *So Does the Nightingale*, 1981; *Don't Worry about Matilda*, 1983.

TELEVISION PLAYS: *Did Your Nanny Come from Bergen?*, 1970; *St. Martin's Summer*, 1974; *The House That Jack Built* series, 1977; *Find Me First*, 1981.

OTHER

Sweetly Sings the Donkey. 1963.

CRITICAL STUDIES: *Anger and After* by John Russell Taylor, 1969; *Feminist Theatre* by Helene Keyssar, 1984; *Look Back in Gender* by Michelene Wandor, 1987.

Judged solely on the plots, Shelagh Delaney's first two plays would seem to place her with her hands firmly in the kitchen-sink world of working-class life: all penny-in-the-slot and gasworks-in-view, Northern grime and vowel sounds. *A Taste of Honey* takes place in a seedy bedsit. Helen, a "semi-whore", leaves with her latest fancy man, abandoning her teenage daughter. The girl, Jo, is an embarrassment: old enough to undermine Helen's perpetual youth, and pregnant by a black sailor. Jo and Geoffrey (a homosexual art student) care for each other, but he leaves when Helen returns, her latest romance in ruins. The two women are left alone, together. There is no suggestion that life will be much different for the unborn child.

Less well known, *The Lion in Love* features a larger cast coping with the same lack of choices. Frank is forever about to leave Kit who, typically, has been arrested for drunk and disorderly behaviour just as the play opens. Both their children dream of a better life. One is set to emigrate, the other is falling in love. Not much hope is suggested for either. A street corner prophet appears from time to time, predicting change. The action demonstrates the unlikeliness of this. Social determinism reigns.

Obviously Delaney was influenced by what came before, but it is a mistake to regard her plays as part of any continuum of social realism.

John Osborne's *Look Back in Anger* is popularly held to have hurled stones through the drawing-room windows of British theatre in the mid-1950's, and a comparison of the depiction of female characters in that play with the protagonists of *A Taste of Honey* and *The Lion in Love* is revealing. Constantly Delaney presents women toughened by circumstance. Frustrated, trapped, and dissatisfied, they are offered only momentary sweetness in a bleak world. Economic dependency is stressed, whether in marriage or prostitution, which Delaney depicts without sentiment or moral judgements. The unsatisfactory nature of sexual relationships is revealed again and again. Peg's careless rapture in *The Lion in Love* is undercut by her mother and father's tormented marriage and the life of Nell, the local street-corner tart. Sex results in unwanted pregnancy. The only tenderness displayed between men and women (other than siblings) is between the pregnant Jo and the homosexual Geoffrey. Even that relationship is doomed; unfortunately, Delaney is of her time in her stereotypical depiction of the feminised and unhappy gay outsider.

Delaney's women's lives and actions are responsive to male behaviour. (Ruth Ellis, the heroine of Delaney's notable screenplay for *Dance with a Stranger*, is perhaps the ultimate example of this.) Nevertheless the very act of representing such lives, of celebrating the strength and endurance of these women, of declaring that such things are an appropriate subject to place centre-stage, is a proto-feminist gesture.

In the same way that Delaney began the reclamation of women's domain that is seen in the work of later, feminist playwrights, her plays anticipate the concern with how a story is told, as much as with what is told. On both sides of the Atlantic, writers such as Megan Terry, Caryl Churchill, and Pam Gems have abandoned traditional (male) theatrical structures in the belief that form *and* content must change to reflect different concerns. Joan Littlewood, who was attempting to establish a new, populist form of theatre saw the potential and significance of the expressionistic, non-naturalistic style of *A Taste of Honey*. The play—first staged by Littlewood's Theatre Workshop—has no fourth wall. A jazz trio accompany and heighten the action. Characters turn from each other mid-sentence, and address the audience directly. In *The Lion in Love*, music is again integral. The structure is episodic, following the various related but separate stories, while the location shifts accordingly between home and street market. (All in all, the play is probably unstageable. Certainly, it met nowhere near the acclaim of *A Taste of Honey* nor has it been revived in the same way.)

It is beyond the brief of this piece to speculate why, after only two plays for the stage and just turned 20 years old, Delaney gave up writing for the theatre in favour of other media. It is tempting to imagine that she was already weary of the patronising amazement of much contemporaneous criticism, which constantly marvelled that a teenage, Northern shop girl could produce art. With hindsight, it is easy to dismiss Delaney's plays as minor period pieces. Like most work which resolutely addresses and reflects the social mores of its time, the plays have not worn well. But Delaney's plays were unique, not to say isolated at the time. Her concern with form and the emphasis she places on working-class women's experience means that Delaney's true significance lies beyond her plays, in her influence.

—Joss Bennathon

See the essay on *A Taste of Honey*.

DEWHURST, Keith.

Born in Oldham, Lancashire, 24 December 1931. Educated at Rydal School, 1945–50; Peterhouse, Cambridge, 1950–53, B.A. (honours) in English 1953. Married 1) Eve Pearce in 1958 (divorced 1980), one son and two daughters; 2) Alexandra Cann in 1980. Yarn tester, Lancashire Cotton Corporation, Romiley, Cheshire, 1953–55; sports writer, Manchester *Evening Chronicle*, 1955–59; presenter, Granada Television, 1968–69, and *Review* arts programme, BBC, 1972; arts columnist, the *Guardian*, London, 1969–72. Writer-in-residence, West Australian Academy of Performing Arts, Perth, 1984. Recipient: Japan prize, for television play, 1968. Agent: Alexandra Cann Representation, 68E Redcliffe Gardens, London SW10 9HE, England.

Publications

PLAYS

Running Milligan (televised 1965). In *Z Cars: Four Scripts from the Television Series*, edited by Michael Marland, 1968.
Rafferty's Chant (produced 1967). In *Plays of the Year 33*, 1967.
The Last Bus (televised 1968). In *Scene Scripts*, edited by Michael Marland, 1972.
Pirates (produced 1970).
Brecht in '26 (produced 1971).
Corunna! (produced 1971).

Kidnapped, adaptation of the novel by Robert Louis Stevenson (produced 1972).
The Miser, adaptation of a play by Molière (produced 1973).
The Magic Island (produced 1974).
The Bomb in Brewery Street (produced 1975).
One Short (produced 1976).
Luggage (produced 1977).
Lark Rise, adaptation of works by Flora Thompson (produced 1978). In *Lark Rise to Candleford*, 1980.
The World Turned Upside Down, adaptation of the work by Christopher Hill (produced 1978).
Candleford, adaptation of works by Flora Thompson (produced 1979). In *Lark Rise to Candleford*, 1980.
Lark Rise to Candleford (includes *Lark Rise* and *Candleford*). 1980.
San Salvador (produced 1980).
Don Quixote, adaptation of the novel by Cervantes (produced 1982). 1982.
Batavia (produced 1984).
Black Snow, adaptation of a novel by Mikhail Bulgakov (produced 1991). 1991.

SCREENPLAY: *The Empty Beach*, 1985.

RADIO PLAYS: *Drummer Delaney's Sixpence*, 1971; *That's Charlie George Over There*, 1972; *Dick Turpin*, 1976; *Mother's Hot Milk*, 1979.

TELEVISION PLAYS: *Think of the Day*, 1960; *A Local Incident*, 1961; scripts for *Z Cars* series, 1962–67; *Albert Hope*, 1962; *The Chimney Boy*, 1964; *The Life and Death of Lovely Karen Gilhooley*, 1964; *The Siege of Manchester*, 1965; *The Towers of Manhattan*, 1966; *Softly Softly* series, 1967, 1975–76; *The Last Bus*, 1968; *Men of Iron*, 1969; *Why Danny Misses School*, 1969; *It Calls for a Great Deal of Love*, 1969; *Helen*, from the play by Euripides, 1970; *The Sit-In*, 1972; *Lloyd-George*, 1973; *End Game*, 1974; *The Great Alfred* (*Churchill's People* series), 1975; *Our Terry*, 1975; *Just William* series, from books by Richmal Crompton, 1977; *Two Girls and a Millionaire*, 1978; *The Battle of Waterloo*, 1983; *What We Did in the Past*, 1986; *Joe Wilson* series, from short stories by Henry Lawson 1987 (Australia); and for *Knight Errant*, *Skyport*, *Love Story*, *Front Page Story*, *The Villains*, *The Emigrants*, *Dominic*, *Juliet Bravo*, *Van der Valk*, *Casualty*, and *Making News* series.

NOVELS
Captain of the Sands. 1981.
McSullivan's Beach. 1985.

Keith Dewhurst comments:

One day in June 1986 I walked into a discount bookshop in Sydney and flicked through an encyclopaedic television guide compiled by Leslie Halliwell, whom I remember with gratitude from my Cambridge days (when he managed the Rex Cinema), and the critic Phillip Purser. Two of my own television plays were accorded entries: *Men of Iron* and *The Siege of Manchester*, which had an asterisk admitting it to "Halliwell's Hall of Fame." This stunned me, in an amiable sort of way, and seems to me to be a classic example of the random fates that await the plays people write.

The Siege of Manchester was a broken-backed epic, for which I have a very soft spot, as I suppose one does for anything half-regretted, and I am delighted that Phillip Purser remembers it, but it does not seem to me to be in the same class as some other television plays I have written, such as *Albert Hope*, *It Calls for a Great Deal of Love*, *Our Terry*, *Lloyd-George*, *Men of Iron* itself, and an episode of *Juliet Bravo* called *Oscar*.

Similarly, *Lark Rise*, which was performed at the National Theatre and subsequently in various countries around the world has, I hazard, been recognised as an interesting piece, and the one in which the director Bill Bryden and myself best expressed a modern genre—the promenade play with music, that tries to make the theatre an event again. Yet the plays by which one arrived at that destination, especially *Corunna!*, aren't even in a vestibule of fame. They're out in the car park, where it's pissing with rain.

This damp obscurity I attribute mainly to the plays in question never having been published. Nor was *The Bomb in Brewery Street*, which additionally suffered from radical chic reviewers who thought that, being set in the Belfast troubles, it should provide solutions that eluded Elizabeth I, Oliver Cromwell, Henry Grattan, Gladstone, Parnell, Lloyd-George, and de Valera. In fact it is a funny and carefully researched work whose sub-text clearly favours colonial disengagement, and I wish I could hustle it into *somebody's* "Hall of Fame," but I don't suppose I will.

I can, however, close with an appropriate "Hall of Fame" reminiscence. There was an extra in *The Siege of Manchester* who was supposed to be dead in a battle scene but kept getting up. Four years later, when the director Herbert Wise and I were working on *Men of Iron*, we met this same extra in the studio corridor, clearly wearing a costume for our new play.

> Herbert gripped my wrist and said: "It's George!"
> George said: "Hello, Mr. Wise. I never thought I'd work for you again!"
> "You wouldn't have," said Herbert, "if I'd remembered your other name."
> Maybe the car park does have consolations, after all.

Keith Dewhurst is a highly skilled and conscientious dramatic craftsman. He has been prepared to write in a number of different dramatic styles, readily accepting the challenges of working for the technically demanding medium of television and of preparing for the stage adaptations of works of fiction which a large proportion of his audience already know well and love in their original form. For television he has adopted the realistic manner which is the current norm for popular entertainment, and his *Van der Valk* detective series has been well received. For the stage, however, he has often preferred to experiment with ideas taken up from Bertolt Brecht's "epic theatre," with the illusion of reality broken in order to facilitate a more direct address to the audience and to accommodate subjects which might prove unduly resistant to conventional treatment. As well as scaling down his work so that it fits comfortably on to the small screen, Dewhurst has used a number of different forms of staging, including arena style, the thrust stage with the audience seated to either side of a long ramp, and what he calls "promenade production" which goes a long way towards abolishing the traditional—or to be more accurate, the 19th-century—distinction between the public and the actors in order to create (if need be at the cost of some spoiling of the sight lines that used to be thought so important) a greater degree of intimacy and involvement. Music is not treated as a mere incidental or just to emphasise atmosphere; it serves as an essential part of the dramatic presentation in many instances. Dewhurst never loses sight of the need for the theatre to entertain, but when he comments on this he is not just repeating a commonplace and far less is he making the facile distinction of some old-fashioned critics between a theatre of entertainment and a theatre of ideas. Instead, he insists that drama can and ought to be an artistic medium which appeals to a wide range of people in a number of different ways. In this, as in his choice of dramatic mentor, Dewhurst proclaims a wide sympathy with the great mass of humanity.

His talents and his sympathy are clearly revealed in *Running Milligan*, an outstanding contribution to the BBC's epoch-making series *Z Cars*. Milligan is shown leaving prison, let out on parole to attend his wife's funeral. The policemen on patrol see him, and their immediate suspicions set the perspectives of a tragedy that is inevitable. At home Milligan predictably finds no support and cannot resist the crazy temptation of trying to run away. It is to no avail, and Barlow, who has presided over the usual police station subplot, arrives to arrest him. To some extent this is conventional enough, but Dewhurst contrives to bring out all the pathetic helplessness of Milligan, suggesting that the blame lies not with him but with his impossible situation and that society's response to his problems is no less bungling and ineffectual than his own efforts at escape. The dialogue is pared down to essentials, but in a scene near the end when Milligan tries to comfort a drink-sodden tramp whose memory is fuddled by memories of fighting in the war by telling him a fairy story, there is a sudden and disturbingly apt touch of poetry.

Rafferty's Chant, which was produced at the Mermaid Theatre, London, has a great deal more humour in its portrayal of the life and downfall of a wonderfully plausible con man in the used car trade. The dialogue is crisp and laconic, but there is a wonderful touch of romance in Rafferty's patter as he sells old bangers as if they were dream machines. The skimpy plot of this play that has more than a touch of farce to it is no more than a thread to hold together closely observed characters in a number of sketches that explore their motivations as they try to cope with one of those vitally important little matters in present-day life, the buying of a car. As we laugh with Rafferty at mankind's foibles there is no more danger of our taking any more seriously than he does the stern words he imagines a judge speaking to him before pronouncing a stiff sentence for preying on gullibility.

Following a line of development that probably owes its origins to the experiments of the French director Jean-Louis Barrault and which was certainly influenced to some extent by the work of Ariane Mnouchkine whose production of *1789* with the Théâtre du Soleil he witnessed at the Cartoucherie de Vincennes, Paris, Dewhurst has done some of his most original work in adaptations. *Corunna!*, for instance, dramatises episodes from the Napoleonic War as a ballad opera with no more than five actors reinforced by a five-piece rock band. *Kidnapped*, after Robert Louis Stevenson, was also notable for its freedom of dramatic treatment. If the problem with *Don Quixote* was an excess of text, that with *Lark Rise*, after Flora Thompson's celebrated portrait of village life in Victorian Oxfordshire, was a lack of narrative and a consequent lack of a clear central focus of attention. Dewhurst does not try to remedy this. His approach is rather to let the images of the village and its people develop before the eyes of the audience so that the succession of glimpses may add together almost as they do when we look in on real life. In this way *Lark Rise* serves as a prelude to the rather more obviously shaped *Candleford*. The texts do not read particularly well, but that criticism is no more just here than when it is levelled at television scripts. Flora Thompson's book, like the novels of Cervantes or Stevenson, remains intact for those who wish to read it. Dewhurst's aim is to find a dramatic representation of these works which functions in performance with all the different means of communication that are available in the theatre when, without the trammels and clutter of old-fashioned realism, the imagination is engaged and provoked into providing whatever may be sensed as needed to colour the pictures that are sketched before our eyes. The success of the productions of *Lark Rise* and *Candleford* is ample justification for the enterprise that Dewhurst has embarked upon.

—Christopher Smith

DONLEAVY, J(ames) P(atrick).

Born in Brooklyn, New York, United States, 23 April 1926; became Irish citizen, 1967. Educated at a preparatory school, New York; Trinity College, Dublin. Served in the United States Naval Reserve during World War II. Married 1) Valerie Heron (divorced), one son and one daughter; 2) Mary Wilson Price in 1970 (divorced), one daughter and one son. Recipient: London *Evening Standard* award, 1961; Brandeis University Creative Arts award, 1961; American Academy award, 1975. Address: Levington Park, Mullingar, County Westmeath, Ireland.

Publications

PLAYS

The Ginger Man, adaptation of his own novel (produced 1959). 1961; as *What They Did in Dublin, with The Ginger Man: A Play*, 1962.
Fairy Tales of New York (produced 1960). 1961.
A Singular Man, adaptation of his own novel (produced 1964). 1965.
The Plays of J.P. Donleavy (includes *The Ginger Man*, *Fairy Tales of New York*, *A Singular Man*, *The Saddest Summer of Samuel S*). 1972.
The Beastly Beatitudes of Balthazar B, adaptation of his own novel (produced 1981).

RADIO PLAY: *Helen*, 1956.

NOVELS

The Ginger Man. 1955; complete edition, 1963.
A Singular Man. 1963.
The Saddest Summer of Samuel S. 1966.
The Beastly Beatitudes of Balthazar B. 1968.
The Onion Eaters. 1971.
A Fairy Tale of New York. 1973.
The Destinies of Darcy Dancer, Gentleman. 1977.
Schultz. 1979.
Leila. 1983.
DeAlfonce Tennis: The Superlative Game of Eccentric Champions: Its History, Accoutrements, Conduct, Rules and Regimen. 1984.
Are You Listening Rabbi Löw. 1987.
That Darcy, That Dancer, That Gentleman. 1990.

SHORT STORIES

Meet My Maker the Mad Molecule. 1964.

OTHER

The Unexpurgated Code: A Complete Manual of Survival and Manners, drawings by the author. 1975.
Ireland: In All Her Sins and in Some of Her Graces. 1986.
A Singular Country, illustrated by Patrick Prendergast. 1989.

BIBLIOGRAPHY: by David W. Madden, in *Bulletin of Bibliography*, September 1982.

CRITICAL STUDIES: *J.P. Donleavy: The Style of His Sadness and Humor* by Charles G. Masinton, 1975; *Isolation and Protest: A Case Study of J.P. Donleavy's Fiction* by R.K. Sharma, 1983.

Although J.P. Donleavy is better known as a novelist, he has adapted his own novels, *The Ginger Man* and *A Singular Man*, into plays which have received fairly successful productions, and his original stage play, *Fairy Tales of New York*, won the *Evening Standard* Most Promising Playwright Award for 1961. In adjusting to the medium of the theatre, Donleavy faced two particular problems. His prose style is rich, idiosyncratic, and of a quality to encourage cult enthusiasms: but to what extent could this verbal power be incorporated into stage dialogue without leaving the impression of over-writing? His novels too are usually written from the standpoint of one man, an anti-hero such as Sebastian Dangerfield or George Smith: but in a play the audience is necessarily aware of other characters, simply because they're on the stage. If the central character talks too much, the audience's sympathy may be drawn towards the reactions of other people to him. A single angle of vision, easy to maintain in a novel, is often hard to achieve in the theatre, which is a multidimensional medium.

Donleavy's first play, *The Ginger Man*, revealed an uncertain control of these difficulties. The story concerns Sebastian Dangerfield, an impoverished

American living with his English wife, Marion, in Dublin. He is supposedly
studying law at Trinity College: but his main efforts are directed towards
staving off creditors, avoiding the responsibilities of fatherhood, and raking
together enough money to get drunk. In the novel Sebastian's sheer wildness,
his refusal to settle down, is exciting: it is an archetypal rebellion against
dreary conformity. But in the play, we are unavoidably aware of the pain
Sebastian causes others — particularly Marion who leaves him, and the genteel
spinster, Miss Frost, whom he seduces. And the fine uninhibited imagination of
Sebastian, which provides so much fun in the book, is in the play relentlessly
controlled by the physical surroundings of the set: the squalid flat at One
Mohammed Road, the prim suburban house at 11 Golden Vale Park. "*The
Ginger Man*," concluded Richard Gilman, "desperately requires: song, dance,
lyrical fragments, voices from nowhere, shapes, apparitions, unexplainable
gestures." In the format of a naturalistic play, it lost many of the qualities
which made the book so remarkable. Even the theme seemed less original: the
relationship between O'Keefe and Sebastian recalled the boozing friendship
between Joxer and "Captain" Boyle in O'Casey's *Juno and the Paycock*.

   Fairy Tales of New York is much more successful: a sequence of four related
anecdotes, which almost seems to continue the ginger man's career. An
American returns to his native city, with his English wife who dies on the
voyage. Cornelius Christian is in the same state of desolation, harassed by
poverty, guilty and grief-stricken, which faced Sebastian at the close of the
earlier play. The four scenes illustrate Cornelius's gradual rehabilitation: the
burial of his wife and his job at the funeral parlour, his entry into the American
business world, his work-outs at a gymnasium and finally his successful
(though imaginary) conquest of a snobbish head-waiter and an embarrassed
girlfriend. Unlike Sebastian, however, Cornelius is a reserved quiet man —
observing others and sometimes poking gentle fun at them: and this changed
role for the central character, together with the much greater flexibility of
form, allows Donleavy's great gifts for caricature, witty dialogue, and buoyant
fun to be more evident. Nor are the episodes as unrelated and superficial as
they may appear. Donleavy stresses the contrast between the democratic ideals
of American society with the rigidly class-structured and snobbish habits:
Christian is employed because he's been to Europe and acquired "breeding" —
he dazzles the head-waiter, who refused to serve him because he wore peach
shoes, by dressing as a visiting Eastern potentate wearing no shoes at all. The
spurious emotionalism of the funeral parlour is related to Christian's moving
grief: and the sheer falseness of an over-commercialized society is exposed with
a delicate skill that only Evelyn Waugh and Edward Albee have matched.

   Although *A Singular Man* lacks some of the moral seriousness (and fun) of
Fairy Tales of New York, it too is a rewarding play: centered around the life of
a fairly successful New York businessman, George Smith, his friendships and
affairs with three women, Ann Martin, Sally Tomson, and Shirl. Smith is a fall
guy, always missing out on the opportunities he dreams about. "The only time
the traffic will stop for me," he confesses to Shirl, "is when I'm dead." His
sexual fantasies focus on Sally Tomson, a gorgeous secretary, protected by her
tough-guy brother and many other lovers. Her death at the end of the play, just
before her marriage to a rich tycoon, crystallizes Smith's sense of cosmic
defeat. But Smith never quite gives up hope: and his resilience through success-

ive embarrassments and failures provides the mainspring for the play. *A Singular Man* is similar in construction to *Fairy Tales of New York*: a sequence of 12 anecdotal scenes, which work both on the level of isolated and very amusing revue sketches, and together as a group, the insights of one episode being carried forward to the next, until the full picture emerges both of the society and the central man. In the first scene, Smith opts out of conversation with a boring friend by answering just "Beep beep"; in the seventh, he tries the same tactics with Shirl, only to discover that his relationship with her is too charged and complex to admit such an evasion.

Donleavy's style of humour is reminiscent both of *New Yorker* cartoons and of the American dramatist Murray Schisgal, whose plays are also popular in Britain. But his jokes are never flippant—although they sometimes seem whimsical. They succeed because they're based on detailed observation and a rich command of language. Although as a dramatist, he may not yet have lived up to the promise of *Fairy Tales of New York*, he remains one of the most potentially exciting dramatists now at work.

—John Elsom

DUFFY, Maureen (Patricia).

Born in Worthing, Sussex, 21 October 1933. Educated at Trowbridge High School for Girls, Wiltshire; Sarah Bonnell High School for Girls; King's College, London, 1953–56, B.A. (honours) in English 1956. Schoolteacher for five years. Co-founder, Writers Action Group, 1972; joint chair, 1977–78, and president, 1985–89, Writers Guild of Great Britain; chair, Greater London Arts Literature Panel, 1979–81; vice-chair, 1981–86, and since 1989 chair, British Copyright Council; since 1982 chair, Authors Lending and Copyright Society; vice-president, Beauty Without Cruelty; fiction editor *Critical Quarterly*, Manchester, 1987. Recipient: City of London Festival Playwright's prize, 1962; Arts Council bursary, 1963, 1966, 1975; Society of Authors travelling scholarship, 1976. Fellow, Royal Society of Literature, 1985. Agent: Jonathan Clowes Ltd., Ironbridge House, Bridge Approach, London NW1 8BD. Address: 18 Fabian Road, London SW6 7TZ, England.

Publications

PLAYS

The Lay-Off (produced 1962).
The Silk Room (produced 1966).
Rites (produced 1969). In *New Short Plays 2*, 1969.
Solo, Olde Tyme (produced 1970).
A Nightingale in Bloomsbury Square (produced 1973). In *Factions*, edited by Giles Gordon and Alex Hamilton, 1974.

RADIO PLAY: *Only Goodnight*, 1981.

TELEVISION PLAY: *Josie*, 1961.

NOVELS

That's How It Was. 1962.
The Single Eye. 1964.
The Microcosm. 1966.
The Paradox Players. 1967.
Wounds. 1969.
Love Child. 1971.
I Want to Go to Moscow: A Lay. 1973; as *All Heaven in a Rage,* 1973.
Capital. 1975.
Housespy. 1978.
Gor Saga. 1981.
Scarborough Fear (as D.M. Cayer). 1982.
Londoners: An Elegy. 1983.
Change. 1987.
Illuminations. 1991.
Occam's Razor. 1993.

VERSE

Lyrics for the Dog Hour. 1968.
The Venus Touch. 1971.
Actaeon. 1973.
Evesong. 1975.
Memorials of the Quick and the Dead. 1979.
Collected Poems. 1985.

OTHER

The Erotic World of Faery. 1972.
The Passionate Shepherdess: Aphra Behn 1640–1689. 1977.
Inherit the Earth: A Social History. 1980.
Men and Beasts: An Animal Rights Handbook. 1984.
A Thousand Capricious Chances: A History of the Methuen List 1889–1989.
    1989.

Editor, with Alan Brownjohn, *New Poetry 3.* 1977.
Editor, *Oroonoko and Other Stories,* by Aphra Behn. 1986.
Editor, *Love Letters Between a Nobleman and His Sister,* by Aphra Behn.
    1987.
Editor, *Five Plays,* by Aphra Behn. 1990.

Translator, *A Blush of Shame,* by Domenico Rea. 1968.

MANUSCRIPT COLLECTION: King's College, University of London.

CRITICAL STUDIES: by Dulan Barber, in *Transatlantic Review 45* Spring 1973;
Guide to Modern World Literature by Martin Seymour-Smith, 1973, as *Funk
and Wagnalls Guide to Modern World Literature,* 1973; *A Female Vision of
the City* by Christine Sizemore, 1989.

Maureen Duffy comments:

(1973) I began my first play in my third year at university, finishing it the next year and submitting it for the *Observer* playwriting competition of 1957–58. I had done a great deal of acting and producing at school and at this stage my aim was to be a playwright as I was already a poet. I wrote several more plays and became one of the Royal Court Writers Group which met in the late 1950's to do improvisations and discuss problems. I have continued to write plays alternately with novels and every time I am involved in a production I swear I will never write anything else. From early attempts to write a kind of poetic social realism I have become increasingly expressionist. *Solo, Olde Tyme* and *Rites* are all on themes from Greek mythology. *Megrim*, the play I am working on at present, is a futurist study of racialism and the making of a society. I believe in theatrical theatre including all the pantomime elements of song, dance, mask and fantasy and in the power of imagery.

Maureen Duffy is firmly established as one of the foremost novelists of her generation. During the past 30 years she has also written plays; the fact that these, with the possible exception of *Rites*, have not yet received the recognition they deserve is due quite as much to an absence of a fortuitous conjunction of circumstance typical of the theatre and necessary for the achievement of success, as to the demands made on the audience by the author.

Duffy's plays are not "easy." They are densely written, pitched between fantasy and realism, and have allegorical undertones. At the centre of her work lie three short plays derived from Greek myths: The Bacchae (*Rites*), Narcissus (*Solo*), and Uranus (*Olde Tyme*).

Rites, which first appeared in an experimental programme of plays presented by the National Theatre, is set in a ladies' public lavatory, presided over by the monstrous Ada (*Agave*). Duffy describes it as a black farce. She use a chorus of modern prototypes—three office girls, a cleaner, an old tramp—and involves them in situations both modern (a girl's attempted suicide in a cubicle) and parallel to the myth. Her Dionysus is a boy doll, brought in by two women and examined with gloating curiosity; her Pentheus a transvestite lesbian, dressed like a man. She is brutally murdered as a consequence of entering this exclusive women's domain, and disposed of in the incinerator for sanitary towels. It helps to know *The Bacchae*, but it is by no means essential. The strength of the play resides in the power of the writing, the violence of its situations, and the deliberate "Peeping Tom" element.

In *Solo* her Narcissus is a man, reflecting on his image in a bathroom mirror: again a deft blending of the modern and the ancient mythical.

Olde Tyme, which deals with the castration of Uranus, is in many ways her most interesting and original play, but dramatically the least convincingly realized. It is studded with brilliant, Pirandellian ideas. Her hero is a television tycoon, keeping his employees in slavish dependence. He sustains his confidence with the help of cherished memories of his mother, a queen of the Music Halls. The slaves get their chance to revolt when he hires a derelict theatre and forces them to recreate an old Music Hall evening, with his mother as the star. This he plans to film and preserve for posterity.

Sexual fantasies are enacted, and at last his "mother" appears and punctures with her revelations the whole basis of the tycoon's life. He is destroyed ("castrated") and his minions take over. There are echoes here of Jean Genet's *The Balcony*, but the play's effectiveness is undermined by the lack of credibility of the characters. To dehumanize a three-dimensional character and make him two-dimensional will engage an audience's emotions, but you cannot flatten caricatures.

Among Duffy's other works for the stage are *The Silk Room*, which chronicles the gradual disintegration of a pop group, and a play about François Villon. The unproduced *Megrim* is an expressionist, futuristic fantasy about a secluded society. It combines the nightmarish quality of Fritz Lang's film *Metropolis* with the intellectual daring of the discussions contained in Shaw's late extravaganzas. To these Duffy has added a human, mainly sexual dimension of her own. It makes a rich but probably undigestible concoction.

More modestly, and entirely successfully, *A Nightingale in Bloomsbury Square* shows us Virginia Woolf going though a lengthy creative stocktaking prior to suicide before a spectral audience consisting of Sigmund Freud and Vita Sackville-West. It is an interrupted monologue, written with great sympathy and power.

Duffy is a writer of fierce originality and imaginative depth; hopefully, she will take the opportunity at some point to prove herself to a wider public as a dramatist, too.

—Frank Marcus

DUNBAR, Andrea.

Born in Bradford, Yorkshire, 22 May 1961. Educated at Buttershaw Comprehensive School, Bradford. Has two daughters and one son. Recipient: George Devine award, 1981. *Died 1991.*

Publications

PLAYS

The Arbor (produced 1980). 1980.
Rita, Sue, and Bob Too (produced 1982). 1982; screen version, 1988.
Shirley (produced 1986). 1988.
Rita, Sue, and Bob Too; The Arbor; Shirley. 1988.

SCREENPLAY: *Rita, Sue, and Bob Too*, 1987.

Andrea Dunbar was unique: an original voice, not waving but shouting from the underclass of the North of England, a class that is jobless, school-less, and money-less. Her plays, not so much slices as hacksaw chunks, expose rough life on a Bradford council estate, where family violence is the norm, drinking and fighting the main entertainments, and you're odd one out if you haven't been sexually abused by the time you are 12. Dunbar wrote, not as a middle-class voyeur, but as an active protagonist, and it is this which gives her plays a bleak truthfulness and rich vein of humour. Dunbar's characters, particularly the women, have a resilience and wit that make their actions funny and moving, as well as shocking.

Her first and still most famous play describes family life on a breezeblock estate, inappropriately named The Arbor by some town planner with a sense of humour. A young girl becomes pregnant and her family react in various ways. Her father, a drunken bully, beats her up; her mother, a put-upon but still spirited woman, tries ineptly to help. Her brothers, sisters, and neighbours join in the family battles, which eventually rage up and down the entire street. The girl is sent away to a mother-and-baby home where she learns sums in the morning and nappy changing in the afternoon and comes up against a very different class of people. Figures of authority punctuate this play, as in all Dunbar's others. Social workers, teachers, policemen all attempt to interfere and alter the course of the girl's life. Dunbar sees them as through the small end of the telescope, not necessarily with hostility but with curiosity. They inhabit another world, strange and distant from the lives of the main protagonists. Some of Dunbar's wittiest scenes lie in the addressing of authority across a major gap in life experience.

In *Rita, Sue, and Bob Too* a married man has sex with two under-aged girls, who then compete with each other and with his wife for his favours. Again, violence is never far (a couple of lagers, usually) from the surface, and often quickly erupts. The men visit it upon the women, the women upon each other. It's a fact of life, no better or worse than any other. A black eye or broken tooth is proof of love. Or at least of possession. Thrills in this environment consist of what comes cheap—beer, glue, and sex, with a preference for the last as it comes cheapest of all. But if a girl falls pregnant, she's on her own and she's a sissy if she can't cope.

In *Shirley* Dunbar examines for the first time the relationship between two women. Shirley and her mother, at violent odds with each other at the start of the play, screaming abuse in the presence of their respective alarmed and embarrassed lovers, end by arriving at a tacit understanding of and agreement with each other. Throughout their desperate rows, fuelled by jealousy and the struggle for power over poor and barren territory, the bond between them is evident. They hate and love each other, and have a whole range of explicit curses to demonstrate their passion.

Passion is the keynote of all Dunbar's plays. There's nothing tame or reasoned about them. The major passions are rage, envy, spite, jealousy, and sexual desire. The action proceeds through emotion in a culture which revolves around grabbing what you can, before you are toothless and hairless and old before your time. The plays rarely move outside the boundaries of the estate with its pubs, chippies, bedrooms, and streets. All of life, for its inhabitants, is contained in this isolated cube. They have little apparent curiosity for the outside world and scorn the ways of those not of their kind. Their life may be brutal but it has its mores and niceties like any other, and strangers ignore them at their peril.

Dunbar was not a prolific writer. She remained devoted to the world which created her, the fights and feuds of which charge her work. Women have no rights in her work other than those they kick and bite for. Above all they respect, no, revere, the power of the male, although it be the power to bruise, impregnate, and terrify them. This was not Ripper country for nothing. Nevertheless, these women rise to challenge the terms of their existence and express their anarchy. They cheek policemen, flout the education officer, spit at the social worker. Andrea Dunbar created a band of bloodied but unbowed women whose raw existence is supported, not by the men in their lives, but by the offer of survival techniques from other women: their friends and mothers who've been there before.

—Carole Hayman

DUNN, Nell (Mary).

Born in London in 1936. Educated at a convent school. Married the writer Jeremy Sandford in 1956 (marriage dissolved); three sons. Recipient: Rhys Memorial prize, 1964; Susan Smith Blackburn prize, for play, 1981; *Evening Standard* award, for play, 1982; Society of West End Theatre award, 1982. Agent: Curtis Brown, 162–168 Regent Street, London W1R 5TB. Address: 10 Bell Lane, Twickenham, Middlesex, England.

Publications

PLAYS

Steaming (produced 1981). 1981.
Sketches in *Variety Night* (produced 1982).
I Want, with Adrian Henri, adaptation of their own novel (produced 1983).
The Little Heroine (produced 1988).

SCREENPLAY: *Poor Cow*, with Ken Loach, 1967.

TELEVISION PLAYS: *Up the Junction*, from her own stories, 1965; *Every Breath You Take*, 1988.

NOVELS

Poor Cow. 1967.
The Incurable. 1971.
I Want, with Adrian Henri. 1972.
Tear His Head Off His Shoulders. 1974.
The Only Child: A Simple Story of Heaven and Hell. 1978.

SHORT STORIES

Up the Junction. 1963.

OTHER

Talking to Women. 1965.
Freddy Gets Married (for children). 1969.
Grandmothers. 1991.

Editor, *Living Like I Do* 1977; as *Different Drummers*, 1977.

Nell Dunn was best known in the 1960s and 1970s as a chronicler of the lives of working-class women. The child of a securely middle-class background, with a convent school education, she became fascinated by the haphazard lives of women who existed without the safety net of money or education to sustain them. In 1963 she published a collection of short stories, *Up the Junction*, which consisted of vignettes of life as she had observed it among the young in Clapham. The book, which she later adapted for television, emphasised the vitality and sharpness of perception of the women, together with their accept-ance of the fate life had mapped out for them—a few short butterfly days, followed by a hopeless and unrewarding existence.

In her first novel, *Poor Cow*, Dunn centred on one woman, Joy, whose life from early on is set on a downward spiral. At 22 she has gone through one broken marriage and has a young son, Jonny. As her own life deteriorates, she transfers her hopes onto her son, trusting that his life, at least, will be better. Her epitaph on her own is: "To think when I was a kid I planned to conquer the world and if anyone saw me now they'd say, 'She's had a rough night, poor cow.'" A film was made of the book by director Ken Loach.

Dunn's stage play, *Steaming*, continues her fascination with working-class women and with the character on whom Joy was based in particular: the woman who lives for freedom and fun, but in reality remains a prisoner of her lack of self-confidence and the hard brutalities of life. Josie, the "Joy" figure, is lively, earthy, enjoys leading her men a dance, but invariably ends up the worse for it. "How come I always get hit on the left side?" she asks, after yet another beating up.

Steaming is set in a London Turkish bath, which provides Dunn with the background for what she is best at—women talking among themselves, with-out the constraints of a male presence. The only male, the caretaker of the Baths, is dimly glimpsed through a glass door, unable to enter the female domain. The six characters are a mixture of age and class. Apart from Josie, there is Mrs. Meadow, a repressive mother, who will not let her retarded, overweight daughter take her "plastics" off, even in the shower. There are two middle-class women—Jane, a mature student with a bohemian past, and Nancy, who shops at Peter Jones and whose husband has just left her after 22 years of marriage. The Baths are presided over by Violet, in her forties, who has worked there as attendant for 18 years and who is threatened with early retirement if the Council goes ahead with its intention to close the building.

Not a great deal happens in the play, but the humour and conversation sustain the evening. Without their clothes, and in the steamy companionship of the Baths, the women develop a sisterhood that transcends class barriers. The new entrant, Nancy, at first nervous of the milieu, is drawn in and at one point breaks down and talks about her broken marriage and the pressures that have kept her dependent on a man. Josie reveals that her seeming sexual freedom is also tied to dependence on a man's finances. Their campaign against the closure of the Baths gives them a new lease of life, and by the end Josie, after making a brilliant, if disregarded, speech at a public meeting, says she is going to get an education; Nancy, the rejected wife, announces she is "going to get fucked"; and Dawn asserts herself against her over-protective mother.

Whether this ending is anything more than a way of giving an upbeat finale to the play is a matter for debate, and Dunn's characters will probably find they are not able to change their lives greatly after their temporary euphoria. The dialogue of the working-class women has far more of a ring of truth about it than the dialogue of the middle-class women, but the author has always found a richness and rhythm in working-class speech that she fails to find in the more educated voice. *Steaming* can be regarded as a gentle piece of female consciousness-raising. It must also be one of the few feminist plays to have brought large numbers of male chauvinists in, attracted by the fact that the cast members are nude for much of the time.

I Want, written in 1972 in collaboration with Adrian Henri, is about a love affair between a well-bred, convent-educated girl but "with the devil in her" and a scholarship boy from a Liverpool terrace home. They meet in the 1920's and the play charts the course of their relationship over the next 60 years. It has moments of humour, but lacks the strength of *Steaming*. Dunn also wrote a book of interviews, *Talking to Women*, published in 1965. It is of interest for its recording of the stirrings of "female consciousness" among divergent women. In 1991 she published a sequel in *Grandmothers*. Dunn, herself a grandmother, drew on her own experiences as well as those of her friends to investigate the pleasures and pains of being a grandmother. Based on conversations with 14 of her female friends, it is particularly interesting because of the variety of backgrounds from which her subjects come, and because of the contrast between the traditional image of a grandmother and present-day reality.

Dunn's play *The Little Heroine*, which deals with a young woman's addiction to heroin, was produced during the same year as Granada Television produced her *Every Breath You Take*. This play deals with the effect on a newly divorced woman, Imogen, of finding her 13-year-old son diagnosed as diabetic. Obsessed with Tom's diet and insulin injection, she is unable to concentrate on anything else. In the end it is Tom, mature and sensible for his age, who restores her sense of proportion and helps her rebuild the life and career which she had seemed ready to abandon.

—Clare Colvin

DYER, Charles (Raymond).

Born in Shrewsbury, Shropshire, 7 July 1928. Educated at the Highlands Boys' School, Ilford, Essex; Queen Elizabeth's School, Barnet, Hertfordshire. Served in the Royal Air Force, 1944–47: flying officer. Married Fiona Thomson in 1959; three sons. Actor and director; chair and artistic director, Stage Seventy Productions Ltd. Address: Old Wob, Gerrards Cross, Buckinghamshire, England.

Publications

PLAYS

Clubs Are Sometimes Trumps (as C. Raymond Dyer) (produced 1948).
Who on Earth! (as C. Raymond Dyer) (produced 1951).
Turtle in the Soup (as C. Raymond Dyer) (produced 1953).
The Jovial Parasite (as C. Raymond Dyer) (produced 1954).
Single Ticket Mars (as C. Raymond Dyer) (produced 1955).
Time, Murderer, Please (as C. Raymond Dyer) (produced 1956). 1962.
Wanted—One Body! (as C. Raymond Dyer) (produced 1956). 1961.
Poison in Jest (as C. Raymond Dyer) (produced 1957).
Prelude to Fury (as C. Raymond Dyer) (produced 1959).

Red Cabbage and Kings (as R. Kraselchik) (produced 1960).
Rattle of a Simple Man (produced 1962). 1963.
Gorillas Drink Milk, adaptation of a play by John Murphy (produced 1964).
Staircase (produced 1966). 1966.
Mother Adam (produced 1971; also director: produced 1971). 1972.
A Hot Godly Wind (produced 1975). In *Second Playbill 3*, edited by Alan
    Durband, 1973.
Futility Rites (produced 1980).
Lovers Dancing (produced 1983). 1984.

SCREENPLAYS: *Rattle of a Simple Man*, 1964; *Staircase*, 1969; *Brother Sun and
Sister Moon*, 1970.

NOVELS

Rattle of a Simple Man. 1964.
Charlie Always Told Harry Almost Everything. 1969; as *Staircase; or, Charlie
    Always Told Harry Almost Everything*, 1969.
Under the Stairs. 1991.

MANUSCRIPT COLLECTION: Manchester Central Library.

THEATRICAL ACTIVITIES

DIRECTOR: **Plays**—in London, Amsterdam, Rotterdam, Paris, and Berlin.
ACTOR: **Plays**—roles in 250 plays; debut as Lord Harpenden in *While the Sun
Shines* by Terence Rattigan, 1947; Duke in *Worm's Eye View* by R.F.
Delderfield, 1948–50; Digger in *The Hasty Heart* by John Patrick, 1950;
Wilkie in *No Trees in the Street* by Ted Willis, 1951; Turtle in *Turtle in the
Soup*, 1953; Launcelot Gobbo in *The Merchant of Venice*, 1954; Freddie
Windle in *The Jovial Parasite*, 1954; Maitre d'Hotel in *Room for Two* by
Gilbert Wakefield, 1955; Keith Draycott in *Pitfall* by Falkland L. Cary, 1955;
Dr. John Graham in *Suspended Sentence* by Sutherland Scott, 1955; Horace
Grimshaw in *The Imperfect Gentleman* by Harry Jackson, 1956; Wishee
Washee in *Aladdin*, 1956; Syd Fish in *Painted Sparrow* by Guy Paxton and
E.V. Hoile, 1956; Flash Harry in *Dry Rot* by John Chapman, 1958; Shylock in
The Merchant of Venice, 1959; Viktor in *Red Cabbage and Kings*, 1960; Percy
in *Rattle of a Simple Man*, 1963; Mickleby in *Wanted—One Body!*, 1966.
Films—include *Cuptie Honeymoon*, 1947; *Naval Patrol*, 1959; *The
Loneliness of the Long Distance Runner*, 1962; *Rattle of a Simple Man*, 1964;
The Knack, 1965; *How I Won the War*, 1967. **Television**—*Hugh and I* series,
1964; Charlie in *Staircase*, 1986.

Charles Dyer comments:

Outside bedtime, no one truly exists until he is reflected through the mind of
another. We exist only as we think others think of us. We are not real except in
our own tiny minds according to our own insignificant measurement of
thought.

Animals adapt to their inadequacies without shame or discernible consciousness. Eventually, they wither to nothing, wagging their minds behind them,

and die unsurprised—like frogs. Man is different, and is measured according to breadth of chest, amount of hair, inside leg, bosom and backside. He is insulted by death. He cares. And he cares more about what is seen than is hidden; yet unseen differences have greatest emotional effect.

Such as loneliness.

And I write about loneliness.

Obviously, Man is progressing towards a life, a world of Mind. Soon. Soon, in terms of creation. But with physicalities dismissed, the mind is lonelier than ever. Mind was God's accident. An unfortunate bonus. We should be more content as sparrows, spring-fluttering by the clock; a sudden day, tail-up; then the cock-bird, and satisfaction matter-of-factually; a search for straw; eggs and tomorrow automatic as the swelling of string in water. It happens for sparrows, that is all! Anything deeper is Mind. And Mind is an excess over needs. Therefore Mind is loneliness.

Rattle of a Simple Man and *Staircase* and *Mother Adam* form a trilogy of loneliness, three plays enacted on Sundays, Bells are so damned lonely. Duologues, they are, because two seems the most sincere symbolic number, especially as man plus woman may be considered physically One. My plays have no plots, as such. Action cannot heal loneliness: it is cured only by *sharing* an action, and is emphasised by reduction of plot. And reduction of stage setting—which should, I feel, be expendable once the play is written. I detail a setting for the preparation of each duologue, that its dialogue may relate to a particular room; then, as a casting reflects its mould, the setting becomes irrevocably welded into and between the lines. The potency of these duologues is greater in drapes.

They reprimand me, occasionally, for handicapping my characters either physically or mentally: Cyrenne the prostitute and Percy, male virgin, in *Rattle of a Simple Man*; schizophrenic Adam and arthritical Mammles in *Mother Adam*; homosexual Charlie and nakedly-bald Harry in *Staircase*. And as the Trilogy grew, I locked them into barber shops and attics, depriving them even of a telephone to outside realities. This was a private challenge; yet what interest in an even face? what fault in a crooked smile? I love the courage of my imperfect characters, I despair with them—so small in a world of mindless faces, and faceless minds driving science to God's borders. In *Staircase*, man plus man situation, Charlie and Harry are lost without one another. But Charlie is too proud to admit such a fatal interdependence. He patronises Harry, taunts him, and drops "exciting" names which are anagrams of his own; he refuses to reflect anything of Harry; thus, Harry becomes an anagram, too; and even me, as their author. Charlie, Harry and me, become one; because there is no reality until we are reflected through someone else's eyes.

My characters have hope with their imperfections. They are dismayed by today's fading simplicity; today's lack of humility—no one ever wrong, always an excuse; kissing footballers without respect for the losers; and people who, from the safety of secret conscience, dismiss others as "them."

Man's disease is loneliness; God's is progress.

The opening performance of Charles Dyer's *Rattle of a Simple Man* was given at the Garrick Theatre on 19 September 1962. I had heard that it consisted of a dialogue between a mug and a tart, and, knowing nothing of Dyer's delicacy and integrity, assumed it would be full of equivocal situations. Before the end of the first act I realized I was in the presence of a new and valid talent, possessed to an astonishing degree of the capacity to find pearls among swine. In drunken football fans, in middle-aged, failing homosexual hairdressers, and the half-paralysed relics of tambourine-banging religiosity, Dyer finds not the débris of humanity, but unforgettable gleams of tenderness and self-sacrifice:

> Cyrenne—Been on holiday?
> Percy—I went to Morecambe. There were lots of married couples at the digs. They took a fancy to me. I was always making them laugh. It was marvellous. I think I'll go somewhere else next year, though.

Dyer shows his skill in changing, by the simplest words, the whole mood of a scene. One can tell the very moment the light went out for Percy.

For many years Dyer travelled the country as an actor in provincial productions of London successes; and in Percy's unhappy seaside memories there may well be recollections of drab theatrical lodgings. The two homosexual barbers in *Staircase* are exceptionally bitter on this subject:

> Charlie—Even me honeymoon was a—a—a holocaust: one night of passion and food-poisoning for thirteen. Maggots in the haddock, she claimed.
> (Harry giggles)
> Oh, I was laughing, dear. Yes. What! Lovely—your blushing bride all shivering and turgid in the promenade shelter; hurricanes whipping the shingle. Couldn't even paddle for a plague of jelly-fish.

Dyer considers and reconsiders every aspect of his work, and does not let it go until he has got out of it everything that it contains. Unlike most other eminent contemporary dramatists he is ready, even delighted, to discuss his work, its meaning, and its origin. It is clear that what he puts into his plays is but a small part of his knowledge of the people he writes about. He has written two novels, which have had considerable success, and both are treatments of themes dealt with in his plays, *Rattle of a Simple Man* and *Staircase*. Most people suppose that the novels are rewritings of the plays, but this is not true. The novels are the original work, and the plays follow after.

Thus, though *Rattle of a Simple Man* has an effect similar to that of the *nouveau roman* in that it leaves the audience with a question unanswered, Dyer is really at the opposite pole from writers like Alain Robbe-Grillet and Marguerite Duras. They leave questions open because their philosophy tells them that human knowledge is limited, whereas Dyer ends with an uncertainly only because the wealth of information with which he could resolve it would blur the clear outline of what he wishes to say.

Long before the end of *Rattle* we understand and love Cyrenne and Percy. They are characters, bruised, resilient, and in their ridiculous way curiously dignified, who make for righteousness, because they manifest sympathy and consideration for others. They are in fact people of honour.

That they are so is the basis of Dyer's outlook on the drama. He writes his plays, which are spare and austere in form, according to a classic formula of abiding power. The question with Dyer is not what his characters appear to be, but what they will do in the circumstances in which he places them. It is in my opinion a mistake to consider *Staircase* as primarily a study of homosexuality. Essentially it is a study of how under great stress a man's character may crumble, and then rebound to a level it never attained before.

Dyer is in fact the complement to Anouilh, whom in many ways he rivals in theatrical expertise. Whereas with bitter distress Anouilh discovers the sordidness of purity, Dyer—in this resembling Maupassant—comes upon purity in sordidness. Against dispiriting odds, people are capable of behaving unexpectedly well. This is one reason why Dyer's work is so much more exhilarating than that of even his most distinguished contemporaries. He is a dramatist who indulges neither in self-pity nor in recrimination.

In *Staircase*, presented by the Royal Shakespeare Company 1966–67, Dyer did a very curious thing. He gave his own name to the character played by Paul Scofield. This was the introduction of his theory that everybody is alone. He carries his theme into *Mother Adam*, but in *Staircase* all characters, on and offstage, are woven into patterns of the name Charles Dyer. It is a dramatic device to pinpoint the lack of substance in a man-man relationship where Charlie could not exist without Harry, nor Harry without Charlie. All is loneliness. And each without the other, says Dyer, would be like "a golfer holing-in-one by himself. Nobody to believe him. Nobody to prove his moment ever truly existed." Dyer is at his best when dealing with commonplace aspects of life, and discerning in them the emotional depths of their apparent shallowness. There is something both ludicrous and touching in the way Harry broods over the distresses he suffered as a scout master. Patrick Magee brought real humanity to his task of making tea for Scofield's Dyer, prissy, pampered, pomaded, a ruined god, awaiting a summons for indecent behaviour. To his lurking terror, Mr. Scofield gave a fine touch of injured vanity.

The actor who plays this splendid part—one of the best in modern drama— can be riveting, revolting, and masterly all at the same time: in his sudden bursts of panic, in his vain boastings of a largely imaginary past as a pantomime dame, in his irritability, and in his readiness, in his own terror, to wound his pitiably vulnerable companion.

Mother Adam is Dyer's most ambitious play. Adam's paralysed mother is a tyrant of extreme power, and she brings it to bear on her son, who longs—he thinks—to escape and marry. Despite its consciousness that, in one of Dyer's shining phrases, "There aren't so many silk-loined years," the play is as full of laughter as it is of heartbreak. Its dialogue is rich in curious eloquence and stirring images.

Fine as these things are, it is not in them that Dyer's mastery is to be found, but in his capacity to hold in his mind two conflicting rights, and to see, with a true compassion, that their confrontation cannot be resolved. It is because of this capacity that he has written in *Mother Adam* one of the few tragedies of our time. Adam cannot be free unless his mother is deserted; his mother cannot be cared for unless her son's life is ruined. It is this situation that Charles Dyer observes with a dancing eye and a riven heart.

I say, with the same absolute confidence with which I wrote of Pinter's *The Birthday Party* in 1958, that in the history of the contemporary theatre *Mother Adam* will rank as a masterpiece.

Dyer had previously written two fine and successful plays: *Rattle of a Simple Man* and *Staircase*. *Mother Adam* is better than either. It is more disturbing; it has deeper resonances; it is more beautifully written, with an imagination at once exotic and desperately familiar; it has a profounder pity, and a more exquisite falling close.

Loneliness haunts Dyer's imagination. Is there any solution to this terrible problem? Dyer says there is. Loneliness is the product of selfishness, and where no selfishness is, there is no loneliness. The condition of unselfishness is not easy to attain. It is within reach only of the saints. But sanctity is not an unattainable goal. We should all aim for it.

In *Mother Adam* Dyer seeks the continuing theme of Oneness. Man and mother, almost to the edges of Oedipus. The moment when Adam falls to his knees at the bedside, hugging his mother, dragging her crippled knuckles to his face, begging "Hug me! hug me! I dream of love. I need love," should represent the climax, not only of *Mother Adam*, but of the whole Loneliness Trilogy.

In two of his plays Dyer deals with subjects which, when the plays were first produced, were considered daring. The Lord Chamberlain made 26 cuts in *Staircase*, including the scene in which Harry explains his hatred of the physical side of life. The *Report on Censorship 1967* mentioned *Staircase* throughout 25 of its two hundred pages. Dyer likes to feel he is ahead of trends, but not excessively so: "In terms of eternity, the interval between Adam and Eve's nakedness and the Moment when God cast them forth in animal skins is but a finger click. The serious, most important period is what happens *after* they put on clothes."

We clothe our inadequacies. This is what Dyer's plays are all about.

—Harold Hobson

E

EDGAR, David.

Born in Birmingham, Warwickshire, 26 February 1948. Educated at Oundle School, Northamptonshire, 1961–65; Manchester University, 1966–69, B.A. (honours) in drama 1969. Reporter, Bradford *Telegraph and Argus*, Yorkshire, 1969–72; Yorkshire Arts Association fellow, Leeds Polytechnic, 1972–73; resident playwright, Birmingham Repertory Theatre, 1974–75; lecturer in playwriting, Birmingham University, 1974–78; literary adviser, Royal Shakespeare Company, 1984–88. Since 1988 honorary senior research fellow, Birmingham University. Recipient: John Whiting award, 1976; Bicentennial Exchange fellowship, 1978; Society of West End Theatre award, 1980; New York Drama Critics Circle award, 1982; Tony award, 1982. Lives in Birmingham. Agent: Michael Imison Playwrights, 28 Almeida Street, London N1 1TD, England.

Publications

PLAYS

Two Kinds of Angel (produced 1970). In *The London Fringe Theatre*, edited by V.E. Mitchell, 1975.
A Truer Shade of Blue (produced 1970).
Still Life: Man in Bed (produced 1971).
The National Interest (produced 1971).
Tedderella (produced 1971).
Bloody Rosa (produced 1971).
Acid (produced 1971).
Conversation in Paradise (produced 1971).
The Rupert Show (produced 1972).
The End (produced 1972).
Excuses, Excuses (produced 1972; as *Fired*, produced 1975).
Rent; or, Caught in the Act (produced 1972).
State of Emergency (also director: produced 1972).
Not with a Bang But a Whimper (produced 1972).
Death Story (produced 1972).
The Road to Hanoi, in *Point 101* (produced 1972).
England's Ireland, with others (produced 1972).
A Fart for Europe, with Howard Brenton (produced 1973).
Gangsters (produced 1973).
Up Spaghetti Junction, with others (produced 1973).

Baby Love (produced 1973). In *Shorts*, 1989.

The Case of the Workers' Plane (produced 1973; shorter version, as *Concorde Cabaret*, produced 1975).

Operation Iskra (produced 1973).

Liberated Zone (produced 1973).

The Eagle Has Landed (televised 1973; produced 1973).

Man Only Dines (produced 1974).

The Dunkirk Spirit (produced 1974).

Dick Deterred (produced 1974). 1974.

The . . . Show (produced 1974).

The Midas Connection (televised 1975). In *Shorts*, 1989.

O Fair Jerusalem (produced 1975). In *Plays 1*, 1987.

The National Theatre (produced 1975). In *Shorts*, 1989.

Summer Sports: Beaters, Cricket, Shotputters, Cross Country, Ball Boys (produced 1975; as *Blood Sports*, produced 1976; revised version of *Ball Boys* produced 1977). *Ball Boys* published, 1978; in *The Best Short Plays 1982*, edited by Ramon Delgado, 1982; as *Blood Sports with Ball Boys*, in *Shorts*, 1989.

Events Following the Closure of a Motorcycle Factory (produced 1976).

Destiny (produced 1976). 1976; revised version (produced 1985), 1986.

Welcome to Dallas, J.C., adaptation of a play by Alfred Jarry (produced 1976).

The Perils of Bardfrod, with Richard Crane (produced 1976).

Saigon Rose (produced 1976). In *Plays 1*, 1987.

Wreckers (produced 1977). 1977.

Ecclesiastes (broadcast 1977). In *Plays 2*, 1990.

Our Own People (produced 1977). With *Teendreams*, 1987.

Mary Barnes (produced 1978). 1979; revised version, 1984.

The Jail Diary of Albie Sachs, adaptation of the work by Sachs (produced 1978). 1978.

Teendreams, with Susan Todd (produced 1979). 1979; revised edition, with *Our Own People*, 1987.

The Life and Adventures of Nicholas Nickleby, adaptation of the novel by Dickens (produced 1980). 2 vols., 1982; in *Plays 2*, 1990.

Maydays (produced 1983). 1983; revised version, 1984.

Entertaining Strangers: A Play for Dorchester (produced 1985; revised version produced 1987). 1986.

That Summer (produced 1987). 1987.

Plays 1 (includes *The Jail Diary of Albie Sachs, Mary Barnes, Saigon Rose, O Fair Jerusalem, Destiny*). 1987.

Vote for Them, with Neil Grant (televised 1989). 1989.

Shorts: Short Plays (includes *Blood Sports with Ball Boys, Baby Love, The National Theatre, The Midas Connection*). 1989.

Heartlanders, with Stephen Bill and Anne Devlin (produced 1989). 1989.

The Shape of the Table (produced 1990). 1990.

Plays 2 (includes *Ecclesiastes, The Life and Adventures of Nicholas Nickleby, Entertaining Strangers: A Play for Dorchester*). 1990.

Plays 3 (includes *Our Own People, Teendreams, Maydays, That Summer*). 1991.

The Strange Case of Dr. Jekyll and Mr. Hyde, adaptation of the story by
   Robert Louis Stevenson. 1991.

SCREENPLAY: *Lady Jane*, 1986.

RADIO PLAYS: *Ecclesiastes*, 1977; *Saigon Rose*, 1979; *A Movie Starring Me*,
1991.

TELEVISION PLAYS: *The Eagle Has Landed*, 1973; *Sanctuary*, from his play
Gangsters, 1973; *I Know What I Meant*, 1974; *The Midas Connection*, 1975;
Censors, with Hugh Whitemore and Robert Muller, 1975; *Vote for Them*,
with Neil Grant, 1989.

OTHER
The Second Time as Farce: Reflections on the Drama of Mean Times. 1988.

CRITICAL STUDIES: *David Edgar, Playwright and Politician* by Elizabeth Swain,
1986; *File on Edgar* edited by Simon Trussler, 1991.

THEATRICAL ACTIVITIES
DIRECTOR: Plays—*State of Emergency*, 1972; *The Party* by Trevor Griffiths
(co-director, with Howard Davies), 1985.

A glance at the titles of David Edgar's many plays of the early 1970s will
suggest readily enough to anyone who was aware of the chief social and
political issues of the time in Britain (and not only there) the nature of his early
work. Edgar himself has described his work with General Will between 1971
and 1974 as "pure unadulterated agit-prop," designed to convey information
in an entertaining way and from a socialist standpoint by using satirically the
forms of popular culture—pantomine, comic strip, and the like. The aim was
to elucidate political and economic conditions in general by reference to
particular incidents. In 1973–74 Edgar turned from agit-prop to "become a
social realist," feeling the necessity to "inculcate consciousness" more forcefully and in so doing to create a truly radical "theatre of public life." Several
documentary plays preceded *Destiny* which, through television and radio
adaptations, brought his work before the widest possible audience (though he
is well aware of the problematic nature of the "mass" audience).
   Edgar describes *Destiny* as having an "agit-prop structure"—the dramatic
unit is, as in Brechtian epic theatre, the presentational scene rather than the
traditional long act—but it is the creation of convincing characters (without
the "psychologism" which is anathema to the socialist playwright) rather than
demonstration-room puppets which enables it to communicate so powerfully a
sense of crisis. Though the play spans in epic fashion the period from 1947 (the
year of Indian Independence and the consequent return home of the colonial
army) to the mid-1970's, its main action takes place against the background of
a West Midland by-election campaign and the concurrent unofficial strike of
Asian workers at a local foundry. The growth of the fascist Nation Forward
party, through the power of its racist rhetoric to manipulate widely differing

groups and individuals into a shallow yet dangerous unit of purpose, is coolly examined, and its relation to Conservatism in its many varieties precisely analyzed. Nation Forward gains increasing popular support and the new, tough Toryism, bitter at the loss of empire, shakes off old-style sentimental-paternalist Conservatism, secretly joining forces with the fascists in order to break the Asian strike and to ensure a formidable economic basis for the hard right. The cruel irony of its final plot-twist crystallizes the play's message in terms of the individual: the pathetic local antique dealer (and before that, soldier in India) whose misdirected bitterness had driven him to join Nation Forward and who—as their adopted candidate in the by-election—has been exploited by the party to such good effect, finds out by accident that his shop was taken away from him not by Jewish property speculators (as his mentors had insinuated) but by the same businessmen who are now concluding a secret agreement with his own party leaders.

Wreckers (written for and with 7:84) and *Teendreams* (written with Susan Todd for the feminist group Monstrous Regiment) confirm Edgar's continuing belief in the validity and usefulness of collectively devised agit-prop-type work in the late 1970's. His best work of this period, however, shows a growing interest in the relation between politics and psychology—especially the psychology of suffering. This interest emerges first in *The Jail Diary of Albie Sachs*, an adaptation yet very much Edgar's own play. For the Jewish lawyer Albie, detained under the "90-day" law in his native South Africa, the suffering inflicted upon him by the state is merely destructive, depriving him of moral strength and crushing his will to political action; yet for the eponymous heroine of *Mary Barnes* the suffering caused by mental illness is something to be gone *through* (in her case in a Christ-like way). Alternative therapy, unlike conventional psychiatry, helps her to "go through" her schizophrenia towards the attainment of a stable self. In this way she becomes capable, as many "normal" people are not, of real human relationships. The play avoids the simplistic rubric of the anti-psychiatry fashion of the 1960's—that only the mad are truly sane—while at the same time allowing an implicit socio-political critique to emerge from Mary's schizophrenia and the treatment of it. Yet it is also honest about the dilemmas and conflicts within the alternative community and the causes of its eventual dissolution. *Mary Barnes* is technically an adaptation, but one which—like the immensely popular and widely seen version of *Nicholas Nickleby*, and the more recent post-Freudian *The Strange Case of Dr. Jekyll and Mr. Hyde*—brings into question the value of conventional distinctions between adaptation and original play.

Since his adaptation of *Nicholas Nickleby* (for the Royal Shakespeare Company), Edgar has continued to work on plays with and for particular groups, most recently with *Entertaining Strangers*. Written as a community play for Dorchester (by a "stranger" and on the subject of the rightness of "entertaining strangers" of different kinds), this is nonetheless a rich dramatic text in its own right, sharing significant formal characteristics with a slightly earlier play, Edgar's most important one of the 1980's, *Maydays*.

By way of an epic structure resembling that of *Destiny* (though without the feel of agit-prop), *Maydays* deals with the course of socialism since World War II. With special concentration on the impact of the crucial dates 1956 and 1968, and ending in the election year of 1979, the play attempts to articulate

the shifting relations between history, ideology, and personal belief and commitment by charting the ironically interconnected progress of three men: the
radical son of a vicar who becomes a Trotskyist but who, in the aftermath of
1968, grows disillusioned, is ejected from the party, and ends up in the 1980's
Tory think-tank; a working-class communist who, feeling himself to have been
born too late and into the wrong class, comes in the 1970's to embrace
unquestioningly the authoritarian nationalism of the hard right; and a Russian
army officer who, having been jolted by his experience in Hungary in 1956, is
imprisoned as a dissident in the 1970's, then exiled to the West—where he
finds his views being co-opted and himself used by the same right-wing
authoritarian grouping. The play ends with two very different acts of protest:
the subtle disruption by the Russian exile, Lermontov, of a public function
organized by the right to honour him; and the stand of the women on
Greenham Common. The many ironies built into the plot(s) are characteristic
of Edgar's drama as a whole. Their pointedness and inevitability are intensified
by the rich pattern of echo and counterpoint—in both phrase and idea—that is
created by the continuous juxtaposition of the three narrative strands. The
intensity is both dialectical and emotional: in a play which (among other
things) examines the opposition in political discourse between thought and
feeling, Edgar succeeds in provoking both.

Despite his advocacy of urban "festivals of the oppressed" as the necessary
future for theatre, Edgar's own creative practice seems to have become, in the
late 1980's and early 1990's, ever more social-realist. His play about the 1984
miners' strike, *That Summer*, is not the wide-ranging public drama that might
have been expected, but an intimate, even domestic piece. Indeed, the miners'
strike—although the desperate reality of it is registered forcefully in an indirect
way—is less the subject of the play than the occasion for a witty and even
poignant revaluation of late 1960's radicalism and its relevance in the
Thatcher era. When a generation-of-'68 Oxford history don and his family
play host in a North Wales holiday house to two teenage girls from the Welsh
coalfields, the class- and culture-clashes which inevitably ensue resolve themselves, through a shift of emphasis away from class towards a shared culture of
dissent, in a modest affirmation of the continuity of a tradition of radical non-
compliance. ("That Summer" is both 1984 and 1968). Gay, feminist and anti-
nuclear protesters are not the closest political cousins of the striking miner.

Edgar's response to revolution in eastern Europe was, dramatically speaking, a direct one. Although *The Shape of the Table* is "based on events in a
number of countries, it draws most from Czechoslovakia, and is thus about a
negotiated, essentially pacific and ultimately decisive overthrow of communist
rule." The focus is on "high politics" rather than popular dissent or events on
the street; the excitement of the play is in the manoeuvrings of the incumbent
party leaders in their negotiations for survival with a radical "Public Platform"
opposition led by a Havel-like dissident writer. It is a play of argument and
debate, which clarifies the differing experiences of oppression on all sides and
quietly qualifies the future delights of Western-style democracy. Yet it is also
Edgar's most "playful" piece. The very inevitability of the outcome promotes
in us the awareness of a pattern and irony which are even more pervasive than
in *Destiny* or *Maydays*. The action is shadowed by the characteristic structures
and motifs of fairy tale which are consistently invoked by the opposition leader

Prus, and the progress of negotiations is imaged wittily by the (literal) change of shape of the table which dominates the set. The ironic reversals of plot and situation are acknowledged by the characters themselves. In the final debate, between dissident-become-president Prus and hard-line ex-first secretary, the bluntly sarcastic ex-Titoite Lutz, Prus offers a deal for Lutz's pardon which echoes the one he himself was offered in the very first scene. (Lutz refuses, thereby accepting individual responsibility and imprisonment.) And when the discrediting of an ambitious younger minister of the old regime reveals a Soviet "master-script" for large-scale liberalisation without loss of party domination, the wryly conciliatory ex-prime minister points out to the Dubček figure— an elderly "ghost" at this table from the projected "New Morning" of 1968 —that "this revolution was set in train by the very people who put paid to yours. As Marx perceptively reminds us, the events of history occurring twice. First time as tragedy, the second time as farce."

—Paul Lawley

ELIOT, T(homas) S(tearns).

Born in St. Louis, Missouri, U.S.A., 26 September 1888; became British citizen, 1927. Educated at Mrs. Lockwood's school, St. Louis; Smith Academy, St. Louis, 1898–1905; Milton Academy, Massachusetts, 1905–06; Harvard University, Cambridge, Massachusetts (board member, *Harvard Advocate*, 1909–10; Sheldon travelling fellowship, 1914), 1906–10, 1911–14, AB 1909, AM in English 1910; the Sorbonne, Paris, 1910–11; Merton College, Oxford, 1914–15. Married 1) Vivien (born Vivienne) Haigh-Wood in 1915 (separated 1933; died 1947); 2) Esmé Valerie Fletcher in 1957. Teacher, High Wycombe Grammar School, Buckinghamshire, 1915–16, and Highgate Junior School, London, 1916; tutor, University of London Extension Board, Southall, 1916–19; clerk in the Colonial and Foreign Department, then in charge of the Foreign Office Information Bureau, Lloyd's Bank, London, 1917–25; assistant editor, the *Egoist*, London, 1917–19; regular contributor, *Times Literary Supplement*, London, from 1919; founding editor, the *Criterion*, London, 1922–39; editor, later director, Faber and Gwyer, 1925–28, and Faber and Faber, publishers, London, 1929–65; Clark lecturer, Trinity College, Cambridge, 1926; Charles Eliot Norton professor of poetry, 1932–33, and Theodore Spencer memorial lecturer, 1950, Harvard University; Page-Barbour lecturer, University of Virginia, Charlottesville, 1933; member of the editorial board, *New English Weekly*, London, 1934–44, and *Christian News Letter*, Oxford, 1939–46; visiting fellow, Institute for Advanced Studies, Princeton University, New Jersey, 1948. Joined Church of England, 1927. Recipient: Nobel prize for Literature, 1948; New York Drama Critics Circle award, 1950; Hanseatic-Goethe prize (Hamburg), 1954; Dante Gold medal (Florence), 1959; order of merit (Bonn), 1959; Emerson-Thoreau medal, 1960; U.S. medal of freedom, 1964. Numerous honorary doctorates from U.S. and European universities. OM (Order of Merit), 1948; Officer, Légion d'Honneur, and Commander, Order of Arts and Letters (France), 1950; honorary member, American Academy; foreign member, Accademia dei Lincei (Rome) and Akademie der schönen Künste. *Died 4 January 1965.*

Publications

PLAYS

Sweeney Agonistes: Fragments of an Aristophanic Melodrama (produced 1933). 1932.
The Rock: A Pageant Play (produced 1934). 1934.
Murder in the Cathedral (produced 1935). 1935; subsequent editions 1936, 1937, 1938.
The Family Reunion (produced 1939). 1939.
The Cocktail Party (produced 1949). 1950; revised edition, 1950.
The Complete Poems and Plays. 1952.
The Confidential Clerk (produced 1953). 1954.
The Elder Statesman (produced 1958). 1959.
Collected Plays: Murder in the Cathedral; The Family Reunion; The Cocktail Party; The Confidential Clerk; The Elder Statesman. 1962; as *The Complete Plays*, 1969.

VERSE

"Prufrock" and Other Observations. 1917.
Poems. 1919.
Ara Vos Prec. 1920; as *Poems*, 1920.
The Waste Land. 1922; *A Facsimile and Transcripts of the Original Drafts Including the Annotations of Ezra Pound*, edited by Valerie Eliot, 1971.
Poems 1909–1925. 1925.
Journey of the Magi. 1927.
A Song for Simeon. 1928.
Animula. 1929.
Ash-Wednesday. 1930.
Marina. 1930.
Triumphal March. 1931.
Words for Music. 1935.
Two Poems. 1935.
Collected Poems 1909–1935. 1936.
Old Possum's Book of Practical Cats. 1939.
"The Waste Land" and Other Poems. 1940.
East Coker. 1940.
Later Poems 1925–1935. 1941.
The Dry Salvages. 1941.
Little Gidding. 1942.
Four Quartets (includes *Burnt Norton; East Coker; The Dry Salvages; Little Gidding*). 1943.
A Practical Possum. 1947.
Selected Poems. 1948.
The Undergraduate Poems. 1949.
Poems Written in Early Youth, edited by John Hayward. 1950.
The Cultivation of Christmas Trees. 1954.
Collected Poems 1909–1962. 1963.

OTHER

Ezra Pound: His Metric and Poetry. 1918.

The Sacred Wood: Essays on Poetry and Criticism. 1920.

Homage to John Dryden: Three Essays on Poetry in the Seventeenth Century. 1924.

Shakespeare and the Stoicism of Seneca. 1927.

For Lancelot Andrewes: Essays on Style and Order. 1928.

Dante. 1929.

Charles Whibley: A Memoir. 1931.

Thoughts after Lambeth. 1931.

Selected Essays 1917–1932. 1932; revised edition, 1950.

John Dryden: The Poet, The Dramatist, The Critic. 1932.

The Use of Poetry and the Use of Criticism: Studies in the Relation of Criticism to Poetry in England. 1933.

After Strange Gods: A Primer of Modern Heresy. 1934.

Elizabethan Essays. 1934; as *Elizabethan Dramatists.* 1963; selection, as *Essays on Elizabethan Drama,* 1956.

Essays Ancient and Modern. 1936.

The Idea of a Christian Society. 1939.

Points of View, edited by John Hayward. 1941.

The Classics and the Man of Letters. 1942.

The Music of Poetry. 1942.

Reunion by Destruction: Reflections on a Scheme for Church Unity in South India Addressed to the Laity. 1943.

What is a Classic? 1945.

Die Einheit der Europäischen Kultur. 1946.

On Poetry. 1947.

Milton. 1947.

From Poe to Valéry. 1948.

A Sermon Preached in Magdalene College Chapel. 1948.

Notes Towards the Definition of Culture. 1948.

The Aims of Poetic Drama. 1949.

Poetry and Drama. 1951.

The Value and Use of Cathedrals in England Today. 1952.

An Address to the Members of the London Library. 1952.

Selected Prose, edited by John Hayward. 1953.

American Literature and the American Language. 1953.

The Three Voices of Poetry. 1953.

Religious Drama, Mediaeval and Modern. 1954.

The Literature of Politics. 1955.

The Frontiers of Criticism. 1956.

On Poetry and Poets. 1957.

Geoffrey Faber 1889–1961. 1961.

George Herbert. 1962.

Knowledge and Experience in the Philosophy of F.H. Bradley (doctoral dissertation). 1964.

To Criticize the Critic and Other Writings. 1965.

Selected Prose, edited by Frank Kermode. 1975.

Letters, edited by Valerie Eliot. 1990.

Editor, *Selected Poems*, by Erza Pound. 1928; revised edition, 1949.
Editor, *A Choice of Kipling's Verse*. 1941.
Editor, *Introducing James Joyce*. 1942.
Editor, *Literary Essays of Ezra Pound*. 1954.
Editor, *The Criterion 1922–1939* (18 vols.). 1967.

Translator, *Anabasis: A Poem*, by Saint-John Perse. 1930; revised edition, 1938, 1949, 1959.

BIBLIOGRAPHIES: *T.S. Eliot: A Bibliography* by Donald Gallup, 1952; revised edition, 1969; *The Merrill Checklist of Eliot* by Bradley Gunter, 1970; *A Half-Century of Eliot Criticism: An Annotated Bibliography of Books and Articles in English, 1916–1965* by Mildred Martin, 1972; *T. S. Eliot: A Bibliography of Secondary Works* by Beatrice Ricks, 1980.

CRITICAL STUDIES (a selection): *T.S. Eliot* by Philip R. Headings, 1964; revised edition, 1982; *T.S. Eliot Between Two Worlds: A Reading of T.S. Eliot's Poetry and Plays* by David Ward, 1973; *T.S. Eliot* by Stephen Spender, 1975; *T.S. Eliot: The Critical Heritage* (2 vols.), edited by Michael Grant, 1982; *T.S. Eliot: A Chronology of His Life and Works* by Caroline Behr, 1983; *T.S. Eliot: A Life* by Peter Ackroyd, 1984; *T.S. Eliot: Modern Critical Views* edited by Harold Bloom, 1985; *T.S. Eliot: Plays: A Casebook* edited by Arnold P. Hinchcliffe, 1985; *A T.S. Eliot Companion: Life and Works* edited by F.B. Pinion, 1986; *T.S. Eliot* by Angus Calder, 1987; *Approaches to Teaching Eliot's Poetry and Plays* edited by Jewel S. Brooker, 1988; *T.S. Eliot's New Life* by Lyndall Gordon, 1988; *Poetic Drama* by Glenda Leeming, 1989.

T.S. Eliot became known as a dramatist when his fame as a poet was already well established. In a certain sense, he had always been seen as a "dramatic" poet, and from the outset his criticism was preoccupied with the relation between drama and poetry. His early dramatic theory was anti-naturalist and Symbolist, taking as its models the ballet and the liturgy. After his conversion to Anglicanism in 1927, however, he came to consider the question, "Is the poetic drama possible for our century?" in different terms. In the essay "A Dialogue on Dramatic Poetry", the theatre is proposed not as an aestheticist substitute for orthodox religion but as a medium for the conscious life of a community, a force for cultural cohesion ancillary to religion.

Eliot's first dramatic effort, *Sweeney Agonistes*, subtitled *Fragments of an Aristophanic Melodrama*, was a coda, in parody music-hall rhythms, to the despairing diagnosis of cultural decline in *The Waste Land*. The characters epitomize a terminal and paralyzing boredom and horror at the heart of life. For all the brilliant vernacular vitality of the language, *Sweeney* represents a static, anti-dramatic spectacle, an imaginative stalemate in Eliot's career as a writer. The use of classical Greek drama as a structural analogy, however, was to remain a constant in his stagecraft.

It was perhaps the writing of choruses for the pageant-play *The Rock* that led to the experiment of *Murder in the Cathedral*, an imaginative reconstruction of the martyrdom of Thomas à Becket. The plot is not theatrical in any

usual sense, centred as it is on the spiritual conflict of one character who is
almost completely defined by the sanctity for which he is destined. The events
of the play do not follow a temporal dramatic logic but an "eternal design" of
"action as suffering" which admits of little development; in his preparation for
martyrdom Thomas is assailed by personified temptations, while the instinctive rhythms of human response to the religious mystery are voiced by the
chorus of the women of Canterbury.

The surprising success of *Murder in the Cathedral*, written for a small
church audience at the Canterbury Festival, encouraged Eliot in his belief that
the theatre might offer a solution to the problem of communication between
poet and audience, if existing forms of theatrical entertainment were utilized.
In the essay "John Marston" he applauded the Jacobean dramatists for
managing to operate simultaneously on the level of the groundlings and on
that of the sensitive minority who could appreciate the quality of the poetry.
This "doubleness in the action, as if it took place on two planes at once", is the
strategy adopted in *The Family Reunion*, as in the plays that followed. A
modern, naturalistic outer plot (a matriarch's attempt to install her son as
master of the family estate) is superimposed on an inner, timeless plot (the
spiritual ordeal and conversion of the son, who has murdered his wife),
signalled by the otherworldly presence of the Eumenides. What appears to the
largely unconscious chorus of uncles and aunts to be a drama of "crime and
punishment" is revealed to the conscious protagonist as a drama of "sin
and expiation".

In Eliot's first two plays, surface naturalism is violated by the protagonist's
calling to religious attainment. With *The Cocktail Party*, however, he made a
bid for a larger audience by turning to drawing-room comedy in the Noël
Coward mode. In keeping with the dictum of *Murder in the Cathedral* that
"humankind cannot bear very much reality", the religious message is, as it
were, conveyed in a sugar-coated pill. "Poetry and Drama" concludes that
poetic drama is possible for our century, as long as the poetic element in the
language is strictly subordinated to dramatic utility, muted to the point of
invisibility or "transparence" except at moments of exceptional intensity.
Crucially, the effect of the verse rhythm ought to be largely unconscious; the
vulgar substance of conventional plot would thus satisfy the demands of the
mass of the audience, while the poetic spirit would work on their emotions
without their awareness.

A frequent criticism of the later plays is that the conventional or prosaic
dilution of Eliot's poetic style, though highly successful on its own terms,
entails a corresponding loss of dramatic power and conviction. In *The Cocktail
Party*, for example, the martyrdom of the spiritual aspirant Celia Coplestone is
relegated to offstage status, but the gruesome details of her suffering return to
haunt the reconciling final scene, where they sound harshly dissonant against
the prevailing note of light entertainment.

The vestiges of ritual choreography in *The Cocktail Party*, such as the
libation of the Guardians, are entirely dispensed with in *The Confidential
Clerk*, a farce of mistaken identity in which the higher, analogical level dealing
with vocation and spiritual fatherhood is all but submerged. In spite of box-
office success, many reviewers noted that the cost of a determination to
sanctify the average in human experience is a bloodlessness of character and

feeling, unredeemed by the rather self-regarding morality—exemplified by the obscure and homely Eggerson—of cultivating individual small gardens in accordance with our sphere in life, the duties of our station, and our paternal inheritance of values. Much the same criticisms were applied to *The Elder Statesman*, where Lord Claverton has to come to terms with his own imperfect past, detach himself from his public persona, and learn to love his children before he can find happiness in old age.

Any discussion of Eliot's success as a dramatist must confront the attitudes of patronage and paternalism towards the audience implicit in his theories. In their desire to avoid the élitism of the avant-garde "anti-theatre", his plays did not avoid the dangers of viewing the community in terms of mass civilization and minority culture—the few conscious and the many unconscious—and thus cannot be said to have given expression, as he had hoped, to the ethical awareness of a people. They did, however, significantly further the debate about the possibility of poetic drama in the 20th century.

—Christina Britzolakis

See the essay on *Murder in the Cathedral*.

ENGLAND, Barry.

Born in London, 16 March 1934. Educated at Downside School, Bath. Served in the British Army, 1950–52. Married Diane Dirsztay in 1967; one son and one daughter. Actor in provincial repertory companies, films, and television. Recipient: Arts Council grant; Author's Club award, 1968. Agent: Patricia Macnaughton, Macnaughton Lowe Representation, 200 Fulham Road, London SW10 9PN, England.

Publications

PLAYS

End of Conflict (produced 1961). 1964.
The Big Contract (produced 1963).
The Damn Givers (produced 1964).
Conduct Unbecoming (produced 1969). 1971.

TELEVISION PLAYS: *The Sweet War Man*, 1966; *The Move after Checkmate*, 1966; *An Experience of Evil*, 1966; *You'll Know Me by the Stars in My Eyes*, 1966; *The Man Who Understood Women*, 1967.

NOVEL

Figures in a Landscape. 1968.

Barry England comments:

I am a storyteller. I revere economy and precision.

Barry England is known for one play, *Conduct Unbecoming*. The play's well-deserved success was no doubt partly due to its unfashionably gripping story, with some help perhaps from its fashionable period setting—British India in the 1880's—and its dashing red uniforms. But, although England's approach to his subject matter is a little reminiscent of the equally unfashionable Rattigan's in *The Winslow Boy*, in that he treats a moral conflict in which there is little doubt from the outset who is right and who is wrong, *Conduct Unbecoming* is more than a simple moral tract as it is more than a thriller.

England's dramatic method is that of "putting the screws on." The dramatist chooses a completely enclosed situation, fills it with mutually conflicting characters and then deftly tightens the situation until the pips squeak. In the form of plotting, this method is inevitably an ingredient in almost every sort of play. But it is a question of where the weight of the play finally rests. Do the characters, the stage images, the philosophical, political, or social themes spill over the framework and more or less conceal it? Are they subservient to it, as in farces, thrillers, and court-room dramas? Or almost miraculously created from it, as in Racine or middle-period Ibsen?

It is quite difficult to decide where the weight falls in *Conduct Unbecoming*. An image such as the pig-sticking episode in the second scene makes a most powerful impression in its own right, but loses force for being meticulously absorbed into the final twists of the plot: there is not enough left over to expand in the mind of the audience. For all the subtlety and unexpectedness of the characters, the plot never ceases to contain them, and its neat finish seems to put them away in a box and shut the lid on them. As for England's theme, it is so organic to his method that one must ask whether he has chosen the method to explore the theme or the theme to suit the method.

His earlier plays *End of Conflict* and *The Damn Givers* argue for the primacy of the theme. *End of Conflict* is another army play, set in the New Territories of China at the time of the Korean War. Like *Conduct Unbecoming* its situation arises from the introduction of a new officer into the Mess. Its plotting is looser than that of the later play, but its theme is almost identical—the clash of an individual, still experimental code of behaviour with a traditional, collective code. For all its apparent rigidity, the army's code is shown to be flexible enough to allow good men to behave well. Indeed in *End of Conflict* the real hero is not the liberal-minded rebel who causes disaster by his inexperienced good intentions, but the liberal-minded and experienced conformist. In *Conduct Unbecoming* this clash and its outcome are more complex, but again it is the officer with "bourgeois principles" of honour who triumphs, saving the rebel from himself at the same time as restoring a true sense of honour to the regiment, whose collective pride and inflexibility had corrupted it.

The Damn Givers is a much less convincing piece, perhaps because a group of pleasure-loving socialites makes a less coherent collective than a regiment. The misfit here is a young sex-starved academic and the clash is between his awakened idea of lasting love—after he has slept with the voracious Lady Jane Moore-Fuller-Bracke—and the collective's idea of sex as one pleasure among others to be taken on the trot. England's own lack of conviction in this variation on his basic theme seems to be reflected both in the shadowy characters and the too predictable plot.

Nevertheless, it does seem clear that England's theme comes first. Because it is well defined—there is no suggestion of the infinite perplexities of life beyond the enclosed societies England studies—it is almost perfectly served by a tightly geared plot. The characters too are emanations of the theme, in the sense that their passions stop at discovering the honourable mode of conduct within a given set of rules. But since, at least in the setting of an officers' Mess in the heyday of the British Raj, such people are entirely credible, they can develop an individuality well beyond the limitations of the morality or the cliffhanger. The real strength of *Conduct Unbecoming* is in its delicately orchestrated character studies.

—John Spurling

EVARISTI, Marcella.

Born in Glasgow, 19 July 1953. Educated at Notre Dame High School for Girls, Glasgow, to 1970; University of Glasgow, 1970–74, B.A. (honours) in English and drama. Married Michael Boyd in 1982; one son and one daughter. Playwright-in-residence, University of St. Andrews, Fife, 1979–80; creative writing fellow, University of Sheffield, Yorkshire, 1979–80; writer-in-residence, universities of Glasgow and Strathclyde, 1984–85. Recipient: BBC Student Verse Competition prize, 1971; Arts Council bursary, 1975–76; Pye award, 1982. Agent: Andrew Hewson, John Johnson Authors' Agent, 45/47 Clerkenwell House, Clerkenwell Green, London EC1R 0HT, England.

Publications

PLAYS

Dorothy and the Bitch (produced 1976).
Scotia's Darlings (produced 1978).
Sugar and Spite (revue), with Liz Lochhead (produced 1978).
Mouthpieces (revue; produced 1980).
Hard to Get (produced 1980).
Commedia (produced 1982). 1983.
Thank You For Not in *Breach of the Peace* (revue; produced 1982).
Checking Out (produced 1984).
The Works (produced 1984). In *Plays Without Wires*, 1989.
Terrestrial Extras (produced 1985).
Trio for Strings in 3 (sketch; produced 1987).
Visiting Company (produced 1988).
The Offski Variations (produced 1990).

RADIO PLAYS: *Hard to Get*, 1981; *Wedding Belles and Green Grasses*, 1983; *The Hat*, 1988; *The Theory and Practice of Rings*, 1992; *Troilus and Cressida and La-di-da-di-da*, 1992.

TELEVISION PLAYS: *Eva Set the Balls of Corruption Rolling*, 1982; *Hard to Get*, 1983.

THEATRICAL ACTIVITIES

ACTOR: **Plays**—roles in *Dorothy and the Bitch*, 1976; *Twelfth Night*, 1979; *Sugar and Spite*, 1981; *Mystery Bouffe*, 1982; *The Works*, 1985; *Terrestrial Extras*, 1985; Rhona Andrews in *Visiting Company*, 1988; *The Offski Variations*, 1990. **Radio**—roles in *The Works*, 1985; *The Hat*, 1988.

A rare but consistently recognizable sensibility marks the work of Marcella Evaristi. To explain it, she has frequently remarked on her heritage; part Italian Catholic, part Jewish, altogether Glaswegian. It is a blend that has kept her a significant part of the Scottish theatre scene since her first play, *Dorothy and the Bitch*, in 1976, although her most important plays have had life south of the border in England as well.

Her qualities are seen at their most harmonious in her emotionally powerful play, *Commedia*. Set partly in Evaristi's native Glasgow and partly in Bologna, the drama marries the passionate domesticity of an Italian home in Scotland to the volatile politics of Italy in 1980. As in all her work, she reveals the most intimate details of her characters' private lives with a coroner's attention to opening up wounds, but her concerns in *Commedia* are also the ways in which the broader world determines the fate of the individual.

The play begins with edgy comedy as the adult sons of the widowed Elena bring their wives to Elena's house for their usual Chianti Hogmanay, a Scottish New Year's Eve full of "pasta, pollo alla cacciatore and wine" and seemingly lacking in the traditional whisky and tall, dark stranger "first-footing it" through the door at midnight. But there is a handsome stranger, Davide, a young teacher from Bologna working in Glasgow schools, and working on Elena's heart.

An affair between Davide and Elena, for all its uncertainties caused by a 20-year age gap, brings up less generational conflict than might be expected: the lovers are prepared to work at their differences. Typically for Evaristi, conflict erupts from within the family, from the jealousy of one of Elena's own sons. The men in Evaristi's plays regularly cling to boyhood, while the women accept whatever responsibility is required.

There are fairy-tale elements that promise a happy ending: Elena is entertainingly eccentric from the first and engages the audience's sympathy. She receives the support of an "outsider": Lucy, the American wife of the jealous son, Stefano. Davide's radical left politics provide a philosophy and a circle of friends that accommodate his relationship with Elena. But there is a bitterness in the writing; when Elena and Davide take a holiday in Bologna, it provokes a family showdown which inadvertently leads to the death of her gentler son, Cesare, one of the innocent people killed in the fascist bombing of Bologna's railway station.

The relationship subsequently fails, Lucy leaves Stefano, Elena's late-life freedom is curtailed when Cesare's widow and her daughter move in and, in effect, all the women return to a world without men. A happy ending will remain a fairy-tale until male and female relationships can survive without illusion.

There is a poetic grace and imagination in the best of Evaristi's writing that elevates the most domestic of themes. In *Commedia* Elena's conflicts are encapsulated in a song, "Tin Mags the Kitchen Witch," which divides her character into disciplinarian mother and libertarian witch, a kind of lady of misrule. In a play such as *Wedding Belles and Green Grasses* she follows two sisters and their half-sister through childhood to puberty and first boyfriends; to jobs, marriage, and divorce, lyrically raising the familiar material into ironic understanding through musical repetition of themes with subtle variations for each character.

In her major radio play, *The Hat*, her poetic imagination makes even greater leaps. The world is full of objects which are given voice; an elegant olde worlde mirror observes the troubled relationship of Marianne and her artist lover, Crispin, and comments on it to Marianne's dismay. Other inanimate characters develop conversational relationships with her, including her compact mirror and most importantly her cloche hat. The hat, despised by Crispin, can be seen symbolically as Marianne's sexuality, but the imagery of the play transcends Freud. Crispin's great achievement as an artist is a collage representing Marianne's free spirit. As Marianne establishes her own independence, the collage in its gallery deteriorates and Crispin's only hope of retaining his artistic reputation is to sexually subjugate her once again.

Women remain at the mercy of men in another of her radio plays, a potent reworking of the Troilus and Cressida story, *Troilus and Cressida and La-di-da-di-da*. Fine elevated sentiments from the two lovers begin the play, beautifully stating a bodily and spiritual commitment from each partner. When war intervenes, Troilus reluctantly becomes a soldier and continually restates his love, but Cressida is deprived of his words by other men who prostitute her. Corruption of ideals is again the natural product of male society.

Evaristi also writes well for herself as a performer, appearing in one-woman shows such as *The Offski Variations* where she further investigates the seemingly endless separations of people, from abandoned child to divorcing parents and departing partners, but her best work transcends the strong persona of her own character. She is a lyric dramatist of intense subjectivity, constantly observing the impact of society on the individual.

—Ned Chaillet

EVELING, (Harry) Stanley.

Born in Newcastle upon Tyne, Northumberland, 4 August 1925. Educated at Rutherford College; Samuel King's School; King's College, Durham University (William Black Noble Student, 1950–51), B.A. (honours) in English 1950, B.A. (honours) in philosophy 1953; Lincoln College, Oxford, D. Phil. 1955. Served in the Durham Light Infantry, 1944–47. Married to Kate Eveling. Assistant lecturer, Department of Logic and Metaphysics, King's College, University of Aberdeen, 1955–57; lecturer, Department of Philosophy, University College of Wales, Aberystwyth, 1957–60. Senior lecturer, 1960–83, and since 1984 teaching fellow in philosophy, University of Edinburgh. Since 1970 television critic, the *Scotsman*, Edinburgh. Recipient: Earl Grey fellowship, 1955. Agent: Lemon, Unna and Stephen Durbridge, 24 Pottery Lane, Holland Park, London W11 4LZ, England. Address: c/o Fettes College, Carrington Road, Edinburgh EH4 1QX, Scotland.

Publications

PLAYS

The Balachites (produced 1963). With *The Strange Case of Martin Richter*, 1970.
An Unspeakable Crime (produced 1963).

Come and Be Killed (produced 1967). With *Dear Janet Rosenberg, Dear Mr. Kooning*, 1971.

The Strange Case of Martin Richter (produced 1967). With *The Balachites*, 1970.

The Lunatic, The Secret Sportsman, and the Woman Next Door (produced 1968). With *Vibrations*, 1970.

Dear Janet Rosenberg, Dear Mr. Kooning (produced 1969). With *Come and Be Killed*, 1971.

Vibrations (produced 1969). With *The Lunatic, The Secret Sportsman, and the Woman Next Door*, 1970.

Dracula, with others (produced 1969).

Mister (produced 1970). In *A Decade's Drama*, 1980.

Sweet Alice (as *Jakey Fat Boy*, produced 1970; as *Sweet Alice*, produced 1971). In *Plays and Players*, March 1971.

Better Days, Better Knights (produced 1971).

Our Sunday Times (produced 1971).

Oh Starlings (produced 1971). In *Plays and Players*, March 1971.

The Laughing Cavalier (produced 1971).

He Used to Play for Hearts, in *Christmas Present* (produced 1971).

Caravaggio, Buddy (produced 1972).

Union Jack (and Bonzo) (produced 1973).

Shivvers (produced 1974).

The Dead of Night (produced 1975).

The Buglar (sic) *Boy and His Swish Friend* (produced 1983). 1983.

RADIO PLAYS: *Dance ti Thy Daddy*, 1964; *The Timepiece*, 1965; *A Man Like That*, 1966; *The Devil in Summer*, with Kate Eveling, from a play by Michel Faure, 1971; *The Queen's Own*, 1976.

TELEVISION PLAY: *Ishmael*, 1973.

VERSE
(*Poems*). 1956.

OTHER
The Total Theatre. 1972.

MANUSCRIPT COLLECTIONS: Brandeis University, Waltham, Massachusetts; National Library of Scotland, Edinburgh.

Stanley Eveling comments:

My plays seem, very roughly speaking, to oscillate between reality and unreality, between moral dramas and plays in the absurdist, or, better, Dickensian, tradition. I hanker after the former and still think that *Mister*, a sort of dramatic interface between the fantastic and the real, is the play that says most, though it doesn't have the inventive duplicity and cunning of *Dear Janet* and some others.

If I had to say what theme hovers around in all, it would be that they all seem to have something to do with beleaguered human beings, most often male ones, in circumstances that precisely don't call for his (or her) particular virtues. In *Mister*'s case these are heroic virtues, Nelsonian virtues; in the case of the Oblomovian Jim in *Come and Be Killed*, it is as if he were called upon to exercise the "wrong" virtues, mundane virtues that go with domesticity and responsibility, like asking Shelley to wash the nappies or the Ford Cortina, or so Jim construes it. Alec, in *Dear Janet*, is asked to play a romantic role in a young girl's dream as she is required to fulfil a dreamed-up bit of him. In *The Buglar Boy and His Swish Friend* (the most complicated play, perhaps), the characters themselves, called down from the eternal library of the imagination, attempt and fail to fulfil the tragic requirements of the play's theme, attempt and fail to take on a tragic role at a time, in an age, and with qualities that belong to comedy. This is as close as I want to get. In an as yet unproduced play, *Impossible People*, I see that the theme is that of a man called upon to perform the last male role, that of being subservient to his wife's genius. Naturally he does not succeed.

What is "ridiculous" or "absurd" is that the wrong qualities are also the right qualities, that tragic predicaments happen in comic circumstances, that is, outside the environment which would give them tragic significance. As Janet says of her own work, at the end of the play, it is carried along on "the last ripple left by the receding impulse of tragedy."

Stanley Eveling is a prolific and at first sight a somewhat baffling playwright: he writes in a variety of styles and almost always adopts a veiled, even blurred approach to his subject matter. But although he is a professional moral philosopher as well as a playwright and although his characters often involve themselves in philosophical argument and speculation, his plays are by no means intellectual, in the sense of being elaborately constructed to act as working models of some abstract thesis. Eveling's approach is veiled not because he is hiding the machinery, but on the contrary because he himself seems to write in the act of watching the machinery at work; he sits almost painfully close to the characters, feels them rather than thinks them, and uses one style or another, as he might use one stage or another, as at most a temporary accommodation for his stubborn and chaotic material.

This material is presented in its simplest versions in the two plays *Come and Be Killed* and *Dear Janet Rosenberg, Dear Mr. Kooning*. The first concerns an abortion, the second an abortive relationship between an ageing novelist and his female fan. The muddled, narrowly confined, squalid situations in which the characters find themselves in both plays are compounded by their own muddled, limited, and selfish reactions. "You're not wicked, you're just ignorant," says one character to another in *Come and Be Killed*: this might be a motto for all Eveling's work. Creation in general is messy, cruel, blind, and the lords of creation are no more and no less: in *The Balachites*, Eveling shows a pair of innocents, a modern Adam and Eve, corrupted not by Satan but by the ghosts of dead men; in his nearest thing to an "absurdist" play, *The Lunatic, The Secret Sportsman, and the Woman Next Door*, he shows the pathetic innocence of mental and sexual aberration.

Naturally the idea of there being such creatures as "heroes" in such a world is a fruitful source of still further pain and confusion. The story of Donald Crowhurst, who made it appear that he was winning the *Sunday Times* single-handed yacht race round the world, but turned out to have disappeared, almost certainly overboard, without ever having sailed beyond the Atlantic, forms the basis of Eveling's play *Our Sunday Times*. But he extends the story, as the title implies, to cover a much more widespread form of bogus heroism, of cheaply bought superiority over trivial circumstances, the vicarious act of reading newspapers or watching television. The play's effect is weakened by this attempt at generalization; Eveling steps back too far from his characters. But *Mister*, in which he again treats a would-be sailor-hero, the owner of an antique shop who acts out his fantasy of being Lord Nelson, with the unfortunate complication of having a Lady Hamilton on the premises who is not content with a sexual relationship confined to fantasy, is perhaps Eveling's best play. It is certainly his saddest and funniest, his finest example of what Janet Rosenberg calls "the curious mixture of farce and misery which is the slight ripple left by the receding impulse of tragedy."

Nevertheless, although Eveling's dramatic outlook is on the whole more sad than angry, reminiscent of those world-weary but intermittently kindly doctors in Chekhov's plays, he has written at least one play in which the mixture of farce and misery is replaced by that of savage humour and despair. In *The Strange Case of Martin Richter* a German industrialist employs three ex-Nazis as household servants, not realizing or not caring what this means for his butler, who is of "Swebish" origin and whose father was murdered during the Third Reich for being "Swebish." The butler's solution is to pretend that he himself was a prominent Nazi, claim acquaintance with Hitler, constitute himself "Leader" of a neo-Nazi party and pretend to eliminate the industrialist for being "Swebish." The play ends, after several twists of fortune and a marvellously composed drunken party, with everything as it was, the industrialist once more on top of the evil heap. *Martin Richter* is the nearest thing in Eveling's work to a straight political and moral fable. It is compact and clear, a powerful and bitterly comic outcry against the nastiness, brutishness, and shortness of human life.

Shivvers, Caravaggio, Buddy, and *The Dead of Night* all deal with suicide in one form or another. The central character of *Shivvers*, having for a time assuaged his own sense of guilt by imposing vicious behaviour on a vicar and a whore, commits suicide when they shake off his domination. *Caravaggio, Buddy* is an ambitious comic fantasy—an episodic quest play somewhat reminiscent of *Peer Gynt*—whose hero fails in many attempts to commit suicide and ends up reconciled with society. The play's complex and carefully controlled shifts of style establish in dramatic rather than intellectual terms the reality and humanity of the misfit as against the unreality and inhumanity of the "organized." It is full of delightful comic inventions, such as the colloquy between Buddy and a Yeti on the slopes of Mount Everest, while just off-stage innumerable international expeditions make more or less disastrous assaults on the summit. *The Dead of Night* is a sombre piece—enlivened by a German general trying to disguise himself as a woman—set beside Hitler's bunker in Berlin and featuring the arch-suicide himself.

All three plays show Eveling sharpening his lines and clarifying his construction without losing his closeness to the characters. His themes remain the same, but his methods of exploring them become more precise and versatile.

—John Spurling

F

FLANNERY, Peter.

Born in Jarrow, Tyne and Wear, 12 October 1951. Educated at the University of Manchester, B.A. (honours) in drama 1973. Director, actor, and stage manager, Manchester, 1974–76; playwright-in-residence, Royal Shakespeare Company, London, 1979–80. Member, North West Arts Association drama panel, 1980–85. Recipient: London *Sunday Times* Student Play award, 1978; Thames Television award, 1979; Arts Council bursary, 1980, 1984; John Whiting award, 1982; Beckett award, 1989. Agent: Stephen Durbridge, Lemon, Unna and Durbridge, 24 Pottery Lane, Holland Park, London W11 4LZ, England.

Publications

PLAYS

Heartbreak Hotel (produced 1975). 1979.
Last Resort (produced 1976).
Are You with Me? (produced 1977).
Savage Amusement (produced 1978). 1978.
The Boy's Own Story (produced 1978).
The Adventures of Awful Knawful, with Mick Ford (for children; produced 1978). 1979.
Jungle Music (produced 1979).
Our Friends in the North (produced 1982). 1982.
Heavy Days (produced 1982).
Silence on My Radio (produced 1983).
Blind Justice: Five Screenplays (includes *Crime and Punishment*; *White Man, Listen*; *The One About the Irishmen*; *A Death in the Family*; *Permanent Blue*) (televised 1988). 1990.
Singer (produced 1989). 1989.

RADIO PLAYS: *Small Talk*, with Elizabeth Gamlin, 1986; *Singer*, 1992.

TELEVISION PLAYS: *Our Friends in the North: Seven Screenplays* (includes *One Man, One Vote*; *Public Relations*; *Honour*; *Conspiracies*; *Pictures*; *Power*; *Mysteries*), 1984; *Warhill*, 1985; *Blind Justice: Five Screenplays*, 1988; *Shoot the Revolution*, 1990.

Peter Flannery, son of two generations of Jarrow shipyard workers, studied drama at Manchester University, planning to be a director. He was soon writing, however: *Heartbreak Hotel*, a rock musical; the 75-minute *Last Resort*, in which a peculiar group of people meet beside the Punch and Judy show on Blackpool beach; the one-character *The Boy's Own Story*, in which a goalkeeper explains himself between saves; and *Jungle Music*, Brecht's *In the Jungle of the Cities* as musical, updated and moved to Manchester.

Flannery first drew attention with *Savage Amusement*, staged by the Royal Shakespeare Company at the Warehouse in 1978. Set in 1982, after a Tory election victory (then in the future), four young drop-outs squatting in Hulme in south Manchester realise their dependence on a strange, detached working-class youth, and, more important, reveal a crumbling, frightening environment. Flannery explained his subject in *The Warehouse Papers*: "I was concerned about what young people in Hulme might grow up thinking and hoping. . . . Whose fault is Hulme? Can or should people from outside get involved with the place? What happens if Hulme continues to deteriorate? . . . If I am living in a society founded on civilised values, then what went wrong? . . . Though I am aware that poverty *is* a political issue, the play attempts no political solutions." Michael Billington noted that, though Flannery sympathized with his characters, he also showed "their powerlessness in the face of disintegration." More than this, Flannery created a unique and disturbing world of fear and threat, of wilderness and concentration camp, of a collapsing social fabric.

Small Talk, a sensitive study of childlessness, for radio in 1986, was followed in 1988 by the five-part *Blind Justice*, among the very few television scripts to be published. Two "alternative" lawyers, a man and a woman, dealt with various cases raising awkward questions about the legal system. Flannery visited Romania in 1990 before writing, again for television, *Shoot the Revolution*, about the fall of Ceausescu in December 1989. Using news film and a narrator, the situation in Romania was illustrated by a secret policeman, his ineffectual liberal teacher brother, a peasant girl, and an actress representing the intellectuals.

In his introduction to the text of *Blind Justice* Flannery says that he belongs "among that small band of writers which still wants to write about the big picture." This is what he has done in his two epic condition-of-England plays, *Our Friends in the North* and *Singer*.

Our Friends, episodic and ambitious, spans 1964 to 1979, with scenes in Newcastle, Soho, Scotland Yard, Parliament, and Rhodesia. Flannery expects his audience to know its British history for this period, and to pick up on his allusions to the scandals around Poulson and Dan Smith in the northeast in the 1960's. The three main plot threads are the ties between an unprincipled architect and a complacent local Labour party; corrupt police failing to act against vice in London; and the pretence that genuine sanctions were imposed on Rhodesia after the unilateral declaration of independence in 1965. The threads are linked by the parallel biographies of two Newcastle boys, one disillusioned after experience of Labour politics, the other somehow educated to understand power through crime and a spell as a mercenary in Rhodesia. The play ends with the latter and a prostitute apparently about to machine-gun a P.R. man as he leaves a restaurant, perhaps also to shoot an M.P., an oil executive, a civil servant, and three top policemen, heard but not seen in the closing minutes. *Our Friends* is about the decline and disappearance of principles and how even innocents become involved in corruption. Parliamentary democracy appears ineffective. *Our Friends* was re-written as an 11-part TV serial for the BBC, but appears to have been blocked because of the possible legal implications of its characters' being based on real people.

Flannery was prompted to write *Singer* by reading Shirley Green's biography of Peter Rachman, who became notorious nationally at the end of the 1950's as an unscrupulous and wealthy slum landlord. From the biography Flannery learned that Rachman was a survivor of the concentration camps. This led him into a year's research, a strong response to the books of Primo Levi, and so to a play about "a man's rapaciousness and the reasons behind it." The scale was Jacobean, five acts with prologue and epilogue, so *Singer* was well suited to be the first modern play staged in the Royal Shakespeare Company's Swan theatre at Stratford-on-Avon.

Chorus speeches give us briefly the dates, from wartime ("a time, and what a time, when war was not a crime but a crusade"), through Harold Wilson's 1960's ("Now the white heat of technological revolution dazzles the eyes and all the youth of England are on fire") to the Thatcherite 1980's, the years of "the Great Housekeeper, with fox-like cunning, lion's strength, and matching crocodile accessories."

Singer, a Polish Jew, is first seen as a prisoner in Auschwitz, already a wheeler-dealer, with his nephew Stefan and the German Communist, Manik, both of whom accompany him to Britain after the war. Soon he is dealing in nylons and frying pans from a public telephone box in Bayswater, charming young women (he resembles Krank in John Arden's *Waters of Babylon*), then rising to riches in property deals, evicting elderly sitting tenants. He obtains British citizenship, entertains the upper classes at a party, and at the end of Act 3 drowns in a Hampstead pond. Reappearing, he woos a girl whose crippled father proves to have been a guard at Auschwitz. He delivers soup to the homeless on the South Bank but then is led into a scheme to provide "camps" for the homeless. He has, meanwhile, found Stefan, now a photographer, who also paints scenes from the camps so that the Holocaust will be remembered: finally Stefan kills himself.

The drama is memorable for the huge title role originally played by Antony Sher. *Singer* explores the immigrant experience, the legacy of Nazism, the need to remember—Auschwitz, the Rachman era, the 1980's failing to learn from Rachman's exploitation. For Neil Taylor *Singer* was "a parable to explain the nature of modern Britain and, at the same time, the moral significance of such universals as memory and guilt."

Flannery's major stage plays require enormous casts, while all his work is controversial and anti-Establishment. One hopes that both the Royal Shakespeare Company and television companies will continue to find a place for his necessary and challenging work.

—Malcolm Page

FORSYTH, James (Law).

Born in Glasgow, Lanark, 5 March 1913. Educated at Glasgow High School, graduated 1930; Glasgow School of Art, diploma in drawing and painting 1934. Married 1) Helen Steward in 1938 (divorced 1953), two sons; 2) Louise Tibble in 1955. Served in the Scots Guards, 2nd Monmouthshire Regiment, 1940–46: captain, battalion adjutant; Bronze Cross of the Netherlands. Worked with the General Post Office Film Unit, 1937–40; dramatist-in-residence, Old Vic Company: worked with the Old Vic School and the Young Vic, 1946–48; dramatist-in-residence, Howard University, Washington, D.C., 1962; guest director and lecturer, Tufts University, Medford, Massachusetts, 1963; distinguished professor-in-residence, Florida State University, Talla-hassee, 1965; director, Tufts University Program in London, 1967–71. Since 1972 artistic director, The Forsyths' Barn Theatre, Ansty, Sussex. Member of the Executive Council, League of Dramatists and Radio Writers Association, 1954–64; founding member, Theatres Advisory Council, Recipient: Arts Council bursary, 1980. Agent: Cecily Ware, 19-C John Spencer Square, London N1 2LZ; or, Harold Freedman, Brandt and Brandt, 1501 Broadway, New York, New York 10036, U.S.A. Address: Grainloft, Ansty, Haywards Heath, Sussex RH17 5AG, England.

Publications

PLAYS

Trog (broadcast 1949; produced 1959).

Brand, adaptation of the play by Ibsen (broadcast 1949; produced 1964). 1960.

The Medicine Man (produced 1950).

Emmanuel: A Nativity Play (broadcast 1950; produced 1960). 1952.

Héloïse (broadcast 1951; produced 1951). In *Three Plays*, 1957.

The Other Heart (broadcast 1951; produced 1952; also director: produced 1963). In *Three Plays*, 1957; revised version, as *Villon*, music by Gardner Read (produced 1981).

Adelaise (broadcast 1951; produced 1953). In *Three Plays*, 1957.

Three Plays. 1957.

The Pier (televised 1957; produced 1958).

The Road to Emmaus: A Play for Eastertide. 1958.

Joshua, music by Franz Waxman (produced 1960). 1959.

Dear Wormwood, adaptation of *The Screwtape Letters* by C.S. Lewis (pro-duced 1965). 1961; as *Screwtape*, 1973.

Fifteen Strings of Money, adaptation of a play by Guenther Weisenhorn based on a story by Chu Su-chen (produced 1961).

Everyman (produced 1962).

Defiant Island (produced 1962). 1975.

Seven Scenes for Yeni (produced 1963).

Cyrano de Bergerac, adaptation of the play by Edmond Rostand (produced 1963). 1968.

If My Wings Heal (produced 1966).

Four Triumphant (televised 1966; as *Festival of Four*, produced 1976).

What the Dickens, adaptation of the novel *The Pickwick Papers* by Dickens
  (produced 1974).
Lobsterback (produced 1975).
No Crown for Herod (as *Christmas at Greccio*, produced 1976). 1977.
The Play of Alban (produced 1977).
"N" for Napoleone (produced 1978).
When the Snow Lay Round About (broadcast 1978; as *Wenceslas*, produced
  1980).
A Time of Harvest (produced 1981; as *The Threshing Floor*, broadcast 1982).

SCREENPLAYS: *The End of the Road*, with Geoffrey Orme, 1954; *Francis of
Assisi*, with Eugene Vale and Jack Thomas, 1961.

RADIO PLAYS: *The Bronze Horse*, 1948; *Trog*, 1949; *Brand*, 1949; *Emmanuel*,
1950; *Seelkie*, music by Brian Easdale, 1950; *The Other Heart*, 1951;
Adelaise, 1951; *Héloïse*, 1951; *The Nameless One of Europe*, 1951; *For He's
a Jolly Good Fellow*, 1952; *Pig*, 1953; *The Festive Spirit*, 1955; *Lisel*, 1955;
Christophe, 1958; *Every Pebble on the Beach*, 1963; *When the Snow Lay
Round About*, 1978; *The Threshing Floor*, 1982.

TELEVISION PLAYS: *Old Mickmack*, 1955; *The Pier*, 1957; *Underground*, from a
novel by Harold Rein, 1958; *Four Triumphant*, 1966; *The English Boy*, 1969;
The Last Journey, 1972; *The Old Man's Mountain*, 1972.

OTHER
Tyrone Guthrie: A Biography. 1976.
Back to the Barn. 1986.
The Clearing Where the Cuckoo Came. 1992.

MANUSCRIPT COLLECTION:
Lincoln Center Library of the Performing Arts, New York.

THEATRICAL ACTIVITIES
DIRECTOR: **Play**—*The Other Heart*, 1963.

James Forsyth comments:

(1982) The plays themselves being the playwright's *more than* personal statement to the public, I am reluctant to make other statements. I say "more
than personal" and I say "play*wright*" (not playwrite) for these reasons: That
Theatre, where it is more than a show for Entertainment or Propaganda
purposes, is an Art—an all-arts Art—and in Art the thing wrought out of the
raw material is a thing in itself and speaks for itself. I *wright* for the Theatre as
a performing place for the Art of Theatre, a tough and practical and popular
art. The *writing* of the playwright is only the recording art which ends up with
a script. The script ends up with "the thing itself" which is the event, the
production. And it is all *wrought* out of the many arts of the playwright in the
fields of sight, sound, touch, etc., realized in any playhouse by all the contribu-
tory arts of those who were once, and accurately, referred to as "artistes."

I had started life as an artist painter and sculptor, and my apprenticeship to the art of the theatre, with the Old Vic Company of Guthrie and Olivier, gave me a taste for the all-arts theatre and also for epic theatre. I am a playwright because I have found that the live event of the play is the best occasion in the world for the communion with—the sharing of artistic experience with—an audience; and the art of Theatre is the best medium for creation of the concepts worth sharing.

But the all-arts theatre is a hard road in a world of theatre brutally constricted by cash considerations, a constriction relieved only a bit by subsidy of certain playhouses and the heroism of "fringe" and "off-off" companies. That is why I have directed, for the last ten years, my own plays in my own barn which is a natural playhouse with an enthusiastic audience and a company of so-called "amateurs" who have become professed to the Art of Theatre to a professional degree. But in turning away in some despair from the world of the professional theatre and showbiz in its present state to this limited but real local success in the art, I have not of course "made a living" from it, which begins to make this statement more "personal" than necessary. But by the subsidy of an Arts Council bursary I have been able to complete what could be my most important play, *The Spanish Captain.*

Craft is fundamental to all art, although not all craftsmen are artists, any more than every artist is a craftsman. Indeed today, as artists are promoted by PRs, craft has become somewhat unfashionable. Hence the well-made play has, of recent years, come to be regarded as something slightly old-fashioned. Yet the virtue of a well-made play is that it knows how to tell a story, how to hold an audience, and this is an essential part of the dramatist's craft.

James Forsyth is such a playwright and this term is perhaps the most pat of all for an author who has himself said (January 1972): "I have yet to wright my best play. And 'wright' is right, I am not a 'dramatist,' I am a 'playwright.' Drama is the stuff, plays are the works, and I am professed to works."

His works are prolific, a steady output over the years, from the Old Vic production of *The Other Heart* to a television series on the patron saints of England, Scotland, Ireland and Wales, to *The Last Journey*, a 90-minute television play on Tolstoy.

The Other Heart is one of Forsyth's strongest and most powerfully constructed plays and full of excellent small character studies such as that of Marthe, the servant, who when asked why she risks her life in coming to Paris during the plague replies, "I need to help." In the character of the romantic poet, François Villon, Forsyth catches marvellously the impetuosity of young love, and the radiant recklessness of the visionary and poet. They are qualities that seem to attract him again and again. While he is drawn to "wrighting" plays about historical characters, it is noticeable how many of them are variations upon the theme of "a pair of starcrossed lovers." In this play we have Villon and Catherine de Vausselles; we have also Francis and Clare in *If My Wings Heal*, Héloïse and Abelard in *Héloïse*; in *The Last Journey*, a study of the last days of Tolstoy, Forsyth has written brilliantly of the tragic gap between a husband and wife.

The clash of the idealist with reality is perhaps, however, the profoundest recurring theme in all Forsyth's work. It has attracted him to a powerful adaptation of Ibsen's *Brand*, and in *If My Wings Heal* he sets out to explore the conflict between St. Francis of Assisi, the creative artist, poet, visionary, and Brother Elias, the ambitious administrative genius of the Franciscan Order. It was Brother Elias who wanted to turn the Friars Minor into the most powerful order within the Church, "for the sake of possession, for the possession of power." As one of the Friars remarks, "It was never Brother Francis's idea that we should be other than small bands, always on the move. We were to be the salt which is scattered."

This is a tougher and less sentimental rendering of the story of Francis of Assisi than the *Little Plays of St. Francis* by Laurence Housman, or the five-act devotional drama by Henri Ghéon, *The Marriage of St. Francis*. Only the scene of the stigmata fails. Perhaps it is an impossibility—to put on the stage a mystical experience. Perhaps only a major poet, such as T. S. Eliot, whose insight into the transcendental was close to that of the great mystics themselves, could really tackle such a scene. If Forsyth is a playwright proven he is, I think, a poet *manqué*. His weakest writing stems almost always from a tendency to poeticize, to lapse into obvious rhyming blank verse. Yet in theatre terms one can see what he is about for the steady beat and rhythm of these passages serve to carry the story forward.

David, *Andrew*, *Patrick*, and *George* (*Four Triumphant*) are four full-length plays, envisaged as a cycle, to be performed over two days. They embody not merely the history of the four patron saints but are a study of the pioneers of Christianity. Each play is self-sufficient, and yet each gains from its relation to the others.

Perhaps Forsyth's most memorable play is *Defiant Island*, the true story of Henri Christophe, the first black king of Haiti. It is a deeply moving tragedy of an idealist who is led astray by his fanatical devotion to his own ideals, so that the man is destroyed at the expense of the image of himself as the first black monarch. Finally, when Napoleon insists on "nothing less than the total extinction of every adult black, male and female," Henri Christophe, who had naively believed that all men could meet in equal justice, has to admit to himself, "I asked too much. It is a fault in me."

Henri Christophe, Brand, Abelard, Villon, Francis of Assisi are all portraits of men of thought suffused with passion; they are the solitary visionaries, the reckless romantics, the uncomfortable reformers; in the true sense of the word they are heroes. Forsyth belongs to that great tradition of bardic poets, who sang the exploits and epics of heroes. It is a tradition that is at present a little out of fashion, but fashions change and the wheel comes full circle. When that happens Forsyth will find he has wrought his best play.

—James Roose-Evans

FRAYN, Michael.

Born in Mill Hill, London, 8 September 1933. Educated at Sutton High School for Boys; Kingston Grammar School, Surrey; Emmanuel College, Cambridge, B.A. 1957. Served in the Royal Artillery and Intelligence Corps, 1952–54. Married Gillian Palmer in 1960 (marriage dissolved 1990); three daughters. Reporter, 1957–59, and columnist, 1959–62, the *Guardian*, Manchester and London; columnist, the *Observer*, London, 1962–68. Recipient: Maugham award, 1966; Hawthornden prize, 1967; National Press award, 1970; *Evening Standard* award, for play, 1976, 1981, 1983, 1985; Society of West End Theatre award, 1977, 1982; British Theatre Association award, 1981, 1983; Olivier award, 1985; New York Drama Critics Circle award, 1986; Emmy award, 1990; *Sunday Express* Book of the Year award, 1991. Honorary fellow, Emmanuel College, 1985. Lives in London. Agent: Elaine Greene Ltd., 37 Goldhawk Road, London W12 8QQ, England.

Publications

PLAYS

Zounds!, with John Edwards, music by Keith Statham (produced 1957).

Jamie, On A Flying Visit (televised 1968). With *Birthday*, 1990.

Birthday (televised 1969). With *Jamie, On a Flying Visit*, 1990.

The Two of Us (includes *Black and Silver, The New Quixote, Mr. Foot, Chinamen*) (produced 1970; *Chinamen* produced 1979). 1970; *Chinamen* published in *The Best Short Plays 1973*, edited by Stanley Richards, 1973; revised version of *The New Quixote* (produced 1980).

The Sandboy (produced 1971).

Alphabetical Order (produced 1975). With *Donkeys' Years*, 1977.

Donkeys' Years (produced 1976). With *Alphabetical Order*, 1977.

Clouds (produced 1976). 1977.

The Cherry Orchard, adaptation of a play by Chekhov (produced 1978). 1978.

Balmoral (produced 1978; revised version, as *Liberty Hall*, produced 1980; revised version, as *Balmoral*, produced 1987). 1987.

The Fruits of Enlightenment, adaptation of a play by Tolstoy (produced 1979). 1979.

Make and Break (produced 1980). 1980.

Noises Off (produced 1981). 1982.

Three Sisters, adaptation of a play by Chekhov (produced 1985). 1983.

Benefactors (produced 1984). 1984.

Wild Honey, adaptation of a play by Chekhov (produced 1984). 1984.

Number One, adaptation of a play by Jean Anouilh (produced 1984). 1985.

Plays I (includes *Alphabetical Order, Donkey's Years, Clouds, Make and Break, Noises Off*). 1986.

The Seagull, adaptation of a play by Chekhov (produced 1986). 1986.

Clockwise (screenplay). 1986.

Exchange, adaptation of a play by Yuri Trifonov (broadcast 1986; produced 1989). 1990.

Uncle Vanya, adaptation of a play by Chekhov (produced 1988). 1987.

Chekhov: Plays (includes *The Seagull, Uncle Vanya, Three Sisters, The Cherry Orchard,* four vaudevilles). 1988.
The Sneeze, adaptation of works by Chekhov (produced 1988). 1989.
First and Last (televised 1989). 1989.
Look Look (as *Spettattori,* produced 1989; as *Look Look,* produced 1990). 1990.
Listen to This: 21 Short Plays and Sketches. 1991.
Plays 2 (includes *Benefactors, Balmoral, Wild Honey*). 1992.
Here (produced 1993). 1993.

Screenplay: *Clockwise,* 1986.

Radio play: *Exchange,* adaptation of a play by Yuri Trifonov, 1986.

Television plays and documentaries: *Second City Reports,* with John Bird, 1964; *Jamie, On a Flying Visit,* 1968; *One Pair of Eyes,* 1968; *Birthday,* 1969; *Beyond a Joke* series, with John Bird and Eleanor Bron, 1972; *Laurence Sterne Lived Here* (*Writers' Houses* series), 1973; *Imagine a City Called Berlin,* 1975; *Making Faces,* 1975; *Vienna: The Mask of Gold,* 1977; *Three Streets in the Country,* 1979; *The Long Straight* (*Great Railway Journeys of the World* series), 1980; *Jerusalem,* 1984; *First and Last,* 1989.

Novels
The Tin Men. 1965.
The Russian Interpreter. 1966.
Towards the End of the Morning. 1967; as *Against Entropy,* 1967.
A Very Private Life. 1968.
Sweet Dreams. 1973.
The Trick of It. 1989.
A Landing on the Sun. 1991.
Now You Know. 1992.

Other
The Day of the Dog (*Guardian* columns). 1962.
The Book of Fub (*Guardian* columns). 1963; as *Never Put Off to Gomorrah,* 1964.
On the Outskirts (*Observer* columns). 1967.
At Bay in Gear Street (*Observer* columns). 1967.
Constructions (philosophy). 1974.
Great Railway Journeys of the World, with others. 1981.
The Original Michael Frayn: Satirical Essays, edited by James Fenton. 1983.
Editor, *The Best of Beachcomber,* by J.B. Morton. 1963.

Critical study: introduction by Frayn to *Plays 1,* 1986.

Michael Frayn deplored the "didactic drive" of the 1970s because it replaced drama by ideology. Like his contemporary Alan Ayckbourn, Frayn consciously distinguished his work from the political drama that was sweeping the English stage at the beginning of the 1970s, asserting a return to traditional comic values. In contrast to Joe Orton, who treated tragic material as farce for shock effect, Frayn makes farce a way of exposing the insensitivity of stock responses through showing potential tragedy beneath the comic surface. Laughter in Frayn is therefore frequently ambiguous, as in *Alphabetical Order*:

Lucy: (. . . *starts to laugh again*) . . . I'm sorry. It's not funny!
Nora: It's not at all funny.
John: It's what one might call tragic irony. (*He starts to laugh*)

Frayn deals with society in terms of organizations—the news media, a manufacturing industry, the commercial theatre—which intrinsically threaten the survival of humanity. Deadening order is always subverted, however unintentionally; and the life force triumphs, though at the expense of what the individuals concerned are striving for. Thus the newspaper library of *Alphabetical Order* is overwhelmed by the accretion of trivia in the piles of yellowing newsprint. While the instant redundancy of all the facts recorded in these clippings satirizes the illusory nature of what our news-fixated culture considers important, the confusion of the library files is presented as organic: a sign of individualism surviving even in what is (taking newspaper-slang literally) a "morgue."

According to Frayn, what his plays "are all about . . . is the way in which we impose our ideas upon the world around us. In *Alphabetical Order* it is by classification, in *Make and Break* by consumption." This approach takes the form of challenging the way audiences perceive what they see on stage, and is closely related to the subjects of his plays: the way news-reportage categorizes events (in *Alphabetical Order*), or the difference between socialist and capitalist views of the world, as in *Clouds* (which reflects Frayn's disorienting experiences as a journalist in Cuba).

His most successful play, *Noises Off*, applies this to the theatre itself, taking as its title the technical term for behind-the-scenes activity that breaks the theatrical illusion. It juxtaposes backstage action with the rehearsal and performance of a mirror text: *Nothing On*, a highly artificial farce that echoes Ben Travers's *Rookery Nook*. The characters are stock figures on two overlapping levels. As actors they are the drunken old-stager, the short-sighted sex symbol, and the fading television star investing in her own show to finance retirement. And they are cast as Shavian Burglar (à la *Heartbreak House*), dumb blonde, and comic servant (duplicating the television soap role in which the aging actress made her name).

The catalyst on both back- and on-stage levels is the director. His casual affairs with both the sex symbol and the assistant stage manager (hired because her father's firm is sponsoring the production), are a real-life version of the on-stage characters' sexual activities. This behind-the-scenes promiscuity progressively disrupts the performance that he has so carefully organized in the rehearsal.

The Act I dress-rehearsal of *Nothing On* demonstrates the fragility of the ordered precision on which the performance of farce depends. Lines are forgotten, entries missed, doors jam at crucial moments or won't close; and the comedy misfires completely. It is the incompetence of the actors, not the antics of the characters, that is funny.

In the second Act—when the perspective is reversed, showing us the set from behind—the humour comes from mistaken motives and a series of emotional crises (typical of farce) that afflict the actors in the wings. The complete silence imposed on them by the ongoing performance just the other side of the thin scenery, magnifies their misunderstandings and frustrations into hysterical comedy. In fact, *Noises Off* outdoes *Nothing On* in every way. The activity behind the scenes results in double the number of men with trousers round their ankles (including the director), and two semi-nude girls instead of the one in *Nothing On*. The chaos distorts the unseen performance, finally eclipsing it, when the assistant stage manager's announcement of her pregnancy rings out through the theatre just after the curtain-lines (which are greeted with a deadly silence from the imaginary audience of *Nothing On*).

As Frayn comments: "The fear that haunts [the cast] is that the unlearned and unrehearsed—the great dark chaos behind the set, inside the heart and brain—will seep back on to the stage. . . . Their performance will break down, and they will be left in front of us naked and ashamed." And this fear is realized in the final Act, some months later in the tour, when the mayhem behind the scenes has indeed spread onto the stage. As the performers hit each other over the head, or are tripped down the backstage stairs from the "bedroom" as they exit, the stage manager is forced to enter as a stand-in for one after another, only to have the injured actor stagger into view while he is still on the set. This culminates in no fewer than three comic burglars appearing when the old soak misses his entry. Believing him to be drunk, the stage manager dashes on stage to say his crucial lines—as does the director, believing the stage manager is already on in another role—followed by the drunken actor himself. Under the pressure of such physical chaos the dialogue, uncertain at the best of times, disintegrates. In desperation the cast drag down the curtain between them and the audience.

This open theatricality—where people are presented as performers, and their social context is a stage set, so that everything relates to drama—is characteristic of the most inventive contemporary comedy, being shared by Trevor Griffiths, Peter Barnes, and Tom Stoppard.

—Christopher Innes

See the essay on *Noises Off.*

FRIEL, Brian (Bernard Patrick Friel).

Born in Killyclogher, County Tyrone, 9 January 1929. Educated at St. Columb's College, Derry, 1941–46; St. Patrick's College, Maynooth, 1946–49, B.A. 1949; St. Mary's Training College (now St. Joseph's College of Education), Belfast, 1949–50. Married Anne Morrison in 1954; four daughters and one son. Schoolteacher in primary and intermediate schools in Derry, 1950–60. Since 1960 full-time writer: founder, with Stephen Rea, Field Day Theatre Company, Northern Ireland, 1980. Observer, for five months in 1963, Tyrone Guthrie Theatre, Minneapolis. Recipient: Irish Arts Council Macauley fellowship, 1963; Christopher Ewart-Biggs Memorial award, 1982; New York Drama Critics Circle award, 1989, 1991; Olivier award, 1991; *Evening Standard* award, 1991; *Plays and Players* award, 1991; Writers Guild of Great Britain award, 1991; Tony award, 1992. D.Litt.: Rosary College, Chicago, 1979; National University of Ireland, Dublin, 1983; University of

Ulster, Coleraine, 1986; Queen's University, Belfast, 1992; Trinity College, Dublin, 1992. Member, Irish Academy of Letters, 1972, Aosdana, 1983, and Irish Senate, 1987. Agent: Curtis Brown, 162–168 Regent Street, London W1R 5TB, England. Address: Drumaweir House, Greencastle, County Donegal, Ireland.

Publications

PLAYS

The Francophile (produced 1960; as *The Doubtful Paradise*, produced 1960).
The Enemy Within (produced 1962). 1979.
The Blind Mice (produced 1963).
Philadelphia, Here I Come! (produced 1964). 1965.
The Loves of Cass McGuire (broadcast 1966; produced 1966). 1967.
Lovers: Part One: Winners; Part Two: Losers (produced 1967). 1968.
Crystal and Fox (produced 1968). 1970; with *The Mundy Scheme*, 1970.
The Mundy Scheme (produced 1969). With *Crystal and Fox*, 1970.
The Gentle Island (produced 1971). 1974.
The Freedom of the City (produced 1973). 1974.
Volunteers (produced 1975). 1979.
Living Quarters (produced 1977). 1978; in *Selected Plays*, 1984.
Faith Healer (produced 1979). 1980; in *Selected Plays*, 1984.
Aristocrats (produced 1979). 1980; in *Selected Plays*, 1984.
Translations (produced 1980). 1981; in *Selected Plays*, 1984.
American Welcome (produced 1980). In *The Best Short Plays 1981*, edited by
    Stanley Richards, 1981.
Three Sisters, adaptation of a play by Chekhov (produced 1981). 1981.
The Communication Cord (produced 1982). 1983.
Selected Plays (includes *Philadelphia, Here I Come!*; *The Freedom of the City*;
    Living Quarters; *Aristocrats*; *Faith Healer*; *Translations*). 1984.
Fathers and Sons, adaptation of a novel by Turgenev (produced 1987). 1987.
Making History (produced 1988). 1989.
Dancing at Lughnasa (produced 1990). 1990.
The London Vertigo, adaptation of a play by Charles MacKlin (produced
    1992).
A Month in the Country, adaptation of the play by Turgenev (produced 1992).
    1992.
Wonderful Tennessee (produced 1993).

SCREENPLAY: *Philadelphia, Here I Come!*, 1970.

RADIO PLAYS: *A Sort of Freedom*, 1958; *To This Hard House*, 1958; *The Founder Members*, 1964; *The Loves of Cass McGuire*, 1966.

SHORT STORIES

The Saucer of Larks. 1962.
The Gold in the Sea. 1966.
A Saucer of Larks: Stories of Ireland (selection). 1969.
Selected Stories. 1979.
The Diviner. 1983.

OTHER
Editor, *The Last of the Name*, by Charles McGlinchey. 1986.

BIBLIOGRAPHY: *Ten Modern Irish Playwrights* by Kimball King, 1979.

CRITICAL STUDIES: *Brian Friel* by D.E.S. Maxwell, 1973; *Brian Friel: The Growth of an Irish Dramatist* by Ulf Dantanus, 1985; *Brian Friel* by George O'Brien, 1990; *Brian Friel and Ireland's Drama* by Richard Pine, 1990.

Brian Friel began as a writer of short stories, and the art of the short story permeates all of his dramatic work. His drama is lyrical, intimate, and understated in ways perhaps more common to the short-story form than to the stage. Yet Friel has proved, during a career spanning 30 years, his theatrical skills in arousing and maintaining audience interest; therefore, his narrative power cannot be described satisfactorily in terms of the short-story writer. One should recall that Chekhov, the writer with whom Friel is most often compared, also had two strings to his bow.

After a few radio plays written for BBC Northern Ireland, Friel's first significant stage play (*The Enemy Within*) was written for the Abbey Theatre. The significance lies less in the play itself, a history play set in the seventh century, than in its introduction of Friel as an Abbey playwright. This tradition (founded by Yeats and Synge and carried on by O'Casey) was by 1962 much attenuated, yet the role it provided for Irish playwrights was still nominally if problematically available, to mediate between individual vision and social or socio-political reality. Friel's originality lay in his perception of the critical state of this relationship in modern Irish life. For Friel, there was an unacknowledged gap between the individual mind (and experience) and a social reality which was crumbling at an alarming rate, so that old beliefs, old values, and settled lifestyles (heretofore rendered coherent by the patriarchal nature of Irish authority) no longer retained a satisfying viability. A major statement on this alienated condition appeared in *Philadelphia, Here I Come!*, one of Friel's best and most enduring plays. Once more significantly, this play was *not* staged at the Abbey Theatre, to which Friel did not return until 1973; in the meantime he worked out his experimental and revolutionary ideas in alternative theatres in Dublin and elsewhere, under the influence of directors not tied to conventional notions of production, such as Tyrone Guthrie.

Philadelphia, Here I Come! might at first sight appear to be just one more Irish peasant play, addressing topics familiar from the canon of Irish drama. But in effect Friel subverts the tradition. His play is not mainly concerned with a conventional theme, such as emigration, the land, or a love-match. Its primary concentration is on the alienated consciousness of a young man, Gareth O'Donnell, whose relationship with his widowed father is an image of a new, privatized awareness of human isolation. Friel divides this character in two, Private and Public, to be played by two actors, "two views of the one man." Private Gar, the "alter ego," is invisible to all on stage but serves to articulate for the audience the inner thoughts and feelings of the young hero. These thoughts and feelings give a Hamlet-like dimension to the characterization, and this is where the real power of the play lies, though it is also supremely well balanced in its use of comedy and pathos.

Friel himself has said that the two plays which followed, *The Loves of Cass McGuire* and *Lovers*, share with *Philadelphia* the common theme of love. It is perhaps truer to observe that they are about loneliness and the futility of communication. Each is also theatrically experimental. After 1972, however, a very different emphasis makes its appearance in Friel's work. In January 1972 the political situation in Northern Ireland took a turn for the worse, as British paratroopers shot 13 civilians on a civil rights march in Derry. Like many another Irish writer Friel was outraged, particularly as Derry was his adopted city. He wrote *The Freedom of the City* to express his anger at the whitewashing Widgery Report, which exonerated the British army. Its premiere at the new Abbey Theatre marked Friel's return to nationalist concerns. The play, while not among Friel's best, is remarkably skilful in its adaptation of Brechtian techniques of storytelling to a current political situation, even though critics in London and New York faulted it on political grounds. On these grounds it is a play to be linked with *Translations* and *Making History*, as Friel became increasingly preoccupied with the crisis in Northern Ireland. *Translations* was staged by the Field Day Theatre Company, established by Friel and actor Stephen Rea to intervene culturally in this crisis by touring with plays which addressed specific issues. To some degree, Friel became a political dramatist.

Translations, a history play set in the year 1833, is one of Friel's best and most internationally performed plays. The action takes place in a hedgeschool and uses two distinct but here interrelated issues to explore skilfully a community in crisis, and a native culture at the point of dissolution. The issues are education and cartography, which in a colonial situation relate specifically to language and identity. Though the implications of the play are far-ranging, there is, as always in Friel, a simple human situation at its core: here, a love story between the English soldier Yolland and the Irish woman Máire (deemed to be speaking only Gaelic throughout). The tragic failure of this affair recounts a whole national disaster.

Dancing at Lughnasa, Friel's most successful play to date, shows how inadequate and even now falsifying it is to categorise him as a political playwright. The fact that it was premiered by the Abbey Theatre rather than by Field Day suggests that Friel himself felt the need to escape the confines of the Field Day ideology. *Dancing at Lughnasa* is a reminder that Friel is first and foremost an artist, a storyteller, a playwright for whom nuances of emotional experience take priority over ideas. Even in the 1970's, when his work seemed to point inevitably to the writing of *Translations*, he could confound the critics with such essentially non-political plays as *The Gentle Island*, *Living Quarters*, *Aristocrats*, and—above all—*Faith Healer*. The latter stands out as one of Friel's most original and poetic plays, occupied with the ambivalent powers of the eponymous artist figure. If *Dancing at Lughnasa* filters the doomed perfection of the past through the imagination of a boy about to develop into a writer, *Faith Healer* goes to the root of the mature artist's guilt for his failure to intervene in that doom.

Faith Healer comprises only four monologues, two from Frank and one each from his wife Grace and his impresario Teddy. In Pirandellian fashion the audience must sift the truth of what these characters contradictorily narrate. The stories they tell not only reinforce Friel's skill, but their climax also returns us to Ballybeg, the village invented for *Philadelphia, Here I Come!*. In a sense the exile of that play returns to his place of birth and is destroyed in *Faith Healer*. Thus Friel's plays inter-relate in patterns which tell not only the story of Ireland and her wounds but also the timeless story of human longing for completion, forgiveness, and love.

—Christopher Murray

See the essay on *Translations*.

FRISBY, Terence.

Born in New Cross, London, 28 November 1932. Educated at Dobwalls Village School; Dartford Grammar School; Central School of Speech Training and Dramatic Art, London, 1955–57. Married Christine Vecchione in 1963 (divorced); one son. Worked as a salesman, capstan lathe operator, factory hand, waiter, chauffeur, chucker-out at the Hammersmith Palais, etc.; since 1957 professional actor; also a producer. Resident director, New Theatre, Bromley, Kent, 1963–64. Recipient: Writers Guild of Great Britain award, for screenplay, 1970; Houston International Film Festival gold award, for comedy, 1991. Agent: Lemon, Unna, and Durbridge, 24 Pottery Lane, Holland Park, London W11 4LZ. Address: 72 Bishops Mansions, Bishops Park Road, London SW6 6DZ, England.

Publications

PLAYS

The Subtopians (also director: produced 1964). 1964.
There's a Girl in My Soup (produced 1966). 1968.
The Bandwagon (produced 1969). 1973.
It's All Right If I Do It (produced 1977). 1977.
Seaside Postcard (also director: produced 1977). 1978.
First Night (produced 1987).
Just Remember Two Things: It's Not Fair and Don't Be Late (broadcast 1988). In *Best Radio Plays of 1988*, 1988.

SCREENPLAY: *There's a Girl in My Soup*, 1970.

RADIO PLAY: *Just Remember Two Things: It's Not Fair and Don't Be Late*, 1988.

TELEVISION PLAYS: *Guilty*, 1964; *Public Eye* series, 1964; *Take Care of Madam*, 1965; *Adam Adamant* series, 1966; *More Deadly Than the Sword*, 1966; *Don't Forget the Basics*, 1967; *Lucky Feller* series, 1976; *That's Love* series, 1988–92.

CRITICAL STUDIES: *Anger and After* by John Russell Taylor, 1962, revised edition, 1969, as *The Angry Theatre*, 1962, revised edition, 1969; *The Season* by William Goldman, 1969, revised edition, 1984.

THEATRICAL ACTIVITIES

DIRECTOR: Plays—in various repertory companies, 1963–64; *The Subtopians*, 1964; *Seaside Postcard*, 1977.

ACTOR (as Terence Holland, 1957–66): Plays—over 200 roles in repertory theatres; London debut as Charlie Pepper in *Gentleman's Pastime* by Marion Hunt, 1958. Television—*Play School*, 1964–66; *It Must Be Something in the Water* by Alan Plater, 1973; *Two Townsmen*, adaptation of Thomas Hardy's work by Douglas Livingstone, 1974; *Leeds—United!* by Colin Welland, 1974; *When the Boys Come out to Play* by Richard Harris, 1975; *The Brothers*, 1976; *The Madness Museum* by Ken Campbell, 1986; *Signals*, 1990; *A Strike Out of Time*, 1991; *That's Love*, 1992.

Terence Frisby's first play, *The Subtopians*, was greeted with eulogies when, in 1964, it was seen for the first time. It was, critics decided, funny but complex, accurately worked out, deeply felt in spite of its genuine comedy, serious in intention but almost painfully hilarious, and it had an unbreakable grip on the realities of social life in the 1960's.

Frisby was 32 when *The Subtopians* arrived to signal a newcomer whose gifts were, to say the least, so interesting that his future activities were sure to demand close attention. Part at least of the technical neatness of his first play was due to his training at the Central School of Speech Training and Dramatic Art and to his work as an actor in repertory, musicals, and films, as an entertainer in night clubs and cabaret, and as a director. There is a solid foundation of technique beneath the sometimes unkind observation and harsh comedy.

In 1966 *There's a Girl in My Soup* brought Frisby one of the greatest commercial successes in the modern theatre, running for six years in the West End and, at the same time, pleasing most of the critics. Like *The Subtopians*, it has beautifully efficient machinery and precision of observation. Its hero has the sort of position in life—he is an expert on food, writing for intellectual periodicals—which once would have pointed him out as a figure of fun but, in 1966, assured an audience that he was a leader of thought and fashion whose familiarity with the best restaurants is intrinsically romantic and enviable. Thus he is in a position to follow an exhausting, eventful career as an amorist whose endless successes are with the young who find his expertise, and the attitude towards him of those whose efforts he criticises, altogether glamorous. It is less the dialogue or anything explicit in the play than the form it takes and the succession of events which indicate that behind the parade of insatiable appetite for change and his pride in his sexual prowess he is at the same time both lonely and uncertain of his attractiveness to those whom he regards as victims. Frisby naturally chooses to study the girl whose victim he becomes, in whose life he is only a pleasant interlude. The "trendiness" and "contemporaneity" of *There's a Girl in My Soup* carried the play round a triumphal tour of the world's theatres, with productions not only throughout the English-speaking theatre but in most European countries as well as in Turkey, Israel, and Mexico.

The course of events which led to the production of Frisby's third play, *The Bandwagon*, rose out of his success as a script writer. *Guilty*, a one-off piece for the BBC in 1964, was followed by a comedy, *Don't Forget the Basics*, for

Independent Television and contributions to various series, notably to *Public Eye*, which at its best gave an almost continental seediness to the activities of a provincial private detective, and *Adam Adamant*, in which adventure stories which might almost have come to birth in a boys' comic were treated with unusual and preposterous elegancies and elaborations. *The Bandwagon*, originally *Some Have Greatness Thrust upon Them*, was to be one of BBC television's socially conscious Wednesday Plays. It chose to imagine the situation of a stupid, ugly, graceless teenage girl, a member of a family of almost appalling fecundity—her mother and her sister are both pregnant when the play begins—who discovers that, though unmarried, she is to become the mother of quintuplets. Her fecundity, before drugs inducing multiple births had won any special attention, reaches the ears of popular newspapers, who make her a heroine, and television, which interviews her. The interview comes to an end when Aurora (the most unfortunately named heroine) explains the physiological misinformation and ignorance that are responsible for her plight. Frisby's refusal to alter a line which, the BBC believed, would give unnecessary offence, led to the Corporation's refusal to produce the play.

The BBC was, perhaps, entirely wrong. The line—"My friend Syl told me it was safe standing up"—is all of a piece—with a matter-of-fact simplicity which makes Aurora almost unexploitable. Aurora is manoeuvred into marriage, and has to be hurried from the church into childbed; and so have her mother and sister. The play belongs to the tradition of broad farce, and its final scene, as the women-folk depart from the altar in agonized haste, sacrifices the precarious dignity and simplicity which have won the sympathy of the audience. *The Bandwagon*, in the good old days of curtain-raisers, could have stopped at its natural end, the silent, almost unnerving confrontation of two essentially pathetic victims of exploitation, Aurora and her husband-to-be, and have retained its integrity.

Although *The Bandwagon* seemed, when it was new, likely to follow Frisby's earlier plays and become an outstanding success, it did not do so. Possibly its depressing social milieu and its unfriendly view of what we have been taught to call the "media," as well as its combination of farce with serious moral concern, simply bothered audiences who found Aurora to be no more than a heroine of farce. In the same way, neither *It's All Right If I Do It*, and *Seaside Postcard* won any startling success. Frisby's gift for comic incident and comic dialogue, obviously rooted in a serious view of society, has not, perhaps, found its audience when it applies to areas outside the provinces and the glossy West End world of *There's a Girl in My Soup*.

—Henry Raynor

FRY, Christopher.

Born Christopher Fry Harris in Bristol, 18 December 1907. Educated at Bedford Modern School, 1918–26. Served in the Non-Combatant Corps, 1940–44. Married Phyllis Marjorie Hart in 1936 (died 1987); one son. Teacher, Bedford Froebel Kindergarten, 1926–27; actor and office worker, Citizen House, Bath, 1927; schoolmaster, Hazelwood School, Limpsfield, Surrey, 1928–31; secretary to H. Rodney Bennett, 1931–32; founding direc-

tor, Tunbridge Wells Repertory Players, 1932–35; lecturer and editor of
schools magazine, Dr. Barnardo's Homes, 1934–39; director, 1939–40, and
visiting director, 1945–46, Oxford Playhouse; visiting director, 1946, and
staff dramatist, 1947, Arts Theatre Club, London. Also composer. Recipient:
Shaw Prize Fund award, 1948; Foyle poetry prize, 1951; New York Drama
Critics Circle award, 1951, 1952, 1956; Queen's Gold medal, 1962; Royal
Society of Literature Heinemann award, 1962. D.A.: Manchester Polytechnic,
1966; D.Litt.: Oxford University, 1988. Honorary Fellow, Manchester
Polytechnic, 1988. Fellow, Royal Society of Literature. Agent: ACTAC Ltd, 15
High Street, Ramsbury, Wiltshire SN8 2PA. Address: The Toft, East Dean,
near Chichester, West Sussex PO18 0JA, England.

Publications

PLAYS

Youth and the Peregrines (produced 1934).

She Shall Have Music (lyrics only, with Ronald Frankau), book by Frank
    Eyton, music by Fry and Monte Crick (produced 1934).

To Sea in a Sieve (as Christopher Harris) (revue; produced 1935).

Open Door (produced 1936). n.d.

The Boy with a Cart: Cuthman, Saint of Sussex (produced 1938). 1939.

The Tower (produced 1939).

Thursday's Child: A Pageant, music by Martin Shaw (produced 1939). 1939.

A Phoenix Too Frequent (produced 1946). 1946.

The Firstborn (broadcast 1947; produced 1948). 1946; revised version (pro-
    duced 1952), 1952.

The Lady's Not for Burning (produced 1948). 1949; revised version, 1950.

Thor, With Angels (produced 1948). 1948.

Venus Observed (produced 1950). 1950.

Ring round the Moon: A Charade with Music, adaptation of a play by Jean
    Anouilh (produced 1950). 1950.

A Sleep of Prisoners (produced 1951). 1951.

The Dark Is Light Enough: A Winter Comedy (produced 1954). 1954.

The Lark, adaptation of a play by Jean Anouilh (produced 1955). 1955.

Tiger at the Gates, adaptation of a play by Jean Giraudoux (produced 1955).
    1955; as *The Trojan War Will Not Take Place* (produced 1983), 1983.

Duel of Angels, adaptation of a play by Jean Giraudoux (produced 1958).
    1958.

Curtmantle (produced in Dutch, 1961). 1961.

Judith, adaptation of a play by Jean Giraudoux (produced 1962). 1962.

The Bible: Original Screenplay, assisted by Jonathan Griffin. 1966.

Peer Gynt, adaptation of the play by Ibsen (produced 1970). 1970.

A Yard of Sun: A Summer Comedy (produced 1970). 1970.

The Brontës of Haworth (televised 1973). 2 vols., 1974.

Cyrano de Bergerac, adaptation of the play by Edmond Rostand (produced
    1975). 1975.

Paradise Lost, music by Penderecki, adaptation of the poem by Milton (pro-
    duced 1978). 1978.

Selected Plays (includes *The Boy with a Cart, A Phoenix Too Frequent, The
    Lady's Not for Burning, A Sleep of Prisoners, Curtmantle*). 1985.

One Thing More; or, Caedmon Construed (produced 1986). 1987.
The Seasons, poems to accompany Julie Cooper's adaptation of Vivaldi's *The Four Seasons* (produced 1990).
A Journey into Light, music by Robert Walker (produced 1992).

SCREENPLAYS: *The Beggar's Opera*, with Denis Cannan, 1953; *A Queen Is Crowned* (documentary), 1953; *Ben Hur*, 1959; *Barabbas*, 1962; *The Bible: In the Beginning*, 1966.

RADIO PLAYS: for *Children's Hour* series, 1939–40; *The Firstborn*, 1947; *Rhineland Journey*, 1948.

TELEVISION PLAYS: *The Canary*, 1950; *The Tenant of Wildfell Hall*, 1968; *The Brontës of Haworth* (four plays), 1973; *The Best of Enemies*, 1976; *Sister Dora*, from the book by Jo Manton, 1977.

VERSE

Root and Sky: Poetry from the Plays of Christopher Fry, edited by Charles E. and Jean G. Wadsworth. 1975.

OTHER

An Experience of Critics, with *The Approach to Dramatic Criticism* by W.A. Darlington and others, edited by Kaye Webb. 1952.
The Boat That Mooed (for children). 1966.
Can You Find Me: A Family History. 1978.
Death Is a Kind of Love (lecture). 1979.
Genius, Talent and Failure: The Brontës (lecture). 1987.
Looking for a Language (lecture). 1992.

Editor, *Charlie Hammond's Sketchbook*. 1980.
Translator, *The Boy and the Magic*, by Colette. 1964.
Translator, with Timberlake Wertenbaker, *Jean Anouilh: Five Plays*. 1986.
Incidental Music:
A Winter's Tale, 1951.

BIBLIOGRAPHY: by B.L. Schear and E.G. Prater, in *Tulane Drama Review 4*, March 1960.

MANUSCRIPT COLLECTION:
Harvard University Theatre Collection, Cambridge, Massachusetts.

CRITICAL STUDIES: *Christopher Fry: An Appreciation*, 1950, and *Christopher Fry*, 1954, revised edition, 1962, both by Derek Stanford; *The Drama of Comedy: Victim and Victor* by Nelson Vos, 1965; *Creed and Drama* by W.M. Merchant, 1965; *The Christian Tradition in Modern British Verse Drama* by William V. Spanos, 1967; *Christopher Fry* by Emil Roy, 1968; *Christopher Fry: A Critical Essay*, 1970, and *More Than the Ear Discovers: God in the*

Plays of Christopher Fry, 1983, both by Stanley M. Wiersma; *Poetic Drama* by Glenda Leeming, 1989.

THEATRICAL ACTIVITIES
DIRECTOR: **Plays**—*How-Do, Princess?* by Ivor Novello, 1936; *The Circle of Chalk* by James Laver, 1945; *The School for Scandal* by Sheridan, 1946; *A Phoenix Too Frequent*, 1950; *The Lady's Not for Burning*, 1971; and others.
ACTOR: **Plays**—in repertory, 1937.

Christopher Fry comments:

The way a man writes for the theatre depends on the way he looks at life. If, in his experience, direction and purpose seem to be all-pervading factors, pattern and shape are necessary to his writing. The verse form is an effort to be true to what Eleanor, in *Curtmantle*, calls "the silent order whose speech is all visible things." No event is understandable in a prose sense alone. Its ultimate meaning (that is to say, the complete life of the event, seen in its eternal context) is a poetic meaning. The comedies try to explore a reality behind appearances. "Something condones the world incorrigibly" says Thomas Mendip in *The Lady's Not for Burning*—in spite of the "tragic" nature of life. The problem, a long way from being solved, is how to contain the complexities and paradoxes within two hours of entertainment: how to define the creative pattern of life without the danger of dogmatic statement. Dogma is static; life is movement. "La vérité est dans une nuance."

Christopher Fry's work was doubtless overrated in the fruitful years of *The Lady's Not for Burning* and *A Sleep of Prisoners*; it is most certainly underrated today. This is in part due to an integrity and consistency in the work of a playwright who has pursued his own style of the serio-comic and chosen to ignore fashion. It is as if Beckett and the theatre of the absurd had not existed, nor Brecht and the practice of epic theatre with its oblique devices of structure and technique, nor the socially and politically committed drama following Osborne's *Look Back in Anger*; and Fry's reputation has paid the price. It remains to be seen whether his neglect of contemporary trends matters in the final verdict.

In *A Yard of Sun*, Fry is still writing in that highly idiosyncratic, all-but-verse idiom of loose pentameters which drew attention to his earliest plays. Characteristically mixing the colloquial and the allusive, a minor character can say, "I pick words gingerly like a rose out of thorns," and at a stroke equalizes his role with that of a major, thus by prosaic kitchen-sink standards making all the parts equally literate and classless. Or Angelino Bruno, one of the two central characters whose families are unexpectedly united after World War II, can come out with a startling turn of expression which fixes and underscores the general statement of the stage:

What a settling-up God's having this week!
Both of us within two days. Well, once
The bit's between His teeth things start to move.

Although it may not bear close analysis as poetry on the page, verbal panache of this kind keeps Fry's stage alive when a situation is static. It is often spendthrift with the necessary economy of the action, and the idiom which refreshed the grim postwar years and dazzled the critics can now seem irrelevant, even facile.

But Fry was seeking a spiritual idiom for a contemporary and unobtrusively Christian verse drama after T.S. Eliot had prepared the ground with *Murder in the Cathedral* (1935) and *The Family Reunion* (1939). Where Eliot was concerned to find a spare and unobtrusive verse form designed to control the speech and movement on a stage of modern martyrs, Fry, in a less certain style but with more sense of the stage, aimed with abandon at a general mood to match his themes. There are moments in *A Sleep of Prisoners*, possibly the best anti-war play of its period, when the verse achieves the richness of both tonal and physical embodiment of the stage moment while exploring a verbal idea:

> How ceaseless the earth is. How it goes on.
> Nothing has happened except silence where sound was,
> Stillness where movement was . . .

These lines are spoken by the figure of Adam just after he has witnessed the murder of Abel his son, and they enact both the father's horror and the scene's meaning.

Where, however, Eliot's profundity of vision carried him through his own inadequacies as a dramatist—notably his inability to create character which did not suffer the atrophy of symbolism—Fry came to lean on an explosive central situation fruitful in itself. This situation might lack the qualities of conflict, tension, and development, yet still be capable of holding attention. Thus *A Sleep of Prisoners* consists of a pattern of re-enacted Old Testament stories chosen to illustrate facets of the idea of violence. Each story is not only informed by the audience's own memories of the Bible, but also, because it is dreamed by a modern soldier held prisoner in a church, is automatically granted a contemporary relevance: within the structure of the play the spectator himself works to supply the missing factor in the dramatic equation, and the teaching element of a morality play is actively deduced by our application of the fiction to the fact. Nevertheless, this play suffers, as only morality plays can, from the static preconception by which morality characters tend to be fixed in their symbolic attitudes.

This play in its time startled and delighted audiences by the free use of its church setting, where at a glance the chancel could be Adam's jungle or the pulpit Abraham's mountain: as they were for *Murder in the Cathedral*, audiences were both theatregoers and congregation, and were unusually exercised by the multiplicity of association felt within the performance. There are no such props for a dramatic experience in Fry's other plays, although in *The Boy with a Cart*, a simple mystery play of spontaneous charm, *The Firstborn*, exploring the tragic dilemma of Moses and the Plagues, and *Curtmantle* he draws upon legend and history in parallel attempts to bring the remote closer to home. *Curtmantle*, too neglected a play, was his most sustained attempt at a serious character study: this chronicle play of Henry II in conflict with his Archbishop Becket is set out in a sequence of vivid episodes more in the simple manner of Bolt's episodic *A Man for All Seasons* than with the prismatic counterpoint of Brecht's epic theatre, the scenes designed to illustrate the wit, the wisdom, and the complex passions of the title part as Henry searches for a rational unity of divine and secular law.

Fry creates a drama of colour and flair, choosing a situation for its imaginative potential, often one of implicit crisis involving a clash of strong, bright personalities. His situation enables him to demonstrate a compassionate affirmation of life—an optimism which inevitably seemed escapist beside the bleak absurdist landscape of the postwar years, in spite of the tragic mode of *The Firstborn*, *Thor*, *With Angels* (the 1948 Canterbury Festival play) and *The Dark Is Light Enough*, plays which exemplify Fry's philosophy of maturing through crisis:

> We reach an obstacle, and learn to overcome it;
> our thoughts or emotions become knotted, and we
> increase ourselves in order to unknot them; a
> state of being becomes intolerable, and, drawing
> upon a hidden reserve of spirit, we transform it.

But he is nevertheless remembered for those early comedies of mood touched with the wit and fantasy by which he could express his most gentle and humane thinking. The prototype for this kind of comedy, and still the most regularly revived, was the one-act, *A Phoenix Too Frequent*. This was taken from the ancient tale of the young Roman widow romantically committed to a fast to the death in her husband's tomb, until she and an equally romantic young soldier agree to substitute the husband's body for the corpse the soldier was guarding with his life. With the lightest of touches, the widow decides for life, and youth and love supplant social convention and death: a joyful illustration of the life-force at work.

The spring-time comedy that made Fry's name and competed for London's attention with Eliot's *The Cocktail Party* in 1949 was his best-known play *The Lady's Not for Burning*, an extension of the style and spirit of *A Phoenix Too Frequent*. His verbal pyrotechnics were at their most assured, and the medieval colour on his stage lifted the play into a rarefied atmosphere that forced comparison with Giraudoux and the lighter Anouilh of *L'Invitation au château* (which Fry was later to translate beautifully as *Ring round the Moon*). A simple crisis again sets the play in motion, when one Thomas Mendip, desiring but denied death, is confronted with Jennet Jourdemayne, who wants to live but must die as a witch. She envies his deathwish, he her "damnable mystery," until, to test his sincerity and her courage, Fry impudently arranges for them one last "joyous" evening together before Jennet's execution. The result is to dramatize with graceful irony Fry's sense of cosmic purpose.

His other plays designed to celebrate the seasons followed irregularly in an unpredictable range of moods, some unexpectedly sombre: *Venus Observed* (autumn), *The Dark Is Light Enough* (winter) and *A Yard of Sun* (summer). *Venus Observed* was a comedy of middle-aged disillusionment, but pleasingly balanced and without fashionable cynicism. However, *The Dark Is Light Enough* selects the year of revolutions, 1848, for its darker setting, and secures its unity in the compassionate and gracious presence of an Austrian countess, a part created by Edith Evans. With the Countess's "divine non-interference" it is demonstrated:

how apparently undemandingly
She moves among us; and yet
Lives make and unmake themselves in her
    neighbourhood
As nowhere else.

Thus the theme is one of providence, and, through the wisdom of the Countess as she recognizes the imminence of death, embodies the necessity of our respect for every human personality in its touch of grace.

To set side by side plays as contrasting as *The Lady's Not for Burning* and *The Dark Is Light Enough* is inescapably to be impressed by Fry's versatility, and by the integrity of a writer who uses his chosen medium as a way of searching out his personal philosophy whether in the vein of farce or tragedy, spring or winter. Eliot notwithstanding, Fry's is the most sustained attempt in English to write an undogmatic Christian drama in modern times.

—J.L. Styan

See the essay on *The Lady's Not for Burning*.

G

GALLACHER, Tom.

Born in Alexandria, Dunbartonshire, Scotland, 16 February 1934. Writer-in-residence, Pitlochry Festival Theatre, Perthshire, 1975–78, and Royal Lyceum Theatre, Edinburgh, 1978–80. Recipient: Scottish Arts Council award, 1986. Agent: Michael Imison Playwrights, 28 Almeida Street, London N1 1TD, England.

Publications

PLAYS

Our Kindness to Five Persons (produced 1969). 1980.

Mr. Joyce Is Leaving Paris (produced 1970; revised version produced 1971). 1972.

Revival! (produced 1972). With *Schellenbrack*, 1978.

Three to Play: Janus, Pastiche, Recital (produced 1972; *Recital* produced 1973).

Schellenbrack (produced 1973). With *Revival!*, 1978.

Bright Scene Fading (produced 1973).

The Only Street (produced 1973). 1980.

Personal Effects (produced 1974).

A Laughing Matter (produced 1975).

Hallowe'en (produced 1975). 1980.

The Sea Change (produced 1976). 1980.

A Presbyterian Wooing, adaptation of the play *The Assembly* by Archibald Pitcairne (produced 1976).

The Evidence of Tiny Tim, with Joan Knight (produced 1977).

Wha's Like Us—Fortunately (produced 1978).

Stage Door Canteen, with John Scrimger (produced 1978).

Deacon Brodie, adaptation of the play by Robert Louis Stevenson and W.E. Henley (produced 1978).

An Enemy of the People, adaptation of a play by Ibsen (produced 1979).

Jenny (produced 1979). 1980.

Natural Causes (produced 1980).

The Father, adaptation of a play by Strindberg (produced 1980).

A Doll's House, adaptation of a play by Ibsen (produced 1980).

The Parole of Don Juan (produced 1981).

The Treasure Ship, adaptation of the play by John Brandane (produced 1981).
The Wild Duck, adaptation of a play by Ibsen (produced 1987).

RADIO PLAYS: *Progress to an Exile*, 1970; *The Scar*, 1973; *Hunting Shadows*, 1975; *The Man with a Hatchet*, 1976; *Portrait of Isa Mulvenny*, 1978; *Perfect Pitch*, 1979; *Store Quarter*, 1983; *The Previous Tenant*, 1986.

TELEVISION PLAYS: *The Trial of Thomas Muir*, 1977; *If the Face Fits*, 1978.

NOVELS
Apprentice. 1983.
Journeyman. 1984.
Survivor. 1985.
The Wind on the Heath. 1987.

SHORT STORIES
Hunting Shadows. 1981.
The Jewel Maker. 1986.

OTHER
The Way to Write for the Stage. 1987.

Tom Gallacher comments:

(1977) Mainly, the plays deal with exceptions. Sometimes the exceptions are artists; sometimes it is another kind of outsider, a genius, a catalyst, or a singular man. All of them are in some way seeking to extend the meaning of their lives or the boundaries of reality.

An illustration of this can be gained from my book *The Jewel Maker* which is a fictional account of a playwright at work. There it is made clear how the work is influenced by people and events, and how the conflict of illusion and reality extends the boundaries of the human spirit. That is the testing ground where human evolution continues to progress.

All the plays celebrate the individual. The protagonists are unmoved by Class, Party, or Movement but they are acutely conscious of the interior actions of emotion, spirit, and reason. The crises—whether sad or funny—are person to person. The conflict in comedy and drama arises from an effort to make a workable connection—between the accepted and the potential, between what we are and what we may be, between what is degrading and what is exalting.

"Only connect" was the motto which E.M. Forster placed as guardian over his novel *Howards End*. I can't think of a better motto for a writer because the motto leads to a concept of great courage and enterprise. The characters in my plays do not always master the concept or gain its acceptance by others. But if they go down they go down knowing which way is forward.

At the end of Tom Gallacher's first play, *Our Kindness to Five Persons*, an alcoholic Glaswegian author pours himself another drink and proposes a solitary toast: "Should auld acquaintance be forgot and *never* brought to mind? Yes. Please God. Yes." The play has just demonstrated a denial of the prayer; but the question, and the artist's special rights of adjudication over it, are the constant threads through the plays Gallacher has written since.

Gallacher's preoccupation with art and artist is immediately obvious on the surfaces of his plays. Writers are the central characters of at least half of them, and Gallacher often points a passage of dialogue towards the epigrammatic use of a quotation, or builds a scene around the recitation of poetry or the singing of ballads. Literary sources and models are of even greater substantive and structural importance for some of Gallacher's work. *The Sea Change* and the short radio play *The Scar* are both dream-plays-within-plays in which the stuff of the central character's imagination comes from Shakespeare. *A Presbyterian Wooing* descends from literary obscurity: *The Assembly*, a Jacobite's dramatic satire on the ecclesiastical politics and personal morals of the Edinburgh Kirk. Trimmed and embroidered into a neo-Restoration comedy of sexual hypocrisy, *A Presbyterian Wooing* demonstrates Gallacher's sensitivity to earlier dramatic modes and his ability to tune his invention and idiom to the same key. The same knack belabours Ibsen's dramaturgy and Kierkegaard's ontology in *Revival!*, the aim of which seems to be to tease the audience into reading the complete works of both Scandinavians. In *Hallowe'en*, on the other hand, Fraser's account of that ritual in pagan times is compactly reincarnated in contemporary Glasgow, and the literary *drame à clé* is cleanly unlocked in the dialogue.

The thematic purposes to which Gallacher puts these and other of his "auld acquaintance" in literature are remarkably repetitive, though the dramatic techniques he uses vary considerably. He is occupied unto the edge of obsession with the dual nature of the remembered past—omnipresent in influence and irretrievable in fact. Every one of his original plays is in large measure focused upon the relationship between dramatic past and present. In some cases, a radical time change is built into the play, its point of departure being the out-of-time introduction of the central character. *The Sea Change, Bright Scene Fading*, and the unproduced *A Lady Possessed* are all constructed as flashbacks in time and space through the consciousness of that character, while *Mr. Joyce Is Leaving Paris* brings the personages of Joyce's past to the front of his present consciousness. The other plays, while preserving naturalistic time schemes and the convention of the fourth wall, investigate events and relationships anterior to the action of the play, reenact them or exorcise them.

For Gallacher the memory that matters is the artistic statement of a perception about personal experience. Such a statement stands for him as evidence of the essentials of observed and observer, and as an imposition of order and connexion among these essentials. "Witness" and "pattern" are the terms which often turn up in the dialogue; another is "signpost," an indication of where someone has been and a directive to those who follow. When the plays incorporate such overt expositions of their author's understanding of art, it is not surprising that several draw attention to their own artificiality, nor that so many celebrate the triumph of artistic insight—over technology, biographical data, time, and the perceptions of the pedestrian majority of mankind.

Though the penultimate victory supplies him with some fairly strong stuff, Gallacher finds his best dramatic material in the last. Only here does he create any real competition, and only here are his aesthetic concerns communicated by more than interpretative glosses and plot gimmickry. The axis along which Gallacher most characteristically depicts these conflicts is that of an intense relationship between a gifted figure and a sympathetic sibling or comrade left behind: James and Stanislaus Joyce in *Mr. Joyce Is Leaving Paris*, Martin and Richard in *The Only Street*, and Otto and Steve in *Bright Scene Fading*. The high price of giftedness also hovers over the presentation of parent-child, husband-wife, and mentor-pupil relationships in these and other plays, but Gallacher plays a better game for higher stakes when he is dealing with doubles and shadows.

Gallacher's own practice of art as witness and as pattern is apparent in his plays and illuminates some of their more idiosyncratic aspects. His writing of dialogue is distinguished on the one hand by an accurate reproduction of spoken rhythms, with particularly precise variations for local, professional, social, and even situational idiom, and on the other hand by a wit which specializes in paradoxes, perfect squelches, and the literalisation of abstractions and figures of speech. Gallacher rarely loses this balance of an attentive ear and orderly invention.

Gallacher's patterning of his materials betrays a taste for symmetry, a mastery of plot mechanics, and an ability to exploit exposition, complication, reversal, and resolution in traditional well-made ways or to invert them for the sake of emphasis. (The exceptions to this rule of flexibility are found in his act-endings; he seems incapable of placing an interval anywhere but on the edge of a cliff in the plot). His fascination with pattern is perhaps most easily perceived in miniature in the tidy and playful plots of his three one-acts for three players (*Janus*, *Recital*, and *Pastiche*). The patterning is, however, so apparent in the full-length plays as well that it is impressively ironic that Gallacher's best and best-known play should be, superficially, his most untidy: *Mr. Joyce Is Leaving Paris*. The second half of this play saw production first. Its order is not dictated by traditional dramaturgy but, as is pointed out by one of the figures which haunt the ageing Joyce, by the order of events at an Irish wake. That the "corpse" is the sole survivor of the wake is a good instance of how Gallacher can plot a joke to great thematic purpose. The order of the first half, set much earlier in Joyce's career but written slightly later in Gallacher's, is one of the playwright's confrontations of gifted and ungifted, moving from mutual challenge, though routines long familiar to both, towards acceptance. Though Stanislaus turns up, much muted, in the second half, the two patterns converge only through the consciousness of Joyce—formal confirmation of his (and, behind him, Gallacher's) claim to sole mastery of the remembered situations.

Mr. Joyce Is Leaving Paris in fact typifies Gallacher's dramatic writing as a whole as well as at its best. The qualitative difference between its parts is the difference between commendably accomplished craftsmanship and irresistibly imaginative insight. An analogous difference may be discerned in the use of theatrical resources. To these Gallacher is always attentive, using them to supplement the scripted action and dialogue in his fourth-wall dramas and pulling off some stunning isolated effects in the process. At best, however, Gallacher makes the technical parts of theatrical production indispensable to his dramatic statement. The lighting in the second half of *Mr. Joyce Is Leaving Paris*, for example, and the set for *The Sea Change* serve as visual indices to the central character's control of his memories and thus as evidence of the truth of his vision. In *The Sea Change* that vision, despite its ingenious presentation, remains derivative and diffuse. But when, as in the second half of *Mr. Joyce Is Leaving Paris*, Gallacher aligns tradition and his individual talent in perfect focus, he creates a resonant work.

—Marion O'Connor

GEE, Shirley (née Thieman).

Born in London, 25 April 1932. Educated at Frensham Heights, Farnham, Surrey; Webber-Douglas Academy of Dramatic Art, London. Married Donald Gee in 1965; two sons. Stage and television actress, 1952–66. Member of the Radio Committee, Society of Authors, 1980–82. Since 1986 member of the Women's Committee, Writers Guild. Recipient: *Radio Times* award, 1974; Pye award, for radio play, 1979; Sony award, for radio play, 1983; Susan Smith Blackburn prize, 1984; Samuel Beckett award, 1984. Agent: John Rush, David Higham Associates, 5–8 Lower John Street, London W1R 4HA. Address: 28 Fernshaw Road, London SW10 0TF, England.

Publications

PLAYS

Typhoid Mary (broadcast 1979; produced 1983). In *Best Radio Plays of 1979*, 1980.
Never in My Lifetime (broadcast 1983; produced 1984). In *Best Radio Plays of 1983*, 1984.
Ask for the Moon (produced 1986). 1987.
Warrior (produced 1989). 1991.

RADIO PLAYS: *Stones*, 1974; *The Vet's Daughter*, from the novel by Barbara Comyns, 1976; *Moonshine*, 1977; *Typhoid Mary*, 1979; *Bedrock*, 1979; *Men on White Horses*, from the novel by Pamela Haines, 1981; *Our Regiment* (documentary), 1982; *Never in My Lifetime*, 1983; *Against the Wind*, 1988; *The Forsyte Chronicles*, co-adaptation of *The Forsyte Saga* by John Galsworthy, 1990.

TELEVISION PLAYS: *Long Live the Babe*, 1984; *Flights*, 1985.

CRITICAL STUDIES: *British Radio Drama* edited by John Drakakis, 1981; *The Way to Write Radio Drama* by William Ash, 1985; *The Feminist Companion to Literature in English*, edited by Virginia Blain, Patricia Clements, and Isobel Grundy, 1990.

THEATRICAL ACTIVITIES

ACTOR: roles with Worthing, Hull, Malvern, and other repertory companies, and in more than 100 television plays and series episodes, 1952–66.

Shirley Gee comments:

I really don't like to make statements about my work; I hope those who see or hear the plays will have the freedom to draw their own conclusions. However, I'll try. I suppose I write to try to understand. To make sense out of chaos. To confront some terrors. I wonder what particular individuals might do trapped in a particular public event or social context. I watch them grapple, try to come to terms, fight to find the meaning of their lives. Often they are in a besieged landscape: the dead in *Stones*; Mary the typhoid carrier, imprisoned, in *Typhoid Mary*; British soldiers and Irish nationals in Belfast in *Never in My Lifetime*; the Victorian laceworkers and present-day sweatshop workers in *Ask for the Moon*. They are tyrannised by fear or poverty or loneliness or war. Their individual needs and desires run counter to the needs and desires of society, and must be sacrificed to that society. Still, they behave with love and courage. They save one another despite themselves. They beam a little light into a dark world. I wonder what I would have done, had I been in their place.

The list of women playwrights who have won major awards is, although increasing daily, not long, and one might expect Shirley Gee's name to be better known. Sadly, it is easy to account for her comparative lack of fame: most of her work has been written for radio, the most critically neglected medium of the past few decades. In Gee's case this is doubly unfortunate, for her radio experience is what gives her work for the stage its special vitality.

The radio playwright enjoys virtually unlimited freedom of approach; as long as he or she can unlock the listener's imagination anything is possible. Radio allows all kinds of spatial and temporal jumps; it is possible to create and instantly change the scenery, flash backwards or forwards in time, simply by the use of a few words or a snatch of song. Gee has always been one of the most technically authoritative of radio writers, and it was perhaps the triple accolade given to her radio play *Typhoid Mary*—a Giles Cooper award, a Pye award, a Special Commendation in the Italia prize—that prompted the Royal Shakespeare Company to stage the play and discover that its darting, fragmented structure worked onstage with verve and power.

Typhoid Mary is Mary Mallon, the tragic Irish immigrant who unwittingly spread the disease around New York at the beginning of the century. Instead of narrating her story straightforwardly, Gee creates a kaleidoscope of fragments: in one brief scene, for example, disembodied voices chant sensationalist newspaper headlines ("Calamity Cook Kills Wholesale"), a lawyer pronounces on her status in dry legal prose, a chorus sings "Molly Malone" to the accompaniment of spoons, and Mary in the midst speaks of her pain and grief as if she was in her own living room.

This lively variety of styles (from naturalism to the surreal) provides an analysis of her plight from several simultaneous angles. The spoon music stresses her background as struggling immigrant desperate to make good in a new world, and the humming of "Molly Malone" counterpoints this; Mary is already enshrined in popular song and in the popular imagination as a killer. The crude unthinking bias against her is fed by the press and allowed by the law. In fact Gee allows us in a few seconds to see Mary with the whole of American society ranged against her, with a vividness and compression naturalistic techniques would never permit.

For all its liveliness *Typhoid Mary* remained a study of a tragic individual without wider resonance. Gee's next ambitious work, also originating in radio, showed her wrestling with political drama. *Never in My Lifetime* opens shatteringly with the shooting of two British soldiers in a Belfast disco, then flashes backwards and forwards in time to explain the motives behind the shooting and its consequences. We follow the lives of the soldiers—Charlie, badly wounded, with a pregnant wife, and Tom, who dies—and the girls who lured them into ambush—the terrorist Maire, and Tess who is sleeping with Tom and joins Maire to save her own life when this becomes known to the IRA. By juxtaposing past and present, snatches of song, and snippets of Belfast life, Gee creates their lives and evokes unforgettably the grief of their loved ones. On a less personal level, however, the play is not so satisfying. The breadth and daring of the structure give the misleading impression that the play is presenting the fullest possible spectrum of Belfast politics. In fact, the cards are stacked. The only voice to speak for the Republican cause, for instance, is the voice of terrorism. Through the violent and twisted Maire, not just this killing but the whole concept of Irish nationhood is associated with a chain of ugly and sexually perverse imagery, contrasting with the wholesome lyricism of the naive Tess. The soldiers are described taking part in a brutal attack, but it is not shown, whereas the disco incident is terrifyingly realised. Essentially the play takes a pro-British stance while presenting itself as a slice of life; it seems that Gee is not fully in control of her material.

Ask for the Moon, however, shows a clearer political direction, and also translates the techniques of radio into striking visual terms. It shows simultaneously two generations of workers, Victorian lacemakers and women in a modern sweat shop. Gee's talent for conveying the texture of working life does more than lament their exploitation; she also shows how working conditions are structured to prevent unionisation. A lacemaker is forced to provide her child with opium so that the group will not slow up production; an old sweatshop hand steals another's piece-work to escape the sack. Gee makes it clear that this is forced on them despite real comradeship and caring and pride in their work. There is a touching moment when time barriers are broken and both groups join in wonder to admire a wedding veil that has cost one woman her eyesight. The women have no illusions about why they betray one another, and in the final anger of one of them, at first blind rage and then quiet planning for her own future, there is a hint that they are learning at last how to change.

—Frances Gray

GEMS, Jonathan (Malcolm Frederick).

Born in London, 7 January 1952; son of Pam Gems, *q.v.* Educated at Stowe School, Buckinghamshire, 1965–67; Holland Park Comprehensive, London, 1967–68; Sandown Grammar, Isle of Wight, 1968–69; Royal Academy of Dramatic Art, London, 1970–71; Exeter College of Art, 1971–72. Married Catherine Hall in 1981. Founder, with Richard Branson, *Student* magazine, 1969–70; managing director, Capricorn Graphics, founder, Jonny and the Gemstones music group, and editor, *It's All Lies* (adult comic), 1970–73; deputy manager, Portobello Hotel, and managing director, Holland Mirrors, both London, 1973–75; stage manager, Open Space Theatre, London, and managing director, Jean Collette Seel fashion company, 1975–76; stage manager, Half Moon Theatre, London, 1976–77. Recipient: George Devine award, 1980; Critics Circle award, 1986; Aspen Film Festival award, 1992. Lives in Los Angeles. Agent: Sebastian Born, Curtis Brown, 161–168 Regent Street, London W1R 5TB, England.

Publications

PLAYS

Jesus Rides Out (produced 1978).
The Shithouse of the August Moon (produced 1978).
Rinni Bootsie Tutti Frutti (produced 1978).
The Dentist (produced 1979).
The Tax Exile (produced 1979). 1986.
The Secret of the Universe (produced 1980).
Naked Robots (produced 1980). With *Susan's Breasts* and *The Paranormalist*, 1989.
The Paranormalist (produced 1982). With *Naked Robots* and *Susan's Breasts*, 1989.
Doom Doom Doom Doom (produced 1984).
Susan's Breasts (produced 1985). With *Naked Robots* and *The Paranormalist*, 1989.
Naked Robots, Susan's Breasts, The Paranormalist. 1989.

SCREENPLAYS: *White Mischief*, with Michael Radford, 1985; *The Dress*, 1990.

THEATRICAL ACTIVITIES

DIRECTOR: Plays—some of his own plays; *The Treat* by Pam Gems, London, 1982 (co-director); *These Foolish Things* by Philip Davis, London, 1983. Film—*The Dress*, 1990.

Jonathan Gems comments:

I wanted to be a great playwright but instead I've ended up writing movie scripts in Los Angeles.

It would seem that Jonathan Gems has become one more in a line of younger British dramatists (Antony Minghella is another instance) wooed away from the theatre by movies. However skilled Gems's screen-writing may be, it would be sad to lose his special talent from the theatre.

Perhaps he became disillusioned by the fact that none of his plays of the 1980's made the breakthrough into the mainstream. However successful he may have been in filling small theatres on the London fringe, he clearly wanted to reach a wider audience, not to mention make a decent living, hardly possible on fringe royalties, even with packed houses. But the fact remains that few dramatists managed to pin down with such lethal accuracy and comedic flair the subcultures of the 1980's.

Gems made a big stir with *The Tax Exile*, a rarity of modern high comedy, tracing the destruction of a decent, middle-aged man by the venality of his family. High comic spirits and a strongly moral core made an unusual combination from a young writer in 1979, and all his plays of the 1980's were fuelled by this fusion. In *Naked Robots*, as he admitted, "I wrote about me and my friends," to subsequent lack of enthusiasm when he started showing the script around, everyone rejecting it on the grounds that the characters were disgusting and the situations unbelievable ("I was baffled. This was my life!"). The RSC rescued the play and its 1980 Warehouse production remains one of the company's key achievements in new writing. Set in a warehouse dominated by a bed comprised of 10 stacked mattresses, its characters are predominantly young, either drifting like the middle-class punk Gemma or trying to carve out careers in fashion or the music industry like the central couple Desna and Nudy, and the play, tracing the shifting relationships that develop, covers a world of squats, casual sex, abortion, pop music, and drugs (Gems's dealer, Ray, is often an hilariously inept figure). He neither judges nor sentimentalises his characters; the play remains one of the most clear-eyed of its period.

The family seems less than a cosy unit in most of Gems's plays; characters like Desna and Gemma seem totally detached from their parents. And initially in *The Paranormalist* we seem again to be in the midst of the post-nuclear family with the paranormalist grandfather Sonny resented by his mixed-up psychiatrist daughter Barbara, at odds in turn with her drop-out daughter Mopsa, who is recovering from an abortion as the play begins. *The Paranormalist* is hardly short on action—it involves several paranormal experiments, Sonny's levitation, and an exorcism. Partly this was Gems's attempt to move beyond the technical restrictions of studio theatres, but it also reflected his sense of the inexplicable and the unknown that underlines most lives. Sonny's serenity casts an increasing spell over the action which ends, after the violence of the exorcism which casts out Barbara's demons, with a beguiling scene of unity as the characters sing a harmonised version of "The Melody Lingers On" as the lights fade.

Gems's most recently produced play is *Susan's Breasts*. He wanted to tackle the theme of love but the play "became predominantly a play about people *not* falling in love," except for the mysterious character of Lemon, a disturbed but passionate young man who gives the play its emotional resonance. The play focuses on another group of young Londoners, some more affluent and distinctly less appealing than those in *Naked Robots*, the men mostly a brutish, sexist lot interested solely in financial and social success. The women—aspiring actress Susan, American model Pookie, and the drug-addict Carol—all seem to connive at the males' sexism in a mid-1980's world where love is sex and relationships are business deals. Opening with a superbly written scene at a picnic in a London park, the play moves into a new gear as Lemon's love for (and obsession with) Susan increases. Susan has been diagnosed as sterile; she casually sleeps once with Lemon and becomes pregnant (the breasts of the title now increase in size), and although Lemon escapes from the asylum in which he has been committed to plead with her, the closing implication is that Susan, faced with the loss of a movie role, will abort the child. The play's final image of Susan being comforted by the increasingly addicted Carol is another instance of Gems's ability to fuse strong theatrical images with his gift for the dialogue of his splendidly varied casts of characters.

—Alan Strachan

GEMS, (Iris) Pam(ela, née Price).

Born in Bransgore, Dorset, 1 August 1925. Educated at Brockenhurst County High School, 1936–41; Manchester University, 1946–49, B.A. (honours) in psychology 1949. Served in the Women's Royal Naval Service, 1944–46. Married Keith Gems in 1949; two sons, including Jonathan Gems, *q.v.*, and two daughters. Research assistant, BBC, London, 1950–53. Agent: ACTAC, 16 Cadogan Lane, London S.W.1, England.

Publications

PLAYS

Betty's Wonderful Christmas (for children; produced 1972).
My Warren, and After Birthday (produced 1973).
The Amiable Courtship of Miz Venus and Wild Bill (produced 1973).
Sarah B. Divine! (additional material), by Tom Eyen, music by Jonathan Kramer (produced 1973).
Go West Young Woman (produced 1974).
Up in Sweden (produced 1975).
Dusa, Fish, Stas, and Vi (as *Dead Fish*, produced 1976; as *Dusa, Fish, Stas, and Vi*, produced 1976). 1977.
The Project (produced 1976).
Guinevere (produced 1976).
The Rivers and Forests, adaptation of a play by Marguerite Duras (produced 1976).
My Name Is Rosa Luxemburg, adaptation of a play by Marianne Auricoste (produced 1976).
Franz into April (produced 1977).
Queen Christina (produced 1977; revised version produced 1982). 1982.
Piaf (produced 1978). 1979.
Ladybird, Ladybird (produced 1979).
Sandra (produced 1979).
Uncle Vanya, adaptation of a play by Chekhov (produced 1979). 1979.
A Doll's House, adaptation of a play by Ibsen (produced 1980).
Sketches in *Variety Night* (produced 1982).
The Treat (produced 1982).
Aunt Mary (produced 1982).In *Plays by Women 3*, edited by Michelene Wandor, 1984.
The Cherry Orchard, adaptation of a play by Chekhov (produced 1984).
Loving Women (produced 1984). In *Three Plays*, 1985.
Camille, adaptation of a play by Dumas fils (produced 1984). In *Three Plays*, 1985.
Pasionaria, music by Paul Sand, lyrics by Gems and Sand (produced 1985).
Three Plays (includes *Piaf, Camille, Loving Women*). 1985.
The Danton Affair, adaptation of a work by Stanislawa Przybyszewska (produced 1986).
The Blue Angel, adaptation of a novel by Heinrich Mann (produced 1991).
Yerma, adaptation of the play by Federico García Lorca (produced 1993).

TELEVISION PLAYS: *A Builder by Trade*, 1961; *We Never Do What They Want*, 1979.

NOVELS

Mrs. Frampton. 1989.
Bon Voyage, Mrs. Frampton. 1990.

THEATRICAL ACTIVITIES

ACTOR: Film—*Nineteen Eighty-Four*, 1984.

Contemporary women playwrights explore areas of experience that the stage has traditionally ignored, and are developing styles designed as a radical contrast to the standard dramatic forms. Indeed, from a feminist viewpoint the category of "woman-writer" defines "a species of creativity that challenges the dominant image," since "the very concept of the 'writer' implies *maleness*." However, like Caryl Churchill, Pam Gems rejected this extreme position, declaring that "the phrase 'feminist writer' is absolutely meaningless because it implies polemic, and polemic is about changing things in a direct political way. Drama is subversive."

Like Churchill too, Gems developed her vision and theatrical techniques through dealing with historical subjects; and their example has been influential, making the history play characteristic of women's drama over the last decade. The tension between received ideas of the past—reinforcing the subservient status of women by relegating them to invisibility—and the very different feminist perspective, contributes to the thematic complexity of such plays.

Like many women dramatists, Pam Gems came to the theatre late, after 20 years of marriage and child-raising. Starting on the fringe, her early work for feminist theatre groups included an autobiographical piece, together with two monologues about female isolation and abortion, and a satiric pantomime. *Queen Christina*, her first major play, struck a new note and established all her central themes.

As in this play, Gems's most characteristic work dramatizes the human reality of women who have been transformed into cultural symbols. These range from the 17th-century Swedish Queen who renounced her crown, and a 19th-century courtesan, to a modern nightclub singer, or most recently *The Blue Angel* image of Marlene Dietrich as vampire sexuality. In each case the character is set against a familiar and highly romanticized picture. The counter-source for the earliest of Gems's historical dramas was the classic Garbo film of an ethereal and intellectual beauty, who abdicates for love, then finds consolation in religion when the man for whom she has sacrificed everything is killed in a duel. *Piaf* turns from Hollywood myth to the sanitized commercial image of a vulnerable street-sparrow, a purely emotional being whose songs are the direct expression "of unhappiness . . . of being made helpless by love . . . of being alone." *Camille* is a reversal of both Dumas's sentimentally tragic *La Dame aux camélias* and Verdi's operatic idealization in *La Traviata*.

The deforming pressures of society are most fully explored in *Queen Christina*, who provides a test-case for issues of sexual definition, biological determinism and social programming. As the sole heir to a kingdom at war, this historical figure has been "reared as a man . . . And then, on her accession, told to marry and breed, that is to be a woman. By which time, of course, like males of her era, she despised women as weak, hysterical, silly creatures." For Gems "It is a confusion which seems as apposite as ever." Forced to abdicate, she searches Europe for a way of life in which she can be herself. She is hailed as "an inspiration" to man-hating feminists (in the shape of 18th-century French "blue-stockings") in their campaign for control over their bodies through abortion. However, she finds herself repulsed by their life-denying warfare against the opposite sex, which she recognizes as the mirror image of male domination. She seeks spiritual emancipation in the Catholic Church, but finding that the Pope is interested only in exploiting her celibacy as religious propaganda, she asserts that "We won't deny the body." Offered the kingdom of Naples, she attempts to return to her masculine role. But when it forces her to kill her lover for betraying her invading armies, she rejects the whole male ethos, setting herself against domination in all its forms, master/servant as well as man/woman. Finally—when too old to bear children—she discovers the value of maternal instincts and affirms her biological nature.

For Gems, "Whichever way we look at it, the old norms won't do any more." The play asks what it means to be "female"; and Christina's example implies that a valid definition can only be reached through "the creation of a society more suited to both sexes"—which Gems has described as her aim in writing. Her concept of drama as subversive, rather than confrontational, means working on public consciousness indirectly. In line with this, her protagonist comes to realize that positive change can only be achieved through the specifically female, undervalued qualities of "weakness," non-violent resilience, and maternal nurture: "Half the world rapes and destroys—must women, the other half, join in?"

Typically, Gems creates an opposition between what is depicted on the stage and the audience's expectations. This is most obvious in *Piaf*, where incidents from the Parisian singer's life are interpolated with renditions of her popular lyrics. The gutter milieu, her prostitution and involvement in murder, drunkenness, and drugs contrast with the glittering public persona. Piaf disintegrates under the contradiction; and when the gap between idol and real woman can no longer be disguised, society preserves the false image by divorcing musical soul from female body.

At the same time, the way the songs rise out of the scenes emphasizes that Piaf's unconventional art and her physical crudity are inseparable. Her rise to stardom is a process of continual exploitation by the men who manage or marry her, and by her public (by extension the audience for Gems's play) who project their desires onto her. Yet it is also her status as a star that enables her to assert a personal autonomy, however provisional. This is expressed through her sexual freedom, which overturns all the moral codes. And the same reversal of conventional values is reflected in the play itself, which shows Piaf not only copulating but ostentatiously pissing on stage. Physicality at its most basic (a stock way of representing reality) demolishes the socially acceptable female stereotype, promoted and imposed by men, and thus provides an example of alternative values.

—Christopher Innes

See the essay on *Piaf*.

GILL, Peter.

Born in Cardiff, Glamorgan, 7 September 1939. Educated at St. Illtyd's College, Cardiff. Actor, 1957–65; associate director, Royal Court Theatre, London, 1970–72; director, Riverside Studios, Hammersmith, London, 1976–80. Since 1980 associate director, National Theatre, London, and since 1984 director, National Theatre Studio. Recipient: Belgrade International Theatre Festival prize, for directing, 1968; George Devine award, 1968; British Theatre Association award, for directing, 1985. O.B.E. (Officer, Order of the British Empire), 1980. Agent: Casarotto Ramsay Ltd., National House, 60–66 Wardour Street, London W1V 3HP, England.

Publications

PLAYS

The Sleepers Den (produced 1965; revised version produced 1969). With *Over Gardens Out*, 1970.

A Provincial Life, adaptation of a story by Chekhov (produced 1966).

Over Gardens Out (produced 1969). With *The Sleepers Den*, 1970.

The Merry-Go-Round, adaptation of the play by D.H. Lawrence (produced 1973). 1973.

Small Change (produced 1976). With *Kick for Touch*, 1985.

The Cherry Orchard, adaptation of a play by Chekhov (produced 1978).

Kick for Touch (produced 1983). With *Small Change*, 1985.

In the Blue (produced 1985). With *Mean Tears*, 1987.

As I Lay Dying, adaptation of the novel by Faulkner (produced 1985).

Mean Tears (produced 1987). In *Plays International*, August 1987; with *In the Blue*, 1987.

THEATRICAL ACTIVITIES

DIRECTOR: **Plays**—all his own plays, and *A Collier's Saturday Night* by D. H. Lawrence, 1965, 1968; *The Dwarfs* by Harold Pinter, 1966; *The Ruffian on the Stair* by Joe Orton, 1966; *O'Flaherty, V. C.* by Shaw, 1966; *The Local Stigmatic* by Heathcote Williams, 1966; *The Soldier's Fortune* by Thomas Otway, 1967; *The Daughter-in-Law* by D. H. Lawrence, 1967, 1968, and 1972; *Crimes of Passion* by Joe Orton, 1967, 1972; *June Evening* by Bill Naughton, 1967; *The Widowing of Mrs. Holroyd* by D. H. Lawrence, 1968; *Life Price* by Michael O'Neill and Jeremy Seabrook, 1969; *Much Ado about Nothing*, 1969; *Hedda Gabler* by Ibsen, 1970; *Landscape and Silence* by Harold Pinter, 1970; *The Duchess of Malfi* by Webster, 1971; *Macbeth*, 1971; *Cato Street* by Robert Shaw, 1971; *A Midsummer Night's Dream*, 1972; *Crete and Sergeant Pepper* by John Antrobus, 1972; *Twelfth Night*, 1974; *Fishing* by Michael Weller, 1975; *The Fool* by Edward Bond, 1975; *As You Like It*, 1975; *The Changeling* by Middleton and Rowley, 1978; *Measure for Measure*, 1979; *Julius Caesar*, 1980; *Scrape Off the Black* by Tunde Ikoli, 1980; *A Month in the Country* by Turgenev, 1981; *Don Juan* by Molière, 1981; *Major Barbara* by Shaw, 1982; *Danton's Death* by Georg Büchner, 1982; *Tales from Hollywood* by Christopher Hampton, 1983; *Venice Preserv'd* by Thomas Otway, 1984; *Antigone*, 1984; *Fool for Love* by Sam Shepard, 1984; *A Twist of Lemon* by Alex Renton, 1985; *The Garden of England* by Peter Cox, 1985;

Bouncing by Rosemary Wilton, 1985; *Up for None* by Mick Mahoney, 1985; *Mrs. Klein* by Nicholas Wright, 1988; *Juno and the Paycock* by Sean O'Casey, 1989. **Opera**—*The Marriage of Figaro* by Mozart, 1987. **Television**—*Girl* by James Robson, 1973; *Grace* by David Storey, 1974; *A Matter of Taste* by Alex La Guma, 1974; *Fugitive* by Sean Walsh, 1974; *Hitting Town* by Stephen Poliakoff, 1976.

ACTOR: **Plays**—Customer in *Last Day in Dreamland* by Willis Hall, 1959; Plato in *The Trial of Cob and Leach* by Christopher Logue, 1959; Mangolis in *The Kitchen* by Arnold Wesker, 1959; Marcus and A Postcard Seller in *This Way to the Tomb* by Ronald Duncan, 1960; Silvius in *As You Like It*, 1962; in *The Caucasian Chalk Circle* by Brecht, 1962. **Films**—*H.M.S. Defiant (Damn the Defiant!)*, 1962; *Zulu*, 1964.

For Peter Gill, playwriting has always been incidental to his profession as director. Indeed, he is still better known as the director who first realised the theatrical potential of D. H. Lawrence's plays than as the author of any of his own works, all of which he has also directed. His special skill, both as director and as dramatist, derives from the naturalistic exploitation of subtext, usually in association with relatively inarticulate proletarian characters, so that the simplest domestic situations are weighted and economically developed for their dramatic potential. *The Sleepers Den* illustrates this method well. The Shannon family, immured in an apparently condemned Cardiff slum flat, suffers variously from claustrophobia and agoraphobia; cornered, defensive, and scared to come to grips with their real dangers, they gradually expose themselves to emotional decomposition until their whole pattern of life collapses. The subtext becomes of paramount importance because of the characters' severely limited capacity even to begin to understand their problems. The Shannons are a fragmented family: an adult brother and sister, their bedridden mother, and a daughter. There is no explanation of how this situation has evolved, and there is no evidence that anyone understands it; across the three generations, power and defense are manipulated by trivial—but effective—gestures of bribery, blackmail, and threatening. Two outsiders—a debt collector and a Catholic social worker—function as catalysts to the situation, but the revelations which are offered seem ridiculous irrelevancies; the brother confesses to the social worker that he has been doing overtime and not telling his sister, and no one seems to understand the seriousness of court action for debt. It is clear that the characters' mental state is a reflection of their environment, that their lethargy and low self-esteem have a century of conditioning behind them. The dramatic crisis comes at the end of the second act, when the sister barricades herself inside the flat as a response to a situation which is too complicated for her to understand, let alone solve; the very short last act consists in her ignoring the pleadings of her brother and the daughter, who are now forced to sleep with friends. In Gill's 1969 production it was clear that old Mrs. Shannon is dead in the last act, so that the sister has shut herself in with the corpse. The interpretation is available that, far from presenting a grotesque family incident, the play suggests a recurrent pattern, with the now insane sister usurping her dead mother's role at the end, where a hereditary family state of introverted lethargy is on the verge of re-enactment. The ambiguous omission of an apostrophe from the play's title, which has been observed in all editions, may be calculated to hint at this.

The single sealed-in set of *The Sleepers Den* is an ideal laboratory for naturalism, but in *Over Gardens Out* Gill developed similar assumptions about character evolution, but set the action in two domestic and several exterior locations. Again, several generations are represented, and surprise and vagueness about the processes of physical decay and growth are intermittently felt; but the structures of authority and rebellion between the generations are relatively unambiguous here, and mindless behaviour, though plentiful, seems attributable to individual characters rather than collective. This means that particular anti-social gestures can be isolated as particular problems, so that even through some of the severities of the action a rich vein of wry comedy persists. The central characters are two adolescent Cardiff boys of widely differing propensities (though both are intellectually limited) whose leisure hours are filled with acts of vandalism which range from the trivial to the alarming. The picaresque tone of this play is more typical of the 1960's than is *The Sleepers Den*, but the play does show an advance in terms of its warmly sympathetic characterisation. A very similar technique is deployed more adventurously in *Small Change*, where two Cardiff boys are again followed through boyhood and adolescence into manhood; for the premiere, Gill even used one of the lead actors from *Over Gardens Out* (and would use him again in *Kick for Touch*). Such an expansive chronology means that the play's naturalistic cogency is not comparable with the earlier plays, and Gill allows himself rather more intelligent and perceptive characters, who deliver nostalgic, poetical monologues, the quality of which has been questioned by critics. However, by 1976 Gill could include a climactic scene of adult anagnorisis and recrimination, in which the boyhood relationship is explicitly perceived as homosexual.

Gill's later plays use very similar material, dissected with increasingly audacious techniques. *Kick for Touch* has two Cardiff brothers, war babies, reminiscing haphazardly across a kitchen table; a woman who is married to one of them and has been the lover of both, is the linking device for a series of interior monologues and duologues, with uninvolved characters simply moving a yard or two away and freezing. Again, there is a bond of something approaching love between the men, but the finale does not pivot on this but on the mystery of a domestic tragedy. *In the Blue* has only two male characters, homosexuals, one of whom is articulate and educated. The technical novelty of this play consists in the hypothetical reinterpretation of scenes, alternative performances introduced just by the word "OR", so that there is some uncertainty as to which version repre sents actuality and which fantasy. Gill's naturalism has here been obscured completely; the play is almost purely expressionistic. In *Mean Tears*, chronological structuring is denied in a collation of short segments of time in which three men and two women intersect, collide, and form fragile relationships.

Gill has also written and directed numerous successful adaptations, but mention should be made of one heroic failure because its technical effrontery resembles that of his original plays. *As I Lay Dying* theatricalises the innovative narrative method of Faulkner's novel, resulting in a pattern of monologues, with varying perspectives being traded across the body of the characters' mother. The jigsaw of monologues epitomises a tendency in Gill's plays, and the maternal catalyst is also recurrent, especially in *Small Change*.

—Howard McNaughton

GODBER, John (Harry).

Born in Upton, Yorkshire, 15 May 1956. Educated at Minsthorpe High School, South Elmsall, Yorkshire; Bretton Hall College, West Bretton, Yorkshire, 1974–78, Cert. Ed. 1977, B. Ed. (honours) 1978; Leeds University, 1978–79, M.A. in theatre 1979, graduate study, 1979–83. Teacher, Minsthorpe High School, 1981–83. Since 1984 artistic director, Hull Truck theatre company. Recipient: Edinburgh Festival award, 1981, 1982, 1984; Olivier award, 1984; Los Angeles Drama Critics Circle award, 1986. Address: Hull Truck, Spring Street Theatre, Spring Street, Hull, Yorkshire HU2 8RW, England.

Publications

PLAYS

A *Clockwork Orange*, adaptation of the novel by Anthony Burgess (produced 1980).
Cry Wolf (produced 1981).
Cramp (produced 1981; revised version, music by Tom Robinson and Hereward K, produced 1986).
E.P.A. (produced 1982).
Happy Jack (produced 1982). In *Five Plays*, 1989.
Young Hearts Run Free: Ideas Towards a Play (produced 1983).
September in the Rain (produced 1983). In *Five Plays*, 1989.
Bouncers (produced 1984). With *Shakers*, 1987.
Up 'n' Under (produced 1984). 1985.
Shakers, with Jane Thornton (produced 1985). With *Bouncers*, 1987.
Up 'n' Under II (produced 1985).
Blood, Sweat and Tears (produced 1986).
The Ritz (televised 1987; as *Putting on the Ritz*, produced 1987).
Teechers (produced 1987). 1989.
Oliver Twist (for children), adaptation of the novel by Charles Dickens (produced 1987).
Salt of the Earth (produced 1988). 1989.
Five Plays (includes *Up 'n' Under, Bouncers, Teechers, September in the Rain, Happy Jack*). 1989.
On the Piste (produced 1990). 1992.
Happy Families (produced 1991). 1992.
The Office Party (produced 1992).
April in Paris (produced 1992).

TELEVISION PLAYS: series scripts for *Grange Hill*, 1981–83, *Brookside*, 1983–84, and *Crown Court*, 1983; *The Rainbow Coloured Disco Dancer*, from work by C.P. Taylor, 1984; *The Ritz* series, 1987; *The Continental*, 1987; *My Kingdom for a Horse*, 1991.

THEATRICAL ACTIVITIES

DIRECTOR: **Plays**—all of his own plays; *Imagine* by Stephen Jeffreys, *Hedda Gabler* by Ibsen, and *The Dock* by Phil Woods, 1987; *Twelfth Night* by Shakespeare, 1989; *Sweet Sorrow* by Alan Plater, 1990.

John Godber is very clear about his particular theatrical style: "the dancer and not the poet is the father of the theatre." Reading his plays gives little sense of the energy and pace of the pieces in performance, an energy and pace deriving from his resolute refusal to separate the role of writer from that of director. His involvement with the Hull Truck Company has been a happy one; their commitment to a theatre based on contemporary and community-related issues and a long pedigree of theatre derived from improvisation and intense collaboration between writer and actors has allowed him the room to experiment with an exhilarating mixture of theatrical techniques. The result has been some of the funniest and most enjoyable evenings spent in a theatre in recent years.

Plot in Godber's work is kept to a minimum, and frequently the plays have a strong if deliberately jokey documentary feel to them. In *Bouncers*, the action takes place at a provincial disco—where the events of a typical night are interspersed with flash-back scenes of anxious preparation for the great night-out by the lads and girls. Nothing particularly unusual occurs. The bouncers rehearse various degrees of aggression towards the punters, copious amounts of tears, beer, and vomit are spilt, and the characters are united in a macabre attempt to shut off the grim realities of their lives—an attempt that will be, as always, doomed. All the many characters (both male and female) are played by the same four male bouncer actors, and the effect is to enlarge the comic potential of the events but also to stress its non-particularity. Godber is not interested in creating unique psychologically-realised characters. They are representative, standing in for an audience who may very well proceed from the theatre to such a disco—the more particularly since he is intent on attracting audiences that would not normally regard theatre as a part of their cultural experience. The club acts then as a gently symbolic location of the contemporary world at play, looking for a dream-world of alcoholic oblivion and easy sex, and finding instead a continuation of the daytime regime, ruled over by arbitrary bouncers free to admit or refuse entrance to a fun palace in which there are strict rules about dress, an expensive bar, and complete limitations on the celebration of any conceivable excess. There are tentative plans to turn the play into a movie, though it is difficult to see how the particular style of the play would mesh with the conventionally naturalistic demands of the film medium.

Shakers, written in collaboration with Jane Thornton, changes the sexual perspective. Set in a provincial wine bar run by four waitresses who again play all the other (male and female) characters, it offers an even bleaker account of the urge to escape. We see four young girls at work in the supermarket, fantasising about the birthday party to come, agonising over the choice of clothes, and seeing as the limit of their dreams the joy of actually working in a cocktail bar. But the life at Shakers presented by the four waitresses is no different from any other work situation. The hours are long, the pay is bad, and sexual harassment is not only rife, but is effectively encouraged by the unseen management. That they are the better able to analyse their situation than their male counterparts in *Bouncers* is typical of Godber's work. His strong feminist line demands this distinction. His plays are all about politically marginalised people, failures and victims of the system; for the women the victimisation is made worse by their sense of being underdogs in a world of underdogs, and they are given a stronger oppositional voice.

The pace of the productions and the constant role-switching does little to disguise, however, a certain literalness of political analysis. Everything fits too neatly into place. His concentration on marginalised characters in an urban wasteland brings with it an inability to look beyond the boundaries of marginalisation—although it must be admitted that in performance it is a weakness that is less apparent than on more sober reflection. For these reasons his most successful play to date is *Up 'n' Under*, for here Godber has been able to use the build-up to and the actual enactment on stage of a Rugby League Sevens match as a far less prosaic metaphor of a modern world of male competition and machismo. Down-at-heel Arthur is conned into a large bet with a bent but successful businessman that he cannot train the worst amateur pub team in Yorkshire to beat the top dogs, the Cobblers Arms from Castleford. Arthur's team are dragged, understrength and unwillingly, into a training programme supervised by (horror of horrors!) a woman, and the scene is set for a *Rocky*-style conclusion—Arthur's favourite movies are the *Rocky* films—in which the underdog gets up off his backside at the last possible moment and wins. The presentation of the game, with seven actors (including their female trainer) acting out play, is the most exciting piece of total theatre I have ever seen, and tension as to the outcome is kept up throughout. This is not Hollywood, however, and our heroes lose by the odd point. But Godber's characters, though inveterate losers, always retain an optimistic strain and the play ends with the team planning a double-or-nothing bet on the result of a further match—a match which duly takes place in *Up 'n' Under II*.

The sporting theme was re-explored in *On the Piste*—the very title proclaiming its seaside postcard antecedence—which played at the Leeds Grand in the summer of 1990, and this was followed by one of the most unusual events in theatrical history. In 1991 the Little Theatre Guild of Great Britain commissioned a play for the first time. Suitably enough they turned to John Godber, and on October 12 his *Happy Families* received 49 simultaneous first performances by different U.K. companies. The story, which follows the rise of John Taylor—small-town bright lad on the make—was a typical Godber mix of sex and class warfare, and it is hard to think of a writer, at the same time both populist and popular, more suited for the Guild's ambitious commission.

—John Bull

GOOCH, Steve.

Born in Surrey, 22 July 1945. Educated at the Emanuel School, London, 1956–63; Trinity College, Cambridge, 1964–67, B.A. (honours) in modern languages 1967; St. John's College, Cambridge (Harper-Wood Scholar), 1967; Birmingham University, 1968–69. Assistant editor, *Plays and Players* magazine, London, 1972–73; resident dramatist, Half Moon Theatre, London, 1973–74, Greenwich Theatre, London, 1974–75, Solent People's Theatre,

Southampton, 1981–82, Theatre Venture, London, 1983–84, and Croydon Warehouse Theatre, Surrey, 1986. Recipient: Arts Council bursary, 1973; Thames Television award, 1974. Agent: Casarotto Ramsay Ltd., National House, 60–66 Wardour Street, London W1V 3HP, England.

Publications

PLAYS

The NAB Show (produced 1970).
Great Expectations, adaptation of the novel by Dickens (produced 1970).
Man Is Man, adaptation of the play by Brecht (produced 1971).
It's All for the Best, adaptation of the novel *Candide* by Voltaire (produced 1972).
Big Wolf, adaptation of a play by Harald Mueller (produced 1972). 1972.
Will Wat; If Not, What Will? (produced 1972). 1975.
Nicked (produced 1972).
The Mother, adaptation of a play by Brecht (produced 1973). 1978.
Female Transport (produced 1973). 1974.
Dick (produced 1973).
The Motor Show, with Paul Thompson (produced 1974). 1975.
Cock-Artist, adaptation of a play by Rainer Werner Fassbinder (produced 1974). In *Gambit 39–40*, 1982.
Strike '26, with Frank McDermott (produced 1975).
Made in Britain, with Paul Thompson (produced 1976).
Landmark (as *Our Land, Our Lives*, produced 1976; revised version, as *Landmark*, produced 1980). 1982.
Back-Street Romeo (produced 1977).
Rosie, adaptation of a play by Harald Mueller (also director: produced 1977).
The Women Pirates: Ann Bonney and Mary Read (produced 1978). 1978.
In the Club (produced 1979).
Future Perfect, with Michelene Wandor and Paul Thompson (produced 1980).
Fast One (produced 1982). 1982.
Fuente Ovejuna, adaptation of the play by Lope de Vega (produced 1982).
Flotsam, adaptation of a play by Harald Mueller (produced 1985). In *Gambit 39–40*, 1982.
Home Work, adaptation of a play by Franz Xaver Kroetz (produced 1990). In *Gambit 39–40*, 1982.
Taking Liberties (produced 1984).
Good for You (produced 1985).
Mister Fun (produced 1986).
Star Turns (produced 1987).
Massa (produced 1989). 1990.
Our Say (produced 1989).
Lulu, adaptation of *Earth Spirit* and *Pandora's Box* by Frank Wedekind (produced 1990).
The Marquis of Keith, adaptation of the play by Frank Wedekind (produced 1990).

RADIO PLAYS: *The Kiosk*, from a play by Ludvík Aškenazy, 1970; *Delinquent*, from a play by Harald Mueller, 1978; *Santis*, from a play by Martin Walser, 1980; *What Brothers Are For*, 1983; *Bill of Health*, 1987.

OTHER
All Together Now: An Alternative View of Theatre and the Community. 1984.
Writing a Play. 1988.

Translator, *Poems and Ballads*, by Wolf Biermann. 1977.
Translator, with Paul Knight, *Wallraff, The Undesirable Journalist*, by Günter Wallraff. 1978.

CRITICAL STUDIES: *Stages in the Revolution* by Catherine Itzin, 1980; "The Surveyor and the Construction Engineer" by Gooch, in *Theatre Quarterly 36*, 1980.

THEATRICAL ACTIVITIES
DIRECTOR: **Plays**— *Work Kills!* by Bruce Birchall, 1975; *Consensus* by Michael Gill, 1976; *Rosie*, 1977; *Night Shift* by John Derbyshire, 1983.

Steve Gooch comments:

My work has developed over the years from an attempt to articulate the voice of working-class and other dispossessed sections of British society towards a general aesthetic in which the personal struggle to take control of one's life is given full emotional value within an open-eyed depiction of the social nexus surrounding it.

This has often been expressed through historical analogy and the portrayal of "hidden history," and frequently by means of multiple protagonists or groups engaged in a common, though variegated, purpose. In these plays I have attempted to reflect the increasingly collective nature of modern life, confronting the dilemma of pluralism within an ordered democratic progress.

Crucial to this "group" aesthetic is the gap between experience and thought, specifically in the way individual characters in groups "think" each other. This has also been important in my smaller-cast plays during the 1980's, where wider social conflict has tended to be treated through the microcosm of man-woman relationships. In each of these contexts language becomes the fine-tuning of communication between conflicting social aspirations and judgements. In exploring this, my translation and adaptation of European works has been invaluable in sensitising my understanding of language as the barometer of social will.

In contrast to other playwrights of the British 1968 generation, Steve Gooch has not, in spite of being a very prolific and versatile writer, found a firm foothold in either the major subsidised theatre companies or the mass media. This is not due to a lack of talent or of successful productions of his plays or even to a decline of the British alternative theatre scene, but rather to Gooch's adherence to a theatre for the community. A great deal of artistic energy, from the beginning of Gooch's career as a writer for the stage, has gone into the mediation, by translations or adaptations, of plays and theatrical ideas from the Romance and German languages. Gooch shows particular skill in his translations of German dramatists of the classical modernist period like the early Brecht and, more recently, Frank Wedekind, and of those contemporary playwrights (Kroetz, Harald Mueller, Martin Walser) whose preoccupation with political aspects of subjectivity mirrors his own, but he has also adapted classics like Dickens, Voltaire, Lope de Vega, and Terence.

In his original work for the stage Gooch early on found a congenial venue in the Half Moon Theatre in London's East End. One of the first results of their workshop projects was Gooch's dramatization, as *Will Wat; If Not, What Will?*, of Wat Tyler's 1381 peasants' uprising, the first proto-socialist movement in English history. In this attempt "to show what the history books usually leave out" Gooch draws on contemporary documents and alternative versions of medieval history to present the peasants' point of view in their opposition to royal militarism and exploitation by old feudal and emerging merchant interests. The play acutely balances the eventual defeat of the peasants led by John Ball and Wat Tyler against the positive growth of self-awareness of an oppressed class. History is brought on stage as a collective process whose dramaturgy has to preempt individual identification by anti-illusionist techniques such as double casting, songs, and quotes from historical documents. Similar Brechtian techniques are employed in Gooch's next historical play, also produced by the Half Moon Theatre, *Female Transport*. Again, it is history from below, this time in the more familiar scenery of early 19th-century Britain. The play gives a realistic account of the voyage to Australia of six female convicts who gradually win through to an insight into the necessity of resistance against a patriarchal class society. This socialist-feminist line in Gooch's work is elaborated in an early text that ended up as a Royal Shakespeare Company production of *The Women Pirates: Ann Bonney and Mary Read*. In this epic portrait of two historical women at the turn of the 18th century, Gooch charts, in a loose configuration of scenes interspersed with many songs, a successful if seemingly peripheral liberation from hegemonic law and morality.

While developing his Brechtian style of historical plays with a socialist, humanist, and feminist slant, Gooch collaborated on some theatrical projects that concerned sections of the contemporary working class in a more direct way. It was here that Gooch came nearest to his declared aim of writing "about working-class experience and history, and for a working-class audience and readership." In *The Motor Show* (written with Paul Thompson) Gooch tried to create a working-class community theatre from within. After local research at the Dagenham Ford plant by the group called Community Theatre, the play turned into a 24-scene documentation, in a deft cartoon-like style mixing documentary, realistic, and music hall elements, of 60 years of struggle between the Ford Company and their workers. The Community Theatre failed to set itself up in Dagenham, but the unashamedly agit-prop techniques— rescued from preachiness by witty dialogue—of *The Motor Show*, largely retained in *Strike '26* and in *Made in Britain* (a documentary about British Leyland, again written with Paul Thompson), became a model for many similar attempts by other writers. In *Our Land, Our Lives* Gooch's concern with issues involving specifically contemporary communities was placed on a more general level by being given a fictional focus in a reunion of young married people in a village barn that had served them as a meeting-place in their schooldays. The play shows the encroachment of agribusiness on traditio-nal village life, but in the reworking of it with Essex University Theatre (under the title *Landmark*) it came to include the theme of nuclear threat. In the revised version the fields against whose sale the young people have been rallying opposition are bought up by the Ministry of Defence to be converted into a site for nuclear missiles.

In the new austerity of the 1980s Gooch has apparently redefined the range of his dramatic themes, even though he has remained faithful to the small companies and theatre groups of the dwindling alternative circuit. The move away from agit-prop didacticism is obvious even in his recent *Taking Liberties*, written in the genre of the historical play which lends itself most readily to political discourse with clear-cut messages. In this play we get an unusually broad social panorama, from patricians to plebeians, bound up in the radical agitation of the late 18th century. The carnivalesque action here focuses on the mock election of a Mayor of Garratt and reflects John Wilkes's creation of a new type of populist politics involving the London masses. The play also indicates a change in the post-1979 political atmosphere in that it does not so much rescue the utopian perspectives from the historical setting but ends in the temporary defeat of plebeian aspirations for political participation. The widen-ing of thematic range and intended appeal finds expression in a reappropria-tion of realist and even naturalist theatrical approaches. This development accompanies the synthesis in Gooch's conception of his own work between John McGrath's purist reliance on popular traditions and David Edgar's more eclectic attitude towards mainstream theatrical codes. The new approach characterizes even a play with a seemingly exotic setting like *Fast One*, in which a merchant seaman is caught up in an international intrigue about the sale of arms in an unspecified South American country.

Mister Fun, written for a Sheffield-based touring group, goes even further in the direction of a naturalist tradition that the author had never completely excluded from his theatre language. The play concentrates on the lives of a young couple working on a traditional fairground. The action shows the inevitable take-over of the fair by the electronics branch of the leisure industry after a local council's abortive attempts to give it a permanent site. This process is traced in its divisive effects on the young couple's lives. In their drifting apart the girl achieves some degree of independence, whereas the eponymous hero becomes a kind of walking ad for what was once popular entertainment but which now usurps people's work and minds.

—Bernd-Peter Lange

GOW, Ronald.

Born in Heaton Moor, near Manchester, Lancashire, 1 November 1897. Educated at Altrincham Grammar School, Cheshire; Manchester University, B.Sc. 1922. Served in the British Army, 1918–19. Married the actor Wendy Hiller in 1937; one daughter and one son. Worked as a chemist and school-master; educational film producer. Agent: Laurence Fitch Ltd., 483 Southbank House, Black Prince Road, Albert Embankment, London SE1 7SJ, England. *Died 27 April 1993.*

Publications

PLAYS

Breakfast at Eight (produced 1920). 1921.

The Sausage (produced n.d.). 1924.

Under the Skull and Bones: A Piratical Play with Songs (produced n.d.). 1929.

Higgins: The Highwayman of Cranford (produced n.d.). 1930.

Henry; or, The House on the Moor (produced n.d.). 1931.

Five Robin Hood Plays (includes *The King's Warrant, The Sheriff's Kitchen, All on a Summer's Day, Robin Goes to Sea, The Affair at Kirklees*). 1932.

The Golden West (produced n.d.). 1932.

The Vengeance of the Gang (produced n.d.). 1933.

O.H.M.S. (produced 1933). 1933.

Gallows Glorious (produced 1933; as *John Brown*, produced 1934). 1933.

My Lady Wears a White Cockade (produced 1934). 1935.

Love on the Dole, adaptation of the novel by Walter Greenwood (produced 1934). 1935.

Compromise. 1935.

The Marrying Sort. 1935.

The Miracle on Watling Street: A Play for the Open Air. 1935.

Men Are Unwise, adaptation of the novel by Ethel Mannin (produced 1937).

Ma's Bit o' Brass, based on the screenplay *Lancashire Luck* (produced 1938; as *Lovejoy's Millions*, produced 1938). 1938.

Scuttleboom's Treasure. 1938.

Grannie's a Hundred. 1939.

The Lawyer of Springfield (broadcast 1940). 1949.

Jenny Jones, music by Harry Parr Davies, adaptation of stories by Rhys Davies (produced 1944).

Tess of the D'Urbervilles, adaptation of the novel by Thomas Hardy (produced 1946).

Jassy, adaptation of the novel by Norah Lofts (produced 1947).

Ann Veronica, adaptation of the novel by H.G. Wells (produced 1949). 1951; revised version, with Frank Wells, music by Cyril Ornadel, lyrics by David Croft (produced 1969).

The Full Treatment, with Robert Morley (produced 1953).

The Edwardians, adaptation of the novel by V. Sackville-West (as *Weekend in May*, produced 1959; as *The Edwardians*, produced 1959). 1960.

Mr. Rhodes (produced 1961).

A Boston Story, adaptation of the novel *Watch and Ward* by Henry James (as *Watch and Ward*, produced 1964; revised version, as *A Boston Story*, produced 1968). 1969.

This Stratford Business, adaptation of stories by Henry James (produced 1971).

The Friendship of Mrs. Eckley (produced 1975).

The Old Jest, adaptation of the novel by Jennifer Johnston (produced 1980).

SCREENPLAYS: *The Man Who Changed His Mind*, 1928; *The Glittering Sword*, 1929; *Southern Roses*, 1936; *Lancashire Luck*, with A.R. Rawlinson, 1937; *Mr. Smith Carries On*, 1937; *Jig Saw*, 1942.

RADIO PLAYS: *The Lawyer of Springfield*, 1940; *Enter, Fanny Kemble*, 1940; *Front Line Family* series, during World War II; *Mr. Darwin Comes Ashore*, 1941; *Patience on a Monument*, 1944; *Westward Ho!* (serialization), from the novel by Charles Kingsley, 1953; *Lorna Doone* (serialization), from the novel by R.D. Blackmore, 1954.

TELEVISION PLAY: *Trumpet in the Clouds*, 1955.

OTHER
Editor, *Plays for the Classroom*. 1933.

Ronald Gow commented:

The question I am being asked is "what makes me tick as a playwright?" I was brought up near Manchester with the strong belief that the Gaiety Theatre was the greatest thing that ever happened there—even greater than the Hallé—and that Brighouse, Monkhouse, and Houghton were not only household words but shining examples. We knew them all and I had even acted with the author of *Hindle Wakes*. I was definitely stage-struck and when we built a theatre in my home town I cared little whether I shifted scenery or acted or took tickets at the door. After many one-act plays and a desperate wish to be a shining example myself I began to look around for something to be angry about. Most of my plays had some compelling obsession in them. When I wrote about Bonnie Prince Charlie it became anti-war and anti-romantic. Result, a mere six weeks at the Embassy. Next play about John Brown, whose soul went marching on, brought the audience cheering to their feet at the old Shaftesbury. But a bitter anti-slavery bias and an austere title (*Gallows Glorious*) were no good in that temple of musical comedy. Two weeks. (Two nights in New York.) I was trying to write an anti-unemployment play (three million of them) but fortunately read Walter Greenwood's *Love on the Dole* and decided to dramatize that instead. Marriage necessitated making money, with no axes to grind, resulting in comedies like *Ma's Bit o' Brass* and various film scripts and a great deal of propaganda radio and film work during the war (*Front Line Family*). Success with adapting novels led to London productions of *Tess of the D'Urbervilles*, *Ann Veronica*, *The Edwardians*, and *A Boston Story* from a Henry James novel.

Ronald Gow was a very modest man. Questioned about his work, he would say that any claim to distinction as a playwright that he may have achieved was due rather to his ability as an adaptor of borrowed plots to stage production than as an inventor of original stories. He would say this with a deprecating air, as of one ready to admit that he is operating on an artistic level rather below the highest.

How he could take this view, seeing that he was following the lead given by the most inveterate plot-borrower of them all, William Shakespeare, was not clear. One suspects Gow of being over-modest; and suspicion becomes certainty when a close critical look at his whole range of dramatic writings reveals that his early original plays were no less distinguished than his subsequent adaptations. Simply, they were less popular.

A reason for this can easily be found. Gow was educated at the grammar school at Altrincham in Cheshire, a town with easy access to Manchester. His subject was science, and his objective a B.Sc. degree at Manchester University; but during his schooldays the institution in that city which chiefly excited his interest was the Gaiety Theatre, where Miss Horniman had installed her famous regime and a whole group of angry young men were writing for her a whole series of realistic plays about social injustices of the time.

Gow, violently stage-struck, worshipped at the feet of these dramatists, came to know some of them (Harold Brighouse, Stanley Houghton, and the older Alan Monkhouse), and made up his mind that when the time came he would follow their example; meanwhile he became an enthusiastic amateur actor.

Fortunately for him, there lay at his very door the means to make the theatre an absorbing hobby without too much encroachment on the more serious business of earning a living. An amateur dramatic society at Altrincham, the Garrick, was fast becoming (and, incidentally, is still) one of the leaders in its own field. In the period after World War I when the professional stage was given over almost wholly to glittering frivolity and the general playgoing public asked for nothing better, the task of keeping a more serious theatre alive fell to amateurs who, organized and led by the newly formed British Drama League, rose nobly to the call.

As the movement gathered force and a large public responded, men like Gow found their hobby growing into something very like a profession. He himself, now a young man with his science degree behind him, working first as research chemist and then as schoolmaster, was in his spare time wholly at the Garrick Theatre's service. He acted for it, wrote for it, shifted scenery, took money at the doors. For several years he was its secretary; and when it decided to build itself its own playhouse, he even laid bricks for it. By the time when, at 33 or so, he decided to try his luck as a professional dramatist, he had had a fuller training for the craft than most.

True to the principles he had learnt as a boy, he now looked for social injustices to write about. This was easy enough so far as themes went, for he had as sharp a sense of the follies and injustices of human life as any of the Horniman dramatists whose disciple he was. Unlike them, however, he had a natural sense of period, and was apt to look to the past for his plots.

From the first, there was no question of the excellence of Gow's writing, and he soon had a play accepted for West End production. This was *Gallows Glorious*, which told the story of that John Brown whose soul, in the song, goes marching on. It was produced at the old Shaftesbury Theatre in 1933, and the first-night audience received it with rapturous applause and a standing ovation. But the Shaftesbury (destroyed by German bombs in World War II) was a big house to fill, and the general public, which was not in the mood for period pieces anyhow, showed no interest in John Brown whatever. The play limped along for two weeks and then had to be taken off.

A rather similar experience in the following year with an anti-romantic and anti-war play about Bonnie Prince Charlie must have taught him the lesson that a man writing a play-with-a-purpose should choose to set his action in the immediate present, for he next sat down to write about unemployment, the chief problem of the moment. While engaged on this he happened to read Walter Greenwood's novel *Love on the Dole*, and decided to dramatize Greenwood's story instead of going on with his own.

The great success of this play changed Gow's whole life. It made a name not only for him but for Wendy Hiller, the aspiring young actress who played his heroine and whom, in 1937, he married. It also brought him sharply to the notice of Pinewood film studios and the BBC, with the ironic result that he was, practically speaking, lost to the stage for nine years or so. Indeed, his next two stage plays, *Ma's Bit o' Brass* and *Tess of the D'Urbervilles* were both adapted to the stage from filmscripts of his own.

Ma's Bit o' Brass, a light-hearted exercise in the Lancashire idiom, ranks rather uneasily among Gow's original pieces. It never quite reached the West End, but it toured successfully and became a favourite among "Reps" and amateurs. Its author regarded it with a kind of rueful gratitude.

He wrote the film version of *Tess* for his wife, who during the war was invited to play this part in Hollywood. He himself did not quite "see" her in the part, and advised her against taking it—and, indeed, it was not one of her greatest successes. But she did well enough for John Burrell to want her to do it on the London stage, and to invite Gow to write the play. His next three West End productions—*Ann Veronica*, *The Edwardians* and the very delightful *A Boston Story*—were adaptations (as was his last play, *The Old Jest*) but *The Friendship of Mrs. Eckley* is an original story about the Brownings.

—W.A. Darlington

GRAY, Simon (James Holliday).

Born on Hayling Island, Hampshire, 21 October 1936. Educated at a school in Montreal; Westminster School, London; Dalhousie University, Halifax, Nova Scotia, 1954–57, B.A. (honours) in English 1957; Trinity College, Cambridge, 1958–61, B.A. (honours) in English 1961, M.A. Married Beryl Mary Kevern in 1965; one son and one daughter. Harper-Wood student, 1961–62, and research student, 1962–63, Trinity College; lecturer in English, University of British Columbia, Vancouver, 1963–64; supervisor in English, Trinity College, 1964–66; lecturer in English, Queen Mary College, London, 1965–85. Since 1964 editor, *Delta* magazine, Cambridge. Recipient; *Evening Standard* award, 1972, 1976; New York Drama Critics Circle award, 1977; Cheltenham prize for literature, 1982. Honorary fellow, Queen Mary College, 1985. Lives in London. Agent: Judy Daish Associates, 83 Eastbourne Mews, London W2 6LQ, England.

Publications

PLAYS

Wise Child (produced 1967). 1972.

Molly (as *Death of a Teddy Bear*, televised 1967; revised version, as *Molly*, produced 1977). In *The Rear Column and Other Plays*, 1978; in *The Rear Column, Dog Days, and Other Plays*, 1979.

Sleeping Dog (televised 1967). 1968.
Spoiled (televised 1968; produced 1970). 1971.
Dutch Uncle (produced 1969). 1969.
Pig in a Poke (televised 1969). With *Close of Play*, 1980.
The Idiot, adaptation of a novel by Dostoevsky (produced 1970). 1971.
Butley (produced 1971). 1971.
Man in a Side-Car (televised 1971). In *The Rear Column and Other Plays*, 1978; in *The Rear Column, Dog Days, and Other Plays*, 1979.
Otherwise Engaged (produced 1975). In *Otherwise Engaged and Other Plays*, 1975.
Plaintiffs and Defendants (televised 1975). In *Otherwise Engaged and Other Plays*, 1975.
Two Sundays (televised 1975). In *Otherwise Engaged and Other Plays*, 1975.
Otherwise Engaged and Other Plays. 1975.
Dog Days (produced 1976). 1976; in *The Rear Column, Dog Days, and Other Plays*, 1979.
The Rear Column (produced 1978). In *The Rear Column and Other Plays*, 1978; in *The Rear Column, Dog Days, and Other Plays*, 1979.
The Rear Column and Other Plays. 1978.
The Rear Column, Dog Days, and Other Plays. 1979.
Close of Play (produced 1979). With *Pig in a Poke*, 1980; published separately, 1982.
Stage Struck (produced 1979). 1979.
Quartermaine's Terms (produced 1981). 1981; revised version, 1983.
Chapter 17 (produced 1982).
Tartuffe, adaptation of the play by Molière (produced 1982). With *The Holy Terror*, 1990.
The Common Pursuit: Scenes from Literary Life (produced 1984; also co-director: produced 1986; revised version, produced 1987; also director: produced 1988). 1984.
Play 1 (includes *Butley, Otherwise Engaged, The Rear Column, Quartermaine's Terms, The Common Pursuit*). 1986.
Melon (produced 1987; revised version, as *The Holy Terror*, broadcast 1989; also director: produced 1992). 1987; as *The Holy Terror*, with *Tartuffe*, 1990.
After Pilkington (televised 1987). 1987.
Hidden Laughter (also director: produced 1990). 1990.
Old Flames and A Month in the Country. 1990.
The Definitive Simon Gray 1 (includes *Butley, Wise Child, Dutch Uncle, Spoiled, The Caramel Crisis, Sleeping Dog*). 1991.
The Definitive Simon Gray 2 (includes *Otherwise Engaged, Dog Days, Molly, Pig in a Poke, Man in a Side-Car, Plaintiffs and Defendants, Two Sundays*). 1992.

SCREENPLAYS: *Butley*, 1976; *A Month in the Country*, 1987.

RADIO PLAYS: *Up in Pigeon Lake*, from his novel *Colmain*, 1963; *The Holy Terror* (revised version of *Melon*), 1989.

TELEVISION PLAYS: *The Caramel Crisis*, 1966; *Death of a Teddy Bear*, 1967; *A Way with the Ladies*, 1967; *Sleeping Dog*, 1967; *Spoiled*, 1968; *Pig in a Poke*, 1969; *The Dirt on Lucy Lane*, 1969; *Style of the Countess*, 1970; *The Princess*, 1970; *Man in a Side-Car*, 1971; *Plaintiffs and Defendants*, 1975; *Two Sundays*, 1975; *After Pilkington*, 1987; *Old Flames*, 1990; *They Never Slept*, 1991; *Running Late*, 1992; *The Common Pursuit*, 1992.

NOVELS

Colmain. 1963.
Simple People. 1965.
Little Portia. 1967.
A Comeback for Stark (as Hamish Reade). 1968.

OTHER

An Unnatural Pursuit and Other Pieces: A Playwright's Journal. 1985.
How's That for Telling 'Em, Fat Lady? A Short Life in the American Theatre. 1988.

Editor, with Keith Walker, *Selected English Prose*. 1967.

CRITICAL STUDY: *Simon Gray: A Casebook*, edited by Katherine H. Burkman, 1992.

THEATRICAL ACTIVITIES

DIRECTOR: **Plays**—*Dog Days*, 1980; *The Common Pursuit* (co-director, with Michael McGuire), 1986; *Hidden Laughter*, 1990.

Cruel notices have dogged Simon Gray's career, but his plays have fared well with audiences, and his best are important by any standard. He is a witty, intelligent, literary playwright with a flair for the topical and gift for creating memorable characters. His genre is the comedy of manners. Frequently he combines elements from the bedroom farce with features of the whodunit. Butley's savage wit, Simon Hench's arch reserve, Quartermaine's kindly vacancy, Melon's mental sufferings, and Ronnie's words about the divine and human spirit and hidden laughter live in the landscape of the mind long after the details of the play have been forgotten. Gray's skillful control of dialogue— witty, derisive, colloquial, syntactically lively, and often irreverent—rarely fails him. His portraits of academics and the life of the literarily inclined belong beside Kingsley Amis's *Lucky Jim*. Some critics fault Gray for his lack of "magnanimity of spirit and largeness of vision." No doubt his often corrosive humor contributes to this judgement, but his poignant depiction of Quartermaine in his Chekhovian play *Quartermaine's Terms* ought to go a long way towards silencing those who argue that he lacks heart. If anything, he feels too keenly and requires humor to make life more tolerable.

Gray's plays have appeared regularly in the West End since *Wise Child* opened in 1967, shocking its London audience. In 1972, *Butley* won the *Evening Standard* Best Play award. Nonetheless, his detractors gave most of the credit to the superior actors and directors—including Alec Guinness, Simon Ward, Alan Bates, and Harold Pinter—who lent their talents to his plays. In 1979, in a particularly nasty review, James Fenton of the *Sunday Times* announced that Gray had committed "public suicide" in his thriller *Stage Struck*, and gloated that *Close of Play*, an "overblown domestic tragedy," had itself closed at the Lyttelton in less than 10 days. *Quartermaine's Terms*, an international success and the only play to win the Cheltenham prize for literature, was similarly savaged by a San Francisco radio reviewer.

Not one quick to forget or forgive slights, Gray opens his playwright's journal, *An Unnatural Pursuit and Other Pieces*, quoting Fenton's words: "Ladies and Gentlemen, the play's the thing, as Shakespeare put it. But Ladies and Gentlemen, there isn't a play here! No play at all, ladies and gentlemen." Later Gray defiantly boasts that his new play, *The Common Pursuit*, like *Quartermaine's Terms*, "has no plot." Ambiguously named after F.R. Leavis's book, the play takes revenge upon Gray's unkindly reviewers and includes a rude joke at the expense of the *Sunday Times*. Gray feared that the joke would cost him dearly and, if his account of the play's reviews and fate is accurate, his fears were warranted. Ultimately, his producers backed out of the plans to move the play from the Lyric in Hammersmith to the West End. Later, the play traveled to the United States where it was performed in New Haven; a revised version was also staged in Los Angeles.

Gray has had more than his share of flops. His adaptation of Dostoevsky's *The Idiot* entertained his audience but left the critics immodestly displaying their expertise on the Russian master while ignoring Gray's talents. *Dutch Uncle* was depressing; the critics deplored its lack of taste. *Spoiled*, with its touching exploration of a homosexual encounter between pupil and teacher— an encounter which is reworked in a number of his plays and films for television—simply failed to stir any interest. *Close of Play* did not work.

Butley was a stunning success, capturing the bitchiness, vanity, and all-too-fragile ego of a thoroughly jaundiced university lecturer. The protagonists of *Otherwise Engaged* and *Stage Struck* possess many of the traits that made Ben Butley unforgettable. Both plays had long runs in the West End. Gray's thrillers do not take advantage of a period setting. Instead they capitalize upon kinky sexuality and psychologically perverse behavior. His BBC screenplay *After Pilkington* shows him at his best. He calls it a Jamesian ghost-thriller and exploits games from childhood to chilling ends. But his stage plays in this genre lack the marvelous visual effects which made Paul Giovanni's Sherlock Holmes play *The Crucifer of Blood* such a favorite. Instead, they depend on the ingenuity of their plots and the psychological intricacies of their characters for their success. Gray's domestic comedies compare favorably with Alan Ayckbourn's, but with the important exception of *Quartermaine's Terms*, they have the same limitations. They pander to popular taste, make too much of sexual peccadilloes, be they between members of the same or of the opposite sex, and often lack love. None equals Peter Shaffer's *Black Comedy*.

In *Otherwise Engaged* and *Dog Days*, as well as in the television plays *Two Sundays* and *Plaintiffs and Defendants*, the characters of one play slip into the others while the situation remains fairly constant. In *Otherwise Engaged* a snobbish, Oxford-educated editor, Simon Hench, lives with his schoolteacher wife, Beth, and their annoying tenant David. On a day when Simon hopes to listen quietly to Wagner while his wife is away on an outing with her foreign students and a colleague, Ned, he is repeatedly interrupted. His tenant stops in, followed by his brother on an unexpected visit. Next his boisterous friend Jeff, and his current mistress Davina, barge in. Finally, Simon is confronted by an old schoolmate who accuses him, rightly, of having an affair with Joanna, a young lady in Simon's office who happens to be betrothed to the schoolmate. In the course of the day the old rivalries between the brothers are explored; Simon is propositioned by the bare-breasted Davina after she quarrels with Jeff; and Simon learns that his wife has been having an affair with Ned and now, pregnant, wants to marry him. At the play's close, Jeff and Simon turn on *Parsifal.*

Dog Days offers a variant of the same situation with different names. Peter is the junior editor whose wife, Hilary, is having an affair that threatens to destroy the marriage. His brother, Charles, is married to a vegetarian earth-mother, Alison, who has produced four children and is expecting more. After accusing Hilary of "replacing mechanical sex with spontaneous frigidity," Peter walks out to join Joanna. When pre-coital depression mars his affair, he returns contrite to Hilary who will no longer have him. Peter and Charles live a dog's life, both grovelling to people they loathe, both dependent on others in ways they had not predicted. Hilary, like Beth, cannot contemplate spending any more years in a marriage with a man who likes neither himself nor her. In the two television plays about Peter and Charles, the marriages withstand Peter's infidelities and Alison's endless cooing.

The Rear Column, a fascinating play, is based on Stanley's march to the relief of Emin Pasha in 1887 and the fate of the rear column and the five white men left behind in the encampment in the Congo with three hundred "niggers" inside and hoards of cannibals without. The play is about Major Barttelot. Left to guard the rear column, he ends up flogging, shooting, and eating the natives while Jameson, the British naturalist left behind with him, also loses all moral purpose. In his final decadence, he watches a "nigger girl" killed, cooked, and eaten so that he can sketch the rite of cannibalism with the same care he devotes to sketching the African birdlife.

Gray's plays are peopled with men discontented with themselves and ill-suited to their roles. Often these men are homosexuals. Transvestitism (*Wise Child*), bondage (*Sleeping Dog*), and sado-masochistic games (*Sleeping Dog, Dutch Uncle,* and *Stage Struck*) are the acts they resort to in their self-loathing. Butley has married to escape his homosexuality only to leave his wife six months later and return to his male student/lover turned colleague. Butley constantly belittles his wife, colleagues, and lover. Ultimately his corrosive humor drives them all away, leaving him too worn out and full of self-dislike to initiate yet another affair with one of his students. Butley uses words to kill. Although he cuts to the quick those who need or love him, ultimately it is he who is the victim. The nasty cut on his chin that he dabs at throughout the play physicalizes the depth of his self-dislike. Mr. Godboy, the protagonist of *Dutch Uncle,* courts punishment at the hands of a police constable noted for his strict ways. Mr. Godboy is unsuccessful in his attempt to gas his wife and upstairs tenant, but he does experience vicariously the humiliations practiced by the constable. In *Molly,* Molly and her lover kill her rich old husband—a man whose habit of spanking his "naughty" wife finally infuriates the lover. In *Sleeping Dog* a retired colonial officer torments a West Indian for being too familiar with his wife. He chains the Jamaican in the cellar of his English house, makes him confess to crimes against his wife and to homosexuality, and finally forces the man to service his wife. *Stage Struck* develops the cat-and-mouse game of *Dutch Uncle* into an extravagant panoply of stage tricks masterminded by the stage-director husband who uses suicide and murder to revenge himself upon his domineering actress wife.

Quartermaine's Terms, Gray's finest play to date, and *The Common Pursuit* depart in significant ways from the mode of *Butley* although both take school teachers and literary types for their characters. Butley and Simon Hench use language and wit trenchantly—Butley to lash out, deflecting his self-hatred against others, Hench more sparingly as an armor to prevent others from touching him. In contrast, Sir John Quartermaine, teacher in a Cambridge public school training foreign boys in English, is a man of halting phrases, few words, and nearly vacant silences. While the play traces the fortunes of the school and its small staff, we witness Sir John's retreat from his world into a drowsy sleep where he can no longer remember when or what he is teaching or even the swans on the pond near his aunt's home. He drifts in and out of reminiscences, weaving the words of Yeats's "The Wild Swans at Coole" with his own vague memories, reproducing in his own diminished way the sense of radical dislocation and displacement of Yeats's poem.

Gray's treatment of Quartermaine and the staff is richly comic. The plotting and character delineation are Chekhovian. Mr. Meadle is the play's Two-and-Twenty-Misfortunes; Quartermaine's yearnings for another era echo Anya's and Gaef's nostalgia in *The Cherry Orchard*; the characters in the play cannot remember each others' names; they murmur reassuring pleasantries while underneath they are confused and hurting. Melanie is a frustrated spinster driven to kill her sickly, hatred-ridden mother and do penance through her Christian conversion. Mr. Meadle, the accident-prone new instructor from the North Country, struggles desperately to secure both a permanent position in the school and a wife. There is a liberal sprinkling of marital infidelities and complications in the play, and it contains the suicide which often figures in Gray's plays. But its texture is different. When Quartermaine is finally dismissed by the new principal on the eve of the Christmas break, it is wrenching. All of Windscape's reasons for the firing are legitimate: Quartermaine has not been teaching for years; the other staff simply carried him on, not having the heart to do anything else. On one level it is unconscionable to pretend that Quartermaine has a role to play in an instructional institution; on another, we want to ask, "why not let him linger in the staff lounge, teaching almost not at all, rather than displace him utterly?" Gray crafts the final scene so skillfully that we are forced to balance the conflicting needs of the situation. The gentle goodnight exchanged between the two men followed by Quartermaine's lapse into silence ends the play. Echoes of Yeats's poem hover in the air. It is Gray's best ending.

The Common Pursuit departs from *Butley* in its treatment of time and its reliance on cinematic techniques for its staging and its plot development. Gray calls it a play about friendship, "English, middle-class, Cambridge-educated friendship." He has remarked that its control of time grew out of the television play *Two Sundays*. It covers 20 years and closes with a scene set 15 minutes later than its opening scene, 20 years before. Critics have anachronistically compared the play to Pinter's *Betrayal*, written a number of years after *Two*

Sundays. *The Common Pursuit* is episodic, tracing the fortunes of the Cambridge friends and their literary enterprise. Many of its characters are the typical academic misfits and literary opportunists that figure in almost all of his plays. Unlike the protagonists of a number of Gray's other plays, Stuart is not the hub around which the action revolves. Stuart is what Gray calls "the spine of the play," but the play's sweeping movement over the lives of the six Cambridge friends is more akin to the structure of Virginia Woolf's novel *The Waves* than it is to the structure of Gray's other plays. Gray rightly sensed that the play might be too precious, too literary, and too elitist to please the public, but it is an effective evening of theatre, and the depiction of the group of writers, editors, scholars, and publishers is adept. Its control of time is superb and its startling epilogue a stunning piece of theatre.

Melon is a memory play presented from the perspective of its protagonist, a successful literary publisher who discovers one day that the ground has opened up under his feet: the entire routine of success around which his life has been fashioned collapses and he finds himself in the midst of a mental breakdown, recounting to his psychiatrist how it all came to be. The themes in the play are familiar: marital infidelity and breakdown, thwarted ambition, and confused sexual identity. Melon's overbearing presence, his infidelities, and his contempt for others finally undo him, but the agony of this all too familiar character-type is intensified as we see the play through his perspective. He has the unbearable task of trying to rebuild himself and trying to speak the moment when his world came apart. Gray is good at this kind of play. He employs a musical metaphor with its capacity to embrace both harmony and discord to unite his protagonist's memories. The play is fluid, evocative, and disturbing. In *Melon*, Gray affords Alan Bates another of the roles he plays so well.

Hidden Laughter is a very funny and yet deeply sad play which teases out T.S. Eliot's treatment of childish laughter and the garden in "The Four Quartets." The play's action covers 13 years, tracing the happenings in the life of a successful literary agent, his novelist wife, and two children as they seek a retreat in the life of the country. The years are full of strange happenings, near-accidents, and near-deaths. The tone moves from that of pastoral idyll to a very tentative, troubled present, full of strained relationships. The most memorable character in the play is the tolerant and yet good vicar whose life touches all the other characters in the play.

Gray is among Britain's most talented playwrights working in the traditional genre of the comedy of manners. He is well schooled in his craft, original, and able to create unforgettable characters.

—Carol Simpson Stern

GREENE, Graham.

Born in Berkhamsted, Hertfordshire, 2 October 1904. Educated at Berkhamsted School; Balliol College, Oxford. Served in the Foreign Office, London, 1941–44. Married Vivien Dayrell-Browning in 1927; one son and one daughter. Joined Roman Catholic church, 1926; staff member, the *Times*, London, 1926–30; film critic, 1937–40, and literary editor, 1940–41, *Spectator*, London; director, Eyre and Spottiswoode, publishers, London,

1944–48, and The Bodley Head, publishers, London, 1958–68. Member, Panamanian Canal Treaty Delegation to Washington, 1977. Recipient: Hawthornden prize, 1941; James Tait Black memorial prize, 1949; Shakespeare prize (Hamburg), 1968; Thomas More medal, 1973; Dos Passos prize, 1980; City of Madrid medal, 1980; Jerusalem prize, 1981; Ruben Dario medal (Nicaragua), 1987. Litt. D.: Cambridge University, 1962; D. Litt.: Edinburgh University, 1967; Oxford University, 1979; honorary doctorate: University of Moscow, 1988. Honorary fellow, Balliol College, 1963; honorary citizen, Anacapri, 1978. Companion of Honour, 1966; Chevalier, Legion of Honour (France), 1967; Grand Cross, Order of Balboa (Panama), 1983; Commandant, Order of Arts and Letters (France), 1984; Companion of Literature, Royal Society of Literature, 1984; O.M. (Order of Merit), 1986. *Died 3 April 1991.*

Publications

PLAYS

The Living Room (produced 1953). 1953.
The Potting Shed (produced 1957). 1957; revised version (produced 1958), 1958.
The Complaisant Lover (produced 1959). 1959.
Three Plays (includes *The Living Room, The Potting Shed, The Complaisant Lover*). 1961.
Carving a Statue (produced 1964). 1964.
The Third Man: A Film, with Carol Reed. 1968; revised version (original script), 1984.
Alas, Poor Maling, from his own story (televised 1975). In *Shades of Greene*, 1975.
The Return of A.J. Raffles: An Edwardian Comedy Based Somewhat Loosely on E. W. Hornung's Characters in The Amateur Cracksman (produced 1975). 1975.
Yes and No, and For Whom the Bell Chimes (produced 1980). 1983.
The Great Jowett (broadcast 1980). 1981.
Collected Plays (includes *The Living Room, The Potting Shed, The Complaisant Lover, Carving a Statue, The Return of A.J. Raffles, The Great Jowett, Yes and No, For Whom the Bell Chimes*). 1985.

SCREENPLAYS: *The First and the Last* (*21 Days*), 1937; *The New Britain*, 1940; *Brighton Rock* (*Young Scarface*), with Terence Rattigan, 1947; *The Fallen Idol*, with Lesley Storm and William Templeton, 1948; *The Third Man*, with Carol Reed, 1950; *The Stranger's Hand*, with Guy Elmes and Giorgio Bassani, 1954; *Loser Takes All*, 1956; *Saint Joan*, 1957; *Our Man in Havana*, 1960; *The Comedians*, 1967.

RADIO PLAY: *The Great Jowett*, 1980.

TELEVISION PLAY: *Alas, Poor Maling*, 1975.

NOVELS

The Man Within. 1929.
The Name of Action. 1930.
Rumour at Nightfall. 1931.
Stamboul Train. 1932; as *Orient Express,* 1933.
It's a Battlefield. 1934; revised edition, 1948.
England Made Me. 1935; as *The Shipwrecked,* 1953.
A Gun for Sale. 1936; as *This Gun for Hire,* 1936.
Brighton Rock. 1938.
The Confidential Agent. 1939.
The Power and the Glory. 1940; as *The Labyrinthine Ways,* 1940.
The Ministry of Fear. 1943.
The Heart of the Matter. 1948.
The Third Man. 1950.
The Third Man, and The Fallen Idol. 1950.
The End of the Affair. 1951.
Loser Takes All. 1955.
The Quiet American. 1955.
Our Man in Havana. 1958.
A Burnt-Out Case. 1961.
The Comedians. 1966.
Travels with My Aunt. 1969.
The Honorary Consul. 1973.
The Human Factor. 1978.
Doctor Fischer of Geneva; or, The Bomb Party. 1980.
Monsignor Quixote. 1982.
The Tenth Man. 1985.
The Captain and the Enemy. 1988.
The Last Word. 1990.

SHORT STORIES

The Basement Room and Other Stories. 1935.
The Bear Fell Free. 1935.
24 Short Stories, with James Laver and Sylvia Townsend Warner. 1939.
Nineteen Stories. 1947; augmented edition, as *Twenty-one Stories,* 1954; selection, as *Across the Bridge and Other Stories,* 1981.
A Visit to Morin. 1959.
A Sense of Reality. 1963.
May We Borrow Your Husband? and Other Comedies of the Sexual Life. 1967.
The Collected Stories. 1972.
How Father Quixote Became a Monsignor. 1980.

VERSE

Babbling April. 1925.
For Christmas. 1951.

OTHER

Journey Without Maps. 1936.
The Lawless Roads: A Mexican Journey. 1939; as *Another Mexico,* 1939.

British Dramatists. 1942; included in *The Romance of English Literature*, 1944.

The Little Train (for children). 1946.

Why Do I Write? An Exchange of Views Between Elizabeth Bowen, Greene, and V. S. Pritchett. 1948.

After Two Years. 1949.

The Little Fire Engine (for children). 1950; as *The Little Red Fire Engine*, 1953.

The Lost Childhood and Other Essays. 1951.

The Little Horse Bus (for children). 1952.

The Little Steamroller: A Story of Adventure, Mystery, and Detection (for children). 1953.

Essais Catholiques, translated by Marcelle Sibon. 1953.

In Search of a Character: Two African Journals. 1961.

The Revenge: An Autobiographical Fragment. 1963.

Victorian Detective Fiction: A Catalogue of the Collection Made by Dorothy Glover and Greene. 1966.

Collected Essays. 1969.

A Sort of Life (autobiography). 1971.

The Virtue of Disloyalty. 1972.

The Pleasure-Dome: The Collected Film Criticism 1935–1940, edited by John Russell Taylor. 1972; as *Greene on Film: Collected Film Criticism 1935–1940*, 1972.

The Portable Graham Greene, edited by Philip Stratford. 1973.

Lord Rochester's Monkey, Being the Life of John Wilmot, Second Earl of Rochester. 1974.

Ways of Escape. 1980.

J'Accuse: The Dark Side of Nice (bilingual edition). 1982.

A Quick Look Behind: Footnotes to an Autobiography. 1983.

Getting to Know the General: The Story of an Involvement. 1984.

Graham Greene Country, paintings by Paul Hogarth. 1986.

Why the Epigraph? 1989.

Yours Etc.: Letters to the Press, edited by Christopher Hawtree. 1989.

Reflections 1923–1988, edited by Judith Adamson. 1990.

Editor, *The Old School: Essays by Divers Hands*. 1934.

Editor, *The Best of Saki*. 1950.

Editor, with Hugh Greene, *The Spy's Bedside Book: An Anthology*. 1957.

Editor, *The Bodley Head Ford Madox Ford*. 4 vols., 1962–63.

Editor, *An Impossible Woman: The Memories of Dottoressa Moor of Capri*. 1975.

Editor, with Hugh Greene, *Victorian Villainies: Four Classic Victorian Tales*. 1984.

BIBLIOGRAPHY: *Greene: A Checklist of Criticism* by J.D. Vann, 1970; *Greene: A Descriptive Catalog* by Robert H. Miller, 1978; *Greene: A Bibliography and Guide to Research* by R.A. Wobbe, 1979; *Greene: An Annotated Bibliography of Criticism* by A.F. Cassis, 1981.

MANUSCRIPT COLLECTION: Humanities Research Center, University of Texas, Austin.

CRITICAL STUDIES: *Greene the Entertainer* by Peter Wolfe, 1972, and *Essays in Greene* edited by Wolfe, 1987; *Greene: A Collection of Critical Essays* edited by Samuel Hynes, 1973; *Greene: An Introduction to His Writings* by Henry J. Donaghy, 1983; *The Other Man: Conversations with Graham Greene* by Marie Françoise Allain, 1983; *Greene* by John Spurling, 1983; *Greene: The Artist as Critic* by Elizabeth Davis, 1984; *Greene* by Richard Kelly, 1984; *The Achievement of Greene* by Grahame Smith, 1986; *Greene: His Mind and Art* by B.P. Lamba, 1987; *Greene's Childless Fathers* by Daphna Erdinast-Vulcan, 1988; *A Reader's Guide to Greene* by Paul O'Prey, 1988; *Greene* by Neil McEwan, 1988; *The Life of Greene 1904–1939* by Vincent Sherry, 1989; *Greene: A Revaluation: New Essays* edited by Jeffrey Meyers, 1990; *Greene: The Dangerous Edge: Where Art and Politics Meet* by Judith Adamson, 1990.

Graham Greene was approaching his fiftieth birthday and generally accepted as one of the few outstanding novelists of the age when, in 1953, his first play, *The Living Room*, was produced. Three years later, John Osborne's *Look Back in Anger* inaugurated a revolution in the English theatre, but Greene's later plays were obviously uninfluenced by the outburst of new activity and the exploration of new styles and themes.

As a novelist, Greene developed new and effective narrative techniques, but his almost cinematic cutting and timing of scenes have been fed into the tradition. When he turned to the theatre, fulfilling ambitions which (he explained in the Preface to *Three Plays*) had been with him since his school days, he turned to the traditional disciplines of the well-made play. He found "a fascination in unity" and designed his plays to preserve traditional theatrical virtues. The results are elegantly made for all their harshness, economical and precise; their interest is always in the matter expressed, not in the development of new means of expression.

Greene's range was always limited; he had a few obsessive themes to which he tended to return always with new and sharper intensities. He was concerned primarily about the relation of man—not generalized, abstract man but whatever individual happens to demand his attention—to God, and secondly about men's relationships to each other.

The Complaisant Lover, a comedy, restricts itself to his secondary theme; its tone is not happy but, at times, distressing; its solution to a difficult moral problem is by no means conventional and its observation of average sensual life is not designed to comfort an audience. For all her clandestine love affair with a possessive bookseller, Mary Rhodes loves her dentist husband (the domestic clown, the practical joker who is most at home in the mental world of his prep-school son) no less than she loves her lover.

The play might easily become a commonplace domestic tragedy; Rhodes might carry out his suicide plan, but it is his wife's needs which persuade him to abandon it: if she wants a husband and a lover, she must have both for the sake of her happiness; it is the adulterer who finds the solution outrageous until Rhodes persuades him that to love is to give the beloved what she needs.

The Complaisant Lover is Greene's *Comédie humaine*; in his first play, T*he Living Room*, he returns to the idea of a Catholic suicide without repeating the ideas of his novel *The Heart of the Matter*. Rose Pemberton, who kills herself because her life can bring only unhappiness to the people she loves, is the centre round which others—her old aunts and her crippled uncle who can no longer function as a priest—revolve in a life which rejects the truth and refuses to acknowledge the fact of death. Rose's suicide compels them to do so; in a sense, it offers them salvation. The rules, the crippled priest explains, are man's rules, man's attempt to make God's will into comprehensible law; decisions rest ultimately with God. It is not only *The Heart of the Matter* but *Brighton Rock* and *The Power and the Glory* which are somehow involved in *The Living Room*, but it is a remarkably gentle, emotionally simple work to have come from a writer so wittily harsh as Greene.

The Potting Shed is harsh in Greene's accustomed way, and it seems that it won less respect than it deserves because it is rooted in a supernatural event. Its central character, as a boy, hanged himself but was restored to life because a priest sacrificed his faith to bring the boy back. Greene's own unsparing criticism of the play is that the "hollowness" of the man who had been dead is less convincingly treated than the "hollow man" he had explored in the novel *A Burnt-Out Case*, but nothing in the novel compares with the tragedy of the priest who finds that God took him quite seriously and destroyed his capacity for faith when the boy was given life again. Greene could have quoted again the line of the old priest at the end of *Brighton Rock*, and offered another reflection on "the appalling strangeness of the mercy of God". Nothing in *A Burnt-Out Case* is so moving as the prospect of warmth returning to the play's spiritually dead central figure.

Carving a Statue, Greene wrote in the Preface to its published version, is neither "symbolic" nor "theological", and he has some caustic fun at the expense of critics who found its symbolism and theology obscure while they should have been regarding it as a play of direct statements which means no more than is seen and heard on the stage. A bad sculptor—Greene was thinking, he wrote, of Benjamin Robert Hayden, who killed himself when he awoke from a dream of impossible greatness—has given his life to the making of a statue of God the Father. Everything except his dreams is sacrificed to his task; he knows that his work—though he does not realize its worthlessness—is a refuge from the pressures he would suffer if he abandoned a task he had no notion of how to complete. His friends, his adolescent son's happiness, a dumb girl's life, are all destroyed. Greene draws no moral and offers no comment.

The Return of A.J. Raffles came as a disappointment after these plays. Witty and lightly treated, almost a sub-Wildean pastiche, it sets E.W. Hornung's upper-class burglar into more imposing social circumstances than his creator envisaged for him; Raffles is involved in the quarrel of Lord Alfred Douglas with the Marquis of Queensberry; Edward VII appears as an unconscious *deus ex machina*. But there is no sense, in this play, that the Society burglar is blaspheming the standards by which he lives; the late-20th century, perhaps, sees nothing outrageous in the idea of a gentleman-thief, and the seamier side of Edwardian society, thus exposed, turns Raffles from a kind of unaltruistic Robin Hood into one of the corrupt in a corrupt society. *Yes and No, and For Whom the Bell Chimes* is another easy-going play in which Greene exploits a certain elegance of technique almost, it seems, for its own sake, without any of the obsessive compulsion which had given force to his earlier works.

Though Greene's plays do not offer technical or stylistic experiments but live as their author's expression in traditional dramatic form of the essential preoccupation of all his work, one thing—and again it is traditional—should be said of them. They create personalities—the crippled priest of *The Living Room*, the hollow man who returned from the dead in *The Potting Shed*, and the sculptor of *Carving a Statue*—which demand and reward fine acting, as do the husband and lover of *The Complaisant Lover*. They translate into terms of theatre the strangeness and haunting power which belong to Greene's novels. Inescapably, they are religious plays in which men are able to see that they live inescapably and often terrifyingly in the presence of God.

—Henry Raynor

GREENWOOD, Walter.

Born in Salford, Lancashire, 17 December 1903. Educated at Langworthy Road Council School, Salford. Married Pearl Osgood (divorced 1940). Worked at various jobs, including pawnbroker's clerk, office boy, stable boy, packing-case maker, sign writer, cab driver, warehouseman, salesman, automobile factory worker, 1916–33. Lived on the Isle of Man for many years. D.Litt.: University of Salford, 1971. *Died 10 or 11 September 1974.*

Publications

PLAYS

Love on the Dole, with Ronald Gow, from the novel by Greenwood (produced 1934). 1935.
My Son's My Son, completion of play by D.H. Lawrence (produced 1936).
Give Us This Day, from his novel *His Worship the Mayor* (produced 1940).
The Cure for Love: A Lancashire Comedy (as *A Rod of Iron*, produced 1945; as *The Cure for Love*, produced 1945). 1947.
So Brief the Spring: A Cornish Comedy (produced 1946).
Too Clever for Love (as *Never a Dull Moment*, produced 1948; revised version, as *Too Clever for Love*, produced 1951). 1952.
Saturday Night at the Crown (produced 1954; revised version produced 1956). 1958.
Happy Days (produced 1958).
Fun and Games (produced 1963; as *This Is Your Wife*, produced 1964).
There Was a Time, from his autobiography (produced 1967; as *Hanky Park*, produced 1971).

SCREENPLAYS: *No Limit*, 1935; *Love on the Dole*, with Barbara K. Emery and Rollo Gamble, 1941; *Six Men of Dorset*, 1944; *The Village That Voted the Earth Was Flat*, 1945; *Eureka Stockade*, 1947; *The Cure for Love*, 1949; *Chance of a Lifetime*, with Bernard Miles, 1950.

TELEVISION PLAY: *The Secret Kingdom* serial, from his own novel, 1960.

NOVELS

Love on the Dole: A Tale of the Two Cities. 1933.
His Worship the Mayor; or, It's Only Human Nature After All. 1934; as *The Time Is Ripe*, 1935.
Standing Room Only; or, A Laugh in Every Line. 1936.
The Secret Kingdom. 1938.
Only Mugs Work: A Soho Melodrama. 1938.
Something in My Heart. 1944.
So Brief the Spring, from his own play. 1952.
What Everybody Wants. 1954.
Down by the Sea. 1956.
Saturday Night at the Crown, from his own play. 1959.

SHORT STORIES

The Cleft Stick; or, It's the Same the Whole World Over. 1937.

OTHER

How the Other Man Lives. 1939.
Lancashire. 1951.
There Was a Time (autobiography). 1967.

Walter Greenwood's first play was an adaptation of his own first best-selling novel. *Love on the Dole*, written in collaboration with Ronald Gow, suffers to some extent from the inevitable loss of dimension in adapting a novel-original for the stage. The novel was a moving, grimly realistic, and at the time eye-opening revelation of how the poor in the North lived during the years of the slump, and the love story of Sally Hardcastle, who compromises with the harsh realities of such a world to become mistress of a prosperous bookmaker after her sweetheart's death in an unemployment demonstration, was only the main thread in the book, which has often and justifiably been compared with Dickens. The necessary reduction in scope for the stage results in a certain gap between the characters and their environment, what Sally's lover Larry Meath describes as "Labour never ending, pawnshops, misery and dirt . . . Grey depressing streets, mile after mile of them". Much of the background of the novel has to be sacrificed to stage exigencies, and key events such as the unemployment demonstrations and the evidence of factory life and conditions, take place in the wings. To a certain extent, the play becomes only the plain story of Sally Hardcastle, but there is more to it than this, for in certain scenes, notably a finely written interlude between Sally and Larry on the moors, the play encompasses without propaganda the central struggle against industrial enslavement so vividly explored in the novel. Moreover, Sally herself remains a memorable study in gradual self-realization and developing hardness as the only escape from her background. The play version also has much of the original's humour underneath grim surface events and retains much of its unsentimentalized viewpoint in its picture of a depressed people growing old with the best part of their lives already gone.

After this first stage success, Greenwood as a playwright concentrated on comedy, with *The Cure for Love* and *Saturday Night at the Crown*. Both are in the familiar-enough vein of North Country comedy, largely lost to the stage since television and "Coronation Street". *Saturday Night at the Crown,* in particular, is a highly skilful re-working of staple material. With no plot to speak of, it is simply a gently moving comedy set in the snug bar of a Northern town pub. Its characters—wife-dominated men, brassy designing widow, faithful barmaid, etc.—are stereotypes, but Greenwood, apart from the caricatured U.S. airman, infuses and animates them with loving and unsentimental observation, especially the vital figure of Ada Thorpe, the most vivid of his gallery of formidable Lancashire matriarch-figures. And for all its apparent looseness, the play, opening with a birth and ending with the aftermath of a funeral party, has a cunning internal rhythm.

After a lengthy absence, Greenwood returned to the theatre with *Hanky Park,* a dramatization of his autobiography *There Was A Time,* and a return to that corner of Salford previously chronicled in *Love on the Dole.* It is an uneven piece, although it has some compelling scenes. The first half in particular, tracing his early life up to the outbreak of World War I, is a fast-moving impressionistic montage, combining documentary background with his stage self's boyhood—clog-shod workers rising, the temporary escape from a world of pawnshops and factories in May Day celebrations, children's games and music-hall songs—and creates, in the figures of his mother and her neighbour Annie Boarder, that matriarchal society which kept his world together. However, the second half of the play, which includes several lengthy autobiographical addresses, is dangerously less intrinsically dramatic; the characters of the opening move out of focus, and the persona of Walter himself, traced through to the beginnings of his impulse to write, is too removed from the play's framework for comfort. For all its structural faults, however, the play hardly deserved its lukewarm and somewhat patronizing reception; one critic described it as an "idyll", although what could be idyllic about Salford in the 1920s is hard to imagine.

Greenwood once wrote that when he died, "Salford" would be found engraved on his heart, and indeed his writing rarely strayed from his home ground. Far from being the limitation this might suggest, it enabled Greenwood to forge a vital link between the Manchester playwrights of the earlier part of the century and more recent Northern dramatists such as Bill Naughton and Alan Plater.

—Alan Strachan

GRIFFITHS, Trevor.

Born in Manchester, Lancashire, 4 April 1935. Educated at St. Bede's College, Manchester, 1945–52; Manchester University, 1952–55, B.A. in English 1955; studied for external M.A. from 1961. Served in the British Army, Manchester Regiment, 1955–57: infantryman. Married Janice Elaine Stansfield in 1960 (died 1977); one son and two daughters. Teacher of English and games in a private school, Oldham, Lancashire, 1957–61; lecturer in liberal studies, Stockport Technical College, Cheshire, 1962–65; further education officer, BBC, Leeds, 1965–72. Co-editor, *Labour's Northern Voice,* 1962–65, and series editor for Workers Northern Publishing Society.

Recipient: BAFTA Writer's award, 1982. Lives in Yorkshire. Agent: Peters, Fraser and Dunlop Group, 503/4 The Chambers, Chelsea Harbour, Lots Road, London SW10 0XF, England.

Publications

PLAYS

The Wages of Thin (produced 1969).
The Big House (broadcast 1969; produced 1975). With *Occupations*, 1972.
Occupations (produced 1970). With *The Big House*, 1972; revised version, 1980.
Apricots (produced 1971). With *Thermidor*, 1978.
Thermidor (produced 1971). With *Apricots*, 1978.
Lay By, with others (produced 1971). 1972.
Sam, Sam (produced 1972; revised version produced 1978). In *Plays and Players*, April 1972.
Gun (also director: produced 1973).
The Party (produced 1973; revised version produced 1974). 1974.
All Good Men (televised 1974; produced 1975). In *All Good Men, and Absolute Beginners*, 1977.
Comedians (produced 1975; revised [women's] version produced 1987). 1976; revised version, 1979.
The Cherry Orchard, adaptation of a play by Chekhov, translated by Helen Rappaport (produced 1977). 1978; revised edition, 1989.
All Good Men, and Absolute Beginners: Two Plays for Television. 1977.
Through the Night, and Such Impossibilities: Two Plays for Television. 1977.
Deeds, with others (produced 1978). In *Plays and Players*, May and June 1978.
Country: A Tory Story (televised 1981). 1981.
Sons and Lovers, adaptation of the novel by D.H. Lawrence (televised 1981). 1982.
Oi for England (televised 1982; produced 1982). 1982.
Real Dreams, adaptation of the story "Revolution in Cleveland" by Jeremy Pikser (also director: produced 1984). 1987 (includes "Revolution in Cleveland" by Pikser).
Judgement over the Dead: The Screenplays of The Last Place on Earth, adaptation of a book by Roland Huntford (as *The Last Place on Earth*, televised 1985). 1986.
Fatherland (screenplay). 1987.
Collected Plays for Television (includes *All Good Men, Absolute Beginners, Through the Night, Such Impossibilities, Country, Oi for England*). 1988.
Piano (produced 1990). 1990.
The Gulf Between Us: The Truth and Other Fictions (also director: produced 1992). 1992.
Thatcher's Children (produced 1993).

SCREENPLAYS: *Reds*, with Warren Beatty, 1981; *Fatherland*, 1987.

RADIO PLAYS: *The Big House*, 1969; *Jake's Brigade*, 1971.

TELEVISION PLAYS: *Adam Smith* series (as Ben Rae), 1972; *The Silver Mask*, from a story by Horace Walpole (*Between the Wars* series), 1973; *All Good Men*, 1974; *Absolute Beginners* (*Fall of Eagles* series), 1974; *Don't Make Waves* (*Eleventh Hour* series), with Snoo Wilson, 1975; *Through the Night*, 1975; *Bill Brand* series, 1976; *Sons and Lovers*, 1981; *Country: A Tory Story*, 1981; *Oi for England*, 1982; *The Last Place on Earth*, 1985.

OTHER

Tip's Lot (for children). 1972.

MANUSCRIPT COLLECTION: British Film Institute, London.

Critical Studies: *Stages in the Revolution: Political Theatre in Britain Since 1968* by Catherine Itzin, 1980; *An Introduction to Fifty Modern British Plays* by Benedict Nightingale, 1982; *Powerplays: Trevor Griffiths in Television* by Mike Poole and John Wyver, 1984.

THEATRICAL ACTIVITIES

DIRECTOR: **Plays**—*Gun*, 1973; *Real Dreams*, 1984; *Saint Oscar* by Terry Eagleton, 1989, 1990; *The Gulf Between Us*, 1992.

Trevor Griffiths is unique for the remarkable consistency with which he has probed into critical phases and issues of the international labour movement. Earlier social and political dramatists portrayed individual labour struggles or dealt with the brutal consequences of fascism, but never before have the crucial questions of socialist strategy and morality been so forcefully examined on the stage. While assuming the desirability of socialism, Griffiths is anxious to distinguish and analyse the different positions hammered out by various brands of socialism and communism, and the personal dilemmas arising out of absorbing engagement in one of these movements.

Significantly, Griffiths started with a number of plays about Continental rather than British points of crisis. *Occupations* is set in Turin at the height of the revolutionary upsurge after World War I when factories were taken over and soviets formed in many Italian cities. The play shows the workers of Turin addressed in two moving speeches by Gramsci, but its focus is less on the confrontation between capital and labour than on the controversy between Gramsci and Kabak, a secret envoy of the Comintern, over the correct estimate and handling of the situation. Kabak, who has the experience and prestige of a successful revolution behind him, stands for a communist *realpolitik*; Gramsci, by contrast, embodies a hesitant, if fervent revolutionary idealism, which is always guided by a consideration, even love, for the people he leads.

The strategic differences between these two exponents of communism are also reflected in their personal outlooks. At the end Kabak leaves behind his mistress, who is dying of cancer; Gramsci goes to Sardinia to attend to his sister on her deathbed. The political and the personal, it is suggested, should not be seen as separate concerns. This dual perspective is also expressed by the play's title (Griffiths has a predilection for succinct, ambiguous titles), which refers not only to the action taken by the Fiat workers, but also to the private undertakings of the protagonists.

One of several future historical developments hinted at towards the end of *Occupations* is Stalinism. It can be seen germinating in Kabak's ruthless pragmatism and is summed up in Gramsci's ominous words: "Treat masses as expendable, as fodder, during the revolution, you will always treat them thus." *Thermidor* gives us a glimpse of Soviet Russia in the throes of Stalinism, during the purges of 1937. This one-act play is named after the summer month of the French revolutionary calendar, in which Robespierre himself fell victim to the Terror he had unleashed in the defence of the Revolution. Here it is Anya, formerly a loyal member of the Communist Party, who will disappear in the cellars of the NKVD. The play shows her at the mercy of her interrogator, Yukhov, who twists her sentences and fabricates absurd charges. Here there is even less doubt than in the altercations between Gramsci and Kabak as to where the author's sympathies lie. Yukhov's phrase "Enemies . . . are no longer people" disqualifies him and a whole system from speaking in the name of a humanist socialism. But when Anya finally pleads innocent and Yukhov asks the rhetorical question "Are you?," this is as much the voice of the author, who cannot absolve a once diligent and influential party member like Anya of historical guilt.

In contrast to these two analytical and descriptive plays *The Party* introduces an ironical note. An assortment of non-communist and almost exclusively non-working-class leftists meet at the instigation of a progressive television producer, Joe Shawcross, to discuss the possibilities of joint revolutionary action in Britain, all against the backdrop of Parisian students mounting the barricades in May 1968. The ironic nature of the whole radical-chic congregation, and the impotence of the British (intellectual) left, are suggested from the beginning through the appearance, in the Prologue, of Groucho Marx musing at a picture of his political namesake, and Joe's masturbation prior to the arrival of the leftist partygoers. Neither of the two conflicting analyses of the situation offered by a sociology lecturer and a veteran Trotskyist respectively (the latter pointing to the necessity of building *the* Party) is entirely wrong, but equally neither is free of empty revolutionary phrase-making and worn-out slogans, as the debunking comments of an accidentally present drunken writer point out.

Occupations, *Thermidor*, and *The Party* were all conceived and written for the stage. So was *Comedians*, which is often regarded as Griffiths's best work. It is certainly his funniest, even though one finds oneself often painfully aware of the impropriety of one's laughs. For this is a comedy about the social uses of stand-up comedy, and of working-class entertainment, a comedy about the proper function of the performer and, by implication, of the dramatist. Humour for Griffiths is too serious a business to be left in the hands of mindless word-jugglers who insult people's intelligence or pander to ethnic and sexual stereotypes.

Since the mid-1970's Griffiths's career has, however, been primarily and deliberately that of a television playwright. Few critics and scholars have appreciated this decision, and some on the left have even accused him of opportunism. The author has sought this medium out of a deep conviction that a socialist dramatist today cannot afford only to address the theatre-goer, whether in the West End or the fringe. While the one kind of theatre reaches only a middle-class audience, the other too often ends by preaching to the converted. For the vast majority of the population "drama in a dramatised society" (Raymond Williams) like ours means television drama, and as one character in *Through the Night* puts it: "whoever does not reach the capacity of the common people and fails to make them listen to him, misses his mark."

Yet what Griffiths has called the "strategic penetration" of the central channel of communication proved initially difficult. *Such Impossibilities*, commissioned by the BBC as part of a series entitled *The Edwardians*, was rejected, ostensibly on grounds of cost, but more probably because its hero, the militant labour leader Tom Mann, and its theme, the 1911 transport strike in Liverpool, a social conflict of almost civil-war like dimensions, fitted awkwardly into an ancestral gallery composed of such establishment figures as Baden-Powell, Horatio Bottomley, and Charles Stewart Rolls.

Not surprisingly, therefore, *All Good Men*, Griffiths's first major produced television play, shows the author fully alert to the power of the medium to forge consensus and to mystify. The television producer who wants to conduct an interview with the elderly Labour politician Edward Waite, a former Cabinet Minister now to be made a peer, is attacked by William, the politician's son, precisely for his seemingly disinterested, value-free pose. William, a left-wing research student, is equally critical of the historical record of the Labour Party, and the dispute between father and son over its successes, as the former sees it, or purely minor reforms ultimately solidifying capitalism, as the latter argues, forms the climax of the play. But true to his now familiar oppositional set-up, Griffiths, though sharing many of William's reservations about "Labourism," distributes the arguments fairly evenly. Moreover, Waite —like so many of Griffiths's totally committed figures—has paid a heavy price for his lifelong dedication to working-class politics. He has been deserted by his wife and is now betrayed by his son, who supplies the interviewer with compromising material about his father's past, not out of personal vindictiveness but in order to bring the internal political machinations of the Labour Party into the open.

All Good Men, like its 11-part successor *Bill Brand*, questions the parliamentary road to socialism, and scrutinises the role of the Labour Party, without writing off either completely. But as the revolutionary optimism of much of the British socialist drama of the 1970's subsided and experienced a definite check under the realities of Thatcher's Britain, Griffiths found other themes more pertinent, among them the situation of unemployed urban youths (*Oi for England*) and the construction of national myths (*The Last Place on Earth*).

Country, Griffiths's strongest play of the 1980's, is about a significant "moment" in the history of British socialism, namely Labour's landslide victory in 1945. But it looks at it from an unexpected angle, an upper-class estate in Kent, where the members of the Carlion dynasty have assembled for the annual family gathering, at which a successor to the ageing Sir Frederic, baronet and Chairman of the Board of the Carlion brewery empire, will have to be found. As the devastating election results come in, and the common people themselves symbolically lay claim to the property by trespassing and occupying a barn, incredulity and consternation alternate with wrath. But Philip, one Carlion not affected by the general stupefaction, an outsider among the pretenders for the succession not least because of his bohemian lifestyle, now energetically assumes responsibility. Philip's victory over the "old gang," his efficient and smooth dealing with the squatters, indicates the capacity of the ruling class to renew itself and adapt to unforeseen circumstances—a point already made in *Occupations*, where the Fiat manager envisages a whole paternalistic welfare programme as a palliative against future social unrest.

Griffiths's work also includes screenplays. Chief among these are *Reds* (directed by Warren Beatty) about the American journalist John Reed's involvement in the October Revolution, and *Fatherland* (directed by Ken Loach), an intriguing story of German partition and a songmaker's search for his father, who left the GDR for the West 30 years before his son.

With *Real Dreams* Griffiths has lately returned to the stage—and to an earlier preoccupation. Like *The Party*, this play about the American student movement in the late 1960's highlights the feelings of isolation and frustration behind the leftward move of many intellectuals. The attempt of a commune of white middle-class students to move out of the protected world of the campus and form a fighting alliance with Puerto Rican working people fails dismally, hampered as it is by all kinds of ethnic, cultural, sexist, and psychic blocks. But the play ends on an optimistic note: the real historical contradictions are dissolved into an anticipatory dream of perfect unity, grace, and victory—all symbolised by a trance-like Tai-Chi exercise. The limitations and self-indulgence as well as the potential power and promise of this phase of radicalism are thus brought alive. If the conclusion appears somewhat forced, the play demonstrates once again Griffiths's masterly building up of tension, and testifies to his continuing concern for the global struggle for liberation.

Perhaps the most important single theatrical influence on the later Griffiths is Chekhov, whose *The Cherry Orchard* he adapted to shrill screams of protest from critics who took issue with the downgrading of the central figure Ranevsky, and the consequent shift of emphasis from plangent sorrow over the loss of property to the acute anticipation of a revolutionary situation. Chekhov also looms large in *Piano*, which is based on the Russian's early unfinished play *Platonov* and equally set in turn-of-the-century rural society, A kindred atmosphere of imminent historical change hangs over the characters, most of them finely graded blasé upper-class, who are enmeshed in a web of failure and frustration, confusion and apathy, stalemate and deadlock—a mental and psychological state not at a great remove from that of radical intellectuals of the present day after the collapse of socialist hopes.

—H. Gustav Klaus

See the essay on *Comedians*.

GRILLO, John.

Born in Watford, Hertfordshire, 29 November 1942. Educated at Watford Boys Grammar School 1954–61; Trinity Hall, Cambridge, 1962–65, B.A. in history 1965. Professional actor: in Lincoln, Glasgow, Farnham, Brighton, London. Resident dramatist, Castle Theatre, Farnham, Surrey, 1969–70; literary associate, Soho Theatre Club, London, 1971. Recipient: Arts Council bursary, 1965. Agent (for acting): Howes and Prior Ltd., 66 Berkeley House, Hay Hill, London W.1, England.

Publications

PLAYS

Gentlemen I . . . (produced 1963).
It Will Come or It Won't (produced 1965).
Hello Goodbye Sebastian (produced 1965). In *Gambit 16*, 1970.
The Downfall of Jack Throb (produced 1967).
The Fall of Samson Morocco (produced 1969).
Oh Everyman Oh Colonel Fawcett (produced 1969).
Mr. Bickerstaff's Establishment (produced 1969; expanded version produced 1972).
History of a Poor Old Man (produced 1970).
Number Three (produced 1970). In *New Short Plays*, 1972.
Blubber (produced 1971).
Zonk (produced 1971).
Food (produced 1971).
Will the King Leave His Tea Pot (produced 1971).
George and Moira Entertain a Member of the Opposite Sex to Dinner (produced 1971).
The Hammer and the Hacksaw, in *Christmas Present* (produced 1971).
Christmas Box, and Civitas Dei (produced 1972).
Snaps (Civitas Dei, Days by the River, MacEnery's Vision of Pipkin) (produced 1973).
Crackers (produced 1973).
Mr. Ives' Magic Punch and Judy Show (produced 1973).

TELEVISION PLAY: *Nineteen Thirty Nine*, 1973.

CRITICAL STUDY: by Germaine Greer, in *Cambridge Review*, 29 May 1965.

THEATRICAL ACTIVITIES
ACTOR: **Plays**—Dabble in *Lock Up Your Daughters* by Bernard Miles, Billy Bones in *Treasure Island* by Jules Eckert Goodman, Poet in *Five to a Flat* by Valentine Kataev, Ingham in *Little Malcolm and His Struggle Against the Eunuchs* by David Halliwell, roles in *Beyond the Fringe*, Andrei in *The Three Sisters* by Chekhov, Clarence in *2 Henry IV*, Max in *The Homecoming* by Harold Pinter, Jopplin in *A Shouting in the Streets* by Elizabeth Dawson, and Rusty Charley in *Guys and Dolls* by Abe Burrows and Jo Swerling, 1966–67; Old Man in *Hello Goodbye Sebastian* and Rasputin in *The Rasputin Show* by Michael Almaz, 1968; Verlaine in *Total Eclipse* by Christopher Hampton, 1968, roles in *Erogenous Zones* by Mike Stott, 1969, Perowne in *AC/DC* by Heathcote Williams, 1970, Reporter and Deaf and Dumb Man in *Lulu* by Peter Barnes, 1971, and Marx in *Anarchist* by Michael Almaz, 1971; Glendower in *1 Henry IV*, 1969; Eddy in *Tango* by Mrozek, Millionaire in *Cliffwalk* by Sebastian Shaw, Fawcett in *Oh Everyman Oh Colonel Fawcett*, and Don Pedro in *Much Ado About Nothing*, 1969–70; Nurse in *Number Three*, 1970, Thug in *Dynamo* by Christopher Wilkinson, 1971, and Recorder in *Inquisition* by Michael Almaz, 1971; Mr. Bickerstaff in *Mr. Bickerstaff's Establishment*, 1972; Doc in *The Tooth of Crime* by Sam Shepard, 1972;

Sergeant Kite in *The Recruiting Officer* by Farquhar, 1972; Dr. Rank in *A Doll's House* by Ibsen, 1972; Poltrone in *The Director of the Opera* by Anouilh, 1973; Gremio in *The Taming of the Shrew*, 1974; Ashley Withers in *The End of Me Old Cigar* by John Osborne, 1975; role in *Bussy d'Ambois* by George Chapman, 1988. **Films**—*The F and H Film*; *Dynamo*; *Firefox*, 1982; *Brazil*, 1985. **Television**—*Brideshead Revisited*, 1981; *Chessgame*, 1983; *Dog Ends*, 1984; *Blott on the Landscape*, 1985; *Mother Love*, 1989.

John Grillo comments:

(1973) Aspects of my work include 1) A writing out of private obsessive fantasies and an attempt to excite the audience by parading on the stage that which is forbidden. 2) The plays are firmly based in the lower-middle-class morality and culture of my childhood. 3) Influence of theatrical innovators and fantasists such as Ionesco and Jarry. 4) Influence of television and film. Before the age of twenty I had visited the theatre perhaps half a dozen times. 5) I do not know how my work will develop but I hope it will become more public, less private, more realistic, less fantastic.

John Grillo is the Alfred Jarry of modern British theatre: a clown dramatist whose plays mingle outrageous solemnity with knockabout comedy and a Rabelaisian relish for dirty jokes. His stories have the simplicity of Punch and Judy shows. Bickerstaff (in *Mr. Bickerstaff's Establishment*) murders his sleep-walking wife as an alternative to committing suicide. Emboldened by this desperate deed, he tries to take over the underworld of pimps, thugs, and prostitutes: but finally the Forces of the Law—and his wife's ghost—catch up with him and condemn him to death. Bickerstaff (like Punch) escapes and decides to "emigrate—to Beirut": where his yearning for the fleshpots of the East can be satisfied. The Nurse (in *Number Three*) is a male fascist orderly in a mental hospital, preserving a solemn repressive dignity before a torrent of sexual insults from his worst patient, Three. The King (in *Will the King Leave His Tea Pot*) retires from the Affairs of State—and his frustrated thinning wife—into a huge womb-like tea-pot: thus causing the utmost consternation among his subjects, who lose all sense of protocol. These anecdotes are told in the style of children's stories. The characters are dressed like cartoons: Bickerstaff is a "fat man with a drooping bedraggled moustache"—like Crippen. The Queen (in *Will the King Leave His Tea Pot*) "wears a long silver dress, which is frayed at the edges, a necklace of pearls, several of which are missing and two or three of which are molars." The dialogue mainly consists of torrential speeches, where wild puns, extreme thought-associations, and an almost innocent scatology provide buoyant, idiosyncratic fun. The characters talk at each other—rather than to or with—and any change in mood is underlined by asides to the audience. When the Nurse, who is trying to persuade Three to go to bed, changes his tactics, he tells the audience that he is doing so. "Poor Nurse is worried because Number Three is such a bad boy. Nurse is a very sensitive man and he cries when Number Three plays him up . . . (aside) This is called 'Making the patient feel guilty.'"

This overtness in handling the story, the dialogue, the bawdiness, and the characters gives Grillo's plays an ingenuous charm. Grillo is an actor—as well as a dramatist—and he has a performer's instinct for bizarre, shock tactics. As an actor, he has worked extensively with fringe theatre in Britain: in the rudimentary pub theatres of London and the student theatre clubs. His plays are designed to require little in the way of staging, but to rely on actor-audience contact, in the style of music hall. He is one of the rare dramatists to exploit the essential roughness, the slapdash circumstances of fringe theatre: and therefore his plays work particularly well in pubs. Nor is the humour as unsophisticated as may appear. Grillo delights in choosing apparently "serious" themes and placing them in comic-strip settings. In his longest and perhaps most ambitious play, *Hello Goodbye Sebastian*, Grillo tells the story of an apprentice gravedigger, Sebastian, who longs for a better life and refuses to fill in a grave, because the old man whose wife occupies it believes in the resurrection of the dead. Sebastian's home life however is an unhappy one. His mother, Mary, and the lodger, Charlie, are living off his earnings: and their sex life dominates the household arrangements. Sebastian can't leave his job—to become a barber—because his mother doesn't want him to: it would destroy the precarious balance of her affair. And so Sebastian finally resigns himself to being a gravedigger: and in the final scene, he fills in the grave of the old man's wife. The allegorical overtones of Grillo's story relate it to the Theatre of the Absurd and to Ionesco's plays in particular. The suppression of innocence and adolescent hope leads to a death-centredness. Sebastian at the end of the play fills up the grave with unnecessary relish: "Half a pound of worms, landlord, down the hatch. Pound of filth, landlord. Coming, sir, down the hatch!" But this "serious" theme is handled with a flippant lightness, which does not, however, prevent the allegory from being both noticeable and important to the success of the play.

Grillo's cheerful irreverence has a habit of misfiring in the wrong surroundings. He was once the resident dramatist/actor with a repertory theatre in Farnham, a quiet country town in the South of England. His comic-strip version of the Everyman story caused the greatest possible local outrage. "They called the play," remembers Grillo, "lavatorial, smutty, schoolboyish, nihilistic, unnecessarily cruel, and what's more my acting stank." Nor was he at ease in the portentous atmosphere of avant-garde theatre clubs, which may be one reason why his plays have been under-rated by British critics. His best productions have perhaps come with the talented fringe group, Portable Theatre, who included *Zonk* and *Food* in their 1971 repertoire. *Zonk* is an extraordinary family comedy, involving a mother, Dora (a man in drag), a domineering father, Bone, a son, and a substitute Dora (an attractive woman in her early forties). The son's antagonism towards his father and his yearnings for sex with his mother provide a comic interpretation of Oedipalism. The son eventually disgusts the father by sucking milk from his mother's artificial penis. Not all of Grillo's plays are, however, equally extreme. His *History of a Poor Old Man* is a mock-melancholic monologue of an old man arrested for soliciting in a lavatory.

Grillo's great quality as a dramatist is that his sense of fun is infectious. The jokes tumble over each other and the uninhibitedness of the bawdry creates an easy relaxation in the theatre. He breaks down the over-solemn atmosphere of playgoing and brings back a childlike delight in trying anything once. His plays are unique, and have stayed fresh and exuberant. His technical range is severely limited, but within these limits his imagination is exhilarating.

—John Elsom

H

HAIRE, Wilson John.

Born in Belfast, Northern Ireland, 6 April 1932. Educated at Clontonacally Elementary School, Carryduff, County Down, 1939–46. Married 1) Rita Lenson in 1955 (marriage dissolved) five children; 2) Sheila Fitz-Jones in 1974 (marriage dissolved);3) Karen Mendelsohn in 1979 (marriage dissolved). Actor, Unity Theatre, London, 1962–67; co-director, Camden Group Theatre, London, 1967–71; resident dramatist, Royal Court Theatre, London, 1974, and Lyric Theatre, Belfast, 1976. Recipient: George Devine award, 1972; *Evening Standard* award, 1973; Thames Television award, 1974; Leverhulme fellowship, 1976. Address: 61 Lulot Gardens, London N19 5TS, England.

Publications

PLAYS

The Clockin' Hen (produced 1968).
The Diamond, Bone and Hammer; and Along the Sloughs of Ulster (produced 1969).
Within Two Shadows (produced 1972). In *Scripts 9*, September 1972.
Bloom of the Diamond Stone (produced 1973). 1979.
Echoes from a Concrete Canyon (produced 1975).
Lost Worlds: Newsflash, Wedding Breakfast, Roost (produced 1978). 1978.
Worlds Apart, with J.P. Dylan (produced 1981).

TELEVISION PLAYS: *Letter from a Soldier*, 1975; *The Dandelion Clock*, 1975.

Wilson John Haire comments:

(1988) I first began writing about Northern Ireland back in 1960. I wrote three short stories for a monthly paper called the *Irish Democrat*. My first story was called "Refuge from the Tick-Man" and I went under the pen name of "Fenian." "Fenian" is a derogatory name for Catholic in Northern Ireland. When I began writing the story of how my family fled the city of Belfast for the countryside to escape the debt collectors I became proud of that name. To me it meant someone who resists corruption and sectarian bullying. The editor of the paper persuaded me to use my real name for my second story "The Screening"—a teenage boy, pretending to be a Protestant, survives interrogation and taunts about Catholicism and gets the job for which he is applying. The third story was "The Beg." "Beg" is bag or sack in Ulster dialect. The local shipyard sheds a quarter of its workers, and the story is told through the eyes of an apprentice carpenter.

I took to writing drama in 1968 with a one-act play *The Clockin' Hen*. A broody hen hatches out her eggs under a darkening sky—in 1968 the Reverend Paisley attempts to lead a demonstration, with protection, through a Catholic ghetto and is resisted. A Catholic and Protestant are put on trial. The Catholic sees no hope of justice in a court that openly loathes him.

After that I wrote *The Diamond, Bone and Hammer, and Along the Sloughs of Ulster*. It is a sort of "Fear and Misery in the Third Reich." This play sequence was produced at the Hampstead Theatre, and later transfered to the Unity Theatre. This was not a professional production, and no reviewer appeared except for D.A.N. Jones of the *Listener*, who gave it an intelligent review. It was this one and only review that made me want to go on writing.

On opening night, Friday, 8 August 1969, the Bogside riots began, and Ulster became a topic of conversation in London. On 12 April 1972 *Within Two Shadows* opened at the Royal Court Theatre. The media said it was the first play on the Ulster crisis to open in London. I come from a parentage of both Catholic and Protestant. I saw this as the "two shadows" in my life, and I told the tale from within the family.

Though I have not had a London production of my work recently it still continues to be alive and well within the colleges and universities in the English-speaking world. At the moment I am hoping to write some drama for radio. I have a love for language and I am hoping that radio will give me the facilities that the old Royal Court Theatre once gave.

Wilson John Haire, born in the Shankill Road, Belfast, the son of a Catholic mother and a Protestant father, has drawn much of the background material for his plays from that stark area of the tortured city. Even when the actual turmoil of Northern Ireland is not part of a play, as in *Echoes from a Concrete Canyon*, we can still feel the claustrophobic atmosphere of an unfriendly town beyond the walls of a lonely flat. Four of Haire's plays, however, are set against the background of sectarian violence, bigotry, and loneliness. He conveys the tragedy of Ulster more directly and vividly than any other contemporary playwright, drawing upon memories which reach far back into his childhood.

Haire is not a polemical writer. Political ideas interest him, particularly as part of the environments from which they come, but he is concerned more with the nature and extent of Ulster's suffering than with easy moralising. His best known play, *Within Two Shadows*, is also the most autobiographical. It deals with a working-class Belfast family, dog-eared with poverty, and torn apart by prejudices which they try to exclude but which gradually eat into their lives. In the play the mother is a Protestant, the father a Catholic, and we feel that both, at some time in their lives, have made conscientious efforts to leap over the religious barriers which divide them. But the pressure of events, the opinions of their neighbours, and the growing violence are too much for them. They try to stay away from conflict, if only to protect their children; but the children are growing up, now teenagers, and quick to enter into the rivalries, as part of their puppy-play but with fangs bared.

In *Bloom of the Diamond Stone* Haire shows what could almost have been the beginnings of that marriage, a Romeo and Juliet love affair, where the young couple from opposite sides fall in love and then have to battle against their families, the restrictions set at work, and the rigid outlooks of their former friends. In both plays Haire conveys a sense of inner honesty and goodness corrupted by circumstance. In that way, he can be an optimistic writer. His characters are not vicious in themselves, only made so by a historical backlog of revenge, fear, and defensiveness. To that extent, Ulster's torment seems the result of a curable mixture of follies, rather than the dark nightmare of the soul as other dramatists, including David Rudkin, have sometimes presented it. The British soldier searching for a "terrorist" in *Bloom of the Diamond Stone* is shown to be a likeable human being, until his fears and his job prompt him to be otherwise.

But the follies extend in all directions. They are sometimes rooted in sheer lack of understanding of the awfulness of the situation. In his first television play, *Letter from a Soldier*, Haire merely describes a soldier's effort to make his family in England understand what a tour of duty in Ulster is like. His second, *The Dandelion Clock*, concerns the particular problems facing a young girl growing up in Belfast. What sort of future can she plan for herself? The problems, however, are not just ones of comprehension. They also stem from the social organisation which is out of touch with the lives people lead.

The Clockin' Hen, Haire's first stage play, concerns a court case in which two shipyard workers of different religions are put on trial, following a Paisleyite demonstration in 1966. How do they react to the presence of the Law? Do they regard Law in any meaningful sense? And if they do not, where does an Ulsterman go? "Emotionally," Haire has said, "I am a Catholic, but intellectually I am a Protestant." This conflict is reflected in his plays. Haire perceives the need for a formal social order, but is sympathetic to the resentments caused by the existing one. To be out of touch with society, to defy, ignore, or simply have an engrained distrust of the ordering forces which are there, is equivalent to "dropping out." Haire's sympathy with Irish drop-outs, tramps, and drunkards is shown in *The Latchicoes of Fort Camden*, an unperformed play set in a London dosshouse.

Haire's skill as a dramatist reveals the strength and weaknesses of someone who chooses subjects so close to his personal experience. He can write vigorously and directly, usually naturalistically, but without the detachment needed to ensure that his plays have a clear form and that each point is made dramatically and concisely. He has indicated an intention to break away from his concentration on Northern Ireland; but in *Echoes from a Concrete Canyon*, which concerns the mental breakdown of a woman living with her daughter in a block of flats and estranged from her husband, the clotted verbosity which often accompanies autobiography is still present. Lightening touches of humour are rare; and the frequent poeticisms add heaviness rather than variety to the language. Haire in time may gain maturity as a dramatist by becoming less dependent on his background, but he may lose the force of reality which adds power to his Ulster plays. He speaks as a witness and a survivor of a continuing drama of stupidity, cruelty, and resentment. That, so far, has been his main role, and not an insignificant one, in contemporary British theatre.

—John Elsom

HALE, John.

Born in Woolwich, Kent, 5 February 1926. Educated at army schools in Egypt, Ceylon, and Malta; Borden Grammar School, Sittingbourne, Kent; Royal Naval College, Greenwich. Served in the Fleet Air Arm, 1941–51: boy apprentice to petty officer, later commissioned. Married Valerie June Bryan in 1950; one son and one daughter. Stage hand, stage manager, and electrician, in variety, touring, and repertory companies, 1952–55; founder, and artistic director, Lincoln Theatre, 1955–58; artistic director, Arts Theatre, Ipswich, 1958–59 and Bristol Old Vic, 1959–61; freelance director, 1961–64; member of the Board of Governors, 1963–71, associate artistic director, 1968–71, and resident playwright, 1975–76, Greenwich Theatre, London. Since 1964 freelance writer and director. Recipient: Golden Globe award, 1970. Agent: (for plays and screenplays), Lemon, Unna and Durbridge, 24–32 Pottery Lane, Holland Park, London W11 4LZ; (for novels), Aitken and Stone Ltd., 29 Fernshaw Road, London SW10 0TG, England.

Publications

PLAYS

The Black Swan Winter (as Smile Boys, That's the Style, produced 1968; as The Black Swan Winter, also director: produced 1969). In Plays of the Year 37, 1970.
It's All in the Mind (also director: produced 1968).
Spithead (also director: produced 1969). In Plays of the Year 38, 1971.
Here Is the News (produced 1970).
Lorna and Ted (also director: produced 1970).
Decibels (produced 1971). In Prompt Three, edited by Alan Durband, 1976.
The Lion's Cub (televised 1971). In Elizabeth R, edited by J.C. Trewin, 1971.
In Memory of . . . Carmen Miranda (also director: produced 1975).
Love's Old Sweet Song (also director: produced 1976).
The Case of David Anderson, Q.C. (produced 1980).

SCREENPLAYS: The Mind of Mr. Soames, with Edward Simpson, 1969; Anne of the Thousand Days, with Bridget Boland, 1970; Mary Queen of Scots, 1972.

RADIO WRITING: Micah Clarke series, 1966.

TELEVISION PLAYS: The Rules That Jack Made, 1965; The Noise Stopped, 1966; Light the Blue Touch Paper, 1966; Thirteen Against Fate series, 1966; Samson and Delilah, Strike Pay, and Her Turn, all from short stories by D.H. Lawrence, 1966–67; The Queen's Traitor (5 parts), 1967; Retreat, 1968; The Picnic, 1969; The Distracted Preacher, 1969; The Lion's Cub, in Elizabeth R series, 1971; The Bristol Entertainment, 1971; Anywhere But England, 1972; Ego Hugo: A Romantic Entertainment, 1973; Lorna and Ted, 1973; The Brotherhood, 1975; An Impeccable Elopement, 1975; Goodbye America, 1976; The Grudge Fight, from his own novel, 1981; Children of the North, 1991.

NOVELS

Kissed the Girls and Made Them Cry. 1963.
The Grudge Fight. 1964.
A Fool at the Feast. 1966.
The Paradise Man. 1969.
Mary, Queen of Scots (novelization of screenplay). 1972.
The Fort. 1973.
The Love School. 1974.
Lovers and Heretics. 1976.
The Whistle Blower. 1984.

THEATRICAL ACTIVITIES

DIRECTOR: **Plays**—about 150 plays in Lincoln, Ipswich, Bristol and elsewhere, including several of his own plays, and *An Enemy of the People* by Arthur Miller, 1958; *Cyrano de Bergerac* by Edmond Rostand, 1959; *The Merry Wives of Windsor*, 1959; *The Tinker* by Laurence Dobie and Robert Sloman, 1960; *The Rehearsal* by Anouilh, 1961; *The Killer* by Ionesco, 1961; *Sappho* by Lawrence Durrell, 1961; *Mother Courage* by Brecht, 1966. **Television**— about 16 plays, 1961–64, including *The Fruit at the Bottom of the Bowl* by Ray Bradbury, and *Drill Pig* by Charles Wood; *The Rules That Jack Made*, 1965. **Recordings**—13 Shakespeare plays, including *The Taming of the Shrew*, *Richard II*, and *Henry V*, FCM Productions.

John Hale comments:

I am both a playwright and a novelist. The plays and novels are written alternately; I buy the time with screenplays for television and films. If I have anything to say only part of it is in the plays: all of it, whatever it is, is in the plays and the novels taken together.

As a playwright, John Hale seems to share what is a common quality of actors, the ability to take up a theme, immerse himself in it, work it out, and leave it: recognizably the same actor is performing, if your concern is to look for him, yet the characters are different creations. Where other writers may work through and within an obsession, in some cases (Strindberg and Tennessee Williams) becoming trapped by it, so that their plays are like a series of studies of some vast central object too large to be contained in any one play, Hale seems to make a fresh start in each case, as if he were to say, "Here is my subject. I give myself to it. I use *this* particular piece of my own experience for it. I build it from inside, and shape it from the outside. I have made a play. I move on."

The Black Swan Winter, Hale's first stage play, was written after his own father's death, and uses memories of his father and himself. In a later play, *Love's Old Sweet Song*, Hale and his father appear again, and his grandfather also, but as supporting characters in what seems to be primarily an appalled examination of two castrating women, mother and daughter jointly devoted to the destruction of all the men around them. His novel *The Grudge Fight* used his experience of the navy, and when he wanted to return to the subject in *Spithead* he used instead the secondary experience of history. *It's All in the Mind* is his only excursion into politics, *Lorna and Ted* the only one into Suffolk, and his one-act monologue *In Memory of . . . Carmen Miranda* the only one into Samuel Beckett country, which is just as well since he seems not to be happy there.

Yet there is a moral being, Hale himself, who made all this work, even though he is modest as well as moral, and requires one to search for him. *Kissed the Girls and Made Them Cry*, *The Black Swan Winter*, and *Love's Old Sweet Song* all share a theme, the attempt to get back into one's past and find out what went wrong. The shadow of his father, a warrant officer in the Regular Army, lies upon his work and is shown in Hale's concern for fairness and his admiration of discipline, most of all self-discipline: if Forster can be boiled down to "Only connect," then Hale's two words are "Soldier on." Fairness for him means most of all fairness to other people, a decent recognition of the right to difference, but it can also mean (*Lorna and Ted*) fairness to oneself, an assertion of one's own rights, and an acceptance of responsibility.

Hale's plays are well-made in the manner, nowadays common, of a television play (or a play by Shakespeare), with a number of scenes running into each other, and a fragmented set. They are thoughtful, observed, humane, and only rarely self-indulgent. Their fault (commonly found in company with these virtues) is an occasional over-explicitness: Hale's characters, like Priestley's, too often say what they should only mean, though this is not a fault of *Lorna and Ted*, which is his most interesting play so far. He seems always to have been happiest when writing duologues (too many characters at once appear to worry him), and in this two-hander, with only a non-speaking voluptuous lady in support, his construction has been most at ease, most relaxed, least stiff.

—John Bowen

HALL, Willis.

Born in Leeds, Yorkshire, 6 April 1929. Educated at Cockburn High School, Leeds. National Service 1947–52: radio playwright for the Chinese Schools Department of Radio Malaya. Married 1) the actress Jill Bennett in 1962 (marriage dissolved 1965); 2) Dorothy Kingsmill-Lunn (marriage dissolved); 3) Valerie Shute in 1973; four sons. Lives in Ilkley, West Yorkshire. Recipient: *Evening Standard* award, 1959; BAFTA award, 1988. Agent: London Management, 235 Regent Street, London W1A 2JT, England.

Publications

PLAYS

Final at Furnell (broadcast 1954). 1956.
Poet and Pheasant, with Lewis Jones (broadcast 1955; produced 1958). 1959.
The Gentle Knight (broadcast 1957; produced 1964). 1966.
The Play of the Royal Astrologers (produced 1958). 1960.

Air Mail from Cyprus (televised 1958). In *The Television Playwright: Ten Plays for BBC Television*, edited by Michael Barry, 1960.

The Long and the Short and the Tall (produced 1958). 1959.

A Glimpse of the Sea, and Last Day in Dreamland (produced 1959). In *A Glimpse of the Sea: Three Short Plays*, 1961.

Return to the Sea (televised 1960; produced 1980). In *A Glimpse of the Sea: Three Short Plays*, 1961.

Billy Liar, with Keith Waterhouse, adaptation of the novel by Waterhouse (produced 1960). 1960.

Chin-Chin, adaptation of the play by François Billetdoux (produced 1960).

A Glimpse of the Sea: Three Short Plays. 1961.

Celebration: The Wedding and The Funeral, with Keith Waterhouse (produced 1961). 1961.

Azouk, with Robin Maugham, adaptation of a play by Alexandre Rivemale (produced 1962).

England, Our England, with Keith Waterhouse, music by Dudley Moore (produced 1962). 1964.

Squat Betty, with Keith Waterhouse (produced 1962). With *The Sponge Room*, 1963.

The Sponge Room, with Keith Waterhouse (produced 1962). With *Squat Betty*, 1963; in *Modern Short Plays from Broadway and London*, edited by Stanley Richards, 1969.

All Things Bright and Beautiful, with Keith Waterhouse (produced 1962). 1963.

Yer What? (revue), with others, music by Lance Mulcahy (produced 1962).

The Days Beginning: An Easter Play. 1964.

The Love Game, adaptation of a play by Marcel Achard, translated by Tamara Lo (produced 1964).

Come Laughing Home, with Keith Waterhouse (as *They Called the Bastard Stephen*, produced 1964; as *Come Laughing Home*, produced 1965). 1965.

Say Who You Are, with Keith Waterhouse (produced 1965). 1966; as *Help Stamp Out Marriage* (produced 1966). 1966.

Joey, Joey, with Keith Waterhouse, music by Ron Moody (produced 1966).

Whoops-a-Daisy, with Keith Waterhouse (produced 1968). 1978.

Children's Day, with Keith Waterhouse (produced 1969). 1975.

Who's Who, with Keith Waterhouse (produced 1971). 1974.

The Railwayman's New Clothes (televised 1971). 1974.

They Don't All Open Men's Boutiques (televised 1972). In *Prompt Three*, edited by Alan Durband, 1976.

Saturday, Sunday, Monday, with Keith Waterhouse, adaptation of a play by Eduardo De Filippo (produced 1973). 1974.

The Card, with Keith Waterhouse, music and lyrics by Tony Hatch and Jackie Trent, adaptation of the novel by Arnold Bennett (produced 1973).

Walk On, Walk On (produced 1975). 1976.

Kidnapped at Christmas (for children; produced 1975). 1975.

Stag-Night (produced 1976).

Christmas Crackers (for children; produced 1976). 1976.

Filumena, with Keith Waterhouse, adaptation of a play by Eduardo De Filippo (produced 1977). 1978.

A Right Christmas Caper (for children; produced 1977). 1978.
Worzel Gummidge (for children), with Keith Waterhouse, music by Denis King, adaptation of stories by Barbara Euphan Todd (produced 1980). 1984.
The Wind in the Willows, music by Denis King, adaptation of the story by Kenneth Grahame (produced 1984).
Treasure Island, music by Denis King, adaptation of the novel by Robert Louis Stevenson (produced 1984).
Lost Empires, with Keith Waterhouse, music by Denis King, adaptation of the novel by J.B. Priestley (produced 1985).
The Water Babies, adaptation of the novel by Charles Kingsley (produced 1987).
Jane Eyre, adaptation of the novel by Charlotte Bronte (produced 1992).
Mansfield Park, adaptation of the novel by Jane Austen (produced 1993).

SCREENPLAYS: *The Long and the Short and the Tall* (*Jungle Fighters*), with Wolf Mankowitz, 1961; with Keith Waterhouse— *Whistle Down the Wind*, 1961; *The Valiant*, 1962; *A Kind of Loving*, 1963; *Billy Liar*, 1963; *West Eleven*, 1963; *Man in the Middle*, 1963; *Pretty Polly* (*A Matter of Innocence*), 1967; *Lock Up Your Daughters*, 1969.

RADIO PLAYS: *Final at Furnell*, 1954; *The Nightingale*, 1954; *Furore at Furnell*, 1955; *Frenzy at Furnell*, 1955; *Friendly at Furnell*, 1955; *Fluster at Furnell*, 1955; *Poet and Pheasant*, with Lewis Jones, 1955; *One Man Absent*, 1955; *A Run for the Money*, 1956; *Afternoon for Antigone*, 1956; *The Long Years*, 1956; *Any Dark Morning*, 1956; *Feodor's Bride*, 1956; *One Man Returns*, 1956; *A Ride on the Donkeys*, 1957; *The Calverdon Road Job*, 1957; *The Gentle Knight*, 1957; *Harvest the Sea*, 1957; *Monday at Seven*, 1957; *Annual Outing*, 1958; *The Larford Lad*, 1958; *The Case of Walter Grimshaw*, with Leslie Halward, 1958.

TELEVISION PLAYS: *Air Mail from Cyprus*, 1958; *Return to the Sea*, 1960; *On the Night of the Murder*, 1962; *The Ticket*, 1969; *The Railwayman's New Clothes*, 1971; *The Villa Maroc*, 1972; *They Don't All Open Men's Boutiques*, 1972; *Song at Twilight*, 1973; *Friendly Encounter*, 1974; *The Piano-Smashers of the Golden Sun*, 1974; *Illegal Approach*, 1974; *Midgley*, 1975; *Match-Fit*, from a story by Brian Glanville, 1976; *A Flash of Inspiration*, 1976; *Secret Army* series, 1977; *The Fuzz* series, 1977; *Hazell Gets the Boot* (*Hazell* series), 1979; *Danedyke Mystery*, from a work by Stephen Chance, 1979; *National Pelmet*, 1980; *Minder* series, 1980–86; *Christmas Spirits*, 1981; *Stan's Last Game*, 1983; *The Road to 1984*, 1984; *The Bright Side* series, 1985; *The Return of the Antelope*, and *The Antelope Christmas Special*, from his own stories, 1986; with Keith Waterhouse— *Happy Moorings*, 1963; *How Many Angels*, 1964; *Inside George Webley* series, 1968; *Queenie's Castle* series, 1970; *Budgie* series, 1971–72; *The Upper Crusts* series, 1973; *Three's Company* series, 1973; *By Endeavour Alone*, 1973; *Briefer Encounter*, 1977; *Public Lives*, 1977; *Worzel Gummidge* series, from stories by Barbara Euphan Todd, 1979; *The Reluctant Dragon* (animated), 1988.

NOVEL

The Fuzz (novelization of TV series). 1977.

OTHER

They Found the World (for children), with I.O. Evans. 1960.
The Royal Astrologer: Adventures of Father Mole-Cricket or the Malayan Legends (for children). 1960.
The A to Z of Soccer, with Michael Parkinson. 1970.
The A to Z of Television, with Bob Monkhouse. 1971.
My Sporting Life. 1975.
The Incredible Kidnapping (for children). 1975.
The Summer of the Dinosaur (for children). 1977.
The Television Adventures [and *More Television Adventures*] *of Worzel Gummidge* (for children), with Keith Waterhouse. 2 vols., 1979; complete edition, as *Worzel Gummidge's Television Adventures*, 1981.
Worzel Gummidge at the Fair (for children), with Keith Waterhouse. 1980.
Worzel Gummidge Goes to the Seaside (for children), with Keith Waterhouse. 1980.
The Trials of Worzel Gummidge (for children), with Keith Waterhouse. 1980.
Worzel's Birthday (for children), with Keith Waterhouse. 1981.
New Television Adventures of Worzel Gummidge and Aunt Sally (for children), with Keith Waterhouse. 1981.
The Last Vampire (for children). 1982.
The Irish Adventures of Worzel Gummidge (for children), with Keith Waterhouse. 1984.
The Inflatable Shop (for children). 1984.
Dragon Days (for children). 1985.
The Return of the Antelope (for children). 1985.
The Antelope Company Ashore [*At Large*] (for children). 2 vols. 1986–87.
Worzel Gummidge Down Under (for children), with Keith Waterhouse. 1987.
Spooky Rhymes (for children). 1987.
Henry Hollins and the Dinosaur (for children). 1988.
Doctor Jekyll and Mr. Hollins (for children). 1988.
The Vampire's Holiday (for children). 1992.
The Vampire's Revenge (for children). 1993.

Editor, with Keith Waterhouse, *Writer's Theatre.* 1967.
Editor, with Michael Parkinson, *Football Report: An Anthology of Soccer.* 1973.
Editor, with Michael Parkinson, *Football Classified: An Anthology of Soccer.* 1975.
Editor, with Michael Parkinson, *Football Final.* 1975.

Willis Hall and Keith Waterhouse have written so many stage plays and television and film scripts over nearly 30 years that critics are wont to regard them as the stand-by professionals of British theatre. Their technical skill has never been doubted—but their artistry and originality often have. They were both born in Leeds in 1929 and have therefore shared a similar Yorkshire background. Both were successful individually before their long-standing collaboration began. Hall's *The Long and the Short and the Tall* was premiered by the Oxford Theatre Group in 1958: and was described by Kenneth Tynan as "the most moving production of the [Edinburgh] festival." Waterhouse's novel, *Billy Liar*, was well received in 1957. The stage version of *Billy Liar* was their first joint effort, and its success in London (where it helped to establish the names of the two actors who played the title role, Albert Finney and Tom Courtenay) encouraged them to continue in the vein of "purely naturalistic provincial working-class comedy," to quote T. C. Worsley's description. *Celebration*, *All Things Bright and Beautiful*, and *Come Laughing Home*, together with the one-act plays *The Sponge Room* and *Squat Betty*, allowed critics to regard them as the true successors of Stanley Houghton and Harold Brighouse: and this convenient label stuck to their work, until 1965, when their farce, *Say Who You Are*, set in Kensington and concerning a middle-class *ménage à quatre*, proved an unexpected success of the season. This lively and (in some respects) ambitious sexual comedy demonstrated that their talents were not confined to one style of humour nor their sense of place to the North of England. When this barrier of mild prejudice was broken, it was remembered that Hall was responsible for perhaps the best British adaptation of a comtemporary French comedy, Billetdoux's *Chin-Chin* (1960), that both had contributed widely to revues and satirical programmes (such as the BBC's *That Was the Week That Was*) and had written modern versions of Greek tragedies (such as Hall's *Afternoon for Antigone*). Their range as writers and their sophistication obviously extended beyond the narrow limits which brought them their reputations.

Nor is technical skill so common a quality among contemporary dramatists that it can be dismissed as unimportant. Hall and Waterhouse have the merits of good professionals. When they write satirically, their polemic is sharp, witty, and to the point. When they write naturalistically—whether about a provincial town in Yorkshire, a seaside amusement arcade, the war in Malaya, or Kensington—they take the trouble to know the surroundings in detail: and this groundwork enables them to discover possibilities which other writers overlook. *Celebration*, for example, presents two contrasting family events—a marriage and a funeral set in a working-class suburb of a Yorkshire town. There is no main story to hold the episodes together, nor a theme, nor even a clearly identifiable climax. But the play triumphs because the distinctive flavour of each "celebration" is captured and because the 15 main characters are each so well drawn. The slender threads of continuity which bind the episodes together reveal a sensitive insight into the nature of the society. The first act is about the wedding preparations in the backroom of a pub: Rhoda and Edgar Lucas are determined to do well by their daughter, Christine, who is marrying Bernard Fuller. But Rhoda has decided to economize by not employing Whittaker's, the firm in the town who specialize in weddings. Her efforts to ensure that the wedding breakfast doesn't let her daughter down are helped and hindered by the other members of the family: but despite the tattiness of the scene, the collapsible tables, the grease-proof paper and the dirty cups, the audience eventually is drawn to see the glowing pride and family self-importance which surround the event. Christine and Bernard survey the transformed room at the end of the act: and their contented happiness justifies the efforts. The second act is about the funeral of Arthur Broadbent, Rhoda's great-uncle and the best known eccentric of the family, who has been living in sin for years with May Beckett. The funeral is over and the pieties continue in the living room of the Lucas's house. But the family doesn't wish to acknowledge May Beckett, until she invades the house both physically (since they try to prevent her from coming) and emotionally, by expressing a grief which the conventional sentiments of the family cannot match. May's nostalgic tribute to her lost lover—so carefully prepared for in the script and emerging with an easy naturalness—is one of the truly outstanding moments of postwar British naturalistic drama: to rank with Beatie's speech at the end of Wesker's *Roots*.

This assured handling of naturalistic details is a feature of all their best plays. What other writers would have used the pub and the telephone box as so important a part of a sex comedy, replacing the more familiar stage props of a settee and a verandah? Or caught the significance of a back yard for a lonely introvert like Billy Liar? Or surrounded the pregnant unmarried girl, Vera Fawcett, in *Come Laughing Home*, with a family whose stultifying complacency offered a convincing example of the waste land from which she is trying unsuccessfully to escape? With this unusual skill in capturing an exact milieu, Hall and Waterhouse are also adept at writing those single outstanding roles which actors love to play. The part of Private Bamforth in *The Long and the Short and the Tall* gave Peter O'Toole his first opportunity—which he seized with relish: Hayley Mills was "discovered" in their film, *Whistle Down the Wind*, with the then underrated actor, Alan Bates. Hall and Waterhouse were once criticized for writing "angry young man" parts without providing the psychological insight or rhetoric of Osborne's Jimmy Porter. John Russell Taylor wrote that

> the central characters, Bamforth and Fentrill [in *Last Day in Dreamland*], are almost identical: the hectoring angry young man who knows it all and stands for most of the time in the centre of the stage, aquiver as a rule (whether the situation warrants it or not) with almost hysterical intensity, berating the other characters, who in each case, rather mysteriously, accept him as a natural leader and the life and soul of the party. The indebtedness to *Look Back in Anger* is unmistakable. . . .

This description may apply to Fentrill, whose anger at the rundown amusement arcade seems somewhat strained since he's not forced to stay there: less so to Bamforth, whose bitterness derives from claustrophobic jungle war: and scarcely at all to the other main characters of their plays. The distinctive strength of their protagonists lies not in their volubility nor their character complexities, but in their reactions to unsympathetic surroundings. Vera Fawcett is not a stock rebel: Billy Liar doesn't rebel at all—he's too satisfied with fantasies about escape. Unlike John Osborne, Hall and Waterhouse rarely offer "mouthpiece" characters, people whose insight and rhetoric about their own problems justify their presence on the stage. Their central characters emerge from their surroundings: the environment shapes the nature of their rebellion. Their dilemmas are a typical part of their societies: and are not superimposed upon their families as a consequence of too much intelligence or education.

A fairer criticism of their work might run along these lines: while their dialogue is always lively and accurate, it rarely contains flashes of intuition.

Much of the humour of *Celebration*, *Billy Liar*, and *Say Who You Are* depends upon carefully calculated repetition. The characters are sometimes given verbal catch-phrases—Eric Fawcett teases his son Brian endlessly for ordering "whisky and Scotch" in a pub—but more frequently are given habits which become irritating after a time. Eric Fawcett's life centres around making model boats (in *Come Laughing Home*); Edgar continually chides Rhoda for not arranging the wedding through Whittaker's, while his son Jack greets every newcomer with the same question, "Lend us a quid?" Often the reiteration makes a valid dramatic point—if only to illustrate the poverty of the relationships: but sometimes it seems just an easy way of establishing a person, by constantly reminding the audience of an obsession. Hall and Waterhouse often fail to reveal any deeper cause behind the nagging habit: and this lack of depth prevents the characters from seeming sympathetic. In *Say Who You Are* the two men, David and Stuart, are both self-opinionated male chauvinists: credible enough but rather uninteresting because they have so little self-knowledge. Valerie, who invents a marriage so that she can have an affair without getting too involved, is a more engaging creation—but she too seems superficial when we learn that her objections to marriage rest on a dislike of "togetherness"—"toothbrushes nestling side by side"—and on little else. Sometimes when Hall and Waterhouse try to give an added dimension to their characters, the effect seems strained: when Vera Fawcett resigns herself to an arid future with her family from whom she cannot escape, she says "I wanted to reach out for something, but I couldn't reach far enough. It's something you need—for living—that I haven't got. I haven't really looked, but I wanted to, I was going to." This statement of her defeat doesn't dramatically match or rise to the opportunity which the play provides for her.

This superficiality has often been explained as the reverse side of the authors' facility; writers who produce so many scripts can't be expected to be profound as well. But there may be another reason. Hall and Waterhouse share a remarkable sense of form and timing, which partly accounts for the success of *Say Who You Are* and *Celebration*. David and Sarah go to two different telephones at the same time, intending to ring each other up—with the result that the numbers are always engaged and they jump to the wrong conclusion. The scenes are based on a clever use of parallels and counterpoint: but this also depends on the characters behaving with a mechanical predictability. We know what they're really going to do, and the fun comes from seeing their stock reactions fail to achieve the expected results. The formalism of the scripts, in short, sometimes prevents the characters from having an independent life: and this is the result, not so much of technical facility, as of an overzealous care in the construction which shortsightedly ignores other possibilities. Despite these limitations, however, Hall and Waterhouse have an expertise which few other writers of the new wave of British drama can match and which accounts for the continuing popularity of their best plays.

—John Elsom

HALLIWELL, David (William).

Born in Brighouse, Yorkshire, 31 July 1936. Educated at Bailiff Bridge Elementary School; Victoria Central Secondary Modern School, Rastrick; Hipperholme Grammar School; Huddersfield College of Art, Yorkshire, 1953–59; Royal Academy of Dramatic Art, London, diploma 1961. Founder, with Mike Leigh, Dramagraph production company, London, 1965; director and committee member, Quipu group, London, 1966–76; visiting fellow, Reading University, 1969–70; resident dramatist, Royal Court Theatre, London 1976–77, and Hampstead Theatre, London, 1978–79. Co-director, Vardo Productions Ltd. Since 1991 director, playwriting workshops, The Actor's Centre, London. Recipient: *Evening Standard* award, 1967; John Whiting award, 1978. Fellow, Royal Society of Literature. Address: 8 Crawborough Villas, Charlbury, Oxford OX7 3TS, England.

Publications

PLAYS

Little Malcolm and His Struggle Against the Eunuchs (produced 1965). 1966; as *Hail Scrawdyke!* (produced 1966), 1967.

A Who's Who of Flapland (broadcast 1967; produced 1969). In *A Who's Who of Flapland and Other Plays*, 1971.

The Experiment, with David Calderisi (also co-director: produced 1967).

A Discussion (produced 1969). In *A Who's Who of Flapland and Other Plays*, 1971.

K. D. Dufford Hears K. D. Dufford Ask K. D. Dufford How K. D. Dufford'll Make K. D. Dufford (produced 1969). 1970.

Muck from Three Angles (produced 1970). In *A Who's Who of Flapland and Other Plays*, 1971.

The Girl Who Didn't Like Answers (produced 1971).

A Last Belch for the Great Auk (produced 1971).

A Who's Who of Flapland and Other Plays. 1971.

An Amour, and A Feast (produced 1971).

Bleats from a Brighouse Pleasureground (broadcast 1972; produced 1972).

Janitress Thrilled by Prehensile Penis (also director: produced 1972).

An Altercation (also director: produced 1973).

The Freckled Bum (also director: produced 1974).

Minyip (also director: produced 1974).

Progs (also director: produced 1975).

A Process of Elimination (also director: produced 1975).

Meriel the Ghost Girl (televised 1976; also director: produced 1982). In *The Mind Beyond*, 1976.

Prejudice (also director: produced 1978; as *Creatures of Another Kind*, produced 1981).

The House (produced 1979). 1979.

A Rite Kwik Metal Tata (produced 1979).

Was It Her? (broadcast 1980; also director: produced 1982).

A Tomato Who Grew into a Mushroom (produced 1987).

RADIO PLAYS: *A Who's Who of Flapland*, 1967; *Bleats from a Brighouse Pleasureground*, 1972; *Was It Her?*, 1980; *Spongehenge*, 1982; *Grandad's Place*, 1984; *Shares of the Pudding*, 1985; *Do It Yourself*, 1986; *Bedsprings*, 1989; *Parts*, 1989; *There's a Car Park in Witherton*, 1992; *Crossed Lines*, 1992.

TELEVISION PLAYS: *A Plastic Mac in Winter*, 1963; *Cock, Hen and Courting Pit*, 1966; *Triptych of Bathroom Users*, 1972; *Blur and Blank via Checkheaton*, 1972; *Steps Back*, 1973; *Daft Mam Blues*, 1975; *Pigmented Patter*, 1976, and *Tree Women of Jagden Crag*, 1978 (*Crown Court* series); *Meriel the Ghost Girl* (*The Mind Beyond* series), 1976; *There's a Car Park in Witherton*, 1982; *Speculating about Orwell*, 1983; *Arrangements*, 1985; *Doctor Who* series (2 episodes), 1985; *The Bill* (1 episode), 1989; *Bonds*, 1990.

CRITICAL STUDY: article in *The Gothic Impulse In Contemporary Drama* by Mary Beth Inverso, 1990.

THEATRICAL ACTIVITIES

DIRECTOR: **Plays**—Quipu group: many of his own plays, and *The Dumb Waiter* by Harold Pinter, *Keep Out, Love in Progress* by Walter Hall, *The Stronger* by Strindberg, and *A Village Wooing* by Shaw, 1966; *The Experiment* (co-director, with David Calderisi), 1967; *A Day with My Sister* by Stephen Poliakoff, 1971; *The Hundred Watt Bulb* by George Thatcher, *I Am Real and So Are You, A Visit from the Family*, and *Crewe Station at 2 A.M.* by Tony Connor, 1972; *The Only Way Out* by George Thatcher, 1973; *We Are What We Eat* by Frank Dux, *The Knowall* by Alan C. Taylor, and *The Quipu Anywhere Show* (co-director, with Gavin Eley), 1973; *The Last of the Feinsteins* by Tony Connor, 1975; *Paint* by Peter Godfrey, 1977; *Lovers* by Brian Friel, 1978; *Jelly Babies* by Glenn Young, 1978.

ACTOR: **Plays**—Vincentio in *The Taming of the Shrew* and Seyton in *Macbeth*, 1962; Hortensio in *The Taming of the Shrew*, 1962; Sydney Spooner in *Worm's Eye View* by R.F. Delderfield, 1962; General Madigan in *O'Flaherty, V.C.* by Shaw, and Jim Curry in *The Rainmaker* by N. Richard Nash, 1962; Hero in *The Rehearsal* by Anouilh, Pozzo in *Waiting for Godot* by Beckett, and The Common Man in *A Man for All Seasons* by Robert Bolt, 1963; Scrawdyke in *Little Malcolm and His Struggle Against the Eunuchs*, 1965; Jackson McIver in *The Experiment*, 1967; Policeman in *An Altercation*, 1973; Botard in *Rhinoceros* by Ionesco, 1974; Frankie in *Birdbath* by Leonard Melfi, 1975. **Films**—*Defence of the Realm*, 1986; *Mona Lisa*, 1986. **Radio**—Landlord in *Spongehenge*, 1982; Interrogator in *Bedsprings*, 1989; Hitler in *The Eagle Has Landed*, 1989, and *The Eagle Has Flown*, 1992, by Jack Higgins; Prison Officer in *Crossed Lines*, 1992.

David Halliwell comments:

Since the last edition of this book I have arrived at the essence of what I want to do as a dramatist. I have developed the means of expressing the conflicts and harmonies between the inner and outer parts of characters that I have been selecting and moving towards from the beginning of my dramatic career.

Means organically centred on actors and performances which, although they can be adapted to any medium, require, in essence, no mechanical or electronic equipment.

David Halliwell's dramatic territory is Flapland; his perennial subject, the Hitler syndrome; the motive force of his central characters, that childish outburst of King Lear's: "I will do such things,/What they are, yet I know not, but they shall be/The terrors of the earth." Malcolm Scrawdyke, the hero of *Little Malcolm and His Struggle Against the Eunuchs*, models himself explicitly on the early Hitler, except that he wears a Russian anarchist's greatcoat in place of Hitler's raincoat. Expelled from art school, Scrawdyke enlists three variously inadequate siblings into his Party of Dynamic Erection, plans a ludicrous revenge (which never gets beyond the fantasy stage) on the man who expelled him, and succeeds only in two petty, but nonetheless unpleasant, acts of terror: the "trial" of his most articulate and independent sibling, and the beating-up of a girl who has taunted him with sexual cowardice. Scrawdyke is only a phantom Hitler, his rabble-rousing speeches are confined to the inside of his Huddersfield garret and his grasp of reality so tenuous as to constitute little danger even to his specific enemies, let alone the community at large. But the hero of Halliwell's other full-length play, *K. D. Dufford Hears K. D. Dufford Ask K. D. Dufford How K. D. Dufford'll Make K. D. Dufford*, who actually wears a raincoat, sets his sights lower than Scrawdyke: his recipe for instant notoriety is to murder a child and he is entirely successful. Halliwell makes an ambitious attempt in this play not simply to suggest the interplay between fantasy and reality, but actually to display it, chapter and verse, on the stage, with several different versions of each scene—the real event compared with the event as imagined to his own advantage by K. D. Dufford and by each of the other main characters.

Halliwell explores the possibilities and limitations of this device in a series of short plays—*Muck from Three Angles*, *A Last Belch for the Great Auk*, *Bleats from a Brighouse Pleasureground*, and *Janitress Thrilled by Prehensile Penis*. The effect is often clumsy and ultimately superfluous since the shades of fantasy and reality pursue one another with such unerring clarity through his virtuoso monologues, that an audience must grow restive at being told by means of explicit technical devices what it has already grasped implicitly through intense dramatic sympathy.

For, however faceless, talentless, witless, loveless, lacking in courage and moral compunction these characters may be, Halliwell's comic view of them makes them irresistibly sympathetic. Something similar happens in the plays of Halliwell's contemporary Joe Orton, as well as in those of the master from whom they both learnt, Samuel Beckett. The fact that these characters would be, if met in real life, virtually sub-human, certainly pitiable or despicable to an extreme degree, is beside the point. In Halliwell's, as in Orton's and Beckett's plays, they are exaggerated dramatic representations of universal human weaknesses; and Halliwell has found and shown that, in this age of overpopulation and social disorientation, we are peculiarly vulnerable to paranoia. In *The Experiment*, partly devised by himself, partly improvised by the actors,

Halliwell acted an avant-garde theatrical director "of international repute" rehearsing his company in "a modern epic translated from the Icelandic entitled *The Assassination of President Garfield*." The efforts of this director to drive his cast towards the nadir of art, to discover in the purposeless murder of a forgotten American politician deeper and deeper levels of insignificance, satirized the gullibility of audiences as much as the inflated self-admiration of certain members of the theatrical profession, but there were above all a direct demonstration of Halliwell's own special subject: the banal striving to be the unique, the insignificant the significant, the squalid reality the dream of power.

In his lightest and most charming play, *A Who's Who of Flapland*, originally written for radio but successfully translated to lunch-time theatre, Halliwell closes the circle by confronting one paranoiac with another, his equal if not his master at the gambits and routines of Flapland. Here, as in *Little Malcolm*, Halliwell relies entirely on his mastery of dramatic speech, using his native industrial Yorkshire idiom as a precision instrument to trace complex patterns of aggression, alarm, subterfuge, humiliation, triumph, surrender. The more recent plays *A Rite Kwik Metal Tata*, *The House*, and *Prejudice*, are all what one might call "polyphonic" developments of this technique, adding, for example, a cockney girl and an upper-class MP to the Yorkshire characters in *Metal Tata* and a Bradford Pakistani and an exiled Zulu to those in *Prejudice*. *The House*, set in a country mansion requisitioned as a hospital during World War I, is the least successful, since Halliwell's command of regional idioms is not matched by any sense of period, and the action is too desultory. But in *Prejudice* and *Metal Tata* the plots are strong enough to allow him to turn his characters all round and inside out in relation to each other without losing the momentum of the play. Of course this is only what the best playwrights have always done, but good methods decay into tired conventions and it is clear that Halliwell's struggle has been to remove the dead wood and reconstitute traditional polyphonic drama in the fresh terms of his own ideas and idiosyncrasies.

—John Spurling

HAMPTON, Christopher (James).

Born in Fayal, the Azores, 26 January 1946. Educated at schools in Aden and Alexandria, Egypt; Lancing College, Sussex, 1959–63; New College, Oxford, 1964–68, B.A. in modern languages (French and German) 1968, M.A. Married Laura Margaret de Holesch in 1971; two daughters. Resident dramatist, Royal Court Theatre, London, 1968–70. Recipient: *Plays and Players* award, 1970, 1973, 1985; *Evening Standard* award, 1970, 1984, 1986; Los Angeles Drama Critics Circle award, 1974, 1989; Olivier award, 1986; New York Drama Critics Circle award, 1987; BAFTA award for television, 1987, for screenplay, 1990; Writers Guild of America award, 1989; Prix Italia, 1989; Academy award, 1989. Fellow, 1976, and since 1984 council member, Royal Society of Literature. Agent: Casarotto Ramsay Ltd., National House, 60–66 Wardour Street, London W1V 3HP. Address: 2 Kensington Park Gardens, London W.11, England.

Publications

PLAYS

When Did You Last See My Mother? (produced 1966). 1967.
Marya, adaptation of a play by Isaak Babel, translated by Michael Glenny and Harold Shukman (produced 1967). In *Plays of the Year 35*, 1969.
Total Eclipse (produced 1968). 1969; revised version (produced 1981), 1981.
Uncle Vanya, adaptation of a play by Chekhov, translated by Nina Froud (produced 1970). In *Plays of the Year 39*, 1971.
The Philanthropist: A Bourgeois Comedy (produced 1970). 1970; revised version, 1985.
Hedda Gabler, adaptation of a play by Ibsen (produced 1970). 1971; with *A Doll's House*, 1989.
A Doll's House, adaptation of a play by Ibsen (produced 1971). 1972; with *Hedda Gabler*, 1989.
Don Juan, adaptation of a play by Molière (broadcast 1972; produced 1972). 1974.
Savages (produced 1973). 1974; revised version, 1976.
Treats (produced 1976; revised version produced 1988). 1976.
Signed and Sealed, adaptation of a play by Georges Feydeau and Maurice Desvallières (produced 1976).
Able's Will (televised 1977). 1979.
Tales from the Vienna Woods, adaptation of a play by Ödön von Horváth (produced 1977). 1977.
Ghosts, adaptation of a play by Ibsen (produced 1978). 1983.
Don Juan Comes Back from the War, adaptation of a play by Ödön von Horváth (produced 1978). 1978.
The Wild Duck, adaptation of a play by Ibsen (produced 1979). 1980.
Geschichten aus dem Wiener Wald (screenplay), with Maximilian Schell. 1979.
After Mercer, based on works by David Mercer (produced 1980).
The Prague Trial, adaptation of a work by Patrice Chéreau and Ariane Mnouchkine (produced 1980).
A Night of the Day of the Imprisoned Writer, with Ronald Harwood (produced 1981).
The Portage to San Cristobal of A.H., adaptation of the novel by George Steiner (produced 1982). 1983.
Tales from Hollywood (produced 1982). 1983.
Tartuffe; or, The Impostor, adaptation of the play by Molière (produced 1983). 1984.
Les Liaisons Dangereuses, adaptation of the novel by Choderlos de Laclos (produced 1985). 1985.
The Ginger Tree, adaptation of the novel by Oswald Wynd (televised 1989). 1989.
Faith, Hope, and Charity, adaptation of a play by Ödön von Horváth (produced 1989). 1989.
Dangerous Liaisons: The Film. 1989.
White Chameleon (produced 1991). 1991.
The Philanthropist and Other Plays (includes *Treats*, *Total Eclipse*). 1991.

Sunset Boulevard, with Don Black, music by Andrew Lloyd Webber, adaptation of the film by Charles Brackett, Billy Wilder, and D.M. Marsham Jr. (produced 1993).

SCREENPLAYS: *A Doll's House*, 1973; *Geschichten aus dem Wiener Wald* (*Tales from the Vienna Woods*), with Maximilian Schell, 1981; *Beyond the Limit* (*The Honorary Consul*), 1983; *The Good Father*, 1986; *Dangerous Liaisons*, 1989.

RADIO PLAYS: *2 Children Free to Wander* (documentary), 1969; *Don Juan*, 1972; *The Prague Trial 79*, from a work by Patrice Chéreau and Ariane Mnouchkine, 1980.

TELEVISION PLAYS: *Able's Will*, 1977; *The History Man*, from the novel by Malcolm Bradbury, 1981; *Hotel du Lac*, from the novel by Anita Brookner, 1986; *The Ginger Tree*, adaptation of the novel by Oswald Wynd, 1989.

CRITICAL STUDIES: *Theatre Quarterly 12*, October–December 1973; *Christopher Hampton: A Casebook*, edited by Robert Gross, 1990.

THEATRICAL ACTIVITIES

ACTOR: **Play**—role in *When Did You Last See My Mother?*, 1966.

Les Liaisons Dangereuses coyly preserves the original French title of an epistolary novel adroitly dramatized by Christopher Hampton—to applause on Broadway, in the West End, and on the screen. The title—French or English—aptly summarizes Hampton's own theatrical focus. Although Hampton is not an overtly political playwright, he suggests that one of the dangers to the self-absorbed partners of their liaison is their very indifference to politics.

At age 18, while still an Oxford undergraduate (reading French and German) Hampton composed his first play, *When Did You Last See My Mother?* It received a bare-boards Sunday night production at the Royal Court Theatre and was immediately snapped up for the West End. Hampton's cruel and articulate protagonist adheres to the Angry tradition established by John Osborne, but all three of Hampton's characters are involved in dangerous liaisons—a love-hate ménage of teenage boys, a brief affair between one of the boys and the mother of the other. Unlike Broadway's *Tea and Sympathy*, the latter emotion is absent from Hampton's stage. In six swift, pitiless scenes, the teenage lovers circle back to their ménage—after the automobile accident in which the self-reproachful mother is killed.

In *Total Eclipse* the cruelly brilliant teenager is the French poet Arthur Rimbaud, who formed a dangerous liaison with Paul Verlaine, a married poet nearly twice his age. Hampton steeped himself in scholarly sources about their two-year relationship, in order to dramatize its tempestuous quality, again in six scenes. This time it is Verlaine who pivots from wife to lover, again and again, until Mme. Verlaine divorces him. Lies, drink, and drugs exacerbate the homosexual liaison, which erupts twice into violence: Rimbaud coolly stabs Verlaine's hands, and on another occasion Verlaine accidentally shoots

Rimbaud in the hand—and is imprisoned for two years. Hampton's final scene bears witness to his title, since both poetic talents suffer total eclipse; a derelict Verlaine is visited by the sister of the dead Rimbaud, and he fantasizes an idyllic liaison.

In spite of Hampton's two productions by the age of 21, he toyed with the idea of graduate study after taking his degree in 1968, whereupon Bill Gaskill created for him the position of resident dramatist at the Royal Court, with a slender income and no duties. Hampton proceeded to work simultaneously on translations, adaptations, and his own *The Philanthropist,* conceived as a rebuttal to Molière's *Le Misanthrope.* As the latter is an aristocratic comedy in rhyme, Hampton's play is a bourgeois comedy in prose. Since the protagonist Philip is a philologist as well as philanthropist, Hampton has marked him thrice as a lover (the translation of philo). True to Hampton's focus, Philip involves himself in dangerous liaisons—with the woman he wants to marry and with a woman who does not attract him. Spurned by both, he starts a wooing letter to still a third woman. By the end of the play, all love rejected, Philip reaches into a drawer for a gun, but when he pulls the trigger, a flame shoots out to light his cigarette. His will be a slower death, with sophisticated London as an analogue of the desert island to which Molière's misanthrope resolved to flee.

Incisive and obliquely moral about the worlds of his experience, Hampton reaches out globally in *Savages.* Triggered by the genocide of Brazilian Indians, *Savages* indicts cultured Europeans and radical South Americans for their complicity in the systematic decimation of the natives in order to acquire their land. Painting on a large canvas, Hampton parallels the public tragedy with a private one. A British Embassy official and minor poet, significantly named West, is taken hostage by Brazilian radicals who hope to trade him for their imprisoned colleagues. As the confinement of West stretches on, Hampton shows us the past in flashback—Embassy dinners, an anthropologist's distress, a pious and callous American mission, mercenaries who kill wholesale, preparations for the ceremonial gathering of Indian tribes, West's poems based on Indian legends. Then abruptly, the two plots coalesce in disaster. A bourgeois radical proves his revolutionary fervor by shooting West. A light plane bombs the Indians at their ceremony, and the pilot descends to shoot survivors. But the pilot burns all trace of the massacre, whereas West, dead, becomes a hero of the media.

Hampton retreated to another lover's triangle in *Treats.* A private term for sexual favors, the title points to the desires of two different men for Ann, married to the psychologically sadistic Dave, and intermittently living with the flaccid Patrick. When the play ends, Ann has replaced Patrick with Dave, and the sado-masochistic merry-go-round will presumably continue.

While producing these plays, Hampton worked on an unusually wide range of translations—Ibsen, Chekhov, Molière, and the lesser-known Austrian playwright Ödön von Horváth, who fired his imagination. Fleeing to Paris after the *Anschluss,* Horváth was killed at the age of 37 when a freak storm felled a tree under which he had taken shelter. In *Tales from Hollywood* Hampton invents a life for Horváth among the anti-Nazi Central European refugees in Hollywood. Mixing both easily and uneasily with the Mann family, Brecht, and others, Horváth is unable to toe any party line, as he is unable to fulfill any woman's needs. Unlike earlier Hampton heroes, Horváth is too humane and compassionate for dangerous liaisons. He withdraws from his putative afterlife, and is killed instantly by the falling tree, as recorded in history.

White Chameleon is a new departure for Hampton, since it is rooted in his own life. Set in Alexandria, Egypt, from 1952 to 1956, the play traces the effect on an English family of Egyptian social conflict. The protagonist Christopher is split in two—a boy of Hampton's own age at that time, and an adult looking back in memory. In White Chameleon a liaison of sympathy between young Christopher and the family servant Ibrahim proves ultimately dangerous to the latter. Little people are devoured by cataclysmic events.

Hampton is a playwright in the old English sense of the word "wright"—a craftsman who hones his tools even as he moulds increasingly large structures. As witty as his contemporaries, Hampton is more serious than most of them in his incisive dramas of cruelties of our private and public lives.

—Ruby Cohn

See the essay on The Philanthropist.

HANLEY, James.

Born in Liverpool, Lancashire, 3 September 1901; brother of the writer Gerald Hanley. Served in the Canadian Army, 1915. Married Dorothy Enid Heathcote; one son. Merchant seaman until 1924; later journalist. Recipient: Welsh Arts Council award, 1979. Died 11 November 1985.

Publications

PLAYS

Say Nothing (broadcast 1961; produced 1962). In Plays of the Year 27, 1963.
The Inner Journey (as Für Immer und Ewig, produced 1966; as Inner Journey, produced 1969). 1965.
Plays 1 (includes The Inner Journey and A Stone Flower). 1968.
Leave Us Alone (produced 1972).

RADIO PLAYS: S.S. Elizabethan, 1941; Freedom's Ferry series, 1941; Open Boat series, 1941; Return to Danger, 1942; Don Quixote Drowned, from his own story, 1953; Sailor's Song, from his own novel, 1954; Man in the Mirror, 1954; The Welsh Sonata, from his own novel, 1956; A Winter Journey, 1957; The Ocean, from his own novel, 1958; I Talk to Myself, 1958; A Letter in the Desert, 1958; Gobbet, 1959; Levine, from his own novel, 1959; The Queen of Ireland, 1960; Miss Williams, 1960; Say Nothing, 1961; A Moment for Reflection, 1961; The Furys, from his own novels, 1961; A Pillar of Fire (for children), 1962; A Walk in the World, 1962; A Dream, 1963; What Farrar Saw, 1963; One Way Only, 1967; The Silence, 1968; The House in the Valley, from his own novel, 1971; A Terrible Day, 1973; A Dream Journey, 1975; Another World, from his own novel, 1980.

TELEVISION PLAYS: *Inner World of Miss Vaughan*, 1964; *Another Port, Another Town*, 1964; *Mr. Ponge*, 1965; *Day Out for Lucy*, 1965; *A Walk in the Sea*, 1966; *That Woman*, 1967; *Nothing Will Be the Same Again*, 1968; *It Wasn't Me*, 1969.

NOVELS

Drift. 1930.
Boy. 1931.
Ebb and Flood. 1932.
Captain Bottell. 1933.
Resurrexit Dominus. 1934.
The Furys:
   The Furys. 1935.
   The Secret Journey. 1936.
   Our Time Is Gone. 1940; revised edition, 1949.
   Winter Song. 1950.
   An End and a Beginning. 1958.
Stoker Bush. 1935.
Hollow Sea. 1938.
The Ocean. 1941.
No Directions. 1943.
Sailor's Song. 1943.
What Farrar Saw. 1946.
Emily. 1948.
The House in the Valley. 1951; as *Against the Stream*, 1982.
The Closed Harbour. 1952.
The Welsh Sonata: Variations on a Theme. 1954.
Levine. 1956.
Say Nothing. 1962.
Another World. 1972.
A Woman in the Sky. 1973.
A Dream Journey. 1976.
A Kingdom. 1978.
Lost. 1979.
Against the Stream. 1981.

SHORT STORIES

The German Prisoner. 1930.
A Passion Before Death. 1930.
The Last Voyage. 1931.
Men in Darkness: Five Stories. 1931.
Stoker Haslett. 1932.
Aria and Finale. 1932.
Quartermaster Clausen. 1934.
At Bay. 1935.
Half an Eye: Sea Stories. 1937.
People Are Curious. 1938.
At Bay and Other Stories. 1944.
Crilley and Other Stories. 1945.

Selected Stories. 1947.
A Walk in the Wilderness. 1950.
Collected Stories. 1953.
Don Quixote Drowned. 1953.
The Darkness. 1973.
What Farrar Saw and Other Stories. 1984.

OTHER

Broken Water: An Autobiographical Excursion. 1937.
Grey Children: A Study in Humbug and Misery. 1937.
Between the Tides. 1939; as *Towards Horizons,* 1949.
John Cowper Powys: A Man in the Corner. 1969.
The Face of Winter. 1969.
Herman Melville: A Man in the Customs House. 1971.
Editor, with Nina Froud, *Chaliapin: An Autobiography as Told to Maxim Gorky.* 1967.

BIBLIOGRAPHY: *Hanley: A Bibliography* by Linnea Gibbs, 1980.

CRITICAL STUDY: *Hanley* by Edward Stokes, 1964.

Diary entry: "Going to visit James Hanley for the first time—'Come at 11 and I'll brew you a strong cup of tea.'" As I approach the house in Camden Town I look up at the topmost window and observe the pale smudge of a face, like some look-out in a lonely lighthouse. I sense that it is Hanley. A hand waves and then the face disappears. I wait at the front door. He is dressed formally in a suit but wears brown carpet slippers. His blue eyes gleam from under wild eyebrows and soft untidy hair which he keeps brushing back off his forehead. He chuckles as though we are about to take part in a conspiracy and then leads me upstairs to the small front room where he hibernates'.

Since that first visit I have often looked back over my many meetings with this unique and lonely artist and I have thought of the words of Antaeus in his play *The Inner Journey*, "My living dream is for the wastes of some high up, remote, lost, shut in and forgotten room. How I love silence, peace", as well as the words of another of his characters, Gareth, in *A Stone Flower*, "I'll find you a nice quiet place at the top of a house, and there'll be a window there, and when you look out you will see the sea and it will be very near."

So many of Hanley's novels are concerned with the sea but increasingly over the past years he turned inland, and inward. Again, as Antaeus says, "I want to live on myself now, with myself, in myself." Yet Hanley was no pale introvert or self-indulgent narcissist. As a novelist he has long been recognised as a major writer—"Too long!" he might grunt. E.M. Forster called him a writer of distinction and originality: John Cowper Powys described him as a genius and C.P. Snow rated him as one of the most important living authors, unsurpassed in qualities of compassion, humility, and sheer power.

Then, for eight years, he stopped writing novels and turned to writing plays for the radio, television, and theatre. Yet he regards the period of writing plays as a delusion. In a *Sunday Times* interview (12 May 1972), he said "Now I know I'm not [a playwright] and I'd better get back to the job that I know . . .".

Although his radio and television plays (bar one) have all been performed, Hanley was singularly unlucky in the theatre. I tried at one point in the history of the Hampstead Theatre Club to mount a season of three of his plays; I also tried, unsuccessfully, to cast his play *The Inner Journey*, and I commissioned a stage play from the television script *A Stone Flower*. His best known play remains *Say Nothing*. Staged at the Theatre Royal, Stratford East, it was highly praised by critics, notably B.A. Young and John Russell Taylor, the latter subsequently describing it as "the most neglected play of the past two decades".

In this wild and fantastical black comedy Hanley portrays three people in the North of England whose attitudes are so fixed that they are incapable of change. They take in a young lodger, Charlie. He tries to draw them out but comes, painfully, to realize that "nothing will get in, and nothing will get out". Mr. Baynes dreams of escaping from Mrs. Baynes but, she tells him, "I know even about your dreams". As Hanley himself says, "*Say Nothing* is a total and final situation for three people lying on the rack of their own limitations in a moral morass—the character of these people is itself their fate. The moral right to drive them an inch further than this (as Charlie attempts to do) does not exist. They dream, but their dreams smoulder, and never catch fire". Yet it is not a dead household. Like Sartre in *Huis Clos*, Hanley portrays a living hell in which these people (as in so many of his plays) are their own judges, prisoners, and warders, unable to climb beyond their own natures. Charlie departs, saddened and bewildered, his idealism shaken. "Nobody can do anything for anybody", he cries. The others remain "drowned in the grey monotones of their tight and hidden lives". Some people belong inside, nourished by their hate, by their pride (like Mair, the young wife in *A Stone Flower*). These are the characters Hanley brilliantly portrays.

In *Say Nothing* Mrs. Baynes says at one point, "I never said this to you before, Baynesy, but sometimes I have a dread of the words that will come out of one's mouth—you never know where their journey ends". And in Hanley's plays people do say terrible and forbidden things, they wound and savage each other, scarring for life.

A Stone Flower is a dramatic poem on pride, carved as it were of granite and slate. Set in mid-Wales at the turn of the century, it is the story of a young wife who will not forgive her husband, a sailor, who has, unwittingly, poxed her. Hanley is brilliant in his creation of smaller characters, and in his play he paints a powerful portrait of Mair's mother, a proud and lonely woman, as well as of the twisted bitterness of the chapel minister, Moesen Davies, who still lusts after her daughter—"she lives in my skull, old woman, and I remember once I split myself wide open so she can look inside". In a superb scene, set in the chapel by night, Hanley brings together Moesen Davies and Gareth, the young sailor husband, pain confronting pain. It has always surprised me that no one has thought of filming this play.

Of his other plays, *The Inner Journey*, (which has been staged in America) is an extraordinary work of flawed genius. I say flawed because in it Hanley created not merely a play requiring titanic actors but wrote one of the roles for a dwarf. It is therefore practically unstageable, at least until such times as a dwarf who is also an actor of magnitude can be found.

The story concerns a 70-year-old vaudeville artist, his dipsomanic wife, and their embittered dwarf son who is made to pose as a ventriloquist's doll in a savage ventriloquist act. Of this play Hanley wrote, "The journeys of Antaeus and Christian are always inward. Their dreams are as desperate as their hopes. Their love/hate relationship will flower either side of the grave, and the chain that holds them will always clang. They are people crucified by their imagination". Once again the play is rich with minor characters, Dickensian in their detail and richness of comedy. For though Hanley wrote savagely—"Would you like me to draw my fingernail slowly round his skull and open the windows in his head?"—he had a pungent, mordant, earthy sense of humour.

Few know that it was James Hanley who discovered the poet R.S. Thomas, and sent his poems to publisher after publisher until they were finally accepted by Rupert Hart-Davis. That first volume is dedicated to James Hanley. It is not surprising that Hanley, living for many years in a lonely Welsh valley, was drawn to Thomas and his poetry, such as the following, from *The Minister*, a radio play:

"Beloved, let us love one another". The words are blown
To pieces by the unchristened wind
In the chapel rafters, and love's text
Is riddled by the inhuman cry
Of buzzards circling about the moor.

Like Thomas, James Hanley was an original whose intense and lonely vision burnt as fiercely and as proudly as that of another great Welsh artist, David Jones, the poet and artist. Though Liverpool-Irish in origin, Hanley regarded himself as wholly Welsh by adoption. When finally the Welsh National Theatre comes to be built, it could do well to stage the works of James Hanley.

—James Roose-Evans

HANNAN, Chris(topher John).

Born in Glasgow, 25 January 1958. Educated at St. Aloysius' College, Glasgow, 1969–75; University College, Oxford, 1975–78. Voluntary worker, Simon Community, Glasgow, 1978–80. Recipient: *Time Out* award, 1991; *Plays and Players* award, 1991; Charrington London Fringe award, 1991. Lives in Edinburgh. Agent: Alan Brodie Representation, 91 Regent Street, London W1R 7TB, England.

Publications

PLAYS

Purity (produced 1984).
Klimkov: Life of a Tsarist Agent (produced 1984).
Elizabeth Gordon Quinn (produced 1985). 1990.
The Orphans' Comedy (produced 1986).
Gamblers, with Christopher Rathbone, adaptation of a play by Nikolai Gogol (produced 1987).
The Baby (produced 1990). 1991.
The Evil Doers (produced 1990). 1991.
The Pretenders, adaptation of the play by Henrik Ibsen (produced 1991).

Chris Hannan comments:

I'm attracted to mess; chaos. I read a couple of books about chaos theory, which I enjoyed. I can get quite into the philosophy of science. I suppose it gives me a way to think about form, patterns, order and disorder.

I like characters who believe in things however ridiculous the belief. Elizabeth Gordon Quinn, for example, is a woman who refuses to believe she's poor. To prove to herself that she's someone grand—an individual—she has a piano. Unfortunately this means she can't eat or pay the rent. She's a ridiculous and destructive woman in conflict with her family and community but also sort of heroic.

Elizabeth Gordon Quinn is quite melodramatic. Whatever I write I like the thing to have a heightened quality, a language. I admire language which is mesmeric even when it's nonsense, like in Gogol or Ben Jonson where words dance in front of the characters' eyes like the fires of hell.

I suppose I write about people who are trying to save themselves, in deformed or exotic ways. Like Macu in *The Baby* who confronts Pompey and the entire Roman State singlehandedly in a misplaced attempt to exorcise her private hurts. Or like Sammy and Tracky in *The Evil Doers* who try to save themselves from the chaos in their lives by creating more chaos.

Chris Hannan's career thus far is already notable for a number of bold and successful variations in genre. His early plays, *Klimkov*, *Elizabeth Gordon Quinn*, and *The Orphans' Comedy*, were all produced at the Traverse Theatre in Edinburgh. Of these it was *Elizabeth Gordon Quinn* that really brought his talent into the limelight. A rich and powerful piece set in a tenement in 1920s Glasgow, it is in some ways reminiscent of other Scottish work of the 1970s and 1980s, much of which has been rooted in passionate socialist convictions. Hannan's play recovers from the past an eloquent voice against historical injustice and oppression. Vivid characterization—especially of the indomitable protagonist—a robust sense of humour, and the precise evocation of period earned Hannan comparisons with Sean O'Casey, and the language of the play continually revealed a daring drive towards high style and burlesque.

The Evil Doers, which was produced at the Bush Theatre in London in 1990, presents itself as a City Comedy, a scathing satire on the pretensions of Glasgow to be European City of Culture. It is also a stunning account of a family desperately trying to stave off fragmentation in the face of alcoholism, debt, and congenital self-delusion. The writing bristles with mordant social observation—comic in the case of the teenage Heavy Metal patter, brutal in the portrayal of a young loan-shark—and contains one of the decade's finest mockeries of the Thatcherite ethic of individual enterprise. Hannan's ear for dialogue, heavily flavoured by Glaswegian slang, pinpoints evasions, blind spots, and emotional tremors with a high-definition precision sometimes equal to David Mamet's. The play deservedly earned Hannan the Most Promising Playwright award from *Plays and Players* and the Charrington Fringe Best Playwright award.

Hannan has come to a wider audience through his version of Ibsen's *The*

Pretenders, produced by the RSC, but perhaps his finest, certainly his most ambitious work so far, is *The Baby*, produced at the Tron Theatre in 1990. This comparatively large-scale play adopts an Imperial Roman setting to pursue a complex meditation on the themes of innocence, violence, love, and political expediency. The structure adheres to no single dramatic model and may never have made the narrative easy to grasp—particularly in the theatre, with parts being doubled by the cast. But the play gives further proof of Hannan's versatility with language and indicates an ability also to write with the visceral effects of spectacle and physical action in mind. Passages of gory and sensational melodrama give way to moments of sudden tenderness or unexpected parallels with contemporary politics—so that one has to adjust one's mode of response continuously and at short notice. At one moment, the play seems almost to wallow in its period, like *Titus Andronicus* exploiting it for a vein of violent extremism. At another, it lurches into pressing and topical allusion, as political in its applications as *Coriolanus* or a piece by Brecht. As a playwright with a natural instinct to make demands both of his audiences and of those who produce his work, Hannan is undoubtedly one of British theatre's brightest prospects for the 1990s.

—Matthew Lloyd

HARDING, John.

Born in Ruislip, Middlesex, 20 June 1948. Educated at Pinner Grammar School; Manchester University, 1966–69, B.A. (honours) in drama 1969. Married Gillian Heaps in 1968; one son. Agent: Michael Imison Playwrights, 28 Almeida Street, London N1 1TD, England.

Publications

PLAYS

For Sylvia, with John Burrows (produced 1972). In *The Best Short Plays 1978*, edited by Stanley Richards, 1978.
The Golden Pathway Annual, with John Burrows (produced 1973). 1975.
Loud Reports, with John Burrows and Peter Skellern (produced 1975).
Dirty Giant, with John Burrows, music by Peter Skellern (produced 1975).
The Manly Bit, with John Burrows (produced 1976).

RADIO PLAY: *Listen to My Voice*, 1987.

TELEVISION PLAY: *Do You Dig It?*, with John Burrows, 1976.

THEATRICAL ACTIVITIES

ACTOR: Plays—all his own plays, and *Jack and Beanstalk*, 1969; Whitaker in *The Long and the Short and the Tall* by Willis Hall, 1970; Pantalone in *Pinocchio* by Brian Way, 1971; James in *My Fat Friend* by Charles Laurence, 1972; Antipholus in *The Comedy of Errors*, 1973; Sir Andrew Aguecheek in *Twelfth Night*, 1974; *Donkeys' Years* by Michael Frayn, 1976; Actors Company: *The Importance of Being Earnest* by Wilde and *Do You Love Me?* by R.D. Laing, 1977–78; *The Circle* by W. Somerset Maugham, 1978; *The*

Double Dealer by Congreve, *Strife* by Galsworthy, *The Fruits of Enlightenment* by Tolstoy, *Undiscovered Country* by Tom Stoppard, *Richard III*, and *Amadeus* by Peter Shaffer, 1978–81; *Miranda* by Beverley Cross, 1987. Film—*Little Dorrit*, 1987. Television—*Man of Mode* by Etherege, 1980; *Baby Talk* by Nigel Williams, 1981.

See the essay on John Burrows and John Harding.

HARE, David.

Born in Bexhill, Sussex, 5 June 1947. Educated at Lancing College, Sussex; Jesus College, Cambridge, M.A. 1968. Married Margaret Matheson in 1970 (divorced 1980); two sons and one daughter. Founding director, Portable Theatre, Brighton and London, 1968–71; literary manager, 1969–70, and resident dramatist, 1970–71, Royal Court Theatre, London; resident dramatist, Nottingham Playhouse, 1973; co-founder, 1973, and director, 1975–80, Joint Stock Theatre Company; founder, Greenpoint Films, 1982. Since 1984 associate director, National Theatre, London. Since 1981 member of the Council, Royal Court Theatre. Recipient: *Evening Standard* award, 1971, 1985; Rhys Memorial prize, 1975; USA/UK Bicentennial fellowship, 1977; BAFTA award, 1979; New York Drama Critics Circle award, 1983; Berlin Film Festival Golden Bear, 1985; *City Limits* award, 1985; *Drama* magazine award, 1988; Olivier award, 1990; *Time Out* award, 1990; *Plays and Players* award, 1990; London Theatre Critics award, 1990. Fellow, Royal Society of Literature, 1985. Lives in London. Agent: Casarotto Ramsay Ltd., National House, 60–66 Wardour Street, London W1V 3HP, England.

Publications

PLAYS

Inside Out, with Tony Bicât, adaptation of the diaries of Kafka (also director: produced 1968).
How Brophy Made Good (produced 1969). In *Gambit 17*, 1971.
What Happened to Blake? (produced 1970).
Slag (produced 1970). 1971.
The Rules of the Game, adaptation of a play by Pirandello (produced 1971).
Deathsheads (sketch), in *Christmas Present* (produced 1971).
Lay By, with others (produced 1971). 1972.
The Great Exhibition (produced 1972). 1972.
England's Ireland, with others (also director: produced 1972).
Brassneck, with Howard Brenton (also director: produced 1973). 1974.
Knuckle (produced 1974). 1974; revised version, 1978.
Fanshen, adaptation of the book by William Hinton (produced 1975). 1976.
Teeth 'n' Smiles, music by Nick Bicât, lyrics by Tony Bicât (also director: produced 1975). 1976.
Plenty (also director: produced 1978). 1978.
Deeds, with others (produced 1978). In *Plays and Players*, May and June 1978.
Licking Hitler (televised 1978). 1978.

Dreams of Leaving (televised 1980). 1980.
A Map of the World (also director: produced 1982). 1982; revised version, 1983.
Saigon: Year of the Cat (televised 1983). 1983.
The Madman Theory of Deterrence (sketch), in *The Big One* (produced 1983).
The History Plays (includes *Knuckle*, *Licking Hitler*, *Plenty*). 1984.
Pravda: A Fleet Street Comedy, with Howard Brenton (also director: produced 1985). 1985.
Wetherby (screenplay). 1985.
The Asian Plays (includes *Fanshen*, *Saigon: Year of the Cat*, *A Map of the World*). 1986.
The Bay at Nice, and Wrecked Eggs (also director: produced 1986). 1986.
The Knife (opera), music by Nick Bicât, lyrics by Tim Rose Price (also director: produced 1987).
Paris by Night (screenplay). 1988.
The Secret Rapture (produced 1988). 1988.
Strapless (screenplay). 1990.
Racing Demon (produced London, 1990). 1990.
Murmuring Judges (produced 1991). 1991.
Heading Home (televised 1991). With *Wetherby* and *Dreams of Leaving*, 1991.
Heading Home, Wetherby, Dreams of Leaving. 1991.
The Early Plays (includes *Slag*, *Teeth 'n' Smiles*, *Dreams of Leaving*). 1992.
The Absence of War (produced 1993).

SCREENPLAYS: *Wetherby*, 1985; *Plenty*, 1985; *Paris by Night*, 1989; *Strapless*, 1990; *Damage*, 1992.

TELEVISION PLAYS: *Man above Men*, 1973; *Licking Hitler*, 1978; *Dreams of Leaving*, 1980; *Saigon: Year of the Cat*, 1983; *Heading Home*, 1991.

OTHER
Writing Left-Handed. 1991.

CRITICAL STUDIES: *The New British Drama* by Oleg Kerensky, 1977; *Dreams and Deconstructions* edited by Sandy Craig, 1980; *Stages in the Revolution* by Catherine Itzin, 1980; *David Hare* by Joan F. Dean, 1990; *David Hare: Theatricalizing Politics* by Judy Lee Oliva, 1990; *File on Hare* edited by Malcolm Page, 1990.

THEATRICAL ACTIVITIES

DIRECTOR: **Plays**—*Inside Out*, 1968; *Christie in Love* by Howard Brenton, 1969; *Purity* by David Mowat, 1969; *Fruit* by Howard Brenton, 1970; *Blowjob* by Snoo Wilson, 1971; *England's Ireland*, 1972; *The Provoked Wife* by Vanbrugh, 1973; *Brassneck*, 1973; *The Pleasure Principle* by Snoo Wilson, 1973; *The Party* by Trevor Griffiths, 1974; *Teeth 'n' Smiles*, 1975; *Weapons of Happiness* by Howard Brenton, 1976; *Devil's Island* by Tony Bicât, 1977; *Plenty*, 1978; *Total Eclipse* by Christopher Hampton, 1981; *A Map of the World*, 1982; *Pravda*, 1985; *The Bay at Nice, and Wrecked Eggs*, 1986; *King*

Lear, 1986; *The Knife*, 1987. **Film**—*Wetherby*, 1985; *Paris by Night*, 1989; *Strapless*, 1990. **Television**—*Licking Hitler*, 1978; *Dreams of Leaving*, 1980; *Saigon: Year of the Cat*, 1983; *Heading Home*, 1991.

David Hare's early plays show a bright young man drawing on his education, writing of Kafka and Blake, and his experience: *Teeth 'n' Smiles*, about a Cambridge May Ball, audaciously linked rock band and serious play, while giving Helen Mirren a memorable part; *Slag*, superficially about women teachers, in fact reflects Hare's view of how institutions shape people. Hare also gained practical theatre experience with Portable in his twenties and accepted invitations to write, collaborating on *Lay By* and *England's Ireland*. Leftwing political convictions (always scrutinized, flexible, and rarely dogmatic) begin to show in *The Great Exhibition*, the study of a Labour M.P. burned out and sold out. His political self-education continues in his adaptation of *Fanshen*, clearly showing the condition of Chinese peasants improved after the Revolution and implying a roughly comparable need for change in Britain (though *Fanshen* was as much a Joint Stock collective effort as a distinct Hare work).

From *Brassneck* on, nearly all Hare's writing engages with the Condition-of-England, and—unusually—his scripts for film and television are also a part of his unfolding, expanding, and increasingly complex view. In a sense, the most recent play at the time of writing, *Murmuring Judges*, becomes about Part 16 of Hare on the State of the World. (With two pieces especially, *A Map of the World* and *Saigon*, Hare's subject broadens from Britain to the whole world.) Co-written with Howard Brenton, *Brassneck* is an epic, the rise of a new style of capitalism in the Midlands from 1945 on, including operating strip-clubs and importing heroin, to a final toast to "the last days of capitalism."*Plenty*, probably his best play (and surviving reasonably faithfully in the film version) also starts with World War II. Young Susan operates in occupied France full of a sense of mission and optimistically looks ahead on a sunny hillside in August: "There will be days and days and days like this." In flashback, this is the last line of the drama, and earlier we have seen Susan's disillusion, counterpointing her private life with such public events as the Festival of Britain in 1951 (changed to the 1953 Coronation in the film) and the British attack on Suez in 1956. Her friend Alice appears to be more successful at discovering a purpose in her life in peacetime. (Hare's preoccupation with how the war shaped post-war Britain is reflected also in his *Licking Hitler*, for television.)

His writing in the 1980's is sometimes tilted towards the personal, notably in the films *Wetherby* (reflecting Hare as Londoner puzzled by middle-class life in the small Yorkshire market-town), *Strapless*, and *Paris by Night*. In the Introduction to the latter, Hare writes: "Although there has been a considerable body of films and plays about the economic results of Thatcherism, there has been almost nothing of consequence about the characteristics and personalities of those who have ruled over us during these last eight years." He remedies this in *The Secret Rapture*, which contrasts a Conservative woman M.P. (a full-scale attempt to understand Margaret Thatcher) and her good sister ("a portrait of absolute goodness," wrote Michael Ratcliffe).

The Secret Rapture is one of his four plays staged at the National Theatre between 1985 and 1991 which engages urgently with the state of British society. (His fifth appearance at the National Theatre in this period was with the modest, more domestic double-bill of *Wrecked Eggs* and *The Bay at Nice*. The first of the four, *Pravda*, again co-authored with Brenton, is a ferocious, brilliant, energetic exposé of newspapers, distinguished on the stage by the powerful playing of Anthony Hopkins as an unprincipled magnate. *Racing Demon* is *about* the Church of England and to some extent about the place of religion in society now, and *Murmuring Judges* is *about* the British legal system, with emphasis on its shortcomings. Yet these are not narrowly documentary; both are theatrical and entertaining as well as thought-provoking.

Each of Hare's mature works has greater resonance when placed in sequence and in context. In his latest plays, more than any other British dramatist, he is scrutinizing the present state of the nation.

—Malcolm Page

See the essay on *Pravda*.

HARRIS, Richard.

Born in London, 26 March 1934. Recipient: London *Evening Standard* award, 1979, for best comedy, 1984; Molière award, Paris, 1990; New York Film and Television Festival gold medal, 1990. Agent: Lemon, Unna, and Durbridge, 24 Pottery Lane, Holland Park, London W11 4LZ, England.

Publications

PLAYS

Partners: A Comedy (produced 1969). 1973.
Albert: A One-Act Comedy (produced 1971). 1972.
You Must Be Virginia (produced 1971).
No, No, Not Yet, with Leslie Darbon (produced 1972).
Two and Two Make Sex, with Leslie Darbon (produced 1973). 1973.
Who Goes Bare?, with Leslie Darbon (produced 1974).
Conscience Be Damned (produced 1975).
Correspondents' Course, with Leslie Darbon (produced 1976). 1976.
The Pressures of Life: Four Television Plays. 1977.
Outside Edge (produced 1979). 1980.
The Dog It Was (produced 1980).
The Business of Murder (produced 1981). 1985.
Is It Something I Said? (produced 1982). 1982.
Local Affairs (produced 1982). 1982.
Stepping Out (produced 1984). 1985.
The Maintenance Man (produced 1986). 1987.
Three Piece Suite (produced 1986).
Visiting Hour (includes *Plaster, Keeping Mum, Show Business, Going Home, Waiting, Magic*) (produced 1987; revised version produced 1990). 1991.
Party Piece (produced 1990). 1990.
Mixed Blessing (musical), with Keith Strachan (produced 1991).

SCREENPLAYS: *Strongroom*, with Max Marquis, 1965; *I Start Counting*, adaptation of the novel by Audrey Erskine Lindop, 1969; *The Lady in the Car with Glasses and a Gun*, adaptation of the novel by Sebastian Japrisot, 1970; *Orion's Belt*, adaptation of the novel by Jan Michelet, 1988; *Stepping Out*, 1991.

RADIO PLAY: *Was It Something I Said?*, 1978.

TELEVISION PLAYS: *Who's a Good Boy Then?* *I Am*; *You Must Be Virginia*; *Saving It for Albie*; *When the Boys Come Out to Play*; *Sunday in Perspective*; *Occupier's Risk*; *Time and Mr. Madingley*; *I Can See Your Lips Move*; *A Slight Formality*; *Jack's Trade*; *Dog Ends*; *Searching for Senor Duende* and *This for the Half, Darling*, in *About Face* series, 1989; *Murder Most English*, adaptation of *The Flaxborough Chronicles* by Colin Watson; *The Prince and the Pauper*, adaptation of the novel by Mark Twain; *Plain Murder*, adaptation of the novel by C. S. Forester; *Sherlock Holmes*, adaptation of the novel by Arthur Conan Doyle; *The Darling Buds of May*, adaptation of the novel by H. E. Bates, 1991; *A Touch of Frost*, adaptation of the novels by R. D. Wingfield; *Shoestring* series; *Man in a Suitcase* series; *The Gamblers* series.

Few playwrights can boast one of the longest-running comedies in London as well as one of the longest-running thrillers. Richard Harris has had both, with *The Business of Murder* and *Stepping Out*. But then Harris has always been a skilled professional. His work delivers exactly what it promises for the most part; but with two plays—*Outside Edge* and *Stepping Out*—he staked a claim to be regarded as an original comic talent, more than the second-league Ayckbourn which he has sometimes been dubbed.

He seems at home in most theatrical genres. He has also written (in collaboration with Leslie Darbon) a clever farce with the misleadingly sniggering title *Two and Two Make Sex*. A typical piece of British farcical comedy—menopausal man pursing younger girl, her boyfriend attracting the older man's wife, both pairs ignorant of the complications until a late scene of near-confrontations—it naturally (being a British farce) featured sex deferred rather than sex consummated, but within the limitations of the genre, some characteristic Harris insights into women's points of view could be glimpsed underneath all the mechanics of telephone calls and close encounters on a split-level set. And *The Maintenance Man*, a fairly formula comedy centred round an eternal triangle, again provided two rounded roles for women.

Women dominated *Outside Edge* and *Stepping Out*. Set in a local cricket club, *Outside Edge* is a deceptively small-scale play; underneath the cricket jokes and sight gags gradually emerges a sense of real pain in the midst of this suburban haven, and cracks in supposedly happy marriages and relationships begin to appear like weeds on the club's lawn. Harris has again written especially good female roles—and he has created an original and endearing double-act in the shape of a role-reversal couple, she tall and lusty (memorably played by Maureen Lipman in London), coping with all the heavy building work at home, he tiny and domestic, taking over cooking and polishing. They are the happiest couple in the play.

Stepping Out has only one male role—the shy widower who is the only man in attendance at the weekly tap dance class in a North London church hall. Mavis, the ex-chorus girl instructor, the redoubtable and temperamental pianist, together with seven very contrasting pupils, comprise the rest of the cast. In the course of the play, following the class through until their appearance at the finale stepping out at a charity performance to Irving Berlin, Harris traces the patterns behind these separate lives, It is obliquely handled—much is revealed in throwaway clues rather than in confessional speeches—especially so in the case of Vera, another Harris original, an apparently brightly confident wife of an older and much-absent businessman husband, given to cheery aphorisms ("It may be February outside but it's always August under the armpits"), whose marriage, we gradually sense, is driving her into increasing isolation. Harris doesn't have room to develop all his characters to the same extent, but the play has an authenticity and sureness of rhythm that make it more than a formula hit; when this core to the play was readjusted, as for the glitzy Broadway version or for the movie, it was much less successful.

More recent Harris work has included the revue-style book for *Mixed Blessings*, a musical on marriage involving several contrasted couples which was poorly staged in its regional premiere, and several reworkings, under various titles, of a comedy now titled *Party Piece*, set in the adjoining back gardens of two socially contrasted couples and with a memorable portrait of a possessive mother. All of this suggests that Harris's drive not to repeat himself is unimpaired.

—Alan Strachan

HARRISON, Tony.

Born in Leeds, Yorkshire, 30 April 1937. Educated at Cross Flatts County Primary, Leeds, 1942–48; Leeds Grammar School, 1948–55; University of Leeds, 1955–60, B.A. in classics 1958, postgraduate diploma in linguistics. Married 1) Rosemarie Crossfield in 1962, one daughter and one son; 2) Teresa Stratas in 1984. Schoolmaster, Dewsbury, Yorkshire, 1960–62; lecturer in English, Ahmadu Bello University, Zaria, Northern Nigeria, 1962–66, and Charles University, Prague, 1966–67; editor, with Jon Silkin and Ken Smith, *Stand* magazine, Newcastle-upon-Tyne, 1968–69; resident dramatist, National Theatre, London, 1977–79. U.K.-U.S. Bicentennial fellow, New York, 1979–80. President, Classical Association of Great Britain, 1987–88. Recipient: Northern Arts fellowship, 1967, 1976; Cholmondeley award, 1969; UNESCO fellowship, 1969; Faber memorial award, 1972; Gregynog fellowship, 1973; U.S. Bicentennial fellowship, 1979; European Poetry translation prize, 1983; Whitbread Poetry prize, 1992. Fellow, Royal Society of Literature, 1984. Agent: Peters, Fraser, and Dunlop, 503/4 The Chambers, Chelsea Harbour, Lots Road, London SW10 0XF, England.

Publications

PLAYS

Aikin Mata, with James Simmons, adaptation of *Lysistrata* by Aristophanes (produced 1965). 1966.
The Misanthrope, adaptation of a play by Molière (produced 1973). 1973.

Phaedra Britannica, adaptation of a play by Racine (produced 1975). 1975.
Bow Down, music by Harrison Birtwistle (produced 1977). 1977.
The Passion, from the York Mystery Plays (produced 1977; with *The Nativity*
and *Doomsday*, as *The Mysteries*, 1985). 1977; in *The Mysteries*, 1985.
The Bartered Bride, adaptation of an opera by Sabina, music by Smetana
(produced 1978). 1978; in *Dramatic Verse*, 1985.
The Nativity, from the York Mystery Plays (produced 1980; with *The Passion*
and *Doomsday*, as *The Mysteries*, 1985). In *The Mysteries*, 1985.
The Oresteia, music by Harrison Birtwistle, adaptation of the plays by
Aeschylus (includes *Agamemnon, Choephori, Eumenides*) (produced 1981).
1981.
Yan Tan Tethera, music by Harrison Birtwistle (produced 1983). In *Dramatic
Verse*, 1985.
The Big H, music by Dominic Muldowney (televised, 1984). In *Dramatic
Verse*, 1985.
Dramatic Verse 1973–1985 (includes *The Misanthrope, Phaedra Britannica,
Bow Down, The Bartered Bride, The Oresteia, Yan Tan Tethera, The Big H,
Medea: Sex War*). 1985; as *Theatre Works 1973–1985*, 1986.
Doomsday, from the York Mystery Plays (with *The Nativity* and *The Passion*,
as *The Mysteries*, produced 1985). In *The Mysteries*, 1985.
The Mysteries, adaptation of the York Mystery Plays (includes *The Passion,
The Nativity, Doomsday*) (produced 1985). 1985.
Medea: Sex War (produced 1991). In *Dramatic Verse*, 1985.
The Trackers of Oxyrhynchus (produced 1988). 1990.
The Common Chorus. 1992.
Square Rounds (also director: produced 1992). 1992.

Television plays: *Arctic Paradise*, 1981; *The Big H*, music by Dominic
Muldowney, 1984; *Loving Memory* series, 1987; *V.*, 1987; *The Blasphemers'
Banquet*, 1989; *The Gaze of the Gorgon*, adaptation of *The Oresteia* and *The
Mysteries*, 1992.

Verse
Earthworks. 1964.
Newcastle Is Peru. 1969.
The Loiners. 1970.
Corgi Modern Poets in Focus 4, with others, edited by Jeremy Robson. 1971.
Ten Poems from the School of Eloquence. 1976.
From the School of Eloquence and Other Poems. 1978.
Looking Up, with Philip Sharpe. 1979.
Continuous: 50 Sonnets from the School of Eloquence. 1981.
A Kumquat for John Keats. 1981.
U.S. Martial. 1981.
Selected Poems. 1984; revised edition, 1987.
The Fire-Gap: A Poem with Two Tails. 1985.
V. (single poem). 1985; with press articles, 1989.
Anno 42. N.p., Michael C. Caine, 1987.
Ten Sonnets from the School of Eloquence. 1987.

V. and Other Poems. 1989.
A Cold Coming: Gulf War Poems. 1991.
The Gaze of the Gorgon. 1992.

OTHER
Translator, *Poems*, by Palladas. 1975.

BIBLIOGRAPHY: *Tony Harrison: A Bibliography 1957–1987* by John R. Kaiser, 1989.

MANUSCRIPT COLLECTIONS: University of Newcastle-upon-Tyne; Newcastle Literary and Philosophical Society.

CRITICAL STUDIES: *Essays on Tony Harrison* edited by Neil Astley, 1990; *Ancient Sun, Modern Light* by Marianne McDonald, 1992; "Postmodern Classics: The Verse Drama of Tony Harrison" by Romana Huk, in *British and Irish Drama Since 1960*, edited by James Acheson, 1993.

Tony Harrison comments:

It seems to me no accident that some of the world's best poetry is to be found in some of the world's best drama, and comes from those periods when poets, and I emphasise poets, worked directly with actors and wrote their pieces for specific players and spaces. This is to be found in the ancient Greek drama, for which I have had a lifelong passion, when the poet was regarded as the "didaskalos" the "teacher" of his work, and the term would involve everything now taken over by the function of director. The relationship is to be found also in the theatre of Shakespeare, the Jacobeans, Molière, Racine, Goethe, Yeats, Brecht, or in the anonymous poets who worked and reworked their texts with their illiterate players in the medieval Mysteries. My at least 25-year quest for a space for myself as a poet in the theatre, involved me in seeking the help of some of these ancients and using their stylistic resources to discover new ones for myself. And I have always thought in terms of "theatre" rather than in the compartmentalised genres of drama, music theatre, opera, remembering that opera originated when artists thought they were rediscovering Greek drama. I have always found working with composers very congenial.

I have never for a moment been interested in antique reproduction only in finding styles and conventions to confront modern issues and conflicts that the predominantly naturalistic styles seemed unable to encompass. When I first started out on my quest I found only what has been called "poetry in the theatre rather than of it" that is in works like Eliot and Fry. And indeed even the great verse classics were often played in pedestrian prose translations so far had the theatre left behind that tradition. What kept verse alive for me as a theatrical medium was not only my immersion in great theatrical poets of the past, whose styles and language I studied and often translated, but also an early appetite and relish for the verse of the music-hall recitation and the pantomime which were still vigorous enough when I was a child for me to have been influenced by them. Indeed they were my earliest experiences of theatre. I have sometimes used the resources I found in these popular forms to "unlock" or "reoriginate" the classics of the past and bring the energy of the so-called "low" art forms into the so-called "high" art forms. Sometimes I believe that there is not that great a difference between the two, and that our culture has falsely made them seem too irreconcilably distinct.

My close work with actors from the beginning of my theatrical career has led me, project by project, deeper into the everyday practicalities of theatrical production until I have reached the position of preferring to direct my own theatre pieces and to collaborate with known actors in known spaces, whether conventional theatres or not. *The Trackers of Oxyrhynchus* was devised in the National Theatre Studio with actors I had worked with on other projects, and was premiered in the unique space of the ancient stadium of Delphi in Greece. When it played subsequently in the Olivier Theatre at the National, it was radically rewritten for the new space. When the production toured to Salts Mill, Saltaire, Art Carnuntum, Vienna, the Gasworks Theatre, Copenhagen, and the Brighton Festival I was with the company for every performance and went on making local variations in the text.

If his status as England's best-known contemporary theatre poet will probably always be controversial, Tony Harrison's achievement as a brilliant and innovative translator can scarcely be contested. Audacity sometimes hovering on the edge of verbal vandalism has characterised some of his verse, both in his collections of poetry and in his plays, but works like his *Misanthrope* and *Oresteia* have satisfied even those with a conservative concept of the translator's role. However, he is also thoroughly conversant with current translation theory, and in other works he extends the logic of transposition and refraction to move far beyond any suggestion of the play as a statement of faith to an original.

From the first, Harrison has been acutely aware of the need to read both the original and the target audience. He always regarded *Aikin Mata*, his Nigerian *Lysistrata*, as unplayable except in West Africa. Though it has been successfully staged even by the Sydney Theatre Company, *The Trackers of Oxyrhynchus* was written for a single performance at Delphi. And even the apparently conventional *The Misanthrope* was written to an audience for whom 1968 was a recent memory. However, it was *Phaedra Britannica* that confronted London with the principle of cultural transposition as an integral function in contemporary translation.

The politicisation of Racine by grounding the play in India just before the Mutiny was a brilliant piece of audience manipulation. Denied the consolation of reading the play as an object "back there" in French literature, or even as an archaeological exhibit from Greek prehistory, London theatre-goers found it folded into their own imperial history, the more fragile because its cultural sequel was already written. Reading Racine by taking a detour through India thus became an ingeniously contrived exercise in Orientalism in the theatre, a point illustrated by the response of unwitting critics who complained of the absence of (consolingly meaningless) Greek gods. In their place, Harrison offered some specifically Indian deities, but also a collective "They," a dark, menacing colonial sense of otherness. Thomas (Hippolytus), a half-caste, is rejected by his father as an "animal," his Indian blood a "lower self" that sooner or later will emerge from its "lair."

Harrison has always been conscious of himself as a Yorkshire poet, and his interest in regional material is combined with his training in comparative linguistics in *Bow Down*, a savage theatricalisation of several treatments of the "Two Sisters" ballad. Here, his technique may be compared with what Walter Benjamin (whom he admires) saw as an ideal in translation, the interlinear: Harrison collates the versions, leaving the Danish, for example, in its original. This inclination to leave "ready-mades" embedded throughout a work is more pronounced in the "sex-war" opera *Medea*, and would itself become the subject of a play in *Oxyrhynchus*.

Defiantly regionalist is *The Mysteries*, where a darts mat represents the palm-strewn road into Jerusalem, and Herod's son reads the York telephone directory before his father tears it to bits, a gesture of macho physicality that has no precedent in the Herod of the Cycle plays. The initial entrance of God on a fork-lift seems appropriate in what Harrison sees as the "post-Christian" era, but the structural awkwardness of the play (an amalgam of all four cycles) reflects the fact that it was written first just as an Easter Passion and eight years later bulked out with a Nativity (which includes a lot of Wakefield material like Cain and Noah) and a Doomsday. Between the two versions, Harrison wrote the television play *The Big H*, a highly stylised treatment of Herod in contemporary Leeds, which incorporates some of the precise stylistic features of the "Slaughter of the Innocents" play from the Cycles; formal boasting speeches from Herod and lamentation sequences from the mothers co-exist with startling liberties, like the fact that all three Herods are local school-teachers with secret selves (called Jekyll and Hyde) with a propensity for fascism and "kiddicide." Though clearly written as a Christmas play, it was premiered by BBC2 on a Boxing Day.

The Trackers of Oxyrhynchus is a work of virtuosity which fittingly combines the proclivities of all of Harrison's best work. Grenfell and Hunt, the pioneer British papyrologists, are digging through Egyptian compost heaps and find the fragments of a satyr play, which is then realised, with themselves in the central roles of Apollo and Silenus. Harrison's keen sense of prosody is wittily indulged here, as his characteristic rhyming couplets are filled out with blanks around the papyrus word fragments, and a Caryatid maiden, a power-lifter carrying a pediment, enters and launches into a pastiche of Victorian translationese. The performance is contextualised within the frame of the Pythian Games which are then synchronised with the world of the audience with the intrusion of "new generation" satyrs as football hooligans. The play thus recreates the co-existence of the high and the low, the sacred and the profane, which Harrison's brilliant introduction argues was integral to classical Greek drama. His detractors, who have called his work kitsch, are given some substance here, in so far as compost is kitsch. But—as Silenus shrewdly observes—the full subtleties of that kitsch are accessible only to readers with a very good reading knowledge of Greek.

—Howard McNaughton

HARWOOD, Ronald.

Born Ronald Horwitz in Cape Town, South Africa, 9 November 1934. Educated at Sea Point Boys' High School, Cape Town; Royal Academy of Dramatic Art, London. Married Natasha Riehle in 1959; one son and two daughters. Joined Donald Wolfit's Shakespeare Company in London, 1953; actor, 1953–59; presenter, *Kaleidoscope* radio programme, 1973, and television series *Read All About It*, 1978–79, and *All the World's a Stage*, 1984; artistic director, Cheltenham Festival, 1975; visitor in theatre, Balliol College, Oxford, 1986. Chairman, Writers' Guild of Great Britain, 1969; member of the Literature Panel, Arts Council of Great Britain, 1973–78. Recipient: Royal Society of Literature Winifred Holtby prize, for fiction, 1974; *Evening Standard* award, 1980; Drama Critics Circle award, 1980. Fellow, Royal Society of Literature, 1974. Agent: Judy Daish Associates, 83 Eastbourne Mews, London W2 6LQ, England.

Publications

PLAYS

Country Matters (produced 1969).
One Day in the Life of Ivan Denisovich (screenplay). 1970.
The Good Companions, music by André Previn, lyrics by Johnny Mercer, adaptation of the novel by J.B. Priestley (produced 1974). 1974.
The Ordeal of Gilbert Pinfold, adaptation of the novel by Evelyn Waugh (produced 1977). 1983.
A Family (produced 1978). 1978.
The Dresser (produced 1980). 1980.
A Night of the Day of the Imprisoned Writer, with Christopher Hampton (produced 1981).
After the Lions (produced 1982). 1983.
Tramway Road (produced 1984). 1984.
The Deliberate Death of a Polish Priest (produced 1985). 1985.
Interpreters: A Fantasia on English and Russian Themes (produced 1985). 1985.
J.J. Farr (produced 1987). 1988.
Another Time (produced 1989). 1989.
Reflected Glory (produced 1992). 1991.

SCREENPLAYS: *The Barber of Stamford Hill*, 1962; *Private Potter*, with Casper Wrede, 1962; *A High Wind in Jamaica*, with Denis Cannan and Stanley Mann, 1965; *Drop Dead Darling* (*Arriverderci, Baby!*), with Ken Hughes, 1966; *Diamonds for Breakfast*, with N.F. Simpson and Pierre Rouve, 1968; *Eyewitness*, 1970; *Cromwell*, with Ken Hughes, 1970; *One Day in the Life of Ivan Denisovich*, 1972; *Operation Daybreak*, 1975; *The Dresser*, 1984; *The Doctor and the Devils*, 1986.

RADIO PLAY: *All the Same Shadows*, from his own novel, 1971.

TELEVISION PLAYS: *The Barber of Stamford Hill*, 1960; *Private Potter*, with Casper Wrede, 1961; *Take a Fellow Like Me*, 1961; *The Lads*, 1963;

Convalescence, 1964; *Guests of Honour,* 1965; *The Paris Trip,* 1966; *The New Assistant,* 1967; *Long Lease of Summer,* 1972; *The Guests,* 1972; *A Sense of Loss* (documentary on Evelyn Waugh), with John Selwyn, 1978; *The Way Up to Heaven,* 1979, *Parson's Pleasure,* 1986, and *The Umbrella Man,* 1986 (all in *Tales of the Unexpected* series); *Evita Péron,* 1981; *Mandela,* 1987; *Breakthrough at Reykjavik,* 1987; *Countdown to War,* 1989.

NOVELS

All the Same Shadows. 1961; as *George Washington September, Sir!,* 1961.
The Guilt Merchants. 1963.
The Girl in Melanie Klein. 1969.
Articles of Faith. 1973.
The Genoa Ferry. 1976.
César and Augusta. 1978.

SHORT STORIES

One. Interior. Day. Adventures in the Film Trade. 1978.

OTHER

Sir Donald Wolfit, C.B.E.: His Life and Work in the Unfashionable Theatre. 1971.
All the World's a Stage. 1984.
Mandela. 1987.

Editor, with Francis King, *New Stories 3.* 1978.
Editor, *A Night at the Theatre.* 1982.
Editor, *The Ages of Gielgud: An Actor at Eighty.* 1984.
Editor, *Dear Alec: Guinness at Seventy-Five.* 1989.

THEATRICAL ACTIVITIES

DIRECTOR: Plays—*The Odd Couple,* 1989; *Another Time,* 1991.
ACTOR: Plays—with Donald Wolfit's Shakespeare Company: roles in *Macbeth, The Wandering Jew* by E. Temple Thurston, *The Taming of the Shrew, 1 Henry IV, Hamlet, Volpone* by Jonson, *Twelfth Night, A New Way to Pay Old Debts* by Massinger, and *The Clandestine Marriage* by Garrick and Colman, 1953; Third Jew in *Salome* by Oscar Wilde, 1954; Captain Arago in *The Strong Are Lonely* by Fritz Hochwalder, 1955; repertory seasons in Salisbury and Chesterfield.

Ronald Harwood is both a popular and populist writer with a most diverse list of works—novels, television plays, screenplays, and stage plays. If there is any theme or common denominator in his work it must focus on his own deep love of the theatre (*The Dresser, After the Lions,* and *Reflected Glory* all have theatrical settings) and his concern to show how people feel rather than how they think. Most of the plays turn on a central anguished relationship, based on conflict, and have an acute sense of character, only to be expected in a novelist and dramatist brought up as an actor.

Harwood came to Britain from South Africa in 1953 and joined Donald Wolfit's Shakespeare Company as an actor and as a dresser to the great man himself. His early work included theatrical adaptations of Alexander Solzhenitsyn (*One Day in the Life of Ivan Denisovich*) and Evelyn Waugh (*The Ordeal of Gilbert Pinfold*) as well as the book for an André Previn-Johnny Mercer musical adaptation of J. B. Priestley's *The Good Companions*. *The Ordeal of Gilbert Pinfold* is probably the best of his early works. It is an excellent adaptation of Waugh's late novel about an invalid on a cruise bedevilled by figments of his own imagination and is based on Evelyn Waugh's actual experiences. *Gilbert Pinfold* was produced at the Royal Exchange Theatre in Manchester in 1977 and reached London in 1979. This Manchester-London progression was repeated in 1978 with *A Family*, which played at the Haymarket Theatre. The play is designed to show that a family, however possessive, has the inner resources to remain true to itself in spite of adversity. Good though the writing is, especially the delineation of character, there is an odd sense that this is another adaptation from a novel—a "hangover" perhaps from earlier work.

The play that established Harwood as an international success was *The Dresser*, which transferred from Manchester to the Queen's Theatre, London in 1980. The play recreates with wonderful detail and fidelity the kind of classical touring theatre which must have all but disappeared when Harwood first joined Donald Wolfit's company in 1953. The play has a wonderful and poignant quality of the end of an era about it. An aging actor/manager, simply called "Sir," struggles to play up to eight major Shakespearean roles a week as his company tours Britain in the middle of World War II. Emotionally and creatively spent, "Sir" performs each night only with the help of his dresser, Norman, who cajoles, bullies, protects, and cossets his highly strung employer. The central relationship between "Sir" and Norman is superbly realized and does much to make *The Dresser* one of the most significant and best-loved plays of the 1980's, in spite of the fact that the play has no overiding social message—an attribute considered essential at the time. It should be stressed that "Sir" is not a portrait of Sir Donald Wolfit, but rather an amalgam of several actor/managers known and read about by the author. The central role of "Sir" is a mosaic, a symbol of the age of actor/managers who were often remarkable men, dedicated not only to the classical repertoire but also to a surprisingly high degree of performance. As "Sir" acts King Lear on what proves to be the last night of his life, other stories of ambition, loyalty, loneliness, and betrayal are played out off-stage, acting as a counterpoint and making this the most moving and empathetic of all Harwood's work. *The Dresser* proved to be a hard act to follow and indeed, although *After the Lions* shares the same backstage setting, it did not transfer to London after its Manchester premiere. This play deals with a grim period in the life of the great Sarah Bernhardt, the point in her career when her leg was amputated. The main focus of the play is the attempt of Pitou, Bernhardt's secretary, to get the great actress to retire and not face a humiliating American tour. Skilful though the writing is, the play does not have the atmospheric immediacy of *The Dresser*, although the major roles must be coveted by the acting establishment.

Tramway Road, seen briefly in London in 1984, is a fine play. Two of its major characters are a married expatriate English couple trapped in a bitter relationship. The man teaches elocution to a South African youth who dreams of a theatre in London. But the boy is "reclassified" as a half-caste and his

future is destroyed. Faced with the boy's dilemma, the husband acts with a
weakness it is difficult to forgive. The play is essentially a clash between the
wistfulness of what might have been and the reality of the cruelty of bigotry.
Written with deep conviction and truth, this play reminds one of the works of
Athol Fugard, so it is interesting to note what Ronald Harwood himself has to
say about the piece in an interview in the April 1992 edition of *Plays and
Players*: "My stand (the condemnation of South Africa) was honourable, and
it was certainly fashionable at the time. But it is easy to pontificate when one is
6000 miles away. I think Athol Fugard is a wonderful writer and a proper
witness to what happened there. I'm not a proper witness, I wasn't there." In
spite of Harwood's protests, *Tramway Road* remains the most undervalued
of all his plays.

The year 1985 was a prolific one. *The Deliberate Death of a Polish Priest*
was presented at the Almeida Theatre in London. This documentary play was
based on the transcripts of a trial and other material arising out of the murder
of Father Jerzy Popieluszko in 1984. The priest was a political activist and all
the words of Father Popieluszko and the witnesses are their own. Disarmingly
simple, the tragic story—and its attempted cover-up—has a deep emotional
impact. On a totally different emotional level, *Interpreters*, which enjoyed a
long London run, also looks at the last days of the Cold War. The play's focus
is the visit to England by the Soviet president. As the itinerary is carefully
examined, the English translator Nadia (who is of Russian descent) and the
Russian, Victor, face each other at the conference table. But Nadia and Victor
were embroiled in a passionate affair a decade earlier and we eagerly watch
the renewal of this romance even though we suspect the rejuvenated liaison
cannot last.

In *Another Time*, presented in London in 1989, Harwood returned both to a
South African setting and to a re-exploration of the themes of the family.
Initially set in Cape Town in the 1950's, the play examines the life of Leonard
Lands, 17 years old, the only child of immigrant parents and a gifted pianist. In
order to achieve success commensurate with his talent, Leonard must study in
Europe. Act Two takes place 35 years later, in London, and Leonard has
reached another turning point in his life. Harwood skilfully examines the price
Leonard has paid for his single-minded devotion to his music and the effect this
has had on his relationship to his family.

Ronald Harwood's latest play, *Reflected Glory*, opened in London in 1992.
Like much of his work, the play turns on a central, troubled relationship. Here,
the struggle is between two brothers: Michael is a playwright whose latest
script exposes the deepest personal secrets of his family: the other brother,
restauranteur Alfred, has tried and failed to injunct the play, causing a long
and acrimonious rift with his sibling. *Reflected Glory* concerns the attempt by
Michael to effect a "so-called" reconciliation—in fact, he is trying to clear the
ground for his latest play which will examine his relationship with Alfred.
Funny, heartfelt, and with autobiographical overtones, *Reflected Glory* is in
many ways Harwood's best play since *The Dresser*.

—David E. Kemp

HASTINGS, Michael (Gerald).

Born in Lambeth, London, 2 September 1938. Educated at Alleyn's School, 1949–53; apprentice, Kilgour French and Stanbury, bespoke tailors, London, 1953–56. Married Victoria Hardie in 1975; two sons and one daughter from previous marriage. Recipient: Arts Council award, 1956; Encyclopaedia Britannica award, 1965; Maugham award, 1972; Writers Guild award, 1972; Emmy award, 1973; British Screenwriters Guild award, 1975; *Evening Standard* award, 1979. Fellow, Royal Geographical Society. Agent: Andrew Hewson, John Johnson Ltd., Clerkenwell House, 45–47 Clerkenwell Green, London EC1R 0HT. Address: 2 Helix Gardens, London S.W.2, England.

Publications

PLAYS

Don't Destroy Me (produced 1956). 1956.
Yes, and After (produced 1957). In *Three Plays*, 1966.
The World's Baby (produced 1965). In *Three Plays*, 1966.
Lee Harvey Oswald: A Far Mean Streak of Indepence Brought on by Negleck (as *The Silence of Lee Harvey Oswald*, produced 1966). 1966.
Three Plays (includes *Don't Destroy Me*; *Yes, and After*; *The World's Baby*). 1966.
The Silence of Saint-Just (produced 1971). 1970.
The Cutting of the Cloth (produced 1973).
For the West (Uganda) (produced 1977). In *Three Plays*, 1980.
Gloo Joo (produced 1978). In *Three Plays*, 1980.
Full Frontal (produced 1979). In *Three Plays*, 1980.
Carnival War (as *Carnival War a Go Hot*, produced 1979). With *Midnite at the Starlite*, 1981.
Midnite at the Starlite (as *Midnight at the Starlight*, televised 1980; as *Midnite at the Starlite*, produced 1981). With *Carnival War*, 1981.
Three Plays. 1980.
Two Fish in the Sky (produced 1982).
The Miser, adaptation of a play by Molière (produced 1982).
Tom and Viv (produced 1984). 1985.
Going to a Party (for children; produced 1984).
The Emperor, with Jonathan Miller, adaptation of a novel by Ryszard Kapuscinski (also co-director: produced 1987). 1988.
A Dream of People (produced 1990).
Three Political Plays (includes *The Emperor*, *For the West (Uganda)*, *Lee Harvey Oswald*). 1990.
Death and the Maiden, adaptation of the play by Ariel Dorfman (produced 1991). 1991.

SCREENPLAYS: *Bedtime*, 1968; *The Nightcomers*, 1972.

TELEVISION PLAYS: *The Game*, from his novel, 1961, revised version, 1973; *For the West (Congo)*, 1965; *Blue as His Eyes the Tin Helmet He Wore*, 1967; *Camille '68*, 1968; *Ride, Ride*, 1970; *The Search for the Nile* (documentary), with Derek Marlowe, 1971; *Auntie Kathleen's Old Clothes*, 1977; *Murder*

Rap, 1980; *Midnight at the Starlight*, 1980; *Michael Hastings in Brixton* (documentary), 1980; *Stars of the Roller State Disco*, 1984.

NOVELS
The Game. 1957.
The Frauds. 1960.
Tussy Is Me: A Romance. 1970.
The Nightcomers. 1972.
And in the Forest the Indians. 1975.

SHORT STORIES
Bart's Mornings and Other Tales of Modern Brazil. 1975.

VERSE
Love Me, Lambeth, and Other Poems. 1961.

OTHER
The Handsomest Young Man in England: Rupert Brooke: A Biographical Essay. 1967.
Sir Richard Burton: A Biography. 1978.

MANUSCRIPT COLLECTIONS: Princeton University, New Jersey; University of Texas, Austin.

THEATRICAL ACTIVITIES
DIRECTOR: Play—*The Emperor* (co-director, with Jonathan Miller), 1987.

Michael Hastings's first play was produced at the now defunct New Lindsey Theatre in Notting Hill when he was only 18, winning him instant fame as one of the youngest dramatists ever to have had his work performed. *Don't Destroy Me* showed an ear for the casual but revealing remark, though the dialogue was never fully controlled. Hastings's second play, *Yes, and After*, was three times as long (i.e., four and a half hours), indicating an increasing ease with the medium. It was also a mature work in many respects. He exploited his ability at dialogue, his minor characters were well observed, and, significantly, the female characters came at least as fully to life as the male ones: the daughter in this play is one of his finest creations. Both these plays were considered significant additions to the new drama of the angry young men.

Hastings returned to the stage only after nine years. For five years he had not written at all, having spent time educating himself while living frugally in France, Germany, and Spain. The education was less digested, in dramatic terms, than was desirable: *The World's Baby* is a sceptical chronicle of British life from the 1920's to the 1950's. The central character, Anna, begins as a Dionysian dispenser of sex. While her Cambridge boyfriends change as a result of wartime experiences, Anna's anti-bourgeois convictions remain intact. Hastings's Jewish and working-class background might lead one to expect sympathy with Anna's views, but their effect is pitilessly to transform her from charming (if childish) impetuousness to menopausal crankiness. Is Anna to be seen as a victim of circumstances, as a symbol of her times, or simply as an individual? She is a little of each but not enough of any to be quite convincing. If Hastings's technique had not grown any more coherent, he certainly had come better to understand how people behave under emotional stress.

Hastings discovered the vein which he was to mine most successfully with his first popular success, *The Silence of Lee Harvey Oswald*. The playwright's background had given him an undeniable instinct for character, his self-education gave him a sense of what is topical, and he rightly focused on the person rather than on history. He had read through the 26-volume Warren Commission Report, but the purpose of his play was to understand what was enigmatic in the alleged assassin. Structured on Oswald's declining marriage, the play's emotional power is generated by the explosive brutality of Oswald's treatment of his wife. When she attempts to desert him, their sense of loneliness and exhaustion, which prompts Oswald to plead with her for her return, is equally tellingly handled. The play moves from verbatim transcripts of evidence by Oswald's wife and mother, to dramatisations of episodes described by them. The two women hold different views of the man, his mother believing him to be a framed CIA agent, his wife thinking that he killed Kennedy to gain notoriety. (The play's popularity may have also come from the perpetually appealing techniques and suspense of cross-examination, which has a key place in the technique of the play.) The two views are, however, presented flatly. Oswald remains impenetrable, and Hastings's concern for truth is precisely what prevents the play from achieving the insight of art.

In his play on Saint-Just, Hastings violently couples the documentary material with invented dialogue about twisted revolutionary heroes. Saint-Just's powerful and mysterious silence for the 30 hours preceding his execution is made into the play's crucial anti-climax, showing Hastings at his technically adventurous best. *For the West*, on Idi Amin, is a better blend of documentary and imaginative material, and it is assisted by a large part of it taking place in Amin's dreams.

In the third stage of his playwriting career, Hastings was preoccupied with racial themes. *Gloo Joo* and *Carnival War* are perhaps the best known of the plays on these themes, but Hastings's undoubtedly serious concern is undercut by the farcical mode in which he chooses to treat strongly divisive issues. *Carnival War* combines larking about the Notting Hill Carnival with buffoonery aimed against the police, reminiscent of some of Hastings's earlier plays, especially the television play *Blue as His Eyes the Tin Helmet He Wore*. Notwithstanding this, Hastings's plays about black people have enjoyed considerable success in Africa and the Caribbean.

Tom and Viv is based on the allegation that T. S. Eliot's first wife Vivien Haigh-Wood was committed to an asylum not because she was a lunatic but because, emotionally troubled as she was, she indulged in behaviour that Eliot and his Bloomsbury friends found embarrassing. The controversial nature of this thesis was compounded by the uncertainty regarding its factual basis. History will reveal the truth of the matter. This satirical and sometimes sickening play succeeds as a startling recreation of the period and of period characters, eloquently portraying the savagery of the two societies that destroyed Viv: the landed merchant class of her origin and her husband's glittering literary set who considered her a boor.

Hastings is a dramatist of ever-widening range (extended even further in his recent *The Emperor*), but he still seems in search of a completely congenial dramatic form; there remains a gulf between the inner and outer worlds of his plays.

—Prabhu S. Guptara

HOLMAN, Robert.

Born in Guisborough, Cleveland, 25 August 1952. Educated at Lawrence Jackson School, Guisborough, 1963–69; Prior Pursglove Sixth Form College, Guisborough, 1969–71. Bookstall assistant, Paddington Station, London, 1972–74; resident dramatist, National Theatre, London, 1978–80, and Royal Shakespeare Company, Stratford-on-Avon, 1984. Recipient: Arts Council bursary, 1974; George Devine award, 1978; Fulbright fellowship, 1988. Agent: Casarotto Ramsay Ltd., National House, 60–66 Wardour Street, London W1V 3HP, England.

Publications

PLAYS

The Grave Lovers (produced 1972).
Progress in Unity (produced 1972).
Coal (produced 1973).
The Natural Cause (produced 1974).
Mud (produced 1974). With *German Skerries*, 1977.
Outside the Whale (produced 1976). With *Rafts and Dreams*, 1991.
German Skerries (produced 1977). With *Mud*, 1977.
Emigres, adaptation of the play by Sławomir Mrozek (produced 1978). In *New Review*, 1979.
Rooting (produced 1980).
Other Worlds (produced 1983). 1983.
Today (produced 1984). 1985.
The Overgrown Path (produced 1985). 1985.
Making Noise Quietly: A Trilogy (includes *Being Friends, Lost, Making Noise Quietly*) (produced 1986). 1987.
Across Oka (produced 1988). 1988.
Rafts and Dreams (produced 1990). With *Outside the Whale*, 1991.

TELEVISION PLAYS: *Chance of a Lifetime*, 1979; *This Is History, Gran*, 1984.

NOVEL

The Amish Landscape. 1992.

Allusive and carefully crafted, Robert Holman's plays explore the inter-penetration of ordinary lives and large historical events. The Great Depression, the Spanish Civil War, World War II, the Holocaust, the destruction of Nagasaki, and the continuation of research on the hydrogen bomb—such realities darken the worlds shaping and shaped by his characters, worlds which in turn illuminate the contradictions and complexities of these realities. History is not a backcloth—nor even a stage—for these characters, but a sense of pattern which reveals, and is revealed by, their actions or inactions. Time and again his protagonists articulate this simple truth: "It's important. History. Our lives."

Perhaps his strongest and most ambitious play to date is *The Overgrown Path*. This opens with a playlet performed by primary-school children in modern-day Nagasaki. It recounts the experience of a girl called Etsuko on the day the atomic bomb was dropped. When the playlet ends, Etsuko is identified as the children's schoolteacher. The rest of the drama takes place on the Greek island of Tinos where Daniel Howarth, a 73-year-old British academic, has retired from the world with Beth, his second wife. Four years his junior, she is American and a doctor. As a member of a medical relief team in Nagasaki in 1945, she had witnessed the effects of the bomb and, during her time there, had befriended a 10-year-old orphan of the blast called Etsuko. Daniel's career had been in atomic physics and he had led the research programme on the hydrogen bomb throughout the 1950s. They met and married in the 1960s. To their escape on Tinos comes Daniel's daughter by his first marriage, and a bright questioning disciple—in his late thirties—who is hesitating before embarking on what clearly could be a brilliant academic career. From the lives of these four people come stories and processes of learning which reveal patterns of design and accident that help to bring both characters and historical "facts" into a felt relationship. As Daniel says to his inquisitive disciple: "I'm not a historian, but it seems to me we look at history in the wrong way. We have to look at ourselves first. At our own stories. When we stop repeating our own failings, and take responsibility for our actions, maybe we have a chance."

This need to "take responsibility" is a recurring motif. It is something Joe Waterman, in an earlier play *Other Worlds*, is running away from. It is something his betrothed, at their last tragic meeting, insists upon:

Joe: It's other people messed it up, not us.
Emma: It's us.

It is something that, by the end of the play, Joe learns to do. *Other Worlds* takes place during the final decades of the 18th century when enclosure by private Acts of Parliament was dividing communities and challenging custom. The barriers of enmity and suspicion raised by one such Act, separating the world of the fishers and the world of the farmers on an isolated stretch of the north Yorkshire coast, are reinforced by the threat of an invasion from France. Fear of the unknown and of the reciprocal violence engendered by enclosure is portrayed through such vivid stage imagery as the unexpected irruption of a shipwrecked gorilla dressed in a blue woollen sailor's jumper, his capture in a fishing net, and his imprisonment and eventual execution as a Frenchman alongside a vagrant girl who, dressed in boy's clothes, is thought to be a French spy and whose protestations of gender are not believed. The absurdity of such images highlights how, in a collision of closed worlds, any sense of identity, shared humanity, or responsibility to otherness becomes constrained. Against these implosive forces are posited a belief in education and learning, hope—

"when you've lost hope, you've lost everything"—and the need not to drift or run away but to take on the responsibility for one's actions.

In all of Holman's work, a care for detail is balanced by an impressionistic style designed to engage an audience in a continual process of inference, surprise, reassessment, and understanding concerning both events and people. In many of his plays events move backwards and forwards in time, as—for example—in *Today*, where they move from 1936 to 1920 to 1922 to 1937 to 1946. In this drama, we are drawn into the experiences of the relatives, friends, and casual acquaintances of Victor Ellison, a Yorkshire music teacher who, struggling to compose something out of his life, goes to fight in Spain. Their experiences articulate differences in opportunities, aspirations, economics, class, and region before and during the Great Depression. The shifts in time sharpen our sense of the choices and restrictions facing these figures as well as highlighting how chance and accident can affect the direction of events. These shifts in perspective involve the audience in seeing and revising why and how these things happened. Holman's approach to characterisation deepens this involvement. New, often contradictory, facets of character are continually juxtaposed, making us modify, even change outright, our sense of what motivates each person.

We get to know Holman's characters through partial and accidental revelations and encounters. This allusive approach is best exemplified in *Lost*, the shortest of the one-act plays comprising the trilogy *Making Noise Quietly*. A young naval lieutenant visits his sister's mother-in-law to commiserate on her son's death in the Falklands. They have not met before. She does not know who he is. The mother has not heard that her son is dead. She does not even know that he was married. These facts—along with details of family relationships, their social backgrounds, and respective pasts—are disclosed in a seemingly haphazard way which exposes an emotional muddle of "little lies" in the front room of a small terraced house in Redcar, a muddle that parallels and illuminates the moral murk of the Falklands War.

—Leslie du S. Read

HOPKINS, John (Richard).

Born in London, 27 January 1931. Educated at Raynes Park County Grammar School; St. Catharine's College, Cambridge, B.A. in English. Served in the British Army (national service), 1950–51. Married 1) Prudence Balchin in 1954; 2) the actress Shirley Knight in 1970; two daughters. Worked as television studio manager; writer, BBC Television, 1962–64. Since 1964 freelance writer. Recipient: two Screenwriters Guild awards. Agent: William Morris Agency, 31–32 Soho Square, London W1V 6AP, England. Address: Hazelnut Farm, R.F.D. 1, Fairfield, Connecticut 06430, U.S.A.

Publications

PLAYS

A Place of Safety (televised 1963). In *Z Cars: Four Scripts From the Television Series*, edited by Michael Marland, 1968.

Talking to a Stranger: Four Television Plays (includes *Anytime You're Ready I'll Sparkle, No Skill or Special Knowledge Is Required, Gladly My Cross-Eyed Bear, The Innocent Must Suffer*) (televised 1966). 1967.
A Game—Like—Only a Game (televised 1966). In *Conflicting Generations: Five Television Plays*, edited by Michael Marland, 1968.
This Story of Yours (produced 1968). 1969.
Find Your Way Home (produced 1970). 1971.
Economic Necessity (produced 1973).
Next of Kin (produced 1974).
Losing Time (produced 1979). 1983.
Absent Forever (produced 1987).

Screenplays: *Two Left Feet*, with Roy Baker, 1963; *Thunderball*, with Richard Maibaum, 1965; *The Virgin Soldiers*, with John McGrath and Ian La Fresnais, 1969; *Divorce—His, Divorce—Hers*, 1972; *The Offence*, 1973; *Murder by Decree*, 1980; *The Holcroft Covenant*, with George Axelrod and Edward Anhalt, 1982; *The Power*, with John Carpenter and Gerald Brach, 1983.

Television plays: *Break Up*, 1958; *After the Party*, 1958; *The Small Back Room*, 1959; *Dancers in Mourning*, 1959; *A Woman Comes Home*, 1961; *A Chance of Thunder* (6 parts), 1961; *By Invitation Only*, 1961; *The Second Curtain*, 1962; *Look Who's Talking*, 1962; *Z Cars* series (53 episodes), 1962–65; *The Pretty English Girls*, 1964; *I Took My Little World Away*, 1964; *Parade's End* (serialization), from the novel by Ford Madox Ford, 1964; *Time Out of Mind*, 1964; *Houseparty* (ballet scenario), 1964; *The Make Believe Man*, 1965; *Fable*, 1965; *Horror of Darkness*, 1965; *A Man Like Orpheus*, 1965; *Talking to a Stranger* (4 parts), 1966; *Some Place of Darkness*, music by Christopher Whelen, 1966; *A Game—Like—Only a Game*, 1966; *The Gambler* (serialization), from a novel by Dostoevsky, 1968; *Beyond the Sunrise*, 1969; *The Dolly Scene*, 1970; *Some Distant Shadow*, 1971; *That Quiet Earth*, 1972; *Walk into the Dark*, 1972; *The Greeks and Their Gifts*, 1972; *A Story to Frighten the Children*, 1976; *Double Dare*, 1976; *Fathers and Families* (6 plays), 1977; *Smiley's People*, with John le Carré, from the novel by le Carré, 1982.

With well over 50 scripts for the television series *Z Cars*, and several short television plays behind him, John Hopkins is not primarily a writer for the stage. It was on the newer medium that his reputation was made, and continues to stand at its highest. Indeed, one important critic called his tetralogy, *Talking to a Stranger*, "the first authentic masterpiece written directly for television," and there must be many others who, though perhaps charier of the word "masterpiece," would agree that no finer dramatic work has yet been seen on it. It is undeniably impressive in itself: it also makes a helpful introduction to the first plays Hopkins was subsequently to write for the theatre, *This Story of Yours* and *Find Your Way Home*.

Each of the four plays involves approximately the same day, and each is written from the stance of a different member of the same family, the father, the mother, and their two grown-up children, Alan and Teresa. All are characterized in striking depth; all, with the possible exception of the son, are thoroughly self-absorbed, more inclined to talk in monologue than dialogue; all, again except for him, stand in danger of being overwhelmed by their own self-destructive feelings; all, including him, are lonely and dissatisfied. The tetralogy opens with Teresa, bustling with frantic neurosis, and ends with the mother, dead by her own hand, and, between the two, Hopkins avoids none of the emotional collisions and unpleasantness that his plot generates. Where most contemporary writers would hedge, or tread warily, or retreat into irony, he strides in wholeheartedly and sometimes repetitively, using straightforward, unpretentious, naturalistic language. Not surprisingly, he has been accused of dramatic overstatement, even melodrama.

But "melodrama" occurs when a writer presents extremes of feeling which are neither justified by his material nor empathetically understood by himself. In *Talking to a Stranger* the emotions on display are no more than the "objective correlative" of the dramatic situation, so painstakingly assembled; and, equally, Hopkins has a thorough grasp of the people he has created. He gives the impression of knowing, instinctively, how they would react to any new event. The question is: can we say as much for his stage plays? And the proper answer would seem to be: not quite.

This Story of Yours seems almost to be accusing Hopkins's scripts for *Z Cars* of romanticizing their subject, the police (though in fact they were widely admired for their wry realism). It is a study of the mind of Detective-Sergeant Johnson, trapped in an unfulfilling marriage and at once disgusted and fascinated by work that, characteristically, Hopkins describes in lurid detail. He breaks, and, in a scene of considerable dramatic intensity, beats to death an alleged child rapist: an act that is doubly self-destructive, since it wrecks his career and since it is clearly a way of sublimating his loathing for his own hideous thoughts and corrupt desires. *Find Your Way Home* mainly concerns two homosexuals, one young, unhappy, and apparently a part-time prostitute, the other a married man, and ends with them settling down seriously to live together, having confessed their mutual love. By bringing on a distraught wife, and by accentuating the crudity and sadness of the homosexual subculture, Hopkins is at pains to make this decision as difficult as possible. But his view evidently is that it is the right one. The older man has "found his way home," to a more honest and fulfilling way of life.

From this, it will be seen that Hopkins's view of the world is bleak: and what seems "melodramatic" in his work is often only his way of emphasizing his belief that people are lonely and perverse, full of black thoughts and longings. If a relationship is capable of any success at all, which is doubtful, it can be only after each partner has accepted his own and the other's emotional inadequacies, as the protagonists of *Find Your Way Home* are beginning to do. It is an outspoken, unfashionable moral stance which, to be persuasive, may need the more thorough characterization we find in *Talking to a Stranger*. There are psychological gaps left open in the stage plays, and notably in *Find Your Way Home*, whose scheme forces Hopkins to the dubious assumption that a young man who has gone very far in self-destructive promiscuity may be capable of sustained affection in a mature relationship. Hopkins achieves his effects by accumulating the emotional evidence as thickly as he can, and may therefore need more space, more time, than other contemporary writers in order to do so.

—Benedict Nightingale

HORSFIELD, Debbie.

Born in Manchester, 14 February 1955. Educated at Eccles Grammar School, Manchester, 1966–73; Newcastle University, B.A. (honours) in English literature 1977. Assistant administrator, Gulbenkian Studio Theatre, Newcastle-upon-Tyne, 1978–80; assistant to the artistic director, Royal Shakespeare Company, London, 1980–83; writer-in-residence, Liverpool Playhouse, Liverpool, 1983–84. Recipient: Thames Television award, 1983. Agent: Sheila Lemon, Lemon, Unna, and Durbridge, 24 Pottery Lane, Holland Park, London W11 4LZ, England.

Publications

PLAYS

Out on the Floor (produced 1981).
Away from It All (produced 1982).
The Next Four Years, Parts 1–2 (produced 1983).
All You Deserve (produced 1983).
Red Devils (produced 1983). In *Red Devils Trilogy*, 1986.
True Dare Kiss (produced 1983). In *Red Devils Trilogy*, 1986.
Command or Promise (produced 1983). In *Red Devils Trilogy*, 1986.
Touch and Go (produced 1984).
Revelations (produced 1985).
Red Devils Trilogy.   1986.
Royal Borough (produced 1987).
In Touch (produced 1988).
Making Out (televised 1989). 1989.

RADIO PLAY: *Arrangements*, 1981.

TELEVISION PLAYS: *Face Value*, in *Crown Court* series, 1982; *Out on the Floor*, 1983; *Making Out* series, 1989–91.

Debbie Horsfield is among the most successful of Britain's young women playwrights, primarily due to the popularity of her television drama writing. Her original idea for *Making Out* was to focus on working-class women's issues. Horsfield sets the series in a factory; thus, rather than putting one woman at the centre of a largely male world, she has created a community of women who live and work with men, yet who are not primarily identified through their relationships (social or sexual) with those men. *Making Out* reached a wide audience eager to see reflections of real women on the screen. Significantly, the series is not only written by a woman (Horsfield) but has tended to be directed and produced by women as well.

The same focus on strong, realistic women is what fuels Horsfield's writing for the theatre. Her best-known theatre work is the *Red Devils Trilogy*. All three plays in the trilogy focus on the same four characters: Alice, Nita, Phil, and Beth. These four young women grow up together and their relationships, careers, hopes, and fears develop as they share their experiences and their love of football (Manchester United, to be precise). Of course, Manchester United is not only the name of a football team, but is also an accurate phrase to describe the relationship between the four central female characters, all from Manchester, all united as friends whose lives develop in different ways but stem from common roots and shared experiences.

In this trilogy of comic plays, the same idea which gives energy to *Making Out* likewise fuels the power of the theatre performance: women working and playing together, women who share interests (non-stereotypically "feminine" interests at that), women who like each other and enjoy each other's company, women who know how to make each other laugh, just as Horsfield clearly knows how to make her audiences laugh. The power of Horsfield's writing is her combination of unusual scenarios and settings for women with a frank, unsentimental, yet playful style. The working-class settings invite men as well as women into the worlds of the plays. Working-class situations are rarely portrayed as well in the theatre. Thus, the *Red Devils Trilogy* has a certain interest, even for those with no interest in football.

In the first play, *Red Devils*, the four central characters are Manchester schoolgirls on their way to the 1979 Cup Final at Wembley Stadium. The action takes place in Manchester before the game, in London during the game, and at a motorway service station between the two cities after the game. The cast of characters is laid out on the page of the published version in the shape of a football formation, with Horsfield's name (as author) in the goal box. This playful presentation of the "facts" of the performance is in keeping with the mood of the play: like much of Horsfield's work (including several of her earlier plays), it emphasizes female friendship and the enjoyment which women, like men, find in each other's company. Petty differences are presented in a humorous rather than a "catty" way.

The same positive spirit enlivens the remaining two plays in the trilogy: *True Dare Kiss* and *Command or Promise*, both staged in London's Cottesloe Theatre (The Royal National Theatre) in 1985. In both of these plays, the same four characters have grown up and remain friends, sharing different aspects of their adult lives, as well as their continued love of football. The plays have been criticized for being "too much like soap opera," a criticism which says as much about our cultural expectations as it does about the plays. It is true that the depiction of the young women's lives in these later plays is channeled through multiple storylines, familiar from televised soap operas and serials (and very effectively utilized in Horsfield's own television success, *Making Out*). But to identify the form of the plays as a fault is misleading: they are episodic and weighted with the conflicting and overlapping stories of four different women's lives. Relationships are represented between women and men, women and work, women and higher education, women and cultural trends (punk culture and football). Yet the uniting thread of the four stories, as they develop and grow in the three plays of the *Red Devils Trilogy*, is the relationship between the four women. That focus on women's friendship is still uncommon on the stage. Debbie Horsfield has begun to make it more acceptable, and has thereby opened the way for other playwrights to experiment with a wide range of common but little-represented experiences in contemporary theatre.

—Lizbeth Goodman

HOWARD, Roger.

Born in Warwickshire, 19 June 1938. Educated at Dulwich College, London; Royal Academy of Dramatic Art, London, 1956–57; Bristol University, 1958; University of Essex, Colchester, M.A. 1976. National Service in Royal Armoured Service Corps, 1958: sentenced to imprisonment for refusal to wear uniform: dishonourable discharge. Married Anne Mary Zemaitis in 1960; one son. Teacher, Nankai University, Tientsin, China, 1965–67; manager, Collets Bookshop, Peterborough, 1967–68, and Bookshop 85, London, 1968–72; teacher, Peking University, 1972–74; playwright-in-residence, Mercury Theatre, Colchester, 1976; Arts Council fellow in creative writing, University of York, 1976–78; Henfield writing fellow, University of East Anglia, Norwich, 1979. Since 1979 lecturer, and founding director, Theatre Underground, and since 1980 editor, New Plays series, University of Essex. Member, Council of Management, Society for Anglo-Chinese Understanding, and editorial committee, *China Now* magazine, London, 1970–72; member of the editorial committee, *Platform* magazine, London, 1978–82; since 1980 founder, Theatre Action Press, Colchester; guest professor, Janus Pannonius University, and visiting director, Pécs Little Theatre, Pécs, Hungary, 1991. Recipient: Arts Council bursary, 1975. Address: Department of Literature, University of Essex, Wivenhoe Park, Colchester, Essex CO4 3SQ, England.

Publications

PLAYS

Bewitched Foxes Rehearsing Their Roles (produced 1968).
New Short Plays 1, with Leonard Melfi and Carey Harrison (includes *The Carrying of X from A to Z, Dis, The Love Suicides at Havering, Seven Stages on the Road to Exile*). 1968.
Fin's Doubts (produced 1969). 1968.
The Love Suicides at Havering (produced 1969). In *New Short Plays 1*, 1968.
The Carrying of X from A to Z (produced 1971). In *New Short Plays 1*, 1968.
Dis (produced 1971). In *New Short Plays 1*, 1968.
Seven Stages on the Road to Exile (produced 1970). In *New Short Plays 1*, 1968.
Season (produced 1969).
Simon Murdering His Deformed Wife with a Hammer (produced 1969).
The Meaning of the Statue (produced 1971). In *Slaughter Night and Other Plays*, 1971.
Writing on Stone (produced 1971). In *Slaughter Night and Other Plays*, 1971.
Slaughter Night and Other Plays: The Meaning of the Statue, The Travels of Yi Yuk-sa to the Caves at Yenan, Returning to the Capital, Writing on Stone, Korotov's Ego-Theatre, Report from the City of Reds in the Year 1970, The

Drum of the Strict Master, The Play of Iron, Episodes from the Fighting in the East, A New Bestiary. 1971.

The Travels of Yi Yuk-sa to the Caves at Yenan (produced 1976). In *Slaughter Night and Other Plays,* 1971; *in Scripts 4,* February 1972.

The Drum of the Strict Master (produced 1976). In *Slaughter Night and Other Plays,* 1971.

Korotov's Ego-Theatre (produced 1978). In *Slaughter Night and Other Plays,* 1971.

Episodes from the Fighting in the East (produced 1978). In *Slaughter Night and Other Plays,* 1971; in *Scripts 4,* February 1972.

Report from the City of Reds in the Year 1970 (produced 1978). In *Slaughter Night and Other Plays,* 1971.

The Auction of Virtues, in *Point 101* (produced 1972). In *Y,* 1977.

Sunrise. 1973.

Klöng 1, Klöng 2, and the Partisan (produced 1976).

Notes for a New History (produced 1976).

The Tragedy of Mao in the Lin Piao Period (produced 1976). In *The Tragedy of Mao in the Lin Piao Period and Other Plays,* 1989.

The Great Tide (produced 1976).

A Feast During Famine (produced 1977).

Travelling Players of the Dawn (produced 1977).

The Play of Margery Kempe (produced 1978). In *The Tragedy of Mao in the Lin Piao Period and Other Plays,* 1989.

Women's Army (produced 1978).

Joseph Arch (produced 1978).

Queen (produced 1979). In *The Tragedy of Mao in the Lin Piao Period and Other Plays,* 1989.

Memorial of the Future: A Rag (produced 1979). With *The Society of Poets,* 1979.

The Society of Poets: A Grotesquery (produced 1979). With *Memorial of the Future,* 1979.

A Break in Berlin (produced 1979). 1981.

The Siege (produced 1981). As *The Violent Irruption and Terrible Convulsions of the Siege During the Late Lamentable Civil War at Colchester in the Year 1648,* 1981.

White Sea (produced 1982). In *The Tragedy of Mao in the Lin Piao Period and Other Plays,* 1989.

Partisans (produced 1983). 1983.

The Speechifier, in *Double Space,* no. 2, 1984–85.

Contact (produced 1985). In *Britannia and Other Plays,* 1990.

The Tragedy of Mao in the Lin Piao Period and Other Plays (includes *The Play of Margery Kempe, White Sea, Queen*). 1989.

Britannia and Other Plays (includes *A Break in Berlin, The Siege, Partisans, The Speechifier, Contact*). 1990.

The Christ-Bringer's Comedy (produced 1992).

NOVELS

A Phantastic Satire. 1960.
From the Life of a Patient. 1961.

SHORT STORIES

Four Stories, with *Twelve Sketches*, by Tony Astbury. 1964.
Ancient Rivers. 1984.

VERSE

To the People. . . . 1966.
Praise Songs. 1966.
Senile Poems. 1988.

OTHER

The Technique of the Struggle Meeting. 1968.
The Use of Wall Newspapers. 1968.
The Hooligan's Handbook: Methods of Thinking and Action. 1971.
Method for Revolutionary Writing. 1972.
Mao Tse-tung and the Chinese People. 1977.
Le théâtre chinois contemporain. 1978; as *Contemporary Chinese Theatre*, 1978.

Editor, *Culture and Agitation: Theatre Documents*. 1972.

CRITICAL STUDIES: "*The Drum of the Strict Master* at the Essex University Theatre" by Howard, in *Theatre Quarterly*, no. 24, 1976; *Contradictory Theatres* edited by Leslie Bell, 1985; "The Dramatic Sense of Life: Theatre and Historical Simulation" by Howard, in *New Theatre Quarterly*, no. 3, 1985.

Roger Howard comments:

(1973) In revolutionary war, plays are performed to show scenes of the struggle in which fighters who actually took part replay their "parts" as examples to other fighters. Their short, instructional plays go back over the battle just ended in order to point out the lesson to be learnt for the next round. They educate by showing the audience—other fighters—the significance of their actions.

Such drama is deeply rooted in the day-to-day work experience of the people. It captures their imagination because it closely expresses themselves. At the same time it is a higher form of artistic expression than mere realism, because it shows the people's actions in their relationship to the new, evolving, and advancing socialist morality. Their plays are agitation in the service of the people's advance and an aid in the overthrow of the old society.

My short plays are part of the same process. Preparing for the situation where there will be open military warfare, they are agitational plays in the wider war which engulfs us all, the war between classes which takes many forms and which will not cease until classes cease. Each play is located at a point where a certain stage of development in struggle has been reached, and where the choices are open as to what the following stage should be.

The point reached at the opening of each play may be either a victory or a defeat for revolutionary advance. The body of the play then develops the initial point by showing the contending sides and conflicting interests, giving visual and verbal guidelines from the particular instance to the wider significance in the form of interpolated screen captions, extended sound words, lyrical or didactic verses, or actual physical combat.

The characters are shown in their class as well as in their individual roles; they are individuals who express class positions in the way they think, speak, act, and interact. Their conflicts therefore elicit humour, grotesquery, poetry, reason, tragedy, and decision.

The resolution of the conflicts between the characters, as of those within one character, is resolution not of a "personality" to his "destiny" or of the "mind" to the "universe," still less of the "underdog" to his "station in life." It is a resolution that will give the revolutionary protagonist, the positive character, his due as the man who has history on his side in an era when capitalism is in decline and the many forces of socialism are in the ascendant. It is therefore a resolution of *ideas*, by which the conscious, active man triumphs over the slave in man, whether it be in himself or in others. For some, the resolution comes as a condemnation: they are the negative characters, the reactionaries, backward rejects of history. For others, the resolution comes too late; for them they have their message to pass on to a new generation. For all our mistakes, man is learning to advance. The point of resolution in each play is therefore an ideological point, to be perceived as such by the audience.

So the characters of the plays are representations of contradictory class position as they appear in individual human beings. This gives the positive characters greater dimensions than those of mere self-contained, alienated individuals at odds with society for their own sake, just as in life itself the activists of revolution are so much greater figures than those who merely talk about it or those who use socialism for their personal advantage.

Our oppression will last for as long as we remain afraid; if only we act, we lose our fear. Oppressors tremble when they lose their grip on our terror. The revolutionary characters in my plays are heroic because they are no longer afraid. And they are no longer afraid because they have become conscious. They know that as active workers, conscious of class, they hold the future in their hands. I warm to those men and women in our century who, raising the people to raise themselves, and growing thus in stature, have reminded mankind of its dignity. My heart is stung when I hear of their deeds; they are few of them famous and most suffered great privation and even death. My plays can hardly emulate their lives but they are some sort of small monuments, not for us to gaze at and pity, but to stir us to action. They rescue from the great killings some memorials of actions that teach us to kill more precisely in future: our killers.

(1977) The idea of people as doers, as much as sufferers, has been pushed into the background in much of recent drama that has become academically respectable, from Ibsen to Beckett. The idea that people are capable of directing their future more completely has been neglected.

In my short plays I have introduced prototypes of such representative men and women. The transition I am now making from short to full-length plays will give the idea of renewal more scope. The first long play, *The Tragedy of Mao in the Lin Piao Period*, is a 19-scene construction of the shifts in the relationship between two men striving to remake men and themselves. Then follows a trilogy on turning points in English history, from tribalism to feudalism, to capitalism, and to socialism.

(1982) The trilogy—*The Earth-Founding, The Force in the Land* and *The Great Tide*—has expanded into a series of full-length historical plays which now includes *Bread, Meat and Higher Learning* about the Marian suppression of the protestants, *The Siege* about clashes of inner self and outer self-interest in the radical debates of the English Civil War at the time of the Siege of Colchester (a play commissioned by the Mercury Theatre), and *Joseph Arch* about the founding of the agricultural workers' union. In these plays and in *A Break in Berlin* I have attempted to develop a method of characterisation that dialectically relates the inner person to his or her outer status in historical change, relying increasingly heavily on a dynamic use of dialogue as "spoken action" to present multi-dimensional and many-layered representations of characters caught in their personal "moments" inside the "movement" of changing societies. I still use a variety of dramatic forms—comic extravaganza in *Queen*, a study of the psychological effects of rule on the personality of Elizabeth II; epic in *Joseph Arch*, now expanded into a 37-scene play retitled *The Weight of Many Masters*; comic grotesquery in *The Society of Poets*; naturalism in *A Break in Berlin*; dynamic verbal-action theatre in *The Siege*. I have developed a notion of socialist tragedy which attempts to use a method of writing plays to show the processes of a person's life in terms of the extent to which he or she must submit to necessity and the extent to which he or she remains free (and willing) to act. *The Force in the Land, The Tragedy of Mao, A Break in Berlin* and *The Siege* are examples of such attempts. Increasingly I have felt the need to bring my critical, scholarly, and theoretical work on theatre, which has appeared largely in journals, together with the practice of production and the teaching of ideas of theatre. My work at Essex University is to do with the idea content of new English theatre writing and I have initiated a New Plays Scheme whereby each year M.A. drama students are given the opportunity of working on the production of a play with a specially commissioned theatre writer. I have founded the Theatre Underground in this connection in order to explore the possibility of a materialist and dialectical method of theatre writing and production practice. Theatre Underground's productions are of new English and overseas plays which have to do with representing, in a variety of theatre forms and by dialectical characterisation, a dramatic appraisal of men and women in their personal and their social lives in the connections of their personae to the wider forces of their time. The Theatre Underground scripts published in Essex University New Plays series—*A Break in Berlin* was the first—are accompanied by production notes and introductory material which provide a discourse about the play both as a piece of dramatic literature and as a theatre piece for performance. In Theatre Underground work my own ideas develop alongside the work of others whose research and practice is in overlapping areas and who have become involved in the concepts embodied by Theatre Underground. My plans for the future include plays about George Stephenson, Hitler, Ernst Toller and early English socialists; and a play about the rise and tribulations of the "alternative" theatre of the 1970's.

(1988) My exploration of socialist tragedy has extended to five new plays. *White Sea*, an ironic drama with music, traces the effects of their labour on the consciousness of a group of theatre workers helping to dig the White Sea Canal in the Soviet Union in the early 1930's. The "tragedy of expediency" occurs where Stalinist social and political euphoria, associated with the Five-Year

Plan, meets the necessities of material reality—and plain human inadequacies. *Partisans* is a series of grotesque and savage scenes in the comic and disturbing life of a freedom-seeking actress in the English "alternative" theatre of the 1960's and 1970's. She turns from drugs to terrorism and goes from prison to a peace camp before gaining a sense of her own identity as that of a victim's mental and emotional dissolution in a surrounding pre-nuclear chaos. The published edition contains a short essay by Charles Lamb on aspects of the play's dramaturgy. This "tragedy of liberation," whose main character, Cindy, bears some resemblance to Gerda in *A Break in Berlin* and Margery in *The Play of Margery Kempe* in her tortured questing, was followed by a tragedy of confinement, *The Speechifier*. Based on *The Orator*, a play by the Lithuanian writer Kazys Saja, the play is set in the family apartment of the ghost-writer of a Leader of a tyrannical state. The writer loses himself in obedience to his master, achieving a most perfect acquiescence rewarded when his family is gassed, trapped in their flat. *Britannia* (unproduced) is a dream play about the state of England. Christian Wager embarks on a journey of self-exposure from early-mediaeval hermetic spirituality, through Tudor state-forming and Victorian empire-building to Thatcherite monetarist opportunism, before learning how an intellectual has to conform to the powers-that-be. This latterday Faust is chided by his female double, Wager 2, for not learning from a regicide who at least had the nobleness to crown with his own suicide his repeated failure through the ages to remove the monarch, while Wager signs a deal with the King ensuring merely his own degenerate survival. *Contact* is a four-hander in 17 scenes, a contemporary tragedy of romantic love in a Europe divided by ideologies and united in opportunism. A young Polish woman and an English poet have a brief affair across the borders, an idealistic contact which collapses in a bitter war of self-interest.

All these plays reflect a new idea of tragedy in which human drives reach the limits imposed on them by necessity in one form or another. They reflect a notion of a tragic moment as resulting from a collision that is socially produced as well as personally motivated. Much of the theory attached to these ideas is published in *Contradictory Theatres*, a collection of essays and documentation about the work of the Theatre Underground at Essex University, which also contains essays by other hands on *A Break in Berlin* and *White Sea*.

(1993) After directing *The Play of Margery Kempe* at Pécs Little Theatre in Hungary, I was commissioned to write *The Christ-Bringer's Comedy*, produced by Theatre Underground at Essex University for the centenary conference on 1492 and for the Essex Festival. The central figure of Columbus commits the *hubris* of taking the name of God in vain in his pursuit of possessions, a lonely questing figure who has features of both Don Juan and Faust. The central act is concerned with Columbus's discoveries, but the first and third acts find him, Faust-like, travelling through time before and after the life-span of the historical figure, when he meets not only Venus but the Spanish Arabian mystic poet Ibn Al-'Arabi, Saint Catherine of Genoa, the poet Lesya Ukrainka, a rabbi of Chernobyl called Menahem Nahum, and the neo-Confucian philosopher Wang Yang-ming. Despite his consultations with such figures, from whom he asks guidance in his longings, he never really understands the nature of either the new world he discovered or of the Europeans and Indians he affected to offer to save. Living by fire, he dies by fire, as Venus prophesises, when he is sucked into the flames of a nuclear power plant at melt-down.

Roger Howard is a genuine original, whose plays combine an essentially Maoist political stance with a range of diverse and eclectic styles, including Brechtian epic theatre, slapstick, music hall, and cartoon theatre. In his intro-ductory essay to his collection *Slaughter Night* he makes the point that, in the present political situation, it is the playwright's task to divide and agitate, not to help in the creation of culture, which is part of the "deep sleep" our rulers want to impose on us. His plays are sharp, clear, and carry out this task of division with an admirable precision, though their form is very far from being conventional agitational socialist realism. This essay, which of necessity con-siders the plays more as cultural objects than as means of heightening political consciousness, is an exercise in contradictions, an example of the dialectical relationship between politics and art; but it is true to say that the best of the plays do work on an artistic and aesthetic level over and above their directly political one.

Howard's plays fall into three distinct phases. First, there are the lyrical pre-China pieces, like *Season* and *Simon Murdering His Deformed Wife with a Hammer*, which propagate a William Morris-type socialism through semi-abstract poetic characters and language. *Season* shows the struggle between urban and rural values; while *Simon* shows a young man trying to educate his wife to his own level of political consciousness, failing and murdering her as a result. Then come more complex plays, like *The Love Suicides at Havering*, which shows a group of people attempting to overcome their psychological inhibitions as a necessary precondition to achieving a revolutionary situation, and *Fin's Doubts*, which shows in symbolist form the full cycle of a revolution. A group of revolutionaries overthrow an era of reactionary repression, achieve the first stages of a revolution, and impose temporary authoritarian measures to consolidate its achievements; by a process of bureaucratic ossification this authoritarianism becomes permanent, and the whole cycle starts off again.

Howard went to China as a teacher for two years and the result can be seen in the artistically and politically more mature plays in *Slaughter Night*. The title play juxtaposes Sauer, the Dog King, and the Writer, a nice, cosy arrange-ment with the Writer reflecting Sauer's interests through his works until two Wolves and an Outlaw show him the error of his ways. *The Meaning of the Statue* shows a young man in conversation with the statue of a general. Essentially, it is about the loss of spontaneity and fluidity in a revolutionary situation occasioned by its bureaucratic organisation, symbolised by the youth being shot by the statue and being put, in the same fixed position, in the statue's place. *Returning to the Capital* uses the characters of Seami Motokiyo and his son, the fashioners of the first Noh plays, to point the differences between and consequences of being a reformist, like Seami, and a revolution-ary. *Writing on Stone* is about a couple romanticising the past in lyrical images and being afraid to face up to the implications of the present. *Korotov's Ego-Theatre* shows the irrelevance and sterility of individualist concepts of art in a revolutionary situation; *Episodes from the Fighting in the East*, the erratic progress of a revolution and the shifts of power that take place within it; while

A New Bestiary hilariously satirises, through animal imagery, types of people pretending to be revolutionaries who are in fact, without realizing it, on the revolutionaries' side. They all use language and sound in a most original way.

The Tragedy of Mao in the Lin Piao Period examines the ideological differences between Mao and the PLA commander-in-chief Lin (who was killed in an air crash in 1971 while fleeing to Moscow) and their origins in the civil war struggles of the 1930's. It is a subtle stylistic mixture of realism and a kind of heightened poetry, which in its totality gives some idea of how China's peasant-based socialism has evolved.

Howard has been little performed as yet; his plays are, however, eminently actable and stageable. They condense more into their brief spans, both in thought and style, than most full-length plays.

—Jonathan Hammond

HOWARTH, Donald.

Born in London, 5 November 1931. Educated at the Grange High School for Boys, Bradford; Esme Church Northern Children's Theatre School, 1948–51. Stage manager and actor in various repertory companies, 1951–56. Literary manager, Royal Court Theatre, London, 1975–76. Recipient: Encyclopaedia Britannica award, 1961; George Devine award, 1971. Agent: Casarotto Ramsay Ltd., National House, 60–66 Wardour Street, London W1V 3HP, England.

Publications

PLAYS

Lady on the Barometer (also co-director: produced 1958; as *Sugar in the Morning*, produced 1959).
All Good Children (produced 1960). 1965.
Secret of Skiz, adaptation of a play by Zapolska (produced 1962).
A Lily in Little India (televised 1962; also director: produced 1965). 1966.
Ogodivelefttthegason (also director: produced 1967).
School Play, in *Playbill One*, edited by Alan Durband. 1969.
Three Months Gone (produced 1970). 1970.
Othello Sleges Blankes, adaptation of the play by Shakespeare (also director: produced 1972).
Scarborough (also director: produced 1972).
The Greatest Fairy Story Ever Told, adaptation of a play by Kathleen Housell-Roberts (also director: produced 1973).
Meanwhile, Backstage in the Old Front Room (produced 1975).
Ibchek (also director: produced 1979).
Adventures of a Black Girl, adaptation of the novel *Adventures of a Black Girl in Her Search for God* by Shaw (also director: produced 1980).

SCREENPLAY: *Gates to Paradise*, 1968.

RADIO PLAY: *Reece*, 1989.

TELEVISION PLAYS: *A Lily in Little India*, 1962; *Stanley*, 1972.

CRITICAL STUDY: introduction by Michael Billington to *New English Dramatists 9*, 1966.

THEATRICAL ACTIVITIES

DIRECTOR: Plays—several of his own plays, and *This Property Is Condemned* by Tennessee Williams, 1960; *Miniatures* by David Cregan, 1965; *Play Mas* by Mustapha Matura, 1974; *Mama, Is Terry Home for Good?* by James Edward Shannon, 1974; *Parcel Post* by Yemi Ajibade, 1976; *Rum an' Coca Cola* by Mustapha Matura, 1976; *Waiting for Godot* by Beckett, 1981.
ACTOR: Plays—roles in reportory, 1951–56; Salvation Army Captain in *Progress to the Park* by Alun Owen, 1959.

Donald Howarth comments:

Art is what you don't do. Less is more.

One of the pleasures of reading through Donald Howarth's earlier plays in sequence—*Sugar in the Morning, All Good Children, A Lily in Little India, Ogodivelefttthegason,* and *Three Months Gone*—is the pleasure of seeing a playwright finding his way to an individual and successful compromise between naturalism and freewheeling expressionism by dint of returning again and again to the same themes and the same characters but never to the same style. He has worked hard, and at its worst his writing is laborious, but he has been capable from the beginning of sustaining passages of comedy which deftly combine truthfulness with elegant and compelling theatrical rhetoric. Finally, in *Three Months Gone*, he achieved a sureness of touch that enables him to tie fantasy material down to solid surfaces and to draw dividends from all his earlier stylistic experiments. *Ogodivelefttthegason* is the play in which he takes the most expressionistic short cuts and spans over the greatest amount of human experience. It is his least successful play, though, not because it is the least comic or the least realistic, but because it is the most shapeless and the least able to gain an audience's sympathy for the characters or sustain its interest in them—partly because their identity keeps changing. *Three Months Gone*, while no less remote from the slow development of the conventional naturalistic three-act play, has a storyline strong enough to keep the colourful balloons of fantasy that both main characters fly tethered securely to a solid matter-of-factness.

Mrs. Broadbent, the sexually frustrated landlady in *Sugar in the Morning*, and Grannie Silk, her obstinately vulgar, cheerful, warm-hearted, interfering mother, are both rough prototypes of Mrs. Hanker in *A Lily in Little India* and *Three Months Gone*, who combines the main characteristics of both of them without having Mrs. Broadbent's pretensions to gentility or her ineptness at finding food for her sexual appetites. A clear picture of suburban life emerges in *Sugar in the Morning* but much of the basic energy is spent on drawing it. Decisions about which lodgers to take, clipping the privet hedge, arguments about noisy radios and washing hung up outside windows, rent collecting, drinking cups of tea in the landlady's room, hurrying for the twenty-to-eight bus, finding a shilling for the gas meter, discussing whether to have a baby—in using episodes like these as its currency, the play makes them all seem equally important. None of the characters in *Sugar in the Morning* reappears in *All Good Children* but Rev. Jacob Bowers and his daughter and son, Anna and Maurice, are in both *All Good Children* and *A Lily in Little India*, which introduces Mrs. Hanker and her son Alvin, who are to reappear in *Three Months Gone*, together with Anna and Maurice. The whole of the action of *All Good Children* is set in a converted farmhouse in South Yorkshire, but the 60-year-old minister is about to retire and to move his family to the suburb where we find them in the two subsequent plays. The new theme introduced in *All Good Children*, which will recur persistently in the later work, is the relationship between Protestant morality and sexual deprivation. Jacob Bowers, now a devout anti-sensualist, has been very different when younger, and became a minister only because of guilt feelings after his affair with a minister's daughter had caused the old man's death. Unlike his younger brother, Clifford, who has been more of a conformist, Maurice has reacted violently against his Puritanic upbringing and becomes a sailor. His letters, with their juicy descriptions of local brothels, have been Anna's main life-line, and the love she feels for Maurice verges on the incestuous, but after her mother's death, caused by an on-stage fall down a staircase, she rejects her chance of breaking out of the family cage and condemns herself, after 20 years of imprisonment, to staying with her father.

The plot of *All Good Children* is developed mostly through speeches that rake over the past. *A Lily in Little India* is a less Ibsenite play, and physical action bulks larger in it. The action, like the stage, is divided between the Bowers' house and the Hankers'. We see Anna waiting on the old father who has spoiled her life by his narrowness, and writing letters to the brother through whom she is still vicariously living; in the other house a selfishly sensual landlady is trapping a reluctant postman into an affair regardless of the harm done to her sensitive son, who finds happiness only in growing a lily and in his encounters with Anna. When the mother, poised on a ladder outside his bedroom window, threatens to destroy his beloved lily, he throws water in her face causing her to fall backwards, and moves into Anna's house when his mother goes to hospital. The characters win considerable sympathy and interest, and there are some very funny and some very touching moments, but the comedy and the seriousness do not quite balance or reinforce each other as one comes to feel they should and, though the dialogue has been praised by Michael Billington (in his Introduction to the Penguin *New English Dramatists* 9) as "a just sufficiently heightened version of ordinary speech," it sinks sometimes into self-consciousness and just occasionally into sentimentality.

But the dialogue of *Three Months Gone* is virtually unflawed. The rapid shifts in and out of Anna's fantasies, and later Alvin's, give Howarth the opportunity to penetrate funnily but compassionately their private views of themselves, each other, and the two other main characters, Maurice and Mrs. Hanker, who are sexually so much more robust. There is a hilarious scene in which Mrs. Hanker, bullying Alvin to find the pluck to make Anna marry him, makes him propose to her while she pretends to be Anna, and this is followed by a sequence in which Maurice makes a pass at him under guise of teaching him how to make a woman submit. The audience's uncertainty about which sequence represents fantasy, which reality, is often an advantage.

The later plays are different and less successful. *The Greatest Fairy Story Ever Told* is a skittish pantomime full of arch chinoiserie. There are characters called Much Too Yin and Too Much Yang and jokes about Pon-Ting's fabric hall and the Royal Courtyard. *Meanwhile, Backstage in the Old Front Room* is highly serious, ambitiously moving further away from naturalism than any of Howarth's earlier works. It leans on both Beckett and Genet: *Endgame* is feminised in the relationship between the dominating old woman who never leaves her wheelchair and the blind younger women, possibly her daughter, who lives with her. The power games and the extremism in making the characters speak out their thoughts are reminiscent of Genet's *The Maids*. The influence is domesticated into a family setting, but not altogether digested.

—Ronald Hayman

HUGHES, Dusty.

Born in Boston, Lincolnshire, 16 September 1947. Educated at Queen Elizabeth Grammar School, Wakefield, Yorkshire, 1957–65; Trinity Hall, Cambridge, 1965–68, M.A. (honours) in English. Has one daughter. Assistant director, Birmingham Repertory Theatre, 1970–72; theatre editor, *Time Out*, London, 1973–76; artistic director, Bush Theatre, London, 1976–79; script editor, *Play for Today* series, BBC Television, 1982–84. Member, Arts Council Drama panel, 1975–80. Recipient: London Theatre Critics award, 1980; Edinburgh Festival award, 1981. Agent: Sebastian Born, Curtis Brown Group, 162–168 Regent Street, London W1R 5TB, England.

Publications

PLAYS

Grrr (produced 1968).
Commitments (produced 1980). With *Futurists*, 1986.
Heaven and Hell (produced 1981).
Molière; or, The Union of Hypocrites, adaptation of a play by Mikhail Bulgakov (produced 1982). 1983.
From Cobbett's Urban Rides, in *Breach of the Peace* (produced 1982).
Bad Language (produced 1983).
Philistines, adaptation of a play by Maxim Gorky (produced 1985). 1985.
Futurists (produced 1986). With *Commitments*, 1986.
Jenkin's Ear (produced 1987). 1987.
Metropolis, music by Joe Brooks, adaptation of the Fritz Lang film (produced 1989).
A Slip of the Tongue (produced 1992).

SCREENPLAYS: *Cries from the South*, 1986; *In Hiding*, 1987; *Tom*, 1991; *Crimes of Passion*, 1992.

TELEVISION PLAY: *The Secret Agent*, adaptation of the novel by Joseph Conrad, 1992.

THEATRICAL ACTIVITIES:

DIRECTOR: **Plays**—*The Soul of the White Ant* by Snoo Wilson, 1976; *Blood Sports* by David Edgar, 1976; *Vampire* by Snoo Wilson, 1977; *Happy Birthday, Wanda June* by Kurt Vonnegut, Jr., 1977; *In at the Death* by Snoo Wilson and others, 1978; *A Greenish Man* by Snoo Wilson, 1978; *Wednesday* by Julia Kearsley, 1978.

Dusty Hughes emerged in the 1980s with several dramatic works to his credit and more to come. An early experience with the left-wing's not having transformed him into a "good Bolshevik" has shaped the subject and concerns of his produced plays. The plays pursue a theme of disenchantment with the Marxist-Socialist ideal turned sour or repressive, as well as with middle-class aspirations which disclose emptiness and produce social and personal inertia.

Standing as immediate examples are Hughes's three best works: *Commitments*, *Futurists*, and an adaptation, *Molière; or, The Union of Hypocrites*.

Commitments introduces a small group of left-wing activists in 1973 using as live-in headquarters the London flat of a tolerant bourgeois dilettant reluctant to join their cause. Forming a focal and substantially dimensionalized triumvirate are the charming but undirected benefactor, an actress strongly committed to "the Party," and her working-class actor-lover. Fellow workers drop in as the group discusses politics and strategies and performs menial Party tasks, while outside the 1974 Labour government comes to power owing little to the Party's efforts or workers. Malaise affects the group's interrelationships: the flat-owner, motivated to become politically active, now ends up returning to his wastrel ways persuaded that the Party is "authoritarian and not a little unrealistic"; and the politically committed actress loses her lover, who returns to his wife. The drama offers a trenchant picture of disillusioned leftists whose cause and commitments have seemed wasted effort.

In *Futurists* Hughes takes us to 1921 post-revolution Petrograd, where great and mediocre artists, journalists, political hacks, striking sailors, and Bolshevik informers mingle in a sweaty nightclub. The drama centers on the Futurist poets—the famous figures of Mandelstam, Mayakovsky, Anna Akhmatova, and others are vividly recreated—who are drawn together by a fervent revolutionary belief that they have something to say but are initially unaware that their individualistic, unconventional thought and expression will eventually doom them. They proclaim their art and reveal their loss of equilibrium in the excitement of revolutionary confusion, while beyond the nightclub the revolution has gone wrong. The poets have relied for protection on their hero Gorky, friend of Lenin, who presides over them like a one-man arts council, but finds he cannot save them from the firing squads or being otherwise silenced. In the new society the artist is an endangered species: the mediocre survive, the talented grow silent or die. Central to the action, the tubercular Gorky becomes a tragic figure losing his self-assured belief that "people don't kill poets" as he becomes increasingly powerless to help his friends and is even warned by Lenin to leave the country. Hughes fills his characters and their world with vibrant life and a dire meaning, tellingly visualized in the 1986 London production as the colorfully grotesque Futurist trappings of the artists' cabaret are progressively stripped away to reveal the ominous black and red banners of Stalin. Yet with Anna Akhmatova's final recitation of a forbidden poem, Hughes reminds us that poetry outlasts revolutions.

That the playwright was drawn to adapt Mikhail Bulgakov's *Molière* is understandable. The play focuses on Molière's relationship to Louis XIV, as a sardonic paradigm of the Russian Bulgakov's position as a writer under Stalin, who in 1936 banned the play after seven performances. Hughes, in portraying a freethinking Molière incurring the wrath of Mother Church in mounting *Tartuffe* and suffering its banishment and his own fall from grace, demonstrates how the artist must demean himself before tyrannical and faction-influenced authority. Rejecting his long-time mistress Madeleine for a disastrous marriage with her supposed younger sister, Molière is informed upon by a dismissed actor in his company. This allows the religious cabal unscrupulously to engineer Molière's fall from favor by extracting Madeleine's confession that his wife is actually their mutual daughter, thus forcing the King's disapproval and his capitulation to their condemnation of the artist. The lively portrait of Molière, who switches from the impetuous actor-manager-writer backstage to a grovelling sycophant when in the presence of his sovereign, is both dramatically powerful, if perhaps historically exaggerated (as is the use of the unproven incest rumor), and thematically lucid. Molière underestimates the power of church and state with its near-omnipotent king and informer-ridden society resembling Stalinist Russia. The play is effective as theatre and as political statement.

Several further works also are underscored by socio-political themes. A critically unsuccessful (yet in its 1989 London production, visually spectacular) musical adaptation of Fritz Lang's 1927 film *Metropolis*, with an uninspired libretto by Hughes, presents a futuristic vision of a city where workers toil in subterranean factories under the dictatorship of an above-ground capitalist élite. A workers' revolt blows up the city, paving the path for a less harsh future whose power structure may or may not be significantly changed for the better. In *A Slip of the Tongue*, the question of whether freedom obligates a sense of responsibility to the political world or gives license to indulge hedonistic impulses is embodied in the actions of a noted dissident and womanizing writer who leaves the long harassment of a unspecified Eastern European country after the Berlin Wall crumbles to become a globe-trotting lecturer rather than a needed helper in framing a new government. This imperfect play drew popular attention in a 1992 Chicago world premiere with John Malkovitch as the anti-hero protagonist. *Jenkin's Ear*, in its focus on a disillusioned ex-foreign correspondent pursuing a missing female friend in a Central American country like Honduras, concerns the moral issue of whether getting a story is worth people's lives. The rapid inertness of middle-class values infecting the generations underlines *Bad Language*, a wryly comic survey of Cambridge undergraduates touched by the malady of sameness, and *Philistines*, an adaptation of Gorky's flawed yet compelling first play in which Hughes incisively presents a blackly comic portrait of a turn-of-the-century *petit bourgeois* Russian provincial family unable to change their ineffectual lives, and foreshadowing the national upheaval.

Productively engaged in turning out new work, Hughes continues to earn recognition as a playwright committed to creating dramas of substance that thoughtfully examine or offer parallels to the socio-political tapestry of this time.

—Christian H. Moe

HUTCHINSON, Ron.

Born near Lisburn, County Antrim, Northern Ireland; brought up in Coventry, Warwickshire. Educated at schools in Coventry. Worked at various jobs, including fish gutter, carpet salesman, scene shifter, and bookseller, all Coventry; clerk, Ministry of Defence and Ministry of Labour, Coventry; social worker and claims investigator, Department of Health and Social Security, Coventry, 5 years. Resident writer, Royal Shakespeare Company, London, 1978–79. Moved to Los Angeles in 1988. Recipient: George Devine award, 1978; John Whiting award, 1984; Emmy award, 1989; Ace award, 1989. Agents: Judy Daish Associates, 83 Eastbourne Mews, London W2 6LQ, England; and Merrily Kane, The Artists Agency, 10000 Santa Monica Boulevard, #305, Los Angeles, California 90067, U.S.A.

Publications

PLAYS

Says I, Says He (produced 1977). Part 1 in *Plays and Players,* March and April 1978; complete play, 1980.
Eejits (produced 1978).
Jews/Arabs (produced 1978).
Anchorman (produced 1979).
Christmas of a Nobody (produced 1979).
The Irish Play (produced 1980).
Into Europe (produced 1981).
Risky City (broadcast 1981; produced 1981).
The Dillen, adaptation of a work by Angela Hewins (produced 1983).
Rat in the Skull (produced 1984). 1984.
Mary, After the Queen, with Angela Hewins (produced 1985).
Curse of the Baskervilles, from a story by Arthur Conan Doyle (produced 1987).
Babbit: A Marriage, adaptation of a novel by Sinclair Lewis (produced 1987).
Pygmies in the Ruins (produced 1991).

RADIO PLAYS: *Roaring Boys,* 1977; *Murphy Unchained,* 1978; *There Must Be a Door,* 1979; *Motorcade,* 1980; *Risky City,* 1981; *Troupers,* 1988; *Larkin,* 1988.

TELEVISION PLAYS: *Twelve Off the Belt,* 1977; *Deasy Desperate,* 1979; *The Last Window Cleaner,* 1979; *The Out of Town Boys,* 1979; *Deasy,* 1979; *The Winkler,* 1979; *Bull Week,* 1980; *Bird of Prey* series, 1982 and 1984; *Connie* series, 1985; *The Marksman,* from the novel by Hugh C. Rae (*Unnatural Causes* series), 1987; *The Murderers Among Us: The Simon Wiesenthal Story,*

1988; *Dead Man Walking*, 1988; *Red King, White Knight*, 1990; *The Josephine Baker Story*, 1990; *Prisoners of Honor*, 1991; *Blue Ice*, 1992.

NOVEL

Connie (novelization of television series). 1985.

The value of Ron Hutchinson's drama derives largely from its consistent concentration on the Irish experience *outside* Ireland—an experience which serves in his plays to crystallize native Irish problems. The focus is only incidentally social in character. *Risky City* offers a forceful account, in the form of deathbed flashbacks, of the wasting of a Coventry—Irish youth by his inner-city environment, but his experience is not presented as a specifically Irish one. More characteristic is Hutchison's first stage play, *Says I, Says He*, in which the "Old Firm" of two picaresque Ulster navvies, the "roaring boy" Hannafin and the "clean-shave" Phelan, leave their terrorist siblings, and the beautiful dancer for whose hand they are rivals, to conquer London. Financial success for Phelan (gained, ironically, not without obscure threats of Ulster-style violence) attracts the attention of the terrorists, but turns out to be illusory, a matter of the "gab." Reunited, the two plan to leave for England again but are gunned down.

With its musical numbers (some of them uproariously obscene, all of them broadly ironic), *Says I, Says He* resembles a navvies' version of Stewart Parker's *Catchpenny Twist*—another Irish play in which the aspiring heroes ultimately fail to escape political violence. Where Parker has musicians, Hutchinson, as his title suggests, has talkers—but they are no less *performers*: the play consists of a series of comic sketch-episodes (in which the humour is not often a matter of inflection) crowned by Phelan's final fibbing performance ("You took *me* in. With *your* act"). However, in this play Hutchinson is content to revel in his characters' gift of the gab rather than to reflect upon it. The comedy is not of the serious kind.

Eejits also focuses on performers. But here the four violently argumentative members of a London-based Ceilidh band are not under threat from terrorists; rather they carry their national(ist) factionalism around with them. The same predicament receives thorough and hilarious treatment, again in connection with a performance, in *The Irish Play*. In a broken-down Midlands Irish club, the embattled President O'Higgins, striving to retain his control and dignity in the face of the machinations of the opposing Roche faction, endorses the presentation of a nationalistic historical play (agit-prop Ferguson) as part of his plan to endow the bibulous membership with a "historical perspective." As to history, he discovers that "it's all around us, that's the trouble," when, in debate, committee, and finally rehearsal, the ancient alignments of civil war emerge: "Constitutionals versus Hill-men"; Collins versus De Valera; Kerry versus Wexford. In a comic metaphor of internecine self-destruction, the building is jointly wrecked by the warring factions, leaving only the bewildered step-dancer who "plays recorder and dances in the rubble."

The playwriter Ruari in *The Irish Play* declares that he is "trying to understand my country . . . my countrymen . . . myself." Hutchinson himself has said of his most successful and best play, *Rat in the Skull*: "I wanted to write this play to sort out my personal reactions to what is going on in Ireland.

. . . You find out who you are in the process." Certainly this feels like a work energized by a personal imperative. For the first time, Hutchinson's abrasively comic dialogue and his preoccupation with performance are concentrated into a sustained scrutiny of the self-awareness and self-understanding catalyzed within an Irishman by his presence in England.

Rather than a plot, *Rat in the Skull* presents a situation and poses a question. The framework is not naturalistic. Under a screen, showing clinical photographs of Michael Patrick De Valera Demon Bomber Roche after his clinical beating-up by Detective-Inspector Nelson of the Royal Ulster Constabulary in Paddington Green police station, are played out the interrogation of Roche by Nelson which led up to the beating, and the consequent interviews, by the Irish "specialist" Superintendent Harris, of Nelson and of the young policeman detailed to be present at the interrogation. The case had been "stitched up," and Nelson had come to London only because of the possibility of the prisoner's turning informer; so why the very deliberative act of violence? The weary Harris reaches for extenuating personal circumstances (an unfaithful wife and a recently dead father), persuading Nelson to accept an "unfit discharge," but neither he nor the baffled, indifferent Constable Naylor can conceive of the complex relation between history and personal identity which renders these Irishmen intimate in conflict—to the exclusion of the Englishman —and which alone points to the explanation. Nelson's fierce parodies of sectarian rhetoric and his sudden changes of tone and address turn the interrogation into a terrible comic performance—one calculated not only to "get inside" and break Roche but also to discomfit an English public which, he senses, stereotypes him in the role of "unclean" Paddy. As Naylor, the "audience" to the interrogation, says: "Roche hasn't said a word the sod, but he's straight man to Nelson . . . it's him and Roche on me." But Nelson is also inflicted with the performer's self-scrutinizing distance. The eponymous rat-in-the-skull images the doubt and self-awareness that persuade him to "break step" for the first time with his Protestant forebears by acknowledging, through this calculated gesture of violence, that he is not a state-sanctioned fighter in a "Holy War" but rather one of "two fellas in a ditch, clubbing each other, till the one dropped dead." *Rat in the Skull* capitalizes thematically on the talent for punchy, stylized dialogue that has always been apparent in Hutchinson's work for both stage and television (*Bird of Prey* and *Connie*), and in so doing enriches that most vital tradition within Irish drama—its concern with the nature and power of rhetoric.

Since the late 1980's, Hutchinson has lived and worked in America, writing scripts for film and television. His most recent stage play could be seen as an apologia, a treatment of the playwright's "quarrel with himself" over his leaving Ireland. For D.I. Nelson there is no way out: his decisive act of violent (self-) confrontation condemns him to inevitable violent death. But for Harry Washburn, in *Pygmies in the Ruins*, an even more intricate acknowledgement of the guilty historical roots of his own personal identity sanctions self-justification and release, so that emigration—a "going *to*" America—can be distinguished from exile—a "running *from*" Ireland. Act I of *Pygmies* "takes place simultaneously in Belfast 1991 and Belfast 1871." Again, a mystery informs the action. When Washburn, a police photographer with artistic pretensions, cracks up after working on yet another (apparently) sectarian murder, he becomes obsessed with the unsolved murder in 1871 of a pathetic domestic servant-girl. In 1871 we see Dr. Mulcahy's investigation of that earlier case; though thwarted, it nonetheless reveals the dark underside of that "Progress" which has earned Belfast prosperity and civic pride. The police-photographer and the physician from Dublin are both examples of the artist as witness, intimate with, yet professionally detached from their surroundings. The double whodunit changes radically when, in Act II, the two "meet" in Washburn's hallucinatory consciousness to play out a nightmare trial-scene. Mulcahy joins with the play's other characters to embody the sick man's feelings of guilt at not only his own life and calling (with its "aesthetic of extinction") but also the "bloody knot of rope" which binds the identity of a whole culture: "the idea of the North," "the mystery of us." They are pygmies in the ruins of a city. Suicide is arrested and recovery begins only when Washburn comes to realize that the very strenuousness of his self-confrontation is a mark of the "voluntary man," the free individual. Reality returns, and Washburn, defying the charge of "quitting," prepares to leave for America with his lover and "a kind of peace."

—Paul Lawley

I

ISITT, Debbie.

Born in Birmingham, 7 February 1966. Educated at Lordswood Girls' School, Birmingham, 1977–82; Coventry Centre for the Performing Arts, 1983–85. Dancer, Unique, Birmingham, 1978–82; receptionist, Hendon Business Association, Birmingham, 1982–83; actor, Cambridge Experimental Theatre Company, European tour, 1985–86; co-founder and since 1986, artistic director, Snarling Beasties Theatre Company, Longford, Coventry; guest director, Coventry Centre for Performing Arts, 1991, Other Theatre of Comedy Trust, London, 1992, and Repertory Theatre, Heilbronn, Germany, 1992. Recipient: *Scottish Daily Express* award, 1988; Independent Theatre award, 1989; Perrier Pick of the Fringe award, 1989, 1990; *Time Out* Theatre award, 1990/91; Edinburgh Fringe Festival first, 1992. Agent: Nick Marston, A. P. Watt Ltd., 20 John Street, London WC1N 2DR. Address: c/o Snarling Beasties Coventry Touring Theatre Co-op Ltd., 36 Sydnall Road, Longford, Coventry CV6 6BW, England.

Publications

PLAYS

Gangsters (produced 1988).
Punch and Judy: The Real Story (also director: produced 1989).
Valentino (also director: produced 1990).
Femme Fatale (also director: produced 1990).
The Woman Who Cooked Her Husband (produced 1991).
You Never Know Who's Out There (produced 1992).
Out of the Ordinary (produced 1993).

TELEVISION PLAY: *The Lodger*, 1992.

THEATRICAL ACTIVITIES

DIRECTOR: **Plays**—all her own plays; *East* by Steven Berkoff, 1986.
ACTOR: **Plays**—all her own plays; *A Midsummer Night's Dream*, 1985–86.

Debbie Isitt comments:

Writing for me has to have a purpose and that purpose is usually to reach people and hopefully make them feel something, see something, hear something, think something, and maybe even do something. In my experience writing for the theatre is vitally important; I am not reliant very often on producers, publicists, marketing machines, sponsors, donors, editors, censors, men in suits and women in shoulder pads to be able to create and get my work seen. Part of this freedom comes from directing and appearing in my own work; I only have to find a willing person to let me have a space, find others willing to push themselves and take a few risks and put it on. This is the most important bit—to put it on and say—this is what I wanted to say and it's how I wanted to say it—it is a truthful interpretation of what I intended and let people take from it what they wish. I could not stand to be part of a system that compromised my plays, that shaped them and bent them and formed them into someone else's. If a writer is not herself behind the words then she is not a writer. She should put herself on the line and create dramas that draw people into her world just for the duration of the play; even if the world is one from her imagination it is HER imagination and no one else's that we should be sharing. So much emphasis is put on criteria for funding, fitting in, opting out. I would like to think I can maintain control of my writing, although as I move some way into film I begin to see that things are very difficult, there seems to be little room for guts, imagination, and risk.

I tend to choose themes that are at once personal and close to home while smacking of larger social issues. Heterosexual relationships and the dark forces seething behind contemporary marriage is a theme that I am drawn to time and again. Social myths and secrets that we hide and disguise and twist to fit in and conform. Domestic violence, tranvestism, betrayal, phobias, lies are the stuff my plays are made of. They are real and surreal fusing together. Music is a massive influence, especially the great works of contemporary heros like Frank Sinatra, Ella Fitzgerald, Patsy Cline. The woman's psyche being put centre stage is another of my interests; I like to put women into certain situations to see how they react and then make them do things and think things and say things that we're not supposed to and see how the men react. It's really a very interesting process. I also like to leave room for movement and mime and visual techniques often influenced by films and incorporate it on the stage. Above all I think I like to be truthful to the characters, the situation, and myself. The plays are usually funny even though they are often dark. I cannot stand to get depressed—we need to recognize the funny side of pain and guilt and grief. We also need fight and spirit and punch and my plays must be performed with pace and vitality. I am not the sentimental type—just the mental type.

Debbie Isitt's plays are inextricably linked to her productions in which she usually also acts. The company was formed in 1986 and called Snarling Beasties (Steven Berkoff's creative slang for testicles) because Isitt fancied the idea of strait-laced bureaucrats unwittingly referring to male genitalia in the course of deciding whether or not to give the company money. After their inaugural production of Berkoff's East at Edinburgh, it fell upon Isitt to come up with some follow-up material. Not for her the luxury of dwelling on every syllable; her best work has been produced under the pressure of the deadline of the Edinburgh Festival. Punch and Judy, Femme Fatale, and The Woman Who Cooked Her Husband are a trio of plays exploring the underbelly of heterosexual relationships on the themes of wife-battering, transvestism, and adultery respectively. In production her words are supported by an expressionistic, mimetic presentation of character, loud popular music, and a set that hits you between the eyes. The effect is intensely theatrical and reminiscent of Berkoff in the aggressive use of rhyming couplets. Such an upfront presentation is exhilarating to watch, although sometimes one wonders whether it is the raucous music that is providing the uplift rather than Isitt's words.

Judging from Isitt's work, she is not a woman in need of courses in assertiveness. Her approach is unashamedly partisan: men appear as boorish, unimaginative wimps with little or nothing to recommend them. *The Woman Who Cooked Her Husband* was inspired by the real-life case of Nicholas Boyce in 1985 in which Boyce chopped his wife up and distributed the pieces because he could no longer stand her nagging. The Judge, summing up, said that Boyce was sorely provoked and he only served six years for manslaughter. In contrast, Sara Thornton is serving life for killing her husband after being abused for years. Such an imbalance of justice fuels Isitt's anger. *The Woman Who Cooked Her Husband* depicts a triangular relationship between Kenneth, his wife Hilary, and Laura, his mistress. Kenneth is torn between Laura's skills in bed and Hilary's in the kitchen. Hilary has devoted her life to serving up tempting delicacies in the belief that a well-fed man will never leave her. Through flashback, we see Kenneth's first encounters with the sulky Laura who can hardly summon up enough energy to open a packet of fish fingers. Cringing, shifty, and a poor liar, Kenneth continues to meander between the two until Laura takes matters into her own hands and spills the beans to Hilary, forcing Kenneth to leave her. At a strange reunion, Kenneth salivates as he anticipates his first good meal for a long time, but Hilary, finally supported by Laura, has other ideas for the menu.

There is no doubt that Kenneth is the most unpleasant character on stage and there can be few audiences who wouldn't cheer Hilary on in her grisly deed. But Isitt also criticises the wife's tendency to blame "the other woman" instead of her spouse. The woman, it seems, is seen as inadequate if she is left and criticised as a homewrecker if she does the leaving. Isitt doesn't see that marriage has much to offer a woman. So one-sided and dogmatic is the approach that it can inspire resistance in an audience. It is the black humour that transforms the bile into something more memorable.

Femme Fatale, the second play in the trilogy, is more complex because for once Isitt doesn't have all the answers. Georgia and Jimmy could be a model couple, with lots of disposable income and a good sex life, only Jimmy is drawn irresistibly towards a black cubicle at the back of the stage where he is transformed into Jessica. Apart from the shock and distaste, what enrages Georgia is that Jessica should be such a paragon of femininity, lying on the sofa painting her nails and eager to do all she can to make their domestic life run smoothly. Her perfection challenges Georgia's refusal to be a slave to the sink or her husband. Jimmy likes to dress up because he says it makes him feel "free from pressure." But being a woman is far from being free of pressure. Isitt tentatively explores why transvestites are drawn to such stereotypical images of femininity, tottering around on high heels and crowned with their beehive hairdos—everything that feminists are trying to escape. As Georgia gets more aggressive, so Jimmy becomes more passive. Beneath the feminist rhetoric, there is some sympathy for the man who feels he has to adopt the clothes of a woman in order to explore the more feminine side of his nature. But Isitt never loses sight of the fact that discovering one's husband dressed in a pair of one's knickers does have a funny side.

Since the trilogy the Other Theatre of Comedy Trust commissioned *You Never Know Who's Out There*, which explores the seedy, racist and misogynist world of the Northern club and is reminiscent of Trevor Griffiths's *Comedians*. A power struggle amongst the performers results in much spilling of blood but little illumination. Snarling is Isitt's hallmark. Now that we know that she is not afraid to show her teeth, it would make a change if she occasionally concealed them.

—Jane Edwardes

J

JEFFREYS, Stephen.

Born in London, 22 April 1950. Educated at Stationers' Company's School, London, 1961–68; Southampton University, B.A. (honours) in English language and literature, 1972, and research student for M.Phil, 1972–74. Driver for Silexeine Paints, London, 1969, and Jeffreys Brothers (Billiards) Ltd., London, 1972–74; teacher, Upton House Comprehensive School, London, 1974–75; lecturer in drama and English, Cumbria College of Art and Design, 1975–78; writer-in-residence, Brewery Arts Centre, and founder, Pocket Theatre, Cumbria, 1978–80; writer-in-residence, Paines Plough, London, 1987–89; since 1991 part-time literary associate, Royal Court Theatre, London. Recipient: *Sunday Times* National Student Drama award, 1977; Edinburgh Fringe first, 1978, 1984; *Evening Standard* award, 1989; Critics Circle award, 1989; *Plays and Players* award, 1989. Agent: Tom Erhardt, Casarotto Ramsay Ltd., National House, 60–66 Wardour Street, London W1V 3HP, England.

Publications

PLAYS

Where the Tide Has Rolled You (produced 1973).
Counterpoint (produced 1975).
Like Dolls or Angels (produced 1977).
Mobile 4 (produced 1978). 1979.
Darling Buds of Kendal (produced 1978).
Year of the Open Fist (for children; produced 1978).
The Vigilante Trail (produced 1979).
Jubilee Too (produced 1980).
Watches of the Night (broadcast, 1981; produced 1981).
Imagine (produced 1981).
Peer Gynt with Gerry Mulgrew, adaptation of the play by Henrik Ibsen (produced 1981).
Hard Times, adaptation of the novel by Dickens (produced 1982). 1987.
Futures (produced 1984).
Carmen 1936, adaptation of the novel by Prosper Mérimée (produced 1984).
Clearing House (produced 1984).
Returning Fire (produced 1985).
Desire (produced 1986).
The Garden of Eden (produced 1986).

Valued Friends (produced 1989). In *First Run 2*, edited by Kate Harwood, 1990.
The Clink (produced 1990). 1990.
A Jovial Crew, adaptation of the play by Richard Brome (produced 1992). 1992.
A Going Concern (produced 1993). 1993.

RADIO PLAYS: *Like Dolls or Angels*, 1979; *Watches of the Night*, 1981; *Absolute Decline*, 1984; *Carmen 1936*, 1992.

THEATRICAL ACTIVITIES

DIRECTOR: **Plays**—*Stone* by Edward Bond, *Games* by James Saunders, *The Vigilante Trail*, all 1979.

Stephen Jeffreys comments:

I think of myself in the widest sense as an entertainer, and I write plays partly out of a desire to create exciting events. I like audiences to laugh, to be moved, and to be confronted—to have a big experience. I am interested in telling stories and use different techniques—naturalism, epic theatre—in the service of narrative. As a playwright working in live theatre I want to give audiences an evening they cannot have in front of the television or in the cinema, an experience which depends on their sharing a space with live actors.

Stephen Jeffreys is one of the most strikingly versatile British playwrights to have come to the fore during the 1980's. His output spans a number of ingenious translations and dramatic adaptations as well as original plays in an impressive variety of genres. The most characteristic features of his work are an unerring comic instinct, a shrewd eye for topical relevance, and a brilliant theatrical nous for turning limited resources to rich account.

After the success of *Like Dolls or Angels*, his "study of a stuntman on the skids," Jeffreys was involved with the setting-up of Pocket Theatre Cumbria, which was to become one of the most successful of the small-scale touring companies. His association with the company continued through the premieres of several of his plays including *Watches of the Night* and *Futures*, and allowed Jeffreys to develop a natural talent for writing with specific requirements in mind. He also began to explore subject matter to which he would return one way or another: his early play about John Lennon, *Imagine*, evinced a fascination with the world of popular music that crops up to telling effect in his later work (it's suggestively used to mark the passage of time in *Valued Friends* and to give one of the characters a secret life in *A Going Concern*, a new play based on the Jeffreys family business of making billiard tables, which is as yet unproduced).

Pocket Theatre also first produced Jeffreys's version of Dickens's *Hard Times*. This model of how to preserve the quintessential flavours of a prose writer in a purely theatrical format has deservedly become a staple for touring companies both in Britain and abroad. Other adaptations to his name are *Peer Gynt* and most recently *A Jovial Crew*, from the original by Richard Brome, for a production by Max Stafford-Clark with the Royal Shakespeare Company that has been applauded for its deft underscoring of modern resonances in pre-Civil War drama.

The same gift for dynamic interpretation of historical material is evident in *Carmen 1936*, his play about the Spanish Civil War produced by the Scottish company Communicado, which won a Fringe First in 1984. In the late 1980s, Jeffreys wrote two fine plays on occasional pretexts: *Returning Fire*, which celebrated the return of Halley's Comet, and *The Garden of Eden*, a large-scale piece for the community of Carlisle that used a cast of 150. The first of these plays was produced by Paines Plough, the new writing company for whom he also wrote *The Clink*. This Jacobean revenge comedy may have felt over-long in the theatre, but it nonetheless displays a vivid control of pastiche and cunningly pitched anachronism.

This body of work displays Jeffreys's impressive knack of finding the right dramatic idiom for each project, his ability to write to the strengths of a particular company or to tease theatrical magic out of the narrowest of briefs. By the mid-1980's Jeffreys had confirmed his potential as a collaborative writer *par excellence*, a strikingly ingenious dramatic craftsman, but not one, perhaps, with a distinctive personal voice. *Valued Friends*, produced at Hampstead Theatre in 1989 and revived there a year later, marked a new leap forward in that it more conspicuously exploited the writer's own experience of the here and now. This superbly written response to the property boom is palpably founded on an insider's observations of the dramatic situation at hand, and manipulates the sympathies of the audience with ironical aplomb. The play tells the story of a group of friends who have shared a flat since they were students. When a property developer tries to buy them out, their attitudes and relationships become subject to a process of erosion. The major decisions of their lives are eventually governed by the housing market and the greed it inexorably instils. Jeffreys's handling of the characters is wry and clear-sighted, but also notably tolerant. Many of his contemporaries, having seized on the same scenario, would have turned in a more two-dimensional issue-drama. It's not that Jeffreys's humour and wit shirk any political responsibility: they're simply deployed with a sure sense of how the audience's desire to identify with the characters will entangle them in the same quagmire of values and commitments. The play deservedly won awards for its author, and interestingly took on new shades and tonalities in its second production, after the boom had turned to bust—a measure of its subtlety and stature, which many a more conventional critique of Thatcherism would never have been able to emulate.

—Matthew Lloyd

JELLICOE, (Patricia) Ann.

Born in Middlesbrough, Yorkshire, 15 July 1927. Educated at Polam Hall, Darlington, County Durham; Queen Margaret's, Castle Howard, Yorkshire; Central School of Speech and Drama, London (Elsie Fogarty prize, 1947), 1944–47. Married 1) C. E. Knight-Clarke in 1950 (marriage dissolved 1961); 2) Roger Mayne in 1962, one son and one daughter. Actress, stage manager, and director, in London and the provinces, 1947–51; founding director,

Cockpit Theatre Club, London, 1952–54; lecturer and director, Central
School of Speech and Drama, 1954–56; literary manager, Royal Court
Theatre, London, 1973–75; founding director, 1979–85, and president, 1986,
Colway Theatre Trust. O.B.E. (Officer, Order of the British Empire), 1984.
Agent: Casarotto Ramsay Ltd., National House, 60–66 Wardour Street,
London W1V 3HP, England.

Publications

PLAYS

Rosmersholm, adaptation of the play by Ibsen (also director: produced 1952;
revised version produced 1959). 1960.
The Sport of My Mad Mother (also co-director: produced 1958). In *The
Observer Plays*, 1958; revised version, 1964; with *The Knack*, 1964.
The Lady from the Sea, adaptation of a play by Ibsen (produced 1961).
The Knack (produced 1961; also co-director, 1962). 1962.
The Seagull, with Adriadne Nicolaeff, adaptation of a play by Chekhov
(produced 1964).
Der Freischütz, translation of the libretto by Friedrich Kind, music by Weber
(produced 1964).
Shelley; or, The Idealist (also director: produced 1965). 1966.
The Rising Generation (produced 1967). In *Playbill 2*, edited by Alan
Durband, 1969.
The Giveaway (produced 1968). 1970.
You'll Never Guess (also director: produced 1973). In *3 Jelliplays*, 1975.
*Two Jelliplays: Clever Elsie, Smiling John, Silent Peter, and A Good Thing or a
Bad Thing* (also director: produced 1974). In *3 Jelliplays*, 1975.
3 Jelliplays (for children; includes *You'll Never Guess*; *Clever Elsie, Smiling
John, Silent Peter*; *A Good Thing or a Bad Thing*). 1975.
Flora and the Bandits (also director: produced 1976).
The Reckoning (also director: produced 1978).
The Bargain (also director: produced 1979).
The Tide (also director: produced 1980).
The Western Women, music by Nick Brace, adaptation of a story by Fay
Weldon (also co-director: produced 1984).
Changing Places (produced 1992).

OTHER

Some Unconscious Influences in the Theatre. 1967.
Devon: A Shell Guide, with Roger Mayne. 1975.
Community Plays: How to Put Them On. 1987.

THEATRICAL ACTIVITIES

DIRECTOR: Plays—*The Confederacy* by Vanbrugh, 1952; *The Frogs* by
Aristophanes, 1952; *Miss Julie* by Strindberg, 1952; *Rosmersholm* by Ibsen,
1952; *Saint's Day* by John Whiting, 1953; *The Comedy of Errors*, 1953;
Olympia by Ferenč Molnár, 1953; *The Sport of My Mad Mother* (co-director,
with George Devine), 1958; *For Children* by Keith Johnstone, 1958; *The
Knack* (co-director, with Keith Johnstone), 1962; *Skyvers* by Barry Reckord,

1963; *Shelley*, 1965; *You'll Never Guess*, 1973; *Two Jelliplays*, 1974; *A Worthy Guest* by Paul Bailey, 1974; *Six of the Best*, 1974; *Flora and the Bandits*, 1976; *The Reckoning*, 1978; *The Bargain*, 1979; *The Tide*, 1980; *The Poor Man's Friend* by Howard Barker, 1981; *The Garden* by Charles Wood, 1982; *The Western Women* (co-director, with Chris Fog and Sally-Ann Lomax), 1984; *Entertaining Strangers* by David Edgar, 1985.

The major plays by new young writers in London between 1956 and 1959 included *Look Back in Anger, The Birthday Party, Roots, Serjeant Musgrave's Dance, A Resounding Tinkle, The Long and the Short and the Tall, Flowering Cherry, Five Finger Exercise, The Hostage, A Taste of Honey*—and Ann Jellicoe's *The Sport of My Mad Mother* at the Royal Court, the heart of this activity.

Since this impressive debut, Jellicoe has written only three other full-length stage plays, two of them slight. The 16 brief scenes of *Shelley* take the poet from his Oxford years, through two marriages, to Harriet Westbrook and Mary Godwin, to his drowning in Italy. *Shelley*, subtitled "the Idealist," is written as though for a 19th-century touring company of twelve: heavy, walking gentleman, juvenile, and so on. Jellicoe remarks that as a writer she is tackling a new set of problems here, working "within a set narrative framework—partly for the sheer technical discipline involved." Shelley interests her because he is very young, and trying to be good: "the problems of goodness which are so much more interesting than those of evil." He is tragic because of "his blindness to the frailty of human nature." *Shelley* is a flat work, with conspicuous explanatory sections in which the poet talks like a letter or tract.

The Giveaway turns on a suburban housewife who wins a competition prize of ten years' supply of cornflakes (which are conspicuously on stage); she has had to pretend to be under 14. While the only production may not have done it justice, *The Giveaway* seems to be a clumsy attempt to write a farce, with a hint of satire on consumerism and a touch of the kind of non-verbal comedy Jellicoe had written earlier.

Jellicoe's best play, *The Knack*, is an exuberant, liberating, youthful comedy. Three young men share a flat: Tolen (he has only this one curious name), who has "the knack" of success with women; likeable Colin, who lacks it and envies Tolen; and the garrulous Tom, half outside the sex war. Enter Nancy, a lost, gawky, 17-year-old Northerner, looking for the YWCA, who will give Tolen a chance to demonstrate his knack. The staccato, repetitive dialogue skims along like jazz, and is sometimes hard to follow on the page. A bed provides comic business (they pretend it is a piano), as do entries through the window. An undercurrent is Tolen's Nazi characteristics, and whether negotiation is possible with such people. (The film, scripted by Charles Wood and directed by Richard Lester, is substantially changed, and also great fun.)

Jellicoe's *succès d'estime, The Sport of My Mad Mother*, is much more unusual and demanding. This is about four London teenagers and three people they come across, a liberal American, a retarded girl of 13, and Greta, an Australian who comes to represent also the Hindu goddess of destruction and creation, Kali. Yet character, plot, dialogue hardly matter. This is a piece to be brought to life by a director, and, to make reading really difficult, stage-directions are few. The form is non-linear; Jellicoe writes in the Preface to the revised text of 1964 that the play "was not written intellectually according to a prearranged plan. It was shaped bit by bit until the bits felt right in relation to each other and to the whole. It is an anti-intellect play not only because it is about irrational forces and urges but because one hopes it will reach the audience directly through rhythm, noise and music. . . . Very often the words counterpoint the action or intensify the action by conflicting with it." *The Sport of My Mad Mother* is highly original (especially for Britain and for the 1950's) in its Artaudian use of ritual, in its stress on physical expressiveness, in its use of speech and drums for rhythms, in its audacious non-literary form and apparent shapelessness, and in its search for the roots of arbitrary violence. Proper recognition and appreciation will require a readily available film version, as yet unmade.

In 1972 Jellicoe told Carol Dix in the *Guardian*: "Directing, as I see it, is an interpretative art, and writing is a creative art, and it's a bloody relief not to have to be creative any longer. The impulse to create is linked with the aggressive instinct."

A ten-year silence ended when in 1978 Jellicoe moved to Lyme Regis, Dorset; she has since staged numerous community plays in the southwest. These ambitious works involve many local people (up to 180 onstage), use the town as the setting and have a promenade production. Jellicoe wrote the first, *The Reckoning*, about the Monmouth Rebellion of 1685. Allen Saddler described it in *Plays and Players*: "It is all action. The mayor and his cronies scramble about in a frenzy, people rush by in terror, beg for mercy or confide strange secrets in your ear. A girl who is pregnant by a Catholic finds herself in a strange dilemma, proclamations are read from various parts of the hall. Soldiers burst in. Bands play. Prisoners are dragged off screaming. Brawls break out just where you are standing. Events proceed so quickly that there is no time to examine the Catholic or the Protestant case." *The Western Women*, about the part played by women in the siege of Lyme in the Civil War, was rewritten by Jellicoe from a script by Fay Weldon. Another local history piece, *The Bargain*, concerned Judge Jeffreys and was commissioned by the Southwest Music Theatre. Jellicoe in her essay in *Women and Theatre* writes of the satisfaction of this community activity: "It was extraordinary, the people of Lyme, in rehearsal and in performance, watching a play about themselves. There is a unique atmosphere. It's partly the promenade style of performance, partly that the play is specially written for the town, but it has never failed, that excitement, they just go wild. . . . What I love about it is slowly building something in the community."

In May 1992 Jellicoe took up the challenge of devising a community play for Woking, Surrey, a place lacking much history or sense of identity. Her *Changing Places* focused on women, on Ethel Smythe, composer and militant suffragette, contrasting her with a working-class woman—outside the middle-class movement for votes-for-women—who achieves self-realisation as a nurse in World War I. Jellicoe appears unlikely to return to the Royal Court, or to the West End, as her fulfilment now comes from her community work in the West Country.

—Malcolm Page

JOHNSON, Terry.

Born 20 December 1955. Educated at Queens School, Bushey, Hertfordshire; University of Birmingham, 1973–76, B.A. in drama 1976. Actor in late 1970's, and director. Recipient: *Plays and Players* award, 1982; *Evening Standard* award, 1983; John Whiting award, 1991. Lives in London. Agent: Phil Kelvin, Goodwin Associates, 12 Rabbit Row, London W8 4DX, England.

Publications

PLAYS

Amabel (produced 1979).
Days Here So Dark (produced 1981).
Insignificance (produced 1982). 1982.
Bellevue (produced 1983).
Unsuitable for Adults (produced 1984). 1985.
Cries from the Mammal House (produced 1984).
Tuesday's Child, with Kate Lock (televised 1985; produced 1986). With *Time Trouble*, 1987.
Time Trouble (televised 1985). With *Tuesday's Child*, 1987.
Imagine Drowning (produced 1991). 1991.
Hysteria; or Fragments of an Analysis of an Obsessional Neurosis (produced 1993). 1993.

SCREENPLAYS: *Insignificance*, 1985; *Killing Time*, 1985.

TELEVISION PLAYS: *Time Trouble*, 1985; *Tuesday's Child*, with Kate Lock, 1985; *Way Upstream*, adaptation of the play by Alan Ayckbourn, 1988.

THEATRICAL ACTIVITIES

DIRECTOR: **Plays**—*The Woolgatherer* by William Mastrosimone, 1985; *I've Been Running* by Clare McIntyre, 1986; *Candy and Shelley Go to the Desert* by Paula Cizmar, 1986; *Bedroom Farce* by Alan Ayckbourn, 1987; *Children of the Dust* by Anne Aylor, 1988; *Rag Doll* by Catherine Johnson, 1988; *Sleeping Nightie* by Victoria Hardie, 1989; *Death of a Salesman* by Arthur Miller, 1989; *Just Between Ourselves* by Alan Ayckbourn, 1991. **Television**— *Time Trouble*, 1985; *Way Upstream* by Alan Ayckbourn, 1988; *Rag Doll* by Catherine Johnson, 1988; *The Lorelei* by Nick Dunning, 1989; *Man in Heaven* (episode 3: *Falling in Love*), 1990; *Ball on the Slates* by Bryan Elsley, 1990.

Boldness of conception and a subtle control in execution are richly combined in Terry Johnson's drama. Thus *Insignificance*, despite all the potential for lurid sensation in a scenario which brings together an Einstein-figure, a Marilyn Monroe-figure, a Joe DiMaggio-figure, and a Senator McCarthy-figure in a New York hotel room in 1953, impresses as a sustained dramatic scrutiny, within a basically naturalistic framework, of the nature of celebrity and of the human need for celebrities. It is a play about wants. The far-from-dumb-blond Actress arrives at the Professor's hotel room wanting to talk to him, to prove her knowledge (of his theories especially), and finally to sleep with him; the Ballplayer wants the Actress to come home and *make* a home; the Senator, meanwhile, wants the Professor to co-operate with him and his committee, and to back an anti-Soviet nuclear programme. The Professor himself wants only to be left alone to retreat with his calculations about the shape of the universe. He it is who articulates a Theory of *existential* Relativity, concerning the need of each individual to feel a centre of identity which in modern Western culture results in the erection of "false gods" as guarantors and measures of personal wholeness—the neon-lit image of the Actress's famous skirt-blown-up pose; the Ballplayer immortalized on a million bubble-gum cards; the omniscient Professor dubbed "True Child of the Universe." Yet the Actress, whose desperate desire for a child is thwarted even within the play itself (she miscarries when the Senator strikes her), ultimately recognizes the despair implicit in the Professor's refusal to confront his own fear—of an impending nuclear devastation for which he feels responsible. The repulsive Senator, self-proclaimed "gentleman and . . . solipsist," is the extreme embodiment of the "madman's scheme of things" that the Professor and the Actress, in their different ways, both diagnose as general: so convinced is he of a self-centred universe that he can claim to have *invented* them all to fulfil his purposes.

The ability of Johnson fully and powerfully to *dramatize* complex ideas and arguments is also evident in *Unsuitable for Adults*. The setting—an upstairs pub-theatre in Soho—is very different from that of *Insignificance*, but the concentration is again upon a vital lack of personal identity in modern culture. The resolution is gender-based. The feminist alternative comedian Kate attempts to convince the asthmatic lunchtime stripper Tish of her unthinking collusion with a culture which turns women into images and potential objects of violence; but Kate's real *experience* of feminism and her extrication from her own hopeless involvement with Nick, a brilliant impressionist whose pretence and avoidance of moral responsibility in his private life are an extension of his act, can take place only with self-acknowledgement and self-understanding. While the other acts—Tish's schoolgirl strip, Nick's impressions, the magician Keith's feeble escapism—provide images of fantasy or compensation for an audience which as a result of that remains "captive," Kate attempts aggressively to confront both them and herself with her scabrous Lenny Bruce-style act (a considerable opportunity for the performer). But her routine gradually falls apart, and verbal violence comes to a cathartic physical climax when she deliberately mutilates a finger: "the body turns against the mind and says, 'Enough. I want to stop this now.'" In the play's Epilogue Kate withdraws to a Dartmoor cottage with Tish (who is recovering from a serious asthma attack). The performances are over, and the stripping is now a discovery of truth, both moral and physical: it reveals an essentially *natural* identity in which both women partake.

The very considerable philosophical ambition of *Insignificance* and *Unsuitable for Adults* is fully disclosed only as the carefully worked dramatic pattern of each play becomes apparent. Each is notable for a stylistic texture which is varied and flexible, natural and uninsistent; climaxes are violent, but there are no shocks of structure or style. In *Cries from the Mammal*

House, however, there is a clear relation between philosophical ambition and theatrical experiment. Hitherto in Johnson's work, metaphor has provided a crucial means of dialectical organization within a broadly naturalistic structure; but now a single, diagnostic dramatic metaphor is proposed at the outset and subsequently explored in a theatrical mode replete with bizarre detail, blackly comic juxtaposition, and stylistic variation. The point of reference is expressionism—in plot as in style. When a half-Celtic bastard bird-conservationist arrives at the zoo kept by his brother for the funeral of their father, the zoo's founder, he finds it in a state of terminal decay. Despite the efforts of his wife, Anne (who falls in love with the visitor), the despairing brother Alan is impotent to reverse the trend of death and morbid preservation begun by the morally corrupt founding father himself, and the zoo is sold. Renewal comes only after the "Birdman" David has undertaken a "dreamlike" journey to Mauritius in search of the pink pigeon and returns to England, having experienced the company of strange colonial survivors and kidnap by a Creole tribe, with a real live Dodo. The zoo animals have by now been killed, prior to his suicide, by Alan; but as the play ends, David and Anne, together with her daughter Sally (formerly traumatized but now released) and his three Mauritian companions, plan a "new lease of life" for the zoo—under the sign not of the decadent Western father but of an Eastern enlightenment (and with the "absurd cry" of the Dodo).

Johnson's recent play, *Imagine Drowning*, also has a richly symbolic setting with much characteristically grotesque detail: a chaotic guest-house on the Cumbrian coast in the shadow (or "glow") of Sellafield Nuclear Power station. Into this modern "haunted house," with its bizarre menagerie, comes a young woman called Jane, who is in search of her radical journalist husband David. An intricately worked double time-scheme enables the intertwined presentation of the crises of self undergone by both David (a few weeks earlier) and Jane. David gives way to a reactionary individualist pessimism and confronts the "cold, black nugget" of the homicidal impulse within himself; Jane experiences the depressive "schism" of mind and body. However, the play's resolution is unconvincing because the full dramatic realization of the "journey of the soul" is limited by the presence of two figures of ethical authority through whom the playwright offers explicit diagnosis and commentary. Both figures are, inevitably, marginal to society, if not actually outside it: the severely disabled Tom, whose political activism is presented with affectionate (self-) irony, attempts to stir the couple to political action, and catalyses Jane's confrontation of her relation to David; Buddy, "grounded" American ex-astronaut and now mystical beach-bum, forces each to be "baptized into the new age" by immersion in the sea, thus effecting a death-and-rebirth consonant with his holistic philosophy. The dominance of these figures inhibits exploration of the play's most interesting character, the mysterious, eccentric survivor, Brenda, "a very slow woman" who keeps the guest house. Buddy's philosophy recognizes "connection," but the causal link made by the playwright between the deathly effects, moral and physical, of Sellafield, and the homicidal activities of Brenda's imprisoned mass-murderer husband, seems rather a matter of ideological correctness than of the fresh perception of the relation between self and society of which we know Johnson to be capable. The large symbolic ambitions of this "dream play about the pain we're all immersed in" are frustrated by the very urgency of the need to deliver a message about the "moral, political and sexual confusion" of the 1980s and the possibility of renewal in the future.

—Paul Lawley

JOHNSTONE, Keith.

Born in Brixham, Devon. Married to Ingrid Johnston. Director of the Theatre Studio, 1965–66, and associate director, 1966, Royal Court Theatre, London; director, Theatre Machine Improvisational Group; taught at Royal Academy of Dramatic Art, London, and Statens Teaterskole, Copenhagen. Currently associate professor of drama, University of Calgary. Co-director, Loose Moose Theatre Company, Calgary. Address: Department of Drama, University of Calgary, Calgary, Alberta T2N 1N4, Canada.

Publications

PLAYS

Brixham Regatta, and For Children (produced 1958).
The Nigger Hunt (produced 1959).
Gloomy Go Round (produced 1959).
Philoctetes, adaptation of the play by Sophocles (produced 1964).
Clowning (produced 1965).
The Performing Giant, music by Marc Wilkinson (also co-director: produced 1966).
The Defeat of Giant Big Nose (for children; also director: produced 1966).
Instant Theatre (produced 1966).
Caught in the Act (produced 1966).
The Time Machine (produced 1967).
The Martians (produced 1967).
Moby Dick: A Sir and Perkins Story (produced 1967).
Wakefield Mystery Cycle (also director: produced 1968).
Der Fisch (also director: produced 1971).
The Last Bird (produced 1973). 1981.
Shot by an Elk (produced 1974).
Robinson Crusoe (produced 1976).

OTHER

Impro: Improvisation and the Theatre. 1979; revised edition, 1981.

THEATRICAL ACTIVITIES

DIRECTOR: **Plays**—*Eleven Plus* by Kon Fraser, 1960; *The Maimed* by Bartho Smit, 1960; *The Triple Alliance* by J.A. Cuddon, 1961; *Sacred Cow* by Kon Fraser, 1962; *Day of the Prince* by Frank Hilton, 1962, 1963; *The Pope's Wedding* by Edward Bond, 1962; *The Knack* by Ann Jellicoe (co-director, with Jellicoe), 1962; *Edgware Road Blues* by Leonard Kingston, 1963; *The Cresta Run* by N.F. Simpson, 1965; *The Performing Giant* (co-director, with

William Gaskill), 1966; *The Defeat of Giant Big Nose*, 1966; *Wakefield Mystery Cycle*, 1968; *Der Fisch*, 1971; *Waiting for Godot* by Beckett, 1972.

Keith Johnstone comments:

(1973) I began writing plays when the Royal Court commissioned me in 1957. They were about physical sensations, often sensations experienced in infancy, expressed in visual images.

When I began writing again in 1966 it was only to provide suitable scripts for improvisors and short "entertainment" pieces. Most of my work from 1965 to 1970 was with my group Theatre Machine. We toured in many parts of England, gave demonstrations to teachers and trainee teachers, and hammered out an effective formula. *Instant Theatre* was the Theatre Machine in an early show. We were the only British group to be invited to Expo 67 in Montreal, and toured in Denmark, Germany, Belgium, Yugoslavia, and Austria.

I am at present writing an account of my improvisational methods, and am returning to writing "real" plays. *Brixham Regatta* was given a Sunday night production at the Mermaid in about 1969 and it looked O.K. to me. This has made me feel that there might be some point in trying a serious work again.

I dislike "sets." I think theatre should be popular. I think theatre should "freak-out" the audience rather than offer conversation pieces. Favourite play — *Do It!* performed by the Pip Simmons Group.

Keith Johnstone's work has been relatively little exposed and it can hardly be claimed that he has had much direct influence on the British theatre; but in a more subtle and pervasive manner, his work played an important role in the British theatre of the 1960's. To a large extent this was initially confined to his work at the Royal Court for the English Stage Company during one of its most creative periods. Associated with the Court from 1957, he was a co-director of the 1965–66 season and director of the Theatre Studio, from which emerged Johnstone's Theatre Machine Group, whose work, based on improvisations, has influenced a large number of younger English actors and writers.

The first efforts of the Court Studio to gain widespread attention consisted of a 1965 Christmas show, *Clowning*. Designed for both children and adults, each performance was unpredictable and different, basing itself on mime and improvisation exercises originated in the Court's acting classes. Its theme, broadly, was the making of clowns, examining whether and how they can be trained. Taking a few basic situations from which the actors could take off into improvisation, the show intriguingly experimented with that sense of the unexpected and dangerous which Johnstone evidently sees as a major clowning skill, in its concentration on the immediacy of the theatrical moment. Some aspects of this work were elaborated in Johnstone's most interesting play to date, *The Performing Giant*, produced in a double-bill with Cregan's *Transcending* at the Court in 1966. The play received a poor reception at the time; critics seemed to lack a critical vocabulary with which to cope with a kind of theatre which later many other experimental groups were to make easier for them. Basically the play is an allegory of the adolescent's attempt to understand the mysteries and puzzles of the outside world as well as the processes of the developing body; a group of pot-holers encounter a giant and explore the terrain of his inside as a potential tourist Disneyland only to have the giant rebel and defeat them with the aid of the female pot-holer with whom he falls in love. To most critics the play seemed merely strange and extravagant; charging it with whimsical obscurity in its initial premise, they missed the denseness of the developing fantasy and the way in which Johnstone's allegory worked, not as a planned series of concepts but as an immediate theatrical experience, using a loose basic structure as a starting-point in a manner parallel to the work of another Court dramatist, Ann Jellicoe, in *The Sport of My Mad Mother*. It would be interesting to see *The Performing Giant* revived, for it is a more important play than was noticed at the time.

Johnstone's other work in England has been mainly in the shape of further Theatre Machine shows, each one progressively more adventurous, or of adaptations (such as his excellent version of Sophocles's *Philoctetes*). His sense of the possibilities of theatre, coupled with his ability to work within the terms of fantasy without sentimentality or whimsy, marks him as an original voice too rarely heard.

—Alan Strachan

K

KEANE, John B(rendan).

Born in Listowel, County Kerry, 21 July 1928. Educated at Saint Michael's College, Listowel, graduated 1947. Married Mary O'Connor in 1955; three sons and one daughter. Chemist's assistant, 1946–51; street sweeper and furnace operator, Northampton, England, 1952–54. Since 1955 pub owner-operator, Listowel. Weekly columnist Limerick *Leader* and Dublin *Evening Herald*. Since 1973 president, Irish PEN. D. Litt: Trinity College, Dublin, 1977; D.F.A.: Marymount Manhattan College, New York, 1984. Address: 37 William Street, Listowel, County Kerry, Ireland.

Publications

PLAYS

Sive (produced 1959). 1959.
Sharon's Grave (produced 1960). 1960.
The Highest House on the Mountain (produced 1961). 1961.
Many Young Men of Twenty (produced 1961). 1961; in *Seven Irish Plays 1946–1964*, edited by Robert Hogan, 1967.
No More in Dust (produced 1962).
Hut 42 (produced 1963). 1963.
The Man from Clare (produced 1963). 1963.
The Year of the Hiker (produced 1964). 1964.
The Field (produced 1965). 1967.
The Roses of Tralee (produced 1966).
The Rain at the End of the Summer (produced 1967). 1967.
Big Maggie (produced 1969). 1969.
Faoiseamh (produced 1970).
The Change in Mame Fadden (produced 1971). 1973.
Moll (produced 1971). 1971, revised edition, 1991.
The One-Way Ticket (produced 1972). 1972.
Values: The Spraying of John O'Dovey, Backwater, and The Pure of Heart (produced 1973; *The Pure of Heart* produced 1985). 1973.
The Crazy Wall (produced 1973). 1974.
Matchmaker (produced 1975).
The Good Thing (produced 1976). 1976.
The Buds of Ballybunion (produced 1979). 1979.
The Chastitute (produced 1980). 1981.
Three Plays (includes *Sive, The Field, Big Maggie*). 1990.

Radio Plays: *Barbara Shearing*, 1959; *A Clutch of Duckeggs*, 1970; *The War Crime*, 1976 (UK); *The Talk Specific*, 1979; *The Battle of Ballybooley*, 1980.

NOVELS
The Bodhrán Makers. 1986.
Durango. 1992.

SHORT STORIES
Death Be Not Proud and Other Stories. 1976.
More Irish Short Stories. 1981.
Love Bites and Other Stories. 1991.
The Ram of God and Other Stories. 1992.

VERSE
The Street and Other Poems. 1961.

OTHER
Strong Tea. 1963.
Self-Portrait. 1964.
Letters of a Successful T.D. [*an Irish Parish Priest, an Irish Publican, a Love-Hungry Farmer, a Matchmaker, an Irish Civic Guard, a Country Postman, an Irish Minister of State*]. 8 vols., 1967–78.
The Gentle Art of Matchmaking. 1973.
Is the Holy Ghost Really a Kerryman? 1976.
Unlawful Sex and Other Testy Matters. 1978.
Stories from a Kerry Fireside. 1980.
Unusual Irish Careers. 1982.
Man of the Triple Name. 1984.
Owl Sandwiches. 1985.

BIBLIOGRAPHY: *Ten Modern Irish Playwrights* by Kimball King, 1979.

CRITICAL STUDIES: in *Seven Irish Plays 1946–1964* edited by Robert Hogan, 1967, and *After the Irish Renaissance* by Hogan, 1967; *Fifty Years Young: A Tribute to John B. Keane* edited by John M. Feehan, 1979; *Festival Glory in Athlone* by Gus Smith, 1979; *The Irish Theatre* by Christopher Fitz-Simon, 1983; *Modern Irish Drama 1891–1980* by D. E. S. Maxwell, 1984.

John B. Keane comments:

I regard the playwright of today as a man who must speak for his people, to speak up and to speak out, to say what vested interests, politicians, and big business are afraid to say. I believe that men should be tried for not speaking out when doing so would benefit their fellows and ultimately save lives. Those guilty of not doing so are criminals in every sense of the word. Most men have moral courage, but moral courage without skill to impose one's views is like a steed without a rider. I feel strongly about exploring the ills of modern Ireland

and the world, for the anguish of our times is the Frankenstein monster that
has been created by our convenient and long silences. We reap this anguish
because we have encouraged its growth by pulling the bedclothes over our
heads, hoping that the ogres might go away and that dawn might purify all.
That is why we are fast approaching a post-Christian era. This is why speaking
out early and often is so essential if there is to be a decent quality of life. I look
to life as it is lived around me and listen to a language that is living. It would be
against my nature to ignore a living speech and a living people. I sometimes feel
I would die without these to sustain me. Playwriting is my life. Just as a tree
spreads its roots into the earth, I spread my recording impulses around the
breasts of my people and often into their very cores. People need to be
recorded, to be witnessed; they expect and deserve it. I feel a responsibility to
my people, a duty to portray them accurately and with dignity lest they are
falsely delineated. There is a lot of love and humour in my plays, for without
love and humour there is nothing. Where there is love there is every virtue you
care to think of: love begets all that is great and constant. Think of that word
"constant." That's what love is. That is the rock to which I have anchored
myself, and I think my best is to come.

In the programme notes to the 1991 Field Day Theatre Company's production
of Thomas Kilroy's *The Madame MacAdam Travelling Theatre*, Christopher
Murray recalls a story about Anew McMaster, the director of an Irish
Shakespearean company which toured Ireland after World War II:

> When the first All-Ireland amateur drama festival took place in Athlone
> in 1953 McMaster played that same week in Galway (some fifty miles
> away) to empty houses. On the last night he came forward dressed as
> King Lear at the end of the play, took out a pair of spectacles and read to
> the sparse audience a few lines of bitter protest at his desertion. Taking
> off his spectacles and putting away the text of his address he delivered his
> parting shot. "I will leave you to the amateurs."

The most detailed record of John B. Keane's early success as a dramatist is
recorded in *Festival Glory in Athlone* (1979), Gus Smith's account of 25 years
of amateur drama in Ireland. The real value of the book lies in its documentation of the relationships and tensions between a resurgent amateur theatre in
Ireland and a moribund professional one during this period. The All-Ireland
Drama Festival culminating in Athlone was, and remains in essence, a circuit
of competitive festivals. Unlike McMaster, many "professionals" were happy
to hire their services as adjudicators for the amateur stage, the broad aim being
to provide some kind of basic training in the form of qualified advice from the
adjudicators and to make awards for merit, which not infrequently provided
the only means for an individual to find confirmation in his or her aspirations
to make a career in the theatre. However, the festivals are, by their nature,
social occasions. Audiences, spurred on by the spirit of festivity, frequently
exceeded those the professional stage could attract, hard pressed as it was by
outmoded stages, inadequate facilities, increasingly large wage bills, and a

largely unimaginative repertoire. Accordingly, the festivals not infrequently occasioned invidious and unnecessary comparisons.

John B. Keane's first stage success, *Sive*, a tragic story of a young illegitimate girl unwillingly matched to marry an old man and who as a consequence takes her own life, started out as an amateur production of a script originally submitted to, and rejected by, both the Abbey Theatre and RTE (the Irish Radio and Television Service). However, Micheal O hAodha, an executive with RTE, suggested that Keane try it out on an amateur company. Subsequently O hAodha was to adjudicate this production in positive terms as "a carbon copy of an Abbey production." Tomas McAnna, an employee of the Abbey and subsequently its artistic director, was less kind. In his adjudication he intimated that the obvious success of the play was due to the fact that it had been "rewritten in the way suggested by the Abbey Theatre," a point which Keane himself has always vigorously rebutted.

Keane's success with the amateurs was quickly followed by interest from professional companies keen to premiere his work (initially the Southern Theatre Group based in Cork; later, Gemini Productions under the direction of Barry Cassin in Dublin). Nevertheless, his initial outstanding success on the amateur stage has over the years consistently been used by critics to undervalue his achievement. The tendency has been to compare him negatively to other writers: "Geographically, but not imaginatively, the locale [of Keane's plays] is George Fitzmaurice's countryside, no longer so evocative of demonic dolls . . . Keane's Kerry is an indecisive countryside which falls short of wider identifications," as D. E. S. Maxwell wrote in *Modern Irish Drama 1891–1980* (1984). "The language of the early plays shares the North Kerry quirkiness of [Fitzmaurice]" according to Christopher Fitz-Simon's *The Irish Theatre* (1983). Neither of these writers is concerned with Keane's continuing ability, certainly with his major plays, to attract and hold his audiences' attention; and recent interest in his work (mainstage productions at the Abbey Theatre and a film of *The Field*, starring Richard Harris) suggest that the significance of his impact on the Irish stage is due for reappraisal.

Most of Keane's published plays were written between 1959 and 1979; since then, the bulk of his output has been poetry or prose, complemented by a substantial contribution to the developing success of the annual Listowel Writers' Festival. His dialogue is characteristically robust and colourful; his sense of the visual is atypically acute in a dramatic tradition that is so wordbound. His images shift easily along the continuum that links the intimate with the primeval, enabling him to move unselfconsciously from moments of domestic tedium to eruptions of mythic energy and ritual power. Hence his characters, while appearing to be larger than life, are at once familiarly real and strangely archetypal. It is this flexibility of definition in his characterisation that keeps the tendency to burlesque and melodrama in check. In *Sharon's Grave* he creates a grotesque double-headed monster which he dismembers in the last scene. At the point where Dinzie Conlee, the malignant cripple and his hulking brother Jack, on whose back he is forcibly borne, are about to mutilate the girl Trassie, Jack sets Dinzie down to settle a score with Peadar, Trassie's fiancé. The apotheosis of the cripple's impotence is an illustration of Keane's ability to exercise remarkable control over the tone of his plays. Again, Maxwell, writing about *The Field*, rationalises a text rather than the performance on which it is predicated when he observes that while Bull McCabe "emanates a brooding menace . . . the play never brings him, its story, and the telling of its story into 'The Present' . . . aircraft, electricity, television . . . remain trappings." Behind this criticism, typical of most, lies an assumption that Keane, unlike the better known Brian Friel (who frequently deals with the same kind of conjunctions, notably in *Translations*) is unequal to the task of writing for the stage.

James N. Healy, who was to create many of Keane's major roles, suggests that the rural background of the plays is something that is part of the "living present" rather than the recent past. This is more perceptive. Keane is at his most Irish when he is dealing with practical metaphysics; the central theme in *The Field* is the foregrounding of an immutable and atavistic relationship between man and the space he inhabits: "When you'll be gone, Father, to be a Canon . . . and the Sergeant to be a superintendent, Tadgh's children will be milking cows and keeping donkeys out of the ditches . . . and if there's no grass there's the end of me and mine."

Paradoxically, the progress of Keane's drama, while it is nearly always set in the present, records a loss of intensity as it withdraws from the elemental conflicts at the outer reaches of civilisation (*The Highest House on the Mountain*) to the contemporary and sentimental perspective of Ireland from a North of England building site (*Hut 42*, Keane's first Abbey premiere). It is a compliment to his genius to say that in the whole of the canon of his dramatic output he strongly resists the temptation to work to a formula while writing around issues about which he feels best qualified to write. His dialogue is assured; he is strongly attracted to local themes. His declared conventional interests (walking, reading, occasional beer-drinking) are, to a degree, at variance with his observations that little in life can be conventional and realistic at the same time. But with John B. Keane there is, as there was with Brecht, a nagging feeling that he owes his considerable success to being comprehensively misunderstood.

—Paul J.A. Hadfield

KEATLEY, Charlotte.

Born in London in 1960. Educated at Manchester University, B.A. in drama 1982; University of Leeds, M.A. in theatre arts 1983. Theatre critic for the Yorkshire *Post, Times Educational Supplement, Plays and Players,* Glasgow *Herald,* 1980–86, and for the *Financial Times*; writer, actor, and director in performance art and community theatre in Leeds and Manchester, 1982–84; teacher in drama in primary and secondary schools around Britain, 1985–86; Judith E. Wilson visiting fellow in English, Cambridge University, 1988–89; lecturer in playwriting and theatre skills, University of London, Royal Court Young People's Theatre and Women's National Touring Theatre, London, University of Birmingham, and Vassar College, Poughkeepsie, New York, 1988–92. Recipient: *Sunday Times* award, for acting, 1980; Manchester *Evening News* award, 1987; George Devine award, 1987; *Plays and Players* award, 1989; Edinburgh Fringe first, for direction, 1991. Agents: Peregrine Whittlesey Agency, 345 East 80th Street, New York, New York 10021,

U.S.A.; and Rod Hall, A.P. Watt, 20 John Street, London WC1N 2DL, England.

Publications

PLAYS

Underneath the Arndale (produced 1982).
Dressing for Dinner (produced 1982).
An Armenian Childhood, with Pete Brooks and Steve Schill (produced 1983).
The Legend of Padgate, music by Mark Vibrans (also director: produced 1986).
Waiting for Martin (produced 1987).
My Mother Said I Never Should (produced 1987). 1988; revised version, 1989.
You're a Nuisance Aren't You, in *Fears and Miseries of the Third Term*, with others (produced 1989).
The Singing Ringing Tree (for children), music by Errollyn Wallen (produced 1991).

RADIO PLAYS: *My Mother Said I Never Should*, 1989; *Citizens* series, with others, 1989–90.

TELEVISION PLAY: *Badger* (for children), 1989.

THEATRICAL ACTIVITIES

DIRECTOR: **Plays**—*The Legend of Padgate*, 1986; *Autogeddon* by Heathcote Williams, 1991.

Charlotte Keatley is one of the youngest playwrights to have a main stage performance at the Royal Court. Her play *My Mother Said I Never Should* received wide-spread acclaim after its run at that theatre. It was compared by reviewers to the work of Sharman MacDonald in its depiction of generations of women learning about themselves and each other. This play is Keatley's primary claim to fame in the theatre, though she has also written *Underneath the Arndale* and *Dressing for Dinner*. In addition, she is known as one of the writers of the television serial *Citizens*. She is currently at work on another full-length play.

In interview in 1989, Charlotte Keatley compared her work to that of the early feminist and alternative theatres. She said: "When you start making plays about your own experiences and in your own language, there is so much to say that the temptation is to say it all quickly and crudely, and so you throw up big signs. After that, you can become more sophisticated and more subtle in the way you say things, which I would say started happening in the late seventies." Keatley's work has developed in a similar way, from the dark humour of *Dressing for Dinner* to the more sophisticated balance of humour and drama which is explored in *My Mother Said I Never Should*.

Keatley performed in her play *Dressing for Dinner*, a visual theatre piece devised and produced by Keatley's own company, The Royale Ballé. The (unpublished) play centred on the image of the feminine woman and her essential item of apparel: the obligatory "little black number." It experimented with images and ideas, movement and gesture, in a form which borrowed both from 1980's feminist thought and the theatrical styles of visual and performance theatre artists such as Clare MacDonald. Visual tricks such as comparing —through innuendo and layered symbolism—the dressing of a woman and the dressing of a fish in aspic were utilized as "shock techniques" which first made the audience laugh, and then made them question the source of their laughter.

Keatley continued to experiment with "shock techniques" in her later work, and most notably in *My Mother Said I Never Should*. But in the latter, the "shock" is primarily directed at audience empathy rather than such radical questioning of audience values and motives. Both *Dressing for Dinner* and *My Mother Said* explore the relations between generations of women and their shared experiences and memories. Yet *My Mother Said I Never Should* is a much more sophisticated piece of writing, and of theatre. It can be studied as a script or literary text, chronicling the lives of four generations of women in war-torn and post-war Britain. It can also be studied in larger terms as a performance of self in society, that is, it can be analyzed as a play informed by feminist politics and theories, played out in the differences between generations of woman.

Keatley, of course, belongs to one of those generations. But her skill as a playwright has transcended the limitations of the author's own perspective, offering instead a play which can be—and often is—seen to be filtered through the perspective of different generations. In fact, as Keatley herself has observed when sitting in the audience of her own play, members of the audience tend to identify with a particular character, and with her generation. The critical conception of "the gaze" is manipulated in terms of generational difference rather than gender difference.

Gender is, though, also a crucial consideration in the play. No male characters appear on stage. Yet unlike many women's plays which are criticized for the lack of men or for "cardboard depictions of men," Keatley seems somehow to have sidestepped that kind of red-herring criticism, partly through humour and partly through a skillful manipulation of audience expectation in regard to the invisible male characters. While no men appear on stage in *My Mother Said I Never Should*, Keatley has incorporated references to male characters in the script: husbands and partners are referred to and seem at times to be present in the wings as the women on stage shout questions and comments to them. This manipulation of audience expectation is used to comic effect, but also has a more serious purpose. In Keatley's words: "I finally decided to do the play without men at all because I wanted to present whole ways of being for women which only happen when the men have gone out of the room."

That introduction to female characters as they appear when no men are present is one of Keatley's greatest contributions. That men seemed to enjoy the plays as well is a tribute to the quality of the writing. With or without male characters, the creation of plays which deal intelligently and evocatively with the performance of gender roles on stage makes Keatley a playwright whose work should be read and seen.

—Lizbeth Goodman

KEEFFE, Barrie (Colin).

Born in London, 31 October 1945. Educated at East Ham Grammar School, London. Married 1) Dee Truman in 1969 (divorced 1979); 2) the writer Verity Bargate in 1981 (died 1981), two stepsons; 3) Julia Lindsay in 1983. Actor, at Theatre Royal Stratford East, London, 1964, and National Youth Theatre, 3 years; reporter, *Stratford and Newham Express*, London, to 1969, and for news agency to 1975; dramatist-in-residence, Shaw Theatre, London (Thames TV Playwright scheme), 1977, and Royal Shakespeare Company, 1978; associate writer, Theatre Royal Stratford East, 1986–1991. Since 1977 member of the Council, National Youth Theatre; since 1978 member of the Board of Directors, Soho Poly Theatre, London. Recipient: French Critics prize, 1978; Mystery Writers of America Edgar Allan Poe award, for screenplay, 1982. Agent: Lemon, Unna, and Durbridge, 24 Pottery Lane, Holland Park, London W11 4LZ; and, Gilbert Parker, William Morris Agency, 1350 Avenue of the Americas, New York, New York 10019, U.S.A. Address: 110 Annandale Road, London SE10 0JZ, England.

Publications

PLAYS

Only a Game (produced 1973).
A Sight of Glory (produced 1975).
Gimme Shelter: Gem, Gotcha, Getaway (*Gem* produced 1975; *Gotcha* produced 1976; trilogy produced 1977). 1977.
My Girl (produced 1975; revised version produced 1989). With *Frozen Assets*, 1989.
A Certain Vincent, with Jules Croiset, adaptation of letters of Vincent Van Gogh (also director: produced 1975).
Scribes (produced 1975).
Here Comes the Sun (produced 1976). In *Act 3*, edited by David Self and Ray Speakman, 1979.
Barbarians: A Trilogy: Killing Time, Abide with Me, In the City (*Abide with Me* produced 1976; trilogy produced 1977). 1978.
Up the Truncheon (produced 1977).
A Mad World, My Masters (produced 1977; revised version produced 1984). 1977.
Frozen Assets (produced 1978; revised version produced 1987). 1978.
Sus (produced 1979). 1979.
Heaven Scent (broadcast 1979). In *Best Radio Plays of 1979*, 1980.
Bastard Angel (produced 1980). 1980.
Black Lear (produced 1980).
She's So Modern (produced 1980).
Chorus Girls, music by Ray Davies (produced 1981).
A Gentle Spirit, with Jules Croiset, adaptation of a story by Dostoevsky (also director: produced 1981).
The Long Good Friday (screenplay). 1984.
Better Times (produced 1985). 1985.
King of England (produced 1988). With *Bastard Angel*, 1989.

Not Fade Away (produced 1990). In *Wild Justice, Not Fade Away, Gimme Shelter*, 1990.
Wild Justice (produced 1990). In *Wild Justice, Not Fade Away, Gimme Shelter*, 1990.
Wild Justice, Not Fade Away, Gimme Shelter: Three Plays. 1990.

SCREENPLAY: *The Long Good Friday*, 1981.

RADIO PLAYS: *Good Old Uncle Jack*, 1975; *Pigeon Skyline*, 1975; *Self Portrait*, 1977; *Heaven Scent*, 1979; *Paradise*, 1989.

TELEVISION PLAYS: *The Substitute*, 1972; *Nipper*, 1977; *Not Quite Cricket*, 1977; *Champions*, 1978; *Hanging Around*, 1978; *Waterloo Sunset*, 1979; *No Excuses* series, 1983; *King*, 1984; *Betty*, 1990.

RECORDING: *A Certain Vincent*; *No Excuses*.

NOVELS
Gadabout. 1969.
No Excuses (novelization of his television series). 1983.

OTHER
Editor, *The 1984 Verity Bargate Award Short Plays*. 1985.
Editor, *The Verity Bargate Award New Plays 1986*. 1987.
Editor, *The Verity Bargate Award New Plays 1988*. 1987.

THEATRICAL ACTIVITIES
DIRECTOR: **Plays**—*A Certain Vincent*, 1975; *A Gentle Spirit*, 1981, 1982.

In the days when Barrie Keeffe worked for a local newspaper in East London, one of his assignments was the astrology column which, even more than most astrology columns, was a piece of total imagination written under the byline of "Kay Sera." The random assignment of different fates to his readers must have given his employers some indication of his developing dramatic gifts, but it was another assignment which profoundly coloured his future work. At the end of an interview with the pro-censorship campaigner Mary Whitehouse, later to be the recognizable target of his satire, *She's So Modern*, he asked her whom the people were that she professed to speak for. With a metaphorical pat on the head, she replied: "Ordinary, decent people; like you and me." The plays which followed that interview, whether comedies or dramas, frequently troubled Mrs. Whitehouse, particularly when broadcast on television, but Keeffe's explorations of British racism and alienated youth certainly followed his own concerns with decency. What is remarkable, for a writer so very much of his time and place, is how successful the plays have been in other countries and how they have endured.

Revivals began in the mid 1980's, when Keeffe found that *Frozen Assets*, his play written for the Royal Shakespeare Company in 1978, was being performed and revalued. His radio version of the play, somewhat less profane but no less powerful than the stage version, was being broadcast by the BBC in his own updated adaptation and stage revivals were being scheduled in acknowledgement that the basic story of a Borstal boy on the run in London had survived with its comical cynicism intact. Indeed, the picture the play paints of East London as a community destroyed by property speculation was provided with additional poignancy in the wake of the yuppie invasion of dockland.

Similarly, 1986 had seen revivals of his 1977 trilogy of one-act plays, *Gimme Shelter*, which included the play *Gotcha* about a schoolboy who held his teachers hostage with matches held over the open petrol tank of a motorcycle. The arguments in that play had not dated, nor had the level of resentment he had first measured in schools where pupils were being dumped, unprepared, into a society which could not provide them with jobs. Another apparently topical play, *Sus*, about a black man arrested under the now abolished "sus" law where people could be held by the police on grounds of suspicion alone, has also survived the progress of time and continues to appear in various productions, both in Britain and abroad, though it was very specifically set on the night of Margaret Thatcher's first electoral victory. At the heart of its survival is the recognizable human pain of the man falsely accused of his wife's death.

Despite the continued interest in his early plays, and the undoubted influence of his plays about disaffected British youth, the flood of his stage plays from the 1970s had subsided to a trickle in the mid-1980s. The plays that appeared in the 1980's were notably different from the scripts of the 1970s, as with the short-lived musical he wrote with Ray Davies of The Kinks, *Chorus Girls*, a political entertain- ment taken from an obscure comedy by Aristophanes, *Thesmophoriazusae*. Similar in some ways to the satirical comedy he wrote in 1977 for the Joint Stock Company, *A Mad World, My Masters* (with the title and the spirit of the free-flowing plot borrowed from the Jacobean writer Thomas Middleton), the play tapped a classical source for a very current inspiration and concerned the kidnapping of Prince Charles by dedicated feminists. Ill-directed, the play had only a local success in London's Theatre Royal, Stratford East, the theatre for which it was designed. None the less it was witty, often uproariously so, with several excellent songs from Davies, and its presentational format marked a breakthrough in Keeffe's technique.

The play which followed four years later, *Better Times*, was another departure, part documentary about East London's historical Poplar Rent Strike and again part East End comedy in the mood of *A Mad World*. Meticulous in its recreation of the courtroom scenes and backroom dramas surrounding an important moment in British socialist history, and admirable for it, the most telling demonstration of Keeffe's talent was in the imaginary scenes with his patented version of an East End Keystone Cop. Though cheered by his East London audiences, the play was received with bemusement by several of his critics. It has often been the wayward force of his comedy which has bewildered reviewers, but the touch of absurdism in his work remains another of the qualities which keeps the apparently topical subject-matter of the plays alive.

Keeffe's work has long benefited from associations with specific companies, beginning with the National Youth Theatre and achieving a major impetus from the late Verity Bargate's support at London's Soho Poly Theatre. It was in that small venue that both his youth trilogies, *Gimme Shelter* and *Barbarians*, were developed, and something of the claustrophobic power of those pictures of aimless young Londoners can probably be ascribed to their original performance space which he exploited to its full. The trilogies boldly gave his inarticulate and angry young men a rich imagistic language, both abusive and tender, which has been much imitated by younger writers. Keeffe, however, has varied his dramatic offerings much more than his followers and his own influences range visibly from Plautus—the twins in *She's So Modern*—to Chekhov.

Bastard Angel was written for the Royal Shakespeare Company. Belying its own gutsy story of a female rock singer rattling painfully through despair in the mansion which she bought in order to humiliate servants who had humiliated her when she was a young singer, the play took its inspiration from Chekhov's *Platonov* and key images from each of the four acts of the Russian play have been retained. More cataclysmic by far than the Chekhov original, with the rock star entering into a sexual relationship with her own son, the play manages to retain autumnal beauty in the midst of violent events and blasting music. The later television version, *No Excuses*, carried the story further but lacked the focus of the stage version which is a major work.

Throughout the 1980's, he developed a successful continuing relationship with London's Theatre Royal, Stratford East, once the home of Joan Littlewood. A split with the theatre came in 1991, but his work with Philip Hedley there produced two of his best later plays, *My Girl* and *Wild Justice*, both written for the actor Karl Howman.

My Girl is a claustrophobic comedy, highly impassioned and often painful, about the relationship between a social worker and his wife. The constant caring for strangers which is his job seems to deprive him of the devotion appropriate to his heavily pregnant wife and their child, but a crisis is reached when his attraction to a client threatens their marriage. Never simply about the relationship, since the fundamental anxiety concerns Sam's inability to reconcile his own ideals with the stress of his underpaid job, it is none the less a powerful love story. *Wild Justice* is a modern revenge play, triggered by the death of a child and as blackly insistent as any Jacobean revenge tragedy. It contains some of the very best of Keeffe's writing.

With the success of his screenplay *The Long Good Friday*, a film which seized the initiative from American crime movies to mingle East End villainy, the IRA, international crime, and a unique political perspective, Keeffe moved into the rank of writers constantly courted by Hollywood, a not altogether happy arrangement given the tendency of moviemakers to demand their Hollywood version of his vision. Prior to that he had contributed notably to British television, particularly with his audacious comedy, *Waterloo Sunset*, with its portrait of an elderly white woman who walks out on an old folks' home and moves in with a black family in South London. (It later became the stage play *Not Fade Away*.)

His short prize-winning radio play *Heaven Scent*, about crime and perfume, is a model of radio technique and beautifully demonstrates his own gift for characterization and storytelling. Radio also saw the premiere of his epic drama about Robespierre, *Paradise*, a play of great power and historical clarity which recognizes, as few other sources do, the extreme youth of the makers of the French Revolution. Vast in its intention and achievement, the play has yet to find a stage performance.

Adept in all areas of drama, he has also written the novel of *No Excuses*, providing interesting commentary on the intentions of the story; losing, however, the touch of Chekhov which made the original play so effective. With his exuberant language and uninhibited vision of the potential of the stage, his greatest gifts are theatrical—few writers have his ability to create searing images through the speech of their characters.

—Ned Chaillet

KEMPINSKI, Tom.

Born in London, 24 March 1938. Educated at Hall School; Abingdon Grammar School; Cambridge University (open scholar). Married. Actor, 1960–71. Recipient: London Drama Critics award, 1980. Agent: Alan Brodie Representation, 91 Regent Street, London W1R 7TB, England.

Publications

PLAYS

The Peasants Revolt (produced 1971).
The English Civil War (produced 1972).
Moscow Trials (produced 1972).
Pageant of Labour History (4 plays; produced 1973).
The Ballad of Robin Hood, with Roger Smith (produced 1973).
October, with Roger Smith (produced 1973).
Sell-Out (1931), with Roger Smith, music by Kempinski and Smith (produced 1974).
Flashpoint (as Gerrard Thomas) (produced 1978).
What about Borneo? (produced 1978).
The Workshop, adaptation of a play by Jean-Claude Grumberg (produced 1979; as *The Workroom*, produced 1982).
Japanese Noh Plays (for children; produced 1979).
Mayakovsky, adaptation of a work by Stefan Schütz (produced 1979).
Duet for One (produced 1980). 1981.
Dreyfus, adaptation of the play by Jean-Claude Grumberg (produced 1982).
The Beautiful Part of Myself (produced 1983).
Life of Karl Marx, with Roger Smith (produced 1984).
Self-Inflicted Wounds (produced 1985).
Separation (produced 1987). 1989.
Sex Please, We're Italian (produced 1991).
A Free Country, adaptation of a play by Jean-Claude Grumberg (produced 1991).
When the Past Is Still to Come (produced 1992).

SCREENPLAY: *Duet for One*, with Jeremy Lipp and Andrei Konchalovsky, 1987.

Tom Kempinski comments:

There are two kinds of oppression in the world: the oppression of one group in society by another, and the oppression of one part of a person by another part of the same person. I write about both kinds, because I have experienced both — and also studied and struggled to change both.

My historical plays are influenced by English radio comedy of the 1950s, and include songs and music which I compose.

My "personal" plays are characterised by attempts to penetrate beneath the surface of people's deeds to their inner, and often concealed motives. These plays are written in a "naturalistic" "style," and — in a country that keeps a stiff upper lip (since 1800?) in order not to show weakness to wogs, niggers, wops, and other human beings which Britain has conquered — are found to be just a touch emotional.

Top people — whether parents or dictators — prefer lies of all kinds, because they invent these lies to maintain their superior status in the world.

Tom Kempinski writes about strong people under unbearable pressure, charting the process of their bravely resisted but inevitable collapse. Stephanie Abrahams in *Duet for One* is a classical musician struck down by multiple sclerosis and compelled to face a life without the music that has been the centre of it; Isaac Cohen in *Self-Inflicted Wounds* is a dedicated Nazi-hunter who finds his courage faltering when it comes time to publish his research; Carter in *Flashpoint* is a wise-cracking soldier whose method of coping with army routine is tested in a crisis.

Given these outlines, it is not surprising that Kempinski's plays sometimes skirt the edge of soap opera and melodrama. *Duet for One*, which consists entirely of Stephanie's sessions with an overly wise psychologist, follows a predictable emotional outline, at least in part: one knows from the minute she enters bravely denying a psychological problem that she will eventually break down and cry, "I-can-never-never-play-the-the-the-violin again" (it happens at the end of Act 1), just as one can predict that the laconic psychologist will eventually make an eloquent pull-yourself-together speech (Act 2). *Self-Inflicted Wounds* is also a bit schematic in the way that Cohen's affair with a young girl and his own family secrets are twisted back on the main plot to be used against him by his enemies. And the action of *Flashpoint*, which involves an armed soldier going berserk and taking his platoon hostage in an attempt to stop the execution of a deserter, threatens to lose sight of its ideas in the melodramatic action.

But these dangers, not always avoided, are almost inevitable, given Kempinski's determination to find the sources and limits of his protagonists' strength. Notably, the process is not simple or direct, and the discoveries made are complex and sometimes surprising. Stephanie Abrahams does not go from bold defiance to simple despair — that predictable breakdown is only the end of the first act. Kempinski sees that despair is a step, not a conclusion; it is followed by self-denial and self-abasement, as Stephanie tries to convince herself that she doesn't care about her loss of dignity and self-control; by self-deceit, as the fear of losing her husband is raised to deflect the psychologist from deeper probing; and only then by the loss of all defenses and the admission of the very elementary fears that everything else was covering, an admission that Kempinski sees as the bravest step of all and the basis for hope.

Similarly, Cohen's perplexing hesitancy to publish the damning results of his research is not explained or exposed simply. Each revelation is a little more true than the one before it, but not itself the entire truth. Even at the end, when Cohen admits that he might have deliberately sabotaged himself by giving his enemies the means to discredit him, his reasons are a subtle mixture of weakness and strength, betrayals of his own morality and higher affirmations of it. And Carter is also shown to be more complex than one might first expect: his wise-guy attitude does not keep him from being the strongest participant in the hostage crisis or bar him from sympathy for his weaker comrades. It is only after the crisis is over and he learns how those outside had manipulated both gunman and hostages that Carter momentarily breaks, showing in his sense of betrayal a core of faith in the military that his sneers had hidden.

Kempinski's one attempt at comedy, *Sex Please, We're Italian*, merely proves that his talents do not lie in that area. This would-be romp about townsfolk trying to hide their many sexual peccadillos from a visiting clergyman is leadenly unfunny, without the manic energy or insane internal logic that successful farce demands.

Duet for One remains the strongest of Kempinski's plays, largely because it is such a successful theatrical piece: its effectiveness as a vehicle for a sensitive actress disguises or counterbalances its weaknesses. It is also the most tightly focused of his plays: making the "enemy" a disease frees Kempinski from having to create melodramatic events and also eliminates any potentially distracting political overtones. Like many well-meaning political writers, Kempinski tends to become less controlled and more simplistic the closer he comes to his own passionate convictions. To the extent that *Self-Inflicted Wounds* is about Nazism, *Flashpoint* about the British military presence in Northern Ireland, or *Dreyfus* about anti-semitism, they are at their weakest and most diffuse; Kempinski's strengths are always in the personal dramas.

—Gerald M. Berkowitz

KILROY, Thomas.

Born in Callan, County Kilkenny, 23 September 1934. Educated at Christian Brothers School, Callan; St. Kieran's College, Kilkenny; University College, Dublin, 1953–59, B.A. 1956, higher diploma in education 1957, M.A. in English 1959. Married 1) Patricia Cobey in 1963 (divorced 1980), three sons; 2) Julia Lowell Carlson in 1981. Headmaster, Stratford College, Dublin, 1959–64; visiting lecturer in English, University of Notre Dame, Indiana, 1962–63; visiting professor of English, Vanderbilt University, Nashville, 1964–65; assistant lecturer, Department of Modern English and American Literature, University College, Dublin, 1965–73; lecturer, School of Irish Studies, Dublin, 1972–73. Visiting professor, Sir George Williams University and McGill University, both Montreal, 1973, University College, Galway, 1975–76 and 1979, Dartmouth College, Hanover, New Hampshire, 1976, University College, Dublin, 1977–78, and Bamberg University, West Germany, 1984; Examiner in Modern English, Trinity College, Dublin, and Thomond College, Limerick, 1983. Recipient: *Guardian* prize, for fiction, 1971; Royal Society of Literature Heinemann award, for fiction, 1972; Irish Academy prize, 1972; American-Irish Foundation award, 1974; Arts Council of Ireland bursary, 1976; Bellagio Study Centre grant, 1986; Rockefeller grant, 1986. Fellow, Royal Society of Literature, 1972; member, 1973, and member of the Council, 1979, Irish Academy of Letters; member, Aosdana, 1986. Lives in Kilmaine, Mayo, Ireland. Agent: Casarotto Ramsay Ltd., National House, 60–66 Wardour Street, London W1V 3HP, England.

Publications

PLAYS

The Death and Resurrection of Mr. Roche (produced 1968). 1969.
The O'Neill (produced 1969).
Tea and Sex and Shakespeare (produced 1976).
Talbot's Box (produced 1977). 1979.
The Seagull, adaptation of a play by Chekhov (produced 1981). 1981.
Double Cross (produced 1986). 1986.
Ghosts, adaptation of the play by Henrik Ibsen (produced 1988).
The Madame MacAdam Travelling Theatre (produced 1991). 1991.

RADIO PLAYS: *The Door*, 1967; *That Man, Bracken*, 1986.

TELEVISION PLAYS: *Farmers*, 1978; *The Black Joker*, 1981.

NOVEL

The Big Chapel. 1971.

OTHER

Editor, *Sean O'Casey: A Collection of Critical Essays.* 1975.

BIBLIOGRAPHY: *Ten Modern Irish Playwrights* by Kimball King, 1979.

CRITICAL STUDIES: articles by Christopher Murray, in *Ireland Today*, 1982, and by Gerald Dawe, in *Theatre Ireland 3* , 1982; "The Fortunate Fall: Two Plays by Thomas Kilroy" by Anthony Roche, in *The Writer and the City* edited by Maurice Harmon, 1984; "A Haunted House: The Theatre of Thomas Kilroy" by Frank McGuinness, in *Irish Theatre Today* edited by Barbara Hayley and Walter Rix, 1985; "Thomas Kilroy" by Anthony Roche, in *Post-War Literatures in English: A Lexicon*, 1989.

Thomas Kilroy is probably best known on both sides of the Atlantic for *The Death and Resurrection of Mr. Roche*, a tragicomedy which demonstrates his flair for funny yet trenchant dialogue in a style reminiscent of O'Casey. In this play, as well as in his historical portraits of Matt Talbot in *Talbot's Box* and

William Joyce and Brendan Bracken in *Double Cross*, his characters are strongly defined, and his sense of dramatic structure is adroit. He is quite eclectic in his dramaturgy; his plays have little in common except an apparent rejection of the strong naturalistic tradition of many Abbey playwrights. His first play, *Mr. Roche*, is basically realistic in style, while his second, *The O'Neill*, is a historical work about Owen Roe O'Neill, the Irish opponent of Queen Elizabeth I. *Talbot's Box* is a penetrating psychological study notable for its use of expressionistic devices. *Tea and Sex and Shakespeare* is a thin comedy which teeters on the edge of absurdist theater. *Double Cross* is a curious dramatic diptych, a study of two political opposites who figured prominently in the propaganda battles of England and Germany in World War II. A decade separated a fine adaptation of Chekhov's *The Seagull* from a brilliant updating of Ibsen's *Ghosts*. Kilroy's most recent work, *The Madame MacAdam Travelling Theatre*, is a meditation on acting and the theatre imposed on a humorous account of a down-at-heel company of actors touring rural Eire in the early 1940s. Some of Kilroy's themes are traditionally Irish; others are universal (e.g., the "aloneness" of spiritual isolation, the theatre as a "doubling" of reality).

In *The Death and Resurrection of Mr. Roche* an all-male drinking party seemingly turns tragic when one of the group dies suddenly, or so it appears. Kelley, a mid-thirties civil servant of peasant background, has extended a casual invitation to assorted patrons of Murray's Bar to return to his small, desolate Dublin flat for further drinking. Last to arrive is Mr. Roche, the oldest of the lot and a known homosexual to whom Kelley is openly hostile. After they are even further into their cups, they begin to torment him, and he "dies" suddenly after they have forced him into a cubbyhole of a cellar. While two of the drinkers, Doc and Kevin, are out attempting to dispose of the body, Kelley and Seamus have what is thematically the most significant scene of the play. In an account of a sexual encounter with Roche, Kelley reveals his homosexual tendencies, and Seamus confesses he is trapped in marriage to a girl whose "sameness is beginning to drive me mad." At a carefully chosen moment, Doc and Kevin reappear with a very live Mr. Roche and an explanation that never quite includes how Doc could have pronounced him dead in the first place.

The central theme is the stultifying effect—the spiritual and cultural sterility —that contemporary urban life has had on young Irish men who were able to leave small family farms and villages and make careers in Dublin. They are descendants of the early "peasant play" characters who, unconsciously at least, longed to leave behind the hard life on the land, the narrow provinciality of the village, and the stifling influence of parents and clergy for the headier life of Dublin, England, or America. Kilroy's Irish are cousins to Brian Friel's Gar who leaves the small family business for the United States in *Philadelphia, Here I Come!* The father-son conflict, the Irish generational gap, is well behind Kilroy's characters; they have made their escape and feel lucky. However, they have, as they sadly admit, lost contact with their families. Kelley thinks he has a very good job, and Seamus, with whom he grew up, is proud of being a teacher and, until he thinks about it, is happily married. Their reunion over several pints becomes a melancholy soul-baring in which Seamus admits that he is not just attempting to recapture the pleasure of their last reunion two years ago. "Twas more like I was trying to get back to ten years ago. What was

healthy then is sick now. . . . Why haven't you changed even a little? . . .
You're in the same situation as you were when you came to Dublin—" Kelley
angrily insists that he's "the success of my family," while Seamus concludes
sadly that he's "as happy as ever I'll be." Their conversation concludes with
Kelley's unwelcome revelation that he had, in fact, invited Roche to the
apartment before and that once they had had sexual relations.

Homosexuality is Kilroy's second theme, along with Irish hypocrisy. Kelley's
hostile attitude toward Roche is made clear quite early to underline his
hypocrisy: "I won't let the likes of him over that step. . . ." After Roche's
"death," Kelley is terrified that their acquaintance will come out: "Prison I can
take. It's the bad name that leaves me wake at the knees." However, Roche is,
in Kevin's words, "not a bad auld skin." In fact, Roche speaks for Kilroy in a
plea for sympathy and understanding for all his characters, for homosexuality
is here the playwright's metaphor for "aloneness." Through Roche, Kilroy
strongly condemns their lifestyle, their drinking bouts to assuage loneliness
and uncertainty, the waste of their lives. When Kelley condescendingly rejects
Roche's sympathy, the homosexual makes a plea for all of them: "We all need
sympathy now and again. . . . There's little comfort as it is, in this world. . . .
Who am I or you to deny someone the single object which makes each day
bearable?" Writing in 1968, Irving Wardle praised *Mr. Roche* as "the most
important new work ever presented by the Dublin Theatre Festival."

Tea and Sex and Shakespeare was Kilroy's contribution to the 1976 Dublin
Festival and has not been published. It involves the fantasies of a blocked
writer named Brien. In one fruitless day spent in his Dublin attic workroom, he
plays out his dreams involving his wife, Elmina, who is, in fact, at work; his
neighbor, Sylvester, who finds him a nuisance but fancies his wife; his comic
landlady and her nubile daughter, Deirdre, to whom he is tutor; and finally
Mummy and Daddy, his in-laws, who might have escaped from a short play by
Edward Albee. Brien's dream world centers around dramatic suicides and
seductions, with dialogue quoted or paraphrased from Shakespeare, the subject of his tutorials with the buxom Deirdre. The plot and characters are
exceedingly thin. The play ends on a poignantly serious note as the long-
suffering wife remonstrates with Brien: "You build your absurd jokes around
you like a high wall so that no one can reach you," she charges. Brien responds
that he is only trying to say "I'm alone." Her reply—"And who in this world
isn't alone?" reiterates the theme of spiritual isolation that Kilroy mined far
more effectively and dramatically in *Talbot's Box*. This comedy of the frustrated, haunted creative person is only moderately successful.

Talbot's Box rarely matches the humor of *Mr. Roche*, but in its central
character there is a highly effective study of religious zealotry, a subject the
dramatist had dealt with in his novel *The Big Chapel* a few years earlier. Matt
Talbot was a Dublin workman and mystic who died in 1925, and as early as
1931 a movement was underway for his canonization. On his death, it was
discovered that for many years he had been wearing heavy chains and cords
around his body, arms, and legs and that some of the rusty chains had sunk
into the flesh. The play is an inquiry into the psyche of Talbot. The action
comes through four actors who portray a variety of different roles, with
costume changes made on stage. The playwright touches a number of social
bases: for example, Talbot's role in the Transport Strike of 1913 sets his

unique vision against the background of labor troubles, just as his encounters with the Church demonstrate that in his zealous humiliation of the flesh he is as unmanageable as Shaw's St. Joan. In the key scene of the play, Talbot tells the priest, "I knows the darkness! . . . 'Tis in every man, woman 'n child born inta the world." For him, "the darkness is Gawd," and "there's no peace till ya walk through it inta some kinda light." The humiliation of the flesh is "only the way for me to know the darkness of me own body." In Kilroy's own words *Talbot's Box* is a play "about aloneness, its cost to the person and the kind of courage required to sustain it."

Kilroy's next work for the stage was a highly effective adaptation of Chekhov's *The Seagull*. Now set on an estate in the West of Ireland, this transplanted Russian classic shows no signs of a sea-change in its passage from one predominantly rural, 19th-century culture to another.

Double Cross is concerned with the problem of "doubleness or doubling, . . . the way things repeat themselves in life or attract their opposites." This is the "basis of acting or role-playing," Kilroy writes in an introduction, as well as the impetus behind "the universal desire . . . to make up and tell stories, thereby inventing a reality which may reflect everyday life but is still distinct from it." *Double Cross* attempts "to move along the lines from role-playing and fiction-making to the act of political treason." William Joyce, born in Brooklyn in 1906, arrived in England (via Ireland and Northern Ireland) in 1921. By 1933 he had become a member of Sir Oswald Mosley's British Union of Fascists. In 1939 he went to Germany where he joined German Radio. Before the year was out, he had become the infamous Lord Haw-Haw, probably Goebbels's best known radio commentator and apologist for the Nazi regime. Kilroy finds Joyce's "opposite" in Brendan Bracken, born 1901 in Tipperary, who by dint of systematic cultivation of the rich, famous, aristocratic, and politically powerful, rose, by 1939, to be Churchill's Parliamentary Private Secretary at the Admiralty and, by 1941, to be Minister of Information, whose responsibility it was to counteract the effect of Lord Haw-Haw's broadcasts.

Double Cross is divided into two halves: "The Bracken Play: London" and "The Joyce Play: Berlin." The first scene of "the Bracken Play" introduces both Joyce and Bracken (played by the same actor) as well as an actor and actress who both narrate and play a variety of characters, most notably Churchill and Lord Beaverbrook and the two women in the lives of Joyce and Bracken. Structurally, each play is made up of a series of free-flowing scenes which chronicle, in the case of Bracken, his political maneuverings and his affair with a woman called Popsie, while still allowing him to look back at his modest beginnings in Ireland and ahead to his own death (by cancer) in 1958. Joyce's "Berlin Play" focuses on his relations with his second wife, Margaret, and an interview (after his capture by the Allies) with Lord Beaverbrook. He was hanged as a war criminal in 1946.

For Kilroy this is a play about "two men who invented themselves," Bracken as an actor on the English political scene of the late 1930's and the war years, and Joyce as "a creator of fictions" driven to an invented self by a "deep, angry impatience," with life. Both came of unremarkable Irish backgrounds; both invented lives for themselves in English society; both tried to imitate his oppressor, Joyce by his anti-British propaganda, and Bracken by his very

"English" attitude toward Ireland. Each of the plays is a tour de force for both the dramatist and the actor, with the first being the better of the two. Yet, as Irving Wardle wrote in the London *Times*, Kilroy's idea that "social play-acting in some way leads to fascism and treason" is not effectively projected. However, the play remains a fascinating study of "doubles/opposites." Kilroy followed *Double Cross* with a radio play on the same subject—or the Bracken half of it—called *That Man, Bracken*, which is an effective distillation of material used in the earlier work.

Kilroy's adaptation of Ibsen's *Ghosts* is a highly effective updating, justifiably received with enthusiasm in its first production at the 1988 Dublin Theatre Festival. The scene is now a provincial Irish town, but most importantly, the time is moved up to the late 1980's. Certain changes, which are both natural and effective, make the play very contemporary. First, Oliver Aylward (like Ibsen's Oswald Alving) has come home to die; he is in the final stages of AIDS. Second, there is a hint that his father introduced him to drugs (probably marijuana) in his childhood (Kilroy's variation on Oswald's story of how, when a small boy, he became ill by smoking his father's pipe). Third, Oliver's rejection of the "ghosts" theme—that the fathers' sins are visited on the children—is more forceful, coupled as it is with his assertion of personal responsibility. Fourth, the euthanasia theme is far more acceptable now than it would have been for much of the life of Ibsen's play, and since Helen Aylward (Ibsen's Helene Alving) seems a more "liberated" woman than her original, there is reason to suppose that Oliver won't be allowed to suffer very long. All four characters—even Father Manning (Pastor Manders)—are drawn with greater precision than in most translations of Ibsen. Kilroy's excoriation of the social hypocrisies surrounding marriage and the family are more trenchant in this adaptation: "There is more evil propagated inside family life than in any other human organisation that I know of," says Oliver. Finally, even the image/symbol of the sun is employed with more resonance in the final moment of the play. This adaptation is so timely and effective that a modern classic becomes a brand-new play.

Kilroy's most recent work for the stage, *The Madame MacAdam Travelling Theatre*, is a highly original play which generated a negative critical response at the 1991 Dublin Theatre Festival. This is not a play that is strong in either plot (quite complex) or characterization (certainly adequate). Set in a very small town in rural Ireland during the Emergency (the World War II years when the country was neutral), *Madame MacAdam* concerns a small, third-rate British travelling theatre company which, by the merest chance, winds up in the Free State. They are depleted in number (only five), and they have run out of petrol. Unable to move on, they become involved in: a crooked greyhound race (through which they hope to obtain petrol); the search for a missing child; the seduction of a local teenager by a young actor in the company; and somewhat incidentally, a performance of an Irish melodrama dealing with the 18th-century patriot Robert Emmet and his love, Sarah Curran.

Interweaving these various strands of plot, Kilroy sometimes satirizes, sometimes parodies, as he employs the most hackneyed materials of melodrama in a setting that only occasionally hints at realism (e.g., the drone of war planes overhead which may be either German or English). As Madame MacAdam says in her first speech: "Tonight we offer the usual fare. A love story. A lost child. Villainy at large. While in the background the drums of war. And at the end, that frail salvation of the final curtain. What else is there?"

Kilroy employs projected scene headings of a melodramatic nature which evoke silent film subtitles but which also recall the scene captions employed (to quite a different end) in Brechtian theater. Their function is, of course, not only to acknowledge and so mitigate the episodic nature of the plot but also to gently tease the banal ingredients. Madame herself begins the play with a speech (above) that finally seems directed more to the audience in the real theater than to the rural Irish who watch Robert Emmet court Sarah.

The various plot strands form a context for a running commentary (by several characters) on the acting profession and the nature and function of the theater. This is really what the play is about: the actor's artistic urge for expression; his triumph in making an audience "believe"; the ephemeral nature of his achievement; the healing and transforming power of theater; "the greatest mystery of all"—becoming another person; "human error and human frailty . . . and the second-rate" as the foundation for "the miracle of theatre." Madame (thought to be based on the famous actor-manager of that period, Anew McMaster) is comically pompous, but she can also be wisely succinct: "To keep at bay the principle of chaos. That is what is urgent." Although not necessarily his best, *Madame MacAdam* is Kilroy's most complex and demanding play.

—Gene A. Barnett

KOPS, Bernard.

Born in London, 28 November 1926. Educated in London elementary schools to age 13. Married Erica Gordon in 1956; four children. Has worked as a docker, chef, salesman, waiter, lift man, and barrow boy. Writer-in-residence, London Borough of Hounslow, 1980–82; lecturer in drama, Spiro Institute, 1985–86, and various educational authorities, 1989–90. Writer-in-residence, Polka Theatre, London, 1991–92. Recipient: Arts Council bursary 1957, 1979, 1985, 1990, 1991; C. Day Lewis fellowship, 1981–83. Agent: David Higham Associates, 5–8 Lower John Street, London W1R 4HA. Address: 35 Canfield Gardens, Flat 1, London N.W.6, England.

Publications

PLAYS

The Hamlet of Stepney Green (produced 1958). 1959.
Goodbye World (produced 1959).
Change for the Angel (produced 1960).
The Dream of Peter Mann (produced 1960). 1960.
Stray Cats and Empty Bottles (produced 1961).
Enter Solly Gold, music by Stanley Myers (produced 1962). In *Satan, Socialites, and Solly Gold: Three New Plays from England*, 1961; in *Four Plays*, 1964.
Home Sweet Honeycomb (broadcast 1962). In *Four Plays*, 1964.
The Lemmings (broadcast 1963). In *Four Plays*, 1964.

Four Plays (includes *The Hamlet of Stepney Green, Enter Solly Gold, Home Sweet Honeycomb, The Lemmings*). 1964.
The Boy Who Wouldn't Play Jesus (for children; produced 1965). In *Eight Plays: Book 1*, edited by Malcolm Stuart Fellows, 1965.
David, It Is Getting Dark (produced 1970). 1970.
Moss (televised 1975; produced 1991).
It's a Lovely Day Tomorrow, with John Goldschmidt (televised 1975; produced 1976).
More Out Than In (produced 1980).
Ezra (produced 1981).
Simon at Midnight (broadcast 1982; produced 1985).
Some of These Days (produced 1990; as *Sophie! Last of the Red Hot Mamas*, produced 1990).
Playing Sinatra (produced 1991). 1992.
Androcles and the Lion (for children; produced 1992).
Dreams of Anne Frank (for children; produced 1992).
Who Shall I Be Tomorrow? (for children; produced 1992).

RADIO PLAYS: *Home Sweet Honeycomb*, 1962; *The Lemmings*, 1963; *Born in Israel*, 1963; *The Dark Ages*, 1964; *Israel: The Immigrant*, 1964; *Bournemouth Nights*, 1979; *I Grow Old, I Grow Old*, 1979; *Over the Rainbow*, 1980; *Simon at Midnight*, 1982; *Trotsky Was My Father*, 1984; *More Out Than In*, 1985; *Kafe Kropotkin*, 1988; *Colour Blind*, 1989; *Congress in Manchester*, 1990; *The Ghost Child*, 1991; *Soho Nights*, 1992; *Sailing with Homer*, 1992.

TELEVISION PLAYS: *I Want to Go Home*, 1963; *The Lost Years of Brian Hooper*, 1967; *Alexander the Greatest*, 1971; *Just One Kid*, 1974; *Why the Geese Shrieked*, and *The Boy Philosopher*, from stories by Isaac Bashevis Singer, 1974; *It's a Lovely Day Tomorrow*, with John Goldschmidt, 1975; *Moss*, 1975; *Rocky Marciano Is Dead*, 1976; *Night Kids*, 1983; *The Survivor* series, 1991–92.

NOVELS
Awake for Mourning. 1958.
Motorbike. 1962.
Yes from No-Man's Land. 1965.
The Dissent of Dominick Shapiro. 1966.
By the Waters of Whitechapel. 1969.
The Passionate Past of Gloria Gaye. 1971.
Settle Down Simon Katz. 1973.
Partners. 1975.
On Margate Sands. 1978.

VERSE
Poems. 1955.
Poems and Songs. 1958.
An Anemone for Antigone. 1959.
Erica, I Want to Read You Something. 1967.

For the Record. 1971.
Barricades in West Hampstead. 1988.

OTHER

The World Is a Wedding (autobiography). 1963.
Neither Your Honey nor Your Sting: An Offbeat History of the Jews. 1985.

Editor, *Poetry Hounslow.* 1981.

MANUSCRIPT COLLECTIONS: University of Texas, Austin; Indiana University, Bloomington.

Bernard Kops's work is informed by tension between the despair—not for himself, but for humanity—from which suicide beckons, and a redeeming joy of life. Contradictions inform such poems as "Shalom Bomb," "Sorry for the Noise—We're Dancing," and "First Poem," which injoins "let's dance upon the desolation." Despite his clarity of vision about the mess we're making of the world and the death which awaits us—necessarily as individuals, with increasing probability collectively as well—Kops's celebratory rejoinder sets to dancing the feet of those high-spirited people who populate his novels and poems and plays.

Although occasionally mislabeled a kitchen-sink realist, Kops writes neither gritty nor cozy domestic drama. More often presentational than representational, offering parables upon human nature, his plays are theatrical poetry employing language—in its rhythms, rhymes, word play, and word choice—and conflicts not so much contemporary as timeless.

Unlike other "poetic" playwrights, however, Kops creates not a rarefied atmosphere but robust crackpots, energetic con-artists and their gullible targets, and colorful characters whose values he satirizes even as he nudges them towards reform and affirmation of life. A writer poised between tears and laughter, Kops has increasingly emphasized palpable passion; of late he leaves spectators more often touched than chuckling.

Kops frequently depicts old people made anxious by mortality, yet he emphasizes the imperative to live. Although such plays as *Just One Kid*, *Change for the Angel*, *Goodbye World*, and *It's a Lovely Day Tomorrow* don't flinch from death snatching people prematurely or tempting them to end their own lives, Kops holds up those characters who harbor a death wish as negative examples not to be emulated. Thus Danny Todd's initial respect for independent lives in *Home Sweet Honeycomb* is commendable, and his ultimate embrace of the firing squad which killed his brother signifies his dehumanization. Sam Levy and Peter Mann both learn through their skirmishes with death to embrace life. Appreciating only on his death bed that he's let life slip by, Sam in *The Hamlet of Stepney Green* returns as a ghost to inspire love of life in his son. Peter Mann grows from a lad convinced nothing's worth living for to exuberance about life. An anti-nuclear and anti-war play, *The Dream of Peter Mann* makes a compelling argument against mass destruction; life is worth living. The remarkable black comedy *The Lemmings* likewise carries in its criticism of suicide implicit affirmation. After Norman and

Iris follow their parents into the water, the sound of seagulls and sea devastates us because they should have lived.

Frequently Kops dramatizes means of surviving bereavement or failure. Moss chooses life in the face of grief for his beloved grandson. Moss survives by taking up painting and giving away his money, while Harry of *Rocky Marciano Is Dead* maintains his independence by nurturing the potential of a black boxer. *The Lost Years of Brian Hooper* and *Simon at Midnight* likewise demonstrate the efficacy of hopes and dreams in combating futility and fear of death; without them, life is meaningless.

Repeatedly interfering with these characters' happiness are their wealth and/or greed. The miser Moss has agonized over the loss of his sweet-shop profits to thieving kids; his salvation lies in divesting himself of his fortune. Sam Levy and Peter Mann have been distracted from life's beauty by pursuit of riches from pickled-herring or shrouds. The successful rightwing writer in *David, It Is Getting Dark* is driven so far as to plagiarize the work of a Jewish writer living in penury. The title character of *Enter Solly Gold*, as he fleeces a family of vulgar snobs, releases them from materialism to enjoyment of life. *The Boy Who Wouldn't Play Jesus* dramatizes a Christmas lesson about giving which turns the boy into a social activist. Distressed that Christianity "hasn't really happened yet," he appeals to the cast members' consciences and cancels the nativity play. As long as children are starving, Jesus cannot be born.

For many years Kops's work displayed ambivalence towards women. Although occasionally rapturous about romantic love, Kops gives David Levy and Peter Mann traditional women who want nothing in life but to sacrifice themselves for their mates. His men most often are hen-pecked or neglected or part of a bickering couple in a marriage not exactly made in heaven. His sons fall victim to overbearing mothers who smother them or even—in *Home Sweet Honeycomb* and *The Lemmings*—send them to their deaths. Such stereotypes of domineering mothers and controlling wives have, however, given way in several recent Kops plays to more fully developed women. The runaway in *Night Kids* who resorts to prostitution to survive inspires compassion both when she's on the streets and as she returns to her indifferent parents. Leading female characters in *Sophie! Last of the Red Hot Mamas* (about Sophie Tucker) and *Kafe Kropotkin* (about an anarchist collective) even show signs of autonomy and competence. Sandra of *Playing Sinatra* survives and escapes, leaving the two men, her friend and her symbiotic sibling, trapped in the creepy South London house obsessing over Sinatra recordings instead of living. The female character in *Who Shall I Be Tomorrow?*, on the other hand, mines herself more deeply in pathetic poverty.

Kops's masterpiece *Ezra* attempts to reconcile Ezra Pound's poetic genius with the fascism and anti-semitism he espoused. Playful in tone and fluid in structure, *Ezra* dramatizes Pound's postwar imprisonment. Mocking his situation and those who accuse him of treason with snatches of pop songs, Pound chats with Mussolini and Vivaldi. Not a one-dimensional villain, Pound argues in his defense: "A poet listens to his own voice." Implicitly, Kops condemns the confiscation of Pound's literary manuscripts as evidence and defends his right to free expression. After his release, troubled by his former views, Pound goes to the Ghetto Vecchio in Venice, where he appeals to the Jews there to vouch for him. As he is answered only by the wind, Pound cannot understand why the houses are empty. Kops appears to forgive the poet's complicity in genocide out of a humanity which the poet cannot discover in himself until too late, when Pound reaches a chilling anagnorisis, a recognition that those Jews he loved have perished because of policies he championed.

—Tish Dace

KUREISHI, Hanif.

Born in London, 5 December 1954. Educated at King's College, University of London, B.A. in philosophy. Writer-in-residence, Royal Court Theatre, London, 1981 and 1985–86. Recipient: George Devine award, 1981; *Evening Standard* award, for screenplay, 1985. Agent: Lemon, Unna, and Durbridge, 24 Pottery Lane, Holland Park, London W11 4LZ, England.

Publications

PLAYS

Soaking the Heat (produced 1976).
The Mother Country (produced 1980).
The King and Me (produced 1980). In *Outskirts, The King and Me, Tomorrow—Today!*, 1983.
Outskirts (produced 1981). In *Outskirts, The King and Me, Tomorrow— Today!*, 1983.
Tomorrow—Today! (produced 1981). In *Outskirts, The King and Me, Tomorrow—Today!*, 1983.
Cinders, from a play by Janusz Glowacki (produced 1981).
Borderline (produced 1981). 1981.
Artists and Admirers, with David Leveaux, from a play by Alexander Ostrovsky (produced 1982).
Birds of Passage (produced 1983). 1983.
Outskirts, The King and Me, Tomorrow—Today! 1983.
Mother Courage, adaptation of a play by Brecht (produced 1984).
My Beautiful Laundrette (screenplay; includes essay "The Rainbow Sign"). 1986.
Sammy and Rosie Get Laid (screenplay). 1988.
London Kills Me (screenplay). 1991.
Mother Courage and Her Children, adaptation of a play by Brecht, lyrics by Sue Davis (produced 1993).

SCREENPLAYS: *My Beautiful Laundrette*, 1985; *Sammy and Rosie Get Laid*, 1988; *London Kills Me*, 1991.

RADIO PLAYS: *You Can't Go Home*, 1980; *The Trial*, from a novel by Kafka, 1982.

NOVEL

The Buddha of Suburbia. 1990.

Hanif Kureishi is often assumed to be a purely Asian writer, but for the most part his earlier plays look at events through the eyes of characters who are white. Kureishi himself was born in London of mixed parentage, with an English mother and Pakistani father. He grew up without feeling that he was different from his classmates and has always thought of himself as an Englishman. However, the need for an Asian voice in contemporary theatre and the current concern with problems that affect Asians have caused him to examine that other aspect of his heritage.

After two early plays produced in 1980, *The Mother Country* at Riverside Studios and *The King and Me* (about a couple's obsession with Elvis Presley) at the Soho Poly, Kureishi's more ambitious play *Outskirts* received a production at the Royal Shakespeare Company Warehouse in 1981. It centres on two men who grew up together in the straggling suburbs around Orpington and on the eventual divergence of their lives. Del, who has always tagged along with the more dominant Bob, makes the break from their dead-end working-class background and trains as a teacher. Bob, who leaves school early for a well-paid job, finds himself on the unemployment scrapheap. In his bitterness, he turns to the National Front where, he says, "We're strong men, together. Men worn down by waiting. Abused men. Men with no work. Our parents made redundant. Now us. . . ." But the racialism he expresses now is a reminder of an evening ten years ago when he and Del had beaten up a Pakistani. On that occasion, Del had taken the initiative in violence, and the shadow of that incident haunts him now that he is a respectable teacher.

Outskirts has an awkwardness of construction in the way it moves from past to present and back again, and the appearance at intervals of Bob's mother is not always successfully dealt with. But nonetheless, Kureishi gets inside the skin of young men who thought, with the end of school and a wage packet each week, that the world was theirs: "I tell you," says Bob, "it's all waiting for a boy like me. Cars, clothes, crumpet." Kureishi also illuminates the lot of the women. Bob's wife, Maureen, returns from having had an abortion rather than bring up a child in a home with no money, to be told by Bob's mother, who is prematurely old, "You did the right thing. Sometimes I wish I'd done the same. I know it's wicked to say that. But I think it. I do."

In *Borderline*, written after a workshop collaboration with Joint Stock and produced at the Royal Court in 1981, Kureishi turns to the problems of Asian immigrants. The idea of writing about Asians in Britain came from the Court's artistic director, Max Stafford-Clark, and Kureishi was at first nervous of writing from outside his own experience. His misgivings proved unnecessary, and with the combination of several weeks of meeting and talking with Asians in Southall, and the inspiration of his imagination and his own past, he was able to write a play about the Asian dilemma in England. For him, writing about Pakistanis in England is also a way of writing about the English and the way England has changed.

Borderline is concerned with the lives of several Asians who are trying to survive in an indifferent or hostile community. An English observer, Susan, a journalist writing an article on Asians in England, takes the role at times of commentator on what Kureishi himself heard during his research: "All the people I've spoken to have been beaten or burnt or abused at some time. You speak to them, they say they like England, it is democratic, or just or good. And then say what's been done to them here. Such viciousness in England." The play also deals with conflict among the Asians—those who try to maintain an Asian way of life, and those who adopt English morals and attitudes. The parents of Amina decide to send her back to an arranged marriage in Pakistan, but she realises that she has become English and, whether she likes it or not, England is her home.

Birds of Passage deals with a lower middle-class family in Sydenham who have fallen on hard times. There are resonances of *The Cherry Orchard* as the family are forced to sell their house to an Asian former lodger. The father of the family, a self-educated Labour councillor, does not realise times have changed until he loses his job. His daughter, despite her education, has taken to prostitution on the side, and his wife's sister and her husband, at one time affluent on the proceeds of selling central heating, suddenly find that the bottom has dropped out of the market. Kureishi writes about his ineffectual characters with affection, and there is what amounts to a hymn of praise to suburbia from the father. "Out here we live in peace, indifferent to the rest of the world. We have no sense of communal existence but we are tolerant, not cruel." The least sympathetic character is the Asian, Asif, the spoilt, indolent son of rich parents. Asif despises poor Pakistani immigrants and is smugly upwardly mobile. The play is not primarily about racial attitudes, but about the effect of the recession on people in Britain who believed in the optimism of the 1960's and then had to face unemployment in the early 1980's.

Kureishi's script for the film *My Beautiful Laundrette* brought him to the attention of a wider public. A small-budget movie, directed by Stephen Frears, it caught the imagination of critics and audiences. Several of the characters and situations of his stage plays are enlarged on here. The outwardly modest but sexually experienced Amina of *Borderline* has her counterpart in the film, as does the amoral young entrepreneur Asif of *Birds of Passage*, while the intense and, in the film's case, homosexual, relationship of the two boys who grew up together echoes the relationship of Del and Bob in *Outskirts*.

Kureishi's second film, *Sammy and Rosie Get Laid*, was larger, more diffuse, and in the end less satisfactory. It featured polemical discussions on drugs, and the gay incidents seemed to be extraneous rather than a development of the story. Sammy, an Asian, and Rosie, English, living in Brixton, have an uneasy relationship. Sammy's Pakistani politician father arrives in London, to find that the pleasant and gentlemanly England he remembers has vanished. He is haunted by the ghost of a man with a battered face, a reminder of his responsibility for torture in Pakistan. The film has raw, strong images, but suffers from Kureishi's ambition to give a dissertation on everything that is wrong in Britain in the Thatcherite 1980's.

Kureishi's next film, which he directed, *London Kills Me*, narrows the theme to the London drug scene. Clint, a young member of a drug-dealing posse, is half in love with a heroin addict Sylvie, but she is stolen from him by the posse leader, Muffdiver. The smalltime posse tries to get in with the bigtime dealers but only end by alienating them. Clint, having been unlucky in love and crime, decides to go straight and takes a job as a waiter in a diner. His first ingratiating smile at a customer implies he will be a success in his new occupation. Although the film is set against the drug scene, it concentrates on the triangular relationship and the symbolic search by Clint for the "true shoe" after his have been stolen when he is beaten up by a couple of dealers to whom he owes money. The ending is ambiguous. The spontaneous street hustler has turned into a paid performer in waiter's costume, yet there is an air of futility about his friends who decide to continue the life of flight and disguise.

Kureishi's novel, *The Buddha of Suburbia*, has an autobiographical element. It is the story of Karim Amir, "an Englishman born and bred—almost," who lives with his English mother and Indian father in a dull South London suburb. It is his dream to escape to London proper and to the world of sex and drugs. Finally his father, "the Buddha of Suburbia," leads the way with his glamorous mistress, Eva, and introduces him to the exciting life of the city. Karim becomes an actor and falls under the influence of the charismatic theatre director Matthew Pike, star of the flourishing alternative theatre. The play Karim is in transfers to New York, where he re-encounters his old schoolfriend Charlie, now a rock star and into sado-masochism. The book is strong on dialogue and characters—some of which are clearly borrowed from real life. It is episodic in construction and reads at times like a source book for the recurring themes in his plays.

—Clare Colvin

L

LAFFAN, Kevin (Barry).

Born in Reading, Berkshire, 24 May 1922. Married Jeanne Lilian Thompson in 1952; three sons. Repertory actor and director until 1950; director of productions, Pendragon Company, 1950–52, and Everyman Theatre Company, 1953–58, both Reading. Recipient: ATV Television award, 1959; Irish Life award, 1969; National Union of Students award, 1969; *Sunday Times* award, 1970. Agent: ACTAC (Theatrical and Cinematic) Ltd., 16 Cadogan Lane, London S.W.1, England.

Publications

PLAYS

Ginger Bred (as Kevin Barry) (produced 1951).
The Strip-Tease Murder (as Kevin Barry), with Neville Brian (produced 1955).
Winner Takes All (as Kevin Barry) (produced 1956).
First Innocent (as Kevin Barry) (produced 1957).
Angie and Ernie, with Peter Jones (produced 1966).
Zoo Zoo Widdershins Zoo (produced 1969). 1969.
It's a Two-Foot-Six-Inches-above-the-Ground World (produced 1969). 1970.
The Superannuated Man (produced 1971).
There Are Humans at the Bottom of My Garden (produced 1972).
Adam and Eve and Pinch Me (produced 1974).
Never So Good (produced 1976).
The Wandering Jew (produced 1978).
The Dream of Trevor Staines (produced 1983).
Adam Redundant (also director: produced 1989).

SCREENPLAYS: *It's a Two-Foot-Six-Inches-above-the-Ground World* (*The Love Ban*), 1973; *The Best Pair of Legs in the Business*, 1973.

RADIO PLAY: *Portrait of an Old Man*, 1961.

TELEVISION PLAYS: *Lucky for Some*, 1969; *The Best Pair of Legs in the Business*, 1969; *You Can Only Buy Once*, 1969; *Castlehaven* series, 1970; *Kate* series, 1970; *A Little Learning*, 1970; *The Designer*, 1971; *Decision to Burn*, 1971; *Fly on the Wall* (trilogy), 1971; *The General*, 1971; *Emmerdale Farm*, 1972, 1977; *Justice* series, 1973; *The Reformer*, 1973; *Getting Up*, 1973; *Beryl's Lot* series, with Bill McIlwraith, 1973, 1977; *After the Wedding Was Over*, 1975; *It's a Wise Child*, 1975; for *Bud Flanagan* programme.

NOVEL

Amos Goes to War with M. Mitchell. 1987.

Anybody leaving the theatre after the first performance of Kevin Laffan's *Zoo Zoo Widdershins Zoo* would probably have been amazed to discover that the writer was a man in his forties. Laffan's study of a group of young people—the eldest are in their early twenties—sharing a house and everything in it while refusing to work and turning to petty crime—shop-lifting, robbing telephone booths, and cheating gas meters—when money is scarce, seems to have come exactly out of the way of life it re-creates.

Laffan, however, was born in 1922 and *Zoo Zoo Widdershins Zoo* was his first real success. It won an award from the National Union of Students, which wanted a play for production in universities. If the occasion of the play suggested its theme, only Laffan's complete understanding of his characters, their idioms, attitudes and rejection of social responsibility, can account for the play's authenticity and for its cool, morally neutral tone. It captures and makes comprehensible a gaiety which seems to grow out of the apparently depressing life-style these people have adopted. Cleverly, it is a play entirely about a minute community, and there is a feeling that the audience, as well as the squatters, is betrayed when the couple whose house has become a home for the group manoeuvre the others out and, suddenly, revert to conventional bourgeois habits.

Zoo Zoo Widdershins Zoo is almost plotless, carefully designed to seem as aimless as the way of life it observes, and its alternations of intensity and relaxation are all conveyed in the limited, inexplicit dialogue which exploits its young people's idiom.

This was by no means Laffan's first play. He began his career in the theatre as an actor; with others, he helped to found the Everyman Theatre Company in Reading and in 1959 won an award from ATV for a television play *Cut in Ebony* which was never produced because it deals, in terms of comedy, with problems of race and colour. Laffan, abandoning acting and direction, earned the time to write plays by undertaking any other writing that would pay, including a not very successful series of television programmes for the comedian Bud Flanagan. His television plays, *Lucky for Some*, *You Can Only Buy Once*, and *The Best Pair of Legs in the Business*, however, established him as a playwright in this medium, and *Castlehaven*, a television serial doing for a Yorkshire community what *Coronation Street* did for Lancashire, became a fixed part of commercial television schedules outside London.

Laffan's stage play *Angie and Ernie* was produced outside London. *The Superannuated Man* won an Irish Life award in 1969 but was produced only in 1971. But *Zoo Zoo Widdershins Zoo*, after its university production, was given a successful commercial production in London and impressed the critics, with the result that *It's a Two-Foot-Six- Inches-above-the-Ground World*, first seen at the Theatre Royal, Bristol, was able to travel to London and make a distinct impression there; it considers, in a very individual tone of toughly angry, affectionate hilarity, the effects on a young Catholic husband and wife of their Church's refusal to permit any means of birth control. Catholics complained that Laffan's play misrepresents the Church's attitude, but in its own terms, as a work for the theatre, it is entirely successful.

The marriage of a young Liverpool Catholic is falling into ruins; his wife, a Protestant girl who was converted to Catholicism only in order to marry him, has provided him with three sons; another child would probably kill her, while sexual abstinence, which suits the wife even less than it suits the husband, is destroying the marriage. The voice of the Church is transmitted by a young priest who expresses the Catholic prohibition at its most extreme and unyielding. A totally permissive view is offered by an outsider—a van driver making a delivery at the middle son's Catholic primary school. The father's prudery had prevented him from teaching his children anything about their physical functions, so that the van driver's use of the school lavatory, arousing the child's interest in an adult masculine body, costs the unfortunate driver—an energetic and undeviating lecher—his job.

These people argue their cases with great energy, and the play dresses the situation in continual high spirits. When all else fails, the wife's surreptitiously acquired and so far unused collection of contraceptive pills comes in useful; they can, for example, be mistaken for aspirins. It would not be fair to accuse Laffan of pulling his punches in the interests of good taste or of scrupulous intellectual fairness in his presentation of opposed points of view. He is, however, far more deeply involved through his emotions than through any desire to solve intellectual arguments, and under the hard-edged hilarity of its presentation, there is a touching awareness of the painful situation of two simple, good, likeable people trapped by the husband's earnest conviction.

Laffan's progress has been slow. *There Are Humans at the Bottom of My Garden* did not rival the success of its predecessor, and his later work for television, notably the skilfully written *Emmerdale Farm* and the more predictable *Justice* series, won a loyal television following without suggesting any of the tougher moral and social implications of his work for the theatre. A handful of television plays and two unusual comedies, differing so widely in tone and aim as *Zoo Zoo Widdershins Zoo* and *It's a Two-Foot-Six-Inches-above-the-Ground World*, suggest that his other plays deserve careful study by some enterprising theatre manager.

—Henry Raynor

LAVERY, Bryony.

Born in Wakefield, Yorkshire, 21 December 1947. Educated at the University of London, 1966–69, B.A. (honours) in English 1969. Artistic director, Les Oeufs Malades, 1976–78, Extraordinary Productions, 1979–80, and Female Trouble, 1981–83, all London. Resident dramatist, Unicorn Theatre for Young People, London, 1986–88; artistic director, Gay Sweatshop, London, 1989–91. Agent: Andrew Hewson, John Johnson Ltd., Clerkenwell House, 45–47 Clerkenwell Green, London EC1R 0HT. Address: 17 Maitland Road, London E15 4EL, England.

Publications

PLAYS

Of All Living (produced 1967).
Days at Court (produced 1968).

Warbeck (produced 1969).

I Was Too Young at the Time to Understand Why My Mother Was Crying (also director: produced 1976).

Sharing (also director: produced 1976).

Germany Calling, with Peter Leabourne (produced 1976).

Grandmother's Footsteps (also director: produced 1977).

Snakes (produced 1977).

The Catering Service (also director: produced 1977).

Floorshow, with others (produced 1978).

Helen and Her Friends (also director: produced 1978).

Bag (also director, produced 1979).

Time Gentlemen Please (cabaret; produced 1979).

The Wild Bunch (for children; produced 1979). In *Responses*, edited by Don Shiach, 1990.

Sugar and Spice (for children; produced 1979).

Unemployment: An Occupational Hazard? (for children; also director: produced 1979).

Gentlemen Prefer Blondes, adaptation of the novel by Anita Loos (produced 1980).

The Joker (for children; also director: produced 1980).

The Family Album (also director: produced 1980).

Pamela Stephenson One Woman Show (cabaret; produced 1981).

Missing (also director: produced 1981).

Zulu, with Patrick Barlow (produced 1981).

Female Trouble (cabaret; produced 1981).

The Black Hole of Calcutta, with Patrick Barlow (produced 1982).

Götterdämmerung; or, Twilight of the Gods, with Patrick Barlow and Susan Todd (produced 1982).

For Maggie, Betty and Ida, music by Paul Sand (produced 1982).

More Female Trouble (cabaret), music by Caroline Noh (produced 1982).

Uniform and Uniformed, and Numerical Man (broadcast 1983). In *Masks and Faces*, edited by Dan Garrett, 1984.

Hot Time (produced 1984).

Calamity (produced 1984).

Origin of the Species (produced 1984). In *Plays by Women: Six*, edited by Mary Remnant, 1987.

The Wandsworth Warmers (cabaret; also director: produced 1984).

The Zulu Hut Club (for children; produced 1984).

The Wandsworth Warmers Christmas Carol Concert (cabaret; also director: produced 1985).

Over and Out (also director: produced 1985).

Witchcraze (produced 1985). In *Herstory*, edited by Gabrial Griffin and Elaine Aston, 1991.

Getting Through (additional lyrics only), by Nona Shepphard, music by Helen Glavin (produced 1985).

The Wandsworth Warmers in Unbridled Passions (cabaret; also director: produced 1986).

Sore Points (for children; produced 1986).

Mummy, with Sally Owen and L. Ortolja (produced 1987).

Madagascar (for children; also director: produced 1987).
The Headless Body, music by Stephanie Nunn (produced 1987).
The Dragon Wakes (for children; produced 1988).
Puppet States (produced 1988).
The Drury Lane Ghost, with Nona Shepphard (produced 1989).
Two Marias (produced 1989). In *Her Aching Heart, Two Marias, Wicked,* 1991.
Wicked (produced 1990). In *Her Aching Heart, Two Marias, Wicked,* 1991.
Her Aching Heart (produced 1990). In *Her Aching Heart, Two Marias, Wicked,* 1991.
Kitchen Matters (produced 1990).
Her Aching Heart, Two Marias, Wicked. 1991.
Flight (produced 1991).
Peter Pan, with Nona Shepphard (produced 1991).
The Sleeping Beauty, with Nona Shepphard (produced 1992).
The Way to Cook a Wolf (produced 1993).

RADIO PLAYS: *Fire the Life-Giver*, 1979; *Changes at Work* series, 1980; *Let's Get Dressed*, 1982; *Uniform and Uniformed*, 1983; *Numerical Man*, 1983; *Magical Beasts*, 1987; *Cliffhanger* series, 1990; *Laying Ghosts*, 1992.

TELEVISION PLAYS: *Revolting Women* series, with others, 1981; *Rita of the Rovers*, 1989; *The Cab Wars*, 1989.
Video: *The Lift*, 1988; *Twelve Dancing Princesses*, 1989.

CRITICAL STUDY: "But Will Men Like It; or, Living as a Feminist Writer Without Committing Murder" by Lavery, in *Women and Theatre* edited by Susan Todd, 1984.

THEATRICAL ACTIVITIES

DIRECTOR: **Plays**—most of her own plays; *More Female Trouble* (revival), 1983; *Homelands: Under Exposure* by Lisa Evans, and *The Mrs. Docherties* by Nona Shepphard (co-director, with Shepphard), 1985; *Hotel Destiny* by Tasha Fairbanks, 1987.

Bryony Lavery's plays are comic in the best sense of the term, funny, and engaging at a popular level. As Lavery's work tends to deal with controversial issues, including the representation of lesbian and gay sexuality and the funding of the theatre itself, its popularity is all the more significant. Lavery has worked in British alternative theatre for many years; she was, for instance, one of the early contributors to the work of both Gay Sweatshop and Monstrous Regiment. In the 1970's, Lavery collaborated with Caryl Churchill and Michelene Wandor on *Floorshow*, the Monstrous Regiment's cabaret. She also worked on the Regiment's cabaret *Gentlemen Prefer Blondes* and on comic shows such as *Female Trouble* and *More Female Trouble*, as well as in writing full-length plays. More recently, she has worked in children's theatre, theatre in education, and in teaching playwriting.

By drawing on this wide range of experience, Lavery has developed a voice which is quite unique in British theatre. Her style is intelligent and comic without being too sarcastic or snide; her writing reveals a certain jolly approach to important topical issues. In this way, Lavery has succeeded in developing a style which reaches beyond the typical middle-class forms of farce and drawing-room humour. Her work is self-consciously aware of those forms, but has found a balance between parody and celebration which is politically effective because it makes the plays so engaging, so enjoyable to read and watch.

Origin of the Species and *Her Aching Heart* are probably Lavery's best-known plays. Both illustrate Lavery's skill for combining humour with serious social commentary.

Origin of the Species was first produced by Monstrous Regiment in 1984, with Gillian Hanna as Molly, the anthropologist looking for said origins, who finds them in Victoria, the living creature-woman she unearths, played by Mary McCusker. Directed by Nona Shepphard, this play was ambitious in its scope (all of history) but remarkably unambitious in its use of resources: two actors, minimal sets and props, a small playing space. The power of the play is in its language and its use of humour. Similarly, *Her Aching Heart* is a sophisticated piece of writing, another two-hander which combines wit and parodies of courtly and poetic language with the representation of social issues in entertaining form.

Her Aching Heart was first produced in 1990 at the Oval House, London, directed by Claire Grove and performed by Nicola Kathrens and Sarah Kevney. The play is a "lesbian historical romance" which casts two modern-day women as the readers of bodice-ripping fiction, and concurrently as the heroines and heroes of that fiction. Modern-day characters Molly and Harriet engage in a budding romance in "real life" which parallels the stories of Molly, the servant girl, and Lady Harriet of Helstone Hall, the fiery aristocrat of the novel. Molly and Harriet read the novel and engage in the fictional romance, while they begin to know each other through telephone conversations. The audience gets to know the story, the highs and lows and misunderstandings of their romance, through the narratives and songs of these two central characters. They sing of love and of longing, and the songs are enriched by their references to stereotyped images of romance lifted from fiction and fairytales. That the two lovers are both women is important, but is not the key to the play's politics. Rather, the interweaving of the modern and the "historical," the real and the fictional, the serious and the silly, results in a complicated play which is a delight to read and to watch.

Her Aching Heart toured twice with the Women's Theatre Group in 1990 and 1991, both times with great success. That the play is so accessible and so amusing, as well as so beautifully constructed, makes the choice of a lesbian story-line all the more significant. Similarly, the play engages with gender, class, and power as issues intrinsic to an informed examination of bodice-ripper as a popular form, and to the expectations involved in reading romantic fiction. Yet all these important considerations are represented as parts of the larger fabric of the play rather than as "politically correct" issues to be evaluated in and of themselves.

Of course, not all Lavery's work is written for two actors. Some of the work has been much larger in scale, and some has been immediately linked to contemporary social issues. In 1990, for instance, Lavery wrote *Kitchen*

Matters, a play for Gay Sweatshop. As a mixed group with feminist politics, Sweatshop has promoted women's work since its founding in 1974. Sweatshop's struggle with viability in the current economic climate of the arts inspired Bryony Lavery to write the play as an "epic comedy." In a humorously self-referential scene. *Kitchen Matters* opens with a narrator (a woman at a typewriter) discussing her decision to write a (the) play:

> . . . There were some kids in a touring theatre company.
> They were Gay they were Poor they were Minority
> but they wanted a show.
> I had to help them out.
> I'm a writer with a Large Soul and Big Bills.
> My brain met up with my heart and they took a walk
> down into my guts to see what was there.
> The place was full of undigested matter.
> I chewed it over.
> A heavenly light shone on my blank A4 paper.
> I lit my two hundred and thirty-fourth cigarette.
> I started to write.

Lavery's enjoyment of and facility with language is evident even in this short extract. So is her dedication to the theatre. The narrator of this scene, like Lavery, wrote for the benefit of the theatre company. The play was highly successful, and reached many people from different communities, of different classes and sexual orientations. It was a political play with a point to make. But the comedy made the point, and the self-conscious nature of the humour made it all the more powerful as a play.

Lavery's current work is even larger in scale. In early 1992, she was at work on another "epic", but one which involves "a cast of 17" and which is "set in the tomb of an 11th-century Chinese Emperor." Whether or not such an ambitious play will find sufficient financial backing in Britain is a large question, and no doubt one which Lavery will weave into the humour of the play itself.

One thing is certain: if there is a contemporary playwright whose work deserves more attention—on theatrical and social grounds—it is Bryony Lavery.

—Lizbeth Goodman

LEIGH, Mike.

Born in Salford, Lancashire, 20 February 1943. Educated at North Grecian Street County Primary School; Salford Grammar School; Royal Academy of Dramatic Art, London, 1960–62; Camberwell School of Arts and Crafts, London, 1963–64; Central School of Art and Design, London, 1964–65; London Film School, 1965. Married the actress Alison Steadman in 1973; two sons. Founder, with David Halliwell, Dramagraph production company, London, 1965; associate director, Midlands Arts Centre for Young People, Birmingham, 1965–66; actor, Victoria Theatre, Stoke-on-Trent, Staffordshire,

1966; assistant director, Royal Shakespeare Company, 1967–68; lecturer, Sedgley Park and De La Salle colleges, Manchester, 1968–69, and London Film School, 1970–73. Recipient: Chicago Film Festival and Locarno Film Festival awards, 1972; George Devine award, 1974; *Evening Standard* award, 1982, 1989; Venice Film Festival Critics award, 1988; Stars de Demain Coup de Coeur, 1989; Peter Sellers Comedy award, 1989; National Society of Film Critics Best Film award, 1991. Agent: Peters, Fraser, and Dunlop Group, 503/4 The Chambers, Chelsea Harbour, Lots Road, London SW10 0XF, England.

Publications

PLAYS

The Box Play (produced 1965).
My Parents Have Gone to Carlisle (produced 1966).
The Last Crusade of the Five Little Nuns (produced 1966).
Waste Paper Guards, (produced 1966).
NENAA (produced 1967).
Individual Fruit Pies (produced 1968).
Down Here and Up There (produced 1968).
Big Basil (produced 1969).
Epilogue (produced 1969).
Glum Victoria and the Lad with Specs (produced 1969).
Bleak Moments (produced 1970).
A Rancid Pong (produced 1971).
Wholesome Glory (produced 1973).
The Jaws of Death (produced 1973).
Dick Whittington and His Cat (produced 1973).
Babies Grow Old (produced 1974).
The Silent Majority (produced 1974).
Abigail's Party (produced 1977). With *Goose-Pimples*, 1983.
Ecstasy (produced 1979). With *Smelling a Rat*, 1989.
Goose-Pimples, (produced 1981). With *Abigail's Party*, 1983.
Smelling a Rat (produced 1988). With *Ecstasy*, 1989.
Greek Tragedy (produced 1989).
It's a Great Big Shame! (produced 1993).

SCREENPLAYS: *Bleak Moments*, 1972; *The Short and Curlies*, 1987; *High Hopes*, 1988; *Life Is Sweet*, 1991; *Naked*, 1993.

RADIO PLAY: *Too Much of a Good Thing*, 1979 (banned).

TELEVISION PLAYS: *A Mug's Game*, 1973; *Hard Labour*, 1973; "Five Minute Films": *The Birth of the 2001 FA Cup Final Goalie, Old Chums, Probation, A Light Snack,* and *Afternoon,* all 1975; *The Permissive Society*, 1975; *Nuts in May*, 1976; *Knock for Knock*, 1976; *The Kiss of Death*, 1977; *Who's Who*, 1979; *Grown-Ups*, 1980; *Home Sweet Home*, 1982; *Meantime*, 1983; *Four Days in July*, 1985.

CRITICAL STUDY: *The Improvised Play: The Work of Mike Leigh* by Paul Clements, 1983.

THEATRICAL ACTIVITIES

DIRECTOR: All his own plays and films.

"My work" said Mike Leigh in a recent interview, "is always very strictly scripted with serious literary considerations."

Such words should be taken into account when assessing Leigh's plays, for a misconception has grown up—caused perhaps by his famous improvisational method—that his work is simply a "slice of life." Nothing could be further from the truth—though, as anyone who has seen his plays will attest, this method does give his pieces a very recognizable form and flavour.

Leigh produces his work through a process that is, broadly speaking, collaborational. A group of actors is selected and each is presented with the germ of a character. They are then asked to go away and develop these characters, using their own experience and imagination. At the end of several weeks, or months, they are reassembled and, under Leigh's direction, a play is put together. The accent here is on "under Leigh's direction": although he welcomes, indeed expects, creative input from his actors, Leigh remains very much in control. "I function as author and director," he has said. "There's no committee involved."

Such a process produces a very particular kind of play. Plots are simple, almost non-existent; language is idiomatic, even vulgar. There are no great dramatic moments, no soaring lyrical flights—little, indeed, that is "theatre" in the usual sense. What there *is* a close and exact study of suburban angst which uses the smallest words and actions to highlight undercurrents of malice and frustration. It's Artaud moved to Pinner, one might say, or Beckett in Brooklyn. What it's not is simply a "slice of life."

Leigh's first major success, and still his most popular play, was *Abigail's Party*. Eponymous Abigail is having a thrash; intimidated, her mother Sue retreats to the lurid drawing room of neighbour Beverley, a former beautician, and of her estate agent husband Laurence. Two other guests arrive; what should be a "lovely evening" then degenerates into a hilariously grotesque nightmare of jealousy, cruelty, and indifference. We laugh at Leigh's characters, but we laugh uneasily: in their material wealth and spiritual poverty they are, perhaps, a little too close for comfort.

Ecstasy, Leigh's next play, stands a little apart from his other pieces. Here the characters are working-class rather than lower middle-class; and, though desperate, Jean and Dawn, and Mike and Len, manifest a clumsy warmth and sympathy quite absent from, say, *Abigail's Party*. Particularly moving are the songs that end the play—songs whose sweetness (and occasional indecency) accentuate the characters' human pathos to an almost unbearable degree.

Two years later came *Goose-Pimples*, a return, at least in tone, to the world of *Abigail's Party*. Jackie, trainee croupier and lodger, brings home Muhammed, a small-time Arab businessman, for a drink. He thinks she's a prostitute; she thinks he's an oil-sheik. Into this misunderstanding barges her landlord, a car dealer, a colleague of his from work, and the colleague's wife. What follows is a parody of West End farce, with exits and entrances and muddles galore. At the end of the piece the two Englishmen, in a fit of drunken and entirely spurious gallantry, assault and humiliate Muhammed—a graphic depiction of the violence and xenophobia undercutting British society. It's a brutal moment; the shadow of Pinter, one feels, is hovering nearby.

After several years of film and television work Leigh returned to the stage with *Smelling a Rat*. More a playlet than a play, it is, perhaps, the slightest of Leigh's pieces. Of greater substance is *Greek Tragedy*, which Leigh directed in Australia in 1989. This project was something of a risk, for by his own admission Leigh knew nothing of Greek-Australian society. Using, however, a cast drawn entirely from this ethnic group he overcame this difficulty, producing by his collaborational method a play every bit as accurate and discomforting as his British pieces. A tragedy in more than one sense (it observes, for example, the classical unities), *Greek Tragedy* portrays the sterile, loveless marriage of Kalliope and Alex, two workers in the rag trade for whom the Australian dream has scarcely come true. Into their stifled lives burst Larry and Vicki, emigrant success stories and monsters *par excellence*; the stage is then set for another of Leigh's studies in suburban cruelty and frustration. If it all sounds a little familiar—*Goose-Pimples*, as it were, translated Down Under—it's still horribly unerring; one waits with interest to see what Leigh will do next.

—John O'Leary

LEONARD, Hugh.

Pseudonym for John Keyes Byrne. Born in Dublin, 9 November 1926. Educated at Presentation College, Dun Laoghaire, 1941–45. Married Paule Jacquet in 1955; one daughter. Civil servant, Dublin, 1945–59; script editor, Granada Television, Manchester, 1961–63; literary editor, Abbey Theatre, Dublin, 1976–77; programme director, Dublin Theatre Festival, 1978–80. Recipient: Italia prize, for television play, 1967; Writers Guild of Great Britain award, 1967; Tony award, 1978; New York Drama Critics Circle award, 1978; Outer Circle award, 1978; Vernon Rice award, 1978; Sagittarius prize. D.H.L.: Rhode Island College, Providence, 1980; D. Litt.: Trinity College, Dublin, 1989. Agent: Lemon, Unna, and Durbridge, 24 Pottery Lane, Holland Park, London W11 4LZ, England. Address: 6 Rossaun, Pilot View, Dalkey, County Dublin, Ireland.

Publications

PLAYS

The Italian Road (produced 1954).
The Big Birthday (produced 1956).
A Leap in the Dark (produced 1957).
Madigan's Lock (produced 1958). With *Pizzazz*, 1987.
A Walk on the Water (produced 1960).
The Passion of Peter Ginty, adaptation of the play *Peer Gynt* by Ibsen (produced 1961).
Stephen D, adaptation of the works *A Portrait of the Artist as a Young Man* and *Stephen Hero* by James Joyce (produced 1962). 1965.

Dublin One, adaptation of the stories *Dubliners* by James Joyce (produced 1963).
The Poker Session (produced 1963). 1963.
The Family Way, adaptation of a play by Eugène Labiche (produced 1964).
The Late Arrival of the Incoming Aircraft (televised 1964). 1968.
A View from the Obelisk (televised 1964; in *Scorpions*, produced 1983).
The Saints Go Cycling In, adaptation of the novel *The Dalkey Archives* by Flann O'Brien (produced 1965).
Mick and Mick (produced 1966; as *All the Nice People*, produced 1976). 1966.
A Time of Wolves and Tigers (televised 1967; produced in *Irishmen*, 1975). In *Suburb of Babylon*, 1983.
The Quick, and The Dead (produced 1967).
The Au Pair Man (produced 1968). In *Plays and Players*, December 1968.
The Barracks, adaptation of the novel by John McGahern (produced 1969).
The Patrick Pearse Motel (produced 1971). 1972.
Da (produced 1973). 1976; revised version, 1978.
Summer (produced 1974). 1979.
Suburb of Babylon (includes *A Time of Wolves and Tigers, Nothing Personal, The Last of the Last of the Mohicans*) (as *Irishmen*, produced 1975). 1983.
Some of My Best Friends Are Husbands, adaptation of a play by Eugène Labiche (produced 1976).
Liam Liar, adaptation of the play *Billy Liar* by Keith Waterhouse and Willis Hall (produced 1976).
Time Was (produced 1976). In *Da, A Life, Time Was*, 1981.
A Life (produced 1979). 1980.
Da, A Life, Time Was. 1981.
Kill (produced 1982).
Pizzazz (produced 1983). 1986.
Scorpions (includes *A View from the Obelisk, Roman Fever, Pizzazz*) (produced 1983).
The Mask of Moriarty, based on characters by Arthur Conan Doyle (produced 1985).
Moving (produced 1992).
Selected Plays. 1992.

SCREENPLAYS: *Great Catherine*, 1967; *Interlude*, with Lee Langley, 1967; *Whirligig*, 1970; *Percy*, with Terence Feely, 1970; *Our Miss Fred*, 1972; *Widows' Peak*, 1986; *Da*, 1989.

RADIO PLAYS: *The Kennedys of Castleross* series.

TELEVISION PLAYS: *The Irish Boys* (trilogy), 1962; *Saki* series, 1962; *A Kind of Kingdom*, 1963; *Jezebel Ex-UK* series, 1963; *The Second Wall*, 1964; *A Triple Irish*, 1964; *Realm of Error*, 1964; *My One True Love*, 1964; *The Late Arrival of the Incoming Aircraft*, 1964; *Do You Play Requests?*, 1964; *A View from the Obelisk*, 1964; *The Hidden Truth* series, 1964; *Undermind* series, 1964; *I Loved You Last Summer*, 1965; *Great Big Blond*, 1965; *Blackmail* series, 1965; *Public Eye* series, 1965; *Simenon* series: *The Lodger* and *The*

Judge, 1966; *Insurrection* (8 parts), 1966; *Second Childhood*, 1966; *The Retreat*, 1966; *Silent Song*, from a story by Frank O'Connor, 1966; *The Liars* series, 1966; *The Informer* series, 1966; *Out of the Unknown* series, 1966–67; *A Time of Wolves and Tigers*, 1967; *Love Life*, 1967; *Great Expectations* (serialization), from the novel by Dickens, 1967; *Wuthering Heights* (serialization), from the novel by Emily Brontë, 1967; *No Such Things as a Vampire*, 1968; *The Corpse Can't Play*, 1968; *A Man and His Mother-in-Law*, 1968; *Assassin*, 1968; *Nicholas Nickleby* (serialization), from the novel by Dickens, 1968; *Conan Doyle* series: *A Study in Scarlet* and *The Hound of the Baskervilles*, 1968; *Hunt the Peacock*, from a novel by H.R.F. Keating, 1969; *Talk of Angels*, 1969; *The Possessed* (serialization), from a novel by Dostoevsky, 1969; *Dombey and Son* (serialization), from the novel by Dickens, 1969; *Somerset Maugham* series: *P & O*, 1969, and *Jane*, 1970; *A Sentimental Education* (serialization), from a novel by Flaubert, 1970; *The Sinners* series, 1970–71; *Me Mammy* series, 1970–71; *White Walls and Olive Green Carpets*, 1971; *The Removal Person*, 1971; *Pandora*, 1971; *The Virgins*, 1972; *The Ghost of Christmas Present*, 1972; *The Truth Game*, 1972; *Tales from the Lazy Acres* series, 1972; *The Moonstone* (serialization), from the novel by Wilkie Collins, 1972; *The Sullen Sisters*, 1972; *The Watercress Girl*, from the story by H.E. Bates, 1972; *The Higgler*, 1973; *High Kampf*, 1973; *Milo O'Shea*, 1973; *Stone Cold Sober*, 1973; *The Bitter Pill*, 1973; *Another Fine Mess*, 1973; *Judgement Day*, 1973; *The Travelling Woman*, 1973; *The Hammer of God*, *The Actor and the Alibi*, *The Eye of Apollo*, *The Forbidden Garden*, *The Three Tools of Death*, and *The Quick One* (*Father Brown* series), 1974; *London Belongs to Me*, from the novel by Norman Collins, 1977; *Bitter Suite*, 1977; *Teresa*, *The Fur Coat*, and *Two of a Kind*, from stories by Sean O'Faolain, 1977; *The Last Campaign*, from the novel *The Captains and the Kings* by Jennifer Johnston, 1978; *The Ring and the Rose*, 1978; *Strumpet City*, from the novel by James Plunkett, 1980; *The Little World of Don Camillo*, from a novel by Giovanni Guareschi, 1981; *Good Behaviour*, from a work by Molly Keane, 1983; *O'Neill* series, 1983; *The Irish R.M.* series, 1985; *Hunted Down*, from a story by Dickens, 1985; *Troubles*, 1987; *Parnell and the Englishwoman* (serialization), from his own novel, 1991.

NOVEL

Parnell and the Englishwoman. 1990.

OTHER

Leonard's Last Book (essays). 1978.
A Peculiar People and Other Foibles (essays). 1979.
Home Before Night: Memoirs of an Irish Time and Place. 1979.
Leonard's Year (journalism). 1985.
Out After Dark (memoirs). 1989.
Rover and Other Cats (memoirs). 1992.

BIBLIOGRAPHY: *Ten Modern Irish Playwrights* by Kimball King, 1979.

THEATRICAL ACTIVITIES
ACTOR: **Play**—in *A Walk on the Water*, 1960.

Hugh Leonard comments:

(1973) Being an Irish writer both hampers and helps me: hampers, because one is fighting the preconceptions of audiences who have been conditioned to expect feyness and parochial subject matter; helps, because the writer can utilise a vigorous and poetic idiom which enables him to combine subtlety with richness. Ireland is my subject matter, but only to the degree in which I can use it as a microcosm; this involves choosing themes which are free of Catholicism and politics, both of which I detest, and which deprive one's work of applicability outside Ireland.

For many years I was obsessed with the theme of betrayal (*A Walk on the Water* and *The Poker Session*)—its effects and its inevitability. My work then began to reflect a preoccupation with defining and isolating the essence of the new prosperity, which I used as the subject for satire (*The Patrick Pearse Motel* and *Thieves*, as yet unproduced). By and large—and after the event—my work reflects Ibsen's observation that to be a writer is to sit in judgment on oneself; and perhaps for this reason I now want to write a play which, like *A Walk on the Water* and *Pandora*, is autobiographical. Like most writers I am involved in seeking a form. A play takes me a long time to write, and my methods involve—partly deliberately, partly because of how I work—various subterranean levels. At times this leads to an excess of cleverness, stemming perhaps from a lack of faith in one's own powers. Now that I have learned both the requirements and the uses of the dramatic form I would like to use a simplicity of style combined with visual situations—the image in my mind is the scene in which Lavinia confronts her mother across her father's corpse in *Mourning Becomes Electra*.

Like all writers who achieve middle-age, I am conscious of having wasted time, and also of having at last arrived at a sense of identity. Ideally, I would now like to write my "failures"; i.e., plays written as pure acts of self-expression, without any hope of their being staged. I am conscious that my main faults are the cleverness (in the structural sense) which I have mentioned and at times an irresponsible sense of comedy, which is not so much out of place as inclined to give my work an unintended lightness. These faults at least I know and can guard against. I regard myself as an optimist, and the theme that emerges from my plays is that life is good if it is not misused. But this is only an impression which—again after the event—I have gleaned from revisiting my work. As Moss Hart has said, one begins with two people on a stage, and one of them had better say something pretty damn quick! One starts to write, and one's own character and beliefs—not consciously defined—shapes, limits, enriches, pauperises, and defines one's work. Choice of subject and form are the cartridge case which contains the bullet. A play is an accident: often one writes the right play at the wrong time in one's life, and vice-versa; often one begins to write it that vital fraction in time before it has ripened in one's skull—or a moment too late, when it has gone cold. One goes on trying.

In the masterful autobiography of his early years, *Home Before Night*, Hugh Leonard tells of his gradual progress into the stifling prize of a job in the Irish civil service. The book is an eloquent statement of reconciliation, exploring his illegitimacy and family relationships, and is a rich lode of characters, full of personalities that are developed further in his plays. There is a passage toward the end where he records his first serious experience of theatre-going, when he visited the Abbey's production of Sean O'Casey's *The Plough and the Stars*. His prose crystallizes that experience, communicating the personal epiphany that made him a playwright. Rushing from the theatre to a train, he found himself in a compartment with a courting couple, sulking at his presence: "The pair of them could strip to their skins for all he cared. He looked away from them through the window and saw his reflection in the dark glass. It was amazing how calm he looked. His breath in the unheated compartment threw a mist upon the glass, but even then he could see, as if it was out there by the tracks, the door he would escape through."

Since O'Casey Irish playwrights have made Ireland their major subject. Leonard has claimed his place in that tradition, but there are essential differences, and he has always looked for broader applicability. He works mainly through the emergent middle classes of Ireland, with conflicts more suburban than urban and politics and religion as mere ghosts in the background. They are, of course, inescapable ghosts.

His best plays explore the characters of his own life, and stretch from *A Walk on the Water* to *A Life*, with 20 years of experience between the plays and a rare, deepening texture that demonstrates his own increased understanding of the past. Memory is also the form of many of his adaptations, including his first international success, *Stephen D*, a dramatization of James Joyce's autobiographical books. Using both *A Portrait of the Artist as a Young Man* and Joyce's earlier, more straightforward version of the book, *Stephen Hero*, Leonard showed his sympathy for the metaphysical flight of Dedalus—Joyce's own exile from church, family, and Ireland—as directly as if telling his own story.

His earliest plays found him more within the Irish dramatic tradition, even showing a concern with politics, but the form of *A Leap in the Dark* suggested his alienation from the violent course Irish politics often took. On a New Year's Eve in Dublin, a father and son fall out over the new troubles in Northern Ireland, with the son opposing the violence so completely that his best friend tries to show the reasoning behind the border raids by confessing his own part in them. The son, Charles, then discovers that another raid is in the making and sets out to inform the police. On his return to the house, he is shot.

It is rare that such scenes are depicted in Leonard's work, but his private path has wandered in many directions. After his start in theatre, writing plays for the Dublin Theatre Festival, he learned the disciplines of prolificacy by writing a serial called *The Kennedys of Castlerosse* for commercial radio. He went from Irish radio to British television, editing scripts, writing dramas and churning out numerous series. In the midst of that work, and while providing a steady stream of original plays for the stage, he continued adapting the work of other writers. Before *Stephen D*, there was the Irish *Peer Gynt*, which he called *The Passion of Peter Ginty*. Flann O'Brien's surreal humour in *The Dalkey*

Archives went to the stage as *The Saints Go Cycling In* and *Billy Liar* was transformed into an Irish play for the Abbey as *Liam Liar*.

Leonard, who is known to most of Ireland as Jack Byrne, or plain Jack, since they reject the pseudonym of Hugh Leonard, is quick to point out that an Irish literary movement is when two playwrights are on speaking terms. Nonetheless he has found himself at the centre of Irish letters on several occasions, including the stormy year he spent as literary manager of the Abbey and during his spell of literary management as one of the directors of the important Dublin Theatre Festival. Those positions were dignified by his presence, for there is no doubt that he is a major playwright of international importance.

For a long time he had a rewarding relationship with a theatre in Olney, Maryland, just outside Washington, D.C. Plays such as *The Patrick Pearse Motel* and *Da* were mounted in Olney well before New York took notice. New York, however, finally did with *Da* what London regularly refused to do with Leonard's critically well-regarded work; it gave him a major popular success.

The play is a joyous one, undisguisedly about the death of Leonard's own stepfather, the Da of the title. At the father's death the son flies from London to Dublin for the funeral, only to find that the old man wanders in to discuss the funeral and claim his place in his stepson's heart and mind. Leonard links past and present with the son's younger self, who is also on hand, reliving the traumas of adolescence, fighting it out with his mother, and getting furiously annoyed with his Da. The memories of the past and the details of the present, which include putting the meagre effects of the father into order, are so ingeniously layered that farce, understanding, and frustrated fury all manage to coexist, and, from Leonard's precise evocation of individuals at different points in time, the love that comes from understanding is conveyed.

A minor figure from *Da* is the character of Drumm, a man who figures in the autobiography as the civil servant who brings Leonard into the civil service. In *Da* he complains of "tummy trouble" which is revealed as cancer in the next memory play, *A Life*. Again, past and present coexist, with Drumm irascibly trying to make his peace with the girl he failed to marry in his youth while witnessing his younger self making all the original mistakes that foretold his old age as a bundle of attitudes and principles. The delicacy of Leonard's imagery and the richness of his comedy deflects the maudlin potential of the story, and the affirmation of life is reflected even in the final sentence when Drumm confronts the imminence of death and says to his wife, "Let's make a start." In those plays, Leonard is a writer at the height of his powers and he confirms his ability to extend the specific to a large audience: it is as if he were a master of the spectator's memories as well as his own.

A spectacular Dublin story about money siphoned out of Leonard's accounts saw to it that Leonard spent the greater part of his time for a few years after *A Life* concentrating on the more lucrative expression of films, but he never abandoned the theatre. His most notable advance was *Kill*, a dinner-party metaphor about Irish politics with some acidly presented characters all too recognizable to the Irish audience. His presentation of the Irish government as covert collaborators with terror alienated some of his audience, but not permanently. His Sherlock Holmes adventure, *The Mask of Moriarty*, was the hit of the 1985 Dublin Theatre Festival despite a notorious interview with the play's leading actor which gave away the twist in the play before it opened.

Although a number of friendly notices greeted an English production of *The Mask of Moriarty* at Leicester's Haymarket Theatre the following year, with the twist that Holmes's enemy Moriarty had had surgery to become Holmes's double being widely publicized again, it failed to find a West End home. Leonard's subsequent successes included a movie version of *Da* and a major television series, *Parnell and the Englishwoman*, a story about the Irish leader Charles Stewart Parnell and an adulterous affair which destroyed his career. Perhaps the lurking point, that without that affair Parnell's leadership might have kept Ireland from later years of bloodshed, was not finely enough expressed, but Leonard's novel of the same story won him the Sagittarius prize for first novel by an author over 60.

His 1992 play, *Moving*, saw him in the familiar geographical territory of the Dublin seaside town of Dalkey, but his attempt to chart an ordinary suburban family's rise over the 30 years from 1957 to 1987 showed its scheme rather too clearly. From childish skipping of mass to gay rights years later, from household pride to high pretension, the family called Noone represent an Ireland which cannot find its way. Overall, however, Leonard's art represents a potent expression of Ireland as he sees it, from where it moulds the individual.

—Ned Chaillet

LESSING, Doris (May, née Tayler).

Born in Kermansha, Persia, 22 October 1919; moved with her family to England, then to Banket, Southern Rhodesia, 1924. Educated at Dominican Convent School, Salisbury, Southern Rhodesia, 1926–34. Married 1) Frank Charles Wisdom in 1939 (divorced 1943), one son and one daughter; 2) Gottfried Lessing in 1945 (divorced 1949), one son. Au pair, Salisbury, 1934–35; telephone operator and clerk, Salisbury, 1937–39; typist, 1946–48; journalist, Cape Town *Guardian*, 1949; moved to London, 1950; secretary, 1950; member of the Editorial Board, *New Reasoner* (later, *New Left Review*), 1956. Recipient: Maugham award, for fiction, 1954; Médicis prize (France), 1976; Austrian State prize, 1981; Shakespeare prize (Hamburg), 1982; W.H. Smith Literary award, 1986; Palermo prize (Italy), 1987; Mondello prize (Italy), 1987; Cavour award (Italy), 1989. Honorary doctorate: Princeton University, New Jersey, 1989, University of Durham, 1990. Associate member, American Academy, 1974; honorary fellow, Modern Language Association (U.S.A.), 1974; distinguished fellow in literature, University of East Anglia, Norwich, 1991. Agent: Jonathan Clowes Ltd., Iron Bridge House, Bridge Approach, London, NW1 8BD, England.

Publications

PLAYS

Before the Deluge (produced 1953).
Mr. Dollinger (produced 1958).
Each His Own Wilderness (produced 1958). In *New English Dramatists*, 1959.

The Truth about Billy Newton (produced 1960).
Play with a Tiger (produced 1962). 1962; in *Plays by and about Women*,
    edited by Victoria Sullivan and James V. Hatch, 1973.
The Storm, adaptation of a play by Alexander Ostrovsky (produced 1966).
The Singing Door (for children), in *Second Playbill 2*, edited by Alan Durband.
    1973.
The Making of the Representative for Planet 8 (opera libretto), music by Philip
    Glass, adaptation of the novel by Lessing (produced 1988).

TELEVISION PLAYS: *The Grass Is Singing*, from her own novel, 1962; *Care and
Protection* and *Do Not Disturb* (both in *Blackmail* series), 1966; *Between
Men*, 1967.

NOVELS

The Grass Is Singing. 1950.
Children of Violence:
    Martha Quest. 1952; with *A Proper Marriage*, 1964.
    A Proper Marriage. 1954; with *Martha Quest*, 1964.
    A Ripple from the Storm. 1958; with *Landlocked*,1966.
    Landlocked. 1965; with *A Ripple from the Storm*. 1966.
    The Four-Gated City. 1969.
Retreat to Innocence. 1956.
The Golden Notebook. 1962.
Briefing for a Descent into Hell. 1971.
The Summer Before the Dark. 1973.
The Memoirs of a Survivor. 1974.
Canopus in Argos: Archives:
    Shikasta. 1979.
    The Marriages Between Zones Three, Four, and Five. 1980.
    The Sirian Experiments. 1981.
    The Making of the Representative for Planet 8.   1982.
    The Sentimental Agents. 1983.
The Diaries of Jane Somers. 1984.
    The Diary of a Good Neighbour (as Jane Somers). 1983.
    If the Old Could—(as Jane Somers). 1984.
The Good Terrorist. 1985.
The Fifth Child. 1988.

SHORT STORIES

This Was the Old Chief's Country. 1951.
Five: Short Novels. 1953.
No Witchcraft for Sale: Stories and Short Novels. 1956.
The Habit of Loving. 1957.
A Man and Two Women. 1963.
African Stories. 1964.
Winter in July. 1966.
The Black Madonna. 1966.
Nine African Stories, edited by Michael Marland. 1968.

The Story of a Non-Marrying Man and Other Stories. 1972; as *The Temptation of Jack Orkney and Other Stories,* 1972.
Collected African Stories. 1981.
   1. *This Was the Old Chief's Country.* 1973.
   2. *The Sun Between Their Feet.* 1973.
(Stories), edited by Alan Cattell. 1976.
Collected Stories: To Room Nineteen and *The Temptation of Jack Orkney.* 2 vols., 1978; as *Stories,* 1 vol., 1978.
London Observed. 1991.
The Real Thing. 1991.

VERSE

Fourteen Poems. 1959.

OTHER

Going Home. 1957; revised edition, 1968.
In Pursuit of the English: A Documentary. 1960.
Particularly Cats. 1967.
A Small Personal Voice: Essays, Reviews, Interviews, edited by Paul Schlueter. 1974.
Prisons We Choose to Live Inside. 1986.
The Wind Blows Away Our Words, and Other Documents Relating to Afghanistan. 1987.
The Doris Lessing Reader. 1989.
African Laughter: Four Visits to Zimbabwe. 1992.

BIBLIOGRAPHY: *Doris Lessing: A Bibliography* by Catharina Ipp, 1967; *Doris Lessing: A Checklist of Primary and Secondary Sources* by Selma R. Burkom and Margaret Williams, 1973; *Doris Lessing: An Annotated Bibliography of Criticism* by Dee Seligman, 1981; *Doris Lessing: A Descriptive Bibliography of Her First Editions* by Eric T. Brueck, 1984.

CRITICAL STUDIES (selection): *Doris Lessing* by Dorothy Brewster, 1965; *Doris Lessing,* 1973, and *Doris Lessing's Africa,* 1978, both by Michael Thorpe; *Doris Lessing: Critical Studies* edited by Annis Pratt and L.S. Dembo, 1974; *Notebooks/Memoirs/Archives: Reading and Re-reading Doris Lessing* edited by Jenny Taylor, 1982; *Doris Lessing* by Lorna Sage, 1983; *Doris Lessing* by Mona Knapp, 1984; *Doris Lessing* edited by Eve Bertelsen, 1985; *Critical Essays on Doris Lessing* edited by Claire Sprague and Virginia Tiger, 1986; *Doris Lessing: The Alchemy of Survival* edited by Carey Kaplan and Ellen Cronan Rose, 1988; *Doris Lessing* by Ruth Whittaker, 1988; *Doris Lessing* by Jeannette King, 1989; *Understanding Doris Lessing* by Jean Pickering, 1990.

In any theatre, a deal of talent must go to waste, especially among playwrights, but it is a great pity that Doris Lessing's career as a playwright should have been abortive. One of the failures of George Devine's successful regime at the Royal Court was its failure to help her to go on from *Each His Own Wilderness,* which was given a Sunday night production in 1958. Though it was dismissed by many of the critics as a novelist's play can so readily be

dismissed, simply by describing it as "a novelist's play," in fact it was remarkably free from the flaws that might have been expected—flat characters, over-
leisurely development, verbal analysis written out as dialogue, lack of dramatic
drive. Lessing had, on the contrary, a very keen instinct for how to ignite a
situation theatrically.

By building the play around a mother–son conflict and empathizing successfully with the son, she steered clear of the pitfall of subordinating all the other
characters to the woman she could most easily identify with. Myra Bolton is an
attractive, middle-aged campaigner for left-wing causes, warm, well-meaning,
but gauche in human relationships, liable to inflict unintended pain not only on
her son but on the three men in the play she has had relationships with—two of
her own generation, one of her son's. The muddles and misunderstandings of
these involvements are all developed in a way that contributes richly to the
play's dramatic texture, and the untidiness we see on the set—the hall of her
London house—contributes visually to the impression of an inability to keep
things under control.

The men are all well characterized—the sad, ageing, lonely politician, the
architect trying to embark on a new marriage with a young girl, the opportunistic 22-year-old son of a woman friend, and above all Tony, the son, who
returns from National Service to find Myra did not know which day to expect
him. His pained anger at his own inability to commit himself to any outside
reality and at the lack of understanding between them mounts effectively
through the play, reaching a climax when he discovers that Myra has sold the
house he loves more than anything, intending to help him by raising money to
set him up on his own in a flat. It may be a well-made play but it is made
remarkably well, with an unusual talent for keeping a number of relationships
simultaneously on the boil, and it catches the flavour of the life of left-wing
intellectuals in the 1950's. Showing private people devoting their lives to
protesting about public issues, Lessing successfully merges personal and political themes. Like the characters in John McGrath's play, these people are all
"plugged-in to history."

Lessing had started writing for the theatre five years earlier, in 1953, and of
the three plays she turned out *Mr. Dollinger* was also produced in 1958, earlier
in the year, at the Oxford Playhouse, and *The Truth about Billy Newton* was
produced in 1960 at Salisbury. But the only play of hers to receive a full-scale
London production was *Play with a Tiger* which was written in 1958 and had
a seven-and-a-half week run at the Comedy in 1962 with Siobhan McKenna as
the central character, who is, unfortunately, very much more central than any
of the characters in *Each His Own Wilderness*.

Lessing was determined to turn her back on both naturalism and realism. "It
is my intention," she wrote in a 1963 note on the play,

> that when the curtain comes down at the end, the audience will think: Of
> course! In this play no one lit cigarettes, drank tea or coffee, read
> newspapers, squirted soda into Scotch, or indulged in little bits of
> "business" which indicated "character." They will realize, I hope, that
> they have been seeing a play which relies upon its style and its language
> for its effect.

But it starts off naturalistically in an underfurnished room with a litter of books and cushions, paraffin heaters, a record player, and a telephone. There are also sound effects of traffic noises. Anna Freeman is a woman of "35 or so" who lives as a literary freelance, has a son by a broken marriage and has recently decided not to marry an Englishman who is about to settle for a safe job on a woman's magazine. She is in love with an American Jew who would never settle and if she had been entertaining ideas of marrying him, these would be killed off in Act 1 by the visit of a nice young American girl who announces that she is going to have Dave's baby.

The play's starting points, in other words, are all naturalistic and there is even a naturalistic cliché neighbour who fusses about an invisible cat. But towards the end of Act 1 the walls disappear, and though the neighbour is going to reappear and the play is still going to make gestures towards satisfying the audience expectations that its first half-hour has aroused, its centre has been shifted. With only a few interruptions from other characters, about 62 pages of the 92-page script are taken up with a dialogue between Anna and Dave. But the language and the style cannot depart completely from those of the naturalistic beginning. Some of the writing in it is very good, some of it bad and embarrassing, especially when they play games reminiscent of the psycho-analytical situation.

Even the best sections of the dialogue, which make a defiant and articulate declaration of rights on behalf of the woman against the male predator, tend to generalize the play away from its roots in the specific predicament of a specific woman. In reacting against naturalism, Lessing is renouncing all its disciplines, some of which were very useful to her in *Each His Own Wilderness*. *Play with a Tiger* may look more like a public statement and it was seized on by feminist groups, whose performances unbalanced the central relationship by failing to give Dave equal weight with Anna. Lessing complained about this in a 1972 postscript, but the fault is basically in the play, which is really more private than *Each His Own Wilderness*, and more self-indulgent, in that the dialogue is spun too directly out of personal preoccupations.

—Ronald Hayman

LEVY, Deborah.

Born in South Africa in 1959. Educated at Dartington College of Arts, Devon, 1978–81, B.A. (hons.) in theatre language 1981; fellow in creative arts, Trinity College, Cambridge, 1989–91. Since 1992 writer and director for MANACT Theatre Company, Cardiff and London. Agent: Leah Schmidt, Curtis Brown, 162–168 Regent Street, London W1R 5TB, England.

Publications

PLAYS

Pax (produced 1984). 1985.
Clam (produced 1985). 1985.
Our Lady (produced 1986).
Heresies (produced 1987). With *Eva and Moses*, 1987.
Eva and Moses. With *Heresies*, 1987.

Blood Wedding, (libretto) adaptation of the play by Federico García Lorca (produced 1992). 1992.
The B File (also director: produced 1992). 1992.
Call Blue Jane (produced 1992).

TELEVISION PLAYS: *Celebrating Quietly*, 1988; *Lickin' Bones*, 1990; *The Open Mouth*, 1991.

NOVEL
Beautiful Mutants. 1987.

SHORT STORIES
Ophelia and the Great Idea. 1986.

VERSE
An Amorous Discourse in the Suburbs of Hell. 1990.

OTHER
Editor, *Walks on Water: Five Performance Texts*. 1992.

Deborah Levy comments:

I now mostly direct my own texts for the theatre, working with ensemble companies who come from diverse arts backgrounds and cultures. I hope to create with them as writer and director, work that is visual, visceral, kinetic, and physical.

A female world without patriarchy can be deduced from Deborah Levy's dramatic work. Its primary substances are bread, fruit, and eggs, its primary symbols are fish, the sea, and the moon, and its religion is a combination of Goddess-worship and the ritual aspects of Catholicism and Judaism. Children (female) are parented by the whole community, which is itself inter-generational and the collective guardian of a herstory of revolutionary élan as well as domestic drudgery. The wisest women are witches and eccentrics like The Keeper in *Pax* and Leah in *Heresies*. Money-making is the most abhorred activity, art-making the best. Even the betrayers can be redeemed, such as Mayonnaise (*Heresies*) who is the beautiful wife and mistress respectively of a securities-dealer (Edward) and a commercial architect (Pimm), and who forces her lover's ex-wife and child to return to Budapest. Her hair falls out and, it is implied, she loses Pimm, but she is welcomed into the circle of women at the end who gather to hear Leah's final composition. The Domesticated Woman's presence in *Pax* is intensely resented by the fiercely independent and autocratic Keeper, but she is accepted by the other younger women, The Mourner (a geologist), and H.D., the hidden daughter of The Keeper, but also a reference, presumably, to the great American Modernist writer Hilda Doolittle. When The Mourner leaves at the end she gives an egg to the Domesticated Woman, a symbol not just of fertility but also of professional expertise. The Mourner specialises in the egg fossils of dinosaurs. The two older women come to look on the younger generation with a wry affection. "We have," observes The Keeper, "two young women between us. Mad as nettles in a storm." In an endnote to the play Levy admits she began by detesting what the Domesticated Woman represented and finished with respect and even liking for her. Perhaps Mary, the devout Catholic servant of Pimm, best sums up the ideal existence: "I'd like a house with a garden and a tree." Active, mobile women are respected in the plays but the settings are all interiors and rapid movements of flight or travel are either in retrospect or prospect.

These, along with emotionally numb men and distracted hunts for fathers and mothers, are the commonplaces of second-wave feminist Utopias; indeed, there are distinct echoes of the first, Edwardian wave. The posed eccentricity of Leah playing the piano in a hat rimmed with lighted candles, and of her companion, Violet, trampling a tub of grapes, recalls the desperate bohemianism of Gudrun and Ursula in *Women in Love*. Mayonnaise's staccato statements of inconsequent desires ("I want to be a Catholic") echo the disjointed utterances of Evelyn Waugh's Agatha Runcible, and H.D., with her fishing-rod and her cigars, can trace her ancestry back to Una Troubridge and Vita Sackville-West. But Levy defamiliarises these themes by a persistent preoccupation with Eastern Europe, as site both of terrible history and of a more humane community. In *Clam* Alice and Harry, a domestic couple, who double as Lenin and Krupskaya, another domestic couple, play out a history of the defeat of revolution. A fishtank, as in *Heresies*, is a key prop. It is a cornucopia of objects to provoke fantasies. Alice imagines the sea bringing in Poland and Latvia and other Eastern bloc countries like fish so that "a little boy kissed the Ukraine . . . a woman in a bikini put Poland on her belly." For Cholla, domestic cleaner and mother of Pimm's child, Hungary is her lost homeland of song and fecundity, a culture she rejected for that of the frozen English and to which she now wishes to return. Leah remembers the Russians as beautiful in their revolution and The Keeper counterpoints a refrain of "I want to go back to Vienna/Prague etc." with horrific recollections of the Holocaust. Cholla fled from Hungary at the age of 17 because of the claustrophobia of family life, but now she dreams of her mother standing on Liberty Bridge "in her red shoes . . . calling me." Cholla sums up East/West relations in a prescient line: "The West only likes Eastern Europe when she cries."

Levy is both of and not of the performance art movement of the 1980's. She has an interest in visual theatre and her symbol for the imagined funeral of H.D.'s father, one bright light on a polished marble column, effectively condenses a multiplicity of signs. Music strains to become a language in its own right under Leah's promptings and the abrupt emotional shifts of Mayonnaise and Krupskaya are typical of the distrust of continuous narrative in much performance art. But Levy also has a traditional interest in plot and character-conflict. The many histories that are recounted indicate a concern for verbal language that many performance artists would consider quite outmoded. One suspects that Levy is still struggling to reconcile her commitment to a distinctive female voice in theatre with her determination to find her own voice. Too often her characters, particularly male, mouth attitudes rather than dramatise situations. With the decline of feminism and the collapse of communism she will be forced back onto her own linguistic resources, although, in true postmodernist fashion, she may find her way to them through the words of others, as her libretto-version of Lorca's *Blood Wedding* for The Women's Theatre Trust would seem to indicate.

—Tony Dunn

LIVINGS, Henry.

Born in Prestwich, Lancashire, 20 September 1929. Educated at Park View Primary School, 1935–39; Stand Grammar School, Prestwich (scholarship), 1940–45; Liverpool University, 1945–47, read Hispanic studies. Served in the Royal Air Force, 1950–52. Married Judith Francis Carter in 1957; one son and one daughter. Worked for Puritex, Leicester, then actor with Theatre Royal, Leicester, and many repertory companies; associated with the BBC programme *Northern Drift*. Recipient: *Evening Standard* award, 1961; Encyclopaedia Britannica award, 1965; Obie award, 1966. Agent: Lemon, Unna, and Durbridge, 24 Pottery Lane, Holland Park, London W11 4LZ. Address: 49 Grains Road, Delph, Oldham, Lancashire OL3 5DS, England.

Publications

PLAYS

Stop It Whoever You Are (produced 1961). In *New English Dramatists 5*, 1962.

Big Soft Nellie (as *Thacred Nit*, produced 1961; as *Big Soft Nellie*, produced 1961). In *Kelly's Eye and Other Plays*, 1964.

Nil Carborundum (produced 1962). In *New English Dramatists 6*, 1963.

Kelly's Eye (produced 1963). In *Kelly's Eye and Other Plays*, 1964.

There's No Room for You Here for a Start (televised 1963). In *Kelly's Eye and Other Plays*, 1964.

The Day Dumbfounded Got His Pylon (broadcast 1963; produced 1965). In *Worth a Hearing: A Collection of Radio Plays*, edited by Alfred Bradley, 1967.

Kelly's Eye and Other Plays. 1964.

Eh? (produced 1964). 1965.

The Little Mrs. Foster Show (produced 1966; revised version, also director: produced 1968). 1969.

Brainscrew (televised 1966; produced 1971). In *Second Playbill 3*, edited by Alan Durban, 1973.

Good Grief! (includes *After the Last Lamp, You're Free, Variable Lengths, Pie-Eating Contest, Does It Make Your Cheeks Ache?, The Reasons for Flying*) (produced 1967). 1968.

Honour and Offer (produced 1968). 1969.

The Gamecock (produced 1969). In *Pongo Plays 1–6*, 1971.

Rattel (produced 1969). In *Pongo Plays 1–6*, 1971.

Variable Lengths and Longer: An Hour of Embarrassment (includes *The Reasons for Flying, Does It Make Your Cheeks Ache?*) (produced 1969).

The Boggart (produced 1970). In *Pongo Plays 1–6*, 1971.

Conciliation (produced 1970). In *Pongo Plays 1–6*, 1971.

The Rifle Volunteer (produced 1970). In *Pongo Plays 1–6*, 1971.

Beewine (produced 1970). In *Pongo Plays 1–6*, 1971.
The ffinest ffamily in the Land (produced 1970). 1973.
You're Free (produced 1970).
GRUP (televised 1970; produced 1971).
Mushrooms and Toadstools (produced 1970). In *Six More Pongo Plays*, 1974.
Tiddles (produced 1970). In *Six More Pongo Plays*, 1974.
Pongo Plays 1–6. 1971; revised versions, music by Alex Glasgow, 1976.
This Jockey Drives Late Nights, adaptation of a play by Tolstoy (produced 1972). 1972; revised version, 1976.
Daft Sam (televised 1972; produced 1976). In *Six More Pongo Plays*, 1974.
The Rent Man (produced 1972). In *Six More Pongo Plays*, 1974.
Cinderella: A Likely Tale, adaptation of the story by Perrault (produced 1972). 1976.
The Tailor's Britches (produced 1973). In *Six More Pongo Plays*, 1974.
Glorious Miles (televised 1973; produced 1975).
Jonah (produced 1974). 1975.
Six More Pongo Plays Including Two for Children (includes *Tiddles*, *The Rent Man*, *The Ink-Smeared Lady*, *The Tailor's Britches*, *Daft Sam*, *Mushrooms and Toadstools*). 1974.
Jack and the Beanstalk, music by Alex Glasgow (produced 1974).
Jug, adaptation of a play by Heinrich von Kleist (produced 1975; revised version produced 1986).
The Astounding Adventures of Tom Thumb (for children; produced 1979).
Don't Touch Him, He Might Resent It, adaptation of a play by Gogol (produced 1984).
This Is My Dream: The Life and Times of Josephine Baker (produced 1987).
The Great Camel Rumbles and Groans and Spits (produced 1988). In *New Plays 1*, edited by Peter Terson, 1988.
The Public, adaptation of a play by Federico García Lorca (produced 1988). In *Lorca, Plays: Three*, edited by Gwynne Edwards, 1991.
The Barber of Seville, adaptation of the play by Beaumarchais (produced 1989).
Stop the Children's Laughter (produced 1990).

RADIO PLAYS: *After the Last Lamp*, 1961; *The Weavers*, from a play by Hauptmann, 1962; *The Day Dumbfounded Got His Pylon*, 1963; *A Public Menace*, from the play by Ibsen, 1964; *Nelson Cape Requests the Pleasure*, 1967; *The Government Inspector*, from a play by Gogol, 1969; *The Dobcross Silver Band* (documentary), 1971; *The Red Cockerel Crows*, from a play by Hauptmann, 1974; *A Most Wonderful Thing*, 1976; *Crab Training*, 1979; *Urn*, 1981; *The Moorcock*, 1981.

TELEVISION PLAYS: *The Arson Squad*, 1961; *Jack's Horrible Luck*, 1961; *There's No Room for You Here for a Start*, 1963; *A Right Crusader*, 1963; *Brainscrew*, 1966; *GRUP*, 1970; *Daft Sam*, 1972; *Glorious Miles*, 1973; *Shuttlecock*, 1976; *The Game*, from the play by Harold Brighouse, 1977; *The Mayor's Charity*, 1977; *Two Days That Shook the Branch*, 1978; *We Had Some Happy Hours*, 1981; *Another Part of the Jungle* and *I Met a Man Who Wasn't There* (*Bulman* series), 1985.

SHORT STORIES
Pennine Tales. 1983.
Flying Eggs and Things: More Pennine Tales. 1986.

OTHER
That the Medals and the Baton Be Put on View: The Story of a Village Band 1875–1975. 1975.

CRITICAL STUDY: *Anger and After* by John Russell Taylor, 1962, revised edition, 1969, as *The Angry Theatre,* 1962, revised edition, 1969.

THEATRICAL ACTIVITIES

DIRECTOR: **Plays**—*Stop It Whoever You Are*; *The Little Mrs. Foster Show,* 1968; *Trinity Tales* by Alan Plater.
ACTOR: **Plays**—with the Century Theatre, the Midland Theatre Company, Coventry, Theatre Workshop, Stratford East, and other repertory and London theatres. **Radio**—*Northern Drift* (miscellany). **Television**—*Cribbins, Livings and Co.,* 1976; *Get the Drift,* 1976; *Night People* by Alan Plater, 1978.

Henry Livings comments:

To me, a show is an opportunity for communal imaginings, actors and audience together, for which I provide the material. When I first wrote plays, I felt there weren't enough plays which were fun, and that plot and naturalism were overwhelming the other aspects (fun, magic, social observation, the sculptural kinetics, the social connection that can be set up in a theatre); I now feel that I neglected story too much: I still feel it's better to know the story beforehand—if we're wondering what happens next, how can we pay attention to what's happening now?—but I try to steal a good story as well. I would like to make plays that are neither a simple narrative nor a flat picture, but a complete experience to carry out of the building, so that we could look around us with new eyes and say "Oh yes, that's right." For this I go mostly for laughter, because for me laughter is the shock reaction to a new way of looking at something: even a pun questions our security in the solidity of words. I also believe that we are what we do, rather than having some kind of permanent identifiable reality: the materials of art, observation, ritual, symbol, gesture, community give us a chance to focus for a moment, and then go forward with fresh hope that we matter and that what we do signifies. For this reason again I try to choose as a principal character or characters someone who isn't normally a big deal in our thinking—not that I'm not interested in power, as we all are, but that I want to see how it works and on whom. I have only once had the worm turning (in *Stop It*), and then only on Mrs. Warbeck, the scold, which is a good gag; but have frequently shown the humble to be indestructible—which I consider to be a fair observation of what goes on: we do survive, in our millions, in spite of famine, war, and pestilence.

Henry Livings's success in presenting "a new way of looking at something" is arguably at the core of the "controversies" over his work. Some critics suggest a lack of compassion, an absence of distinction between victims and oppressors, and a neglect in providing "positive action and solution." They suggest that a playwright who focuses on the underdog is required, at the least, to invest his underdog with momentary glory, preferably illustrating a victory for the individual over authority.

Livings lets them down by rejecting the conventional approaches. As he says, his characters are people not "normally a big deal," or, as he describes Perkin Warbeck, "very insignificant." None exhibits particularly redeeming personal characteristics or grows in our affections. Those who attempt revenge do so in inept and insignificant ways. Perkin Warbeck in *Stop It Whoever You Are* is an old, cantankerous lavatory cleaner brow-beaten by his wife for never having attained the social heights of schoolmate Alderman Oglethorpe. His seduction by precocious 14-year-old Marilyn inspires Warbeck with enough energy to express his resentment by attempting to soak Oglethorpe when the official entourage, on discovering that the new library they are opening has no public convenience, is forced to use the factory lavatory. Perkin back-handedly soaks his boss, and is sacked. He collapses and is taken home to die, only to return through a medium to haunt his wife.

Warbeck's revenge is something of an own-goal. Stanley, in *Big Soft Nellie*, a stuttering milksop electrician, unable to elicit the acknowledgement that the business depends on his ability to repair electrical goods, temporarily steals his employers' television and cannot even get himself arrested. Livings avoids the usual manner of dealing with the humble and ignored. He neither heroicises them nor elaborates personal detail to elicit sympathy. For Livings, the fact of their existence is justification enough and merits attention. What his characters all have in common, besides their indisputable insignificance, is their inability or unwillingness to play that game that doles out significance, to acknowledge the importance of the construct that those around them take for granted as the source of relevance and social cohesion. Their lack of participation, rather than elevating them to "heroic" heights, exposes the essential arbitrariness of the construct itself. Thus, it is not "authority" but the system justifying it that is in the dock.

Livings has often been linked with the Irish playwright Brendan Behan. Some of the common aspects of their work may well be the effect of their experiences with Joan Littlewood at Theatre Workshop (Livings acted in Behan's *The Quare Fellow*). Livings's plays are constructed of a series of short music-hall skits, each relatively complete in itself. Both his frequent use of a compere-type narrator and his broad seaside-postcard-like characters retain an aura of the music hall. However, he also shares with Behan a fundamental respect and fondness for the natural anarchy of human life, the inherent, chaotic unreasonableness of human emotion and day-to-day ingenuity, and a moral resistance to attempts to control and categorise through the imposition of organised hierarchical structures. Like Behan, he sees the systems of institutional ordering as destructive to the anarchic, unpredictable spirit and innate dignity which express the irreducible value of human life.

In his straight-talking northern manner, Livings does not attempt to elevate the humble or to invest the insignificant with glory. Rather, he insists dignity is inviolable and concentrates on exposing the constructs that attempt to make it negotiable by denying the many and augmenting the few, exposing their arbitrariness through highlighting their ludicrousness. Once seen as arbitrary, they might lose their power and become changeable if not dispensable.

We find Livings's characters in ludicrous situations. Viewed from an unquestioning everyday perspective, however, these situations, on the face of it, are fairly ordinary and mundane. It is the perspective created through the dogged unchangeability of his characters' worm's-eye view that renders the circumstances ridiculous. In *Eh?*, for example, a young man obsessed with growing mushrooms acquires a job in a factory which requires only that he turn the central machine on and off. From the point of view of the employer or the factory staff one can safely assume that there would be little remarkable about the situation. The machine is the heart of their purpose; the lad, the smallest cog in their impressive wheel. Onstage, however, even the visual image of the individual dwarfed by the immense machine necessitates an assessment of fundamental values. The obsessive technology that surrounds him (including a musical door) compounds the appalling waste of human energy and renders the situation ludicrous. The "unresolved" ending in which the young man, his girlfriend, and the mushrooms rise in a cloud of smoke as the machine explodes offers no practical solutions, but sustains the question of where our values should lie and compounds the instigating assumption of the original image: that the constructs we embrace to organise and assess our lives are arbitrary, ludicrous, and demeaning.

The central characters of the plays are ordinary, unremarkable people who can't, won't, or don't know how to play the game that seems to occupy and give importance to those around them. Their denial is not the expression of heroic integrity, nor is it a moral stand, but arguably the source of their insignificance: they simply don't seem able to see the Emperor's New Clothes. Unacknowledged, the structures themselves lose their inevitability and the behaviour sustaining them appears ludicrous—at worst, destructive to human nature, at best, arbitrary and bemusing.

Nil Carborundum, whose title sums up the main thrust of Livings's work ("Don't let them grind you down"), provides perhaps the clearest example of his argument. Neville is serving out his National Service as a cook. He arrives in camp as a war game is about to commence. ("It is assumed for the purpose of the Surprise Enterprise that the Home Counties have been dislocated by ground-to-ground nuclear missiles. . . . Umpires will wear yellow armbands.") Because Neville doggedly refuses to acknowledge any role except that of cook, every possible attitude towards the war game is played out, from total engagement to the embittered irony of the Commander, to Neville's refusal to recognise its existence. Neville's denial exposes the game as a ludicrous construction and a waste of human energy and ingenuity. In contrast with Arnold Wesker, whose *Chips with Everything* poses National Service and the army as a metaphor for human life, Livings presents it as exemplary of the arbitrariness of social constructs and their denial of human value. Neville's resistence is never heroic, but his behaviour suggests that, faced with such ludicrous, demeaning demands, the best one can do—even the most positive act possible —is to deny one's participation, not on self-aggrandised principle, but in fact, thus exposing the construct itself to evaluation.

In *There's No Room for You Here for a Start* (a television play), the tentative relationship between Lily, a lonely aging landlady and her lodger,

Len, a one-armed semi-tramp, is sharply contrasted with the obsessive, offi-cious demands of the council that she cut her hedge to the regulation height. It is not difficult to assess the relative importance of the emotional needs of two lonely, isolated people (the play is possibly the first to deal with the effects of child abuse) and regulation-size hedges. Nor is it difficult to understand how Len's desperate desire to protect Lily leads him to meet the council's authori-tarian aggression with a gun. The excessiveness of his response highlights the ludicrousness of theirs. The hedge is, unsurprisingly, cut to council regulation height. However, Len and Lily are condemned to lonely futures.

Livings's most serious piece is the disturbing, poetic *Kelly's Eye*. Set in 1939, it is a Conradian story of a man, self-isolated as a result of a guilty, painful past, drawn back into social interaction and inevitable destruction through emotional engagement. Livings makes no attempt to exonerate Kelly for the murder of his friend; at best, it is indicative of a growing violence and chaos, as well as Kelly's lack of self-knowledge. Kelly's constant memories of soldiering in World War I give us more insight into the deed than Kelly can.

Kelly meets young Anna on an isolated beach when he rescues her from her callous boyfriend. Love grows between them. Reluctantly, Kelly moves into town with her where, as he feared, Anna's wealthy father and the law soon track him down. Kelly commits suicide. Kelly's story, however, is never permitted the vestiges of special significance; the murder, his and Anna's love for each other, his capture, and his suicide are overshadowed by news that war has been declared, another man-made construct that overlooks the value and dignity of the "insignificant" man.

Livings's writing has been described as "comic strip," but the broad, colour-ful, and splendidly bizarre style presents a difficult vision suggesting that the systems by which we order and evaluate are not "natural" formations but arbitrary constructs that might be reassembled, changed, or dispensed with in favour of simple compassion and respect, or even a wholehearted embracing of the fundamental anarchy of human nature.

—Elaine Turner

LOCHHEAD, Liz.

Born in Motherwell, Lanarkshire, 26 December 1947. Educated at Dalziel High School, Motherwell, 1960–65; Glasgow School of Art, 1965–70, dip-loma in art. Art teacher at Bishopbriggs High School, Glasgow, and other schools in Glasgow and Bristol. Recipient: BBC Scotland prize, 1971; Scottish Arts Council award, 1973, and fellowship, 1978. Address: 11 Kersland Street, Glasgow G12 8BW, Scotland.

Publications

PLAYS

Blood and Ice (produced 1982; revised version, produced 1984). 1982.
Tickly Mince (revue), with Tom Leonard and Alisdair Gray (produced 1982).
The Pie of Damocles (revue), with others (produced 1983).
A Bunch of Fives, with Tom Leonard and Sean Hardie (produced 1983).
Silver Service. 1984.

Dracula, adaptation of the novel by Bram Stoker (produced 1985). With *Mary Queen of Scots Got Her Head Chopped Off*, 1989.
Tartuffe, adaptation of the play by Molière (produced 1985). 1985.
Mary Queen of Scots Got Her Head Chopped Off (produced 1987). With *Dracula*, 1989.
The Big Picture (produced 1988).
Patter Merchant (produced 1989).
Jock Tamson's Bairns, with Gerry Mulgrew (produced 1990).
Quelques Fleurs (produced 1991).
The Magic Island, adaptation of Shakespeare's *The Tempest* (for children; produced 1993).

SCREENPLAY: *Now and Then*, 1972.

RADIO PLAY: *Blood and Ice*, 1990.

TELEVISION PLAY: *Sweet Nothings* in *End of the Line* series, 1984.

VERSE
Memo for Spring. 1972.
The Grimm Sisters. 1981.
Dreaming Frankenstein, and Collected Poems. 1984.
True Confessions and New Clichés. 1985.
Three Scottish Poets: MacCaig, Morgen, Lochhead. 1992.

CRITICAL STUDY: "Feminist Nationalism in Scotland: *Mary Queen of Scots Got Her Head Chopped Off*" by Ilona S. Koren-Deutsch, in *Modern Drama*, September 1992.

THEATRICAL ACTIVITIES
ACTOR: **Play**—*The Complete Alternative History of the World, Part 1*, 1986.

Once upon a time there were *twa queens* on the wan green island, and the wan green island was split inty two kingdoms. But no equal kingdoms, naebody in their richt mind would insist on that.
—La Corbie, *Mary Queen of Scots
Got Her Head Chopped Off*

Liz Lochhead is a teller of tales, the author of strongly narrative plays, dramatic monologues, and poetry. The stories she recounts are often drawn from popular memory and folk culture but are retold with a distinctively female voice. History, myth, and memory interconnect and are analysed and deconstructed in a body of work that finds reference in both literary and popular culture. In common with other contemporary women writers Lochhead has been attracted to the images and the conventions of the Gothic and has discovered in fairytales and in childhood rhymes a new set of metaphors for the role of women in society. Like Angela Carter, Lochhead twists the familiar to find a dark and bloody unconscious with new perspectives on the assumed truths of our society.

Lochhead's plays retell the stories of Mary Shelley and Frankenstein, Mary Queen of Scots and Elizabeth I, Tartuffe, and Dracula with a compelling mix of traditional Scots, contemporary vernacular dialogue, and a subtle lyricism that contemporary theatre writing often effaces in favour of bald realism. Lochhead is not afraid to mix the prosaic and the poetic in one play, one scene, one speech. This combination brings to her already credible and recognisable characters new heights of tragedy or pathos. In *Quelques Fleurs* the extended monologues of Verena and her oilrig-worker husband, Derek (characters as recognisable in a Scottish context as Mike Leigh's characters are within English culture), are written in a mordantly idiomatic and scathingly witty prose to blackly comic effect.

Across a range of genres and subjects Lochhead writes about women and about monsters. Rarely, however, does she write about monstrous women. Focusing on the experiences of women in history, in literature, and in our contemporary world, Lochhead's writing uncovers society's fears of the *unheimlich* aspects of the feminine. Her plays foreground the social and domestic, sexual and creative roles of women within societies which politically and culturally marginalise and devalue their work and their lives. Lochhead takes the common view of these women—Mary as *femme fatale* and Elizabeth as scheming politician in *Mary Queen of Scots Got Her Head Chopped Off*, Mary Shelley as daughter of Mary Wollstonecraft and William Godwin and lover and wife of Percy Bysshe Shelley, with Elise as mere downtrodden maid, in *Blood and Ice*—and peels back the mythology, drawing out the essential humanity of the person. She strives to find in each of her creations a more empowering identity than has traditionally been projected.

Lochhead's plays reset the role of women within both historical and contemporary society with a ubiquity of language that draws on her skills as poet and performer. The subjects of her plays may be historically diverse but they are united by an energetic, vibrant, and precise use of language.

Blood and Ice, her first full-length play, achieved after several revisions, is essentially a memory play with characters and spirits emerging from the life and imagination of Mary Shelley. Time, place, and degree of "reality" are all signalled in the prose and the verse of the text. In a play dealing with Mary Shelley's creativity and the writing process, with commentary on the lives of both Shelley and Byron, there is a deliberate overemphasis on the importance of words. Language is used to mark shifts in time and space, memory and imagination. Variations in tone suggest in turn the lyricism of the idyll of Lake Geneva, the artificiality of the conversation and society of Mary's Romantic companions, the prosaic language of domestic duties and responsibilities, and the obsessive and violent nature of her imagination and her creativity.

The nature and value of creativity is also examined by presenting alternative visions of Mary Shelley as mother and author. The process of writing the novel is mirrored in her role as mother (to her children and in her increasingly maternal relationships with Shelley and her half-sister Claire) and as creator of the fiction of *Frankenstein*. This is further compared to the character of Frankenstein bringing life to his monster. Society's restricting expectations of roles of wife/lover and mother are described as problematic—particularly to the creative and powerful woman. *Blood and Ice* shows that society demands a heavy price from the woman who steps outside the framework of family and wants to be more than muse to another's imagination. At the end of the play Mary Shelley may be left isolated and alone but Lochhead has recovered her and her life from a distraction of myths and received ideas to posit an impression of her heroine as a person, as a mother, and as a writer in her own right.

As with *Blood and Ice*, the demands of society upon woman to be wife and mother is a central theme of *Mary Queen of Scots Got Her Head Chopped Off*. In this play, however, the dramatic conflict is not played out in private places or in the psyche of one woman but in the public sphere and the political conflicts of two nations. The play's narrator, chorus, and sometime conscience La Corbie poses the central riddle of the play: ". . .I ask you, when's a queen a queen/And when's a queen juist a wummin?"

Plays like *Blood and Ice*, *Mary Queen of Scots Got Her Head Chopped Off*, and *Dracula*, although written with a strongly narrative spine, are structurally dense—with complex layerings of temporal, geographic, and psychological spaces. Lochhead uses doubling with psychological intent, actors being required to play two, three, or even four different but fundamentally linked characters. Mary and Elizabeth are matched at each step by parallel and complimentary characters, each time played by the same actors. The pairings of the maids Marian and Bessie, the beggars Mairn and Leezie, and the children Marie and Wee Betty each reveal another facet of Lochhead's project to show the similarities in the problems faced by Mary and Elizabeth in particular, but also by other women both in the time-frame of the drama and in our own age.

Scottish theatre writing is often criticised for its essential nostalgia and preoccupation with the nation's history, and certainly *Mary Queen of Scots Got Her Head Chopped Off* is a play about a privileged moment in Scotland's political development. Typically of Lochhead, however, the play energises the discourse of nostalgia through the use of rhymes and games. Using *Doppelgänger* for all the main players in the drama and an omnipresent narrator who speaks in an eclectic version of 16th-century Scots, and introducing parallel scenes within contemporary culture, her use of the past is very much more precise and focused than is the case with plays that offer a more straightforward version of historical drama. Lochhead sets out to reinterpret the past and to draw out a new and political agenda for the contemporary audience. She mixes the introspection of much of Scottish culture with a desire to develop a new set of images and a new system of metaphors for the depiction of domestic and psychological drama. The activation of memory as well as history is again reflected in her use of language. The play ends with the characters of the drama transformed into children playing a demonic game in which Mary/Marie is again the victim of prejudice and group hysteria.

Just as the received images society holds of Mary Shelley are dissected in *Blood and Ice*, so in *Mary Queen of Scots Got Her Head Chopped Off* Lochhead re-examines the mythology associated with both Mary and Elizabeth and again finds disturbing parallels between the demands made of the women in the play and the prejudices that still limit their expectations and ambitions. The play functions as an explicit metaphor for contemporary society.

Lochhead's plays re-examine the deeply rooted prejudices and assumptions held by our culture. Using the conventions of historical drama in *Mary Queen of Scots Got Her Head Chopped Off*, restoring the real horror and tragedy of *Dracula*, and revealing the isolation of women as different as Mary Shelley and Verena, Lochhead rewrites the myths of our culture to reinstate the experiences and the voices of women.

—Adrienne Scullion

LOWE, Stephen.

Born in Nottingham, 1 December 1947. Educated at the University of Birmingham, 1966–70, B.A. (honours) in English 1969. Actor and director, Stephen Joseph Theatre-in-the-Round, Scarborough, Yorkshire, 1975–78; senior lecturer, Dartington College of Arts, Devon, 1978–82; resident playwright, Riverside Studios, London, 1984. Since 1984 artistic director, Meeting Ground Theatre Company, Nottingham. Recipient: George Devine award, 1977. Agent: Judy Daish Associates, 83 Eastbourne Mews, London W2 6LQ, England.

Publications

PLAYS

Comic Pictures (includes *Stars* and *Cards*) (produced 1972; revised version produced 1976). *Cards* published 1983; *Stars* included in *Moving Pictures: Four Plays*, 1985.

Touched (produced 1977). 1977; revised version (produced 1981), 1981.

Shooting, Fishing and Riding (produced 1977).

Sally Ann Hallelujah Band (produced 1977).

The Ragged Trousered Philanthropists, adaptation of the novel by Robert Tressell (produced 1978). 1978; revised version (produced 1983), 1983.

Fred Karno's Bloody Circus (produced 1980).

Moving Pictures (as *Glasshouses*, produced 1981; as *Moving Pictures*, produced 1985). In *Moving Pictures: Four Plays*, 1985.

Tibetan Inroads (produced 1981). 1981.

Strive (produced 1983). In *Moving Pictures: Four Plays*, 1985.

The Trial of Frankenstein (produced 1983).

Seachange (produced 1984). In *Moving Pictures: Four Plays*, 1985.

Keeping Body and Soul Together (produced 1984). In *Peace Plays 1*, edited by Lowe, 1985.

Moving Pictures: Four Plays. 1985.

Desire (produced 1986).

Demon Lovers (produced 1987).

The Storm, adaptation of a play by Alexander Ostrovsky (produced 1987).

Divine Gossip (produced 1988). With *Tibetan Inroads*, 1988.

William Tell, adaptation of the play by Schiller (produced 1989).

Paradise (musical; produced 1990).

TELEVISION PLAYS: *Cries from a Watchtower*, 1979; *Shades*, 1982; *Kisses on the Bottom*, 1985; *Albion Market* series, 1986; *Coronation Street* series, 1989; *Families* series, 1990; *Ice Dance*, 1990; *Flea Bites*, 1992; *In Suspicious Circumstances*, 1992; *Tell-Tale Hearts*, 1992; *Scarlet and Black*, 1993.

OTHER

Editor, *Peace Plays 1*. 1985.
Editor, *Peace Plays 2*. 1989.

CRITICAL STUDIES: "Letters from a Workshop: *The Ragged Trousered Philanthropists*," in *Dartington Papers 2*, 1978, and "Peace Plays: Peace as a Theatrical Concern," in *Englische Amerikanische Studien*, nos. 3–4, 1986, both by Lowe.

Stephen Lowe comments:

The best introductions to my work are, of course, the plays. But some central concerns, or obsessions, are clear even to me, and have taken me into plays set in the past, and into plays set on the other side of the world—in Tibet. One concern is to explore moments of real change in society, to discover perhaps an optimistic vision that might inspire us through the present moment of change. A large number of them *I* would call political love stories; these have often led me into an exploration of "inner language" through dreams and fairy and folk tale elements.

As Joyce pointed out, there are probably only three subjects worth writing about—politics, religion, and sex. I have discovered in my work that the clear divisions between these create a false perspective, and the interrelation of all these elements is, to me, a crucial theatrical concern, in both form and content.

Stephen Lowe's career as a professional playwright started with a production of two short plays, *Cards* and *Stars* at the Library Theatre in Scarborough while Lowe was employed there as an actor. Since then, his plays have been regularly premiered and performed on all the major British stages, on radio, and on television.

His work as a playwright is characterised by a sustained interest in exploration and experiment, both in dramatic technique and in the process of production. Largely because of this, his work is hard to classify. Much of his work deals with material derived from being born in, and spending most of his life around, Nottingham. His plays not uncommonly cover issues that broadly characterise the texture of D.H. Lawrence's work: local dialect, intense interest in sexuality, the preoccupations of working-class people, and, most distinctively, a powerfully subjective view of the artistic imagination as the means to free the individual from the social and personal myths that circumscribe the actions in their daily lives. In Lowe, as in Lawrence, it is this distinctive voice that gives, to the broadly provincial tone of his work, a resonance and allusiveness that make him undoubtedly one of the most significant British writers of the last decade. As a complement to this, his theatrical interests and activities challenge his own residual prejudices about "the spirit of place," sustained by a concern to balance the subjective elements of his writing against a wider, universal perspective.

Nowhere are these tensions more explicit than in his first major successful play, *Touched*, first directed at the Nottingham Playhouse by Richard Eyre, taken on tour and then revived by Bill Gaskill for the Royal Court in 1981. The play is set in the 100-day period between May and August 1945, between the end of the war in Europe and the dropping of the atomic bomb on Hiroshima. Against a collage of sounds and images which document the processes of a world adjusting with difficulty to peace, Lowe reveals the quiet, relentless tragedy of an extended family, through a structured defoliation of the private hopes and fears of the women left at home to sustain the life of a community unmanned by the war.

The burden of the play rests on Sandra, a married woman in her mid-thirties who sees the chance to confront the old hierarchies with her decision to carry a child begotten in an opportunistic relationship with an Italian prisoner of war. The plot is complicated by an 18-year-old epileptic boy's unsolicited declaration to Sandra's family that he is the father of her child. It transpires that his admission of paternity arises from a wish to offer her a measure of protection from the stigma of straying outside the tribe, and to expiate his sin of spying on Sandra's illicit lovemaking with the prisoner of war. In gratitude, Sandra presents herself to Johnny, but he cannot "touch" her. Like all the men in the play, he cannot function as a man where the traditional myths based on a male-orientated world are challenged. This desolate vision of the impending return of the men at the end of the war is unrelieved throughout the play. The nature of the ambiguous peace is reflected in our final realisations that Sandra's pregnancy is an illusion, and ratified in the final ironies in General MacArthur's voice-over: "Men everywhere walk upright in the sun . . . The entire world is at peace . . . The Holy Mission is completed."

Touched is an important play in that it prefigures most of Lowe's thematic concerns, not the least of which is a belief that, in order to deal with the myths it embodies, history cannot be treated like a "theme park," detached from the present. For Lowe, the historic "moment" is often the mainspring of dramatic action; it is inevitable that while the "moments" he employs to test out his hypotheses are generally accessible ones, they invariably have personal resonances for him. In *Touched*, the interest in 1945 grew out of extended discussion with his aunt and his mother and his father's trials in the 8th Army. In *Moving Pictures*, perhaps the most autobiographical of his plays, the "moment" is 1963–64, the age of mobility and the growth of the nuclear family: the shift from street community to high-rise flat. *Strive* is a short play based on the Falklands War, a "moment" he develops with more complexity in *Seachange*, also based on the Falklands War, but again linked to a personal odyssey Lowe made some years earlier across the Aegean Sea. His grandfather, who had fought in the Gallipoli campaign during World War I, was killed when the ship he was on went down after aerial bombardment. In the introduction to the play, Lowe recalls how on his odyssey he imagined how he might have "passed over the clear waters of his grandfather's grave," re-enacting "the uncertain intimacy of those who love each other through blood, but [who] are only too aware of the sea of time that divides them."

The link between history and the imagination is understated in *Touched*. It is given more detailed examination in *Tibetan Inroads*, *Moving Pictures*, *Demon Lovers*, and *Divine Gossip*. *Demon Lovers* is, in effect, on an imaginative constructive of the love story between the Moors Murderers Ian Brady and Myra Hindley, and the gothic horror of an art (in this case, a video) worked out of the suffering they inflicted on their victims, Lowe is powerfully interested in the relationship between imagination, creativity, and art. In *Demon Lovers*, and earlier in *The Trial of Frankenstein*, he alludes to the negative power of an imagination denied expression. *Divine Gossip* reveals the more positive, though no less potent, manifestation of creativity in action. The play has an historical setting: 1929, the year in which three of Lowe's heroes (George Orwell, Harry Crosby, and D.H. Lawrence) were all in Paris. It juxtaposes aspects of maleness—in art, sexuality, and the desire for death— upon a story of Louise Brooks's *Pandora's Box* and a French prostitute aspiring to be Louise Brooks.

Through *Touched*, Lowe earned an early reputation for being a writer of women's plays. *The Ragged Trousered Philanthropists* and *Divine Gossip* clearly prove this is not the case. Between these poles lies *Shooting, Fishing and Riding*, a play about rape, inspired by the feminist writer Susan Brownmiller's book, *Against Our Will*. While he considers this piece to have been unsuccessful, his most recent work for television, *Tell-Tale Hearts*, a psychological thriller set in Edinburgh and Glasgow, returns to this early theme of sexual abuse within relationships.

Lowe is at his most articulate and assured in writing about inter-personal relationships. *Tibetan Inroads* is an exemplary work from a number of perspectives. The play is based around the vicissitudes of natural love and the penalties and consequences of disrupting social convention. If *Tibetan Inroads* makes any single statement about people it is that they are endlessly unknowable, possessing in equal measure the mystical, intangible capacities for compassion and abuse. But above all, his characterisations reveal a care for, and love of, the extraordinary richness, diversity, and complexity across the spectrum of human behaviour. Characteristic of this is the uproariously comic, plangent scene from *Moving Pictures* in which adolescent brothers and sisters try to construct a Lawrentian sex-movie in a studio improvised out of the parent's front parlour.

Lowe's evocations of mood and period are wrought with great skill and economy. It is germane to note how his progress as a dramatist has been paralled by his continuing workshop and community projects. Those workshops aimed to politicise the imagination of the participants—on the one hand to give responsibility denied them in their ordinary lives, on the other, to discover new ways of understanding history and art.

—Paul Hadfield

LUCIE, Doug.

Born in Chessington, Surrey, 15 December 1953. Educated at Tiffin Boys'
School, 1965–72: Worcester College, Oxford, 1973–76, B.A. (honours) in
English 1976. Resident playwright, Oxford Playhouse Company, 1979–80;
visiting playwright, University of Iowa, Iowa City, 1980. Recipient: *Time Out*
award, 1988. Agent: Michael Imison Playwrights, 28 Almeida Street, London
N1 1TD, England.

Publications

PLAYS

John Clare's Mad, Nuncle (produced 1975).
Rough Trade (also director: produced 1977).
The New Garbo (produced 1978).
We Love You (also director: produced 1978).
Oh Well (also director: produced 1978).
Heroes (also director: produced 1979).
Fear of the Dark (produced 1980).
Poison (also director: produced 1980).
Strangers in the Night (produced 1981).
Hard Feelings (produced 1982). With *Progress*, 1985.
Progress (produced 1984). With *Hard Feelings*, 1985.
The Key to the World (produced 1984).
Force and Hypocrisy (produced 1986).
Fashion (produced 1987). 1987.
Doing the Business (produced 1990).
Grace (produced 1993).

TELEVISION PLAYS: A *Class of His Own*, 1984; *Funseekers*, with Nigel Planer,
1987.

THEATRICAL ACTIVITIES

DIRECTOR: **Plays**—some of his own plays; student productions of *The Duchess
of Malfi* by Webster, *The Comedy of Errors*, and *Hitting Town* by Stephen
Poliakoff.
ACTOR: **Plays**—*We Love You*, 1978; *Oh Well*, 1978.

Wherever people congregate there will be rich pickings for those with an ear
for the nuances of speech and a nose for the ridiculous. Since comedy of
manners was invented, the drawing room has provided the playwright with a
suitable microcosm for bourgeois society. Where once there were drawing
rooms there are now communal living spaces. At some point in the 1970's
Doug Lucie moved into yours or mine. He has captured the social mores
and hypocrisies of a particular social strata—at university and beyond—and
pilloried us on stage for our general amusement and embarrassed recognition.
  Lucie has not dealt exclusively with the cynicism, power games, and capacity

for self-delusion of his contemporaries. *The New Garbo* anticipated the interest in the actress Frances Farmer. *Strangers in the Night* flirted with a lurid expressionism redolent of mid-period Sam Shepard. But it is as the persistent chronicler of his peers that Lucie has gained his reputation. *We Love You* dealt with adolescent rebel posturing. *Heroes* showed six undergraduates in a shared house in Oxford and contrasted them with a different group living there ten years before. *Hard Feelings* is set in Brixton in 1981. Inside another shared house they bicker and pose. Outside, they riot. *Progress* is marriage and careers and sexual politics. Will is a Channel 4 researcher; Ronee is a social worker. What with the lodger, the battered wife they adopt, the phone calls from Ronee's lesbian lover, and Will's men's group ("We're trying to change our attitudes by being open and supportive without resorting to traditional, hierarchical structures"), their living room achieves honorary communal status.

Lucie's plays unfold with an ease and grace which belie a precise construction and rigorous comic technique. Lucie has an insidious way with his exposition; scenes end at precisely the right moment—the structure never sags; the comic effect derives from incongruous juxtaposition and savage undercutting. With a good designer to capture the latest nuances of interior decor and personal accessories, an evening at a Lucie play can provide an irresistible but excruciating portrait of the way we carry on, as our foibles are exposed in a relentlessly funny and viciously acute way.

Is it replication or exaggeration? There are those who say Lucie lacks subtlety. True, he assembles predictable characters in unsurprising combinations. *Progress* is a title with heavy-handed irony. In *Hard Feelings* the living room blinds are always down, which is perhaps an overemphatic metaphor. But unless Lucie aspires to subtlety, lack of it is neither here nor there. One cannot scourge discreetly. Yet who is being scourged and why? It may be that Lucie feels himself an interloper in the world he describes, but his sympathies are always with the outsider, regardless of their actions and attitudes. When Tone, the outsider in *Hard Feelings*, bellows, "people aren't kind of things, they're people," he articulates the author's—and the audience's—outrage. But in *Progress* the outsiders are Mark and Lenny. Mark is a gutter-press journalist with a spectacular line in sexist banter. Lenny uses his wife "as a sparring partner and she doesn't box." He also rapes her. Being bereft of privilege or pretense does not accord integrity by default, and it seems untypically naïve of Lucie even to hint that this is the case.

I do not think, as some do, that Lucie is trivial, but he often trivialises. Comedy of manners is, almost by definition, concerned with surfaces. Too often the dictates of this comic form constrain Lucie. When human beings are reduced to plot functionaries, however brilliantly, it is difficult to care much about what happens to them. Points are half-raised then abandoned, lest the pace slacken. Despite his huge talent, Lucie often seems wilfully insubstantial.

It is possible that Lucie will transcend the civilising parameters he has set himself and attain the corroscating heights of great satire. Interestingly, his 1984 play *The Key to the World* moved out of the drawing room and towards a more humane and less comic vision. Whatever direction Lucie takes, he is a dramatist of rare wit and exceptional powers of observation.

—Joss Bennathan

LUKE, Peter (Ambrose Cyprian).

Born in St. Albans, Hertfordshire, 12 August 1919. Educated at Eton College; Byam Shaw School of Art, London; Atelier André Lhote, Paris. Served in the Rifle Brigade, in the Western Desert, Italy, and Northwest Europe, 1940–46: Military Cross, 1944. Married 1) Carola Peyton-Jones (died); 2) Lettice Crawshaw (marriage dissolved), one son (deceased) and one daughter; 3) the actress June Tobin in 1963, two sons and three daughters. Sub-editor, Reuters, 1946–47; worked in the wine trade, 1947–57; book critic, *Queen* magazine, London, 1957–58; story editor, *Armchair Theatre* programme, 1958–60, and editor, *Bookman* programme, 1960–61, and *Tempo* arts programme, 1961–62, all for ABC Television, London; drama producer, BBC Television, London, 1963–67. Since 1967 freelance writer, producer, and director: director, Gate Theatre, Dublin, 1977–80. Recipient: Italia prize, for television production, 1967; Tony award, 1969. Agent: Lemon, Unna, and Durbridge, 24 Pottery Lane, Holland Park, London W11 4LZ, England.

Publications

PLAYS

Hadrian VII, based on *Hadrian the Seventh* and other works by Frederick Rolfe, "Baron Corvo" (produced 1967). As *The Play of Hadrian VII*, 1968.
Bloomsbury (produced 1974). 1976.
Rings for a Spanish Lady, adaptation of a play by Antonio Gala (also director: produced 1977).
Proxopera, adaptation of the novel by Benedict Kiely (produced 1978).
Married Love: The Apotheosis of Marie Stopes (produced 1985).
Yerma, adaptation of the play by Federico García Lorca (produced 1987). In *Lorca, Plays: One*, edited by Gwynne Edwards, 1987.

RADIO PLAYS: *Nymphs and Satyrs Come Away*, 1985; *The Last of Baron Corvo*, 1989; *The Other Side of the Hill* (includes *The Road to Waterloo* and *It's a Long Way to Talavera*), 1991.

TELEVISION: *Small Fish Are Sweet*, 1959; *Pig's Ear with Flowers*, 1960; *Roll On, Bloomin' Death*, 1961; *A Man on Her Back*, from a story by William Sansom, 1966; *The Devil a Monk Wou'd Be*, from a story by Daudet, 1967; *Anach Cuan: The Music of Sean O Riada*, 1967; *Black Sound—Deep Song: The Andalusian Poetry of Federico García Lorca*, 1968; *Honour, Profit, and Pleasure*, with Anna Ambrose, 1985.

NOVEL
The Other Side of the Hill. 1984.

SHORT STORIES
Telling Tales: The Short Stories of Peter Luke. 1981.

OTHER
Sisyphus and Reilly: An Autobiography. 1972.
Paquito and the Wolf (for children). 1981.

The Mad Pomegranate and the Praying Mantis: An Andalusian Adventure. 1984.

Editor, *Enter Certain Players: Edwards-MacLiammóir and the Gate 1928–1978.* 1978.

CRITICAL STUDIES: by Ronald Bryden in *Observer*, 21 April 1968; by Harold Hobson in *Sunday Times*, 21 April 1968; "Peter Luke Used to Be a Television Producer. Then He Escaped" by Luke, in *Listener*, 12 September 1968; by Clive Barnes in *New York Times*, 9 January 1969; "*Hadrian VII* Is Alive and a Hit" by John Chapman, in *San Francisco Examiner*, 5 October 1969.

THEATRICAL ACTIVITIES

DIRECTOR: Plays—*Hadrian VII*, 1970; *Rings for a Spanish Lady*, 1977. Television—*Hamlet at Elsinore*, 1963; *A Passage to India*, 1966; *Silent Song*, 1967; *Anach Cuan: The Music of Sean O Riada*, 1967; *Black Sound—Deep Song: The Andalusian Poetry of Federico García Lorca*, 1968.

Peter Luke comments:

(1977) To write an introduction to my work as a playwright is difficult because to date there is relatively little of it. I did not write my first play until I was nearly forty. The oeuvre, such as it is to date, consists of four original plays for television and one dramatization of a novel by William Sansom for the same medium. In addition there are two films d'auteur commissioned by the BBC. They are respectively, and perhaps significantly, about a musician and a poet. Then there is the stage play, *Hadrian VII*, which was first written in 1961 but was not produced until 1967. *Bloomsbury*, produced by Richard Cottrell in 1974, ran for only five weeks due to the American recession as it affected Throgmorton Street and the tourist trade and a petulant notice from Harold Hobson (anagram: Dora Snobhol). (1988: Since then *Married Love* has had an airing, but has not yet reached the West End.)

I would like to be able to give some indication of the direction in which I think I am going, but this is difficult. Certainly I am more than ever interested in poetry, which is not to say that I am immediately contemplating a play in verse. But if I can see a development in my work, it is towards the articulate. Language is my preoccupation and I feel that the theatre, now as in the past, and quite irrespective of present day vogues and trends, should be the place to use it in.

The choice of medium was made for me. My father, Harry Luke, was a writer but early on I decided that I wanted to paint and I had already spent two years studying when the war broke out in 1939. Nineteen—nearly twenty—years later, in 1959, my first television play, *Small Fish Are Sweet*, starring Donald Pleasence and Katherine Blake, was produced. Several others followed hard upon. What happened in between is told in an essay in autobiography, *Sisyphus and Reilly*.

I did not intend to become a playwright. It happened by accident. I do not even now consider myself to be solely a writer of plays, though I suppose few writers can have been so fortunate as to have had an international success on the scale of *Hadrian VII*. Indeed, how many playwrights have had a major success which began as a flop? Thanks to Hadrian, however, I am now free to write what I want to and my intention for the foreseeable future is to alternate plays with books. This I find very therapeutic and my one concern now is that the results will justify the therapy, and that the therapy will give me a long life in which to write a great deal more.

Peter Luke was almost 40 when, in 1958, he became a story editor for ABC Television, and began writing television plays. In 1963, he joined the BBC, with whom he stayed until 1967. Since then he has worked as a freelance writer, producer, director, and translator, as well as writing a historical novel, short stories, and two autobiographical reminiscences.

In 1967 Luke adapted Frederick Rolfe's novel, *Hadrian the Seventh*, for the stage. In an otherwise faithful rendering, he made one major change. In the novel, the protagonist is a young man called George Arthur Rose. Luke has described his play as "a biography of Rolfe himself in terms of his 'Hadrian' fantasy."

Hadrian VII begins with Rolfe being visited by two bailiffs. They present him with a writ, resulting from a series of petty debts, which he refuses to sign. Left alone to his "imagining," he fantasizes that the two bailiffs are a Bishop and a Cardinal come to persuade him to accept ordination. They invite him to Rome, where he learns that he has been elected Pope. He calls himself Hadrian VII, and immediately announces his intention of dissolving the "temporal" Church and selling the Vatican's treasure and real estate. The cardinals are outraged. Meanwhile, Jeremiah Sant, who knew Rolfe before his election, tries to wheedle money out of him. Hadrian refuses to give him any, but offers to help save his soul instead. Sant thereupon draws a revolver and shoots Hadrian, who dies requesting that Sant be forgiven his crime. The final scene shows the bailiffs confiscating Rolfe's belongings, among them the manuscript of his masterpiece. The play's enormous success in the late 1960's can be attributed to two factors. The contrast between the "real" Rolfe in his seedy garret and Rolfe as he imagines himself is dramatically very effective; and the theme—individuality vs. authority—is perennial.

Luke's next play, *Bloomsbury*, portrays the group of friends which surrounded Lytton Strachey, as seen through the eyes of Virginia Woolf. Towards the end of the play, she says: "Yes, I have created an art form out of them all. . . . I have orchestrated their movements like the waves." Although the concept is clever, the various relationships and attitudes explored lack the dramatic interest of his previous work.

Proxopera—a coinage for "operation proxy"—is adapted from a novel by Benedict Kiely, who described his story as "a condemnation of the interference by violent men in the lives of the innocent." A group of IRA gunmen are holding a family at gunpoint. They threaten to kill the women and child if Binchey, a retired schoolmaster, does not drive a bomb into town for them. He agrees, and sets off to do so, but when he sees his town in the early morning light, he can't bring himself to aid in the murder of any of its citizens. He tells two soldiers what he is carrying. They rescue his family, but Binchey dies of a heart attack after safely exploding the bomb.

Married Love: The Apotheosis of Marie Stopes opens lightheartedly, contrasting Stopes's academic brilliance and her emotional immaturity. After chasing a Japanese professor to no avail, she marries a man who is impotent. As a result, she comes to think that contraception could be used to produce a better species. George Bernard Shaw persuades her that it would be better employed to help women to avoid unwanted pregnancies. Her subsequent achievement in promoting contraception is set against her sense of personal emptiness. Early in the play, she tells Shaw: "I only know that I haven't got something that I feel I ought to have." She never acquires it. She never settles; is never satisfied. The play maintains a fine balance between comedy and domestic tragedy. It is certainly Luke's best work since *Hadrian VII*.

Ez, commissioned by the Hampstead Theatre Company (and not yet produced), is about the non-trial for treason of Ezra Pound. The first act is set in a cage in a Pisan prison; the second, in St. Elizabeths hospital in Washington where Pound spent more than a decade. Some of Pound's best work belongs to this period, but Luke is more concerned with the contradictions inherent in his character: an egotist, he would share his scraps of food with a cat; a racist, he made friends easily with blacks. He emerges as a victim of a genius inseparable from irresponsibility. But when he is eventually released, he is no longer so sure that what he believed in was right. His confession that he was at fault brings the play to a close. It is a plea for tolerance.

Luke has also written many successful television plays and documentaries, from *Small Fish Are Sweet* in 1959, to *Honour, Profit, and Pleasure*, about Handel, co-written with Anna Ambrose, in 1985. And he has made two excellent translations from the Spanish. *Rings for a Spanish Lady*, from a prize-winning play by Antonio Gala, is the story of how El Cid's widow, who represents Spain, is compelled by the king to forego her love for Don Minaya and accept her widowhood. Luke describes his translation of Lorca's *Yerma* as "the first unbowdlerized version."

Although Luke's subjects vary widely, their themes are closely related. In all his plays, the main character's dreams or plans are threatened by a society which has no place for his or her kind of individuality. His work is a call for greater understanding between individuals.

—Terence Dawson

M

MacDONALD, Sharman.

Born in Glasgow, Scotland in 1951. Educated at Edinburgh University. Married to Will Knightley; two children. Thames Television writer-in-residence, The Bush Theatre, London, 1984–85. Recipient: *Evening Standard* award, 1984. Agent: Patricia MacNaughton, MacNaughton Lowe Representation, 200 Fulham Road, London SW10 9PN, England.

Publications

PLAYS

When I Was a Girl, I Used to Scream and Shout . . . (produced 1984). 1985.
The Brave (produced 1988). In *When I Was a Girl, I Used to Scream and Shout . . ., When We Were Women*, 1990.
When We Were Women (produced 1988). In *The Brave, When I Was a Girl, I Used to Scream and Shout . . .*, 1990.
When I Was a Girl, I Used to Scream and Shout . . ., The Brave, When We Were Women: Three Plays. 1990.
All Things Nice (produced 1991). 1991.
Shades (produced 1992). 1992.
Winter Guest (produced 1993).

TELEVISION PLAY: *Wild Flowers*, 1990.

NOVELS

The Beast. 1986.
Night, Night. 1988.

Familial bonds, the confusions of adolescence, a Celtic heritage—all are powerfully recurrent themes in Sharman MacDonald's work, which deals with mother/child relationships with an emotional charge and engaging comedy that mark her as a distinctive voice in the British theatre. Celtic writers seem especially strong on this territory—many of the scenes between MacDonald's adolescent girls Fiona and Vari in *When I Was A Girl, I Used To Scream and Shout . . .* recall the Edna O'Brien of *A Pagan Place*. But MacDonald's landscape of small Scottish towns where the climate seems to be predominantly grey and rainy is very much her own.

She made an electrifying debut with *When I Was A Girl, I Used To Scream and Shout . . .*, which transferred from the tiny Bush Theatre to enjoy a long

West End run with Julie Walters initially starring. MacDonald was an actress for some years before becoming a full-time writer, and this play—like the work of many actor-dramatists—had refreshingly lively dialogue which at once stamped her as an original. The play may have relatively little plot, but as it swings across time (it moves between 1983, when it was written, 1955, and 1960), a complex web of family tensions and bonds is built up.

It opens on a rocky beach on the east coast of Scotland in 1983, with the 32-year-old Fiona, unmarried and childless, revisiting a childhood haunt with her mother Morag, one of MacDonald's outstanding creations—a garrulous, warm, but often sharp-tongued woman, much given to commenting on the lack of a grandchild ("A woman's body is a clock that runs down very rapidly," she is prone to remark). Later in the play it transpires that Fiona was pregnant at 15—the scenes in flashback involving the 17-year-old Ewan who fathers the child are superbly written—a deliberate move on Fiona's part, in the complicated emotional relationship between Fiona and Morag, to prevent her mother going abroad with a new man, ending in an abortion with Morag remaining at home. All the 1983 scenes between Morag and Fiona beautifully convey the loving but acerbic relationship between them, and equally assured are the time-shifts to 1955, with Fiona and her friend Vari giggling through their first sexual fumblings and comparing notes on boys, and to 1960 with Fiona's decision, made with the devastating candour of adolescence, to use Ewan to father her child. Tough and tender as well as funny, it was a remarkable first play.

There was a cooler reaction to MacDonald's subsequent work; it is not an uncommon pattern for British critics to moderate their enthusiasm for dramatists to whose early work they awarded high praise. But it must be admitted that *The Brave* and *When We Were Women*, both produced in 1988, were somewhat disappointing. *The Brave* was an admirable effort to break away from a Scottish setting; set in Morocco, it had a startling opening sequence by an hotel poolside with Ferlie, a Scottish woman in her mid-thirties, lumbered with what transpires to be the dead body of a Moroccan whom she has killed in self-defence. She and her sister Susan, a political terrorist who has jumped bail and fled to Morocco where Ferlie has been visiting her, spend most of the play trying to get rid of the body, finally burying it in the desert on the site of the crumbling movie-set for *Samson and Delilah*, with the help of two engineers working in Morocco and taking a brief vacation at the hotel. This pair—the spaced-out Robert, endlessly strumming his guitar, and his friend Jamie, a Scottish exile with false teeth and an abrasive wit—provide much of the vitality in a play which only fitfully sparks into life. There are some splendid scenes, specially Susan's efforts to steal a spade from the poolside with which to bury the body while her sister distracts the barman, and Jamie gives the play energy whenever he is on stage, his raw Scottish vigour reminding both the sisters and the audience that geography cannot fundamentally alter cultural heritage, but too often the play remains obstinately arid.

When We Were Women, which came out of work at the National Theatre Studio, may bear some of the hallmarks of laboratory conditions, but it was a significant technical experiment for MacDonald too. Again, the background is Scotland—this time during World War II—and centres round another of MacDonald's young heroines. Isla lives with her mother, the indomitable

Maggie, and her common-law husband Alec. Written in a series of short scenes, alternating between Isla's life at home and her encounters with a serviceman, Mackenzie, the play subtly evokes the sense of time suspended during war. Isla becomes pregnant by Mackenzie, who marries her only for the marriage to be revealed as bigamous. At the close the family is left turned in on itself.

All Things Nice also covered familiar MacDonald terrain while she continued to experiment technically. The play inhabits two worlds. Scotland again provides one, with another adolescent heroine in 15-year-old Moira, staying with her Gran and her "paying guest," the Captain, and becoming aware of life in the company of her best friend Linda. Parallel with these scenes, earthy and funny, we also focus on the isolated figure of Rose, Moira's mother, absent with Moira's father who is working for a Middle-Eastern oil company. Rose's increasingly revealing letters disclose a woman trapped in an unhappy marriage and beginning to seek refuge in drink and affairs. MacDonald traces the tension between the two worlds with delicate precision, and the scenes between Moira and Linda have all the insight into the closed world of adolescence that distinguished *When I was a Girl. . .*, whilst the figure of the bedridden Captain, cajoling and frightening, reveals again her ability to create rich male roles as well as female ones.

MacDonald returned to the embrace of the commercial theatre with *Shades*, with Pauline Collins starring in what is perhaps the richest role MacDonald has yet written. Once again, a mother/child relationship is at the heart of the play, which begins with a widowed mother in her forties dressing to go out to a dance with a new man friend and which, for virtually the entire first act, consists of a dialogue between the woman, Pearl, and her 10-year-old son. This act delicately probes the unusual relationship—flirtatious as well as possessive —between a single parent and a sensitive child, while the second act contains a beautifully-handled scene with Pearl's new man backing off from further commitment once he realises how strong her love remains for her husband, who died young. The play is fundamentally a chamber piece and suffered to a degree from the commercial pressures of playing in a large West End theatre. The experience of the production seems to have been tricky for MacDonald, who announced shortly before the play's opening that she would not be writing for the theatre again. It is to be hoped she will change her mind.

—Alan Strachan

MANKOWITZ, (Cyril) Wolf.

Born in London, 7 November 1924. Educated at East Ham Grammar School, London; Downing College, Cambridge, M.A. in English 1946. Served as a volunteer coal miner and in the British Army during World War II. Married Ann Margaret Seligmann in 1944; four sons. Play and film producer: with Oscar Lewenstein, 1955–60; independently, 1960–70; with Laurence Harvey, 1970–72. Owner, Pickwick Club restaurant, London, 1963–70; also antique and art dealer. Moved to Ireland in 1971. Since 1982 adjunct professor of English, and adjunct professor of theatre arts, 1987–88, University of New Mexico, Albuquerque. Honorary consul to the Republic of Panama in Dublin,

1971. Exhibition of Collages, Davis Gallery, Dublin, 1990. Recipient: Society
of Authors award, for poetry, 1946; Venice Film Festival prize, 1955; BAFTA
award, 1955, 1961; Oscar, for screenplay, 1957; Film Council of America
golden reel, 1957; Evening Standard award, 1959; Cork Film Festival
International Critics prize, 1972; Cannes Film Festival grand prize, 1973.
Address: The Bridge House, Ahakista, Durrus, near Bantry, County Cork,
Ireland; or, 2322 Calle Halcon, Sante Fe, New Mexico 87505, U.S.A.

Publications

PLAYS

Make Me an Offer, adaptation of his own novel (televised 1952; revised
    version, music and lyrics by Monty Norman and David Heneker, produced
    1959).
The Bespoke Overcoat (produced 1953). 1954.
The Baby, adaptation of a work by Chekhov (televised 1954; produced 1981).
    In *Five One-Act Plays*, 1955.
The Boychik (produced 1954).
It Should Happen to a Dog (televised 1955; produced 1967). In *Five One-Act
    Plays*, 1955.
Five One-Act Plays. 1955.
The Mighty Hunter (produced 1956). In *Five One-Act Plays*, 1955.
The Last of the Cheesecake (produced 1956). In *Five One-Act Plays*, 1955.
Expresso Bongo, with Julian More, music and lyrics by David Heneker and
    Monty Norman (produced 1958). 1960.
Belle; or, The Ballad of Dr. Crippen, with Beverley Cross, music by Monty
    Norman (produced 1961).
Pickwick, music and lyrics by Cyril Ornadel and Leslie Bricusse, adaptation of
    the novel by Dickens (produced 1963). 1991.
Passion Flower Hotel, music and lyrics by Trevor Peacock and John Barry,
    adaptation of the novel by Rosalind Erskine (produced 1965).
The Samson Riddle (produced 1972; as *Samson and Delilah*, produced 1978).
    1972.
Jack Shepherd, music by Monty Norman (produced 1972; as *Stand and
    Deliver*, produced 1972).
Dickens of London (televised 1976). 1976.
The Hebrew Lesson (screenplay). 1976.
The Irish Hebrew Lesson (produced 1978).
Iron Butterflies (produced 1985). Two acts in *Adam International Review*,
    1984.

SCREENPLAYS: *Make Me an Offer*, with W.P. Lipscomb, 1954; *A Kid for Two
Farthings*, 1955; *The Bespoke Overcoat*, 1955; *Trapeze*, 1955; *Expresso
Bongo*, 1959; *The Two Faces of Dr. Jekyll (House of Fright)*, 1960; *The
Millionairess*, with Ricardo Aragno, 1960; *The Long and the Short and the
Tall (Jungle Fighters)*, with Willis Hall, 1961; *The Day the Earth Caught Fire*,
with Val Guest, 1961; *Waltz of the Toreadors*, 1962; *Where the Spies Are*,
with James Leasor and Val Guest, 1965; *Casino Royale*, with others, 1967; *La
Vingt-cinquième Heure (The Twenty-fifty Hour)*, 1967; *The Assassination
Bureau*, with Michael Relph, 1969; *Bloomfield (The Hero)*, with Richard

Harris, 1970; *Black Beauty*, with James Hill, 1971; *The Hebrew Lesson*, 1972; *Treasure Island*, with Orson Welles, 1973; *The Hireling*, 1973; *Almonds and Raisins* (documentary), 1983.

TELEVISION PLAYS: *Make Me an Offer*, 1952; *The Baby*, 1954; *The Girl*, 1955; *It Should Happen to a Dog*, 1955; *The Killing Stones*, 1958; *Love Is Hell*, 1966; *Dickens of London* series, 1976; *Have a Nice Death*, from the story by Antonia Fraser (*Tales of the Unexpected* series), 1984.

NOVELS

Make Me an Offer. 1952.
A Kid for Two Farthings. 1953.
Laugh Till You Cry: An Advertisement. 1955; included in *The Penguin Wolf Mankowitz*, 1967.
My Old Man's a Dustman. 1956; as *Old Soldiers Never Die*, 1956.
Cockatrice. 1963.
The Biggest Pig in Barbados: A Fable. 1965.
Raspberry Reich. 1979.
Abracadabra! 1980.
The Devil in Texas. 1984.
Gioconda. 1987.
The Magic Cabinet of Professor Smucker. 1988.
Exquisite Cadaver. 1990.
A Night with Casanova. 1991.

SHORT STORIES

The Mendelman Fire and Other Stories. 1957.
Expresso Bongo: A Wolf Mankowitz Reader. 1961.
The Blue Arabian Nights: Tales of a London Decade. 1973.
The Days of the Women and the Nights of the Men: Fables. 1977.

VERSE

XII Poems. 1971.

OTHER

The Portland Vase and the Wedgwood Copies. 1952.
Wedgwood. 1953; revised edition, 1980.
Majollika and Company (for children). 1955.
ABC of Show Business. 1956.
A Concise Encyclopedia of English Pottery and Porcelain, with R.G. Haggar. 1957.
The Penguin Wolf Mankowitz. 1967.
The Extraordinary Mr. Poe: A Biography of Edgar Allan Poe. 1978.
Mazeppa: The Lives, Loves, and Legends of Adah Isaacs Menken: A Biographical Quest. 1982.

MANUSCRIPT COLLECTION: Mugar Memorial Library, Boston University.

THEATRICAL ACTIVITIES
DIRECTOR: Film—*The Hebrew Lesson*, 1972.

Wolf Mankowitz comments:

There have been some quite good notes and notices on odd works of mine from time to time, but I really could not give details. Let's just say that they all agreed that I was somewhat over-diversified and altogether too varied, and generally speaking, pragmatic, which means, I suppose, opportunistic in the way one tends to be if one is a professional writer. Lately my writing has been described as erudite, sophisticated, always funny, sometimes bizarre—so whether I'm getting better or worse, I am certainly continuing. I have never considered myself to be a playwright. I think of myself as a storyteller, and I tend to use whatever form the story seems to me to require.

In his early novels and short stories Wolf Mankowitz displayed a sure grasp of the dramatic, that sense of character and situation which makes for good theatre. *Make Me an Offer* and *A Kid for Two Farthings* are both simple, direct narratives, sensitive and funny; it was natural enough to see them transcribed for the stage and the screen. Since then, Mankowitz has joyfully embraced show biz at all levels; he has become an impresario, he is a screenwriter who adapts his own scripts and those of others, and he has put every form of popular entertainment on celluloid. The films to which he has contributed range in their appeal from the glamorous (*The Millionairess*) to the horrific (*The Two Faces of Dr. Jekyll*), from adventure (*The Day the Earth Caught Fire*) to schmaltz (*Black Beauty*).

Mankowitz has certainly found his spiritual home in Shaftesbury Avenue but that hasn't shaken his allegiance to the basic principles of storytelling first learnt in the East End; he still employs a powerful mixture of cynicism and sentiment, still reveres the past, still delights in patterns of speech and idiosyncrasies of behaviour. At a guess, his central character in *Make Me an Offer* is something of a self-portrait. "Who knew better than he that nothing is given, that everything passes, the woods decay. He was the ultimate human being. He resigned himself to make a profit." *Expresso Bongo* is a further comment on commercialisation, a musical set in Soho, where the promoters of pop live in the continued hope of overnight successes, sudden fortune.

Of Mankowitz's one-act plays, *The Bespoke Overcoat* has always attracted praise for its technical skill and depth of feeling. It is published together with four smaller pieces, one entitled *It Should Happen to a Dog*, another, *The Last of the Cheesecake*. As one might expect, these are anecdotes of Jewish life, poignant, comic, and shrewd. *The Bespoke Overcoat* is something more, a celebration of that stubborn reverence for life which the good adhere to, however desperate their circumstances. Morry the tailor ("a needle like Paganini") can never give his friend the longed-for overcoat, since Fender has died in poverty. But human values are not negated by death: this truth is triumphantly stated in Morry's speeches and, at the close of the play, in his chanting of the Kaddish. Pathos is the dominant mood in another early play, *The Boychik*; this is a study of hopeless ambition, that of an elderly actor who, with his son, dreams of reopening the decaying theatre where he was once a star.

Mankowitz has made an important contribution to postwar drama, which is not always acknowledged by those who distrust box office success. His picture of Jewish life is convincing for its realism and memorable for its use of symbolism, as in *A Kid for Two Farthings*. He has eschewed the avant garde but is nevertheless a highly sophisticated playwright who understands the traditions of the European theatre and has worked against the parochialism of the English stage.

—Judy Cooke

MARCHANT, Tony.

Born in London, 11 July 1959. Educated at St. Joseph Academy School. Recipient: Edinburgh Festival award, 1982; *Drama* award, 1982. Agent: Lemon, Unna, and Durbridge, 24 Pottery Lane, Holland Park, London W11 4LZ, England.

Publications

PLAYS

Remember Me? (produced 1980).
Thick as Thieves (includes *London Calling* and *Dealt With*) (produced 1981). 1982.
Stiff (produced 1982).
Raspberry (produced 1982). In *Welcome Home, Raspberry, The Lucky Ones*, 1983.
The Lucky Ones (produced 1982). In *Welcome Home, Raspberry, The Lucky Ones*, 1983.
Welcome Home (produced 1983). In *Welcome Home, Raspberry, The Lucky Ones*, 1983.
Welcome Home, Raspberry, The Lucky Ones. 1983.
Lazydays Ltd. (produced 1984).
The Attractions (produced 1987). 1988.
Speculators (produced 1987). 1988.

TELEVISION PLAYS: *Raspberry*, 1984; *Reservations*, 1985; *This Year's Model*, 1988; *The Money Men*, 1988; *Death of a Son*, 1989; *The Attractions*, 1989; *Take Me Home*, 1989; *Goodbye Cruel World*, 1992.

Tony Marchant comments:

I started writing at 20, and for the past seven or eight years I have written about my generation in various situations—unemployed, trapped in office conformity, at war, in a state of sexual confusion. The experiences of my characters differ vastly: from having fought in the Falklands (*Welcome Home*) to confronting the "stigma" of infertility (*Raspberry*). Generally the plays are about people attempting to confound the expectations of their environment. They are mostly excluded from the mainstream of society, but suffer from its judgement. They all question these judgements and ultimately defy them. Theirs is a plea for dignity.

Tony Marchant's work so far marks him as the spokesman for people not normally given a voice. His earliest plays toured schools and youth clubs and he has tended to work in theatres which have a strong sense of community, such as the Theatre Royal at Stratford East, a regular clientele, such as the now closed Soho Poly, or for touring companies like Paines Plough—in short in intimate locations which allow his greatest strengths free play. He has a sharp eye for the minutiae of characterisation, allied to the ability to endow his characters with a high level of articulacy that still seems to keep within the bounds of naturalism. *Thick as Thieves*, for example, shows a group of unemployed London teenagers; the first part, *London Calling*, depicts them merely wandering about flirting with the notion of casual violence; but there is also a clear sense that at least some of them are thinking out their situation in a remarkably organised way. They take on the unthinking prejudices of Pimple, a mate who is toying with the ideas of the National Front; but while they are clear about who not to blame for their situation, they cannot conceive of a way out and their very real linguistic energy is dissipated in destructive self-parody. They are only too aware that they are prime subjects for well-meaning, ineffectual documentary: when Pimple remembers bonfires on the tatty dump that is now their social space, Paul responds sardonically "Our heritage— building things with rubbish and setting light to 'em." The idea of waste is made overt in the second play, *Dealt With*, in which Paul and the others confront a personnel officer who has rejected him; they harass him without much effect and the play ends with the boys on the run from the security guard, except for Paul, now on the verge of suicide. Here the focus is split: on the one hand there is a simple clash between the deprived and the prosperous, on the other a contrast between the dreams with which Paul invests this confrontation and the inadequacy of the personnel officer as a target for his rage. Marchant sometimes seems lost between the two and the somewhat melodramatic ending looks like a way of dodging the issue.

In his play about the Falklands aftermath, *Welcome Home*, we are shown a group of young men who have found at least a temporary alternative—the Army. Marchant gives a scrupulous account of both the benefits and the cost of that alternative on a personal level. In the discipline of the "cherry berets" the boys have found both self-image and self-respect. They have developed a comradeship which can show itself in uproarious horseplay but also in their care that a comrade's funeral shall turn out well. In return the Army demands not just their lives but also the right to control their self-expression. As the Corporal points out, the funeral is part of their public duty to be heroes "as advertised on TV"; when one of them messes up the discipline of the procession he isn't simply punished by the Army for violating its image—he assists the process, breaking down from pure shame. The Corporal treats him with savage violence, but his motivation is not the reflex action of a man addicted to "bull"; it is rather a clumsy attempt at shock therapy, an attempt to help while staying within the permitted boundaries of the Para image; this, Marchant implies, is the real cost of the Army as an outlet for youthful energy and courage—the damage it does to the best human instincts.

Raspberry is perhaps the clearest celebration of the human ability to trans- cend immediate oppression. Two women share a gynaecological ward—one for an abortion, the other for yet another operation for her infertility. Despite the insensitivity of the system that has flung them together, symbolised by the hostility of the nurse towards the young abortion patient, they achieve a close and mutually comforting relationship. Lacking any common ground, they unite against their surroundings in an almost surreal spirit. What starts as a near-quarrel turns, in the face of an angry nurse, to a mischievous assertion that they have been playing games; this then becomes something like fact as they improvise a "party" to transform the grimness of the pre-operation evening; this leads in turn to a genuine relationship; the moment when they hold each other in the face of their shared pain is a touching moment of theatre. This ability to show the play instinct at work in the unlikeliest settings, and the comradeship arising out of it, is perhaps Marchant's major strength. At present the naturalism of his sets and plots precludes a close analysis of the underlying politics. One simply accepts that, unjust as it is, this is the present situation. However, he shows clearly the resources that are there to fight it; the linguistic energy of his characters is a lively symbol of human energy in the face of oppression. For change to occur, Marchant implies, that energy needs only to be harnessed.

—Frances Gray

MARCUS, Frank (Ulrich).

Born in Breslau, Germany, 30 June 1928; emigrated to England in 1939. Educated at Bunce Court School, Kent (evacuated to Shropshire), 1939–43; St. Martin's School of Art, London, 1943–44. Married Jacqueline Sylvester in 1951; one son and two daughters. Secretary, salesman, and manager, T.M.V. Ltd., London, 1944–54; manager, Marshal's Antiques (Silver), London, 1954–65. Actor, director, and scenic designer, Unity Theatre, Kensington, London; founder, International Theatre Group. Theatre critic, the *Sunday Telegraph*, London, 1968–78; regular contributor to *Plays and Players*, London, *London Magazine*, and *Dramatists Guild Quarterly*, New York. Since 1984 television critic, *Plays International*, London. Recipient: *Evening Standard* award, 1965; *Plays and Players* award, 1965; *Variety* award, 1966. Agent: Casarotto Ramsay Ltd., National House, 60–66 Wardour Street, London W1V 3HP. Address: 8 Kirlegate, Meare, near Glastonbury, Somerset BA6 9TA, England.

Publications

PLAYS

Minuet for Stuffed Birds (also director: produced 1950).
Merry-Go-Round, adaptation of a play by Schnitzler (as *Reigen—La Ronde*, produced 1952). 1953.
The Man Who Bought a Battlefield (produced 1963).
The Formation Dancers (produced 1964; revised version, produced 1971). In *Plays of the Year 28*, 1965.
The Killing of Sister George (produced 1965). 1965.
Cleo (produced 1965). Excerpt, as *Cleo and Max*, in *London Magazine*, February 1966.
The Window (televised 1966; produced 1969). 1968.
Studies of the Nude (produced 1967).
Mrs. Mouse, Are You Within? (produced 1968). In *Plays of the Year 35*, 1969.

The Guardsman, adaptation of a play by Ferenc Molnár (produced 1969). 1978.
Blank Pages: A Monologue (televised 1969; also director: produced 1972). 1973; in *The Best Short Plays 1974*, edited by Stanley Richards, 1974.
Notes on a Love Affair (produced 1972). In *Plays of the Year 42*, 1973.
Christmas Carol (produced 1972; as *Carol's Christmas*, produced 1975).
Keyholes (produced 1973).
Beauty and the Beast (produced 1975). In *Plays of the Year 46*, 1978.
Anatol, adaptation of the play by Schnitzler (produced 1976). 1982.
Portrait of the Artist (mime; produced 1976).
Blind Date: An Anecdote (produced 1977). 1977; in *The Best Short Plays 1979*, edited by Stanley Richards, 1979.
The Ballad of Wilfred II (produced 1978).
The Merman of Orford (mime; produced 1978).
The Weavers, adaptation of a play by Gerhart Hauptmann (produced 1980). 1980.
La Ronde, with Jacqueline Marcus, adaptation of a play by Schnitzler (televised 1982; produced 1991). 1982.
From Morning to Midnight, adaptation of a play by Georg Kaiser (produced 1987).

SCREENPLAYS: *The Snow Tiger*, 1966; *The Formation Dancers*, 1972.

RADIO PLAYS: *The Hospital Visitor*, 1979; *The Beverley Brooch*, 1981; *The Row over La Ronde*, 1982.

TELEVISION PLAYS: *Liebelei*, 1954; *The Window*, 1966; A *Temporary Typist*, 1966; *The Glove Puppet*, 1968; *Blank Pages*, 1969; *Carol's Story*, 1974; *La Ronde*, with Jacqueline Marcus, 1982.

MANUSCRIPT COLLECTION: Boston University Libraries.

CRITICAL STUDIES: "The Plays of Frank Marcus" by Irving Wardle, in *London Magazine*, March 1966; "The Comedy is Finished" by Marcus, in *London Magazine*, June–July 1971.

THEATRICAL ACTIVITIES
DIRECTOR: **Plays**—*House of Regrets* by Peter Ustinov, 1948; *The Servant of Two Masters* by Carlo Goldoni, 1949; *Minuet for Stuffed Birds*, 1950; *The Broken Jug* by Heinrich von Kleist, 1950; *Husbands and Lovers* by Ferenc Molnár, 1950; *The Man of Destiny* by Shaw, 1950; *Reigen* (*La Ronde*) by Arthur Schnitzler, 1952; *Georges Dandin* by Molière, 1953; *This Property Is Condemned* by Tennessee Williams, 1953; *The Killing of Sister George*, toured, 1967; *Blank Pages*, 1972.
ACTOR: **Plays**—The General in *House of Regrets* by Peter Ustinov, 1948; Silvio in *The Servant of Two Masters* by Carlo Goldoni, 1949; title role in *The Man with the Flower in His Mouth* by Pirandello, 1950; Priest in *The Broken Jug* by Heinrich von Kleist, 1950; Napoleon in *The Man of Destiny* by Shaw, 1950; Orlando in *Angelica* by Leo Ferrero, 1951; The Son in *My Friend, The Enemy* by Sheila Hodgson, 1952.

A quality that has distinguished all Frank Marcus's mature plays is his sympathetic, though not sentimental, understanding of the behaviour of women in love, using the word "love" in its widest possible sense. The examination of feminine amatory practice in its various forms has been his theme in play after play. In two of them, Cleo and Notes on a Love Affair, it furnishes virtually the whole material of the plot.

Marcus's first play to achieve any kind of commercial success was The Formation Dancers, a light-hearted foursome in which one man borrows another man's mistress for a brief episode. His wife, to reclaim his fidelity, feigns an affair with this other man. The plot, in fact, is triviality itself; but two points are worth observing. One is the insistence that it is the two women who are always in command. The other is the drawing of the mistress, a Chelsea demi-beatnik of a type more common in 1964 (the date of the play) than now, who recurs several times in later work.

A much more detailed portrait of what is pretty well the same character appears in Cleo. This play is a theme and variations; the protagonist, that same demi-beatnik, as intelligent as she is footloose, is observed in a series of encounters with assorted men. (It may be significant that in 1953 Marcus published a translation of Schnitzler's Reigen, best known as the film La Ronde.) In this play it is clear that woman is unarguably the dominant sex, even if her dominance cannot always insure her against disaster. A later play, Studies of the Nude, was a developed version of one of the episodes from Cleo. Schnitzler's Anatol, adapted by Marcus ten years after Cleo, gives an idea of where he got the story from, only here the sexes are reversed.

Between The Formation Dancers and Cleo came what is certainly Marcus's most imaginative play so far, The Killing of Sister George. This is a penetrating study of a lesbian love affair. The "masculine" woman of the association is a once-successful actress whose career has dwindled to a steady part in a radio soap opera from which the producers now intend to drop her. She shares her life with a girl who appears to be merely young and silly, but who is later revealed as not so young and mentally retarded, the object not only of love but of a genuinely charitable beneficence. It is the younger girl, however, who at the end of the play has moved into a greater happiness and left the older woman on the brink of despair: the dominance is once again attributed to the weaker vessel. This play, in which the events mark an almost uninterrupted sequence of sadness, is nevertheless hilariously funny throughout: an imaginative masterpiece. Its sensitivity was somewhat obscured in a subsequent film version, in which Marcus did not have a hand.

After Sister George, Marcus's next piece dealt with characters almost defiantly ordinary. This was Mrs. Mouse, Are You Within?, once more a comedy of which the storyline is unrelieved tragedy. It is set among mildly trendy middle-class people in London, and once again there is a strong female part at the core, though on this occasion, for once, she is a character to whom things happen rather than a character who makes things happen. What happens is that she becomes pregnant by a passing association with a black neighbour. The lover decamps; the boring man to whom she has been engaged for eight years is so stuffy that she sends him away; and her Marxist landlord, in whom she has never felt much interest, makes a proposal of marriage to which she agrees from the depths of her despair.

The ordinariness of the characters is an asset to the play, in that vast misfortunes seem vaster when they light on little people. But *Mrs. Mouse* has not quite the imaginative spark of *Sister George* nor the wit of *The Formation Dancers*, though there is plenty of good comedy and real pathos in it. The *Cleo* character is once more recognisable in the heroine's younger sister.

Notes on a Love Affair is more romantic and less comic than any of Marcus's previous work. In this, a woman novelist stuck on a play sets up a love affair between a former lover of hers and a colourless girl who works for her dentist, so that she may observe their mutual reactions. As so often, the experiment progresses through realms of comedy to final heartbreak. The play does not mark any advance on Marcus's part, unless in his willingness to adopt the Pirandellian shift of having his heroine explain directly to the audience what she is doing. But it is a moving play, and contains two fine parts for actresses.

Marcus has also made several adaptations, including a stylish translation of Molnár's *The Guardsman*, and written several plays for television, one of which, a short two-hander called *The Window*, has also been seen in the theatre. There is some significance in the Molnár translation. If there is any detectable influence in Marcus's work, it is in Molnár and Schnitzler that you will find it.

—B.A. Young

McCABE, Eugene.

Born in Glasgow, Scotland, 7 July 1930. Educated at Castleknock College, Dublin; University College, Cork, B.A. 1953. Married Margôt Bowen in 1955; one daughter and three sons. Since 1955 farmer in County Monaghan. Chair Patrick Kavanagh Society, 1970–73. Recipient: *Irish Life* award, 1964; Prague Festival award, for television play, 1974; Irish Critics award, for television play, 1976; Royal Society of Literature Winifred Holtby prize, for fiction, 1977; Reading Association of Ireland award, for children's book, 1987. Agent: Macnaughton Lowe Representation, 200 Fulham Road, London SW10 9PN, England. Address: Drumard, Clones, County Monaghan, Ireland.

Publications

PLAYS

The King of the Castle (produced 1964). 1978.
Breakdown (produced 1966).
Pull Down a Horseman (produced 1966). With *Gale Day*, 1979.
Swift (produced 1969).
Victims (trilogy; includes *Cancer, Heritage, Victims*), adaptation of his own fiction (televised 1976; produced 1981). 1976; *Cancer* published 1980.
Roma, adaptation of his own story (televised 1979). 1979.
Gale Day (televised 1979; produced 1979). With *Pull Down a Horseman*, 1979.

TELEVISION PLAYS: *A Matter of Conscience*, 1962; *Some Women on the Island*, 1966; *The Funeral*, 1969; *Victims* (trilogy), 1976; *Roma*, 1979; *Gale Day*, 1979; *Music at Annahullion*, from his own short story, 1982; *The Year of the French*, with Pierre Lary, from the novel by Thomas Flanagan, 1983.

NOVELS
Victims: A Tale from Fermanagh. 1976.
Death and Nightingales. 1992.

SHORT STORIES
Heritage and Other Stories. 1978.
Christ in the Fields. 1993.

OTHER
Cyril: The Quest of an Orphaned Squirrel (for children). 1986.

Eugene McCabe's output is small: one could wish for more plays from such a talent. In the 1980s he turned more to fiction and television as his media, winning much acclaim for his adaptation of Thomas Flanagan's best-selling historical novel *The Year of the French.* As playwright, McCabe belongs to the 1960s, when he was instrumental, together with such dramatists as Brian Friel, Thomas Murphy, and John B. Keane, in revitalizing the moribund Irish theatre (symptomatic of which was the Abbey Theatre's ultra-conservatism at this period).

McCabe's plays have a forthrightness that must be seen in the context of theatrical and cultural conditions in an Ireland emergent from isolationism and about to come to terms with changes and challenges brought by television, the EEC, air travel, and an affluence deriving from unprecedented industrial development. *The King of the Castle* challenged certain taboos in Irish society by presenting for contemplation the spectacle of a childless couple goaded by social attitudes towards sex and fertility into hiring a surrogate father. The setting is a farm in County Monaghan, where Scober Mac Adam is harvesting and has many hired hands and petty farmers in assistance. A proud and powerful figure, Scober is all too sensitive to the mocks and jeers of those who look on his pretty wife Tressa and fault Scober for her childlessness. The imagery and atmosphere of the harvest reinforce Scober's bitter sense of sterility, and unknown to Tressa he encourages a young labourer, Matt Lynch, to think of her as in need of him. When she discovers the monstrous notion that Scober has planned, Tressa, a sympathetic character, is shattered. Ironically, Scober has succeeded only in driving her further away from him than ever, while the mockery of the "chorus" of Hardy-esque locals is not silenced but increased. Written with sensitivity as well as appropriate frankness, this play is McCabe's greatest claim to attention as a dramatist. It is, one might say, an Irish *Desire under the Elms.* It won for McCabe the prestigious *Irish Life* award.

Two unpublished plays followed: *Breakdown* and *Swift.* Neither was a success. *Breakdown,* a play about the new Ireland of big business deals and shady ethical standards, could nevertheless be regarded as rather old-fashioned in its moral approach, "pure Ibsen through the idiom," as the *Irish Times* reviewer put it. *Swift* was a major production at the Abbey with Tyrone Guthrie directing, Tanya Moisiewitch designing, and Micheál MacLiammóir from the Gate Theatre starring as Swift. The *Irish Times* reviewer described the play as "an episodic, impressionistic chronicle" and found it somewhat tedious, in spite of (or can it have been because of?) the stars descending amid the homely Abbey company. The subsequent television adaptation of *Swift* indicated that the proper medium for McCabe's main theme, Swift's madness, was film rather than theatre. But in tackling the theme for the stage he was joining a long and distinguished line of Irish dramatists fascinated by the mysteries of Swift's biography: Yeats, Lord Longford, and Denis Johnston, for example.

The greater success on television of *Swift* may have inclined McCabe towards that medium and away from the stage. Yet he did, in fact, write once more for the stage with *Gale Day*, a short play about Patrick Pearse. This was written at a time when revisionist historians were depicting Pearse as less than heroic, and, indeed, seriously flawed. *Gale Day* puts Pearse on trial and presents him as sympathetic and courageous in spite of the charges laid against him. This play makes a pendant to an earlier short piece in which Pearse and James Connolly hold a debate over the true nature of Irish republicanism, *Pull Down a Horseman*. McCabe does not take sides between the romantic idealist and the socialist.

With his three-part television drama on the Northern Ireland situation, *Cancer*, *Heritage*, and *Victims*, McCabe reached a wider audience with enormous success. Using fiction that McCabe had either already published or was about to publish, these plays carried a documentary quality that was both new and powerful on Irish television. From his native vantage point in the border county of Monaghan adjoining the rural population of Fermanagh that is sharply divided on sectarian lines, McCabe can communicate through codes of language and skilful subtext startling and even shocking insights into the ways violence blasts through coexistence and undermines human feeling. As one character puts it in *Heritage*: "men who don't want to hate are pushed to it" and must take sides. McCabe probably said all he wanted to say about the Northern Ireland tragedy in these three plays. Subsequently, he wrote a simple study of a tramp figure, an Irish Mad Tom, in *Roma*, based on a story with the same title already published in *Heritage and Other Stories*. The confused mind of the old man could be seen as an image of Irish consciousness strained by the twin forces of loyalty to traditional pieties and the necessity to see and accept changes in moral standards when doors are opened to foreign influences. The concern with "breakdown" under one kind of strain or another has been McCabe's enduring theme as a playwright, and it is found again even in so minor a piece as *Roma*.

—Christopher Murray

McGRATH, John (Peter).

Born in Birkenhead, Cheshire, 1 June 1935. Educated at Alun Grammar School, Mold, Wales; St. John's College, Oxford (Open Exhibitioner), 1955–59, Dip.Ed. Served in the British Army (national service), 1953–55. Married Elizabeth MacLennan in 1962; two sons and one daughter. Farm worker, Neston, Cheshire, 1951; play reader, Royal Court Theatre, London, and television writer and director, 1959–65. Founder and artistic director, 7:84 Theatre Company, 1971–88 (divided into Scottish and English companies, 1973); since 1983 founding director, Freeway Films. Since 1989 director, Channel Four Television, London. Judith E. Wilson fellow, Cambridge University, 1979. Agent: Casarotto Ramsay Ltd., National House, 60–66 Wardour Street, London W1V 3HP, England. Address: c/o Freeway Films, 67 George Street, Edinburgh EH2 2JG, Scotland.

Publications

PLAYS

A Man Has Two Fathers (produced 1958).

The Invasion, with Barbara Cannings, adaptation of a play by Arthur Adamov (produced 1958).

The Tent (produced 1958).

Why the Chicken (produced 1959; revised version 1960).

Tell Me Tell Me (produced 1960). In *New Departures*, 1960.

Take It (produced 1960).

The Seagull, adaptation of a play by Chekhov (produced 1961).

Basement in Bangkok, music and songs by Dudley Moore (produced 1963).

Events While Guarding the Bofors Gun (produced 1966). 1966.

Bakke's Night of Fame, adaptation of the novel *A Danish Gambit* by William Butler (produced 1968). 1973.

Comrade Jacob, adaptation of the novel by David Caute (produced 1969).

Random Happenings in the Hebrides; or, The Social Democrat and the Stormy Sea (produced 1970). 1972.

Sharpeville Crackers (produced 1970).

Unruly Elements (includes *Angel of the Morning, Plugged-in to History, They're Knocking Down the Pie-Shop, Hover Through the Fog, Out of Sight*) (produced 1971; *Plugged-in to History*, produced 1971; *Out of Sight, Angel of the Morning, They're Knocking Down the Pie-Shop*, and *Hover Through the Fog*, produced 1972). *Angel of the Morning, Plugged-in to History* and *They're Knocking Down the Pie-Shop*, published as *Plugged-in*, in *Plays and Players*, November 1972.

Trees in the Wind (also director: produced 1971).

Soft or a Girl (produced 1971; revised version, as *My Pal and Me*, also director: produced 1975).

The Caucasian Chalk Circle, adaptation of a play by Brecht (produced 1972).

Prisoners of the War, adaptation of the play by Peter Terson (produced 1972).

Underneath (also director: produced 1972).

Serjeant Musgrave Dances On, adaptation of the play *Serjeant Musgrave's Dance* by John Arden (produced 1972).

Fish in the Sea, music by Mark Brown (produced 1972; revised version produced 1975). 1977.

The Cheviot, the Stag, and the Black, Black Oil (also director: produced 1973). 1973; revised version, 1975; revised version, 1981.

The Game's a Bogey (also director: produced 1974). 1975.

Boom (also director: produced 1974; revised version produced 1974). In *New Edinburgh Review*, August 1975.

Lay Off (also director: produced 1975).

Little Red Hen (also director: produced 1975). 1977.

Oranges and Lemons (also director: produced 1975).
Yobbo Nowt, music by Mark Brown (also director: produced 1975; as *Mum's the Word*, produced 1977; as *Left Out Lady*, produced 1981). 1978.
The Rat Trap, music by Mark Brown (also director: produced 1976).
Out of Our Heads, music by Mark Brown (also director: produced 1976).
Trembling Giant (English version) (produced 1977).
Trembling Giant (Scottish version) (also director: produced 1977).
The Life and Times of Joe of England (also director: produced 1977).
Big Square Fields, music by Mark Brown (produced 1979).
Joe's Drum (also director: produced 1979). 1979.
Bitter Apples, music by Mark Brown (produced 1979).
If You Want to Know the Time (produced 1979).
Swings and Roundabouts (also director: produced 1980). In *Two Plays for the Eighties*, 1981.
Blood Red Roses (also director: produced 1980; revised version produced 1982). In *Two Plays for the Eighties*, 1981.
Two Plays for the Eighties. 1981.
Nightclass, music by Rick Lloyd (also director: produced 1981).
The Catch, music by Mark Brown (produced 1981).
Rejoice!, music by Mark Brown (produced 1982).
On the Pig's Back, with David MacLennan (produced 1983).
The Women of the Dunes (produced in Dutch, 1983).
Women in Power; or, Up the Acropolis, music by Thanos Mikroutsikos, adaptation of plays by Aristophanes (also director: produced 1983).
Six Men of Dorset, music by John Tams, adaptation of a play by Miles Malleson and Harry Brooks (produced 1984).
The Baby and the Bathwater: The Imperial Policeman (produced 1984; revised version produced 1985).
The Albannach, music by Eddie McGuire, adaptation of the novel by Fionn MacColla (produced 1985).
Behold the Sun (opera libretto), with Alexander Goehr, music by Goehr (produced 1985).
All the Fun of the Fair, with others (produced 1986).
Border Warfare (also director: produced 1989).
John Brown's Body (also director: produced 1990).
Watching for Dolphins (produced 1991).
The Wicked Old Man (produced 1992).

SCREENPLAYS: *Billion Dollar Brain*, 1967; *The Bofors Gun*, 1968; *The Virgin Soldiers*, with John Hopkins and Ian La Fresnais, 1969; *The Reckoning*, 1970; *The Dressmaker*, 1989.

RADIO PLAY: *The Game's a Bogey*, 1979.

TELEVISION PLAYS: scripts for *Bookstand* series, 1961; *People's Property* (*Z Cars* series), 1962; scripts for *Tempo* series, 1963; *Diary of a Young Man* series, with Troy Kennedy Martin, 1964; *The Entertainers* (documentary), 1964; *The Day of Ragnarok*, 1965; *Mo* (documentary), 1965; *Shotgun*, with Christopher Williams, 1966; *Diary of a Nobody*, with Ken Russell, from the novel by George and Weedon Grossmith, 1966; *Orkney*, from stories by

George Mackay Brown, 1971; *Bouncing Boy*, 1972; *Once upon a Union*, 1977; *The Adventures of Frank*, from his play *The Life and Times of Joe of England*, 1979; *Sweetwater Memories* (documentary), 1984; *Blood Red Roses*, 1986; *There Is a Happy Land*, 1987.

OTHER

A Good Night Out: Popular Theatre: Audience, Class and Form. 1981.
The Bone Won't Break: On Theatre and Hope in Hard Times. 1990.

Translator, with Maureen Teitelbaum, *The Rules of the Game* (screenplay), by
  Jean Renoir. 1970.

BIBLIOGRAPHY: by Malcolm Page, in *New Theatre Quarterly*, November 1985.

MANUSCRIPT COLLECTION: University of Cambridge.

CRITICAL STUDIES: *Disrupting the Spectacle* by Peter Ansorge, 1975; *British Theatre since 1955* by Ronald Hayman, 1979; *Stages in the Revolution* by Catherine Itzin, 1980; *Dreams and Deconstructions* edited by Sandy Craig, 1980; "Three Socialist Playwrights" by Christian W. Thomsen, in *Contemporary English Drama* edited by C.W.E. Bigsby, 1981, and "The Politics of Anxiety" by Bigsby, in *Modern Drama*, December 1981; *Modern Scottish Literature* by Alan Bold, 1983; interview with Oscar Moore, in *Plays and Players*, April 1983.

THEATRICAL ACTIVITIES

DIRECTOR: **Plays**—many of his own plays, and *Bloomsday* by Allan McClelland, 1958; *The Birds* by Aristophanes, 1959; Live New Departures series of plays, 1961–64; *The Eccentric* by Dannie Abse, 1961. **Television**— *Bookstand* series, 1961; *The Compartment* by Johnny Speight, 1961; *Z Cars* series (8 episodes), 1962; *The Fly Sham* by Thomas Murphy, 1963; *The Wedding Dress* by Edna O'Brien, 1963; *The Entertainers* (documentary), 1964; *The Day of Ragnarok*, 1965; *Mo* (documentary), 1965; *Shotgun* by McGrath and Christopher Williams, 1966; *Double Bill* by Johnny Speight, 1972; *Z Cars: The Final Episode*, 1978; *The Adventures of Frank*, 1979; *Come to Mecca* by Farrukh Dhondy, 1983; *Blood Red Roses*, 1986.

John McGrath comments:

(1973) My plays, I now realize, have been from the beginning about the relationship of the individual to other individuals and thence to history. They have pursued this theme in many ways, poetic, comic, tragic, realistic, and latterly more and more freely. Music is now coming to play a more important part in my plays, to help break through the barriers of naturalism which I can no longer tolerate. My work has never suited London (West End) audiences or ways of thinking: it is now being seen by working-class audiences from Orkney to Plymouth, and by young audiences all over the country in the new university theatres and art labs and studio theatres, via the 7:84 Theatre Company. I have also benefited from a thriving relation with the Everyman Theatre, Liverpool, under the direction of Alan Dosser, as previously from working with directors as perceptive and helpful as Ronald Eyre, Anthony Page, and Richard Eyre in Edinburgh.

My plays are not difficult to approach, although they tend to have many levels of meaning embedded fairly deeply under them as well as on the surface. The key, if key is needed, is a growing political consciousness allied to a growing feeling for individual human beings, with all the contradictions that alliance involves.

The enormity of John McGrath's contribution to the field of contemporary drama will probably never be fully realised, largely because of the way in which he has latterly chosen to direct his energies. Active in the theatre as an undergraduate writer, he immediately went on to earn a place in history as one of the key developers of the dominant mode of modern television naturalism — during his time with the BBC he was jointly responsible for the hugely influential Z Cars series. Rejecting a full-time career in television, he turned first to the conventional professional theatre. After *Events While Guarding the Bofors Gun*, a play deriving from his own experience in Army National Service in the 1950s, linkable thematically and in stature with Arnold Wesker's *Chips with Everything*, he produced *Bakke's Night of Fame*, an adaptation of a novel, as well as working on a number of screenplays, including that for his own *The Bofors Gun*.

Interest in the political consciousness of his characters was apparent from the outset but the demands of television and the conventional professional theatre for a well-crafted play with a resolved narrative proved inhibiting. The sense of class confrontation and ideological moulding in *The Bofors Gun*, for instance, is never matched by any strand in the play which suggests a way out of the fatalistically conceived framework of plot and society. What McGrath sought was a way of presenting individuals in conflict with their social context, but in ways which suggested the possibility of change through self-education and experience. This was to involve him in a conscious turning-away from the conventional theatre with what he saw as, at best, its minimally questioning analysis of capitalist society. The problem for him was as much that of audience as theatrical style: "the audience has changed very little in the theatre, the social requirements remain constant, the values remain firmly those of acceptability to a metropolitan middle-class audience, with an eye to similar acceptability on the international cultural market."

The real break with his past — and a consistent turning away from the politically restricting naturalistic mode — came in 1968. McGrath had started work on the first of a long series of plays about Scotland's history and its struggles, *Random Happenings in the Hebrides*. The play was to deal with the attempts of a young Scottish Labour MP to work for change for his island community within the confines of the parliamentary system. In the middle of writing the play, the barricades went up in Paris. McGrath went over and rethought the play, placing a greater emphasis on a non-parliamentary oppositional strategy, but seeing all the time the conflict between the need for political organisation and the immediacy of action that he had witnessed in

France. It was a theme that was to dominate much of his later work, taking him progressively further away from naturalism and into various models of agit prop theatre in pursuit of an audience that could be defined in terms of its political potential rather than its interest in the theatre as such.

By 1970, when *Random Happenings* was first produced, McGrath had started a formative period of work with the Liverpool Everyman—including a series of playlets about contemporary Britain, *Unruly Elements* (later retitled *Plugged-in to History*). In 1971 McGrath founded 7:84, a socialist theatre group intent on taking plays into the kind of non-theatrical venues shunned by the conventional theatrical establishment. Since then he has worked largely in Scotland, producing a string of plays dealing with Scottish socialist strategy in a variety of historical and contemporary contexts—with the occasional production for the English offshoot of 7:84. Productions have varied from the didactic intensity of the first 7:84 piece, *Trees in the Wind*, to offerings, such as the political pantomime *Trembling Giant*, that make use of the loosest of narrative structures to put across a deliberately crude analysis. McGrath's clear awareness of the dangers of arguing for an impossibly simple solution to a highly complex problem—the dilemma of all revolutionaries living in a non-revolutionary age—is brilliantly articulated in the humour and wit of the plays, frequently inviting the audience into the never self-contained discourse. The general method is summed up well by Joe's tongue-in-cheek invitation to the audience to take its seats again after the interval in *Joe's Drum*, a play written in response to the election of a Conservative administration and the failure of the Scottish Assembly vote. They are assured that they should not be frightened off by the fear of weighty material. "It's yer ain true story told in biased argument, highly selective history and emotional folksong. Are ye all back that's comin' back? Right—lock the doors."

McGrath's—and 7:84's—insistence on a theatre that should not only offer enlightenment but entertainment is a key part of the play's acceptance. McGrath has moved progressively away from the kind of consumer society cultural parody that has proved a staple of so much agit prop theatre—as in the "Beat the System" TV show in *The Game's a Bogey*—in search of popular cultural roots that oppose those offered by the consumerist system. The use of the Highland ceilidh form for the first Scottish 7:84 tour in 1973, of *The Cheviot, the Stag, and the Black, Black Oil*, gave McGrath the structure of a traditional evening entertainment through which to tell the story of Scottish exploitation through history to the, then, oil boom. In subsequent plays he was to make the link between the music as part of an oppositional cultural history and the need to question contemporary representations a major part of the shows' dynamics.

McGrath's is a questioning development of agit prop, and his conclusions are usually open-ended, witnessing a small personal achievement perhaps but not proclaiming the imminence of revolutionary change. And in this context, his depiction of the particular dilemma of women caught in the dual webs of capitalism and a male-oriented ideology has emerged as a major theme in his work. In *Joe's Drum* his wife is a continual presence, chipping away at masculine vanities, and in a play such as *Yobbo Nowt* all the emphasis is placed on the struggles of a wife after she has ejected an unfeeling husband. Her discovery of the way in which the system operates against the "have-nots" parallels her own discovery of individual potential, and the play ends with a small personal leap forward.

McGrath has continued to produce work at a prolific rate—always with a central interest in the way in which the individual can operate against the increasingly sophisticated and endlessly elastic models of late capitalist society. The overall effect is to suggest the way in which the various manifestations of authority and oppression are a part of a single system and thus linkable, as they are from one play to another—each then becoming just one in a series of views through the different windows of a part of the same enormous construction. In *Blood Red Roses*, he traced the political struggles of Bessie from the 1950s to the present day; she is just one of what is by now a very large political family assured of an audience away from the subsidised and commercial theatres of London where reputations are made. However, his insistence on the continual tracing of that struggle has itself been a great struggle and, as McGrath recounts in *The Bone Won't Break*, the establishment, and in particular that part of the establishment holding the purse-strings of the Arts Council, has continually opposed the efforts of McGrath and 7:84—to the extent that the company has at last ceased to operate. As a result, stage productions from McGrath have become less frequent of late—although the 1990 *John Brown's Body* at Glasgow's Tramway, in which the dominant stage feature was a huge platform along three walls from which the ruling-class characters controlled and directed the workers and audience on stage level, saw him continue unabashed. More energy has inevitably gone into work for film and television, but no let-up in activity is to be anticipated. A popular writer in a genuine sense, McGrath will continue to be active long after the reputations of many participants in what he sees as an integral part of the capitalist system have been forgotten.

—John Bull

McGRATH, Tom.

Born in Rutherglen, Lanarkshire, 23 October 1940. Educated at Glasgow University, degree in drama and English. Married; four daughters. Director, Third Eye Centre, Glasgow; founding editor, *International Times* underground newspaper, London, 1960s; writer-in-residence. Traverse Theatre, Edinburgh, and University of Iowa, Iowa City. Since 1990 associate literary director, Scottish Arts Council, Edinburgh. Also a jazz pianist. Agent: Michael Imison Playwrights, 28 Almeida Street, London N1 1TD, England.

Publications

PLAYS

Laurel and Hardy (produced 1976; as *Mr. Laurel and Mr. Hardy*, produced 1976).
The Hard Man, with Jimmy Boyle (produced 1977). 1977.
The Android Circuit (produced 1978).
Sisters (produced 1978; revised version produced 1985).
Animal (produced 1979).
The Innocent (produced 1979).

1–2–3: Who Are You Anyway?, *Very Important Business*, *Moondog* (produced 1981).
The Phone Box (for children; 1983).
Pals (produced 1984).
Kora (produced 1986).
Thanksgiving (produced 1986).
Private View, with Mhairi Grealis (produced 1987).
Trivial Pursuits (produced 1988).

RADIO PLAY: *The Silver Darling*, from the novel by Neil Gunn, 1982.

TELEVISION PLAYS: *The Nuclear Family*, 1982; *Blowout*, 1984; *The Gambler*, 1984; *End of the Line*, 1984.

COMPOSER: music for *The Great Northern Welly Boot Show*, book by Tom Buchan, lyrics by Billy Connolly, 1972.

For a long time, the original success of Tom McGrath's most completely achieved play, *Animal*, kept it out of circulation in England. Although the hit of the 1979 Edinburgh Festival, when it was presented as an official offering by the Traverse Theatre, it was snapped up by American entrepreneurs and the English rights were blocked. The absurdity of such absolute control was reflected by its middling success when it was finally produced south of the Scottish border long after its ecstatic notices. None the less, it remains his most dazzling theatrical conceit.

Originally mounted in an ascending structure of scaffolds and platforms, the play observed the drama of life in a colony of apes, with the intrusive presence of zoologists observing them. The real spectacle and abiding image of the play was the movement and inter-relationships of the apes themselves. With the animals portrayed by loose-limbed actors and actresses, the effect was of life observed through a series of mirrors. The animals were watched by the humans, while the apes aped the humans they were watching. Insights and comedy came through the parallel dramas, and, ironically, dramatic communication was hindered most by the necessity of speech among the humans.

Before becoming a dramatist, McGrath was himself an outside observer of sorts. He edited Britain's most influential counter-cultural periodical, *International Times*, part of the exploding drug culture of the 1960s. That experience was brought to his play for the Royal Shakespeare Company, *The Innocent*, which followed a progression from the use of drugs for pleasure to addiction and withdrawal in an attempt to consider the implications of a selfish pursuit of pleasure on the dreams of the lost "alternative society." It was the first of his plays even to suggest personal experience and observation, and most of his work through the 1970s was notable for his wide-ranging interests. Science fiction and dramatized biography were perhaps the strongest elements.

His first play, which appeared at the Edinburgh Festival in 1976 and later transferred to London, was *Mr. Laurel and Mr. Hardy*, a private view of the off-screen life of the best comic team of the first Hollywood era. McGrath takes the ambitious route of showing both lives independently as well as matching his two actors for some of the on-screen routines. For McGrath, the attraction of Stan Laurel is obviously his Glasgow beginnings, but Oliver Hardy is given equal biographical substance. The play is notable for its contemplation of the team's pathetic final years, with Laurel alone, still writing routines for himself and his old partner, but speaking both parts.

McGrath's second play, a violent dramatization of the life of a reformed Glasgow gangster, appeared the following year. *The Hard Man* was written with Jimmy Boyle, who told the story under his own name in the book *A Sense of Freedom*, which McGrath had a hand in. The story is essentially an odyssey through childhood and gang warfare in the Glasgow slums, culminating in a criminal career which included brutal murder. There is a further dimension to the story, which could tell of Boyle's rehabilitation in prison and his emergence as a sculptor. The play does not go that far; rather it provides a form of ritual re-enactment of the street violence which accentuates key moments in the life of Johny Byrne, the fictional Boyle. Inside prison, jailed for murder, Byrne remains the fiercely proud street-fighter, resisting the regimentation and sadism of the prison and finally reaching a peculiar transcendence in a cramped cage where he squats and smears excrement over himself.

That power was missing from McGrath's fantasy *The Android Circuit*, and from his portrait of three girls growing up in London's East End, *Sisters*. Moments of that force are again visible in a trilogy which he wrote for the Traverse and BBC radio, *1–2–3*, which McGrath described as "plays about male identity written from a feminist viewpoint by a man." The plays are chiefly connected by a cast of three (two men and a woman), and the first play, *Who Are You Anyway?*, blazes a trail of gender confusion as male love and bonding are transferred to love of a woman. The final play appears to pick up the thread of *The Innocent* and shows the two men and woman reinventing a myth about woman as witch, or specifically as priestess of the moon. *Moondog* begins with a drop-out Scot pictured in his chosen solitude in the Highlands, greeting the morning with a chant before being interrupted by an old friend who comes bearing unwanted business propositions. A further interruption is in the form of the woman who arrives with a different purpose, in the nature of human sacrifice.

The trilogy failed in London, but found an audience for the same production at the Toronto Theatre Festival of 1981 and McGrath himself spent a year at the University of Iowa directing the Playwrights' Workshop there. Returning to Scotland, he returned to Scottish themes, notably with *Kora*, a documentary drama about the struggle of tenants in a Dundee housing estate to improve conditions, but filled with flashes of McGrath's theatrical invention and optimism. The American experience was satirically reflected through his short play, *Thanksgiving*, written for Glasgow's Tron Theatre. As part of a trilogy including plays by other Glasgow-based writers, it was designed to accommodate original music by Edward McGuire, but rather more theatrically made use of the spectral presence of the musicians as he dissected the consumerism of America's Thanksgiving Day, with a bossy television set and a woman reasonably declaring her love for two men during "the year of the Ayatollah." It passes more as amused observation than enlightening comment, and if his work in the 1980s is less visible than his work of the 1970s, it is similarly diverse and sympathetic.

While he continued to supply original plays and adaptations to the Scottish theatre, from the Edinburgh Lyceum to Cumbernauld Theatre Company, by the 1990's McGrath had moved into a new role with perhaps even more influence on the future of Scottish drama. As associate literary director of the Scottish Arts Council he masterminded training and astute subsidy to become regarded as a "guru" of Scottish playwrights. His own work still represented a major part of his time, but perhaps reverting to his early days, when as a founder member of the *International Times* he was concerned with enfranchising the disaffected into an alternative society, his inspiration to others is proving to be a major achievement.

—Ned Chaillet

McGUINNESS, Frank.

Born in Buncrana, Donegal, 29 July 1953. Educated at Carndonagh College, Donegal, 1966–71; University College of Dublin, 1971–76, B.A., and M.Phil in medieval studies. Lecturer, University of Ulster, Coleraine, Londonderry, 1977–79, University College of Dublin, 1979–80, and since 1984 St. Patrick's College, Maynooth, County Kildare. Since 1992 director, The Abbey Theatre, Dublin. Member of Aosdanna, from 1991. Recipient: Rooney prize, 1985; Harvey's award, 1985; *Evening Standard* award, 1986; *Plays and Players* award, 1986; Cheltenham prize, 1986; Charrington award, 1987; Ewart-Biggs Peace prize, 1987; Edinburgh Fringe first, 1988; Prague prix des journalists, 1989. Agent: Sheila Lemon, Lemon, Unna, and Durbridge, 24 Pottery Lane, Holland Park, London W11 4LZ, England.

Publications

PLAYS

The Factory Girls (produced 1982). 1983; revised edition, 1988.

Borderlands (produced 1984). In *Three Team Plays*, edited by Martin Drury, 1988.

Observe the Sons of Ulster Marching Towards the Somme (produced 1985). 1986.

Baglady (produced 1985). With *Carthaginians*, 1988.

Gatherers (produced 1985).

Innocence: The Life and Death of Michelangelo Merisi Caravaggio (produced 1986). 1987.

Yerma, adaptation of the play by Federico García Lorca (produced 1987).

Rosmersholm, adaptation of the play by Henrik Ibsen (produced 1987).

Carthaginians (produced 1988). With *Baglady*, 1988.

Times in It (produced 1988).

Peer Gynt, adaptation of the play by Henrik Ibsen (produced 1988). 1990.

Mary and Lizzie (produced 1989). 1989.

Beautiful British Justice (sketch) in *Fears and Miseries of the Third Term* (produced 1989).

The Bread Man (produced 1990).

Three Sisters, adaptation of the play by Anton Chekhov (produced 1990). 1990.
Threepenny Opera, adaptation of the play by Bertolt Brecht (produced 1991).
Someone Who'll Watch over Me (produced 1992). 1992.

TELEVISION PLAYS: *Scout*, 1987; *The Hen House*, 1990.

MANUSCRIPT COLLECTION: National Library of Ireland.

Frank McGuinness comments:

After 20 years or more of civil war, Ireland still stumbles forward, keeping its head just above water. I want my plays to trace the steps of that stumbling, to be steeped in that unholy water. Having lost the certainness of faith and fatherland, this country is in the business of finding new languages, new laws. Theatre is likewise radically shaken. *Someone Who'll Watch over Me*, *Mutabilitie*, and another project will, I hope, form a contingently linked trilogy, giving what are new lives to those lies, the conflict of Ireland and England, the edging of Ireland to Europe.

"It is possible that there is no other memory than the memory of wounds." The epigraph to *Carthaginians*, taken from Czesław Milosz, could stand as epigraph to the whole of Frank McGuiness's work. The characteristic Irish preoccupation with (in his own words) "the effect that the past has on our present" finds distinctive form in his plays through an exploration of the relationship between culture (whether local or national) and personal identity in which the past is experienced as both a burden and a source of energy. McGuinness has described his plays as "attempts to give what was lost a voice," and the constant formal and stylistic experimentation of his work evidences his continuing effort to articulate the relationship between the personal and the cultural spheres as part of a project of recuperation and regeneration. The necessity to *give voice* also guarantees the essentially theatrical nature of the work. McGuinness's plays find their resolutions in acts of *utterance*, of a ritual or quasi-ritual nature: song, recitation, oratory, incantation, or naming. Above all, these plays are shaped by the imperative of *confession*, which, though sacramental in feeling, is valued as an act of *human* reciprocity. By giving voice we keep our words to the voiceless.

McGuinness's first play, *The Factory Girls*, prefigures the dramatic movement of his later ones. The confrontational response of a group of five women to the threat of redundancy leaves them in an apparently hopeless situation, but it also catalyses a realisation in each of an independence gained through bonding. In this terminal situation, individuality and collectivity are found to be mutually sustaining. This realisation, in a much more richly contextualised form, assumes a pivotal position in McGuinness's best-known (and best) play, the award-winning *Observe the Sons of Ulster Marching Towards the Somme*. As a piece in which a writer from a Catholic background addresses empathetically the experience of Protestant Ulstermen at one of the vital symbolic moments of Loyalist historical memory, the play was, quite properly, regarded as a significant act of fellowship. Yet it is the perception of "something rotten" at the heart of a "dying" Unionist culture that prompts the characters to question, in their different ways, both the idea of inevitable death as "sacrifice" and the familiar rhetoric of blood which embodies that idea. The play is in four named parts, each evoking a ritual of a secular character. Part 1, "Remembrance," is a monologue set in the present, in which the elderly, blind Kenneth Pyper affirms his fidelity to the sacrifice of "the irreplaceable ones," his immediate comrades on the Somme in 1916, then calls up their ghosts to help him answer the question of "why we let ourselves be led to extermination." The "ghosts," including Pyper's own very different younger self, play out the events leading up to 1 July 1916. In "Initiation," the eight young Ulstermen gather in a makeshift barracks where the homosexual Pyper, failed sculptor and "black sheep" of an ascendancy family, with a disastrous French marriage behind him and a death-wish driving him on, mocks Unionist culture —by fierce parody—as only an insider could, and vows "I'll take away your peace." In "Pairing" the stage is divided to evoke four numinous locations: Boa Island, a church, a rope-bridge, and the Twelfth Field. The men are home on leave, but "the guns are home" too, and the realisation that "we *are* the sacrifice" brings about within each of the four pairings a dissolution of identity, personal and cultural. Yet the same moment also yields a visionary clarity of understanding. The fellowship and even (homosexual) love that enables each man to refashion himself as an independent being is finally tested and proven in Part 4, "Bonding." As they wait in the trenches to go over the top in this "last battle," their ritual preparations affirm the potency of Protestant rhetoric not as triumphalist threat and self-justification but as common inheritance and shared medium of identity. It is Pyper, remade in the bond, who delivers the final prayer; the battle-cry of "Ulster" reaches paroxysm and his younger and elder selves join hands to "Dance in this deserted temple of the Lord."

The symbolic mode developed through *Sons of Ulster*, *Innocence* (a play about Caravaggio, another homosexual artist-figure), and the densely powerful monologue *Baglady*, finds its most daring embodiment—both visual and verbal—in McGuinness's play about Northern Catholic culture, *Carthaginians*. Once again the focus is on an isolated group of individuals in crisis, but here the isolation is self-imposed and the situation even more openly symbolic. This is a play of waiting. Although the setting is a real place in real time, and the dialogue-style predominantly naturalistic, the action is largely internalised, articulated not through conventional narrative but through image, symbol, and quasi-ritual utterance. Six people—three women and three men—are camped out in Derry city graveyard awaiting the fulfilment of a vision of the dead rising in the burial ground. The world they create for themselves, in this place of ancient resonances, is one which effects strange inversions and suspensions of normal experience by the attempt to mediate between the living and the dead. The group is anchored to everyday fact and reality only through the kind offices of Dido Martin, "patriot and poof," the queen of this particular Carthage and the representative of quite another kind of camp. As with Pyper and Caravaggio, homosexuality here constitutes not a social "issue" but a perspective offering clarification and insight. By virtue of his gender position and through his theatricality (he even writes a parodic play for them) Dido delivers a criticism of the culture of the living even as he is mediating it to the group. Each of the graveyard dwellers nurses the "wound" of a deep personal loss or torment of political conscience, but these are subsumed in the overshadowing memory of a great communal wound: Bloody Sunday, a day in 1971 when British troops shot dead several civilians during a protest march in Derry. The confessional rites of personal release are finally sealed by the communal invocation, as Sunday dawns, of the names of the victims of the atrocity. The dead are present as silent "Listeners," and the living are enjoined to include themselves in a general forgiveness. As "they sleep in the graveyard," the vigilant Dido affirms the survival of the city ("Carthage has not been destroyed"), discards the accumulated detritus of Northern Catholic culture, and leaves Derry to "walk the earth."

Where the symbolic intensities of *Carthaginians* seem indebted to Lorca, the fantastic narrative of *Mary and Lizzie*, with its constant reference to "popular forms of English art" (pantomime and television comedy) and Irish folk tradition (ballad and myth), announces its affiliation to *Peer Gynt* (which McGuinness has translated). This is the playwright's most direct treatment of voicelessness. "Frederick Engels lived with two Irishwomen, Mary and Lizzie Burns"; they showed him the "Condition of the Victorian Working Class" in Manchester. For this reason they are, for McGuinness, "probably the most important Irish people of the 19th century, in terms of world history." Yet they are remembered only by the single line in Engels's Life: they *are* their name(s). Neither fully "historical" nor fully "mythical," Mary and Lizzie, like Pyper, Caravaggio, and Dido, move between two distinct realms. In the world of Myth, a nameless shadowy territory projected by Irish song, folklore, and ritual, and defined by darkness and the earth, they are first sent out from the arboreal City of Women to "kiss and tell," then shown the future, in the forms of a Magical Priest (son of Mother Ireland), representing both Protestantism and Catholicism in a "killing combination," and a ritual Feast of Famine— complete with balladeering Pig. They escape to England and the realm of History, where, after "passing the time" with the young Queen Victoria (a pantomime dame), they descend to the "open sewer" of Manchester. There they agree to guide a fearful Engels through the nameless "dark" of the "dangerous poor," and so become silent collaborators in his project to "change the world." The sisters' insistence on sexuality and the body disrupts the philosophical double-act of Engels and Karl Marx, and at "Dinner with Karl and Jenny" (Marx's wife—herself tormented by the suppression of her contribution) the reason and abstraction of "scientific" socialism is posed against the instinctive physicality and lyrical utterance of Mary and Lizzie. As Jenny reads Engels's terrible account of the Manchester Irish, the illiterate sisters counter his betrayal by singing the folk-song "She Moved Through the Fair." Finally, the regenerative power of song and the earth is decisively affirmed in the face of a vision of the "night to come," brought about in the name of political ideologies and attested to by nameless "Women of the Camps" in choric song. Even after Mary's "death," song can unite the sisters with their mother to wander the earth (like McGuinness's other mediator-figures) and "sing the songs of those who were never sung about." The linkage of myth, song, and the earth bears witness to the endurance of the voiceless.

The Bread Man returns to the (historical) present to address the problematic relationship between southern and Northern Ireland. The experience of guilt, distrust, dispossession, and despair surrounding a fraternal bereavement is given wider symbolic resonance through a dramaturgy of the interior recalling that of *Innocence.* This play met with general critical disappointment, but the consistency of thematic focus and the variety of formal treatment to be found in McGuinness's drama as a whole combine to inspire confidence in the quality of his future work.

—Paul Lawley

McINTYRE, Clare.

Member, Nottingham Playhouse TIE Company, 1977–78, The Women's Theatre Group, London, 1979–81, and Common Stock, London, 1981. Recipient: Beckett award, 1989; *Evening Standard* award, 1990; London Drama Critics award, 1990. Agent: Leah Schmidt, Curtis Brown Group, 162–168 Regent Street, London W1R 5TB, England.

Publications

PLAYS

Better a Live Pompey than a Dead Cyril, with Stephanie Nunn, adaptation of the poems and writings of Stevie Smith (produced 1980).
I've Been Running (produced 1986).
Low Level Panic (produced 1988). In *First Run,* edited by Kate Harwood, 1989.
My Heart's a Suitcase (produced 1990). 1990.

RADIO PLAY: *I've Been Running,* 1990.

THEATRICAL ACTIVITIES

ACTOR: **Plays**—role in *Better a Live Pompey than a Dead Cyril,* by McIntyre with Stephanie Nunn, 1980; Mrs. Kendal in *The Elephant Man* by Bernard Pomerance, 1982; Dawn in *Steaming* by Nell Dunn, 1985; Gwendolen in *The Importance of Being Earnest* by Oscar Wilde, 1985; Jane in *Crystal Clear,* 1986; Jan in *Bedroom Farce* by Alan Ayckbourn, 1987; Linda in *Kafka's Dick* by Alan Bennett, 1988. **Films**—*The Pirates of Penzance,* 1981; *Krull,* 1982; *Plenty,* 1984; *Empire State,* 1986; *Security,* 1987; *A Fish Called Wanda,* 1988. **Television**—*Hotel du Lac,* 1985; *Splitting Up,* 1990.

Clare McIntyre was an actress working in theatre and film for several years before she turned full-time to writing. As a member of the Women's Theatre Group she produced a delightful compilation of the work of Stevie Smith. Her first original play was *I've Been Running,* directed by Terry Johnson and performed at the Old Red Lion in London. It focuses on a female health freak whose fears are kept at bay by feverish activity. McIntyre is one of a long line of female playwrights whose work has been encouraged and nurtured by a combination of the Women's Playhouse Trust and Max Stafford-Clark at the Royal Court. Both *Low Level Panic* and *My Heart's a Suitcase* reveal an uncanny ability to reflect the obsessions and anxieties of contemporary women. Like Caryl Churchill, her plays attract a huge female following, but there is no reason why men shouldn't also enjoy her wit and shrewd observation.

The panic in *Low Level Panic* is engendered in a couple of female flat-sharers when confronted with the images of women peddled by advertising and pornography. The territory is similar to Sarah Daniels's but without her aggression. Mary, Jo, and Celia are preparing for a party. McIntyre cleverly sets all but two of the play's scenes in the bathroom, the very place where women minutely examine their bodies and almost invariably find them wanting. Lying in the bath, Jo imagines herself as the heroine of a sexual fantasy, a leggy model gliding through the cocktail bars of London's hotels, clinking glasses of Martini and meeting the admiring eyes of a rich handsome stranger across a crowded room. Such glacial perfection and anonymity is in complete contrast with Jo's vision of herself as overweight and over-talkative, especially when confronted with a roomful of people at a party. Far from being an expression of her own sensuality, her fantasy makes her feel both humiliated and undesirable. It is also in sharp contrast with the reality experienced by Mary when, in one of just two scenes set outside the bathroom, she is stopped on her way home and raped. As a result she can no longer dress up for a party without feeling she is asking to be attacked again. The pornographic magazine she discovers in their dustbin appears to her to be a legal incitement to men to attack women. In contrast, Celia, the third member of the flat and the least developed as a character, dishes out advice on the right colour of eyeshadow as though life simply consists of trapping the right man. The intimate dialogue about spots, herpes, and even unattractive clitorises is sharply observed and very amusing. But above all it is the confusion and naïvety of her characters that McIntyre captures so accurately.

Anxiety is also a theme in *My Heart's a Suitcase*. Chris is 30 years old, a waitress and distinctly unhappy about it: "What's wrong with being a waitress is that it's a shit job with shit money, no shitting pension and zero fucking prospects." She has a capacity to complain that rivals Jimmy Porter's in Osborne's *Look Back in Anger*. *My Heart's a Suitcase* is a play of the 1980s, a time when everybody was supposed to be getting richer but Chris, who is middle-class, articulate, has a degree, and could presumably earn money if she set her mind to it, is paralysed. Her life is drifting by while she is obsessed with the horrors of the world, an obsession intensified after being attacked by a man with a gun on the tube. Her more placid friend Hannah faces the possibility of real paralysis in the form of multiple sclerosis. The two of them travel down to the seaside together, invited to spend the weekend in an empty flat belonging to a rich ex-boyfriend of Chris's. Thus Chris is given plenty of opportunity to rail against the injustice of some people having money while she has a pittance. She is confronted with real riches when Colin's wife, Tunis, arrives at the flat trailing her consumer goods behind her and throws a tantrum when she discovers her specially made curtains don't fit. Tunis doesn't even have to work for her money but fritters her time away in endless shopping sprees. McIntyre, however, avoids drawing too neat a moral; Tunis is indolent but not a villain and is discontented without being wildly unhappy. It is not that Chris is particularly greedy; it is more that she imagines that wealth would make her happy, although a strange religious phantom called Luggage suggests that it is a woman's role in life to make do with her lot. This phantom, together with that of the man who attacked her, are the least engaging aspects of the play. Most enjoyable is Chris's ability to articulate her discontent with such ferocious gusto. She may be maddening but it is hard to dislike her, and McIntyre makes a rare attempt to present the rich complexities of female friendship onstage. She is a humorous, observant playwright with a deep understanding of the female psyche, and, if she is not diverted into television, could well produce a major play in the future.

—Jane Edwardes

MERCER, David.

Born in Wakefield, Yorkshire, 27 June 1928. Educated at King's College, Newcastle upon Tyne, BA (honours) in fine art (Durham University) 1953. Married twice; one daughter. Laboratory technician, 1942–45; served as a laboratory technician in the Royal Navy, 1945–48; lived in Paris, 1953–54; supply teacher, 1955–59; teacher, Barrett Street Technical College, 1959–61. Recipient: Writers Guild award, for television play, 1962, 1967, 1968; BAFTA award, 1966; French Film Academy César award, 1977; Emmy award, 1980. *Died 8 August 1980.*

Publications

PLAYS

The Governor's Lady, (broadcast 1960). In *Stand,* Spring 1962; revised version (produced 1965), 1968.
Where the Difference Begins (televised 1961). In *The Generations,* 1964.
The Buried Man (produced 1962).
A Climate of Fear (televised 1962). In *The Generations,* 1964.
The Generations: A Trilogy of Plays (includes *Where the Difference Begins; A Climate of Fear; The Birth of a Private Man*). 1964; as *Collected TV Plays 1,* 1981.
A Suitable Case for Treatment (televised 1962). In *Three TV Comedies,* 1966.
The Birth of a Private Man (televised 1963). In *The Generations,* 1964.
For Tea on Sunday (televised 1963). In *Three TV Comedies,* 1966.
And Did Those Feet (televised 1965). In *Three TV Comedies,* 1965.
Ride a Cock Horse (produced 1965). 1966.
Belcher's Luck (produced 1966). 1967.
Three TV Comedies (includes *A Suitable Case for Treatment; For Tea on Sunday; And Did Those Feet*). 1966.
In Two Minds (televised 1967; produced 1973). In *The Parachute with Two More TV Plays,* 1967.
The Parachute with Two More TV Plays: Let's Murder Vivaldi; In Two Minds. 1967.
The Parachute (televised 1968). In *The Parachute with Two More TV Plays,* 1967.
Let's Murder Vivaldi (televised 1968; produced 1972). In *The Parachute with Two More TV Plays,* 1967; in *The Best Short Plays 1974,* edited by Stanley Richards, 1974.

On the Eve of Publication and Other Plays (television plays; includes *The Cellar and the Almond Tree* and *Emma's Time*). 1970.
Robert Kelvin trilogy: *On the Eve of Publication* (televised 1968); *The Cellar and the Almond Tree* (televised 1970); *Emma's Time* (televised 1970). All in *On the Eve of Publication and Other Plays*, 1970.
White Poem (produced 1970).
Flint (produced 1970). 1970.
After Haggerty (produced 1970). 1970.
Blood on the Table (produced 1971).
The Bankrupt (televised 1972). In *The Bankrupt and Other Plays*, 1974.
You and Me and Him (televised 1973). In *The Bankrupt and Other Plays*, 1974.
An Afternoon at the Festival (televised 1973). In *The Bankrupt and Other Plays*, 1974.
The Bankrupt and Other Plays (includes *You and Me and Him; An Afternoon at the Festival; Find Me*). 1974.
Find Me (televised 1974). In *The Bankrupt and Other Plays*, 1974.
The Arcata Promise (televised 1974; produced 1982). In *Huggy Bear and Other Plays*, 1977.
Duck Song (produced 1974). 1974.
Huggy Bear (televised 1976). In *Huggy Bear and Other Plays*, 1977.
Huggy Bear and Other Plays (includes *The Arcata Promise* and *A Superstition*). 1977.
Shooting the Chandelier (televised 1977). With *Cousin Vladimir*, 1978.
Cousin Vladimir (produced 1978). With *Shooting the Chandelier*, 1978.
Then and Now (produced 1979). With *The Monster of Karlovy Vary*, 1979.
No Limits to Love (produced 1980). 1981.
Collected TV Plays 1–2 (includes *Where the Difference Begins; A Climate of Fear; The Birth of a Private Man; A Suitable Case for Treatment; For Tea on Sunday; And Did Those Feet; The Parachute; Let's Murder Vivaldi; In Two Minds*). 2 vols., 1981.
Plays 1 (includes *Where the Difference Begins; The Governor's Lady; A Suitable Case for Treatment; On the Eve of Publication; The Cellar and the Almond Tree; Emma's Time; After Haggerty*). 1990.

SCREENPLAYS: *90 Degrees in the Shade* (English dialogue), 1965; *Morgan! A Suitable Case for Treatment*, 1966; *Family Life* (*Wednesday's Child*), 1972; *A Doll's House*, with Michael Meyer, 1973; *Providence*, 1978.

RADIO PLAYS: *The Governor's Lady*, 1960; *Folie à Deux*, 1974.

TELEVISION PLAYS: *Where the Difference Begins*, 1961; *A Climate of Fear*, 1962; *A Suitable Case for Treatment*, 1962; *The Birth of a Private Man*, 1963; *A Buried Man*, from the stage play, 1963; *For Tea on Sunday*, 1963; *A Way of Living*, 1963; *And Did Those Feet*, 1965; *In Two Minds*, 1967; *The Parachute*, 1968; *Let's Murder Vivaldi*, 1968; *Robert Kelvin* trilogy: *On the Eve of Publication*, 1968, *The Cellar and the Almond Tree*, 1970, *Emma's Time*, 1970; *The Bankrupt*, 1972; *You and Me and Him*, 1973; *An Afternoon at the Festival*, 1973; *Barbara of the House of Grebe*, from a story by Thomas Hardy, 1973; *Find Me*, 1974; *The Arcata Promise*, 1974; *Huggy Bear*, 1976; *A Superstition*, 1977; *Shooting the Chandelier*, 1977; *The Ragazza*, 1978; *A Rod of Iron*, 1980; *A Dinner of Herbs*, 1988.

BIBLIOGRAPHY: *The Quality of Mercer: A Bibliography of Writings by and About David Mercer* by Francis Jarman, John Noyce, and Malcolm Page, 1974.

CRITICAL STUDIES: *The Second Wave: British Drama for the Seventies* by John Russell Taylor, 1971; *David Mercer: Where the Difference Begins*, edited by Paul Madden, 1981; *Days of Vision: Working with David Mercer* by Don Taylor, 1990.

The tensions between utopia and defeat in David Mercer's major plays can be regarded as a triangle whose points are North, South, and East. Heroes of Yorkshire or Midlands working-class origin struggle to reconcile their fame among the London literati with their commitment to a socialism that may have been born in the Marxist East. Their guilt at growing away from their inarticulate origins is underscored by the sceptical or indifferent women with whom they live or whom they divorce.

Children, in some form or another, are an obsessive presence, although Mercer never creates a conventional nuclear family. Peter, a successful Yorkshire novelist, shuttles between three women in *Ride A Cock Horse*. His wife, Nan, a doctor, cannot have children; his actress girlfriend, Myra, is past the menopause; he impregnates his other girlfriend, Fanny, but she aborts the child, which is what Peter really wanted. Bernard Link's flat, in *After Haggerty*, is invaded by an aggressive American, Claire, with an infant, Raskolnikov, who is never seen but who, like his absent father, Haggerty, comes increasingly to dominate the household. Ossian Flint, a 70-year-old communist vicar, motorcycles off to Rome and Greece with 19-year-old Dixie, pregnant by Arthur the anarchist, in *Flint*. Lucy, the serving-girl, is pregnant by Belcher, the handyman, from start to finish in *Belcher's Luck* (1966), but Belcher has only contempt for his living son, Victor, who has been adopted and cosseted by the asexual lord of the manor, Catesby.

Such an emphasis on birth and children is unusual for a Marxist writer; it can be read as a further intensification, at the domestic level, of Mercer's contradictory emotions towards radicalism in the political sphere. The exchange between Nan and Peter in Act II, Scene 1 of *Ride A Cock Horse* dramatically freezes the opposing impulses of female and male:

Nan: . . . Well. I want to go back up there—
Peter: I shall go abroad. I shall go to Warsaw.

Earlier Peter has tried to resolve his stasis by appropriating the language of birth for males and for adults only: "I am the proud father of a lovely, bouncing wife", he shouts at his passive wife. He follows up with, "Clever people know that the hip thing is to give birth to adults". Peter's attempts at self-birthing fail. Both his mistresses finish up at Nan's hospital, and Peter is reduced, at the end of the play, to a sobbing wreck, clinging like a child to his father who has come down from his Yorkshire pit to try and save the marriage.

The play reads like *Look Back in Anger* with an extra female character. Nan is accused of the same passivity as Alison, and Peter's fantasy and vituperation descend from Jimmy Porter. Rooms trap and offer solace to both Peter and Jimmy. But Peter has an outlet, the East, that Osborne does not give Jimmy. The description of the death of Jimmy's father is an occasion for harrowing pathos, and his allegiance to the International Brigade gets much less emphasis.

Parents in Mercer's plays are alive and are perceived as great boulders across the highway to internationalist self-fulfilment. Bernard Link, in *After Haggerty*, cannot get past the opening lines of his lectures in Paris, Prague, or Havana—key cities for the international Left of the 1960's—before lapsing into mental dialogues of love and hate with his parents in Yorkshire. Peter, at moments of acute crisis, addresses interior letters to his parents. Victor Belcher, to evade his father's contemptuous presence, invents imaginary conversations with Kant, Hegel, and Marx.

Only Flint combines paternity with freedom, but the child is not his, and he himself is a caricature of an English stereotype, the Red Dean. His bid for liberty takes him, not to Moscow, but to the centres of classical culture, Rome and Athens, and he dies a futile death, in the flames of the tanker into which his motorcycle crashes. He has been an arsonist anyway in his life, pursuing a politics as gestural as Peter's firing of his own flat to try to cut through the contradictions of desire, fatherhood, and artistry.

When Link Senior visits his son's ménage, he sits there like a pillar of common-sense refuting the flighty radicalism of Claire and Bernard. When Bernard says, "The question of the father will have to be gone into at some time", he is speaking about Raskolnikov, but implicitly also circling around the central question of Mercer's work—what does an artist father?

On the Eve of Publication, *The Cellar and the Almond Tree*, and *Emma's Time*, a trilogy of plays for television, concentrates on this issue with great dramatic bravura and foreshadows the next radical question for the 1970s— what does a woman mother? The trilogy traces the slow death of Robert Kelvin, a quarrelsome and distinguished Marxist novelist, through an alternation of narratives set in publishing London, in a central European country after communist takeover and, less extensively, in Nottingham and Paris. Stock film footage from Wajda's *Ashes and Diamonds*, the unemployed in the 1930s, and Lenin's funeral points up the political dimension in Kelvin's work, but its "realism" is designed to emphasise the fragility of Kelvin's writing. We know now how profoundly the East failed to deliver socialism. Kelvin is as sardonic about the possibility of its success as his Czech friend, Sladek, who is tortured by Nazi and Stalinist alike, and humiliated by an aristocratic Countess. But it is still a possibility, the dull, battered apex to Mercer's triangle.

Working slowly beneath this history, however, and barely surfacing at the end of the trilogy, is an alternative radicalism for the future, that of women. Obsessed as he is with plots and metaphors of birth and inheritance, Mercer gives considerable space to women in his plays. Even in their misery they are articulate. "I co-operate in my own humiliation", says Myra. "There's no limit to what men can do to me, because I'd sooner be tortured than ignored". And

Fanny is clear about her situation: "I—feel meaningless without a man. And I resent it. I feel humiliatingly feminine".

By 1970 Claire is cussing Bernard in the opening lines of *After Haggerty* and she has something of the *hauteur* of Helen Rawston in *Belcher's Luck*. But American heiresses and English upper-class bitches have dominatrix histories long pre-dating feminism. Much more interesting is Emma in the trilogy. She is a middle-class Cambridge graduate, aged 24, and is constant companion to the 64-year-old Kelvin. She services him in every way and has no interest in politics, indeed no interests of her own. She appears to everyone as a passive, beautiful receptacle. She has the language to estimate her own failings: "My sort of . . . sensitive, erudite . . . inertia of self-pity . . . the refuge of feeling masochistic, of only being an object". But she lacks even the self-dramatization that supports Myra in her suicide attempt. Mercer gives her the same kind of coolness and assurance without depth that Maitland inveighs against in Osborne's *Inadmissible Evidence*.

Sladek tracks her down at the end, silent in her bare, white room. He wants them, together, to write up his memoirs and dedicate them to Robert. Emma's role, we can imagine, will be that of amanuensis and typist to another Marxist hero. Yet the last play is entitled *Emma's Time*. Mercer is right. It will be Emma's time. She sums up, with sensitive prescience, everything that the feminists will theorize and fight against. But she is of exactly the class and education from which those feminists will derive. When Emma says to Sladek, just before she agrees to the memoirs, "I'm—blank", she signifies both the nadir of female self-abasement, and a nothingness which will be fruitful, a space to be inscribed with dozens of configurations of new female selves in the years to come. Emma is not pregnant. She is a "zero" waiting to be politicised. If men cannot father themselves, women will mother themselves. David Mercer's work is as apposite to the 1990s as it was to the 1960s.

—Tony Dunn

MILLAR, (Sir) Ronald (Graeme).

Born in Reading, Berkshire, 12 November 1919. Educated at Charterhouse School, Surrey; King's College, Cambridge. Served in the Royal Naval Volunteer Reserve, 1940–43: sub-lieutenant. Since 1977 deputy chair, Theatre Royal, Haymarket, London. Knighted, 1980. Agent: Ian Bevan, 37 Hill Street, London W1X 8JY. Address: 7 Sheffield Terrace, London W.8, England.

Publications

PLAYS

Murder from Memory (produced 1942).
Zero Hour (produced 1944).
The Other Side, adaptation of the novel by Storm Jameson (produced 1946).
Frieda (produced 1946). 1947.
Champagne for Delilah (produced 1949).
Waiting for Gillian, adaptation of the novel *A Way Through the Wood* by
    Nigel Balchin (produced 1954). 1955.
The Bride and the Bachelor (produced 1956). 1958.

A Ticklish Business (produced 1958; as *The Big Tickle*, produced 1958). 1959.
The More the Merrier (produced 1960). 1960.
The Bride Comes Back (produced 1960). 1961.
The Affair, adaptation of the novel by C.P. Snow (produced 1961). 1962.
The New Men, adaptation of the novel by C.P. Snow (produced 1962). In *The Affair, The New Men, The Masters*, 1964.
The Masters, adaptation of the novel by C.P. Snow (produced 1963). In *The Affair, The New Men, The Masters*, 1964.
The Affair, The New Men, The Masters: Three Plays Based on the Novels and with a Preface by C.P. Snow. 1964.
Robert and Elizabeth, music by Ron Grainer, lyrics by Millar, adaptation of the play *The Barretts of Wimpole Street* by Rudolf Besier (produced 1964). 1967.
On the Level, music by Ron Grainer (produced 1966).
Number 10, adaptation of the novel by William Clark (produced 1967). 1967.
They Don't Grow on Trees (produced 1968). 1969.
Abelard and Heloise, based on *Peter Abelard* by Helen Waddell (produced 1970). 1970.
Parents' Day, adaptation of the novel by Edward Candy (produced 1972).
Odd Girl Out, adaptation of the novel by Elizabeth Jane Howard (produced 1973).
The Case in Question, adaptation of the novel *In Their Wisdom* by C.P. Snow (produced 1975). 1975.
Once More with Music (produced 1976).
A Coat of Varnish, adaptation of the novel by C.P. Snow (produced 1982). 1983.

SCREENPLAYS: *Frieda*, with Angus Macphail, 1947; *So Evil My Love*, with Leonard Spiegelgass, 1948; *The Miniver Story*, with George Froeschel, 1950; *Train of Events*, with others, 1950; *The Unknown Man*, with George Froeschel, 1951; *Scaramouche*, with George Froeschel, 1951; *Never Let Me Go*, with George Froeschel, 1953; *Rose Marie*, 1954; *Betrayed*, with George Froeschel, 1954.

THEATRICAL ACTIVITIES

ACTOR: **Plays**—in *Swinging the Gate* (revue), 1940; Prince Anatole Kuragin in *War and Peace* by David Lucas, 1943; Cully in *Mr. Bolfry* by James Bridie, 1943; David Marsden in *Murder for a Valentine* by Vernon Sylvaine, 1944; Flight Lieutenant Chris Keppel in *Zero Hour*, 1944; Penry Bowen in *Jenny Jones* by Ronald Gow, 1944; Roy Fernie in *We Are Seven* by Ian Hay, 1945; Colin Tabret in *The Sacred Flame* by W. Somerset Maugham, 1945; Smith in *Murder on the Nile* by Agatha Christie, 1946. **Films**—*The Life and Death of Colonel Blimp*, 1943; *Beware of Pity*, 1945.

Ronald Millar was born in Reading in 1919. When he was a small boy his mother, an actress, wishing him to be protected from the glamorous uncertainties of stage life, sent him to a good preparatory school to receive a classical education. At the end of his time there he sat for scholarships at several of the great public schools. He was offered one at Harrow, but refused it on the advice of his headmaster, who had his eye on Winchester. At the Winchester examination, however, he happened to be out of sorts and narrowly missed an award; but he did gain one at Charterhouse.

From his mother's point of view this was an unhappy accident; for at that time Charterhouse, of all the great public schools, had the closest connection with the theatre and the largest number of old boys who were actors. And from there young Ronald went on to King's, which of all the colleges in Cambridge had the strongest theatrical tradition.

The outcome was fairly predictable. Millar joined various University acting clubs, showed talent, gained experience—incidentally, he was given the leading part in the triennial Greek play which is traditionally a great dramatic event at Cambridge—and was inevitably attracted to the professional stage. Then service in the Royal Navy delayed his final decision; but by the time he was invalided out he had made up his mind. He did not return to Cambridge to take his degree, but turned actor at once.

However, the years spent with the classics were not wasted. There are many worse forms of training for a writer, and Millar's ambition to be a dramatist was at least as strong as his desire to act, and was to prove much more lasting. His second play, *Zero Hour*, was produced at the Lyric in June 1944, with himself in the cast, and his third, *Frieda* (about a girl escaped from Nazi Germany), at the Westminster in 1946. This had a fair success on the stage and a bigger one as a film.

In 1949 Millar suffered a deep disappointment. Returning to England after an interlude spent writing filmscripts in Hollywood, he brought with him a light comedy, *Champagne for Delilah*, which was instantly accepted for West End production. To all the experts who handled it, it seemed certain to have a huge success, and it was received with acclaim on its prior-to-London tour. But on arrival at the New Theatre it proved a dead failure, and nobody has ever been able to suggest why. Seven years later, however, Millar must have felt compensated by an ironic twist of fate when another play, *The Bride and the Bachelor*, ran for more than 500 performances after having been given a hostile reception by nearly all the critics. Later still, in 1960, a sequel to this piece, *The Bride Comes Back*, also ran very well.

By this time Millar had enough successful work to his credit to prove that one of his outstanding qualities was his versatility. From the seriousness of *Frieda* to the frivolity of the two "Bride" plays was a big step and a vivid contrast in styles; and he now proceeded to demonstrate further uses to which his versatility might be put.

The year 1961 saw the beginning of a whole series of plays adapted by Millar from novels or other literary sources, the first of them being a stage version of C.P. Snow's story of college life at Cambridge, *The Affair*. As a Cambridge man himself, Millar was familiar with the atmosphere so truthfully rendered by the book, and, given a free hand, matched that atmosphere quite perfectly. Then came a setback. Manager after manager refused to believe that a play so local in its application could interest the general public. At last Henry Sherek, who had been Millar's backer for *Frieda* and *Champagne for Delilah*, accepted the risk, and was rewarded with critical favour and a year's run.

A second play from a Snow novel, *The New Men*, followed in 1962 and had no success; but a second Cambridge piece, *The Masters*, was staged in 1963 and ran even longer than *The Affair* had, and in 1975 yet another, *The Case in Question*, ran very well.

The particular talent which carried Millar to his notable successes in this field is an ability to turn a novelist's narrative prose into dialogue without losing his personal flavour, added to which is an ability where necessary to write in scenes of his own invention in a style to fit in with the rest.

This was perhaps not an especially difficult task in the case of the two Cambridge plays, where novelist and adapter had in common a detailed knowledge of and feeling for the atmosphere they wished to convey; but it became a problem of much delicacy in the case of Millar's next, and much more serious play, *Abelard and Heloise*. The main materials for this play were Helen Waddell's book about Peter Abelard and the famous letters, and the task was to find an idiom which would convey both these elements. This was done with such skill that the play drew not only the more serious playgoers but also the general public. Produced in May 1970, it ran into 1972.

One other proof of Millar's versatility should be noted. In 1964 he wrote both the book and lyrics for *Robert and Elizabeth*, the musical version of *The Barretts of Wimpole Street*, which ran for two and a half years.

—W.A. Darlington

MINGHELLA, Anthony.

Born in Ryde, Isle of Wight, 6 January 1954. Educated at the University of Hull, Yorkshire (Reckitt Travel Award), B.A. (honours) 1975. Lecturer in drama, University of Hull, 1976–81. Recipient: London Theatre Critics award, 1984, 1986. Lives in London. Agent: Judy Daish Associates, 83 Eastbourne Mews, London W2 6LQ, England.

Publications

PLAYS

Mobius the Stripper, adaptation of the story by Gabriel Josipovici (also director: produced 1975).

Child's Play (also director: produced 1978).

Whale Music (also director: produced 1980). In *Whale Music and Other Plays*, 1987.

A Little Like Drowning (produced 1982). In *Whale Music and Other Plays*, 1987.

Two Planks and a Passion (produced 1983). In *Whale Music and Other Plays*, 1987.

Love Bites (produced 1984).

What If It's Raining? (televised 1986). In *Interior: Room, Exterior: City*, 1989.

Made in Bangkok (produced 1986). 1986.

Whale Music and Other Plays. 1987.

Hang Up (broadcast 1987). In *Interior: Room, Exterior: City*, 1989.

Cigarettes and Chocolate (broadcast 1988). In *Interior: Room, Exterior: City*, 1989.
Interior: Room, Exterior: City (includes *Cigarettes and Chocolate, Hang Up, What If It's Raining?*). 1989.
Living with Dinosaurs and One-Act Plays and Sketches. 1991.
Plays 1 (includes *Made in Bangkok, Whale Music, A Little Like Drowning, Two Planks and a Passion*). 1992.
Truly, Madly, Deeply (screenplay). 1992.

SCREENPLAYS: *Truly, Madly, Deeply*, 1991; *Mr. Wonderful*, 1993.

RADIO PLAYS: *Hang Up*, 1987; *Cigarettes and Chocolate*, 1988.

TELEVISION PLAYS: *Studio* series, 1983; *What If It's Raining?* 1986; *Inspector Morse*, from a novel by Colin Dexter, 1987; *Storyteller* series, 1987; *Signals* (opera), music by John Lunn and Orlando Gough, 1989; *Driven to Distraction*, episode in *Inspector Morse* series, 1990.

NOVELS
On the Line (novelization of television series). 1982.
The Storyteller (novelization of television series). 1988.

THEATRICAL ACTIVITIES
DIRECTOR: **Plays**—some of his own plays. **Film**—*Truly, Madly, Deeply*, 1991.

Anthony Minghella emerged as one of the most consistently adventurous younger British dramatists of the 1980s. He is a writer refreshingly prepared to tackle a wide variety of subjects, and his plays have been marked by an unsentimental humanism and steadily growing technical confidence as he moved from relatively small-scale work in studio and fringe theatres to wider exposure in the commercial sector.

Whale Music was an early indication of Minghella's original voice; with an all-female cast (Minghella has continued to write superb roles for actresses), it is structured round a diverse group of women waiting in a seaside town for a student friend to have her baby. While the play at times seems over-schematic and, in its succession of short scenes, at points jerkily constructed (the dissolving scenes worked much more surely in a later television version), it still creates a recognisable milieu with understated precision. Tender, ironic, and funny, it contains some memorable writing, particularly a long speech from the drifting Stella, giving room to the pregnant Caroline, savagely corrosive in its picture of the men she encounters in her one-night stands.

A Little Like Drowning is also written in a succession of short scenes, but here ambitiously spanning the years with its fulcrum in the break-up of an Anglo-Italian couple's marriage. Moving between the present on an English beach where the old Leonora recalls her life to her granddaughter, to her 1920s marriage to Alfredo in Italy and Alfredo's affair and later life in Dublin with Julia, the play seamlessly links time and space—a scene in 1939 with Alfredo packing to leave Leonora has both Leonora and Julia on stage, unaware of each other, the scene playing as if their dialogue is totally independent. Minghella continued to explore and celebrate his own Anglo-Italian inheritance, this time on a more epic scale, in *Love Bites*. The first act is set in wartime England, concentrating on two Italian-immigrant brothers, Angelo and Bruno, establishing themselves in the ice-cream business. Particularly impressive in this act is Minghella's handling of Angelo's affair with Elizabeth, a schoolteacher who becomes pregnant by him and to whose love he cannot finally respond; his suggestion of the curiously suspended quality of time during wartime is especially evocative. The second act leaps into the present, set in a convention hotel with Angelo about to be inaugurated as President of the Ice Cream Group of Great Britain. Minghella handles his large cast and canvas here with a sharp sense of focus, painting a vivid picture of the family's tribal relationships among the different generations. Bruno, in disappointed middle age, realises that he has let himself be trapped by the past but comes to realise in a powerfully written late scene that he and Angelo are essentially alike after all; in such scenes, Minghella's control of the play's changes of mood is continuously sure.

He moved completely away from such material in *Two Planks and a Passion*, set in late 14th-century York, where a troubled Richard II, his wife, and his friend the Earl of Oxford have escaped the court's pressures while the workmen's guilds prepare the Mystery Plays for the Feast of Corpus Christi. The play weaves several strands—the royals' mischievous exploitation of local bourgeois snobbery, rivalry among the artisans for patronage, and the workers rehearsing the Crucifixion—including some scenes of high comedy (especially that involving the King mercilessly teasing the fawning mayor during an innovative golf game), gradually drawing them together as the rehearsal becomes a moving performance witnessed by the royal party. The play may occasionally suffer from the lack of one truly dynamic central character but it remains an engaging, grave, and totally individual play.

Two Planks and a Passion gradually brought Minghella into the critical spotlight and a "Most Promising Playwright" award rightly came his way in 1984. That promise was amply confirmed by his first major West End play, *Made in Bangkok*. The play covers a group of English tourists and businessmen in Bangkok; often sharply and satirically funny, its moods keep boldly changing, emerging as a very dark comedy indeed about personal as well as cultural exploitation. He again created a challengingly complex leading female role in Frances, wife of a devious and finally frightening businessman, the only character not tainted by some form of exploitation, and he again demonstrates his ability to handle a multi-scene and intricately interlocking play with accomplished control. He also reaffirmed the theatre's ability to shock, to jolt an audience's moral attitude, as in the scene in which Edward, a repressed homosexual dentist, finally makes a sickeningly pathetic bid for the favours of the hotel-worker guide who has helped him. Minghella's dispassionate (and compassionate) handling of all his characters gave the play a depth of texture that made one intrigued to see in what direction he will travel next.

—Alan Strachan

MITCHELL, Adrian.

Born in London, 24 October 1932. Educated at Greenways School, Wiltshire; Dauntsey's School, West Lavington, Wiltshire; Christ Church, Oxford (editor, *Isis* magazine, 1954–55), 1952–55. Served in the Royal Air Force, 1951–52. Reporter, Oxford *Mail*, 1955–57, and *Evening Standard*, London, 1957–59; columnist and reviewer, *Daily Mail*, *Woman's Mirror*, the *Sun*, the *Sunday Times*, *Peace News*, *Black Dwarf*, *New Statesman*, and the *Guardian*, all London. Instructor, University of Iowa, Iowa City, 1963–64; Granada fellow in the arts, University of Lancaster, 1967–69; fellow, Wesleyan University Center for the Humanities, Middletown, Connecticut, 1971–72; resident writer, Sherman Theatre, Cardiff, 1974–75; visiting writer, Billericay Comprehensive School, Essex, 1978–80; Judith E. Wilson fellow, Cambridge University, 1980–81; resident writer, Unicorn Theatre for Young People, London, 1982–83. Recipient: Eric Gregory award, 1961; P.E.N. prize for translation, 1966; Tokyo Festival award, for television, 1971. Fellow, Royal Society of Literature, 1988. Agent: Peters, Fraser, and Dunlop Group, 503–504 The Chambers, Chelsea Harbour, Lots Road, London SW10 0XF, England.

Publications

PLAYS

The Ledge (libretto), music by Richard Rodney Bennett (produced 1961).

The Persecution and Assassination of Jean-Paul Marat as Performed by the Inmates of the Asylum of Charenton under the Direction of the Marquis de Sade [*Marat/Sade*], adaptation of a play by Peter Weiss (produced 1964). 1965.

The Magic Flute, adaptation of the libretto by Schikaneder and Giesecke, music by Mozart (produced 1966).

US, with others (produced 1966). As *US: The Book of the Royal Shakespeare Production US/Vietnam/US/Experiment/Politics . . .*, 1968; as *Tell Me Lies*, 1968.

The Criminals, adaptation of a play by José Triana (produced 1967).

Tyger: A Celebration of the Life and Work of William Blake, music by Mike Westbrook (produced 1971). 1971.

Tamburlane the Mad Hen (for children; produced 1971).

Man Friday, music by Mike Westbrook (televised 1972; produced 1973). With *Mind Your Head*, 1974.

Mind Your Head, music by Andy Roberts (produced 1973). With *Man Friday*, 1974.

The Government Inspector (as *The Inspector General*, produced 1974; revised version, as *The Government Inspector*, produced 1985). 1985.

A Seventh Man, music by Dave Brown, adaptation of the book by John Berger and Jean Mohr (produced 1976).

White Suit Blues, music by Mike Westbrook, adaptation of works by Mark Twain (produced 1977).

Houdini: A Circus-Opera, music by Peter Schat (produced 1977). 1977(?).

Uppendown Mooney (produced 1978).

The White Deer (for children), adaptation of the story by James Thurber (produced 1978).

Hoagy, Bix, and Wolfgang Beethoven Bunkhaus (produced 1979).

In the Unlikely Event of an Emergency, music by Stephen McNeff (produced 1979).

Peer Gynt, adaptation of the play by Ibsen (produced 1980).

The Mayor of Zalamea; or, The Best Garrotting Ever Done, adaptation of a play by Calderón (produced 1981). 1981.

Mowgli's Jungle, adaptation of *The Jungle Book* by Kipling (pantomime; produced 1981).

You Must Believe All This (for children), adaptation of "Holiday Romance" by Dickens, music by Nick Bicât and Andrew Dickson (televised 1981). 1981.

The Wild Animal Song Contest (for children; produced 1982).

Life's a Dream, with John Barton, adaptation of a play by Calderón (produced 1983).

A Child's Christmas in Wales, with Jeremy Brooks, adaptation of the work by Dylan Thomas (produced 1983).

The Great Theatre of the World, adaptation of a play by Calderón (produced 1984).

C'mon Everybody (produced 1984).

Animal Farm (lyrics only), book by Peter Hall, music by Richard Peaslee, adaptation of the novel by George Orwell (for children; produced 1984). 1985.

The Tragedy of King Real (screenplay), in *Peace Plays 1*, edited by Stephen Lowe.1985.

Satie Day/Night (produced 1986).

The Pied Piper (for children), music by Dominic Muldowney (produced 1986). 1988.

Mirandolina, adaptation of a play by Goldoni (produced 1987).

The Last Wild Wood in Sector 88 (produced 1987).

Love Songs of World War Three (produced 1988).

Fuente Ovejuna, adaptation of the play by Lope de Vega (produced 1988).

Woman Overboard, adaptation of a play by Lope de Vega, music by Monty Norman (produced 1988).

The Patchwork Girl of Oz, adaptation of the story by L. Frank Baum (for children; produced 1988).

Anna on Anna (produced 1988).

The Tragedy of King Real (produced 1989).

Triple Threat (produced 1989).

Greatest Hits (produced 1992).

A New World and the Tears of the Indians, adaptation of works by Lope de Vega and Bartholome de las Casas (produced 1992).

SCREENPLAYS: *Marat/Sade*, 1966; *Tell Me Lies* (lyrics only), 1968; *The Body* (commentary), 1969; *Man Friday*, 1976; *The Tragedy of King Real*, 1983.

RADIO PLAY: *The Island* (libretto), music by William Russo, 1963.

TELEVISION PLAYS: *Animals Can't Laugh*, 1961; *Alive and Kicking*, 1971; *William Blake* (documentary), 1971; *Man Friday*, 1972; *Somebody Down There Is Crying*, 1974; *Daft As a Brush*, 1975; *The Fine Art of Bubble Blowing*, 1975; *Silver Giant, Wooden Dwarf*, 1975; *Glad Day*, music by Mike Westbrook, 1979; *You Must Believe All This*, 1981; *Juno and Avos*, from a libretto by Andrei Voznesensky, music by Alexei Rybnikov, 1983.

OTHER: Initiated and helped write student shows: *Bradford Walk*, Bradford College of Art; *The Hotpot Saga, The Neurovision Song Contest*, and *Lash Me to the Mast*, University of Lancaster; *Move Over Jehovah*, National Association of Mental Health; *Poetry Circus*, Wesleyan University; *Mass Media Mash* and *Mud Fair*, Dartington College of the Arts, 1976 and 1977.

NOVELS
If You See Me Comin'. 1962.
The Bodyguard. 1970.
Wartime. 1973.
Man Friday. 1975.

VERSE
(Poems). 1955.
Poems. 1964.
Peace Is Milk. 1966.
Out Loud. 1968; revised edition, as *The Annotated Out Loud*, 1976.
Ride the Nightmare: Verse and Prose. 1971.
Cease-Fire. 1973.
Penguin Modern Poets 22, with John Fuller and Peter Levi. 1973.
The Apeman Cometh. 1975.
For Beauty Douglas: Collected Poems 1953–1979. 1982.
Nothingmas Day (for children). 1984.
On the Beach at Cambridge: New Poems. 1984.
Love Songs of World War Three (collected song lyrics). 1989.
Greatest Hits (collected song and lyrics). 1992.

RECORDING: *Poems*, with Stevie Smith, 1974.

OTHER (for children)
The Adventures of Baron Munchausen. 1985.
The Baron Rides Out [*on the Island of Cheese, All at Sea*]. 3 vols., 1985–87.
Leonardo, The Lion from Nowhere. 1986.
Our Mammoth [*Goes to School, in the Snow*]. 3 vols., 1987–88.
Rhinestone Rhino. 1989.

Editor, *Strawberry Drums*. 1989.

OTHER
Naked In Cheltenham (miscellany). 1978.
Tourist Snapshots of Chile. 1985.

Editor, with Richard Selig, *Oxford Poetry 1955*. 1955.
Editor, *Jump, My Brothers, Jump: Poems from Prison*, by Tim Daly. 1970.

THEATRICAL ACTIVITIES

ACTOR: **Plays**—*C'mon Everybody*, 1984; *Love Songs of World War Three*, 1988; *Triple Threat*, 1989; *Greatest Hits*, 1992.

"A truthful colour supplement. As you turn the pages, conflicting images hit you." Adrian Mitchell's description of his stage show *Mind Your Head* may to some extent be applied to all his dramatic creations. Impossible to pigeon-hole into any one form, they mingle genres indiscriminately, juxtaposing pathos with horror and ribald humour. Instead of adhering to the norms of dramatic artifice, Mitchell appears to seize the chaos and disturbance of modern life and transfer it whole to the stage. Constants of his work are its anarchic individualism and the opposition of its author to establishment mores.

Irony lies at the root of Mitchell's dilemma. A notable "performance" poet, adept in a structured, concentrated medium, he nevertheless strives continually to dispense with the formal restraints of language. Equally, as a playwright, he attempts to eschew established theatrical conventions. Overall, Mitchell's work recalls the 1960s and its legacy of protest, which had a profound influence on his thinking. Together with his contemporary Christopher Logue, he featured prominently in anti-Vietnam War demonstrations, taking part in the famous public poetry readings and contributing to the radical stage show *US*.

All the same, this aspect of Mitchell's writing may be over-stressed. His plays are perhaps more traditional and less unorthodox than they appear at first glance. Centuries ago, Aristophanes combined fantasy, social comment, satire, and personal invective against establishment figures, the action interspersed with song and dance routines. In much the same way, Mitchell's dramas blend the 1960s "happening" with elements of pantomime and old-time music hall, their seemingly random progress broken by songs and comic patter from various members of the cast. *Mind Your Head* typifies this approach, a surreal revamping of the Hamlet legend, built around the passengers and crew of a London bus. Mitchell allows his humour a free rein, using parodies of comic and pop song styles for some of the key passages—Hamlet's Soliloquy, for example, is performed as a Frankie Howerd monologue—and bestowing the names of jazz musicians on his characters. The pantomime atmosphere of the show, with its songs and jokes, provides for audience participation, which accords with Mitchell's "performance" style. A similar work is *Tyger*, where scenes from the daily life of the poet William Blake are expanded to include a fantasy moon-voyage, and several establishment "names" are mercilessly caricatured in song-and-dance form. Mitchell's affinity with Blake is spiritual rather than stylistic, and he is able to evoke the nature of the man by judicious quotation, while retaining his own mixed-genre method of presentation.

Mitchell's television plays tend to show more formal organization than his stage dramas. *Glad Day* is an exception, another Blake tribute where Mitchell manages to transfer some of the spontaneous energy of *Tyger* to the small screen. Like several of Mitchell's dramas, *Glad Day* involved the close co-

operation of Mike Westbrook, whose musical accompaniments gave an added
power to Blake's poetry, not least in the memorable "Song of the Slave" whose
lyrics are intensified by the jazz arrangement. More typical of the television
plays is *Man Friday*, a significant work which Mitchell later adapted for the
stage and as a novel. It embodies many of Mitchell's most profound beliefs on
the theory of white supremacy, which he contrasts with the foundations of so-
called "primitive" societies. In a series of dialogues between Crusoe and the
"savage" Friday, Mitchell adroitly ridicules not only the white man's "civiliz-
ing" mission, but also popular concepts of nationalism, crime and punishment,
and property ownership. The stage version, which allows for more audience
interaction, is a strong work, but the original television play is the more
enduring. Ironically, as with other Mitchell creations, its organized structure
ensures its success.

The throwaway "instant" quality of some of Mitchell's writing, his ability to
create for specific occasions, may perhaps explain his skill in adapting the
work of other writers. His earliest success in this field came in the 1960s, with
his verse translation of Weiss's *Marat/Sade*, whose blend of social comment
and gallows humour evidently appealed to him. Since then, he has produced
versions of works by Dickens, Gogol, Calderón, Goldoni, and—more recently
—Baum and Lope de Vega. *You Must Believe All This*, taken from a Dickens
original, shows Mitchell to be an adept writer for children, to whom audience
participation is a natural response, a skill which is further confirmed by his
rearrangement of L. Frank Baum's fables in *The Patchwork Girl of Oz*, and
outside the field of drama by his growing number of illustrated books for
younger readers. Mitchell fractures the original texts to obtain the desired
result, altering language and adding or deleting scenes, usually to good effect.
His adaptation of Gogol's *The Government Inspector* inserts the famous
"troika" scene and speech from *Dead Souls*, and provides Khlestakov with a
startling airborne departure, both of which work dramatically and are in
keeping with the lurking unease that underlies this particular "comedy."
Similarly, his versions of Calderón's *Life's a Dream* and *The Mayor of
Zalamea* break with the fluency of their Spanish originals in favour of a
popular, slangy English verse-form which conveys greater impact than a strict
translation. Calderón's exploration of the major human themes, his matching
of sentiment with grim humour, is clearly to Mitchell's taste, and thus far the
results have been interesting. The same may be said of *Woman Overboard*, his
highly individual reworking of Lope de Vega's play *The Dog in the Manger*.
This gift for adaptation is far from being the least of Mitchell's talents, and his
efforts in this field deserve comparison with the best of his original plays,
which continue unabated. Recent examples of the latter include his one-act
musical satire on the world's worst airline, *In the Unlikely Event of an
Emergency*, and three longer productions which Mitchell describes as "compilation shows of songs and poems," namely *Triple Threat*, *Love Songs of World
War Three*, and *Greatest Hits*. These last have Mitchell appearing as a leading
performer onstage as well as in his customary role of author, and are proof
that he has lost none of his power and drive. If anything his creative energy
seems to have increased, with fresh concepts and approaches being constantly
sought in his latest dramas. *Anna on Anna*, his one-woman show portraying
the life of poetess Anna Wickham, and specially written for the actress Illona

Linthwaite, is a perfect example in this respect. While it remains to be seen where these explorations will lead Mitchell in future, one suspects that the answers will be well worth waiting for.

—Geoff Sadler

MITCHELL, (Charles) Julian (Humphrey).

Born in Epping, Essex, 1 May 1935. Educated at Winchester College, Hampshire, 1948–53; Wadham College, Oxford, B.A. 1958; St. Antony's College, Oxford, M.A. 1962. Served in the Royal Naval Volunteer Reserve, 1953–55: midshipman. Member, Arts Council Literature Panel, 1966–69; formerly, Governor, Chelsea School of Art, London. Chair, Welsh Arts Council Drama Committee, 1988–92. Recipient: Harkness fellowship, 1959; Rhys Memorial prize, 1965; Maugham award, 1966; International Critics prize, for television play, 1977; Christopher award, for television play, 1977 (U.S.A.); Florio prize, for translation, 1980; Society of West End Theatre award, 1982. Lives in Newport, Gwent, Wales. Agent: Peters, Fraser, and Dunlop Group, 503–504 The Chambers, Chelsea Harbour, Lots Road, London SW10 0XF, England.

Publications

PLAYS

A Heritage and Its History, adaptation of the novel by Ivy Compton-Burnett (produced 1965). 1966.
A Family and a Fortune, adaptation of the novel by Ivy Compton-Burnett (produced 1966). 1976.
Shadow in the Sun (televised 1971). In Elizabeth R, edited by J.C. Trewin, 1972.
Half-Life (produced 1977). 1977.
Henry IV, adaptation of the play by Pirandello. 1979.
The Enemy Within (produced 1980).
Another Country (produced 1981). 1982.
Francis (produced 1983). 1984.
After Aida; or, Verdi's Messiah (produced 1986). 1986.
The Evils of Tobacco, adaptation of a work by Chekhov, translated by Ronald Hingley (produced 1987).

SCREENPLAYS: Arabesque, with Stanley Price and Pierre Marton, 1966; Another Country, 1984; Vincent and Theo, 1990.

RADIO DOCUMENTARY: Life and Deaths of Dr. John Donne, 1972.

TELEVISION PLAYS: Persuasion, from the novel by Jane Austen, 1971; Shadow in the Sun, 1971; The Man Who Never Was, 1972; A Perfect Day, 1972; Fly in the Ointment, 1972; A Question of Degree, 1972; The Alien Corn, from a story by W. Somerset Maugham, 1972; Rust, 1973; Jennie, 1974; Abide with Me, from the book A Child in the Forest, by Winifred Foley, 1976; Staying On, from the novel by Paul Scott, 1980; The Good Soldier, from the novel by

Ford Madox Ford, 1981; *The Weather in the Streets*, from the novel by
Rosamond Lehmann, 1984; episodes for *Inspector Morse* series, 1987–92; *All
the Waters of Wye* (documentary), 1990; *Survival of the Fittest*, 1990.

NOVELS

Imaginary Toys. 1961.
A Disturbing Influence. 1962.
As Far as You Can Go. 1963.
The White Father. 1964.
A Circle of Friends. 1966.
The Undiscovered Country. 1968.

SHORT STORIES

Introduction, with others. 1960.

OTHER

Truth and Fiction (lecture). 1972.
Jennie, Lady Randolph Churchill: A Portrait with Letters, with Peregrine
    Churchill. 1974.

Editor, with others, *Light Blue, Dark Blue: An Anthology of Recent Writing
    from Oxford and Cambridge Universities*. 1960.

Julian Mitchell's success as a playwright makes nonsense of claims that the
well-made play is dead. He is a skilful craftsman whose work fits well into a
British theatrical tradition as defined by, say, Terence Rattigan. Dialogue is all
in his work, and the plays offer audiences an invitation into a world of polite
discourse in which, if voices are occasionally raised, there is always someone
present to push the argument forward into its next phase. He is not an
innovative writer but he is always a polished one, as might be expected from
someone who came late to the stage after an extensive literary apprenticeship.
The 1990s have seen him embark in yet another direction with his screenplay
for *Vincent and Theo*, but his reputation as a writer in the 1960s rested solely
on his activities as a novelist. The 1970s saw him established as a regular
writer and adapter for television—his work included dramatisations of
Austen's *Persuasion*, Paul Scott's *Staying On*, and Ford Madox Ford's *The
Good Soldier*, as well as a contribution to the *Elizabeth R* series—and it was
only in the 1980s that he really began to receive serious attention as a stage
dramatist. Indeed, two of his earliest stage plays, *A Heritage and Its History*
and *A Family and a Fortune*, were both adapted from novels by Ivy Compton-
Burnett, and it is always apparent that he writes as a novelist converted to
the stage.
  His first novel was compared by one critic with the work of Aldous Huxley,
and his plays all have a dedicated commitment to a series of theatrical debates
that makes the comparison only too inviting. At worst, the characters serve as
convenient mouth-pieces for opposing views—in *Half-Life*, for instance, that
most predictable of all West End formats, a country-house weekend, is the

venue for a political discussion with an assorted bunch of over-articulate people, and there is scarcely any sense of theatre about the events depicted. All is wit and verbal sword-play. But at best the debate is more open, and nowhere more so than in his most successful play to date, *Another Country*.

In *Another Country* Mitchell offers one of many recent analyses of the "betrayal" of their class by the Cambridge Communist school of the 1930s. What makes his account interesting is that he transfers the action back to the penultimate year of their public-school days, placing the thoughts of the pro-Stalinist Judd and the flamboyantly gay Bennett (Guy Burgess in thin disguise, as is made explicit in the film version) in the context of that institution which is intended to mould them for their future roles as statesmen and administrators. The familiar use of the school as metaphor of the state, not of the country at large but of its ruling-class, allows Mitchell to show how an essentially apolitical Bennett might be led into the world of espionage both as a reaction to the brutal punishing of his sexual appetites by an institution which serves only to heighten their appeal, and as an extension of the need to be continually in disguise, leading a double life, which he sees as his fate.

The economic need to restrict the size of the cast (although the play eventually transferred to the West End, it started its life at the Greenwich Theatre) does much to increase the sense of enclosure, of claustrophobia, that confronts any boy who cannot, or will not, fit into the system ready created for him. Bennett actually spends a great deal of time in the play acknowledging the attention of his off-stage and never-seen young lover and peering through binoculars at what is happening outside the particular room he is in—including the early sighting of the removal of the body of a boy who has hanged himself in the bell tower, a victim of the sexual double-standards of the school.

After Aida presents a similarly enclosed stage, in this instance to consider the events leading up to Verdi's agreement to compose *Otello*. It is difficult not to compare the play with Shaffer's *Amadeus*, but it stands up very well to the exercise, being a much less pretentious re-animation of musical history. A preoccupation with the past is also evident in Mitchell's earlier play, *Francis*, which takes a long sweep through the life of St. Francis and his attempts to hang on to his ideal of poverty in the face of pressure from both the established church and his increasingly wealthy new order. As a character Francis is Mitchell's most successful creation, with a stronger sense of internal conflict apparent than in most of his protagonists who are allowed to dominate the action simply by the superiority of their wit and rhetoric. Francis's attempt to relive the Spartan life of his Christ unites the rebellious instincts of Bennett with the puritan discipline of Judd in *Another Country*, and here the corrupt oppression of church and papacy take the place of the school. As in all his plays, the voice of the rebel is allowed a place—as it is with the young Prue Hoggart in *Half-Life*—but the resolution of the plays, having suggested a plausible reason for the rebellion, is always to suggest the impossibility of real change.

History, for Mitchell, teaches a lesson of conflict in which the terms of reference remain essentially unchanged. In all his plays there is little sense of new ground being broken, either theatrically or intellectually, but if the mainstream is to continue to demand a steady diet of well-made plays then at least there is always evidence of an articulate intelligence behind Mitchell's work; and that is certainly to be welcomed in the increasingly dull world of contemporary West End theatre.

—John Bull

MOLLOY, M(ichael) J(oseph).

Born in Milltown, County Galway, 3 March 1917. Educated at St. Jarlath's College and in a seminary for 4 years. Farmer, 1950–72. Recipient: Irish Arts Council award, 1972. Address: Milltown, Tuam, County Galway, Ireland.

Publications

PLAYS

Old Road (produced 1943). 1961.
The Visiting House (produced 1946). In *Seven Irish Plays 1946–1964*, edited by Robert Hogan, 1967.
The King of Friday's Men (produced 1948). 1954; included in *Three Plays*, 1975.
The Wood of the Whispering (produced 1953). 1961; included in *Three Plays*, 1975.
The Paddy Pedlar (produced 1953). 1954; included in *Three Plays*, 1975.
The Will and the Way (produced 1955). 1957.
A Right Rose Tree (produced 1958).
Daughter from over the Water (produced 1962). 1963.
The Wooing of Duvesa (produced 1964).
The Bitter Pill, in *Prizewinning Plays of 1964*. 1965.
Three Plays. 1975.
Petticoat Loose (produced 1979). 1982.
The Bachelor's Daughter (produced 1985).

M.J. Molloy may be Ireland's most genuine folk-dramatist. He is certainly the most distinguished contributor to this genre since Synge. Unlike Synge, who was a stranger to rural Ireland and had to be educated about its culture, Molloy is a native of County Galway and still lives there, in simple circumstances very like those he describes in his plays. Most of his plays have been produced either at the Abbey Theatre or by the Abbey Theatre Company. They represent a 45-year effort to provide for the Irish theater the sort of play Yeats said was needed to make Irish people conscious of their own history. Molloy has singlemindedly written plays which deal with the experience of the Irish countryman. A broadly educated man himself, he has witnessed and understood the changes which in the past 40 years have moved rural Ireland away from what Molloy regards as its feudal traditions and toward a society less certain of its values and more vulnerable to the exploitation of its land and its people.

In all of Molloy's plays there is nostalgia for a time when men had a proper regard for each other and for the land, a time when depopulation had not reduced rural Ireland to a gaggle of testy and self-righteous bachelors, a time before technology and an unscrupulous middle class purloined the land. Not surprisingly, since he is a dramatist rather than an historian, Molloy's plays do not deal with that ancient age of social order, but rather with periods of conflict, of moments when one can observe the old order passing. A self-confessed romantic, Molloy can see no good coming out of this change.

Two of Molloy's early plays, *The King of Friday's Men* and *The Visiting House*, might be regarded as paradigms of the worlds that have been lost. Set in late 18th-century Mayo and Galway, *The King of Friday's Men* reveals a large society still responsive to the old feudal structure of lord and peasant. The play concerns a lord's obsession with his right to have as his mistresses the unmarried daughters of his tenant farmers. His exploitation of a feudal right provokes disorder in the land and leads ultimately to the violent death of the lord. Molloy is not naive in his romantic attachment to Ireland's feudal past. As a Catholic, he believes that human nature has been self-seeking and violent since the Fall and can never change. Nevertheless, all the characters in *The King of Friday's Men* share the same social and moral values. Lord and tenant both know when privilege has been exploited.

The Visiting House has a contemporary setting and reveals a shrunken social order. Unlike *The King of Friday's Men* in which action ranges all over Galway and Mayo, and an heroic Bartley Dowd wipes out a contingent of the lord's men with a few swipes of his shillelagh, *The Visiting House* is confined to the single setting which Molloy has used for most of his plays. The heroics are rhetorical rather than physical as characters called The Man of Learning and The Verb-to-Be nightly take their positions by the fire and engage in a merry flyting match. Within these narrowed circumstances, however, *The Visiting House* does reveal a social order based on ownership of the land. A once flourishing institution barely more than a memory when Molloy wrote his play, the visiting house was the place where small farmers gathered and where each had respect and a social identity.

Molloy's other plays deal more directly with the breakdown of traditional Irish rural life. *Old Road* is about the depopulation caused by farmers being unable to divide their small farms any further. Only the oldest son may inherit the land. Others must leave the community for Dublin or England. *The Wood of the Whispering* also has depopulation for its theme. Molloy assembles an array of zany and impotent old bachelors who lust after the one or two girls left in the village. Their lives pass in the shadow of ancient Castle D'Arcy, a reminder to Molloy's audience of a time when society was stable. *The Will and the Way* has to do with a rural community whose visiting house is threatened by the arrival of a city-type who has no feeling for community life and nearly succeeds in destroying it.

In his more recent plays Molloy has been unable to maintain the gentle comic spirit and ironic distance which characterize his earlier work. The last traces of genuine rural Irish life are being destroyed by technology, especially by television which gives the Irish a false sense of being a national community while at the same time imposing a radical isolation of one man from another. *A Right Rose Tree* presents a rural Ireland so fraught with social problems that the play is more like documentary than drama. It deals with the period 1921–23, when the Irish countryside rises up against the English only to witness even more bloody battles of brother against brother when the Black and Tans have left. The utter lawlessness which results permits the base to inherit the earth. The lines from Yeats which give the play its title assert the purposefulness of violence—"There's nothing but our own red blood/Can make a right Rose tree." For Molloy violence has no such creative energy. The final horror of *A Right Rose Tree*, the symbolic killing of a landlord by insensitive, ignorant, and cowardly men, leaves nothing of value after it.

—Arthur E. McGuinness

MORNIN, Daniel.

Born in Belfast, 10 January 1956. Educated at Orangefield Primary School, 1961–67, and Orangefield Secondary, 1967–71, both Belfast. Served in the Royal Navy as ordinary seaman, 1974–77. Married Aine Beegan in 1991; one son. Agent: Judy Daish, Judy Daish Associates, 83 Eastbourne Mews, London W2 6LQ, England.

Publications

PLAYS

Mum and Son (produced 1981).
Kate (produced 1983).
Getting Out (as *Short of Mutiny*; produced 1983).
Comrade Ogilvy (produced 1984).
By the Border (produced 1985).
The Murderers (produced 1985).
Built on Sand (produced 1987).
Weights and Measures (produced 1987).
At Our Table (produced 1991).

TELEVISION PLAY: *Border Country*, 1991.

NOVEL
All Our Fault. 1991.

Daniel Mornin comments:

I seem to be attracted to themes that are, I hope, more enduring than they are fashionable, themes that lie beneath "the passing scene" to give strength to a play between the lines. I have always hoped that this provokes thought, incites curiosity so that the play remains with the audience a good while longer than the length of time they have sat in their seats: even if they dislike the play (my plays are often not likeable) I hope they remember it. Recently I have become interested in "morality," the fragile, fictive morality of the intellect, the "the what should be" and the human morality of "what is" of experience, often the violent experience that comes when society (as in Northern Ireland for a time) breaks down, or as with my new play a man fights in a war.

Daniel Mornin's work to date clearly illustrates the instinct to retreat from the images that shaped the experience of his early life in Belfast. At the same time, the public acts of brutality and intolerance that have come to symbolise the divided city in which he grew up, are frequently discovered in the landscapes of his plays. This paradox is resolved in his treatment of his material. The violence that lies at the heart of the sectarian divisions in his native city is central to much of his work, though his instinct is not to deal with it as a purely local phenomenon. Rather, he presents a world view in which metaphysical degeneracy and moral corruption appear to be the inevitable concomitants of what "being human" is all about. *Mum and Son* (directed at the Riverside Studios by David Leveaux), his professional début, documents a welter of emotional screw-ups inflicted on a dutiful son by his intense, isolated, insecure, possessive, predatory, massively irritating mother. The situation is aggravated by an aura of mystery concerning the boy's father and further notched up, first by the presentation of apparently incontrovertible facts surrounding the mystery of the father, then by the subsequent contradiction of these "facts."

Mornin's obsession with the darker, hardly performable, aspects of behaviour is mediated through his intuitive flair for writing dialogue and his masterly control of tone. His working method is to return to themes and rework situations. He is rarely content to set aside a plot or a dramatic structure until he has exhausted the possibilities inherent in them. His best work exemplifies his extraordinary control over the imaginative and technical demands made by the, largely, realistic situations he depicts. Yet his work as a whole suggests that he cannot readily meet the need to devise structures of sufficient formal complexity to match the brilliance of his dialogue.

There are two aspects of Mornin's one-act play, *By the Border*, which illustrate the tensions underlying his thematic and structural preoccupations. The first is the employment of the brother-sister theme which, over the span of plays he has written, has increasingly been overlaid with the archetypal and symbolic resonances of Greek tragedy. This theme initially appeared in *Kate* (widely regarded as one of the best of his plays), a focused, painful, thought-provoking, and accurate study of an incestuous relationship between the son and daughter of a "mixed" marriage. The second is a "delaying" device which, in *By the Border*, takes the form of a character who remains onstage for a large part of the play without saying anything, thus raising questions in the audience's mind over the character's reasons for being there.

The reference to Greek tragedy is clearly intended to heighten the universality of Mornin's dramas, though there is no wide agreement that the plays subjected to this treatment are either more focused or more accessible than those which are not. It is worth noting that Mornin's best dialogue is contained in scenes with the structural simplicity of Greek drama; specifically in the interplay between two (or three) actors. It therefore seems superfluous to emphasise structural principles at the expense of dramatic action.

Roland Barthes encapsulates the generic problems of imposing the patterns of tragedy on the close, psychological perspectives of modern drama in his essay "Putting on the Greeks" (*Critical Essays*, 1972). He reminds us: "the sentiments (of characters in the Greek drama) are not at all psychological in our modern sense of the word . . . pride is not a sin here, a marvelous and complicated disease; it is an offence against the city, it is a political excess."

Mornin's developing fondness for classical themes may to some extent be a response to the ethos of the theatre that has encouraged his writing. Yet his promise and potential as a playwright stem from his ability to evaluate his achievements with fastidious care, and to see the art of playwriting essentially as a provisional and experimental one.

His latest play, *At Our Table* (directed at the Royal National Theatre by Jenny Killick), represents an attempt to reconcile the distinctions Barthes draws between modern and classical Greek theatre. Again, Mornin's major structural device (developed out of *By the Border*) is to delay the revelation which will confirm the full horror of the apparently ordinary domestic drama played out before us. The characters grow in significance throughout the play through a conscious finessing of the distinction between the "public" and "private" sentiments of the characters.

Virtually all of Mornin's plays underline the provisionality of his dramaturgy. *Weights and Measures* (directed at the National Theatre Studio by John Burgess) is a striking example of a play that shows how complex is the relationship between the expansion of Mornin's thematic interests and his developing technical skill. Based on the life of Denis Nilssen, the serial killer, it is set in a house, stratified to reveal activities on various levels. In the upper part of the house there are scenes between a "yuppie" and two women who, in the course of the play, spiritually destroy him. In the lower level, the Nilssen figure plays out a number of brilliant scenes with an actor who appears, in various guises, as different people. The play, however, is caught between the theoretical compactness of its formal symmetry and the practical problems of reconciling an audience to the confusing demands of dividing the stage space equally between scenes of widely differentiated dramatic interest. *Weights and Measures* is an important play, however, in that Mornin is consciously working to consolidate his practical achievements as a writer of taut, psychologically threatening dialogue while shifting the emphasis of his muse away from personal experience towards imagination and research.

Built on Sand (directed at the Royal Court Theatre Upstairs by Lindsay Posner), has an imaginative setting on the island of Crete; but the additional device of refracting the topical evils of Belfast, in a reworking of *The Murderers*, through the mirror of classical mythology is neither felicitous nor efficient.

The Murderers is generally regarded as one of his best plays. It appears (though Mornin does not acknowledge this) to be based on an account of the Shankill Butchers, a group of Protestant paramilitaries who achieved notoriety in the 1970's through a series of indiscriminate and bestial murders. Its formal achievement is to extend the play's climax (the mutilation, in the back room of a public house, of a young man culled from the street) to an unbearable pitch. The play is a detailed anatomy of the clash of working-class men, not as an undifferentiated mass, but as a complex of interdependent relationships initiated in blood and tribal fealty and compacted in the thrall of unmitigated horror. In *The Murderers*, more than in any other of Mornin's plays, there is a distinctive and malodorous atmosphere. The darkness exemplifies Mornin's ability to sustain the tension between character and action in a way that is deeply shocking.

As *The Murderers* illustrates, Mornin's depiction of women is overshadowed by his brilliant observation and astute handling of situations in which men are thrown together, by design or accident. Mornin shows consummate skill in dramatising homophile relationships, not as narrowly homoerotic and homosexual, but centring rather on the dark, secretive interdependence of men as members of a group. *Short of Mutiny* is set mainly below decks of a Royal Navy destroyer, and casts a cold eye over the behaviour of predominantly young seamen, working to discharge themselves dishonourably from the service so as to avoid paying themselves "out." Set against them are the ship's officers who, realising the game and also trapped themselves, cannily avoid the predicted confrontation. As a counterpoint to the main action, there are intensely disturbing scenes involving the time-hardened older men, reduced to making ships to go in bottles.

Short of Mutiny requires over 20 people to perform it, one of the reasons for the long delay in its production. Mornin's willingness to adapt to the demands of modern theatrical production is subsequently reflected in plays of smaller casts. He has written for radio, and a first novel, *All Our Fault*, is being filmed for television. In 1992 he was working on a new play for the Royal National Theatre. His unschematic view of his function as an artist, coupled with an ability to attract actors and directors of the highest calibre to stage his work, indicates that, in the foreseeable future, his playwriting career is assured.

—Paul Hadfield

MORRISON, Bill.

Born in Ballymoney, County Antrim, Northern Ireland, 22 January 1940. Educated at Dalriada Grammar School, Ballymoney, 1951–58; Queen's University, Belfast, 1958–62, LL.B. (honours) 1962. Married Valerie Lilley in 1968. Actor in Belfast, Dublin, and London, from 1963; resident writer, Victoria Theatre, Stoke-on-Trent, Staffordshire, 1969–71; radio drama producer, BBC, Belfast, 1975–76; resident writer, Everyman Theatre, 1977–78, lecturer in creative writing, C.F. Mott College, 1977–78, drama producer, Radio City, 1979–81, and associate director, 1981–83, and artistic director, 1983–85, Playhouse Theatre, all Liverpool. Since 1978 board member, Merseyside Young People's Theatre, Liverpool, since 1981 board member, Playhouse Theatre, and since 1985 chair, Merseyside Arts Drama Panel. Recipient: Ford Foundation grant, 1972; Arts Council bursary, 1975; Pye award, for radio feature, 1981. Agent: Michael Imison Playwrights, 28 Almeida Street, London N1 1TD, England.

Publications

PLAYS

Love and a Bottle, adaptation of the play by George Farquhar (produced 1966).
Laugh But Listen Well (produced 1967).
Conn and the Conquerors of Space (for children; also director: produced 1969).
Please Don't Shoot Me When I'm Down (produced 1969).
Jupiter-5 (for children; produced 1970).

Aladdin and His Magic Lamp (for children; also director: produced 1971).
Tess of the d'Urbervilles, adaptation of the novel by Hardy (produced 1971). 1980.
Sam Slade Is Missing (broadcast 1971; produced 1972). In *The Best Short Plays 1973*, edited by Stanley Richards, 1973.
The Time Travellers (for children; produced 1971).
Patrick's Day (produced 1972).
The Love of Lady Margaret (broadcast 1972; produced 1973).
Ellen Cassidy (broadcast 1974; produced 1978).
The Emperor of Ice-Cream, adaptation of the novel by Brian Moore (broadcast 1975; produced 1977).
The Irish Immigrants Tale (produced 1976).
Flying Blind (produced 1977). 1978.
Time on Our Hands (produced 1979).
Dr. Jekyll of Rodney Street (produced 1979).
Scrap! (produced 1982).
Cavern of Dreams, with Carol Ann Duffy (produced 1984).
Run, Run, Runaway (for children; produced 1986).
Be Bop a Lula (musical; produced 1988).
O Love Song for Ulster: The Marriage, The Son, The Daughter (produced 1993).

RADIO PLAYS: *Sam Slade Is Missing*, 1971; *The Love of Lady Margaret*, 1972; *The Great Gun-Running Episode*, 1974; *Ellen Cassidy*, 1974; *Crime and Punishment*, from a novel by Dostoevsky, 1975; *Crow's Flight*, from a play by Dimitri Kehaidis, 1975; *The Emperor of Ice-Cream*, 1975; *Simpson and Son*, 1977; *The Big Sleep, The High Window, The Lady in the Lake, The Little Sister*, and *The Long Goodbye*, all from the novels by Raymond Chandler, 1977; *Maguire*, 1979; *The Spring of Memory* (feature), 1981; *Blues in A-Flat*, 1989.

TELEVISION PLAYS: *McKinley and Sarah*, 1973; *Joggers*, 1978; *Potatohead Blues*, 1982; *Shergar*, 1986; *A Safe House*, 1990.

THEATRICAL ACTIVITIES
DIRECTOR: Plays—*On Approval* by Frederick Lonsdale, 1967; *The Lion in Winter* by James Goldman, 1969; *Two Gentlemen of Verona*, 1969; *Conn and the Conquerors of Space*, 1969; *Aladdin and His Magic Lamp*, 1971; *A Doll's House* by Ibsen, *Ladies in Waiting* by Ellen Fox, *These Men* by Mayo Simon, *Skirmishes* by Catherine Hayes, *Walking on Walter* by Claire Luckham, *A Lesson from Aloes* by Athol Fugard, *I Want* by Nell Dunn and Adrian Henri, *Breezeblock Park* by Willy Russell, *Alfie* by Bill Naughton, *Cavern of Dreams*, and *The Divvies Are Coming* by Eddie Braben, 1981–85; *The Beastly Beatitudes of Balthazar B* by J.P. Donleavy, 1983.
ACTOR: Plays—roles at Arts Theatre, Belfast, and with Ulster Theatre Company, 1963–65; Nick in *Who's Afraid of Virginia Woolf?* by Edward Albee, 1966; Barney Muldoon in *Illuminatus!* by Robert Anton Wilson, 1978.
Film—*Sinful Davey*, 1969.

Bill Morrison comments:

(1982) I was born in Ireland but I was born in the British part of it. I was born during a war and have lived in the shadow of war since. I am more an Ulster writer than an Irish one. My language has the particular rhythms of that place, my characters and subjects are violently shaped by it, my use of comedy is dictated by it. I write in order to try to make sense of what happens to me and what I see around me and I hope by that to make a record of how people felt and lived in a particular time and place, which I take to be the job of the writer in any society.

I also write for an audience. I am proud of the fact that my work has been performed in twelve countries. The excitement and persistence of theatre is that it is the form which depends on the creative participation of the audience to complete it. The audience always affects and often profoundly alters the quality of the artistic event. To me the theatre is a laboratory of human communication, a place of constant experiment. The glory of the nature of it is that it has to be on the human scale. Technology does change and improve but it barely affects the essential experience. Writing for radio, TV, or film is rewarding because of the audience it reaches but it is not the same. Theatre is the only human activity I have found which embraces and needs all levels of skill and talent in its making and where, despite all its internal conflicts, the need and advantage of co-operating always wins. The event is always greater than the individual. It is always communal.

That is how it should be. It is why I now run a theatre with other writers. However, I regret the fact that, apart from a community tour of a show *Time on Our Hands* which I devised with a company, my work remains unperformed in Northern Ireland.

(1988) The purpose of the writer in society is to record how people feel about the time they live in and the events in it. I try to make sense of what I feel and see around me, and mostly fail—which is why I write comedy and farce. The story of my time is the story of murder exposed as farce.

Following up his own proposition that since 1969 "the trouble with being an Ulster playwright has been trouble," Bill Morrison wrote in 1977: "the best of my work, or at least the most important to me, has been about my country and the people who try to survive in it. The plays have been about my struggle to understand the disease in my society which caused its intense, unbearably prolonged and homicidal breakdown. But they have also been about my struggle to find a form which would encompass it." This comment conveniently suggests the characteristics which give Morrison's drama its force: his exploration of the problematic relation between cultural and personal spheres in the Ulster context, and the formal experimentation from play to play that such an exploration necessarily entails. Moreover, in a writer who believes, as Morrison does, that "the theatre is ultimately the only way of fully discovering oneself," the "struggle to find a form" makes itself felt as a moral as well as an artistic imperative.

The struggle was complicated for Morrison in the early 1970's by a lack of sympathy he encountered in theatre (and television) for his exploratory treatment of the Ulster situation. Finding an outlet instead in radio, he experimented with the use of stereo in adaptations (notably *Crime and Punishment*) and, in his first original radio play, *The Love of Lady Margaret*, satisfyingly exploited the potential of the medium for narrative ambiguity in the rendering of an isolated consciousness and its labyrinth of ultimately self-thwarting fictions.

The aptness of the radio medium to the playwright's concerns is powerfully (though perhaps not consistently) apparent in *Ellen Cassidy*—a later stage version of which the author considers to have been unsatisfactory. Here the troubled consciousness belongs to the 34-year-old Armagh-born Protestant Ellen. Now in London, estranged from yet still haunted by her Irish husband, and awaiting the arrival of her young lover, she engages with the constraints and outcomes of an Ulster upbringing in a fluid series of recollections, reflective monologues, and flashbacks. The writing is often richly imaged, and at the heart of the play is the symbolic opposition of blood—the issue of menstruation, of sexual and sectarian violence, the pulsing badge of cultural belonging, something *inside* the self and controlling it—and water, an element outside the self which for Ellen promises cool, free-floating identity. As a woman, Ellen has experienced in both her upbringing and her relationships the stifling cultural consequences of the evolutionary determinism expatiated upon by her older lover, the biologist Gorman. When it becomes clear that the men in her life are, in their different ways, all pathetically enslaved by their cultural conditioning and its "stories," she finally proclaims her independence of all three and of "the old old days of pain": "My name is Ellen Cassidy and I live all alone."

Because of—or perhaps despite—the lyrical power of its monologues, *Ellen Cassidy* cannot help but bring to mind Morrison's admission that at this time he was "using plays as a form of psychoanalysis." *Flying Blind* signals a breakthrough for Morrison in its achievement of a decisively *im*personal form for the articulation of his characteristic preoccupations. The brooding and often painful energies of *Ellen Cassidy* are here gathered, shaped, and endowed with a bitter comic trajectory by the crisp dialogue and coolly contrived sudden mayhem of farce. The result is, as one critic has put it, "a world where the laws of farce and tragedy are interchangeable."

The increasingly fevered comings and goings of *Flying Blind* take place in and around the "imaginatively furnished" living room of an Ulster medical rep, Dan Poots, a supplier of "happy pills" who has dedicated himself to survival in an environment he considers to be in the grip of a "perversion of the spirit." He retreats between stereo headphones, listening to the music of his hero, Charlie "Bird" Parker, who "found the terms of membership unacceptable"—as Dan now does. Even before the darkly funny (and, for him, bladder-stretching) incursions of two groups of terrorists—a Protestant murder-squad and vengeful Catholics—Dan's strategy for survival is seriously disturbed by the demands of his concerned wife Liz, and by her old flame the sociologist Michael, who has returned to his native Ulster, laden with simplistic socio-political solutions and a desperation born of childlessness, determined to "save" Liz (or, failing that, her babysitter). Meanwhile the lawyer Boyd, recently forced out of politics by terrorist death-threats, is alarmed to find his sexual impulses arising only in the revolver he brandishes—and even that fails to go off at the climactic moment. In fact sex, that generic stipulation of farce, is here ingeniously invested with a pivotal diagnostic function. The pathetic impotence of the men in the play is symptomatic of a diseased society in which, as Dan realizes, potency exists not in sexual relationships but in the self-destructive violence of history's "blind men," the terrorists. Hence the moral force behind the farce when Dan and his generous (though unfulfilled) neighbour Bertha confront imminent death by undressing to make love right in front of the panic-stricken terrorists who are threatening them. In the end a fatal mêlée (graced by a bucket of piss and a purblind terrorist called Magoo) disrupts the reconciliation of friends and neighbours, and happy ending gives way to familiar stalemate.

Following the success of *Flying Blind* and after a group of Raymond Chandler adaptations for radio, Morrison worked on radio scripts in the U.S.A. and on a number of television projects, most of them either abortive or disappointing, in Britain. His last important stage play before his spell as director at the Liverpool Playhouse (1981–85) was *Scrap!* Here again farce is the formal basis, but the action is rather less riotous than in *Flying Blind*, and there are interwoven elements of the thriller-mode—or even of whodunnit.

Scrap! is centrally concerned with betrayal—personal, cultural, and political. The high-ranking English policeman Cleaver (a.k.a. Butcher) aims "to solve the problems of a whole country" by an appeal to what he considers to be the "eternal verities"—"bribery, blackmail, and betrayal." His plan is to lure the key Protestant terrorist organizer Sidney Mulligan out of Belfast to Liverpool and to deliver him over to the Catholic terrorist leader Madigan as part of a deal involving the military-strategic co-operation with Britain of a prospective non-neutral "new" united Ireland. To this end Cleaver brings over to Liverpool Mulligan's schoolgirl daughter Kate, who has gone to the police with her father's operational notebooks in her possession. Kate, ironically, is glad to escape Belfast, and with it the childhood innocence that makes her a potential blood-sacrifice on the altar of Ulster's history, yet at the same time she is torn at the prospect of betraying her father and all that he stands for. She manages to deposit the vital documents with his cousin, the English scrap-dealer Tommy Atkins (who is unaware of the fact). When Mulligan himself arrives in Liverpool, impelled less by his concern for the notebooks than by the desperation and "black pain" he feels at the disappearance of the child in whose innocence he invests all his surviving values, he is drawn into a deadly, yet also farcical, pattern of intrigue and betrayal. The plainly allegorical design of the play is reinforced by the co-ordination of symbolic structure and setting: the mirror-lined basement bar of the second half realizes visually the darkly oppressive phantom-world of Ulster history which shuts out the "sweet day-light" of freedom and reduces the Protestants to the contorted scrap of Britain. At the climax, Cleaver's underhand plans go grotesquely wrong, and the powerful Protestant Mulligan, having wrapped himself in a waistcoat of dynamite and lit the fuse, grasps the disarmed Catholic Madigan under one arm and the crooked Englishman Cleaver under the other, as he asks: "which among us deserves to be saved?" This final stage-image crystallizes the dead-lock Morrison has always sought to confront and to understand through his drama—in the belief that such understanding would also constitute a kind of self-discovery.

A further strand of Morrison's work is constituted by his imaginative realizations of "true stories" which are in some way enigmatic or remarkable. Into this category fall the television films *Shergar* (about the kidnap of the racehorse), and *A Safe House* (about the Maguire case), and the stage play *Be Bop a Lula*. Based on research by Spencer Leigh, *Be Bop a Lula* tells the story of rock n rollers Gene Vincent and Eddie Cochran on their 1960 British tour, during which the latter died in a car crash. The narrative, woven around no less than 30 songs (performed live), concentrates on the relationship between the broodingly violent and self-destructive Vincent, with his crippled leg and black leathers, and the fresh but fated Cochran. Cochran is the rising star, but the final image of the play is of the already fading Vincent sitting on his friend's coffin. The play is a kind of requiem, a contribution to (pre-Beatles) rock mythology rather than an exploration of it. "Great drama it isn't," wrote one reviewer, "but it is good rock and roll."

—Paul Lawley

MORTIMER, John (Clifford).

Born in Hampstead, London, 21 April 1923. Educated at Harrow School, Middlesex, 1937–40; Brasenose College, Oxford, 1940–42, B.A. 1947; called to the bar, 1948; Queen's Counsel, 1966; Master of the Bench, Inner Temple, 1975. Served with the Crown Film Units as scriptwriter during World War II. Married 1) Penelope Dimont in 1949 (divorced 1971), one son and one daughter; 2) Penny Gollop in 1972, two daughters. Drama critic, *New Statesman*, *Evening Standard*, and *Observer*, 1972, all London; member of the National Theatre Board, 1968–88; president, Berkshire, Buckinghamshire, and Oxford Naturalists' Trust, from 1984; chair, League of Dramatists; chair of the council, Royal Society of Literature, from 1989; chair, Royal Court Theatre, from 1990; president, Howard League for Penal Reform, from 1992. Recipient: Italia prize, for radio play, 1958; Screenwriters Guild award, for television play, 1970; BAFTA award, for television series, 1980; *Yorkshire Post* award, 1983. D. Litt.: Susquehanna University, Selinsgrove, Pennsylvania, 1985; University of St. Andrews, Fife, 1987; University of Nottingham, 1989; LL.D.: Exeter University, 1986. C.B.E. (Commander, Order of the British Empire), 1986. Lives in Henley-on-Thames, Oxfordshire. Agent: Peters, Fraser, and Dunlop Group, 503–504 The Chambers, Chelsea Harbour, Lots Road, London SW10 0XF, England.

Publications

PLAYS

The Dock Brief (broadcast 1957; produced 1958). In *Three Plays*, 1958.
I Spy (broadcast 1957; produced 1959). In *Three Plays*, 1958.
What Shall We Tell Caroline? (produced 1958). In *Three Plays*, 1958.
Three Plays: The Dock Brief, What Shall We Tell Caroline?, I Spy. 1958.

Call Me a Liar (televised 1958; produced 1968). In *Lunch Hour and Other Plays*, 1960; in *The Television Playwright: Ten Plays for B.B.C. Television*, edited by Michael Barry, 1960.

Sketches in *One to Another* (produced 1959). 1960.

The Wrong Side of the Park (produced 1960). 1960.

Lunch Hour (broadcast 1960; produced 1960). In *Lunch Hour and Other Plays*, 1960.

David and Broccoli (televised 1960). In *Lunch Hour and Other Plays*, 1960.

Lunch Hour and Other Plays (includes *Collect Your Hand Baggage, David and Broccoli, Call Me a Liar*). 1960.

Collect Your Hand Baggage (produced 1963). In *Lunch Hour and Other Plays*, 1960.

Sketches in *One over the Eight* (produced 1961).

Two Stars for Comfort (produced 1962). 1962.

A Voyage round My Father (broadcast 1963; produced 1970). 1971.

Sketches in *Changing Gear* (produced 1965).

A Flea in Her Ear, adaptation of a play by Feydeau (produced 1966). 1967.

A Choice of Kings (televised 1966). In *Playbill Three*, edited by Alan Durband, 1969.

The Judge (produced 1967). 1967.

Desmond (televised 1968). In *The Best Short Plays 1971*, edited by Stanley Richards, 1971.

Cat among the Pigeons, adaptation of a play by Feydeau (produced 1969). 1970.

Come As You Are: Four Short Plays (includes *Mill Hill, Bermondsey, Gloucester Road, Marble Arch*) (produced 1970). 1971.

Five Plays (includes *The Dock Brief, What Shall We Tell Caroline?, I Spy, Lunch Hour, Collect Your Hand Baggage*). 1970.

The Captain of Köpenick, adaptation of a play by Carl Zuckmayer (produced 1971). 1971.

Conflicts, with others (produced 1971).

I, Claudius, adaptation of the novels *I, Claudius* and *Claudius the God* by Robert Graves (produced 1972).

Knightsbridge (televised 1972). 1973.

Collaborators (produced 1973). 1973.

The Fear of Heaven (as *Mr. Lucy's Fear of Heaven*, broadcast 1976; as *The Fear of Heaven*, produced with *The Prince of Darkness* as *Heaven and Hell*, 1976). 1978.

Heaven and Hell (includes *The Fear of Heaven* and *The Prince of Darkness*) (produced 1976; revised version of *The Prince of Darkness*, as *The Bells of Hell* produced 1977). *The Bells of Hell* published 1978.

The Lady from Maxim's, adaptation of a play by Feydeau (produced 1977). 1977.

John Mortimer's Casebook (includes *The Dock Brief, The Prince of Darkness, Interlude*) (produced 1982).

When That I Was (produced 1982).

Edwin (broadcast 1982). In *Edwin and Other Plays*, 1984.

A Little Hotel on the Side, adaptation of a play by Feydeau and Maurice Desvalliers (produced 1984). In *Three Boulevard Farces*, 1985.

Edwin and Other Plays (includes *Bermondsey, Marble Arch, The Fear of Heaven, The Prince of Darkness*). 1984.

Three Boulevard Farces (includes *A Little Hotel on the Side, A Flea in Her Ear, The Lady from Maxim's*). 1985.

Die Fledermaus, adaptation of the libretto by Henri Meilhac and Ludovic Halévy, music by Johann Strauss (produced 1989). 1989.

SCREENPLAYS: *Ferry to Hong Kong*, with Lewis Gilbert and Vernon Harris, 1959; *The Innocents*, with Truman Capote and William Archibald, 1961; *Guns of Darkness*, 1962; *I Thank a Fool*, with others, 1962; *Lunch Hour*, 1962; *The Running Man*, 1963; *Bunny Lake Is Missing*, with Penelope Mortimer, 1964; *A Flea in Her Ear*, 1967; *John and Mary*, 1969.

RADIO PLAYS: *Like Men Betrayed*, 1955; *No Hero*, 1955; *The Dock Brief*, 1957; *I Spy*, 1957; *Three Winters*, 1958; *Lunch Hour*, 1960; *The Encyclopedist*, 1961; *A Voyage round My Father*, 1963; *Personality Split*, 1964; *Education of an Englishman*, 1964; *A Rare Device*, 1965; *Mr Luby's Fear of Heaven*, 1976; *Edwin*, 1982; *Rumpole*, from his own stories, 1988; *Glasnost*, 1988.

TELEVISION PLAYS: *Call Me a Liar*, 1958; *David and Broccoli*, 1960; *A Choice of Kings*, 1966; *The Exploding Azalea*, 1966; *The Head Waiter*, 1966; *Hughie*, 1967; *The Other Side*, 1967; *Desmond*, 1968; *Infidelity Took Place*, 1968; *Married Alive*, 1970; *Swiss Cottage*, 1972; *Knightsbridge*, 1972; *Rumpole of the Bailey*, 1975, and series, 1978, 1979, 1987, 1988; *A Little Place off the Edgware Road, The Blue Film, The Destructors, The Case for the Defence, Chagrin in Three Parts, The Invisible Japanese Gentlemen, Special Duties*, and *Mortmain* all from stories by Graham Greene, 1975–76; *Will Shakespeare*, 1978; *Rumpole's Return*, 1980; *Unity*, from the book by David Pryce-Jones, 1981; *Brideshead Revisited*, from the novel by Evelyn Waugh 1981; *Edwin*, 1984; *The Ebony Tower*, from the story by John Fowles, 1984; *Paradise Postponed*, from his own novel, 1986; *Summer's Lease*, from his own novel, 1989; *The Waiting Room*, 1989; *Titmuss Regained*, from his own novel, 1991.

BALLET SCENARIO: *Home*, 1968.

SON ET LUMIÈRE SCRIPTS: *Hampton Court*, 1964; *Brighton Pavilion*, 1965.

NOVELS

Charade. 1948.

Rumming Park. 1948.

Answer Yes or No. 1950; as *The Silver Hook*, 1950.

Like Men Betrayed. 1953.

The Narrowing Stream. 1954.

Three Winters. 1956.

Will Shakespeare: The Untold Story. 1977.

Paradise Postponed. 1985.

Summer's Lease. 1988.

Titmuss Regained. 1990.
The Rapstone Chronicles (includes *Paradise Postponed, Titmuss Regained*)
   1991.
Dunster. 1992.

SHORT STORIES

Rumpole. 1980.
*Rumpole of the Bailey.*1978.
The Trials of Rumpole. 1979.
Regina v. Rumpole. 1981.
Rumpole's Return. 1980.
Rumpole for the Defence. 1982.
Rumpole and the Golden Thread. 1983.
The First Rumpole Omnibus (includes *Rumpole of the Bailey, The Trials of
   Rumpole, Rumpole's Return*). 1983.
Rumpole's Last Case. 1987.
The Second Rumpole Omnibus (includes *Rumpole for the Defence, Rumpole
   and the Golden Thread, Rumpole's Last Case*). 1987.
Rumpole and the Age of Miracles. 1988.
Rumpole à la Carte. 1990.
Rumpole on Trial. 1992.

OTHER

No Moaning of the Bar (as Geoffrey Lincoln). 1957.
With Love and Lizards (travel), with Penelope Mortimer. 1957.
Clinging to the Wreckage: A Part of Life. 1982.
In Character (interviews). 1983.
The Liberty of the Citizen (lecture), with Franklin Thomas and Lord Hunt of
   Tanworth. 1983.
Character Parts (interviews). 1986.

Editor, *Famous Trials*, edited by Harry Hodge and James H. Hodge. 1984.
Editor, *Great Law and Order Stories.* 1990.
Editor, *The Oxford Book of Villains.* 1992.

MANUSCRIPT COLLECTIONS: Boston University; University of California, Los
Angeles.

CRITICAL STUDY: *Anger and After* by John Russell Taylor, 1962, revised edition, 1969, as *The Angry Theatre*, 1962, revised edition, 1969.

John Mortimer comments:

(1982) Comedy, I remember saying when my plays were first performed, is the
only thing worth writing in this despairing age. Twenty years later the world
has offered no call for a change of attitude. It may be that only in the most

secure and optimistic ages can good tragedies be written. Our present situation, stumbling into a misty future filled with uncertainty and mistrust, is far too serious to be described in terms that give us no opportunity to laugh.

As a barrister, John Mortimer has been a doughty advocate of the freedom of the stage from censorship, and as a public figure he is respected as a staunch left-wing intellectual, albeit with an uninhibited taste for the good life and a hearty dislike of what he is wont to call the "nanny state." His own most successful plays, however, have been agreeable and witty middle-class entertainments. They are deftly crafted and beautifully scripted, with well-observed characters who are presented, sometimes, in plots of such simplicity as to be little more than a single extended situation, and his theatrical style departs from traditional realistic canons only in a certain fluidity of staging. His remarkable expertise in the difficult form of the one-act play has tempted some critics to suggest that Mortimer is less at home with longer plays, but this is not entirely fair, for he does know how to develop ideas and characters. Mortimer's skilled theatrical craftsmanship is exemplified particularly well in his translations of *A Flea in Her Ear*, *Cat among the Pigeons*, and *The Lady from Maxim's*, three French farces by Georges Feydeau. Above all, however, Mortimer is associated in the public mind with the *Rumpole* television series. Rumpole is, in Mortimer's phrase, an Old Bailey hack, and each of the many half-hour episodes presents an entertaining if undemanding intertwining of three elements: the battles of a bumbling but liberal-minded barrister to defend the flawed individuals who are his clients against the English legal system; the everyday squabbles between the oddly assorted partners in chambers in London; and Rumpole's domestic difficulties with his harridan of a wife, Hilda, or, as the British public has come to call her, "She Who Must be Obeyed."

The Dock Brief, which was Mortimer's first play to be produced, contains much that is to be found again and again in his work. Set in the cells beneath the courtroom, it is economical to produce, but imagination and the provision of acting opportunities compensate for any lack of extravagance in staging. Hilariously funny yet sad in all its implications, the play juxtaposes a very human prisoner charged with killing his wife and a totally incompetent ageing barrister who dreams that presenting the case for the defence will win him the reputation for which he has always yearned. In the cell he attempts to play out the court room drama which he foresees, but in court, we are told, he fails dismally. A happy paradox, however, results in an unexpected happy ending.

Another of Mortimer's early plays, the very popular one-act *Lunch Hour* illustrates two more characteristic aspects of his work. As a barrister specialising in divorce cases, Mortimer was well acquainted with the world of sleazy hotels and the clientele that used them for their assignations. With an attractive blend of wit and sympathy, *Lunch Hour* shows what this may well mean in personal terms. Sex, it turns out, is really only a secondary consideration here, and once again, as in *The Dock Brief*, there are beguiling episodes which raise the question of the relationship between individuals' true selves and the roles that they are called upon to assume in life. Mortimer is also interested, in what some might regard as a very English way, with life in English private schools, and this is represented for the first time in the sensitive and closely observed early play *What Shall We Tell Caroline?*, in which, of course, it transpires that putting the question in quite those terms represents a fundamental misunderstanding of the headmaster's 18-year-old daughter.

Many theatre-goers regard *A Voyage round My Father* as Mortimer's greatest achievement, and both on stage, with Alec Guinness in the lead, and on television with Laurence Olivier, it made a great impression. Mortimer's father was a noted figure in the courts, both for the style of his advocacy and for the fact that he was blind, and *A Voyage* is a marvellously rich portrayal of this impossibly difficult character in counterpoint to John Mortimer's life from childhood through adolescence to maturity. The situations can become hilarious as the blind barrister deliberately flouts every bourgeois convention; the dialogue has all the brilliance one might expect from men whose stock-in-trade is the ability to speak well; the social observation is sharp; and with all this there is also great sympathy for a wounded human being who fights to retain his dignity. Symbolic of the blind barrister's determination not to be daunted by his affliction is his passionate concern for the beauty of his garden. By the end the audience feels almost guilty for enjoying looking at the summer flowers he cannot see.

The Judge also explores the legal world, this time from the angle of a judge who, at the end of his career, returns not only to his home town in the provinces but to unresolved aspects of his past. The tone is more serious than in many of Mortimer's plays, and the public has generally preferred rather lighter fare, such as *Collect Your Hand Baggage*, with its whimsically deflating ending, *Two Stars for Comfort*, set in a modest hotel, and clever short plays like those collected in *Come As You Are* which reveal, in a form and with an attitude that demands little of the audience, an acute awareness of just what makes people tick.

—Christopher Smith

MOTTON, Gregory.

Born in London, 17 September 1961. Lives with Lotta Kjellberg; one daughter. Recipient: Arts Council bursary, 1989; Royal Literary Fund grant, 1991. Agent: Rod Hall, A.P. Watt, 20 John Street, London WC1N 2DR, England.

Publications

PLAYS

Chicken (produced 1987). With *Ambulance*, 1987.

Ambulance (produced 1987). With *Chicken*, 1987.

Downfall (produced 1988). With *Looking at You (Revived) Again*, 1989.

Looking at You (Revived) Again (produced 1989). With *Downfall*, 1989.

The Ghost Sonata, adaptation of the play by August Strindberg (produced 1989).

The Pelican, adaptation of the play by August Strindberg (produced 1989).

Picture of Dorian Gray, adaptation of the novel by Oscar Wilde (produced 1990).
Woyzeck, adaptation of the play by Georg Büchner (produced 1992). 1992.
A Message for the Broken Hearted (produced 1993).
The Terrible Voice of Satan (produced 1993).

SCREENPLAY: *Kleptophilia*, 1992.

RADIO PLAYS: *The Jug*, 1991; *Lazy Brién*, 1992.

In a 1988 *Guardian* review of *Downfall*, Gregory Motton's third drama in two years, Michael Billington detected "the birth of a new genre: Urban Impressionism." Occasioned by the congruent staging of Nick Ward's *The Strangeness of Others* (to which many reviewers unfavourably compared Motton's work), the label is no less useful than many another—"surrealism," Billington went on to suggest; "tragi-farcical nightmare," opined Paul Taylor of the *Independent*. Motton "[is] fast making a name for himself," Sheridan Morley ventured in *Punch*, as "the dramatic poet of urban disintegration." A drama wilfully (if not always clearly) focused on social damage and dissidence and at the same time fashioning an expressionist, sometimes symbolist mode of address does not lend itself easily to shorthand account: abrupt shifts of mood and register, dialogue gracelessly demotic then poetically or portentously inflected, violence and comedy charged by incipient wandering and waste make clear that dramatic naturalism is as residual a feature of Motton's stagecraft as his characters are the residues and casualties of psychosocial "development."

A break with naturalism is hardly apparent from the settings of the earlier plays, *Chicken*—"an abandoned working men's cafe" and "a street outside [a] doorway"—and *Ambulance*—"Ellis's room" and "the street, outside a launderette"; however, the interplay between road and room, as it were, shapes a series of narratives which, in both plays, elliptically explore what have become Motton's ruling concerns: commitment and communication, power and loss. Indeed, the title *Ambulance* has much to do with the impairment of characters' motor functions: the crippled Clivey, locked into a relation with Louise, is then mothered by Mary who is herself unable to carry her legs beyond a certain radius of Holloway Prison; meanwhile, the uncertainly gendered Ellis injures herself jumping from a stifling room onto the pavement outside, thus prompting the ambulance's arrival. Ambulancemen figure as anonymous powers of capture and disablement, much as, in *Chicken*, the "party" that Pat (the patriarch) menacingly invokes and the role he assumes of Secretary of State for Sanitation and Education (to include "secrecy"), suggest individual disempowerment by bureaucracy and factional interests. Commitment, along with individual desire for personal and professional growth, is readily transmuted into involuntary committal.

Indeed, individuals (periodically but always problematically forming couples) wander through an increasingly fractured narrative line across the plays, forcing out an ever more compacted set of dramatic co-ordinates: lost, abandoned, imagined children, for example—with the sense of continuity, history, and relation they suggest—are repeatedly invoked. The killing of the chicken in the play of that title is a matricidal act (no eggs), the breaking of a food chain by a usurping father. The "pain of separation," as Johnny terms it in *Ambulance* (on occasions, from that which one never possessed) includes loss of memory, relation, and aspiration, of visible and attainable goals, even as seekers with binoculars search the skies and invoke the "cosmos." The same play's Pedro, increasingly wracked with bodily spasms, can still claim, however, that "Life goes on" even when, at the play's close, the "battering ram" (an ambulance crew) hoves into view.

Downfall, a drama divided into 56 brief scenes, is forbiddingly dense and oblique with its networks of verbal and circumstantial patterning, its snatches of biblical and occult narrative, its characters (Tower Man, Spanish Lover, Violent Man) emblematically rather than socially situated. More so than in the earlier drama, dialogue swings from the barely articulate outburst or stumbling exchange to outpourings of garrulous but vacuous energy or fitfully focused portentousness; pointed concentration slides off into offhand non-sequitur. At the same time, despite—perhaps because of—having each scene titled as an episode, Motton's dramatic—but more especially visual—imagination has developed to incorporate wildly different modes and circumstances: the Violent Man hounded by a swooping helicopter, Hetty and Rolo itinerant but grounded beneath the choric Tower Man, Secret Service man Geronimo progressively losing power and position in respect of the "sides" which the play, as carnival, insists on dislocating. Such circumstances recur and are refashioned to punctuate material which might otherwise overreach itself.

A moment of tender (if not quite literally touching) intimacy between "two strays" just before the play's close ("There are lots of people in the world," Clancy, not for the first time, remarks) serves to highlight Motton's emphasis on permissive rather than repressive commitment in a world open to surveillance, institutional power, and false prophets, all emanating from on high upon a falling world. In a shadowing of the Christian story (with "skulduggery" as Gethsemane and Dover "the nation's Calvary" at the play's end) *Downfall* enacts the struggle to remain upright (in every sense of that word) along a modern *via dolorosa* of betrayal, suffering, guilt, and despair. Along the way there are any number of false epiphanies (and a conspicuously unachieved annunciation) ending with "a long road stretching out" before three figures themselves stretched across the skyline and Motton's concluding dance (of death?).

The debt to Strindberg (several of whose plays Motton has translated for production) is most evident in his more tightly worked, economically constructed "ghost" play *Looking at You (Revived) Again*. It presents a triangle of figures—a man, Abe, "dark woman" Mrs. James (the wife whom, it seems, from reconstructed dramas of the past, Abe has abandoned and whose children he affects to be seeking) and "Peragrin's daughter" whom Abe consorts with as "the dark side . . . the invisible side of (his) soul." "p.d." (as she is known) finally overshadows not only the crippled Mrs. James, now upstanding, and transforms herself into a figure of mannikin beauty, but also overshadows Abe (who claims to have been "eclipsed" entirely) with the promise of a child which will stir him to a sense of responsibility. Inset narrated stagings of a wedding, threats from landlords and bailiffs, desolate settings, and sickness notwithstanding, the lack of social specificity and the more tightly worked psychodramas of repression, transference and working through make this, Motton's most recent play, a studied rejection of naturalism. One might indeed be forgiven for seeking the play's public concerns less with "urban disintegration" and contemporary British culture than with European Jewry and for locating its dramatic kinship within European Expressionism.

—James Hansford

MOWAT, David.

Born in Cairo, Egypt, 16 March 1943. Educated at Bryanston School, 1956–60; New College, Oxford, 1961–64, B.A. (honours) in English language and literature 1964; University of Sussex, Falmer, 1964–66. Cilcennin fellow, University of Bristol, 1973–75; director of the Playwrights Workshop, University of Iowa, Iowa City, 1978; fellow, Virginia Center for Creative Arts, 1979. Since 1984 director of the Playwriting Workshop, Actors Centre, London. Recipient: Arts Council bursary, 1970, 1971, 1976, 1977, 1983. Agent: Casarotto Ramsay Ltd., National House, 60–66 Wardour Street, London WIV 3HP. Address: 7 Mount Street, Oxford OX2 6DH, England.

Publications

PLAYS

Jens (produced 1965). In Anna-Luse and Other Plays, 1970.
Pearl (produced 1966).
1850 (produced 1967).
Anna-Luse (produced 1968). In Anna-Luse and Other Plays, 1970.
Dracula, with others (produced 1969).
Purity (produced 1969). In Anna-Luse and Other Plays, 1970.
Anna-Luse and Other Plays. 1970.
The Normal Woman, and Tyyppi (produced 1970).
Adrift, with others (produced 1970).
The Others (produced 1970). 1973.
Most Recent Least Recent (produced 1970).
Inuit (produced 1970).
Liquid (produced 1971).
The Diabolist (produced 1971).
John (produced 1971).
Amalfi, based on The Duchess of Malfi by Webster (produced 1972).
Phoenix-and-Turtle (produced 1972). In The London Fringe Theatre, edited by Victor Mitchell, 1975.
Morituri (produced 1972).
My Relationship with Jayne (produced 1973).
Come (produced 1973).
Main Sequence (produced 1974).
The Collected Works (produced 1974).
The Memory Man (produced 1974).
The Love Maker (produced 1974).
X to C (produced 1975).

Kim (produced 1977).
Winter (produced 1978).
The Guise (produced 1979).
Hiroshima Nights (produced 1981).
The Midnight Sun (produced 1983).
Carmen (produced 1984).
The Almas (produced 1989).

RADIO PLAYS: *To Die in Africa*, 1989; *Singing and Dancing in Kanpur*, 1991.

SHORT STORIES
New Writers 11, with others. 1974.

The name of David Mowat is familiar to those who frequent experimental fringe theatres. He began his career as one of the band of writers who provide much of the repertoire of short plays produced on the lunch-time circuit.

Many of these playwrights seem almost indistinguishable from each other: indeed, some half dozen of them indulge occasionally in corporate efforts. Their methods are freewheeling, their subject matter often sensational, and their intention to subvert the existing social structure by means of shock effects. They command respect on account of their talent and seriousness of purpose, although their playing out of sadistic and erotic fantasies induces doubt as often as cheers.

From these writers, Mowat stands conspicuously apart. There is present in his work an obsessive search for truth: "What information, useful information for the living of our lives, are we getting from this person?" asks the Narrator in a direct address to the audience in *Phoenix-and-Turtle*. In the same play he also observes "There's no obscenity so obscene as the horrid spectra of untruth lurking in the centre of one's home." The speaker is a Lecturer in English who has been sacked as a result of a liaison with a student; who has just burnt the manuscript of his book on the subject of the eponymous Shakespeare poem; who feels compelled to tell his wife that she has not long to live; and who—after an incestuous attack on his daughter—discovers that the girl is already pregnant. All these lies are brought into the open but, characteristically, the very act of telling the truth by means of the basic lie of theatre is also questioned. The author likens art to putting a frame around lies and, by making them scan or rhyme, pretending to give them a moral purpose.

Fat-Man (from the same period but not yet produced), deals allegorically with the rifts in the political left. Using as a motto a dictum of Mao Tse-tung's —"When the body is healthy, the feelings are correct"—the scene is set in a gymnasium threatened with demolition. The name of three of its four characters—Fatman, Cripple, and Little-Boy—indicate the satirical nature of the problem: each one has passionate convictions regarding the desired use of the gymnasium. The play is subtitled "the exercise of power"; needless to say, Mowat offers no easy solutions. His adaptation of *The Duchess of Malfi* and his approving quotation of Webster's remark that all life is a torture chamber may point to a vein of pessimism, but this, too, could be misleading. There is a quality of nagging obsession in Mowat's plays. His zeal for uncovering the truth has an echo of Ibsen, his haunted, nightmarish fantasies remind one of

Strindberg. Of living authors, only Pinter comes to mind: Mowat, too, is a master of mystery and economy and his plays, though often difficult to comprehend at first sight, share with Pinter's the power to keep an audience spellbound.

He has travelled a long way since he wrote *Jens*: a comparatively straight-forward piece of symbolism in which animals and humans mingle surrealisti-cally. His most impressive early play was *Anna-Luse*. Here, a blind young girl gets up in the morning, goes through a ritual of stock-taking of her body and her possessions, and is visited by a girlfriend (also blind), a confused young man, and a dubious P.T. instructor. The last was the victim of a gang of thugs on the way over. Drenched but undaunted, he proceeds to give the girls some strange therapy, which induces in Anna-Luse a phantom pregnancy and childbirth. It is, however, the Instructor who is revealed most surprisingly: he ends, curled up like a baby, at Anna-Luse's breast.

Mowat's plays are by no means solemn. In *The Diabolist*, for example, a worried mum is introduced to her daughter's new boyfriend. He is the epitome of the ordinary bloke, but turns out unexpectedly to be a devil-worshipper. Apart from a macabre and not altogether unsuccessful ending, this sketch is as funny as anything produced by the absurdists.

The surface of these plays is in most cases shabbily suburban and lower middle class. They gain from being staged with absolute naturalism; the tension between manner and matter becomes then increasingly menacing. The rug is slowly and unnervingly pulled from under our feet, and we leave the theatre with our heads buzzing with questions which have no easy or formal solutions but which demand to be asked, if not answered.

Mowat's full-length play *John* belongs in this category. Its hero spends the entire play in a catatonic trance. The unease engendered by his silence, and its effect on the other, superficially "ordinary" characters, provides an exciting evening. Sudden irruptions of extreme violence occur regularly in Mowat's work, but they never appear gratuitously.

The short play *Come* seems to me wilfully enigmatic. Here a distraught father attempts to persuade his estranged daughter to return to him. He lies in wait for her in a room adjoining an intellectual party which becomes an orgy. Nothing is achieved, and neither the motives nor the narrative makes any comprehensible sense.

The full-length play *The Collected Works* is Mowat's most lucid and fully realized to date. The setting is a library; the books, like the eyes of accumulated wisdom and disillusion, stare down at the turbulent emotional tangle involving a researcher, a love-sick girl, the sterile Chief Librarian, and his beautiful wife. Taking as his theme the tensions between life and art, Mowat contrasts the messiness and unexpectedness of the former with the unalterable composure of the latter. There is much sly comedy as the characters explain themselves in lengthy monologues. Once again, he writes in a deliberate undertone, but the surface simmers with unease and bubbles with incipient volcanic explosions.

With his sensitivity, his depth, and his increasing technical assurance, there is every chance that he will emerge from his present, somewhat esoteric, milieu and give us a play of real significance, with "useful information for the living of our lives."

—Frank Marcus

MUNRO, Rona.

Born in Aberdeen, 7 September 1959. Educated at Mackie Academy, Stonehaven; Edinburgh University, 1976–80, M.A. in history (honours). Married Edward Draper in 1981; one son. Writer-in-residence, Paines Plough Theatre Company, London, 1985–86. Recipient: McClaren award for radio, 1986; Susan Smith Blackburn prize, 1991; *Evening Standard* award, 1991; London Theatre Critics Circle prize, 1992; *Plays and Players* award, 1992. Agent: Casarotto Ramsay Ltd., National House, 60–66 Wardour Street, London W1V 3HP, England.

Publications

PLAYS

The Salesman (produced 1982).
The Bang and the Whimper (produced 1982).
Fugue (produced 1983). 1983.
Touchwood (for children; produced 1984).
The Bus (for children; produced 1984).
Ghost Story (for children; produced 1985).
Piper's Cave. In *Plays by Women: Five*, edited by Michelene Wandor and Mary Remnant, 1985.
The Biggest Party in the World (produced 1986).
Dust and Dreams (produced 1986).
The Way to Go Home (produced 1987).
Winners (produced 1987).
Off the Road (produced 1988).
Saturday at the Commodore (produced 1989). In *Scot Free*, edited by Alasdair Cameron, 1990.
Bold Girls (produced 1990). In *First Run 3*, edited by Matthew Lloyd, 1991.
Your Turn to Clean the Stair (produced 1992).

RADIO PLAYS: *Kilbreck* series, 1983–84; *Watching Waiters*, 1986; *Dirt under the Carpet*, 1987; *Citizens* series, 1988; *Elsie*, 1990; *Elvis*, 1990; *Eleven*, 1990; *Three Way Split*, 1992.

TELEVISION PLAYS: *Hardware*, 1984; *Biting the Hands*, 1989; 3 episodes in *Dr. Who* series, 1989; *Say It with Flowers* in *Casualty* series, 1990.

Rona Munro comments:

I am a Scottish playwright, a woman playwright, and an Aberdonian playwright, not necessarily in that order. All of these facts inform my writing but don't define it. Up till now a lot of my writing has concerned itself with issues around gender and sexual politics and as yet there's no sign of that preoccupation wearing off. I'm concerned to address these issues from a broad, human perspective, and as far as possible to write entertainingly and honestly, reflecting women's and men's lives as I perceive them rather than as I would choose them to be. I'm concerned to assert my place as part of a living tradition, a distinctive Scottish culture, and to explore the possibilities of writing in Scots as well as in English. I am also apparently incapable of writing anything without slipping a few gags in and will probably always choose to write drama that is liberally laced with comedy.

Rona Munro is one of Scotland's most innovative young playwrights. Her use of language and particularly of Aberdonian dialect in some of her work, and her creative weaving of Celtic myth into her contemporary scenarios, both serve to enrich her theatre writing immensely. Her own experiences as a student, cleaner, and experienced traveller have also influenced her work, lending it a voice which is at once true to her working-class origins and informed by world affairs and global issues.

An early play, *Fugue*, was commissioned in 1982 and staged at the Traverse Theatre, Edinburgh in 1983. Another early work, *Ghost Story*, was staged at the Tron Theatre, Glasgow, in 1985. She has also written for television and radio, but her theatre work is her true forte, and has been influenced by her work with (and has been influential upon the work of) both Paines Plough Theatre Company and her own women's comedy duo, the Msfits, founded with colleague Fiona Knowles. But her best-known plays—and deservedly so—are *Piper's Cave* and *Saturday at the Commodore*.

Piper's Cave is a curiously surreal play, a two-hander between a young woman (Jo) and a mysterious man who appears to be older than his 30-odd years (Alisdair). A third "character" of sorts is the unseen spirit of the landscape. Munro gives this spirit a "local habitation and a name," as well as a good number of lines in the script: the landscape is called "Helen." Helen is present from the opening of the play, but she comes into her own about half-way through, when she speaks as frequently as do the two "real" characters. Whether or not she is speaking, however, Helen's presence is crucial throughout, for this is a play about the power of the environment, and one which challenges ingrained essentialist notions about "Mother Nature." At the same time, it addresses the issues of gender and power, sex and violence.

Piper's Cave, as Rona Munro reveals in the published afterword to the play, "actually exists," though she exercised some creative licence in terms of its location. Similarly, the issues which Munro deals with in the play are quite real. Yet the play experiments with reality and myth by combining them, drawing on one to enrich the other. The play introduces young Jo as a modern woman, and Alisdair as a version of the legendary "piper who walked into the hill and never came out." Helen is the natural world, and she has a mighty wit. But Jo and Alisdair also have their "other-worldly" sides: Alisdair is, or thinks he is, the legendary piper; Jo becomes, or thinks she becomes, the Selky, the seal woman of Celtic myth. At the play's end, we hear splashing: the sound of waves which could be made by Jo, or by Helen, or which might be the sound of curtains closing on a thought-provoking play.

While in *Piper's Cave* only Alisdair spoke regularly in dialect, all of *Saturday at the Commodore* is written to be performed in a strong Aberdonian. The play is quite short (only five pages in the published version); a one-woman monologue of sorts, commissioned by 7:84 Scotland as part of a series of short pieces by "Voices of Today's Scotland." The use of dialect is crucial, due to the

setting of both the play and its performances (it was first performed at the Isle
of Skye in 1989).

Lena is the 30-year-old central character, or narrator, who relates the story
of *Saturday at the Commodore*, a story of one woman's memories of childhood and adolescence in Scotland. The play is a story, a narrative which
somehow conjures up vivid images of other places and people, most notably
Nora, Lena's "best mate" and the girl she fancied as well. The development
into womanhood, from being a student to being a teacher, through one
heterosexual relationship to a life of independence—all this is told in a
narrative which is relaxed, wry, witty, and immensely engaging. The dialect
makes it Lena's story, and a uniquely Scottish story. Yet Munro's ability to
create likeable characters and familiar, evocative situations makes it a larger
story as well, one worth staging and re-staging to see what different communities and different audiences may make of it.

—Lizbeth Goodman

MURDOCH, (Jean) Iris.

Born in Dublin, Ireland, 15 July 1919. Educated at the Froebel Education
Institute, London; Badminton School, Bristol; Somerville College, Oxford,
1938–42, B.A. (first class honours) 1942; Newnham College, Cambridge
(Sarah Smithson student in philosophy), 1947–48. Married the writer John
Bayley in 1956. Assistant principal in the Treasury, London, 1942–44; admi-
nistrative officer with the United Nations Relief and Rehabilitation
Administration (UNRRA) in London, Belgium, and Austria, 1944–46; fellow,
St. Anne's College, Oxford, and university decturer in philosophy, Oxford
university, 1948–63; honorary fellow of St. Anne's College from 1963; lec-
turer, Royal College of Art, London, 1963–67. Recipient: James Tait Black
Memorial prize, 1974; Whitbread award, 1974; Booker prize, 1978;
Shakespeare prize (Hamburg), 1988; National Arts Club (U.S.A.) medal of
honor, 1990. D. Litt.: Oxford University, 1987. Member, Irish Academy,
1970; honorary member, American Academy, 1975, and American Academy
of Arts and Sciences, 1982; honorary fellow, Somerville College, 1977, and
Newnham College, 1986. Companion of literature, Royal Society of
Literature, 1987. C.B.E. (Commander, Order of the British Empire), 1976;
D.B.E. (Dame Commander, Order of the British Empire), 1987. Lives in
Oxford. Agent: Ed Victor Ltd., 162 Wardour Street, London W1V 3AT,
England.

Publications

PLAYS

A Severed Head, with J.B. Priestley, adaptation of the novel by Murdoch
(produced 1963). 1964.
The Italian Girl, with James Saunders, adaptation of the novel by Murdoch
(produced 1967). 1969.
The Servants and the Snow (produced 1970). With *The Three Arrows*, 1973.
The Three Arrows (produced 1972). With *The Servants and the Snow*, 1973.

Art and Eros (produced 1980). In *Acastos*, 1986.

The Servants (opera libretto), adaptation of her play *The Servants and the Snow*, music by William Mathias (produced 1980).

Acastos: Two Platonic Dialogues (includes *Art and Eros* and *Above the Gods*). 1986.

The Black Prince, adaptation of her own novel (produced 1989). In *Three Plays*, 1989.

Three Plays (includes *The Servants and the Snow, The Three Arrows, The Black Prince*). 1989.

RADIO PLAY: *The One Alone* (in verse), music by Gary Carpenter, 1987.

NOVELS

Under the Net. 1954.
The Flight from the Enchanter. 1956.
The Sandcastle. 1957.
The Bell. 1958.
A Severed Head. 1961.
An Unofficial Rose. 1962.
The Unicorn. 1963.
The Italian Girl. 1964.
The Red and the Green. 1965.
The Time of the Angels. 1966.
The Nice and the Good. 1968.
Bruno's Dream. 1969.
A Fairly Honourable Defeat. 1970.
An Accidental Man. 1972.
The Black Prince. 1973.
The Sacred and Profane Love Machine. 1974.
A Word Child. 1975.
Henry and Cato. 1976.
The Sea, The Sea. 1978.
Nuns and Soldiers. 1980.
The Philosopher's Pupil. 1983.
The Good Apprentice. 1985.
The Book and the Brotherhood. 1987.
The Message to the Planet. 1989.
The Green Knight. 1993.

VERSE

A Year of Birds. 1978.

OTHER

Sartre, Romantic Rationalist. 1953; as *Sartre, Romantic Realist*, 1980.
The Sovereignty of Good over Other Concepts (lecture). 1967.
The Sovereignty of Good (essays). 1970.

The Fire and the Sun: Why Plato Banished the Artists. 1977.
Reynolds Stone (address).   1981.
*The Existential Political Myth.*1989.
Metaphysics as a Guide to Morals. 1992.

BIBLIOGRAPHY: *Iris Murdoch and Muriel Spark: A Bibliography* by Thomas T. Tominaga and Wilma Schneidermeyer, 1976; *Iris Murdoch: A Reference Guide* by Kate Begnal, 1987.

MANUSCRIPT COLLECTION: University of Iowa, Iowa City.

CRITICAL STUDIES: *Iris Murdoch* by Rubin Rabinovitz, 1968, *Iris Murdoch* by Frank Baldanza, 1974; *Iris Murdoch* by Donna Gerstenberger, 1974; *Iris Murdoch: The Shakespearian Interest,* 1979, and *Iris Murdoch,* 1984, both by Richard Todd, and *Encounters with Iris Murdoch* edited by Todd, 1988; *Iris Murdoch: Work for the Spirit* by Elizabeth Dipple, 1981; *Iris Murdoch's Comic Vision* by Angela Hague, 1984; *Iris Murdoch: The Saint and the Artist* by Peter J. Conradi, 1986; *Iris Murdoch* edited by Harold Bloom, 1986; *A Character Index and Guide to the Fiction of Iris Murdoch* by Cheryl K. Bove, 1986; *Iris Murdoch* by Deborah Johnson, 1987; *Iris Murdoch: Figures of Good* by Suguna Ramanathan, 1990.

Iris Murdoch has published one volume of plays, *Three Plays,* which includes *The Servants and the Snow, The Three Arrows,* and her adaptation of her novel *The Black Prince.* In addition, she has published *Acastos,* a volume containing two philosophical plays in the form of Platonic dialogues, *Art and Eros* and *Above the Gods.* The drama critic Harold Hobson praised Andrew Cruickshank's performance of *Art and Eros,* saying that he conducted "a Socratic enquiry with philosophic zeal and illuminating theatrical skill." *Above the Gods* inquires into the differences between morality and religion. Murdoch wrote both her Platonic plays so that they could be performed either in modern dress or in period costume. In a period version of *Above the Gods,* she suggests casting the servant as a black man born of a Nubian mother. This choice on her part shows her willingness to unsettle a modern British audience, questioning religion, values, British ideas of empire, and slavery. Before Murdoch tried her own playwriting, she collaborated with J.B. Priestley in the stage adaptation of her novel *A Severed Head,* and with James Saunders on the adaptation of *The Italian Girl.* The experienced hands of her collaborators made these plays more actable than her own later ones—indeed, *A Severed Head* was a theatrical success. Her play *The Black Prince* is her first attempt to adapt one of her own novels into a play without the benefits of an experienced theatrical collaborator. It is a witty, fast-paced drama, about love, death and art that testifies to her sure hand as a master of the dramatic as well as the narrative mode.

The play version of *A Severed Head* diminishes the complexity and obscurity of Murdoch's novel while it preserves its zany, quick-paced, very British high comedy. Physical farce, unexpected entrances, surprise discoveries, and unanticipated twists of plot all contribute to the effect. In "Against Dryness," Murdoch described her own novel as one in which Sartre's "facile idea of sincerity" is tested against the "hard idea of truth." When Martin is confronted by his wife's affair with her analyst, he tries broadmindedly to take it in his stride. Unwilling to confess his own affair, and himself attracted to the American analyst, he suffers passively as his wife flaunts her infatuation and asks his approval of her plan to move into her lover's home. It takes Honor Klein, the half-sister of the analyst and a Cambridge anthropologist, to function as the "dark god" of this play. Manipulating all the other characters, she forces Martin to submit to irrational and primitive forces, to understand the "hard idea of truth," and to give himself over to his love for her, however temporary and however imperfectly understood. The play rivals Restoration comedy in the variety of its sexual pairings. Martin passes through the stages of the outraged husband, latently homosexual lover to his wife's lover, complacent cuckold, violent lover, and lover surrendering to a higher, more mysterious, primitive love. Variations of incest are explored in the relationship between Honor and her half-brother and Antonia and her brother-in-law. In many ways *A Severed Head* is a modern *The Cocktail Party*. T. S. Eliot's one-eyed Reilly becomes Murdoch's Honor Klein. Both plays examine religious feeling and neurotic obsessions.

Murdoch's other plays, with the exception of *The Black Prince*, confirm that her gifts are as a novelist; nevertheless, they are also interesting in their own right. In her novels, Murdoch the storyteller and Murdoch the moral philosopher, struggling with ideas of freedom and contingency and accident and pattern, live fairly comfortably together. In her plays, the two fight each other and conspire to flatten her characters in ways that the novel can accommodate or avoid. She is often unable to find the dialogue that believably captures her hybrid characters—half-mythic, half-natural. She strikes the best balance in *The Black Prince* but she does so at the expense of her intellectual inquiry into the nature of art, love, and ethics.

The Servants and the Snow is a compact play which, like Strindberg's *Miss Julie*, depends for its effect on the pressure that the environment and past exert on the characters. The snow madness imprisons the characters; it covers and holds the blood guilt of the past. Basil, a landowner who returns to the isolated country house of his father who has died six months earlier, finds himself accountable for his father's crimes. He feels unequal to the task of being master to his 200 or more servants. Too anxious to play benevolent master, and too scrupulously "sincere" in his efforts to examine his own situation and motives, he finds himself forced to atone for his father's affair with a servant girl, Marina, which led to the death of the girl's husband at the hand of her jealous master. To prevent the erosion of his own authority, Basil is persuaded to re-enact his father's crime—to deflower the servant girl on her nuptial night. Neither Marina nor Oriane can tolerate weak men. Like the girl in Sylvia Plath's poem "Daddy," they prefer the "boot in the face" administered by the brute Daddy/husband. Marina consents to the marriage because it will figuratively give her back her dead master and dead husband. Oriane loathes Basil's sentimentality and misguided sense of guilt and cannot abide the injury to her pride posed by Marina. In a jealous rage, Oriane kills her husband during Marina's wedding vows and welcomes the arrival of her brother, the General, who knows how to treat servants as swine and give commands. The play examines the nature of power and the relationship of past to present. It also examines moral character. The final action fulfills Murdoch's ideas about accident and free will, but it cannot wholly contain the ideas. The characters in the play are too reductive.

The Three Arrows depends heavily for its effect upon ritual action and theatricality. Some of its moments are brilliant. Set in medieval Japan, the play explores the choices available to Prince Yorimitsu, a political prisoner held captive by the Emperor and a pawn of the Shogun, the real ruler. Yorimitsu's avowed ambition is to be a leader of the forces of the North and seize the power of the Shogun. The play abounds with deceits and stratagems. Necessity conspires to defeat moral purpose and free will. Yorimitsu is forced to choose between the contemplative life, an honorable death, love, or his ambition for power. The choices he ultimately exercises are constrained: he acts without properly knowing the motives of those who act against him, or understanding the meaning of the choices put to him. At the end of the play he is free, the Shogun dead, the princess he loved dead, and the young Emperor the willing accomplice in his escape. Intellectually the play is fascinating, but its plot unfolds too slowly and the motives behind certain actions are incompletely conceptualized.

Murdoch's most recent play, presented at the Aldwych Theatre in 1989 to considerable critical acclaim, is adapted from one of her finest and most difficult novels, a novel more novelistic than any she has written. Offering her most protracted and penetrating examination of aesthetics and the relation of art to human behavior, The Black Prince is a highly self-reflexive and elaborately mediated novel. It tells the story of Bradley Pearson, a fussy, aging, recently retired taxman and blocked writer, and his ordeal with love and art. It is introduced by two forewords and concluded by five postscripts, four written by the principal dramatic characters: Christian, Pearson's ex-wife; Francis, his "unfrocked" physician brother-in-law; Rachel, the battered and vengeful wife of Pearson's literary rival, Arnold Baffin, and mother of Julian; and Julian, the Baffin's 20-year-old daughter with whom the 58-year-old Pearson (53 in the play version) falls absolutely in love. The fifth postscript is written by Pearson's mysterious editor and cell-mate, Loxias, his alter ego and muse, the god Apollo in disguise, who finally compels Pearson to answer to Apollonian truth and goodness, replacing the dark creative god Eros with the higher god Apollo. Murdoch's play could hardly do justice to the intricacy of the novel's struggle with form and formlessness. She does, in her play version, combine the dramatic and narrative modes, allowing Pearson to step forward and address the audience directly, with veiled references to his final transformation. She also concludes the play with an epilogue where four characters offer their highly eschewed and self-serving interpretations of the play's central action, the murder of Baffin. Notably missing from the play is any reference to Loxias, the editor and Apollo figure. No doubt Murdoch's instincts were right in this regard. The novelistic techniques and the ambiguous, often tortuous structure, could not but damage the play. She does treat the theme of The Black Prince in her play version, developing the relationship between Julian, decked out in her Hamlet costume, and Hamlet, and also enabling the audience to understand the relationship of Bradley Pearson's struggle to write with Shakespeare's. However, without a familiarity with the novel these references in the play may not adequately convey the theme. What does succeed, and very well, is her highly comic and ironic treatment of the three interwoven crises: Pearson's struggles with his sister's failed marriage and suicide; his rivalry with Baffin, over both women and art; and his immersion in his love for Julian which leads to the play's denouement, Rachel's murder of Baffin for which Pearson is tried and convicted.

Murdoch's wit and irony and gift for character, her fondness for patterning and artifice, serve her well when she adapts her novels for the stage.

—Carol Simpson Stern

MURPHY, Tom (Thomas Murphy).

Born in Tuam, County Galway, 23 February 1935. Educated at Vocational School, Tuam; Vocational Teachers' Training College, Dublin. Married Mary Hippisley; three children. Apprentice fitter and welder, Tuam, 1953–55; engineering teacher, Vocational School, Mountbellow, County Galway, 1957–62. Actor and director, 1951–62. Member of the Board of Directors, 1972–83, and since 1986 writer-in-association, Irish National Theatre (Abbey Theatre), Dublin; Regents lecturer, University of California, Santa Barbara, 1981; writer-in-association, Druid Theatre, Galway, 1983–85. Founding member, Moli Productions, Dublin, 1974. Recipient: Irish Academy of Letters award, 1972; Independent Newspapers award, 1983; Harvey's award, 1983, 1986; *Sunday Tribune* award, 1985. Member, Irish Academy of Letters, 1982, and Aosdána, 1984. Agent: Alexandra Cann Representation, 68E Redcliffe Gardens, London SW10 9HE, England; and, Bridget Aschenberg, International Creative Management, 40 West 57th Street, New York, New York 10019, U.S.A. Address: 46 Terenure Road West, Dublin 6, Ireland.

Publications

PLAYS

On the Outside, with Noel O'Donoghue (produced 1961). With *On the Inside*, 1976; in *A Whistle in the Dark and Other Plays*, 1989.
A Whistle in the Dark (produced 1961). 1971; in *A Whistle in the Dark and Other Plays*, 1989.
Famine (produced 1966). 1977; in *Plays: One*, 1992.
The Fooleen (as *A Crucial Week in the Life of a Grocer's Assistant*, televised 1967; as *The Fooleen*, produced 1969). 1970; as *A Crucial Week in the Life of a Grocer's Assistant*, in *A Whistle in the Dark and Other Plays*, 1989.
The Orphans (produced 1968). 1974.
The Morning after Optimism (produced 1971). 1973.
The White House (produced 1972).
On the Inside (also director: produced 1974). With *On the Outside*, 1976; in *A Whistle in the Dark and Other Plays*, 1989.
The Vicar of Wakefield, adaptation of the novel by Goldsmith (produced 1974).
The Sanctuary Lamp (produced 1975). 1976; revised version, 1984.
The J. Arthur Maginnis Story (produced 1976).
Conversations on a Homecoming (televised 1976; produced 1985). 1986; in *After Tragedy*, 1988.

Epitaph under Ether (also director: produced 1979).
The Blue Macushla (produced 1980). In *Plays: One*, 1992.
The Informer, adaptation of the novel by Liam O'Flaherty (also director: produced 1981).
She Stoops to Conquer, adaptation of the play by Goldsmith (produced 1982).
The Gigli Concert (produced 1983). 1984; in *After Tragedy*, 1988.
Bailegangáire (produced 1985). 1986; included in *After Tragedy*, 1988.
A Thief of a Christmas (produced 1985). In *Plays: Two*, 1993.
After Tragedy: Three Irish Plays (includes *The Gigli Concert, Conversations on a Homecoming, Bailegangáire*). 1988.
A Whistle in the Dark and Other Plays (includes *A Crucial Week in the Life of a Grocer's Assistant, On the Outside, On the Inside*). 1989.
Too Late for Logic (produced 1989). 1990
The Patriot Game (produced 1991). In *Plays: One*, 1992.
Plays: One (includes *Famine, The Patriot Game, The Blue Macushla*). 1992.
Plays: Two (includes *Bailegangáire, Conversations on a Homecoming, A Thief of a Christmas*). 1993.

TELEVISION PLAYS: *The Fly Sham*, 1963; *Veronica*, 1963; *A Crucial Week in the Life of a Grocer's Assistant*, 1967; *Snakes and Reptiles*, 1968; *Young Man in Trouble*, 1970; *The Moral Force, The Policy, Relief* (trilogy), 1973; *Conversations on a Homecoming*, 1976; *Speeches of Farewell*, 1976; *Bridgit*, 1981; *Fatalism*, 1981.

BIBLIOGRAPHY: *Ten Modern Irish Playwrights* by Kimball King, 1979.

CRITICAL STUDIES: "Thomas Murphy Issue" of *Irish University Review*, Spring 1987; *The Politics of Magic: The Work and Times of Tom Murphy* by Fintan O'Toole, 1987.

THEATRICAL ACTIVITIES
DIRECTOR: **Plays**—*On the Outside/On the Inside*, 1974; *Famine*, 1978; *The Well of the Saints* by J.M. Synge, 1979; *Epitaph under Ether*, 1979; *The Informer*, 1981.

Tom Murphy comments:

My plays attempt to recreate the feeling or the mood of life rather than to represent it: they attempt to create something that can be identified with, felt or recognised. The emotional and/or spiritual truth is, if anything, more important than the intellectual truth. The mood can be the theme of the play.

Apart from *A Whistle in the Dark*, which made Kenneth Tynan and other notables sit up in the early 1960s, Tom Murphy's plays have not won the international recognition they deserve. It is significant that when *Conversations on a Homecoming* was staged by the Galway Druid Theatre Company at the Pepsico International Arts Festival in New York in 1986 he was spoken of in reviews as if he were new on the scene.

The main reason for this unwarranted neglect internationally seems to lie in Murphy's exploration of themes that are particularly (though not exclusively) Irish, in a form that uncompromisingly makes strenuous demands on audiences. A typical Murphy play, while not necessarily set in Dublin and possibly as vague in setting as the dreamlike forest in *The Morning after Optimism*, is occupied with a spiritual deprivation and a social humiliation that are endemically Irish. The grounding, the "objective correlative," is invariably a situation potentially explosive, deriving from feelings powerfully responsive to defects in a particular community, society, or national institution. Unless one is familiar with the grounding, the plays may appear obscure or the level of feeling inexplicably intense, and the language (Murphy's strongest weapon) perhaps in excess of the apparent facts. This is to say that atmosphere and mood are of primary importance. For example, *The Sanctuary Lamp*, to the puzzlement of some British reviewers covering the Dublin Theatre Festival in 1975, caused disturbance among its first audiences at the Abbey Theatre, and comparison was made with the initial impact of O'Casey's *The Plough and the Stars* (1926), when riots occurred. Murphy's play was regarded by some as highly blasphemous. The satiric and iconoclastic feelings released in it arise out of a church setting, taken over by three outcast characters, Harry and Francisco, who used to have a circus act of a sleazy nature, and Maudie, a runaway orphan frightened into believing that Jesus has taken away her baby because she is bad. Francisco has pursued Harry for defecting, and to spring upon him the shattering news that Harry's wife, who formed part of their dubious circus act in rich people's houses, is dead from an overdose of drugs. Harry, for his part, is heart-sick at the death of his little daughter Teresa, and is burning with feelings of revenge against life and God. He takes the job of sacristan and custodian of the lamp that signifies the divine presence. When Francisco arrives pursuing the fugitive from himself, they argue in the locked church at night over the effects on their lives of the "metaphysical monster" the Catholic Church. With a bottle of altar wine in one hand Francisco delivers from the pulpit his bitter jeremiad against contemporary Catholicism. But when all passion's spent, the three characters settle down for the night in a confession box, forming a fellowship against the dark, and tending the lamp as a gesture of human rather than of divine presence.

Murphy's plays, besides being uncompromising as passionate indictments of hypocrisy of every kind, are also theatrically demanding. Some, such as the historical drama *Famine*, are almost unrelieved Theatre of Cruelty. One of his best and most ambitious plays, *The Gigli Concert*, ran for three and a half hours at the Abbey Theatre, and Murphy refused at that time to cut it. The director and cast of such plays face huge problems, but overcoming them has provided the Irish theatre with some of its greatest achievements in the 1970s and early 1980s. *The Gigli Concert* may be described as a fantastic reworking of the Faust story so as to explore and express in contemporary terms the nature of damnation and of magical release. The plot centres on a self-made Irish millionaire's visit during a mental breakdown to one J.P.W. King, a professed "dynamatologist," actually an abandoned practitioner of an American quasi-science. The "patient" wants to sing like Beniamino Gigli. It is an obsession arising from recurring depression caused by guilt. In this regard he could be compared with Ibsen's Solness (*The Master Builder*) and

Osborne's Maitland (*Inadmissible Evidence*). King gets caught up in the pursuit of this impossible ambition and Gigli's voice, on record, begins to fascinate him also. "He's the devil!" the Irish Man warns him. But when the latter backs away, preferring to return to society with all his neuroses intact, and King's Gretchen figure has told him she is dying of cancer, while Helen accuses him of making obscene telephone calls, King feels compelled to go on with the mad scheme of trying himself to sing like Gigli. He turns to conjuring and in a theatrically challenging scene he manages to bring off the impossible: the "magic" of theatre and its illusion allows the audience to believe that this hopeless case has transcended the barriers of the normal. King then plugs in the cassette player once more and pressing the repeat button lets Gigli sing on forever while he takes off elsewhere.

Bailegangáire, another extraordinary play, breaks new ground. Written when Murphy was playwright-in-association at the Druid Theatre in Galway, it has a good deal of Irish (i.e., Gaelic) words and phrases and it deals with Irish tragic material in a style that seems to marry Synge and Beckett. The play combines two levels and two situations in two time periods. On one level an old woman, Mommo, raves in a senile manner in bed, endlessly telling a story of a tragic event in her history, but never finishing the tale. On another level her granddaughters, Mary and Dolly, while caring for her try at the same time to come to terms with their own lives. Often their conversations take place while Mommo raves on at the same time. Each of the women is in fact trying to seize hold of her life, but it happens that Mommo holds the key to the happiness of all three. Mary, the nurse, realising that Mommo's obsession with the story relates to her own need to shape her life, forces her to finish the tale for the first time. It concerns a laughing contest in which Mommo's husband won over a local champion but caused his death and subsequently the death of another grandchild. The full facts have the effect of drawing Mary and Dolly closer to Mommo, and, rather like the three characters who settle down for the night at the end of *The Sanctuary Lamp*, these three women settle down in Mommo's bed and, in knowledge and understanding, find peace. The beautiful and moving ending was powerfully rendered by Siobhan McKenna as Mommo in the first production, which travelled to the Donmar Warehouse, London, in 1986. The play, while being well received, was found to be somewhat mystifying to some English reviewers, who could make sense of it only as allegory, with Mommo as Ireland obsessed with her history.

Too Late for Logic tried to consolidate the new direction Murphy began to take with *The Gigli Concert*, towards what he calls "after tragedy." These later plays tend to move beyond tragedy into a mood of acceptance. A new attitude towards women, now dramatised as holding the key to sanity and survival, is still developing in Murphy's work. *Too Late for Logic* is in one sense merely a play about the suicide of an academic too bound up in Schopenhauer; but in a wider sense the play explores how Christopher might have learned from the women in his life. Instructive as this learning process may be it lacks the dramatic fire of Murphy's earlier plays, since the form chosen is to begin with the suicide of Christopher and make him the observer of his own self-defeat. It remains to be seen if Murphy can move beyond this self-obsessed phase and integrate his new quasi-feminist sympathies with dramatic inventiveness.

Murphy's only serious rival among his Irish contemporaries is Brian Friel, who in a programme note for *The Blue Macushla* paid tribute to Murphy's unique talent, his restless and uncompromising imagination. By his refusal to write the popular play, and by his digging afresh every time into the daunting recesses of passion and folly, Murphy has shown himself to be one of the best, if the most unpredictable, of modern Irish dramatists.

—Christopher Murray

N

NEWMAN, G(ordon) F.

Born in Kent in 1947. Married to Rebecca Hall; two children. Recipient: BAFTA award, 1992. Agent: Elaine Steel, 21 Brookfield, 5 Highgate Hill West, London N6 6AS. Address: Wessington Court, Woolhope, Hereford, HR1 4QN, England.

Publications

PLAYS

Operation Bad Apple (produced 1982). 1982.
An Honourable Trade (produced 1984). 1984.
The Testing Ground, from his own novel (produced 1989).

SCREENPLAY: *Number One*, 1985.

TELEVISION PLAYS: *Law and Order* series, 1978; *Billy*, 1979; *The Nation's Health*, 1984; *1996*, 1989; *Here Is the News*, 1990; *For the Greater Good*, 1991; *Black and Blue*, 1992.

NOVELS

Sir, You Bastard. 1970; as *Rogue Cop*, 1973.
Billy: A Family Tragedy. 1972.
The Player and the Guest. 1972.
The Abduction. 1972.
You Nice Bastard. 1972.
Three Professional Ladies. 1973.
The Split. 1974.
The Price. 1974.
You Flash Bastard. 1974.
The Streetfighter. 1975.
A Detective's Tale. 1977.
The Guvnor. 1977; as *Trade-Off*, 1979.
A Prisoner's Tale. 1977.
A Villain's Tale. 1977.
The List. 1979.
The Obsession. 1980.
Charlie and Joanna. 1981.
The Men with the Guns. 1982.

The Nation's Health. 1983.
Law and Order. 1983.
Set a Thief. 1986.
The Testing Ground. 1987.
Trading the Future. 1992.

G.F. Newman comments:

I declare myself to be a radical vegan (pure vegetarian), one who has hitherto
sought to change corrupt and oppressive institutions through political ideas.
But lately I've realised that change comes only from the heart of man (and
woman), rather than as a consequence of the political clothes he wears. It
comes when we recognise a true ideal and are brave enough to run with it;
when we see truth and are strong enough to stand and defend it. Recognising
that the exploitation of one species paves the way to the exploitation of all
others is such a truth; acknowledging the interconnectedness of all living
creatures on this planet is such an ideal. If we want to change society, if we
want a fairer, more just, more compassionate society, first we must extend
justice and compassion beyond our immediate family and our own kind to
every living creature. Until we do so we will never be without racial or national
or sexual strife; we will never sustain lasting beneficial change. To every action
there is reaction; our troubled human condition is largely the result of what we
do to the "other nations" who share this earth with us. If there were political
solutions to be had we would almost certainly have them by now, and all of
our problems would have been legislated away. Due process is part of the
problem, not the solution; only when we gain self-recognition will we start to
approach solutions. In my work I strive to create mirrors that reflect some of
the problems that confront us to help me gain self-recognition.

G.F. Newman is known above all as the author of fiction, and though he has
turned to dramatic form from time to time, it is not in the theatre that he has
made his name. On television, his *The Nation's Health* and *Law and Order*,
for instance, created quite a stir, but that was more on account of their highly
controversial content than because of specifically dramatic qualities, and the
published versions take the form of novels.

  Operation Bad Apple, which was given its first performance at the Royal
Court Theatre, London, on 4 February 1982, reveals both the strengths and
weaknesses of Newman as a dramatist. There is a sense of commitment which
has to be respected, and the action moves speedily to make its points. The play
shares with several of Newman's novels the central character of Detective
Chief Inspector Terry Sneed, and indeed the whole work might be well thought
of as a deft dramatisation of an episode from his chronicles of the world of
"bent" London coppers, which had special relevance at the time. The first
scene introduces the theme of the investigation, by police drafted in from
Wiltshire, of complaints about possible misconduct in the Metropolitan Police.
It is not long before we come to appreciate that there is indeed genuine cause
for concern. As the investigators fret about the impact on their family lives of a
lengthy absence from home in the debilitating moral atmosphere of the capital,

they come into contact with corruption at every level, with brutal policemen abusing their power both in their relationships with brother officers and with the criminal classes. What becomes increasingly plain, however, is the fact that the powerful and cynical Sneed is the most guilty of all the policemen, though his subordinates too are portrayed as disreputable, grasping, and cowardly. To conclude this disheartening drama Newman offers a scene in which two pillars of the establishment are seen out on a golf-course organising a totally immoral cover-up in an effort to avert any criticism of the status quo.

The effect is certainly striking, but there is no escaping the feeling that Newman is rather too keen to shock by exposing what he plainly feels are the disgraceful inadequacies of the police force. No doubt he has a point, but a little more balance and perspective might be fairer and would certainly make for better drama because the audience would not have quite the same feeling of being pushed in one direction.

The dramatic style of the play is fluid, cutting swiftly from one brief scene to the next, almost in cinematic style, and with the audience largely left to make sense of the juxtapositions without formal explanations. Characters are used functionally, rather than developed for their own sake, and there is a certain reliance on social type which is in harmony with the general thrust of a play that shows, in many ways, more interest in groups and classes than in people as such. Some quite lengthy speeches are the expression of the way certain individuals impose their will on those around them. The incessant use of bad language, which some might regard simply as realistic, also serves as an effective and constant reminder of moral degradation.

—Christopher Smith

NICHOLS, Peter (Richard).

Born in Bristol, 31 July 1927. Educated at Bristol Grammar School, 1936–44; Bristol Old Vic Theatre School, 1948–50; Trent Park Teachers' Training College, Hertfordshire, 1955–57. Served in the Royal Air Force, 1945–48. Married Thelma Reed in 1959; three daughters (one deceased) and one son. Actor, in repertory, television, and films, 1950–55; teacher in primary and secondary schools, 1957–59; has also worked as a park keeper, English language teacher in Italy, cinema commissionaire, and clerk. Visiting playwright, Guthrie Theatre, Minneapolis, 1977. Governor, Greenwich Theatre, London, 1970–76; member, Arts Council Drama Panel, 1972–75. Recipient: Arts Council bursary, 1961; *Evening Standard* award, 1967, 1969, 1978, 1982, 1985; John Whiting award, 1968; Ivor Novello award, 1977; Society of West End Theatre award, 1978, 1982; Tony award, 1985; New York Drama Critics Circle award, 1989. Fellow, Royal Society of Literature, 1983. Agent: Casarotto Ramsay Ltd., National House, 60–66 Wardour Street, London W1V 3HP. Address: The Old Rectory, Hopesay, Craven Arms, Shropshire SY7 8HD, England.

Publications

PLAYS

Promenade (televised 1959). In *Six Granada Plays*, 1960.
Ben Spray (televised 1961). In *New Granada Plays*, 1961.

The Hooded Terror (televised 1963; produced 1964).
A Day in the Death of Joe Egg (produced 1967). 1967; as *Joe Egg*, 1967.
The Gorge (televised 1968). In *The Television Dramatist*, edited by Robert Muller, 1973.
The National Health; or, Nurse Norton's Affair (produced 1969). 1970.
Hearts and Flowers (televised 1970). In *Plays 1*, 1987.
Forget-Me-Not Lane (produced 1971). 1971.
Neither Up nor Down (produced 1972). In *Plays 1*, 1987.
The Common (televised 1973). Revised version in *Plays 1*, 1987.
Chez Nous (produced 1974). 1974.
The Freeway (produced 1974). 1975.
Harding's Luck, adaptation of the novel by E. Nesbit (produced 1974).
Privates on Parade (produced 1977). 1977.
Born in the Gardens (also director: produced 1979). 1980.
Passion Play (produced 1981). 1981; as *Passion* (produced 1983), 1983.
Poppy, music by Monty Norman (produced 1982). 1982.
Privates on Parade (screenplay). 1983.
A Piece of My Mind (produced 1987).
Plays 1 (includes *Forget-Me-Not Lane, Hearts and Flowers, Neither Up nor Down, Chez Nous*, The *Common* revised version, *Privates on Parade*). 1987; revised edition, as *Plays: One* (includes *A Day in the Death of Joe Egg, The National Health, Forget-Me-Not Lane, Hearts and Flowers, The Freeway*), 1987.
Plays: Two (includes *Chez Nous, Privates on Parade, Born in the Gardens, Passion Play, Poppy*). 1990.

SCREENPLAYS: *Catch Us If You Can (Having a Wild Weekend)*, 1965; *Georgy Girl*, with Margaret Forster, 1966; *A Day in the Death of Joe Egg*, 1972; *The National Health*, 1973; *Privates on Parade*, 1983; *Changing Places*, 1984.

TELEVISION PLAYS: *Walk on the Grass*, 1959; *After All*, with Bernie Cooper, 1959; *Promenade*, 1959; *Ben Spray*, 1961; *The Big Boys*, 1961; *The Reception*, 1961; *The Heart of the Country*, 1962; *Ben Again*, 1963; *The Hooded Terror*, 1963; *The Continuity Man*, 1963; *The Brick Umbrella*, 1964; *When the Wind Blows*, 1965; *The Gorge*, 1968; *Majesty*, from a story by F. Scott Fitzgerald, 1968; *Winner Takes All*, from a story by Evelyn Waugh, 1968; *Daddy Kiss It Better*, 1968; *Hearts and Flowers*, 1970; *The Common*, 1973.

OTHER
Feeling You're Behind: An Autobiography. 1984.

CRITICAL STUDIES: *The Second Wave* by John Russell Taylor, 1971; interview in *Playback 2* by Ronald Hayman, 1973; *The New British Drama* by Oleg Kerensky, 1977; *British Television Drama* edited by George W. Brandt, 1981; *Landmarks of Modern British Drama: The Seventies* edited by Roger Cornish and Violet Ketels, 1986.

THEATRICAL ACTIVITIES
DIRECTOR: **Plays**—*A Day in the Death of Joe Egg*, 1971; *The National Health*, 1977; *Born in the Gardens*, 1979; *Forget-Me-Not Lane*, 1990.

Few dramatists have had more success than Peter Nichols in making their characters reveal their attitudes towards a problem, towards each other, towards society; and in this media age, when everyone's opinion is solicited, known, and categorized, the writer who is an artist at encapsulating attitude is likely to achieve wide popularity.

In, for example, *A Day in the Death of Joe Egg*, Nichols demonstrates admirably his ability to deal with a forbidden subject (in 1967), that of the paraplegic, the spastic, the "vegetable" (referred to in many ways during the course of the play). There was a surge of approval as a new barrier of inhibition was swept away: this is very flattering to an audience. Nichols manages to present an uncomfortable subject in a kind of hectic, hectoring way that is contrived not to offend. He incorporated every possible range of emotional response. We come away feeling there's something in the problem for all of us.

Nichols's jokes always cut near the bone, and in the revival of *Joe Egg*, directed by the author himself, one sometimes had the feeling there was no bone left to cut near. Possibly there may be something too quiescent at the back of the parents' games. They constantly exercise their instantly dismissable feelings at the expense of their "problem." Sometimes, one feels, a sustained and heartfelt cry of pain might be more cathartic. But pain is not an attitude. The main reservation concerns the theme. One looks in vain for some guiding idea to capture the imagination. Here and there Nichols throws in a possibility, as when, for instance, he points out that we are all cripples in some way, all limited. While the peripheries of the problem never relax their hold, a central issue obstinately fails to materialize. Nichols's method is to touch upon all, moving forward with brittle and lightning force in case he loses his audience.

The National Health, produced at the National Theatre in 1969, combines many Anouilhesque qualities and shortcomings. Half of this play is a comic comment on the human race, the conclusion being that each of us is entitled to his own death—half a gallop through every known attitude to health. The result has a lively spontaneous progress, is well-organized, but, ultimately, on the thin side.

In *Forget-Me-Not Lane* the debt to Anouilh appears even greater, as a middle-aged man asks himself what went wrong in his marriages and re-examines his childhood and his life with his parents during World War II. The device of shuttling the action back and forth between past and present results in much high comedy and some sharp theatrical moments. *Chez Nous* presents the much-trodden situation of two friendly married couples, Dick and Liz, Diana and Phil, on holiday in the Dordogne, who are driven to the brink of splitting up. The marital tug of war that we have already seen in *Joe Egg* and *Forget-Me-Not Lane* is organized in greater depth and comic intensity than Nichols has used previously, and in his presentation of the boulevard twist of fate—that Dick's daughter has given birth to Phil's son—Nichols pulls off a memorable *coup de théâtre*. Some critics found it highly improbable, but the combination of artificiality and the earthy—even squalid—way the couples express themselves towards each other produces an enjoyable, if not exactly profound, sense of truth.

In *Passion Play* Nichols drives even more relentlessly down the path of adultery by a device of splitting the main characters, Eleanor and James, into double identities (a device similar to that of Brian Friel in *Philadelphia, Here I Come!*). Again it's the many-sidedness of life he attempts to pay tribute to, but what promises much by way of exploring the inner states of the pair never lives up to expectations. No larger vision appears than that of lost apes in pursuit of ultimate sexiness: this may, of course, be sound comment, or may equally point to the shortcoming that virtuosity has become an end in itself.

With minor plays such as *The Freeway* Nichols returns to the episodic comic style of *The National Health*, though with less success. A great motorway (the FI) has been built running North to South, and in a week-end jam a number of marooned motorists commingle in the form of a glorified variety entertainment. Though there is some sharply observed satire, we seem, like the cars themselves, not to arrive anywhere in particular. But by the same token, *Privates on Parade* succeeds admirably. It is a mixture of cynical squaddie comment and concert routines of an army entertainment troupe around 1950, and in it Nichols again demonstrates his skill as pure entertainer. *Harding's Luck* is a straightforward adaptation of E. Nesbit's children's novel, using the author as narrator. The central character is Dickie, the crippled urchin from Deptford. He is elevated by the hospitality of a genteel family, finds out he is well-connected, and finally is submitted to a magical transformation backwards in time—from an Edwardian childhood into a Jacobean youth.

Poppy is an ambitious attempt to do with pantomime convention what *Privates on Parade* did with the concert party, but it is much less successful. Taking as his subject the Opium Wars in mid-19th-century China, Nichols satirizes British imperial commercialism in a mixture of styles, and reveals, ultimately, that he has little that is vitally comic or original to add to what became a hackneyed target for entertainers in the 1980s.

—Garry O'Connor

See the essay on *A Day in the Death of Joe Egg*.

NKOSI, Lewis.

Born in Durban, South Africa, 5 December 1936. Educated at public schools in Durban; Zulu Lutheran High School; M.L. Sultan Technical College, Durban, 1961–62; Harvard University, Cambridge, Massachusetts (Nieman Fellow), 1962–63. Married Bronwyn Ollerenshaw in 1965; twin daughters. Staff member, *Ilanga Lase Natal* (Zulu newspaper), Durban, 1955–56, *Drum* magazine and *Golden City Post*, Johannesburg, 1956–60, and *South African Information Bulletin*, Paris, 1962–68; radio producer, BBC Transcription Centre, London, 1962–64; National Education Television interviewer, New York, 1963; literary editor, *New African* magazine, London, 1965–68; Regents lecturer on African Literature, University of California, Irvine, Spring 1971. Currently professor of English, University of Zambia, Lusaka. Recipient: Dakar Festival prize, for essays, 1965; C. Day Lewis fellowship,

1977; Macmillan Silver Pen award, 1987. Agent: Deborah Rogers, Rogers, Coleridge, and White Ltd., 20 Powis Mews, London W11 1JN, England. Address: Department of English, University of Zambia, P.O. Box 31338, Lusaka, Zambia.

Publications

PLAYS

The Rhythm of Violence (produced 1963). 1964; in *Plays from Black Africa*, edited by Fredric M. Litto, 1968.
Malcolm (televised 1967; produced 1972).
The Chameleon and the Lizard (libretto; produced 1971).

SCREENPLAY: *Come Back Africa*, 1959.

RADIO PLAYS: *The Trial*, 1969; *We Can't All Be Martin Luther King*, 1971.

TELEVISION PLAY: *Malcolm*, 1967.

NOVEL
Mating Birds. 1983.

OTHER
Home and Exile (essays). 1965; revised edition, 1983.
The Transplanted Heart: Essays on South Africa. 1975.
Tasks and Masks: Themes and Styles of African Literature. 1981.

THEATRICAL ACTIVITIES
ACTOR: **Play**—Father Higgins in *No-Good Friday* by Athol Fugard, 1958.

When Lewis Nkosi's *The Rhythm of Violence* was published in 1964 it was hailed as the first play by a black South African to appear in print since Herbert Dhlomo's *The Girl Who Killed to Save* (1935). Because of its sensitive handling of the explosive issues of South African racism the play was widely acclaimed and Nkosi was seen by some as being in the vanguard of a new black South African theatre. Since then Nkosi has published short stories and essays (a form in which he seems to excel), but his visible dramatic output has been limited to three radio and television plays.

Since the mid-1960s the immediacy of the South African situation, the terrific tensions it creates (which Nkosi himself has noted in his speculations on the dearth of recent plays and novels from South Africa), have made it difficult for the black South African writer to do anything other than the personal forms of essay, short story, and autobiography. Drama is written for an audience, and the stricter, though more subtle, laws which developed after the Sharpeville Massacre made it difficult for a mixed audience to come together in South Africa.

Thus we are left with only one major work in theatre on which to judge Nkosi, *The Rhythm of Violence*, an outstanding first play, an important one. There are some weaknesses in the play. Certain of the scenes tend to drag and some of the characters seem static, almost unreal—especially Tula and Sarie, the Zulu boy and Boer girl who are caught in the web of destruction. Nkosi's moral, however, that violence is mindless, that it destroys both the guilty and the innocent, and that violence begets more violence, is effectively acted out. Nkosi also does an excellent job in presenting the two Boer policemen, Jan and Piet, in such a way that we see beyond the harshness of their exterior into their confused souls. They are the most fully realized characters in the play and in one masterful scene, when Jan pretends to be a black politician and is carried away in his part ("You spoke just like a native communist," says Piet in a shocked voice), Nkosi makes it clear that the possibility for understanding between men does exist—unless the rhythm of violence prevents such understanding from developing.

—Joseph Bruchac

O

O'CASEY, Sean.

Born John Casey in Dublin, Ireland, 30 March 1880. Educated at schools in Dublin; lived in extreme poverty as a child. Married Eileen Carey Reynolds in 1927; two sons and one daughter. Worked in the stockroom of a hardware company from age 14; intermittently employed in clerical jobs; manual worker, Great Northern Railway, Ireland, 1901–11 (dismissed for union activities); wrote for nationalist and labour journals from 1907; member, Gaelic League, then Irish Republican Brotherhood, in the early 1900's; involved in the Dublin transport strike, 1913; resigned from the Irish Republican Brotherhood when they failed to support locked-out workers, and helped form the Irish Citizen Army, 1913–14 (primarily supported socialist, rather than nationalist, goals); associated with the Abbey Theatre, Dublin, 1923–28; moved to England, 1926; drama critic, *Time and Tide*, London, in the 1930s. Recipient: Hawthornden prize, 1926. *Died 18 September 1964.*

Publications

PLAYS

The Shadow of a Gunman (produced 1923). In *Two Plays*, 1925.
Cathleen Listens In: A Phantasy (produced 1923). In *Feathers from the Green Crow*, 1962.
Juno and the Paycock (produced 1924). In *Two Plays*, 1925.
Nannie's Night Out (produced 1924). In *Feathers from the Green Crow*, 1962.
Two Plays: Juno and the Paycock, The Shadow of a Gunman. 1925.
The Plough and the Stars (produced 1926). 1926.
The Silver Tassie (produced 1929). 1928.
Within the Gates (produced 1934). 1933; revised version in *Collected Plays 2*, 1949.
The End of the Beginning (produced 1937). In *Windfalls*, 1934.
A Pound on Demand (produced 1939). In *Windfalls*, 1934.
Five Irish Plays (includes *Juno and the Paycock; The Shadow of a Gunman; The Plough and the Stars; The End of the Beginning; A Pound on Demand*). 1935.
The Star Turns Red (produced 1943). 1940.
Purple Dust: A Wayward Comedy (produced 1943). 1940.
Red Roses for Me (produced 1943). 1942.
Oak Leaves and Lavender; or, A World on Wallpaper (produced 1947). 1946.

Cock-a-Doodle Dandy (produced 1949). 1949.
Collected Plays (4 vols.). 1949–51; augmented edition, as *The Complete Plays* (5 vols.), 1984.
Bedtime Story: An Anatole Burlesque (produced 1952). In *Collected Plays 4*, 1951.
Hall of Healing: A Sincerious Farce (produced 1952). In *Collected Plays 3*, 1951.
Time to Go: A Morality Comedy (produced 1952). In *Collected Plays 4*, 1951.
Selected Plays. 1954.
The Bishop's Bonfire (produced 1955). 1955.
Three Plays (includes *Juno and the Paycock; The Shadow of a Gunman; The Plough and the Stars*). 1957.
The Drums of Father Ned: A Mickrocosm of Ireland (produced 1959). 1960.
Behind the Green Curtains; Figuro in the Night; The Moon Shines on Kylenamoe: Three Plays. 1961.
The Moon Shines on Kylenamoe (produced 1962). In *Behind the Green Curtains . . .*, 1961.
Behind the Green Curtains (produced 1962). In *Behind the Green Curtains . . .*, 1961.
Figuro in the Night (produced 1962). In *Behind the Green Curtains . . .*, 1961.
Three More Plays. 1965.
The Harvest Festival. 1979.

SCREENPLAYS: *Juno and the Paycock* (*The Shame of Mary Boyle*), with Alma Reville and Alfred Hitchcock, 1929.

VERSE

Songs of the Wren (2 vols.). 1918.
More Wren Songs. 1918.

OTHER

The Story of Thomas Ashe. 1917(?).
The Sacrifice of Thomas Ashe. 1918.
The Story of the Irish Citizen Army. 1919.
Windfalls: Stories, Poems, and Plays. 1934.
The Flying Wasp (on theatre). 1937.
Mirror in My House: The Autobiographies (2 vols.). 1956; as *Autobiographies* (2 vols.), 1963. Individual volumes:
  1. *I Knock at the Door: Swift Glances Back at Things That Made Me.* 1939.
  2. *Pictures in the Hallway.* 1942.
  3. *Drums under the Windows.* 1945.
  4. *Inishfallen, Fare Thee Well.* 1949.
  5. *Rose and Crown.* 1952.
  6. *Sunset and Evening Star.* 1954.
The Green Crow (essays and stories). 1956.
Feathers from the Green Crow 1905–1915 (miscellany), edited by Robert Hogan. 1962.

Under a Colored Cap: Articles Merry and Mournful with Comments and a Song. 1963.
Blasts and Benedictions: Articles and Stories, edited by Ronald Ayling. 1967.
The Sean O'Casey Reader, edited by Brooks Atkinson. 1968.
The Sting and the Twinkle: Conversations with O'Casey, edited by E. H. Mikhail and John O'Riordan. 1974.
Letters, edited by David Krause. 1975–
Seven Plays, edited by Ronald Ayling. 1985.

BIBLIOGRAPHIES: *Sean O'Casey: A Bibliography of Criticism* by E.H. Mikhail, 1972; *Sean O'Casey: A Bibliography* by Ronald Ayling and Michael J. Durkan, 1978; supplement in *O'Casey Annual*, 2, 1983; *Sean O'Casey and His Critics: An Annotated Bibliography 1916–1982* by E.H. Mikhail, 1985.
Critical Studies(a selection): *Paycocks and Others: Sean O'Casey's World* by Bernard Benstock, 1976; *Sean O'Casey* by John P. Frayne, 1976; *Sean O'Casey* by Doris Da Rin, 1976; *Sean O'Casey's Tragi-Comic Vision* by Donald D. Wilson, 1976; *Sean O'Casey* by James R. Scrimgeour, 1978; *O'Casey's Satiric Vision* by B.L. Smith, 1978; *Sean O'Casey: Politics and Art* by C. Desmond Greaves, 1980; *Sean O'Casey* (biography) by Hugh Hunt, 1980; *O'Casey: Centenary Essays* edited by David Krause and Robert G. Lowery, 1980; *The Essential O'Casey: A Study of the Twelve Major Plays* by Jack Mitchell, 1980; *The O'Casey Enigma* edited by Micheál O hAodha, 1980; *Essays on Sean O'Casey's Autobiographies* edited by Robert G. Lowery, 1981; *O'Casey: From Times Past* by Brooks Atkinson, edited by Robert G. Lowery, 1982; *O'Casey's Autobiographies: An Annotated Index* by Robert G. Lowery, 1983; *Sean O'Casey* by James Simmons, 1983; *A Guide to O'Casey's Plays* by John O'Riordan, 1984; *Sean O'Casey: The Dublin Trilogy: A Casebook* edited by Ronald Ayling, 1985; *O'Casey the Dramatist* by Heinz Kosok, 1985; *File on O'Casey* by Nesta Jones, 1986; *Sean O'Casey: Modern Critical Views* edited by Harold Bloom, 1987; *O'Casey and Expressionism* (book and slide set) by Nesta Jones, 1988; *Sean O'Casey: A Life* by Garry O'Connor, 1988.

In the course of his long career, the Irish playwright Sean O'Casey wrote a large number of plays characterized by a remarkably all-embracing range of techniques. A typical O'Casey play combines in varying proportions vaudeville turns, melodramatic discoveries, sentimental song, strange noises, tired clichés, poetic speeches, angry polemics, romantic encounters, circling dancers, flamboyant costumes and miraculous transformations.

This "inclusiveness" is in part the result of O'Casey's delight in creating hybrid dramatic forms and styles. For example, in the "Dublin Trilogy" (*The Shadow of a Gunman, Juno and the Paycock*, and *The Plough and the Stars*), O'Casey successfully mixed tragedy and comedy to create a theater of bittersweet ironies, not exactly comic and not precisely tragic, but a union of the two that has overwhelming dramatic force. In *The Silver Tassie*, elements of naturalism and expressionism co-exist and amplify the perspectives from which the horrors of World War I assault the audience. And in late works like *Cock-a-Doodle Dandy* and *The Drums of Father Ned*, O'Casey blends realism and fantasy to create a world of promise and wonder in which all things are possible, even an enchanted bird whose anarchic sexual power can release the rebelliousness of the young and thereby threaten and subvert the repressive forces of an authoritarian Church and a conservative State.

O'Casey's use of language is another source of variety. O'Casey's characters share a malleable speech that ranges from the cadences of the King James Bible to the coarseness of the local "snug". The colloquial Hiberno-English that flows effortlessly from the lips of many characters is so enriched with colorful imagery, persistent alliteration, unexpected turns of phrase, and quotations from Shakespeare, Milton, Pope, and Shelley, that it is often described as "Elizabethan".

Some characters use highly individualized idioms and verbal idiosyncrasies: no one else in an O'Casey play sounds like either Fluther Good in *The Plough and the Stars*, with his repeated comic assurances that he does not mean anything "derogatory", or like Joxer Daly in *Juno and the Paycock*, with his grab-bag of tag endings and clichés. Such peculiarities of speech are more than just verbal decorations. Specialized vocabularies such as Donal Davoran's heightened poetic constructions (in *The Shadow of a Gunman*), O'Dempsey's insistent references to Celtic mythology (in *Purple Dust*), Mrs. Gogan's habitual elaborations on the details of death (in *The Plough and the Stars*) and the Croucher's ironic reversals of Ezekial (in *The Silver Tassie*) delineate character and advance plot.

Variety also characterizes O'Casey's manipulation of all the other resources of the theater. For example, O'Casey used lighting in his stage directions to suggest a world of multiple and fluctuating realities. By literally blotting out and obliterating the foolishness of the characters, the sudden darkness that engulfs the stage towards the end of *Purple Dust* severs the dead past from the emergent future. In Act III of *Red Roses for Me*, the mauve and bronze lighting that gradually drenches the stage reveals the previously concealed beauties of the disinherited.

O'Casey used directions for sets in the same dynamic way as he used lighting. Walls crumble (in *Purple Dust*), houses are transformed into factories (in *Oak Leaves and Lavender*), furniture is added and subtracted (in *Juno and the Paycock*), characters appear and disappear through windows (in *Juno and the Paycock*), doors (in *The Plough and the Stars*) and ceilings (in *Purple Dust*). In plays like *The Plough and the Stars*, *Oak Leaves and Lavender*, *Purple Dust*, *Cock-a-Doodle Dandy*, and *The Drums of Father Ned*, O'Casey manipulated stage space so that noises, shouts, songs and speeches from the outside blend insistently with the action going on indoors. Through this layering effect, O'Casey demonstrated that his stage reality is embedded in a more comprehensive external reality.

O'Casey's all-embracing theatre expressed his profound sense of the palpable richness of life. At the same time, his plays recognize that social and political conditions (often conveyed by the intrusive world outside) frequently prevent that richness from being realized. They also explore the ways by which society may be transformed and humanized to accommodate the expansive needs of the human spirit, and the reasons why such social change is often frustrated. O'Casey's plays do not, however, offer characters and audiences the easy fatalism of defeat by immutable forces. Inherent in the life of his impoverished but resilient characters is the possibility for revolutionary change, and he judged the characters by their ability to respond positively to this political challenge.

O'Casey's dramatic techniques and political preoccupations reflected his socialist perspective. Although the early plays (*The Shadow of a Gunman, Juno and the Paycock, The Plough and the Stars, The Silver Tassie,* and *Within the Gates*) are frequently viewed as being hostile to politics *per se*, O'Casey was, in fact, only critical of those political activities that ignored the reality of poverty, in which most of his characters live out their lives. He was also critical of the anti-political attitudes of many of his characters, particularly those of such otherwise admirable women as Juno (in *Juno and the Paycock*) and Nora (in *The Plough and the Stars*): their devotion to irrelevant and unachievable private strategies of salvation in a time of political and economic collapse is understandable, yet evidently completely inappropriate. O'Casey judged both political and private activities to be failures because they did not address what were, for him, the destructive manifestations of poverty—tuberculosis, unemployment, chronic drunkenness, and premature death.

In the plays of the middle period (*The Star Turns Red, Purple Dust, Red Roses for Me,* and *Oak Leaves and Lavender*), sometimes referred to as the "coloured plays", O'Casey dramatized more explicitly than elsewhere the challenge to entrenched power by radical change. *The Star Turns Red,* for example, unashamedly presents the red star (communism) supplanting the Star of Bethlehem. In the late plays (*Cock-a-Doodle Dandy, The Bishop's Bonfire, The Drums of Father Ned, Behind the Green Curtains, Figuro in the Night*), O'Casey attacked the dominant ideology of Ireland for what he regarded as its stultifying combination of political conservatism, clerical domination, and sexual and artistic repression. At the same time, and often with great comic abandon, he dramatized the power of unrestrained sexuality to challenge the repressive authority of the Establishment.

O'Casey's plays, particularly the "Dublin Trilogy", continue to be performed throughout the world.

—Bernice Schrank

See the essay on *Juno and the Paycock*.

O'MALLEY, Mary (Josephine).

Born in Bushey, Hertfordshire, 19 March 1941. Resident writer, Royal Court Theatre, London, 1977. Recipient: *Evening Standard* award, 1978; Susan Smith Blackburn prize, 1978; Plays and Players award; Pye award, for television play. Address: c/o Salmon Publishing, The Bridge Mills, Galway, Republic of Ireland.

Publications

PLAYS

Superscum (produced 1972).
A 'nevolent Society (produced 1974).
Oh If Ever a Man Suffered (produced 1975).
Once a Catholic (produced 1977). 1978.
Look Out . . . Here Comes Trouble (produced 1978). 1979.
Talk of the Devil (produced 1986; revised version produced 1986).

TELEVISION PLAYS: *Percy and Kenneth*, 1976; *Oy Vay Maria*, 1977; *Shall I See You Now?*, 1978; *On the Shelf*, 1984.

OTHER
A Consideration of Silk. 1990.

Mary O'Malley came into the public eye with her mischievous play *Once a Catholic*, which premiered at the Royal Court Theatre in 1977, and then transferred to the West End. The play won awards from the London *Evening Standard* and *Plays and Players*. The play is a warm but sharply retrospective look at a Catholic girls' convent in the 1950s, with the youth rebellion of that decade given added edge by the repressiveness of the nuns. All the girls are called "Mary," and the play is a witty and perceptive extended sit-com, which is such good fun that it would undoubtedly offend no-one. In its way it even was able to test the taboos of the commercial theatre, in a scene where one of the shocked nuns discovers a packet of Tampax hidden in the lavatory, and a final act of sacrilege when one of the girls affixes a plasticine penis to a statue of Christ in the school chapel—for which Mary the scape-goat (the only one who genuinely wants to become a nun) is blamed.

There is a satirical edge to O'Malley's writing which derives from a sensitivity to the very ordinary pains and ironies of daily life—and also to the iconography of domestic experience, which is so important to people. This latter was the main feature of her play *Look Out . . . Here Comes Trouble*, staged by the Royal Shakespeare Company at the Warehouse in London in 1978. The play was set in a psychiatric ward, but floundered in the material detail, and although the comic pain was a feature in the lives of the characters, it never became part of the structural fabric of the play. Somehow O'Malley appears to be caught between the potentialities of a more ruthless satirical approach and a familiar, lightly comic sit-com approach.

—Michelene Wandor

O'NEILL, Michael.

Educated at Northampton Grammar School; Cambridge University. Teacher. Agent: Curtis Brown, 162–168 Regent Street, London W1R 5TB, England.

Publications

PLAYS (with Jeremy Seabrook)
Life Price (produced 1969).
Morality (produced 1971).
Millennium (produced 1973).
Our Sort of People (produced 1974).
Sex and Kinship in a Savage Society (produced 1975).
Sharing (produced 1980).
Black Man's Burden (produced 1980).

RADIO PLAYS: *The Bosom of the Family*, 1975; *Living Private*, 1978; *Our Children's Children*, 1980; *Life Skills*, 1985.

TELEVISION PLAYS: *Skin Deep*, 1971; *Soap Opera in Stockwell*, 1973; *Highway Robbery*, 1973; *A Clear Cut Case*, 1973; *A Stab in the Front*, 1973; *Children of the Sun*, 1975; *Beyond the Call of Duty* (*Crown Court series*), 1976; *A State of Welfare*.

It was Genet whose beliefs about society radically changed when he discovered that, according to the most advanced and accurate statistics available, the percentage of criminals remained the same whichever class or system held power at a particular moment. Michael O'Neill and Jeremy Seabrook's early work suffers from the widespread delusion that it is only as a result of capitalism, the "ceaseless gutting of their body and spirit in the name of enterprise, profits, efficiency," that there is a social sediment at the bottom of society, providing both aggressors and victims for horrible crime. For in their first performed play, *Life Price*, the pre-destined victim, Debbie, and the typical child murderer, George Reginald Dunkley, are both observed against a landscape of "neglected mounds of detritus, crumbling terraces, derelict buildings, and the housing estate itself, all cabbage-stalks and dilapidated creosote fences, maculated concrete, rusting bed-springs and motor-bikes, dead chrysanthemums and dingy paintwork."

A State of Welfare, a television play, is a much better organized work about an American scent spray firm moving into England, and its impact on the household of an average worker. Here the theme of a working-class boy bettering himself, by taking French lessons with an executive's wife, and so coming into conflict with his father—the two sides of industry get together over dinner in a powerful scene reminiscent of Ibsen's *The League of Youth*—forms a substantial and colourful central thread.

Morality is an even more domestic story than *A State of Welfare*. A family called the Pargeters are trying to make their son Nick "get on" by passing his A-level exams and winning a place at university. When it is discovered that Nick is having a homosexual affair with his progressive and sensitive teacher, Larry, the family is up in arms at the scandal this will cause in the neighbourhood. However, when Nick's parents manage to summon up the courage to go and see Larry, Larry calms them down with a hypocritical assertion of "morality." The psychology—and morality—may be crude compared with other plays about divided loyalty, but *Morality* is a lively portrayal of family conflict. As in *Life Price* the authors would seem to be saying it is society which is to blame for the cynicism and destructiveness of young people towards their elders. This is an attitude supported by concrete, almost documentary writing, not by the continual assertion of a doctrinaire point of view.

In *Millennium*, set in a semi-detached house on a Northampton estate, there's a gap of 53 years between the first part and the second. The authors present for comparison the life-style of Florrie's family, and that of Doll her granddaughter, in a broader and more sentimental way than in the earlier plays. In Florrie's family one of the girls is dying of scarlet fever, while about her rage the violences of poverty, the stringencies of life caused by the father's status as a hired man. The rebel son, common to both generations, in the first part merely burns his sister's boots (cost, 8/6), while in the second he has, as part of a gang, tied up a boy, cut his hair, and tried to extort money from his parents. The boot-burning satisfies the instinct for anger at the circumstances, and it is punished and purged within the family unit. The second misdemeanour is a matter for the courts, showing the impersonality of justice and how the family has broken down. The time gap achieves a neat and forceful comparison.

Dramatically striking, too, is the Pirandellian twist by which Florrie's family advance on their petty-minded materialist descendants and engage in a battle of wits. The author's sympathies clearly lie with the earlier brood, on whom a huddled statuesque dignity is conferred. Grim and monochrome as they appear, they have the virtue of discipline and look to the after-life for their reward.

Sex and Kinship in a Savage Society is a less successful treatment of the same theme of family disintegration. In *Black Man's Burden* the family is Jamaican. We hear imposing astral voices with Jamaican accents telling the heroine Melvita her child-to-be is the New Messiah. The family settles in England and the problems of assimilating such a striking notion into a society with a National Health service intent on imposing its own solution on visionaries gives the authors opportunity, once more, for striking contrasts, this time comic, beguiling speech rhythms, and exact evocations of place.

—Garry O'Connor

ORTON, Joe.

Born John Kingsley Orton in Leicester, 1 January 1933. Educated at Clark's College, Leicester, 1945–47; Royal Academy of Dramatic Art, London (Leicester Educational Committee grant), 1951–53, diploma 1953. Lived with Kenneth Halliwell, from 1953. Amateur actor, Leicester and London, 1949–51; assistant stage manager, Ipswich Repertory Company, Suffolk, 1953; worked part-time in Cadbury's chocolate factory, London, 1957–59; served six-month prison term with Halliwell (for theft of and malicious damage to library books), Wormwood Scrubs Prison, London, and Eastchurch Prison, Sheerness, Kent, 1962; travelled with Halliwell to Morocco, 1967. *Died (murdered by Halliwell), 9 August 1967.*

Publications

PLAYS

Entertaining Mr. Sloane (produced 1964).
Loot (produced 1965; revised version produced 1966). 1967.
The Ruffian on the Stair (broadcast 1964). In *New Radio Drama*, 1966; revised version (produced as part of *Crimes of Passion*, 1967), in *Crimes of Passion*, 1967.
The Erpingham Camp (televised 1966; produced as part of *Crimes of Passion*, 1967). In *Crimes of Passion*, 1967.
The Good and Faithful Servant (televised 1967; produced 1971). With *Funeral Games*, 1970.
Crimes of Passion: The Ruffian on the Stair, and The Erpinghman Camp (produced 1967). 1967.
Funeral Games (televised 1968: produced 1970). With *The Good and Faithful Servant*, 1970.

What the Butler Saw (produced 1969). 1969.
Until She Screams (sketch), in *Oh! Calcutta!* (produced 1970). In *Evergreen Review*, May 1970.
The Complete Plays. 1976.
Up Against It: A Screenplay for the Beatles (produced 1985). 1979.

RADIO PLAYS: *The Ruffian on the Stair*, 1964.

TELEVISION PLAYS: *The Erpingham Camp*, 1966; *The Good and Faithful Servant*, 1967; *Funeral Games* (*The Seven Deadly Virtues* series), 1968.

NOVEL

Head to Toe. 1971.

OTHER

The Diaries, edited by John Lahr. 1986.

CRITICAL STUDIES: *Prick Up Your Ears: The Biography of Joe Orton* by John Lahr, 1978; *Joe Orton* by C.W.E. Bigsby, 1982; *Joe Orton* by Maurice Charney, 1984; "An Acquired Taste: Joe Orton and the Greeks" by Peter Walcot, in *Legacy of Thespis*, edited by Karelisa V. Hartigan, 1984; *Because We're Queers: The Life and Crimes of Kenneth Halliwell and Joe Orton* by Simon Shepherd, 1988; *Modern British Farce* by Leslie Smith, 1989.

As a consequence of journalists' insistence on viewing his life and work as an emblem of the anarchic spirit of the "Swinging Sixties", Joe Orton's brief but meteoric career as a comic playwright is still the subject of serious misinterpretation. Voyeuristic interest in the more exotic details of his homosexual exploits has coloured critical responses to his plays, leading critics to treat them as the mischievous clowning of an egocentric immoralist. This persona was, in fact, assiduously cultivated by Orton himself as an ironic rejoinder to the puritanical outcries which his unsparing exposure of middle-class prejudice and hypocrisy habitually provoked.

A heavily biographical interpretation of the plays not only runs counter to Orton's overt statements of satiric intent, but also ignores the social criticism which motivates the structure of every play from *Entertaining Mr. Sloane* to *What the Butler Saw*. The truth is that, as with most satirical writers, Orton's work is the product of a kind of righteous anger at personal and social hypocrisy, revealing him as something of a moralist, albeit an unconventional one. As a homosexual man, he was inevitably forced to confront the homophobia and misogyny produced by a patriarchal culture, and was not content merely to dramatise the spectacle of an absurd universe in an apparent state of entropy. The shocking counterpoint of witty speech and violent action in the plays constitutes a calculated and often savage attack on the false moralisms of post-war British society. Although the style of the plays may encourage critics to treat them as examples of "camp", in fact they represent a consistent comic strategy aimed at exposing the contradictions inherent in Western capitalist societies.

Orton was quite conscious of what he was doing: "To be destructive, words

must be irrefutable. Print was less effective than the spoken word because the
blast was greater. . . . But if you could lock the enemy into a room somewhere,
and fire the sentence at them you could get a sort of seismic disturbance" (from
"The Vision of Gombold Proval", published posthumously as *Head to Toe*).
These words almost constitute a programme for his work as a commercial
playwright creating subversive comedies for middle-brow audiences.

While many plays of the early 1960s—the so-called "angry young men"—
were following John Osborne's in launching direct rhetorical broadsides
against the class inequalities and hypocrisies of a Britain struggling to find a
post-colonial role in world affairs, Orton's first two plays, *The Ruffian on the
Stair* (written for radio) and *Entertaining Mr. Sloane* revealed him as a disciple
of Harold Pinter. The detailed naturalistic evocation of a shabby middle-class
milieu in each play, and the blend of menace and comedy characteristic of the
stage thriller, inevitably remind one of Pinter's early plays.

But it is characteristic of Orton that, even when most obviously influenced
by the already established Pinter, a certain tendency towards conscious parody
manifests itself. Here the traditions of witty writing absorbed through Orton's
close reading of Wilde and the camp satirical novelist, Ronald Firbank, are
noticeable. By choosing to engineer a comic collision between the working-
class, or lower-middle-class, style and milieu of early Pinter, and the upper-
class comedy-of-manners idiom, Orton invented his own entirely original
comic form. The manner in which his "wide boy" characters rationalise their
louche behaviour in the epigrammatic style of Welfare State dandies produces
explosive comedy; likewise, the banal pseudo-morality of his respectable
middle-aged, middle-class hypocrites and megalomaniac authority figures is
funny because their idiom—the debased language of the tabloid press—
is revealed to be morally bankrupt and in a perpetual state of self-
contradiction. The more energetically these characters attempt to repress or
conceal their real motives through pseudo-Wildean witticisms, the more
nakedly is their cupidity and lust exposed for what it is. These middle-aged
hypocrites are 1960s versions of Wilde's Lady Bracknell, jealously devoting
themselves to censuring in others the ruthless egotism they cultivate in
themselves.

In his second play, *Entertaining Mr. Sloane* (his first stage play), Orton
developed this technique of subverting the stylistic expectations evoked by the
opening milieu to create a parody of middle-brow entertainment (well-made
West End thriller), which so closely approximates to the real thing that the
subversion of middle-class values is often either perceived as genuinely
immoral or, alternatively, as a light-hearted pastiche. The proprieties of
middle-class commercial theatre are maintained throughout the play in respect
of the naturalistic setting and stage business. But from the opening conversation between the landlady, Kath, and her prospective lodger, Sloane, which
plays with the relationship between social politeness and sexual flirtation
("The bedroom was perfect", remarks Sloane), the dialogue teases the
audience into a comic recognition of the gulf separating the characters' true
motives from their reflexes of social behaviour.

By the end of the play, everything in this lower-middle-class world is the
opposite of what it had appeared to be: the innocent young lodger is a callous
murderer and bisexual prostitute; the kind and matronly landlady is his

mistress, prepared to use blackmail to retain his sexual favours; her brother, the apparently respectable and macho businessman, Ed, is revealed as homosexual and totally without scruple in concealing Sloane's murder of his father from the police; even the seemingly pathetic old father, Kemp, is shown to be malicious and potentially violent. The ending, in which Kath and Ed unceremoniously agree to share Sloane, is a calculated affront to the sentimental expectation that in the real world such criminal immorality would be discovered and punished.

With *Loot*, *The Erpingham Camp* (made for television), and *What the Butler Saw*, Orton made a distinctive contribution to modern British drama by fusing his unique linguistic style with the structure of farce. Characters and situation combine in each of the plays to generate action which serves as a wild kinetic and visual accompaniment to the explosive effects of the dialogue.

Loot makes the drab milieu of shabby lower-middle-class gentility the scene of a black farce whose dynamic arises from the contradiction between the surface respectability of the McLeavy household and the anarchic stage business which works as so many permutations of the basic gag, involving the substitution of the stolen cash for the corpse of Mrs. McLeavy in the coffin. While replacing the well-made-play/comedy-of-manners formula of *Entertaining Mr. Sloane* with a farce plot, Orton's master-stroke is the introduction of an actual representative of institutional authority in the person of Inspector Truscott. Unlike Ed, in that he is a member of the CID, and therefore *does* represent the repressive force of social order, Truscott is as arbitrary as Ed in employing the mask of authority to hide his own corrupt motives. Farce conventions allow Orton the possibility of elaborating the contradictions within each character so that the action assumes the surrealistic playfulness of *The Importance of Being Earnest* while maintaining a wholly naturalistic anchor in the banal clichés of the lower-middle-class suburban scene.

The highly original holiday camp setting of *The Erpingham Camp* permits the development of the *Loot* formula in an even more anarchic manner: in running his camp, Erpingham aims to control the way every holidaymaker achieves pleasure. Society's tendency towards rampant authoritarianism extends to include every aspect of social life. The absurd and degrading attempts of the camp officers to entertain the campers become pointless strategies for social control, the officers collaborating to reinforce Erpingham's megalomaniacal vision of himself as a peculiarly British tyrant. The terrible, though more-or-less unintentional, revenge wrought on the camp authorities by the campers constitutes a hilarious parody of Euripides' *The Bacchae*. The camper's anarchic individualism is expressed through a mask of self-righteous moralism, just as the puritanical desire of the institutional authority to discipline and punish is presented as respect for a civilised order.

Orton's experiment with epic form prepared him for *What the Butler Saw*, which is generally regarded as his masterpiece. His last play is a summation of all he had previously achieved—an end-of-the-pier peepshow version of *The Importance of Being Earnest*. The farce formula is here explicitly indicated by the insane-asylum setting, the doors of which function brilliantly to enhance the accelerating confusion that alludes to the type of plot-complication associated with a classic Feydeau farce. The choice of setting is also clearly emblematic of the madness that Orton presents as a function of institutional authority.

Motifs used in previous plays are multiplied. One authority figure, the corrupt and psychologically unstable psychiatrist, Dr. Prentice, is set up to be replaced by another psychiatrist, Dr. Rance—who turns out to be an insane megalomaniac who has pretended to be investigating Dr. Prentice as a pretext for gaining scandalous material for a best-seller he is writing!

The exposure of authority figures is reduced to its most primitive slapstick roots by the treatment of the traditional figure of popular entertainment, the policeman, as a ludicrous fall guy. Sergeant Match's complete incompetence is signalled by the loss of his trousers, which causes him, at the end of the play, to have to lead the characters—drugged and weary and bearing aloft the missing parts of a statue of Sir Winston Churchill—out of the locked asylum through a skylight, attired in a leopard-skin dress in a parody of a Dionysian ritual of liberation. By the end of the play, conventional gender categories have been shown to conceal the complexities of sexual identity, just as the normal distinction between sanity and madness has been revealed as totally unreliable. The implication of the ending is highly ambiguous: if Orton is savage in his satirical attack on the structures of society, he is also as sceptical as Euripides with regard to the liberating effects of orgy.

By the age of 34 Orton had achieved wide-ranging re-interpretations of the forms and values of West End theatre. It is tantalising to speculate on how his dramaturgy may have developed had he lived longer.

—Robert Gordon

See the essay on *What the Butler Saw.*

OSBORNE, John (James).

Born in London, 12 December 1929. Educated at Belmont College, Devon. Married 1) Pamela Lane in 1951 (marriage dissolved 1957); 2) the actress Mary Ure in 1957 (marriage dissolved 1963); 3) the writer Penelope Gilliatt in 1963 (marriage dissolved 1968), one daughter; 4) the actress Jill Bennett in 1968 (marriage dissolved 1977); 5) Helen Dawson in 1978. Journalist, 1947–48; toured as an actor, 1948–49; actor-manager, Ilfracombe Repertory, 1951; also in repertory, as actor and stage manager, in Leicester, Derby, Bridgewater, and London; co-director, Woodfall Films, from 1958; director, Oscar Lewenstein Plays Ltd., London, from 1960. Member of the Council, English Stage Company, London, 1960–82. Recipient: *Evening Standard* award, 1956, 1965, 1968; New York Drama Critics Circle award, 1958, 1965, Tony award, 1963; Oscar, for screenplay, 1964; Writers Guild Macallan award, for lifetime achievement, 1992. Honorary Doctor: Royal College of Art, London, 1970. Member, Royal Society of Arts. Address: c/o Faber and Faber Ltd., 3 Queen Square, London WC1N 3AU, England.

Publications

PLAYS

The Devil Inside Him, with Stella Linden (produced 1950).
Personal Enemy, with Anthony Creighton (produced 1955).
Look Back in Anger (produced 1956). 1957.
The Entertainer, music by John Addison (produced 1957). 1957.
Epitaph for George Dillon, with Anthony Creighton (produced 1957). 1958.

The World of Paul Slickey, music by Christopher Whelen (also director: produced 1959). 1959.
A Subject of Scandal and Concern (as *A Matter of Scandal and Concern*, televised 1960; as *A Subject of Scandal and Concern*, produced 1962). 1961.
Luther (produced 1961). 1961.
Plays for England: The Blood of the Bambergs, Under Plain Cover (produced 1962). 1963.
Tom Jones: A Film Script. 1964.
Inadmissible Evidence (produced 1964). 1965.
A Patriot for Me (produced 1965). 1966.
A Bond Honoured, adaptation of a play by Lope de Vega (produced 1966). 1966.
The Hotel in Amsterdam (produced 1968). With *Time Present*, 1968; in *Four Plays*, 1973.
Time Present (produced 1968). With *The Hotel in Amsterdam*, 1968; in *Four Plays*, 1973.
The Right Prospectus (televised 1970). 1970.
Very Like a Whale (televised 1980). 1971.
West of Suez (produced 1971). 1971; in *Four Plays*, 1973.
Hedda Gabler, adaptation of the play by Ibsen (produced 1972). 1972.
The Gift of Friendship (televised 1972). 1972.
A Sense of Detachment (produced 1972). 1973.
Four Plays: West of Suez, A Patriot for Me, Time Present, The Hotel in Amsterdam. 1973.
A Place Calling Itself Rome, adaptation of *Coriolanus* by Shakespeare. 1973.
The Picture of Dorian Gray: A Moral Entertainment, adaptation of the novel by Oscar Wilde (produced 1975). 1973.
Jill and Jack (as *Ms.; or, Jill and Jack*, televised 1974). With *The End of Me Old Cigar*, 1975.
The End of Me Old Cigar (produced 1975). With *Jill and Jack*, 1975.
Watch It Come Down (produced 1976). 1975.
You're Not Watching Me, Mummy (televised 1980). With *Try a Little Tenderness*, 1978.
A Better Class of Person (An Extract of Autobiography for Television), and *God Rot Tunbridge Wells*. 1985.
The Father, adaptation of a play by Strindberg (produced 1989). With *Hedda Gabler*, 1989.
Déjàvu (produced 1992). 1992.

SCREENPLAYS: *Look Back in Anger*, with Nigel Kneale, 1959; *The Entertainer*, with Nigel Kneale, 1960; *Tom Jones*, 1963; *Inadmissible Evidence*, 1968; *The Charge of the Light Brigade*, with Charles Wood, 1968.

TELEVISION PLAYS: *Billy Bunter*, 1952, and *Robin Hood*, 1953 (*For the Children* series); *A Matter of Scandal and Concern*, 1960; *The Right Prospectus*, 1970; *The Gift of Friendship*, 1972; *Ms.; or, Jill and Jack*, 1974; *Almost a Vision*, 1976; *You're Not Watching Me, Mummy*, 1980; *Very Like a Whale*, 1980; *A Better Class of Person*, 1985; *God Rot Tunbridge Wells*, 1985.

OTHER

A Better Class of Person: An Autobiography 1929–1956. 1981.
Too Young to Fight, Too Old to Forget. 1985.
Almost a Gentleman: An Autobiography 1956–1966. 1991.

BIBLIOGRAPHY: *John Osborne: A Reference Guide* by Cameron Northouse and Thomas P. Walsh, 1974.

CRITICAL STUDIES: *Anger and After* by John Russell Taylor, 1962, revised edition, 1969, as *The Angry Theatre*, 1962, revised edition, 1969, and *Look Back in Anger: A Casebook* edited by Taylor, 1968; *John Osborne* by Ronald Hayman, 1968; *Osborne* by Martin Banham, 1969; *The Plays of John Osborne: An Assessment*, 1969, and *John Osborne*, 1969, both by Simon Trussler; *John Osborne* by Alan Carter, 1969; *Theatre Language: A Study of Arden, Osborne, Pinter, and Wesker* by John Russell Brown, 1972; *John Osborne* by Harold Ferrar, 1973; *Anger and Detachment: A Study of Arden, Osborne, and Pinter* by Michael Anderson, 1976; *Coping with Vulnerability: The Achievement of John Osborne* by Herbert Goldstone, 1982; *John Osborne* by Arnold P. Hinchliffe, 1984; *File on Osborne* edited by Malcolm Page, 1988.

THEATRICAL ACTIVITIES

DIRECTOR: **Plays**—with the Huddersfield Repertory Company, 1949; *The World of Paul Slickey*, 1959; *Meals on Wheels* by Charles Wood, 1965; *The Entertainer*, 1974; *Inadmissible Evidence*, 1978.
ACTOR: **Plays**—Mr. Burrells in *No Room at the Inn* by Joan Temple, 1948; on tour and in repertory in Ilfracombe, Bridgwater, Camberwell, Kidderminster, Derby, 1948–56; Antonio in *Don Juan* by Ronald Duncan, 1956, Lionel in *The Death of Satan* by Ronald Duncan, 1956, roles in *Cards of Identity* by Nigel Dennis, 1956, Lin To in *The Good Woman of Setzuan* by Brecht, 1956, The Commissionaire in *The Apollo de Bellac* by Giraudoux, 1957, and Donald Blake in *The Making of Moo* by Nigel Dennis, 1957; Claude Hicket in *A Cuckoo in the Nest* by Ben Travers, 1964. **Films**—*First Love*, 1970; *Get Carter*, 1971; *Tomorrow Never Comes*, 1978; *Flash Gordon*, 1980. **Television**—*The Parachute* by David Mercer, 1968; *The First Night of Pygmalion* by Richard Huggett, 1969; *Lady Charlotte*, 1977.

The staging of *Look Back in Anger* in May 1956 is frequently cited as the start of a dramatic renaissance in Britain. While Beckett's *Waiting for Godot* had been praised the previous year and Brendan Behan's *The Quare Fellow* was to open two weeks later, the statement is broadly true. *Look Back in Anger* established the English Stage Company at the Royal Court as a writers' theatre and because of its success, many young authors turned to plays instead of fiction, or found it easier to have their work performed.

Look Back in Anger presents Jimmy Porter, an eloquent young man running a sweet stall in a provincial town. He is a graduate of a university which was not even redbrick, but white tile. His wife Alison is upper-middle-class, as he often reminds her; later her ex-Indian Army father appears. Cliff, a young

Welshman, shares the flat; an actress, Helena, moves in, eventually sharing Jimmy's bed, and his wife moves out, returning—with whimsical talk of bears protecting squirrels—at the end.

I was one of the young people in the gallery at the Royal Court in the summer of 1956. For the first time ever I saw people similar to people I knew on the stage, talking in the same way—though none could sustain wit and raciness in the way Jimmy did. These characters talked about the same subjects. I scribbled memorable lines from the play all over my programme: the diplomat who was "the platitude from outer space"; "I must say it's pretty dreary living in the American Age—unless you're an American of course"; "There aren't any good, brave causes left. If the big bang does come, and we all get killed off, it won't be in aid of the old-fashioned grand design."

Jimmy Porter was angry at the apathetic mid-1950s. Five months later he could have joined protests at the British invasion of Suez and less than two years later he might have marched to Aldermaston with the newly-formed Campaign for Nuclear Disarmament. I remember too from the Royal Court gallery Mary Ure as Alison in her slip: the play had a sexiness almost unknown on the British stage at the time. Kenneth Tynan's review in the *Observer* had drawn me to the drama: Osborne had presented "post-war youth as it really is" in "the best young play of the decade."

While *Look Back in Anger* is a key document to the mood of the 1950s, it survives for its presentation of class, male versus female, and the generation gap in terms of pre- and post-war, and especially for the eloquence of Jimmy.

The Entertainer followed, a more ambitious work looking at three generations and picturing the state of England through the metaphor of the decline of the music-hall. Archie Rice, third-rate comedian, who sings "Why should I bother to care?" finally refuses to flee to Canada, publicly because "you can't get draught Bass in Toronto," in fact because being English is still so important to him. His proudest moment was when two nuns looked at him and crossed themselves. His neglected wife looks back to the heyday of the music-halls when she sings "The boy I love he's up in the gallery." Archie points to the analogy with England with "Don't clap too hard, we're all in a very old building." Archie's son is kidnapped, then killed, at Suez, and his daughter cries out, in the most subversive speech heard till then in a London theatre: "What's it all in aid of—is it really just for the sake of a gloved hand waving at you from a golden coach?"

Both *Look Back in Anger* and *The Entertainer* were quite well presented in films made at the time.

Five more substantial Osborne plays were staged in the 1960s. *Inadmissible Evidence*, about a lawyer whose public and private lives are disintegrating, was a drama of forceful, inimitable invective rivalling that of Jimmy Porter. *Luther* turned to history, to the roots of protest, for a spectacular stage piece which finally focused on psychological explanations for Luther's revolt. *A Patriot for Me*, also with a big cast, examined a homosexual scandal in Austro-Hungary before World War I, a theme which challenged the Lord Chamberlain's censorship. *The Hotel in Amsterdam*, a quiet conversation piece, has six people in the film business escaping their boss for a weekend. *Time Present*, which contrasts sisters—an actress and an earnest Labour MP—facing the approaching death of their father, has been undervalued. These last two plays are ensemble work, in contrast to the earlier ones: lesser characters are granted a right-of-reply.

Osborne's output in a long career includes other full-length plays: an ill-fated musical, *The World of Paul Slickey*; adaptations and translations; and short plays and work for television.

Osborne's work comes full cycle, and possibly concludes, with *Déjàvu* in 1992. He returns to Jimmy Porter 36 years later, living in comfort in Shropshire, still accompanied by Cliff. An Alison is still at the ironing board (his daughter by a failed second marriage) while the men read the Sunday papers. The new Helena is a friend of the daughter. The older Jimmy is even more prone to extended monologue than he was in *Look Back in Anger*, and Osborne seems to enjoy annoying his audience by non-stop attacks on progressives, gays, feminists, Australians, the lower-middle-class, and change in the Church of England. *Déjàvu* has two strengths: intriguing oblique comment on *Look Back in Anger*, as play and myth, and the pain seen in Jimmy, sinking with claret, his teddy bear, and the Book of Common Prayer.

Angered by the critical reception of *Déjàvu*, Osborne wrote in the *Spectator* (London): "No more plays, no more journalism for me" (20 June 1992). As his most polished and entertaining work in recent years has been two volumes of autobiography (*A Better Class of Person* vividly recreates a pre-1939 upbringing), this choice of words allows us to expect more non-fiction.

—Malcolm Page

See the essay on *Look Back in Anger*.

OWEN, Alun (Davies).

Born in Liverpool, Lancashire, 24 November 1925. Educated at Cardigan County School, Wales; Oulton High School, Liverpool. Married Mary O'Keeffe in 1942; two sons. Stage manager, director, and actor, 1942–59. Recipient: Screenwriters and Producers Script of the Year award, 1960; Screenwriters Guild award, 1961; *Daily Mirror* award, 1961; Golden Star, 1967; Banff International Television Festival prize, 1985. Lives in London. Agent: Julian Friedmann, Blake Friedmann Agency, 37–41 Gower Street, London WC1E 6HH, England.

Publications

PLAYS

The Rough and Ready Lot (broadcast 1958; produced 1959). 1960.
Progress to the Park (broadcast 1958; produced 1959). In *New English Dramatists 5*, 1962.
Three T.V. Plays (includes *No Trams to Lime Street*; *After the Funeral*; *Lena, Oh My Lena*). 1961.
The Rose Affair (televised 1961; produced 1966). In *Anatomy of a Television Play*, 1962.
Dare to Be a Daniel (televised 1962). In *Eight Plays: Book 1*, edited by Malcolm Stuart Fellows, 1965.
A Little Winter Love (produced 1963). 1965.
Maggie May, music and lyrics by Lionel Bart (produced 1964).

The Game (includes *The Winner* and *The Loser*) (produced 1965).
The Goose (produced 1967).
The Wake (televised 1967). In *Theatre Choice: A Collection of Modern Short Plays*, edited by Michael Marland, 1972.
Shelter (televised 1967; produced 1971). 1968.
George's Room (televised 1967). 1968.
There'll Be Some Changes Made (produced 1969).
Norma, in *We Who Are About to . . .*, later title *Mixed Doubles* (produced 1969; revised version produced 1983). 1970.
Doreen (televised 1969). In *The Best Short Plays 1971*, edited by Stanley Richards, 1971.
The Male of the Species (televised 1969; produced 1974). In *On Camera 3*, edited by Ron Side and Ralph Greenfield, 1972.
Lucia (produced 1982).

SCREENPLAYS: *The Criminal* (*The Concrete Jungle*), with Jimmy Sangster, 1960; *A Hard Day's Night*, 1964; *Caribbean Idyll*, 1970.

RADIO PLAYS: *Two Sons*, 1957; *The Rough and Ready Lot*, 1958; *Progress to the Park*, 1958; *It Looks Like Rain*, 1959; *Café Society*, 1982; *The Lancaster Gate End*, 1982; *Colleagues*, 1982; *Kisch-Kisch*, 1983; *Soft Impeachment*, 1983; *Tiger*, 1984; *Halt*, 1984; *Earwig* series, 1984; *Widowers*, 1985.

TELEVISION PLAYS: *No Trams to Lime Street*, 1959; *After the Funeral*, 1960; *Lena, Oh My Lena*, 1960; *The Ruffians*, 1960; *The Ways of Love*, 1961; *The Rose Affair*, 1961; *The Hard Knock*, 1962; *Dare to Be a Daniel*, 1962; *You Can't Win 'em All*, 1962; *The Strain*, 1963; *Let's Imagine* series, 1963; *The Stag*, 1963; *A Local Boy*, 1963; *The Other Fella*, 1966; *The Making of Jericho*, 1966; *The Fantasist*, 1967; *The Wake*, 1967; *Shelter*, 1967; *George's Room*, 1967; *Stella*, 1967; *Thief*, 1967; *Charlie*, 1968; *Gareth*, 1968; *Tennyson*, 1968; *Ah, There You Are*, 1968; *Alexander*, 1968; *Minding the Shop*, 1968; *Time for the Funny Walk*, 1968; *The Ladies*, 1969; *Doreen*, 1969; *Spare Time*, 1969; *Park People*, 1969; *You'll Be the Death of Me*, 1969; *The Male of the Species* (U.S. title: *Emlyn, MacNeil, Cornelius*), 1969; *Joan*, 1970; *Hilda*, 1970; *And a Willow Tree*, 1970; *Just the Job*, 1970; *Female of the Species*, 1970; *Joy*, 1970; *Ruth*, 1971; *Funny*, 1971; *Pal*, 1971; *Giants and Ogres*, 1971; *The Piano Player*, 1971; *The Web*, 1972; *Ronny Barker Show* (3 scripts); *Buttons*, 1973; *Flight*, 1973; *Lucky*, 1974; *Left*, 1975; *The Vandy Case*, 1975; *Forget-Me-Not* (6 plays), 1976; *The Fetch*, 1977; *The Look*, 1978; *Passing Through*, 1979 (Ireland); *The Runner*, 1980; *Sealink*, 1980; *Lovers of the Lake*, from the story by Sean O'Faolain, 1984; *Unexplained Laughter*, from the novel by Alice Thomas Ellis, 1989; *Come Home Charlie and Face Them*, from the novel by R.F. Delderfield, 1990.

THEATRICAL ACTIVITIES

ACTOR: **Plays**—with the Birmingham Repertory Company, 1943–44; Gotti in *The Lonely Falcons* by P.N. Walker-Taylor, 1946; Jepson in *Humoresque* by Guy Bolton, 1948; Rolph in *Snow White and the Seven Dwarfs*, 1951; with Sir Donald Wolfit's Company at the Old Vic, 1951: in *Tamburlaine the Great* by

Marlowe, Charles in *As You Like It*, Curan and Herald in *King Lear*, Officer in *Twelfth Night*, Salarino in *The Merchant of Venice*, Sexton in *Macbeth*, Gonzales Ferera in *The Wandering Jew* by J. Temple Thurston, a Lord and Joseph in *The Taming of the Shrew*; with the English Stage Company at the Royal Court, 1957; Clifford in *Man with a Guitar* by Gilbert Horobin, and Smith in *The Waiting of Lester Abbs* by Kathleen Sully, 1957; Reader in *The Samson Riddle* by Wolf Mankowitz, 1972. Films—*Valley of Song (Men Are Children Twice)*, 1953; *Every Day Except Christmas*, 1957; *In the Wake of a Stranger*, 1959; *I'm All Right Jack*, 1959; *Jet Storm*, 1959; *The Servant*, 1963.

The main strengths of Alun Owen's work have always been its accuracy of observation, its depth of characterization, and the power and fluency of its dialogue, sometimes reaching the level of poetry. *Progress to the Park*, set in the Liverpool of the late 1950s, is a vivid and detailed portrait of working-class life in that town at the period. The play's central theme is the vice-like grip that religious intolerance has on the city's inhabitants; and is expressed through the central relationship between Bobby Laughlin, a Protestant boy, and Mag Keegan, a Catholic girl. Their potential love is stifled and destroyed by the bigoted attitudes of their elders. There are a number of sharply defined character studies, including members of the Laughlin and Keegan families; and of Teifion Davies, the detached, ironic young Welshman who has a love-hate relationship to his home town, which is reflected in his commentary on the action. The play teems with vitality and power, each episode flowing effectively and relentlessly into and out of each other but related strongly to the central theme.

The Rough and Ready Lot is set in monastery in a Spanish colony in South America a few years after the end of the American Civil War and revolves around four "soldiers of fortune"—Kelly, O'Keefe, Morgan, and the Colonel. They are in a lull between fighting, ostensibly on the side of the Indians in their bid to free themselves from their Spanish oppressors; in the meantime, the four men talk. O'Keefe is a fanatical Catholic; Morgan an equally fanatical political revolutionary; the Colonel is a "realist," who thinks he knows the motives for people's actions but is, in fact, incredibly blinkered; while Kelly just takes life as it comes. They argue and try to impose their views on the others, sometimes in bursts of magnificent rhetoric; but in the end only Kelly survives. As Irving Wardle said in a review, "Its dialogue flows beautifully; its characters are conceived in depth and, as embodiments of conflicting principles, they are disposed in a pattern of geometric symmetry; the plot is constructed solidly and attaches itself tenaciously to the governing theme."

In the musical *Maggie May*, written with Lionel Bart, Owen returns to the Liverpool scene and gives us another teeming, vital slice of life. The early and mid-1960s was also the time of his award-winning television plays, also set on Merseyside, *No Trams to Lime Street*, *Lena, Oh My Lena*, and *After the Funeral*; and his sharp and witty script for the Beatles' first and best film, the semi-documentary *A Hard Day's Night*. By contrast, *The Rose Affair*, also a television award-winner, was a modernized version of the fairy-tale *Beauty and the Beast*, the Beast-figure an isolated, high-powered businessman, the Beauty a girl he falls in love with from afar; stylistically, it had some bold innovations for its time and also had some pithy things to say on the split between being a public and a private person.

In recent years, most of Owen's work has been for television, and includes *Shelter*, a play about the confrontation between an aggressive working-class man and an alienated young middle-class woman, and *Dare to Be a Daniel*, in which a young man with a grudge against his former schoolteacher returns to the small town where he comes from to gain his revenge.

Owen adapted his 1969 television play *The Male of the Species* for the stage in 1974. Consisting of three short plays, this work purports to show how women are exploited by men. Mary MacNeil is shown in her encounters with three crucial male figures: her father, a master carpenter; her employer, a suave, urbane barrister; and the "office cad." The trouble is, however, that the men are all depicted as attractive, while Mary is portrayed as the willing victim. The perhaps unconscious male chauvinism of the play is disappointing in a writer of Owen's talent.

—Jonathan Hammond

P

PAGE, Louise.

Born in London, 7 March 1955. Educated at High Storrs Comprehensive School, Sheffield; University of Birmingham, 1973–76, B.A. in drama and theatre arts 1976; University of Wales, Cardiff, 1976–77, post-graduate diploma in theatre studies 1977. Yorkshire Television fellow in creative writing, University of Sheffield, 1979–81; resident playwright, Royal Court Theatre, London, 1982–83; associate director, Theatre Calgary, Alberta, 1987. Recipient: George Devine award, 1982; J.T. Grein award, 1985. Agent: Phil Kelvin, Goodwin Associates, 12 Rabbit Row, London W8 4DX. Address: 6–J Oxford and Cambridge Mansions, Old Marylebone Road, London NW1 5EC, England.

Publications

PLAYS

Want-Ad (produced 1977; revised version produced 1979).
Glasshouse (produced 1977).
Tissue (produced 1978). In *Plays by Women 1*, edited by Michelene Wandor, 1982.
Lucy (produced 1979).
Hearing (produced 1979).
Flaws (produced 1980).
House Wives (produced 1981).
Salonika (produced 1982). 1983.
Falkland Sound/Voces de Malvinas (produced 1983).
Real Estate (produced 1984). 1985.
Golden Girls (produced 1984). 1985.
Beauty and the Beast (produced 1985). 1986.
Goat (produced 1986).
Diplomatic Wives (produced 1989). 1989.
Plays: One (includes *Tissue, Salonika, Real Estate, Golden Girls*). 1990.
Adam Was a Gardener (produced 1991).
Like to Live (produced 1992).
Hawks and Doves (produced 1992).

RADIO PLAYS: *Saturday, Late September,* 1978; *Agnus Dei,* 1980; *Armistice,* 1983.

TELEVISION PLAY: *Peanuts* (*Crown Court* series), 1982.

Although Louise Page's work may lack the strident militancy expected of modern women writers, her contribution lies in her singling out the experiences of women as keystones to an examination of social conditioning. These women are unexceptional, lacking in unique personality traits. Their right to be the centre of the drama stems from the situations they are in, unremarkable situations in themselves, but personal crises to the characters through whom we see the contradictions between our socially conditioned expectations and our private experience of life. By isolating these ordinary women and their mundane crises, Page explores and exposes the social preconceptions by which people define and judge, analysing the ways in which these assumptions limit our lives, complicate our decisions, and contradict our experiences.

Page adopts different theatrical styles to highlight this tension between socially conditioned expectations and private experience. In plays as different in form as *Tissue*, *Salonika*, and *Real Estate*, the most frequent single word is "expect," and the action of the plays is played out against a background of expectations, making the audience aware of the contradictions and distortions these ingrained preconceptions place upon individual behaviour. *Tissue*, for example, is not so much a play about breast cancer as a play in which the crisis of breast cancer serves as a focus for the examination of assumptions about female sexuality and value.

A straight narrative about a woman fighting breast cancer would, by definition, imply themes of personal heroism. The structure of *Tissue* changes the emphasis from personality and the fact of cancer to the associated ideas that make facing breast cancer more difficult for both victim and associates. Scenes from Sally's life, unconnected by time or space, irrelevant in themselves, are magnetized by Sally's cancer; their juxtaposition highlights the complex socially conditioned assumptions which create the feminine mystique. Their sequence has the logic of memory, setting each other off through association of word, image, or emotional logic and building an analysis of the obsessive connections between breasts and sexuality, sex and love, and the evaluation of women by physical appearance we absorb from childhood. Sally herself is barely a character at all. She displays no individual personality traits; her thoughts and reactions are not so much personal as situational, the responses of a woman who has breast cancer.

Breasts define womanhood. They are assumed to be the measure of attractiveness, synonymous with sexuality and prerequisites for love, happy partnership, and future. The mystique created round the female body is shown through the play to prevent realistic and healthy attitudes towards oneself and others. Sally's mother, who treated Sally's growing breasts as objects of magical impurity, is afraid to touch her own to test for cancer. Sally's boss tells of his wife who "wrecked her life trying to keep her body whole. I did not ask her to be beautiful but to be there." Although we would consciously reject the evaluation of a woman solely on the size of her breasts, the progress of the play illuminates the way these assumptions infiltrate our lives and inform our behaviour.

Through stylistic choices, Page depersonalizes the characters in order to accentuate their situations and responses. All the men and women, except

Sally, are meant to be played by the same actor and actress. Direct speeches to the audience and other theatrical devices like the content-related sequence of scenes and the quick-fire lists (the "possible causes" of cancer in Scene 28) serve to demystify by removing the personal elements and emphasizing the situational behaviour and its constriction through preconceptions. The construction of the play encourages audiences to go beyond their fear of cancer and recognize the social conditioning which exacerbates their fears but which, through unravelling and understanding, can be overcome. Cancer, terrifying as it is, becomes not the end of the road, but a pathway through distorted preconceptions of femininity and the examination of the taboos of both cancer and sexuality.

Sally's greatest fear when she finds she has cancer is not that she will die, but that she will cease to be attractive to men and thus be unable to love and be loved. Only at the end, when she has a new lover, and after she has confronted, with us, the moments of her life which make up the fearful, complex confusion between her appearance and her value as a woman does she take joy in the very fact of living.

Salonika, too, celebrates the indefatigable life force which defies physical limitation, while making us aware of our assumptions and their limiting effect on our lives. The play's dream-like quality not only stems from the World War I soldier's ghost rising from the sands; the situation itself flies in the face of expectation. The mother and daughter on holiday to visit the father's grave are 84 and 64 years old. The mother has a 74-year-old lover who has hitch-hiked to Greece to be with her. In a world where love is assumed to be the reserve of the young and beautiful, these very facts cause a sense of unreality and demand that we take note of our preconceptions.

Within the play, too, the characters are constantly evaluating the expectations they held in the light of experience:

Ben—(the ghost)—I didn't think you'd be a daughter.
Enid—Didn't you?
Ben—No. That's why I said to call a girl Enid. Because I thought you'd be a boy.
Leonard—You expect everything in you to shrivel. All the hate and the longing. The lust. You don't expect to have them any more. But there isn't much else so you have them all the more. I could kill now. If I had the strength. . . . That's not what you expect.

Life as we live it defies expectation. The young man on the beach suddenly dies, leaving the old to bury him.

This dichotomy between social preconceptions and personal experience is elaborated in a more realistic form in *Real Estate*. Here Gwen, a middle-aged woman, lives with Dick, her second husband, outside Didcot where she runs a small estate agency. Her daughter Jenny, a successful London buyer, returns for the first time since she ran away 20 years before. Jenny is pregnant and has come to claim the care and attention mothers are expected, automatically, to provide. Gwen, conventional as she appears, does not revert to type. Although she dreads losing contact with Jenny again, she resists her intrusion into her life.

We assume, without thinking, that the younger, modern woman would introduce a life-style free from preconceptions and conventions. But Jenny, the very image of the modern independent woman, demands conventional responses from others. The "modernness" she brings with her is calloused, self-centred, and totally material. She carelessly lets the dog out; she refuses to marry Eric, the child's father, while demanding his attention. When she insinuates herself into the business Gwen has founded on honesty, loyalty, and personal concern, Jenny's first act is to encourage a client to gazump.

Almost by definition, we expect a middle-aged, middle-class woman's life to be circumscribed by convention and socially approved roles, but, without proselytizing, Gwen and Dick have evolved a life-style that suits them both: "I can't ask you to stay for supper because I don't know if there's enough. Are you expecting to be asked to stay? Dick's province, not mine. He's the one who knows how long the mince has been in the freezer. How many sheets there are which haven't been turned edge to edge." Dick even embroiders tapestries! Indeed, the men in the play could not be more amenable. Eric, though divorced, appears sympathetic to his wife and is actively committed to the care of his daughter. Jenny considers this a liability; when her needs conflict with the child's, she demands priority although she refuses Eric her commitment. While Gwen has no desire to be a mother, again, nor a grandmother, Dick longs for a baby on whom to lavish loving care.

Gwen cannot share her life with Jenny. Their expectations and values are mutually exclusive. Without fuss, leaving to Dick the traditional role she once imagined for herself, Gwen takes the little acorn she planted at the play's start and plants it in the forest; like Jenny, it is well able to continue its growth on its own, though probably more willing. The placing of Gwen at the centre of the play challenges our assumptions. We are led to consider the limitations these preconceptions force upon individual lives and their lack of validity as bases for judgement and the evaluation of human behaviour. While retaining our sympathy, Gwen foils our expectations, setting them in relief so we might evaluate them.

Page structures her plays to call into question our assumptions about character, behaviour, and role and to stress that the roots of these automatic expectations and responses are in social conditioning rather than personality and psychology. Her choice of unexceptional women in unexceptional circumstances places emphasis on the way these preconceptions infiltrate the very fabric of our lives, laying bases for misunderstanding and regret and corrupting moments of crisis and decision.

—Elaine Turner

PARKER, (James) Stewart.

Born in Belfast, Northern Ireland, 20 October 1941. Educated at Queen's University, Belfast, B.A. 1963, M.A. 1965. Married Kate Ireland in 1964. Instructor in English, Hamilton College, Clinton, New York, 1964–67, and Cornell University, Ithaca, New York, 1967–69. Recipient: *Evening Standard* award, 1977; Christopher Ewart-Biggs Memorial prize, 1979; Banff International Television Festival prize, 1985. *Died 2 November 1988.*

Publications

PLAYS

The Iceberg (broadcast 1974). In *Honest Ulsterman*, 1975.
Spokesong, music by Jimmy Kennedy (produced 1975). 1980.
The Actress and the Bishop (produced 1976).
Catchpenny Twist (televised 1977; produced 1977). 1980.
Kingdom Come, music by Shaun Davey (produced 1978).
The Kamikaze Ground Staff Reunion Dinner (televised 1979). In *Best Radio
   Plays of 1980*, 1981.
Tall Girls Have Everything (produced 1980).
Nightshade (produced 1980). 1980.
Pratt's Fall (produced 1983).
Northern Star (produced 1984).
Heavenly Bodies (produced 1986).
Pentecost (produced 1987).

RADIO PLAYS: *Speaking of Red Indians*, 1967; *Minnie and Maisie and Lily
Freed*, 1970; *Requiem*, 1973; *The Iceberg*, 1974; *I'm a Dreamer, Montreal*,
1976; *The Kamikaze Ground Staff Reunion Dinner*, 1979; *The Traveller*,
1985.

TELEVISION PLAYS: *Catchpenny Twist*, 1977; *I'm a Dreamer, Montreal*, 1979;
The Kamikaze Ground Staff Reunion Dinner, 1981; *Iris in the Traffic, Ruby in
the Rain*, 1981; *Joyce in June*, 1982; *Blue Money*, 1984; *Radio Pictures*, 1985;
Lost Belongings, 1987.

VERSE

The Casualty's Meditation. 1967.
Maw. 1968.

OTHER

Editor, *Over the Bridge*, by Sam Thompson. 1970.

CRITICAL STUDIES: "Metaphor as Dramatic Structure in Plays by Stewart
Parker" by Andrew Parkin in *Irish Writers and the Theatre*, edited by Masaru
Sekine, 1986; "The Will to Freedom: Politics and Play in the Theatre of
Stewart Parker" by Elmer Andrews in *Irish Writers and Politics*, edited by
Okifumi Komesu and Masaru Sekine, 1990.

With its witty alertness to the unconscious felicities and incongruities of
everyday speech, Stewart Parker's dialogue embodies that resilience and energy
in the midst of routine and deadness which is the chief concern of his plays.
Form and stagecraft reinforce this impression, for Parker typically establishes
and develops his themes less by soberly discursive means than by a constant
play of allusion, symbol, and metatheatrical reference operating within a fast-

moving, eventful narrative. (Music and song frequently enhance the charm and energy of the action.) Parker's is a virtuoso stagecraft, joyfully unafraid of self-display.

This was a comic writer at home with serious subjects. The Troubles are, not unnaturally for a Northern Irish playwright, ominously present either within or behind most of Parker's work. He saw himself as preoccupied "with the challenge of forging a unifying dramatic metaphor for the Northern Irish human condition". His interest was in cultural and psychological consequences, rather than political causes or solutions: the pressures of circumstances created by sectarian violence and a military presence are shown, in such pieces as *I'm a Dreamer, Montreal* and the "Caribbean-Irish Musical Comedy" *Kingdom Come* (which, like the radio play *The Iceberg*, allegorizes the situation), to stifle the energy of the individual.

Parker's best-known piece, *Spokesong*, was intended as "a play about violence which would ambush the audience with pleasure". It is typical of his work in its (oblique) treatment of the Troubles and in its clever stagecraft. Frank's attempt to woo Daisy (in competition with his "implacably bitter" brother Julian) and to preserve the family bicycle-shop in Belfast from the ravages of urban "development" and terrorist bombs is presented concurrently with his grandparents' courtship and his grandfather's service in World War I. The "bicycle-philosophy" of Frank's family is shown to represent physical energy, freedom, health and beneficial social change amidst the chaos and constriction of the "diseased", car-dominated city. Frank is driven almost to despair by the surrounding pressures, but Daisy steps in to save the shop and stand with him. Their united resolve promotes an affirmation not so much of the eccentric bicycle-philosophy, as of human energy and independence *per se*.

By remaining in Belfast, Frank and Daisy acknowledge and confront the historical past and its consequences. But the catchpenny songwriters of *Catchpenny Twist* find themselves with little choice in the same matter. When their exuberance gets them the sack from their teaching jobs, Ray and Martyn are forced to leave Belfast because of terrorist death-threats. The threats pursue them, through growing emotional turmoil (caused largely by their singer, Monagh), first to Dublin, and then to London. The "twist" comes when, having missed their chance of a break in a European song-contest, they are blown up by a parcel-bomb at a foreign airport. Their Republican "friend" considers their endeavour puerile because of its lack of connection with the serious business of their country's political past; yet the final effect of the play's wit and the energy of its songs is to question the moral adequacy of a seriousness that inhibits feeling and destroys life.

It would be misleading to suggest that Parker's work is concerned exclusively with Northern Ireland and its problems. For example, both *Nightshade*, a vivid, whirling piece about the need to confront the reality of death, and *Pratt's Fall*, a poignant late comedy which opposes the truths of reason and science with those of imagination and belief, meditate entertainingly on the necessity for art and the artist, and in doing so handle characteristic themes outside the characteristic Troubles-context. Nevertheless it was to the North of Ireland and its cultural past that Parker turned for what was to be his final project, a "triptych" of history plays, "dealing roughly with the struggle between the individual will and the forces of the Age in which it operates". These plays present (in the author's own words), "three self-contained groups of figures, from the eighteenth, nineteenth and twentieth centuries respectively, hinged together in a continuing comedy of terrors".

The dramatic format of the first two plays of the triptych is that of a man near or at the point of death reviewing his life and actions in a series of key flashbacks which counterpoint or parody various dramatic styles or scenes. The central figure of the first, *Northern Star*, is the great Protestant United Irishman, Henry Joy McCracken. After the "stillborn" attempt of the 1798 rising to create a united Irish nation, McCracken is on the run and being sheltered by his toughly commonsensical mistress, Mary Bodle, in a semi-ruined farm labourer's cottage outside Belfast. The time is "the continuous past", with "deliberate anachronisms and historical shifts". "McCracken's Night Thoughts" (the play's original subtitle) are presented by him, in modern idiom, in a sequence of dramatic scenes which chart the course through Seven (ironic) Ages of his attempt to forge a united Ireland. Each "Age" is a pastiche of the style of a famous Irish playwright: Innocence (Sheridan); Idealism (Boucicault); Cleverness (Wilde); Dialectic (Shaw); Heroism (Synge); Compromise (O'Casey); Shame (Behan)—and a terminal monologue after Beckett. The ambition is Joycean—nothing less than an attempt to transform an individual's history, through a virtuoso theatrical digest, into a nation's, and thus to suggest how an escape from the dungeon of history might be effected by way of moral and creative, rather than physical, force.

In the less interesting second play of the triptych, *Heavenly Bodies*, the Victorian Irish playwright Dion Boucicault has been metamorphosed from object of pastiche to central character. He is put on trial for his afterlife and found guilty of a self-serving opportunism that has led him to exploit his suffering fellow-countrymen for the sake of showbusiness and a glittering career ("You *are* the Age", he is told). The trial is conducted by Boucicault's "Mephistophelean sparring partner", the Irish singing clown Johnny Patterson, who was murdered by his audience. He is the most impressive of Parker's many artist-performers. His belief in the "commingling of the Orange and the Green", and his fatal efforts to bring it about, place him alongside McCracken as a symbol of the possibility of creative reconciliation.

The "climactic piece" of the triptych, *Pentecost*, is Parker's last play, and his best. The time is 1974 and the setting Belfast—specifically a *"respectable working class 'parlour' house"*, described as "slap bang in the firing line", and "eloquent with the history of this city". When Marian, a Catholic, moves into the house in an attempt to take refuge from life, she is (literally) haunted by the ghost of the only previous tenant, Lily Matthews, whose life the house and its hoarded contents plainly embody ("she never threw anything away"). As the "lingering tribal suicide" of the Loyalist workers' protest strike takes its course on the streets outside, Marian discovers evidence of the life-denying price of Lily's Protestant "godliness": an abandoned illegitimate child which, together with Marian's own dead baby, Christopher ("he was a kind of Christ to me"), comes to symbolize not just loss of personal hope, but the absence of a cultural future. Yet "the ways of life" are finally affirmed when Marian and her "holy family" of fellow refugees—her childhood friend Ruth, her "free-spirited" estranged husband Lenny, and his friend Peter (the names are significant)—gather in a passionate impromptu wake for the province. As Pentecost Sunday dawns, a visionary and prophetic flame lights on story, recitation, song, and confession, prompting a painful celebration of the human love and self-delight that is being corrupted by a barren culture.

—Paul Lawley

PHILLIPS, Caryl.

Born in St. Kitts, West Indies, 13 March 1958; brought to England in 1958. Educated at schools in Leeds to 1974, and in Birmingham, 1974–76; Queen's College, Oxford, 1976–79, B.A. (honours) 1979. Founding chair, 1978, and artistic director, 1979, *Observer* Festival of Theatre, Oxford; resident dramatist, The Factory, London 1981–82; writer-in-residence, Literary Criterion Centre, Mysore, India, 1987, and Stockholm University, Sweden, 1989. Since 1990 visiting writer, Amherst College, Massachusetts. Member of the Board of Directors, Bush Theatre, London, 1985–88; member, British Film Institute Production Board, London, 1985–88. Recipient: Arts Council bursary, 1983; Malcolm X prize, 1985; Martin Luther King Memorial prize, 1987; *Sunday Times* Young Writer award, 1992. Lives in London. Agent: Judy Daish Associates, 83 Eastbourne Mews, London W2 6LQ; or, Curtis Brown, 162–168 Regent Street, London W1R 5TB, England.

Publications

PLAYS

Strange Fruit (produced 1980). 1981.
Where There Is Darkness (produced 1982). 1982.
The Shelter (produced 1983). 1984.
The Wasted Years (broadcast 1984). In *Best Radio Plays of 1984*, 1985.
Playing Away (screenplay). 1987.

SCREENPLAY: *Playing Away*, 1986.

RADIO PLAYS: *The Wasted Years*, 1984; *Crossing the River*, 1986; *The Prince of Africa*, 1987; *Writing Fiction*, 1991.

TELEVISION PLAYS: *The Hope and the Glory*, 1984; *The Record*, 1984; *Lost in Music*, 1985.

NOVELS

The Final Passage. 1985.
A State of Independence. 1986.
Cambridge. 1991.

SHORT STORIES

Higher Ground. 1986.

OTHER

The European Tribe (travel). 1987.

Caryl Phillips comments:

My dominant theme has been cultural and social dislocation, most commonly associated with a migratory experience.

Few British dramatists have been equally at home in fiction and in the theatre, but Caryl Phillips is a playwright well on his way to a reputation that overlaps a variety of categories. Most of his work has been concerned with the immigrant experience of blacks in Britain, but his perspective is both historical and international and he has applied his talent with success to drama for the stage, television, radio, and cinema. In addition, with his first two books he made a mark in the demanding form of the novel. Journalism, too, has proved a fruitful form, provoking thoughtful essays on such significant predecessors as James Baldwin. Indeed, Baldwin is an unmistakeable model and inspiration and the clear, passionate view of the United States which was seen in Baldwin's early essays, when he was able to combine a knowledge of the American South with a European perspective, is reflected in Phillips's view of Britain, though Phillips goes further and applies Baldwin's measures to Europe as well. For Phillips, it is Europe that has made him a "black" writer. In the preface to his play in two parts, *The Shelter*, he says: "In Africa I was not black. In Africa I was a writer. In Europe I am black. In Europe I am a black writer. If the missionaries [for which read critics] wish to play the game along these lines then I do not wish to be an honorary white."

Although born in St. Kitts in the West Indies, and very conscious of his Caribbean heritage, he is a child of Leeds in England where he was reared, and his accent is Yorkshire. His plays have persistently explored the conflicts of immigration, looking at the yearning for a homeland which has achieved mythological significance and at the reality of life in a society which views the immigrant as an outsider because of colour. While immigration has remained his major theme, he has maintained an ironic distance that sees slavery as the first immigration, and that it was very much an immigration imposed on the African by Europeans and North Americans.

His perspective is finally more mid-Atlantic than Caribbean, and the title of his first play, *Strange Fruit*, is drawn directly and knowingly from the Billie Holiday song about lynching. As in much of his later work, the subject is a West Indian family held together by a single parent but pulled between two hemispheres. Although Vivien has educated her sons in England, they feel drawn to the black culture of the Caribbean.

In his next and more ambitious play, *Where There Is Darkness*, the pull of the islands is felt by a West Indian man, Albert, who 25 years earlier fled his home for the promises of England, first making a girl pregnant so her father would pay their passage to the "motherland." Phillips sets the play on the eve of Albert's return to the Caribbean, during and after a farewell party for the white friends and colleagues he has gathered in his years as a social worker. In his London garden Albert confronts the guilt of his betrayals, including the sacrifice of his first wife to his ambition, and his inability to bring the son he loves into his vision of success.

While remembering that his own father had advised him that the only way out of the gutters and up to the mountains was through exile, and foreign wealth, the sacrifice he was prepared to make was the gift of his son to England. When he took his father-in-law's money for the passage it was to the admonition that: "The child belongs to England." His disappointment when his son announces that he is leaving university to marry his pregnant black girlfriend proves the final blow in his struggle for self-justification. At the beginning of the play, Albert's confrontation with his accommodations to white society has driven him into the garden with a raging headache. At the end of the play he has stripped down to his trousers to plunge into an imaginary sea. His Faustian bargain has torn his spirit apart.

Everywhere in Phillips's work he is concerned with the price paid for admission into the white man's world, "the price of the ticket" in Baldwin's phrase. In his novel, *The Final Passage*, as in his plays of immigration, it is confrontation with the bitter reality of England that is the revelation. But the final passage is not really a voyage made by choice. It is rather the completion of a journey that began with the "middle passage," the crossing of the Atlantic from Africa to the New World in English slave ships. For the black men and women of his dramas, every choice is the result of a desperate search for a homeland to replace the Africa which they lost in generations past when their ancestors were ripped from their tribes. The final passage for the black people of the Commonwealth is the attempt to complete the voyage to English society.

In *The Shelter*, a play which takes on the potent image, taboo for so long, of black men with white women, he first imagines a shipwreck which throws together a freed slave and a white widow on a desert island at the end of the 18th century. His use of the period language is too fussy to wholly express his ideas and the ex-slave is so demonstrably superior to the English woman in thought and poetic speech that his slow transformation in her mind from ape to man is devalued, but it does nicely prepare the way for the second act: an examination of a sexual relationship between a black immigrant and a white woman in the London of the 1950s. At that key moment in the history of immigration, the man and woman can only meet in a pub by pretending to be strangers. When their relationship is revealed by a kiss they sacrifice their right to sit together but a more fundamental decision is being made. The woman has chosen to bear the man's child despite his announcement that he wants to return "home," alone.

Radio is a medium which has allowed Phillips the means to explore his ideas with greater ambition, beginning with his prize-winning play, *The Wasted Years*. In that piece he was able to recreate the pressures of school and family life on two brothers, products of the wave of immigration so ironically reflected by "news reports" describing the original arrival of the previous generation, "these dashing chaps in their colourful hats and big smiles." His starkly refined short radio play, *Crossing the River*, looked at the triangle of the slave heritage, from Africa to the United States and Britain, and his most powerful radio piece, *The Prince of Africa*, was the richly imagined story of the crossing of a slave ship. Although the destination of the ship was Boston,

Massachusetts, it was a play which was firm in its condemnation of England as a nation of slavers and gave little sympathy to the guilty captain who refused to take personal responsibility for his cargo.

With a finely disciplined command of language, and wide experience of a world well beyond the triangle of the slave heritage, Phillips promises to be a dramatist who will continue to broaden the understanding of his audiences, particularly when he is allowed to drop the burden of his label as a "black" writer.

—Ned Chaillet

PINNER, David.

Born in Peterborough, Northamptonshire, 6 October 1940. Educated at Deacon's Grammar School, Peterborough; Royal Academy of Dramatic Art, London, 2 years. Married the actress Catherine Henry Griller in 1965; one daughter and one son. Has acted with repertory companies in Sheffield, Coventry, Windsor, and Farnham, and in London. Playwright-in-residence, Peterborough Repertory Theatre, 1974. Recipient: 4 Arts Council bursaries. Agent: Elspeth Cochrane Agency, 11–13 Orlando Road, London SW4 0LE. Address: 18 Leconfield Avenue, London SW13 0LD, England .

Publications

PLAYS

Dickon (produced 1966). In *New English Dramatists 10*, 1967.
Fanghorn (produced 1967). 1966.
The Drums of Snow (televised 1968). In *New English Dramatists 13*, 1968; revised version (produced 1970), in *Plays of the Year 42*, 1972.
Marriages (also director: produced 1969).
Lightning at the Funeral (produced 1971).
The Potsdam Quartet (produced 1973; revised version produced 1980). 1980.
Cartoon (produced 1973).
An Evening with the GLC (produced 1974).
Hereward the Wake (produced 1974).
Shakebag (produced 1976). In *Green River Review*, 1976.
Lucifer's Fair (produced 1976).
The Last Englishman (broadcast 1979; also director: produced 1990).
Screwball (produced 1982).
Revelations (produced 1986).
The Teddy Bears' Picnic (produced 1988).
Skin Deep (produced 1989).

RADIO PLAYS: *Dickon*, 1966; *Lightfall*, 1967; *Cardinal Richelieu*, 1976; *The Ex-Patriot*, 1977; *Keir Hardie*, 1978; *The Square of the Hypotenuse*, 1978, *Talleyrand*, 1978; *Drink to Me Only*, 1978; *The Last Englishman*, 1979; *Fings Ain't What They Used to Be*, 1979.

TELEVISION PLAYS: *The Drums of Snow*, 1968; *Strange Past*, 1974; *Juliet and Romeo* (Germany), 1976; *The Potsdam Quartet*, 1979; *Leonora*, 1981, *The Sea Horse*, 1982.

NOVELS
Ritual. 1967.
With My Body. 1968.
There'll Always Be an England. 1985.

MANUSCRIPT COLLECTION: Grinnell College, Iowa.

THEATRICAL ACTIVITIES
DIRECTOR: **Plays**—*Marriages*, 1969; *All My Sons* by Arthur Miller, 1976; *The Three Sisters* by Chekhov, 1976, *The American Dream* by Edward Albee, 1977; *Suddenly Last Summer* by Tennessee Williams, 1977; *The Last Englishman*, 1990; *Macbeth*, 1992; *Andromache* by Euripides, 1992.
ACTOR: **Plays**—Hornbeck in *Inherit the Wind* by Jerome Lawrence and Robert E. Lee, 1960; Ross in *Macbeth* and Magpie in *Naked Island* by Russell Bladdon, 1961; Gratiano in *The Merchant of Venice*, 1963; title role in *Billy Liar* by Keith Waterhouse and Willis Hall, 1964; Cassius in *The Man Who Let It Rain* by Marc Brandel, 1964; Laertes in *Hamlet*, Bassanio in *The Merchant of Venice*, and Edmund in *King Lear*, 1964–65; Lopahin in *The Cherry Orchard* by Chekhov, 1965; Sergeant Trotter in *The Mousetrap* by Agatha Christie, 1966; Joseph in *Revelations*, 1986. **Film**—*Robbery*, 1967. **Television** —*The Growing Pains of P. C. Penrose* by Roy Clarke, 1975; *The Prince Regent* by Robert Muller, 1979, *Henry V*, 1979; *Fame Is the Spur*, by Howard Spring, 1982; *A Murder Is Announced* by Agatha Christie, 1985.

David Pinner's *Fanghorn* may have misfired in the 1967 production and it may fail to sustain the comic impact and inventiveness of the first two acts in the third, but the talent is unmistakable. What is remarkable about the writing is its energy. It begins with a middle-aged man beheading roses with a sword, then fencing flirtatiously with his 16-year-old daughter, before switching to making her jump by slashing at her legs. And it sustains a brisk pace in visual surprises and twists in the plot. Occasionally an uncertain note is struck with deliberately over-written lines like "Look at that gull battering his whiteness against the hooks of the wind!" But there are also some very funny lines and plenty of intriguing changes of direction in the dialogue, which builds up to the entrance of Tamara Fanghorn, a tough-talking, leather-clad sophisticate, who arrives before she is expected, and from upstairs. Subsequent developments make it look as though she is in league with the wife to humiliate the husband, who is First Secretary to the Minister of Defence. Act 2 ends with him naked except for his pants, his hands tied with his belt and his feet with the telephone wire. As the curtain falls Tamara is brandishing a cut-throat razor and threatening "Now I am going to cut off what offends me most!" When the curtain rises on Act 3, we find him denuded only of his moustache. The crucial twist comes when his disillusioned wife has walked out on him and we find that this is what he and Tamara had wanted all along.

Dickon is centred more ordinarily on family relationships. It is vitiated by perfunctoriness and superficiality in most of its characterisation, but there is a glowingly affectionate portrait of a lower-middle-class father trying to fight off the awareness of cancer, and then later fighting with pain. But the end piles on the drama too heavily, with one son powdering morphine tablets to put the dying man out of his agony, the other son giving them to him and then the two of them fighting and laughing hysterically.

There is a curious reprise of these themes in *The Potsdam Quartet*. Act 1 ends with the leader revealing to the cellist that for ten years he has been suffering from Parkinson's Disease, and the cellist, who had thought he was going mad, reacts with a joyful demonstration of relief. How the cellist could have remained ignorant of his own condition is never adequately explained and there are only cursory references to the illness in Act 2, in which the biggest climax is provided by a quarrel between the second violin and the viola player, who are lovers, John (second violin) threatens Ronald (viola) that he is going to have the boyfriend of the leader's daughter, and Ronald responds by swallowing a succession of sleeping pills.

The play is set in an ante-room at the Potsdam Conference in 1945. The string quartet (which is based on the Griller Quartet) play two quartets to Churchill, Stalin, and Truman. Act 1 takes place immediately after the first quartet and Act 2 immediately after the second. Apart from the four musicians the only character is a Russian guard who hardly ever speaks. The characters are well contrasted and there is some amusing dialogue, but it is a realistic play in which the action is limited to what can go on in one room between four men who know each other extremely well. Act 1 cannot always avoid the pitfall of making them tell each other things they all know in order to give information to the audience and Act 2 resorts to making them all drunk in order to increase the ratio of action to talk. It lacks the energy and the courage of *Fanghorn* but after writing many unproduced plays in the six intervening years, Pinner cannot be blamed for playing safe, though the theatre can be blamed for failing to nourish the talent he originally showed.

Perhaps his two best plays are two one-acters produced at the Soho Poly. *Cartoon* is about an alcoholic cartoonist drying out in a clinic just up the road from the pub where he customarily spends his lunch-hour drinking grapefruit juice and weeping as he regularly wins money out of the fruit machine. *An Evening with the GLC* is set in a television studio where a Labour Councillor and his wife are exposed to a live interview conducted by their son. They both walk a little too willingly into the traps which are set for them, but the exposure of political dishonesties is nonetheless effective. Written when Pinner was resident playwright at Peterborough, *Hereward the Wake* is another historical play with dialogue in the modern idiom.

—Ronald Hayman

PINNOCK, Winsome.

Born in London in 1961. Educated at Goldsmiths' College, London, B.A. (honours) in English and drama 1982. Playwright-in-residence, Tricycle Theatre, London, 1989–90, and since 1991 Royal Court Theatre, London. Recipient: Unity Theatre Trust award, 1989; George Devine award, 1991; Thames Television award, 1991. Agent: Lemon, Unna, and Durbridge, 24 Pottery Lane, Holland Park, London W11 4LZ, England.

Publications

PLAYS

The Wind of Change (produced 1987).
Leave Taking (produced 1988). In *First Run*, edited by Kate Harwood, 1989.
Picture Palace (produced 1988).
A Rock in Water (produced 1989). In *Black Plays: Two*, edited by Yvonne Brewster, 1989.
A Hero's Welcome (produced 1989).
Talking in Tongues (produced 1991).

TELEVISION PLAYS: episode in *South of the Border* series, 1988; episode in *Chalkface* series, 1991.

Winsome Pinnock is widely acknowledged as one of the leading young talents currently writing for the British theatre. She is also known as one of a very small circle of black women playwrights whose work is regularly produced at mainstream theatres in Britain, most notably at the Royal Court.

Though Pinnock was born and educated in London, her work is influenced by an awareness of the role of a Caribbean heritage in the lives of black communities in England. Some of her most recent work has also dealt with the theme of civil rights. These two interests combine and enrich the language, as well as the themes, of her plays.

One of Pinnock's best-known plays is *A Hero's Welcome*, first presented as a rehearsed reading at the Royal Court in 1986, and given a full production—in a revised version—at the Theatre Upstairs in 1989 (produced by the Women's Playhouse Trust). The play is set in Jamaica and tells a story of family tension and young love, framed in the traditions and expectations of West Indian culture but informed by the British context of its writing and production. It centres on three young women, Minda, Sis, and Ishbel. All three grow up in a small Caribbean community in 1947. All are looking for a way out of poverty, for better lives, and Len, the returning "hero" (charged with a strong sexual drive which is exciting and enticing to the young women) seems to symbolize that kind of possibility and hope. Only the two older women characters, Nana and Mrs. Walker, are able to offer the wisdom of age and experience which keeps the girls in line, in their community. That such a play found a wide and diverse audience is itself an achievement, but more important was the national recognition which this production brought to Pinnock.

Also in 1989—in fact, one month before *A Hero's Welcome* was given its full production—the Theatre Upstairs premiered Pinnock's *A Rock in Water*. This play broke new ground for Pinnock and for London audiences, in its powerful evocation of a recent historical figure: Claudia Jones, the founder of the Notting Hill Carnivals in the mid-1950s and a dedicated worker at one of the first black presses, the *West Indian Gazette*. In bringing Jones to public attention, Pinnock engaged in a process of "writing [black] women into history." And as Jones was not just any woman, the play also engaged audiences in a recognition of the importance of location and cultural identity in the lives of black women and men. The play chronicles the life of Claudia Jones in Trinidad and Harlem as well as in London, where she lived only after she was exiled to England after being accused of "un-American activities."

A Rock in Water was commissioned by the Royal Court's Young People's theatre and was developed through workshops with actors. But Pinnock also did her own research by interviewing people who had known Claudia Jones: she brought the woman to life through the memories of contemporaries and co-workers, including the actress Corinne Skinner-Carter (who was featured in *A Hero's Welcome*). The play was performed by 14 members of the Young People's Theatre, all of whom had been closely involved in the development of the ideas which Pinnock wove into the play.

Leave Taking was first produced at the Liverpool Playhouse Studio in 1988, the same year which saw the national tour of *Picture Palace*, produced by the Women's Theatre Group. While *Picture Palace* focused on the roles which women play and the images which are used in advertising and the media in Britain, *Leave Taking* followed on from *A Hero's Welcome* in its cross-cultural focus. *Leave Taking* was given a revival in 1990, when it was directed by Jules Wright and produced by the Women's Playhouse Trust at the Royal Court. The play's popularity is related to its scope and its intelligent yet humorous view of relationships between individuals and their cultural identities. *Leave Taking* also introduced the theme of cultural difference in the coming of awareness of individuals and groups of black women and men, a topic which is rarely dealt with in British theatre. *Leave Taking* was revived for a run at the Belgrade Theatre, Coventry in May 1992.

Pinnock's most recent play, *Talking in Tongues*, was performed at the Royal Court Theatre (directed by Hetty MacDonald), when Pinnock was writer-in-residence there in 1991. In this play, Pinnock's concern with the intermingling of cultures, identities, and voices is further developed within the story of a number of black and white friends and colleagues who come together at a New Year's Eve party. Sexuality and inter-racial relationships are represented, as are the themes of competition and identification between blacks and whites, women and men. As in her other work, the use of dialect frames the play with the sound and rhythm of another language. The film adaptation of *Talking in Tongues* is already underway.

In these plays, as in most of Pinnock's work to date, the realist drama focuses on the central dilemma of the black woman coming to terms with (predominantly) white British society. Pinnock's talent as a playwright is enriched in all of her work by her keen awareness of the nuances of language, and by her ability to reach out to and communicate with the many different "communities" and individuals who make up the audiences of her plays.

—Lizbeth Goodman

PINTER, Harold.

Born in Hackney, London, 10 October 1930. Educated at Hackney Downs Grammar School, 1943–47; Royal Academy of Dramatic Art, London, 1948. Conscientious objector: no military service. Married 1) the actress Vivien Merchant in 1956 (divorced 1980), one son; 2) the writer Lady Antonia Fraser in 1980. Professional actor, 1949–60, and occasionally since then; also a director; associate director, National Theatre, London, 1973–83; director, United British Artists, 1983; since 1988 editor and publisher Greville Press,

Warwick, and since 1989 member of the editorial board, *Cricket World*. Recipient: *Evening Standard* award, 1960; Newspaper Guild of New York award, 1962; Italia prize, for television play, 1962; Berlin Film Festival Silver Bear, 1963; Screenwriters Guild award, for television play, 1963, for screenplay, 1963; New York Film Critics award, 1964; BAFTA award, 1965, 1971; Tony award, 1967; Whitbread award, 1967; New York Drama Critics Circle award, 1967, 1980; Shakespeare prize (Hamburg), 1970; Writers Guild award, 1971; Cannes Film Festival Golden Palm, 1971; Austrian State prize, 1973; Pirandello prize, 1980; Commonwealth award, 1981; Donatello prize, 1982; British Theatre Association award, 1983, 1985; Bobst award, 1984. D.Litt.: universities of Reading, 1970, Birmingham, 1971, Glasgow, 1974, East Anglia, Norwich, 1974, Stirling, 1979, Hull, 1986, and Sussex, 1990; Brown University, Providence, Rhode Island, 1982. Honorary fellow, Modern Language Association (USA), 1970; fellow, Royal Society of Literature; honorary member, American Academy and Institute of Arts and Letters, 1984, and American Academy of Arts and Sciences, 1985; honorary fellow, Queen Mary College, London, 1987. C.B.E. (Commander, Order of the British Empire), 1966. Lives in London. Agent: Judy Daish Associates, 83 Eastbourne Mews, London W2 6LQ, England.

Publications

PLAYS

The Room (produced 1957; also director). In *The Birthday Party and Other Plays*, 1960.

The Birthday Party (produced 1958). 1959; in *The Birthday Party and Other Plays*, 1960; revised version, 1965.

Sketches in *One to Another* (produced 1959). 1960.

Sketches in *Pieces of Eight* (produced 1959). In *A Slight Ache and Other Plays*, 1961; in *The Dwarfs and Eight Revue Sketches*, 1965.

A Slight Ache (broadcast 1959; produced 1961). In *A Slight Ache and Other Plays*, 1961; in *Three Plays*, 1962.

The Dumb Waiter (produced 1959). In *The Birthday Party and Other Plays*, 1960.

The Dwarfs (broadcast 1960; also director: produced 1963; revised version produced 1966). In *A Slight Ache and Other Plays*, 1961, in *Three Plays*, 1962.

The Birthday Party and Other Plays (includes *The Dumb Waiter* and *The Room*). 1960; as *The Birthday Party and The Room* (includes *The Dumb Waiter*), 1961.

The Caretaker (produced 1960). 1960; with *The Dumb Waiter*, 1961.

Night School (televised 1960). In *Tea Party and Other Plays*, 1967; in *Early Plays*, 1968.

A Night Out (broadcast 1960; produced 1961). In *A Slight Ache and Other Plays*, 1961; in *Early Plays*, 1968.

A Slight Ache and Other Plays (includes *The Dwarfs, A Night Out*, and sketches). 1961.

The Collection (televised 1961; also co-director; produced 1962; revised version, televised 1978). 1962; in *Three Plays*, 1962.

Three Plays. 1962.

The Lover (televised 1963; also director: produced 1963). In *The Collection, and The Lover,* 1963.

The Collection, and The Lover (includes the prose piece *The Examination*). 1963.

The Compartment (unreleased screenplay), in *Project 1,* with Samuel Beckett and Eugène Ionesco. 1963.

Dialogue for Three, in *Stand,* vol. 6, no. 3, 1963.

Tea Party (televised 1965; produced 1968). 1965; revised version, 1968.

The Homecoming (produced 1965). 1965; revised version, 1968.

The Dwarfs and Eight Revue Sketches (includes *Trouble in the Works, The Black and White, Request Stop, Last to Go, Applicant, Interview, That's All, That's Your Trouble*). 1965.

The Basement (televised 1967; produced 1968). In *Tea Party and Other Plays,* 1967; in *The Lover, The Tea Party, The Basement,* 1967.

Tea Party and Other Plays. 1967.

The Lover, The Tea Party, The Basement. 1967.

Early Plays: A Night Out, Night School, Revue Sketches. 1968.

Sketches by Pinter (produced 1969). In *Early Plays,* 1968.

Landscape (broadcast 1968; produced 1969). 1968; in *Landscape, and Silence,* 1969.

Silence (produced 1969). In *Landscape, and Silence,* 1969.

Landscape, and Silence (includes *Night*). 1969.

Night, in *Mixed Doubles* (produced 1969). In *Landscape, and Silence,* 1969.

Five Screenplays (includes *The Caretaker, The Servant, The Pumpkin Eater, Accident, The Quiller Memorandum*). 1971; modified version, omitting *The Caretaker* and including *The Go-Between,* 1971.

Old Times (produced 1971). 1971.

Monologue (televised 1973; produced 1973). 1973.

No Man's Land (produced 1975). 1975.

Plays 1–4. 1975–81; as *Complete Works 1–4,* 1977–81.

The Proust Screenplay: A la Recherche du Temps Perdu. 1977.

Betrayal (produced 1978). 1978.

The Hothouse (also director: produced 1980). 1980; revised version (produced 1982), 1982.

Family Voices (broadcast 1981; produced 1981). 1981.

The Screenplay of The French Lieutenant's Woman. 1981.

The French Lieutenant's Woman and Other Screenplays (includes *Langrishe, Go Down, The Last Tycoon*). 1982.

Other Places (includes *Family Voices, Victoria Station, A Kind of Alaska*) (produced 1982). 1982; revised version, including *One for the Road* and omitting *Family Voices* (produced 1984).

Precisely (sketch), in *The Big One* (produced 1983).

One for the Road (also director: produced 1984; in *Other Places,* produced 1984). 1984; revised version, 1985.

Mountain Language (also director: produced 1988). 1988.

The Heat of the Day, adaptation of the novel by Elizabeth Bowen (televised 1989). 1989.

The Comfort of Strangers and Other Screenplays (includes *Reunion, Turtle Diary, Victory*). 1990.
Party Time (also director: produced 1991). With *Mountain Language*, 1991.
The New World Order (also director: produced 1991).
Moonlight (produced 1993).

SCREENPLAYS: *The Servant*, 1963; *The Guest (The Caretaker)*, 1964; *The Pumpkin Eater*, 1964; *The Quiller Memorandum*, 1966; *Accident*, 1967; *The Birthday Party*, 1968; *The Go-Between*, 1971; *The Homecoming*, 1973; *The Last Tycoon*, 1976; *The French Lieutenant's Woman*, 1981; *Betrayal*, 1982; *Turtle Diary*, 1985; *The Trial*, 1989; *Reunion*, 1989; *The Handmaid's Tale*, 1990; *The Comfort of Strangers*, 1990; *The Remains of the Day*, 1991.

RADIO PLAYS: *A Slight Ache*, 1959; *The Dwarfs*, 1960; *A Night Out*, 1960; *Landscape*, 1968; *Famiˡ Voices*, 1981; *Players*, 1985.

TELEVISION PLAYS: *Night School*, 1960; *The Collection*, 1961, revised version, 1978; *The Lover*, 1963; *Tea Party*, 1965; *The Basement*, 1967; *Monologue*, 1973; *Langrishe, Go Down*, from the novel by Aidan Higgins, 1978; *Mountain Language*, 1988; *The Heat of the Day*, 1989; *Party Time*, 1992.

NOVEL
The Dwarfs. 1990.

VERSE
Poems, edited by Alan Clodd. 1968; revised edition, 1971.
I Know the Place. 1979.
Ten Early Poems. 1992.

OTHER
Mac (on Anew McMaster). 1968.
Poems and Prose 1949–1977. 1978; revised edition, as *Collected Poems and Prose*, 1986.

Editor, with John Fuller and Peter Redgrove, *New Poems 1967: A PEN Anthology*. 1968.
Editor, with Geoffrey Godbert and Anthony Astbury, *100 Poems by 100 Poets*. 1986.

BIBLIOGRAPHY: *Pinter: A Bibliography: His Works and Occasional Writings with a Comprehensive Checklist of Criticism and Reviews of the London Productions* by Rudiger Imhof, 1975; *Harold Pinter: An Annotated Bibliography* by Steven H. Gale, 1978.

CRITICAL STUDIES (a selection): *Harold Pinter*, by Arnold P. Hinchliffe,1967, revised edition 1981; *Harold Pinter* by Ronald Hayman, 1968, revised edition, 1980; *Harold Pinter* by John Russell Taylor, 1969; *Stratagems to Uncover Nakedness: The Dramas of Harold Pinter* by Lois Gordon, 1969; *Harold Pinter: The Poetics of Silence* by James H. Hollis, 1970; *Harold Pinter* by Alrene Sykes, 1970; *The Peopled Wound: The Plays of Harold Pinter* by Martin Esslin, 1970, revised edition, as *Pinter: A Study of His Plays*, 1973, revised edition, 1977, revised edition, as *Pinter: The Playwright*, 1982; *The Dramatic World of Harold Pinter: Its Basis in Ritual* by Katherine H. Burkman, 1971; *Pinter: A Collection of Critical Essays* edited by Arthur Ganz, 1972; *The Plays of Harold Pinter: An Assessment* by Simon Trussler, 1973; *The Pinter Problem* by Austin E. Quigley, 1975; *The Dream Structure of Pinter's Plays: A Psychoanalytic Approach* by Lucina Paquet Gabbard, 1976; *Where the Laughter Stops: Pinter's Tragi-Comedy*, 1976, and *Harold Pinter*, 1982, both by Bernard F. Dukore; *Butter's Going Up: A Critical Analysis of Harold Pinter's Work* by Steven H. Gale, 1977, and *Harold Pinter: Critical Approaches* edited by Gale, 1986; *Harold Pinter: A Critical Evaluation* by Surendra Sahai, 1981; *Canters and Chronicles: The Use of Narrative in the Plays of Samuel Beckett and Harold Pinter* by Kristin Morrison, 1983; *Harold Pinter* by Guido Almansi and Simon Henderson, 1983; *Pinter: The Player's Playwright* by David T. Thompson, 1985; *Pinter's Comic Play* by Elin Diamond, 1985; *Harold Pinter: You Never Heard Such Silence* edited by Alan Bold, 1985; *Making Pictures: The Pinter Screenplays* by Joanne Klein, 1985; *Harold Pinter: The Birthday Party, The Caretaker, and The Homecoming: A Casebook* edited by Michael Scott, 1986; *Pinter's Female Portraits: A Study of Female Characters in the Plays of Pinter* by Elizabeth Sakellaridou, 1988; *Harold Pinter: Towards a Poetics of His Plays* by Volker Strunk, 1989; *Pinter in Play* by Susan Merritt, 1990; *Harold Pinter: A Casebook* by Lois Gordon, 1990; *File on Pinter* by Malcolm Page, 1992.

THEATRICAL ACTIVITIES

DIRECTOR: **Plays**—*The Birthday Party*, 1958; *The Room*, 1960; *The Collection* (co-director, with Peter Hall), 1962; *The Lover*, 1963; *The Dwarfs*, 1963; *The Birthday Party*, 1964; *The Man in the Glass Booth* by Robert Shaw, 1967; *Exiles* by James Joyce, 1970; *Butley* by Simon Gray, 1971; *Next of Kin* by John Hopkins, 1974; *Otherwise Engaged* by Simon Gray, 1975, 1977; *Blithe Spirit* by Noël Coward, 1976; *The Innocents* by William Archibald, 1976; *The Rear Column* by Simon Gray, 1978; *Close of Play* by Simon Gray, 1979; *The Hothouse*, 1980; *Quartermaine's Terms* by Simon Gray, 1981; *Incident at Tulse Hill* by Robert East, 1981; *The Trojan War Will Not Take Place* by Jean Giraudoux, 1983; *The Common Pursuit* by Simon Gray, 1984; *One for the Road, and Victoria Station*, 1984; *Sweet Bird of Youth* by Tennessee Williams, 1985; *Circe and Bravo* by Donald Freed, 1986; *Mountain Language*, 1988; *Vanilla* by Jane Stanton Hitchcock, 1990; *Party Time*, 1991; *The New World Order*, 1991; *Oleanna* by David Mamet, 1993. **Film**—*Butley*, 1976. **Television**—*The Rear Column* by Simon Gray, 1980; *The Hothouse*, 1981.

ACTOR (as David Baron and Harold Pinter): **Plays**—with Anew McMaster's theatre company in Ireland, 1950–52; with Donald Wolfit's theatre company,

Kings Theatre, Hammersmith, London, 1953; numerous provincial repertory companies, 1953–60; Mick in *The Caretaker*, 1964; Goldberg in *The Birthday Party*, 1964; Lenny in *The Homecoming*, 1969; Deeley in *Old Times*, 1985; Hirst in *No Man's Land*, 1992. Radio—*Monologue*, 1975; *Rough for Radio* by Samuel Beckett, 1976; *Two Plays* by Václav Havel, 1977. Films—*The Servant*, 1963; *Accident*, 1967; *The Rise and Rise of Michael Rimmer*, 1970. Television—*Rogue Male*, 1976; *Langrishe, Go Down*, 1978; *The Birthday Party*, 1986.

In a remarkably prolific period between 1957 and 1965, Harold Pinter established himself as the most gifted playwright in England and the author of a unique dramatic idiom. Popularly labelled "the Pinteresque," Pinter's theater is not "of the absurd"; nor is it a "drama of menace," both of which portray the gratuitous visitation upon innocent victims of external forces of terror or "the absurd." Actually, "the Pinteresque" consists of a much more frightening visitation: Pinter's comfortable people (at least through *Silence* and *Landscape*), unlike the innocents of Kafka's or even Beckett's worlds, are besieged by their own internal fears and longings and their own irrepressible guilts and menacing sexual drives, and it is these which invariably wage successful war against the tidy life-styles they have constructed in order to survive from day to day.

Pinter's characters, usually enclosed in a room, organize their lives with the "games people play." But in their games or role-playing—where each has agreed to a specific scenario with implicit limits and taboos—they often say one thing but really feel and often communicate another. During their exchanges, in fact, the verbal is only the most superficial level of communication. The connotations of their words and their accompanying gestures, or pauses, or *double-entendres*—and their hesitations and silences—really communicate a second level of meaning often opposed to the first. Pinter himself has said of language: "The speech we hear is an indication of that which we don't hear. It is a necessary avoidance, a violent, sly, and anguished or mocking smoke screen which keeps the other in its true place. When true silence falls we are left with echo but are nearer nakedness. One way of looking at speech is to say that it is a constant stratagem to cover nakedness." Indeed, one way of looking at Pinter's plays is to say that they are dramatic stratagems that uncover nakedness.

Into his characters' rooms, and into their ritualized and verbal relationships, a stranger invariably enters, whereupon language begins to disintegrate, and the protection promised by the room becomes threatened. The commonplace room, in fact, becomes the violent scene of mental and physical breakdown. What occurs, in effect, is that the characters *project on to* the stranger—an intruder into their precarious, psychic stability—their deepest fears. The so-called victimizers—Goldberg and McCann in *The Birthday Party*; Riley in *The Room*; the blind, mute matchseller in *A Slight Ache*; the visiting, unfamiliar sister-in-law in *The Homecoming*; the old, garrulous, and admittedly opportunistic Davies in *The Caretaker*; and even the mechanical dumb waiter in *The Dumb Waiter*—all function as screens upon which the characters externalize their own irrationality, that side of themselves which the games have ultimately been inadequate to hide. Pinter's "intruders" are, in a sense, his technique for leading his characters to expose their true identities. What is, of course, simultaneously funny and horrific is that the games constructed—and even the "intruders" or screens, which are mirror images of the characters— contain within themselves the boring lives already lived *and* the violence struggling for expression.

In Pinter's first play, *The Room*, Rose coddles, feeds, clothes, and emascu- lates her silent husband, Bert, fittingly portrayed as a child (he has agreed to play the passive child in their relationship), wearing a silly hat and reading comic books. Protective of her precarious stability she admits: "This is a good room. You've got a chance in a place like this. . . . It's cold out. . . . It's murder." When a young couple enters (a mirror of Rose and Bert many years before), thinking her flat free, she actually experiences them as potential "murderers." This is exacerbated by her landlord's (Kidd's) retaliatory remarks (because of her earlier putdown) and his mention that a blind, black man in the basement (an obvious image of her subterranean mind) is waiting to "see" her. For the rest of the play, Rose acts out her rage, sexual appetite, and then guilt toward the black Riley, as though re-enacting an earlier Oedipal crime. From her "You're all deaf and dumb and blind, the lot of you," she succumbs to his "Sal [a childhood name]. . . . I want you to come home" and caresses his eyes and head. With Bert's return, following this enactment of her most basic instinctual/tabooed behavior, she becomes blind.

In *The Birthday Party* a young man has similarly secluded himself in order to hide from some lingering childhood guilt. When the two strangers Goldberg and McCann enter his seaside retreat, Stanley becomes violent and projects upon them his own fantasies and guilts: "You stink of sin"; "you contaminate womankind. . . . Mother defiler. . . . You verminate the sheet of your birth." Later at a "celebration," his landlady, Meg, with whom Stanley has structured a safe though flirtatious child-lover relationship, and the neighbor, Lulu, along with Goldberg and McCann, act out both Stanley's taboo Oedipal impulses and his repulsion and guilt toward these drives. As Rose became blind, Stanley becomes mute. In *The Dumb Waiter* two hitmen lose control when some actually very funny messages descend on the building's dumb waiter and the w.c. misfunctions, whereupon their carefully measured roles are upset. In *The Caretaker* the intrusion of a harmless (though manipulative and highly verbal) old man threatens the carefully designed relationship of two brothers. In *The Homecoming* a presumably stable all-male household is exposed in all its rage, confused sexuality, and utter precariousness when an unknown woman (the visiting wife of a third son) appears. Her mere presence threatens everyone's identity. In *The Basement* and *Tea Party* Pinter returns to his earlier triangular patterns, and focuses on the breakdown of orderly and controlled behavior for displays of cuckoldry and homosexuality.

Silence and *Landscape* indicate a new direction. The same childless couples inhabit these plays, but they have long ago learned that playing games will not assure their relationship. Nothing is certain in their isolated rooms, and least of all, identity or connection. Each not only fails to understand himself (unable to distinguish fantasy from experience) but he can never know the stranger who calls himself his spouse. There is a kind of finality in these plays but also a poignancy about these people so inextricably locked within themselves.

The plays demand a more poetic reading—for the lyrical sense of the characters' rationalizations, hopes, fears, and fantasies, which are true at one and the same time. Still in the tradition of Joyce, Woolf, and Beckett, Pinter has now moved from earlier explorations of the underside of self (and what Freud called "the seething cauldron" beneath logical thought and act) to a dramatic rendering of the simultaneous levels of fantasy and real experience that equally occupy the individual. He has said of the complexities and ultimate mystery of human behavior: "The desire for verification on the part of us all, with regard to our own experience and the experience of others, is understandable, but cannot always be satisfied. I suggest there can be no hard distinctions between what is real and what is unreal, nor between what is true and what is false. A thing is not necessarily either true or false; it can be both true and false."

The details, characters, and images of *Silence* and *Landscape* are similar, as though each were two halves of a whole. Poetic images of growing old, they tell of brief and unfulfilled love affairs. Their details are of walks in the country, moments in pubs, and flights of birds; recollections are illuminated by memories of fading sunlight or grey clouds or gusts of rain. Speakers interrupt their wistful thoughts with lusty outbursts about the most mundane of matters. Every word, gesture, color, and mood reverberates, and each character's reveries define the others; although their conversations are not directed to the other, each one explains the way in which life has passed the other by, although to him that insight remains unfathomable. Just as these people fail to connect, their poetically connected insights, their common pain and joy, and their repetition of words and gestures suggest a universality about human nature. Pinter has clearly moved toward new, poetic dimensions; interestingly, he also published his first volume of poems at this time, although they were written as early as his first plays.

Old Times returns to issues of possible and real homosexual and heterosexual commitment, fidelity, and friendship. Pinter's triangle (two women and a man) suggests any number of possibilities and combinations: "There are some things one remembers even though they may never have happened. There are things I remember which may never have happened but as I recall them so they take place." *No Man's Land* recreates a male world of potential comforters and predators with each man locked in a precarious linguistic world of identity. "No man's land" is that mysterious realm of truth and self-knowledge, of one's comprehension of oneself and one's world that "never moves, which never changes, which never grows older, but which remains forever, icy and silent."

Almost as though Pinter had begun with a line from *Old Times* (where one man tells another he "proposed" that his wife "betray" him), *Betrayal* treats multiple betrayals among friends, spouses, lovers (and even within the self)—in a fascinating structural manipulation of time. Perhaps inspired by his screenplay of Proust's *A la recherche*, it begins two years after an affair ended and in nine scenes moves back in time. Humor, banality, poetry, violence, diluted passion, and pain merge in a poignant evocation of time and one's eternal separation from both innocence and responsibility.

The Hothouse, written in 1958 but not published until 1980, focuses on the sanatorium in which the mute Stanley in *The Birthday Party* might have been committed. Staff members chatter in banal, funny, and threatening conversations about sex and the variations of power and control. Playing with traditional symbolism—there has been both a birth and death; the play occurs on Christmas; the characters (in this hothouse) are named Roote, Cutts, Lush, and Lamb—Pinter raises serious and ambiguous issues about sanity and insanity, "leaders" and "followers." At the end, a gratuitous mass murder of the staff is committed, but the perpetrator remains ambiguous: is it one of the patients? Is it one of the staff?

The London production of *Other Places* included *Victoria Station*, *A Kind of Alaska*, and *Family Voices*; in New York, *One for the Road* replaced *Family Voices*, originally a radio play. There is a curious unity in the three remaining works, as they anatomize primitive responses to menace and loyalty. *Tours de force* in concreteness, they are finely chiselled portraits of the contingency of human experience; they simultaneously evoke the most abiding of human encounters with evil or kindness.

The very short *Victoria Station* portrays the conversation between a taxi despatcher and a driver who, after picking up a female passenger, loses all sense of place and identity. The despatcher becomes his brother's keeper. *One for the Road* conveys a series of frightening confrontations between a banal, Goldberg-like torturer (vaguely representative of God and country) and his victims—a tortured man, his brutally assaulted wife, and their eventually murdered son. In the most affecting of the group, *A Kind of Alaska*, a woman in her mid-forties "erupts to life" after nearly 30 years of sleeping sickness. Pinter depicts her rebellious, bewildered, foolish, angry, and gallant responses in a combination of hallucination, childlike language, and erotic wish fulfilment. The reality of her lost youth and lost love, along with her sister's and doctor's unshakable loyalty, create a powerful work.

Pinter's work since the late 1980's has been political in the extreme. He has announced, repeatedly, that he feels a responsibility to pursue his role as "a citizen of the world in which I live, [and] insist upon taking responsibility." This responsibility consists of both speaking out publicly and writing about the political oppression of the individual through the subversive function of language. As such, *Mountain Language* treats the oppression of an unnamed people in an unspecified totalitarian state for the crime of retaining their own (mountain) language. In the first of four brief scenes, Pinter portrays a mother and wife who wait an entire day before being permitted to visit their imprisoned husband and son—each man apparently arrested for retaining his now-outlawed language. As one officer reminds the women: "Your language is forbidden. It is dead. No one is allowed to speak your language." Already terrorized by two guards and their dogs, the women, even when permitted to see the prisoners, are subjected to additional ridicule and sexual menace. As the elderly mother visits her son—and both are forbidden to speak in their native language—a "voice over" (tape) plays out their thoughts; but the guards' double-talk destroys any possibility of communication. In the next of these stark, rapid scenes, a young woman sees the hooded figure of her badly tortured husband and is told she can save him only if she sleeps with an administrator. In the final scene, when the state arbitrarily changes the law and the mother is told she "can speak in her own language. Until futher notice," she has become too terrorized to do so, and her son collapses before her eyes. The play is a frightening image, as Pinter explained, of what happens when people are deprived of "expressing their own identity through their own language."

The New World Order, billed as "a short satiric response to the Gulf War," is a 10-minute play whose title is taken from one of George Bush's political phrases. It portrays the gratuitous torture two men inflict upon an innocent. In a small room two captors stand and discuss what to do with their victim, who sits silent and blindfolded before them. As they play word games punctuated by Pinter's meticulous pauses, they increase the prisoner's apprehension of his impending torture. In essence, the two men play ironic variations on the theme "He has no idea what we are going to do with him," and the victim, like the audience, has "some idea," "a faint idea," "a little idea" and constructs any series of possible tortures. The guards also remind each other about their power in language—for example, they tease their victim with contradictory and vulgar sexual epithets (He is "a cunt" and then "a prick"); they proceed to question whether he is a peasant or theologian. At one point, the more vocal terrorist becomes silent. "I feel pure," he says, as if through sheer power and authority he had reached a transcendent state. In Pinter's somewhat mysterious climax, we are told that not only will his partner but the prisoner as well will shake his hand "in about thirty-five minutes." It would appear that what was the peasant, theologian, or just plain Pinter innocent has either been driven entirely mad or has totally capitulated to authority. The new world order has reduced all dissent or individuality to blind conformity.

—Lois Gordon

See the essay on *The Homecoming*.

PLATER, Alan (Frederick).

Born in Jarrow-on-Tyne, County Durham, 15 April 1935. Educated at Pickering Road Junior and Infant School, Hull, 1940–46; Kingston High School, Hull, 1946–53; King's College, Newcastle upon Tyne (University of Durham), 1953–57; qualified as architect (Associate, Royal Institute of British Architects), 1961. Married 1) Shirley Johnson in 1958 (divorced 1985), two sons and one daughter; 2) Shirley Rubinstein, three stepsons. Worked in an architect's office, Hull, 1957–60. Since 1960 full-time writer. Co-founder, Humberside Theatre (formerly Hull Arts Centre), 1970; co-chair, Writers Guild of Great Britain, 1986–87. Recipient: Writers Guild award, for radio play, 1972; Sony award, for radio play, 1983; Royal Television Society award, 1984, 1985; New York and San Francisco film festival awards, 1986; Broadcasting Guild award, 1987; BAFTA writers and drama series award, 1988; Variety Club of Great Britain award, 1989. D. Litt.: Hull University, 1985. Honorary Fellow, Hull College of Higher Education, 1983; Fellow, Royal Society of Literature, 1985. Lives in London. Agent: Alexandra Cann Representation, 68E Redcliffe Gardens, London SW10 9HE, England.

Publications

PLAYS

The Referees (televised 1961).
The Mating Season (broadcast 1962; produced 1963). In *Worth a Hearing: A Collection of Radio Plays*, edited by Alfred Bradley, 1967.

A Smashing Day (televised 1962; revised version, music by Ben Kingsley and Robert Powell, produced 1965).

The Rainbow Machine (broadcast 1962; produced 1963).

Ted's Cathedral (produced 1963).

A Quiet Night (televised 1963). In *Z Cars: Four Scripts from the Television Series*, edited by Michael Marland, 1968.

See the Pretty Lights (televised 1963; produced 1970). In *Theatre Choice: A Collection of Modern Short Plays*, edited by Michael Marland, 1972.

The Nutter (televised 1965; revised version, as *Charlie Came to Our Town*, music by Alex Glasgow, produced 1966).

Excursion (broadcast 1966). In *You and Me*, 1973.

The What on the Landing? (broadcast 1967; produced 1968).

On Christmas Day in the Morning (*Softly, Softly* series; televised 1968). Included in *You and Me*, 1973.

Hop Step and Jump (produced 1968).

Close the Coalhouse Door, music by Alex Glasgow, adaptation of stories by Sid Chaplin (produced 1968). 1969.

Don't Build a Bridge, Drain the River!, music by Michael Chapman and Mike Waterson (produced 1970; revised version, music by Mike O'Neil, produced 1980).

Simon Says!, music by Alex Glasgow (produced 1970).

And a Little Love Besides (produced 1970). In *You and Me*, 1973.

King Billy Vaudeville Show, with others (produced 1971).

Seventeen Per Cent Said Push Off (televised 1972). In *You and Me*, 1973.

The Tigers are Coming—O.K.? (produced 1972).

You and Me: Four Plays, edited by Alfred Bradley. 1973.

Swallows on the Water (produced 1973).

When the Reds Go Marching In (produced 1973).

Annie Kenney (televised 1974). In *Act 3*, edited by David Self and Ray Speakman, 1979.

Tales of Humberside, music by Jim Bywater (produced 1975).

Trinity Tales, music by Alex Glasgow (televised 1975; produced 1975).

Our Albert (produced 1976).

The Fosdyke Saga, with Bill Tidy (produced 1977). 1978.

Drums along the Ginnel (produced 1977).

Fosdyke 2, with Bill Tidy (produced 1977).

Short Back and Sides (televised 1977). In *City Life*, edited by David Self, 1980.

Well Good Night Then . . . (produced 1978).

Skyhooks (produced 1982).

On Your Way, Riley!, music by Alex Glasgow (produced 1982).

A Foot on the Earth (produced 1984).

Prez, music by Bernie Cash (produced 1985).

Rent Party, from an idea by Nat Shapiro (produced 1989).

Sweet Sorrow (produced 1990). 1990.

Going Home (produced 1990). 1990.

I Thought I Heard a Rustling (produced 1991). 1991.

SCREENPLAYS: *The Virgin and the Gypsy*, 1970; *Juggernaut*, 1974; *It Shouldn't Happen to a Vet* (*All Things Bright and Beautiful*), 1976; *Priest of Love*, 1982; *The Inside Man*, 1984.

RADIO PLAYS: *The Smokeless Zone*, 1961; *Counting the Legs*, 1961; *The Mating Season*, 1962; *The Rainbow Machine*, 1962; *The Seventh Day of Arthur*, 1963; *Excursion*, 1966; *The What on the Landing?*, 1967; *Fred*, 1970; *The Slow Stain*, 1973; *5 Days in '55* (*The Gilberdyke Diaries*), 1976; *Tunes*, 1979; *Swallows on the Water*, 1981; *The Journal of Vasilije Bogdanovic* (*In a Strange Land* series), 1982; *Toɩpuddle*, with Vince Hill, 1982; *Who's Jimmy Dickenson?*, from his play *Well Good Night Then . . .*, 1986.

TELEVISION PLAYS: *The Referees*, 1961; *A Smashing Day*, 1962; *So Long Charlie*, 1963; *See the Pretty Lights*, 1963; *Z Cars* series (18 episodes), 1963–65; *Ted's Cathedral*, 1964; *Fred*, 1964; *The Incident*, 1965; *The Nutter*, 1965; *Softly, Softly* series (30 episodes), 1966–76; *To See How Far It Is* (trilogy), 1968; *The First Lady* series (4 episodes), 1968–69; *Rest in Peace, Uncle Fred*, 1970; *Seventeen Per Cent Said Push Off*, 1972; *The Reluctant Juggler* (*The Edwardians* series), 1972; *Tonight We Meet Arthur Pendlebury*, 1972; *It Must Be Something in the Water* (documentary), 1973; *Brotherly Love*, 1973; *The Land of Green Ginger*, 1974; *The Needle Match*, 1974; *Goldilocks and the Three Bears*, 1974; *Wish You Were Here* (documentary), 1974; *Annie Kenney* (*Shoulder to Shoulder* series), 1974; *The Loner* series, 1975; *The Stars Look Down*, from the novel by A.J. Cronin, 1975; *Trinity Tales* series, 1975; *Willow Cabins*, 1975; *Practical Experience*, 1976; *Oh No—It's Selwyn Froggit* series, 1976; *A Tyneside Entertainment* (documentary), 1976; *Seven Days That Shook Young Jim* (*Going to Work* series), 1976; *We Are the Masters Now*, 1976; *There Are Several Businesses Like Show Business*, 1976; *The Bike*, 1977; *Short Back and Sides*, 1977; *Middlemen* series, 1977; *By Christian Judges Condemned*, 1977; *For the Love of Albert* series, 1977; *Give Us a Kiss, Christabel*, 1977; *The Eddystone Lights* (documentary), 1978; *The Party of the First Part*, 1978; *Curriculee Curricula*, music by Dave Greenslade, 1978; *Night People*, 1978; *Flambards*, from works by K.M. Peyton, 1979; *The Blacktoft Diaries*, 1979; *Reunion*, 1979; *The Good Companions*, from the novel by J.B. Priestley, 1980; *Get Lost!* series, 1981; *Barchester Chronicles*, from novels by Trollope, 1981; *The Clarion Van*, from a work by Doris Neild Chew, 1983; *Feet Foremost*, from a story by L.P. Hartley, 1983; *Bewitched*, from the story by Edith Wharton, 1983; *The Consultant*, from the novel *Invitation to Tender* by John McNeil, 1983; *Pride of Our Alley*, 1983; *The Crystal Spirit: Orwell on Jura*, 1983; *Thank You, Mrs. Clinkscales*, 1984; *The Solitary Cyclist*, from a story by Arthur Conan Doyle, 1984; *Edward Lear: On the Edge of the Sand*, 1985; *The Beiderbecke Affair* series, 1985; *A Murder Is Announced*, from the novel by Agatha Christie, 1985; *Coming Through*, 1985; *The Man with the Twisted Lip*, from a story by Arthur Conan Doyle, 1986; *Death Is Part of the Process*, from a novel by Hilda Bernstein, 1986; *Fortunes of War*, from novels by Olivia Manning, 1987; *The Beiderbecke Tapes*, 1987; *A Very British Coup*, from the novel by Chris Mullin, 1988; *The Beiderbecke Connection*, 1988; *Campion*, from the works of Margery Allingham, 1989; *A Day in Summer*, from the novel by J.L. Carr, 1989; *Misterioso*, from his own novel, 1991; *The Patience of Maigret*, from the novel by Georges Simenon, 1992; *Maigret and the Burglar's Wife*, from the novel by Georges Simenon, 1992.

NOVELS

The Beiderbecke Affair. 1985.
The Beiderbecke Tapes. 1986.
Misterioso. 1987.
The Beiderbecke Connection. 1992.

OTHER

The Trouble with Abracadabra (for children). 1975.

CRITICAL STUDIES: introduction to *Close the Coalhouse Door*, 1969; "What's Going On Behind the Coalhouse Door,"in *Sunday Times*, 9 February 1969; "The Playwright and His People," in *Theatre Quarterly 2* , April–June 1971; "One Step Forward, Two Steps Back," in *New Statesman*, 3 November 1972; "Views," in *Listener*, 29 November 1973, and "Twenty-Five Years Hard," in *Theatre Quarterly 25* , 1977, all by Plater; "The London Show" by Yorick Blumenfeld, in *Atlantic*, August 1969; *The Second Wave* by John Russell Taylor, 1971; "Trinity Collage" by Peter Fiddick, in *Guardian*, 12 December 1975; article by Albert Hunt, in *British Television Drama* edited by George W. Brandt, 1981.

Alan Plater comments:

(1973) Authors introducing their work fill me with gloom, like people explaining jokes: if I didn't laugh or cry before the explanation, nothing is likely to change afterwards. Therefore all I can do is look down the laundry list of my work to date and try to work out why I bothered, apart from what Mr. Perelman calls "the lash of economic necessity."

The clue lies in the place of birth and the present address: I was born and have always lived in industrial communities. I live in a place that works for a living. I never ran barefoot other than from choice. I have always eaten well and have never been deprived of anything that mattered: but I have always been close enough to the inequalities and grotesque injustices of our society to get angry about them.

(1977) Essentially I am writing a segment of the history of a society that was forged by the Industrial Revolution. This is less earnest and painful than it sounds; if an idea is important enough it is worth laughing at and one professional associate defined my method as taking fundamentally serious concepts like Politics and Religion and Life and Death and kicking the Hell out of them with old jokes. At any rate, the evidence of the more-or-less knockabout shows we've done around the regions is that people laugh the louder if the fun is spiced with a couple of centuries of inherited prejudice.

The other thought prompted by the laundry list is that not many writers have tangled with as rich and diverse a company of people and subjects: D.H. Lawrence, Mrs. Pankhurst, Sandy Powell, and Les Dawson would look good on any music-hall poster, though there might be some dispute over billing. At any rate, it underlines my feeling that it's the job of the writer at all times to head for the nearest tightrope and, in the words of Max Miller, Archie Rice, or both: "You've got to admit, lady, I do have a go."

(1982) Very little changes. The inequalities and injustices of 1973 are still there and I'm still heading for the tightrope as in 1977. We've got a new dog called The Duke (after Ellington) and I've had a programme banned by the BBC, which is a distinction of a sort. I copied some words by Jean Rhys and pinned them on the wall behind my desk. She says: "All of writing is a huge lake. There are great rivers that feed the lake, like Tolstoy and Dostoevsky. And there are trickles, like Jean Rhys. All that matters is feeding the lake. I don't matter. The lake matters. Nothing else is important. . . ."

(1988) After all that worthy stuff about living in an industrial community, here I am writing this paragraph in downtown N.W.3. In the famous words of Mr. Vonnegut: so it goes. We grow older, we change, we pursue happiness and sometimes find it. Professionally, I still head for the tightrope and Jean Rhys is still with me. So, for that matter, is The Duke.

Alan Plater is one of several dramatists whose work has done much to further the cause of British regional theatre. Although some of his plays have been seen in London and he has written widely for national television and the cinema, for many years his energies were directed towards ensuring the success of the ambitious Hull Arts Centre, a small 150-seat theatre. This physical home was also apparently a spiritual one, for his plays are set in the northeast of England and are largely concerned with the particular problems and history of the area. "Central to the greater part of my writing," he once stated, "is man's relationship to his work": and work in this context means particularly coal-mining and deep-sea fishing, two regional industries. Plater admires the "genuine solidarity and craft-consciousness" of those whose jobs involve "hideous physical working conditions": and he has captured the sheer pride in overcoming fear and danger which distinguishes the miners in his highly successful musical documentary, *Close the Coalhouse Door*. Plater identifies wholeheartedly with the community he describes: he shares the passion for football, and once, when he was asked about his literary influences, he replied by mentioning the popular music-hall names of his youth—Norman Evans, Mooney and King. He also expresses with great fire many of the social and political attitudes (some might call them prejudices) which characterize the region: a hatred of the bosses, who are usually portrayed as effete Southerners, a respect for Trade Union tradition, a somewhat over-generalized call for revolution which is coupled with a suspicion of change, a brashly extrovert dismissal of all forms of theatre which lack working-class appeal and a socialism which refuses to accept that Labour politicians are better than stooges for capitalistic con-men.

His work falls into two main categories. Plater has written several carefully observed naturalistic plays, such as *See the Pretty Lights* and *A Smashing Day*, which were both rewritten for the stage from television scripts. In 1966 Plater met the composer and songwriter Alex Glasgow and together they have collaborated on several musical documentaries, among them *Charlie Came to*

Our Town and *Close the Coalhouse Door*. The documentaries, unlike the naturalistic plays, combine many styles of writing—cross-talk sketches, songs, impassioned oratory, summaries of historical incidents, and much satire— which are all loosely brought together by a general theme, the history of Hull or the struggle of miners to gain decent living standards.

These two styles reveal different qualities. *See the Pretty Lights* is a gentle, warm, and moving account of a meeting between a middle-aged man and a teenage girl at the end of a pier. Both lead dull lives: and the bright lights of the seaside and their momentary friendship helps to relieve—but also to underline —their social frustrations. The hero of *A Smashing Day* is a young man, Lennie, who suffers from bored aimlessness: he meekly accepts his job, the odd nights at the palais with his mates who never become friends, and the routine drink. But he senses that a more exciting life awaits him somewhere if only he could find out where. He goes steady with a girl, Anne, and drifts towards marriage, which he doesn't want: and the social pressures are such that he persists in marrying her even after meeting Liz, an independent and sensitive girl with whom he falls in love. Many critics felt that the increased length of the stage play failed to achieve the concentrated power of the television script, and *A Smashing Day* was not successful in London. But it did provide an excellent part for the then unknown actor, Hywel Bennett, and revealed Plater's ability to describe an apparently uninteresting person in some depth. Lennie is never allowed to be either a pathetic person or an angry young man: and despite his shy insecurity which leaves an impression of spinelessness, his situation is both moving, credible, and strong enough to hold the play together.

If the naturalistic plays are distinguished by restraint and accuracy, the documentaries have entirely the opposite qualities: panache, a cheerful display of class bias, and loose, anything-goes technique. The best known is *Close the Coalhouse Door*, which was remarkably successful in Newcastle but received only a limited run in London, a fact which could be interpreted in several ways. The episodes of mining history are told within the context of a golden "wedding" reception in the Millburn family, who step out of a photograph to tell stories of strikes and hardships. Some scenes were particularly powerful: the death of a miner, the rivalry between families and men, the bitterness against the blackleg miners who went back to work too soon after the General Strike. Plater stressed the complicated mixture of affection and fear for the pits, together with a scorn of modernization programmes whose effect was to send miners back on the dole. The songs by Alex Glasgow caught the friendly liveliness of music halls and pubs, and in Newcastle it became a cult show. "Workers turned up in their thousands once the word got round," recalled Plater: the large Playhouse Theatre was filled to capacity night after night—the audiences would sit in the aisles, even on the steps to the stage.

Why did the show receive such a tepid reception in London? The answer is a complex one, revealing much about Plater's work. Plater has offered two reasons—that London audiences are prejudiced against working-class plays and that in any case they could not be expected to share the associations of the North. Both may be true: but isn't it the job of a dramatist to convey the importance of his theme to those who do not belong to the background? London critics generally commented on the superficial characterization of the play, on the rather simplistic dialogue and form, and on the one-sided in-

terpretations of history. These objections to Plater's documentaries were confirmed by two subsequent shows which didn't come to London: *Simon Says!*, a
wholesale attack on the British ruling classes represented by Lord Thing, the
Chairman of the MCC (the governing board of English cricket), and *And a
Little Love Besides*, a scathing account of the uncharitable Church. The critical
charge against both these plays was that the satire was too sweeping and naïve
to hit any real targets. Plater's documentaries are seen at their best perhaps
either when the subject contains real and deeply felt observations or when the
general sense of fun takes over. *Charlie Came to Our Town*, Plater's first
documentary with Alex Glasgow, is a delightfully light-hearted musical about
an eccentric anarchist.

Plater's two styles complement each other: and it is sad perhaps that they
haven't been combined in one play. The naturalistic plays are small-scale and
lack the passionate energy of the documentaries: the documentaries are too
vaguely polemical and lack the construction of the naturalistic plays. Plater is a
prolific writer, whose talents seem hard to control. But his adaptability is
shown by the skill with which he has adjusted to the various media: his
contributions to the *Z Cars* detective series on television and his screenplay for
D.H. Lawrence's *The Virgin and the Gypsy* have been rightly praised. This
energetic eagerness to tackle any task which interests him helped revitalize the
theatre in the northeast and suggests that in future his many abilities may be
contained within undeniably good plays.

—John Elsom

POLIAKOFF, Stephen.

Born in London, 1 December 1952. Educated at Westminster School, London;
King's College, Cambridge, 1972–73. Married Sandy Welch in 1983; one
daughter. Writer-in-residence, National Theatre, London, 1976–77.
Recipient: *Evening Standard* award, 1976; BAFTA award, 1980; Venice Film
Festival prize, 1989; Bergamo Film Festival prize, 1991. Agent: Casarotto
Ramsay Ltd., National House, 60–66 Wardour Street, London W1V 3HP,
England.

Publications

PLAYS

Granny (produced 1969).
Bambi Ramm (produced 1970).
A Day with My Sister (produced 1971).
Lay-By, with others (produced 1971). 1972.
Pretty Boy (produced 1972).
Theatre Outside (produced 1973).
Berlin Days (produced 1973).
The Carnation Gang (produced 1974).
Clever Soldiers (produced 1974). In *Plays: One*, 1989.
Heroes (produced 1975).
Hitting Town (produced 1975). In *Hitting Town, and City Sugar*, 1976.
City Sugar (produced 1975). In *Hitting Town, and City Sugar*, 1976.

Hitting Town, and City Sugar. 1976; revised edition 1978.
Strawberry Fields (produced 1977). 1977.
Shout Across the River (produced 1978). 1979.
American Days (produced 1979). 1979.
The Summer Party (produced 1980). 1980.
Caught on a Train (televised 1980). With *Favourite Nights*, 1982.
Favourite Nights (produced 1981). With *Caught on a Train*, 1982.
Soft Targets (televised 1982). With *Runners*, 1984.
Breaking the Silence (produced 1984). 1984.
Runners (screenplay). With *Soft Targets*, 1984.
Coming in to Land (produced 1987). 1987.
Playing with Trains (produced 1989). 1989.
She's Been Away, and Hidden City (screenplays). 1989.
Plays: One (includes *Clever Soldiers, Hitting Town, City Sugar, Shout Across the River, American Days, Strawberry Fields*). 1989.
Sienna Red (produced 1992). 1992.
Close My Eyes (screenplay). 1992.

Screenplays: *Runners*, 1983; *Hidden City*, 1988; *She's Been Away*, 1989; *Close My Eyes*, 1991.

Television plays: *Stronger Than the Sun*, 1977; *Bloody Kids*, 1980; *Caught on a Train*, 1980; *Soft Targets*, 1982.

Theatrical activities

Director: **Films**—*Hidden City*, 1988; *Close My Eyes*, 1991.

Stephen Poliakoff first achieved recognition with the two related plays *Hitting Town* and *City Sugar* in 1975. The plays attacked a series of readily identifiable targets—the tackiness and squalor of new inner-city developments, the alienating effects of fast-food shops and discos, the banality of pop radio D.J.s. But here, as so often subsequently, the rather crude political context is less the real subject of the drama than a convenient backdrop against which a series of strangely vulnerable oddball characters rehearse their particular desperation. Poliakoff's is a theatre of individual gesture rather than generalised political analysis. Although his plays appear to offer a series of thematically related attacks on contemporary society in loosely political terms. it is the emotional subtext that is most important.

In *Hitting Town*, it is the awkward movement of a lonely woman and her waywardly embittered younger brother through a desolate provincial night on the town and towards an incestuous bed that creates most of the dramatic tension, just as in the more recent screenplay for *Runners* it is the tentative efforts of the father to achieve some kind of relationship with his young runaway daughter that holds the audience's attention, rather than the more general theme of hopelessness in the face of mass youth unemployment that the film presents as its primary concern. And indeed the daughter is not presented as a passive victim of circumstances. Like so many of Poliakoff's central protagonists she is a survivor, shell-shocked but still in possession of a tentative resilience, surviving in a half-glimpsed London world of the dispossessed by distributing advertising literature.

Poliakoff returns continually to city nightlife. It is when his characters can be displayed at their loneliest—a situation which brings about the very existence of the all-night radio phone-in which provides the structural continuity of *City Sugar*. And it is this pervading sense of isolation in supposedly crowded locations that gives his plays their peculiar clarity, for Poliakoff's stage city is a curiously unpopulated one. In *Hitting Town* the sister and brother first visit a Wimpy Bar in which the only other person present is a waitress who will again be the sole witness to their dialogue in the shopping precinct. Whether other people are assumed to be present, and thus a further cause of the sister's worry at her brother's deliberately provocative behaviour, is deliberately left unclear, but no such ambiguity exists by the time the three of them arrive at a disco in which the only direct evidence of the presence of others comes from the voice of the unseen D.J.

Again, in *Favourite Nights*, Catherine, language teacher by day and escort by night, takes her German businessman student and her sister to a casino in which we otherwise see only a croupier, an American punter, and Alan, an official of the club. The absence of characters who must be understood to be present in night spots such as discos and casinos intensifies the way in which Poliakoff's characters see themselves as a part of, and yet separate from, the contemporary world. Catherine's manic attempts to beat the bank yet again in order to avoid the sexual compromise potentially involved in letting her client pay for their evening out is seen as if in a filmic close-up from which all the extras are excluded; and the attempts to communicate with her lover, Alan, in a locale in which contact between staff and punters is banned, is given a curious intensity by the presence of spy cameras unsupported by any other realised members of the casino management.

It is not surprising, given all this, that the medium of film has come to seem increasingly attractive to Poliakoff. In *Hidden City*, the first film he directed, the fascination with the city as secret world is still evident. A bored mathematical psychologist meets up with a strange young woman who reveals a literal underworld of tunnels and hidden chambers in pursuit of officially dead newsreel film footage, stumbling by accident on evidence of a long-since buried nuclear scandal. But afterwards it is the image of the "hidden city" rather than the concern with the hidden scandal that remain in the mind.

Even when Poliakoff moves out of a city environment, as in *Strawberry Fields*, he takes his characters from London and up the motorway vertebrae of England, in and out of service stations and lay-bys which are as unpopulated as his all-night bars and casinos. Kevin and Charlotte set off to meet at pre-arranged points others members of the fascist group to which they belong. In this instance, the lack of contact with any other characters—with the exception of a police constable and a hitchhiker, who are shot dead at the ends of the first and second acts respectively—stresses their lack of contact with any reality, other than Kevin's half-remembered images of the 1960's, to support their ideology. They see themselves increasingly as latter-day Bonnies and Clydes, but the paranoia of persecution and pursuit on which their stance is built is undercut by the non-appearance of the police who are supposedly chasing them.

This thematic use of the journey is another manifestation of the characters as socially and politically rootless and unconnected to the details of everyday life. In his 1980 television play, *Caught on a Train*, Poliakoff uses a railway journey across Europe in which a series of characters—from a collection of anarchically politicised football hooligans to a young American thoroughly disenchanted with Europe—meet in transit without ever properly communicating as an informing metaphor for an account of the contemporary malaise. This film marked a major development in his work and, interestingly, he was to return to the central motif of the train journey in his most impressive stage play to date—*Breaking the Silence*.

For the first time since his earliest work Poliakoff moves the action into the past, Russia in the immediate aftermath of the revolution. Nikolai, a wealthy Jewish aristocrat based loosely on the playwright's own Russian grandfather, is turned out of his spacious accommodation and is made telephone surveyor of the Northern Railway. To this end he is given a train to patrol a region where telephone poles have yet to be erected, all the time working singlemindedly towards his life's ambition of producing the first synchronised talking pictures. He is to be thwarted, and the play finishes as he prepares for exile in England, his pictures as silent as the northern region's telephone system. It is again a journey of isolation, in which all attempts at communication are literally and metaphorically denied; but it is also another story of a survivor. Poliakoff has for the first time properly united the individual concerns of the narrative with a larger thematic structure. His concern with the links between the political worlds of the east and west, and thus with his own sense of cultural duality, was continued in *Coming in to Land*, which opened at the National Theatre in 1987, and in *Playing with Trains*, and certainly, given the rapidly changing nature of the political map of Europe, there is good reason to hope that he will continue to be preoccupied by this larger social arena.

—John Bull

POTTER, Dennis (Christopher George).

Born in Joyford Hill, Coleford, Gloucestershire, 17 May 1935. Educated at Christchurch Village School; Bell's Grammar School, Coleford; St. Clement Danes Grammar School, London; New College, Oxford (editor, *Isis*, 1958), B.A. (honours) in philosophy, politics and economics 1959. Married Margaret Morgan in 1959; one son and two daughters. Member of the Current Affairs Staff, BBC Television, 1959–61; feature writer, then television critic, *Daily Herald*, London, 1961–64; leader writer, the *Sun*, London, 1964; television critic, *New Statesman*, London, 1967, 1972, 1974–75; book reviewer, the *Times*, London, 1967–73 and the *Guardian*, London, 1973; television critic, *Sunday Times*, London, 1976–78. Labour candidate for Parliament, East Hertfordshire, 1964. Recipient: Writers Guild award, 1965, 1969; Society of Film and Television Arts award, 1966; BAFTA award, 1979, 1980; Italia prize, 1982; San Francisco Film Festival award, for television play, 1987; Broadcasting Press Guild award, for television play, 1987. Agent: Judy Daish

Associates, 83 Eastbourne Mews, London W2 6LQ. Address: Morecambe
Lodge, Duxmere, Ross-on-Wye, Herefordshire HR9 5BB, England.

Publications

PLAYS

Vote Vote Vote for Nigel Barton (televised 1965; revised version produced
  1968). In *The Nigel Barton Plays*, 1968.
*The Nigel Barton Plays: Stand Up, Nigel Barton, Vote Vote Vote for Nigel
  Barton: Two Television Plays*. 1968.
Son of Man (televised 1969; produced 1969). 1970.
Follow the Yellow Brick Road (televised 1972). In *The Television Dramatist*,
  edited by Robert Muller, 1973.
Only Make Believe (televised 1973; produced 1974).
Brimstone and Treacle (produced 1978). 1978.
Blue Remembered Hills (televised 1979; produced 1991). In *Waiting for the
  Boat*, 1984.
Sufficient Carbohydrate (produced 1983). 1983.
Waiting for the Boat: Dennis Potter on Television (includes *Joe's Ark, Blue
  Remembered Hills*, and *Cream in My Coffee*). 1984.
The Singing Detective (televised 1986). 1986.
Christabel (televised 1988). 1988.

SCREENPLAYS: *Pennies from Heaven*, 1982; *Brimstone and Treacle*, 1982;
Gorky Park, 1983; *Dreamchild*, 1985; *Track 29*, 1988; *Secret Friends*, 1991.

TELEVISION PLAYS: *The Confidence Course*, 1965; *Alice*, 1965; *Stand Up, Nigel
Barton*, 1965; *Vote Vote Vote for Nigel Barton*, 1965; *Emergency—Ward 9*,
1966; *Where the Buffalo Roam*, 1966; *Message for Posterity*, 1967; *The
Bonegrinder*, 1968; *Shaggy Dog*, 1968; *A Beast with Two Backs*, 1968;
Moonlight on the Highway, 1969; *Son of Man*, 1969; *Lay Down Your Arms*,
1970; *Angels Are So Few*, 1970; *Paper Roses*, 1971; *Traitor*, 1971; *Casanova*
(series of six plays), 1971; *Follow the Yellow Brick Road*, 1972; *Only Make
Believe*, 1973; *A Tragedy of Two Ambitions*, from a story by Hardy, 1973;
Joe's Ark, 1974; *Schmoedipus*, 1974; *Late Call*, from the novel by Angus
Wilson, 1975; *Double Dare*, 1976; *Where Adam Stood*, from the book *Father
and Son* by Edmund Gosse, 1976; *The Mayor of Casterbridge*, from the novel
by Hardy, 1978; *Pennies from Heaven*, 1978; *Blue Remembered Hills*, 1979;
Blade on the Feather, 1980; *Rain on the Roof*, 1980; *Cream in My Coffee*,
1980; *Tender Is the Night*, from the novel by F. Scott Fitzgerald, 1985; *The
Singing Detective*, 1986; *Visitors*, from his play *Sufficient Carbohydrate*,
1987; *Brimstone and Treacle*, 1987; *Christabel*, 1988; *Blackeyes*, from his
novel, 1989; *Lipstick on Your Collar*, 1993.

NOVELS

Hide and Seek. 1973.
Pennies from Heaven (novelization of television series). 1981.
Ticket to Ride. 1986.
Blackeyes. 1987.

OTHER

The Glittering Coffin. 1960.
The Changing Forest: Life in the Forest of Dean Today. 1962.

THEATRICAL ACTIVITIES
DIRECTOR: **Film**—*Secret Friends*, 1991. Television—*Blackeyes*, 1989.

Dennis Potter presents, albeit with a great deal of brittle humour and some
acerbic comments on present-day life in Britain, an arrestingly grim view of
mankind's eternal plight. He shows how beings are condemned to journey
through lives which are often physically or psychologically painful as they
more or less consciously search for a glory that has departed, for a god whose
existence they vaguely intuit though he remains tantalisingly aloof and who
might release them from their agonising and incurable sense of disinheritance.
Only human relationships can sometimes assuage man's grief, but all too often
they only make it worse. Education may well have served to increase Potter's
feeling of alienation from certain traditional values that might have supported
him, and his attitudes have no doubt been shaped to some degree by prolonged
and distressing ill-health. But if he had been a French intellectual, critics would
have had little hesitation in referring to Jansenism with its uncompromising
condemnation of moral laxness and, above all, to Pascal's doctrine of fallen
man's perennial and insatiable craving to know a god who remains hidden
despite all the efforts of the reason to discover him. Within such a context, the
combination of metaphysical despair with a heartfelt attachment to socialist
values would not seem in the least unusual either.

For the most part Potter has written for television, scoring several notable
successes, among them the famous *Pennies from Heaven* and *The Singing
Detective*, which aroused very considerable public interest. *Christabel* is a
powerful and effective reworking for the small screen of *The Past Is Myself*, an
autobiographical work by Christabel Bielenberg, an intelligent and articulate
woman who married a German lawyer in 1934 and witnessed at first-hand the
horrors of the Nazi period in Germany in the 1930s and during World War II.
Television is a medium that Potter handles with great skill, notably paring
down his dialogue and leaving it to the screen image to convey much of what
he has to say about the characters. Even such early works as *The Nigel Barton
Plays* show many of his constant themes. *Stand Up, Nigel Barton*, presents the
agonies of the bright boy at school, squirming with embarrassment when he
finds he is becoming teacher's pet and realising that he is, in two senses,
becoming alienated from the fellow members of his class. At home things are
little better as Nigel's father, a Nottinghamshire miner, tries to make sense of
his son's education, and Oxford is presented more as Babylon than as the new
Jerusalem which it had seemed when viewed as the goal of every educational
ambition. *Vote Vote Vote for Nigel Barton* takes idealism down another peg,
going behind the scenes of contemporary British politics as Nigel stands as
Labour candidate in a by-election which he knows he cannot win. Party loyalty
and the sheer impossibility of denying the recent past impel him to go forward
until at last despair wins the upper hand. Only then are human values
reasserted, and in his hour of deepest self-doubt his wife Anne sees that, in a
world where compromise is the pre-condition of such limited success as will

ever be possible, Nigel has personal qualities that matter. Another television play, *Follow the Yellow Brick Road*, takes disillusionment further. Jack is an actor, and the sense that authenticity has departed from his life is neatly conveyed by his paranoid illusion that he is being continuously photographed, while his disgust at materialist values is expressed by reference to the futile banalities of the dog-food commercials in which he has to play a ridiculous part. In *Cream in My Coffee* the familiar device of juxtaposing two time-sequences as a couple visit a seaside hotel before their marriage and return 30 years later neatly demonstrates, in a play also notable for its evocation of period, another failure in human relations. With *Joe's Ark* Potter tackles the issue of death with a directness uncommon in television drama. As Lucy lies dying of cancer she talks the matter over with her doctor; he admits he has no cure, or explanation either; then he adds that "every doctor eventually expects his patient to *collude* with him," and in the acceptance of the inevitable there is some comfort.

Brimstone and Treacle was written for television in the mid-1970s, but the BBC refused to screen it until 1987. Potter was naturally outraged, but it is not too hard to see why there were doubts about screening a play in which a girl who has long lain in a coma tended by her distraught parents recovers consciousness after being assaulted and raped by a young man with a whiff of Satanism about him. All the same, as well as revealing Potter's theatrical skills, the stage version of the play bravely tackles a taboo subject and offers some paradoxical optimism at the end.

So too does *Sufficient Carbohydrate*. On a Greek island an English couple are holidaymaking with an ill-assorted American couple who are accompanied by their callow son. The Englishman, Jack, has been forced into selling his food processing company to an American conglomerate, and now manoeuvres are going on to force him to resign the post he was fobbed off with after the merger. Junk food, summed up in vitriolic attacks on sodium monoglutamate, the additive that brings out the flavour, and on efforts to regulate the genes of mushrooms so that they breed identical in shape for easy marketing, is the focus for Jack's attacks on all that the modern world has to offer him. He drinks more than is good for him and equally often gets drunk on words, indulging himself in torrents of abuse about the sins and follies of the modern world. All the frustration of an existence that seems to have no solid purpose is brought out in the sexual tensions that are created, when Jack's wife, her patience exhausted, turns to the American while his wife casts her eyes on his son by a former marriage. Exceedingly funny in its lashing, highly articulate, and allusively literate humour, *Sufficient Carbohydrate* is deftly constructed for the stage, not betraying in any way that its author has had much of his experience in television. Played out amid the beauties of the setting on a Greek island and in a situation where, as it would in a classical drama, no outside force will come to complicate or solve the characters' problems, the human dilemmas hold our attention because the characters are so well observed. At first Jack irritates because of his self-pity, and his idealism seems close to self-indulgence and wishful thinking. Gradually his struggle becomes something grander as he sees, however dimly, a vision of values that will serve to nourish the human spirit in a materialistic age.

—Christopher Smith

POWNALL, David.

Born in Liverpool, 19 May 1938. Educated at Lord Wandsworth College, Long Sutton, Hampshire, 1949–56; University of Keele, Staffordshire, 1956–60, B.A. (honours) 1960. Married 1) Glenys Elsie Jones in 1961 (divorced 1971), one son; 2) Mary Ellen Ray in 1972, one son. Personnel officer, Ford Motor Co., Dagenham, Essex, 1960–63; personnel manager, Anglo-American, Zambia, 1963–69; resident writer, Century Theatre touring group, 1970–72, and Duke's Playhouse, Lancaster, 1972–75; founder and resident writer, Paines Plough Theatre, Coventry, 1975–80. Recipient: John Whiting award, for drama, 1982, 1986. Fellow, Royal Society of Literature, 1976. Agent: Andrew Hewson, John Johnson Ltd., 45–47 Clerkenwell Green, London EC1R 0HT, England.

Publications

PLAYS

As We Lie (produced 1973). 1969.
How Does the Cuckoo Learn to Fly? (produced 1970).
How to Grow a Guerrilla (produced 1971).
All the World Should Be Taxed (produced 1971).
The Last of the Wizards (for children; produced 1972).
Gaunt (produced 1973).
Lions and Lambs (produced 1973).
The Dream of Chief Crazy Horse (for children; produced 1973). 1975.
Beauty and the Beast, music by Stephen Boxer (produced 1973).
The Human Cartoon Show (produced 1974).
Crates on Barrels (produced 1974).
The Pro (produced 1975).
Lile Jimmy Williamson (produced 1975).
Buck Ruxton (produced 1975).
Ladybird, Ladybird (produced 1976).
Music to Murder By (produced 1976). 1978.
A Tale of Two Town Halls (produced 1976).
Motocar, and Richard III, Part Two, music by Stephen Boxer (produced 1977). 1979.
An Audience Called Édouard (produced 1978). 1979.
Seconds at the Fight for Madrid (produced 1978).
Livingstone and Sechele (produced 1978).
Barricade (produced 1979).
Later (produced 1979).
The Hot Hello (produced 1981).
Beef (produced 1981). In *Best Radio Plays of 1981,* 1982.
Master Class (produced 1983). 1983.
Pride and Prejudice, adaptation of the novel by Jane Austen (produced 1983).
Ploughboy Monday (broadcast 1985). In *Best Radio Plays of 1985,* 1986.
The Viewing (produced 1987).
Black Star (produced 1987).
The Edge (produced 1987).

King John's Jewel (produced 1987).
Rousseau's Tale (produced 1991).
My Father's House (produced 1991).
Nijinsky: Death of a Faun (produced 1991).
Dinner Dance (produced 1991).
Elgar's Rondo (produced 1993).

RADIO PLAYS: *Free Ferry*, 1972; *Free House*, 1973; *A Place in the Country*, 1974; *An Old New Year*, 1974; *Fences*, 1976; *Under the Wool*, 1976; *Back Stop*, 1977; *Butterfingers*, 1981; *The Mist People*, 1981; *Flos*, 1982; *Ploughboy Monday*, 1985; *Beloved Latitudes*, from his own novel, 1986; *The Bridge at Orbigo*, 1987; *A Matter of Style*, 1988; *Plato Not Nato*, 1990; *The Glossomaniacs*, 1990; *Bringing Up Nero*, 1991.

TELEVISION PLAYS: *High Tides*, 1976; *Mackerel Sky*, 1976; *Return Fare*, 1978; *Follow the River Down*, 1979; *Room for an Inward Light*, 1980; *The Sack Judies*, 1981; *Love's Labour* (*Maybury* series), 1983; *The Great White Mountain* (*Mountain Men* series), 1987; *Something to Remember You By*, 1991.

NOVELS
The Raining Tree War. 1974.
African Horse. 1975.
God Perkins. 1977.
Light on a Honeycomb. 1978.
Beloved Latitudes. 1981.
The White Cutter. 1988.
The Gardener. 1990.
Stagg and His Mother. 1991.
The Sphinx and the Sybarites. 1993.

SHORT STORIES
My Organic Uncle and Other Stories. 1976.

VERSE
An Eagle Each: Poems of the Lakes and Elsewhere, with Jack Hill. 1972.
Another Country. 1978.

OTHER
Between Ribble and Lune: Scenes from the North-West, photographs by
   Arthur Thompson. 1980.
The Bunch from Bananas (for children). 1980.

Editor, with Gareth Pownall, *The Fisherman's Bedside Book*. 1980.

David Pownall has written prolifically in the 1970s, 1980s, and early 1990s: nine novels, and numerous plays for the stage, radio, and television. Partly because few of the plays are published. he had little attention until the success of *Master Class* at the Old Vic in 1984. A second well-known stage work is an adaptation of Jane Austen's novel *Pride and Prejudice*.

A few of Pownall's plays are conventional pieces of storytelling, for instance, *Ladybird, Ladybird*, which shows Miriam's return to Liverpool after 50 years in the United States. A young war widow, she had escaped her environment, leaving a baby son behind. Now she comes back for a first meeting with her grandchildren, two men and a girl in a wheelchair, and the play shows the twists, turns, shifts, and complexities in these new relationships. Other stories set in the present are *Fences*, for radio, in which an upper-class girl falls in love with a stable-boy, and two for television, *Return Fare*, in which a discharged mental patient goes to live with his brother, and *Follow the River Down*, where an old man relives his life as he follows a river to its mouth.

In Pownall's most distinctive plays, something quite unexpected breaks through, identifiable reality changing to fantasy or taking on ritualistic aspects. In the early, strange *How to Grow a Guerrilla* an English garden has run wild and turned to jungle. A moronic youth plays soldiers, and a take-over by gangsters is followed by one by black police. *Motocar* is set in Rhodesia ten days before independence (indefinitely in the future when Pownall wrote it in 1976), in a mental hospital run by whites for blacks. A suspected black terrorist, named Motocar, is brought in for psychiatric examination. A poetic ritual eventually develops in which the blacks force the four whites to relive aspects of the black experience of oppression.

Most of this group of plays uses historical events and changes and adapts them. *Richard III, Part Two* ingeniously weaves together George Orwell in 1984 and Richard III in 1484 by way of a board game about Richard, called Betrayal. Games and men must both be properly marketed for success — Richard failed in this, while Orwell knew it. The 30-character *Seconds at the Fight for Madrid* is set in November 1936. The audience meets English, Americans, Germans, a Russian, peasants, beggars, who discuss the fate of three showgirls and a musician who have blundered into this military zone. The picture of the Spanish Civil War is completed with appearances by the king, Franco, Hitler, and, since Pownall is ever imaginative, Don Juan and Don Quixote. *Barricade*, set in the Spanish countryside in May 1937, has anarchists joined by two gypsies and a young English army officer on a cycling holiday. The gypsies, in curious stylized scenes, attempt to awaken the Englishman politically. *An Audience Called Édouard* starts with the pose of two men and two women as in *Le Déjeuner sur l'herbe*; Manet, unseen, is imagined painting this somewhere among the audience. The chatter of the foursome is disturbed by two intruders from the river, one of whom is Karl Marx, indeed a disruptor of the harmony of La Belle Époque. In *The Bridge at Orbigo*, for radio, a referee and a footballer retracing the pilgrim route to Santiago de Compostela are guided into the past by a priest. Most difficult of all, in *Music to Murder By* a Californian woman musicologist conjures up the ghosts of Gesualdo, an Italian Renaissance composer, and Philip Heseltine, alias Peter Warlock, a scholar and composer who killed himself in 1930, as an illustration of links between creativity and violence.

A third group of plays treats historical subjects more objectively. *All the World Should Be Taxed* emphasises political elements in the Nativity story. *The Dream of Chief Crazy Horse*, written for schools with 70 parts, surveys ten thousand years of Red Indian history. In *Livingstone and Sechele* the young missionary David Livingstone makes his first convert, Sechele, chief of the Crocodile people, in South Africa, and is obliged to scrutinize his own faith. The other characters are their wives, submissive Mary and Mokoton, a fifth wife, scheming to keep her man from the outsiders. *Black Star* takes a really obscure subject, Ira Aldridge, the black American actor touring in Shakespeare in Poland in 1865. *Bringing Up Nero*, for radio, is a discussion between the young Nero and his tutor, the playwright Seneca, so the theme is whether a writer can influence a tyrant.

Two plays of 20th-century local history were written for Lancaster. *Buck Ruxton* deals with two brutal murders by a Parsee doctor in 1935. *Lile Jimmy Williamson* looks at the man who was the "uncrowned king" of Lancaster from the 1880's to the 1920's. He was a millionaire linoleum manufacturer, and Liberal MP from 1892 on. Pownall explained that Williamson "monopolised the city's industry so that he could pay subsistence wages and control the movement of employment. . . . I wasn't grinding any particular political axe. I was fascinated to find out what happened and why. Especially why it was allowed."

Birmingham Repertory Theatre commissioned *My Father's House*, about Joseph Chamberlain and his sons Neville and Austen, the most famous family in British politics. Pownall remarks that writing about real people "is a relief from creating fictional characters. It gives you a new flavour and uses a different part of your mind."

Pownall has also written three unique "danceplays." *Nijinsky: Death of a Faun*, set on the day Nijinsky hears of the death of Diaghilev, was written for Nicholas Johnson, a dancer who had never acted before. The others were for the Kosh company: *The Edge*, for one voice, about a mother estranged from her daughter, and *Dinner Dance*, which brings seven people into a kitchen. Pownall's work here is pioneering and original.

The wide-ranging historical interests and the musical aspect of *Music to Murder By* come together in *Master Class*, set in the Kremlin in 1948. Stalin, shown as a subtle manipulator, and Zhdanov, a bully, summon two famous composers to condemn their kind of music and to require them to meet Communist Party expectations in future. Shostakovich wants to be loyal, to work within the Soviet system, while Prokofiev feels himself outside it. As Stalin has all the power, the conflict is uneven, and, from outside the drama, audiences may know that the composers survived this confrontation. The second half has additional interest when the men try to compose a Georgian folk-cantata to show their conformity. Though some critics have argued that Pownall trivializes the issues, *Master Class* poses important questions about art and politics, elitism and social purpose, and the distance between modern music and the general public.

Pownall is a man overflowing with ideas, eagerly moving on to the next work rather than perfecting the previous one. His difficulty in gaining wider recognition, though, arises from the demands he makes on his audiences, whether to care about controversy in Russia in 1948 or to go more than halfway towards him in the strange world of *Richard III, Part Two, An Audience Called Édouard* and *Music to Murder By*.

—Malcolm Page

PRIESTLEY, J(ohn) B(oynton).

Born in Bradford, Yorkshire, 13 September 1894. Educated at Belle Vue Grammar School, Bradford, to age 16; Trinity Hall, Cambridge, 1919–21, B.A. in history 1921, M.A. Served in the Duke of Wellington's and Devon regiments, 1914–19. Married 1) Patricia Tempest (died 1925), two daughters; 2) Mary Wyndham Lewis in 1926 (divorced 1952), two daughters and one son; 3) the writer and archaeologist Jacquetta Hawkes in 1953. Employee, Clerk, Helm & Co., wool firm, Bradford, 1911–14; freelance journalist and reviewer, and reader for Bodley Head publishers, London, 1922–29; director, Mask Theatre, London, 1938–39; radio lecturer on BBC programme "Postscripts", 1940; regular contributor, *New Statesman*, London. President, PEN, London, 1936–37; United Kingdom delegate, and chair, Unesco International Theatre Conference, Paris, 1947, and Prague, 1948; chair, British Theatre Conference, 1948; president, International Theatre Institute, 1949; member, National Theatre Board, London, 1966–67. Recipient: James Tait Black Memorial prize, 1930; Ellen Terry award, 1948. LL.D: University of St. Andrews, Fife; D.Litt: University of Birmingham; University of Bradford. Honorary freeman, City of Bradford, 1973; honorary student, Trinity Hall, Cambridge, 1978. Order of Merit, 1977. *Died 14 August 1984.*

Publications

PLAYS

The Good Companions (book only), with Edward Knoblock, lyrics by Harry Graham and Frank Eyton, music by Richard Addinsell, from the novel by Priestley (produced 1931). 1935.

Dangerous Corner (produced 1932). 1932.

The Roundabout (produced 1932). 1933.

Laburnum Grove: An Immoral Comedy (produced 1933). 1934.

Eden End (produced 1934). 1934.

Cornelius: A Business Affair in Three Transactions (produced 1935). 1935.

Duet in Floodlight (produced 1935). 1935.

Three Plays and a Preface (includes *Dangerous Corner; Eden End; Cornelius*). 1935.

Bees on the Boat Deck: A Farcical Tragedy (produced 1936). 1936.

Spring Tide, with George Billam (produced 1936). 1936.

The Bad Samaritan (produced 1937).

Time and the Conways (produced 1937). 1937.

I Have Been Here Before (produced 1937). 1937.

People at Sea (as *I Am a Stranger Here*, produced 1937; as *People at Sea*, produced 1937). 1937.

Two Time Plays (includes *Time and the Conways* and *I Have Been Here Before*). 1937.

Mystery of Greenfingers: A Comedy of Detection (produced 1938). 1937.

The Rebels (produced 1938).

When We Are Married: A Yorkshire Farcical Comedy (produced 1938). 1938.

Music at Night (produced 1938). In *Three Plays*, 1943.

Johnson over Jordan (produced 1939). As *Johnson over Jordan: The Play, and All About It (An Essay)*, 1939.

The Long Mirror (produced 1940). In *Three Plays*, 1943.

Good Night Children: A Comedy of Broadcasting (produced 1942). In *Three Comedies*, 1945.

Three Plays (includes *Music at Night; The Long Mirror; They Came to a City*). 1943.

Desert Highway (produced 1943). 1944.

They Came to a City (produced 1943). In *Three Plays*, 1943.

Four Plays (includes *Music at Night; The Long Mirror; They Came to a City; Desert Highway*). 1944.

How Are They at Home? A Topical Comedy (produced 1944). In *Three Comedies*, 1945.

The Golden Fleece (as *The Bull Market*, produced 1944). In *Three Comedies*, 1945.

Three Comedies (includes *Good Night Children; The Golden Fleece; How Are They at Home?*). 1945.

An Inspector Calls (produced 1945). 1947.

Jenny Villiers (produced 1946).

Ever Since Paradise: An Entertainment, Chiefly Referring to Love and Marriage (produced 1946). 1949.

The Rose and Crown (televised 1946). 1947.

Three Time Plays (includes *Dangerous Corner; Time and the Conways; I Have Been Here Before*). 1947.

The Linden Tree (produced 1947). 1948.

Home is Tomorrow (produced 1948). 1949.

The High Toby: A Play for the Toy Theatre. 1948.

Summer Day's Dream (produced 1949). In *Plays 3*, 1950.

The Olympians, music by Arthur Bliss (produced 1949). 1949.

Plays. 3 vols., 1948–50; vol. 1 as *Seven Plays*, 1950.

Bright Shadow: A Play of Detection (produced 1950). 1950.

Treasure on Pelican (as *Treasure on Pelican Island*, televised 1951; as *Treasure on Pelican*, produced 1952). 1953.

Dragon's Mouth: A Dramatic Quartet, with Jacquetta Hawkes (produced 1952). 1952.

Private Rooms: A One-Act Comedy in the Viennese Style. 1953.

Mother's Day. 1953.

Try it Again (produced 1965). 1953.

A Glass of Bitter. 1954.

The White Countess, with Jacquetta Hawkes (produced 1954).

The Scandalous Affair of Mr. Kettle and Mrs. Moon (produced 1955). 1956.

Take the Fool Away (produced 1955; produced in English, 1959).

These Our Actors (produced 1956).

The Glass Cage (produced 1957). 1958.

The Thirty-First of June (produced 1957).

A Pavilion of Masks (produced 1962; produced in English, 1963). 1958.

The Rack (produced as *Die Tortur*, 1959).

A Severed Head, with Iris Murdoch, from the novel by Murdoch (produced 1963). 1964.

SCREENPLAYS: *Sing as We Go*, with Gordon Wellesley, 1934; *Look Up and Laugh*, with Gordon Wellesley, 1935; *We Live in Two Worlds*, 1937; *Jamaica Inn*, with Sidney Gilliat and Joan Harrison, 1939; *Britain at Bay*, 1940; *Our Russian Allies*, 1941; *The Foreman Went to France (Somewhere in France)*, with others, 1942; *Last Holiday*, 1950.

RADIO PLAYS: *The Return of Jess Oakroyd*, 1941; *The Golden Entry*, 1955; *End Game at the Dolphin*, 1956; *An Arabian Night in Park Lane*, 1965.

TELEVISION PLAYS: *The Rose and Crown*, 1946; *Whitehall Wonders*, 1949; *Treasure on Pelican Island*, 1951; *You Know What People Are*, 1953; *The Stone Faces*, 1957; *Now Let Him Go*, 1957; *Lost City* (documentary), 1958; *The Rack*, 1958; *Doomsday for Dyson*, 1958; *The Fortrose Incident*, from his play *Home is Tomorrow*, 1959; *Level Seven*, from the novel by Mordecai Roshwald, 1966; *The Lost Peace* series, 1966; *Anyone for Tennis*, 1968; *Linda at Pulteney's*, 1969.

NOVELS

Adam in Moonshine. 1927.
Benighted. 1927; as *The Old Dark House*, 1928.
Farthing Hall, with Hugh Walpole. 1929.
The Good Companions. 1929.
Angel Pavement. 1930.
Faraway. 1932.
I'll Tell You Everything, with Gerald Bullett. 1933.
Wonder Hero. 1933.
They Walk in the City: The Lovers in the Stone Forest. 1936.
The Doomsday Men. 1938.
Let the People Sing. 1939.
Black-Out in Gretley: A Story of—and for—Wartime. 1942.
Daylight on Saturday: A Novel About an Aircraft Factory. 1943.
Three Men in New Suits. 1945.
Bright Day. 1946.
Jenny Villiers: A Story of the Theatre. 1947.
Festival at Farbridge. 1951; as *Festival*, 1951.
The Magicians. 1954.
Low Notes on a High Level: A Frolic. 1954.
Saturn over the Water. 1961.
The Thirty-First of June. 1961.
The Shapes of Sleep: A Topical Tale. 1962.
Sir Michael and Sir George. 1964.
Lost Empires. 1965.
Salt is Leaving. 1966.
It's an Old Country. 1967.
The Image Men: Out of Town and *London End* (2 vols.). 1968.
Found, Lost, Found; or, The English Way of Life. 1976.

SHORT STORIES

The Town Major of Miraucourt. 1930.
Albert Goes Through. 1933.

Going Up: Stories and Sketches. 1950.
The Other Place and Other Stories of the Same Sort. 1953.
"The Carfitt Crisis" and Two Other Stories. 1975.

VERSE
The Chapman of Rhymes (juvenilia). 1918.

OTHER
Brief Diversions, Being Tales, Travesties, and Epigrams. 1922.
Papers from Lilliput. 1922.
I for One. 1923.
Figures in Modern Literature. 1924.
The English Comic Characters. 1925.
George Meredith. 1926.
Talking. 1926.
(Essays). 1926.
Open House: A Book of Essays. 1927.
Thomas Love Peacock. 1927.
The English Novel. 1927; revised edition, 1935.
Apes and Angels: A Book of Essays. 1928; as *Too Many People and Other Reflections,* 1928.
The Balconinny and Other Essays. 1929.
English Humour. 1929.
Self-Selected Essays. 1932.
Four-in-Hand (miscellany). 1934.
English Journey, Being a Rambling But Truthful Account of What One Man Saw and Heard and Felt and Thought During a Journey Through England During the Autumn of the Year 1933. 1934.
Midnight on the Desert: A Chapter of Autobiography. 1937.
Rain upon Godshill: A Further Chapter of Autobiography. 1939.
Britain Speaks (radio talks). 1940.
Postscripts (radio talks). 1940; as *All England Listened,* 1968.
Out of the People. 1941.
Britain at War. 1942.
British Women Go to War. 1943.
Manpower: The Story of Britain's Mobilisation for War. 1944.
Here Are Your Answers. 1944.
Letter to a Returning Serviceman. 1945.
The Secret Dream: An Essay on Britain, America, and Russia. 1946.
Russian Journey. 1946.
The New Citizen (address). 1946.
Theatre Outlook. 1947.
The Arts under Socialism (lecture). 1947.
Delight. 1949.
The Priestley Companion: A Selection from the Writings. 1951.
Journey down a Rainbow (travel), with Jacquetta Hawkes. 1955.
All about Ourselves and Other Essays, edited by Eric Gillett. 1956.

The Writer in a Changing Society (lecture). 1956.
Thoughts in the Wilderness (essays). 1957.
The Art of the Dramatist: A Lecture Together with Appendices and Discursive Notes. 1957.
Topside; or, The Future of England: A Dialogue. 1958.
The Story of Theatre (for children). 1959; as *The Wonderful World of the Theatre*, 1959.
Literature and Western Man. 1960.
William Hazlitt. 1960.
Charles Dickens: A Pictorial Biography. 1961; as *Charles Dickens and His World*, 1969.
Margin Released: A Writer's Reminiscences and Reflections. 1962.
Man and Time. 1964.
The Moments and Other Pieces. 1966.
The World of Priestley, edited by Donald G. MacRae. 1967.
Essays of Five Decades, edited by Susan Cooper. 1968.
Trumpets over the Sea, Being a Rambling and Egotistical Account of the London Symphony Orchestra's Engagement at Daytona Beach, Florida, in July–August 1967. 1968.
The Prince of Pleasure and His Regency 1811–1820. 1969.
The Edwardians. 1970.
Anton Chekhov. 1970.
Snoggle (for children). 1971.
Victoria's Heyday. 1972.
Over the Long High Wall: Some Reflections and Speculations on Life, Death, and Time. 1972.
The English. 1973.
Outcries and Asides. 1974.
A Visit to New Zealand. 1974.
Particular Pleasures, Being a Personal Record of Some Varied Arts and Many Different Artists. 1975.
The Happy Dream: An Essay. 1976.
English Humour (not the same as 1929 book). 1976.
Instead of the Trees: A Final Chapter of Autobiography. 1977.
Seeing Stratford. 1982.
Musical Delights. 1984.

Editor, *Essayists Past and Present: A Selection of English Essays*. 1925.
Editor, *Fools and Philosophers: A Gallery of Comic Figures from English Literature*. 1925.
Editor, *Tom Moore's Diary: A Selection*. 1925.
Editor, *The Book of Bodley Head Verse*. 1926.
Editor, *Our Nation's Heritage*. 1939.
Editor, *Scenes from London Life, from Sketches by Boz*, by Dickens. 1947.
Editor, *The Best of Leacock*. 1957; as *The Bodley Head Leacock*, 1957.
Editor, with Josephine Spear, *Adventures in English Literature*. 1963.

BIBLIOGRAPHY: *J.B. Priestley: An Annotated Bibliography* by Alan Edwin Day, 1980.

CRITICAL STUDIES: *J.B. Priestley: Portrait of an Author* by Susan Cooper, 1970; *J.B. Priestley* by John Atkins, 1978; *J.B. Priestley* by A.A. DeVitis and Albert E. Kalson, 1980; *J.B. Priestley: The Last of the Sages* by John Atkins, 1981.

Priestley was a writer of remarkably wide talents, being dramatist, novelist, travel writer, literary critic, essayist, political commentator, and journalist. It was the dramatisation of his own highly successful novel *The Good Companions*, in 1931, that first took him into the theatre, and he soon became a proficient playwright, able to supply the British theatre throughout the 1930s and 1940s with nearly a play a year.

His work in drama is as various as his general writing, and included domestic comedy, social problem plays, psychological and philosophical drama, melodrama, and plays of detection. Perhaps inevitably, with so varied an output, his writing is very uneven, and many of the weaknesses of his first independent pieces, like *The Roundabout* and *Cornelius*, including crude characterisation and run-of-the-mill plotting, recur even in late work, But he had an instinctive theatrical sense and a good feel for stage dialogue. He was unwilling, too, to settle just for commercial success, as he might easily have done following the popularity of his plays of the early 1930s, like *Dangerous Corner* and *Eden End*: having won a reputation, he proceeded to attempt more demanding subject matter and to explore more experimental dramatic forms.

His early successes show something of his versatility: the first, *Dangerous Corner*, was a psychological melodrama; this he followed with something wholly different, a popular comedy of lower-middle-class, suburban, domestic life, *Laburnum Grove*, which nonetheless managed to achieve a wide social appeal, and is still revived today; third, and likewise still holding the stage, was *Eden End*, an effective attempt to dramatise the kind of material Priestley had handled in his late-1920s novel, *The Good Companions*, in that it is set in the drab world of theatre before World War I and admirably recreates the sleazy atmosphere of the provincial stage, its practitioners and "stage-struck" aspirants, and their families.

But Priestley was content neither to settle just for commercial success, nor to be a mere observer and chronicler; he had serious artistic aspirations, and saw himself, too, as a social and political commentator of moderately radical inclination. Unlike many of his contemporaries he took the business of writing for the theatre seriously, and even in light-entertainment pieces, like *Bees on the Boatdeck*, a mixture of fantasy, comedy, and topical comment, he introduced an element of reflection on, and mild criticism of, the prevailing social order.

More manifestly reaching for a serious dimension were the "time and space" plays, like *Time and the Conways, I Have Been Here Before*, and *I Am a Stranger Here*. In these, Priestley was much influenced, indeed rather too obviously so, by the contemporary popularisers of scientific ideas, like Dunne and Ouspensky. The plays, actually have little philosophical depth, and perhaps too much has been made of them as plays of "ideas"; rather, the idea functions simply as a *donné* on which the dramatist builds the real substance of his play, the fortunes of individuals living out their lives in a particular time and place, with specific interests and aspirations, and subject to recognisable human and social pressures. If Priestley is now considered to be one of the very few British dramatists of significance to write between the wars, this is less, one suspects, for the intellectual substance of his best work, than for his ability to craft plays which, when realised by actors, retain their felt humanity and persuade as truthful, credible reflections of life. This in part accounts for the fact that although the "philosophical" and "experimental" plays are the ones critics feel they ought, perhaps, to admire most, those they prefer are mainly those endorsed by audiences and still found on the contemporary stage—not "ideas" pieces like the quasi-expressionistic *Johnson over Jordan* or the socially polemical *They Came to a City*, but the plays rooted in recognisable worlds, treating recognisable characters and situations, like *Laburnum Grove*, *The Linden Tree*, and *When We are Married* (hence, too, the fact that the most enduring of Priestley's "time" plays on the stage is *An Inspector Calls*).

Priestley was not a major dramatist, but he became a very fine craftsman (as Iris Murdoch found when she collaborated with him on the stage adaptation of her novel *The Severed Head*), able to engage the interest of mainstream London theatre audiences in plays of human and social concern—no mean feat in an inter-war-years' theatre that had seemingly relegated anything looking remotely like serious drama to the "little theatre" fringe. Artistically he was not radically innovative, nor indeed was he conspicuously radical in his social and political concerns. His stance was that of the socially aware, liberal-humanist reformer. His strategy in the theatre was to vary his more serious drama with solid, often run-of-the-mill, pieces carpentered for commercial stage managements, although, as said, some of these last, like *When We Are Married*, a Yorkshire domestic farce, must be ranked among his most stage-worthy pieces. He was a writer in whom the boundary between the creative artist and the workaday journalist was thin, and it is easy to complain that his output is more conspicuous for quantity than quality; but he was a fine story-teller, could fashion a character, had a keen theatrical sense, and was not afraid to spice a play with argument and polemic.

Today his work is perhaps more frequently seen on the television screen than in the theatre; television has exploited his skill at crafting character and plot line, his ability to create a sense of period and, more particularly, his intimate knowledge of the early 20th-century theatre and its social ambience, most recently in the 1980s television dramatisations of his novels *Lost Empires* and *The Good Companions*.

Twenty-five years after he ceased to write for the theatre, and 40 years or more after his theatrical heyday, at least four or five of his plays remain securely in the performed repertory. That cannot be said of many dramatists in the English theatre—or any other for that matter.

—Kenneth Richards

See the essay on *An Inspector Calls*.

R

RANSLEY, Peter.

Born in Leeds, Yorkshire, 10 December 1931. Educated at Pudsey Grammar School, Yorkshire, 1942–49; Queen Mary College, University of London, 1950–52. Married 1) Hazel Rew in 1955 (divorced 1970); 2) Cynthia Harris in 1974, one son. Journalist, social worker, and development manager of a publishing company, then freelance writer. Recipient: First Commonwealth Film and TV Festival Gold medal, 1980. Agent: Sheila Lemon, Lemon, Unna, and Durbridge, 24 Pottery Lane, Holland Park, London W11 4LZ, England.

Publications

PLAYS

Disabled (produced 1969; as *Dear Mr. Welfare*, televised 1970; revised version, as *Disabled*, produced 1971). In *Plays and Players*, June 1971.
Ellen (produced 1970). In *Plays and Players* (London), April 1971.
The Thomson Report (produced 1972).
Runaway (produced 1974).
Nothing Special (produced 1981).

TELEVISION PLAYS: *Dear Mr. Welfare*, 1970; *Black Olives*, 1971; *Night Duty*, 1972; *Blinkers*, 1973; *A Fair Day's Work*, 1973; *Bold Face Condensed*, 1974; *Mark Massey Is Dead*, 1974; *Big Annie*, 1974; *Jo and Ann*, 1974; *The House on the Hill*, 1975; *The Healing Hand*, 1975; *Henry and Jean*, 1975; *To Catch a Thief*, 1978; *Couples*, 1978; *Hospital Roulette*, 1979; *Minor Complications*, 1980; *Kate*, 1980; *Bread of Blood*, from the book *A Shepherd's Life* by W.H. Hudson, 1981; *Shall I Be Mother?*, 1983; *The Best Chess Player in the World* (*Tales of the Unexpected* series), from a story by Julian Symons, 1984; *The Price*, 1985; *Inside Story*, 1986; *Sitting Targets*, 1989; *Underbelly*, 1992.

NOVELS

The Price (novelization of television series). 1984.
The Hawk. 1988.
Bright Hair About the Bone. 1991.

Peter Ransley's first two plays, *Ellen* and *Disabled*, are based upon actual persons. For a period Ransley was a social worker, and in his first play, *Disabled*, he writes about one particular old man. In *Ellen* he depicts a playwright from the North who is writing a play about Ellen, a tramp who lives on his doorstep. When the play was staged at the Hampstead Theatre Club the real-life Ellen came to see the play about herself.

The central character in *Disabled*, Barker, is a problem case, dirty, smelly, cantankerous; further, he is in a disputed area where three welfare districts meet, so that responsibility for him is passed from department to department. He alienates all who try to help him, task force, home help, male nurse. But, as Ted, a character in *Ellen*, remarks, "Help is a cruel word." Both plays are concerned with the need to consider individuals as people, and not as "cases." Again, as Ted says in *Ellen*, "Labels. That's what makes people acute cases. The labels people stick on them."

At the end of the first act of *Disabled* a young man enters, an unidentified social worker called Mike. Barker gets him to talk about his marriage, which is on the rocks. He has not had intercourse with his wife for three years (the same length of time that Barker has been without sex since his accident), and after her last miscarriage Mike's wife took up social work. Like the wife Clare in *Ellen*, she is a frigid and sterile person. When she appears at the end of the play she says to Barker, "You are my case," to which he replies, "I am my own case."

Disabled is about the reversal of roles; it probes and poses such questions as who is the helper and who the helped. As Barker begins to tap Mike's dilemma we realize that it is Mike who, psychologically, is disabled. And when at the final curtain Barker is left alone saying "Poor bastard," it is perhaps less of himself that he is thinking than of Mike. In another sense it is also both of them, for in this play, not wholly successfully, Ransley attempts to merge two styles, naturalism and fantasy. In a central scene (finely directed at the Hampstead Theatre Club by Vivian Matalon with Leonard Rossiter as Barker and Peter McEnery as Mike), Barker gets Mike to make up his face like a woman. (Barker used to be a ventriloquist and do an act on the halls with his wife, Maisie.) Empathetically, almost mediumistically, Barker begins to take on the voice of Mike's wife (whom he has never met). By assuming the persona of Mike's wife he is able to uncover Mike's neurosis. At the climax of this curious scene he persuades Mike to lift him out of his wheel chair and to dance with him. As they dance so "Barker's limbs come to life" (author's stage directions). The moment the wife enters the room Barker collapses and falls to the floor.

What the author is trying to convey is that it is Mike whose psychological limbs have been brought to life by Barker's insight and understanding. And in the process of having to think about another human being, Barker finds a role for himself—he, too, comes to life.

Ransley described, in an audience discussion about the play, how at one point in his relationship with the particular old man who provided the play's genesis, he lost his temper and hit the old man. He was at once ashamed of himself but the old man laughed and laughed. For the first time someone had responded to him not as a "case," as a disabled person requiring a special attitude, but as a human begin. By losing his temper Ransley had revealed a true involvement with the old man, they had begun to relate to each other as people.

Ellen is a considerable advance in complexity and skill. While developing further the major theme of *Disabled*, it also touches upon the dilemma of the provincial artist. At one point Ted says to the playwright "We've both come a long way since those old Brummy days. I wasn't sure it was right for you to come to London because it is more of a challenge in the provinces, and you do lose contact with the source of your material—aren't you losing contact with your sources, cockalorum?" to which the playwright replies, "Trust you to go straight to the heart of my neuroses."

One of the arguments for "Drama-in-Education" is that it provides an additional teaching medium, and as such enables any subject from history to geography to English or science, to be taught, or handled, dramatically. Similarly, Ransley's plays are essays in sociology presented through the medium of drama. Carefully and sensitively he dissects aspects of our society. In *Runaway* he brings under his microscope a working-class family in a remote part of Yorkshire who have fallen under the shadow of cancer. The father is an old trade union man who failed to expose the risks of a dangerous chemical used in the manufacture of car tyres in the local factory. The resulting cancer which has crippled his best friend Charlie now threatens him. His 11-year-old grandson, the runaway of the title, and the best written part, is at the centre of the conflicts within this family. The writing is spare, pared to the bone, and beautifully understated.

Ransley's is a quiet and thoughtful talent but one which has a way of lingering on in the memory, of exercising one's conscience in everyday life.

—James Roose-Evans

RATTIGAN, (Sir) Terence (Mervyn).

Born in Kensington, London, 10 June 1911. Educated at Sandroyd School, Cobham, Surrey, 1920–24; Harrow School, Middlesex (scholar), 1925–30; Trinity College, Oxford (history scholar), 1930–33, BA 1933. Served in the Coastal Command of the Royal Air Force, 1939–45: flight lieutenant. Recipient: Ellen Terry award, 1947, 1948; New York Drama Critics Circle award, 1948. CBE (Commander, Order of the British Empire), 1958. Knighted, 1971. *Died 30 November 1977.*

Publications

PLAYS

First Episode, with Philip Heimann (produced 1933).
French Without Tears (produced 1936). 1937; revised version, music by Robert Stolz, lyrics by Paul Dehn, as *Joie de Vivre* (produced 1960).
After the Dance (produced 1939). 1939.
Follow My Leader, with Anthony Maurice (produced 1940).
Grey Farm, with Hector Bolitho (produced 1940).
Flare Path (produced 1942). 1942.
While the Sun Shines (produced 1943). 1944.
Love in Idleness (produced 1944). 1945; as *O Mistress Mine* (produced 1946), 1949.
The Winslow Boy (produced 1946). 1946.
The Browning Version (produced 1948). With *Harlequinade* as *Playbill*, 1949.
Harlequinade (produced 1948). With *The Browning Version* as *Playbill*, 1949.

Adventure Story (produced 1949). 1950.
Who is Sylvia? (produced 1950). 1951.
The Deep Blue Sea (produced 1952). 1952.
The Sleeping Prince (produced 1953). 1954.
Collected Plays (4 vols.). 1953–78.
Plays (2 vols.). 1981:
1. *French Without Tears; The Winslow Boy; The Browning Version; Harlequinade.*
2. *The Deep Blue Sea; Separate Tables; In Praise of Love.*
Separate Tables (includes *Table by the Window* and *Table Number Seven*; produced 1954). 1955.
The Prince and the Showgirl: The Script for the Film. 1957.
Variation on a Theme (produced 1958). 1958.
Ross: A Dramatic Portrait (produced 1960). 1960.
Heart to Heart (televised 1962). In *Collected Plays 3*, 1964.
Man and Boy (produced 1963). 1963.
A Bequest to the Nation, from the television play *Nelson* (produced 1970). 1970.
All on Her Own (televised 1968; produced 1974; as *Duologue*, produced 1976). In *The Best Short Plays 1970*, edited by Stanley Richards, 1970.
High Summer (televised 1972). In *The Best Short Plays 1973*, edited by Stanley Richards, 1973.
In Praise of Love: Before Dawn, and After Lydia (produced 1973). 1973; revised version of *After Lydia* (as *In Praise of Love*, produced 1974), 1975.
Cause Célèbre (broadcast 1975; produced 1977). 1978.

SCREENPLAYS: *The Belles of St. Clement's*, 1936; *Gypsy*, with Brock Williams, 1937; *French Without Tears*, with Anatole de Grunwald and Ian Dalrymple, 1939; *Quiet Wedding*, with Anatole de Grunwald, 1941; *The Day Will Dawn (The Avengers)*, with Anatole de Grunwald and Patrick Kirwan, 1942; *Uncensored*, with Rodney Ackland and Wolfgang Wilhelm, 1942; *English Without Tears (Her Man Gilbey)*, with Anatole de Grunwald, 1944; *The Way to the Stars (Johnny in the Clouds)*, with Anatole de Grunwald, 1945; *Journey Together*, with John Boulting, 1945; *Brighton Rock (Young Scarface)*, with Graham Greene, 1947; *While the Sun Shines*, with Anatole de Grunwald, 1947; *The Winslow Boy*, with Anatole de Grunwald, and Anthony Asquith, 1948; *Bond Street*, with Rodney Ackland and Anatole de Grunwald, 1948; *The Browning Version*, 1951; *The Sound Barrier (Breaking the Sound Barrier)*, 1952; *The Final Test*, 1953; *The Deep Blue Sea*, 1955; *The Man Who Loved Redheads*, 1955; *The Prince and the Showgirl*, 1957; *Separate Tables*, with John Gay, 1958; *The VIPs*, 1963; *The Yellow Rolls-Royce*, 1964; *Goodbye Mr. Chips*, 1969; *A Bequest to the Nation (The Nelson Affair)*, 1973.

RADIO PLAYS: *A Tale of Two Cities*, with John Gielgud, from the novel by Dickens, 1950; *Cause Célèbre*, 1975.

TELEVISION PLAYS: *The Final Test*, 1951; *Heart to Heart*, 1962; *Ninety Years On*, 1964; *Nelson*, 1966; *All on Her Own*, 1968; *High Summer*, 1972.

CRITICAL STUDIES: *Terence Rattigan: The Man and His Work* by Michael Darlow and Gillian Hodson, 1979; *Terence Rattigan* by Susan Ruskino, 1983; *The Rattigan Version: Sir Terence Rattigan and the Theatre of Character* by B.A. Young, 1986.

The fortunes of Terence Rattigan fluctuated during his lengthy career from his youthful West End debut in 1936 with *French Without Tears* through his war-time successes (*Flare Path* and *While the Sun Shines*) to his post-war heyday (*The Winslow Boy, Playbill,* and *The Deep Blue Sea*), his eclipse in the wake of Royal Court "kitchen-sink" drama, and finally, his eventual rehabilitation towards the end of his life (with *In Praise of Love* and *Cause Célèbre*). Despite these vicissitudes (due both to changes in public taste and the variable quality of his work) Rattigan displayed a remarkable continuity in technical skill and theme.

In his preface to the second volume of his *Collected Plays* in 1953, Rattigan confessed that the plays "are all . . . 'well-made', which means that they have a beginning, a middle and an end". Although the virtues of such craftsmanship were generally acknowledged during the first two decades of Rattigan's career, they were later disparaged as what Rattigan himself termed "French Window Drama". In his own defence Rattigan asserted that "Ibsen had French windows", and even Kenneth Tynan, an uncompromising critic of Rattigan's plays, conceded that "whatever his shortcomings as a theorist, nobody can deny Rattigan's supreme agility as a craftsman. His mastery of exposition is complete: give one of his characters a telephone, and within a minute, imperceptibly, the essentials of the situation will have been clearly sketched in".

Rattigan's dependence upon these modern props was evident when he ventured beyond contemporary subjects, as in *Adventure Story* (about Alexander the Great), in which he essayed a looser (more epic) form, but without real success. A similar structural experiment in *Ross* (about T. E. Lawrence) also failed, and it was not until his last play, *Cause Célèbre* (revised from a radio script), that he showed mastery of a freer form.

Tynan's strictures on Rattigan's "shortcomings as a theorist" would hardly have troubled the dramatist, who in a controversial article entitled "Concerning the Plays of Ideas" in *The New Statesman* (4 March 1950) wrote: "I believe that the best plays are about people, and not about things . . . from Aeschylus to Tennessee Williams the only theatre that has ever mattered is the theatre of character and narrative". Much of Rattigan's best work was derived from personal experience. *French Without Tears* dramatises his visit, as an Oxford undergraduate, to an intensive study course in France; *Flare Path* incorporates his own war-time experience in the R.A.F; *The Browning Version* is based on an incident during his school days at Harrow; the opening scene (with the apparently gassed Hester Collyer) of *The Deep Blue Sea* recalls the suicide of his friend Kenneth Morgan; *Separate Tables* evokes the Kensington hotel in which his mother lived; *Variation on a Theme* explores aspects of actress Margaret Leighton's relationship with Laurence Harvey; and *After Lydia* is based on Rex Harrison's experience with his terminally ill wife Kay Kendall. The relative failure of Rattigan's historical plays (*A Bequest to the Nation*, about Nelson and Lady Hamilton, as well as *Adventure Story* and *Ross*) underlines the importance of personal experience to his inspiration.

Although Rattigan proclaimed his rejection of the "play of ideas", there is in fact a thematic consistency running through his *oeuvre*. As Rattigan's biographers Michael Darlow and Gillian Hodson pointed out, "the conflict between emotion and reason which is a motif in all Rattigan's plays surfaces repeatedly in *French Without Tears*". In play after play, Rattigan explored the triangular situation of a character torn between the rival claims of potential lovers. Of the rival lovers, one invariably embodies the "higher love" (rational; socially and intellectually compatible), such as Sir William Collyer, Hester's husband and a judge in *The Deep Blue Sea*; the other (e.g. Freddie Page in the same play) embodies irrational attraction based on sexual gratification and little else.

Except for *Variation on a Theme*, in which Ron has forsaken his male partner for Rose, these relationships are heterosexual, or at least apparently so. However it is generally accepted that often Rattigan was, as one critic put it "depicting homosexual characters or relationships . . . in the guise of heterosexual ones". Rattigan's own relationships ranged from that with the infamous Chips Channon (*The Winslow Boy* is dedicated to his son Paul, in later life a Minister for the Arts) to the young actor Kenneth Morgan, whose suicide provided the seed for *The Deep Blue Sea*. It has been suggested that Hester Collyer in that play should be portrayed as a male character, but the evidence of *Separate Tables* (in *Table Number Seven*) shows that such a transference is not straightforward. In his draft, Rattigan made Major Pollock's offence homosexual (as Mr. Miller's had originally been in *The Deep Blue Sea*), but he changed it to importuning a woman in the cinema. When the play was staged in the more liberal sexual climate of New York it was intended to revert to the earlier version, but in practice this did not work and the revision was retained.

Rattigan's diffidence was based partly on personal discretion and the pre-Wolfenden Report (1957) laws, but it was also in deference to the archetypal theatre-goer whom Rattigan created in his preface to Volume Two of his *Complete Plays* (p.xi) — Aunt Edna, "a nice respectable, middle-class, middle-aged maiden lady . . . She is universal and immortal, and she has lived for two thousand years". Rattigan's detractors accused him of deferring too much to Aunt Edna, not only in his treatment of sexual themes, but in his willingness to compromise in the endings to his plays. The professional and matrimonial uncertainty of Crocker Harris's fate in *The Browning Version* is tenable (Rattigan had considered dispatching him with a heart attack), but many critics felt that he should not have forestalled Hester Collyer (in *The Deep Blue Sea*) from the suicide to which the play seemed to be inexorably moving. In *After Lydia* (by which time Aunt Edna was effectively pensioned off) Rattigan had the courage to deny his audiences a sentimental ending.

Rattigan himself avowed that there was no incompatibility between popular success and quality: "I am not in the least tempted to believe that the failure of a play with an audience means that it must therefore possess some special artistic merit". Tynan was not convinced, concluding his dialogue review of *Separate Tables* with the following exchange between Aunt Edna and the Young Perfectionist:

Aunt Edna: Clearly, there is something here for both of us.
Young Perfectionist: Yes. But not quite enough for either of us.

Posterity will deliver its verdict on Rattigan, but in the years since his death,

enough of his plays (ranging from *French Without Tears* to—pre-eminently—
The Browning Version) have received successful (both critically and commercially) revivals to indicate that his place in the living canon of 20th-century
drama is assured.

—Richard Foulkes

See the essay on *The Browning Version*.

REID, Christina.

Born in Belfast, 12 March 1942. Educated at Everton Primary School,
1947–49, Girls Model School, 1949–57, and Queens University, 1982–83, all
Belfast. Married in 1964 (divorced 1987); three children. Worked in various
office jobs in Belfast, 1957–70; writer-in-residence, Lyric Theatre, Belfast,
1983–84, and Young Vic Theatre, London, 1988–89. Recipient: Ulster
Television Drama award, 1980; Thames Television Playwriting award, 1983;
George Devine award, 1986. Agent: Alan Brodie Representation, 91 Regent
Street, London W1R 7TB, England.

Publications

PLAYS

Did You Hear the One About the Irishman . . .? (produced 1982). With *The
    Belle of Belfast City*, 1989.
Tea in a China Cup (produced 1983). With *Joyriders*, 1987.
Joyriders (produced 1986). With *Tea in a China Cup*, 1987.
The Last of a Dyin' Race (broadcast 1986). In *Best Radio Plays of 1986*, 1986.
My Name, Shall I Tell You My Name (broadcast 1987; produced 1990).
The Belle of Belfast City (produced 1989). With *Did You Hear the One About
    the Irishman . . .?*, 1989.
Les Miserables, adaptation of the novel by Victor Hugo (produced 1992).

RADIO PLAYS: *The Last of a Dyin' Race*, 1986; *My Name, Shall I Tell You My
Name*, 1987; *The Unfortunate Fursey*, adaptation of the novel by Mervyn
Wall, 1989; *Today and Yesterday in Northern Ireland*, for children, 1989.

TELEVISION PLAY: *The Last of a Dyin' Race*, 1987.

Christina Reid comments:

I come from a long line of Irish storytellers. The women of my mother's family
didn't just sit still and tell tales, they dressed up and enacted a mixture of fact
and fiction through song, dance, and dialogue, as much for their own enjoyment as to entertain us children. It is my earliest memory of theatre. In my
plays, characters often tell their story as naturally in song and dance as they do
in words, and much of my writing to date has been about the women and
children of Northern Ireland. There are strong parts for men in the plays, but
there are usually more women in the cast, and the main storyline tends to be
mostly theirs. I don't set out to do this in any causal way; it is simply how I
write, but I do think that too often Northern Ireland is portrayed on stage and

screen as if "the troubles" and male violence is the whole rather than a part of life there, and that this leaves too many songs unsung.

Much as the weaver of homespun interlaces strands of yarn, Christina Reid alternates the tragedies of Belfast life with her ironic humor. Her plays are at once soft and abrasive, delicate and resilient, and they blanket us in warmth. Her portraits of working-class people are well crafted, their characters revealed quickly and neatly by series of humble incidents. Woven into the comfort of the ordinary is the horror of the extraordinary; entwined in the pain is the ache of laughter. The effect is outrageous: prejudice, deprivation, and death are reduced to commonplace events that we can understand, no matter where we live.

Outrage is a natural reaction to Reid's first play, the one-act *Did You Hear the One About the Irishman . . .?*. It is a 1980's romance à la Victor Hugo in that "the sublime and the grotesque" co-exist. Allison, a Protestant, and Brian, a Catholic, are idealists in an imperfect world. Neither can understand why it could be dangerous for them to marry, even though Brian's father was murdered and both have relatives in the Long Kesh prison where political prisoners are held. Their dialogue is witty and gentle, in contrast to the pleading of their families and the warnings of the prisoners. Periodic appearances are made by an Irishman who reads from a list of "Permitted Christmas Parcels" for the prison, thereby injecting reality, and by a comedian whose anti-Irish jokes are increasingly ominous. In counterpoint to Allison's and Brian's joke about forming their own peaceful "Apathy Party," the comedian talks of the inevitable violent deaths the Irish must suffer. The tragic conclusion is expected, yet the theatrical impact is not diminished. Reid makes effective use of black humor.

Tea in a China Cup is a lovely, quiet play. Though it takes place during the Troubles, it is concerned more with pride—making the proper impression and not airing dirty linen in public. It is the maintenance of dignity that obsesses Beth's working-class Protestant family, and fear of becoming caught in the same domestic trap that motivates Beth. In the first scene Beth must buy a grave plot for her mother, Sarah, who is dying of cancer. Reid's ironic faculty is evident immediately as Beth must decide between the Catholic and Protestant sections of the new cemetery, lest her mother stand out "like a sore thumb." Always aware of tradition, Sarah hopes only to live until 12th of July, when the Orangemen will again march past her window. She cautions Beth to remember all the family stories after she is gone, and Beth tells us about the men who went to war, the women who laid out the dead, her own friendship with a Catholic girl, and the importance of having what her grandmother called "a wee bit of fine bone china." But the china which to Sarah symbolizes the last vestige of civilization in a city of soldiers and Catholics is a bane to Beth. As Reid leads us through 30 years in the life of this family, Beth matures. In the end, still loving them all, she is able to break free of the restrictions which bound the women to home and custom. Superstition, prejudice, and tradition are cast aside in one last ironic act; hope is possible.

Less optimistic is *Joyriders*, a spirited evocation of what it means to be a poor Catholic teenager in Belfast. Sandra, Maureen, Arthur, and Tommy are four residents of the deplorable Divis Flats housing development who are given a chance to prove themselves in a youth training program. Two are young offenders, one was scarred when the army accidentally shot him, and one lives alone with her glue-sniffing brother. Reid first places these characters in a theatre, watching the end of Sean O'Casey's *Shadow of a Gunman* with their social worker Kate. By their reactions to the dialogue, their characters are instantly defined. Tommy, possibly a half-caste, is defensive; the disfigured Arthur is a joker; Sandra is practical; Maureen is a romantic. Together, they form a kind of family which Kate leads through various vicissitudes to a conclusion even she cannot control. The startling reversal is reminiscent of the well-made play. *Joyriders* is a particularly ironic title, since the activity brings this group only momentary joy and lasting misery. More ironic still is Kate's realization that the entire training course is the ultimate joyride because, when it ends, the participants have little chance of finding jobs. The course itself is constantly threatened with extinction. Sandra, Maureen, Arthur, and Tommy will all rejoin the cycle of hopelessness. In several ways, the play ends by coming full circle. Reid creates a sensitive portrait of teenagers trying to find their identities in a society that has no place for them. The issue is the fate of children from what Reid quotes as "the worst housing development in Western Europe."

The Belle of Belfast City takes its title from a music-hall song sung by Dolly, the ageing child star and matriarch of this play's family. As three generations gather, their reunion is marred by Jack, a loyalist who protests against the Anglo-Irish Agreement with the Reverend Ian Paisley. All of Dolly's women— Belle, the half-caste granddaughter; niece Janet, the victim of her brother Jack's incestuous attentions; the brave Vi and the idealistic Rose, Dolly's daughters—are subject to the males in power. Jack, the conservative Protestant zealot, and Tom, a strong-arm English "businessman," both harass the women. Each copes in her own valiant way, but is swept along on the political undercurrent which ripples through this play. Eventually Vi is persuaded to sell her shop. Rose fears the right-wing Catholic stand, so like Jack's, which limits women's rights. Reid is more straightforward about her politics than usual.

Reid's themes are women and their submissive role in Northern Ireland, their families, and the damage caused to both by the Troubles. She speaks sympathetically yet unsentimentally, and with the authority of one who knows the people and the customs about which she writes. It is a tribute to her skill that we can receive her message while being entertained. In no sense do we feel we have been subjected to a lecture, and yet we are filled with rage. In the midst of a lovely story is the inescapable presence of oppression, of a cycle of hopelessness despite courage. It is Reid's humor which gives resilience to her characters and provides a fascinating contrast to degradation and horror. Her frequent use of music also adds texture to her plays.

—Carol Banks

RIDLER, Anne (Barbara, née Bradby).

Born in Rugby, Warwickshire, 30 July 1912. Educated at Downe House School; King's College, London, diploma in journalism 1932. Married Vivian Ridler in 1938; two sons and two daughters. Member of editorial department, Faber and Faber publishers, London, 1935–40. Recipient: Oscar Blumenthal prize, 1954, and Union League Civic and Arts Foundation prize, 1955 (*Poetry*, Chicago). Address: 14 Stanley Road, Oxford OX4 1QZ, England.

Publications

PLAYS

Cain (produced 1943). 1943.
The Shadow Factory: A Nativity Play (produced 1945). 1946.
Henry Bly (produced 1947). In *Henry Bly and Other Plays*, 1950.
Henry Bly and Other Plays. 1950.
The Mask, and The Missing Bridegroom (produced 1951). In *Henry Bly and Other Plays*, 1950.
The Trial of Thomas Cranmer, music by Bryan Kelly (produced 1956). 1956.
The Departure, music by Elizabeth Maconchy (produced 1961). In *Some Time After and Other Poems*, 1972.
Who Is My Neighbour? (produced 1961). With *How Bitter the Bread*, 1963.
The Jesse Tree: A Masque in Verse, music by Elizabeth Maconchy (produced 1970). 1972.
Rosinda, translation of the libretto by Faustini, music by Cavalli (produced 1973).
Orfeo, translation of the libretto by Striggio, music by Monteverdi (produced 1975). 1975; revised edition, 1981.
Eritrea, translation of the libretto by Faustini, music by Cavalli (produced 1975). 1975.
The King of the Golden River, music by Elizabeth Maconchy (produced 1975).
The Return of Ulysses, translation of the libretto by Badoaro, music by Monteverdi (produced 1978). In *The Operas of Monteverdi*, edited by Nicholas John, 1992.
The Lambton Worm, music by Robert Sherlaw Johnson (produced 1978). 1979.
Orontea, translation of the libretto by Cicognini, music by Cesti (produced 1979).
Agrippina, translation of the libretto by Grimani, music by Handel (produced 1982).
La Calisto, translation of the libretto by Faustini, music by Cavalli (produced 1984).
Così fan Tutte, translation of the libretto by da Ponte, music by Mozart (produced 1986; broadcast, 1988). 1987.
Don Giovanni, translation of the libretto by da Ponte, music by Mozart (produced 1990).
The Marriage of Figaro, translation of the libretto by da Ponte, music by Mozart (produced 1991).

The Coronation of Poppea, translation of the libretto by Busenello, music by Monteverdi (produced 1992). In *The Operas of Monteverdi*, edited by Nicholas John, 1992.

TELEVISION PLAY: *Così fan Tutte*, 1988.

VERSE

Poems. 1939.
A Dream Observed and Other Poems. 1941.
The Nine Bright Shiners. 1943.
The Golden Bird and Other Poems. 1951.
A Matter of Life and Death. 1959.
Selected Poems. 1961.
Some Time After and Other Poems. 1972.
Italian Prospect: Six Poems. 1976.
Dies Natalist: Poems of Birth and Infancy. 1980.
Ten Poems, with E.J. Scovell. 1984.
New and Selected Poems. 1988.

OTHER

Olive Willis and Downe House: An Adventure in Education. 1967.
A Victorian Family Postbag. 1988.
Profitable Wonders: Aspects of Thomas Traherne, with A.M. Allchin and Julia Smith. 1989.

Editor, *Shakespeare Criticism 1919–1935*. 1936.
Editor, *A Little Book of Modern Verse*. 1941.
Editor, *Time Passes and Other Poems*, by Walter de la Mare. 1942.
Editor, *Best Ghost Stories*. 1945.
Editor, *The Faber Book of Modern Verse*, revised edition. 1951.
Editor, *The Image of the City and Other Essays*, by Charles Williams. 1958.
Editor, *Selected Writings*, by Charles Williams. 1961.
Editor, *Shakespeare Criticism 1935–1960*. 1963.
Editor, *Poems and Some Letters*, by James Thomson. 1963.
Editor, *Thomas Traherne: Poems, Centuries, and Three Thanksgivings*. 1966.
Editor, with Christopher Bradby, *Best Stories of Church and Clergy*. 1966.
Editor, *Selected Poems of George Darley*. 1979.
Editor, *The Poems of William Austin*. 1983.
Editor, *A Victorian Family Postbag*. 1988.
Editor, *A Measure of English Poetry: Critical Essays*. 1991.

MANUSCRIPT COLLECTION: Eton College Library, Buckinghamshire.

CRITICAL STUDY: *The Christian Tradition in Modern British Verse Drama* by William V. Spanos, 1967.

Anne Ridler comments:

(1977) It is a great advantage for a dramatist to know the cast and place he is writing for, the audience he is addressing. Only rarely have I had this oppor-

tunity, and this is perhaps why *Thomas Cranmer*, commissioned for performance in the church where Cranmer was tried, has been judged my best play.

Writing words for music, however, gives a rare opportunity for a contemporary poet to use his particular talents in the theatre, and it is in this field
(whether by original words, or fitting a translation to a musical line) that I
prefer to work at present. Libretto-writing, as W.H. Auden said, gives the poet
his one chance nowadays of using the high style.

Although Anne Ridler has to her credit a number of plays which have their
place in the postwar revival of blank verse drama, it is more likely that she will
be remembered for her volumes of poetry than for her work in the theatre. She
began by tackling the forbidding theme of Cain, presenting the characters from
Genesis with the archangels Michael and Gabriel serving as chorus to the
tragedy. *The Shadow Factory*, a most unusual nativity play, is altogether more
interesting as it juxtaposes reflections on the birth of Christ and some sharp
criticisms of contemporary issues. In the factory the workers are reduced
almost to robots, endlessly repeating the same pointless actions in the production line. The jingle "The Piece-Work Way/Means Better Pay" sums up the
futility of it all, and the director is no doubt intentionally something of an
Orwellian Big Brother. He has, however, had the idea of commissioning a large
mural painting as an example of corporate sponsorship which will enhance the
company's image. The artist who undertakes the work soon sizes up the
situation and, having taken the precaution of obtaining a promise that nobody
shall see what he is doing until it is finished, paints a picture which portrays the
director as a masked figure playing chess heartlessly with the lives of his work
people. Meantime, a parson, who is also admitted to the factory as part of a
policy of good treatment for the staff, rehearses a nativity play with the
workers. The two strands come together as the director swallows his pride and
accepts the mural and its message, or rather the message of the nativity. With
its concern for social injustice the play strikes a chord, and if the director is a
little too wooden in his attitudes and expression, there is certainly life in the
portrayal of the workers, especially William, whose reactions to the birth of his
first child are observed with affectionate accuracy. All the same, the mixture of
realism and allegory is not altogether persuasive, and the optimism, as with
many nativity plays, is a little difficult to swallow except on Christmas Eve.

Henry Bly is more successful because its engaging plot, based on the Grimm
Brothers' fairy tale "Brother Lustig," is realistic only in its depiction of
characters, not of milieu. Henry is a picaresque rogue, always keen to enjoy a
drink or to cadge a coin. On his feckless way through life he falls in with a
Tramp who never explains himself very fully but whom we soon come to
recognise as some sort of Christ-figure when he works miracles without hope
of any material reward. For Henry he is at first merely a simpleton to be
exploited, but by the end the ne'er-do-well comes to realise that what he is
being offered is his chance for salvation. Folklore is also used as the basis for
The Mask which takes the form of a reworking of the moving Somerset
folksong "The Shooting of His Dear" and manages to modernise the tale
without destroying its charm.

Ridler turned to history with *The Trial of Thomas Cranmer*, written to mark the 400th aniversary of his death. When played in the University Church, Oxford, near so many of the sites mentioned by the characters, the tragedy must have been particularly moving, but even without local knowledge this simple and yet very sympathetic chronicle of inhumanity strikes home. Ridler's method is first to show Cranmer as a complete human being, naturally anxious to avoid the challenge of martyrdom, so that she can enlist all our sympathies as he goes to his death. His persecutors seem all the more ignoble since he is not cast in the heroic mould, and his courage and faith impress us all the more since we know he would sooner not be tested. There is, of course, also Cranmer's magnificent control of language, and this, perhaps as much as an obvious Oxford connection and reverence for one of the martyrs of the English church, must have attracted Ridler.

For her, verse drama is not a matter of grand phrases and extravagant imagery. Instead she prefers a sober style, rarely enlivened by metaphor and spiced with just occasional dry wit. She knows the power of monosyllables and has enough confidence in the power of her verse to avoid gross effects. It is the rhythm, close to that of prose yet subtly more strict, that repeatedly lifts the speeches she puts into the mouths of her characters above the mundane matters they may be discussing and gives her dialogue the extra strengths of poetry. In her plays her constant concern is to present images of redemption within contexts which portray the pains, problems, and little joys of mankind. Her verse serves as one more element in the bridge that she seeks to build between two worlds.

After her verse plays, Anne Ridler did not only continue to write poetry herself and edit a variety of other works; she also turned towards the world of opera. For the composer Elizabeth Maconchy, for instance, she provided the libretto for *The Departure* and for *The King of the Golden River* (after Ruskin), and for Robert Sherlaw Johnson she refashioned a popular County Durham folktale for his opera *The Lambton Worm*. In recent years she has also produced translations—or, as she significantly prefers to call them, "singing versions"—of the texts of Monteverdi's *The Return of Ulysses*, Cavalli's *La Calisto*, Handel's *Agrippina*, and Mozart's *Così fan Tutte*. These meticulously worked versions, which reveal a rare combination of verbal and musical sensitivity, have set high standards in this very testing art form. They have made an important contribution to the growing trend, exemplified at its best by Kent Opera, of performing, both in the theatre and on television, the masterpieces of the operatic repertory in English.

—Christopher Smith

ROCHE, Billy (William Michael Roche).

Born in Wexford, 11 January 1949. Educated at Mercy Convent School, Wexford, 1954–57; Christian Brothers, Primary and Secondary, 1957–66. Married Patti Egan in 1973; three daughters. Barman, Shamrock Bar, Wexford, 1967–69; upholsterer, Smiths Car Factory, Wexford, 1969–73 and 1978–80; builders' labourer, London, 1973–75; barman, Stonebridge Lounge, Wexford, 1976; factory worker, Wexford, 1976–78. Singer with The Roach Band, 1975–80; playwright-in-residence, The Bush Theatre, London, 1988.

Recipient: *Plays and Players* award, 1988, 1989; John Whiting award, 1989; George Devine award, 1990; Edinburgh Fringe first, 1990; Thames Television award, 1990; London Theatre Fringe award, 1992; *Time Out* award, 1992. Lives in Wexford. Agent: Leah Schmidt, Curtis Brown Group, 162–168 Regent Street, London W1R 5TB, England.

Publications

PLAYS

Johnny Nobody (produced 1986).
A Handful of Stars (as *The Boker Poker Club*, produced 1987; as *A Handful of Stars*, produced 1988). In *First Run*, edited by Kate Harwood, 1989.
Amphibians (produced 1987; revised version produced 1992).
Poor Beast in the Rain (produced 1989). 1990.
Belfry (produced 1991). In *The Wexford Trilogy*, 1992.
The Wexford Trilogy (includes *A Handful of Stars, Poor Beast in the Rain, Belfry*) (produced 1992). 1992.
The Cavalcaders (produced 1993). 1994.

NOVEL

Tumbling Down. 1986.

THEATRICAL ACTIVITIES

ACTOR: **Plays**—Spud Murphy in *Johnny Nobody*, 1986; Stapler in *The Boker Poker Club*, 1987; Eagle in *Amphibians*, 1987; Willy Diver in *Aristocrats* by Brian Friel, 1988; role in *The Cavalcaders*, 1993. **Films**—role in *Strapless* by David Hare, 1990. **Television**—*The Bill*, 1992.

Billy Roche comments:

It is my fascination with my hometown of Wexford in Ireland that forms the basis of all my work so far. I had hoped that I'd be over it all by now but instead I find my fascination deepens with every play I write. It is mainly the language of the people of Wexford that I'm after—poetic, strange, sly language that can be so devastatingly economic, particularly in the affairs of the heart, and yet has the knack of going right to the core of the matter. Like many other writers before me I keep returning to the place of my birth like a salmon swimming home perhaps because I just long to see my own face in the water or at the very least I really wouldn't mind finding the little fellow I used to be once upon a time.

"The play is set in Wexford, a small town in Ireland." The thematic territory of Billy Roche's *The Wexford Trilogy* is as economically defined and focused as its geographical setting. What is presented in each of the plays is less a plot than a situation of stagnation in which the thwarted energies and desires of the individual continually seek expression—or even resolution in action. The paralysis of a provincial milieu in which, although "it's nobody's fault," "everyone's to blame," is familiar from Joyce's *Dubliners* and the stream of Irish writing that emerges from it, but Roche's treatment is distinctive in its particularity and resonance. Indeed, his writing is notable (especially in view of its themes) for its deep and unembarrassed relation to its artistic roots: not only Joyce and the Irish short story, but Chekhov—mediated perhaps through the 1970s plays of Brian Friel. The affection manifest in the presentation of many of the characters, and the fullness with which the Wexford context is suggested, tend to pull against the astringencies of a Joycean or Chekhovian irony, but the sense of small-town stagnation is nevertheless potent. Not the least Joycean feature of Roche's writing is the pervasive reference to popular culture—film and pop song—which functions as ironic counterpoint to the action. Also noticeable is the way that stereotypes familiar from O'Casey are displaced and rotated. In all three plays, those who ultimately constrain, command, influence, or stand as symbols are versions of the stoical, forebearing mother and the feckless, extravagant father. But these figures are always unseen, offstage: their determining presence is made all the more apparent by their physical absence.

A Handful of Stars, the first play of the Trilogy, is set in a "scruffy pool hall," the favourite haunt of local teenage rebel and self-styled "King of the Renegades," Jimmy Brady. For Jimmy, to "grow up" would be for him to join the "livin' dead," wrapped up in a "nice neat little parcel." Progressively isolated by the loss of his girlfriend (who leaves him because he is "not going to change") and the impending marriage of his best friend, Jimmy realises that he has not "a ghost of a chance" of avoiding the fate of his drunken ne'er-do-well father. He "wages war on everybody," and seals his alienation from local society by attempting to hold up a shop. Taking refuge in the pool hall, he wrecks the privileged preserve of its "élite" members. Before the Garda arrives, the over-the-hill local boxer, Stapler, a surrogate father for Jimmy, steadies him, but can offer only weary words: "Most of us wage war on the wrong people." Jimmy would "rather be an ejit than a creep," and there seems no other option. His parents' momentary happiness now appears like a "mirage," and his arrest will, he knows, consign his mother to further silent torment. Among other things, the play is a tribute to the "young rebels" of 1950s and 1960s Hollywood—"Brando and Dean, Newman, Clift and McQueen." Yet the rebel here represents not a "misunderstood" generation posed against a smug "adult" orthodoxy but a culture split against itself and "screamin'."

For his second play Roche originally projected a piece which was to focus on a Jimmy-like rebel who would refuse his cultural identity, "run for the hills," and join the Carnival. But the Bush Theatre prevailed on the playwright to reconsider and he turned this scenario inside out, effecting in the process a decisive shift of thematic emphasis. Poor Beast in the Rain centres not on departure but on that most pervasive trope of Irish literature—return. According to Roche himself, this is "a rainy day sort of a play which is held together by an ancient Irish Myth as Danger Doyle returns like Oisín to the place of his birth, 'just because he wanted to see his auld mates again.' Danger Doyle, who is a sort of grown-up Jimmy Brady, ran away with another man's wife ten years ago and the play is really about all the people the pair of them left behind." The setting is an "old fashioned betting shop"—owned by the abandoned husband, Steven, and run by him and his daughter Eileen—on the weekend of the All-Ireland Hurling Final, in which the local team is successful. For the frequenters of the betting shop, "the ranks of the left behind," the commonest strategy of consolation is the mythologisation of the past and the veneration of its "characters," be they local wild boys or hurling heroes. Danger Doyle has escaped only to a depressed and workaday existence in England. Yet when he returns, feeling "like a fugitive," it is not to "kiss the past's arse" but to persuade Eileen to go back with him to visit her dejected mother. He also tries to set his "auld mates" free from their devotion to glamorised memories of himself. This entails not a demythologisation (which is revealed as the other, disillusioned, side of the rhetorical coin) but an assurance that, as he says to an embittered old flame, "I don't have what you seem to think I took from yeh." Only when his name is "washed away" will she cease to conceive of herself as a "poor beast" left out "in the rain": to those "reachin' for the moon," the here-and-now can only ever be an "auld snare."

The third play of the *Trilogy*, *Belfry*, signals an interesting formal shift. A split stage and retrospective structure permit a fluidity of action and promote an intimacy with the consciousness of a single individual. Events are framed, punctuated, and indeed ordered, by an expansive and occasionally lyrical narrative addressed "to the audience" in which the "little sacristan"' Artie O'Leary discloses why, in his "queer auld whisperin' world," the "only life he's ever known," he now has "a story to tell." His story is of a furtive, though passionate, adulterous affair with the church helper Angela, and of how she "tapped a hidden reservoir" by releasing him from a life dominated by a tyrannical mother and bounded by his necessary involvement with the rites of birth, marriage, and death. On his mother's death, the illegitimate Artie can become his "father's son again"—a wild "Jack-the-lad" in his free time. It is a small enough victory in a "small enough life," but a not insignificant one when those around him are so thwarted. The young priest Pat laments a life "surrounded by dead and dying," and turns to drink again; Angela attempts to mend her continuing sense of exclusion from her husband's life by moving on to another affair; and the husband himself, Donal, having confronted Artie and then resumed their friendship, broods over his fading status as local handball star. Only Dominic, the backward and endearingly sparky altar boy for whom Artie is a surrogate father, stands apart. He is beaten by Artie, who believes (wrongly) that he has revealed the affair to Donal, and he is killed in an accident whilst escaping from the special school to which he has been sent. But it is his surprise birthday party that Artie's narrative poignantly revisits; it is Dominic who, ringing out "I Can't Get No Satisfaction" on the church bells, and announcing his ambition to make people happy, embodies the "capacity" for happiness in the play. In *Belfry*, as elsewhere in *The Wexford Trilogy*, Roche manages to avoid not just the sentimentality of a facile hope but the equally insidious sentimentality of a self-pitying despair.

—Paul Lawley

RUDKIN, (James) David.

Born in London, 29 June 1936. Educated at King Edward's School, Birmingham, 1947–55; St. Catherine's College, Oxford, 1957–61, M.A. 1961. Served in the Royal Corps of Signals, 1955–57. Married Alexandra Margaret Thompson in 1967; two sons and two daughters. Assistant master of Latin, Greek and music, County High School, Bromsgrove, Worcestershire, 1961–64. Recipient: *Evening Standard* award, 1962; John Whiting award,

1974; Obie award, 1977; New York Film Festival gold medal, 1987; Society of Authors scholarship, 1988; European Film Festival Special Jury award, 1990. Agent: Casarotto Ramsay Ltd., National House, 60–66 Wardour Street, London W1V 3HP, England.

Publications

PLAYS

Afore Night Come (produced 1960). In *New English Dramatists 7*, 1963.
Moses and Aaron, translation of the libretto, music by Schoenberg (produced 1965). 1965.
The Grace of Todd, music by Gordon Crosse (produced 1969). 1970.
Burglars (for children; produced 1970). In *Prompt Two*, edited by Alan Durband, 1976.
The Filth Hunt (produced 1972).
Cries from Casement as His Bones Are Brought to Dublin (broadcast 1973; produced 1973). 1974.
Ashes (produced 1973). 1978.
Penda's Fen (televised 1974). 1975.
No Title (produced 1974).
The Sons of Light (produced 1976). 1981.
Sovereignty under Elizabeth (produced 1977).
Hippolytus, adaptation of the play by Euripides (produced 1978). 1980.
Hansel and Gretel (produced 1980).
The Triumph of Death (produced 1981). 1981.
Peer Gynt, adaptation of the play by Ibsen (produced 1982). 1983.
Space Invaders (produced 1984).
Will's Way (produced 1985).
The Saxon Shore (produced 1986). 1986.
Deathwatch, and The Maids, adaptations of plays by Jean Genet (produced 1987).
When We Dead Awaken, adaptation of the play by Ibsen (produced 1990). 1990.
Screenplays (additional dialogue, uncredited): *Fahrenheit 451*, 1966; *Mademoiselle*, 1966; *Testimony*, 1987; *December Bride*, 1989.

RADIO PLAYS: *No Accounting for Taste*, 1960; *The Persians*, from the play by Aeschylus, 1965; *Gear Change*, 1967; *Cries from Casement as His Bones Are Brought to Dublin*, 1973; *Hecuba*, from the play by Euripides, 1975; *Rosmersholm*, from the play by Ibsen, 1990.

TELEVISION PLAYS: *The Stone Dance*, 1963; *Children Playing*, 1967; *House of Character*, 1968; *Blodwen, Home from Rachel's Marriage*, 1969; *Bypass*, 1972; *Atrocity*, 1973; *Penda's Fen*, 1974; *Pritan* and *The Coming of the Cross* (*Churchill's People* series), 1975; *The Ash Tree*, from the story by M.R. James, 1975; *The Living Grave* (*Leap in the Dark* series), 1981; *Artemis 81*, 1981; *Across the Water*, 1983; *White Lady*, 1987; *Gawain and the Green Knight*, from the Middle English poem, 1991.

BALLET SCENARIO: *Sun into Darkness*, 1966.

THEATRICAL ACTIVITIES

DIRECTOR: **Television** — *White Lady*, 1987.

David Rudkin's *Afore Night Come* is one of the most mature and assured first plays of the postwar period, though in retrospect it can be seen to contain its author's chief dramatic preoccupations only (as it were) in solution, uncrystallized. Primitive chthonic forces long repressed by culture and individual psychology reassert themselves with great violence when a group of fruit-pickers on a Midlands farm single out a casual worker—a strange, "educated" Irish tramp—as scapegoat for their personal, moral, and economic failings and carry out his ritual murder in the sinister, though apparently numinous presence of a crop-spraying helicopter. Thematic elements which are to become central in Rudkin's later work—homosexuality, sexual infertility, the threat of nuclear devastation, England's Irish problem—are present but not developed. Indeed, thematic coherence seems less important to Rudkin at this stage of his career than the recognizably Pinteresque menace which can be generated by the rhythms of a judiciously charged dialogue. It is perhaps for this reason that, though the crucial sacrificial event of *Afore Night Come* is obviously two-edged, the energy of the play makes itself felt as essentially negative.

By contrast, Rudkin's work after his 12-year self-imposed apprenticeship is energized by his passionate commitment to a powerful central *idea*. The primitive impulses of *Afore Night Come* reveal their creative aspect in the concentration on the reintegration and realization of the self that occurs in the gradual, painful liberation from a complex web of repression. On the evidence of his work, Rudkin believes that the power-wielders of modern civilization, and especially the various Christian churches with their capacity for psychological conditioning, function only by burying or perverting for their own dark ends original, natural forces and beliefs. His dramatic response is to affirm the continuity of these forces, on several different levels simultaneously—psychological, sexual, cultural, historical—using those forms which many modern artists have regarded as the enduring repositories of non-rational or even anti-rational values: image, fable, and myth. The quasi-physical impact of Rudkin's dramatic language, with its intense compression and often eccentric syntax, itself reflects these values. Hence also the importance to Rudkin of dialect, the concrete, poetic language of the authentic, geographically rooted self which he repeatedly sets against abstract discourse, the rootless, "Flat Urban Academic" that "will bury our theatre." (The Norwegian acts of his *Peer Gynt* are translated into the "stylized rural Ulster speech" of his own childhood.)

Ashes is a harrowing autobiographical play which rotates the theme of sexual infertility through a series of wider perspectives, political, anthropological, and existential, in handling the problem of free will and determinism. However, the roughly contemporaneous television play *Penda's Fen* offers a more satisfying dramatic realization of his preoccupations. The growth of an adolescent boy in Worcestershire away from social, religious, educational, and sexual constraints into mature selfhood is articulated through images of a local landscape in which the natural forces of Penda's Fen are being perverted, in the modern Pinvin, to menacing scientific ends, through suggestive sequences of music (which, together with sound-effects, has always been more important to Rudkin than scenery or props), and through a series of dream-images which reveal to the boy his homosexuality. Here, as elsewhere in Rudkin's work, homosexuality is important less as a social reality than as an idea: it is the humane "mixed" state which stands as a critique of the conventional phallic "manliness" of society's power-wielders. Having realized that Christianity has "buried" the authentic Jesus—just as "Pinvin" (a real place) has buried Penda's Fen—the boy Stephen rejects power and inherits, in a vision of Penda himself (the last of the English pagan kings) "the sacred demon of ungovernableness."

The key work in Rudkin's oeuvre, at which he worked from 1965 to 1976, is *The Sons of Light*, a massive, multi-layered fable with science-fiction elements and a tripartite mythic structure: "The Division of the Kingdom," "The Pit," "Surrection." The ancient paradigm drawn on by Rudkin is perhaps most familiar from the Christian *Harrowing of Hell*, but the play's fundamental design (as well as its title) is indebted above all to the heresy of Manichaeanism, with its characteristic cosmological dualism. A new pastor and his three sons arrive on a remote Scottish Atlantic island to find it (literally) divided and in the grip of a patriarchal religion of wrath. The island's subterranean industrial complex, an obscene dystopia masterminded by an expressionist-style German scientist, dehumanises and mechanises its workers, allaying any residual stirrings with the (purely functional) promise of religious transcendence. Two of the pastor's sons are killed, but amid terrible violence and purgative suffering, the third son, the "cold" burning "angel" John, descends into this "pit," initiates a fresh consciousness of self in the workers, and destroys the complex, thus uniting the body of the island and reclaiming it for its inhabitants. Simultaneously the identity of a schizophrenic girl, hitherto an outcast, is reintegrated and she is made whole. The structural parallel is underscored by the destruction on several levels of the baneful Father, the figure who, as always in Rudkin, holds in place the structures of repression: sexual, familial, and political. This extraordinary conjunction of Reichian psychotherapy and Artaudian theatre within the arena of myth is a distinctive and powerful achievement.

Rudkin's fiercely idiosyncratic brand of psycho-history is most clearly embodied in *The Triumph of Death*, an extravagant Gothic panorama which dramatises the annihilation or demonisation of natural modes of being and worship by medieval Christianity in its perverted ("Crosstian") project of ideological self-definition and cultural domination (in the name of "Salvation"). With its insistently excremental symbolism, its appropriation of Christian imagery for the evocation of polymorphous ("natural") sexuality and its reconception of Christian mythological figures (most notably "Jehan-"/Joan of Arc), this is undoubtedly Rudkin's riskiest and most challenging work. Indeed, its oddity is a strength (the epigraph insists that the past both is and is not "another country"). Its gravest limitation is a degree of schematisation which *The Sons of Light*, despite shared concerns and imagery, and the fundamental dualism of its structure, largely avoids. *The Triumph of Death*, for all its anti-rationalist primitivism and its fluid Artaudian dramaturgy, is a thesis play: "Our fracture is our fall," and civilisation is founded on repression.

The Saxon Shore attempts to combine an individual's quest for selfhood with an historical vision. The context is also implicitly political, and in Rudkin this means (as in *Ashes*, *Cries from Casement as His Bones Are Brought to Dublin*, and *Across the Water*) the Irish problem. The play is set in Britain in AD 410. The Roman empire is crumbling fast; on the North Sea coast, the displaced native British Celts and a "plantationer" Saxon community face each other across Hadrian's Wall in the presence of a disgruntled and demoralised colonial army. The allegory of the Ulster situation (a Saxon Defence Regiment aids the scornful Roman soldiers and Saxons-turned-nocturnal-werewolves compulsively perpetrate acts of terror) serves as framework for the story of Athdark, a "child growed stale" from mother-domination, who shows "the beginnings of a man" by the end of the play. The structure of the story recalls that of a fable or folktale, whilst resemblances of narrative pattern and tone, as well as verbal echoes, indicate Rudkin's continuing creative-critical engagement with *Peer Gynt*. (*The Dream of Gerontius* and *King Lear* are also, as ever in Rudkin, important intertexts.) But despite the play's variety of English (and a speculative version of Celtic), its dramatic language is disappointingly thin and lacking in resonance. Moreover, the relation between the historical conditions and the development of the individual is never as fully or coherently articulated as it is in Rudkin's best work.

—Paul Lawley

RUSSELL, Willy (William Martin Russell).

Born in Whiston, Lancashire, 23 August 1947. Educated at schools in Knowsley and Rainford, Lancashire; Childwall College of Further Education, Lancashire, 1969–70; St. Katharine's College of Higher Education, Liverpool, 1970–73, Cert.Ed. Married Ann Margaret Seagroatt in 1969; one son and two daughters. Ladies' hairdresser, Liverpool and Kirkby, 1963–68; labourer, Bear Brand warehouse, 1968–69, and teacher, Shorefields Comprehensive, 1973–74, Liverpool. Since 1974 freelance writer. Associate director, 1981–83, and since 1983 honorary director, Liverpool Playhouse; since 1982 founding director, Quintet Films, London. Writer-in-residence, C.F. Mott College of Education, Liverpool, 1976; fellow in creative writing, Manchester Polytechnic, 1977–79. Also folk song composer and singer: performances (with group Kirbytown Three) in clubs and on radio and television since 1965. Recipient: Arts Council bursary, 1974; *Evening Standard* award, 1974; London Theatre Critics award, 1974; Society of West End Theatre award, 1980, 1983, 1988; Golden Globe award, 1984; Ivor Novello award, 1985. M.A.: Open University, Milton Keynes, Buckinghamshire, 1983. Agent: Casarotto Ramsay Ltd., National House, 60–66 Wardour Street, London W1V 3HP. Address: W.R. Ltd., 43 Canning Street, Liverpool L8 7NN, England.

Publications

PLAYS

Keep Your Eyes Down (produced 1971).
Blind Scouse (includes *Keep Your Eyes Down, Playground, Sam O'Shanker*)

(produced 1972; revised version of *Sam O'Shanker*, music by Russell, produced 1973).

Tam Lin (for children), music by Russell (produced 1972).

When the Reds, adaptation of the play *The Tigers Are Coming—O.K.?* by Alan Plater (produced 1973).

Terraces, in *Second Playbill 1*, edited by Alan Durband. 1973; collection published as *Terraces*, 1979.

John, Paul, George, Ringo and Bert (produced 1974).

The Cantril Tales, with others (produced 1975).

Breezeblock Park (produced 1975). 1978.

Break In (televised 1975). In *Scene Scripts 2*, edited by Michael Marland, 1978.

I Read the News Today (broadcast 1976). In *Home Truths*, 1982.

One for the Road (as *Painted Veg and Parkinson*, produced 1976; as *Dennis the Menace*, produced 1978; as *Happy Returns*, produced 1978; as *One for the Road*, produced 1979). 1980; revised version (produced 1986), 1985.

Our Day Out (televised 1977). In *Act 1*, edited by David Self and Ray Speakman, 1979; revised version, songs and music by Bob Eaton, Chris Mellors, and Russell (produced 1983), 1984.

Stags and Hens (produced 1978). 1985.

Lies (televised 1978). In *City Life*, edited by David Self, 1980.

Politics and Terror (televised 1978). In *Wordplays 1*, edited by Alan Durband, 1982.

The Boy with the Transistor Radio (televised 1980). In *Working*, edited by David Self, 1980.

Educating Rita (produced 1980). 1981.

Blood Brothers (produced 1981; revised version, music and lyrics by Russell, produced 1983). 1986.

Educating Rita, Stags and Hens, and Blood Brothers. 1986.

Shirley Valentine (produced 1986). With *One for the Road*, 1988.

SCREENPLAYS: *Educating Rita*, 1983; *Shirley Valentine*, 1989; *Dancin' thru the Dark*, from *Stags and Hens*, 1990.

RADIO PLAY: *I Read the News Today*, 1976.

TELEVISION PLAYS: *King of the Castle*, 1973; *Break In*, 1975; *The Death of a Young, Young Man*, 1975; *Our Day Out*, 1977; *Lies*, 1978; *Politics and Terror*, 1978; *The Daughters of Albion*, 1979; *The Boy with the Transistor Radio*, 1980; *One Summer* series, 1983.

VERSE

Sam O'Shanker: A Liverpool Tale. 1978.

OTHER

PUBLISHED MUSIC: *I Will Be Your Love and OOee boppa OOee boppa*, RSO, 1974; *Dance the Night*, Paternoster, 1980; *Blood Brothers*, Paternoster-Russell Music, 1983; *The Show*, Timeact-Russell Music-Paternoster, 1985; *Mr. Love*, Russell Music-Warner Brothers, 1986.

FILM MUSIC: *Shirley Valentine*, with George Hatzinassios, 1989.

CRITICAL STUDY: "Willy Russell: The First Ten Years" by Timothy Charles, in *Drama*, Summer 1983.

THEATRICAL ACTIVITIES
DIRECTOR: **Play**—*Educating Rita*, 1981.
ACTOR: **Plays**—Narrator in *Blood Brothers*, 1985, and *Shirley Valentine*, 1986. Film—*Educating Rita*, 1983.

Willy Russell comments:

I am loath to make any specific statement on the nature of my work as I reserve the right to dismiss on Thursday the statement I made on Wednesday. However, in a letter of 1984, written to a BBC producer to explain why I would not be writing a play I wrote the following (I think for me it will remain as true on a Thursday as it is on a Wednesday):

To write a play one must passionately believe in something which one wants to communicate. The writer might want to tell of the ills of the world, or of his love for another, of society's folly, of mankind's goodness and baseness. He may want to argue a political cause or just show off his wit. Whatever, it is something which requires a passionate belief in telling what one has to tell. I heard David Edgar say recently that (to paraphrase) writing becomes more difficult as one gets older because as one gets older one gets less certain. Perhaps what he meant was that with age one sees the corollary to every argument, that the radical turns merely liberal. I don't want to be liberal. But *what* do I, personally, want to communicate? What is it that I am deeply concerned with at present? Am I being too heavy on myself? When going through this pre-play torture have I *ever* felt concerned with anything? Is total emptiness a necessary condition in the prelude to writing a play?

I don't want to write what I've already written. I want to learn. I want to write a play which forces me to develop the talent I have. Talent must not go back on itself and stagnate. It is a nerve-wracking process but truly it is better to write nothing than to write something which one has already written. It's only with pushing against the barriers, stretching the boundaries, staring at the abyss that the imagination soars and poetry can be achieved. I believe that no great play was ever written at any significant distance from the abyss—they are all written on the edge. Think of Moss Hart saying that one never learns to be a playwright, only how to write one particular play. The next play, no matter how "successful" the playwright, is something about which he knows nothing. He cannot know how to write it, has no guidelines because, before he has written it, it has never existed. Every play is a trip back to the beginning and a walk through hell all over again.

What do I want to say? What moves me? What story do I want to tell? I believe that every play I have ever written has, ultimately, been one which celebrates the goodness of man; certainly, the plays have included emptiness, despair, possibly even baseness. But it is the goodness that I hope the audience is left with. I really don't want to write plays which are resigned, menopausal, despairing, and whingeing. I don't want to use any medium as a platform for displaying the smallness and hopelessness of man. Man is man because madly, possibly stupidly but certainly wonderfully, he kicks against the inevitability of life. He spends his life looking for answers. There probably are no answers but the fact that man asks the questions is the reason I write plays.

What happens when you grow beyond the class and the culture you were born into? When is freedom real and when is it a fake? What is true knowledge? These are the central questions posed by Willy Russell's major plays since the mid-1970s.

Breezeblock Park is set in the houses of two sisters, Betty and Reeny. It is Christmas and therefore a time for competitive consumption. Betty and Reeny try to outdo each other over costly furniture, bathroom fittings, and central-heating systems. Betty's husband Ted is obsessed with his new car and sees himself as an intellectual with his knowledge of *Mastermind* and his ambitions as an author. Betty's brother Tommy represents a vulgar alternative to this working-class gentility when he gives Betty a vibrator as a Christmas present and prefers to celebrate in the pub rather than in his sister's tasteful front room. Gender roles are strictly defined. The women's territory is the home, particularly the kitchen. Their talk is of clothes, food, children, and relationships. The men work away from the home and their talk is of sport, politics, and general knowledge. Everyone, however, closes ranks over the play's central issue—the pregnancy of Betty's daughter Sandra. Their code demands that she marry the father. There's no shame in "being in the club." As Tommy explains: "It's a bloody secret society they've got goin'. They have a great time." But Sandra is different. She reads, she's interested in ideas, she hangs around with students; in fact, her lover, Tim, is a student. After a strong talking-to by the men, Tim is ready to do the decent thing, but Sandra stands firm. She'll have the child, but she'll live with Tim, unmarried, in a student house. "I want a *good* life, Mother," she shouts at Betty. "I want to sit around and talk about films and—and music." And Betty replies, "You begrudge me every bit of pleasure I have ever had." The two cultures, gentility and bohemianism, are irreconcilable. In a skilful last scene Sandra breaks through the menacing circle of her relations, but only because her mother steps aside. Tim meekly follows her.

Another wedding fails and another escape takes place in *Stags and Hens*. It is stag night for Dave and hen night for Linda before they get married. But both parties have booked into the same dance-hall in Liverpool. On a single set, which consists of the Ladies' and Gents' loos side by side, the differing codes of sex, drink, and clothes are enacted in dialogue which is witty, vulgar, sentimental, and bitter. Linda, we discover, is uneducated but discontented with her girlfriends' cheerful acceptance of the conventions of their class. It isn't so much the consumer world of *Breezeblock Park* that is satirised as the competitive world of grabbing a girl or keeping a man. In a shrewd theatrical move, Dave, the groom at tomorrow's "wedding," stays dead drunk throughout the play, which puts the spotlight even more fiercely on Linda. She finally rejects her world by leaving with Peter, lead singer of the band and an old

flame who's made good in London. But the last word is given to Eddy, the
leader of Dave's friends. It is he, like Tommy in the earlier play, who organises
local solidarity against the outsider. "Don't you come makin' people
unhappy," he warns Dave. "She's our mate's tart. We look after our mates. We
stick with them." Eddy, however, is younger than Tommy. He has to construct
a myth of freedom for his class and culture in the dead wastes of Merseyside.
Peter may be a successful artist but Eddy assures everyone, "You could do that,
what he does if you wanted to. You can do anythin' he can do. We all can." All
they can do is get drunk, draw their names on the toilet walls, and try to chat
up women. Eddy is furious when Linda gets out, but still optimistic for the
future. The play ends with his staggering out of the Gents carrying the still-
oblivious Dave over his shoulder and muttering, "She's gone. Well y've got no
baggage weighin' y' down. There's nothin' holdin' us back now Dave. We
can go anywhere."

With *Educating Rita* all these themes are very sharply expressed and focused
by Rita herself. She's already outpaced Sandra and Linda by enrolling on an
Open University course, but the early encounters between her directness and
the cultured evasiveness of her tutor Frank reveal real cultural gulfs. But, as she
shows in a series of brilliant observations in Act 1, Scene 4, she knows very
well what she's leaving behind and why she wants to change. Her class may
have a certain level of affluence but it hasn't got meaning, it hasn't got culture
as meaningful life. "I just see everyone pissed, or on the Valium, tryin' to get
from one day to the next." Since Rita doesn't believe in a distinct working-
class culture—"I've read about that. I've never seen it though"—she wants the
knowledge and skills that Frank can give her. "What do you want to know?"
he asks her at their first tutorial. "Everything," she replies. By the end she's
certainly acquired a poise, a sophistication—"I know what clothes to wear,
what plays to see"—and a contempt for Frank she didn't have at the beginning. She's escaped her origins and she knows how much everyone resents this
kind of mobility. "They hate it when one of them tries to break away."

In the musical *Blood Brothers*, Russell shifts to men and their life chances.
Twin brothers, separated at birth, are brought up by natural and fake mothers,
in working-class and middle-class environments. Another Linda shuttles between the two. Each sees advantages in the other's situation, but it is working-
class Mickey who suffers unemployment, depression, and jealousy over Linda.
Edward goes to university and becomes a local politician. He helps his brother
with housing and a job but, in a melodramatic ending, Mickey shoots his
brother because he thinks Linda has slept with him and gets shot down himself
by the police. So, once again, the women progress as the men go under.

The pattern is repeated with *Shirley Valentine* but this is the least complex of
Russell's plays. It is a monologue in two acts by a 42-year-old Liverpool
housewife who moves from her downbeat kitchen to a downmarket *taverna* in
Greece. With typical Scouse wit she tells her tale of taking off for a holiday in
Greece with a feminist friend, leaving her boorish husband and her two
layabout children. She has an affair with a Greek waiter and although she
knows he seduces all his clients she gains new confidence in herself from his
flattery. She gives us sharp verbal sketches of oafish English families abroad
and a self-portrait in which stoicism and romanticism are equally mixed.
Shirley is pre-Rita in her self-awareness but she has made a decisive break in

her life-pattern by going to Greece and staying there although her linguistic and cultural resources are still so slender that we have to doubt whether she really has achieved a breakthrough. The play ends with her waitressing at the *taverna* and waiting for her husband who is desperate to get her back. It's a fantasy that she could stay on—she would be ostracised by all the local women as a whore—but the hope is that her husband will treat her with new respect at home. *Shirley Valentine* is an entertaining piece, which had a long London run, but it represents a step backward from Russell's earlier successes.

—Tony Dunn

S

SAUNDERS, James A.

Born in Islington, London, 8 January 1925. Educated at Wembley County School; University of Southampton. Married Audrey Cross in 1951; one son and two daughters. Formerly taught English in London. Since 1962 full-time writer. Recipient: Arts Council bursary, 1960, 1984; *Evening Standard* award, 1963; Writers Guild award, 1966. Lives in Twickenham, Middlesex. Agent: Casarotto Ramsay Ltd., National House, 60–66 Wardour Street, London W1V 3HP, England.

Publications

PLAYS

Cinderella Comes of Age (produced 1949).

Moonshine (produced 1955).

Dog Accident (broadcast 1958; revised version produced 1969). In *Ten of the Best*, edited by Ed Berman, 1979.

Barnstable (broadcast 1959; produced 1960). 1965.

Alas, Poor Fred: A Duologue in the Style of Ionesco (produced 1959). 1960.

The Ark, music by Geoffrey Wright (produced 1959).

Ends and Echoes: Barnstable, Committal, Return to a City (produced 1960). *Return to a City* in *Neighbours and Other Plays*, 1968.

A Slight Accident (produced 1961). In *Neighbours and Other Plays*, 1968.

Double, Double (produced 1962). 1964.

Next Time I'll Sing to You, suggested by a theme from *A Hermit Disclosed* by Raleigh Trevelyan (produced 1962; revised version produced 1963). 1963.

Who Was Hilary Maconochie? (produced 1963). In *Savoury Meringue and Other Plays*, 1980.

The Pedagogue (produced 1963). In *Neighbours and Other Plays*, 1968.

Neighbours (produced 1964). In *Neighbours and Other Plays*, 1968.

A Scent of Flowers (produced 1964). 1965.

Triangle, with others (produced 1965).

Trio (produced 1967). In *Neighbours and Other Plays*, 1968.

The Italian Girl, with Iris Murdoch, adaptation of the novel by Murdoch (produced 1967). 1969.

Neighbours and Other Plays (includes *Trio*; *Alas, Poor Fred*; *Return to a City*; *A Slight Accident*; *The Pedagogue*). 1968.

Haven, later called *A Man's Best Friend*, in *We Who Are about to . . .*, later called *Mixed Doubles* (produced 1969). 1970.

The Travails of Sancho Panza, based on the novel *Don Quixote* by Cervantes (produced 1969). 1970.
The Borage Pigeon Affair (produced 1969). 1970.
Savoury Meringue (produced 1971). In *Savoury Meringue and Other Plays* 1980.
After Liverpool (broadcast 1971; produced 1971). 1973.
Games (produced 1971). 1973.
Opus (produced 1971).
Hans Kohlhaas, adaptation of the story by Heinrich von Kleist (produced 1972; as *Michael Kohlhaas,* produced 1987).
Bye Bye Blues (produced 1973). In *Bye Bye Blues and Other Plays,* 1980.
Poor Old Simon (in *Mixed Blessings,* produced 1973). In *Savoury Meringue and Other Plays,* 1980.
Random Moments in a May Garden (broadcast 1974; produced 1977). In *Bye Bye Blues and Other Plays,* 1980.
A Journey to London, completion of the play by Vanbrugh (produced 1975).
Play for Yesterday (produced 19753). In *Savoury Meringue and Other Plays,* 1980.
The Island (produced 1975). In *Bye Bye Blues and Other Plays,* 1980.
Squat (produced 1976).
Mrs. Scour and the Future of Western Civilisation (produced 1976).
Bodies (produced 1977). 1979.
Over the Wall (produced 1977). In *Play Ten,* edited by Robin Rook, 1977.
What Theatre Really Is, in *Play Ten,* edited by Robin Rook. 1977.
Player Piano, adaptation of the novel by Kurt Vonnegut (produced 1978).
The Mountain (produced 1979).
The Caucasian Chalk Circle, adaptation of a play by Brecht (produced 1979).
Birdsong (produced 1979). In *Savoury Meringue and Other Plays,* 1980.
The Girl in Melanie Klein, adaptation of the novel by Ronald Harwood (produced 1980).
Savoury Meringue and Other Plays, 1980.
Bye Bye Blues and Other Plays (includes *The Island* and *Random Moments in a May Garden*). 1980.
Fall (produced 1981). 1985.
Nothing to Declare (broadcast 1982; produced 1983).
Menocchio (broadcast 1985). In *Best Radio Plays of 1985,* 1986.
Redevelopment, adaptation of a play by Václav Havel (produced 1990). 1990.
Making It Better (broadcast 1991; produced 1992). 1992.

RADIO PLAYS: *Love and a Limousine,* 1952; *The Drop Too Much,* 1952; *Nimrod's Oak,* 1953; *Women Are So Unreasonable,* 1957; *Dog Accident,* 1958; *Barnstable,* 1959; *Gimlet* (version of *Double, Double*), 1963; *It's Not the Game It Was,* 1964; *Pay As You Go,* 1965; *After Liverpool,* 1971; *Random Moments in a May Garden,* 1974; *The Last Black and White Midnight Movie,* 1979; *Nothing to Declare,* 1982; *The Flower Case,* 1982; *A Suspension of Mercy* (*Murder for Pleasure* series), from the novel by Patricia Highsmith, 1983; *Menocchio,* 1985; *The Confidential Agent,* from the novel by Graham Greene, 1987; *Headlong Hall,* from the novel by Thomas Love Peacock, 1988; *Making It Better,* 1991.

TELEVISION PLAYS: *Just You Wait* (version of *Double, Double*), 1963; *Watch Me I'm a Bird*, 1964; *The White Stocking, New Eve and Old Adam, Tickets Please, Monkey Nuts, Two Blue Birds, In Love,* and *The Blue Moccasins,* all from works by D.H. Lawrence, 1966–67; *The Beast in the Jungle,* from the story by Henry James, 1969; *Plastic People,* 1970; *The Unconquered,* 1970; *Craven Arms,* from a story by A.E. Coppard, 1972; *The Mill,* 1972; *The Black Dog,* 1972; *Blind Love,* from the story by V.S. Pritchett, 1977; *The Healing Nightmare,* 1977; *People Like Us,* with Susan Pieat and Ian Curteis, from the novel by R.F. Delderfield, 1978; *Bloomers* series, 1979; *The Sailor's Return,* from the novel by David Garnett, 1980; *The Captain's Doll,* from the story by D.H. Lawrence, 1983; *The Magic Bathroom,* 1987.

James Saunders's work is characterized by a diversity of style which is unusual even among the more eclectic of his contemporaries. He can be compared to a startling variety of other writers, and, should his scripts survive without attribution, future generations of scholars might assign them in something like this fashion: to Harold Pinter the revue sketch investment of the commonplace with interest found in *Double, Double* and the schematic exploration of open marriage found in *Bye Bye Blues;* to John Mortimer the charming coincidence of complementary handicaps which permits two self-pitying people to unite in *Blind Love;* to Samuel Beckett the seemingly plotless philosophizing of *Next Time I'll Sing to You;* to John Arden and Margaretta D'Arcy the episodic structure and satire of inept and hypocritical public officials in *The Borage Pigeon Affair;* to Eugène Ionesco or N.F. Simpson the absurdist farce of such one-acts as *Who Was Hilary Maconochie?, Alas, Poor Fred,* and *A Slight Accident;* to Simon Gray the mutual torment inflicted by sophisticates in extremis found in *Bodies;* to Peter Handke the invitation to spectators to reject the play found in the fragmented *Games;* to Henry Livings the music-hall flavor of *Savoury Meringue;* and to any one of dozens of realistic dramatists the belligerence and bewilderment of the interracial psychological study *Neighbours.*

Although Saunders's stylistic range is breathtaking our 21st-century literary detectives might discover his authorship by recognizing his distinctive situations and themes. His dramatis personae are frequently couples, and he is constantly investigating how people can relate to others, care about others, commit themselves to others, and sustain the relationship long term. The alienated Saunders character often lives close to the edge. He or she finds difficulty wrenching meaning from a life rendered pointless by death and unbearable by loneliness or, paradoxically, by the proximity of people. He probes the false values exemplified in various interpersonal relations, and illuminates the responsibility people assume or evade for the choices they make. He's a humanist sympathetic to the underdog or the rebel, and deeply suspicious of the games people play to keep their emotions at bay or to score points off others. Yet he's expert at dramatizing those often urbane games, and such is the ambiguity of his situations—particularly in his more recent work—that spectators may be forgiven for wondering whether his commiseration for the losers isn't balanced by a certain admiration for the victor's skill.

Saunders has created a constellation of wonderfully ineffectual characters. There's the driver in *Gimlet* whose bus passes through—but is really bypassed by—life. There's the befuddled actor in *Triangle* who's "not quite sure whether I'm trying to play myself or trying not to play myself." There are the musicians in *Trio* who can't perform because they're under attack by flies. There's the teacher in *The Pedagogue* who loses control of his pupils as well as his faith in mankind. There are the men and women in *After Liverpool* who often botch their desultory attempts to talk to each other. There's the wife in *A Slight Accident* who's flustered by her husband's failure to get up off the floor after she's murdered him and poor Pringle's confusion when he's reminded that he killed the title character in *Alas, Poor Fred*. There's the deceased protagonist of *A Scent of Flowers* whose inability to inspire in her family any accessible love has led her to suicide. In *Next Time I'll Sing to You* there's little Lizzie who's lost because she's replacing her twin sister in the role without benefit of either rehearsal or script. There are the ridiculous attempts of the macho men in *The Island* to bully their superiors (the women) into liking them. ("If I had been expecting anything," quips one of the gals, "they'd be a disappointment.") And there are those archetypal sufferers of indignity in *The Travails of Sancho Panza*.

Repeatedly Saunders has dramatized the tension between such poles as independence and dependence or our responsibility for choices versus our lack of control over events. In an early radio play which later became the street theatre piece *Dog Accident*, for instance, Saunders confronts passersby with a dispute between—seemingly—two of their number over a dog who's just been run over. They disagree over whether the dog's demise was its own fault and, later, over whether the dog's really dead or still suffering. Why, argues the indifferent one, should they care about a dying dog when large-scale catastrophe strikes people every day? The other momentarily opts for bothering, then either can't sustain or can't stomach the pain and prefers to go to lunch. Our mutual interdependence and the complex determinants of an event also inform *Bye Bye Blues*, in which three separate couples discuss one or more automobile accidents in which they're all somehow involved or implicated.

Saunders's best-known play, *Next Time I'll Sing to You*, picks as its subject a hermit, Jimmy Mason, who died in Essex in 1942. Another writer might have considered Mason's solitary life and death more conventionally and sentimentally. But Saunders suggests the aimlessness of life with a form which itself rambles. This presentational style and non-linear "plot" may communicate subliminally that life is disordered suffering. Ostensibly, however, the play is a comedy in which the characters are actors making disconnected attempts to put on a play about Mason. They crack jokes, discuss whether they're asleep, and confuse the actress who is supposedly a substitute for her sister. Perhaps five minutes is devoted to conveying the facts of Mason's life. Gradually such philosophical issues as the nature of man and the purpose of life are raised. *Next Time I'll Sing to You*, like *Waiting for Godot*, employs off-beat characters and structure to raise fundamental human questions. After we wonder why Mason lived alone—or, indeed, why he lived—we come to wonder whether his solitude differs only superficially from our own. If we're better off than Mason, the reason may only be "One thing about us—at least we're not dead."

Although well known, *Next Time I'll Sing to You* has been regarded by some critics as pretentious or incomprehensible. Neither charge could be

levelled at Saunders's best play, *Bodies*. Though seemingly more realistic—
because it's set in recognizable contemporary homes—*Bodies* is one of
Saunders's many plays which combine presentational and representational
styles. It also epitomizes his highly verbal work; hearing it is much more
important than seeing it.

In *Bodies* Saunders portrays two couples who many years before had affairs
with each others' mates. Act 1 intercuts monologues, in which each of the four
recalls the affairs, with duologues on their approaching reunion with their ex-
lovers. Act 2 brings them, at that reunion, into present confrontation with their
pasts. The couples have handled their mid-life crises—or passages—quite
differently. Anne and Merwyn—who have considered themselves unromantic
pragmatists—muddle along experiencing their anxiety at reaching middle age,
their panic at disillusionment in the things they once held dear, their terror at
lack of self-esteem. David and Helen, on the other hand, have reached, by
means of a new therapy, a state untroubled by emotions of any kind. They
insist people are only bodies, and happiness and unhappiness don't exist.

We are meant to wonder whether feelings are valuable. Especially if these
passions are painful, is it preferable, like tranquil and twitchless David and
Helen, to be therapeutically freed from suffering, from the insistence on
finding meaning in experience? Or is that insensitive, unresponsive to life, and
is one therefore better off—as Peter Shaffer's *Equus* and innumerable other
contemporary British plays suggest—with one's neuroses intact? But if
Saunders initially sets up a dichotomy between detached David and Helen and
the troubled teacher Merwyn, he subtly suggests that the latter also escapes his
emotional traumas, though his means is not therapy, but mental agility liberally laced with alcohol. An off-stage student, meanwhile, has left Merwyn's
English seminar and fled his feelings still more effectively by killing himself.
Ultimately what Saunders has dramatized, then, is alternative routes to wasting one's personal emotional riches.

Saunders has been blessed with sufficient royalties from his German productions to earn a living and the long-term willingness of two London groups
(the Questors and the Richmond Fringe at the Orange Tree) to try whatever he
happens to write. Free from worry over whether each new work will prove a
commercial success, Saunders has been able to write to please himself. Perhaps
this has encouraged self-indulgence in scenes sometimes simultaneously cerebral and long-winded. Yet when he avoids verbosity, Saunders succeeds with
versatility, ingenuity, whimsy, suspense, wit, and an emotional sensitivity
which permits him to touch us without growing maudlin. Both in depth and in
range, his plays continue to intrigue longer than might the work of a more
uniform playwright.

—Tish Dace

SEABROOK, Jeremy.

Born in Northampton in 1939. Educated at Northampton Grammar School; Gonville and Caius College, Cambridge; London School of Economics, diploma in social administration 1967. Teacher in a secondary modern school for two years; social worker, Inner London Education Authority, 1967–69, and with Elfrida Rathbone Association, 1973–76. Agent: Curtis Brown, 162–168 Regent Street, London W1R 5TB, England.

Publications

PLAYS

Life Price with Michael O'Neill (produced 1969).
Morality, with Michael O'Neill (produced 1971).
Millennium, with Michael O'Neill (produced 1973).
Our Sort of People, with Michael O'Neill (produced 1974).
Sex and Kinship in a Savage Society, with Michael O'Neill (produced 1975).
Yesterday's News, with Joint Stock (produced 1976).
Sharing, with Michael O'Neill (produced 1980).
Black Man's Burden, with Michael O'Neill (produced 1980).
Heart-Throb, with Caroline Hutchison and Anna Mottram (produced 1988).

RADIO PLAYS: *Birds in a Gilded Cage*, 1974; *A Change of Life*, 1979; *A Mature Relationship*, 1979; *Golden Opportunities*, 1982; with Michael O'Neill—*The Bosom of the Family*, 1975; *Living Private*, 1978; *Our Children's Children*, 1980; *Life Skills*, 1985.

TELEVISION PLAYS, with Michael O'Neill: *Skin Deep*, 1971; *Soap Opera in Stockwell*, 1973; *Highway Robbery*, 1973; *A Clear Cut Case*, 1973; *A Stab in the Front*, 1973; *Children of the Sun*, 1975; *Beyond the Call of Duty* (*Crown Court* series), 1976; *A State of Welfare*.

OTHER

The Unprivileged: A Hundred Years of Family Life and Tradition in a Working-Class Street. 1967.
City Close-Up. 1971.
Loneliness. 1971.
The Everlasting Feast. 1974.
A Lasting Relationship: Homosexuals and Society. 1976.
What Went Wrong? Working People and the Ideals of the Labour Movement. 1978.
Mother and Son: An Autobiography. 1979.
Working-Class Childhood. 1982.
Unemployment. 1982.
The Idea of Neighbourhood: What Local Politics Should Be About. 1984.
A World Still to Win: The Reconstruction of the Post-War Working Class, with Trevor Blackwell. 1985.
Landscapes of Poverty. 1985.
Life and Labour in a Bombay Slum. 1987.

The Politics of Hope: Britain at the End of the Twentieth Century, with Trevor
   Blackwell, 1988.
The Leisure Society. 1988.
The Race for Riches: The Human Cost of Wealth. 1988.
The Myth of the Market. 1990.

See the essay on Michael O'Neill and Jeremy Seabrook.

SELBOURNE, David.

Born in London, 4 June 1937. Educated at Manchester Grammar School;
Balliol College, Oxford, B.A. (honours) 1958; Inner Temple, London, called to
the Bar, 1959. Lecturer, University of Aston, Birmingham, 1963–65; Tutor in
Politics, Ruskin College, Oxford, 1965–86. Recipient: Aneurin Bevan
Memorial fellowship, 1975; Southern Arts Association award, 1979; Indian
Council of Social Science research award, 1979; Social Science Research
Council award, 1980; Periodical Publishers Association award, 1986.
Address: c/o Xandra Hardie, 9 Elsworthy Terrace, London NW3 3DR,
England.

Publications

PLAYS

The Play of William Cooper and Edmund Dew-Nevett (produced 1968).
   1968.
The Two-Backed Beast (produced 1968). 1969.
Dorabella (produced 1969). 1970.
Samson (produced 1970). With *Alison Mary Fagan*, 1971.
Alison Mary Fagan (produced 1972). With *Samson*, 1971.
The Damned. 1971.
Class Play (produced 1972). In *Second Playbill 3*, edited by Alan Durband,
   1973.
Three Class Plays (for children; produced 1973).
What's Acting? and Think of a Story, Quickly! (for children; produced 1977).
   1977.
A Woman's Trial (produced in Bengali, as *Shrimatir Bichar*, 1982).

OTHER

Brook's Dream: The Politics of Theatre. 1974.
An Eye to China. 1975.
An Eye to India: The Unmasking of a Tyranny. 1977.
Through the Indian Looking-Glass: Selected Articles on India 1976–1980.
   1982.
*The Making of A Midsummer Night's Dream: An Eye-Witness Account of
   Peter Brook's Production*. 1982.
Against Socialist Illusion: A Radical Argument. 1985.
Left Behind: Journeys into British Politics. 1987.
Death of the Dark Hero: Eastern Europe 1987–1990. 1990.
The Spirit of the Age. 1993.

Editor, *In Theory and in Practice: Essays on the Politics of Jayaprakash Narayan.* 1985.
Editor, *A Doctor's Life: The Diaries of Hugh Selbourne M.D., 1960–1963.* 1989.

CRITICAL STUDIES: introductions by John Russell Brown to *The Play of William Cooper and Edmund Dew-Nevett*, 1968, by Stuart Hall to *An Eye to China*, 1975, and by Selbourne to *What's Acting? and Think of a Story, Quickly!*, 1977.

David Selbourne writes with consistent strategy. He chooses simple actions that involve basic motives with the minimum of complication through story or the representation of the process of everyday living. So he is free to move his characters into ever-changing relationships with each other, and with their own reactions. In the one-act *Samson* a boy tries to break away from his father in twelve short scenes. In *Dorabella* a spinster is attracted to the boyfriend of her hairdresser. In *The Play of William Cooper and Edmund Dew-Nevett* a simpleton and would-be artist seeks happiness and finds corruption.

These are intellectual plays in that they are based on a clear view of how time, power, imagination, thought, and passions work together. But they are realized with a sensual awareness that seeks to create brilliant juxtapositions, activity and language that can take actors and audiences directly to total, undisguised confrontations.

Almost all the dialogue is in a verse form that serves to accentuate thrust and concision. It also holds attention for the echoes from mystical poets and the Old Testament that play a large part in creating the overall impression of the plays. The echoes are purposefully easy to catch and, more than this, they live together with a lively response to ordinary talk and responses. This style with its radiant images offsets the restricted nature of the play's actions, where man is repeatedly shown caught by his own conditions of living. *The Damned* presents self-deception and domination with calculated ruthlessness, but even in this painful drama the words spoken show how the hope of free life is still the characters' true source of energy. At the end of *William Cooper* the simpleton can "fly no more," but he has only just recognized again "Light blazing into my head."

Two plays are in a separate category, for in the one-act *Alison Mary Fagan* and the short *Class Play* Selbourne has placed real people in dramatic forms: in the first an actress who faces herself, her life and her career, and in *Class Play* three pupils and a teacher facing school and life. These are difficult plays to perform, for the dialogue is still shockingly direct and the situations continually changing, but at the centre of the drama is a person who performs or children who are manipulated, and these are to be seen without artifice, recognized as if outside a theatre.

Selbourne is a writer of teeming imagination and clear determination. He has never fallen in with a fashionable mode of writing for the stage. He has worked on his own, confident in the validity of his purpose. He stakes everything he knows; to share that risk is an exhilarating and demanding enterprise that leaves a permanent mark.

—John Russell Brown

SHAFFER, Anthony (Joshua).

Born in Liverpool, Lancashire, 15 May 1926; twin brother of Peter Shaffer, q.v. Educated at St. Paul's School, London; Trinity College, Cambridge (co-editor, Granta), graduated 1950. Conscript coalminer, Kent and Yorkshire, 1944–47. Married 1) Carolyn Soley, two daughters; 2) the actress Diane Cilento in 1985. Barrister, 1951–55; journalist, 1956–58; partner in advertising film production agency, 1959–69. Recipient: Tony award, 1971; Mystery Writers of America Edgar Allan Poe award, for screenplay, 1973. Lives in Wiltshire. Agent: Peters, Fraser, and Dunlop Group, 503–504 The Chambers, Chelsea Harbour, Lots Road, London SW10 0XF, England.

Publications

PLAYS

The Savage Parade (produced 1963; as This Savage Parade, produced 1987).
Sleuth (produced 1970). 1970.
Murderer (produced 1975). 1979.
Widow's Weeds (produced 1977).
Whodunnit (as The Case of the Oily Levantine, produced 1977; revised version, as Whodunnit, produced 1982). 1983.

SCREENPLAYS: Mr. Forbush and the Penguins, 1971; Frenzy, 1972; Sleuth, 1973; The Wicker Man, 1974; Masada, 1974; The Moonstone, 1975; Death on the Nile, 1978; Absolution, 1981; Evil Under the Sun, 1982; Appointment with Death, 1988.

TELEVISION PLAY: Pig in the Middle.

NOVELS

How Doth the Little Crocodile? (as Peter Antony, with Peter Shaffer). 1952; as Peter and Anthony Shaffer, 1957.
Withered Murder, with Peter Shaffer. 1955.
The Wicker Man (novelization of screenplay), with Robin Hardy. 1978.
Absolution (novelization of screenplay). 1979.

BIBLIOGRAPHY: Peter and Anthony Shaffer: A Reference Guide by Dennis A. Klein, 1982.

It is not often that a writer has the opportunity to create a literary fashion and even a new genre, but theatrical thrillers and mysteries can legitimately be divided into pre-Sleuth and post-Sleuth, indicating more than their date of composition. The traditional stage or film mystery is a variant on the classic English Country House mystery novel, a whodunnit in which a crime is committed and the audience tries to guess which of several suspects is the criminal, while the author carefully directs our suspicions in the wrong directions. In Sleuth Anthony Shaffer created the whodunwhat, where not only the identity of the criminal but the nature of the crime—indeed, the reality and reliability of everything we've seen with our own eyes—is part of the mystery.

Sleuth begins in an orthodox way, as a man enlists the aid of his wife's lover in a complex plot to rob himself; this way lover and wife can afford to run off, husband will be free to marry his own mistress, and the insurance company will pay for everything. No sooner has the audience settled in to see whether they'll pull it off and whether one will doublecross the other than we discover that this isn't what has been going on at all; the whole project is a convoluted cover for a murder. And no sooner is that fact absorbed than we are told that the murder we thought we watched happening didn't really happen. (Oh yes it did, we're told a moment later. Oh no it didn't, we're shown a bit after that.) A policeman has come to arrest the murderer. (Oh no he hasn't. Oh yes he has.) In fact, a second murder entirely has happened offstage (Oh no . . .) and the murderer has planted clues implicating the innocent party, which he dares him to find because the police are really coming this time (Oh no . . .). Even the program and cast list can't be trusted.

Of course *Sleuth* has its antecedents, among them Patrick Hamilton's *Gas Light* and the Hitchcock film *Suspicion* (Is the man really trying to kill his wife or is she imagining it?) and the Clouzot film *Diabolique* (Who of the three main characters are the murderers and who the victims?). But Shaffer concentrates and multiplies the questions and red herrings, and dresses them in an entertaining mix of psychology (the husband is a compulsive games-player), social comment (husband is a snob, lover working class), in-jokes (husband writes mysteries of the classic whodunnit kind), and black humor (one plot twist somehow requires a character to dress as a clown). And everything moves so quickly and effortlessly that there is added delight in the author's skill and audacity in so repeatedly confusing us. *Sleuth* was an immense worldwide success that quickly bred dozens of other thrillers of the new genre, notable among them Ira Levin's *Deathtrap* and Richard Harris's *The Business of Murder*. The Agatha Christie-type whodunnit, with corpses who didn't get up again and a murderer who was Someone In This Room, seemed hopelessly old-fashioned when compared to plays in which the audience had to figure out what was really happening before moving on to the question of who was guilty.

Oddly, Shaffer's own follow-ups in the genre he created are rather limp. *Murderer* opens with a 30-minute silent sequence during which we watch a particularly gruesome murder and dismemberment, followed by the arrival of a policeman, the discovery of the grisly evidence and the confession of the criminal—only to be told then that it was all a fake, the pastime of a crime buff reenacting a famous murder. So far, so good, but when the buff then turns his hand to an actual murder, the plot twists are less inevitable and less delightful than in *Sleuth*. Two actual murders take place, one with the wrong victim and one with the wrong murderer, but everything seems forced and unlikely, and requires extensive advance set-ups or after-the-fact explanations. It is ultimately an unpleasant play, working too hard to shock and surprise, and thus removing the pleasure of shock and surprise.

The Case of the Oily Levantine (revised for America as *Whodunnit*) is openly labelled "A Comedy Thriller," and is lighter and more entertaining than *Murderer* though sometimes just as strained and self-conscious. Its first act is a high-spirited parody of the whodunnit genre, with the title character blackmailing everyone in sight—titled dowager, retired officer, debutante, even the butler—until an unidentified one of them murders him. The best touch, with some of *Sleuth*'s flair, is that we periodically hear the disguised voice of the murderer giving teasing clues; it will refer, for example, to lighting a cigarette, only to have each character onstage light up as our hope of catching the criminal fades. As one might predict by now, Act 2 begins with the discovery that nothing we saw in Act 1 was real, except the murder. This twist owes a debt to the 1973 film *The Last of Sheila*, and the working-out of the new version of the murder is unconvincing and unengrossing, despite forced in-jokes both literary and theatrical. There is a satisfying final joke, though, as the solution is shown to be a twist on one of the traditional whodunnit's oldest clichés.

Shaffer's continuing skill as a craftsman of mystery and thrills is seen in his film work, notably for the film version of *Sleuth* and Hitchcock's *Frenzy*. In the theatre, however, his reputation must rest on *Sleuth* and on the genre it created.

—Gerald M. Berkowitz

SHAFFER, Peter (Levin).

Born in Liverpool, Lancashire, 15 May 1926; twin brother of Anthony Shaffer, *q.v.* Educated at a preparatory school in Liverpool; Hall School, London; St. Paul's School, London; Trinity College, Cambridge (co-editor, *Granta*), 1947–50, B.A. in history 1950. Conscript coalminer, Chislet colliery, Kent, 1944–47. Worked in Doubleday bookstore, an airline terminal, at Grand Central Station, Lord and Taylors department store, and in the acquisition department, New York Public Library, all New York, 1951–54; staff member, Boosey and Hawkes, music publishers, London, 1954–55; literary critic, *Truth*, London, 1956–57; music critic, *Time and Tide*, London, 1961–62. Recipient: *Evening Standard* award, 1958, 1980, 1988; New York Drama Critics Circle award, 1960, 1975; Tony award, 1975, 1981; Outer Critics Circle award, 1981; Vernon Rice award, 1981; New York Film Critics Circle award, 1984; Los Angeles Film Critics Association award, 1984; Oscar, for screenplay, 1985; Hamburg Shakespeare prize, 1989; William Inge award, 1992. C.B.E. (Commander, Order of the British Empire), 1987. Lives in New York City. Agent: Macnaughton Lowe Representation, 200 Fulham Road, London SW10 9PN, England; or, Robert Lantz, The Lantz Office, 888 Seventh Avenue, New York, New York 10106, U.S.A.

Publications

PLAYS

Five Finger Exercise (produced 1958). 1958.

The Private Ear, and The Public Eye (produced 1962). 1962.

Merry Roosters' Panto, music and lyrics by Stanley Myers and Steven Vinaver (produced 1963; as *It's about Cinderella*, produced 1969).

Sketch in The Establishment (produced 1963).

The Royal Hunt of the Sun: A Play Concerning the Conquest of Peru (produced 1964). 1965.

Black Comedy (produced 1965). In *Black Comedy, Including White Lies,* 1967.
White Lies (produced 1967). In *Black Comedy, Including White Lies,* 1967; as *White Liars* (produced 1968), 1967; revised version (produced 1976), 1976.
Black Comedy, Including White Lies: Two Plays. 1967; as *White Liars, Black Comedy: Two Plays,* 1968.
Shrivings (as *The Battle of Shrivings,* produced 1970; revised version, as *Shrivings,* produced 1975). 1974; with *Equus,* 1974.
Equus (produced 1973). 1973; with *Shrivings,* 1974.
Amadeus (produced 1979). 1980; revised version (produced 1980), 1981.
The Collected Plays of Peter Shaffer (revised texts; includes *Five Finger Exercise, The Private Ear, The Public Eye, The Royal Hunt of the Sun, White Liars, Black Comedy, Equus, Shrivings, Amadeus*). 1982.
Black Mischief (produced 1983).
Yonadab (produced 1985). Revised version, with *Lettice and Lovage,* 1989.
Lettice and Lovage (produced 1987; revised version, produced 1988). 1988; revised version, with *Yonadab,* 1989.
Whom Do I Have the Honour of Addressing? (broadcast 1989). 1990.
The Gift of the Gorgon (produced 1992). 1993.

SCREENPLAYS: *Lord of the Flies,* with Peter Brook, 1963; *The Public Eye (Follow Me!),* 1972; *Equus,* 1977; *Amadeus,* 1984.

RADIO PLAYS: *Alexander the Corrector,* 1946; *The Prodigal Father,* 1957; *Whom Do I Have the Honour of Addressing?,* 1989.

TELEVISION PLAYS: *The Salt Land,* 1955; *Balance of Terror,* 1957.

NOVELS
The Woman in the Wardrobe (as Peter Antony).1951.
How Doth the Little Crocodile? (as Peter Antony, with Anthony Shaffer). 1952; as Peter and Anthony Shaffer, 1957.
Withered Murder, with Anthony Shaffer. 1955.

BIBLIOGRAPHY: *Peter and Anthony Shaffer: A Reference Guide* by Dennis A. Klein, 1982; *Peter Shaffer: An Annotated Bibliography* by Thomas Eberle, 1991.

CRITICAL STUDIES: *Peter Shaffer* by John Russell Taylor, 1974; *Peter Shaffer* by Dennis A. Klein, 1979; *File on Shaffer* edited by Virginia Cooke and Malcolm Page, 1987; *Peter Shaffer: Roles, Rites and Rituals in the Theater* by Gene A. Plunka, 1988; *Peter Shaffer: A Casebook,* edited by C.J. Gianakaris, 1991.

In 1958, when Peter Shaffer's *Five Finger Exercise* achieved critical acclaim in London, it was difficult to reconcile its middle-class tone and formal elements with the breed of theatre of Britain's Angry Young Men then flourishing. A well-made drawing-room drama set in a weekend cottage in Suffolk, *Five*

Finger Exercise probed the Harringtons' marital strife and its devastating effects upon their nervous, literary son and the secretive, young German tutor brought into the household to educate their volatile 14-year-old-daughter. The intricately wrought monologues of the five characters are played and replayed against a background of music. The family relationships are dangerously out of balance and the intrusion of the outsider threatens to destroy them. Only after numerous variations of the same theme does the play find resolution.

Five Finger Exercise placed Shaffer in the traditions of the well-made play while he was also compared briefly with John Osborne and Harold Pinter. Other plays by Shaffer show his flair for the highly theatrical spectacle and epic theatre. His use of framing and narration derive from dramatists such as Thornton Wilder, Tennessee Williams, Robert Bolt, and Bertolt Brecht. His narrators control the prism through which the work is viewed and provide a structure which offers his play of intellect a wider range.

Shaffer's use of the conventions of presentational aesthetics emerge clearly in *The Royal Hunt of the Sun, Equus, Amadeus,* and *Yonadab*. His narrators interrupt the play's action and dart backwards and forwards, violating the conventions of the fourth wall and addressing the audience directly, inviting them to participate in the experience of epic theatre as it was articulated by Brecht. The epic mode provides solutions to some of the technical problems apparent in *Five Finger Exercise* and very much evident in *Shrivings*, a play marred by too much ideological talkiness and an inadequate objective correlative for the play's ideas. His brilliantly conceived narrators—Old Martin in *The Royal Hunt of the Sun*, the analyst Dysart in *Equus*, Salieri in *Amadeus*, and Yonadab in the eponymous play—rivet the audience's attention, offering a self-conscious examination of the play's narration and story line without diminishing its nakedly dramatic elements.

His two recent works, the stage play *Lettice and Lovage* and the play for broadcast *Whom Do I Have the Honour Of Addressing?*, more nearly resemble his comedies of the 1960s. Abandoning the conventions of the frame and epic theatre, they nonetheless display his interest in narrative technique.

Lettice, a whimsical tour guide, has been hired by the Preservation Trust (a thinly disguised National Trust) to show parties around Britain's historical houses. A devotee of history and invention, Lettice's creative spirit is too restless to allow her merely to recite her official text. The play opens with her regaling a group of tourists with stories about a great staircase constructed from Tudor oak that dominates the grand hall of the all-too-dreary Fustian House. After several more recitations, she constructs ever more melodramatic accounts of the stairs and the house's inhabitants, introducing the Virgin Queen herself, Gloriana, into her tale. She thrives on her own theatrical romanticizing and role-playing, deviating wildly from historical fact in her desperate attempts to make one of the dullest Elizabethan houses in England more interesting. The first act concludes with her being fired by the severe, duty-bound Lotte. Act II finds Lotte befriending Lettice, and the two women quaff Lovage, an herbal brew, enlarging, enlivening, and enlightening their souls, spirits, and eyes as they share their pasts and rebel against the drabness of their lives. In the third act, Lettice coaxes her apparent accuser, Lotte, into allowing her to replay their enactment of Charles the First's beheading in front of Bardolph, an attorney who has come to defend Lettice from Lotte's charges

of attempted murder. In both the first and third act, Shaffer breaks the fourth
wall with entrances from the auditorium and with addresses to both an on-
stage and off-stage audience. Throughout the play, there are readings of letters
as well as constant variations upon an official, transcribed text. Both devices
thicken the play's texture. In all these small ways, Shaffer manipulates techniques of narrative to interrupt the dramatic mode.

Angela Parsons, the deeply self-deluded monologist of his radio play *Whom
Do I Have the Honour of Addressing?*, similarly interweaves readings of her
correspondence into her stage narration as she speaks her supposed last and
only words about her life and death into a tape-recorder. Shaffer sets both of
these later works in the present and abandons the use of flashbacks and the
presence of a narrator. In the radio play, he offers another level of mediation of
the play's dramatic action through the device of the tape-recorder used in a
manner reminiscent of Beckett in *Krapp's Last Tape*.

Two other elements have been staples of almost all Shaffer's plays. Music is
an integral aspect of their soundscape, and elements from detective fiction
figure prominently in his treatment of plot and character. He served for a
number of years as music critic for *Time and Tide* in London. Before he
became a successful playwright, he co-authored two detective novels with his
brother, Anthony Shaffer, author of *Sleuth*. Shaffer's light and playful one-act
play *The Public Eye* presents Julian Christoforou, a raisin-and-yogurt-eating
private eye, who meddles in the domestic life of Charles and Belinda Sidley,
prying in a detective-like way into their souls and psyches. Ultimately, this
British eccentric teaches the couple how to experience love again and how to
play. Shaffer uses the character of the detective and the devices of detective
fiction—disguised identities, the dreary business of sleuthing, the perfunctory
discovery scene, the interrogation scene, the establishing of fees—to structure
his frivolous one-act play. Many of the same devices can be found in Shaffer's
superbly crafted farce *Black Comedy* as well as in *Equus, Amadeus, Lettice
and Lovage*, and *Whom Do I Have the Honour of Addressing?*

Black Comedy depends for its comic effect on a clever theatrical trick of the
eye and mind. While the stage is lit, its fictive world is dark; when the stage is
black, the characters are inhabiting a fully lit fictive world. Because of this
simple reversal, the audience relishes the delight of watching a stage full of
characters groping around in the darkness but actually flooded with light as a
result of a blown fuse in the London flat of Brindsley Miller in early evening.
Miller, a young sculptor, is trying to impress his debutante fiancée's father,
Colonel Melkett, by selling one of his sculptures to an elderly, deaf millionaire
art collector. To insure the evening's success, Brindsley and his fiancée have
swiped numerous pieces of elegant Regency furniture from the flat of his
modish neighbor, a closet homosexual and owner of an antique china shop. As
the evening advances towards its complete dissolution, Brindsley is forced to
drag the furniture from his apartment back to its owner's, right before the
darkened eyes of the owner, his father-in-law-to-be, his mistress who has paid
a surprise visit, a spinster, his alcoholic upstairs neighbor, and his silly, spoilt
fiancée. The scene is hilarious. Comic timing is essential to its success.
Brindsley's misstep which causes him to fall neatly down the entire flight of
stairs as he attempts to return calmly from his bedroom requires that the actor
display no trace of the knowledge that he is facing an uncomfortable fall. The

moment when Brindsley passes under the outstretched arms of his father-in-law and fiancée as they are exchanging a glass of lemonade and he is holding a Regency chair in one hand and a Wedgwood bowl in the other is another brilliant comic moment. All the deft timing of exits and entrances, sudden falls, rapid movements of almost all the major pieces of stage furniture, combined with the sharp white light which glaringly exposes the goings-on to the audience, testify to the importance of the genre of detective fiction and film in Shaffer's imagination. The exposed light bulb and the interrogation scenes of detective fiction probably contributed to the game of hide-and-seek executed in this delightful farce.

In *Amadeus* the debt is even more apparent. The play opens with the word "assassin" hissed and savagely whispered by the chorus of rumour on the stage, rising to a crescendo, and punctuated with the names of Mozart and Salieri. By the end of the second scene Salieri, the narrator, promises the audience one final performance, to be entitled, "The Death of Mozart; or, Did I Do It?" The audience is plunged into a world of a whodunnit in which they are the detective and Salieri is the villain. Shaffer's revised version clarified the London version's dramatic structure, implicating Salieri more directly in Mozart's death and replacing Greybig with Salieri as the Masked Figure and Messenger of Death who appears to Mozart in the penultimate scene of the play.

Yonadab continues in this tradition. Yonadab, the cousin of Amnon and Absalom, David's sons, is the treacherous confidant of both brothers. He plays the one against the other, abetting the scene of Tamar's incestuous rape by her half-brother Amnon and later assisting Absalom in the slaying of Amnon. He is also the reporter of the lurid scene to the audience. Again, the play's focus on reporters and news, on a lurid tale of intrigue, ambition, incest, and murder, on the cunning ways such plots transpire, and on the way villains are punished all reflect the sure hand of a writer familiar with detective fiction.

In both *Lettice and Lovage* and *Whom Do I Have the Honour of Addressing?* the protagonists are guilty of assault; in one case, accidentally, in the other, the justifiable albeit violent reaction to the sordid happenings resulting from Angela's infatuation with a Hollywood stage idol half her age. Both plays can be seen as the confessions of confused, romantic souls—their crimes being an over-active imagination in a colourless world.

Music is also an essential aspect of Shaffer's theatrical talent. In *White Lies*, later revised as *White Liars*, Shaffer used a tape-recording to surround the audience with the inner monologues and dialogues of Sophie, his fortune-telling protagonist. In *The Private Ear* Bob's great passion is music and the gramophone; his failed romance is with a girl he met at a concert. *Five Finger Exercise* depends on the music of Bach and Brahms and the stuck recording of a gramophone repeating over and over a portion from Mahler's Symphony No. 4 to dramatize the suicide attempt of the young German tutor whose father's participation in the Nazi party has driven him to England. Shaffer described *The Royal Hunt of the Sun*'s brilliant score written by Marc Wilkinson: "To me its most memorable items are the exquisitely doleful lament which opens Act II, and, most amazing of all, the final Chant of Resurrection, to be whined and whispered, howled and hooted, over Atahuallpa's body in the darkness, before the last sunrise of the Inca Empire."

Amadeus soars with the music of Mozart and Salieri and a score that reflects how Salieri probably imagined Mozart's music. *Lettice and Lovage* opens with lugubrious Elizabethan music. In its final farcical act, Bardolph is marching about the stage banging upon an invisible drum and calling out his "PAM-TITITI-PAMS," joined by Lettice's soprano doubling of his cries in imitation of the martial music that accompanied King Charles I's execution in 1649.

Finally, Shaffer is a playwright of ideas. Perhaps his eloquent exposition of them failed in *Shrivings*, but the battle between Dysart and Alan Strang in *Equus*, Pizarro and Atahuallpa in *The Royal Hunt of the Sun*, Salieri and Mozart in *Amadeus*, and Yonadab and David's brothers all intelligently explore man's struggle for meaning in a world in which death dominates and religion holds no salvation. Alan Strang, the boy who blinded six horses, knows a savage god; Atahuallpa is the Son of the Sun God; Pizarro has no faith, nor, until the very end, love or passion. East and west collide; faithfulness is played against faithlessness; passion and violence against impotence; passivity and Eastern love against skepticism and violence; and passionate creativity against classical balance and duty.

Some have criticized Shaffer's recent plays for owing too much of their success to the brilliance of their leading actors and too little to their themes and plots. *Lettice and Lovage* was written for Maggie Smith who brilliantly captured Lettice's extravagance of nature. The third act is slightly forced, even in its revised version. Originally the play concluded with Lettice and Lotte setting out to bomb a select number of London's most abominable post-World War II municipal monstrosities. In the revised version, they set out to create their own "E.N.D. Tours" to London's aesthetically disgusting buildings. The radio play also exploits Dame Judi Dench's voice and relies upon the eccentricities of its protagonist and the lurid details of its close to carry it. But both are plays for women, a departure for Shaffer whose earlier plays have lacked major women's roles, and both have a whimsicality and winning poignancy.

It is to Shaffer's credit that he excels in creating plays with stunning spectacles, lavish soundscapes, dramatic action, and a powerful artillery of rhetoric as well as more theatrically modest ones in which it is the delicious play of words and invention that charms us.

—Carol Simpson Stern

See the essay on *Equus*.

SIMPSON, N(orman) F(rederick).

Born in London, 29 January 1919. Educated at Emanuel School, London, 1930–37; Birkbeck College, University of London, 1950–54, B.A. (honours) 1954. Served in the Royal Artillery, 1941–43, and the Intelligence Corps, 1943–46. Married Joyce Bartlett in 1944; one daughter. Staff member, Westminster Bank, London, 1937–39; teacher, College of St. Mark and St. John, London, 1939–41, and City of Westminster College, London, and extra-mural lecturer, 1946–62; literary manager, Royal Court Theatre, London, 1976–78. Address: c/o Simon Brett, 12 Blowhorn Street, Marlborough, Wiltshire SN8 1BT, England.

Publications

PLAYS

A Resounding Tinkle (produced 1957). In *The Observer Plays*, 1958; shortened version included in *The Hole and Other Plays and Sketches*, 1964.

The Hole (produced 1958). 1958.

One Way Pendulum (produced 1959). 1960.

Sketches in *One to Another* (produced 1959). 1960.

Sketches in *You, Me and the Gatepost* (produced 1960).

Sketches in *On the Avenue* (produced 1961).

Sketches in *One over the Eight* (produced 1961).

The Form (produced 1961). 1961.

Oh (produced 1961). In *The Hole and Other Plays and Sketches*, 1964.

The Hole and Other Plays and Sketches (includes shortened version of *A Resounding Tinkle*, and *The Form, Gladly Otherwise, Oh, One Blast and Have Done*). 1964.

The Cresta Run (produced 1965). 1966.

We're Due in Eastbourne in Ten Minutes (televised 1967; produced 1971). In *Some Tall Tinkles*, 1968; in *The Best Short Plays 1972*, edited by Stanley Richards, 1972.

Some Tall Tinkles: Television Plays (includes *We're Due in Eastbourne in Ten Minutes, The Best I Can Do by Way of a Gate-Leg Table Is a Hundredweight of Coal, At Least It's a Precaution Against Fire*). 1968.

Playback 625, with Leopoldo Maler (produced 1970).

SE2How Are Your Handles? (includes *Gladly Otherwise, Oh, The Other Side of London*) (produced 1970; *Gladly Otherwise* produced 1988).

Was He Anyone? (produced 1972). 1973.

In Reasonable Shape (produced 1977). In *Play Ten*, edited by Robin Rook, 1977.

Anyone's Gums Can Listen to Reason, in *Play Ten*, edited by Robin Rook. 1977.

Inner Voices, adaptation of a play by Eduardo De Filippo (produced 1983). 1983.

Napoli Milionaria, adaptation of a play by Eduardo De Filippo (produced 1991).

SCREENPLAYS: *One Way Pendulum*, 1964; *Diamonds for Breakfast*, with Pierre Rouve and Ronald Harwood, 1968.

RADIO PLAYS: *Something Rather Effective*, 1972; *Sketches for Radio*, 1974.

TELEVISION PLAYS: *Make a Man*, 1966; *Three Rousing Tinkles* series: *The Father by Adoption of One of the Former Marquis of Rangoon's Natural Granddaughters, If Those Are Mr. Heckmondwick's Own Personal Pipes They've Been Lagged Once Already*, and *The Best I Can Do by Way of a Gate-Leg Table Is a Hundredweight of Coal*, 1966; *Four Tall Tinkles* series: *We're Due in Eastbourne in Ten Minutes, In a Punt with Friends Under a Haystack on the River Mersey, A Row of Potted Plants*, and *At Least It's a*

Precaution Against Fire, 1967; *World in Ferment* series, 1969; *Charley's Grants* series, 1970; *Thank You Very Much*, 1971; *Elementary, My Dear Watson*, 1973; *Silver Wedding*, 1974; *An Upward Fall* (*Crown Court* series), 1977; *Wainwrights' Law* series, 1980.

NOVEL

Harry Bleachbaker. 1976; as *Man Overboard: A Testimonial to the High Art of Incompetence*, 1976.

MANUSCRIPT COLLECTIONS: Indiana University, Bloomington; University of Texas, Austin; University of California, Berkeley.

CRITICAL STUDIES: *The Theatre of the Absurd* by Martin Esslin, 1961, revised edition, 1968; *Curtains* by Kenneth Tynan, 1961; *Dramatic Essays* by Nigel Dennis, 1962.

N.F. Simpson comments:

The question that, as a writer, one is asked more frequently than any other is the question as to why of all things it should be plays that one has chosen to bring forth rather than, say, novels or books about flying saucers. The answer in my own case lies, I think, in the fact that there is one incomparable advantage which the play, as a form, has over the novel and the book about flying saucers; and this is that there are not anything like as many words in it. For a writer condemned from birth to draw upon a reservoir of energy such as would barely suffice to get a tadpole from one side of a tea-cup to the other, such a consideration cannot but be decisive. Poetry admittedly has in general fewer words still, and for this reason is on the face of it an even more attractive discipline; but alas I have even less gift for that than I have for writing plays, and if I had the gift for it, it would be only a matter of weeks before I came up against the ineluctable truth that there is just not the money in it that there is in plays. Not that, the way I write them, there is all that much money in those either.

As for methods of work, what I do is to husband with jealous parsimony such faint tremors of psychic energy as can sometimes be coaxed out of the permanently undercharged batteries I was issued with at birth, and when I have what might be deemed a measurable amount, to send it coursing down the one tiny channel where with any luck it might do some good. Here it deposits its wee pile of silt, which I allow to accumulate, with the barely perceptible deliberation of a coral reef to the point where it may one day recognise itself with a start of surprise as the small and unpretentious magnum opus it had all along been tremulously aspiring to.

As for why one does it there are various reasons—all of them fairly absurd. There is one's ludicrously all-embracing sense of guilt mainly. I walk the streets in perpetual fear and trepidation, like someone who expects, round the very next corner, to meet his just deserts at the hands of a lynch mob carried away by fully justified indignation. To feel *personally* responsible not only for every crime, every atrocity, every act of inhumanity that has ever been perpetrated since the world began, but for those as well that have not as yet been so much as contemplated, is something which only Jesus Christ and I can ever have experienced to anything like the same degree. And it goes a long way to account for what I write and why I write it. For not only must one do what one can by writing plays to make amends for the perfidy of getting born; one must also, in the interests of sheer self-preservation, keep permanently incapacitated by laughter as many as possible of those who would otherwise be the bearers of a just and terrible retribution. One snatches one's reprieve quite literally laugh by laugh.

My plays are about life—life as I see it. Which is to say that they are all in their various ways about a man trying to get a partially inflated rubber lilo into a suitcase slightly too small to take it even when *un*inflated. Like most Englishmen, of which I am proud to be one, I have a love of order tempered by a deep and abiding respect for anarchy, and what I would one day like to bring about is that perfect balance between the two which I believe it to be peculiarly in the nature of English genius to arrive at. I doubt very much whether I ever shall, but it is nevertheless what I would like to do.

N. F. Simpson is perhaps the most typical English exponent of the so-called Theatre of the Absurd (a term introduced by Martin Esslin to describe the drama of a world without God: "cut off from his religious metaphysical and transcendental roots, man is lost, all his actions become senseless"—his position in the universe is essentially absurd). The roots of such drama lie in the French theatre, in the work of Jarry and Artaud, and may be seen today in the plays of Ionesco and Genet. Simpson indeed has many affinities with Ionesco, not least a stage on which anything can happen and, however bizarre, be taken as normal by the actors. Describing the Paradock couple in a foreword to *Some Tall Tinkles*, Simpson commented: "Nothing is so preposterous that it may not happen here before the day is out."

Simpson's English precedents are the fantasy and nonsense worlds of Lewis Carroll and Edward Lear. Simpson's absurd world contains, however, a strong vein of social criticism; a manic sense of humour cloaks a satirical and often savage commentary on British institutions and suburban life.

Simpson first came to public notice with *A Resounding Tinkle*, which won the *Observer* play competition for 1957. It was first performed in a shortened version in December 1957. The original version takes place in the Paradocks' home. Two comedians explore Bergson's theory of laughter and an apologetic author-figure commiserates with the audience:

I agree. A pretty epileptic start. We're going to see what we can do in the next scene about pulling the thing together.

In Act Two an over-large elephant has been delivered to the Paradocks' back garden; they decide to swap it for their neighbour's snake, which is "too short" for her (it arrives in a pencil box). The Paradocks' son appears, dressed as a woman ("Why, you've changed your sex"). A parody of the BBC's *Critics' Forum* ensues, with the critics (Mustard Short, Denzil Pepper, Miss Salt, and Mrs. Vinegar) discussing "The performance we have all been watching"—after which the author exits, dazed. A man in a bowler hat tells the producer the audience have "had about as much as they can take of this" and the play ends with the full cast toasting the audience.

The second version is tighter and less conscious of itself as a play, cutting the author and comics and concentrating on the Paradocks, their animal interests, and the fact that Mr. Paradock has been asked to form a government by someone "working through the street directory." This version was performed in a double bill with *The Hole*, a play in which the action centres on a hole in the road. A "visionary" sits by the hole, awaiting a spiritual happening; a crowd gathers round him and each member presents differing philosophical speculations as to the purpose of the hole, until a workman emerges from it, stating that it contains an electrical junction box. The visionary is finally left alone, still awaiting his miracle; as a crowd member comments: "it is upon this cavity that we build our faith."

One Way Pendulum, "a farce" set in another suburban household, established Simpson's popularity with audiences. Mabel Groomkirby "takes in her stride most of what happens around her," including son Kirby's ambition to teach several hundred speak-your-weight machines the Hallelujah Chorus. Since they can speak, they should be capable of singing, thinks Kirby, who has "a very logical turn of mind." He is moreover, a Pavlovian—unable to eat until a cash register "pings"—and feels compelled to wear black. Needing "a logical pretext" for this, he commits 43 murders! Kirby intends his singing weighing machines to act as sirens to lure large crowds to the North Pole, where they will all jump—and, in landing, alter the tilt of the world's axis, provoking a new ice age, guaranteed to cause sufficient regular deaths for Kirby's sartorial purposes.

Such details emerge gradually, via his father's obsession with the law, which leads him to build a replica of the Old Bailey in his living room. This becomes the focus of Act Two, when a judge appears and Kirby's trial ensues—a brilliant satire of the legal system. The judge finally discharges Kirby because, in sentencing him:

We may be putting him beyond the reach of the law in respect of those other crimes of which he might otherwise have become guilty. The law, however, is not to be cheated in this way. I shall therefore discharge you.

The Cresta Run, an equally hilarious satire of espionage, was followed in 1972 by *Was He Anyone?*, a merciless exposure of bureaucracy and the social services. It demolishes the committees and departments responsible for rescuing Albert Whitbrace, a bookie's runner, who ran off a liner and is still in the Mediterranean after two and a half years awaiting rescue. A piano is flown out to keep him occupied and he is finally proficient enough to give a concert with the Leningrad Symphony Orchestra, who join him for the purpose. His rescue becomes more urgent as his lifejacket becomes waterlogged and he begins to sink. Finally some "woolly-minded do-gooder" throws him a lifebelt, knocking him unconscious, and he drowns. "Was he anyone?" someone enquires, with the chilling response: "I don't think he was, fortunately." The play is perhaps Simpson's strongest satirical statement about society, and he reworked and enlarged these ideas into his only novel, *Harry Bleachbaker*.

—Rosemary Pountney

SMITH, Dodie (Dorothy Gladys Smith).

Born in Whitefield, Lancashire, 3 May, 1896. Attended Whalley Range High
School, Manchester; St Paul's Girls' School, London; studied acting at Royal
Academy of Dramatic Art, London, 1914–15. Married Alec Macbeth Beesley
in 1939 (died 1987). Actor, 1915–22; buyer, Heal and Son, London,
1923–32; then full-time writer. *Died 24 November 1990.*

Publications

PLAYS

British Talent (as C.L. Anthony) (produced 1923).
Autumn Crocus (as C.L. Anthony) (produced 1931). 1931.
Service (as C.L. Anthony) (produced 1932). 1932.
Touch Wood (as C.L. Anthony) (produced 1934). 1934.
Call It a Day (produced 1935). 1936.
Bonnet over the Windmill (also co-director: produced 1937). 1937.
Dear Octopus (also co-director: produced 1938). 1938.
Lovers and Friends (produced 1943). 1947.
Letter from Paris, adaptation of the novel *The Reverberator* by Henry James
  (produced 1952). 1954.
I Capture the Castle, adaptation of her own novel (produced 1954). 1955.
These People, Those Books (produced 1958).
Amateur Means Lover (produced 1961). 1962.

SCREENPLAYS: *Schoolgirl Rebels* (as Charles Henry Percy), 1915; *The
Uninvited,* with Frank Partos, 1944; *Darling, How Could You!,* with Lesser
Samuels, 1951.

NOVELS

I Capture the Castle. 1948.
The New Moon with the Old. 1963.
The Town in Bloom. 1965.
It Ends with Revelations. 1967.
A Tale of Two Families. 1970.
The Girl from the Candle-Lit Bath. 1978.

FICTION (for children)

The Hundred and One Dalmations. 1956.
The Starlight Barking: More about the Hundred and One Dalmations. 1967.
The Midnight Kittens. 1978.

OTHER

AUTOBIOGRAPHY:
1. *Look Back with Love: A Manchester Childhood.* 1974.
2. *Look Back with Mixed Feelings.* 1978.
3. *Look Back with Astonishment.* 1979.
4. *Look Back with Gratitude.* 1985.

THEATRICAL ACTIVITIES

DIRECTOR: **Plays**—*Bonnet over the Windmill* (co-director, with Murray Macdonald), 1937; *Dear Octopus* (co-director, with Glen Byam Shaw), 1938. ACTOR: **Plays**—in the sketch *Playgoers* by Pinero, 1915; *Kitty Grey* by J.S. Piggott and *Mr Wu* by H.M. Vernon and Harold Owen, 1915; *Ye Gods* by Stephen Robert and Eric Hudson, and *Jane and Niobe*, 1916–17; *When Knights Were Bold* by Charles Marlowe, 1917; in music-hall sketches and in a concert party, 1918; Claudine in *Telling the Tale*, 1919–20; *French Leave* by Reginald Berkeley, 1921; *The Shewing Up of Blanco Posnet* and *You Never Can Tell* by Shaw, 1921; Ann in *The Pigeon* by Galsworthy, 1922.

> Cynthia—Is that a teddy-bear there (Taking it.) Why, it's Symp.
> Scrap—(Following Her). Symp?
> Cynthia—We called him that because he was extra sympathetic. We used to hug him whenever we were miserable—when we were in disgrace or the rabbits died or when nobody understood us.

The quotation is from Dodie Smith's best-known play, *Dear Octopus*, a play about a family, its feuds and friendships, first performed in 1938 with one of those casts publicists call "glittering" (with good reason—included in the Queen's Theatre company were Marie Tempest, John Gielgud, Madge Compton, Angela Baddeley, among others). The theme of sympathy in fact might be Smith's principal key—in all her plays she seems to comprehend the very well-springs of her characters. She builds them surely and with understanding; they emerge as palpable beings, ordinary people who are more-than-ordinarily believable. And that's quite a talent.

Starting with an early screenplay written while studying at RADA (*Schoolgirl Rebels*—written under a male pseudonym) the playwright first went on stage in 1915 at the age of 19, but it did not bring her the golden fruits her pen was later to harvest for her—after a series of depressing tours she left the stage and became a buyer for Heal's. Fortunately while shopping for toys and pictures for middle-class kids she did not stop writing, and in 1923 *British Talent* was given an amateur airing. In 1931 came *Autumn Crocus*—a huge success—and she was launched. She wrote a number of plays in the 1930s, a gilded era when style and construction were of supreme value and audiences expected a well-made play. Smith constructed her plays like boxes, solid, secure, each line leading to another line, each situation growing and blossoming within the classic three-act mould. In fact as one reads them now it is the strong sense of craftsmanship that still comes across—a professional and enviable ability to forge a story so that the shape of the play, from opening curtain to closing line, is all of a piece. You can read her plays like novels—and with a little imagination see the situations developing before you. It isn't surprising that she turned to novel writing, and her first, *I Capture the Castle*, was later turned into a play. She also adapted a Henry James story, *The Reverberator*, to become *Letter from Paris*. It is a play that, unlike some of the others, has a musty air of datedness, and the characters, although still firmly handled and well presented, have a slight edge of melodrama—which may of course be a Jamesian legacy.

It's not just a lucky chance that makes Smith's work so often the choice of enthusiastic amateur groups, for perhaps more than professional actors they seize quickly onto these ready-formed characters which are so near completion on the printed page. Smith liked to write about good, middle-class homes and people with values—taking that sensible but often ignored advice, to write about what one knows. She undoubtedly knew her people and put them into human situations which cleverly avoid being sentimental. Her ear for the comfortably-off family in *Dear Octopus* is very sound; indeed her dialogue has an authentic natural running ring that rarely bogs down.

—Michael T. Leech

SPEIGHT, Johnny.

Born in Canning Town, London, 2 June 1920. Educated at St. Helen's School. Married Constance Barrett in 1956; two sons and one daughter. Worked in a factory, as a jazz drummer and insurance salesman; then writer for BBC radio and television. Recipient: Screenwriters Guild award, 1962, 1966, 1967, 1968; *Evening Standard* award, 1977; Pye award, for television writing, 1983. Address: Fouracres, Heronsgate, Chorleywood, Hertfordshire, England.

Publications

PLAYS

Mr. Venus, with Ray Galton, music and lyrics by Trevor H. Stanford and Norman Newell (produced 1958).
Sketches in *The Art of Living* (produced 1960).
The Compartment (televised 1961; produced 1965).
The Knacker's Yard (produced 1962).
The Playmates (televised 1962; as *Games*, produced 1971).
If There Weren't Any Blacks You'd Have to Invent Them (televised 1965; produced 1965). 1965.
Sketches in *In the Picture* (produced 1967).
The Salesman (televised 1970; produced 1970).
Till Death Us Do Part. 1973.
The Thoughts of Chairman Alf (produced 1976).
Elevenses (sketch), in *The Big One* (produced 1983).

SCREENPLAYS: *French Dressing*, with others, 1964; *Privilege*, with Norman Bogner and Peter Watkins, 1967; *Till Death Us Do Part*, 1968; *The Alf Garnett Saga*, 1972.

RADIO WRITING: For the *Edmondo Ros, Morecambe and Wise*, and *Frankie Howerd* shows, 1956–58; *Early to Braden* show, 1957–58; *The Deadly Game of Chess*, 1958; *The April 8th Show* (*7 Days Early*), 1958; *Eric Sykes* show, 1960–61.

TELEVISION WRITING: For the *Arthur Haynes* show; *The Compartment*, 1961; *The Playmates*, 1962; *Shamrot*, 1963; *If There Weren't Any Blacks You'd Have to Invent Them*, 1965; *Till Death Us Do Part* series, 1966–75, 1981; *To Lucifer a Sun*, 1967; *Curry and Chips* series, 1969; *The Salesman*, 1970; *Them* series, 1972; *Speight of Marty* series, 1973; *For Richer . . . For Poorer*, 1975; *The Tea Ladies* series, with Ray Galton, 1979; *Spooner's Patch* series, with

Ray Galton, 1980; *The Lady Is a Tramp* series, 1982; *In Sickness and in Health*, 1985.

OTHER

It Stands to Reason: A Kind of Autobiography. 1973.
The Thoughts of Chairman Alf: Alf Garnett's Little Blue Book; or, Where England Went Wrong: An Open Letter to the People of Britain. 1973.
Pieces of Speight. 1974.
The Garnett Chronicles: The Life and Times of Alf Garnett, Esq. 1986.
For Richer . . . For Poorer: A Kind of Autobiography. 1991.

THEATRICAL ACTIVITIES
ACTOR: **Films** — *The Plank*, 1967; *The Undertakers*, 1969; *Rhubarb*, 1970.

Johnny Speight is one of those writers whose success in television has become a trap. Unlike almost every other writer of comic series for peak-hour viewers, he has been a source of controversy, scandal, and outrage as well as having been rewarded with a popularity which has proved to be less than totally advantageous to him. He was a factory worker before World War II, and it was not until 1955 that his determination to succeed as a writer bore any fruit. His first work was writing scripts for such comedians as Frankie Howerd, Arthur Askey, Cyril Fletcher, Eric Sykes, and others. When he began to write for Arthur Haynes, he showed an ability to create unusual material rather than the power to exploit the familiar gifts of an established comedian. For Haynes, Speight created the character of a tramp whose aggressive, rebarbative personality had a striking originality.

It was through a series of programmes for BBC television, *Till Death Us Do Part*, that Speight became a household name. His work became a battleground over which "permissive" liberals fought the old-fashioned viewers who believe in verbal restraint, the importance of good taste and the banishment of certain topics, notably religion, from light entertainment. What Speight wrote was originally in essence a cartoon, a cockney version of the north country Andy Capp, in which attitudes almost everybody would condemn as anti-social were derided. Four people — husband and wife, their daughter and son-in-law — inhabit the sitting room of a slum house; they have nothing in common except their bitter dislike for each other. The father, Alf Garnett, is barely literate, full of misconceived, misunderstood, and ignorant prejudices about race, politics, and religion; his language is atrocious. His wife is reduced almost to the state of a vegetable, coming to life only when her detestation of her husband finds some opportunity of expressing itself. The son-in-law, as ignorantly and stupidly of the left as Garnett is of the right, is a Liverpool-Irish Roman Catholic, who dresses flamboyantly, wears his hair long, and does no work whatever; his only spell of activity was an inefficient attempt to swindle social security officials. The daughter agrees in all things with her husband, but it is plain that her agreement is the result of his effectiveness as a lover rather than of any intellectual processes of argument.

Through these appalling people, Speight was able for a time to lambast senseless racial and political prejudices while making cheeky fun of the Royal Family, the church, and anything else which drifted into what passes in the Garnett household for conversation, and Garnett for a time was a very effective weapon against bigotry and stupidity. Unfortunately, his effectiveness as a vehicle for satire tended to diminish as the monstrous energy with which he was created slipped out of control and allowed him to take possession of each episode of a series which continued long after the original impetus had exhausted itself and which began to show something dangerously ambivalent in Speight's attack on racialism. The creation of two Garnett films demonstrated that Speight's monsters were at their most popular when there was nothing left to say about them, so that *Till Death Us Do Part* seemed to turn into an incubus from which the author was unable to escape.

Curry and Chips, another effort to stifle racial prejudice by allowing it to be voiced in its most extreme forms by the stupid, lacked the vitality of *Till Death Us Do Part*, and a later series, *Them*, in which two tramps dreamed of grandeur, their dreams contrasted sharply with the reality of their way of life, was notable only for the gentleness of its comedy, proving that Speight was capable of more than the stridency of life with the Garnett family.

Such work, for all the energy of Garnettry, and the strength with which the leading monster had been created, made it seem that Speight had moved a long way in the wrong direction. In 1961, his first television play proper, *The Compartment*, had nothing to do with the sort of writing which later made him notorious. In a compartment of an old-fashioned train which has no corridor, a businessman is alone with a practical joker who persecutes him for the length of the journey; it becomes the joker's amusement to convince his pompous, easily frightened companion that he is helpless in the company of an armed, murderous psychopath. There are no motives, no explanations, no rationalisations; the events simply happen with a sort of uneasy humour. A year later, the same joker, selling "jokes" and tricks from door to door, finds himself sheltered for a night by a strange, psychopathic girl who is the only inhabitant of a big house. *The Playmates*—for the girl wants to join in fun with the traveller's samples—shares the disregard for motives and explanations already shown by *The Compartment*. A third play, offering, it seems, another aspect of the experience of the joker, was equally effective. The ideas were fashionable at the time when it was avant garde and exciting to offer allegiance to The Theatre of the Absurd, but Speight produced his genuine shocks and *frissons*.

Both *The Compartment* and a later television play, *If There Weren't Any Blacks You'd Have to Invent Them*, were adapted for stage performances but, despite some success, proved to belong to the screen rather than the stage. *If There Weren't Any Blacks* exploited Speight's reputation, won from the Garnett series, as a passionate opponent of racialism, and makes its point amusingly and convincingly with none of the ambivalence which crept into *Till Death Us Do Part* when Garnett took control of the series and began to speak as a character in his own right rather than as an instrument designed by his creator to ridicule the politically idiotic. Speight's only genuine play for the theatre, not adapted from television material, *The Knacker's Yard*, won some praise for the vigour and imaginativeness of its dialogue.

It is impossible not to think of Speight as a creator of grotesque, disturbing characters who is trapped by television into a situation which demands that he repeat, with diminishing returns, a success which rapidly lost its inventiveness. Thus, he pays the penalty of his originality.

—Henry Raynor

SPENCER, Colin.

Born in London, 17 July 1933. Educated at Brighton Grammar School, Selhurst; Brighton College of Art. Served in the Royal Army Medical Corps, 1950–52. Married Gillian Chapman in 1959 (divorced 1969); one son. Paintings exhibited in Cambridge and London; costume designer. Chair, Writers Guild of Great Britain, 1982–83. Agent: (plays) Casarotto Ramsay Ltd., National House, 60–66 Wardour Street, London W1V 3HP; (novels) Richard Scott Simon, 43 Doughty Street, London WC1N 2LF. Address: 2 Heath Cottages, Tunstall, near Woodbridge, Suffolk IP12 2HQ, England.

Publications

PLAYS

The Ballad of the False Barman, music by Clifton Parker (produced 1966).
Spitting Image (produced 1968). In *Plays and Players*, September 1968.
The Trial of St. George (produced 1972).
The Sphinx Mother (produced 1972).
Why Mrs. Neustadter Always Loses (produced 1972).
Keep It in the Family (also director; produced 1978).
Lilith (produced 1979).

TELEVISION PLAYS: *Flossie*, 1975; *Vandal Rule OK?* (documentary), 1977.

NOVELS

An Absurd Affair. 1961.
Generation:
   Anarchists in Love. 1963; as *The Anarchy of Love*, 1967.
   *The Tyranny of Love.*1967.
   Lovers in War. 1969.
   The Victims of Love. 1978.
Asylum. 1966.
Poppy, Mandragora, and the New Sex. 1966.
Panic. 1971.
How the Greeks Kidnapped Mrs. Nixon. 1974.

OTHER

Gourmet Cooking for Vegetarians. 1978.
Good and Healthy: A Vegetarian and Wholefood Cookbook. 1983; as *Vegetarian Wholefood Cookbook*, 1985.
Reports from Behind, with Chris Barlas, illustrated by Spencer. 1984.
Cordon Vert: 52 Vegetarian Gourmet Dinner Party Menus. 1985.
Mediterranean Vegetarian Cooking. 1986.

The New Vegetarian: The Ultimate Guide to Gourmet Cooking and Healthy Living. 1986.

The Vegetarian's Healthy Diet Book, with Tom Sanders. 1986; as *The Vegetarian's Kitchen,* 1986.

One-Course Feasts. 1986.

Feast for Health: A Gourmet Guide to Good Food. 1987.

Al Fresco: A Feast of Outdoor Entertaining. 1987.

Summer Cooking. 1987.

The Romantic Vegetarian. 1988.

The Adventurous Vegetarian. 1989.

Which of Us Two? The Story of a Love Affair. 1990.

The Heretic's Feast: A History of Vegetarianism. 1993.

Editor, *Green Cuisine: The Guardian's Selection of the Best Vegetarian Recipes.* 1986.

CRITICAL STUDY: interview with Peter Burton, in *Transatlantic Review* 35, 1970.

THEATRICAL ACTIVITIES

DIRECTOR: **Play**—*Keep It in the Family,* 1978.

Harold Hobson, reviewing Colin Spencer's musical play *The Ballad of the False Barman* in the *Sunday Times,* referred to "Mr. Spencer's great and complicated skill unified by [his] overwhelming sense of evil. This is its aesthetic strength." Certainly there is something in the play that both attracts and alienates. I recall that, as artistic director of the Hampstead Theatre Club where it was premiered, I sent it to nine directors before the tenth, Robin Phillips, accepted it. Yet re-reading it now for what must be about the twelfth time I find that my first impression is unchanged. The play still seems to me like an impassioned sermon by John Donne, written with the sensuality of Genet, the cogency (especially in the lyrics) of Brecht, and the high camp of Ronald Firbank. If this sounds like mirroring too many influences it should be remembered that it is, after all, a play about disguises. The setting is a bar in Brighton to which come all the so-called "dregs of society." They are welcomed by an enigmatic barman (played by a woman) who fulfills their needs:

> Give me the right to exploit you,
> Tell me your private dream,
> I can fix anything, just leave it to me.

The play's central theme is the opposition of corruption, in the person of the barman, and goodness, in the person of Josie. As the Barman says to Josie. "Your goodness is a thorn in our flesh."

When Josie's lover, a gigolo and burglar called Bill, is thrown into prison, Josie is shown out of the bar. No one will help her. (En route Spencer makes a scathing attack on conventional morality, on the inhumanity of the professional clergyman, the police, and the judiciary.) Josie is driven to accept the hospitality of a mysterious Duke whose advances she has long resisted. But now she says, "I am too tired to do anything else."

She enters the Duke's house with its many rooms. "Explore them," says the

Duke, "I will give you thoughts like new children. I will uncover areas of feeling, of rhythm, and motion, which will astonish, amaze, excite. . ." to which Josie replies, "You have shown me things in myself that I never dreamt were there. . . . You have shown me mirrors." The Duke answers, "The more you know, the greater you will grow."

No critic at the time realized what Spencer was doing here. Brilliantly, more alarmingly than in any Mystery play of York or Wakefield, he has updated the story of the serpent in the Garden of Eden, the temptation to eat of the Tree of Knowledge of good *and* evil. The death of Josie's baby comes in this context as a brutal, dream-potent image of death of innocence, the expulsion from Eden. At the end of the play Josie says to the Duke, "You are all the terror in my soul. You are the darkness that I have always feared but when I was laid in your arms I knew such peace." Throughout Spencer is dealing with the metaphysic of evil, with what Jung calls the *shadow* side of experience. Anyone who has read Jung's *Answer to Job* will recognise that ultimate goodness cannot be separated from the question of ultimate evil. And though there is undoubtedly a force of evil, the powers of darkness, just as there is a force of good, Spencer questions whether what we call evil is necessarily always evil. And whether what we call good is necessarily always good. We have first to come to terms with our shadow side and only then is a transformation possible. It is only when Prospero ceases to call Caliban "a devil, a demi-devil," and says "This thing of darkness I acknowledge as my own," that Caliban, his shadow side, is enabled to say, "Henceforth I'll seek for grace."

Josie comes to see that her goodness was no more than "simplicity, easily destroyed and now quite worthless." She becomes a whore. "I began to do what you all do because I thought you'd understand. How does sin destroy what's good?" Yet she is not corrupted. She merely sheds the shell of naïvety which we, all too often and mistakenly, call innocence. For, as Amanda, the militant Christian in the play, remarks, "It's difficult to go naked in this world."

What Josie finally learns is that "You can't act being good. It just exists in itself. Goodness is a thing apart. It is itself." And because she believes this she will not accept the only society she knows, that of the Bar. She cries out, "Are we in this modern world trapped so vilely in our flesh? No, no, no, no!"

It is with this affirmation that the play ends. And it seems to me in retrospect that no production has yet done the play credit. It is all too easy to be carried away by the surface camp (admittedly a part of the play's fabric) and to neglect its deep moral purpose.

For, fundamentally, Spencer is a moralist. What he does, more urgently than any other contemporary writer, more wittily and with refreshing humour, is to question accepted conventions. In *The Sphinx Mother* (a modern version of the Oedipus story) there is a moving scene at the beginning of the second act between Clare (the Jocasta figure) and Owen (the Oedipus figure):

Clare—There has never been such a partnership of power and goodness.
Owen—How can that be! Goodness based on corruption?
Clare—Where was the corruption? I have experienced no cruelty or violence from you, nor given you any. We trod softly through each other's lives and gave freely.

Clare challenges Owen's terrible self-mutilation, "all that he showed was his pathetic weakness." Through her, Spencer challenges,

> our abstract ideas of what life and love ought to be. It is these abstract ideas that cause violence and aggression. Can you not accept that we did love each other, totally? If a son has lain with his mother for a quarter of a lifetime is that as grotesque as we think it is?

In other plays, notably the comedies *The Fruiting Body* (not yet produced) and *Spitting Image*, Spencer continues to question and probe. *Spitting Image*, a "happy play" as Spencer had it billed, revealed, as John Russell Taylor observed in a brilliant review, that the author has learnt from a writer like Firbank that camp nonsense can sometimes cut deep. And though, on the surface, *Spitting Image* is about two homosexuals one of whom gives birth to a baby by the other, he has used this fantastic particular instance in order to illuminate a believable, disturbing reality. "If the birth is fantastic," writes Taylor,

> the opposition Gary and Tom encounter, the ways and means by which the authorities seek to suppress the awkward individual, the special case which obstinately refuses to fit into the nearest convenient pigeon-hole, are too unforgettably credible. The fantastic particular is made to stand effectively for the host of less eye-catching realities, and the social comment reaches its target unerringly.

If sometimes, as in certain passages from *The Sphinx Mother*, or *The Ballad of the False Barman*, Spencer seems almost florid, baroque in his writing, it is because in these passages (such as Bill's loneliness speech in prison and the Duke's long arias) he is trying to pierce below the external observable reality to that anguish of spirit that cannot really be put into words. In these passages he employs, deliberately, a convoluted, imagistic, surreal style of writing, digging out the kind of uncomfortable and embarrassing images that perhaps occur only in dreams. He is concerned to articulate the lost areas of human experience. In the unproduced *Summer at Camber—39* (the setting is the outbreak of World War II) he has Hester say,

> I feel trapped, Maud. I'm thirty-nine and I feel trapped. I don't think I'll ever get free . . . so many things there are battering begging to speak, not just from inside of me, but . . . so much . . . I don't quite understand. You don't understand. Eddy can't understand, ever . . . what am I doing? How long must I stay without . . . being able to know . . . more?

The intensity of emotion conveyed by those dots, those broken phrases, is what increasingly concerns theatre. As Stanislavsky wrote at the turn of the century, "It is necessary to picture not life itself as it takes place in reality, but as we vaguely feel it in our dreams, our visions, our moments of spiritual uplift." Virginia Woolf said that she wanted to write "books about silence; about the things people do not say," but because she, like Spencer, was a writer, she had to try to use words. How to reach the centre is the shared concern of many different artists. One cry rings through all these explorations, the cry of Josie in *The Ballad of the False Barman*, "Who among you cares enough? Stop all this deceit, please, oh, please. Stop all these disguises!"

—James Roose-Evans

SPURLING, John.

Born in Kisumu, Kenya, 17 July 1936. Educated at Dragon School, Oxford, 1946–49; Marlborough College, Wiltshire, 1950–54; St. John's College, Oxford, 1957–60, B.A. 1960. Served in the Royal Artillery (national service), 1955–57. Married Hilary Forrest (i.e., the writer Hilary Spurling) in 1961; one daughter and two sons. Plebiscite officer for the United Kingdom in Southern Cameroons, 1960–61; announcer, BBC Radio, London, 1963–66; radio and book reviewer, the *Spectator*, London, 1966–70, and other publications. Henfield fellow, University of East Anglia, Norwich, 1973, art critic, *New Statesman*, London, 1976–88. Lives in London. Agent: Patricia MacNaughton, MacNaughton Lowe Representation, 200 Fulham Road, London SW10 9PN, England.

Publications

PLAYS

Char (produced 1959).
MacRune's Guevara As Realised by Edward Hotel (produced 1969). 1969.
Romance, music and lyrics by Charles Ross (produced 1971).
In the Heart of the British Museum (produced 1971). 1972.
Shades of Heathcliff (produced 1971). With *Death of Captain Doughty*, 1975.
Peace in Our Time (produced 1972).
Death of Captain Doughty (televised 1973). With *Shades of Heathcliff*, 1975.
McGonagall and the Murderer (produced 1974).
On a Clear Day You Can See Marlowe (produced 1974).
While Rome Burns (produced 1976).
Antigone Through the Looking Glass (produced 1979).
The British Empire, Part One (produced 1980). 1982.
Coming Ashore in Guadeloupe (produced 1982).
The Butcher of Bagdad (produced 1993).

RADIO PLAYS: *Where Tigers Roam*, 1976; *The Stage Has Nothing to Give Us* (documentary), 1980; *The British Empire: Part One: Dominion over Palm and Pine*, 1982, *Part Two: The Christian Hero*, 1982, *Part Three: The Day of Reckoning*, 1985; *Daughters and Sons*, from the novel by Ivy Compton-Burnett, 1985; *Fancy Pictures: A Portrait After Gainsborough*, 1988; *Discobolus*, 1989.

TELEVISION PLAYS: *Hope*, 1970; *Faith*, 1971; *Death of Captain Doughty*, 1973; *Silver*, 1973.

NOVEL
The Ragged End. 1989.

OTHER
Beckett: A Study of His Plays, with John Fletcher. 1972; revised edition, 1978; revised edition, as *Beckett the Playwright*, 1985.
Graham Greene. 1983.

Editor, *The Hill Station: An Unfinished Novel, and An Indian Diary*, by J.G. Farrell. 1981.

John Spurling comments:

(1977) *MacRune's Guevara* was written from a desire to create an event in space rather than to turn out something recognisable as a play (I imagined it being performed in an art gallery rather than a theatre): at the same time I wanted to represent to myself my own conflicting reactions to Che Guevara and to attack certain forms of artistic and political cant which were dominant in the theatre at the time—perhaps still persist.

I found the idea for the more complex structure of *In the Heart of the British Museum* in Frances Yates's book on Renaissance theories of *The Art of Memory*, but after completing five scenes I put the play away. I took it up again as a commission for the Traverse Workshop Theatre, under Max Stafford-Clark's direction. The piece, with its emphasis on song and dance, was finished with this particular company in mind, but since I had felt the need for just such a company to perform it even before I knew of the company's existence, the original structure did not have to be altered. The subject matter comprises Aztec and Chinese legend, the recent Chinese Cultural Revolution, the exile of the Roman poet Ovid, and some of the subject matter of Ovid's own poems. The central theme is also Ovid's, the idea of Metamorphosis, and this is an important element in the structure.

Shades of Heathcliff grew directly out of being commissioned for Ed Thomason's Crucible Vanguard Theatre in Sheffield. A play for Sheffield seemed to call for a version of *Wuthering Heights*; the company consisted only of three actors and one actress, and, performing in a small space, dictated that it be a chamber piece and that the characters of the four Brontë children and of the novel itself be melted together.

Peace in Our Time was commissioned by the Crucible Theatre, Sheffield. It is the first part of a larger work called *Ghosts and Monsters of the Second World War*, which I have yet to finish. This first part is set in Hell, where the characters (Hitler, Stalin, Mussolini, Chamberlain, et al.) replay some of the political games of 1935–39.

McGonagall and the Murderer is a short play commissioned by the Pool Theatre, Edinburgh. A man who has failed to assassinate Queen Victoria and is now confined in Broadmoor tries to win a second chance by entering the mind of the poet McGonagall, himself on the road to Balmoral. *On a Clear Day You Can See Marlowe* was first written in 1970 and revised in 1974 for the Major Road Company. The play is something of a companion piece to *MacRune's Guevara*—a collage of the few known facts about the playwright Marlowe, much speculation (both reasonable and ludicrous), and versions of his own work in modern rehearsal.

(1988) *While Rome Burns*, commissioned by the Marlowe Theatre,

Canterbury under its then director, David Carson, is a futuristic version of Edgar Allan Poe's story "The Masque of the Red Death." A company of travelling players visits an island off the coast of Britain, the last refuge of a group of well-heeled, middle-class people who have fled from a major catastrophe on the mainland. *Antigone Through the Looking Glass*, also commissioned by David Carson for a production at the King's Head, Islington, London, is roughly the same length as Sophocles' *Antigone* which is being acted off-stage, while we watch the performers coming and going in the green-room.

The British Empire trilogy, covering the period 1820–1911, with a cast of over 200 characters, was intended for the stage. Part One was performed in the studio at Birmingham Rep as a promenade production (directed by Peter Farago with a cast of only 9) and then adapted for BBC Radio 3, which also commissioned Parts Two and Three. I am still hoping to see the whole seven-hour work on the stage, preferably performed in one day or at least on successive evenings.

Coming Ashore in Guadeloupe was started in 1973 for a Dutch company which folded, but substantially revised in 1982 for the Cherub Theatre Company and its director Andrew Visnevski. It is a panorama (in fairly concise form) of the European discovery and conquest of America, featuring Columbus, Cortes, Pizarro, Raleigh, Verrazzano, and others, but viewed much of the time through the eyes of the Indian inhabitants.

John Spurling's work has veered from the technically innovative and exciting to the commonplace, and some of it is probably best forgotten—for example, the sentimental musical drawing-room comedy *Romance*. However, he has produced three plays which will almost certainly survive: *MacRune's Guevara*, *In the Heart of the British Museum*, and *While Rome Burns*.

There is in most of Spurling's plays a profound concern with history and experience. And indeed with what happens to history. In *MacRune's Guevara* it is suggested that the real Guevara was an enigmatic figure of whom we are unlikely to know anything that finally matters. History, present in the play in the form of press reports, and problematic enough by itself, is only one of the ways in which the audience sees Guevara. Other viewpoints come from the actors in the play, as well as from the narrator, Edward Hotel, who is the supposed dramatist. Hotel has recently occupied a room in which the failed Scots-Irish artist MacRune lived just before his death. MacRune had covered the walls of this room with pencil sketches of some 17 scenes of Guevara's Bolivian campaign. These sketches, now faint and sometimes indistinguishable from other marks on the wall, are a parallel to the press reports about Guevara; and these are thrown into a discussion on the nature of history, with Hotel's own views of the subject, and MacRune's supposed views of it—which we are told, with questionable reliability, are heretical from a Marxist point of view. From all this, Guevara emerges as partly ineffectual and partly valiant, guerrilla hero but also a dupe of higher powers, on the one hand an inspirer of love who does not allow himself to be swayed by it from his cause, and on the other a merely simple-minded killer of bourgeois Belgians in an interlude located in the Congo. At the end of his life, he appears disillusioned, though as brave as ever, a man who did not amount to much in life but who has acquired mythic dimensions in death. One critic called this play "an honest magnification of the author's own confusion"; it is, in fact, the exact opposite: a sophisticated attempt to say "No clothes" about a king. Through Guevara, Spurling is also making a point about all contemporary heroes.

The multi-viewpoint technique of *MacRune's Guevara*, of which Spurling was one of the pioneers, was further elaborated in his next notable play, *In the Heart of the British Museum*. Three narratives are interwoven here: the disgrace and rehabilitation of a Chinese professor during the Cultural Revolution, the exile and death of Ovid, and the temptation and fall of the Aztec god Quetzalcoatl and his succession by the grimmer god Texcatlipoca. These themes elaborate and comment on each other. In contrasting power and war with culture and intelligence, in setting history against myth, reputation against reality, Spurling does not take sides. He makes it quite clear that he is not quarrelling with others: it is of his quarrel with his own multitudinous and contradictory responses to Guevara, myth, history, power, and intelligence, that Spurling makes his artistic work. By his omnivorous, witty plays he hopes to make us experience all of reality and thus progress to that profound understanding which is at the heart of all things.

Yet the understanding towards which he stretches his hands is nothing if not radically critical, especially of contemporary fads and blind spots—witness the concern in the title of *While Rome Burns* (loosely structured on Poe's "The Masque of the Red Death"). In this, a privileged few escape from Britain to an island fortress where they are burdened neither with incomes nor with taxes, and are cottoned from news of the world without. War games and cricket, costume balls and leisured adultery, suggestive of a luxury cruise without a destination, are what constitute their concerns. This island sanctuary is approached by an assassin. Disconnected set-pieces provide mannered comic moments which reveal the butterfly character of the protagonists, and their growing sense of dread. We identify with their fear, and yet we cannot help seeing that this beauty is terrible and deserves to be destroyed.

Spurling has written conventional plays with competence; at his best, however, he avoids the comforts of security. Melodrama and the music hall, comedy and tragedy, the neat plot and the predictable one, are alike eschewed. Sometimes Spurling pares away, peels off layer after layer; at other times he takes strange or unexpected angles, comparing like with what appears at first glance to be wholly unlike. Finally, his work functions as parable, icon, mystic text; and, at his finest, he persuades drama to aspire to the condition of poetry.

—Prabhu S. Guptara

STOPPARD, Tom.

Born Tom Straussler in Zlin, Czechoslovakia, 3 July 1937; moved to Singapore, 1939, Darjeeling, India, 1942, and England, 1946. Educated at Dolphin School, Nottinghamshire, 1946–48; Pocklington School, Yorkshire, 1948–54. Married 1) Jose Ingle in 1965 (marriage dissolved 1971), two sons; 2) Miriam Moore-Robinson (i.e., the writer Miriam Stoppard) in 1972, two sons. Journalist, *Western Daily Press*, Bristol, 1954–58, and Bristol *Evening*

World, 1958–60; then freelance journalist and writer: drama critic, *Scene*, London, 1962–63. Member of the board, Royal National Theatre, London, from 1989. Recipient: Ford grant, 1964; John Whiting award, 1967; *Evening Standard* award, 1967, 1973, 1975, 1979, 1983; Italia prize, for radio play, 1968; Tony award, 1968, 1976, 1984; New York Drama Critics Circle award, 1968, 1976, 1984; Shakespeare prize (Hamburg), 1979; Outer Circle award, 1984; Drama Desk award, 1984. M.Lit.: University of Bristol, 1976; Brunel University, Uxbridge, Middlesex, 1979; University of Sussex, Brighton, 1980; honorary degrees: Leeds University, 1980; University of London, 1982; Kenyon College, Gambier, Ohio, 1984; York University, 1984. Fellow, Royal Society of Literature. C.B.E. (Commander, Order of the British Empire), 1978. Lives in Iver, Buckinghamshire. Agent: Peters, Fraser, and Dunlop Group, 503–504 The Chambers, Chelsea Harbour, Lots Road, London SW10 0XF, England.

Publications

PLAYS

A Walk on the Water (televised 1963; produced 1964); revised version, as *The Preservation of George Riley* (televised 1964); as *Enter a Free Man* (produced 1968). 1968.

The Dissolution of Dominic Boot (broadcast 1964). In *The Dog It Was That Died and Other Plays*, 1983.

"M"Is for Moon among Other Things (broadcast 1964; produced 1977). In *The Dog It Was That Died and Other Plays*, 1983.

The Gamblers (produced 1965).

If You're Glad I'll Be Frank (broadcast 1966; produced 1969). With *Albert's Bridge*, 1969; revised version, 1978.

Tango, adaptation of a play by Slawomir Mrozek, translated by Nicholas Bethell (produced 1966). 1968.

A Separate Peace (televised 1966). 1977; in *Albert's Bridge and Other Plays*, 1977.

Rosencrantz and Guildenstern Are Dead (produced 1966; revised version produced 1967). 1967; screenplay published as *Rosencrantz and Guildenstern Are Dead: The Film*, 1991.

Albert's Bridge (broadcast 1967; produced 1969). With *If You're Glad I'll Be Frank*, 1969; in *Albert's Bridge and Other Plays*, 1977.

Teeth (televised 1967). In *The Dog It Was That Died and Other Plays*, 1983.

Another Moon Called Earth (televised 1967). In *The Dog It Was That Died and Other Plays*, 1983.

Neutral Ground (televised 1968). In *The Dog It Was That Died and Other Plays*, 1983.

The Real Inspector Hound (produced 1968). 1968.

After Magritte (produced 1970). 1971.

Where Are They Now? (broadcast 1970). With *Artist Descending a Staircase*, 1973; in *Albert's Bridge and Other Plays*, 1977.

Dogg's Our Pet (produced 1971). In *Ten of the Best*, edited by Ed Berman, 1979.

Jumpers (produced 1972). 1972; revised version, 1986.

Artist Descending a Staircase (broadcast 1972; produced 1988). With *Where Are They Now?*, 1973; in *Albert's Bridge and Other Plays*, 1977.

The House of Bernarda Alba, adaptation of the play by García Lorca (produced 1973).

Travesties (produced 1974; revised version produced 1993). 1975.

Dirty Linen, and New-found-land (produced 1976). 1976.

The Fifteen Minute Hamlet (as *The [Fifteen Minute] Dogg's Troupe Hamlet*, produced 1976). 1978.

Albert's Bridge and Other Plays (includes *Artist Descending a Staircase, If You're Glad I'll Be Frank, A Separate Peace, Where Are They Now?*). 1977.

Every Good Boy Deserves Favour: A Play for Actors and Orchestra, music by André Previn (produced 1977). With *Professional Foul*, 1978.

Professional Foul (televised 1977). With *Every Good Boy Deserves Favour*, 1978.

Night and Day (produced 1978). 1978; revised version, 1979.

Albert's Bridge Extended (produced 1978).

Undiscovered Country, adaptation of a play by Schnitzler (produced 1979). 1980.

Dogg's Hamlet, Cahoot's Macbeth (produced 1979). 1980.

On the Razzle, adaptation of a play by Johann Nestroy (produced 1981). 1981.

The Real Thing (produced 1982). 1982; revised version (produced 1984), 1984.

The Dog It Was That Died (broadcast 1982). In *The Dog It Was That Died and Other Plays*, 1983.

The Love for Three Oranges, adaptation of the opera by Prokofiev (produced 1983).

The Dog It Was That Died and Other Plays (includes *The Dissolution of Dominic Boot, "M" Is for Moon among Other Things, Teeth, Another Moon Called Earth, Neutral Ground, A Separate Peace*). 1983.

Rough Crossing, adaptation of a play by Ferenc Molnár (produced 1984; revised version produced 1989). 1985.

Squaring the Circle: Poland 1980–81 (televised 1984). With *Every Good Boy Deserves Favour* and *Professional Foul*, 1984.

Four Plays for Radio (includes *Artist Descending a Staircase, Where Are They Now?, If You're Glad I'll Be Frank, Albert's Bridge*). 1984.

Dalliance, adaptation of a play by Schnitzler (produced 1986). With *Undiscovered Country*, 1986.

Largo Desolato, adaptation of the play by Václav Havel (produced 1986). 1987.

Brazil (screenplay), in *The Battle of Brazil* by Jack Mathews. 1987.

Hapgood (produced 1988). 1988.

The Radio Plays 1964–1983. 1990.

Arcadia (produced 1993). 1993.

SCREENPLAYS: *The Romantic Englishwoman*, with Thomas Wiseman, 1975; *Despair*, 1978; *The Human Factor*, 1980; *Brazil*, with Terry Gilliam and Charles McKeown, 1985; *Empire of the Sun*, 1988; *Rosencrantz and Guildenstern Are Dead*, 1990.

RADIO PLAYS: *Dissolution of Dominic Boot*, 1964; *"M" Is for Moon among Other Things*, 1964; *If You're Glad I'll Be Frank*, 1966; *Albert's Bridge*, 1967; *Where Are They Now?*, 1970; *Artist Descending a Staircase*, 1972; *The Dog It Was That Died*, 1982; *In the Native State*, 1991.

TELEVISION PLAYS: *A Walk on the Water*, 1963 (revised version, as *The Preservation of George Riley*, 1964); *A Separate Peace*, 1966; *Teeth*, 1967; *Another Moon Called Earth*, 1967; *Neutral Ground*, 1968; *The Engagement*, from his radio play *The Dissolution of Dominic Boot*, 1970; *One Pair of Eyes* (documentary), 1972; *The Boundary* (*Eleventh Hour* series), with Clive Exton, 1975; *Three Men in a Boat*, from the novel by Jerome K. Jerome, 1975; *Professional Foul*, 1977; *Squaring the Circle*, 1984.

NOVEL

Lord Malquist and Mr. Moon. 1966.

SHORT STORIES

Introduction 2, with others. 1964.

BIBLIOGRAPHY: *Tom Stoppard: A Reference Guide* by David Bratt, 1982.

CRITICAL STUDIES: *Tom Stoppard* by C.W.E. Bigsby, 1976, revised edition, 1979; *Tom Stoppard* by Ronald Hayman, 1977, 4th edition, 1982; *Beyond Absurdity: The Plays of Tom Stoppard* by Victor L. Cahn, 1979; *Tom Stoppard* by Felicia Hardison Londré, 1981; *Tom Stoppard: Comedy as a Moral Matrix* by Joan Fitzpatrick Dean, 1981; *The Stoppard Plays* by Lucina Paquet Gabbard, 1982; *Shakespearean Parallels and Affinities with the Theatre of the Absurd in Stoppard's Rosencrantz and Guildenstern Are Dead* by Anja Easterling, 1982; *Tom Stoppard's Plays* by Jim Hunter, 1982; *Tom Stoppard* by Thomas R. Whitaker, 1983; *Stoppard: The Mystery and the Clockwork* by Richard Corballis, 1984; *Tom Stoppard: An Assessment* by Tim Brassell, 1985; *File on Stoppard* edited by Malcolm Page, 1986, *Tom Stoppard* by Susan Rusinko, 1986; *Stoppard the Playwright* by Michael Billington, 1987; *The Theatre of Tom Stoppard* by Anthony Jenkins, 1987, revised edition, 1989; *Tom Stoppard: A Casebook* edited by John Harty, III, 1987; *Tom Stoppard: The Artist as Critic* by Neil Sammells, 1988; *Tom Stoppard: Rosencrantz and Guildenstern Are Dead, Jumpers, Travesties: A Casebook* edited by T. Bareham, 1990; *Tom Stoppard: The Moral Vision of the Major Plays* by Paul Delaney, 1990; *Rosencrantz and Guildenstern Are Dead, Jumpers, The Real Thing* (Text and Performance series), edited by Robert Gordon, 1991; *Tom Stoppard and the Craft of Comedy* by Katherine Kelly, 1991.

THEATRICAL ACTIVITIES

DIRECTOR: **Play**—*Born Yesterday* by Garson Kanin, 1973; *The Real Inspector Hound*, 1985. **Film**—*Rosencrantz and Guildenstern Are Dead*, 1990.

Tom Stoppard vaulted to international renown in 1967 with *Rosencrantz and Guildenstern Are Dead*. It remains undoubtedly his best-known and most often produced work, although it can now be seen as juvenilia within the context of a dramatic talent that has matured steadily in both craft and thematic scope. A characteristic—if somewhat self-conscious—verbal agility has anchored his *oeuvre* as he developed his craft by exploring a variety of dramatic modes, writing for radio, television, and motion pictures as well as for the stage, both mainstream and experimental. Exercising his stylistic virtuosity upon other writers' plot structures, he has also made a number of free adaptations of plays from other languages.

After several years as a journalist and sometime theatre reviewer, in 1960 Stoppard wrote his first play, *A Walk on the Water*, which did not reach the legitimate stage until 1968 (in a revised version, titled *Enter a Free Man*). Meanwhile, it was a series of radio and television plays that launched him as a professional dramatist. Several of those early radio plays—notably *If You're Glad I'll Be Frank*, *Albert's Bridge*, and *Artist Descending a Staircase*—have in recent years been brought to the stage. Their creative use of the radio medium, however, tends to gimmickry at the expense of character, as in *Artist Descending a Staircase*, an ingenious search backward and forward in time for the truth about the circumstances of the artist's death, which had been captured on a tape recording that lends itself to clever ambiguity of interpretation. In the 1991 radio play *In the Native State*, a more subtle and graceful exploitation of the medium's unique properties fuels the story's implicit eroticism and places the focus on an intriguing web of human interactions, between English and Indian people, between people in 1930 and in the present. The radio plays' trajectory from artifice to interest in characters with real emotions parallels the development of Stoppard's writing for the stage.

The title characters of *Rosencrantz and Guildenstern Are Dead* are the school chums of Shakespeare's Hamlet, who have been summoned to Elsinore without knowing what is expected of them. Stoppard's play shows the two characters adrift in somebody else's plot, just as the Absurdists focused upon modern man's rudderlessness in a world he cannot control. While the action of *Hamlet* proceeds in the background, the two innocents play games to pass the time in a manner clearly inspired by Beckett's *Waiting for Godot*. Their desire to overcome the fixity of the work of art in which they must function echoes the premise of Pirandello's *Six Characters in Search of an Author*. The complex interrelationships of life and art are demonstrated with particular theatrical flair in the pair's scenes with the Players who come to perform for Claudius at Elsinore.

Two recurring themes in Stoppard's short plays of the 1960's and early 1970's, as well as in his novel *Lord Malquist and Mr. Moon*, are the relativity of truth and the urge to discern some pattern in the world's chaos. In *Albert's Bridge*, a well-educated young man opts to spend his life painting a suspension bridge, because it sets him above the fray of daily existence which can now be perceived as "dots and bricks, giving out a gentle hum." *The Real Inspector Hound* amusingly toys with the boundary between art and life by having two theatre critics get caught up in the murder mystery drama they are watching. The stage picture at the beginning of *After Magritte* is like a surrealist painting, but the action of the play reveals a kind of manic logic behind the visual nonsense.

The same concerns reappear in Stoppard's two major mid-career full-length plays *Jumpers* and *Travesties*. Although the philosophical discourse may become a bit heavy-handed in *Jumpers*, it must still be counted among his best plays for the brilliance of its theatrical conceits. The intellectual argument of the play, a dialectic between moral philosophy and logical positivism, is reified in stage metaphors like the human pyramid of middle-aged philosophers in jump suits, whose shaky performance inadvertently demonstrates the false logic of a relativistic philosophical system. However, the search for absolutes by philosopher George Moore is constantly subverted by events in his own household that cannot be understood at face value.

Travesties is a dazzling foray into a crucial moment in political and cultural history—filtered through the self-serving memory of a senile minor figure, Henry Carr, who worked at the British Consulate in Zurich during World War I. He comes into contact with Lenin, who is preparing the way for a revolution in Russia; Tristan Tzara, who seeks through Dada to overthrow 25 centuries of artistic convention; and James Joyce, who is already working on the novel that will revolutionize modern literature. Fitting these characters into the borrowed structure of Wilde's *The Importance of Being Earnest* (which was produced by the English Players under Joyce's direction in Zurich in 1917), Stoppard examines the responsibility of the artist to society.

As a kind of busman's holiday from his West End fare, Stoppard wrote a few short pieces for various "alternative theatre" projects undertaken by director Ed Berman, who had premièred *After Magritte*. Berman's community service organization Inter-Action included a children's theatre company called Dogg's Troupe, for which Stoppard wrote the one-act farce *Dogg's Our Pet*. In this play, as in the later paired one-acts *Dogg's Hamlet/Cahoot's Macbeth*, Stoppard makes fun of the arbitrariness of language by having some of his characters speak Dogg's language, which is composed of English words used to mean different things. The stage action in these plays is the construction of a speaker's platform, a stage, or a wall, using slabs, planks, bricks, and cubes— just as language uses the various parts of speech to construct a meaning. *Dogg's Hamlet* incorporates an earlier playlet, *The [Fifteen-Minute] Dogg's Troupe Hamlet*, which is a very funny condensation of Shakespeare's *Hamlet*, followed by a two-minute version as an encore.

In 1976 the American-born Berman asked Stoppard to write a play that would celebrate both the American bicentennial and Berman's naturalization as a British citizen. Stoppard responded by sandwiching the brief sketch, *New-found-land*, into his longer farce, *Dirty Linen*. Set in a House of Commons meeting room, *Dirty Linen* shows the foibles of members of the Select Committee on Promiscuity in High Places; they finally come to accept the common-sense opinions of the attractive Maddie Gotobed who has been sexually involved with most of them. When the Committee adjourns for 15 minutes, two new characters enter and use the room for a discussion of Berman's citizenship application, which leads to a long and cleverly evocative panegyric monologue about America as seen through foreign eyes.

Some of Stoppard's best writing has come from his moral outrage at totalitarian violations of human rights. Invited by André Previn to write a play that would involve a collaboration of actors and a live orchestra on the stage, Stoppard realized that by making the orchestra a figment of one character's imagination, he could set the play in an insane asylum and write about the Soviet practice of confining political prisoners there along with genuine lunatics. For all its serious subject matter, *Every Good Boy Deserves Favour* contains some supremely witty dialogue. It also features a child, Sacha, whose observation of the system's injustice and of his dissident father's integrity has matured him beyond his years. A boy named Sacha also plays a crucial role in the television play *Professional Foul*, which draws its metaphors from a soccer match that is played in Czechoslovakia while British philosophers attend a conference there. In the course of the tense drama, Sacha courageously helps one of them to smuggle his dissident father's doctoral thesis to England for publication. Another television play, *Squaring the Circle*, traces the 1980–81 workers' Solidarity movement in Poland and makes of that complex history a clear and absorbing narrative for the layman. Stoppard's premise is that the concept of a free trade union like Solidarity is as irreconcilable with the Communist bloc's definition of socialism as is the mathematical impossibility of turning a circle into a square with the same area. The brilliantly theatrical short piece *Cahoot's Macbeth* must also be classed as one of Stoppard's "plays of commitment."

Night and Day is a play of transition in Stoppard's development, for it continues his concern for human rights in the face of totalitarianism while it branches into a tentative exploration of romantic emotion. It is above all a play about journalism, a lively demonstration of the pros and cons of a free press. Ruth Carson is the wife of a British mine owner in a fictitious African country where a British-educated black dictator's rule is challenged by a Soviet-backed rebel countryman. The most idealistic of the three journalists who converge upon the Carson home becomes Ruth's fantasy-lover.

In *The Real Thing*, for the first time in Stoppard's canon, the human story is allowed to take precedence over ideological concerns or stylistic conceits. Yet there is a bit of everything in this romantic comedy that does not shy away from either human pain or politics; there is perhaps even a touch of autobiography in that the protagonist Henry Boot is a playwright. His speech, using a cricket-bat metaphor to uphold standards in language and thought, is dramatic writing at its best, a stylistic high point in the work of a writer for whom style has always been the strong suit.

Hapgood, too, may be seen as a compendium of earlier Stoppardian features: a small boy, political intrigue, a glimmer of romantic interest, attempts to discern a pattern in seemingly random events, and a complicated plot illustrating the premise that the truth depends upon where you are standing. Just as Stoppard had mastered certain philosophical arguments in order to write *Jumpers*, he learned particle physics in order to write his espionage comedy-thriller *Hapgood*, in which a Russian-born physicist may be a double or triple agent. Using the behavior of subatomic particles as a metaphor ("there is *no such thing* as an electron with a definite position and a definite momentum"), Stoppard's plot employs two real sets of twins and one fake pair to give dramatic shape to the notion that there is no fixity in human affairs.

During the increasingly long periods between his plays, Stoppard has devoted himself to writing screenplays, directing, and adapting plays in translation. He regards his adaptations as a crucial component of his work, and the liberties he takes with the originals establishes his versions in a category apart from literary translation. *Rough Crossing*, for example, borrows some of the characters and the situation from Ferenc Molnár's *The Play at the Castle* (also known as *The Play's the Thing*), but moves them from a castle on the Italian Riviera to a transatlantic ocean liner. By imposing spatial and temporal boundaries on the action, Stoppard heightens the dramatic tension even as he indulges in a variety of comic distractions. Certainly, Stoppard is long past needing such projects as short refresher courses in the craft of playwriting. They might be seen as tributes to his peers from one who has attained the status of world-class dramatist.

—Felicia Hardison Londré

See the essay on *Rosencrantz and Guildenstern Are Dead*.

STOREY, David (Malcolm).

Born in Wakefield, Yorkshire, 13 July 1933; brother of the writer Anthony Storey. Educated at Queen Elizabeth Grammar School, Wakefield, 1943–51; Wakefield College of Art, 1951–53; Slade School of Fine Art, London, 1953–56, diploma in fine arts 1956. Married Barbara Rudd Hamilton in 1956; two sons and two daughters. Played professionally for the Leeds Rugby League Club, 1952–56; associate artistic director, Royal Court Theatre, London, 1972–74. Fellow, University College, London, 1974. Recipient: Macmillan award (U.S.) for fiction, 1960; Rhys Memorial award, for fiction, 1961; Maugham award, for fiction, 1963; *Evening Standard* award, 1967, 1970; New York Drama Critics Circle award, 1971, 1973, 1974; Faber Memorial prize, 1973; Los Angeles Drama Critics Circle award, 1973; Obie award, 1974; Booker prize, for fiction, 1976. Address: c/o Jonathan Cape Ltd., 20 Vauxhall Bridge Road, London SW1V 2SA, England.

Publications

PLAYS

The Restoration of Arnold Middleton (produced 1966). 1967.
In Celebration (produced 1969). 1969.
The Contractor (produced 1969). 1970.
Home (produced 1970). 1970.
The Changing Room (produced 1971). 1972.
The Farm (produced 1973). 1973.
Cromwell (produced 1973). 1973.
Life Class (produced 1974). 1975.
Mother's Day (produced 1976). 1977.
Sisters (produced 1978). In *Early Days, Sisters, Life Class*, 1980.
Early Days (produced 1980). In *Early Days, Sisters, Life Class*, 1980.
Early Days, Sisters, Life Class. 1980; (produced 1984).
The March on Russia (produced 1989). 1989.
Stages (produced 1992). In *Plays 1*, 1992.
Plays 1 (includes *The Contractor, Home, Stages, Caring*). 1992.

SCREENPLAYS: *This Sporting Life*, 1963; *In Celebration*, 1976.

TELEVISION PLAY: *Grace*, from the story by James Joyce, 1974.

NOVELS
This Sporting Life. 1960.
Flight into Camden. 1960.
Radcliffe. 1963.
Pasmore. 1972.
A Temporary Life. 1973.
Saville. 1976.
A Prodigal Child. 1982.
Present Times. 1984.

VERSE
Storey's Lives: Poems 1951–1991. 1992.

OTHER
Writers on Themselves, with others. 1964.
Edward, drawings by Donald Parker. 1973.

MANUSCRIPT COLLECTION: Boston University, Massachusetts.

CRITICAL STUDIES (a selection): *The Second Wave*, 1971, and *David Storey*, 1974, both by John Russell Taylor; *The Plays of David Storey: A Thematic Study* by William Hutchings, 1988; *British Drama 1950 to the Present* by Susan Rusinko, 1989.

THEATRICAL ACTIVITIES
DIRECTOR: **Television**—*Portrait of Margaret Evans*, 1963; *Death of My Mother* (D.H. Lawrence documentary), 1963.

David Storey's achievement as a dramatist has to be measured alongside the contribution made by Lindsay Anderson, who directed several of Storey's productions at London's Royal Court Theatre. Anderson may well have inspired Storey to branch out into the theatre following his auspicious beginning as a realistic novelist in the early 1960's. Anderson was certainly largely responsible for transforming Storey's most minutely detailed scripts into viable theatrical experiences.

Storey began as a playwright with *The Restoration of Arnold Middleton*, concerning a free spirit who rebels against conventional suburban mores. Both in style and in outlook, this resembled a number of other plays at the time by Tom Stoppard, David Mercer, and John Antrobus, and, though competent, was not truly indicative of Storey's main direction in the theatre.

In Celebration and *The Contractor* were far more distinctive. Each drew from their original novels a quality that was completely Storey's own in the matter-of-fact rendering of Northern working-class life. As grim as Lawrence's earlier evocations of Nottinghamshire mining communities, these were more subdued in tone, seeking simply to render a portrait of the way industrial life had fragmented family relationships, though the undercurrents of almost tribal unity and custom remained. *In Celebration* provides pointed comparisons with Mercer's *Ride a Cock Horse* in its refusal to let migration southward develop into Mercer's celebrated Northern chip on the shoulder. Storey's family of working-class lads return home for their parents' wedding anniversary. The scars of upbringing are manifest; so are the recriminations. But the protest is muted, less by inertia than by the sheer inability to come to terms with transition, even to the point of articulating that something is wrong.

It was an impressive feat, not least because Storey had dared to present something "internal" and "reflective" on a London stage and at a time when the waves of agitprop were beginning to break. Anderson's production concentrated on ensemble playing to underscore the theme of kinship, and Alan Bates and Constance Chapman gave memorable performances in an unglamorous evening that was, for all that, compelling.

The Contractor developed these strands as far as they can go, one feels from Storey's career afterwards. Each of the untoward elements of the earlier play were now fully exploited. Storey refined narrative to the point where there were no dramatic cruces to be explored. Several itinerant labourers appear on stage in desultory fashion to assemble a marquee for a wedding. The audience watches as actors simulate the very business their characters are required to do. They remain in role, but most of the theatricality is provided by their common initiative in successfully performing a set task by the time the act concludes. After the break the actors repeat the process in reverse, and when the marquee is finally dismantled the play ends, as unceremoniously as it begins.

For ensemble playing, this could only be matched by an audience being invited to attend a workshop of actors working with a given group in some highly organized game-playing. As a piece of scripted theatre, it bypassed areas of sleight-of-hand to emerge as a genuine piece of naturalism, closer to real experience than Arnold Wesker's *The Kitchen* had been, because the suspension of disbelief was "unnecessary." Life and art mirrored each other as they had never done before.

To say Storey had set himself an impossible task by trying to move on from this point is to give a far more rounded picture of Storey's career than he does himself. He continued to write plays interspersed with as many novels. Most of them, too, reveal a ready ability to experiment. All of the subsequent plays are at least watchable, and even when he has relied too heavily on existing models, including his own, he has done so with the clear aim of creating something new.

The Changing Room and *Home*, for example, closely followed *The Contractor* in Anderson productions at the Royal Court. But if the one suggested that writer and director were working to a formula (with a still-life depiction of a Northern amateur rugby team), the other compelled audiences to look at Storey anew. *Home*'s lingering achievement—it has to be said—is likely to be as a vehicle for a Gielgud–Richardson double act late in their careers when non-specialist audiences were eager to see two lions of the London stage performing the epitome of their talents. The production duly transferred into the West End and enabled the English Stage Company, at the Royal Court, to enter a turbulent decade of fringe production at least financially solvent. As a play, *Home* now bears too many traces of Beckett's influence to be seen as a development of Storey's canon. *Mother's Day* is, similarly, Ortonesque, while *Sisters* (an early play staged at Manchester) betrays so many uncomfortable similarities to *A Streetcar Named Desire* that it is tempting to wonder why the author did not simply write a transatlantic version of the Williams play.

On more native ground, however, Storey has enjoyed both critical and popular success with further examples of working-class life. If one is perplexed by the apparent absence of a centre to Storey's work, it is worth recalling that he trained as an artist at the Slade, and that the point of a play like *Early Days*, about a politician living out his retirement in bemused and gentle autocracy, may be less to raise searching questions about the condition of England than to offer an impressionistic pastoral better suited to comparison with John Constable's landscapes than with the crazy-quilt landscape of left-wing drama. (The play, incidentally, enabled Richardson to end his career on a note of triumph.)

Painting (and art generally) was the theme of the earlier *Life Class*, which presents a group of faintly-motivated art students, tutored by Alan Bates, trying to create something out of ubiquitous drabness, and failing, as the play fails, to catch hold of anything substantial.

The Farm, Cromwell, The March on Russia, and *Stages* complete Storey's dramatic output to date. He has said that he used the Brontës as inspiration in writing the first of these, and although the information is of tangential significance, this return to the theme of Northern family life, with women at the centre, is a solid achievement. *Cromwell* with its epic structure and its distance on passion, is more circumspect, though Brian Cox held the production together and revealed the author's mordant wit. *The March on Russia* was very much a reprise. At work again with a now-U.S.-domiciled Anderson, Storey seemed content to revive their earliest collaboration under a new title. It is hard, anyway, to see *The March on Russia* as very much more than that. In it, as well, Storey may have been searching, himself, for a centre to his dramatic work. More likely this is to be found, however, in the one milestone of *The Contractor*.

—James MacDonald

See the essay on *Home*.

STOTT, Mike.

Born in Rochdale, Lancashire, 2 January 1944. Attended Manchester University. Stage manager, Scarborough Library Theatre, Yorkshire, and playreader, Royal Shakespeare Theatre, 3 years; script editor, BBC Radio, London, 1970–72; Thames Television resident writer, Hampstead Theatre Club, London, 1975. Agent: Michael Imison Playwrights, 28 Almeida Street, London N1 1TD, England.

Publications

PLAYS

Mata Hari (produced 1965).
Erogenous Zones (produced 1969).
Funny Peculiar (produced 1973). 1978.
Lenz, adaptation of the story by Georg Büchner (produced 1974). 1979.

Plays for People Who Don't Move Much (produced 1974; section produced as
    Men's Talk, 1974).
Midnight (produced 1974).
Other People (produced 1974).
Ghosts, adaptation of a play by Wolfgang Bauer (produced 1975).
Lorenzaccio, adaptation of the play by Alfred de Musset (produced 1976).
Followed by Oysters (produced 1976; as *Comings and Goings*, produced
    1978).
The Scenario, adaptation of a play by Anouilh (produced 1976).
Soldiers Talking, Cleanly (televised 1978). 1978.
The Boston Strangler (produced 1978).
Grandad (produced 1978).
Strangers (produced 1979).
Ducking Out, adaptation of a play by Eduardo De Filippo (produced 1982).
Dead Men (produced 1982).
Pennine Pleasures (produced 1984).
The Fling, adaptation of a work by Asher (produced 1987).
The Fancy Man (broadcast 1987; produced 1988). In *Plays International*,
    November 1988.

RADIO PLAYS: *Lucky*, 1970; *When Dreams Collide*, 1970; *Early Morning
Glory*, 1972; *Lincoln*, 1973; *Richard Serge*, 1973; *The Bringer of Bad News*,
1973; *The Doubting Thomases*, 1973; *The Fancy Man*, 1987.

TELEVISION PLAYS: *The Flaxton Boys*, 1969; *Susan*, 1973; *Thwum*, 1975; *Our
Flesh and Blood*, 1977; *Pickersgill People* series, 1978; *Soldiers Talking,
Cleanly*, 1978; *One in a Thousand*, 1981; *The Last Company Car*, 1983; *The
Practice* series, 1985–86.

Mike Stott's 1976 West End success with his comedy *Funny Peculiar* may well
represent the culmination of his search for an ideal, or at least clinching,
formula for the permissive sex comedy.
    His search began with *Erogenous Zones*, a collection of sketches for per-
formance by a company of six, centred round the twin themes of love and
homicide. The mixture here is one of strip cartoon wit and woman's magazine
cliché, the main charm residing in the way passion is reduced to absurdity
through being couched in dumb and deadpan phrases. The types are instantly
recognizable—the doughy sweetheart, the sadistic cop, the clean-limbed officer
doing press-ups, the big beefy success, the mad gunman, the obsessive lawyer
—with the point always clear before the pay-offs. Stott shows cleverness in
catching the comedy of the obvious, while managing to avoid repetition.
    In *Other People* the form is sometimes laboured though the dialogue is often
sharp. It begins with an arresting image of a "flasher" naked under his plastic,
see-through mac, and a pretty Czech girl who frightens him away by her
eagerness to participate in anything he might suggest. But an arresting image
does not make a play, and the web of relationships Stott establishes—between
a successful businessman, Dave, who ends by taking an overdose, an out-of-
work Italian father-of-five who is given a cheque by the dying man to solve all
his problems, a lonely widow of 51 who lacks love, and her daughter, married

to Dave's friend Geoff—fails to form a coherent pattern of comic interest. The writing is often vivid, as in the Italian's fantasy of selling underwear to Arabs in hair-covered boxes—"We buy the hair, we comb it, shampoo, and we stick it on the boxes. And those Arabs, those Greeks, they go CRAZY in the shops, just to stroke our sexy hairy boxes. Believe me, Mr. Brock, I know those men, the foreigners, the Aristotles, the Ahmeds. They KILL each other to be stroking a hairy English box." The theme of sexual permissiveness is provocatively explored, with the sound of couples making love upstairs and one couple trying to initiate group sex. But it's hard to make out what Stott's intention is, whether he's attempting genuine social observation or merely exploiting current fashion.

Funny Peculiar has a mock moral ending. The hero, Trevor, a North Country grocer proclaiming the virtues of sexual freedom, falls down into his cellar, pursued by a sex-hungry puritan lady of advanced years, and is consequently rendered helpless in plaster and straps on a hospital bed. There he becomes the passive object of wife and mistress's oral lust. A new and up-to-date version of the "tu l'a voulu, Georges Dandin" idea, Trevor's obsession with sex is kept simmering in naked cavorting among the council-estate flower beds and in his attempts to preach to the unconverted customers of his shop (losing custom as a result).

The best writing is found in the scenes when he tries to convince his wife to leap on to the freedom bandwagon and when he upbraids her for sexual ordinariness. Her defence is so heartfelt and real it really seems that her subsequent conversion to his way of thinking is engineered for the sake of the plot. There's one piece of slapstick—a fight with confectionary between a visiting confectionary salesman and Trevor—which must rate as one of the best scenes of comic anarchy ever seen on the West End stage.

In his versions of Büchner's *Lenz* and Wolfgang Bauer's *Ghosts* Stott demonstrates more fragmented skills as an adaptor and translator from the German. *Lenz*, originally a short story about a Strasbourg intellectual who believes he can raise a girl from the dead, is written in numerous short scenes (in Büchner's own expressionistic manner) which fail to come to grips with any central issue. The original of *Ghosts* is a roughed up rewrite of Brecht's satire on a lower-middle-class wedding party, using socially more sophisticated though dramatically more crude characters.

In later plays Stott has not shown he can move beyond formula writing. *The Boston Strangler*, for all its rape and murder in intended subtle variations—ensuring constant changes of wigs and underwear in the actress playing all the victims—cumulatively diminishes interest in the crimes of a psychopath. *Comings and Goings* promises to be better. Jan, a teacher, married to a cream-cracker executive, deserts him and arrives in the household of a pair of homosexuals. But development is lost in favour of generalized encounters confirming the rule of licence and ending with vapid literary parallels. The characters have little genuineness and the comings and goings lack dramatic direction. Stott seems to have come to the position of despising the people he writes about. *Grandad*, too, displays a tawdry lack of charity, becoming unrelievedly tedious. Stott returned to formula writing in the television series *The Practice*, an examination of life in a medical centre.

—Garry O'Connor

T

TABORI, George.

Born in Budapest, Hungary, 24 May 1914. Educated at Zrinyl Gymnasium. Served in the British Army Middle East Command, 1941–43; lieutenant. Married 1) Hanna Freund (divorced 1954); 2) the actress Viveca Lindfors (divorced), one son, one daughter, and one stepson. Former artistic director, Berkshire Theatre Festival, Stockbridge, Massachusetts. Recipient: British Film Academy award, 1953. Address: 172 East 95th Street, New York, New York 10028, U.S.A.; or, c/o Suhrkamp Verlag, Lindenstrasse 29–35, Postfach 4229, 6000 Frankfurt am Main, Germany.

Publications

PLAYS

Flight into Egypt (produced 1952). 1953.
The Emperor's Clothes (produced 1953). 1953.
Miss Julie, adaptation of a play by Strindberg (also director: produced 1956).
Brouhaha (produced 1958).
Brecht on Brecht (produced 1962).
The Resistible Rise of Arturo Ui: A Gangster Spectacle, adaptation of the play by Brecht (produced 1963). 1972.
Andorra, adaptation of the play by Max Frisch (produced 1963).
The Guns of Carrar, adaptation of a play by Brecht (produced 1963). 1970.
The Niggerlovers: The Demonstration, and Man and Dog, music by Richard Peaslee (produced 1967).
The Cannibals (produced 1968). In *The American Place Theatre*, edited by Richard Schotter, 1973.
Mother Courage, adaptation of a play by Brecht (produced 1970).
Pinkville, music by Stanley Walden (produced 1970).
Clowns (also director: produced 1972).
Talk Show (produced 1976).
Changes (produced 1976).
Mein Kampf: A Farce (produced 1989).
Weisman and Copperface (produced 1991).

SCREENPLAYS: *I Confess*, with William Archibald, 1953; *The Young Lovers*, with Robin Estridge, 1954; *The Journey*, 1959; *No Exit*, 1962; *Secret Ceremony*, 1968; *Parades*, 1972; *Insomnia*, 1975.

NOVELS

Beneath the Stone the Scorpion. 1945; as *Beneath the Stone,* 1945.
Companions of the Left Hand. 1946.
Original Sin. 1947.
The Caravan Passes. 1951.
The Journey: A Confession. 1958.
The Good One. 1960.

OTHER

*Ich wollte, meine Tochter läge tot zu meinen Füssen und hätte die Juwelen in
den Ohren: Improvisationen über Shakespeares Shylock: Dokumentationen
einer Theaterarbeit.* 1979.

THEATRICAL ACTIVITIES

DIRECTOR: **Plays**—*Miss Julie* by Strindberg, 1956; *Brecht on Brecht,* 1962;
Hell Is Other People, 1964; *The Cannibals* (co-director, with Marty Fried),
1970; *Pinkville,* 1971; *Clowns,* 1972; *Kohlhaas,* 1974; *Emigrants,* 1975;
Afore Night Come by David Rudkin, 1975; *The Trojan Women* by Euripides,
1976.

George Tabori's world recalls the Sherwood Anderson title *Dark Laughter.*
What a world—betrayal, repression, violence, cannibalism, and, unlike the
Greeks', no redemption. And envisioned more and more as a black comedy.
But not quite. The flavor is sardonic, tongue-in-cheek, but beneath this is
absolutely no acceptance of the world as is. Beneath the sardonic tone we can
apprehend the eyes of an anguished, lacerated soul who has seen mankind in
one perversion, one degradation after another, seen Hungary in its fascistic
period earlier in the century, Germany in the Nazi era, and America in its
growing role as police-butcher of the world, has seen it all, and yet whose
outcry marks him as one who still believes in the impossible dream of brotherhood. I have the sense that Tabori is too angry, too disgusted to *want* to
believe, but that past his disgust, past his disillusionment, there is a tremendous
yearning, a cavernous yearning to believe in the possibility of a decent society.
    Early Tabori is represented by *The Emperor's Clothes,* the tale of a "fuzzy-
headed idealist" intellectual (my quotes) in Budapest who appears to renounce
all his beliefs when he falls into the hands of the secret police, but who emerges
as a man with backbone. Under torture he rediscovers his manhood. In short,
Tabori at his most idealistic.
    But then the world grows darker and Tabori begins to shift from naturalism
toward a more abstract, less lyrical, and far harsher theatre. He began adapting Brecht, e.g., *Brecht on Brecht* and *Arturo Ui,* and his own work became
more detached, more sardonic, more abstract, more song-and-dance oriented.
By the time of *The Cannibals* in 1968, the work was very dry, very dark, very
bitter, very removed. In a Nazi concentration camp, the prisoners decide to
cook and eat their friend Puffi, the fat man who has just died. Hirschler says:

> (To Uncle who is protesting the cannibalism) Listen, Uncle, let's have
> some perspective. The cake is too small. Whenever you eat, you take a
> crumb out of someone else's mouth. At this very moment, while you're

making such a fuss, millions are starving to death in India; but today we may have stumbled on the most elegant solution. The graveyards are full of goodies; the chimneys are going full blast, and nice fat suicides come floating down every river and stream. All that perfectly good stuff going to waste.

Shades of Swift's *A Modest Proposal*. And the cannibalism, which Tabori treats both literally and as a metaphor, is painted as inexorable. At the end of the play, The Loudspeakers place the action in historic context:

... some savages eagerly desire the body of a murdered man
So that his ghost may not trouble them,
For which reason I recommend, dear brethren in Christ,
The Jew's heart, in aspic or with sauce vinaigrette,
So soft it will melt in your mouth.

In The *Niggerlovers* Tabori views the racial tensions that afflict the U.S., but any sympathy is sublimated. No one comes off with any saving grace, the white liberals are stupid or saccharine or slightly perverted, the blacks are corroded with cynicism. No action seems to be of any help, there is no way out.

Pinkville studies the development of an American killer—specifically how the U.S. army takes a non-violent, righteous young man, and using his very righteousness, subverts him into the killer it needs to massacre Vietnamese. Again the action is inexorable. Everything becomes grist for the army's purpose. Again the world is so self-enclosed that there is no way out.

And yet the way out is through the action of Tabori's art. For the very work is a cry. The sardonic element has within it a taint of satisfaction, as if the worst is always somehow satisfying, but the worst is also an indictment of us, ultimately a call. For the early heroes are gone, no heroes left in the later plays, nothing for us to emulate. You and I become the only possible heroes left to Tabori and to the world.

—Arthur Sainer

TAYLOR, Cecil P(hilip).

Born in Glasgow, Scotland, 6 November 1929. Educated at Queen's Park Secondary School, Glasgow. Married Irene Diamond in 1955; Elizabeth Screen, 1967; four children. Worked as an electrician; engineer; salesman; journalist; literary adviser, for the Northumberland Youth Theatre Association, Shiremoor, 1968–81, and for the Tyneside Theatre Trust and the Everyman Theatre, Liverpool, 1971–81. Director of the Writers' Workshop, Northumberland, 1969–81. Script editor, *Burns* series of television plays; writer for BBC Educational Television. Recipient: Arts Council bursary, 1965; Scottish Television Theatre award, 1969. *Died 1981.*

Publications

PLAYS

Aa Went te Blaydon Races, music by Cecil P. Taylor (produced 1962).
Happy Days Are Here Again (produced 1965). In *New English Dramatists* 12, 1968.

Of Hope and Glory (produced 1965).
Fable (produced 1965). In *Traverse Plays*, 1967.
Allergy (produced 1966). In *Traverse Plays*. 1966.
Bread and Butter (produced 1966). In *New English Dramatists 10*, 1967.
Who's Pinkus? Where's Chelm? music by Monty Norman (produced 1966).
Mister David (produced 1967).
The Ballachulish Beat: A Play with Songs. Music by Cecil P. Taylor, 1967.
Oil and Water (televised, 1967; produced 1972).
What Can a Man Do (produced 1968).
Happy Anniversary (televised, 1968; produced 1972).
Thank You Very Much (produced 1969). 1970.
Lies about Vietnam/truth about Sarajevo (produced 1969). Published as *The Truth about Sarajevo: A Play for the Traverse Theatre*, 1970.
Brave (produced 1970).
Revolution (televised, 1970). Section entitled *Charles and Cromwell*, in *Making a Television Play*, 1970.
The Cleverness of Us (produced 1971).
Bloch's Play (televised, 1971; produced 1971). 1971.
Grace Darling Show (produced 1971).
Passion Play, in Christmas Present (produced 1971).
Em'n Ben (produced 1971).
Ginger Golly and the Fable Men (for children: produced 1972).
The Black and White Minstrels (produced 1972).
Me (produced 1972).
Words (televised, 1972). In *Second Playbill 2*, edited by Alan Durband, 1973.
Peer Gynt, adaptation of the play by Ibsen (produced 1972; as *Gynt*, produced 1975.
Antigone, adaptation of the play by Sophocles (produced 1972).
Threepenny Opera, adaptation of a play by Brecht, music by Kurt Weill (produced 1972).
You Are My Heart's Delight (produced 1973).
The Grand Adultery Convention (produced 1973).
Next Year in Tel Aviv (produced 1973).
Drums in the Night, adaptation of a play by Brecht (produced 1973).
5P Opera (produced 1973).
Waiting for Lefty, adaptation of the play by Clifford Odets (produced 1973).
Apples (produced 1973). In *Prompt One*, edited by Alan Durband, 1976.
Columba (produced 1973).
Carol O.K. (produced 1974).
Schippel, adaptation of the play *Sternheim* (produced 1974; as *The Plumber's Progress*, produced 1975).
So Far So Bad (produced 1974).
Spital Tongue Plays (produced 1974).
Pilgrim (produced 1975).
The Killingworth Play (produced 1975).
All Change, with Alex Glasgow (produced 1975).
Aladdin (produced 1976).
Bandits (produced 1976).
Goldberg (produced 1976).

Walter (produced 1977).
Ophelia (produced 1977).
Peter Pan and Emily (produced 1977).
Geordie Jubilee (produced 1977).
Withdrawal Symptoms (produced 1978).
A Nightingale Sang in Eldon Square (produced 1978).
Not by Love Alone (produced 1978).
Magic Island (produced 1978).
Give Us a Kiss (produced 1978).
Open the Big Box (produced 1978).
Cyrano (produced 1978).
Ali Baba (produced 1978).
Operation Elvis (produced 1979).
Peter Pan Man (produced 1979).
Rainbow Coloured Disco Dancer (produced 1980).
To Be a Farmer's Boy (produced 1980).
Give Me Sunshine, Give Me Smiles (produced 1980).

RADIO PLAY: *Love Story*, 1966.

TELEVISION PLAYS: *Lone Rider*, 1966; *Myopia*, 1967; *Oil and Water*, 1967;
Friends, 1967; *Happy Anniversary*, 1968; *Thank You very Much for the
Family Circle*, 1968; *In Case*, 1969; *Street Fighter*, 1969; *Revolutionary*
(trilogy: *Charles and Cromwell, Lenin, Castro*), 1970; *Bloch's Play*, 1971;
Adam Smith series, 1972); *Words*, 1972; *King and Cuthbertson*, 1974; *Izzie*
(*Nightingale's Boys* series), 1975; *The First Train Now Arriving*, from work
by Hunter Davies, 1975; *For Services to Myself*, 1976.

OTHER

*Making a Television Play: A Complete Guide from Conceptions to B.B.C.
Production, Based on the Making of the Play "Charles and Cromwell" for
B.B.C. "Thirty Minute Theatre."* 1970.

MANUSCRIPT COLLECTIONS: National Library, Edinburgh; Central Library,
Newcastle upon Tyne.

CRITICAL STUDIES: *Anger and After* and *The Second Wave* by John Russell
Taylor, 1962, 1971; prefaces to *New English Dramatists* 10, 12, 14, 1967,
1968, 1969; "The Plays of Cecil P. Taylor" by Alastair Cording in *Scottish
Theatre*, iii, 4, 1971.

Cecil P. Taylor wrote:

A gradual scaling down of ambition is the best description of my development
as a playwright. Starting with the aim of the theatre as a potent instrument of
the revolution, I have been beaten down to theatre as another of the communication arts. I used to write plays, such as *Blaydon Races*, genuinely convinced
they would move the workers, by the insights the plays gave into great political
truths, to the revolution. I now write plays as a novelist writes novels or a poet

poetry—to communicate my narrow, odd vision of the world as I am seeing it at the time of writing. Always in the hope that my hang-ups, flaws, insecurities and so on will cross at times those of my audience and they might feel a bit less on their own in this big world, as I do when I read a real book or see a real play.

I don't accept categories in writing, "expressionist," "naturalist," etc. The content, if it is a real play, determines form. I don't like to see actors acting or "plays" in the theatre. I have to be caught up completely in the world of the play, or the play has failed. I suppose it's an arbitrary kind of rule but I tend to think and work to it: if it's true, it's good, if it's false, it's bad.

Cecil P. Taylor's best plays are naturalistic comedies, often set in the Gorbals district of Glasgow, Taylor's home town, but the implications of these stories are neither local nor particularly Scottish. Taylor was a socialist but his plays derive their distinctive humour from the wry recognition that people who profess socialist ideals are rarely able to carry them out in daily life. Taylor had a wonderful ear for inappropriate political jargon. In *Allergy*, his one-act play, Jim, the editor of *Socialist Reflection* (circulation 150 copies), seduces Barbara by saying that "you're the first woman I've met who's sparked off insights in me" —insights (that is) about the course of world revolution. Morris (in *Bread and Butter*) is convinced that Hitler (in the early 1930s) is really taking part in the glorious class struggle by only menacing rich Jews. Taylor's comedies have sometimes been interpreted as concealed attacks on socialism, simply because the characters who talk most about the revolution are obviously incapable of running anything—either an affair, a small newspaper or a car. When a journalist like Christopher (in *Allergy*) gets a decent job, his revolutionary fervour dwindles away. Taylor (it has been suggested) celebrates a sell-out to capitalism: and for this reason his plays in Glasgow—such as *Me* at the Citizens Theatre—have suffered from two types of attack, from those who are distressed by the "bad language" and "immorality" of his plays and from those who deplore the images of comic self-deception among socialists, from the political left and right.

But Taylor was not primarily a political dramatist—in the sense that his plays are not concealed polemic. "The first thing a play has to be about . . ." he wrote, "is people: their relationships to one another and to the society they live in". *Bread and Butter*, his first major success, concerns two Scottish-Jewish couples, Morris and Sharon, and Alec and Miriam, as they grow up and grow old together in Glasgow. The play covers a time-span from 1931 to 1965, a fact which suggests that *Bread and Butter* is a historical documentary. But, in fact, the external history is incidental to the main story which is about the way in which they adjust to one another and to life. Morris, the son of a rich man, is an incurable optimist, believing that the socialist revolution is round the corner: Alec is his working-class friend, poor but doggedly surviving through dreary jobs, until by the end of World War II their financial situations have changed. Morris is ruined: Alec is doing well, although Miriam his wife keeps a tight hand on the purse. From these slight biographies of apparently uninteresting people, Taylor manages to construct a play which is both funny and absorbing: and his skill is shown by the way in which the superficial incidents of the first act gain a depth of significance in the second. The play moves with an easy relaxation towards greater profundity. Morris's optimism becomes a domineering control over his wife: Alec's peaceful acceptance of hardship becomes a sort of masochism, from which he makes only tentative efforts to escape. The dialogue throughout contains this gentle irony, somewhat similar to Bernard Malamud's style, which pokes fun at hope without disavowing it.

The Black and White Minstrels is again an ambitious play which moves from small incidents to major themes. It does not however spread over a wide span of time. Two couples live together in a Glasgow house, sharing partners by rota system to prove their togetherness. A black girl, renting a room in the same house, causes trouble: and the couples gang up against her, partly because she's a puritan and aggressive and partly out of sheer loyalty to each other. But they're socialists too, and therefore to defend the landlord (who is one of them) against a black tenant in a Rent Tribunal court causes them much private anguish. Their cause succeeds: but from the tension between the ideals they profess and the problems they face, the community spirit, fragile enough at the best of times, starts to disintegrate. Taylor manages to balance many themes around this pivot—the impotency of Harry, the harassment of Cyril, an impoverished writer, the earnest maternalism of Pat, and the quieter affection of Gill: and the play accumulates meanings and interest as it progresses, always the sign of a good play.

Allergy is a delightful one-act play: about a journalist, Christopher, who is allergic to adultery but can't avoid seducing girls, and an editor, Jim, who takes over his unconsummated affairs. In Gynt, 1975, his adaptation of Ibsen's Peer Gynt, performed by the Traverse Theatre, Edinburgh, Taylor presents three different stages in Peer Gynt's life as three characters, each of whom alternately play the scenes and watch the others doing so. By that means, Taylor tries to show that Gynt is continually making the choices which lead to his death at the hands of the button-moulder. Death is present in the first scene, as well as the last: and so is Gynt's youth. Time does not pass, but rather repeats itself. Gynt is perhaps the most successful of Taylor's allegories. He did, however, written several non-naturalistic plays: notably documentary for the Northumberland Youth Theatre, Thank You Very Much, and several allegories, Happy Days are Here Again, Who's Pinkus? Where's Chelm? and his first play, Mister David (written in 1962). But Taylor's great talent for discovering humour and relevance within small totally plausible incidents tends to get lost in the broader, more slapdash style of his documentaries and allegories. In one scene from Thank You Very Much, a father meets his daughter's suitor believing that the young man wants to buy his greyhound, and the cross-talk between them provides a good revue sketch—but quite without the Glasgow-Yiddish humour of his naturalistic plays. In Who's Pinkus? Where's Chelm?, a fool leaves a city of fools to seek his fortune in the neighbouring town of Mazeltov (Yiddish for good luck): he fails in his quest, but returns to his home town with tales of success, thus establishing a legendary reputation for business acumen. Pinkus is an amusing central character but the play seems loosely strung together and rather superficial. Taylor's best political plays, such as Lies about Vietnam, are basically naturalistic and two-edged in their attacks.

—John Elsom

TERSON, Peter.

Pseudonym for Peter Patterson. Born in Newcastle upon Tyne, Northumberland, 24 February 1932. Educated at Heaton Grammar School; Newcastle upon Tyne Technical College; Redland Training College, Bristol, 1952–54. Served in the Royal Air Force, 1950–52. Married Sheila Bailey in 1955; two sons and one daughter. Draughtsman, 1948–50; games teacher, 1953–65. Resident writer, Victoria Theatre, Stoke-on-Trent, Staffordshire, 1966–67; associated with the National Youth Theatre. Recipient: Arts Council bursary, 1966; John Whiting award, 1968; Writers Guild award, 1971. Agent: Lemon, Unna, and Durbridge, 24 Pottery Lane, Holland Park, London W11 4LZ, England.

Publications

PLAYS

A Night to Make the Angels Weep (produced 1964). In *New English Dramatists 11*, 1967.
The Mighty Reservoy (produced 1964). In *New English Dramatists 14*, 1970.
The Rat Run (produced 1965).
All Honour Mr. Todd (produced 1966).
I'm in Charge of These Ruins (produced 1966).
Sing an Arful Story, with others (produced 1966).
Jock-on-the-Go, adaptation of the story "Jock-at-a-Venture" by Arnold Bennett (produced 1966).
Holder Dying (extracts produced 1966).
Mooney and His Caravans (televised 1966; produced 1968). With *Zigger Zagger*, 1970.
Zigger Zagger (produced 1967). With *Mooney and His Caravans*, 1970.
Clayhanger, with Joyce Cheeseman, adaptation of the novel by Arnold Bennett (produced 1967).
The Ballad of the Artificial Mash (produced 1967).
The Apprentices (produced London, 1968). 1970.
The Adventures of Gervase Beckett; or, The Man Who Changed Places (produced 1969). Edited by Peter Cheeseman, 1973.
Fuzz (produced 1969).
Inside-Outside (produced 1970).
The Affair at Bennett's Hill, (Worcs.) (produced 1970).
Spring-Heeled Jack (produced 1970). In *Plays and Players*, November 1970.
The 1861 Whitby Lifeboat Disaster (produced 1970). 1979.
The Samaritan, with Mike Butler (produced 1971). In *Plays and Players*, July 1971.
Cadium Firty (produced 1971).
Good Lads at Heart (produced 1971).
Slip Road Wedding (produced 1971).
Prisoners of the War (produced 1971).
But Fred, Freud Is Dead (produced 1972). In *Plays and Players*, March 1972.
Moby Dick, adaptation of the novel by Melville (produced 1972).
The Most Cheerful Man (produced 1973).

Geordie's March (produced 1973).
The Trip to Florence (produced 1974).
Lost Yer Tongue? (produced 1974).
Vince Lays the Carpet, and Fred Erects the Tent (produced 1975).
The Ballad of Ben Bagot (televised 1977). In *Prompt 2*, edited by Alan Durband, 1976.
Love Us and Leave Us, with Paul Joyce (produced 1976).
The Bread and Butter Trade (produced 1976; revised version produced 1982).
Twilight Joker (produced 1977).
Pinvin Careless and His Lines of Force (produced 1977).
Family Ties: Wrong First Time; Never Right, Yet Again (produced 1977). In *Act 2*, edited by David Self and Ray Speakman, 1979.
Forest Lodge (produced 1977).
Tolly of the Black Boy (produced 1977).
Rattling the Railings (produced 1978). 1979.
The Banger (produced 1978).
Cul de Sac (produced 1978).
England, My Own (produced 1978).
Soldier Boy (produced 1978).
VE Night (produced 1979).
The Limes, and I Kid You Not (produced 1979).
The Pied Piper, adaptation of the poem by Robert Browning, music by Jeff Parton (produced 1980). 1982.
The Ticket (produced 1980).
The Night John (produced 1980).
We Were All Heroes (produced 1981).
Aesop's Fables, music by Jeff Parton (produced 1983). 1986.
Strippers (produced 1984). 1985.
Hotel Dorado (produced 1985).
The Weeping Madonna. In *New Plays 1: Contemporary One-Act Plays*, edited by Terson, 1988.

RADIO PLAYS: *The Fishing Party*, 1971; *Play Soft, Then Attack*, 1978; *The First Flame*, 1980; *The Rundle Gibbet*, 1981; *The Overnight Man*, 1982; *The Romany Trip* (documentary), 1983; *The Top Sail at Imberley*, 1983; *Madam Main Course*, 1983; *Poole Harbour*, 1984; *Letters to the Otter*, 1985; *When Youth and Pleasure Meet*, 1986; *The Mumper*, 1988; *Blind Down the Thames*, 1988; *Stones, Tops, and Tarns*, 1989; *Tales My Father Taught Me*, 1990.

TELEVISION PLAYS: *Mooney and His Caravans*, 1966; *The Heroism of Thomas Chadwick*, 1967; *The Last Train Through the Harecastle Tunnel*, 1969; *The Gregorian Chant*, 1972; *The Dividing Fence*, 1972; *Shakespeare—or Bust*, 1973; *Three for the Fancy*, 1973; *Dancing in the Dark*, 1974; *The Rough and the Smooth*, 1975; *The Jolly Swagman*, with Paul Joyce (*Crown Court* series), 1976; *The Ballad of Ben Bagot*, 1977; *The Reluctant Chosen*, 1979; *Put Out to Grass*, 1979; *Atlantis*, 1983; *Salvation Army* series.

OTHER

The Offcuts Voyage. 1988.

Editor, *New Plays 1: Contemporary One-Act Plays.* 1988.
Editor, *New Plays 2: Contemporary One-Act Plays.* 1988.
Editor, *New Plays 3: Contemporary One-Act Plays.* 1989.

Peter Terson has been called a "primitive," a term which (in its complimentary sense) is intended to mean that his technique is artless, his observation fresh and original, and his naturally prolific talent untainted by too much sophistication. This somewhat backhanded tribute, however, belittles his ability. Few dramatists have the sheer skill to write successfully for both the small "in the round" theatre company at the Victoria, Stoke-on-Trent, and the large casts of the British National Youth Theatre, whose London productions take place in conventional proscenium arch theatres. Nor is Terson unknowledgeable about recent trends in the theatre. He insisted, for example, that Harry Philton in *Zigger Zagger*, the boy who escapes from the mindless enthusiams of a football crowd to learn a trade, should not "mature or have a *Roots*-like vision of himself"—thus pushing aside one cliché of contemporary naturalistic drama. One under-rated aspect of Terson's style is the way in which he either avoids an idea which has become too fashionable or twists it to his own ends. In *The Mighty Reservoy* he plays with the Lawrentian theme of the dark, elemental forces of nature and makes it seem both credible as a psychological obsession and (through this haunting power over the mind) a force indeed to be feared. Terson is, however, ruthless with the pretentiousness of middle-class theatre: on receiving a Promising Playwright's Award from Lord Goodman, he enquired whether Green Shield stamps went with it. This latent cheekiness is also part of his plays. Although he rarely ventures into the class polemic of some of Alan Plater's documentaries, he usually caricatures people in authority: magistrates and social workers (in *Zigger Zagger*), scientists and business tycoons (in *The Ballad of the Artificial Mash*) and the paternalistic firm (in *The Apprentices*). He chooses working-class rather than middle-class themes and environments, and writes with particular passion about his own childhood in Newcastle upon Tyne, the poverty and unemployment of the 1930's. This refusal to accept the normal attitudes of the West End coupled with his strong regional loyalties, may help to account for his reputation as a "primitive": but for this very reason the term is misleading. He doesn't write popular West End comedies because he doesn't choose to do so; he doesn't write about middle-class families in the grip of emotional dilemmas because the problems which he tackles seem to him more important. He is a highly skilled writer with a particular insight into Northern working-class societies and whose plays have, at best, a richness of imagination and an infectious humour.

Terson's first plays were produced at the Victoria Theatre, Stoke-on-Trent, a pioneering Midlands company directed by Peter Cheeseman whose work concentrates on "in the round" productions, plays with local associations and documentary plays. Terson caught immediately the company style and became their resident playwright in 1966. His first plays, *A Night to Make the Angels Weep* and *The Mighty Reservoy*, were naturalistic comedies but with strong underlying themes. *The Mighty Reservoy* is set in the Cotswolds, on a large reservoir built on a hill, which is guarded by Dron. The reservoir is presented as a passionate force of water, which might at any time swamp the surrounding villages. Dron has an affectionate pride towards it: and he introduces his friend Church to its mysteries, among them that the water demands one human sacrifice before it will be satisfied. Church eventually becomes this sacrifice. But the dialogue between the two men ranges from intimate, slightly drunken chat about their dissatisfactions about life to a passionate yearning for union with nature. *Mooney and His Caravans*, another two-person play written for the Victoria Theatre, represents a different type of "drowning": a couple on a caravan site are gradually driven away from their home by the aggressive commercialism of Mooney, whom they admire and who owns the site. With these small cast, tightly knit naturalistic plays, Terson also wrote several looser, more flexible and easy-going works, such as *Jock-on-the-Go*, a picaresque tale about a lad on the make in 19th-century Yorkshire, and *The Ballad of the Artificial Mash*, a horror story about the effect of hormone poultry foods on a salesman, one of the first and most effective plays about environmental pollution. Both these plays were in the style of the Stoke documentaries: short scenes, mainly satirical, brought together by songs and dances written and performed by the company. Although Terson left the Victoria Theatre in 1967, the influence of its informal atmosphere, the economy of means and the easiness of story-telling (using a narrator and props to indicate change of locale) remained with Terson as a formative inspiration. He has since written other plays for the company, including *But Fred, Freud Is Dead*, an amusing Northern comedy.

In 1966 Michael Croft, the director of the National Youth Theatre, invited Terson to write a play for his largely amateur group of schoolchildren and young adults. Terson's first play for the company, *Zigger Zagger*, was enormously successful, although its story seems flimsy and episodic. Harry Philton leaves school without distinction, and drifts from one job to another, from his unhappy home to his well-intentioned brother-in-law, sustained at first by his love of football. Eventually, however, this craze for football leaves him and he settles down to a proper trade apprenticeship. Terson sets this story against a background of a (pre-hooligan) football terrace, with fans whose songs and attitudes comment on the main events of the story. The exuberance of the production, the nostalgia and fervour of the football crowds provide an unforgettable image of surging humanity, charged with a youthful energy which only heightened the sad frustrations of Harry's career. *The Apprentices* tackled a somewhat similar theme, but more naturalistically. Bagley, a young tearaway, works reluctantly in a local factory—playing football whenever he has the opportunity. He deliberately scorns all opportunities for promotion, determined to leave the town and his job as soon as he can: but he is trapped into an unwise marriage and at the end of the play he is resigned to a dull frustrating future. *Spring-Heeled Jack* and *Good Lads at Heart*, two other plays written for the National Youth Theatre, explore the frustrations of the misfits in an impoverished society.

Although Terson's plays have a much greater variety and range than is often supposed, he usually limits himself to social surroundings with which he is familiar: and perhaps the least satisfactory part of this limitation is that he shares some stock reactions, say, about the awfulness of progress and the craftsmanship of the past which are expressed rather too often in his plays. He also fails to pare down his documentary plays to the dramatic essentials. But his influence in British regional theatre has been considerable, and more than any other contemporary dramatist he carries forward the ideas of social drama pioneered by Joan Littlewood.

—John Elsom

TOWNSEND, Sue (Susan Lilian Townsend).

Born in Leicester, 2 April 1946. Educated at South Wigston Girls High School, Leicestershire. Married 1) in 1964 (divorced 1971), two sons and one daughter; 2) Colin Broadway in 1985, one daughter. Member of the Writer's Group, Phoenix Arts Centre, Leicester, 1978. Recipient: Thames Television bursary, 1979. Lives in Leicester. Agent: Anthony Sheil Associates, 43 Doughty Street, London WC1N 2LF, England.

Publications

PLAYS

In the Club and Up the Spout (produced 1979).
Womberang (produced 1980; as *The Waiting Room*, produced 1982). In *Bazaar and Rummage, Groping for Words, and Womberang*, 1984.
The Ghost of Daniel Lambert, music by Rick Lloyd (produced 1981).
Dayroom (produced 1981).
Bazaar and Rummage (produced 1982). In *Bazaar and Rummage, Groping for Words, and Womberang*, 1984.
Captain Christmas and the Evil Adults (produced 1982).
Groping for Words (produced 1983; revised version, as *Are You Sitting Comfortably?*, produced 1986; as *Groping for Words*, produced 1988). In *Bazaar and Rummage, Groping for Words, and Womberang*, 1984.
Clients (produced 1983).
Bazaar and Rummage, Groping for Words, and Womberang. 1984.
The Great Celestial Cow (produced 1984). 1984.
The Secret Diary of Adrian Mole Aged 13³/₄, songs by Ken Howard and Alan Blaikley (produced 1984). 1985.
Ear, Nose and Throat (produced 1988). 1989.
Ten Tiny Fingers, Nine Tiny Toes (produced 1989). 1990.
Disneyland It Ain't (produced 1990).

RADIO PLAYS: *The Diary of Nigel Mole Aged 13³/₄*, 1982; *The Growing Pains of Adrian Mole*, 1984; *The Great Celestial Cow*, 1985; *The Ashes*, 1991.

TELEVISION PLAYS: *Revolting Women* series, 1981; *Bazaar and Rummage*, 1984; *The Secret Diary of Adrian Mole* series, 1985; *The Growing Pains of Adrian Mole*, 1987; *The Refuge* series, with Carole Hayman, 1987; *Think of England* series, 1991.

NOVELS

The Adrian Mole Diaries. 1985.
The Secret Diary of Adrian Mole Aged 13³/4. 1982.
The Growing Pains of Adrian Mole. 1984.
Rebuilding Coventry: A Tale of Two Cities. 1988.
Adrian Mole from Minor to Major. 1991.
The Queen and I. 1992.

OTHER

*The True Confessions of Adrian Albert Mole, Margaret Hilda Roberts, and
   Susan Lilian Townsend.* 1989.
Mr. Bevan's Dream. 1989.

Sue Townsend comments:

I suppose I write about people who do not live in the mainstream of society.
My characters are not educated; they do not earn high salaries (if they work at
all). I look beneath the surface of their lives. My plays are about loneliness,
struggle, survival, and the possibility of change.

   Strangely, they are also comedies. Comedy is the most tragic form of
drama.

Sue Townsend writes compassionate comedy whose power comes from its
intermittently hard edge. A comedy with serious intentions is nothing new. But
what is distinctive about the sometimes gentle, sometimes tough comedy
Townsend writes is her ability to balance buoyant laughter with biting social
commentary. In what she has called "problem plays," Townsend presents
groups whose troubles are conventionally ignored: agoraphobics, adult illiterates, Asian women immigrants. In her most recent work, she has written
increasingly on politically volatile issues like national health and institutional
attitudes to childbearing and children. She is optimistic that by comically
encouraging awareness of such groups and issues in a diverse audience (she
hopes to attract working-class people back to the theatre) her theatre can
contribute to social change.

   In *Bazaar and Rummage* genial comedy cushions the revealing and disturbing study of three agoraphobics and their two social workers. Here Townsend
refines the tendencies already apparent in her early theatre script *Womberang*,
tendencies which characterize most of her plays: a group and not an individual
is at the center of the action, the play refuses conventional descriptions of its
plot, and the comedy is generated by community and concern. Townsend
describes plays like *Bazaar*, which offer a "group against the world," as "closet
plays," "enclosed plays," to emphasize her focus on neglected social problems.
In *Bazaar* she engages her predilection for dealing with "the change in [such] a
group" by presenting a trio of agoraphobics venturing from home for the first
time in years, flanked by the two amateur social workers attempting to aid
them. Instead of focusing on one of the characters and her progress toward
health, Townsend balances the advances and setbacks in the lives of all five

women; progress toward self-understanding is not a function of individual awareness but of group members supporting one another through crises. The plot which such communal character development creates is more circular than linear. There is a passing of awareness from one character to another until the group's collected courage allows for a collective exit onto an Acton street. Townsend's approach to comedy in this play occasioned a notable critical debate. The marriage of very funny lines to a feminist message moved some reviewers to dismiss the effort as "glib," "quirky," or "not too seriously meant," and motivated Michael Billington to warn the playwright that laughter "can't be used simply to decorate." But Townsend herself describes the combination of comedy and women as natural. Laughter, she explains, is "how women cope and have coped for centuries." She sees comedy as the most powerful tool available to her as an aid in reaching people; and in *Bazaar*, by allowing her audience to laugh with the agoraphobics, she encourages compassion and enables reflection. While theatre critics have found comedy variously revolutionary or reactionary, Townsend uses it to approach tough social issues and sees it—perhaps for that reason—as "a basic need of the human body."

Townsend's concern turns from women's special problems to the class issue of illiteracy in *Are You Sitting Comfortably?* (an earlier version was called *Groping for Words*). The play shares its class-conscious focus with *The Secret Diary of Adrian Mole Aged 13³/4*, the play version of Townsend's successful novel. Both plays portray working-class characters seeking personal and social validation, but to the very light touch of *Adrian Mole* Townsend adds, in *Are You Sitting Comfortably?*, a pointed political message—a condemnation of the British class structure which seems to require illiterates. The play's class conflict is manifest in the encounter of the well-positioned, middle-class Joyce—the novice literacy instructor—and her three working-class students, George, Thelma, and Kevin. As in *Bazaar*, Townsend again keys the play's action to the symbiotic developments within this group. By the end of the play Joyce must acknowledge that her liberalism effects little social change, but Kevin vocalizes what all the others are scared to. In the play's chilling ending, he realizes that the world doesn't "want us to read! There ain't room for all of us is there?" This painful truth gels not just in Kevin, however, but also in the group. The audience, too, must join in this difficult collective realization, for as it laughs, it is being asked, 'are *you* sitting comfortably?" This play may be the clearest example of Townsend's comic gifts, but also evidence of her commitment to using comedy to urge re-thinking and re-considering.

In two recent works, Townsend moves further in her engagement with political issues. *Ten Tiny Fingers, Nine Tiny Toes* is set in a future where two couples are curiously joined in their attempt to maintain some control over their offspring. In a right-wing society strictly compartmentalized by class, Lucinda and Ralph, the equivalent of an upper-working-class couple, conceive a baby in a government-sanctioned laboratory procedure. In distinct contrast, Dot and Pete, unskilled labourers relegated to perish on the fringes of organized society, conceive naturally—and illegally. When the two mothers meet, awaiting childbirth in a shared hospital room, they bond through recognition of how much the institutions around them devalue both women and the life they produce. Their connection empowers them to challenge the government hegemony. When Lucinda's daughter is destroyed by the authorities because of a deformity (a missing toe), the two conspire to share the breastfeeding and rearing of Dot's baby boy. With both husbands rejected (for their failure to behave admirably to the stress of births gone wrong), the two women face an uncertain future together; yet, as in previous plays, Townsend provides an upbeat ending in which these women brave the future on their own terms. In the one-act *Disneyland It Ain't*, children again provide the focus as Maureen pleads with "Mr. Mouse" to visit her dying 10-year-old daughter. As the British mother and the American carnival worker puzzle through his reluctance to help, her rage and his fear frame a discussion which ranges from national health insurance to consumerism to religious apostasy. All the while, the grim specter of the dying child shadows the caustic and clever dialogue. In theatrical shorthand, Townsend displays her ability to combine the trials of day-to-day survival with a hope she and her most burdened characters manage to eke out.

In fiction as well as in drama, Townsend continues to fuse comedy and serious matter. In her novel *Rebuilding Coventry*, Townsend creates a slightly bizarre, often comic, but deadly serious narrative centered on a woman who discovers she has options in her life only as a result of unintentionally murdering a man strangling his wife. Townsend's feminism and class consciousness—active in both genres—are leading her on a constant quest for new forms and formats. But it is in her plays especially where she has worked, through her comedy, to bring people together both inside and outside of the play's frame.

—Susan Carlson

TRAVERS, Ben(jamin).

Born in Hendon, Middlesex, 12 November 1886. Educated at the Abbey School, Beckenham, Kent; Charterhouse, Godalming, Surrey, until 1904; studied in Dresden, 1904. Served in the Royal Naval Air Service, 1914–17: squadron commander; transferred to the Royal Flying Corps as major, 1918: Air Force Cross, 1920; joined the Royal Air Force, 1939: squadron leader, attached to Ministry of Information, 1940. Married Violet Mouncey in 1916 (died 1951); one daughter and two sons. Worked in the family wholesale grocery business, John Travers and Sons, in London, 1904 and 1909–11, and in Singapore and Malacca, 1905–08; staff member, Bodley Head, publishers, London, 1911–14; full-time writer from 1919: wrote nine 'Aldwych farces,' 1925–33. Prime warden, Fishmongers Company, London, 1946; president, Dramatists Club, 1956–60. Recipient: Evening Standard award, 1975. CBE (Commander, Order of the British Empire), 1976. *Died 18 December 1980.*

Publications

PLAYS

The Dippers, from his novel (produced 1922).
The Three Graces, from the play by Carl Lombardi and A.M. Willner, music by Franz Lehar (produced 1924).
A Cuckoo in the Nest, from his novel (produced 1925). 1938.
Rookery Nook, from his novel (produced 1926). 1930.

Thark (produced 1927). 1932.
Plunder (produced 1928). 1931.
Mischief, from his novel (produced 1928).
A Cup of Kindness (produced 1929). 1934.
A Night Like This (produced 1930).
Turkey Time (produced 1931). 1934.
Dirty Work (produced 1932).
A Bit of a Test (produced 1933).
Chastity, My Brother (produced 1936).
Nun's Veiling (as *O Mistress Mine*, produced 1936; revised version, as *Nun's
    Veiling*, produced 1953). 1956.
Banana Ridge (produced 1938). 1939.
Spotted Dick (produced 1939).
She Follows Me About (produced 1943). 1945.
Outrageous Fortune (produced 1947). 1948.
Runaway Victory (produced 1949).
Wild Horses (produced 1952). 1953.
Corker's End (produced 1968).
The Bed Before Yesterday (produced 1975). In *Five Plays*, 1977.
Five Plays (includes *A Cuckoo in the Nest; Rookery Nook; Thark; Plunder;
    The Bed Before Yesterday*). 1977.
After You with the Milk. 1985.

SCREENPLAYS: *A Little Bit of Fluff (Skirts)*, with Ralph Spence and Wheeler
Dryden, 1928; *Rookery Nook (One Embarrassing Night)*, with W.P.
Lipscomb, 1930; *Thark*, 1932; *A Night Like This*, 1932; *Just My Luck*, 1933;
Turkey Time, 1933; *A Cuckoo in the Nest*, with A.R. Rawlinson, 1933; *Up to
the Neck*, 1933; *Dirty Work*, 1934; *Lady in Danger*, 1934; *A Cup of
Kindness*, 1934; *Fighting Stock*, 1935; *Stormy Weather*, 1935; *Foreign
Affaires*, 1935; *Pot Luck*, 1936; *Dishonour Bright*, 1936; *For Valour*, 1937;
Second Best Bed, 1938; *Old Iron*, 1938; *So This is London*, with others, 1939;
Banana Ridge, with Walter C. Mycroft and Lesley Storm, 1941; *Uncle Silas
(The Inheritance)*, 1947; *Fast and Loose*, with A.R. Rawlinson, 1954.

TELEVISION PLAYS: *Potter*, 1948; *Picture Page*, 1949.

NOVELS
The Dippers. 1920.
A Cuckoo in the Nest. 1922.
Rookery Nook. 1923.
Mischief. 1925.
The Dippers, Together with Game and Rubber and The Dunkum Jane. 1932.
*Hyde Side Up.*1933.

SHORT STORIES
The Collection Today. 1929.

OTHER
Vale of Laughter (autobiography). 1957.
A-Sitting on a Gate (autobiography). 1978.
94 Declared: Cricket Reminiscences. 1981.

Editor, *The Leacock Book.* 1930.
Editor, *Pretty Pictures, Being a Selection of the Best American Pictorial Humour.* 1932.

CRITICAL STUDY: *Modern British Farce* by Leslie Smith, 1989.

In a remarkably long career as a prolific dramatist, screenwriter, and novelist, Ben Travers enjoyed two distinct periods of fame and popularity. From 1925 to 1933 his series of nine farces delighted audiences at London's Aldwych Theatre. 50 years later, much to his own amazement, Travers was "rediscovered". In 1976 his highly successful new comedy *The Bed Before Yesterday* was running simultaneously in London with two farce revivals, *Plunder* and *Banana Ridge*. In the last six years of his life Travers became a much-feted theatrical personality, celebrated for his longevity and sprightliness and once more in favour with producers and audiences who, tired of social-realist plays, embraced the survivor of an earlier popular-theatre tradition. Ironically, the "rediscovery" had been launched by the Royal Court Theatre which had, uncharacteristically, revived *A Cuckoo in the Nest* in 1964; but in reality, many of the early farces had maintained their position in the repertoires of provincial and amateur theatres, and something akin to a folk-memory had formed around the Aldwych farces. Bearing scant relation to the political and social conditions of their time of writing they existed, like P.G. Wodehouse's novels with which they have much in common, in a timeless comic world.

Travers's theatrical roots reached back to Pinero, whose farces Travers studied for their construction, and to the acting styles of Seymour Hicks, Charles Hawtrey, and Gerald du Maurier. Travers stated his farce formula simply: "Act II—the sympathetic and guileless hero is landed in the thick of some grievous dilemma or adversity. Act I—he gets into it. Act III—he gets out of it". The best of his farces—*A Cuckoo in the Nest*, *Rookery Nook*, *Thark*, *Plunder*, and *A Night Like This*—are more loosely plotted and less urgent than Feydeau's, and rely on wordplay, nonsense, insults, set routines and eccentrically named characters who muddle through in peculiarly English fashion.

Almost invariably the plots feature a sympathetically raffish hero and his naive, flapping friend who press-gang a grotesquely hen-pecked husband into helping them out of a scrape involving an often scantily clad young woman in difficulties. Although nothing improper ever occurs, the men are panicked by the presence of sweet but suspicious fiancées and wives, or by middle-aged termagants in the shape of mothers-in-law, cleaning ladies, or hotelkeepers who patrol the plays sniffing out improprieties. Despite gross male incompetence, these mountainous guardians of respectability are ultimately trounced, the situation retrieved, and morality upheld.

Formulaic he may have been, but Travers was superbly served by the Aldwych company headed by Tom Walls and Ralph Lynn. Walls produced, and alternated portrayed irascible old buffers with an eye for a trim ankle with younger racy men-about-town, while monocled Lynn exercised precise vocal and physical comic timing as the silly-ass friends. A *Times* review of *Turkey Time* singled out Lynn's trick of "dropping verbal bricks and retrieving them an inch from the ground". The central male trio was completed by Robertson Hare as the gormless hen-pecked, put-upon friend, ruthlessly bullied by his co-conspirators. Among others in the regular team were Mary Brough, specialist in formidable matrons with a touch of vulgarity, and Winifred Shotter, who supplied the love interest in many of the farces. Something of their ensemble quality can be glimpsed in the filmed versions of these farces, despite their wooden direction.

So successful was Travers's formula that he rarely departed from it. One measure of the popularity of the Aldwych series is Travers' convention of having the principals speak their opening lines off-stage, allowing audiences their moment of recognition and applause without holding up the action. As the sequence progressed, audiences carried expectation and goodwill from one play to the next. Travers was in no position to deny them their favourite sequences: the two heroes acting incompetently in concert or warily in competition for the girl; the inveigling of the Hare character into some dubious escapade; the rehearsed excuses which founder disastrously when deployed. Playful language, which encompasses cross-talk, running gags, silly puns, comic vocal mannerisms and broken-backed insults, may look leaden on the page, but proved eminently performable. Modern revivals, however, have sometimes struggled to capture Travers' idiom, substituting over-elaborate business for the honed skills of the original players and the unscripted rapport they enjoyed with their audiences.

The sexual content of the farces is now so tame as to be almost non-existent. Bedroom scenes demonstrate the hero's discomfort rather than sexual prowess, and provide opportunities for extended comic routines. In *Cuckoo*, Wykeham (originally played by Lynn) attempts to snuggle down on the floor of a cramped bedroom of an inn, while his untroubled lady companion luxuriates in the bed, in a scene reminiscent of W.C. Fields's vaudeville sketch "A Night on the Porch". In *Thark* the two heroes uneasily share a bed in a haunted room. A bedroom becomes the scene of a fumbled jewel robbery in *Plunder*, while in the remaining farces, as *Rookery Nook*'s cleaning lady Mrs. Leverett says, "the other bedrooms is elsewhere". None of the early farces poses any real threat to conventional morality, with the exception of *Plunder*, a suspenseful mix of farce and thriller, described by Travers as "a nice study in ethics". It has the two leads murder one of the characters, and subversively proposes that all property is theft, a challenge muffled by Travers's manipulation of audience sympathy and his adoption of the gentleman crook format. *Plunder* alone anticipates later reworkings of the genre, notably Orton's *Loot*. Nevertheless, in Travers' farces, beneath the froth one can detect a muted plea for guilt-free sexual enjoyment which he finally voiced in his 90th year in *The Bed Before Yesterday*.

This comic and unexpectedly touching portrayal of the sexual awakening of a middle-aged woman reverses the conventions of his farces, which depict such women as unpleasured and unpleasurable and allow the men all the running; but the play carries a plot old-fashioned even for its 1930's setting. The later *After You with the Milk* entertainingly distinguishes between married love and sexual pleasure, but failed to gain comparable success. *Malacca Linda* remains unproduced. Travers' reputation seems certain to rest on his first, rather than last, flowering of talent.

—Ronald W. Strang

TREVOR, William.

Pseudonym for William Trevor Cox. Born in Mitchelstown, County Cork, 24 May 1928. Educated at St. Columba's College, Dublin, 1942–46; Trinity College, Dublin, B.A. 1950. Married Jane Ryan in 1952; two sons. History teacher, Armagh, Northern Ireland, 1951–53; art teacher, Rugby, England, 1953–55; sculptor in Somerset, 1955–60; advertising copywriter, Notley's, London, 1960–64. Recipient: *Transatlantic Review* prize, for fiction, 1964; Hawthornden prize, for fiction, 1965; Society of Authors travelling fellowship, 1972; Allied Irish Banks prize, for fiction, 1976; Heinemann award, for fiction, 1976; Whitbread award, 1976, 1983; Irish Community prize, 1979; BAFTA award, for television play, 1983. D. Litt.: University of Exeter, 1984; Trinity College, Dublin, 1986; D. Litt.: Queen's University, Belfast, 1989; National University, Cork, 1990. Member, Irish Academy of Letters. C.B.E. (Commander, Order of the British Empire), 1977. Lives in Devon, England. Agent: Peters, Fraser, and Dunlop Group, 503–504 The Chambers, Chelsea Harbour, Lots Road, London SW10 0FX, England; and Sterling Lord Literistic Inc., 1 Madison Avenue, New York, New York 10010, U.S.A.

Publications

PLAYS

The Elephant's Foot (produced 1965).
The Girl (televised 1967; produced 1968). 1968.
A Night with Mrs. da Tanka (televised 1968; produced 1972). 1972.
Going Home (broadcast 1970; produced 1972). 1972.
The Old Boys, adaptation of his own novel (produced 1971). 1971.
A Perfect Relationship (broadcast 1973; produced 1973). 1976.
The 57th Saturday (produced 1973).
Marriages (produced 1973). 1973.
Scenes from an Album (broadcast 1975; produced 1981). 1981.
Beyond the Pale (broadcast 1980). In *Best Radio Plays of 1980*, 1981.
Autumn Sunshine, adaptation of his own story (televised 1981; broadcast 1982). In *Best Radio Plays of 1982*, 1983.

RADIO PLAYS: *The Penthouse Apartment*, 1968; *Going Home*, 1970; *The Boarding House*, from his own novel, 1971; *A Perfect Relationship*, 1973; *Scenes from an Album*, 1975; *Attracta*, 1977; *Beyond the Pale*, 1980; *The Blue Dress*, 1981; *Travellers*, 1982; *Autumn Sunshine*, 1982; *The News from Ireland*, from his own story, 1986; *Events at Drimaghleen*, 1988; *Running Away*, 1988.

TELEVISION PLAYS: *The Baby-Sitter*, 1965; *Walk's End*, 1966; *The Girl*, 1967; *A Night with Mrs. da Tanka*, 1968; *The Mark-2 Wife*, 1969; *The Italian Table*, 1970; *The Grass Widows*, 1971; *O Fat White Woman*, 1972; *The Schoolroom*, 1972; *Access to the Children*, 1973; *The General's Day*, 1973; *Miss Fanshawe's Story*, 1973; *An Imaginative Woman*, from a story by Thomas Hardy, 1973; *Love Affair*, 1974; *Eleanor*, 1974; *Mrs. Acland's Ghosts*, 1975; *The Statue and the Rose*, 1975; *Two Gentle People*, from a story by Graham Greene, 1975; *The Nicest Man in the World*, 1976; *Afternoon Dancing*, 1976; *The Love of a Good woman*, from his own story, 1976; *The Girl Who Saw a Tiger*, 1976; *Last Wishes*, 1978; *Another Weekend*, 1978; *Memories*, 1978; *Matilda's England*, 1979; *The Old Curiosity Shop*, from the novel by Dickens, 1979; *Secret Orchards*, from works by J.R. Ackerley and Diana Petre, 1980; *The Happy Autumn Fields*, from a story by Elizabeth Bowen, 1980; *Elizabeth Alone*, from his own novel, 1981; *Autumn Sunshine*, from his own story, 1981; *The Ballroom of Romance*, from his own story, 1982; *Mrs. Silly* (*All for Love* series), 1983; *One of Ourselves*, 1983; *Broken Homes*, from his own story, 1985; *The Children of Dynmouth*, from his own novel, 1987; *August Saturday*, from his own novel, 1990.

NOVELS

A Standard of Behaviour. 1958.
The Old Boys. 1964.
The Boarding-House. 1965.
The Love Department. 1966.
Mrs. Eckdorf in O'Neill's Hotel. 1969.
Miss Gomez and the Brethren. 1971.
Elizabeth Alone. 1973.
The Children of Dynmouth. 1976.
Other People's Worlds. 1980.
Fools of Fortune. 1983.
The Silence in the Garden. 1988.
Two Lives (includes *Reading Turgenev* and *My House in Umbria*). 1991.

SHORT STORIES

The Day We Got Drunk on Cake and Other Stories. 1967.
Penguin Modern Stories 8, with others. 1971.
The Ballroom of Romance and Other Stories. 1972.
The Last Lunch of the Season. 1973.
Angels at the Ritz and Other Stories. 1975.
Lovers of Their Time and Other Stories. 1978.
The Distant Past and Other Stories. 1979.
Beyond the Pale and Other Stories. 1981.
The Stories of William Trevor. 1983.
The News from Ireland and Other Stories. 1986.
Nights at the Alexandra (novella). 1987.
Family Sins and Other Stories. 1990.
Juliet's Story (for children). 1991.
Collected Stories. 1992.

OTHER

Old School Ties (miscellany). 1976.
A Writer's Ireland: Landscape in Literature. 1984.

Editor, *The Oxford Book of Irish Short Stories.* 1989.

MANUSCRIPT COLLECTION: University of Tulsa, Oklahoma.

A successful novelist and prolific television and radio dramatist before turning in any real measure towards the theatre, William Trevor has been somewhat unlucky in his career as far as his full-length plays are concerned. *The Elephant's Foot* closed during its prior-to-London tour, and *The Old Boys* had a particularly unfortunate opening in London with its star's first-night nerves hindering the flow of a play whose full effect depended on the subtleties of its verbal nuances; and although the central performance improved immeasurably during its original limited Mermaid Theatre run and throughout a subsequent provincial tour, sadly the play did not find a West End theatre.

The Elephant's Foot (along with his early one-acter *The Girl*) represents something of a false start for Trevor. Both reveal his unusual gift for dialogue, particularly that of characters enmeshed in their own sense of failure and for those verging on the sinister or seedy, but both remain somewhat inert, heavily relying as they do on a central situation, of strange intruders entering domestic scenes, itself something of a cliché-situation in the theatre of the early 1960's. In *The Girl*, set in suburban London (one of Trevor's favourite locales, both in novels and plays), a mysterious teenage girl descends on the Green household, convincingly claiming to be Mr. Green's daughter, the result of a single drunken escapade with a prostitute. Her arrival, not surprisingly, divides the family, until it is revealed, with the near-curtain arrival of the girl's violent young friends, that Green is only the latest in a long list of prostitute mother's clients, to be descended on and terrorised in turn by the loutish teenage gang. It is adroit and suspenseful enough to sustain its length, although the ghost of Pinter looms heavily over the play, even to some extent over the dialogue, particularly in the opening sections between the Green family, laden with pauses and the reiteration of the clichés of suburban small-talk. *The Elephant's Foot* is similarly burdened with a top-heavy plot and reliance on a closing "surprise." An elderly couple, Colonel and Mrs. Pocock, who live apart except for their Christmas reunion with their twin children, in the midst of preparing their Christmas meal are invaded by the bizarre stranger Freer (first-cousin to the splendid con-man Swingler in *The Old Boys*) and his mute associate Tiger. Freer gradually unsettles the Pococks, frightening them by anticipating the non-arrival of their children, but he fails to insinuate Tiger into the household in the twins' place and the play closes with the Pococks again alone preparing to resume their old domestic battle. After a promising opening, with a very funny verbal tussle between the Pococks over the unfortunate selection of the Christmas brussels sprouts, the play collapses in the second act, only sustaining itself to the final curtain by resorting to coincidence and unconvincing metaphysical overtones. Nevertheless, *The Elephant's Foot* revealed that Trevor was capable of an individual dramatic verbal style (which his early novels, largely in dialogue, had pointed towards), a stylized counterpointing of the colloquial with the rhetorical which owes a little to Ivy Compton-Burnett but essentially remains very much his own.

This was further developed in *The Old Boys*, his own adaptation of his Hawthornden prize-winning novel of the same name, which revealed too Trevor's special understanding of elderly characters, particularly in those scenes set in a London residential hotel populated entirely by old boys of the same minor public school and tyrannised over by a dragoness of a Matron-surrogate. In its study of an old schoolboy rivalry extending from out of the past to influence a struggle over the presidency of the Old Boys' Association, the play is by turns hilarious and deeply touching, although the first act never satisfactorily solves some problems of construction in the adaptation process. But the climatic scene as old Mr. Jaraby at last realises the futility of his grudges and ambitions and, now a widower preparing to join the other old men at the Rimini Hotel, launches into a speech of life-affirming anarchy at the expense of the bullying proprietrix, stands as one of Trevor's finest achievements. Since *The Old Boys* Trevor has enjoyed considerable success with one-act plays often adapted from previous television and radio plays or from short stories. Most of these are acutely observed and tightly written duologues between different kinds of victims—the lonely, deserted, or repressed characters Trevor reveals so compassionately. Some of these, such as *A Night with Mrs. da Tanka*, a hotel encounter between a sad drunken divorcée and a shy bachelor, suffer in the transition to the stage and seem curiously artificial. But the best of them—especially *Going Home*, in which a precocious schoolboy and a spinster Assistant Matron, travelling in a train compartment together for the holidays, painfully realise their mutual loneliness—capture moments of crisis in their characters' lives and give them a genuine life on stage beyond the confines of the original medium from which they were adapted. Likewise, some of the best scenes in *The Old Boys* are those not in or most freely adapted from the original novel; hopefully before long Trevor may emerge with a new full-length play original in all senses of the word.

—Alan Strachan

TURNER, David.

Born in Birmingham, Warwickshire, 18 March 1927. Educated at Moseley Grammar School; Birmingham University, B.A. 1950. Served in an army educational theatre unit, 1945–47. Married Joan Wilson (died 1983); two adopted children. Teacher for 9 years. *Died 11 December 1990.*

Publications

PLAYS

The Bedmakers (produced 1962).
Semi-Detached (produced 1962). 1962; revised version, 1971.
Believe It or Not, with Edward J. Mason (produced 1962).
Trevor (produced 1963).
The Antique Shop (produced 1963).
Slap in the Middle, with others (produced 1965).
Bottomley (produced 1965).

Way Off Beat (televised 1966). In *Conflicting Generations: Five Television Plays*, edited by Michael Marland, 1968.
The Begger's Opera, music edited by Benjamin Pearce Higgins, adaptation of the play by John Gay (produced 1968). 1982.
The Servant of Two Masters, with Paul Lapworth, music by Benjamin Pearce Higgins, adaptation of a play by Carlo Goldoni (produced 1968). 1973.
Quick Quick Slow, music and lyrics by Monty Norman and Julian More (produced 1969).
The Prodigal Daughter (produced 1973). 1976.
The Miser, adaptation of a play by Molière (produced 1973).
The Only True Story of Lady Godiva, with Paul Lapworth (produced 1973).
The Girls (produced 1975).

RADIO PLAYS: *Grantham's Outing*, 1956; . . . *And Tomorrow*, 1956; *Change of Plan*, 1957; *Me, Me Dad and His'n*, 1957; *Mind Your Own Business*, 1958; *Family Business*, 1959; *Come Back* Jack, 1959; *Any Other Business*, 1961; *Now More Than Ever*, 1961; *The Wizard Who Worked Wonders*, from a play by Calderón, 1977.

TELEVISION PLAYS AND SERIALIZATIONS: *Fresh as Paint*, 1956; *The Train Set*, 1961; *Cry from the Depths*, 1961; *The Final Result*, 1961; *On the Boundary*, 1961; *Summer, Autumn, Winter, Spring*, 1961; *Choirboys Unite!*, 1961; *The Chem Lab Mystery*, 1963; *Swizzlewick*, 1964; *This Man Craig* series, 1966; *Way Off Beat*, 1966; *North and South*, from the novel by Elizabeth Gaskell, 1966; *Angel Pavement*, from the novel by J.B. Priestley, 1967; *Treasure Island*, from the novel by Robert Louis Stevenson, 1968; *Père Goriot*, from the novel by Balzac, 1968; *Cold Comfort Farm*, from the novel by Stella Gibbons, 1968; *Olive*, 1970; *Germinal* from the novel by Zola, 1970; *The Roads to Freedom*, from novels by Jean-Paul Sartre, 1972; *Daisy* (*The Edwardians* series), 1973; *Neighbours*, 1973; *Father*, 1973; *Requiem for a Crown Prince*, 1974; *Harold*, 1975; *Prometheus*, from the novel by André Maurois, 1975; *C2H5OH*, 1980.

CRITICAL STUDY: *Anger and After* by John Russell Taylor, 1962, revised edition, 1969, as *The Angry Theatre*, 1962, revised edition, 1969.

David Turner's plays are all firmly rooted in the Midlands, where he lived, and nearly all are closely observed pictures of lower-middle-class life and values. *Semi-Detached* is his best known play and satirizes those values accurately and cruelly. Fred Midway is a middle-aged insurance agent, living with his family in a semi-detached house in a Midlands town, absolutely obsessed with his status in life and "what the neighbours think". He imposes these preconceptions with near-disastrous results on his wife Hilda, his son Tom, and his daughters Eileen and Avril. Eileen is knocking about with a married man, while Avril's husband, Nigel Hadfield, is in disgrace because he went with a prostitute on his visit to London for a football match.

The play is Jonsonian in almost every particular. The author has an unmitigated loathing and contempt for his characters, whose real-life prototypes he has clearly spent many hours observing, and portrays them as caricatures with a grotesquerie arising from their essential social and individual truth. The names of the characters are a clear guide to their personalities—*Mid*way, *Free*man, Make*piece*—and the plot is beautifully constructed and worked out. The play is also excoriatingly witty and funny; witness lines like Fred's "If only I could have a grandchild who actually went to a Public School" and the behaviour of everyone involved in the row between Avril and Nigel, pretending to be acmes of morality but actually basing their behaviour on the most sordidly commercial considerations.

Bottomley is a portrait of another character from the same social and class background as Mid*way*, this time the real-life Horatio Bottomley, the notorious early 20th-century swindler. Bottomley rises meteorically to fame as a businessman and as a politician. A right-wing populist with a strong appeal to the working-class, not unlike Enoch Powell in some aspects, he comes unstuck only because of his tendency to megalomania. The play convincingly reveals Bottomley within his particular political and social context and, by implication, shows how easy it is for a cunning right-wing demagogue to carve a very powerful niche for himself in our society.

The Bedmakers is a sad picture of an elderly workman, Bill Summers, left behind by the march of technology, unable to adjust himself to the new, more sophisticated demands of society for more trendy goods, geared to a quick obsolescence. He determines to make an old-fashioned iron bed for his grandson and the grandson's wife-to-be, fatally unaware that it will be totally useless to them. Both the bed and Bill end up symbolically on the scrapheap. The play is occasionally moving in the way it depicts the conflicts between Bill, his family, and his bosses (who are keeping him on for sentimental reasons); but overall it is a little too heavy-handed and obvious.

By contrast, *The Antique Shop* is a study in corruption. A successful young shop-owner, Don Newman, is corrupted by his desire for money without really realizing the source of his infection. He has three girlfriends in tow and plays off one against the other. Predictably, two of them ditch him and the third, the Jonsonianly-named Judy Trader, only makes a fresh start with him when he inadvertently ruins himself and has to start all over again. The play is an ironic and effective picture of the dehumanizing effect of the narrow, commercially based attitudes of lower-middle-class capitalism.

Come Back Jack, a radio play, shows Jack, a lower-middle-class man, unsuccessfully struggling to keep his family firm from going bust, hampered by his idle, useless partner, his brother-in-law Donald. Jack married into the family essentially because his shrewd father-in-law realized his potential as a businessman. The basically commercial attitudes of the family towards Jack distort their inter-relationships, twisting Jack's character and desires, so that he spends his life fulfilling their objectives and not his. It is only when an ex-girlfriend forces Jack to face up to the cipher he has become that he manages to free himself, breaking away from the doomed family firm and starting afresh on a new basis with his wife.

The Train Set, for television, is a wry, well-observed study of the relationship between a working-class father and his young son and how it can be affected and twisted by lack of money. *Quick Quick Slow*, a musical written with Monty Norman and Julian More, is a satirical tilt at the ersatz cultural values, in this case represented by ballroom dancing.

At his best, Turner was a keen and truthful observer of the narrowing, repressive effects that the values of modern industrial capitalism have on human beings, and expressed them in suitably socially based styles.

—Jonathan Hammond

U

USTINOV, Peter (Alexander).

Born in London, 16 April 1921. Educated at Gibbs Preparatory School, London; Westminster School, London, 1934–37; London Theatre Studio, 1937–39. Served in the Royal Sussex Regiment, Royal Army Ordnance Corps, 1942–46; with Army Kinetograph Service, 1943, and Directorate of Army Psychiatry. Married 1) Isolde Denham in 1940 (divorced 1950), one daughter; 2) Suzanne Cloutier in 1954 (divorced 1971), two daughters and one son; 3) Hélène du Lau d'Allemans in 1972. Actor, writer, and director. Co-director, Nottingham Playhouse, 1963. Rector, University of Dundee, 1968–73. Since 1969 Goodwill Ambassador, Unicef. Recipient: Golden Globe award, 1952; New York Drama Critics Circle award, 1953; Donaldson award, 1953; *Evening Standard* award, 1956; Royal Society of Arts, Benjamin Franklin medal, 1957; Emmy award, for acting, 1957, 1966, 1970; Oscar, for acting, 1961, 1965; Peabody award, for acting, 1972; Unicef award, 1978; Jordanian Independence medal, 1978; Prix de la Butte, 1978; Variety Club award, for acting, 1979; City of Athens gold medal, 1990; Greek Red Cross medal, 1990; medal of honour, Charles University, Prague, 1991. D.M.: Cleveland Institute of Music, 1967; D.L.: University of Dundee, 1969, University of Ottawa, 1991; D.F.A.: La Salle University, Philadelphia, 1971; D. Litt.: University of Lancaster, 1972; University of Toronto, 1984; D.H.L.: Georgetown University, Washington, D.C., 1988. Fellow, Royal Society of Arts; Fellow, Royal Society of Literature, 1978. C.B.E. (Commander, Order of the British Empire), 1975; Commander, Order of Arts and Letters (France), 1985; Order of Istiglal, Hashemite Kingdom of Jordan; Order of the Yugoslav Flag; elected to the Académie des Beaux-Arts, Paris, 1988; knighted, 1990; Chancellor, University of Durham, 1992. Agent: William Morris Agency, 31–32 Soho Square, London W1V 5DG, England. Address: 11 rue de Silly, 92110 Boulogne, France.

Publications

PLAYS

The Bishop of Limpopoland (sketch: produced 1939).
Sketches in *Swinging the Gate* (produced 1940).
Sketches in *Diversion* and *Diversion 2* (produced 1940).
Fishing for Shadows, adaptation of a play by Jean Sarment (also director: produced 1940).
House of Regrets (produced 1942). 1943.

Beyond (produced 1943). 1944; in *Five Plays*, 1965.
Blow Your Own Trumpet (produced 1943). In *Plays about People*, 1950.
The Banbury Nose (produced 1944). 1945.
The Tragedy of Good Intentions (produced 1945). In *Plays about People*, 1950.
The Indifferent Shepherd (produced 1948). In *Plays about People*, 1950.
Frenzy, adaptation of a play by Ingmar Bergman (produced London, 1948).
The Man in the Raincoat (also director: produced 1949).
Plays about People. 1950.
The Love of Four Colonels (also director: produced 1951). 1951.
The Moment of Truth (produced 1951). 1953; in *Five Plays*, 1965.
High Balcony (produced 1952).
No Sign of the Dove (also director: produced 1953). In *Five Plays*, 1965.
Romanoff and Juliet (produced 1956). 1957; revised version, as *R Loves J*, music by Alexander Faris, lyrics by Julian More (produced 1973).
The Empty Chair (produced 1956).
Paris Not So Gay (produced 1958).
Photo Finish: An Adventure in Biography (also director: produced 1962). 1962.
The Life in My Hands (produced 1964).
Five Plays: Romanoff and Juliet, The Moment of Truth, The Love of Four Colonels, Beyond, No Sign of the Dove. 1965.
Halfway Up the Tree (also director: produced 1967). 1968.
The Unknown Soldier and His Wife: Two Acts of War Separated by a Truce for Refreshment (also director: produced 1967). 1967.
Who's Who in Hell (produced 1974).
Overheard (produced 1981).
The Marriage, adaptation of an opera libretto by Gogol, music by Mussorgsky (also director: produced 1981).
Beethoven's Tenth (produced 1982).
An Evening with Peter Ustinov (produced 1990).

SCREENPLAYS: *The New Lot* (documentary), 1943; *The Way Ahead*, with Eric Ambler, 1944; *The True Glory* (documentary), with others, 1944; *Carnival*, with others, 1946; *School for Secrets* (*The Secret Flight*), 1946; *Vice Versa*, 1948; *Private Angelo*, with Michael Anderson, 1949; *School for Scoundrels*, with others, 1960; *Romanoff and Juliet*, 1961; *Billy Budd*, with Robert Rossen and De Win Bodeen, 1962; *Lady L.*, 1965; *Hot Millions*, with Ira Wallach, 1968; *Memed, My Hawk*, 1984.

TELEVISION PLAYS: *Ustinov ad lib*, 1969; *Imaginary Friends*, 1982.

NOVELS
The Loser. 1961.
Krumnagel. 1971.
The Old Man and Mr. Smith. 1990.

SHORT STORIES
Add a Dash of Pity. 1959.
The Frontiers of the Sea. 1966.
The Disinformer. 1989.

OTHER
Ustinov's Diplomats: A Book of Photographs. 1961.
We Were Only Human (caricatures). 1961.
The Wit of Peter Ustinov, edited by Dick Richards. 1969.
Rectorial Address Delivered in the University, 3rd November 1972. 1972.
Dear Me (autobiography). 1977.
Happiness (lecture). 1980.
My Russia. 1983.
Ustinov in Russia. 1987.
Ustinov at Large (articles). 1991.

RECORDINGS: **Writer and performer**—*Mock Mozart, and Phoney Folk Lore,* Parlophone; *The Grand Prix of Gibraltar,* Orpheum; **Narrator**—*Peter and the Wolf; The Nutcracker Suite The Soldier's Tale; Háry János; The Little Prince; The Old Man of Lochnagar; Grandpa; Babar and Father Christmas.*

CRITICAL STUDIES (includes filmographies and bibliographies): *Peter Ustinov* by Geoffrey Willans, 1957; *Ustinov in Focus* by Tony Thomas,1971.

THEATRICAL ACTIVITIES
DIRECTOR: **Plays**—*Fishing for Shadows,* 1940; *Squaring the Circle* by Valentine Katayev, 1941; *The Man in the Raincoat,* 1949; *Love in Albania* by Eric Linklater, 1949; *The Love of Four Colonels,* 1951; *A Fiddle at the Wedding,* by Patricia Pakenham-Walsh, 1952; *No Sign of the Dove,* 1953; *Photo Finish,* 1962; *Halfway up the Tree,* 1967; *The Unkown Soldier and His Wife,* 1968, 1973. **Films**—*School for Secrets* (*The Secret Flight*), 1946; *Vice Versa,* 1948; *Private Angelo,* with Michael Anderson, 1949; *Romanoff and Juliet,* 1961; *Billy Budd,* 1962; *Lady L.,* 1965; *Hammersmith Is Out,* 1972, *Memed, My Hawk,* 1984. **Operas**—*L'Heure Espagnole* by Ravel, *Gianni Schicchi* by Puccini, and *Erwartung* by Schoenberg (triple bill), 1962; *The Magic Flute* by Mozart, 1968; *Don Quichotte* by Massenet, 1973; *Don Giovanni* by Mozart, 1973; *Les Brigands* by Offenbach, 1978; *The Marriage* by Mussorgsky, 1981, 1982; *Mavra* and *The Flood* by Stravinsky, 1982; *Katja Kabanowa* by Janáček, 1985; *The Marriage of Figaro* by Mozart, 1987. ACTOR: **Plays**—Waffles in *The Wood Demon* by Chekhov, 1938; in *The Bishop of Limpopoland,* 1939; Aylesbury Repertory Company: in *French Without Tears* by Terence Rattigan, *Pygmalion* by G.B. Shaw, *White Cargo* by Leon Gordon, *Rookery Nook* by Ben Travers, and *Laburnum Grove* by J.B. Priestley, 1939; Reverend Alroy Whittingstall in *First Night* by Reginald Denham, 1940; *Swinging the Gate* (revue), 1940; M. Lescure in *Fishing for Shadows,* 1940; *Hermione Gingold Revue,* 1940; *Diversion and Diversion 2* (revues), 1940, 1941; Petrovitch in *Crime and Punishment* by Rodney Ackland, 1946; Caligula in *Frenzy,* 1948; Sergeant Dohda in *Love in Albania*

by Eric Linklater, 1949; Carabosse in *The Love of Four Colonels*, 1951; The General in *Romanoff and Juliet*, 1956, 1957; Sam Old in *Photo Finish*, 1962, 1963; Archbishop in *The Unknown Soldier and His Wife*, 1968, 1973; Boris Vassilevitch Krivelov in *Who's Who in Hell*, 1974; title role in *King Lear*, 1979, 1980; Stage Manager in *The Marriage*, 1981, 1982; Ludwig in *Beethoven's Tenth*, 1982, 1983, 1984; *An Evening with Peter Ustinov*, 1990, 1991. **Films**—*Hullo Fame!*, 1941; *Mein Kampf, My Crimes*, 1941; *One of Our Aircraft Is Missing*, 1941; *The Goose Steps Out*, 1942; *Let the People Sing*, 1942; *The New Lot*, 1943; *The Way Ahead*, 1944; *The True Glory* 1945; *School for Secrets (The Secret Flight)*, 1946; *Vice Versa*, 1947; *Private Angelo*, 1949; *Odette*, 1950; *Quo Vadis*, 1951; *Hotel Sahara*, 1951; *The Magic Box*, 1951; *Beau Brummell*, 1954; *The Egyptian*, 1954; *Le Plaisir (House of Pleasure)* (narrator), 1954; *We're No Angels*, 1955; *Lola Montès (Lola Montez, The Sins of Lola Montes)*, 1955; *I girovaghi (The Wanderers)*, 1956; *Un angel paso sobre Brooklyn (An Angel over Brooklyn, The Man Who Wagged His Tail)*, 1957; *Les Espions (The Spies)*, 1957; *The Adventures of Mr. Wonderful*, 1959; *Spartacus*, 1960; *The Sundowners*, 1960; *Romanoff and Juliet*, 1961; *Billy Budd*, 1962; *La donna del mondo (Women of the World)* (narrator), 1963, *The Peaches* (narrator), 1964; *Topkapi*, 1964; *John Goldfarb, Please Come Home*, 1964; *Lady L.*, 1965; *The Comedians*, 1967; *Blackbeard's Ghost*, 1967; *Hot Millions*, 1968; *Viva Max!*, 1969; *Hammersmith Is Out*, 1972; *Big Truck and Sister Clare*, 1973; *Treasure of Matecumbe*, 1976; *One of Our Dinosaurs Is Missing*, 1976; *Logan's Run*, 1976; *Robin Hood* (voice in animated film), 1976; *Un Taxi mauve (The Purple Taxi)*, 1977; *The Last Remake of Beau Geste*, 1978; *The Mouse and His Child* (narrator), 1978; *Doppio delitto (Double Murders)*, 1978; *Death on the Nile*, 1978; *Tarka the Otter* (narrator), 1978; *Winds of Change* (narrator), 1978; *Ashanti*, 1979; *Charlie Chan and the Curse of the Dragon Queen*, 1981; *The Great Muppet Caper*, 1981; *Grendel, Grendel, Grendel* (voice in animated film), 1981; *Evil under the Sun*, 1982; *Memed, My Hawk*, 1984; *Appointment with Death*, 1988; *The French Revolution*, 1989; *Lorenzo's Oil*, 1991. **Television**—*The Life of Dr. Johnson*, 1957; *Barefoot in Athens*, 1966; *In All Directions* series; *A Storm in Summer*, 1970 (USA); *Lord North*, 1972; *The Mighty Continent* (narrator), 1974; *A Quiet War*, 1976 (USA); *The Thief of Bagdad*, 1978; *Jesus of Nazareth*, 1979; *Einstein's Universe* (narrator), 1979; *Imaginary Friends* (5 roles), 1982; *The Well-Tempered Bach*, 1984; *13 at Dinner*, 1985; *Dead Man's Folly*, 1986; *Peter Ustinov's Russia*, 1986 (Canada); *World Challenge*, 1986 (Canada); *Murder in Three Acts*, 1986; narrator for *History of Europe*, *The Hermitage* and *The Ballerinas*; *Peter Ustinov in China*, 1987; *Around the World in Eighty Days*, 1988–89; *The Secret Identity of Jack the Ripper*, 1989–90; *The Mozart Mystique*, 1990; *Ustinov on the Orient Express*, 1991–92.

Peter Ustinov comments:

I believe that theories should emerge as a logical consequence of practice, and not be formulated in a coldly intellectual climate for eventual use. I therefore regard myself as a practical writer who began to write in the period of the proscenium arch, but who survived into the epoch of the arena and platform stages. The theatre, to survive, must do what film and television cannot do, and that is to exploit the physical presence of the audience. Naturalism was the logical reaction against romanticism, but the poetry inherent in all valid works of any school emerges more easily on film and even more easily on television than on the stage, and the time of the "fourth wall" has passed. Also, with the extraordinarily graphic quality of current events diffused by the news media, and the growing public sense of irony and scepticism about the nature and possibilities of government, tragedy and comedy have been chased for ever from their ivory towers. This is the time of the tragic farce, of the comic drama, of the paradox, of the dramatized doubt. In my plays as in my non-dramatic works I have always been interested in the comic side of things tragic and in the melancholy side of things ribald. Life could not exist without its imperfections, just as the human body could not survive without germs. And to the writer, the imperfections of existence are life-blood.

Like Noël Coward, with whose versatility his own was often compared when he was establishing himself, Peter Ustinov had a dazzling early break in his career. While he was appearing in a Herbert Farjeon revue, Farjeon gave one of Ustinov's manuscripts to James Agate, then at the height of his influence on the *Sunday Times*. Following Agate's lavish praise of *House of Regrets*, it was produced in 1942. It is very much a young man's play; its story of Russian émigrés living in genteel poverty in wartime London is an often self-consciously "atmospheric" piece, but it shows already Ustinov's sympathetic identification with eccentrics and the aged in his picture of the old Admiral and General plotting their coup to re-enter Russia. In the immediately following period Ustinov's plays appeared with impressive frequency, perhaps too frequently for their own good. Too many could be described in the terms he uses to label *Blow Your Own Trumpet*, a fantasy set in an Italian restaurant—"An idea rather than a play in the ordinary sense of the word." *The Tragedy of Good Intentions*, a chronicle play about the Crusades, is unfocused and verbose; *The Indifferent Shepherd*, his closest approach to a conventional well-made West End play, centred round a clergyman's crisis of conscience, is lacklustre despite its sincerity; and *No Sign of the Dove*, a resounding critical failure, a re-working of the Noah legend, despite a fine neo-Firbankian opening of high style, dwindles into a tepid mixture of late Shaw and bedroom-door farce. The initial impetus in these earlier plays is rarely sustained consistently.

At the same time, Ustinov's unique gift for the fantastic was developing more surely. *The Banbury Nose*, tracing a great military family through three generations in reverse order (a kind of *Milestones* backwards), is a technical tour de force, but in the scenes between the wife and the men who have loved her Ustinov also reveals a sure understanding of the threads of response between people. Although his 1950's work produced some oddly muffled efforts—such as *The Moment of Truth*, an over-inflated political drama—he also produced *The Love of Four Colonels* and *Romanoff and Juliet*, at his inventive best in both. *The Love of Four Colonels*, set in a European state disputed by the Allies, enjoyably satirizes national characteristics as the four Colonels try to awaken the Sleeping Beauty's love in pastiche scenes in which they play out their own hopes and ideals, while *Romanoff and Juliet* adapts the

Romeo and Juliet story in the Cold War context of rival Russian and American embassies in "the smallest country in Europe." Underneath the fairy tales and Ruritanian trappings there is a shrewd core of humanist understanding of contemporary problems, although with Ustinov's polyglot ancestry this inevitably emerges in an international rather than a local context.

His later output continued to develop earlier themes. *Photo Finish* recalls *The Banbury Nose* in its flashback time-sequence, presenting a famous writer in confrontation with his younger selves as he contemplates the mirror of the past. *The Unknown Soldier and His Wife* is a further exploration of some material in *The Tragedy of Good Intentions* but a much surer play. It sweeps in time from ancient Rome to medieval England to modern times, linked by the same recurring characters who emerge whenever war comes and who control its course. Occasionally it threatens to become a series of admittedly amusing anti-war sketches, but it contains some of Ustinov's most pungent writing.

Certainly few of Ustinov's plays have a tight plot progression; as in his novels he is happier in a more picaresque style. His ancestry perhaps partly explains his drawing on the Russian literary tradition blending tragedy and comedy and his best plays have a strong tension between the two. He once stressed the influence of music on his work and there is indeed a Mozartian strain which informs his best plays which, despite an apparent surface plotlessness, have an internal rhythm which gives them strong theatrical movement. This could hardly be said of a string of disappointing work in more recent years. *Halfway up the Tree*, a tired comedy of the drop-out generation, was sadly jaded, but still not so distressingly feeble as *Who's Who in Hell*. This has a splendid initial idea; it is set in an anteroom of Hell where the ultimate destination of new arrivals (including the U.S. President and the Russian Premier) is decided. But the promise of a sharp political comedy is torpedoed by stale jokes and a woefully jejune level of intellectual argument. *Overheard*, a lachrymose comedy of diplomatic life, was similarly thin, while *Beethoven's Tenth* was not entirely a return to form. Again, there is a hugely promising initial premise—Beethoven materialises as the result of a trance by a psychic au pair in the house of a London music critic and is shortly cured of his deafness, also speaking perfect English. The play seems poised to take off into an exhilarating comedy of ideas but apart from a closing scene to the first act in which the critic's wife, an ex-singer, sings "An die ferne Geliebte" to the composer's accompaniment—as good a scene as anything Ustinov has written —the rest of the play never recovers the buoyancy of the opening.

—Alan Strachan

W

WALCOTT, Derek (Alton).

Born in Castries, St. Lucia, West Indies, 23 January 1930. Educated at St. Mary's College, Castries, 1941–47; University College of the West Indies, Mona, Jamaica, 1950–54, B.A. 1953. Married 1) Fay Moyston in 1954 (divorced 1959), one son; 2) Margaret Ruth Maillard in 1962 (divorced), two daughters; 3) Norline Metivier in 1982. Teacher, St. Mary's College, Castries, 1947–50 and 1954, Grenada Boy's Secondary School, St. George's, Grenada, 1953–54, and Jamaica College, Kingston, 1955; feature writer, *Public Opinion*, Kingston, 1956–57; feature writer, 1960–62, and drama critic, 1963–68, *Trinidad Guardian*, Port-of-Spain. Co-founder, St. Lucia Arts Guild, 1950, and Basement Theatre, Port-of-Spain; founding director, Little Carib Theatre Workshop (later Trinidad Theatre Workshop), 1959–76. Assistant professor of creative writing, 1981, and since 1985 visiting professor, Boston University. Visiting professor, Columbia University, New York, 1981, and Harvard University, Cambridge, Massachusetts, 1982, 1987. Recipient: Rockefeller grant, 1957, 1966, and fellowship, 1958; Arts Advisory Council of Jamaica prize, 1960; Guinness award, 1961; Ingram Merrill Foundation grant, 1962; Borestone Mountain award, 1964, 1977; Royal Society of Literature Heinemann award, 1966, 1983; Cholmondeley award, 1969; Audrey Wood fellowship, 1969; Eugene O'Neill Foundation fellowship, 1969; Gold Hummingbird medal (Trinidad), 1969; Obie award, for drama, 1971; Jock Campbell award (*New Statesman*), 1974; Guggenheim award, 1977; *American Poetry Review* award, 1979; Welsh Arts Council International Writers prize, 1980; MacArthur fellowship, 1981; Los Angeles *Times* prize, 1986; Queen's gold medal for poetry, 1988; W.H. Smith award, for poetry, 1991; Nobel prize, for literature, 1992. D. Litt.: University of the West Indies, Mona, 1973. Fellow, Royal Society of Literature, 1966; Honorary Member, American Academy, 1979. O.B.E. (Officer, Order of the British Empire), 1972. Agent: Bridget Aschenberg, International Famous Agency, 1301 Avenue of the Americas, New York, New York 10019, U.S.A. Address: 165 Duke of Edinburgh Avenue, Diego Martin, Trinidad.

Publications

PLAYS

Cry for a Leader (produced 1950).
Senza Alcun Sospetto (broadcast 1950; as *Paolo and Francesca*, produced 1951?).

Henri Christophe: A Chronicle (also director: produced 1950). 1950.
Robin and Andrea, published in *Bim*, December 1950.
Three Assassins (produced 1951?).
The Price of Mercy (produced 1951?).
Harry Dernier (as *Dernier*, broadcast 1952; as *Harry Dernier*, also director: produced 1952). 1952.
The Sea at Dauphin (produced 1954). 1954; in *Dream on Monkey Mountain and Other Plays*, 1970.
Crossroads (produced 1954).
The Charlatan (also director: produced 1954?; revised version, music by Fred Hope and Rupert Dennison, produced 1973; revised version, music by Galt MacDermot, produced 1974; revised version produced 1977).
The Wine of the Country (also director: produced 1956).
The Golden Lions (also director: produced 1956).
Ione: A Play with Music (produced 1957). 1957.
Ti-Jean and His Brothers (produced 1957; revised version, also director: produced 1958). In *Dream on Monkey Mountain and Other Plays*, 1970.
Drums and Colours (produced 1958). In *Caribbean Quarterly*, vol. 7, nos. 1 and 2, 1961.
Malcochon; or, The Six in the Rain (produced 1959; as *The Six in the Rain*, produced 1960; as *Malcochon*, produced 1969). In *Dream on Monkey Mountain and Other Plays*, 1970.
Jourmard; or, A Comedy till the Last Minute (produced 1959).
Batai (carnival show; also director: produced 1965).
Dream on Monkey Mountain (also director: produced 1967). In *Dream on Monkey Mountain and Other Plays*, 1970.
Franklin: A Tale of the Islands (produced 1969; revised version, also director: produced 1973).
In a Fine Castle (also director: produced 1970). Excerpt, as *Conscience of a Revolutionary*, published in *Express*, 24 October 1971.
Dream on Monkey Mountain and Other Plays (includes *Ti-Jean and His Brothers*, *Malcochon*, *The Sea at Dauphin*, and the essay "What the Twilight Says"). 1970.
The Joker of Seville, music by Galt MacDermot, adaptation of the play by Tirso de Molina (produced 1974). With *O Babylon!*, 1978.
O Babylon!, music by Galt MacDermot (also director: produced 1976). With *The Joker of Seville*, 1978.
Remembrance (also director: produced 1977). With *Pantomime*, 1980.
The Snow Queen (television play), excerpt published in *People*, April 1977.
Pantomime (produced 1978). With *Remembrance*, 1980.
Marie Laveau, music by Galt MacDermot (also director: produced 1979). Excerpts published in *Trinidad and Tobago Review*, Christmas 1979.
The Isle Is Full of Noises (produced 1982).
Beef, No Chicken (produced 1982). In *Three Plays*, 1986.
Three Plays (includes *The Last Carnival*; *Beef, No Chicken*; *A Branch of the Blue Nile*). 1986.
The Last Carnival (produced 1992). In *Three Plays*, 1986.
To Die for Granada (produced 1986).
Viva Detroit (produced 1990).

Steel (produced 1991).
The Odyssey, adaptation of the epic by Homer (produced 1992).

RADIO PLAYS: *Senza Alcun Sospetto*, 1950; *Dernier*, 1952; *Pantomime*, 1979.

VERSE
25 Poems. 1948.
Epitaph for the Young: XII Cantos. 1949.
Poems. 1951.
In a Green Night: Poems 1948–1960. 1962.
Selected Poems. 1964.
The Castaway and Other Poems. 1965.
The Gulf and Other Poems. 1969; as *The Gulf*, 1970.
Another Life. 1973.
Sea Grapes. 1976.
The Star-Apple Kingdom. 1979.
Selected Poetry, edited by Wayne Brown. 1981.
The Fortunate Traveller. 1981.
The Caribbean Poetry of Derek Walcott and the Art of Romare Bearden.
  1983.
Midsummer. 1984.
Collected Poems 1948–1984. 1986.
The Arkansas Testament. 1987.
Omeros. 1989.

OTHER
The Poet in the Theatre. 1990.

BIBLIOGRAPHY: *Derek Walcott: An Annotated Bibliography of His Works* by
Irma E. Goldstraw, 1984.

CRITICAL STUDIES: *Derek Walcott: Memory as Vision* by Edward Baugh, 1978;
Derek Walcott: Poet of the Islands by Ned Thomas, 1980; *Derek Walcott* by
Robert D. Hamner, 1981; *The Art of Derek Walcott* edited by Stewart Brown,
1989.

THEATRICAL ACTIVITIES
DIRECTOR: Many of his own plays.

Although primarily a poet—and as such, one of the best writing in English
today—Derek Walcott is also an accomplished playwright, whose interest in
drama was kindled at an early age. A youthful stage designer, he has for some
time supervised acting workshops in Trinidad, where he has also campaigned
for the establishment of a national Caribbean theatre. His plays afford
dramatic treatment to themes expressed in his poetry, exploring concepts of
personal and racial identity, the brooding presence of evil, and the inevitability
of exile and separation. Walcott's efforts to comprehend and utilize the nature
of his own mixed ancestry in his writing explain much of the tension and
conflict that underlies his work. The descendant of European masters and
African slaves officially denied a history of their own, he strives in poems and

dramas alike to maintain a balance between the two. Walcott's affection for European literature, demonstrated clearly in his mastery of poetic and dramatic styles, is genuine but wary, and in his recent play, *The Last Carnival*, he indicates the dangers of wholesale acceptance of European models by Caribbean artists. At the same time he strongly asserts the heritage of his black forebears, drawing on patterns of Caribbean speech, and African-derived chanting, drumming, and dance in many of his plays. His vision focuses powerfully on the quest for self-knowledge and self-realization in a world where, as the child of two conflicting cultures, he might fairly claim with his fictional character Shabine: "I had no nation now but the imagination."

Walcott's early dramas present native Caribbean figures in heroic and tragic roles, countering the accepted European pantheon of "greats." For a writer trying to recreate a history with meaning for his black compatriots, the Haitian revolution offers evident attractions. *Henri Christophe: A Chronicle* portrays the life, ambition, and eventual downfall of the rebel who became Emperor of Haiti, and Walcott has returned more recently to the events of this period with *Haitian Earth* (as yet unproduced). More typical of his work as a dramatist are those plays which have lowly, downtrodden peasants as their leading characters. In *Malcochon*, *The Sea at Dauphin*, and *Dream on Monkey Mountain* woodcutters, charcoal-burners, and fishermen take centre stage, their subsistence lifestyles presented in the bleakest possible light. Walcott strips away all heroic pretensions from them, revealing his creations as squalid, vulnerable individuals. Makak, for instance, whose nightmare vision provides the core of the play in *Dream on Monkey Mountain*, bears a name which invites comparison with the simian macaque. This allusion to mankind's prehuman ancestry is clear in the text itself: "In the beginning was the ape, and the ape had no name, so God called him man." A further, sinister dimension is also suggested, in the dehumanizing racist stereotype of all blacks as monkeys. Makak, in his dream, struggles to free himself from the power of the White Goddess, whiteness here—as in *Moby Dick*—symbolizing death and negation. With its bleak, compelling insights, its presentation of "the wretched of the earth," *Dream on Monkey Mountain* ranks among Walcott's strongest dramatic statements. Another significant work, *Ti-Jean and His Brothers*, makes effective use of drumming and chanting as background to a play whose dialogue is imbued with Creole speech patterns. Ti-Jean, the untutored peasant, holds the central role in a Caribbean morality play, encountering and overcoming the Devil in his many guises by a combination of luck and mother-wit. His victory, achieved at tragic cost, is given a native context by its "chorus" of chants and drum-rhythms. *The Joker of Seville* reveals talent of another kind, being a remarkable reworking of the Don Juan legend from Molina's Spanish original in which Walcott reshapes the classic material to a valid creation of his own. Following Juan, the amoral, heartless lecher-hero, to his final destruction, he sets the action not in Spain but Trinidad, where Latin and African cultures fuse uneasily together. The stage is devised as a symbolic bull-ring where stick-fighters and masked dancers echo the dialogue with comments and chanted choruses. *O Babylon!* has a more modern setting, its action centring on a confrontation between developers and Rastafarian squatters on the eve of Haile Selassie's visit to Jamaica. Walcott presents scenario and players in a manner at once comic and profound, the complex natures and motives of his characters displayed in speeches which make inspired use of Rastafarian, Jamaican, and English languages. Music and dance again complement the inevitable irony of the play's conclusion.

Three Plays, an impressive triptych from the 1980s, shows Walcott once more exploring major themes in a contemporary Trinidadian setting. *The Last Carnival* traces the shared relationships of a land-owning Creole family and their "adopted" English sibling as colonialism gives way to independence, and the trauma of revolution. The image of the carnival—at once a vain attempt by the thwarted artist Victor to impose the canons of European culture on his unresponsive audience, and a symbolic final gesture of the old order—is effectively contrasted with the surface radicalism of the young revolutionaries, for whom war is another kind of carnival, and one equally doomed to failure. The gradual change in Agatha, the working-class English woman who renounces her own radical politics on Victor's death to become the mainstay of the establishment, is convincingly shown, as is her tense relationship with the isolated, unbalanced Victor and his earthy Creolised brother Oswald. In the end, the one hope for salvation is the exile chosen by Clodia, the Agatha of a new generation. *Beef, No Chicken*, like *O Babylon!*, presents the conflict of developers and "little men" in terms of comic farce. Its central theme is the struggle of small-time restaurateur Otto Hogan to fight off the efforts of a corrupt council to bypass his premises with a major highway. Modern reality is represented by the shopping-mall magnate Mongroo, who regards bribery and coercion as an integral part of "civilization," and a mayor who sees pollution as evidence of progress. Otto's futile attempts to hold up the road by "haunting" workmen in the guise of a female ghost are complicated by a hilariously varied cast which includes a television crew, Cuban revolutionaries, and the members of the council. In the end, he is forced to abandon his principles and join the rat-race, running for mayor as the council and Mongroo are exposed on television. *A Branch of the Blue Nile* is set in a small theatre workshop in Port-of-Spain, and follows the lives of actors and director as they examine their relationships through rehearsals, improvisations, and performance in a modern version of *Antony and Cleopatra*. Walcott depicts players and setting superbly in a powerful, moving drama where acting is presented as a holy or profane transformation, a state of grace or possession which defines and limits the continuing flux of life. The poetic strength of his dialogue—in blank verse speeches, taped conversations, and island dialect—lends an individual voice to all three plays, and in particular to the last, which is surely one of his most impressive achievements.

—Geoff Sadler

See the essay on *Dream on Monkey Mountain*.

WANDOR, Michelene (Dinah).

Born in London, 20 April 1940. Educated at Chingford Secondary Modern School, 1954–56, and Chingford County High School, 1956–59, both Essex; Newnham College, Cambridge, 1959–62, B.A. (honours) in English 1962; University of Essex, Colchester, 1974–75, M.A. in sociology 1975. Married the literary agent Ed Victor in 1963 (divorced 1975); two sons. Poetry editor, *Time Out* magazine, London, 1971–82; regular contributor, *Spare Rib* magazine, London, 1972–77; reviewer, *Plays and Players*, *Listener*, and *New Statesman*, all London, and *Kaleidoscope* programme, BBC Radio. Playwright-in-residence, University of Kent, Canterbury, 1982–83. Currently student, performers' course in Renaissance and Baroque music, Trinity College of Music, London. Recipient: Arts Council bursary, 1974, 1983; Emmy award, 1987. Address: 71 Belsize Lane, London NW3 5AU, England.

Publications

PLAYS

You Too Can Be Ticklish (produced 1971).
Brag-a-Fruit (produced 1971).
The Day after Yesterday (produced 1972).
Spilt Milk, and Mal de Mère in *Point 101* (produced 1972). In *Play Nine*, edited by Robin Rook, 1981.
To Die among Friends (includes *Mal de Mère, Joey, Christmas, Pearls, Swallows*) (produced 1974). In *Sink Songs*, 1975.
Friends and Strangers (produced 1974).
Sink Songs, with Dinah Brooke. 1975.
Penthesilia, adaptation of the play by Heinrich von Kleist (produced 1977).
The Old Wives' Tale (produced 1977). In *Five Plays*, 1984.
Care and Control (produced 1977). In *Strike While the Iron Is Hot*, edited by Wandor, 1980.
Floorshow, with others (produced 1978).
Whores d'Oeuvres (produced 1978). In *Five Plays*, 1984.
Scissors (produced 1978). In *Five Plays*, 1984.
Aid Thy Neighbour (produced 1978). In *Five Plays*, 1984.
Correspondence (broadcast 1978; produced 1979).
Aurora Leigh, adaptation of the poem by Elizabeth Barrett Browning (produced 1979). In *Plays by Women 1*, edited by Wandor, 1982.
Future Perfect, with Steve Gooch and Paul Thompson (produced 1980).
The Blind Goddess, adaptation of a play by Ernst Toller (produced 1981).
Five Plays (includes *To Die among Friends, The Old Wives' Tale, Whores d'Oeuvres, Scissors, Aid Thy Neighbour*). 1984.
The Wandering Jew, with Mike Alfreds, adaptation of a novel by Eugène Sue (produced 1987). 1987.
Wanted (produced 1988). 1988.

RADIO PLAYS AND SERIALS: *Correspondence*, 1978; *The Unlit Lamp*, from the novel by Radclyffe Hall, 1980; *Precious Bane*, from the novel by Mary Webb, 1981; *Lolly Willowes*, from the novel by Sylvia Townsend Warner, 1983; *An Uncommon Love*, 1984; *Kipps*, from the novel by H.G. Wells, 1984; *Venus Smiles*, from the story by J.G. Ballard, 1985; *The Brothers Karamazov*, from a novel by Dostoevsky, 1986; *The Nine Tailors*, from the novel by Dorothy L. Sayers, 1986; *Persuasion*, from the novel by Jane Austen, 1986–87; *Helbeck of Bannisdale*, from the novel by Mrs. Humphry Ward, 1987; *Gardens of Eden*, 1987; *Whose Body?*, from the novel by Dorothy L. Sayers, 1987; *The Dwelling Place*, from the novel by Catherine Cookson, 1988; *Frenchman's Creek*, from the novel by Daphne du Maurier, 1989; *Ben Venga Maggio*,

1990; *The Courtier, the Prince and the Lady*, 1990; *The Mill on the Floss*, from the novel by George Eliot, 1991; *A Summer Wedding*, 1991; *Killing Orders*, from the novel by Sara Paretsky, 1991; *A Question of Courage*, from the novel by Marjorie Darke, 1992; *The King's General*, from the novel by Daphne du Maurier, 1992; *Deadlock*, from the novel by Sara Paretsky, 1993.

TELEVISION PLAYS: *The Belle of Amherst*, from the play by William Luce, 1987; *The Story of an Hour*, adaptation of a story by Kate Chopin, 1988.

NOVEL
Arky Types, with Sara Maitland. 1987.

SHORT STORIES
Tales I Tell My Mother, with others. 1978.
Guests in the Body. 1986.
More Tales I Tell My Mother, with others. 1987.

VERSE
Upbeat: Poems and Stories. 1982.
Touch Papers, with Judith Kazantzis and Michèle Roberts. 1982.
Gardens of Eden: Poems for Eve and Lilith. 1984.
Gardens of Eden: Selected Poems. 1990.

OTHER
The Great Divide: The Sexual Division of Labour; or, Is It Art?, with others. 1976.
Understudies: Theatre and Sexual Politics. 1981; revised edition, as *Carry On, Understudies*, 1986.
Look Back in Gender: Sexuality and the Family in Post-1956 British Drama. 1987.
Wandor on Women Writers: Antonia White, Elizabeth Barrett Browning, Hannah Culwick, Dorothy Richardson, Jean Rhys. 1988.
Once a Feminist: Stories of a Generation. 1990.

Editor, *The Body Politic: Writings from the Women's Liberation Movement in Britain 1969–1972*. 1972.
Editor, with Michèle Roberts, *Cutlasses and Earrings* (poetry anthology). 1977.
Editor, *Strike While the Iron Is Hot: Three Plays on Sexual Politics*. 1980.
Editor, *Plays by Women 1–4*. 4 vols., 1982–85.
Editor, *On Gender and Writing*. 1983.

CRITICAL STUDIES: "The Personal Is Political: Feminism and the Theatre" by Wandor, in *Dreams and Deconstructions* edited by Sandy Craig, 1980; *Feminist Theatre* by Helene Keyssar, 1984.

Michelene Wandor comments:

I began writing plays in 1969, when the "fringe" began. I also was writing poetry and theatre reviews. For me the activities of fiction/non-fiction have always been complementary. At that time I became aware of, and developed, socialist and feminist convictions. For about ten years I wrote plays just for the stage, in a variety of forms—social realism, collage, surreal, comedy, abstract: whatever. Since 1979 I have written extensively for radio, a stimulating medium. I have dramatised/transposed a number of texts for radio—a way of working with the voices and styles of other writers that is both exciting and rewarding. I have absolutely no pre-conceived ideas about the appropriateness or otherwise of dramatic form. For me the appropriate form arrives as a combination of content and my approach to it. Having said that, I can also be lured by any subject. I have written a lot of female-centred work and male-centred work, and am always as aware as I can be of the way an inevitable (though variable) gender-bias operates in every drama.

Michelene Wandor is a playwright who is also known for her poetry and fiction, and for her writing about the theatre. In her theatre writing, Wandor established her reputation with two key texts: *Understudies: Theatre and Sexual Politics* and *Look Back in Gender: Sexuality and the Family in Post-1956 British Drama*. These books, and others to which she has contributed, have earned her a reputation as one of England's most flexible writers, adept at producing critical essays and overviews of the state of the theatre and at writing plays for theatre, radio, and television.

As a playwright, Wandor has worked in a wide variety of different contexts, from her early work with feminist collectives and fringe theatre companies, to her work for the Royal National Theatre and the BBC. Some of her plays have been published in anthologies with playwrights such as Howard Brenton and Frank Marcus, marking her as one of the most notable "political playwrights" of her generation. She is also one of the few women—along with more "mainstream" playwrights such as Caryl Churchill, Pam Gems, and Louise Page—who was in on the watershed of women's alternative theatre in the 1970s. She has worked with and for Monstrous Regiment, Mrs. Worthington's Daughters, and Gay Sweatshop, as an independent playwright, and as a commissioned writer of radio and television drama.

Wandor is best known for a few early stage plays and for a number of highly successful radio dramas. She attributes the high profile of her radio plays to the fashion in contemporary theatre for "conservative" forms, styles, and themes, including the current popularity of dramatic adaptations. In her words:

> If theatre had not become so conservative so quickly, and if the theatre had retained its early 1970s openness, more of my work would be done in the theatre. Basically, to be successful in the theatre as a woman playwright, you need to have patrons who will bandwagon you. To work well in radio some similar things apply, but I genuinely believe that there are more radio producers whose commitment is to the work rather than to the fashion.

The comment reflects on the nature of Wandor's writing, which is always informed by politics; whether social, cultural, sexual, or personal. Thus, it has been Wandor's adaptations which, on the whole, have best suited the "conservative" trend of theatre production. Her best radio work includes *Ben*

Venga Maggio, a dramatic poem in the voice of the popular character Columbina; it is a play which blends spoken language and Italian carnival music. Another notable radio play of the same period is *The Courtier, the Prince and the Lady*, which is set in Renaissance Italy and draws on Machiavelli and Castiglione as source material, while incorporating the music of Josquin and his contemporaries. In 1991, Wandor adapted George Eliot's *The Mill on the Floss* in a five-part serial dramatization. She has since adapted feminist detective stories by Sarah Paretsky and some of the writings of Marjorie Darke.

Wandor has also had considerable success in television drama. She won an Emmy award for her television adaptation of William Luce's play about the life of Emily Dickinson, *The Belle of Amherst*. In 1988, she wrote a short film adaptation of Kate Chopin's *The Story of an Hour*. *The Well Woman*, her television adaptation of Radclyffe Hall's *The Well of Loneliness*, has yet to be produced.

Yet Wandor's most characteristic work is found in her own original stage plays. One important contribution to British theatre was her scripting, from devised and group-researched material, of Gay Sweatshop's *Care and Control* in 1977. That play was among the first political theatre pieces to address the issue of the state and motherhood. It had a considerable social impact as well as theatrical and critical success, as did *Aid Thy Neighbour*, produced at London's New End Theatre in 1978. The latter play offered a frank treatment of the process of artificial insemination by donor, another crucial issue for contemporary women. In these and many of her other stage plays, Wandor combined her feminist politics and social activism in her writing for the stage. While some of her work could be described by labels such as "agitprop" or "social realism," Wandor herself would be the first to qualify and explain these terms. In fact, analysis of the influence of politics on the theatre of the 1970s and 1980s is one of the threads running through Wandor's critical writing about the theatre. For Wandor, playwriting and political involvement (real and representational) tend to go hand in hand.

Partly for reasons related to the politics (and "fashionability") of radio and theatre production, Wandor wrote more and more adaptations in the 1980s, including *Aurora Leigh*—an adaptation of Elizabeth Barrett Browning's poem —produced by Mrs. Worthington's Daughters in 1979 and revived at the Royal National Theatre in 1981. Her major mainstage theatre success was also an adaptation: *The Wandering Jew*, co-written with Mike Alfreds and adapted from Eugène Sue's novel about the Jesuits, given a mainstage production at the Royal National Theatre in 1987.

Yet in the late 1980s and early 1990s, Wandor's stage plays have begun to convey more of her own distinct voice. In *Wanted*, for instance, she took an experimental tack in her depiction of a mixed bag of characters (an angel, an unborn being, and the biblical Sarah), all engaged in a witty and topical theatrical representation of the issue of surrogacy. Here, as in her earlier plays *Care and Control* and *Aid Thy Neighbour*, the concern for gender relations and family structure are central themes. Yet the style of *Wanted* reveals a developmental shift in Wandor's work, a move away from social realism and the structure of adaptations, to the refinement of a distinctive personal voice. That voice, fractured in *Wanted* into three, is still shifting too quickly to predict the next phase in Wandor's career as a playwright. Yet it does seem clear that her current work is developing in conjunction with (and sometimes in a challenging opposition to) current debates about post-modernist and post-structuralist theatres.

—Lizbeth Goodman

WATERHOUSE, Keith (Spencer).

Born in Leeds, Yorkshire, 6 February 1929. Educated at Osmondthorpe Council Schools, Leeds. Served in the Royal Air Force. Married 1) Joan Foster in 1951 (divorced 1968), one son and two daughters; 2) Stella Bingham (divorced 1989). Since 1950 freelance journalist and writer in Leeds and London; columnist, *Daily Mirror*, 1970–86, and *Daily Mail* since 1986, both London. Member, Kingman Committee on Teaching of English Language, 1987–88. Recipient (for journalism): Granada award, 1970, and special award, 1982; IPC award, 1970, 1973; British Press award, 1978; *Evening Standard* award, for play, 1991. Honorary fellow, Leeds Polytechnic. Fellow, Royal Society of Literature. Agent: London Management, 235 Regent Street, London W1A 2JT. Address: 29 Kenway Road, London, S.W.5, England.

Publications

PLAYS

Billy Liar, with Willis Hall, adaptation of the novel by Waterhouse (produced 1960). 1960.

Celebration: The Wedding and The Funeral, with Willis Hall (produced 1961). 1961.

England, Our England, with Willis Hall, music by Dudley Moore (produced 1962). 1964.

Squat Betty, with Willis Hall (produced 1962). In *The Sponge Room, and Squat Betty*, 1963.

The Sponge Room, with Willis Hall (produced 1962). In *The Sponge Room, and Squat Betty*, 1963; in *Modern Short Plays from Broadway and London*, edited by Stanley Richards, 1969.

All Things Bright and Beautiful, with Willis Hall (produced 1962). 1963.

The Sponge Room, and Squat Betty, with Willis Hall. 1963.

Come Laughing Home, with Willis Hall (as *They Called the Bastard Stephen*, produced 1964; as *Come Laughing Home*, produced 1965). 1965.

Say Who You Are, with Willis Hall (produced 1965). 1966; as *Help Stamp Out Marriage* (produced 1966), 1966.

Joey, Joey, with Willis Hall, music by Ron Moody (produced 1966).

Whoops-a-Daisy, with Willis Hall (produced 1968). 1978.

Children's Day, with Willis Hall (produced 1969). 1975.

Who's Who, with Willis Hall (produced 1971). 1974.

Saturday, Sunday, Monday, with Willis Hall, adaptation of a play by Eduardo De Filippo (produced 1973). 1974.

The Card, with Willis Hall, music and lyrics by Tony Hatch and Jackie Trent, adaptation of the novel by Arnold Bennett (produced 1973).

Filumena, with Willis Hall, adaptation of a play by Eduardo De Filippo (produced 1977). 1978.

Worzel Gummidge (for children), with Willis Hall, music by Denis King, adaptation of stories by Barbara Euphan Todd (produced 1980). 1984.

Steafel Variations (songs and sketches), with Peter Tinniswood and Dick Vosburgh (produced 1982).

Lost Empires, with Willis Hall, music by Denis King, adaptation of the novel by J.B. Priestley (produced 1985).

Mr. and Mrs. Nobody, adaptation of *The Diary of a Nobody* by George and Weedon Grossmith (produced 1986). With *Jeffrey Bernard Is Unwell* and *Bookends*, 1992.

Budgie, with Willis Hall, music by Mort Shuman, lyrics by Don Black (produced 1988).

Jeffrey Bernard Is Unwell (produced 1989). With *Mr. and Mrs. Nobody* and *Bookends*, 1992.

Bookends, adaptation of *The Marsh Marlowe Letters* by Craig Brown (produced 1990). With *Mr. and Mrs. Nobody* and *Jeffrey Bernard Is Unwell*, 1992.

Our Song, adaptation of his novel (produced 1992).

*Jeffrey Bernard Is Unwell, Mr. and Mrs. Nobody, Bookends.*1992.

SCREENPLAYS, with Willis Hall: *Whistle Down the Wind*, 1961; *The Valiant*, 1962; *A Kind of Loving*, 1963; *Billy Liar*, 1963; *West Eleven*, 1963; *Man in the Middle*, 1963; *Pretty Polly* (*A Matter of Innocence*), 1967; *Lock Up Your Daughters*, 1969.

RADIO PLAYS: *The Town That Wouldn't Vote*, 1951; *There Is a Happy Land*, 1962; *The Woolen Bank Forgeries*, 1964; *The Last Phone-In*, 1976; *The Big Broadcast of 1922*, 1979.

TELEVISION PLAYS: *The Warmonger*, 1970; *The Upchat Line* series, 1977; *The Upchat Connection* series, 1978; *Charlie Muffin*, from novels by Brian Freemantle, 1979; *West End Tales* series, 1981; *The Happy Apple* series, from a play by Jack Pulman, 1983; *This Office Life*, from his own novel, 1984; *Charters and Caldicott*, 1985; *The Great Paper Chase*, from the book *Slip Up* by Anthony Delano, 1988; *Andy Capp* series, 1988; with Willis Hall—*Happy Moorings*, 1963; *How Many Angels*, 1964; *Inside George Webley* series, 1968; *Queenie's Castle* series, 1970; *Budgie* series, 1971–72; *The Upper Crusts* series, 1973; *Three's Company* series, 1973; *By Endeavour Alone*, 1973; *Briefer Encounter*, 1977; *Public Lives*, 1979; *Worzel Gummidge* series, from stories by Barbara Euphan Todd, 1979.

NOVELS

There Is a Happy Land. 1957.

Billy Liar. 1959.

Jubb. 1963.

The Bucket Shop. 1968; as *Everything Must Go*, 1969.

Billy Liar on the Moon. 1975.

Office Life. 1978.
Maggie Muggins; or, Spring in Earl's Court. 1981.
In the Mood. 1983.
Thinks. 1984.
Our Song. 1988.
Bimbo. 1990.
Unsweet Charity. 1992.

OTHER

The Café Royal: Ninety Years of Bohemia, with Guy Deghy. 1955.
How to Avoid Matrimony: The Layman's Guide to the Laywoman, with Guy
     Deghy (as Herald Froy). 1957.
Britain's Voice Abroad, with Paul Cave. 1957.
The Future of Television. 1958.
How to Survive Matrimony, with Guy Deghy (as Herald Froy). 1958.
The Joneses: How to Keep Up with Them, with Guy Deghy (as Lee Gibb).
     1959.
Can This Be Love?, with Guy Deghy (as Herald Froy). 1960.
Maybe You're Just Inferior: Head-Shrinking for Fun and Profit, with Guy
     Deghy (as Herald Froy). 1961.
The Higher Jones, with Guy Deghy (as Lee Gibb). 1961.
O Mistress Mine: or, How to Go Roaming, with Guy Deghy (as Herald Froy).
     1962.
The Passing of the Third-Floor Buck (Punch sketches). 1974.
Mondays, Thursdays (Daily Mirror columns). 1976.
Rhubarb, Rhubarb, and Other Noises (Daily Mirror columns). 1979.
The Television Adventures [and *More Television Adventures*] *of Worzel
     Gummidge* (for children), with Willis Hall. 2 vols., 1979; complete edition,
     as *Worzel Gummidge's Television Adventures,* 1981.
Worzel Gummidge at the Fair (for children), with Willis Hall. 1980.
Worzel Gummidge Goes to the Seaside (for children), with Willis Hall. 1980.
The Trials of Worzel Gummidge (for children), with Willis Hall. 1980.
Worzel's Birthday (for children), with Willis Hall. 1981.
New Television Adventures of Worzel Gummidge and Aunt Sally (for chil-
     dren), with Willis Hall. 1981.
Daily Mirror Style. 1981; revised, edition as *Waterhouse on Newspaper Style,*
     1989.
Fanny Peculiar (Punch columns). 1983.
Mrs. Pooter's Diary. 1983.
The Irish Adventures of Worzel Gummidge (for children), with Willis Hall.
     1984.
Waterhouse at Large (journalism). 1985.
The Collected Letters of a Nobody (Including Mr. Pooter's Advice to His Son).
     1986.
The Theory and Practice of Lunch. 1986.
Worzel Gummidge Down Under (for children), with Willis Hall. 1987.
The Theory and Practice of Travel. 1989.
English Our English (and How to Sing It). 1991.

Sharon and Tracy and the Rest: The Best of Keith Waterhouse in the Daily Mail. 1992.

Editor, with Willis Hall, *Writers' Theatre.* 1967.

See the essay on Willis Hall and Keith Waterhouse.

WERTENBAKER, (Lael Louisiana) Timberlake.

Educated at schools near St. Jean-de-Luz, France; attended university in the United States. Journalist in London and New York; teacher of French in Greece, one year. Resident writer, Shared Experience, 1983, and Royal Court Theatre, 1985, both London. Recipient: Arts Council of Great Britain bursary, 1981, grant, 1983; Thames Television bursary, 1984, 1985; *Plays and Players* award, 1985; *Evening Standard* award, 1988; Olivier award, 1988; John Whiting award, 1989; London Theatre Critics Circle award, 1991, 1992; Writers Guild Macallan award, 1992. Lives in London. Agent: Michael Imison Playwrights, 28 Almeida Street, London N1 1TD, England.

Publications

PLAYS

This Is No Place for Tallulah Bankhead (produced 1978).
The Third (produced 1980).
Second Sentence (produced 1980).
Case to Answer (produced 1980).
Breaking Through (produced 1980).
New Anatomies (produced 1981). In *Plays Introduction*, 1984.
Inside Out (produced 1982).
Home Leave (produced 1982).
False Admissions, adaptation of a play by Marivaux (produced 1983).
Successful Strategies, adaptation of a play by Marivaux (produced 1983).
Abel's Sister, based on material by Yolande Bourcier (produced 1984).
The Grace of Mary Traverse (produced 1985). 1985.
Léocadia, adaptation of the play by Jean Anouilh (broadcast 1985). In *Five Plays*, by Anouilh, 1987.
Mephisto, adaptation of the play by Ariane Mnouchkine, based on a novel by Klaus Mann (produced 1986).
Our Country's Good, adaptation of *The Playmaker* by Thomas Keneally (produced 1988). 1988; revised edition, 1990.
The Love of the Nightingale (produced 1988). With *The Grace of Mary Traverse*, 1989.
Pelléas and Mélisande, adaptation of the play by Maeterlinck (broadcast 1988; produced 1989).
Three Birds Alighting on a Field (produced 1991). 1991.
The Thebans, adaptation of three plays by Sophocles (includes *Oedipus Tyrannos, Oedipus at Colonus, Antigone*) (produced 1992). 1992.

RADIO PLAYS: *Léocadia*, 1985; *La Dispute*, from the play by Marivaux, 1987; *Pelléas and Mélisande*, from the play by Maeterlinck, 1988.

TELEVISION PLAYS: *Do Not Disturb*, 1991; *The Children*, adaptation of a novel by Edith Wharton, 1992.

Timberlake Wertenbaker comments:

I like monologues. I think they are an unused and rather beautiful form of communication. I do not like naturalism. I find it boring. My plays are an attempt to get away from the smallness of naturalism, from enclosed rooms to open spaces, and also to get ideas away from the restraints of closed spaces to something wider. My plays often start with a very ordinary question: If women had power, would they behave the same way as men? Why do we seem to want to destroy ourselves? Is the personal more important than the political? If someone has behaved badly all of their lives, can they redeem themselves? Parallel to this will be some story I may have heard, some gossip about somebody, a sentence heard or read. A friend of mine once told me his mother had been taught how to be a good hostess by being made to talk to empty chairs. I used that as the opening scene of *The Grace of Mary Traverse*. I once heard about a young couple where the woman, for no apparant reason, had come out of the bath and shot herself. That became *Case to Answer*. Somebody showed me a print of the Japanese courtesan Ono No Komachi. I wrote a play about her. Everything gets collected and used at some point. I'm sure it's the same for all writers, but I haven't asked. Once I have the idea and the people, I do a lot of research. I think plays should be accurate, whatever their subject. Then the imagination can be let free, but only after a solid knowledge of the world, the people, the age, whatever is the world of the play.

I don't think you can leave the theatre and go out and make a revolution. That's the naïvety of the 1970s. But I do think you can make people change, just a little, by forcing them to question something, or by intriguing them, or giving them an image that remains with them. And that little change can lead to bigger changes. That's all you can hope for. Nor do I think playwrights should have the answers. A play is like a trial: it goes before the jury, the audience, and they decide—to like or not like the people, to agree or not to agree. If you really have the answers, you shouldn't be a writer but a politician. And if you're only interested in slice of life, then you should make documentaries. The theatre is a difficult place, it requires an audience to use its imagination. You must accept that and not try to make it easy for them. You must give them language, because it is best heard in the theatre and language is a potent manifestation of hope. In some theatres in ancient Greece, the number of seats corresponded to the number of adult males with voting rights. I think that is right: theatre is for people who take responsibility. There is no point in trying to attract idiots. Theatre should never be used to flatter, but to reveal, which is to disturb.

Timberlake Wertenbaker's plays range from the domestic to the mythic within the duration of each single drama. In their social expositions, these plays identify dispossession and restriction of human potential. Moreover, they demonstrate how these phenomena are the deliberate and intrinsic effects of linguistic systems and terms of reference which define the rights of the individual in exclusively patriarchal terms. But the plays also depict how public experience, and individual communication of that experience, challenge these prescribed definitions. Wertenbaker identifies language as a means not simply of communicating, but of constituting knowledge, both of the self and of the world.

Wertenbaker characteristically locates the seeds of crisis in patriarchal-imperial impositions of definition. Her plays strive towards the discovery of respect for human variety. Her protagonists are in conflict with an authoritarianism specifically paternalistic in nature: it pretends provident fostering care whilst seeking to erode systematically any belief in a possible separateness and difference of individual interests. In Wertenbaker's plays, the ultimate threat of this governing system is to dispossess the individual of speech, and of the right to expression of selfhood. But hope resides in the defiant reactions of her marginalised protagonists.

Wertenbaker's early plays *Case to Answer* and *Abel's Sister* identify blind spots in self-righteous characters who find convenient relief in not deigning to translate their abstract social idealisms into practical dealings with individuals; indeed, they seem to feel their ideological postures permit them a degree of separation, aloof from human untidiness.

In *New Anatomies*, the protagonist Isabelle is dislocated from her childhood idyll with brother Antoine, and she travels through turn-of-the-century Europe and Algeria seeking to elude imposed definitions. Isabelle's intoxicated appetite for life and her naive tendency to see things in terms of inappropriate mythological parallels anticipate the heroine of *The Grace of Mary Traverse*. Mary's hunger for personal knowledge offends her father's sense of her social utility; so begins her odyssey of inquisitive transgression, in search of "grace", in individually reformulated definitions.

Wertenbaker's *Our Country's Good*, based on Thomas Keneally's 1987 novel *The Playmaker*, follows the fortunes of 18th-century convicts deported to Australia. The penal colony governors argue as to whether the convicts are capable of speaking literary language in order to perform a play; Wertenbaker celebrates their discovery of resources through this language. Her most complex play, *The Love of the Nightingale*, is a version of the Philomel myth, enquiring as to the essences of myth and love, through highlighting the activity of questioning. This drama seems the culmination of Wertenbaker's own questionings of the terms and conditions of using language, making moral judgements, and being human—all demonstrated to be irrevocably linked. Its exhortations of metaphorical insight and moral revaluation distinguish Wertenbaker as one of the most promising dramatists to emerge in the 1980s.

—David Ian Rabey

See the essay on *Our Country's Good*.

WESKER, Arnold.

Born in Stepney, London, 24 May 1932. Educated at Upton House Technical School, Hackney, London, 1943–48; London School of Film Technique, 1955–56. Served in the Royal Air Force, 1950–52. Married Doreen Bicker in 1958; two sons and two daughters. Furniture-maker's apprentice and carpenter's mate, 1948; bookseller's assistant, 1949 and 1952; plumber's mate, 1952; seed sorter on farm, 1953; kitchen porter, 1953–54; pastry cook, London and Paris, 1954–58; founder and director, Centre 42, 1961–70. Chair of the British Centre, 1978–83, and president of the Playwrights Permanent Committee, 1981–83, International Theatre Institute. Recipient: Arts Council grant, 1958; *Evening Standard* award, 1959; Encyclopaedia Britannica award, 1959; Marzotto prize, 1964; Best Foreign Play award (Spain), 1979; Goldie award, 1987. Fellow, Royal Society of Literature, 1985. Litt.D.: University of East Anglia, Norwich, 1989. Lives in London. Agent: Ian Amos, Duncan Heath Associates, Oxford House, 76 Oxford Street W1R 1RB, England.

Publications

PLAYS

The Wesker Trilogy. 1960.
> *Chicken Soup with Barley* (produced 1958). In *New English Dramatists 1*, 1959.
> *Roots* (produced 1959). 1959.
> *I'm Talking about Jerusalem* (produced 1960; revised version produced 1960). 1960.
The Kitchen (produced 1959). In *New English Dramatists 2*, 1960; expanded version (produced 1961), 1961.
Chips with Everything (produced 1962). 1962.
The Nottingham Captain: A Moral for Narrator, Voices and Orchestra, music by Wilfred Josephs and Dave Lee (produced 1962). In *Six Sundays in January*, 1971.
Menace (televised 1963). In *Six Sundays in January*, 1971; in *The Plays of Arnold Wesker 2*, 1977.
Their Very Own and Golden City (produced 1965; revised version produced 1966). 1966; revised version (also director: produced 1974), in *The Plays of Arnold Wesker 2*, 1977.
The Four Seasons (produced 1965). 1966; in *The Plays of Arnold Wesker 2*, 1977; revised version in *The Plays of Arnold Wesker 2*, 1990.
The Friends (also director: produced 1970). 1970; in *The Plays of Arnold Wesker 2*, 1977.
The Old Ones (produced 1972). 1973; revised version, edited by Michael Marland, 1974; in *The Plays of Arnold Wesker 2*, 1977.
The Wedding Feast, adaptation of a story by Dostoevsky (produced 1974; revised version produced 1980). In *The Plays of Arnold Wesker 4*, 1980.
The Journalists (produced 1977). 1975.
Love Letters on Blue Paper, adaptation of his own story (televised 1976; produced 1977). 1978.

The Plays of Arnold Wesker:
1. *The Kitchen, Chips with Everything, The Wesker Trilogy.* 1976; revised edition as *The Wesker Trilogy* (includes *Chicken Soup with Barley, Roots, I'm Talking About Jerusalem*), 1979.
2. *The Four Seasons, Their Very Own and Golden City, Menace, The Friends, The Old Ones.* 1977; revised edition as *The Kitchen and Other Plays* (includes revised version of *The Four Seasons; The Kitchen; Their Very Own and Golden City*), 1990.
3. *Chips with Everything, The Friends, The Old Ones, Love Letters on Blue Paper.* 1980; revised edition as *Chips with Everything and Other Plays,* 1990.
4. *The Journalists, The Wedding Feast, The Merchant.* 1980; revised edition as *Shylock and Other Plays* (includes *The Journalists, The Wedding Feast, The Merchant* as *Shylock*), 1990.
5. *One Woman Plays: Yardsale, Whatever Happened to Betty Lemon?, Four Portraits of Mothers, The Mistress, Annie Wobbler.* 1989.
6. *Lady Othello and Other Plays: One More Ride on the Merry-Go-Round, Caritas, When God Wanted a Son, Lady Othello, Bluey.* 1990.

The Merchant (produced 1976; revised version produced 1977; revised version produced 1978).In *The Plays of Arnold Wesker 4,* 1980; revised version published 1983; revised version as *Shylock* included in *The Plays of Arnold Wesker 4,* 1990.

Caritas (produced 1981). 1981.

Mothers: Four Portraits (produced 1982; as *Four Portraits of Mothers,* produced 1984). As *Four Portraits of Mothers,* in *The Plays of Arnold Wesker 5,* 1989.

Annie, Anna, Annabella (broadcast 1983; as *Annie Wobbler,* also director: produced 1983). As *Annie Wobbler,* in *The Plays of Arnold Wesker 5,* 1989.

Sullied Hand (produced 1984).

Yardsale (broadcast 1984; produced 1985). In *The Plays of Arnold Wesker 5,* 1989.

Bluey (broadcast 1985). In *The Plays of Arnold Wesker 6,* 1990.

One More Ride on the Merry-Go-Round (produced 1985). In *The Plays of Arnold Wesker 6,* 1990.

Whatever Happened to Betty Lemon? (produced 1986). In *The Plays of Arnold Wesker 5,* 1989.

Little Old Lady (for children) (produced 1988). In *New Plays 1,* edited by Peter Terson, 1988.

Beorhtel's Hill (produced 1989).

Shoeshine (for children). In *New Plays 3,* edited by Peter Terson, 1989.

The Mistress (also director: produced 1991).In *The Plays of Arnold Wesker 5,* 1989.

When God Wanted a Son (produced 1989). In *Lady Othello and Other Plays,* 1990.

Three Woman Talking (produced 1992).

Letter to a Daughter (televised 1992; produced 1992).

SCREENPLAY: *The Kitchen,* 1961.

RADIO PLAYS: *Annie, Anna, Annabella*, 1983; *Yardsale*, 1984; *Bluey*, 1985.

TELEVISION PLAYS: *Menace*, 1963; *Love Letters on Blue Paper*, from his own story, 1976; *Diary of a Good Neighbour*, adaptation of Doris Lessing's *The Diary of Jane Somers*, 1989; *Letter to a Daughter*, 1992.

SHORT STORIES

Love Letters on Blue Paper. 1974.
Said the Old Man to the Young Man: Three Stories. 1978.
Love Letters on Blue Paper and Other Stories. 1980; revised edition, 1990.

OTHER

Labour and the Arts: II, or, What, Then, Is to be Done? 1960.
The Modern Playwright; or, "O Mother, Is It Worth It?" 1961.
Fears of Fragmentation (essays). 1970.
Six Sundays in January (miscellany). 1971.
Say Goodbye—You May Never See Them Again: Scenes from Two East-End Backgrounds, paintings by John Allin. 1974.
Words as Definitions of Experience. 1976.
Journey into Journalism. 1977.
Fatlips (for children). 1978.
The Journalists: A Triptych (includes the play *The Journalists, A Journal of the Writing of "The Journalists,"* and *Journey into Journalism*). 1979.
Distinctions (essays, lectures, journalism). 1985.

CRITICAL STUDIES (a selection): *Mid-Century Drama* by Laurence Kitchin, 1960, revised edition, 1962; *The Writer and Commitment* by John Mander, 1961; *Anger and After* by John Russell Taylor, 1962, revised edition, 1969, also as *The Angry Theatre*, 1962, revised edition, 1969; "Two Romantics: Arnold Wesker and Harold Pinter" by Clifford Leech, in *Contemporary Theatre*, edited by John Russell Brown and Bernard Harris, 1962; *Arnold Wesker* by Harold U. Ribalow, 1966; "Arnold Wesker, The Last Humanist?" by Michael Anderson, in *New Theatre Magazine*, vol.8, no.3, 1968; *Arnold Wesker* edited by Michael Marland, 1970; *Arnold Wesker* by Ronald Hayman, 1970, revised edition, 1973; *The Plays of Arnold Wesker: An Assessment* by Glenda Leeming and Simon Trussler, 1971, and *Arnold Wesker*, 1972, and *Wesker the Playwright*, 1983, both by Leeming, and *Wesker on File* edited by Leeming, 1985; *Theatre Language: A Study of Arden, Osborne, Pinter, and Wesker* by John Russell Brown, 1972; *Stages in the Revolution* by Catherine Itzin, 1980; *Wesker the Playwright* by Glenda Leeming, 1983; *File on Wesker*, edited by Glenda Leeming, 1985; *Arnold Wesker* by Klaus and Valeska Lindemann, 1985; *Understanding Arnold Wesker* by Robert Wilcher, 1991.

THEATRICAL ACTIVITIES

DIRECTOR: **Plays**—*The Four Seasons*, 1968; *The Friends*, 1970; *The Old Ones*, 1973; *Their Very Own and Golden City*, 1974; *Love Letters on Blue Paper*, 1978; *Annie Wobbler*, 1983; *Yardsale*, 1985; *Whatever Happened to Betty*

Lemon, 1987; *The Merry Wives of Windsor* by Shakespeare, 1990; *The Kitchen*, 1990; *The Mistress*, 1991.

Arnold Wesker comments:

(1982) It is really for others to write about me. I try every so often to explain myself in lectures, articles, interviews. Never satisfactorily. Certain themes and relationships seem to pre-occupy me: the relationship between lovers, husband and wife, parent and child, friends, state and the individual; the themes of injustice, defiance, the power of knowledge.

I have no theories about the theatre writing through which I pursue these themes and relationships. Each play comes to me with its own metaphor, dictates its own form, creates its own atmosphere. All literature contains a mixture of poetry and journalism. Poetry in the theatre is that indefinable *sense* of truth which is communicated when two dissimilar or unrelated moments are placed side by side. "Sense" of truth, not *the* one and only truth. I would like to think my plays and stories have a larger proportion of poetry than journalism, and that if I have any talent it is for identifying the metaphors which life contains for the purpose of illuminating itself.

One day I hope someone may write as generously of me as Ruskin did of Turner:

> This you will find is ultimately the case with every true and right master; at first, while we are tyros in art, or before we have earnestly studied the man in question, we shall see little in him; or perhaps see, as we think, deficiencies; we shall fancy he is inferior to this man in that, and to the other man in the other; but as we go on studying him we shall find that he has got both that and the other; and both in a far higher sense than the man who seemed to possess those qualities in excess. Thus in Turner's lifetime, when people first looked at him, those who liked rainy weather said he was not equal to Copley Fielding; but those who looked at Turner long enough found that he could be much more wet than Copley Fielding when he chose. The people who liked force said that "Turner was not strong enough for them; he was effeminate; they liked De Wint,—nice strong tone;—or Cox—great, greeny, dark masses of colour—solemn feeling of the freshness and depth of nature; they liked Cox—Turner was too hot for them." Had they looked long enough they would have found that he had far more force than De Wint, far more freshness than Cox when he chose,—only united with other elements; and that he didn't choose to be cool, if nature had appointed the weather to be hot . . . And so throughout with all thoroughly great men, their strength is not seen at first, precisely because they united, in due place and measure, every great quality . . .

In an interview in the *Tribune* in 1978 Arnold Wesker characterised himself as "world-weary." "over-whelmed with a sense of frustration and impotence." "For reasons which I don't understand, I do seem to arouse hostilities and irritations." Nevertheless, Wesker continues to write and if he can find no place, or small room, in the British theatre, his plays enjoy a considerable success in other countries. The paradox of a major British writer continually premiering his work abroad, in translation, is heightened when one considers the obsessive concern, in the earlier plays, with the necessity of acting in community to transform and transcend the immediate environment in order to live authentically and fully.

Wesker's plays are plays of ideas, dramatising a debate, expressed in passionate terms, about the complexity and necessity of moral choices, when there is no clear precept to follow. In the earlier plays these moral dilemmas are often laid out in set pieces. In *Roots* Beatie tells the story of the girl in love with one man who deserts her, and loved by another who rejects her because she has given herself to the first. Idealism is seen very early to contain its own negative dialectic. "Tell me your dreams," says Peter, in *The Kitchen*, and unleashes the dream of the man who wants to drop a bomb on the CND marchers, because they hold up the buses.

Ironically, Wesker enjoyed much more success with the earlier plays, in which the dialectics between idealism and frustration were presented more simply, than with the later plays, where the issues are much more complex. Often values which had been seen positively in the earlier plays are revealed to be illusory. The search for "words" through which to apprehend the world, express one's thoughts and feelings, and build "bridges" fails to achieve those aims and becomes a way of obscuring or evading the issues. The realisation of self, through education and culture, which is to be the means of Beatie's liberation, becomes in *The Friends* a source of frustration, isolation, and contempt for others.

Wesker's stature in the theatre declined during the 1960s and 1970s. Until 1964 his battle against apathy and purely materialist values, for the individual's right to life, liberty, and the pursuit of happiness through the orderly and gradual reform of society, could be seen as a feasible, and socialist, course of action. The political and economic crises of the mid-1960s through the 1970s called for either a cynical withdrawal from these aims, a dropping out into anarchistic individualism, or a commitment to a programme, however vague, for mass revolution. Wesker's concern with values that surmount the material has embarrassed his opponents. His concern with the individual has led those who share his own passionate concern for the realisation of working-class potential to brand his work as elitist, subjective, and, ultimately, conformist.

It is very easy to select from Wesker's plays quotations which support a critique of counter-revolutionary idealism. After all, in *The Friends* Manfred has a speech in which he says, "The working class! Hate them! It's coming, Macey. Despise them! I can hear myself, it's coming. Hate them! The working class, my class, offend me. Their cowardly acquiescence, their rotten ordinariness—everything about them—Hate them! There!" Wesker leaves himself open to such criticisms, not because he necessarily agrees with such views but because, recognising that such thoughts and feelings are part of the dialectics of his own make-up, he allows his characters to express them with extreme feeling, without explicitly denying them by suppressing them or taking a committed authorial stance against them. Examined closely, Wesker's later plays present a complex dialectical discourse of contrasting and often contradictory views as to what the central issue involves. Friend and foe alike might condemn this as nit-picking over dead ground of a perverse adherence to idealism in the stern face of reality. Politicos may call for a sword to cut through the Gordian knots with which Wesker becomes enmeshed. He himself relentlessly pursues metaphysical values in an increasingly materialistic world, charting as he goes the deepening frustrations of compromise and the high price exacted for sticking to your beliefs.

What is clear from the line of development through his plays is the continual decrease of the spatial area in which the individual can act. The major shift in his work occurred in the mid-1960s and coincides with his withdrawal from public action, as expressed through his involvement with CND, the Committee of 100, and Centre 42. There are fewer scenes of concerted action in the later plays to mark the potential power of the working-class shown in the first act of *The Kitchen* or the coal-stealing scene in *Chips with Everything*. The size of the community participating in the ritual celebrations becomes smaller and more enclosed. In the first act of *Chicken Soup with Barley* the setting is a room, but there is constant reference to the world outside. The streets of the East End and the battlefields of Spain are arenas of political action. Education will make the world Beatie Bryant's oyster. In *The Old Ones* both the streets and the classroom are potential areas of mindless violence. In *The Merchant* Shylock's actions are confined within the space and rules of the ghetto. The line culminates in the walling up of the nun, Christine, in *Caritas* while she repeats "This is a wall, this is a wall. . . ." The area of the action shrinks and the concerns become more metaphysical.

Wesker's world-weariness and his sense of isolation and impotence are nihilistic only if he sees them subjectively. A move out into the world would reveal them as a common feature of the contemporary human condition. If it is harder to keep faith with Sarah Kahn's injunction to "care," her corollary still stands, "if you don't care you'll die." The struggle might be harder and the issues less clear-cut than they appeared before but the battle must still be waged. But to do this the ghetto has to be broken out of, and being walled up for your beliefs is too high a price to pay for integrity.

Since 1981 Wesker's work has marked time with no major play coming from him. However, there are signs that there is some resurgence of light-heartedness and fun if not optimism. *One More Ride on the Merry-Go-Round* is Wesker's attempt at writing pure comedy but, not unexpectedly, serious themes intrude. The main action of the comedy is the revival of energy and purpose in a 50-year-old academic and his wife. Two further plays, *When God Wanted a Son* and *Lady Othello*, continue the theme of a middle-aged academic in affairs with younger women. Through these plays, Wesker explores further the process first encountered in *Roots*, the education and culturalization of women by an auto-didactic male. In these plays the issues become more complex. In *When God Wanted a Son*, the play centres on the wife, separated from her husband, who returns obsessively to exasperate and infuriate her. In *Lady Othello*, Wesker's finest play for some time, but so far unperformed, the couple in the relationship are incompatible in terms of age, colour, race, and his feelings of guilt. In both of these plays the destructive and divisive effects of education and learning are explored as well as the positive. Alongside these plays, Wesker has written a a series of one-woman plays, the best known and most often performed being *Annie Wobbler*. These serve to remind that Wesker is, above all, a great writer of character parts. His reputation internationally remains unabated but at home he remains bitter and alienated by the lack of respect and production for his plays.

—Clive Barker

See the essay on *The Wesker Trilogy*.

WHELAN, Peter.

Born in Newcastle-under-Lyme, 3 October 1931. Educated at Hanley High School, Stoke-on-Trent, 1941–49; Keele University, Staffordshire, 1951–55. National Service, 1950–51. Married Ffrangcon Price in 1958; two sons and one daughter. Assistant surveyor, Town Planning Office, Stoke-on-Trent, 1949–50; farm worker, Endon Farm, Staffordshire, 1950; manservant, Uffington Hall, Lincolnshire, and demolition worker, Staffordshire, both 1955; hall porter, English Speaking Union Hotel, London, 1956; advertising copywriter, A.S. Dixon Ltd., London, 1956–57; English teacher, Berlitz School, Bergen, Norway, 1957–58; teacher, West London College, London, 1958; advertising copywriter and director, various agencies in London, 1959–90. Recipient: Ford Foundation grant, 1964; Sony Radio award, 1990. Lives in London. Agent: Lemon, Unna, and Durbridge, 24 Pottery Lane, Holland Park, London W11 4LZ, England.

Publications

PLAYS

Lakota, with Don Kincaid (produced 1970).
Double Edge, with Les Darbon (produced 1975). 1976.
Captain Swing (produced 1978). 1979.
The Accrington Pals (produced 1981). 1982.
Clay (produced 1982). 1983.
A Cold Wind Blowing Up, with Les Darbon (produced 1983).
World's Apart, adaptation of a work by Jose Triana (produced 1986).
The Bright and Bold Design (produced 1991). 1991.
The School of Night (produced 1992). 1992.
Shakespeare Country (produced 1993).

Peter Whelan comments:

I feel that any play I embark on must take me into the mysterious areas of human connection. The forces released must be beyond my absolute control. I must never know all the answers. The wastage of human conflict—often seen against a background of larger conflict—is, I suppose, my preoccupation.

I was a late starter, 40 before my first play, *Captain Swing*. I was drawn to it by wishing to counteract despairing visions of humanity as innately violent or socially brutalised. *The Accrington Pals*, *The Bright and Bold Design*, and *Clay* form almost a trilogy, drawing on my extended family background in the potteries and Salford. At the centre of it is the force of attraction and repulsion between people swept along by the times they live in and yearning for some peace in one another. I greatly regret that I have not so far been able to turn this into out-and-out comedy—but there is still time.

I am always impressed by Henry Moore's statement: "If I knew too clearly what I was doing I might not be able to do it." I am influenced by: Yeats, "Hammer your thoughts into a unity"; Tennessee Williams and Chekhov, for humanity; Miller, Brecht, and Ibsen, for structure; and Beckett, for defining where we are now.

Autumn 1830. Within sight of the harvest they have gathered, the farm labourers of Britain are starving while the gentry rejoice in their new threshing machines. Fires flare in Kent. In a small Sussex village, Mathew Hardness, wheelwright and committed democrat ("It's the people who keep the law . . . let those who govern break it. . . . No making revolution but restoring our natural right") encourages peaceful confrontation between labourers and landowners. Meanwhile, the gentry receive threatening letters from "Captain Swing, avenger of the people."

The gentry are engulfed by terror, their guilt sowing fear of anarchy in dynamic contrast to the reason and restraint of the local Swing rebels. However, the infiltration of an Irishman, O'Neil, professional revolutionary hot from the fires of France, greedy for power and violent rebellion, creates factions and confusion amongst the workers, and the arrival of a badly burned soldier, Farquare, on the run from the Dragoons and near death, inflames revolutionary zeal. Gemma, barmaid and town whore, in a passion for Farquare, embraces the revolution with fanatical fervour, vows celibacy, and proclaims Farquare to be Captain Swing.

Flails strike against the bare stage; tri-colour and black flags fly; the menacing presence of giant corn men provides a dark sense of historical and metaphysical necessity setting the immediate moment of history ringing with the energy of unresolved patterns of historical and imminent crisis.

Captain Swing is an impressive stage debut. The scope of the action, the impressive use of stage space, and the powerful construction of dramatic image herald an exciting new writer.

Peter Whelan gives even the most minor characters distinction by activating their personal demands in relation to the historical situation. From Mathew to Agnes, who seeks justice from the committee for her husband's murder of their child, each character is unmistakably both a private individual with personal needs and concerns and an active, unavoidable member of the social context.

On the one hand, this economic approach to character development creates the sensation that every possible attitude toward the immediate crisis and its implications has been argued for our assessment. On the other, it forms the very core of Whelan's structure and themes. The tension between the characters' individual and social identities and responsibilities provides the central dynamic of his work and arguably its most dramatically powerful element.

In *The Accrington Pals* the interdependence between the individual and the community is created by presenting World War I from the perspective of the Home Front. May, a fiercely independent woman who runs a fruit and vegetable stall, is unable to confess her love for Tom, an artist, partly because she knew him as a child, partly because she is older than he, but mainly because, against her deepest fears, he has enlisted. Whelan describes the play as "a story of a class-cum-love relationship between a strong-minded, rugged individualist woman and a dreamy, Utopian idealist young man." This relationship provides the framework for an intense discussion about personal will and success, community responsibility and, as in *Captain Swing*, the personal and social consequences of social and historical power struggles. Occasional letters from the Front and a remarkable scene where May meets Tom's corpse bring the war onto the stage, and when the town learns of the deaths of the Accrington Pals they turn on their own leaders. However, the relationship between the individual and the social context is, typically, ambiguous and complex. Despite its futile waste of human resources, the war affords May the chance to achieve her dream of owning a shop.

Whelan's plays are most successful when his overt question—"How shall we live?"—is set in the conundrum of incorporating private needs and expression with the recognition and responsibility of social demands. His attempt to explore these themes in the drawing-room through the discussion of personal experience is both less engaging and less revealing. *Clay* lacks the social context and social commitment of the first two plays and, hence, both their dramatic dynamism and their complexity. Micky and her husband Ben, Staffordshire potters, are visited by old friends, Win and Pat, recently returned from West Germany. A close foursome as teenagers, the middle-class, middle-aged couples struggle to recapture their relationships, both group and personal (Win and Pat's marriage has nearly failed). Although "How shall we live?" is still on the tip of Whelan's tongue, it is literally and simplistically stated here. The translation of the question to personal angst reduces the discussion to specific personal experience, the issues, like the characters, are limited and hypothetical. The four characters never take on the weight that would allow them to stand as analogous examples. Win doesn't come to "stand for all of us who have ever looked for a refuge from that future"; rather, her obsessive idealizing suggests a pathetic, private pathology. Whelan's occasional insistence on extended relevance—"(clay's) tough. You can't get rid of it. It looks fragile but in five thousand years they'll still be digging lots of it up. . . . When everyone's gone and the churchyard's empty. And that's the ultimate satisfaction of being a potter. Finally, you get buried in your work"—are self-conscious and literary. Separate from the necessities of social interaction and responsibility, the characters are credible but rather unengaging stage people whose personal problems may be viewed with detached sympathy and discarded when the curtain descends.

In *The Bright and Bold Design*, however, a return to historical context seems to re-inspire Whelan's courageous dramatization of unresolved complexities. In his introduction, Whelan implies that he intends to celebrate individualism, and in a manner unusual to his work, isolates Jessie, a talented freehand painter and designer working in a Staffordshire pottery in the 1930s, focusing on her personal experience and emotions. But the effect of the play is more complex. Jessie seeks recognition and self-expression through painting and eventually leaves the factory to stay with an aunt, help in the aunt's shop, and paint. She braves the pressures of Jack, the new design manager (who recognizes her talent and promotes her designs but demands that she amend them to his ideas), and of the community, represented by the other painters and Jack's ideal of bringing beautiful tableware to the workers. However, Whelan's unwillingness to simplify the issues at stake make the intended celebration of individualism ambivalent and more dramatic, demanding further contemplation of the relationship between community and individual. Jack's ideals are tinged and distorted by his personal desires. Simultaneously. Jessie's isolation and the drabness of her "self-fulfilment" makes her apparent victory less glitteringly absolute, especially since she is still, willy-nilly, dependent on others for that independence. It is notable that we last see Jessie back in the community for Jack's funeral. The play asks whether individuality and talent cannot be better used by the community, or even, more pertinently, how we might organize our world so both society and the individual might benefit and grow.

Whelan is constantly exploring how the values in conflicting ideals might be synthesized to mutual advantage; given that we are both uniquely ourselves and inescapably members of our world and responsible to it: "How shall we live?"

—Elaine Turner

WHITEHEAD, Ted
(Edward Anthony Whitehead).

Born in Liverpool, Lancashire, 3 April 1933. Educated at St. Francis Xavier's Jesuit College; Christ's College, Cambridge, B.A. (honours) in English 1955, M.A. Served in the King's Regiment, 1955–57. Married 1) Kathleen Horton in 1958 (marriage dissolved 1976), two daughters; 2) Gwenda Bagshaw in 1976. Milkman, postman, bus conductor, sales promotion writer, salesman, and teacher, 1959–65; advertising copywriter and account executive, 1965–71; resident dramatist, Royal Court Theatre, London, 1971–72; fellow in creative writing, Bulmershe College, Reading, Berkshire, 1975–76. Recipient: George Devine award, 1971; *Evening Standard* award, 1971. Agent: Casarotto Ramsay Ltd., National House, 60–66 Wardour Street, London W1V 3HP, England.

Publications

PLAYS

The Foursome (produced 1971). 1972.
Alpha Beta (produced 1972). 1972.
The Punishment (televised 1972). In *Prompt Three*, edited by Alan Durband, 1976.
The Sea Anchor (produced 1974). 1975.
Old Flames (produced 1975). 1976.
Mecca (produced 1977). 1977.
The Man Who Fell in Love with His Wife, adaptation of his television series *Sweet Nothings* (produced 1984). 1984.
Dance of Death, adaptation of a play by Strindberg (produced 1984).

RADIO PLAY: *The Old Goat Gone*, 1987.

TELEVISION PLAYS: *Under the Age*, 1972; *The Punishment*, 1972; *The Peddler*, 1976; *The Proofing Session*, 1977; *The Irish Connection* (*Crown Court* series), 1979; *Sweet Nothings* series, 1980; *World's End* series, 1981; *The Detective* serial, from the novel by Paul Ferris, 1985; *The Life and Loves of a She-Devil* serial, from the novel by Fay Weldon, 1986; *First Born*, from a novel by Maureen Duffy, 1988; *Jumping the Queue*, from the novel by Mary Wesley, 1989; *The Free Frenchman*, from the novel by Piers Paul Read, 1989; *Murder East Murder West*, 1990.

NOVEL

World's End (novelization of television series). 1981.

Ted Whitehead's chosen dramatic territory is marriage and the impossible demands the institution makes on love and fidelity. His principal characters are most often drawn from the white-collar working class. They are witty and articulate but not intellectuals. His dialogue is a rapid verbal sparring, which frequently breaks down into hysteria or physical violence. His writing drives towards as plain a style as possible in the exposition of his emotional and sexual themes, although he is capable of occasional passages of lyrical beauty. "Escape" and "freedom" are key positives in his vocabulary, but they turn out to be chimeras for both men and women. His plays chart accurately the major debates around the family, sex, and marriage since the early 1960s and, while he has little interest in plot or character-development, his ear is very sharp for the changing discourses of male and female in this area.

A comparison between his first stage success, *Alpha Beta*, and his latest original play, *The Man Who Fell in Love with His Wife*, is immediately instructive. *Alpha Beta* has only two characters, Mr. and Mrs. Elliot, and covers the years 1962 to 1971. Mr. Elliot is a manager on the Liverpool docks and his wife is a housewife. When the play opens he is 29 and she is 26. They have two children who remain as an off-stage audience to the bickering, fighting, violence, and hysteria which make up the play. Mr. Elliot already has a mistress, Eileen, and wants a divorce. His wife won't give him one. Although marriage has turned into a bitter trap for both of them, Mrs. Elliot stands by the moral law of until death us do part. For Mr. Elliot they're dead already. He wants the freedom to "fuck a thousand women." He's no different, he claims, from all his male friends, except they sublimate their desires in blue movies and dirty jokes. "I'm sick of fantasy," he says, "I want reality." Elliot's view is that he married too young and too early for the permissive 1960s. Marriage is changing, he warns his wife, and even a woman like her, in the future, will "want a bit of what's going, for herself." A mutual enslavement like theirs shouldn't last. "Man and women are going to share free and equal unions that last because they want them to last. Not because they're forced!" Mrs. Elliot has only contempt for his "honesty" and his sociology. In her view he's retarded. He's never grown out of the role of working-class bucko, tomcatting around after eternal youth. She won't let him escape his duties as head of the household. Over the years of the play they evolve a kind of compromise. Mr. Elliot pays the bills and resides in the house but pursues his extra-marital affairs. His wife runs the house and just about hangs onto her sanity. The play ends with a suicide threat by Mrs. Elliot which her husband takes half seriously but which fires no buried love or affection in him. It's an unsatisfactory ending because there can be no ending to a war on these terms. As the title suggests, this couple must go down through the alphabet of their hatred and then start all over again.

The Man Who Fell in Love with His Wife begins with just that change in women's status that Mr. Elliot foresaw. Mary Fearon, in her late thirties, has got her first job, in the Civil Service. Her husband Tom, aged 41, is also employed as a dock manager in Liverpool. Mary's office life causes him extreme jealousy but also refuels his sexual passion for her. Suspender-belts and instamatic photos play their part in maintaining an ardour that Mary, who still loves him deeply, cannot match. Love in marriage can be as stifling as hatred. Tom wants to replay their adolescence and courtship. The Platters and Ike and Tina Turner are his favourite music. He drags his wife out to a freezing session on a favourite beach near Liverpool. Mary wants to move on and eventually she moves out. By then Tom has given up his job to monitor his wife throughout the day. The roles and emotions of *Alpha Beta* have been reversed, and there is now a chance for the kind of freedom for both sexes that Mr. Elliot prophesied. For this is the 1980's, and between the Fearons and their daughter intervenes a new role-model, the divorcée in her thirties. She is Julia, an office friend of Mary's, who supports her bid for independence and counters Tom's arguments with reason and confidence. "Is it selfish for me to want my wife to love me?" he asks. "It's selfish to demand it regardless of what she wants," Julia replies. In the end they have to settle for separate lives, although old connections can't be broken. "I love you—even if I can't live with you," says Mary, and Tom, now a cab driver, has to become adult out of his own resources.

Glimpses of this comparative optimism can be seen in other Whitehead plays in the 1970s. In *The Sea Anchor* men and women friends wait, on Dublin Bay, for the arrival of daredevil Nick after his solo voyage across the Irish Sea for Liverpool in a ten-foot dinghy. The play is also about the other side of marriage, since all the characters are engaged in adulterous relationships. Nick is their hero since he "does exactly what he wants to do" while the others all cover up in various ways. Whitehead's theme of the trapped, randy male is complemented by that of the calculating, randy female and in the character of Jean we see a coarser precursor to Julia. The backchat is vulgar and witty, but Andy is given two lyrical passages, when he recalls a shoal of mackerel at night, "a giant ripple, V-shaped . . . it came hissing along beside the boat," and the time he and Nick heard black bodies barking in the silver sea and discovered they were porpoises, which sharply contrast with the brutality of the sexual relationships. Nick's boat comes in, empty. His sea anchor, "a kind of parachute, keeps you steady," hasn't saved him. A lost hero is useless and the sea is a false escape from domestic complexity.

Nor is abroad any solution. The group of English tourists in *Mecca* brings its marital conflicts and emotions intact to Morocco. Middle-aged Andrew sublimates his desire for the 20-year-old Sandy into a false fatherly protectiveness. His wife, Eunice, isn't fooled, but her verbal barbs have an articulacy which Mrs. Elliot lacked. Ian is young and fancy-free and Martin is the gay protector for the defensive bravado of Jill, 38, divorced, and feeling herself caught between the insouciance of Sandy and the certainties of Eunice. "She's not afraid of sex," says Jill to Eunice, "and neither is her generation. That's why they don't get used-up like us." But Sandy's innocence leads her, dressed only in a towel, outside the compound where the tourists live into the poor and violent world of Arab North Africa. She gets raped, a boy who hangs round the compound is suspected, and when he's cornered Andrew beats him to death. His menopausal desire is displaced into murderous aggression. The police and courts are finally bought off, and the tourists take off with relief for "civilization." But back home, as Whitehead's other plays show, the war goes on.

—Tony Dunn

WHITEMORE, Hugh (John).

Born in Tunbridge Wells, Kent, 16 June 1936. Educated at Judd School, Tunbridge Wells, 1945–51; King Edward VI School, Southampton, 1951–55; Royal Academy of Dramatic Art, London, 1956–57. Married 1) Jill Brooke in 1961 (marriage dissolved); 2) Sheila Lemon in 1976; one son. Freelance writer: drama critic, *Harpers and Queen*, London, 1970. Recipient: Emmy award, 1971, 1984; Writers Guild award, 1971, 1972; RAI prize, 1979; Italia prize, 1979; Neil Simon Jury award, 1984. Lives in London. Agent: Judy Daish Associates, 83 Eastbourne Mews, London W2 6LQ, England; or, Phyllis Wender, Rosenstone and Wender, 3 East 48th Street, 4th Floor, New York, New York 10017, U.S.A.

Publications

PLAYS

Horrible Conspiracies (televised 1971). In *Elizabeth R*, edited by J.C. Trewin, 1972.
Stevie: A Play from the Life and Works of Stevie Smith (produced 1977). 1977.
Pack of Lies (produced 1983). 1983.
Breaking the Code, adaptation of the book *Alan Turing: The Enigma of Intelligence* by Andrew Hodges (produced 1986). 1987.
The Best of Friends (produced 1987). 1988.
The Towers of Trebizond (produced 1991).
It's Ralph (produced 1991). 1991.

SCREENPLAYS: *Decline and Fall . . . of a Birdwatcher!*, with Ivan Foxwell and Alan Hackney, 1968; *All Neat in Black Stockings*, with Jane Gaskell, 1968; *Man at the Top*, with John Junkin, 1973; *All Creatures Great and Small*, 1975; *The Blue Bird*, 1976; *Stevie*, 1978; *The Return of the Soldier*, 1983; *84 Charing Cross Road*, 1987.

TELEVISION PLAYS: *The Full Chatter*, 1963; *Dan, Dan the Charity Man*, 1965; *Angus Slowly Sinking*, 1965; *The Regulator*, 1965; *Application Form*, 1965; *Mrs. Bixby and the Colonel's Coat*, from a story by Roald Dahl, 1965; *Macready's Gala*, 1966; *Final Demand*, 1966; *Girl of My Dreams*, 1966; *Frankenstein Mark II*, 1966; *Amerika*, from the novel by Kafka, 1966; *What's Wrong with Humpty Dumpty?*, 1967; *Party Games*, 1968; *The Last of the Big

Spenders, 1968; *Hello, Good Evening, and Welcome*, 1968; *Mr. Guppy's Tale*, from a story by Dickens, 1969; *Unexpectedly Vacant*, 1970; *The King and His Keeper*, 1970; *Killing Time*, 1970; *Cider with Rosie*, from the book by Laurie Lee, 1971; *Horrible Conspiracies (Elizabeth R series)*, 1971; *An Object of Affection*, 1971; *Act of Betrayal*, 1971; *Breeze Anstey (Country Matters* series), from the story by H.E. Bates, 1972; *The Strange Shapes of Reality*, 1972; *The Serpent and the Comforter*, 1972; *At the Villa Pandora*, 1972; *Eric*, 1972; *Disappearing Trick*, 1972; *Good at Games*, 1972; *Bedtime*, 1972; *Intruders*, 1972; *The Adventures of Don Quixote*, from a novel by Cervantes, 1973; *Deliver us from Evil*, 1973; *The Pearcross Girls*, 1973; *A Thinking Man as Hero*, 1973; *Death Waltz*, 1974; *Outrage*, 1974; *David Copperfield*, from the novel by Dickens, 1974; *Trilby*, from the novel by George du Maurier, 1975; *Goodbye*, 1975; *84 Charing Cross Road*, from the book by Helene Hanff, 1975; *Moll Flanders*, from the novel by Defoe, 1975; *The Eleventh Hour*, with Brian Clark and Clive Exton, 1975; *Censors*, with David Edgar and Robert Muller, 1975; *Brensham People*, from novels by John Moore, 1976; *William Wilson*, from the story by Poe, 1976; *Moths*, from the novel by Ouida, 1977; *Exiles*, from the book by Michael J. Arlen, 1977; *Dummy*, 1977; *Mrs. Ainsworth*, from a novel by E.F. Benson, 1978; *Losing Her*, 1978; *Rebecca*, from the novel by Daphne du Maurier, 1979; *Contract*, 1981; *A Dedicated Man*, from the story by Elizabeth Taylor, 1982; *I Remember Nelson*, 1982; *A Bit of Singing and Dancing*, from the story by Susan Hill, 1982; *Lovers of Their Time*, from the story by William Trevor, 1982; *My Cousin Rachel*, from the novel by Daphne du Maurier, 1983; *Office Romances*, from stories by William Trevor, 1983; *Down at the Hydro*, from a story by William Samsom, 1983; *Concealed Enemies*, 1984; *The Boy in the Bush*, from a story by D.H. Lawrence, 1984; *The Final Days*, from a novel by Bob Woodward and Carl Bernstein, 1989.

Hugh Whitemore is best known as a writer for television, and from 1963 he has had a long list of plays to his credit both as parts of series and as individual efforts. His adaptation of Laurie Lee's *Cider with Rosie* won him a Writers Guild award, as did his contribution to *Country Matters* in 1972; and *Elizabeth R*—a series of six plays, one of which, *Horrible Conspiracies*, was provided by Whitemore—received an Emmy award. *Horrible Conspiracies* deals with events surrounding the execution of Mary Queen of Scots, and its fascination with the world of spying and conspiracy was to become a recurrent theme in his work. Gloriana is presented as an aging ruler, ruled by superstition and fear, fixated on thoughts of death, and her court as far from magnificent.

The predominant style of *Horrible Conspiracies* is that of conventional television naturalism—although the play is prefaced by a grim masque portending death—and the piece jumps quickly through a series of locations which suggests the complexities of espionage and counter-espionage that lurk immediately beneath the outward display of power. Little interest is shown in the intricacies of psychological behaviour or in any larger political context, and the play seems very much a part of a larger series in which each individual writer is considerably restrained by the overall structure. Over the years,

Whitemore has shown himself as adept at meeting the strictures of such demands, and as able to turn out a consistently well-crafted piece.

The influence of his work on television is evident in his belated stage entrance. *Stevie: A Play from the Life and Works of Stevie Smith* makes few bows in the direction of the stage. Information is given in the conventional format of recalled anecdotes raised in the course of a series of conversations between Stevie and the aunt she lived with for most of her life. The atmosphere of suburban London comes across well, as does Stevie's delight in the absurdity of her life there, but we gain little insight into her obsession with death and her failed attempt at suicide. It is a well-made play, offering the kind of "coffee-table" approach to biography so frequently to be found on television. Its chief virtue lies in Whitemore's success in creating in the central character a plausible human being, even if we learn little more than superficial things about her. That this was done in a beautifully realized suburban set does little to take the edge off a feeling that *Stevie* is essentially a television play put on stage.

His next stage play, *Pack of Lies*, was exactly this, having started life as the successful BBC television "Play for Today," *Act of Betrayal*. The play concerns the intrusion into a suburban family of the British Secret Service, intent on trapping as Russian spies their close friends and neighbours, the Krogers. The play, which is based on real events in 1960–61, again captures well the restrictions and niceties of suburban life and builds to a traditional theatrical climax as the host family become increasingly and ambivalently involved in the enquiry; but again it is difficult to see what exactly is added to the piece by its adaptation to the stage. The direct narrative asides to the audience apart, its predominant tone is still that of a safe naturalism. It asks no questions that cannot be contained within the confines of plot and set, and it is hard not to think that the chief reason for its appearance in London's West End is the latest bout of interest in Burgess, Philby, et al. One obvious attraction to theatrical managements is that it is a cheap production in a theatrical world currently dominated by excessively expensive musicals.

However, Whitemore's fourth stage-play, *Breaking the Code*, does succeed in making the break from the small screen to the stage. Far more ambitious than his two earlier efforts, it presents the story of Alan Turing, the man who broke the German Enigma code in World War II and pioneered the development of computers. Taking on board the difficult task of elucidating the theory behind Turing's work—and succeeding surprisingly well—the play blends the theme of scientific exploration with its depiction of an establishment England that could have the scientist's name obliterated from the record book because he was a practising homosexual—the two sets of broken codes in conflict. Whitemore has been fortunate in having Derek Jacobi play his protagonist, but it says much for the play's superiority to its predecessors that the actor is able to fill the part so well. *Breaking the Code* is, no less than all Whitemore's work, a classically well-made play, produced to a given West End formula, but the difference is that here, for the first time, the formula has been stretched to fit what the writer wants to say rather than acting as a straitjacket.

Although Whitemore has continued to work for television, the commercial success of his first stage plays has led to three further productions, *The Towers of Trebizond*, produced in Edinburgh, and two more products for London's

West End—*The Best of Friends*, and *It's Ralph*. The latter fitted a familiar pattern of small-cast, single-set domestic dramas. The rural home of a successful journalist and his music-publisher wife is invaded by the unwelcome Ralph, an old friend of the husband—a guest whose presence, in the traditional manner, allows the even greater articulation of mid-life crisis and marital depression. With this play Whitemore was compared inevitably to Ayckbourn, although the sudden removal of the by now emotionally involved Ralph towards the end promises, without properly delivering, a new permutation of the theme.

—John Bull

WHITING, John (Robert).

Born in Salisbury, Wiltshire, 15 November 1917. Educated at Taunton School, Somerset, 1930–34; Royal Academy of Dramatic Art, London, 1935–37. Served in the Royal Artillery, 1939–44: lieutenant. Married Asthore Lloyd Mawson in 1940; two sons and two daughters. Actor in repertory, and in London, 1936–38, 1944–52; drama critic, *London Magazine*, 1961–62. Member, Arts Council Drama Panel, 1955–63. Recipient: Festival of Britain award, 1951. John Whiting award for promising young playwrights established, 1965. *Died 16 June 1963.*

Publications

PLAYS

A Penny for a Song (produced 1951). In *Plays*, 1957; revised version (produced 1962), 1964.
Saint's Day (produced 1951). In *Plays*, 1957.
Marching Song (produced 1954). 1954.
Sacrifice to the Wind, from a play by André Obey (televised 1954; produced 1955). In *Plays for Radio and Television*, edited by Nigel Samuels, 1959.
The Gates of Summer (produced 1956). In *Collected Plays 2*, 1969.
Plays (includes *Saint's Day*; *A Penny for a Song*; *Marching Song*). 1957.
Madame de . . . , from a play by Anouilh (produced 1959). With *Traveller Without Luggage*, 1959.
Traveller Without Luggage, from a play by Anouilh (produced 1959). With *Madame de . . .*, 1959.
A Walk in the Desert (televised 1960). In *Collected Plays 2*, 1969.
The Devils, from an account by Aldous Huxley (produced 1961). 1961.
No Why (produced 1964). 1961.
Conditions of Agreement (as *The Conditions of Agreement*, produced 1965). In *Collected Plays 1*, 1969.
The Nomads (produced 1965). In *Collected Plays 2*, 1969.
Paul Southman from the radio play (produced 1965).
The Collected Plays 1–2, edited by Ronald Hayman. 2 vols., 1969.
No More A-Roving (broadcast 1979; produced 1987). 1975.

SCREENPLAYS: *The Ship That Died of Shame*, with Michael Relph and Basil Dearden, 1955; *The Good Companions*, with T.J. Morrison and J.L. Hodgson, 1957; *The Captain's Table*, with Bryan Forbes and Nicholas Phipps, 1959; *Young Cassidy*, 1965.

RADIO PLAYS: *Paul Southman*, 1946; *Eye Witness*, 1949; *The Stairway*, 1949; *Love's Old Sweet Song*, 1950; *No More A-Roving*, 1979.

TELEVISION PLAYS: *Sacrifice to the Wind*, 1954; *A Walk in the Desert*, 1960.

OTHER

John Whiting on Theatre. 1966.
The Art of the Dramatist and Other Pieces, edited by Ronald Hayman. 1970.

CRITICAL STUDIES: *John Whiting* by Ronald Hayman, 1969; *The Plays of John Whiting: An Assessment* by Simon Trussler, 1972; *The Dark Journey: John Whiting as Dramatist* by Eric Salmon, 1979; *A Private Mythology: The Manuscripts and Plays of John Whiting* by Gabrielle Robinson, 1989.

Although a writer whose talents as a dramatist and theatre critic were admired in the 1950s and 1960s, John Whiting and his work receive little attention today, and even the best of his plays are now infrequently performed. Yet his current neglect cannot be accounted for solely in terms of critical and theatrical fashion, for he was, and remains, something of a maverick figure. From the first, his plays ran against both the mainstream and avant-garde tastes of his time. Although they were seen by many in the early and mid-1950s to presage the resurgence of a drama more serious in philosophical and social import, and more technically demanding and innovative than the prevailing quasi-poetic verse and bourgeois drawing-room drama, Whiting's work never managed to establish itself any more firmly when a concerted reaction against the theatrical *status quo* occurred after the Royal Court production of John Osborne's *Look Back in Anger* in 1956.

The most successful with reviewers and theatre audiences alike was his play *The Devils*, an intelligent adaptation, in a somewhat Brechtian manner, of Aldous Huxley's *The Devils of Loudun*. Commissioned by Peter Hall for the Royal Shakespeare Company, it concerns personal corruption, political manoeuvring, and self-destruction against a historical background illustrating the effects of demonic possession in a 17th-century French nunnery. But it is an earlier piece, *Marching Song*, completed in 1952 and first performed and published in 1954, that is now considered his best play, although it was widely thought at the time to break the cardinal rule that a work so public must "communicate". The questions it raises today, however, are less to do with accessibility than with the extent of its verbal and thematic adequacy, and the persuasiveness of its action and characters. Whiting appears to have sought an austerity of form and language by eliminating all suggestion of melodrama, and by stripping dialogue of verbal exuberance and the casual "fillers" charac- teristic of idiomatic speech. This economy and eschewing of the expected— Whiting himself characterised *Marching Song* as "an anti-theatrical play" —unfortunately results in a loss of dramatic excitement, and a reduction of much of the dialogue to overly portentous generalisations about life, love, solitude, destruction, and the nature of the military man. If he was reacting against the English stage-drawing-room world of what the critic Kenneth Tynan dubbed "Loamshire", Whiting came dangerously close to retreating into that favourite post-war setting for reflective, quasi-philosophical Continental drama (like that of, say, Ugo Betti)—Centraleuropia.

Rupert Foster, a former army general released after seven years of imprisonment, returns to the house of his wealthy former mistress in the hills above an unspecified European city, and there meets up with an odd collection of characters, which includes a faded, bouncy American film director (Harry Lancaster), and a local girl (Dido Morgen), a drifter picked up by Lancaster in a bar on the promise that he put her into his next film. He finds, too, that the democratic government now in power has released him only as a prelude to his standing trial as a scapegoat for past national military defeat. After flirting with defiance under the influence of the life-affirming Dido, he opts for suicide, philosophically embracing his own disposition to self-destruction. Rather too much in this situation lacks persuasion and seems overly contrived: the characters are more ciphers than credible stage figures, their juxtaposition often seems rather forced, with exits and entrances too obviously orchestrated to set up discussion, and the "war crime" committed by Forster sounds more like fiction than real life. The conclusion, with Forster's mistress persuading Dido to stay with her in the house and teach her resignation, is sentimental and overly neat. Notwithstanding its commendable ambitiousness of subject and approach, the play leaves one with the impression of a writer reaching for significant issues, but failing to dramatise them adequately.

Disintegration and destruction, and the sudden arbitrary incursion of violence into lives, are also features of the earlier, and highly controversial, *Saint's Day*, which first brought Whiting to national notice. Awarded the first prize in an Arts Council competition, held in conjunction with the 1951 Festival of Britain, it bewildered most critics and audiences, its seemingly wilful obscurities fuelling a hostility already aroused by the very notion of the Council setting itself up—albeit through a panel of judges (Alec Clunes, Christopher Fry, and Peter Ustinov)—as an arbiter of theatrical excellence. In fact, the judges were not so very misguided. Completed in 1947, and later revised for the Festival competition, it is a young man's play—loose, wordy, and ill-focused—yet for all that has a stage energy and verbal buoyancy wanting in *Marching Song*, and it still comes across as a powerful study of a disintegrating way of life. It is set in the house of a highly respected octogenarian writer, Paul Southman, a still much-admired grand old man of letters who has long been marginalised by the publishing industry for daring to publish a pamphlet entitled "The Abolition of Print". The play provides a sprawling elusive image of the condition of things, more particularly perhaps of Britain, embracing by implication the whole state of culture—not just of the arts, but of political, social, and personal relations. Southman lives in a retirement that is a kind of exile, along with his grand-daughter, Stella, who dreams of the family's financial, and her grandfather's artistic, resurrection. Sharing this retreat with them are Stella's rather feckless husband, Charles, an artist whose work has lost direction, and an independent-minded and oddly threatening house-servant, John Winter. At the play's opening, the family is awaiting the arrival of a young poet, Robert Procathren, calling in order to take the old writer to a London literary dinner, and Winter is despatched to get food from the local villagers. The villagers are hostile to Southman's household, partly for its inability to settle its bills, partly because it represents something different and non-conformist. Southman seems to revel in this hostility, ever disposed to thrive on embattlement, whether with publishers, the literary world, or the local community. When renegade soldiers threaten the village he sides with them, and the violence that eventually erupts leads to the accidental death of his grand-daughter, and the destruction of the village and its church. The young poet, Robert, takes over, and Southman and Charles are condemned to death.

Saint's Day, for all the surface familiarity of its setting and character depiction, is essentially non-naturalistic, and critics have rightly seen in it presages of the later work of Pinter, and even Bond. It is a wordy piece, as loose and rambling in its language as in its structure. But although the dialogue is rarely direct and idiomatic, it has a fluency and naturalness which make it engaging and, much more than *Marching Song*, the play establishes a firm relationship between character and speech. What never adequately cohere, however, are the complex social, political, and spiritual themes. Critics have frequently remarked on Whiting's indebtedness to the verse plays of T.S. Eliot and Christopher Fry, but where their engagement with social and spiritual issues was rooted in their Christian commitment, Whiting's ideological positioning here, as in his other plays, is far from clear. In fact, much of Whiting's work, and notably *Marching Song*, is perhaps even more firmly embedded in the drama of the 1940s and early 1950s than the Eliot–Fry analogy alone suggests, for behind it there is, too, something of the post-war French drama then popular on London stages, particularly that of Sartre and Anouilh (whose *Le Voyageur sans bagage* Whiting translated in 1959 for a London production). Unfortunately, Whiting lacked the intellectual bite, philosophical depth, and gift for the striking phrase and image of the former writer, and the deftness in play construction and sharp sense of stage effectiveness of the latter.

Whiting wrote several other plays, all of considerable interest, from the early *Conditions of Agreement*, through the comedies of the 1950s, *Penny for a Song* and *The Gates of Summer*, to a comedy found among his papers and published in 1975, *No More a-Roving*. Since his early death, academic critical commentary has given some attention to these, and this has been more sympathetic than were the plays' first reviews. That attention is well merited, even if occasionally tending to allow explication to shade into speculative elaboration, and to pay more attention to the issues the plays sought to engage with rather than to their effectiveness as theatrical works on their own. Some of the reasons for their continuing failure to find a wider theatre public are perhaps indirectly evident in Whiting's theatre criticism, which often seems to lament the failure of the drama under review to observe the concerns and artistic high seriousness of the minority intellectual drama, English and Continental, of the 1930s and 1940s. This tends to suggest the extent to which Whiting, as a dramatist, was a transitional figure, engaged with 1950s concerns, but rooted artistically and intellectually in the austere, even patrician, values of an earlier age. Ultimately one must agree with the general critical view that his work remained forever on the level of the promising; it must be thought significant less for its own intrinsic merits, considerable as they are, than for the example it set a younger generation of British playwrights, who saw a dramatist striving bravely and imaginatively—if ultimately only with partial success—to explore new possibilities for the English stage.

—Kenneth Richards

WILKINSON, Christopher.

Born 4 May 1941. Address: 33 Yates Lane, Milnsbridge, Huddersfield HD3 4NW, England.

Publications

PLAYS

Their First Evening Alone Together (produced 1969).
Wally, Molly and Polly (produced 1969).
Teasdale's Follies, with Frank Hatherly, music by Jeremy Barlow (produced 1970).
Strip Jack Naked (produced 1970).
Dynamo (produced 1971).
Plays for Rubber Go-Go Girls (produced 1971).
I Was Hitler's Maid (also director: produced 1971).
Sawn Off at the Knees, with Veronica Thirlaway (produced 1978).

THEATRICAL ACTIVITIES

DIRECTOR: **Play**—*I Was Hitler's Maid*, 1971.

Christopher Wilkinson is best known for his work with two fringe companies —the touring Portable Theatre, and the Vanguard Theatre Club (now the Crucible Theatre-in-Education group), which is attached to Sheffield's main repertory theatre, the Crucible. These close associations have influenced his work. Wilkinson has written ordinary scripts, such as *Strip Jack Naked*, which revealed his wit, his ear for a good line of dialogue, and his delight in a Grand Guignol situation. But he later chose not to write formal scripts, but rather to suggest themes and games for the acting companies to explore—in improvisation and other ways. *I Was Hitler's Maid* is an example of this non-scripted play. Wilkinson offered the actors some stories taken from semi-pornographic men's magazines: blood, sex, and action. These magazines were of a type distributed to American troops in Vietnam, and were therefore considered to relate in some way to a real political situation. The stories were all exceptionally violent. Some were set in World War II—among SS officers and patriots of the French resistance—others in South America—among guerrilla bands and the forces of Law and Order. But the settings were almost irrelevant, for the situations were pointedly similar. A girl was tortured and repeatedly raped by the Enemy, before being rescued by the Hero. In the opening scene, she is whipped by "Hitler"; in a later scene, she becomes "Calamity Jane," the whipping Wild West heroine. The dialogue is based on the clichés of the genre: and the actors were encouraged to break up the story patterns, the snatches of rehearsed scenes, even the moments of violence, in order to emphasize the arbitrary lack of logic of the fantasies. The production progresses towards two main climaxes—an orgy scene (three men raping one girl) and a disembowelling scene, where three soldiers attack a lifelike (female) doll hanging in a cupboard.

Some critics thought that *I Was Hitler's Maid* was not so much a comment on pornography as pornography itself, while others deplored the deliberate lack of construction. But few productions could have achieved such a telling diatribe against sex-and-violence comics without seeming lofty and puritanical. Wilkinson, by presenting the stories on stage—where actors leapt up in astonishing health after being beaten senseless—and by denying the elementary logic which kept the stories credible, brought out the full sado-masochistic absurdity of the genre. A somewhat similar production, *Dynamo*, was less successful perhaps because Wilkinson's moral intentions had to be more overtly expressed. *Dynamo* is set in a strip club, and the first section consists of ordinary dull strip routines performed by gum-chewing, bored girls. We watch them preparing to go on stage, collecting their props and records, adjusting their hair: then we see the routines. But after a time the strip club becomes an interrogation cell, where a girl is tortured by a police chief, kicked around the floor, and finally hung up naked. Wilkinson wished to draw the parallel between ordinary pornographic fantasies and the political torture of an Algerian suspect by the French police: but the play failed because the association between the two events seemed at best clichéd and at worst tenuous and unconvincing. If Wilkinson meant to imply that in both cases women were treated like mere objects of male desire, the theme is convincing enough but rather obvious and could have been developed in many other ways. If he was suggesting that pornography leads to political violence, then the fact that there was no logical connecting link between the scenes damaged his argument.

Wilkinson's most successful work, however, is *Plays for Rubber Go-Go Girls*. These are sketch sequences, loosely linked by an attack on American imperialism and on the sexual fantasies supporting repression. The first half of the production consists of various sex-and-violence stories in the style of *I Was Hitler's Maid*: but the deliberate disorganization of the earlier plays is replaced by a solemn burlesque treatment—high camp. The stories could come from an outrageous adventure story, in the style of James Bond, with beautiful girls from Vietnam and Latin America, submitting with delight to Commie-hating G.I.s. The second half is an amusing skit on childhood training in America. A cop warns his daughter, Fuzz Child, against everything, from drugs to long hair, which might threaten the purity of American middle-class life. The juxtaposition of the repressed fantasies with the formal teaching are related to the Vietnam war, until the war itself is shown to be an effect of various cultural forces. Among these forces is perhaps Wilkinson's most typical preoccupation —the maltreatment of women by men. Women are presented as rubber girls who can be endlessly stabbed either with a phallus or a bayonet. This serious theme is treated with an immense satirical verve and accuracy: the fantasies are funny, familiar, and, shocked out of their usual contexts, have been presented to the public as grotesque art objects, as representative of our civilization as the pyramids were of ancient Egypt. Wilkinson's great achievement as a writer is to make us look afresh at the clichés surrounding our lives.

—John Elsom

WILLIAMS, Heathcote.

Born in Helsby, Cheshire, 15 November 1941. Associate editor, *Transatlantic Review*, London and New York; founding editor, *Suck*, Amsterdam. Recipient: *Evening Standard* award, 1970; George Devine award, 1970; John Whiting award, 1971; Obie award, 1971. Agent: Judy Daish Associates, 83 Eastbourne Mews, London W2 6LQ, England.

Publications

PLAYS

The Local Stigmatic (produced 1966). In *Traverse Plays*, 1965; with *AC/DC*, 1973.
AC/DC (produced 1970). 1972; with *The Local Stigmatic*, 1973.
Remember the Truth Dentist, music by Bob Flagg (produced 1974). With *The Speakers*, 1980.
The Speakers (produced 1974). With *Remember the Truth Dentist*, 1980.
Very Tasty—A Pantomine (produced 1975).
An Invitation to the Official Lynching of Michael Abdul Malik (produced 1975).
Anatomy of a Space Rat (produced 1976).
Hancock's Last Half-Hour (produced 1977). 1977.
Playpen (produced 1977).
The Immortalist (produced 1977). 1978.
At It, in *Breach of the Peace* (produced 1982).
Whales (produced 1986).

SCREENPLAY: *Malatesta*, 1969.

TELEVISION PLAY: *What the Dickens!*, 1983.

VERSE
Whale Nation. 1988.
Falling for a Dolphin. 1988.
Sacred Elephant. 1989.
Autogeddon. 1991.

OTHER
The Speakers. 1964.
Manifestoes, Manifesten. 1975.
Severe Joy. 1979.
Elephants. 1983.

CRITICAL STUDY: "Heathcote Williams Issue" of *Gambit 18–19*, 1971.

THEATRICAL ACTIVITIES

ACTOR: **Films**—*The Tempest*, 1980; *Little Dorrit*, 1987; *Orlando*, 1993.

Often regarded as a one-play dramatist, Heathcote Williams merits praise not only for his acknowledged counter-culture classic of the 1960s, *AC/DC*, but also for plays that have received only cursory critical treatment. All his plays center on social misfits, who either hope for the reformation of a corrupt society or erect barriers against the void that threatens to engulf them.

The spectacular setting and visceral (and often unintelligible) dialogue of *AC/DC* dazzled audiences of the 1960s. In an amusement arcade, three hippies meet two schizophrenics, Maurice and Perowne; all are trying to shed media-induced personalities. Maurice helps Perowne achieve this goal by speaking long fantastic monologues. Maurice's monologues so intimidate two of the hippies, a couple, that, silenced, they drop out of the play altogether.

Such bludgeoning dialogues thread through *AC/DC*, though they are not of thematic importance. Sadie, the remaining hippie, competes with Maurice for control of Perowne. Like Maurice, she relies on long, unrelated fantasies to free Perowne from his enslavement to the video-screens, television, and radio, which are the environment for the second half of the play. Besides fantasizing to Perowne, she also trepans him, thus freeing him from media personalities. Sadie thereby overwhelms Maurice, and she dismisses him for being "into the same territory-sex-adrenalin-bullshit" as everyone else. Sadie looks for a revolution that will destroy such alienation.

Like *AC/DC*, *The Local Stigmatic*, an earlier play, dramatizes a Pinteresque struggle for dominance. Ray often contradicts and challenges Graham, but ultimately he accedes to the latter's game of assaulting strangers. These games lend form to their otherwise pointless existence.

Hancock's Last Half-Hour, like *The Local Stigmatic*, pits an individual against meaninglessness, but in this play the individual loses. Hancock, a former clown, desperately performs comedy to keep the silence from deafening him. He has locked himself in a hotel-room and there engages in the performance that is the play. The performer's fear of audience indifference drives Hancock and accounts for the desperation of his monologue that includes jokes, readings from encyclopedias, Freud's *Jokes*, and press clippings, and parodies of such set-pieces as Hamlet's soliloquy. This fear also accounts for his self-mockery and for his final suicide.

The Immortalist is not as compressed or exciting a play as *AC/DC*, nor does it question existence as do *The Local Stigmatic* and *Hancock's Last Half-Hour*. The play is essentially and atypically didactic. The Immortalist will not die of natural causes, but he *can* be killed. Consequently, he would preserve the earth and its inhabitants from human desecration. He argues against passivity: "Listen, people foul up because they stay in the same place. They've traded Utopia for reality . . . Consuming as a substitute for being . . . You have radio as a substitute for telepathy, television as a substitute for astral projection. Aeroplanes are a substitute for inner fire."

Williams's freaks indict a society that fosters passivity and consumerism through its mass media. As individuals, they can find no structures or values by which to order and give meaning to their lives.

—Frances Rademacher Anderson

WILLIAMS, Nigel.

Born in Cheadle, Cheshire, 20 January 1948. Educated at Highgate School, London; Oriel College, Oxford. Married; three sons. Recipient: Somerset Maugham award, for fiction, 1978. Agent: Judy Daish Associates, 83 Eastbourne Mews, London W2 6LQ. Address: c/o Faber and Faber, 3 Queen Square, London WC1N 3AU, England.

Publications

PLAYS

Double Talk (produced 1976).
Snowwhite Washes Whiter, and Deadwood (produced 1977).
Class Enemy (produced 1978). 1978.
Easy Street (produced 1979).
Sugar and Spice (produced 1980). With *Trial Run*, 1980.
Line 'em (produced 1980). 1980.
Trial Run (produced 1980). With *Sugar and Spice*, 1980.
W.C.P.C. (produced 1982). 1983.
The Adventures of Jasper Ridley (produced 1982).
My Brother's Keeper (produced 1985). 1985.
Deathwatch, adaptation of a play by Jean Genet (produced 1985).
Country Dancing (produced 1986). 1987.
As It Was, adaptation of a book by Helen Thomas (produced 1987).
Nativity (produced 1989).

TELEVISION PLAYS: *Talkin' Blues*, 1977; *Real Live Audience*, 1978; *Baby Talk*, 1981; *Let 'em Know We're Here*, 1981; *Johnny Jarvis* series, 1983; *George Orwell* (documentary), 1983; *Charlie*, 1984; *Breaking Up*, 1986; *Centrepoint*, 1990; *The Last Romantics*, 1991.

NOVELS

My Life Closed Twice. 1977.
Jack Be Nimble. 1980.
Charlie (novelization of television play). 1984.
Star Turn. 1985.
Witchcraft. 1987.
Breaking Up (novelization of television play). 1988.
Black Magic. 1988.
The Wimbledon Poisoner. 1990.
They Came from SW19. 1992.
East of Wimbledon. 1993.

OTHER

Johnny Jarvis (for children). 1983.

THEATRICAL ACTIVITIES

DIRECTOR: Television—*George Orwell*, 1983; *Cambodian Witness* (documentary) by James Fenton, 1987.

Each of Nigel Williams's early plays (1977–80) explores the interaction of and relations between a handful of sharply distinguished individuals who have been isolated by some circumstance, or who isolate themselves, to form a closed group. A convincing (and relishful) rendering of Cockney speech rhythms enables Williams to generate considerable claustrophobic intensity within this dramatic framework. The intensity, however, is largely negative. The plays are dominated by variations on one particular figure: an overbearingly voluble and physically aggressive embodiment of destructive energy. He (or she) stands outside every recognizable position, whether social, sexual, or political, and aims to discredit and destroy those positions (represented by the other characters) by violence both verbal and physical. Though the theme of each play, be it class, race, or sex, is at least *implicitly* political, the presence of this central figure ensures that the dramatic treatment is less political than psychological. The figure catalyzes and externalizes hidden tensions, sometimes with self-destructive consequences, tearing away "civilized" constraints in such a way as to lay bare not political or economic causes but atavistic, tribal impulses.

The tribal emerges clearly in *Class Enemy*. The growing tension and final conflict here take place not between groups but within a single group. Six fifth-formers in a London school fill up an unsupervised afternoon by each "teaching a lesson" on his pet subject. The friction between Iron, the voluble, violent representative of inner-city despair who cherishes his pessimism and seems to relish debasement, and Sky-Light (the nicknames are of course significant), who despite the social circumstances retains trust in the essential goodness of human nature and a radiant perception of the world, erupts into a fight for leadership of the group. Iron wins the fight but, as Sky-Light realizes, the self-directed violence of his moral nature and the frustration of his fevered demand for an indefinable "knowledge" reveal him as the real victim, the "loser."

Sky-Light stands against and illuminates the moral collapse of Iron, but in *Sugar and Spice*, which focuses on sex-hatred as *Class Enemy* focuses on class-hatred, neither the prostitute Suze nor the lovers Carol and Steve are strong enough to counter the disruptive force of the lesbian Sharon and her male counterpart, the Iron-like John. Each contrives the ritual sexual humiliation (by stripping) of a member of the other sex and each addresses a savage climactic speech to the naked victim's genitals. The hatred embodied in Sharon and John represents not just a critique of society's distortion of sexuality but a mutual revulsion of the sexes which seems to extend to a revulsion from sexuality itself.

Though they are no less bleak in tone than the previous plays, *Trial Run* and *Line 'em* both conclude more decisively. In *Trial Run* a young Sikh, Gange, and Billy who is of mixed parentage, stage a mock trial with hostages they have taken while holed up waiting for the police to surrender a Special Patrol Group man upon whom Gange wants revenge. But the disruptive Billy, with his hatred of society in general, wants more than *personal* revenge. After Gange has been killed by police marksmen Billy mysteriously (and unexpectedly) assumes that posture of inner stillness and blank patience of his Eastern ancestors. His abandonment of the social will makes itself felt as an affirmation, yet in *Line 'em* it is precisely this social will, represented by a solidarity that seems less political than tribal, which is finally affirmed. The anarchistic Foreman mocks and undermines the picket line organized by the old-style union man Sam, yet when soldiers arrive to break the picket he reunites his own ranks by causing insubordination in those of the enemy, and by questioning the validity of the Commanding Officer's values. In the final tableau the two "armies" confront one another.

It will be apparent from these accounts that the power of Williams's drama is cumulative: each play concentrates on a single situation and builds up to an explosive climax. His two comic-satiric plays of the early 1980s, W.C.P.C. and The Adventures of Jasper Ridley (Williams's most explicitly political play), depart from this pattern in adopting a more obviously scenic form for the presentation of the experiences of their naïve-innocent central figures within their respective milieux. However My Brother's Keeper again focuses intensely on a single—but this time familial and significantly middle-class—situation. As an old actor lies dying in hospital after a severe stroke, he is visited by his immediate family. His will to live is insistently provoked by his playwright son Tony, whose own thwarted energy arises out of a sense of life wasted through the withholding of feelings, especially love, within this "ordinary" middle-class family. Though vehemently opposed by his brother Sam, a successful businessman with an enduring sense of exclusion from the aesthetic side of the family, Tony attempts to break the maternal domination which he sees as having crippled the family emotionally by encouraging a confrontation (between his parents especially) and a purgation, a speaking out. A point of resolution is reached only when the dying actor-father stumblingly articulates the necessity for mutual acceptance within a family of relationships as "states of conflict." Unusually for Williams—and this could be seen as a significant shift of emphasis in his drama—the energies of the play, and of its central figure Tony, make themselves felt as positive. Yet one does suspect here, more strongly than with Williams's previous work, that a great deal of dramatic heat is being expended in the generation of a rather ordinary light.

In Country Dancing Williams's work takes on an historical focus. Within a narrative framework provided by an encounter in 1914 between folk-song collector Cecil Sharp and an ancient village fiddler born in the year of Waterloo, the story of the fiddler's life and relationships is played out. It is a story of deprivation, love, betrayal, oppression, and abandonment, but one in which the fate of the individual is shown to be inextricably linked to— even determined by—the enormous social shifts occurring in the century between the two moments of "pointless slaughter." The experience and consequences of rural protest and depopulation, and of urbanization and mass industrialization, are suggested with point and ingenuity by the songs and dances which punctuate the action. Dance functions as invocation, provocation, counterpoint, and above all as a complex metaphor of social, personal, and labour relations—larger patterns shaping the lives of individuals. As life becomes a "business" and political economy triumphs, the cosmopolitan individualism of the waltz displaces the rooted community of country dance, and the uprooted fiddler loses both his wife and his musical gift. But music is "the only certain thing," and the gift revives, just at this moment of impending European holocaust. In its formal fluidity and lucid stylization—quite different from the dense naturalism with which Williams originally made his mark—*Country Dancing* seems to represent a significant shift in his writing for the stage.

—Paul Lawley

WILLIS, Ted (Edward Henry Willis; Baron Willis of Chislehurst).

Born in Tottenham, Middlesex, 13 January 1918. Educated at state schools, including Tottenham Central School, 1923–33. Served in the Royal Fusiliers, 1940; writer for the War Office and Ministry of Information. Married Audrey Hale in 1944; one son and one daughter. Artistic director, Unity Theatre, London, 1945–48. Director, World Wide Pictures since 1967, and Vitalcall since 1983. Executive member, League of Dramatists, London, 1948–74; chair, 1958–63, president, 1963–68 and 1976–79, and since 1988 life president, Writers Guild of Great Britain; president, International Writers Guild, 1967–69. Since 1964 governor, Churchill Theatre Trust, Bromley, Kent; member of the Board of Governors, National Film School, London, 1970–73. Recipient: Berlin Festival award, for screenplay, 1957; Edinburgh Festival award; Writers Guild award, 1964, 1967; Royal Society of Arts Silver medal, 1967; Variety Guild of Great Britain award, 1976; Willis Trophy, for television writing, 1983. Fellow, Royal Society of Arts; fellow, Royal Television Society. Life Peer, 1963. Agent: Elaine Greene Ltd., 31 Newington Green, London N16 9PU; and, Lemon, Unna, and Durbridge, 24 Pottery Lane, Holland Park, London W11 4LZ. Address: 5 Shepherds Green, Chislehurst, Kent BR7 6PB, England.

Publications

PLAYS

Sabotage (as John Bishop) (produced 1943).
Buster (produced 1943).
All Change Here (produced 1944).
"God Bless the Guv'nor": A Moral Melodrama in Which the Twin Evils of Trades Unionism and Strong Drink are Exposed, "After Mrs. Henry Wood" (produced 1945). 1945.
The Yellow Star (also director: produced 1945).
What Happened to Love? (produced 1947).
No Trees in the Street (produced 1948).
The Lady Purrs (produced 1950). 1950.
The Magnificent Moodies (produced 1952).
The Blue Lamp, with Jan Read (produced 1952).
A Kiss for Adele, with Talbot Rothwell, adaptation of the play by Barillet and Grédy (produced 1952).
Kid Kenyon Rides Again, with Allan Mackinnon (produced 1954).
George Comes Home. 1955.
Doctor in the House, adaptation of the novel by Richard Gordon (produced 1956). 1957.

Woman in a Dressing Gown, (televised, 1956). In *Woman in a Dressing Gown and Other Television Plays*, 1959; (revised version, produced 1963); 1964.

The Young and the Guilty (televised, 1956). In *Woman in a Dressing Gown and Other Television Plays*, 1959.

Look in Any Window (televised, 1958). In *Woman in a Dressing Gown and Other Television Plays*, 1959.

Hot Summer Night (produced 1958). 1959.

Woman in a Dressing Gown and Other Television Plays (includes *The Young and the Guilty* and *Look in Any Window*). 1959.

Brothers-in-Law, with Henry Cecil, adaptation of the novel by Cecil (produced 1959). 1959.

When in Rome, with Ken Ferry, music by Kramer, lyrics by Eric Shaw, adaptation of a play by Garinei and Giovannini (produced 1959).

The Eyes of Youth, adaptation of the novel *A Dread of Burning* by Rosemary Timperley (as *Farewell Yesterday*, produced 1959; as *The Eyes of Youth*, produced 1959). 1960.

Mother, adaptation of the novel by Gorky (produced 1961).

Doctor at Sea, adaptation of the novel by Richard Gordon (produced 1961). 1961.

The Little Goldmine. 1962.

A Slow Roll of Drums (produced 1964).

A Murder of Crows (produced 1966).

The Ballad of Queenie Swann (televised, 1966; revised version, music by Dick Manning and Marvin Laird, lyrics by Willis, produced 1967; as *Queenie*, produced 1967).

Dead on Saturday (produced 1972).

Mr. Polly, music by Michael Begg and Ivor Slaney, lyrics by Willis, adaptation of the novel by H.G. Wells (produced 1977).

Stardust (produced 1983).

Tommy Boy (produced 1988).

Intent to Kill (produced 1990).

Screenplays: *The Waves Roll On* (documentary), 1945; *Holiday Camp*, with others, 1947; *Good Time Girl*, with Muriel and Sydney Box, 1948; *A Boy, A Girl, and a Bike*, 1949; *The Huggetts Abroad*, with others, 1949; *The Undefeated* (documentary), 1950; *The Blue Lamp*, with others, 1950; *The Wallet*, 1952; *Top of the Form*, with John Paddy Carstairs and Patrick Kirwan, 1953; *Trouble in Store*, with John Paddy Carstairs and Maurice Cowan, 1953; *The Large Rope*, 1953; *One Good Turn*, with John Paddy Carstairs and Maurice Cowan, 1954; *Burnt Evidence*, 1954; *Up to His Neck*, with others, 1954; *It's Great to Be Young*, 1956; *The Skywalkers*, 1956; *Woman in a Dressing Gown*, 1957; *The Young and the Guilty*, 1958; *No Trees in the Street*, 1959; *Six Men and a Nightingale*, 1961; *Flame in the Streets*, 1961; *The Horsemasters*, 1961; *Bitter Harvest*, 1963; *Last Bus to Banjo Creek*, 1968; *Our Miss Fred*, with Hugh Leonard, 1972; and other documentaries.

Radio plays: *Big Bertha*, 1962; *And No Birds Sing*, 1979; *The Buckingham Palace Connection*, from his own novel, 1981; *The Left-Handed Sleeper*, from his own novel, 1982; *Obsession*, 1983; *Death May Surprise Us*, from his own novel, 1984.

TELEVISION PLAYS: *The Handlebar*, *The Pattern of Marriage*, *Big City*, *Dial 999*, *The Sullavan Brothers*, *Lifeline*, and *Taxi* series; *Dixon of Dock Green* series, 1954, and later series; *The Young and the Guilty*, 1956; *Woman in a Dressing Gown*, 1956; *Look in Any Window*, 1958; *Strictly for the Sparrows*, 1958; *Scent of Fear*, 1959; *Days of Vengeance*, with Edward J. Mason, 1960; *Flowers of Evil* series, with Mason, 1961; *Outbreak of Murder*, with Mason; *Sergeant Cork* series, 1963; *The Four Seasons of Rosie Carr*, 1964; *Dream of a Summer Night*, 1965; *Mrs. Thursday* series, 1966; *The Ballad of Queenie Swann*, 1966; *Virgin of the Secret Service* series, 1968; *Crimes of Passion* series, 1970–72; *Copper's End* series, 1971; *Hunter's Walk* series, 1973, 1976; *Black Beauty* series, 1975; *Barney's Last Battle*, 1976; *Street Party*, 1977; *Man-Eater*, from his own novel, 1980; *Einetleim für Tiere*, series (from 1984, Germany); *Mrs. Harris, M.P.*, 1985; *Mrs. Harris Goes to New York*, 1987; *The Iron Man*, 1987; *Mrs. Harris Goes to Moscow*, 1987; *Racecourse* series, 1987; *The Valley of Dream*, 1987; *Mrs. Harris Goes to Monte Carlo*, 1988; *Vincent Vincent*, 1989; *Mrs. Harris Goes to Majorca*, 1990.

NOVELS

The Blue Lamp. 1950.
Dixon of Dock Green: My Life, with Charles Hatton. 1960.
Dixon of Dock Green: A Novel, with Paul Graham. 1961.
Black Beauty. 1972.
Death May Surprise Us. 1974; as *Westminster One*, 1975.
The Left-Handed Sleeper. 1975.
Man-Eater. 1976.
The Churchill Commando. 1977.
The Buckingham Palace Connection. 1978.
The Lions of Judah. 1979.
The Naked Sun. 1980.
The Most Beautiful Girl in the World. 1982.
Spring at the Winged Horse: The First Season of Rosie Carr. 1983.
The Green Leaves of Summer: The Second Season of Rosie Carr. 1988.
The Bells of Autumn: The Third Season of Rosie Carr. 1990.
The Plume of Feathers. 1993.

OTHER

Fighting Youth of Russia. 1942.
The Devil's Churchyard (for children). 1957.
Seven Gates to Nowhere (for children). 1958.
Whatever Happened to Tom Mix? The Story of One of My Lives. 1970.
A Problem for Mother Christmas (for children). 1986.
Evening All: Fifty Years over a Hot Typewriter. 1991.

MANUSCRIPT COLLECTION: Boston University.

THEATRICAL ACTIVITIES

DIRECTOR: Plays—*The Yellow Star*, 1945; *Boy Meets Girl* by Bella and Sam Spewack, 1946; *All God's Chillun Got Wings* by Eugene O'Neill, 1946; *Golden Boy* by Clifford Odets, 1947; *Anna Christie* by Eugene O'Neill.

Ted Willis comments:

I am a good example of what can be done by hard work. I've taken a small talent, honed and sharpened it into a good professional instrument. Might have been a better writer if I'd stuck to one area and kept out of politics (both writing and national) but that's the way I am.

There is no doubt in my mind that Ted Willis owes his success in life to his quite extraordinary power of concentration. At a very early age he decided that he was going to be a writer. When he left school finally at 15 and confided to the Headmaster his determination to write, the crisp comment was "Don't be a fool. You've no literary gift whatever. Much better learn a trade." But to waste time and energy in learning a trade was no part of the Willis plan. He was teaching himself one, and making progress. His intensive study of the cinema was encouraging him to try his hand at that medium, and television; so he took the kind of ill-paid jobs that were open to an unskilled man, and went on writing.

His pen was by now a very well-tempered instrument; but it was through his politics, not his fiction, that this first became publicly known. His views were of the extreme left-wing order, and he expressed them with a force and pungency that made him a valuable asset to the Labour Party. But it was during army service in World War II that he was given the chance to write his first screenplays. This decided his future—for when he went back into civil life in 1945 and was invited to stand for a safe Labour seat in Parliament, he refused. He was still a writer.

He is an inventive storyteller, and his high standard of craftsmanship and severe self-discipline have lead inevitably to success, especially in such compositions as his television series *Dixon of Dock Green* and *Mrs. Thursday*. What it does not necessarily lead to is artistry; and one gathers that Willis knows this very well himself, for he once said modestly to an interviewer, "There are hundreds of better writers with much greater talent than mine. But less ability to work hard."

That honest, if overstated, attempt at self-assessment has a modicum of truth in it, and it is remarkable that not one of his productions has ever induced West End audiences to show much enthusiasm. Even *Woman in a Dressing Gown* (by common consent his best play) caused little stir.

So evident an effect must have a definable cause; but to say simply that Willis has a better talent for screen and television plays than for stage plays is merely to define the matter without explaining it. There could be a dozen explanations but one is fundamental. The world of the living theatre was unknown to the boy who played truant from school to revel in the glories of the cinema. When Willis first encountered the stage in his mid-twenties it was in the spirit not of a lover but of an immensely industrious student. He learned much; but it is not thus that a dramatist acquires that mysterious sense of the theatre which enables him to serve the art of the actor. The hard-working student may well deserve success, but in the theatre he cannot command it.

—W.A. Darlington

WILSON, Snoo (Andrew Wilson).

Born in Reading, Berkshire, 2 August 1948. Educated at Bradfield College, Berkshire, 1962–66; University of East Anglia, Norwich, 1966–69, B.A. (upper second) in English and American studies 1969. Married Ann McFerran in 1976; two sons and one daughter. Founding director, Portable Theatre, Brighton and London, 1968–75; script editor, *Play for Today* series, BBC Television, 1972; dramaturge, Royal Shakespeare Company, 1975–76; director, Scarab Theatre, 1975–80. Henfield fellow, University of East Anglia, 1978. Recipient: John Whiting award, 1978; US Bicentennial fellowship, 1980; San Diego Theater Critics Circle award, 1988. Agent: Casarotto Ramsay Ltd., National House, 60–66 Wardour Street, London W1V 3HP. Address: 41 The Chase, London SW4 0NP, England.

Publications

PLAYS

Girl Mad as Pigs (produced 1967).

Ella Daybellfesse's Machine (produced 1967).

Between the Acts, adaptation of the novel by Virginia Woolf (produced 1969).

Charles the Martyr (produced 1970).

Device of Angels (produced 1970).

Pericles, The Mean Knight (also director: produced 1970).

Pignight (also director: produced 1971). With *Blowjob*, 1975.

Blowjob (produced 1971). With *Pignight*, 1975.

Lay By, with others (also director: produced 1971). 1972.

Reason (as *Reason the Sun King*, produced 1972; as *Reason: Boswell and Johnson on the Shores of the Eternal Sea*, in *Point 101* produced 1972; as *Reason*, produced 1975). In *Gambit*, vol. 8, no. 29, 1976.

England's Ireland, with others (also director: produced 1972).

Vampire (produced 1973). In *Plays and Players*, July 1973; revised version (produced 1977), 1979.

The Pleasure Principle: The Politics of Love, The Capital of Emotion (produced 1973). 1974.

The Beast (produced 1974). In *Plays and Players*, December 1974 and January 1975; revised version, as *The Number of the Beast* (produced 1982), with *Flaming Bodies*, 1983.

The Everest Hotel (also director: produced 1975). In *Plays and Players*, March 1976.

A Greenish Man (televised 1975; produced 1978). 1979.

The Soul of the White Ant (produced 1976). 1978.

Elijah Disappearing (produced 1977).

England-England, music by Kevin Coyne (produced 1977).

The Glad Hand (produced 1978). 1979.
In at the Death, with others (produced 1978).
The Language of the Dead Is Tongued with Fire (produced 1978).
Flaming Bodies (produced 1979). With *The Number of the Beast*, 1983.
Magic Rose (produced 1979).
Spaceache, music by Nick Bicât (produced 1980).
Salvation Now (produced 1981).
The Grass Widow (produced 1982). 1983.
Our Lord of Lynchville (produced 1983; as *Lynchville* produced 1990).
Loving Reno (produced 1983).
La Colombe, music by Gounod, adaptation of the libretto by Barbier and
    Carré (produced 1983).
Hamlyn (produced 1984).
Orpheus in the Underworld, with David Pountney, music by Offenbach,
    adaptation of the libretto by Crémieux and Halévy (produced 1985).
More Light (also co-director: produced 1987). 1990.
80 Days, music and lyrics by Ray Davies (produced 1988).
Walpurgis Night, adaptation of a work by Venedict Erofeyev (produced
    1992).

SCREENPLAY: *Shadey*, 1986.

TELEVISION PLAYS: *The Good Life*, 1971; *Swamp Music*, 1972; *More about the
Universe*, 1972; *The Barium Meal*, 1974; *The Trip to Jerusalem*, 1975; *A
Greenish Man*, 1975; *Don't Make Waves* (*Eleventh Hour* series), with Trevor
Griffiths, 1975.

NOVELS
Spaceache. 1984.
Inside Babel. 1985.

CRITICAL STUDY: Interview in *Theatre Quarterly*, Spring 1980.

THEATRICAL ACTIVITIES
DIRECTOR: **Plays**—*Pericles, The Mean Knight*, 1970; *Pignight*, 1971; *Lay By*,
1971; *England's Ireland*, 1972; *Bodywork* by Jennifer Phillips, 1974; *The
Everest Hotel*, 1975; *Loving Reno* (co-director, with Simon Callow), 1983;
More Light (co-director, with Simon Stokes), 1987.
ACTOR: **Plays**—*Lay By*, 1971; The Porpoise in *Fresh-water* by Virginia Woolf,
1983; Andy Warhol in *Warhola!*, 1990.

Snoo Wilson comments:

(1973) More than anything else the proscenium arch theatre suggests the
success of drawing room conversation as a mirror for a mature civilization. In
these mirrors, the even keel of the state slices through the waters of uncon-
sciousness, and very few playwrights have managed to knock any holes in the
boat, though a number have suggested that the ship was sinking without their

assistance, and others, like the stewards on the *Titanic*, bicycle gaily round the first-class gym, declaring that there is no list to the ship. These last are the ones most likely to be rewarded by the first-class passengers for their élan vital, even while the bilge water is rising round the ankles of the steerage families. The bicycling stewards are most likely to be able to command support that is quite independent of anything except people's gratitude at being amused, and many of them die peacefully in their beds declaring that there was always a slight list to port anyhow, and their reward was plainly a just one since people came and gave willingly, and were briefly happy.

A different brand of steward feels considerable unease at the condition of the ship, and his actions are likely to be much less popular at first than the bicyclists, though as time passes and his costume becomes charmingly archaic his pieces will be revived as Art, safe now from the Life he tried to redirect, which will have moved on in a lateral, unexpected direction. Television in Britain created a brand of "responsible" playwrights whose reputations at first were large and abrasive but now have stabilised in characteristic and therefore unsurprising because recognisable positions of social dynamism, and there the matter rests, a compromise acceptable both to producers who would like to produce more radical plays but have taken "Grandmother's footsteps" as far as they think the head of drama will let them, and to an audience stunned by tedium and kept alive by a feeling they ought to watch plays, sustained by tiny whiffs of excellence that occur in the smog of apathy. Both television and the theatre with one or two exceptions had failed either to make any formal advances in technique or to investigate areas of emotion which would force advances on them: I say "failed" because I believe that there must always be a technical evolution in theatre if only to remind audiences that they are watching a particular genre: playwrights who are adept at naturalism can take the edge off the most workmanlike oeuvre by making its naturalism subliminal.

The small groups who started with very little assistance at first—sometimes none—from the Arts Council in the late 1960s had a different sort of audience, a different sort of motive, and were a growth outside the conventional structure of theatre in Britain largely because it was dull and extremely conservative and did not provide outlets for the sort of things they wanted to do, or, in the case of Portable Theatre, a writer's theatre first, to write. Since there was very little money anyway the opportunity to write what the writer wanted to write and put it on in the way he wanted was possible, and a series of one night stands provided continuous platforms for plays which in the beginning we were prepared to take anywhere.

Now, there are a large number of studio theatres, almost a circuit, round the country. The success of *Lay By*, a group play written round a newspaper story, at the Edinburgh Festival, suggested that it was desirable and possible to launch a play about contemporary events to tour large theatres round England and Scotland. After six months of extreme difficulty we managed to set up a tour of a play about Northern Ireland, called *England's Ireland*, which had its first three weeks in Holland because we were unable to find theatres in England in sufficiently large numbers prepared to take the risk of an unknown play by a previously, quote, experimental group.

When we did bring the play to England, sadly it was in Chalk Farm at the Roundhouse rather than in Glasgow where it drew a significant response, and

Lancaster and Nottingham were the only large repertory companies which
would have it.

   This demonstrates, among other things, the self-stultifying conservatism of
the control of British theatre boards who believe that their audiences should be
fed what they are accustomed to consume, either the costume drama of Ibsen's
Choice, or on plays which by ignoring all but the most trivial of human
difficulties and miseries close minds rather than open them in a stuffy two
hours at the theatre.

   The title I would choose for this essay, *The Freudian Landscape and the
Proscenium Mind*, suggests that the middle-class mind is firmly ensconced on
stage; this is true only by its being a self-perpetuating situation: it is not true
that if we want to widen the range of theatrical experience we have to abandon
the theatre. The theatre has always been a whore to safe fashion, but at the
moment there is a pressure for a particular sort of awareness and articulacy
which hopefully may lead to the good lady opening her legs to a different
position, and renewed and enlarged clientele being the result. The plangent
cries of either the affronted audience or management should not be an
invitation to a secondary dialogue, whose end is respectability. Nor should this
secondary dialogue be mistaken for a play, for the theatre is not that self-
sufficient, being old, and bloated with the worst vices of time serving and
sycophancy: and these will show through shallow devices. It is ourselves,
finally, rather than the civilisation, who we have to prove mature; so, paradoxically, the struggle for exposure which shapes the ideas must not dent them,
any more than an achieved articulacy within theatrical convention supplants
the need for further thought.

Snoo Wilson began his writing career in the late 1960s with Portable Theatre,
of which he was a founding director along with two friends from Cambridge,
David Hare and Tony Bicât—Wilson himself studied at the then new
University of East Anglia. His earlier plays, particularly *Pignight* and *Blowjob*,
are extremely clever and dark works which reflect a good many of Wilson's
general preoccupations. Though never an overtly "political" dramatist Wilson
has always been concerned with problems of individual psychology, in particular schizophrenia, with moral anarchy, and most specifically with the threat of
pollution on a planet which, like the absurdists with whom he has so much in
common, he shows to be in direct if often comic opposition to man's dreams
and aspirations. In *Pignight* a Lincolnshire farm is taken over by a sinister
gangster and turned into a machine for the organized butchering and processing of the animals in question. Underneath this surface violence runs a thread
of eerieness—Smitty, a psychopathic farm labourer inherited by the new
owners, is a running reminder of the war (he suffers from mysterious brain
damage) and takes delight in committing acts of savagery (including the
blowing up of the farm dog, Robby). *Blowjob* is an equally violent exercise in
alienation, with two skinheads planning to blow up a safe in a factory, an act
which they bungle. During their travels they meet up with a homosexual
security guard who tries unsuccessfully to pick them up and with a girl student
who, typically for the time of the play, is alienated from her academic

environment—the whole play acting as a caustic comment on role-playing and its stultifying effect on personality.

Both *Vampire* and *The Pleasure Principle* are plays which further develop Wilson's preoccupation with external ethical codes and their effect on individual freedom. *Vampire*, which has been both revived and revised by Wilson, has a conventional three-act structure which moves from a late 19th-century Presbyterian parsonage and a scene of astral sex in an Edwardian cricket pavilion to a contemporary scene of youthful disquiet (the setting has been altered in a subsequent version from a secular funeral parlour to the pagoda in Kew Gardens), and finishes with Enoch Powell, risen vampire-like from the coffin and delivering his famous "Rivers of Blood" speech. The second act of *Vampire* is a neat example of Wilson's developing style.

In tune with a belief that the stage is the freest medium, he concentrates on sharp juxtapositions which transcend conventional unities of time and place, and—despite Wilson's often underestimated gift for composition—continually upstage the dialogue spoken by his characters. Sarah, an upper-class girl, is wooed by a handsome young cricketer called Henry, killed in World War I. He returns in his astral form to try and make love to Sarah who is frightened of being seen—Freud and Jung suddenly appear on stilts to discuss her hang-up in their own jargonistic fashion, while a talking ox grunts "Let's go to my place and fuck." *The Pleasure Principle* concentrates on the almost undefined relationship between two characters whose opposing ideas of pleasure prevent them from consummating their mutual attraction until the last act. Robert and Gale in fact make it after a seduction sequence played out in a cardboard swan, while the nervous breakdown of Robert, an aggressive businessman with a great belief in capitalism, is prefigured by the entrance of a pair of dancing gorillas bearing messages.

Wilson is by now something of grand old man of the British fringe but still refuses or is unable to be assimilated into the mainstream despite a belief on his own part that his plays are designed to be both popular and fun. Indeed he has developed an eclectic and mercurial interest in occult subjects and in trendy pseudo-science. In *The Beast* and *The Soul of the White Ant*, the latter a quite breathtaking short play, he has explored the worlds of two dead cult figures, the satanist Aleister Crowley and the South African naturalist Eugène Marais, whose reputation, part visionary's, part charlatan's, is tested by the methods of free association that characterise Wilson's work at its best. The title of the play derives from one of Marais's works about the corporate soul which Wilson employs as a metaphor for the collective insanity of his characters, a group of white South Africans who congregate in and around a bar run by a boozy eccentric, Mabel. In typical Wilsonian fashion, the bar is mud-caked and threatened by etymological disaster while Marais himself enters as a back-street abortionist, white-suited, visionary, and also corrupt, a combination of killer and life-giver, as symbolized by an act which he performs when Mabel goes mad and shoots her houseboy, whose carefully collected sperm is now filling her freezer. When the stuff is thrown into the local river two of Mabel's friends, Edith and June, are impregnated and it is Marais who saves them, but only after Mabel's bizarre act of racial and sexual mutilation.

Wilson's most ambitious and perfectly realised play to date is probably *The Glad Hand* which works on many levels both as a political thriller and as a bizarre and often whacky study in synchronisation. On the surface the piece concerns the attempt of one Ritsaat, a South African fascist, to locate and confront the anti-Christ whom Ritsaat claims to have been present on earth during a cowboy strike in Wyoming in 1886. Ritsaat's plan is simple: he will charter an oil tanker and by time-travel via the Bermuda Triangle confront the anti-Christ in person. In fact Ritsaat, through ingenuously offering "cowboy fun" in his recruiting advertisement, acquires two camp actors as part of the crew, along with a family of stock "Paddy" Irish, a portly American script-writer, a Cuban cook, a CIA agent, and a dubious psychic surgeon who performs an operation on board. Indeed the ship acts as setting for the recreated cowboy strike which includes passages of riveting documentary description of conditions prevailing at the time of the "real" incident (which did in fact happen). There's also the arrival on board of a raunchy American lesbian who sparks off several more of the play's coincidences until a final mutiny against Ritsaat's rule develops into an alliance of Cuban cook and chauvinist Irishman. Before dying Ritsaat manages to utter: "Between you and your perceptions is the mirror which you think reflects reality." It's a comment which sums up a good deal of Wilson's own intentions. Indeed in showing that "reality" is something which can be changed or at least rearranged he is making both a theatrical point about naturalism and a political point about the world as it exists, although how much real substance there is behind the technique is open to serious questioning.

In *A Greenish Man* Wilson employs his associative powers on the subject of Northern Ireland. Troy Phillips, a half-Irish Liverpudlian, is sent to Kilburn on an errand of revenge and encounters an IRA dinner being organized by the local Irish publican and a bedraggled factory owner who has perfected a formula for green paint made entirely from grass clippings, as well as a battered divorcée with a liberal conscience and a tax lawyer. It's a play which fell down in production because the knots with which Wilson tied up the different strands of his ideas didn't survive the tug of live performance.

Flaming Bodies is set in the smart and characterless office of a Los Angeles film producer, whose overweight, compulsively hungry script editor, Mercedes, has just been sacked but refuses to leave the office. Again, Wilson uses this Hockneyesque setting as a launching pad for a trip in which Mercedes rediscovers herself, but only after experiencing such events as a Chevy from another film crashing through the window of the office block, King Herod discovering his love of small boys (the film she's working on at the time of her sacking is a life of Christ), Mary and Joseph (both pregnant) turning up on an inflatable donkey, and her mother's ashes turning up in a film producer's lunch! Indeed Mercedes spends a good deal of the time on the phone, talking to her mother to whom she protests her lesbianism, and to her psychiatrist, to whom she protests her sanity. In the flip, weight-conscious world of California film production, Mercedes is attacked on all sides—even by her dead father who hovers in the air outside the office's huge picture window.

In the cartoon play *Spaceache* Wilson created an Orwellian world where the unwanted and unemployed are cryogenically freeze-dried and reduced to milk-bottle size before being sent into orbit until their time comes for resurrection. This play certainly does not exhibit Wilson's talents at their most representative, unlike those in which surface organization is being continually broken up

and recreated and, in an often mundane theatrical terrain, supernatural forces
or natural powers are often the real arbiters of the proceedings.

Unfortunately as he reaches maturity Wilson's refusal to compromise on his
chosen artistic progression has continued to cause him problems. Though he
has moved with some success into novels, films, and opera, his work refuses to
find a home on the main stages of any of Britain's premier subsidised companies despite initial plans and interest from both the National and the Royal
Shakespeare Company. His last play for the Royal Court, *The Grass Widow*,
was a rather unsuccessful jumble of ideas and effects inspired by a year's
sabbatical in California. *The Number of the Beast* was an effectively reworked
version of *The Beast*. Wilson's obsession with Aleister Crowley still produces
dividends, and the piece was an immensely entertaining essay on Crowley's
bizarrely revolutionary life. Wilson's film, *Shadey*, with Antony Sher as the
eponymous sexually confused character, was well reviewed. But his single
most stunning recent success was the libretto for David Pountney's production
of Offenbach's *Orpheus in the Underworld*, a much-seen version for the
English National Opera. Here it seemed that Wilson's ability to challenge
accepted notions of taste and presentation, his impressive grasp of theatrical
metaphor, were welded to a firm base. Sadly, though his work is increasingly
produced abroad, notably in America, he remains an exciting playwright still
to realise his enormous potential at home.

—Steve Grant

WOOD, Charles (Gerald).

Born in St. Peter Port, Guernsey, Channel Islands, 6 August 1932. Educated
at Chesterfield Grammar School, 1942–45; King Charles I School,
Kidderminster, Worcestershire, 1945–48; Birmingham College of Art,
1948–50. Served in the 17/21st Lancers, 1950–55: corporal. Married Valerie
Elizabeth Newman in 1954; one son and one daughter. Factory worker,
1955–57; designer, scenic artist, and stage manager, Theatre Workshop,
London, 1957–59; staff member, Bristol *Evening Post*, 1959–62. Recipient:
Evening Standard award, 1963, 1973; Screenwriters Guild award, 1965; prix
Italia Rai, 1988; BAFTA award, 1988. Fellow, Royal Society of Literature,
1985. Agent: Jane Annakin, William Morris Agency, 31–32 Soho Square,
London W1V 5DG. Address: Long Barn, Sibford Gower, Near Banbury,
Oxfordshire OX15 5RT, England.

Publications

PLAYS

Prisoner and Escort (televised 1961; produced in *Cockade*, 1963).
Cockade (includes *Prisoner and Escort*, *John Thomas*, *Spare*) (produced
1963). In *New English Dramatists 8*, 1965.
Tie Up the Ballcock (produced 1964). In *Second Playbill 3*, edited by Alan
Durband, 1973.
Don't Make Me Laugh (produced 1965).
Meals on Wheels (produced 1965; shortened version produced 1971).
Fill the Stage with Happy Hours (produced 1966). In *New English Dramatists
11*, 1967.

Dingo (produced 1967). 1969.
Labour (produced 1968).
H, Being Monologues at Front of Burning Cities (produced 1969). 1970.
Colliers Wood (produced 1970).
Welfare (includes *Tie Up the Ballcock, Meals on Wheels, Labour*) (produced 1971).
Veterans; or, Hair in the Gates of the Hellespont (produced 1972). 1972.
The Can Opener, adaptation of a play by Victor Lanoux (produced 1974).
Jingo (produced 1975).
The Script (produced 1976).
Has "Washington" Legs? (produced 1978). With *Dingo*, 1978.
The Garden (produced 1982).
Red Star (produced 1984).
Across from the Garden of Allah (produced 1986).
Tumbledown: A Screenplay (televised 1988). 1987.
The Plantagenets, adaptation of Shakespeare's *Henry VI* plays (produced 1988).
Man, Beast and Virtue, adaptation of a play by Pirandello (produced 1989).
The Mountain Giants, adaptation of an unfinished play by Pirandello (produced 1993).

SCREENPLAYS: *The Knack*, 1965; *Help!*, with Mark Behm, 1965; *Tie Up the Ballcock*, 1967; *How I Won the War*, 1967; *The Charge of the Light Brigade*, with John Osborne, 1968; *The Long Day's Dying*, 1968; *The Bed-Sitting Room*, with John Antrobus, 1969; *Fellini Satyricon* (English dialogue), 1969; *Cuba*, 1980; *Vile Bodies*, 1981.

RADIO PLAYS: *Cowheel Jelly*, 1962; *Next to Being a Knight*, 1972.

TELEVISION PLAYS: *Prisoner and Escort*, 1961; *Traitor in a Steel Helmet*, 1961; *Not at All*, 1962; *Drill Pig*, 1964; *Drums along the Avon*, 1967; *A Bit of a Holiday*, 1969; *The Emergence of Anthony Purdy, Esq.*, 1970; *A Bit of Family Feeling*, 1971; *A Bit of Vision*, 1972; *Death or Glory Boy*, 1974; *Mützen ab*, 1974; *A Bit of an Adventure*, 1974; *Love Lies Bleeding*, 1976; *Do As I Say*, 1977; *Don't Forget to Write!* series, 1977, 1979; *Red Monarch*, from stories by Yuri Krotkov, 1983; *Wagner*, 1984; *Puccini*, 1984; *Dust to Dust (Time for Murder* series), 1985; *Company of Adventurers* series, 1986 (Canada); *My Family and Other Animals*, from the book by Gerald Durrell, 1987; *Tumbledown*, 1988; *The Setting of the Sun (Inspector Morse* series), 1989; *On the Third Day*, from the novel by Piers Paul Read, 1992.

CRITICAL STUDIES: *The Second Wave* by John Russell Taylor, 1971; *Revolutions in Modern English Drama* by Katharine J. Worth, 1973.

THEATRICAL ACTIVITIES
DIRECTOR: Film—*Tie Up the Ballcock*, 1967.
ACTOR: Film—*The Knack*, 1965.

Charles Wood grew up in a theatrical family. He served five years as a regular soldier. In both theatre and war he sees a sordid reality sold to the public as glamorous. A line from one of his earliest plays, *Spare*, epitomizes his vision: "he . . . wet hisself grotesque at Waterloo." His most interesting works—and, perhaps, his most and least successful respectively—are those where the interest in theatre and war come together, *Dingo* and *H, Being Monologues at Front of Burning Cities*.

The two acts of *Dingo* give two equally desolate views of World War II. The first is in a desert emplacement during the North African campaign. various soldiers drop in on its two occupants, Dingo and Mogg, most notably a Comic who attempts to entertain the troops. Some of the same characters are in the internment camp of the second act, including the Comic. This time he functions as Master of Ceremonies for a camp entertainment that provides cover for an escape by the officers. The play ends with the liberation of the camp; even Churchill arrives, to "urinate on the West Wall of Hitler's Germany."

In *Dingo*, Wood protests against the glamorization of World War II and even suggests that its conduct was affected by how it could be sold to the public. Its grim reality is all the more horrific for being constantly counterpointed against culturally approved and sanitized images of war. For example, at the end of the play Tanky—whose screams as he burns to death in his tank have come right after the opening dialogue of the play, and whose charred, seated form has been carried around like a ventriloquist's dummy by his mate—keeps repeating "He killed me" through the camp's liberation and the beginning of the glorification of the now-finished war. While the stubborn fact of the phrase and the charred corpse are unchanging, "he" seems to shift reference from N.C.O. to officer to Churchill, so that the simple statement seems to become an indictment of a system. The phrase, thrice repeated, is the last line of the play. It is appropriate that the dead should have the last word.

H, in rough and often awkward verse, dramatizes the Indian Mutiny in spectacular Victorian style with set-piece battles, *tableaux vivants* with actors in the positions of Imperial paintings, painted backdrops, and front cloths which fall as charging officers stagger or slide beneath them. Extraordinary staging demands are made: sepoys advance from beneath an elephant, "five men are mutilated in a horrible manner," a rebel soldier is tied over the mouth of a cannon and blown to bits, raining pieces of flesh in the form of rose petals into the audience. But as that last stage direction suggests, all is subverted by Wood's mid-20th-century theatrical consciousness. The dramatic interest lies in the different characters of the commanders and officers, and in a captain's wife who is raped by an Indo-Irish rebel and bears his child at the end of the play. One can admire the play's ambitiousness and ingenuities, but there are too many assaults and at the end too long a deathbed scene.

The sense that we are watching theatrical "turns" is strong in all Wood's plays. Wood's characters often try out attitudes on each other, particularly in *Veterans*, or parody beliefs they do not share, as in *Dingo*, so the audience is more than usually aware of the transitions from one unit or "beat" to the next. In addition, Wood brings theatrical performance into the script itself. To take *Dingo* as an example, as well as the corpse who is treated as a ventriloquist's dummy, there is also the comedian who attempts to entertain the soldiers stuck in their desert emplacement, sits on a toilet with Churchill and Eisenhower glove-puppets arguing about Arnhem, and M.C.s a climactic POW camp concert with the men in drag. There is nothing so scabrous in *How I Won the War*, directed by Richard Lester with John Lennon in the lead role, for which Wood was scriptwriter in the same year that *Dingo* was produced, but he brought to it a similar presentational style: as men are killed, each is dyed a different colour and continues marching with his platoon.

Wood has twice written plays about making films about war, *Veterans* and *Has "Washington" Legs?* The former was inspired by Wood's experience as scriptwriter for *The Charge of the Light Brigade*. We see the ageing stars engaging in sometimes bitchy banter and in reminiscence while waiting for their call. The overall tone is nostalgic, even elegiac. In contrast, *Has "Washington" Legs?* deals with the business of making movies, and shows the emptiness not of the performers' assumed or faked emotions but of American corporate happy talk, of manipulative psychobabble, as various financial or artistic claimants to a piece of the action jockey over a lamentably unclear project to film the American Revolution. Wood's fierceness is undiminished, and his mockery of the mythification of war continues, but his target has changed to the mediators and middle managers of a service-industry society.

Wood's one play directly about the theatre, *Fill the Stage with Happy Hours*, may be one of the sourest comedies ever written. The characters, especially Albert, the manager of a tatty rep company, and his wife Maggie, whose acting career has given way to managing the bar, try on various attitudes as though to see if they fit the situation. For example, at one point Albert affects moral indignation at the juvenile lead's supposed seduction of his son, at another offers his son a man-to-man chat about seizing career opportunities when the sexual interest of a visiting *grande dame* of the stage is evident. Genuine emotion is either no longer possible for them or, ironically, can only be shown through the adoption of an appropriate borrowed attitude. At the end of the play Maggie tells Albert what he has refused to recognize: that she is dying of cancer. The curtain falls slowly as she sings "Smiling Through" and he turns heroic: "By God, I'll do *Ghosts*, I'll show this bloody town . . . . Isn't she marvellous, your mother—that's what it's about, son— that's how to use it. . . . It's given us a good life, hasn't it Maggie . . .?" Her reply ends the play: "Shut up, dear—you're not very good at it are you?" In the original production the actors stopped the fall of the curtain to bow and blow kisses to the audience, game troupers all.

—Anthony Graham-White

WRIGHT, Nicholas.

Born in Cape Town, South Africa, 5 July 1940. Educated at Rondebosch Boys' School, Cape Town; London Academy of Music and Dramatic Art. Director, Theatre Upstairs, Royal Court Theatre, London, 1970–75; joint artistic director, Royal Court Theatre, 1976–77; associate director of new writing 1984, literary manager, 1987, and since 1992 associate director, Royal National Theatre, London. Recipient: Arts Council bursary, 1981. Agent: Judy Daish Associates, 83 Eastbourne Mews, London W2 6LQ. Address: 33 Navarino Road, London E.8, England.

Publications

PLAYS

Changing Lines (also director: produced 1968).
Treetops (produced 1978).
The Gorky Brigade (produced 1979).
One Fine Day (produced 1980).
The Crimes of Vautrin, adaptation of a novel by Balzac (produced 1983). 1983.
The Custom of the Country (produced 1983). 1983.
The Desert Air (produced 1984). 1985.
Six Characters in Search of an Author, adaptation of a play by Pirandello (produced 1987).
Mrs. Klein (produced 1988). 1988.
Thérèse Raquin, adaptation of the novel by Zola (produced 1990).

OTHER

99 Plays (essays). 1992.

Nicholas Wright's first play appeared as far back as 1968, but although he has spent most of his professional life in the theatre, he has not produced a large body of work. It is not yet possible to speak of a development in his writing, yet certain definite shifts of emphasis can be discerned within a drama which is notable for combining a careful eclecticism of form and mode with steady concentration on a large but well-defined thematic territory.

Wright's work focuses on periods of social and political change or transition and seeks to explore, in a wide range of ways, the relation of the individual, whether as agent or as victim, to the large historical movement. *Treetops*, his earliest success, is typical in its (South) African setting—Cape Town in the year of the death of George VI and of the accession of Elizabeth II, 1952. The action is basically naturalistic, but the sunstroke-induced hallucination which prompts the disillusioned English liberal "Rusty" Walker to leave home and family, secede from the reactionary Torch Commando organization for ex-servicemen, and make an illegal gesture is presented surrealistically: Rusty realizes that he is standing within the footprint of a giant, and a chimpanzee on a bicycle brings an enigmatic message from the dead king which nonetheless makes it clear that the giant is the British Empire, within whose soon-to-be-dismembered body Rusty has been living. Rusty's political activism is a matter of quasi-physical impulse rather than of "correct analysis," but his liberal gestures serve to awaken the hitherto dormant energies of the friend to whom he appeals for help and advice, Leo Skiba, an émigré Lithuanian socialist ideologue and organizer. The personal and political symbiosis which moves Leo finally to action and which affords Rusty "moments of the most intense joy" is throughout paralleled, indeed partly articulated, by the movingly realized relationship—one of affection and provocation, need and violence—between Rusty's son Rupert and Leo's son Mark.

The debt to Brecht evident in Wright's formal strategies throughout his work is most clearly felt in *The Gorky Brigade*, which again scrutinizes the relation between political organization, energy for action, and individual dissent at a time of historical change. In Year Three of the Soviet revolution (1920–21), the revolutionary teacher Ekaterina undertakes the supervision and instruction of a colony of teenage "bourgeois anarchists." In Act 1 her initial despair, her new "scientific" (dialectical) teaching methods, and her eventual success in enabling the colonists to form themselves into the "Gorky Brigade" (under which banner they rob rich peasants in order to further their own revolutionary purposes), are presented in a series of scenes after the Brechtian epic model, some of them attached to rubrics taken from Gorky. However, the Gorky sentences are rotated ironically in Act 2 when Ekaterina's star student Minnie, who has been away at university for six years, returns to the colony. Gorky himself is at last to visit his admirers, and she has come to request his help and influence in the case of a professor of hers who is being condemned and persecuted for his work in genetics. The colony, once in the vanguard of the revolution but now isolated and out of touch by virtue of its very idealism, humiliates and rejects Minnie; and Gorky, feeling himself (after his sojourn in Italy) "europeanized" into doubt and non-commitment, can respond to her appeals, despite his climactic public reaffirmation of Soviet aims and thinking, only with gestures of impotence and bad faith. Yet Minnie will not *retreat* into individual dissent. She refuses to leave the colony again, and as the play ends she is trying to call a meeting of all the colonists in order to regalvanize revolutionary principles and action.

In both *Treetops* and *The Gorky Brigade*, different though they are formally and stylistically, the exploration of the role of individual dissent in the process of political change is clearly shaped and underwritten by a commitment to socialism. In his plays of the 1980s, however, Wright's dramatic attitude towards the individual as a motive force in history is firmly ironic, and his treatment less direct than in those of the late 1970s. The tendency, already apparent in the earlier plays, to make a character represent or embody an attitude or class or group emerges with increasing strength through a more obvious stylization of action. In reference to *The Desert Air*, "embody" is emphatically the word. The enormous central figure (memorably incarnated in the Royal Shakespeare Company production by Geoffrey Hutchings), a carica- ture on a heroic scale, is Colonel—later Brigadier—"Hippo" Gore, a "vulgar toad" in whose "swollen and distended" gut is embodied a whole social movement and moral attitude. Put in charge of a Secret Service unit in wartime Cairo (1942–43), the Hippo dedicates himself to "wangling" his way up through the class-determined hierarchy of the British army, a "stumpy" intent on toppling "those long, tall, *pointy* bastards." Thus the class war cuts across and usurps in importance the World War, and the transference of British support in occupied Yugoslavia from the royalist Chetniks to the communist- led Partisans is effected not by principle or decisive strategic thinking but by the Hippo's self-interested wangling. The physical state figures forth the moral one, often hilariously, sometimes painfully, in the Hippo and his agents, and although he is eventually disgraced, Gore is allowed a final "apotheosis" through a self-interested self-sacrifice, his distended body blown apart at last for the sake of glory in posterity as the man who had "the *guts* to change" British policy—literally.

Wright's handling of the ironic interaction of representative figures is even more impressive in *The Custom of the Country*—all the more so as it is negotiated within the strict generic framework of romantic comedy. Title and plot both derive from Fletcher and Massinger, and there is an authentically Jacobean relish of pace and event in the conduct of a narrative charged with the pathos of yearning and unfulfilment. Wright's decision to set the play in the cultural melting-pot of the southern Africa of the 1890's (mostly Johannesburg) serves to introduce a political dimension into the comedic action. It is the plot's several plotters, rather than the young-married lovers they manipulate, who are the central representative figures: the self-deluding "entrepreneuse," brothel-keeper Daisy Bone, who is persuaded to cast the missionary hero Paul as her "perfect love"; her business manager, the Eastern European Jewish intellectual Lazarus, who looks forward to a moral apocalypse and finds union in death with Daisy; the Afrikaner goldmine owner Henrietta van Es, whose hitherto frustrated femininity finds its sexual object in Paul's "gentleman of leisure" brother Roger, and its maternal project in the reclamation of her errant "zombie" son Willem; and Dr. Jamieson, the agent of British imperialist designs on the African interior whose ultimate success ensures the preparation and impending dispatch of a Pioneer Column to the territory which will eventually become Rhodesia. Happy ending and historical implication are thus posed in an ironic counterpoint which is emphasized by the innocently portentous curtain speech of Paul's African bride Tendai. Such precision of dramatic nuance is characteristic of this play, and indeed of Wright's work at its best.

The historical and political dimensions hitherto characteristic of Wright's work are effectively absent from *Mrs. Klein*. But although this play is not a satire, its dominating, egotistical central figure could be seen as a distant cousin of the Hippo. In *Mrs. Klein* an irony which is at once astringent and sympathetic operates within a tightly patterned and witty meditation upon the complexity of maternal-filial relationships. Set in London in 1934, it is an intimate trio which dramatizes an episode in the life of the emigrée psychoanalyst Melanie Klein. The journey through the "primitive jungle" of mourning for the death of her son triggers a crisis in the relationship of Mrs. Klein with her daughter Melitta—who is also an analyst. Their encounters play out in real terms the familiar categories of analysis. The confrontation turns on rival interpretations of the son's apparent suicide. But Mrs. Klein's assistant, Paula, extricates herself from this conflict, gathers the available facts, and constructs an alternative narrative. The truth of the son's death is a truth not of the suicidal energy of transference of feeling—as Mrs. Klein and Melitta, despite their conflict, both believe—but of freedom and contingency. The death was the result of an accident which befell a happy man. This truth forces a self-confrontation on Mrs. Klein, which in turn lifts the veil of mourning and enables a reaffirmation of her professional calling. The end is open, understated, and intriguingly poised.

—Paul Lawley

WORKS

THE BROWNING VERSION
by Terence Rattigan.

First Publication: 1949.
First Production: 1948.

The plot of this play focuses on Andrew Crocker-Harris, a classics master at an English public school, who is retiring prematurely because of ill-health, and who is confronted by his wife's infidelity and his failure in his chosen profession. Like much of Rattigan's work, *The Browning Version* is drawn from his own experience; in this case as a pupil at Harrow School. The prototype for Crocker-Harris was one of Rattigan's teachers, Mr. Coke Norris, and the central incident of the pupil, Taplow, presenting Crocker-Harris with a copy of Browning's translation of the *Agamemnon* of Aeschylus is based on fact (although there is some doubt as to whether Rattigan himself was the boy involved). Certainly Taplow's interest in cricket and golf reflect Rattigan's enthusiasm for those games.

The action of *The Browning Version* is set in the Crocker-Harris's sitting-room, replete with a stained-glass door leading to the garden as well as an internal door, concealed by a screen. Appropriately, in view of its classical associations, the play observes the unities of time, place, and action demonstrating Rattigan's renowned craftsmanship at its best. Although the dialogue is characteristically everyday (with Taplow's school-boy slang) Rattigan imbues Crocker-Harris with a distinctive turn of speech (reflecting his classical education) and an articulateness, enabling him to comment upon his predicament (though not to express his feelings), which are consistent with naturalistic drama.

As the title implies, Rattigan seeks to establish parallels between his play and its classical source, thus Taplow remarks to Frank Hunter, a science master and Muriel Crocker-Harris's current lover: "It's rather a good plot, really, a wife murdering her husband and having a lover and all that . . .". Of course, Crocker-Harris's fate is not the (literal) blood-bath which awaited Agamemnon on his return from the Trojan War, but Mrs. Crocker-Harris uses the no less deadening battery of psychological warfare as she relentlessly humiliates and degrades her husband. In terms of exploration of character and motive *The Browning Version* is closer to Euripides and his treatment of that other archetypal triangle (Theseus, Phaedra, and Hippolytus) in *Hippolytus* than to Aeschylus's bloody chain of murder and revenge.

The eternal triangle was a favourite formula for Rattigan. Although the central character, torn between two lovers, is usually a woman, it has been suggested that Rattigan on occasion depicted homosexual relationships under the guise of heterosexual ones. For Rattigan, the essence of a triangular relationship was that it enabled him to polarise the conflict between two types of love—on the one hand, the "higher love" (social and intellectual companionship and compatibility) and on the other, merely sexual gratification. Thus Muriel Crocker-Harris is caught between her 18-year-old, increasingly arid, marriage and her passionate affair (one of many) with Frank Hunter, in which she is the helpless and undignified pursuer. Crocker-Harris's classical knowledge facilitates Rattigan's exploration of what Plato in *The Symposium*

763

characterised as "the two Aphrodites . . . common love and the other Heavenly love". He does this with an erudition which makes the following speech central not only to this play but to Rattigan's work as a whole:

> Two kinds of love. Hers and mine. Worlds apart, as I know now, though when I married her I didn't think they were incompatible. In those days I hadn't thought that the kind of love—the love she requires and which I was unable to give her—was so important that it's absence would drive out the other kind of love—the kind of love that I require and which I thought, in my folly, was by far the greater part of love. . . .

Although this exploration of the two loves is the major theme of *The Browning Version*, there are others. Alongside the emotional repression of his marriage Crocker-Harris has sought the popularity of his pupils—"by pandering to their delight in his mannerisms and tricks of speech he has tried to compensate for his lack of natural ability to make himself liked" (Michael Darlow and Gillian Hodson, *Terence Rattigan*, 1979). This might be seen as a reflection of Rattigan's willingness as a dramatist to court popular success in the form of the endorsement of Aunt Edna the "nice, respectable, middle-class, middle-aged, maiden lady", who made her debut as Rattigan's representative playgoer in his Preface to Volume Two of his *Complete Plays* (in which *The Browning Version* appears). Such an identification of author and character would imply a sense of failure on Rattigan's part even at this, the most commercially and critically successful period of his career.

Rattigan was taken to task for flinching from unhappy endings to his plays, preferring to send theatregoers home in a reassured state of mind. *The Deep Blue Sea* is susceptible to this criticism, but not so *The Browning Version*. Rattigan contemplated a tragic outcome (probably Crocker-Harris's death from his heart condition), but instead left his protagonist facing an uncertain future both professionally (at a crammer's) and matrimonially (will Muriel accompany him?). Crocker-Harris does, however, assert his right to make his valedictory speech at the end of the next day's prize-giving. In the film version, Rattigan's old friend Anthony Asquith prevailed upon him to open up the action of the play and to extend it to conclude with Crocker-Harris (Michael Redgrave) making his speech. The film thus finishes on a sentimental, "Mr. Chips" note which betrays the integrity of the original play.

Lasting about 80 minutes in the theatre, *The Browning Version* required a companion piece for which Rattigan provided one of his most ebullient comedies *Harlequinade*, about a performance of *Romeo and Juliet* in a Midland town. As a double-bill the two plays provide opportunities for the actors to demonstrate their versatility. Although John Gielgud (rather tactlessly) turned down Rattigan's invitation to create the part of Crocker-Harris it has since become one of the recognised classic roles of the modern stage, drawing fine performances from Eric Portman (1948), Nigel Stock (1976), Alec McCowan (1980), and Paul Eddington (1987).

—Richard Foulkes

COMEDIANS
by Trevor Griffiths.

First Publication: 1976; revised edition, 1979.
First Production: 1975.

The structure of *Comedians* is that of every backstage movie of the 1930s: setting up the show (in this case, a club night that provides the culmination of a Workers Educational Association course in standup comedy), doing the show, and responses to the show that will launch some of its members to stardom. Here, however, the structure also interrogates the politics of laughter, and through this the dialectic between reform and revolution. The course tutor, Eddie Waters, is an old-fashioned, Northern comedian who teaches humanist, comic values: "We work *through* laughter, not *for* it . . . A true joke, a comedian's joke, has to do more than release tension, it has to *liberate* the will and the desire, it has to *change the situation*". He steers his class away from the racist and sexist stereotypes of the club comic. The group comprises several of these potential stereotypes—two Irishmen (from North and South), a Jew, a milkman. The comic style Eddie teaches them helps them to celebrate their ethnic roots and personal individuality. Faced with the chance of performing in front of Bert Challenor, a manager with the entrée to the professional, showbiz world, some of them sell out, slipping into the timeworn routine of jokes about Pakistanis and smutty innuendo, with varying degrees of confidence and success, while Mick Connor, the Irishman, sticks to his gently ironic routine about being an Irishman abroad and is told by Challenor that "people don't learn, they don't want to, and if they did, they won't look to the likes of us to teach 'em".

The play is not a straightforward confrontation between Eddie's values and Challenor's, however. There is a third way, personified in the act of Eddie's most brilliant and wayward pupil, Gethin Price. Dressed as a combination of skinhead and whiteface clown, he performs a series of complex Kung Fu exercises punctuated by football chants and finally confronts a pair of expensively dressed dummies with an aggression that grows ever greater with his frustration at their continuing silence. "You can laugh, you know, I don't mind you laughing . . . I'm *talking* to you . . . there's people who'd call this *envy*, you know, it's not, it's hate". He ends with an attack on the female dummy, pinning a flower on her which slowly forms a dark, red stain spreading over her. Challenor, predictably, dismisses this in seconds, but the subsequent debate between Eddie and Gethin is at the centre of the third act. Eddie accuses Gethin of "drowning in hate", although he admits that the act was "brilliant". Gethin accuses Eddie of forgetting his roots in the class war that made him a great comedian in the first place: "We're still caged, exploited, prodded and pulled at, milked, fattened, slaughtered, cut up, fed out. We still don't belong to ourselves. Nothing's changed. You've just forgotten, that's all". Eddie can only counter this with a story of his personal failure as a comedian: after visiting a concentration camp just after the war he found there were "no jokes left"; he also admits that "I got an erection in that place", an admission whose implications neither he nor Gethin seems fully to understand.

The frequent stage directions describing Price's delivery as "perfect"—he's the only one who can manage the loaded tonguetwister "The Traitor Distrusts Truth"—his ability to anticipate Eddie's points in class, his slick parody of him, and his final exit, in which he declares his intention to "wait for it to happen", suggest that Griffiths' sympathies lie with his revolutionary energy. There is, however, a deeply disturbing sexism about Gethin which is never fully articulated. At the beginning of the play he improvises an obscene limerick that sparks off Eddie's sermon on stereotypes. At the end of his act he talks across, not to, the female dummy before literally "penetrating" her. If Eddie has gone soft on old-style revolution, Gethin remains true to its failure to question gender roles. Interesting dynamics were created by an all woman version of *Comedians* at the Liverpool Festival of Comedy in 1985, devised by Griffiths and a group of experienced female comedians. Gethin/Glenys' act remained much the same, but its meaning altered simply by virtue of her sex; the obscenities became a measure of a sexual consciousness only partially raised; her attack on the male dummy became not an act of rape but the revenge of a flower-seller, a member not just of an oppressed class but of a sex relegated to the bottom of that class.

—Frances Gray

A DAY IN THE DEATH OF JOE EGG
by Peter Nichols.

First Publication: 1967.
First Production: 1967.

The title character of *A Day in the Death of Joe Egg*, Peter Nichols' first London stage play, is a severely spastic ten-year-old girl whose father, mimicking a doctor with a music-hall German accent, aptly but cruelly terms a "wegetable". *Joe Egg* has very little plot as such. Act I is in effect a two-hander, focusing on Joe's parents, Bri and Sheila, with Joe and the audience as essentially silent (but constantly addressed) spectators. We learn a great deal about the couple in this act: their personality quirks, the fragile state of their marriage, and, especially, the various stratagems they have devised in order to bear the appalling tragedy of Joe. Act II opens up the action with the introduction of the couple's friends Freddie and his wife Pam, and then later Bri's mother Grace, all of whom (however caricatured) have definite opinions about the best way to deal with Joe. The play ends with Bri, having failed in a half-hearted attempt at euthanasia, packing up his bags and running out on Sheila (who remains oblivious to his departure) and on Joe (who is always oblivious) in a denouement left deliberately ambiguous—either an act of supreme cowardice, or a brave bid to achieve salvation.

Like almost all of Nichols' plays, *Joe Egg* is specifically rooted in auto-biography: the dramatic situation, though obviously transmuted into art, mirrors Peter and Thelma Nichols' experience with their eldest child Abigail. Out of this personal pain Nichols has forged a play that is not only intensely moving, as might be expected, but also—unexpected and, to some critics, unacceptable—wildly funny. *Joe Egg*, again like almost all of Nichols' plays, is written in what the author has termed a "comic-strip style", a style greatly influenced by Thornton Wilder's *The Skin of Our Teeth* and closely related to English music-hall or American vaudeville. Like music-hall performers, the characters in *Joe Egg* are constantly breaking the fourth wall—by repeated direct address to the audience, by self-conscious acknowledgements that they are in a theatre (when Bri calls Freddie "a pain in the arse", Grace mutters "I hate a play with language"), or, most frequent of all, by stepping out of character to do a comic routine, like Bri's German doctor or his impersonation of a staggeringly inept vicar. Nichols' original title for the play—and one he now wishes he had kept—was "Funny Turns", simultaneously evoking both Joe's spastic fits, graphically dramatized for us throughout the play, and Bri's and Sheila's way of responding to those fits and to their pain generally, through the anodyne of the music-hall performer's comic acts.

This breaking of the proscenium functions as a kind of "alienation" technique for the audience, although Nichols claims it is the opposite of Brecht's: "[my] alienation techniques . . . are supposed to involve you, draw you in, make the experience more intense". The specific example he cites is the Act I curtain, in which the actor playing Joe suddenly skips on stage and announces the intermission, blissfully healthy and "normal". This is indeed an intensely moving moment, the "magical" fulfillment of her parents' dream ("Wouldn't she be lovely if she was running about?"). But it also provides the audience with an important release, a surprisingly necessary reminder that Joe is not a *real* spastic child but an actor, and therefore "alienates" us in the Brechtian sense as well. An audience needs that Brechtian distancing; it allows us to be sufficiently detached from the horror of Joe's plight so that we can permit ourselves to laugh without guilt at Nichols' comic treatment of her. And it further allows us, again as in Brecht, to be sufficiently detached so that we can *think*, form opinions, make judgments about the "problem" of Joe, for when the play's characters address us directly, they are often attempting to "appeal" to us as in a courtroom, to persuade us of the morality of their views concerning Joe; the audience is being cast as "jury", expected to ponder issues of "right" and "wrong". Nor is it only the audience who requires such Brechtian distancing. Nichols' characters similarly need it, especially Bri and Sheila: breaking through the fourth wall by breaking into music-hall "funny turns" is their way of coping with their pain.

A Day in the Death of Joe Egg raises some highly relevant social issues. Perhaps humour used as an "anaesthetic", is ultimately dangerous. "Isn't that the whole fallacy of the sick joke?", Freddie wonders. "It kills the pain but leaves the situation just as it was?". How, then, do we alter the situation? Bri argues for euthanasia, and on one level Nichols' play is a lively debate about the merits of that particular solution (among others). But on another level, the play is not primarily about Joe at all: Joe becomes a metaphor for the "illness" of Bri and Sheila's marriage, the prism through which we see reflected the character flaws each brings to the relationship. The name "Joe Egg" can thus be read as symbolizing the state of their marriage, which the full title of the play informs us is a "death"; maybe Bri is therefore justified in seeking to escape. For all its thematic interest, however, the importance of *Joe Egg* rests ultimately on its stylistic innovations. Nichols took an enormous risk in dramatizing this sad saga of a profoundly disabled child as a comedy: might not audiences feel they were being encouraged to laugh *at* Joe? The play constantly walks a very thin tightrope, but the risk pays off. *Joe Egg* is black humour at its blackest but also its most redemptive.

—Hersh Zeifman

DREAM ON MONKEY MOUNTAIN
by Derek Walcott.

First Publication: In *Dream on Monkey Mountain and Other Plays*, 1970.
First Production: 1967.

Dream on Monkey Mountain is set in a jail on the island of St. Lucia. Most of the action takes place within the dreams of Makak, a black peasant charcoal-burner, during a night when he has been imprisoned for his own self-protection, after being violently drunk and destructive in the local market. He had a vision of a white woman, an apparition variously called the white goddess, muse, and the moon, who tells him to return to Africa. The jailer (Corporal Lestrade) and the criminals at first speak approvingly or ambivalently about the white man's law while Makak hates himself for being black. Makak dreams of leading the local black people back to Africa where, in one of many transformations within his dream, he becomes a famous warrior. His jailer becomes one of his followers. Makak, after a reversal of historical white-black power relations (he is sent a "floral tribute of lilies from the Ku Klux Klan") ritualistically beheads the white goddess. This frees him from his love-hate obsession with whiteness, he wakes and for the first time in the play says his real name, Felix Hobain. He resolves to return to his home on Monkey Mountain which is compared to Eden, paradise, a new begining, and is symbolic of the New World.

   Dream on Monkey Mountain has been acted in many versions including the New York Negro Ensemble production of 1970 which, while winning the 1971 Obie, is known to have disturbed Derek Walcott for its strong anti-white emphasis. As in most of his plays a conflict between two opposing strengths leads to resolution. Here, as in most of Walcott's writing of this period, the resolution is the rediscovery of the West Indian black that he belongs in the New World and that the islands, which could be paradise despite their history and poverty, are a new beginning. The play sees genesis in the greenery of St. Lucia and not in Africa from which the New World black has become distinct. This means accepting a mixing of cultures and races, recognizing that a new society and culture has been and is being, created, rather than being obsessed with the Manichaean polarities of white and black and the burden of past injustices.

   An advantage of using a dream for most of the play is the rapid transformations of scene and character. The play is swift-moving and full of surprises, disguises, and powerful scenes. In the dream, Makak's friend Moustique, like a hanger-on or parasite of Roman comedy, becomes a con-man and hopes to get money by impersonating his buddy Makak as leader of a back-to-Africa movement. He is unmasked and killed. At the beginning of Part Two there is a scene in the jail which seems like a return to reality but is a dream within the dream and initiates a secondary plot as the two characters Tigre and Souris decide to escape and pretend to become followers of Makak so as to rob him of money they foolishly assume he has hidden. From now on the dream exists on two levels, part of Makak's psychosis, as he imagines he is returning to Africa while the others in the dream think he is deluded and are humouring him while going to Monkey Mountain. Increasingly the play becomes violent with contradictory plots eliding into each other. Then there is the shock of the beheading on stage of the white goddess, immediately followed by a return to the jail where Makak wakes surrounded by a sympathetic, helpful jailor and Moustique.

Walcott moves his themes and symbols through various layers of significance. These include Walcott's coming to terms with his own half-white family background, his love of the English language and its poetry (the muse or white goddess), and the relationship of the English culture of the St. Lucian brown, protestant, middle class to the francophonic Catholicism and Vodunism of the St. Lucian black majority with its patois. Walcott's "A Note on Production" invites us to see Makak's dream as a part of the author's own psyche. Indeed the various characters in the play and their transformations—such as Corporal Lestrade's change from a strong defender of white law to the most violent exponent of black racial assertion—should probably be seen as conflicting aspects of both the author's feelings and of the West Indian personality. It is the Mimic Men, those most filled with self-hate and in love with whiteness, who become the most violent converts to an inverted racism in which white is evil.

Walcott's quotations prefacing parts of *Dream on Monkey Mountain* and various allusions within the play show that Frantz Fanon's *The Wretched of the Earth* is one of the influences. That play examines the way white dominance in colonialism makes blacks want to become whites. A sense of inferiority turns to self-hate and then seeks an outlet through the reversal of roles and a liberating violence against the white oppressor. According to Fanon this is the only way to create a new national culture in contrast to imitation of the colonizer, or nostalgic idealization of the past. Makak's self-hatred, belief that he is ugly, drunkenness and his dream follow Fanon's pattern. After the fantasy of returning to Africa Makak must liberate himself from his obsession with whiteness, especially as represented by white women, through violence. But unlike the radical culture born out of destruction and blood that Fanon assumes, Walcott suggests that this is a dream, a fantasy, and that the future must be built on oneself, on the various contradictions and influences, including the European heritage, that are part of the West Indies.

While the racial and cultural themes are obvious and shaped by the plot, the play also concerns West Indian theatre. It has strong folk elements, such as a black peasant as the main character, the use of song and dance, and various forms of English and French. Some characters have such symbolic names as Moustique, Tigre, Souris, and Lestrade. As in a fable, or in Walcott's earlier *Ti-Jean and His Brothers*, the plot is illustrative. From fable the play develops into ritual drama like that of Genet and Soyinka. But, as Walcott observes in "What the Twilight Says: An Overture" prefacing *Dream on Monkey Mountain and Other Plays*, when the Trinidad Theatre Workshop produced Soyinka's *The Road*, the kind of possession by the god Ogun that the play demanded from an actor was impossible for the West Indian, Afro-Christian. "We could pretend to enter his power but he would never possess us . . . The actor's approach could not be catatonic but rational; expository, not receptive". If the plot of Walcott's play is a racial and cultural allegory, it is also an allegory of West Indian theatre and acting. The influences, like Caribbean culture, range broadly. As with Walcott's poetry of the period the play gives classical European form—its European sources are probably as much in Roman drama and Ben Jonson, as in Strindberg and Genet—to folk culture in which its use of West Indian speech and culture is part of its meaning, its return to genesis, and not merely local colour, in contrast to the confused melange of Africanisms in the African scenes. The mixture of verse and prose, music, drumming, dance, switching of roles, dialect, plays within plays, trials, apparitions and the contrast between the apparently impoverished characters and the rich, grand themes they contain within themselves make the play extraordinarily effective theatre.

—Bruce King

EAST
by Steven Berkoff.

First Publication: In *East; Agamemnon; The Fall of the House of Usher*, 1977; revised edition, 1978.
First Production: 1975; revised version, 1976.

Berkoff has written of *East* that it "takes place within my personal memory and experience and is less a biographical text than an outburst of revolt against the sloth of my youth and a desire to turn a welter of undirected passion and frustration into a positive form".

The "positive form" Berkoff chose is that of a highly stylised theatre piece, more a series of vignettes and monologues than a play in the traditional sense. It combines several disparate elements, from music hall and mime to Shakespeare and Classical Greek drama. The acting, according to Berkoff, "has to be loose and smacking of danger", which is also a perfect description of the play itself.

East opens with the stage completely bare except for five empty chairs and a large screen across the back. (This bare stage is typical of Berkoff. He has written that by "eliminating the junk of sets" and "freeing the stage and giving it space", the spectator becomes more involved because his own imagination and interpretation become a necessary part of the production.) As images of the real East End are projected onto the screen the five characters, Mike, Les, Sylv, Mum, and Dad, enter and take their seats. Then, accompanied by an off-stage piano, they launch into a chaotic rendition of "My Old Man Says Follow the Van".

In the curious mix of Shakespearian allusion and Cockney argot that characterises much of the speech throughout the play, Mike and Les explain to the audience that though they are now the best of friends, the first time they met they nearly killed each other in a fight over Mike's girlfriend, Sylv. This is followed by a gruesome description of the actual fight: Mike tells about his "raziory which danced about his face like fireflies . . . " and rhapsodises about "that soft thud, thwat, as knife hits flesh . . . ". The two men relate how they made their way together to hospital, finally "thick as tealeaves in a pot that's stewed too long", and united in their mutual hatred of the girl they were just fighting over.

Time continually moves backwards and forwards in *East*; one moment we are in the present, the next we are reliving some moment from the past—many of these time changes are brought about by one character telling a story directly to the audience, while the others act as chorus.

Following a flashback to her first sexual encounter with Mike, Sylv bemoans the fact that she wasn't born a man, able to enjoy sexual freedom without being referred to as "an old scrubber-slag-head". A similar sentiment is echoed by Mum during her recollection of an incident in a cinema where, in the darkness, she engaged in mutual masturbation with a stranger only to discover, when the lights went up, that he was her son.

Les speaks with great bitterness about the time he worked in a clothing store, "that charnel house of gabardine and worsted hell", and was arrested for rape. In another monologue he tells of a bus ride during which he ogled a beautiful woman and came to the realisation that he would never have the nerve to speak to her. He will spend his life with what he calls "dirty scrubbers", because of his own low self-image: " . . . it tumbled then—it dropped—the dirty penny—that we get what we ARE".

East concludes with two speeches of resolution; one spoken by Mike and Les in unison, the other a monologue by Sylv. The men speak of anger: "I'm sick of my house, I'm sick of my family, in fact they make me sick". They fantasise about a life of crime: "We'll threaten and murder, connive and rob, the law's on our side, we'll pay the slobs . . . We'll get fat, we'll kill and we'll knife. I hate you pseudo bastards, I hate you with my life".

Sylv's speech concerns the indignity of poverty: " . . . fill in forms at dole queues and stand behind the sacks of skin that are called men and women, translated into numbers crushed in endless files . . . waiting, while ma and pa makes little noughts and crosses upon coupons called hope—or—death . . . ". Sylv's final words are her resolution: "We will not end our days like this".

However, it doesn't seem likely that Sylv's resolution will be realized. *East* ends as it began, with Les and Mike repeating their first three lines, word for word. The implication is that no matter what they resolve and no matter what they try, for these characters, trapped by their poverty and lack of education, nothing will ever change. Like the Red Queen in *Through the Looking Glass*, they will continue to run and run as fast as they can just so they can stay in the same place.

—Molly Brown

EQUUS
by Peter Shaffer.

First Publication: 1973.
First Production: 1973.

A chance remark by a friend at the BBC led Peter Shaffer to write *Equus*. The friend recounted a news story about a youth in a provincial town outside London who, seemingly without cause, struck out the eyes of several horses in a stable. From that sketchy account, the author had the skeletal plot for what has become a modern classic. Two discrete but intertwined stories make up the plot. At the surface is the puzzle involving Alan Strang, an apparently unexceptional youth, who has been ordered to a psychiatric hospital in Southern England because of a heinous crime: the blinding of six horses at the stables where he worked. The courts could determine no justifiable reason for the abhorrent deed; so it becomes the task of the psychiatrists to figure out—and treat—the cause. Hesther Salomon, a magistrate and confidante, asks Martin Dysart to take on young Strang since the other doctors are too repulsed by the boy's act to provide him with objective care. Against his better judgement, Dysart agrees.

Most of the 21 scenes which comprise the first act are given over to Dr. Dysart's investigation of the conflicts that led to the incident. Shaffer's earlier predilection for detective tales is evident here, because in any overview *Equus* closely resembles the suspense thriller. Dysart is the sleuth who tracks down, step by step, those factors in Alan Strang's life that eventually led him to destroy the animals. Through hypnosis, abreaction, and alleged "truth drugs", Dysart ultimately isolates the psychic sources for Alan's aberrant behaviour, a form of psychosexual disfunction: and the shorter second act (14 scenes) embodies the psychiatrist's regimen—a carefully staged abreaction—which relieves the boy of his problem. In Shaffer's dramatic construct, however, concurrent with his discovering Alan's underlying problems, Dysart comes to realise his own dilemma—the second story in the plot. The psychiatrist is undergoing a crisis of conscience growing out of disillusionment with himself, his profession, and contemporary society. Despite his reservations, Dysart does "cure" Alan as the play ends. Yet it is obvious that ridding the boy of his mental conflicts only reverts them onto Dysart himself. *Equus* ends with Shaffer's patented resolution—that is, no resolution in a rudderless universe.

Equus does not enjoy the large cast and multiple plots of some of Shaffer's other important works such as *Royal Hunt of the Sun* and *Amadeus*. But a conciseness and tight focus are gained. The central theme of *Equus* concerns Shaffer's favourite subject, man's aspiring to reach a knowable god whose existence implies a universal order. As is typical with Shaffer, the full story in the plot requires at least two, conflicting protagonists, and in fact, here, there are three. Alan Strang is the nominal center of the story since it is the diagnosis and curing of his psychological problems that constitute the main action of the play. Yet a greater drama arises in the soul of Dr. Dysart whose spiritual anguish is even greater than Alan's. Shaffer frames a three-part puzzle at the play's outset. On stage, in the background, stands a living tableau of a teenage boy nuzzling a horse-figure; in the foreground sits Dysart at his desk in a hospital. Dysart points to the pair behind him, noting that the boy, not the horse, holds the key to Dysart's own dilemma. Dysart directly addresses the audience: "I'm lost . . . I'm desperate . . . In a way, it has nothing to do with this boy. The doubts have been there for years". From the play's first lines, the playwright establishes that the play involves the interlocked lives of these three figures—the ailing boy, the purportedly healing physician, and the mysterious horse-deity.

Dysart's investigations show that part of Alan's mental aberration concerns a bizarre personal worship he initiates with a horse—*Equus*—as god. Alan's father is a confirmed agnostic who undercuts the Christian religious beliefs which Dora, the boy's mother, insists on. At the same time, the youth's first horse ride proved sexually stimulating to him. In a primitive, natural fashion, Alan fuses the two chief forces in his life—worship and sex—into a single figure: the god Equus. By sneaking horseback rides at night in the nude, Alan ritualises his adoration of the horse-god while also experiencing a form of auto-eroticism. The curtain scene for the first act depicts Strang's amazing form of religio-sexual worship when Dysart gets the boy, in hyposis, to expose his hidden desires. In highly stylised fashion, Alan—naked—rides on the shoulders of the "horse"—actually an actor wearing a metallic headpiece denoting a horse's head. As "horse" and rider frenetically circle the stage space, Alan cries out in religious and sexual ecstacy at the moment of climax.

Dysart then understands the basis for the boy's strange behaviour. Now the dilemma begins to be a professional one for the doctor: whether to permit Alan his personal form of worship or to destroy his home-made religion in order to return him to society's conventions. Moreover, Dysart begins to see how tepid his own life is compared to Alan's. Dysart tells Hesther, "Without worship you shrink, it's as brutal as that . . . I shrank my *own* life. No one can do it for you. I settled for being pallid and provincial, out of my own eternal timidity . . . . But that boy has known a passion more ferocious than I have felt in any second of my life. And let me tell you something: I envy it". But Hesther convinces Dysart to do his professional duty. As a paid agent of society, he is expected to mend his patients's minds and souls, allowing them to live in harmony with society. A final scene of abreaction near the end of *Equus* shows Alan stabbing out the eyes of the stylised horse figures; the boy thereby purges himself of his nightmares for good. For freeing Alan from his self-made spiritual world, however, Dysart is forced into a life of self-doubt. The gripping drama ends with the doctor announcing to the audience in horror, "There is now, in my mouth, this sharp chain. And it never comes out".

Equus marks the perfecting of Shaffer's use of narrative frame in his dramas. Dysart plays a dual-role as participant in the inner story concerning Alan's psychological conundrum but is also a narrator who can step outside the plot's action to address the audience directly. The prime benefit of such a dual-level format is its flexibility in moving the plot through space and time. Even more urgent in *Equus* is the perfecting of Shaffer's concept of Apollonian and Dionysian characteristics in human nature. Alan Strang epitomises the Dionysian—that which is creative, intuitive, inspirational. Dysart is the

Apollonian—ordered, premeditated, systematic. Like Shaffer's other major works, *Equus* provides playgoers with provocative themes and gripping theatrical images on stage.

—C. J. Gianakaris

FORTY YEARS ON
by Alan Bennett.

First Publication: 1969.
First Production: 1968.

Bennett's play is set in a minor English public school, Albion House, where staff and pupils are presenting the end of term play, "Speak for England, Arthur", a chronological revue of British political and cultural history from the turn of the century to the end of World War II. The revue comprises readings from actual and fictional literary memoirs, historic radio broadcasts, poems, parodic sketches, slide lectures and songs, most of which are filtered through the memories of Hugh, an upper-class, Conservative Member of Parliament, and his wife, Moggie (suggested by the real-life partnership of Harold Nicolson and Vita Sackville-West). With Nursie, their elderly nanny, they reminisce, grumble, and comment on the conduct of war from the safety of their refuge in the basement of Claridge's Hotel. The play-within-the-play marks the occasion of the Headmaster's retirement and the transfer of office to his senior housemaster, Franklin. The parts in the school entertainment are taken variously by the Headmaster, Franklin, a junior housemaster Tempest, the bursar's secretary Miss Nisbitt, and Matron. Other parts are played by the boys of Albion House who also sing and provide musical accompaniment.

Bennett's first stage play owes much to his experience as writer and performer of cabaret, revue, and television satirical comedy. What started as a stockpile of sketches for a projected revue became in turn a radio play (unproduced) and, with the addition of the school framework, the stage play which enjoyed great success when first produced in 1968 with Sir John Gielgud as the Headmaster and Bennett himself as Tempest. Bennett has disarmingly described his comedy as "an elaborate life-support system for the preservation of old jokes".

The location of *Forty Years On* undoubtedly allows the dramatist to recycle and renew some stock jokes and routines—the many disasters attending amateur performance, schoolboy mayhem, the peculiar language of educational and moral control, and the clichés of an (almost) all-male institution. Bennett seizes these opportunities gleefully and unashamedly, furnishing the Albion House scenes with ripe examples of schoolboy humour and schoolmaster sarcasm with an added undercurrent of homosexual jokes. A Confirmation Class, for example, slides inexorably into a sex lesson conducted too eagerly by a master with roving hands. Elsewhere, Tempest delivers the old joke, "I wish I could put my hands on the choir's parts". The historical and cultural snippets of "Speak for England, Arthur" not only provide fuel for a running battle between Franklin and the Headmaster, who views the former's production with deep suspicion as a radical departure from the past successes of *Samson Agonistes* and *Dear Octopus*, but allow Bennett scope for a range of comic forms. The loose structure easily accomodates set pieces of literary parody, as in the sketch on the Abdication Crisis in the style of "Sapper" or John Buchan. A grotesque romantic encounter on Primrose Hill between Bertrand Russell and Lady Ottoline Morrell, the latter impersonated as a giantess by two boys in outrageous costume, verges on pantomime, while a mock memoir of T. E. Lawrence, whose girlish giggle is said to have earned him the nickname Tee Hee Lawrence, is gloriously silly.

Bennett's characteristically diffident estimate of the play, however, does scant justice to his technical abilities, his precise mimicry of speech styles or to the delicate balance he achieves of low comedy, sharp satire and affectionate homage to a British past which, by 1968, seemed thoroughly outdated and yet still exercised a strong nostalgic pull.

Bennett's method of provoking laughter is best exemplified by the Headmaster's opening address. His high-minded speech is constantly interrupted and subverted by inopportune aircraft noises, coughs, nose blowings and schoolboy misdemeanours, or by his own sudden swoops into prayer. This interruptive technique becomes Bennett's main comic tactic throughout the play. The entertainment, episodic by nature, is further punctuated by the Headmaster's policing for smut, by unscheduled eruptions of the victorious rugby team into the performance, and by the on-stage presentation of the interval of "Speak for England, Arthur". Bennett consistently generates a double laughter: that which savours the exactness of language, character, and situation (both in the school scenes and the parodic re-creations), and that which greets the bathos occasioned by the mundane or ludicrous interruption.

This comic strategy, modulating erratically in tone from the touching to the absurd, the noble to the crass, suffuses the play and gives life to Bennett's overall metaphor of the school as post-war Britain. Albion House, "this little huddle of buildings in a fold of the downs", exhibits in microcosm the symptoms of Britain's 20th-century decline. Poised on the verge of bankruptcy, ripe for change but still clinging to the old values of privilege, order, and gentlemanliness, it mounts a public performance in a "gloomy Victorian Gothic" hall in celebration of the past. (In a typically double-edged image Bennett has the old Headmaster being made up swathed in a prop Union Jack.) The performance, however, is barely under control and is in any case being subverted from within by the new man, Franklin.

The conceit is by no means novel, and in the hands of Brenton or Hare has been more abrasively pursued, but Bennett has the courage to play it for all it is worth, granting equal weight to nostalgic evocation and to ridicule. In the original production Gielgud lent genuine dignity to the Headmaster's fading world, employing his lyrical voice in sly awareness of its potential for grandeur as well as triteness, in contrast to the more waspish notes of Bennett's own Tempest. The play defies interpretation along narrow, ideological lines; rather it encourages an amused observation of the British and their institutions, noting their hypocrisy, amateurishness, and philistinism as well as their innocence, idealism, and love of tradition.

—Ronald W. Strang

HOME
by David Storey.

First Publication: 1970.
First Production: 1970.

From the inconsequential yet worldly conversations between two middle-aged men, Harry and Jack, and then the earthy and innuendo-laden exchanges between two women, Marjorie and Kathleen, it gradually emerges that all four are in a mental home. Manoeuvring for chairs round the metal garden-table, the men and women meet up and tentatively pair up. Albert, a younger inmate, shows off to the others by lifting up a chair, then the table, with one hand. The women mock him and the men are unimpressed. Harry and Jack repeat, with subtle variations, their opening conversation, but finish the play in tears.

Home forces us, because of its minimal action, to pay great attention to the dialogue. Clichés, isolated by skilful pauses, or emphasised by repetition, acquire a resonance and even a metaphorical force. "Well", "still", "mind", "really" are the small-change of ordinary conversation. As the "home" of the title is gradually shown to be a mental institution, these innocent language-counters become charged with deeper meanings. Questions about health, calmness, mental stability and reality itself are being posed. Harry and Jack, however, until challenged by the women, refuse to move beyond cliché. Well-dressed and, apparently, fit and well, they present themselves as the epitomes of two gentlemen of the world in the early years of retirement. Jack, in particular, recalls a wide range of incidents and acquaintances in his life and provides sage reflections on politics. "The ideals of life, liberty, freedom could never have been the same—democracy—well, if we'd been living on the Continent, for example". Harry is more the appreciative listener and prompter. His cliché is "oh, yes", which remains a simple positive until the end when he switches to "oh, no", then begins weeping. World War II is a focal point for shared experience:

> Harry: Ah, yes . . . Couldn't have got far, in our job, I can tell you, without the Royal Air Force.
> Jack: No. No.
> Harry: Britannia rules the waves—and rules the skies, too. I shouldn't wonder.

Families provide opportunities for anecdote and reflection, jobs for display of technical expertise. The whole first act reads like a dramatisation of Flaubert's *Dictionnaire des idées reçues*, and the women demolish these pretensions in Act II. But Storey's point is that, in or out of home, this is how men of a certain age and class speak. Language is a shield, not a probe. Madness should be kept at bay by ritual and convention. The style seems Pinteresque but the ethic derives from Hemingway.

"You all right?" is the cliché of Marjorie and Kathleen, which they ask everyone and which contrasts in its mutuality and wholeness with the staccato conversations of the men. They hate secrets and are realistic about where they are and why they are there. Marjorie and Kathleen are compulsive exhibitionists. In a central exchange between Marjorie and Jack it is the working-class woman's realism that counters the gentleman's fantasy. "Home tomorrow" explains Jack enthusiastically. "Set up here for good" states Marjorie flatly. They have no regrets about incarceration since their real home-lives are unbearable. "'S not like home" states Marjorie. Kathleen responds, "Thank Gawd". The women are vulgar and body-centered, finding sexual innuendo in everything the two men say on their first encounter and asking quite bluntly "What you in for?". Marjorie stands no nonsense from Arthur, for whom coherent language has been reduced to idiotic gestures of physical strength. She challenges him to a mock-fight and, in a baby-like exchange of "won't" and "will", language signifies no more than primitive power. The women are much more conscious than the men of the imagistic possibilities of speech. Kathleen goes into uncontrollable screeches as, discussing the film *Up the Amazon*, Jack remarks: "The canoe, now, was not unlike my own little boat". But the women's referential range—sex, food, the body—is much more limited and their view of "home" is stripped of any fantasy. Their earthy realism is, in fact, as stereotypical as the men's bufferish sophistication. They are cockney "girls", killing themselves with laughter at men and work. They are as desperate as Jack and Harry and, for all four of them, home is not a place where you can be yourself, but a theatre for games of language.

Storey combines naturalist and absurdist techniques in this play as if trying to test the strengths of the two conventions against each other at a time (1970) when each had produced a significant body of post-war work, and in a theatre, the Royal Court, which had staged much of the best of such work. The distinguished cast for the first production—Ralph Richardson, John Gielgud, Dandy Nichols and Mona Washbourne—ensured comic timing of vicious hilarity and a projection of the theatricality of it all. Storey has explored at length, in subsequent works of fiction and drama, the revolt of the imagination against the constraints of domesticity. He never dramatised the theme with such wit and concentration as in *Home*.

—Tony Dunn

THE HOMECOMING
by Harold Pinter.

First Publication: 1965; revised edition, 1968.
First Production: 1967.

The playwright himself has said that *The Homecoming* is the only one of his plays that comes "near to a structural entity which satisfies me". Yet of Pinter's major plays, this is the one that has provoked the sharpest critical disagreements. It is perhaps not surprising that claim and counter-claim should surround a play that so persistently and disturbingly thwarts the naturalistic expectations that its domestic setting and familial subject habitually raise. The briefest account of the action will serve to suggest the play's potential to generate heated debate.

The setting is "an old house in North London" which is the home of an all-male family. Its patriarch is an irascible retired butcher called Max. With him are his benign brother Sam, who is a chauffeur, and his sons Lenny and Joey—the former apparently a pimp, the latter a demolition man by day and an aspiring boxer by night. A third son, the academic philosopher and teacher Teddy, returns to the house from America after six years absence, bringing with him his (English) wife Ruth, who is a stranger to the family. Having, in the first act, been viciously tested by Lenny and abusively received by Max, Ruth is, in the second act, claimed by the men of the house in an explicitly sexual fashion, and, as Teddy prepares to leave again for America, they plan—and negotiate with Ruth herself—to set her up as a prostitute. Uncle Sam protests but drops down dead. Teddy leaves. Ruth stays. The action has spanned just 24 hours.

For its most forceful detractor, Simon Trussler, *The Homecoming* is a "modishly intellectualized melodrama", "a succession of isolated effects", complete with "a yawning probability gap", arrived at by "imposing a formula upon a form". "Pinter's enterprise is sick" and "the writing is becoming automatic". The points are well made. It is easy to feel that the characteristic Pinter manner, in which language becomes strategy, a mode of attack and defence within the ebb-and-flow of subtextual hostilities, has here become mannerism; that the typically high level of indeterminacy is enabling legitimate questions of plausibility to be sidestepped. This *locus classicus* of the Pinteresque is certainly open to the charge of self-parody. Helpful points of reference for a more positive evaluation of the play might be the drama of Strindberg or the films of Buñuel. *The Homecoming*, with its sudden violent juxtapositions, verbal and visual, and its frequent, almost surreal grotesquerie, readily calls to mind their stylistic modes. All three artists, in their different ways, provoke naturalistic expectations only to violate them. And each does so in his attempt to address the issues of power and sexuality within the domestic-familial context. If *The Homecoming* reveals—as has been claimed—"the naked animal", it is with this central purpose.

Ruth claims to have been "a photographic model for the body". When she is introduced into the male household she is perceived as a sexual threat—and rightly so, for firmly defined conceptions of gender and sexuality are at the foundation of existing power-relations in the house. The blustering Max attempts to maintain intimidatory sway over his family by persistently invoking memories of "real" men—either his erstwhile friend, the omnicompetent, Aberdonian street-fighter "Mac", or his father, "a number one butcher" ("I commemorated his name in blood"). In comparison with these sanguineous paragons, Lenny, Sam and Teddy are all "bitches", and Sam a queer, a "tit" and a "wet wick". Yet Max is also anxious to assign to himself the role of biological mother: "I gave birth to three grown men. All on my own bat"; "I suffered the pain, I've still got the pangs". Although he commemorates his dead wife Jessie as an ideal mother, he routinely refers to her as a "slutbitch" and a whore, and when he resolves to take his new daughter-in-law into his house, it is within a projected scenario involving the same dual role for her. The potential domestic power of the woman as matriarch is to be cancelled out by her economic subjection as whore.

But the enigmatic Ruth subverts the intention. When the disturbing sexual power with which she had countered Lenny's verbal intimidation in Act I seems finally to have been harnessed by the prostitution scheme, she shows cold efficiency in the negotiations concerning her "professional" position, and in the play's closing moments assumes the attitude and absolute authority of a matriarch. As her husband leaves, she sits "relaxed on her chair", the head of the pathetic Joey cradled in her lap and the crumbled, stammering Max kneeling at her feet. The displaced patriarch seems to be entering second childhood.

Max has in any case only ever been the nominal head of the household. The real controlling figure has been Lenny. His verbal dexterity and confidence—apparent in his fierce subtextual onslaughts on Max, Ruth, and Teddy—mark him out as such. Yet, paradoxically, it is as a silent watcher of the others, as bearer of a controlling gaze, that his status is most potently established. In the concerted finales of both acts the activity comes from Max, and Ruth is the centre of attention, but it is the silent observing presence of Lenny that matters. The text's final stage direction is "Lenny stands, watching".

Yet the enigma of the play will not easily yield to the model of pimp-son controlling whore-matriarch and through her the whole household. Although the gaze of power is Lenny's, the claim to knowledge-through-seeing comes, odd as it may seem, from Teddy, the strangely acquiescent victim. Asserting, in self-defence, the inaccessibility of his "critical works" to the family, he says: "It's a question of how far you can operate on things and not in things . . . To see, to be able to *see*! I'm the one who can see . . . I can observe it . . . But you're lost in it". The *emigré's* position of *exteriority* is simultaneously his weakness and his strength. Ruth rules the house, and Lenny rules Ruth. But, with Ruth as his agent, Teddy may now be the real power-holder—the outsider *in*. As the play's first director, Peter Hall, put it: "the biggest bastard in a house full of bastards is actually the man who at first sight appears to be the victim". That the text licenses such a perceptual peripeteia without ever permitting confirmation of its truth only serves to underline the indeterminacy of *The Homecoming*.

—Paul Lawley

THE HOSTAGE
(An Giall)
by Brendan Behan (with Joan Littlewood).

First Publication: As *An Giall* [Gaelic version] in *Poems and a Play in Irish*, 1981; as *The Hostage* [in collaboration with Joan Littlewood], 1958; revised edition, 1962.
First Production: As *An Giall*, 1958; as *The Hostage*, 1958; revised version, 1969.

The play is set in a seedy, Dublin lodging house-cum-brothel owned by Monsewer, a dotty, Oxford-educated Englishman who has adopted an outlandish Irish nationality, complete with bagpipes. The house is run by Patrick, lame veteran of the Irish Rebellion, and his as-good-as-wife, Meg. These two preside over the *outré* and lunatic occupants like indulgent parents. A British soldier has been kidnapped and is to be brought to the house as a hostage; he will be killed if the Belfast execution of an Irish youth convicted of an IRA bombing is carried out. When the young, English soldier arrives he is liked and looked after, especially by the servant girl Teresa. The two 19-year-olds fall in love, but the soldier's hopes that Teresa will help him escape are thwarted when, tipped off by one of the occupants, the police raid the house to free the hostage. Caught in the crossfire, the soldier is killed.

Such a plot summary conveys only a small part of the action, for the play is constructed on the lines of music hall entertainment. Scenes are interrupted by characters breaking into song or dance, ranging from Irish jigs and ballads to deliberately shocking, mock-cabaret numbers such as "We're here because we're queer/Because we're queer because we're here", performed by a collection of male, homosexual prostitutes. The audience is regularly addressed from the stage and characters frequently digress into story-telling, at which times the rest of the characters often drift on stage on listen.

The play's ending epitomises its mixture of styles. As the police attack the house, a highly theatricalized battle erupts on the stage, full of shots, screams, drum-rolls, smoke, and hurtling bodies. When the air clears, the hostage lies dead. The servant girl, mourning, kneels to give him her forlorn blessing. There is a pause, then sudden green light on the soldier, who rises and sings raucously:

The bells of hell,
Go ting-a-ling-a-ling,
For you but not for me.
Oh death, where is thy sting-a-ling-a-ling?
Or grave thy victory?

The stage brightens and the entire cast sing the refrain to the audience.

The play as we have it is the product of a collaboration between Behan and Joan Littlewood, the remarkable director of The Theatre Workshop in London. Behan's earlier The Quare Fellow had been staged straightforwardly by the same company. In 1958, Behan agreed to write a piece for an Irish language group using a small, Dublin theatre. This play, An Giall, written in Gaelic, is the early version of The Hostage. Littlewood asked for a translation, which Behan promised but delivered only intermittently and incompletely. Meanwhile, creation of the play proceeded in rehearsals. Through this process, a simple, realistic drama was transformed into a multi-layered piece of theatre. This was Joan Littlewood's method. "Joan took a play to pieces and she put it back together again with actor's inserts, ad libs and catch phrases". Behan was a willing collaborator. "Joan Littlewood has the same views on the theatre that I have", he later wrote, "which is that music hall is the thing to aim at . . . While they were laughing their heads off, you could be up to any bloody thing behind their backs".

What Behan was up to behind their backs is not entirely what was expected of a playwright born and bred into the IRA and who had spent time in jail for it. For all the play's professional Irish charm, it is less a celebration of Irish nationalism than might appear. The serious scenes point up sharply differing attitudes towards the cause. The sentimental fanaticism of the elders is contrasted with the political disengagement of the young lovers, who are the victims in the end. And when Monsewer spouts Gaelic, Pat turns to the audience and says, "Do you hear that? That's Irish. It's a great thing, an Oxford education! Me, I'm only a poor Dublin man. I wouldn't understand a word of it". Yet the sympathy for those who believe and suffer for the freedom of Ireland still works in the play.

One critic called Behan "more a player than a playwright". Certainly the huge success of *The Hostage* was greatly assisted by unpredicted appearances of the author on stage to joke and sing with the actors. His style owes much to the time he spent in various pubs and prisons. Nonetheless, he was a serious writer who admired, and frankly emulated, O'Casey, just as Joan Littlewood learned much from Brecht. *The Hostage* contains many echoes of *Juno and the Paycock* and *The Threepenny Opera*. More importantly, however, it is a genuine attempt to combine the power of realism with that of political cabaret. The critic who remarked, "it's magnificent, but it isn't drama" was right. It is a piece of theatre, one of the few works of the post-war period that truly brought text and performance into collaboration and confrontation.

—Lesley Anne Soule

AN INSPECTOR CALLS
by J.B. Priestley.

First Publication: 1947.
First Production: 1946.

In 1912 a family celebration in the home of factory owner Arthur Birling, to celebrate impending knighthood and his daughter Shiela's engagement to Gerald, is interrupted by an Inspector Goul, apparently investigating the suicide of an impoverished young woman, Eva Smith. The Inspector confronts each member of the party with incidents of their crass, heartless treatment of the girl: Mr. Birling's refusal to increase her meagre wage and dismissal of her for going on strike; Shiela's unjustified insistence the girl be dismissed from her shop-assistant post; Gerald's casual affair with her; brother Eric's abandonment of her when she became pregnant; and Mrs. Birling's refusal to allow her charity committee to assist Eva. When the Inspector leaves, Birling phones the police and discovers, to his relief, they know of no Inspector Goul. Moments later, the phone rings to report the suicide of a young woman.

J.B. Priestley was constantly rattling the cage of realism so that he might deal with concepts beyond the immediate moment. *An Inspector Calls* is arguably his most successful attempt at breaking the boundaries of time and space confining the conventional drawing-room drama, while still achieving an effortless bonding between form and content.

On the surface, the play appears to be a conventional drawing-room play. Certainly, the action is contained in the Birlings' sitting-room and interaction takes place through discussion. However, even with this simple setting, Priestley gently stretches the limits of the form, edging his audience to a wider, and less complacent perspective. Although the action is permanently settled in the same room, safely confined within the three walls of the permenent set, the furniture is rearranged for each act, enforcing (within the limits of the convention) a slightly different perspective, and consequently slightly unsettling a spectator.

In the same manner, Priestley employs other components of the well-made realist play to extend the limits of form and expand the possible references of the play. Setting the play in 1912 allows the audience obvious foreknowledge. Mr. Birling's arrogant assertions of his unshakable superiority, an implied moral superiority justified by a linking of wealth, position, and, apparently, intelligence (for example, in his claims that war is not inevitable, and that the ship, the Titanic is "absolutely unsinkable") flatter the audience, make a clear ironic point, and reveal that both Mr Birling's confident position and his secure world, like his judgement, are not as unassailable as they appear.

At the height of this celebration of moral rectitude confirmed by wealth and position, the strange, uninvited, Inspector Goul arrives. So confident are the characters of their righteousness and position, they do not even ask for credentials, but rather seek to impress their credentials on him: "I was an alderman for years—and Lord Mayor two years ago—and I'm still on the bench—as I know the Bromley police officers pretty well—and I thought I'd never seen you before". Thus, the insulated, self-satisfied complacency of the Birlings' home is invaded by the larger, outside world through the Inspector. The middle-class drawing-room, that private fortress against the unstable dangers of public confusion and interaction, has become vulnerable.

As the Inspector confronts each member of the family with the abused history of Eva Smith, Priestley involves the audience on several levels at once. The members of the family reveal their attitudes towards Eva and the outside world, elaborating their concepts of their place in the world and their varying degress of callousness towards those "less fortunate" than themselves. Secondly, these perspectives and their responses to the Inspector's story set the characters against each other, creating a drama within the family. At the same time, however, the action moves beyond the personal responses of the Birlings. The "drama" of the piece cannot be contained within those three permanent, protective walls of the sitting-room. The Inspector's story, the extremities of Eva's life and the implications of the Birlings' responses render these walls transparent, exposing their inhabitants. And Eva Smith and the multitude she represents come streaming in to create metaphorically the visual and dramatic focus of the play.

In the same way that Mr. Birling's judgements on the Titanic implied more than mere personal opinion, the Birlings' attitudes toward the poor and their own relationship to the social hierarchy become more than personal attitudes. Through the story of Eva Smith, social attitude transcends mere deliniation of character and becomes a platform of action with concrete consequences. So here, too, the conventional drawing-room where one might express one's opinions safely with the decorated, unchanging walls loses its magical safety. These "opinions" are revealed to be powerful instigators of action. The weight of the consequences of that action has caused them to rebound back into the cosy living-room and taint its isolated comfort.

Much of the power of the play rests in Priestley's demand, through Inspector Goul and his story, for the imaginative participation of the audience. To the function of dialogue as a means for transmitting information, Priestley has added the active function of stimulating and directing a visual and imaginative context. Without that creation in the audience's mind of the incidents of Eva's tormented story, the play loses both impact and meaning.

By the end of the play, the scenes of her despair—the strike, the department story, her love affair with Gerald, her relationship with Eric, and her desperate appeal to the charity committee and (most horrible of all), her suicide, seen from *her* point of view—outweigh the Birlings' consternation. Their denials, regrets, and self-defence seem petty in comparison with the apalling struggle we have witnessed. And yet, it is the Birlings who have been onstage; Eva has been, with Priestley's help, our own construction.

Mr. and Mrs. Birling's efforts to discredit the Inspector, like Mr. Birling's prophecies, are petty, selfish, arrogant, and insignificant. Shiela's insistence on breaking off her engagement with Gerald and her genuine repentance give some hope for the future. It is a fitting irony that Mr. Birling's phone call to the police, made to discredit the Inspector, ties him to the young woman's death.

It matters less to us than to the Birlings what the true nature of the Inspector's status might be. Hopefully, we have, for the time of the play, at least, become less attached to information, fact, and material credibility and more concerned with the intangible questions of moral responsibility and emotional integrity. The process of the play is meant to detach the audience from the demands of verisimilitude. It is impossible, also, to determine with any certainty whether Eva Smith is really the same woman who changed her name to survive, or a series of different women. This dual possibility is not merely a clever trick to tantalize, nor only the suggestion that Eva is the representative of a multitude, but also another effort to move the drawing-room drama out of the confines of the specific and the individual to the representative and to abstract moral concepts.

Priestley has gracefully dissipated the specificity of the naturalistic stage conventions so that Eva and the Birlings emerge as representatives, creating a larger concept in which abstract concepts have weight and significance. The images of Eva's life transcend the limits of the stage. Each incident is a moral parable, an example to carry out into the street, and the Birlings' exposure becomes a fable of social ethics and moral responsibility.

The Inspector's "Sermon on the Mount" preaches basic, Christian values of charity, compassion, kindness, and, above all, the responsibility of privilege. Although the mildness of its "message", its acceptance of social hierarchy and its avoidance of the idea of social change may seem inadequate for the present day and certainly dates the play, *An Inspector Calls* merits credit and interest, not least for the skill with which Priestley fills the conventional drawing-room drama with the teeming world it is traditionally fortressed against.

—Elaine Turner

JUNO AND THE PAYCOCK
by Sean O'Casey.

First Publication: In *Two Plays*, 1925.
First Production: 1924.

In a tenement house in Dublin during the Civil War of 1922, "Captain" Boyle's wife, Juno, struggles to support her family while her work-shy husband goes "strutting about the town like a paycock" with his sycophantic crony, Joxer Daly. Their daughter, Mary, is on strike for her "principles" (learnt from her admirer, Jerry Devine, a Labour supporter) while the son, Johnny, who fought in the 1916 Easter Rising and lost his arm in the O'Connell Street fighting, broods in his room, fearful of some unnamed threat. When Boyle is told by Mary's new suitor, the English schoolteacher, Charlie Bentham, that he has been left money in a cousin's will, he proceeds to an orgy of spending on credit, displaying his new possessions, including vulgar furniture, at a party, which is cut short when a funeral procession passes. The bereaved mother, Mrs. Tancred, pauses in the doorway to lament the killing of her Republican son (once Johnny's commandant) and to pray for an end to the murderous hate between Republicans and Free Staters. Juno repeats her words at the end of the play after everything has gone wrong for the Boyles. There will be no money, because of Bentham's careless wording of the will. Mary, whom he has made pregnant, is abandoned, and as the unpaid-for furniture is being reclaimed by removal men, Johnny is taken away by his former comrades, to be shot for betraying Tancred. Juno goes to identify his body; she and Mary, who is now disowned by her father, leave the home, to bring up Mary's child elsewhere. The curtain falls on Boyle and Joxer groping drunkenly for the missing furniture, while the Paycock reflects grandiloquently "The whole worl's . . . in a terr . . . ible state o' chassis".

Juno and the Paycock is the second play in O'Casey's Dublin trilogy, and of the three, it was the overwhelming success. The first of the Abbey plays to have its run extended for a second week, it has remained the most popular and frequently revived of all O'Casey's plays. The vigour of the comedy intertwined with its tragedy has helped to assure this, along with the rich characterisation, which extends to minor parts like that of Mrs. Madigan as well as the great central roles. The characters are made at once larger than life and convincingly natural by language that slips easily from the colloquial into high rhetoric or lyrical minglings of the comic and nostalgic, as in the Paycock's "Them was days, Joxer, them was days. Nothin' was too hot or heavy for me then". Lady Gregory was much affected on the first night by Sara Allgood's repetition of Mrs. Tancred's prayer, "Take away our hearts o' stone . . . an' give us hearts o' flesh", telling Yeats, "This is one of the evenings at the Abbey that makes me glad to have been born".

The sense of immediacy in *Juno and the Paycock* fascinated the play's early audiences and is one cause of its continuing vitality in the theatre. O'Casey was writing remarkably, even dangerously, close to the events of the Civil War. When Mrs. Tancred's moving lines were first heard on the Abbey stage, notes Gerard Fay (in *The Abbey Theatre*, 1958), "a tremor ran through the audience unlike anything felt since the first works of Synge had burst upon Dublin". Though the political terror is off-stage, it casts a sinister shadow, from the opening line, when Mary casually reads out from the newspaper, "On a little bye-road, out beyant Finglas he was found". This first cryptic reference to the murdered Tancred gradually gathers weight and meaning as Johnny is shown reacting with desperate fear to any mention of killings or of his former Republican connections and, at the end of Act II, "seeing" Tancred's ghost kneeling by the Virgin's statue. The arrival of the gunmen creates an impression of tragic inevitability, though O'Casey has kept the audience partly in the dark about the reason for Johnny's seeming neuroticism, so increasing suspense and irony.

The comedy of *Juno and the Paycock* is one of its chief glories but presents directors with some problems. The Paycock and Joxer, if over-played for comedy, as they sometimes are, too easily dominate the play, distorting the balance of sympathy and obscuring larger issues (O'Casey thought *The Plough and the Stars* a better play because it had no such dominating figures). But the Falstaffian pair's zestful bantering provided actors like Barry Fitzgerald and F.J. McCormick, who first played them, with glorious parts: it is refreshing, in the cramped, degraded slum environment to hear the Paycock fantasising about sailing the seas and asking himself "what is the stars, what is the stars?" while Joxer fishes up the right "darlin' word" to suit his patron's mood. Juno is earth-bound in comparison, distrusting romanticists of all varieties. "You lost your best principle when you lost your arm" is her realistic view of her son's commitment to an ideal. As in the rest of the trilogy, she and the women generally are the victims of men's vanity. She does make her own mistakes (Boyle is sharper in recognising Bentham's shoddiness); but as the action moves further into tragedy, her unselfishness casts an increasingly strong light on the darker side of the Paycock's irresponsibility (Joxer is clearly a rat from the start). Boyle's reaction to Mary's pregnancy is, as Ronald Ayling says (in *Continuity and Innovation in Sean O'Casey's Drama*, 1976), savage and "meant to sicken us". Juno is not felt to be exaggerating when she comforts Mary, upset that her child will have no father, with the brave assurance, "It'll have what's far betther—it'll have two mothers".

Juno and the Paycock was written out of O'Casey's hard personal experience of tenement life. Some of its characters had real-life prototypes: Juno, notably, owes much to O'Casey's hard-working, devoted mother. A good production captures the look and feel of a Dublin tenement in the 1920s, bringing out the factors which have contributed to making the 45 year old Juno look strained and older than her years: the lack of privacy and the constant intrusions, from coal block vendors to funerals, from Joxer to debt collectors and gunmen.

The technique is not purely realistic, however. O'Casey detested the craze for "real, real life" on the stage. He creates a poetry of theatre through his poignantly musical language, and through atmospheric sound and visual effects like the votive light which goes out as Johnny's doom approaches or the telling contrast in the party scene between the melody sung with moving simplicity by Juno and Mary and Joxer's incoherent attempts to sing "in a querulous voice". Mundane realities acquire symbolic force. By the time she stands on a stage that has been stripped of home-like comforts, speaking Mrs.

Tancred's lines and reproaching herself for not feeling enough pity for her when her son was found riddled with bullets, as now her own son has been, Juno has become a figure of fate, telling the audience what they should carry into their own lives: "Ah, why didn't I remember that then he wasn't a Diehard or a Stater, but only a poor, dead son". With supreme genius, O'Casey closes his play, not on this high, emotional note, but on the comedy that has gone sour and is now seen clearly to be a factor in the tragedy. The Paycock, along with Joxer, confusedly groping for the chairs that were never paid for, mumbling drunken fantasies about "Easter Week" ("had no business to be there . . . but Captain Boyle's Captain Boyle") tells a truth greater than he knows, in his maudlin moralising: "the whole worl's . . . in a terr . . . ible state o' chassis".

—Katharine Worth

THE LADY'S NOT FOR BURNING
by Christopher Fry.

First Publication: 1949; revised version, 1950; further revised version, 1958.
First Production: 1948.

Thomas Mendip, a discharged but nobly born soldier, and Jennet Jourdemayne, a suspected witch, are unwelcome guests at the house of Hebble Tyson, mayor of the small market-town of Cool Clary. Mendip claims he has killed Matthew Skipps, the local rag-and-bone man, and demands to be executed. Jennet, daughter of an alchemist, is accused by the medieval mob of turning Skipps into a dog. Instead of celebrating his nephew Humphrey's marriage to sweet young Alizon Eliot, Tyson and Justice Tappercoom find themselves caught up in establishing the guilt of Mendip and Jennet. Alliances shift as Alizon falls in love with Richard, Tyson's young clerk, Humphrey and his brother Nicholas with Jennet, and Jennet and Mendip with each other. At the last minute Skipps is delivered, alive, to Tyson's house by Alizon and Richard who then elope, to be pursued by Tyson. Mendip goes free and leaves Cool Clary with Jennet. As a witch her property is forfeit to the town, but Mendip will take her off to his father's castle.

"What a wonderful thing is metaphor" exclaims the tiresomely self-dramatizing Mendip in the opening scene, and it is indeed through his metaphorical usuage that Fry distinguishes himself from the other verse dramatists (Eliot and Duncan) in the period of post-war austerity. But too often the comparisons only half-succeed. Mendip declares his father has a castle "as draughty as a tree". Castles can be draughty but neither in shape nor solidity do they resemble trees. Jennet says she has to hurry because she hears "the pickaxe voice of a cock beginning/To break up the night". The sharpness of sound may be accurate but why should dawn be like a labourer attacking a pavement? The images here are arbitrary. This imprecision particularly detracts from the force of Mendip's long speech to Richard ("I've been cast adrift on a sea of melancholy") at the beginning of Act III. He's trying to explain his self-disgust as the emotional uncertainty of a man caught between animist and scientific views of the world. This clash is, in fact, the plot, in which the superstitious Cool Clary community wants to destroy the witch/ scientist Jennet. Mendip's metaphors logically progress from raft and sea to shore and pastureland. But the edge of the concrete image is blurred by abstraction — "raft of melancholy", "the little oyster-shell of this month of April", "the night's a boundless pastureland of peace". This language is not a parody of bad Edwardian verse any more than unflappable, middle-class Margaret and her two wilful, puppyish sons are pastiche Forster. The turn of the century echoes throughout the play because Fry has interpolated fictional types elaborated then (there is even a Canon Chasuble type chaplain) into the Middle Ages.

With Jennet, however, Fry has created a contemporary figure, more current even in the 1990s than in the 1940s. She continues her father's scientific studies, lives alone, faces death, and falls in love with an accomplished mixture of rationality and passion. She is a beautiful alchemist and therefore in every sense a bewitcher. She doesn't deny her difference, but she sees men as different too. When Humphrey offers to free her if she will sleep with him she debates his offer with a freedom from hysteria unusual in the period. As she and Thomas, thrown together in Tyson's house, reveal themselves to each other, her self-knowledge and character-perception ring much truer than Mendip's rhetoric. She needs no metaphors to describe her life:

I live alone, preferring loneliness
To the companionable suffocation of an aunt.
I still amuse myself with simple experiments
In my father's laboratory. Also I speak
French to my poodle. Then you must know
I have a peacock which on Sundays
Dines with me indoors . . .

This speech echoes the tone and social range of Alexander Pope. She pricks Mendip's bombast but since love is the motive she is not satirical. Beneath his egotism she detects a fear of companionship. "You are making yourself", she remarks, "a breeding ground for love and must take the consequences" — As she herself must, which she recognises in a speech ("Sluts are only human . . .") towards the end of Act II which could have been written by a present-day feminist. Mendip is "decay and a platitude/ Of flesh". He is even, "Evil, Hell, the Father of Lies". Nevertheless he can "drag upon a woman's heart" so that her rationality, which she expresses to the end, recognises its limits: "What is to be done? Something compels us into/The terrible fallacy that man is desirable/And there's no escaping into truth". Fry's Jennet may represent woman as Other, but he has her speak positively and frequently throughout the play.

—Tony Dunn

LOOK BACK IN ANGER
by John Osborne.

First Publication: 1957.
First Production: 1956.

Look Back in Anger is a play dominated by its central character, Jimmy Porter. Jimmy is a product of post-war educational reform, a working-class graduate who had ideals (though these are never clearly articulated) that have been frustrated by the apparent inertia of British life in the 1950s. He marries into the upper-middle classes almost as an act of revenge and subjects his wife, Alison, to a continuous onslaught of bullying and abuse. Alison is weak, passive, and fence-sitting, and she absorbs his insults lamely, with the implication that he is emasculated by the soggy, genteel values of the English middle classes. The cramped flat in the English Midlands where they live is shared with Cliff, a mutual friend, who provides another unresponsive target for Jimmy's tirades.

In Act II, Alison's actor friend Helena arrives and encourages Alison to leave Jimmy, who is unaware that Alison is now pregnant. Helena's presence creates a new sexual dynamic. She is more able to stand up to Jimmy's abuse and her resistance to him is presented as the sexual charge that he needs to find some meaning in his life. Cliff leaves, the comfortable *ménage-à-trois* having been broken up, and Jimmy and Helena stay together for a time. However, much to Jimmy's fury, Helena is shown to believe in traditional moral values; she sees their relationship as wrongful and when Alison conveniently returns to the flat she makes way for Jimmy and Alison to be reconciled. Alison has now been through the pain of losing her baby. The experience is presented, ironically, as something positive. As she puts it, "This is what he's been longing for me to feel . . . I'm in the mud at last! I'm grovelling! I'm crawling!". Jimmy had earlier expressed the view that "anyone who's never watched someone die is suffering from a pretty bad case of virginity", he too has witnessed death, and a renewal of their relationship is now possible.

In 1956, when the play was first performed at the Royal Court Theatre in London, the character of Jimmy had a startling potency as the representative of a generation of disaffected British youth. His anger could be seen to capture a prevalent mood of the period as hopes for peace and plenty after the war faded into the drabness of the 1950s. However, part of the drabness here seems to be an inability to look back and pinpoint the cause of all the anger with any precision, or to look forward with any conviction or vision. Despite his university education, Jimmy chooses to run a sweet stall. This can be understood as a gesture of protest against a society that has introduced reforms, such as wider access to education, without fundamentally altering its power base. The dominant values of society are still those of the old establishment, albeit in a state of terminal decline. This sense of social malaise was made all the more resonant, when the play was first performed in 1956, by Britain's bungling intervention in the Suez crisis that same year.

Since then, the play has been accorded an almost legendary status as a major landmark in post-war, British theatre, defining the beginning of a period of writing by new, young playwrights, who often had a strong sense of social injustice. Such a view is certainly tendentious and liable to discount the work of companies like Unity Theatre Workshop who had consistently given voice to left-wing views from the 1930s onwards. Certainly, though, *Look Back in Anger* marks the emergence of the Royal Court Theatre, under the general direction of George Devine, as a major London venue for new writing. When, in 1956, an extract from the play was shown on television, box-office takings suddenly took off and the consequent commercial success of the play (it was later made into a film with Richard Burton) showed that there was money to be made in new drama.

In retrospect the play seems fairly conventional despite the apparent new-ness of the subject matter, and Osborne himself admitted as much when he described it as "a formal, rather old-fashioned play". It is a three act drama written in the manner of the English well-made play. The dialogue is domi-nated by Jimmy, the action by naturalistic devices like ironing and reading the Sunday papers, and the location by the permanent setting of Jimmy's flat. Jimmy's marriage to Alison sets up a class conflict, but this is not really explored in any depth. It is an implicit assumption of the play that Jimmy's background makes him a person more vital and alive than Alison. By virtue of her class and gender, the latter is created as a character too weak to defend herself. Today the play has a glaring pre-feminist look to it; there is a total absence of any depth to female perspectives and Jimmy's mysogynistic views often seen suspiciously like those of Osborne himself.

In 1989 Osborne granted performance rights for the play to be revived by the English Renaissance Company in a production directed by Judi Dench, with Kenneth Branagh and Emma Thompson playing the parts of Jimmy and Alison. Critics tended to be divided about the success of the play's revival after 33 years. Jimmy was described by some as a self-pitying sentimentalist and, more heroically by Michael Billington, as "a man driven to madness by the unresponsive cool of those around him". The theme of anger and frustration had become less significant than the exploration of a power struggle between the sexes, for which a debt to Strindberg was suggested, and the influence of Eugene O'Neill was detected in the notion that pain and suffering validates human existence.

—Andy Piasecki

MURDER IN THE CATHEDRAL
by T.S. Eliot.

First Publication: 1935 (special acting edition); complete edition, 1935;
    second edition, 1936; third edition, 1937; fourth edition, 1938.
First Production: 1935.

T.S. Eliot's *Murder in the Cathedral* takes place during December 1170 in Canterbury. Thomas Beckett, Archbishop of England, returns to England against the King's orders after seven years exile in France. He knows that King Henry II will have him murdered because of a continuing conflict between their strong personalities over whether church or state will be supreme in England. The play consists of two parts with an interlude. As the play opens, a Chorus of the Women of Canterbury feel drawn towards the cathedral to bear witness to the coming tragic events. Soon after his return, Beckett by himself faces four tempters representing four aspects of his personality—enjoyment of the world, enjoyment of power, compromise to achieve his ends, and, the most powerful temptation, pride in doing right for the wrong motive. The interlude is a sermon given by Beckett on Christmas morning concerning Mass as a re-enactment of the "Passion and Death of Our Lord". In the second part of the play, on 29 December, four knights threaten Beckett. Refusing to compromise with the knights or accept the advice of his priests to seek safety, he resigns himself to God's will and is killed in the cathedral. The knights then turn to the audience treating it as a jury before whom they attempt to justify themselves and the rights of the state. The play ends with the return of the Chorus which claims Beckett as a martyr whose blood has enriched the earth and created a holy place at Canterbury.

Sharing in the verse and religious drama and Anglo-Catholic movements of its time, *Murder in the Cathedral* was originally written for production at the Canterbury Cathedral Festival in 1935, before it transferred to the commercial stage in London, went on various tours, and was made into a film by George Hoellering (for whom Eliot revised the play, adding additional background information at the beginning). While *Murder in the Cathedral* can be acted on a large stage, it was written for the small enclosed space available in Canterbury Cathedral and is still most theatrically effective in a church, small theatre, or theatre in the round. The effects of various entrances of the characters and the playing areas should contrast with the focus on Beckett's spiritual drama without losing a sense of the action being compressed around and within him. In reacting against realism and the seeming shapelessness of English plays, Eliot wanted a drama closer to French classicism than to Shakespearean abundance.

Murder in the Cathedral remains the finest, English, ritual drama from the period, blending modernist experimentation in non-realistic verse theatre, an anthropological view of culture, a mythic structure, and Eliot's own concern with the need for humility, faith, and obedience to divine will. The Chorus, with its allusions to the dying vegetation and passing year, creates a sense of a community threatened, a wasteland needing the sacrificial blood of a martyr for renewal. Similarly to the knights' breaking of the theatrical frame to address the audience, the Chorus creates a continuity between play and spectators. They greet Beckett's arrival in language which often echoes biblical accounts of Christ's passion and sacrifice, an evocation strengthened by Beckett's Christmas Day sermon. Throughout the play, as in Eliot's poetry of this period, the language is rich in biblical and liturgical echoes. The Mass re-enacts the Sacrifice; the play imitates the Mass. This is in keeping with Eliot's comments that the Catholic Mass is the most intense, richest form of drama. The play thus provides a symbol of the basis of its archetype, it assumes that the origins of drama lie in myth and ritual and that drama is a secularization of religious drama. The concern with symbol, type, and figure is further brought out by such means as the Chorus (speaking of itself as "type of the common man") and the four tempters who appear before Beckett, recalling the temptations of Christ. Like Milton's *Samson Agonistes*, which is also an influence on the varied versification, formalized speeches, and portrayal of a change in will, there is little in the way of action and event; Beckett's change from pride in his forthcoming martyrdom to emptying his will so that he may accept the destiny God has ordained is, like Samson's, offered without expressionistic or realistic psychology. Any action—whether to save himself or to court martyrdom—would be a matter of pride and self-love rather than obedience to God's will. While Eliot commented that the versification was influenced by *Everyman*, *Murder in the Cathedral* might be seen as a classical foreshortening of the famous morality play: from a journey through life to the last days of a man when, still faced by temptations, he must reconcile himself to death. As in *Everyman*, the essential problem is the state of mind in which one dies. Although *Murder in the Cathedral* often shares the same mood and language as *Ash-Wednesday*, and belongs to the period when Eliot converted to the Church of England and began abandoning former worldly ambitions, the play's conflict between church and state clearly belongs to the 1930s when the Catholic revival of the previous 50 years was challenged from both the political right and left.

The usual problem with plays involving inner drama, rather than external conflict, is lack of tension and the absurdities that result from trying to externalize spiritual decisions. Eliot avoids such problems by a formality of manner, and the intensity that comes from concentration and focus on Beckett's spiritual state, the decision he must make, and the results (as celebrated by the Chorus). The internal drama is externalized in the form of the four temptations (as aspects of Beckett's own life and personality), the debate with the knights, the decision not to seek safety, and in the way the Chorus directs the audience's responses to the play's events.

While lacking in external (rather than spiritual) drama, *Murder in the Cathedral* is highly theatrical. It has the elevation, tension, and suspense of awaiting the expected found in classical Greek tragedy. The versification is varied according to the speaker and situation. A high proportion of monosyllabic words makes for clarity while Eliot's less frequent use of unusual polysyllabics sharpens attention on themes and elevates the mood. The severely limited cast of characters, the use of the Cathedral and grounds for the scenes, the few scene changes, the many references to the threat facing Beckett, and the limiting of confrontations to those between Beckett and the tempters, three priests, and the knights create a classical intensity and concentration unusual in English drama. The play is filled with theatrical surprises ranging from the sermon to the clever, witty speeches of the four tempters; the parallelism between the four tempters and the four knights; the shock of the knights after the murder suddenly breaking the theatrical frame and addressing the audience in prose. *Murder in the Cathedral* demands the full use of the theatre's resources in any production.

—Bruce King

NEAPTIDE
by Sarah Daniels.

First Publication: 1986.
First Production: 1986.

Neaptide is one of the most important plays to be produced in the past few decades, in terms of both its dramatic and social impact. Set in an outer London suburb, the play takes place in March 1983. The setting and time frame are significant, as the play deals with legal and social attitudes towards lesbian rights and child custody with specific relevance to the cultural context of England in the early 1980s. It focuses with humour and wit on the subtle varieties of violence done to women by the legal system, particularly when it comes to custody of children.

The main character, Claire, is a teacher and a mother, who is faced with a very public dilemma: whether to come out as a lesbian at school in a show of solidarity with some of the pupils or to stay in the closet in order to protect her job. Meanwhile, Claire is involved in a child custody case, sued by her ex-husband Lawrence for "care and control" of their daughter, Poppy. The play skirts two worlds: the private space of Claire's home, continually invaded by family and the threatening presence of her ex-husband, and the public world of the school, where Claire must continually renegotiate her own identity both as a role model for others and as a person in her own right. This conflict is the central tension of the play.

Despite her serious circumstances Claire finds time to read the myth of Persephone to her daughter who clearly sees the relevance of the abducted daughters' plight to her own life. Here is the source for the play's title. "*Neaptide*" refers to: "the lowest tide, when the sun and the moon are in opposition." This term is entirely appropriate to the content and the intent of the play, which takes the myth of Persephone as its framing device: a myth which incorporates a story of the seasons, the sun and the moon, in a tale about the abduction of a young woman and her forced initiation into hetero-sexual union, necessitating a separation from her mother and the women who love and try to protect her. The myth functions both as a bedtime story (Poppy is seven years old) and as an allegorical subtext to the play: Demeter and her four daughters are paralleled by Joyce (Claire's mother) and her three daughters, with young Poppy as the fourth; Claire is clearly Persephone and Poppy is Artemis, the daughter who stays with her mother. Yet their roles reverse in the course of the play, as the impending custody trial forces them both to contemplate losing each other. Here Poppy is a potential Persephone, about to be abducted by the "warring" father/god, Lawrence. The role of the male in the play is sometimes threatening but more often comic; while the women are argumentative, infuriating, and also remarkably supportive when need be.

There is no artificial happy ending: Claire does not win the custody battle, nor is the state apparatus which discriminates against women overthrown. Even towards the end of the play when Claire is advised to run away to America with Poppy since the legal system is clearly stacked against her, she stays to face the trial. The judge awards care and control to the father. In the final scene a note arrives with the message that "Poppy and Claire have arrived safely . . . ." Thus we know that Claire has joined her sister in America; the new world where Poppy will be free to live with Claire till she's old enough to make her own choice.

Sarah Daniels has subsequently criticised *Neaptide* seeing it as an issue play in which concern to represent Claire positively may have stood in the way of depicting her as a fully rounded character: "I didn't allow myself the luxury of making that woman [Claire] more real and that was my mistake. I didn't let *her* make mistakes. I forgot in the pressure of trying to put her beyond reproach that we most identify with others mistakes" (in *Contemporary Feminist Theatres*, 1993).

Claire is more than a character; she is a means through which Daniels can articulate her political position on feminism and the representation of women. Claire is a representative of "womanhood" and "motherhood". Her lesbianism is incidental to her other roles, but is the lens through which her situation is focused precisely because it is the element which most disturbs and frightens the other characters. Lesbian plays are still under-represented and *Neaptide* is the only British lesbian play to have been produced in a mainstream venue. It is a well-crafted work that deals with serious issues and uses comedy as a subversive strategy to grip the audience.

—Lizbeth Goodman

NOISES OFF
by Michael Frayn.

First Publication: 1982.
First Production: 1982.

Noises Off, a farce, is also *Nothing On*, another farce. Michael Frayn's most popular play is so intricately constructed that it had to be beautifully written twice.

There have been backstage comedies before and since, but never has a play so exactly integrated character and the mechanics of the theatre. In the first act the curtain opens on what seems to be a performance of a standard farce, with elements of Ray Cooney and Ben Travers. A classic befuddled housekeeper arrives with a plate of sardines and picks up a ringing telephone. In time-honoured fashion, she muddles her words, tells the caller everything about the house, including that it is the home of "Mr Philip Brent . . . the one who writes the plays" and that he writes them in Spain now. What more could a housebreaker, or an audience in Weston-Super-Mare, wish to know?

Within seconds, however, we know considerably more, because we are no longer watching *Nothing On* by Robin Housemonger, but Mr Frayn's *Noises Off*, where they are rehearsing *Nothing On* in Weston-Super-Mare. The housekeeper, Mrs Clackett, is, we discover, the actress, Dotty Otley, who is hopeless with her props, movements, and lines, and she is appealing to her director for help.

It isn't very long before we discover that Dotty is the show's principal backer, a fading television star hoping to add to her nest egg with a stage vehicle, and that she is having an affair with the much younger leading man (Garry Lejeune) who plays a lascivious estate agent in the Housemonger play, and, that, indeed, the company is riddled with jealousies, secret relationships and anxieties. Everyone in the Frayn play spends their time worrying about Selsdon, a once roistering older actor who plays an elderly housebreaker in *Nothing On*, when he is the most solidly professional and concerned of the troupe. Their concern would be better placed with their director, who is sexually entertaining the play's short-sighted sex symbol, Brooke, and the assistant stage manager, Poppy. But all the characters are provided with seeds of chaos and the hysterical comedy of the dress rehearsal provided for the audience in the first act is gentle preparation for a second act of such choreographed catastrophe that it could hardly take place away from the rigid necessities of a stage performance.

Frayn, who had previously delighted in exploring the arbitrary order of the world as revealed through a newspaper library in his play *Alphabetical Order*, has also regularly dealt with the duality of human nature in his novels and plays, holding up mirrors to his audiences as well as his characters. In *Noises Off* he found the perfect mirror of behaviour by contrasting the behaviour of actors playing a farce to the actual farce of their own human relations.

In doing so, he achieved something rare in farce. The first act of the play is genuinely funny. In revealing to us the entire production team, from director and stars to stage manager and assistant stage manager, with their responsibilities for building sets and understudying on top of everything else, he somehow manages to slip in the entire first act of the play they are rehearsing. But, although that is funny, it is pale preparation for the frantic revelations of Act Two.

In that act, we are backstage watching the performance of the play in the Theatre Royal, Goole. Nearly every relationship has reached a crisis, with Dotty driving Garry mad with her flirtations, and with the director visiting the tour to try to snatch two hours with Brooke while hiding from the A.S.M., Poppy.

From the actors' side of the stage, we witness them diving through doors to make their entrances. We see them catching sight of easily misinterpreted clinches as contact lenses pop out, and then trying to react before their next cue. In virtual mime, we share the backstage traumas of assaults with a cactus and struggles with costumes. And while we hear the entire act on stage in all its incoherence, we concentrate on the tangled lives of the actors, resonantly summed up with Poppy's line to the director just as silence descends: "I'm pregnant!"

The director has stated the theme: "That's what it's all about. Doors and sardines. Getting on—getting off. Getting the sardines on—getting the sardines off. That's farce. That's the theatre. That's life."

For three hours it is. Frayn provides a final act, truncated into laughter from an original third act that consciously cooled the mirth. Utter and complete chaos is the result, with three burglars suddenly and simultaneously appearing on a set where the sardines rule, the doors are broken and the personal fallibility of every character is on display. That too is life.

Elsewhere in his work Frayn exploits his gift for visual comedy, in a mimed adaptation of Chekhov such as *The Sneeze*, for instance. His more natural habit might be thought to be the Chekhovian comic melancholy of a play such as *Benefactors*, where property and its value has a direct relation to the people of London in the 1980s. But *Noises Off* is unmatched in Frayn's generation for its rigorous theatrical construction and comic sensibility. Although he himself has not returned to the form, it remains a master class in the construction of farce with a mind.

—Ned Chaillet

THE NORMAN CONQUESTS
Table Manners
Living Together
Round and Round the Garden
by Alan Ayckbourn.

First Publication: 1975.
First Production: 1973.

Like just about all of Alan Ayckbourn's work *The Norman Conquests* started life at the Scarborough Library Theatre, before transferring to London in 1974. It is a trilogy of plays in which each makes narrative and dramatic sense separately, but when considered together, they create a vision of a world of faded middle-class gentility. In this vision, the very real laughter provoked by the events of a disastrously enforced weekend "house party" comes to take on a progressively greyer feel as the real significance of events is deciphered by the audience.

The trilogy's overall title is explained by reference to the antics of Norman, an impossible, would-be Lothario who figures large in Ayckbourn's glorious catalogue of impossible, male figures. Norman is a scruffy but thoroughly safe, bohemian assistant-librarian set loose in a world of estate agent husbands and charity-organising mothers. He dreams of torrid romances and heady week-ends in a series of provincial scenarios that transfer rather unconvincingly from the pages of library books. The letter would need to be in large-print format to fully alert his wife, Ruth—an actively careerist woman, whose vanity prevents her from wearing the glasses that just might force her to see what really goes on in the world according to Norman.

The action in all three plays overlaps, dealing simultaneously with the consequent events of the weekend in three different locations—in *Table Manners* the dining-room of the large and run-down Victorian house in the country inhabited by the unmarried Annie and her bed-ridden and never seen mother (an off-stage ogre whose previous sexual precosity has now been converted sadly into having her daughter read her steamy romances, the contents of which are probably closer to Norman's dreams than the Romeos and other classical romancers he himself cites); in *Living Together* we learn what was happening in the sitting-room during and between-times; and finally, in *Round and Round the Garden*, the action is taken outside. In the final play there is a preface and an epilogue to events in the two internal locations.

As so often with Ayckbourn—in *Absurd Person Singular* and *How The Other Half Loves*, in particular—it was the technical invention which first attracted its contemporary audiences. Much of the audience interest is centered on observing the skill with which the playwright knits together the many complexities of a plot which is only properly revealed after three separate bites at the same story. And indeed many critics complain that the dexterity is all. Ayckbourn's many admirers would, however, cite the emotional subtext of his work—which shows that these plays are more than mechanically contrived farces, and that they are populated by characters capable of shedding real blood, as well as tears—and the increasingly dark side to his comedy; pointing in particular to the sympathetic treatment of the loneliness of women in a married world ruled over by incompetent, inadequate, and unfeeling men. That the impossible Norman should seem to offer hope not just to one but to all of the female characters in the trilogy is a measure not of his attractions as a conquering knight-errant but of the awfulness of their own situations.

The events of the weekend are initiated by Norman's plan to take his sister-in-law, the mother-burdened Annie, away for a weekend of passion; not in the Hastings that is all booked up but in the East Grinstead that is all that is available (and is, at best, only on the way to what would anyway have been a somewhat unexotic setting for library romance). To the house come Ruth's brother, Reg, and his wife Sarah to administer pills and sympathy to mother while Annie has what they believe will be a long-overdue fling with Tom, a dim and dithering vet. He has been visiting Annie for so long that she is no longer certain whether it is to prevent the need for him opening a tin of food at home, to offer her unnamed and not-much-loved cat constant medical attention, or to declare a passion for her that she is not sure she wishes to hear about. The ultra-organised Sarah worms Annie's pathetic little secret out of her in a matter of moments and immediately sets about wrecking the weekenders' plans in a mixture of moral outrage and, as it later becomes apparent when the unstoppable Norman makes her the same offer for the changed resort of Eastbourne, sexual jealousy. Add to this tangle the arrival of a Ruth intent on recovering Norman in much the same way as one might search for an overdue library book, and the stage is set for a demolition of middle-class proprieties that is Ayckbourn's special field.

In the end it is the magnificently collapsed set-pieces of social ritual that stick in the memory, disturbing in their only slightly distorted and exaggerated relationship to the world of polite discourse inhabited by the plays' audience. Two moments in particular suggest themselves for close attention. The first surrounds the desperate attempts made by Sarah to pull the family back to civilisation around a dinner-table in *Table Manners*; attempts which rapidly decline through an argument about who should sit where (as if the affair were a formal dinner engagement) into a macabre feast presided over by a manic Norman who has dressed for the occasion in the ill-fitting clothes of his dead father-in-law. The second is in *Living Together* when Reg, the estate agent and disposer of property, caught forever in the trivial escapisms of his childhood in the house, attempts to persuade the assembled company to try out his latest, home-made board-game of attempted robberies of commercial properties. Dinner-parties and party-games: these are the territories where Ayckbourn's special talents for social observation come most fully into play.

—John Bull

OUR COUNTRY'S GOOD
by Timberlake Wertenbaker.

First Publication: 1988; revised edition, 1990.
First Production: 1988.

Set in Sydney Cove in 1789, *Our Country's Good* depicts the trials of Ralph Clark, army lieutenant and aspiring theatre director, as he attempts to stage a production of George Farquhar's comedy *The Recruiting Officer* for the entertainment and edification of the convict colonists he and his fellow soldiers are guarding. And trials he does face: not merely are his actors felons (one of his leading ladies, Liz Morden, is in danger of being hanged) but his whole enterprise is subject to constant attack from fellow officers (notably from Major Robbie Ross, the militaristic marine commander) who maintain that any form of diversion for the convicts is an incitement to disorder. Fortunately, however, Ralph is supported by the Governor of New South Wales, Captain Arthur Phillip, who believes in the redemptive powers of art; he receives another sort of support from one of his actors, Mary Brenham, with whom he falls passionately in love. Eventually, despite all difficulties (including an attack on the settlement by Black Caesar, a huge escaped Madagascan who insists on being in his play), Ralph succeeds in staging *The Recruiting Officer*; its opening lines provide the closing ones of *Our Country's Good*.

While not necessarily superior to her other pieces, Timberlake Wertenbaker's *Our Country's Good* has attracted much attention, partly because it deals with an event that is intrinsically fascinating (the first staging of a European drama in the antipodes), partly because it debates in a precise and vivid way one of the enduring mysteries of the human condition, that is, whether we are born wicked or whether we are made that way by circumstance. If Wertenbaker herself has views on this (and the prefatory paragraph from Rosenthal's and Jacobsen's *Pygmalion in the Classroom*, to the effect that children do well if treated well by their teachers, suggests she aligns herself with the liberal side in this matter) she nevertheless allows her various characters to argue the subject fully and persuasively. That there isn't, in the end, a simple answer is no failure of Wertenbaker's for in the course of her play she has succeeded in her stated aim "which is to reveal . . . to disturb".

The Playmaker, Thomas Keneally's 1987 novel on which *Our Country's Good* is based, is a clever and capacious work that describes in great and fascinating detail the events, personalities and environment surrounding Ralph Clark's production of *The Recruiting Officer*. If it exceeds Wertenbaker's play in range and depth, this is perhaps because a novel has far more space in which to work. Plays (especially Wertenbaker's plays) are far more condensed; for

Wertenbaker, in fact, they are trials in which a simple, even ordinary question is debated by a series of characters who take up opposing positions. Thus, in *Our Country's Good*, we have on the liberal side Ralph and Governor Phillip, who believe that involving the convicts in a theatre production may improve their morals; against them stand the Reverend Johnson and Major Ross, representatives of Church and State who maintain that theatre (at least for felons) will lead to disorder and vice. If this dialectic occasionally leads to the creation of excessively diagrammatic, one-dimensional characters (Wertenbaker's Governor Phillip, especially, tends to be no more than a mouthpiece for liberal ideas, and entirely lacks the complex scepticism and plain eccentricity of Keneally's Governor), on the whole Wertenbaker avoids mere arid argument by the vividness (even, sometimes, coarseness) of her language. This is particularly true of the convicts' speech, which is full of the peculiar slang of 18th-century criminal life, and which brings a grotesque and powerful immediacy to the play. *Our Country's Good*, in fact, contains many different modes of speech all working with and against one another, from the dry, rational discourse of Governor Phillip and his officers, to Farquhar's poised and balanced lines, to the haunting choruses, poetic and poignant, of the aboriginal observer who witnesses the arrival of the Europeans and the subsequent destruction of his race. Each level of society, in effect, has its own language; for the convicts the possibility of redemption occurs when they are permitted, or permit themselves, to learn a speech (Farquhar's) other than their own.

It would be wrong to claim *Our Country's Good* is a masterpiece. But it is, undoubtedly, a very, very good play, one which exhibits all the qualities—vividness, clarity, poise—that one has come to expect in Wertenbaker's work.

—John O'Leary

THE PHILANTHROPIST
by Christopher Hampton.

First Publication: 1970.
First Production: 1970.

The Philanthropist, Christopher Hampton's witty and elegant satire of English life, opens with a man literally blowing his brains out—a definite *coup de théâtre*, but an event that appears to have nothing to do with the scenes that follow. Hampton creates this seeming disjunction deliberately; in the Oxbridge circle so brilliantly anatomized in this "Bourgeois Comedy" (the play's subtitle), all the violence and perversity swirling around it in the "external" world is simply ignored. And that external world is *drenched* in violence: the Prime Minister and most of the Cabinet have been assassinated by a retired lieutenant-colonel masquerading as an innocuous granny; a disillusioned student sets fire to his college; and a lunatic group called F.A.T.A.L.—Fellowship of Allied Terrorists Against Literature—is poised to murder 25 of the most eminent English writers. With the exception of the opening-scene bloodbath, however, the "external" violence in the play is all narrated rather than directly enacted—and rightly so, for this gaggle of academics seem to view the world outside their cosy college rooms as a kind of fiction, a tall tale that is never really permitted to impinge on their own egocentric concerns.

Hampton's central character, the philanthropist of the title (appropriately named *Phili*p), is a lover not only of humanity but also of words (he lectures in philology). During the course of the play, all of which is set in Philip's room at college, his philanthropy manages, paradoxically, to alienate almost everyone he encounters: the aspiring student dramatist, John; the crudely obnoxious, right-wing novelist, Braham Head; Araminta, "quickest drawers in the faculty", who cajoles Philip into bed with disastrous results; and, most crucially of all, his fiancée, Celia, who breaks off their engagement because of Philip's weakness ("I haven't even got the courage of my lack of convictions", Philip confesses). At the play's close, this lover of humanity is left utterly alone on stage with a pistol in his hand and, as he informs his colleague Don on the telephone, "about to do something terrible". He then turns the pistol towards him and pulls the trigger—an event that brings the play full circle. But Philip doesn't blow his brains out; instead, "a small flame springs from the hammer", with which Philip lights a cigarette. This is the "something terrible" this reformed smoker has warned of—a suitably bland "suicide" for such a nonentity.

As a satire both of bourgeois decadence and of a desire to please so profound that it becomes a crippling liability, *The Philanthropist* works wonderfully as a self-contained comedy. But the play becomes infinitely richer when seen as a sardonic riposte to Molière's 17th-century masterpiece, *Le Misanthrope*. Hampton cunningly provides a number of subtle clues to his play's French "parentage": thus all of his seven characters have specific counterparts in Molière, and sometimes similar names (Celia, for example, is an updated Célimène); and Braham at one point tells of encountering an American tourist at the Comédie Française who plaintively asks him what the play they are watching is about: "So I said, 'Well, madam, it's about a man who hates humanity so much that he would undoubtedly refuse to explain the plot of a world-famous play to an ignorant tourist'".

Like *Le Misanthrope*, *The Philanthropist* satirizes a corrupt, hermetic, monstrously vain and bitchy world in which hypocrisy and back-stabbing exist under a shell of clever repartee. And like an inverted Alceste, Molière's misanthrope, it is the philanthropist Philip who acts as primary satiric agent: his guilelessness and essential sweetness unconsciously expose the moral bankruptcy of the others (Hampton has stated that he conceived of each of his characters as embodying one of the seven deadly sins). But Hampton's satire, again like Molière's, is a double-edged sword: like Alceste, Philip is both agent and *victim* of the satire. Alceste's punctilious honesty, while clearly exposing the duplicitousness of his society, is so rigid and inflexible that it too begins to strike us as a flaw; and the same can be said of Philip's virtues. On one level, of course, the two protagonists are at opposite extremes, but like all opposites they ultimately begin to merge. Philip's philanthropy is as foolish, in its own way, as Alceste's misanthropy: bred not out of genuine love for humanity but out of a profound loneliness, a desire to be liked so intense that Philip refers to it as a "terror". This compulsion to please forces him to suppress his own ego so ruthlessly that finally there is no real "self" left. Philip's refusal to engage in critical judgment in order to embrace everybody is thus ironically parallel to, and equally absurd as, Alceste's refusal to suspend critical judgment in order to embrace nobody: both characters end up as emotional hermits.

For all its lightness of wit, *The Philanthropist* is, in some ways, an even "darker" comedy than *Le Misanthrope*. All that violence in the play's background, however humorously treated, inevitably begins to "bleed" into the foreground: whereas social tension in Molière leads only to endless litigation, in Hampton it results in murder (literal assassination rather than simply character assassination). Equally grim is Hampton's handling of his counterpart's to Molière's *raisonneurs*, Philinte and Eliante, those exemplars of sense and moderation in a corrupt world; Hampton's Philinte (Don) is utterly cynical and apathetic, while his Eliante (Liz), in the single scene in which she appears, is totally silent: in Hampton's mordant satire, goodness no longer has a voice. Finally, and most ironically, the tone is considerably darkened with the switch in title character from misanthropist to philanthropist. "I wanted to create a character", Hampton has noted, "who was exactly the opposite of Molière's—but exactly the same things happen to him, which shows how times have changed. A different kind of man is unpopular now". Molière's characters understandably became angry when faced with Alceste's constant carping and criticism; Hampton's characters, by contrast, become angry when faced with Philip's gentleness and lack of guile, assuming there *must* be a hidden "knife" somewhere.

—Hersh Zeifman

PIAF
by Pam Gems.

First Publication: 1979.
First Production: 1978.

Pam Gems' most popular play, *Piaf* traces the life of the famous Parisian singer from her start on the streets in the 1930s to her premature death. But the opening underlines that this is not a story of glittering triumph: introduced to her nightclub audience (and us), Piaf falters after the first lines of her song, swaying at the microphone, her act degenerates into an undignified fight with the manager.

In a swift series of short, episodic scenes we are shown the reality behind the public facade of a "star". Although the haunting music of her songs forms an intermittent backdrop, keying in the mood for each incident, and almost every scene ends with Piaf singing one of her well-known lyrics, she is only presented in an on-stage performance twice, and each time it is a spectacle of personal disaster. The introduction is replayed and elaborated on in one of the last scenes, in musical terms "*a reprise*", marking the ignominious end of her career. Reduced to one-night stands, she successively "*breaks down*" after the first bars of her opening number, then "*stands, as if unaware of her surroundings. Misses opening*" and finally, "*frail and trembling . . . lost onstage, and terrified by the lights*" she falls unconscious as she reaches the microphone. Piaf's artistic strength—and her weakness—is the total honesty of her singing. As she declares, "When I go on to do a song, it's me that comes on . . . They see what they're getting—everything I got". The play illustrates the corrupting, depersonalizing effects of showbusiness. A fellow singer and boxing-champion lover both warn her that the only point of any public performance is the money. But to Piaf the direct contact with her audience is all that matters; and driven from man to man, her sexual relationships form the core of action. From the start of the second act—the beginning of the American tour that put her at the top of the international charts—it is all downhill. Unable to meet the hypocritical demands of being a celebrity, she resorts to her earlier habits as a prostitute, picking up a pair of American sailors in a back-street bar, and the barman too. A husband who beats her up, and two smash-ups in the expensive cars with which she bribes ever younger men, put her in hospital. Alcohol and drug addiction lead to her forcible institutionalization. Reduced to a wheelchair, she dies reminiscing with an old prostitute friend about an early tour when, after a wild night with a whole troupe of Chinese acrobats in Milan, Piaf tried to slash her wrists and her friend was so drunk she almost let her commit suicide. Piaf's response is "Pity you didn't." But in the closing black-out after her death we hear her voice in the song that for millions embodied Piaf's personality "Non, je ne regrette rien"; and throughout her gritty humour offsets the tragedy.

Perhaps the most impressive aspect of this play is its harsh objectivity, which mirrors Piaf's image. The dialogue is minimal—bare sentences, no long speeches or moralizing—as are the settings, and only hairstyles or accessories mark the change in decades from the 1930s to the 1960s. The most frequent scenes are an empty cafe, chairs upended on tables and a piano for Piaf's first tryout; a dressing room or a rehearsal hall, which graphically represent her displacement. Gems' point emerges solely through the selection of episodes from Piaf's biography. From the fourth scene, where she is pressed against an alley wall "servicing" a Legionnaire—whom she hands over to her friend Toine in mid-coitus—she is shown with (in all) 13 sexual partners, all but one of whom abuse or exploit her, though she expects no less. Others, a police inspector and a nightclub manager, casually strike her across the face as the normal way of getting women to do what they want. In the original Royal Shakespeare Company production, while each woman character was played by an individual actress, the 26 male parts were split among nine actors— a doubling that indicates the generic nature of the masculine response to a woman like Piaf.

Indeed, even if self-destructively dependent on the men who manage her, take her money or use her fame for their own musical advancement, in simply being herself Piaf threatens the social (and by implication patriarchal) order; just as the open way her behaviour is portrayed was designed to shock Gems' audience. Not only is her sexual activity as a prostitute physically represented on stage, but when a waiter criticizes her lack of manners, Piaf's riposte is to squat and piss in full view at the table. Notably however, in the second half of the play, when fame and the demands of the system have sapped her personality, the only on-stage sex act comes in a scene where a protégé masturbates her while reading out the adulatory reviews of her latest concert in a striking image of the way celebrity degrades the individual and substitutes narcissistic titillation for real feeling.

Piaf is the most explicit exploration of a characteristic theme in Gems' mature drama: the harmful dichotomy between women's experience and the female stereotypes imposed on them, which is most blatant in the case of those "stars" who become sex symbols. The unique power of this play comes from its objectivity, and the combination of crude physicality with the theatricality in which the singer's on-stage performance overlaps with the dramatic presentation. Piaf's natural behaviour challenges all standard images of femininity, while also being the basis of her stardom. At the same time, the audience find themselves cast as the nightclub or concert public whose desires, projected onto Piaf, destroy her. The songs form a compelling historical tribute, yet the performance makes us aware of our complicity in a system that is no less sexist today.

—Christopher Innes

PRAVDA
by Howard Brenton and David Hare.

First Publication: 1985; revised edition, 1986.
First Production: 1985; revised version, 1986.

Pravda is a political satire centred on Fleet Street, about a rich South African business man who purchases two daily British National newspapers—an up-market "quality" paper and a down-market popular paper. In controlling their output, Lambert Le Roux then hires and fires staff at will, always remaining several steps ahead of the many people whom he upsets and who seek revenge. Most obviously, the play attacks the nature of a press which is entirely compliant to a right-wing government, suppressing opposition and helping to impose its ideology even while professing to be free. The focal point occurs when the editor of the quality paper obtains a leaked document proving that a senior government minister has been lying, and is sacked by Le Roux before he can print it. By the end of the play, Le Roux is in a position of absolute power, and even the sacked editor sacrifices his principles by begging for his job back, accepting with delight the editorship of the down-market paper.

Like Richard III, the more evil and manipulative Le Roux becomes, the more he is also attractive and enjoyable for an audience. This is a double irony since the play focuses not just on Le Roux himself, but on why he is allowed to succeed. As Brenton asks: "How can we all convince ourselves that brutal ugliness is charming, witty and intelligent?". Written when the Left in Britain felt that newspapers were becoming increasingly concentrated in the hands of fewer and fewer wealthy proprietors, and the use of government briefings and contrived leaks allowed their cynical manipulation by the Government, the title refers ironically to the nature of the "truth" peddled throughout the British press. It implicitly invites comparison with newspapers of the Eastern bloc which more *obviously* reproduce the Government line, asking why it is that if our press has more freedom it remains similarly subservient. The word "Pravda" is used sarcastically by a journalist after his carefully researched account of police breaking up a Scottish peace camp is re-written by a deputy editor ("Peace on this paper is always in inverted commas . . . call it a peace—inverted commas—squat . . .") and the play ends with Le Roux welcoming us "to the factory of lies". Even the first scenes of the play, in the office of a small provincial newspaper, show journalists forging readers' letters, and refusing to print apologies for errors because it is vital that the public trust without question what they read. Le Roux, supporting the political status quo, introduces his South African formula, commenting on the pointlessness of producing good newspapers when bad ones sell better:

Page one, a nice picture of the Prime Minister. Page two, something about actors. Page three, gossip . . . a rail crash if you're lucky. Four, high technology. Five, sex, sex crimes, court cases . . . Then letters. All pleasingly like-minded, all from Kent . . . Then six pages of sport. Back page, a lot of weather and something nasty about the Opposition.

However, *Pravda* is not just about the press. Le Roux, who delights in frightening people by exaggerating rather than hiding high unemployment figures, epitomises the rampant and aggressive confidence of the New Right which had (in the 1980s) replaced in government the benevolent paternalism of an older tradition of Conservatism. He breaks into the British establishment against the opposition of such Conservatives who find him not "a proper person", through arrogance, money, and the weakness of opposition. Le Roux succeeds because he knows exactly what he wants, and is contemptuous both of those who get trodden underfoot and of the very notion of morality. For Le Roux, making money is "a natural thing" and moral feelings to be compared only to feelings of indigestion which pass over night. By contrast, those who oppose him are hopelessly woolly and vague in their beliefs, as no one realises better than Le Roux himself: "You are all weak because you don't know what you believe", he tells his sacked editor, contemptuously dismissing the irrelevance of attacks carried on through letters to newspapers, books which don't sell, and even questions in the House. He alone recognises that only strength, even violence, can defeat him: "You should hit a man in the face to make his face disappear . . . I don't know why they don't have the manhood to shoot me".

The only other character who understands the futile naïvety of the opposition to Le Roux is Rebecca, who offers an alternative to both the childish plotting for revenge and the violence which Le Roux suggests. She argues vehemently for the need to fight the ideas of the Right with genuine ideas from the Left, and although within the play she is alone and powerless, it is she, significantly the play's only prominent female character, who carries all the weight of possibilities for positive change in the future.

Theatrically, *Pravda* delights in striking images, drawing on the facilities and technology of the theatre for which it was written; it demands a large cast and luxuriates in the opportunity to shift scenes between newspaper offices, an English garden, a Frankfurt Exhibition Hall, the Irving Club, a greyhound track, the Yorkshire Moors, and a Japanese bungalow in Weybridge complete with water garden. The play's considerable success during its year-long run at London's National Theatre was probably due to its visual and verbal wit as much as to its politics, and also to the monstrous, central role it created for Anthony Hopkins. Though some critics thought its humour crudely undergraduate, others found it Jonsonian, and the writers themselves characterised the play as a "comedy of excess". *Pravda* is without doubt a genuinely funny play, which offers an unusual mix of broad satire and scathing political attack.

—Steve Nicholson

PRIVATE LIVES
by Noël Coward.

First Publication: 1930.
First Production: 1930.

Noël Coward's quarrelsome quartet—Elyot, Amanda, Sibyl, and Victor—inhabits the play that is most closely associated with the Coward milieu. The brickbat is tossed as effortlessly as the *bon mot*, marriage vows are broken, old flames rekindled, and no one seems to care about anything significant or important. The play opens at a Riviera hotel, the adjoining terraces of a particularly smart set of suites revealing two couples on their respective honeymoons. Marital bliss proves fleeting however when we learn that Amanda was once married to Sibyl's new husband, Elyot. The once-wedded pair happen to meet, rapidly convince themselves that their divorce was a mistake, and run off to Paris together. As far as the plot goes, that is really about it. The second act is taken up with billing and cooing alternating with wrestling bouts, the curtain coming down on the entrance of the avenging spouses, Sibyl and Victor. The final act is a brittle and stunning "morning after", during which Elyot and Amanda once again realize that they are inseparable. They quietly exit, leaving Victor and Sibyl to their own nettlesome devices.

The play is celebrated for such lines as "certain women should be struck regularly, like gongs". There is though, beneath the shimmer of Coward's *badinage*, a coherent world view that enables his comic world to function. In Act I Amanda speaks the words which give the play its title:

> I think very few people are completely normal really, deep down in their private lives. It all depends upon a combination of circumstances. If all the various cosmic thingummys fuse at the same moment, and the right spark is struck, there's no telling what one mightn't do . . .

Indeed, for Coward, "complete normality" is often a superficial excuse for the cut and parry of his comic interplay. In Act II when the telephone rings, interrupting their extra-marital idyll, Amanda and Elyot are momentarily discomposed, fearing it may be Sibyl and Victor. They quickly recover themselves though, by determining to "behave exquisitely".

The humor of the third act depends entirely upon the audience recognizing along with Elyot that: "this situation is entirely without precedent. We have no prescribed etiquette to fall back on". By stating bluntly the basic premise of the comedy of manners—the existence of "prescribed etiquette"—Coward perfectly positions himself to subvert etiquette's prescriptions. The small talk and "polite conversation" that Amanda attempts to make are juxtaposed with

Victor's attempts at fisticuffs with Elyot—both are, after all, traditional ways of dealing with unwanted situations. However, Victor's choice of violence is easily overcome by Elyot's level-headed lightheartedness, and Amanda is reduced to muffled silence when Elyot's frivolous reply to her drivelling disquisition on the wonders of travel causes her to choke on a croissant.

Throughout his career, Coward attempted to give the play its dramaturgical due. In his introduction to it in *Play Parade 1*, he candidly appraises the quality of the love scene between Amanda and Elyot in the first act, describing it as being "well-written", and claims that there is a "certain amount of sound sex psychology underlying the quarrel scenes" in the second act. Later in his life Coward described the play as: "the lightest of light comedies, based upon a serious situation which is two people who love each other too much. I wouldn't say it's a tragedy, but there's a sadness below it".

Elyot indeed has a rather a low moment in the third act when he bemoans his fate and declares that no one would care in the slightest if he dropped dead at that very instant. Of course, Victor sees this as Elyot's relentless flippancy asserting itself. And the objective of Elyot's gloom is not so much to make him appear suddenly serious, as it is an enabling device that keeps him within the audiences's sympathies. The situation is almost getting "serious", the legally married couples are on the verge of possibly patching things up. This would totally undo everything that the audience has been led to expect and, more importantly, what Coward has directed it to desire.

One of Coward's especial skills as a dramatist is his ability to keep his audience fascinated by his characters. The virtual plotlessness of *Private Lives* demands that we continue to be interested in what the characters say, precisely because there is so little for them to do.

Frequently acknowledged as Coward's masterpiece, *Private Lives* endures because it is so peculiarly mannered that it transcends manners *per se*; it explains itself so carefully as it goes along that the glittering society that it reflects needs not be understood by the audience. The Great Depression wiped out that society forever a few years after the play's premiere anyway. Thus *Private Lives* is a mirror not so much held up to nature, as it is beyond nature, reflecting not a particular society but rather more primal, social impulses.

—Thomas F. Connolly

ROAD
by Jim Cartwright.

First Publication: 1986.
First Production: 1986.

Set in a grim Lancastrian street which is located midway between an unidentified industrial town and its slagheap, *Road* records the events of a single night and their effect on the lives of its inhabitants. Narrator and guide for the audience is the disreputable, boozy but engaging down-and-out Scullery, who weaves an individual path through the various incidents, chatting to passing characters and commenting in brief asides. In the course of the night, each of those depicted—among them an ex-R.A.F. conscript, an old woman, tarts and out-of-work youngsters looking for a pick-up—is forced to confront the bleak reality of his or her existence, and finds or fails to find a means of coping with it. From the total muster of their lives Jim Cartwright constructs a compelling picture of a Northern community struggling to come to terms with the deprivation and seeming lack of purpose in the industrial wasteland created by the ruthless policies of the 1980s.

In the first act Scullery directs our attention to the four young people— Carol, Louise, Brink and Eddie—whose chance encounter provides the eventual climax of the play, while at the same time calling on a variety of other figures whose speeches lend additional perspective. Here Cartwright stresses the blighted hopes of his creations, their confusion and despair. The ageing Molly, and Jerry, the unemployed former airman of the 1950s, have no recourse but nostalgic yearnings for better, vanished days. Their inability to comprehend the reason for the terrible change in their lives is poignantly expressed by Jerry's *cri de coeur*: "I can't see how that time could turn into this time." Similarly, the Professor with his tape-recorder and useless files of information is an embodiment of human failure to impose any pattern on the meaningless, destructive flux of events.

Most tragic of all are the teenage couple Joey and Clare, who having found no purpose in their miserable lives, choose to die by starvation, in the vain hope that death itself will provide an answer. Their mutual suicide closes the act, but although the emphasis is on blight and squalor, Cartwright leavens the mix with continual glints of gallows humour, mostly from Scullery himself. Whether riding a stolen shopping trolley, or looting an apparently derelict house whose owner appears to demand return of the filched articles, he relieves the pervading gloom with his trickery and wisecracks. The bizarre Skin-lad, too, offers hope of a kind. A violent skinhead, his recent conversion to Buddhism reveals a fundamental human need for spiritual nourishment, so lacking in the Road itself.

Cartwright pursues these positive signs in the second act. To be sure, most of the efforts at escape through seduction or drunken oblivion prove futile in the end, but from the meeting of the four young people comes a memorable scene where, listening (inebriated) to Otis Redding's "Try a Little Tenderness", they pour out their secret feelings in a series of personal statements, eventually joining to chant the hopeful mantra that "somehow a somehow might escape." This message of defiant affirmation contrasts with Joey's tragedy of the previous act, and brings the play to a fitting conclusion.

Road was Cartwright's first play, and rapidly established his reputation as a leading original talent of the 1980s. It demonstrated his ability to create a moving communal portrait by the adroit use of loosely linked episodes and diverse characters, a skill further strengthened by utilising familiar Northern social venues—bar, disco, and chip shop, as well as the street itself—for his scenes. An optional pre-show and interval sequence featuring bar and disco ensure further atmosphere and audience participation, and at the same time reveal his talent as a comic writer. Cartwright's sympathy with the futile, bungled lives of his creations is always evident, matched by an ability to squeeze a startlingly poetic dialogue from their coarse, everyday speech. His choice of "Try a Little Tenderness" as the music to spark the revelations of his four characters is a signally appropriate rejoinder to the brutal policies that have laid waste so many communities in the 1980s. Such feelings are most powerfully expressed in the fierce, impassioned soliloquies he gives to his central speakers, and which draw the audience deeper into the action.

A powerful, original voice, Cartwright delineates the Northern working (or unemployed) class experience in human terms. It is a "warts and all" portrayal, with no attempt to glamorise the squalid, desperate efforts of his characters to escape the meaningless nature of their lives. Yet the humour of his writing is always present, and *Road* has, in spite of everything, a celebratory aspect. Hope glimmers through the reek of vomit and piss, and the final utterances are of defiance and strength. By examining his Lancastrian roots, Cartwright recreates an experience relevant to us all. The location may be Northern, but the deep emotions—anger, despair, elation and hope—are feelings we can and ought to share.

—Geoff Sadler

ROSENCRANTZ AND GUILDENSTERN ARE DEAD
by Tom Stoppard.

First Publication: 1967; revised edition, 1968.
First Production: 1966 (abbreviated version); 1967.

In *Rosencrantz and Guildenstern are Dead* Tom Stoppard constructed a play both comic and absurd around the independent lives of two marginal characters in Shakespeare's *Hamlet*. In Shakespeare's play, Rosencrantz and Guildenstern are little people, continually made to seem irrelevant and unimportant. Their very presence is a consequence of their subordination: the King and Queen have sent for them to spy on Hamlet. This they do very badly, and Hamlet continually makes fools of them. They almost always appear together, and their characters are almost indistinguishable. They try to manipulate Hamlet, but Hamlet manipulates them. The King sends them to take Hamlet to England, with a message to the English King requiring that the prince be executed. Hamlet changes the letter so that Rosencrantz and Guildenstern are executed in his place.

Stoppard puts these two marginal characters into the foreground of his play: they are its "heroes". The same things happen to them as happen in Shakespeare's *Hamlet*: they have no autonomy, being pushed and pulled here and there by other people; they have no individuality—no one remembers which of them is which; they are made fools of by Hamlet; and the play ends with their execution, contrived almost as a practical joke. The difference is that in Stoppard's play, the main concern is with the "private" lives of Rosencrantz and Guildenstern: with what they do when they are not on stage, when they are waiting "in the wings" for their appearances in Shakespeare's play. So the interest and sympathy of the audience lies with *them*, not with the major characters of *Hamlet*.

The main dramatic and thematic business of the Shakespeare play—the appearance of the ghost, Hamlet's task of revenge, the hero's tortured and divided personality—are all marginalised in Stoppard's play. We see Hamlet in this play in exactly the same way as Rosencrantz and Guildenstern see him: as a man who comes in and talks in an extraordinary language, behaves in ridiculous ways without any obvious reason, and fools and humiliates Rosencrantz and Guildenstern who are helpless victims of his practical jokes. The King and Queen also talk in this mysterious fashion (one of the play's characteristics is the movement from ordinary, modern conversation to Elizabethan blank verse) and give Rosencrantz and Guildenstern absurd commands, without explanation, manipulating and humiliating them unmercifully.

Most contemporary reviewers saw *Rosencrantz and Guildenstern are Dead* as a drama of the "Absurd", similar to Beckett's *Waiting for Godot*. John Russell Taylor voiced this majority opinion in his book *The Second Wave*: "We know from Beckett that Godot will not come, nothing will ever change, the two figures will remain waiting in the wings of life for the rest of their lives, never quite grasping what is happening centre-stage of life". In this interpretation, the action of the play is a simple parable of the nature of human existence; a demonstration of life's essential meaninglessness, its absence of choice or purpose, its lack of any direction or significance. Ronald Hayman concurs with this view of the play as an absurdist metaphor for the futility of life, but simultaneously proposes a radically different approach: "The theatrical situation is used as an image of the human condition. Birth, growth and death come to seem like the fatalistic web of text that holds the actor stuck". It is one thing to be trapped by a human condition, quite another to be trapped by a *text*, which is after all quite obviously a man-made construction. If the dramatic narrative of the play enacts not a general human condition, but the subjection of human beings to particular social and ideological forces, then it is perhaps closer to Brecht than to Beckett. If the point of Beckett's plays is to say that life is absurd and uncontrollable, the point of Brecht's plays is to say that we, the audience, have the power to change our lives and to make them less absurd, more meaningful.

If we ask what it is that in this play limits and constrains human freedom, the answer is not a universal condition, but a specific cultural object—a play (*the* play) by Shakespeare. *Rosencrantz and Guildenstern are Dead* can be read as a play about Shakespeare, and about the ways in which culture can become a powerful, ideological force helping to oppress and determine our lives. The play *Hamlet* is shown by Stoppard to be exactly such an enormously potent, cultural token, forcing compliance with its ideological hegemony. At many points in the play Rosencrantz and Guildenstern try to act spontaneously, try to escape from the determining pressures of the *Hamlet*-play. They attempt to intervene, to change things, to acquire some control over the process they are caught in. But their actions are never free. At one point one of them shouts into the wings, "I forbid anyone to enter!". Immediately the entire Danish court sweeps onto the stage. Whenever they try to do something spontaneous, they find that it fits into the predetermined pattern of the *Hamlet*-play. "If we just began to suspect", Guildenstern ominously suggests, "that our spontaneity was part of their order, we'd be finished". As indeed, of course, they are.

Rosencrantz and Guildenstern are Dead is not necessarily then, an absurdist drama, for the force which determines and shapes the lives of the characters is not some mysterious, alien power, never seen and never understood; it is nothing more than a play, but the most celebrated play of our most famous national playwright. Whatever power that play, as a cultural token, may possess, it cannot be regarded as invincible or impervious to change.

—Graham Holderness

SAVED
by Edward Bond.

First Publication: 1966; corrected version, in *Bond: Plays, 1*, 1977.
First Production: 1965.

Controversy surrounded the first production of *Saved* at the Royal Court in 1965: there were demonstrations, visits to the theatre by the police, letters to the press, a prosecution brought against the theatre, and theatre censorship debated in parliament. The reason for all this was the play's coolly graphic depiction of violence in everyday surroundings.

The play traces the relationship of a young, working-class couple, Pam and Len. What starts as a casual pick-up quickly turns into something more as Len moves into the South London house of Pam's parents, Harry and Mary. Pam loses interest in Len, and when she has a baby she assumes that the father is Len's friend Fred, whom she now prefers and sees regularly. She neglects the baby, and when she leaves it in the local park after an argument with Fred (who is no longer interested in her), he and the gang of youths of which he is the leader stone it to death in its pram. Fred alone is imprisoned for the killing. Pam grows increasingly frantic at his absence, blaming everything on Len, who nevertheless doggedly sticks by both her and Fred. Meanwhile the living death of Pam's parents' marriage is galvanized into momentary domestic violence, Mary having sexually compromised the willing Len in the presence of Harry. Yet when Len finally decides to leave the house, it is Harry who persuades him to stay and help make the best of their lives. In the almost-wordless, final scene, Len addresses himself to the task of mending a chair broken in the earlier family quarrel, whilst Harry, Mary, and Pam sit in the silence of stalemate.

This summary suggests a busy plot, but the effect is quite the opposite. Bond dramatizes his story in a sequence of 13 scenes, each carefully shaped so as to claim a measure of rhythmic self-sufficiency. Because the focus is on the minutiae of interrelation between characters rather than on events, the effect is of a narrative *edged* along rather than freely flowing. The underlying concern of the play—environmental determinism—is that of classic Naturalism, as is the rhetoric of linguistic authenticity in the phonetic rendering of a version of London working-class speech, with its grim, elliptical reserve. However, the precision and economy of the dramaturgical demands and the ability to extract an entirely unsentimental lyricism from a rich orchestration of dialogue and sound are features that—though entirely characteristic of Bond—evoke Pinter's drama. And the effect of the scenic form, on a stage "as bare as possible", is decidedly post-Brechtian. We are invited to scrutinize rather than identify. In this way Bond's declared aim to teach "moral scepticism and analysis, and not faith" is inscribed within the very form of Saved. Even so, the play would never have been controversial were it not for its sudden power to compel the strongest feelings at those points where events *are* dramatized: the family argument and, above all, the stoning of the baby.

In a 1981 interview, Bond pointed out that his earlier plays were concerned not with solutions but with the presentation of problems. The problem in Saved is environment, social and domestic. It is seen as a trap, and every place seems palled in a kind of deadness. In the house, each individual impinges constantly and irritatingly on the living space of the others, and the blaring television is used to drown out the crying baby. The café is likewise dominated by a desensitizing, electronic medium, the juke-box. The quiet park is a place of lingering threat and explosive violence: a wartime bomb there killed Harry's and Mary's first baby, and now their daughter's child is the victim of the wanton, eruptive violence of the youths ("might as well enjoy ourselves"). All three places are always *cold*. Everyday living in and around them generates a repressed fury which is constantly seeking an outlet. Harry's memory of the war aptly describes the rhythm of present experience: "Once or twice the 'ole lot blew up. Not more. Then it went quiet. Everythin' still". Under these circumstances moral life degenerates into varieties of childishness: melodramatic petulance, sulky brooding, egotism, and ethical myopia.

In the world of Saved, reserve is a terminal symptom. Characters are afflicted not with inarticulateness so much as by an *unwillingness* to articulate. (We may recall one of William Blake's "Proverbs of Hell": "Sooner murder an infant in its cradle than nurse unacted desires".) This is why Len's constant curiosity is vitally important. His very obtuseness is part of his strength, enabling him as it does to *irritate* others into expression. At various times he presses Pam about her parents, Fred about what killing the baby was like, and Harry about Mary's sexual responsiveness and (again) killing in wartime. The preoccupations are, as Bond himself has pointed out, morbid or prurient (and Len tells Fred that he secretly observed the baby-killing). Yet this seems to be a necessary stage in Len's experience. A similar ambiguity must surround his ability to catalyse argument within the dead marriage of Pam's parents. The release of repressed anger and resentment "clears the air", but the energy provoked is manifested in violence: Mary hits Harry with a teapot and he wields a breadknife.

The last two scenes of the play carry a pivotal significance, but the ambiguity concerning positives extends to them also. In the strange, even ghostly, nocturnal encounter between Len and Harry in Scene 12, the men finally make meaningful contact across the generation gap when Harry speaks about his marital and war experiences and assures Len that "yer fit in now. It'll settle down". Yet the male bond that constitutes their "*shared* victory" (the author's own phrase) is achieved at the expense of, and in spite of, the women. "Don't speak to 'em at all", counsels Harry, "It saves a lot a misunderstandin'". The chill choreography of the final scene makes it amply apparent that this is no solution to the impasse which occasions Len's frustration: "I don't give a damn if they don't talk, but they don't even listen t'yer". "He lives with people at their worst and most hopeless . . . and does not turn away from them", says the author's note on this scene. Yet to speak—as Bond goes on to—of Len's heroic optimism does as little justice to the play as his implicitly political comment of 1981, that at the end the characters "are still fighting, still resisting". The unsentimental poise of *Saved* disdains this kind of uplift, as indeed it resists the seductions of despair. The play's title is problematic, but not ironic.

—Paul Lawley

SERJEANT MUSGRAVE'S DANCE
by John Arden.

First Publication: 1959; revised edition, 1972.
First Production: 1959.

Serjeant Musgrave's Dance is set in a Northern mining town, (resembling Barnsley, Arden's home town), in a cold winter of about 1880. Musgrave arrives with three soldiers: disillusioned old Attercliffe and two young men, one tough and the other joking to conceal fear. Ostensibly they are a recruiting party. In the town they find a bitter conflict, with striking miners, led by Walsh, facing three authority figures: the mayor—also the mine-owner—the parson, and the constable. The soldiers lodge at the inn, where Mrs. Hitchcock is the landlady, hardboiled but kindly, and Annie, strange and withdrawn, the barmaid. The remaining character, the bargee, crooked Joe Bludgeon, takes the soldiers to town. Constantly whistling "Michael Finnegan", he always schemes to be on the winning side.

Through scenes at the inn, a churchyard (where Musgrave plots melo-dramatically), and a stable, we gradually realise that the soldiers have been involved in a colonial atrocity and want to bring the message—and "wild-wood madness"—back to England. But their purposes are confused: Attercliffe is a complete pacifist, the second soldier believes that "it's time we did our *own* killing", and the third mourns his dead friend. Musgrave is against colonial wars, relying on God to guide him when the time comes, for "the new, deserter's duty" is "God's dance on this earth".

One soldier is accidentally killed in a drunken fight before Musgrave calls his recruitment meeting. Here he switches abruptly from praising army life to telling of its horrors, then dances and chants as a skeleton of a youth from the town (who had left after making Annie pregnant) is hoisted in the air. Musgrave announces that by his logic 25 people from the town must be killed (or possibly taken as hostages); dragoons then enter, shooting one soldier, and arresting the two survivors. Beer is served; the colliers' leader decides "We're back where we were"; spring is coming and everyone joins in a round dance.

The final scene has Musgrave and Attercliffe in prison awaiting execution, visited by Mrs. Hitchcock, who brings grog. Attercliffe offers an explicit moral, "You can't cure the pox by further whoring": you can't end violence by violence. Attercliffe's wife had left him for a greengrocer, who "sold good green apples and ... fed the people"—more useful than soldiering, and Attercliffe's curtain-line is: "D'you reckon we can start an orchard?".

Arden's language is often vivid and unusual, and he frequently uses fragments of 19th-century songs. He also requires stage colour: red versus black and white, writing: "In the ballads the colours are primary. Black is for death, and for the coal mines. Red is for murder, and for the soldier's coat the collier puts on to escape from his black". He continues that if social criticism is "expressed within the framework of the traditional poetic truths it can have a weight and an impact derived from something more than contemporary documentary facility". Arden subtitles his work "an un-historical parable", set in plausible past time, but not based on an actual event; he observes that he succeeded in creating an "ambiance of English lower-class life in the Victorian period".

The subject of *Musgrave* is violence and the response to it—more violence or turning the other cheek? Originally the reference was to the British occupation of Cyprus, but Arden is anxious to transcend the specific: "I wrote a play attacking the complacency with which the British public was prepared to regard actions undertaken by the British Army in foreign parts. The play becomes famous . . . and the British Army continues to do exactly the same things in Ireland, and has been doing so for ten years". Arden explores both the necessity of non-violence and the mixed and inadequate motivations of those who try to pursue it. He asserts a preference for simple individual goodness over all abstractions. He speaks up powerfully for life and love— sought eagerly and pathetically by Annie—and anarchy: people should scribble on the book of rules of Musgrave, the parson, and the constable.

—Malcolm Page

A TASTE OF HONEY
by Shelagh Delaney.

First Publication: 1959.
First Production: 1958.

The play opens as Helen, a "semi-whore", and her teenage schoolgirl daughter, Josephine, are moving into a shabby flat in a slum area of Manchester. Soon Helen becomes engaged to her latest boyfriend Peter, a "brash car-salesman" who is ten years her junior. Left to fend for herself even before Helen is married, Jo invites her boyfriend Jimmy, a black naval rating, to stay with her over Christmas. The first act closes with Helen departing to get married, leaving Jo alone in the flat. In the second act Jo invites Geoff, a young homosexual art-student who has been thrown out by his landlady, to move in with her. When he discovers that Jo is pregnant and that her boyfriend has returned to sea, Geoff adopts the role of surrogate mother. He is however ejected rudely by Helen who, after Peter has left her for a "bit of crumpet", returns to her daughter's side.

A summary of the plot of *A Taste of Honey* conveys nothing of its contemporary impact and significance. It was written by a 19-year-old working-class girl from Lancashire, directed by Joan Littlewood, and opened at the Theatre Royal, Stratford East, in May 1958. A play written by one woman and directed by another was still a somewhat unusual circumstance even in the "new" British theatre of the 1950s. Although *A Taste of Honey* is basically realistic in approach and accorded with the current fashion for seedy locations and regional settings and accents, in production the fourth wall convention was abandoned and, during the first act, Helen occasionally addressed comments directly to the audience in the manner of a music-hall entertainer. In addition a live jazz-band played during the scene changes.

More significant than these stylistic devices was, however, the fact that the action of the play was seen solely from the viewpoint of women. Untypically for the theatre of the period the male characters are not the focus of the plot but are introduced when necessary to contribute to the play's exploration of the meaning of motherhood, a theme in itself uncharacteristic of a theatre dominated almost exclusively by male concerns. Centering on this subject, the play constantly questions and re-evaluates social roles and assumptions. In the opening minutes of Act I Helen asserts that children owe a debt to their parents but later, when she is about to leave for a holiday with her boyfriend Peter, she absolves herself from the need to reciprocate by denying ever having "laid claim to being a proper mother". In one way or another each of the play's relationships is linked with motherhood and even Peter, with his one eye and his fondness for older women, is identified with Oedipus. Jo herself is set to become a mother in consequence of the Christmas spent alone with her boyfriend, but her initial response to pregnancy is that she wants to be neither a mother nor even a woman. She realises that, whatever Helen says to the contrary, mothers do have a responsibility for their children's upbringing, and contends that some women are so irresponsible that they should not be allowed to have any children at all. Indeed, underpinning this examination of motherhood is a belief, expressed repeatedly by Jo, in the sanctity of the individual, and a recognition that the role of mother is not one which all women necessarily find natural. In one of the play's characteristic reversals of role assumptions Geoffrey, in fact, proves to be far more supportive to Jo than was her biological mother, Helen.

Delaney's sympathetic portrayal of such social "outsiders" as gays or blacks differed markedly from their normally comic or patronising treatment by the contemporary British theatre. That is not to say however that homosexuality or race are explored in their own right. Indeed it is significant that, although Jo questions Geoff about what he does with other men, no reference is made to his lovers and he is kept away from any sexual activity during the action of the play. Jo's black lover is presented predominantly as a figure of fantasy—Prince Ossini—; an escape from loneliness. "It was only a dream I had", Jo later admits to Geoff. Nevertheless, in contrast to the caricatured figure of Peter, both Geoff and Jimmy are presented as sensitive and caring human beings; a fact which, in itself, must be seen as a positive feature uncharacteristic of the period.

The play was well-received by both critics and the public and transferred in February 1959 to Wyndham's Theatre in London's West End. It was acknowledged as an unsentimental, honest, and vital expression of contemporary relationships: Kenneth Tynan applauded it in the *Observer* for its "smell of living" and called Shelagh Delaney, in retrospect rather prematurely, "a portent". The play offers no explicit message, and the absence of any wider reference to the world outside the flat serves to lead the audience's attention away from ideas and instead focuses it upon the interrelationship between the characters. The play's conclusion, although by no means a resolution of the problematic relationship between Jo and Helen (which one assumes will continue to be dominated by Helen's sexuality and their constant bickering), nevertheless does leave Jo with the understanding and confidence to carry on, and perhaps in time become a better mother than Helen. "For the first time in my life I feel really important", she tells her mother towards the end of the play, "I feel as though I could take care of you, too!". The play has moved full circle from the uneasy relationship between the two women, through the ultimately unsatisfactory experiences with men, back to the unsentimental recognition that, however fraught it may occasionally be, there is some comfort in the shared bonds of blood and gender.

—D. Keith Peacock

TOP GIRLS
by Caryl Churchill.

First Publication: 1982; revised edition, 1984.
First Production: 1982.

For a writer who considers herself, as Caryl Churchill does, "both a socialist and a feminist", the phenomenon of Margaret Thatcher poses a problem. The most successful woman politician in British history, the dominant political figure of a whole decade, is a radical—and openly ideological—Conservative. *Top Girls* is Churchill's first response to Thatcherism. It is a play which explores the relation between female success and political positions. In dramatic terms it does so by enacting a *peripeteia*: Churchill wanted the play to seem at first "to be celebrating the extraordinary achievements of women. Then it would cut another way and say that this sort of movement is useless if you don't have a socialist perspective on it".

The long first scene appears, technically and narratively, to be almost self-contained. In it, the dynamic Marlene hosts a party to celebrate her promotion to the managing directorship of the "Top Girls" employment agency. However, the guests are not her immediate friends and colleagues but successful women from history or legend. The personal stories of Victorian traveller Isabella Bird, of Lady Nijo (the 13th-century Japanese Emperor's concubine and Buddhist nun), and of Pope Joan, are interwoven in a rich counterpoint which touches upon the themes of fathers, religion, lovers, and turning-points in life. When Patient Griselda arrives (late) the talk turns to child-bearing, husbands, and personal loss. As the increasingly intoxicated gathering brings up memories of dissent and rebellion against male power, the hitherto monosyllabic Dull Gret (from the painting) delivers a climactic account of how she led her Flemish women in the harrowing of Brueghel's surreal (though politicized) hell.

The remainder of the play's action is split between two locations and involves an important time-shift. At the employment agency itself (in London), we see Marlene and her colleagues talking among themselves and interviewing a number of women clients—all different, but all representative types. Marlene's niece Angie, who at 16 is physically and psychologically underdeveloped (if not actually backward), and who idolizes her aunt, turns up unannounced at the agency and looks on in admiration as Marlene rebuffs the irate and harrassed wife of her former rival for the big post. The final scene takes place "a year earlier" in the house of Marlene's sister Joyce, who has stayed in the country and struggled to bring Angie up there. This long scene balances the opening one by developing an argument between the sisters which invites consideration of the success of women in the context of the political climate of the 1980s. The argument is polarized: Marlene is a Thatcherite whose ultimate point of reference is Reaganite America; Joyce has inherited the entrenched left-wing views of her father. Marlene has left home and become successful; Joyce has stayed and stagnated. When it is revealed that Angie is actually Marlene's daughter (Joyce has been married, but is childless), the final irony takes shape: the ethic of acquisitive individualism which has been the foundation for Marlene's success is one that would condemn her own pathetic child to a life of deprivation and wretchedness. As Marlene says, Angie is "not going to make it".

Churchill's minute concern for speech rhythms and her large-scale use of precisely-notated overlap in dialogue seem together to imply a scrupulously naturalistic intention. Yet the effect in the opening scene is somewhat abstract, musical—a kind of fugue for voices. More generally, a species of *Verfremdungseffekt*, a "making-strange", is achieved through various strategies of discontinuity: historical, in the gathering of famous women for Marlene's party; theatrical, in the space opened up between actor and role by the specified doubling of roles (inviting cross-referencing of characters) and by having Angie and her 12 year old friend Kit played by adults; narratival, in the chronological shift of the final scene. Such strategies invite an awareness in the audience of the play's status as artifact, thereby encouraging scrutiny and debate rather than identification. We are always aware of a group of women playing a script.

The dramatic debate hinges, to a large extent, on the way the first and last scenes engage with one another. The central office scenes evoke the culture for which Marlene is spokesperson—one within which a woman can succeed if she subscribes to an ethic of competitive individualism, whereby the shape of society is seen to be determined by individual energy and initiative, with little or no reference being made to constraints of class or culture. By contrast, both Joyce's life and her arguments bear witness to determining forces of class and culture. For her, Marlene's challenge is merely to a superstructure rather than to a prevailing social base. How, then, does the opening scene enter the debate?

The great women who gather at Marlene's party have all, in their different ways, been "top girls" within male-fashioned and male-dominated cultures. The remarkable sustained energy and tenacity of each of them would seem to stand as an endorsement of Marlene's position. Yet it is less their resemblances that make for the scene's richness of texture and passing comic disharmonies than the extent to which they *differ* from one another. Each has her concerns or obsessions—Isabella her illnesses, her sister, and her Victorian, moral muscularity; Nijo her "thin silks"; Joan her theological disquisition; Gret her sensory instincts (potatoes, cake, and big cocks). These are not just personal idiosyncracies but indelible marks of *cultural* identity. For Marlene their shared gender is the overriding factor, but each of the women is firmly embedded within the culture of her origin. It is precisely because the scene rejects any sentimental idea of an automatic sisterhood (with the concomitant implied narrative, in which a series of heroic individual women, all just like Mrs. Thatcher, are seen to prefigure a triumphant "post-feminist" present) that its climax, at which each of the women comes to realize the perniciousness of her position within her culture, is so powerful and so convincing.

In this way the debate of *Top Girls* is dramatized rather than merely stated. The case for subsuming concerns of gender within a larger radical politics is made not through a mouthpiece (despite the presence of Joyce), not in a polemic against the "bad dream" of Thatcherism, but in the densely orchestrated realization of a particular cultural situation.

—Paul Lawley

TRANSLATIONS
by Brian Friel.

First Publication: 1981.
First Production: 1980.

Set "in the townland of Baile Beag/Ballybeg, an Irish-speaking community in County Donegal" in the summer of 1833, *Translations* tells the story of how British army engineers carried out their assignment to remap and rename all of Ireland after its integration into the United Kingdom. Friel shows the effects of this geographic and linguistic dislocation on a small community of rural Irish who are "invaded" by a detachment of English officers accompanied by Owen, a former citizen of the town. Owen's father Hugh is the master of the tiny hedge-school where people congregate in the evening to learn, for a tiny fee, such subjects as Latin, Greek, and mathematics. After Lieutenant Yolland falls in love with Marie, a local farm woman, and then mysteriously disappears, the English commander, suspecting murder, orders his army to destroy the entire village and evict the people if the Lieutenant isn't found. The play concludes quietly showing Hugh, Marie, and filthy Jimmy, another member of the "community", awaiting the threatened conflagration, and with the two old men, well-liquored, rhapsodizing multilingually about past civilizations' glory and how they fell.

Translations is a wonderful example of how a playwright can take a political issue and dramatize it for maximum theatrical effect. According to Seamus Deane, Friel's colleague in the founding of Field Day Theatre in 1980 (for which *Translations* was first produced), the play is a "tragedy of English imperialism as well as of Irish nationalism", played out in terms of language. In performance, the audience is asked to *hear* an assortment of competing languages in the same play, underscoring the theme of how failing to protect the language of a culture inevitably leads to the destruction of all of that culture. There are, in fact, two distinct ways of speaking and hearing the

English language in the performance of the play, each contrasting with the other to dramatize and press home Friel's political statement. At one moment in Act II, Scene I, Hugh speaks English-accented English to Yolland (who doesn't understand Irish), Irish-accented English to Owen (to conceal his words from the Lieutenant), and precedes both with a quotation in Latin from Ovid. Thus, the dynamic *use* of language by the characters speaking differently-accented English (as well as classical Greek, Latin, and Irish) to each other, creates both the image of one culture overtaking another and the pressure on the inhabitants of this community to confront and deal with the socio-political conflict at the center of their lives.

The most moving yet trenchant scene (Act II, Scene 2) describes how Yolland and Marie manage to fall in love without knowing each other's language until finally, frustrated by their mutual incomprehension and incomprehensibility, they discard language entirely and allow their bodies to "talk" for them. They declare love for the "sound" of each other's speech, but must learn to set aside its literal meaning which, in personal and political circumstances says Friel, is open to constant misinterpretation. (At the play's conclusion, Yolland's disappearance, because it is intended to serve only as the pretext for raising these themes, is neither solved nor even remembered.)

The lovers' sentimental interlude is but the soft underside of a steely political vision concerning how language gives power to the person who speaks it, reads and writes it, and who finally insists on its dominance above all others. (The first action of the play shows Sarah, a woman with a severe speech defect, learning to speak her name for the first time.) In an astonishing turn from the previously benign events of the geographical "renaming", the ordinance survey's Captain Lancey returns in the third act to announce publicly the names of the places he will destroy in his search for his English comrade. As Lancey reads the landscape's newly assigned names, Owen speaks them in their Irish original, and the inevitable clash between cultures is powerfully *sounded*.

As imperialism's loutish and destructive power lays waste to a way of life and thought, we come to feel the brutal effect of how (in Deane's words) "divorcing power from eloquence" can lead to cultural impoverishment and/or quaint but useless romantic fantasy in a subjugated people. (Another response is armed resistance, implied by Owen's final departure to look for his comrades, and although we do not see the results of his meeting, insurrection is, historically speaking, a definite option.) As one of the helpless folk, unable to withstand the verbal and martial onslaught of the vigorous, pragmatic English, the schoolmaster Hugh articulates one reason of his failure: "a civilization can be imprisoned in a linguistic contour which no longer matches the landscape of . . . fact" (Act II, Scene 1).

Truly, the success of a production of *Translations* lies in how forcefully it demands we listen to it. Most of us have visited "foreign" countries, including those "at home", and we know the discomfiture of both not understanding another's language and our need to "translate" the language into one we can comprehend. Around the world, terrible cultural disputes among communities and nations flare into fatal violence. In the universities, debate is intense and prolific concerning the nature of language (linguistics and philosophy), the meaning of language (semiotics and literary criticism), and the politics of language (anthropology, sociology, multicultural education, and law). *Translations* contributes to the full range of these discussions by dramatizing them with passionate, voluble theatricality. The number of personal and geographical analogies we can make to the situation in Baile Beag/Ballybeg in 1830 is only one reason to applaud the way this play "loses nothing in translation".

—Robert Skloot

WAITING FOR GODOT
(En Attendant Godot)
by Samuel Beckett.

First Publication: As *En Attendant Godot* [in French], 1952; as *Waiting for Godot*, 1955.
First Production: As *En Attendant Godot*, 1953; as *Waiting for Godot*, 1955.

On a country road at evening Vladimir and Estragon (nicknamed Didi and Gogo) meet by a solitary tree for a rendezvous with a Mr. Godot whom neither has seen. Vladimir, however, claims to have had instructions from him and assures Estragon that when he comes they will be "saved". They fill in the time with reminiscences, complaints, reflections, comic routines, and many varieties of witty "blathering". A diversion is created when a second pair arrives, en route for a fair, where Pozzo intends to sell his slave, Lucky, whom he drives by a rope round his neck. Lucky is made to dance by Pozzo, and then "think"; his tirade of thinking is brought to a stop when Vladimir follows Pozzo's advice to remove his hat. When the Pozzo/Lucky pair return in Act II, Pozzo has gone blind and Lucky dumb, but they continue relentlessly on their way. At the end of each act, a moon rises and a boy appears with a message from Godot: he is not coming, but will come the next day. Vladimir and Estragon contemplate hanging themselves, using the tree (which has astonishingly leafed in Act II) and the rope that holds up Estragon's trousers. The attempt ends in farce, with Estragon's trousers round his feet and, as in Act I, him saying "Let's go"—and neither moving.

Waiting for Godot is the play above all others which changed the face of modern drama. First performed in its original French at the tiny Théâtre de Babylone, directed by Roger Blin, it demolished all conventional expectations of what theatre should be. Rhythms of ordinary life were suspended. Beckett advised Peter Hall, who directed the first British production, to lengthen the many pauses and bore the audience more, implying that he wanted them drawn more fully into the bafflement, uncertainty, and boredom the characters experience in the course of waiting for Godot: "Nothing happens, nobody comes, nobody goes, it's awful".

Deliberate rejection of obvious suspense was one of the play's liberating effects. Another was the minimal set, a stage bare except for a single tree (given distinctively slender, stylised form by Giacometti in a production of 1961). Beckett later added a stone to which earth-bound Estragon gravitates whenever he can. The country road where the hypothetical meeting is to take place reflects, in dream-like form, the journey during the war made by Beckett and his wife, members of the Resistance, into the French countryside, travelling by night to avoid notice from the Gestapo. The road also serves as a theatre space where the characters pass the time with a great variety of "turns", from the conversational "canters" of Vladimir and Estragon to Lucky's spectacularly fractured "think". In another aspect the empty stage is the road into the "void" along which the Boy comes, at twilight, bearing tantalising messages from Godot.

The abandonment of a conventional plot structure was an important element in the play's liberating influence. The structure (often described as musical) is circular rather than linear. Variations are played on a cluster of powerful themes ("We're waiting for Godot", "why will you never let me sleep?", "Nothing to be done"). Everything repeats itself, changing just enough to suggest that bigger changes are possible. These seem to happen in Act II, the briefer and more sombre of the two acts: the tree has leafed, Lucky has been struck dumb and Pozzo is "blind as Fortune". But change may be an illusion, for memory cannot be relied on. From one act (or evening) to the next, Estragon forgets about Lucky, despite having been bitten by him, and the Boy denies having spoken with Vladimir before, though we saw him doing so. And in both acts the end is the same: Estragon says "Let's go" and the pair do not move. "Being there" is their role and they cannot escape it.

The metatheatrical trend in modern drama and theatre was given an enormous boost by Beckett's artful play with the idea of play in *Waiting for Godot*. All the characters perform (Pozzo needs an audience to support his unstable identity) and Didi and Gogo slyly display their awareness of being in a theatre. Estragon directs Vladimir to the Gents ("End of the corridor on the left") and declares to the auditorium, "Charming spot . . . Inspiring prospects". In the 1984 production by the San Quentin Company (partly directed by Beckett) Larry Held's Estragon looked out to the auditorium on the line "Where are all these corpses from?", a gesture in tune with the company's belief that Beckett wanted to "smash that fourth wall".

Jean Anouilh summed up the play's extraordinary mix of knockabout, banter, and philosophical reflection when he called it "a music-hall sketch of Pascal's *Pensées* played by the Fratellini clowns". Roger Blin, who shared Beckett's fondness for silent comedians like Laurel and Hardy, cast a music-hall comedian, Lucien Raimbourg, as Vladimir, and Alan Schneider directed the first American production with Bert Lahr as Estragon. When Beckett directed his play in 1975 at the Schiller-Theater in West Berlin, the physical contrast between Stefan Wigger's tall, thin Vladimir and Horst Bollmann's dumpy Estragon highlighted the presentation of character as a matter of complementary opposites. Everything is in balance: Vladimir suffers from urinary trouble, Estragon from bad feet (his trouble with his boots is a major leitmotif). Vladimir the reasoner needs Estragon the dreamer and vice versa, while Pozzo and Lucky are equally interdependent in their complex sado-masochistic relationship. Links between the unlike pairs, suggesting a universal human likeness, are hinted at in comic routines like the hat swapping (derived from the Marx Brothers' film *Duck Soup*) and Pozzo's fall, which results in the collapse of all four.

Waiting for Godot made an enormous impact on the collective unconscious. Godot has commonly been equated with God but has also been seen simply as the unknown future. Vladimir's preoccupation with the gospel story of the thieves crucified with Christ ("one of the four says one of the two was saved") has encouraged interpretation along Christian lines, while Godot's failure to appear has been taken as evidence for a nihilistic view. The play has received an astonishing number of different explanations. It has been seen as a mystical search for a *deus absconditus*, a Cartesian probe into the body/mind divide, a Buddhist "journey", an existentialist drama, and in many other ways. The diversity and passion of the critical reaction shows what a deep vein of imagination Beckett has struck with his haunting image of the two friends, waiting in the void in the hope of being saved . . .

Beckett's production notebook, the basis for the revised edition published after his death, illuminates the cryptic text. Lucky's "think" proves, like so much else in the play, to be a lamentation for humanity. Uncertainty may be the ruling principle of the action ("Nothing is certain") but one or two certainties emerge all the same. Vladimir and Estragon will remain "faithful" even if Godot never comes. And Vladimir will respond, if erratically, to the cries for help which have been seen by some as the real meaning of the play. It is one of the most searching as well as poignant moments in all theatre when the nightmare-ridden Estragon falls asleep and Vladimir puts his coat over him, reflecting as he does so, "Was I sleeping while the others suffered? Am I sleeping now?".

—Katharine Worth

THE WESKER TRILOGY
Chicken Soup with Barley
Roots
I'm Talking About Jerusalem
by Arnold Wesker.

First Publication: 1960.
First Production: 1960.

Arnold Wesker audaciously began his playwriting career in his twenties with this trilogy. *Chicken Soup with Barley* introduces the Kahn family in the East End of London. The parents are Hungarian-born Jews and Communists— energetic Sarah and timid Harry—with two children, teenage Ada and the child Ronnie. In the first act, in October 1936, the Kahns and friends take part in successfully breaking up a Fascist march and a youth asserts: "There's no turning back now—nothing can stop the workers now". The mood in Act 2, ten years later, is more of post-war exhaustion than hope, and Harry has a stroke on stage. The third act moves on to 1955–6 and again incorporates the decline of the family and the decline of the hopes of the Left. Monty, active in the 1930s, visits and says: "There's nothing I can do any more. I'm too small; who can I trust?". With the truth about Stalin revealed and the suppression of the rising in Hungary, even Ronnie is disillusioned. Yet the curtain-line— always important for Wesker—is Sarah's: "If you don't care, you'll die", and the image of the title is of caring: a neighbour brought chicken soup for young Ada when she was ill.

Roots is the most admired play of the three (partly because of Joan Plowright's success in the first production). The East-Enders of *Chicken Soup* are contrasted here with a farming family in Norfolk that is wholly unpolitical. Beatie, the daughter, has escaped to work in kitchens in Norwich and London, where she has fallen in love with Ronnie Kahn. She returns home for two weeks and Wesker riskily communicates the boredom of rural life. Ronnie does not appear (so is ingeniously created through Beatie's quotations and imitations), but writes near the end to break off their engagement. After tears and a quarrel with her mother, Beatie finds her own voice, no longer quoting Ronnie: "We don't fight for anything, we're so mentally lazy we might as well be dead . . . The whole stinkin' commercial world insults us and we don't care a damn". Though the family ignores her, she grasps the fact that she is now thinking and feeling for herself: "It does work, it's happening to me, I can feel it's happened, I'm beginning, on my own two feet—I'm beginning". Though this is a breakthrough only for Beatie, Wesker has commented on the others, "everyone of them could have been a Beatie". Some critics have perversely refused to identify with Beatie, preferring the uneducated, unambitious locals. Yet Beatie's final breakthrough is exciting, theatrical, and convincing.

I'm Talking About Jerusalem is the story of Ada and her husband, Dave, from 1946 to 1959. Dave has fought in the Spanish Civil War and then in the Far East in World War II. They are living in a cottage deep in the country, and Dave making furniture there, attempting to integrate his home and his working life. But few can afford his expensive work and his apprentice chooses to earn more in a factory. So, at the end, they move to London; but Dave does not see this as a defeat, and Ronnie closes the play with: "We must be bloody mad to cry". Wesker makes fuller use of the possibilities of the stage in *Jerusalem* than previously: the singing of Yiddish folk songs and dancing a Zanny Hora; a silent scene in which Dave apologises to Ada by doing homage to her; Dave as "Mr. Life" putting "the fire of life" into his child with a "touch of magic and of clowning".

Wesker's programme note (never reprinted) for the first staging of the full trilogy at the Royal Court in 1960 states:

> Basically it is a family; on another level it is a play about human relationships; and on a third, and most important level, it is a story of people moved by political ideas in a particular social time. There are many theories about socialism. *Chicken Soup with Barley* handles the Communist aspect. *Roots* handles the personal aspect, that is, Ronnie feels you can only teach by example. *I'm Talking About Jerusalem* is a sort of study in a William Morris kind of socialism. If you like, the three

plays are three aspects of socialism, played out through the lives of a Jewish family.

Wesker acknowledges the strong autobiographical element in the plays, with only the cynical visitor in *Jerusalem* entirely his creation.

Wesker shows the joys, miseries, richness, complexity, changeability of working-class family life. He sketches in, equally, a history of socialism from the idealism of the 1930s to withdrawal or disenchantment at the end of the 1950s (the last scene of *Jerusalem* is the day after the Conservatives win the election). Yet in different ways Sarah, Ada, Dave, Ronnie, and Beatie are keeping the faith or finding their way to new ones.

—Malcolm Page

WHAT THE BUTLER SAW
by Joe Orton.

First Publication: 1969.
First Production: 1969.

What the Butler Saw turned out to be Joe Orton's final play, a magnificently comic celebration of excess that for the first time properly, or perhaps improperly, united his interest in the comic potential of language with his wonderment at the absurdities of the physical manifestations of behaviour. It is not only quite easily his best play, it heralds the arrival of what would have been one of the major post-war playwrights.

The plot is not readily summarised, its many and intricate complications being themselves a major part of the play's concern with the way in which rationalising words are ultimately always betrayed by the stronger imperatives of the body. Suitably enough the play is set in an asylum presided over by a psychiatrist, Dr. Prentice, whose intended sexual adventures and his continual attempts to lie his way out of the frustrated consequences are themselves a part of the tension between the desire for liberation and the protective retreat into repression which lies at the heart of the play.

At the outset Prentice is interviewing a candidate for a secretarial position, an interview which inevitably concludes with a demand that the girl, Geraldine, undress for a complete physical examination. Surprised by the unexpected arrival of Prentice's wife, the naked girl is first hidden and then easily persuaded to borrow the clothes of Nicholas, a porter from the Station Hotel who has arrived bearing Mrs. Prentice's luggage.

Add to this initial sexual confusion the potential for chaos afforded by the introduction of, first, Rance, a visiting psychiatrist intent on examining the suitability of Prentice and his clinic for the treatment of the insane, and then a Sergeant Match in pursuit of anything remotely illegal—which covers just about everything that subsequently occurs to the characters or is revealed about their pasts—and one has a fair idea of the kind of revelations to follow. Incest is added to adultery and tranvestitism when it transpires that Geraldine and Nicholas are, unknown to all parties concerned, the twin children of the

Prentices, conceived in the linen cupboard of the Station Hotel—Orton's equivalent of Oscar Wilde's abandoned handbag in *The Importance of Being Earnest*.

It is obvious that the further the plot proceeds, the less Orton is concerned with anything like a moral evaluation of the characters' actions or motivations. Farce here is more than a technique; it is a way of life. On his first entrance Dr. Rance asks, "Why are there so many doors? Was the house designed by a lunatic?". It is a question that not only emphasises the function of the psychiatric clinic—a madhouse with openings for all tastes—but also recalls the play's epigram, from Tourneur's *The Revenger's Tragedy*: "Surely we're all mad people, and they whom we think, are not". Orton's redefinition of farce allowed for a complete abandonment of the naturalistic trappings of plot and character in favour of a world in which the repressions and sublimations of life are allowed a fully-articulated play.

The world of *What the Butler Saw* is a true Freudian nightmare of unleashed sexual repression. It is civilisation without its clothes. Indeed it is Dr. Prentice's inability to admit to the only comparatively straightforward heterosexual act in the entire play that sets things in motion. The wife he would deceive has just returned from a meeting of a club "primarily for lesbians", during the proceedings of which she has availed herself of the body of the young porter Nick, who has actually arrived at the asylum intent on demanding money for the photographs taken during the event; and Nick himself spent a large part of the previous evening sexually harrassing an entire corridor of schoolgirls.

Normality is never the norm in this play; as in the brothel in Genet's *The Balcony*, the asylum converts dreamed fantasy into actable reality. "Marriage excuses no-one the freaks' roll-call", Sergeant Match assures Prentice when he attempts to protest his absolute innocence. What follows is a sort of sexual *Bartholemew Fair* in which clothing is first removed and then redistributed in a confusion of sexual roles—the whole business being observed and interpreted by the lunatic inspector Rance, who offers a succession of psychoanalytical explanations of the characters' behaviour, the unlikelihood of which is only surpassed by the truths of the various cases.

It is a flawed play. It needs, and would certainly have received, considerable rewriting—in particular, the tedious running gag about the lost penis from the statue of Winston Churchill, which is eventually used to bring proceedings to a close, is a part of an interest in the over-facile shooting of sacred cows that characterised Orton's earliest work, and could easily be removed. However, what it promises is a redefinition of farce, a complete liberation of libido in a glorious celebration of chaos and *fin-de-civilisation*. "'It's the only way to smash the wretched civilisation', I said, making a mental note to hot-up *What the Butler Saw* when I came to rewrite . . . Yes. Sex is the only way to infuriate them. Much more fucking and they'll be screaming hysterics in no time", noted Orton.

But sex is both the subject of the play and the vehicle which suggests potentially more serious matters. The tradition of farce inherited by Orton was diluted and trivial, confirming rather than questioning the assumptions of its audience. His awareness of the proximity of farce and tragedy—as seen, for instance, in the scene of the mad King Lear and the blind Gloucester on the beach at Dover—both as theatrical modes and as mirrors of psychological reaction to chaos, points to what he was really attempting. While the plays of those such as Tourneur and Webster move easily from farce to tragedy, the presentation of chaos counterpointed by the articulation of a sense of a moral order, in this play there is no possibility of a transition to a tragic definition of farce. The characters end the play bloodied but unbowed; the ending is, however, purely mechanical. As Orton argued, farce had become an escapist medium, on the run from precisely that which it had originally presented—the disturbing manifestation of the human consciousness which threatens the stability of the social order.

Orton has frequently been compared to Oscar Wilde, and in this play in particular it is a useful comparison. But here more than ever there is a key distinction. Where Wilde invites us to look beyond the brittle and studied brilliance of his characters' dialogue to the hollowness underneath, Orton presents all his cards directly to the audience. What we are being shown *is* the underneath. What Orton was moving towards was the presentation of a pre-civilised world in which the awakened subconscious, at large in a decadent society, makes everyone a "minority group". Had he lived, his redefinition of the boundaries of comedy would have been a major feature of the modern theatre.

—John Bull

TITLE INDEX

The following list includes the titles of all stage, screen, radio, and television plays cited in the entries. The name in parenthesis directs the reader to the appropriate entry where fuller information is given. Titles appearing in **bold** are subjects of individual essays in the Works section. The date is that of first production or publication. These abbreviations are used:

s screenplay
r radio play
t television play

A la Recherche du Temps Perdu (Pinter), 1977
Aa Went te Blaydon Races (Taylor), 1962
A-A-America (E. Bond), 1976
Abelard and Heloise (Millar), 1970
Abel's Sister (Wertenbaker), 1984
Abide with Me (Keeffe), 1976
Abide with Me (t J. Mitchell), 1976
Abigail's Party (Leigh), 1977
Able's Will (t Hampton), 1977
Abortive (r Churchill), 1971
About Face (t Harris), 1989
Above the Gods (Murdoch), 1986
Absence of Emily (t Cannan), 1982
Absence of War (Hare), 1993
Absent Forever (Hopkins), 1987
Absent Friends (Ayckbourn), 1974
Absolute Beginners (t Griffiths), 1974
Absolute Decline (r Jeffreys), 1984
Absolute Hell (Ackland), 1987
Absolution (s A. Shaffer), 1981
Absurd Person Singular (Ayckbourn), 1972
Acapulco (Berkoff), 1986
Acastos (Murdoch), 1986
Access to the Children (t Trevor), 1973
Accident (s Pinter), 1967
According to the Book (Campton), 1979
Accrington Pals (Whelan), 1981
AC/DC (H. Williams), 1970
Ace of Clubs (Coward), 1950
Aces High (s Barker), 1976
Achilles Heel (t Clark), 1973
Acid (Edgar), 1971
Across from the Garden of Allah (Wood), 1986
Across Oka (Holman), 1988
Across the Water (t Rudkin), 1983
Act of Betrayal (t Whitemore), 1971
Act Without Words (Beckett), 1958
Act Without Words II (Beckett), 1959
Acte sans paroles (Beckett), 1957
Activists Papers (E. Bond), 1980
Actor (Berkoff), 1993
Actor and the Alibi (t Leonard), 1974
Actress and the Bishop (Parker), 1976
Adam Adamant (t Frisby), 1966
Adam and Eve and Pinch Me (Laffan), 1974
Adam Redundant (Laffan), 1989
Adam Smith (t Griffiths, Taylor), 1972
Adam Was a Gardener (Page), 1991

Adelaise (r Forsyth), 1951
Adrift (Mowat), 1970
Adventure Story (Rattigan), 1949
Adventures of a Black Girl (Howarth), 1980
Adventures of Awful Knawful (Flannery), 1978
Adventures of Don Quixote (t Whitemore), 1973
Adventures of Frank (t J. McGrath), 1979
Adventures of Gervase Beckett (Terson), 1969
Adventures of Jasper Ridley (N. Williams), 1982
Aesop's Fables (Terson), 1983
Affair (Millar), 1961
Affair at Bennett's Hill (Terson), 1970
Affair at Kirklees (Gow), 1932
Afore Night Come (Rudkin), 1960
After Aida (J. Mitchell), 968
After All (t Nichols), 1959
After Birthday (P. Gems), 1973
After Dinner Joke (t Churchill), 1978
After Haggerty (Mercer), 1970
After-Life (r Bermange), 1964
After Liverpool (r Saunders), 1971
After Lydia (Rattigan), 1973
After Magritte (Stoppard), 1970
After Mercer (Hampton), 1980
After Midnight, Before Dawn (Campton), 1978
After October (Ackland), 1936
After Pilkington (t Gray), 1987
After the Ball (Coward), 1954
After the Dance (Rattigan), 1939
After the Funeral (t Owen), 1960
After the Last Lamp (r Livings), 1961
After the Lions (Harwood), 1982
After the Party (t Hopkins), 1958
After the Rain (Bowen), 1966
After the Wedding Was Over (t Laffan), 1975
After Tragedy (Murphy), 1988
After You with the Milk (Travers), 1985
After-Life (Bermange), 1969
Afternoon (t Leigh), 1975
Afternoon at the Festival (t Mercer), 1973
Afternoon at the Seaside (Christie), 962
Afternoon Dancing (t Trevor), 1976
Afternoon for Antigone (r Hall), 1956
Afternoon Off (t Bennett), 1979
Against the Wind (r Gee), 1988

No Man's Land (Pinter), 1975
No More A-Roving (Whiting), 1975
No More in Dust (Keane), 1962
No More Sitting on the Old School Bench
(Bleasdale), 1977
No, No, Not Yet (Harris), 1972
No One Sees the Video (Crimp), 1990
No One Was Saved (Barker), 1971
No Quarter (r Bermange), 1962
No Room at the Inn (John Arden, D'Arcy),
1976
No Sign of the Dove (Ustinov), 1953
No Skill or Special Knowledge Is Required
(Hopkins), 1966
No Such Things as a Vampire (t Leonard),
1968
No Surrender (Bleasdale), 1986
No Telegrams, No Thunder (r Abse), 1962
No Title (Rudkin), 1974
No Trams to Lime Street (t Owen), 1959
No Trees in the Street (Willis), 1948
No Why (Whiting), 1961
Nobody Here But Us Chickens (Barnes), 1989
Noise Stopped (r Hale), 1966
Noises Off (Frayn), 1981
Nomads (Whiting), 1965
Non-Stop Connolly Show (John Arden,
D'Arcy), 1975
Noonday Demons (Barnes), 1977
Norma (Owen), 1969
Normal Service (Byrne), 1979
Normal Woman (Mowat), 1970
Norman Conquests (Ayckbourn), 1973
North and South (t Turner), 1966
Northern Star (Parker), 1984
Not as Bad as They Seem (t Barnes), 1989
Not at All (t Wood), 1962
Not by Love Alone (Taylor), 1978
Not Fade Away (Keeffe), 1990
Not I (Beckett), 1972
Not, Not, Not, Not, Not Enough Oxygen
(r Churchill), 1971
Not Now Comrade (s Cooney), 1977
Not Now, Darling (Cooney), 1967
Not Quite Cricket (t Keeffe), 1977
Not the Nine O'Clock News (t Burrows),
1980
Not with a Bang But a Whimper (Edgar),
1972
Not with My Wife You Don't (s Barnes),
1966
Notes for a New History (Howard), 1976
Notes on a Love Affair (Marcus), 1972
Nothing Personal (Leonard), 1975
Nothing Special (Ransley), 1981
Nothing to Declare (Saunders), 1982
Nothing Will Be the Same Again (t Hanley),
1968
Nottingham Captain (Wesker), 1962
Now and Then (Campton), 1970
Now and Then (s Lochhead), 1972
Now Let Him Go (t Priestley), 1957

Now More Than Ever (r Turner), 1961
Now That It's Morning (s Bartlett), 1992
Now You Know (r Campton), 1971
Nuclear Family (t T. McGrath), 1982
Nude with Violin (Coward), 1956
Number of the Beast (Wilson), 1982
Number One (Frayn), 1984
Number One (s Newman), 1985
Number Seventeen (s Ackland), 1931
Number 10 (Millar), 1967
Number Three (Grillo), 1970
Numerical Man (Lavery), 1983
Nuncle (t Bowen), 1962
Nun's Veiling (Travers), 1953
Nurse Norton's Affair (Nichols), 1969
Nuts in May (t Leigh), 1976
Nutter (t Plater), 1965
Nymphs and Satyrs Come Away (r Luke),
1985

O Babylon! (Walcott), 1976
O Fair Jerusalem (Edgar), 1975
O Fat White Woman (t Trevor), 1972
O Love Song for Ulster (Morrison), 1993
O Mistress Mine (Rattigan), 1946
O Mistress Mine (Travers), 1936
Oak Leaves and Lavender (O'Casey), 1946
Oak Tree Tea Room Siege (Bowen), 1990
Object of Affection (t Whitemore), 1971
Objections to Sex and Violence (Churchill),
1975
Objects of Affection (t Bennett), 1982
Observe the Sons of Ulster Marching Towards
the Somme (McGuinness), 1985
Obsession (r Willis), 1983
Occupations (Griffiths), 1970
Occupier's Risk (t Harris), 1989
Ocean (r Hanley), 1958
October (Kempinski), 1973
Odd Girl Out (Millar), 1973
Odyssey (Walcott), 1992
Oedipus at Colonus (Wertenbaker), 1992
Oedipus Tyrannos (Wertenbaker), 1992
Of All Living (Lavery), 1967
Of Hope and Glory (Taylor), 1965
Off the Road (Munro), 1988
Off-Beat (s Barnes), 1961
Offence (s Hopkins), 1973
Office Party (Godber), 1992
Office Romances (t Whitemore), 1983
Office Suite (Bennett), 1981
Offski Variations (Evaristi), 1990
Ogodiveleftthegason (Howarth), 1967
Oh (Simpson), 1961
Oh! Calcutta! (Beckett, Orton)
Oh Everyman Oh Colonel Fawcett (Grillo),
1969
Oh If Ever a Man Suffered (O'Malley), 1975
Oh Les Beaux Jours (Beckett), 1963
Oh No – It's Selwyn Froggit (t Plater), 1976
Oh Starlings (Eveling), 1971
Oh Well (Lucie), 1978